Dietary Reference Intakes: RDA, AI*

Life Stage Group	Calcium (mg/d)	Chromium (µg/d)	Copper (µg/d)	Fluoride (mg/d)	Iodine (µg/d)	Iron (mg/d)	Magnesium (mg/d)	Manganese (mg/d)	Molybdenum (µg/d)	Phosphorus (mg/d)	Selenium (µg/d)	Zinc (mg/d)	Potassium (g/d)	Sodium (g/d)	Chloride (g/d)
Infants															
0–6 mo	200*	0.2*	200*	0.01*	110*	0.27*	30*	0.003*	2*	100*	15*	2*	0.4*	0.12*	0.18*
6–12 mo	260*	5.5*	220*	0.5*	130*	**11**	75*	0.6*	3*	275*	20*	**3**	0.7*	0.37*	0.57*
Children															
1–3 y	**700**	11*	**340**	0.7*	**90**	**7**	**80**	1.2*	**17**	**460**	**20**	**3**	3.0*	1.0*	1.5*
4–8 y	**1,000**	15*	**440**	1*	**90**	**10**	**130**	1.5*	**22**	**500**	**30**	**5**	3.8*	1.2*	1.9*
Males															
9–13 y	**1,300**	25*	**700**	2*	**120**	**8**	**240**	1.9*	**34**	**1,250**	**40**	**8**	4.5*	1.5*	2.3*
14–18 y	**1,300**	35*	**890**	3*	**150**	**11**	**410**	2.2*	**43**	**1,250**	**55**	**11**	4.7*	1.5*	2.3*
19–30 y	**1,000**	35*	**900**	4*	**150**	**8**	**400**	2.3*	**45**	**700**	**55**	**11**	4.7*	1.5*	2.3*
31–50 y	**1,000**	35*	**900**	4*	**150**	**8**	**420**	2.3*	**45**	**700**	**55**	**11**	4.7*	1.5*	2.3*
51–70 y	**1,000**	30*	**900**	4*	**150**	**8**	**420**	2.3*	**45**	**700**	**55**	**11**	4.7*	1.3*	2.0*
>70 y	**1,200**	30*	**900**	4*	**150**	**8**	**420**	2.3*	**45**	**700**	**55**	**11**	4.7*	1.2*	1.8*
Females															
9–13 y	**1,300**	21*	**700**	2*	**120**	**8**	**240**	1.6*	**34**	**1,250**	**40**	**8**	4.5*	1.5*	2.3*
14–18 y	**1,300**	24*	**890**	3*	**150**	**15**	**360**	1.6*	**43**	**1,250**	**55**	**9**	4.7*	1.5*	2.3*
19–30 y	**1,000**	25*	**900**	3*	**150**	**18**	**310**	1.8*	**45**	**700**	**55**	**8**	4.7*	1.5*	2.3*
31–50 y	**1,000**	25*	**900**	3*	**150**	**18**	**320**	1.8*	**45**	**700**	**55**	**8**	4.7*	1.5*	2.3*
51–70 y	**1,200**	20*	**900**	3*	**150**	**8**	**320**	1.8*	**45**	**700**	**55**	**8**	4.7*	1.3*	2.0*
>70 y	**1,200**	20*	**900**	3*	**150**	**8**	**320**	1.8*	**45**	**700**	**55**	**8**	4.7*	1.2*	1.8*
Pregnancy															
14–18 y	**1,300**	29*	**1,000**	3*	**220**	**27**	**400**	2.0*	**50**	**1,250**	**60**	**12**	4.7*	1.5*	2.3*
19–30 y	**1,000**	30*	**1,000**	3*	**220**	**27**	**350**	2.0*	**50**	**700**	**60**	**11**	4.7*	1.5*	2.3*
31–50 y	**1,000**	30*	**1,000**	3*	**220**	**27**	**360**	2.0*	**50**	**700**	**60**	**11**	4.7*	1.5*	2.3*
Lactation															
14–18 y	**1,300**	44*	**1,300**	3*	**290**	**10**	**360**	2.6*	**50**	**1,250**	**70**	**13**	5.1*	1.5*	2.3*
19–30 y	**1,000**	45*	**1,300**	3*	**290**	**9**	**310**	2.6*	**50**	**700**	**70**	**12**	5.1*	1.5*	2.3*
31–50 y	**1,000**	45*	**1,300**	3*	**290**	**9**	**320**	2.6*	**50**	**700**	**70**	**12**	5.1*	1.5*	2.3*

Note: This table (taken from the DRI reports, see www.nap.edu) presents Recommended Dietary Allowances (RDAs) in **bold type** and Adequate Intakes (AIs) in ordinary type followed by an asterisk (*). An RDA is the average daily dietary intake level sufficient to meet the nutrient requirements of nearly all (97–98 percent) healthy individuals in a group. It is calculated from an Estimated Average Requirement (EAR). If sufficient scientific evidence is not available to establish an EAR, and thus calculate an RDA, an AI is usually developed. For healthy breast-fed infants, an AI is the mean intake. The AI for other life stage and gender groups is believed to cover the needs of all healthy individuals in the groups, but lack of data or uncertainty in the data prevent being able to specify with confidence the percentage of individuals covered by this intake.

Data from: DIETARY REFERENCE INTAKES series, National Academies Press. Copyright ©1997, 1998, 2000, 2001, 2005, and 2011, by the National Academy of Sciences. These reports may be accessed via www.nap.edu. Courtesy of the National Academies Press, Washington, DC. Reprinted with permission.

Dietary Reference Intakes: RDA, AI*

Vitamins

Life Stage Group	Vitamin A (µg/d)[a]	Vitamin C (mg/d)	Vitamin D (µg/d)[b,c]	Vitamin E (mg/d)[d]	Vitamin K (µg/d)	Thiamin (mg/d)	Riboflavin (mg/d)	Niacin (mg/d)[e]	Vitamin B_6 (mg/d)	Folate (µg/d)[f]	Vitamin B_{12} (µg/d)	Pantothenic Acid (mg/d)	Biotin (µg/d)	Choline (mg/d)[g]
Infants														
0–6 mo	400*	40*	10*	4*	2.0*	0.2*	0.3*	2*	0.1*	65*	0.4*	1.7*	5*	125*
6–12 mo	500*	50*	10*	5*	2.5*	0.3*	0.4*	4*	0.3*	80*	0.5*	1.8*	6*	150*
Children														
1–3 y	**300**	**15**	**15**	**6**	30*	**0.5**	**0.5**	**6**	**0.5**	**150**	**0.9**	2*	8*	200*
4–8 y	**400**	**25**	**15**	**7**	55*	**0.6**	**0.6**	**8**	**0.6**	**200**	**1.2**	3*	12*	250*
Males														
9–13 y	**600**	**45**	**15**	**11**	60*	**0.9**	**0.9**	**12**	**1.0**	**300**	**1.8**	4*	20*	375*
14–18 y	**900**	**75**	**15**	**15**	75*	**1.2**	**1.3**	**16**	**1.3**	**400**	**2.4**	5*	25*	550*
19–30 y	**900**	**90**	**15**	**15**	120*	**1.2**	**1.3**	**16**	**1.3**	**400**	**2.4**	5*	30*	550*
31–50 y	**900**	**90**	**15**	**15**	120*	**1.2**	**1.3**	**16**	**1.3**	**400**	**2.4**	5*	30*	550*
51–70 y	**900**	**90**	**15**	**15**	120*	**1.2**	**1.3**	**16**	**1.7**	**400**	**2.4**[h]	5*	30*	550*
>70 y	**900**	**90**	**20**	**15**	120*	**1.2**	**1.3**	**16**	**1.7**	**400**	**2.4**[h]	5*	30*	550*
Females														
9–13 y	**600**	**45**	**15**	**11**	60*	**0.9**	**0.9**	**12**	**1.0**	**300**	**1.8**	4*	20*	375*
14–18 y	**700**	**65**	**15**	**15**	75*	**1.0**	**1.0**	**14**	**1.2**	**400**[i]	**2.4**	5*	25*	400*
19–30 y	**700**	**75**	**15**	**15**	90*	**1.1**	**1.1**	**14**	**1.3**	**400**[i]	**2.4**	5*	30*	425*
31–50 y	**700**	**75**	**15**	**15**	90*	**1.1**	**1.1**	**14**	**1.3**	**400**[i]	**2.4**	5*	30*	425*
51–70 y	**700**	**75**	**15**	**15**	90*	**1.1**	**1.1**	**14**	**1.5**	**400**	**2.4**[h]	5*	30*	425*
>70 y	**700**	**75**	**20**	**15**	90*	**1.1**	**1.1**	**14**	**1.5**	**400**	**2.4**[h]	5*	30*	425*
Pregnancy														
14–18 y	**750**	**80**	**15**	**15**	75*	**1.4**	**1.4**	**18**	**1.9**	**600**[j]	**2.6**	6*	30*	450*
19–30 y	**770**	**85**	**15**	**15**	90*	**1.4**	**1.4**	**18**	**1.9**	**600**[j]	**2.6**	6*	30*	450*
31–50 y	**770**	**85**	**15**	**15**	90*	**1.4**	**1.4**	**18**	**1.9**	**600**[j]	**2.6**	6*	30*	450*
Lactation														
14–18 y	**1,200**	**115**	**15**	**19**	75*	**1.4**	**1.6**	**17**	**2.0**	**500**	**2.8**	7*	35*	550*
19–30 y	**1,300**	**120**	**15**	**19**	90*	**1.4**	**1.6**	**17**	**2.0**	**500**	**2.8**	7*	35*	550*
31–50 y	**1,300**	**120**	**15**	**19**	90*	**1.4**	**1.6**	**17**	**2.0**	**500**	**2.8**	7*	35*	550*

Note: This table (taken from the DRI reports, see www.nap.edu) presents Recommended Dietary Allowances (RDAs) in **bold type** and Adequate Intakes (AIs) in ordinary type followed by an asterisk (*). An RDA is the average daily dietary intake level sufficient to meet the nutrient requirements of nearly all (97–98 percent) healthy individuals in a group. It is calculated from an Estimated Average Requirement (EAR). If sufficient scientific evidence is not available to establish an EAR, and thus calculate an RDA, an AI is usually developed. For healthy breast-fed infants, an AI is the mean intake. The AI for other life stage and gender groups is believed to cover the needs of all healthy individuals in the groups, but lack of data or uncertainty in the data prevent being able to specify with confidence the percentage of individuals covered by this intake.

[a] As retinol activity equivalents (RAEs). 1 RAE = 1 µg retinol, 12 µg β-carotene, 24 µg α-carotene, or 24 µg β-cryptoxanthin. The RAE for dietary provitamin A carotenoids is two-fold greater than retinol equivalents (RE), whereas the RAE for preformed vitamin A is the same as RE.

[b] As cholecalciferol. 1 µg cholecalciferol = 40 IU vitamin D.

[c] Under the assumption of minimal sunlight.

[d] As α-tocopherol. α-Tocopherol includes RRR-α-tocopherol, the only form of α-tocopherol that occurs naturally in foods, and the 2R-stereoisomeric forms of α-tocopherol (RRR-, RSR-, RRS-, and RSS-α-tocopherol) that occur in fortified foods and supplements. It does not include the 2S-stereoisomeric forms of α-tocopherol (SRR-, SSR-, SRS-, and SSS-α-tocopherol), also found in fortified foods and supplements.

[e] As niacin equivalents (NE). 1 mg of niacin = 60 mg of tryptophan; 0–6 months = preformed niacin (not NE).

[f] As dietary folate equivalents (DFE). 1 DFE = 1 µg food folate = 0.6 µg of folic acid from fortified food or as a supplement consumed with food = 0.5 µg of a supplement taken on an empty stomach.

[g] Although AIs have been set for choline, there are few data to assess whether a dietary supply of choline is needed at all stages of the life cycle, and it may be that the choline requirement can be met by endogenous synthesis at some of these stages.

[h] Because 10 to 30 percent of older people may malabsorb food-bound B_{12}, it is advisable for those older than 50 years to meet their RDA mainly by consuming foods fortified with B_{12} or a supplement containing B_{12}.

[i] In view of evidence linking folate intake with neural tube defects in the fetus, it is recommended that all women capable of becoming pregnant consume 400 µg from supplements or fortified foods in addition to intake of food folate from a varied diet.

[j] It is assumed that women will continue consuming 400 µg from supplements or fortified food until their pregnancy is confirmed and they enter prenatal care, which ordinarily occurs after the end of the periconceptional period—the critical time for formation of the neural tube.

Data from: DIETARY REFERENCE INTAKES series, National Academies Press. Copyright ©1997, 1998, 2000, 2001, 2005, and 2011, by the National Academy of Sciences. These reports may be accessed via www.nap.edu. Courtesy of the National Academies Press, Washington, DC. Reprinted with permission.

Bring Nutrition Into Focus

Bring Nutrition
INTO
FOCUS

Bring Nutrition **into Focus**

The Third Edition of *Nutrition: From Science to You* provides students with the tools that they need to effectively learn and master nutrition concepts and to apply those concepts to their daily lives.

UPDATED Visual Chapter Summaries tied to Learning Outcomes

Each chapter ends with a Visual Chapter Summary. These are now structured to mirror the organization of the chapter content and are numbered to correspond with the chapter learning outcomes. They contain important art and photos from the chapter and serve as concise study and review tools, with accompanying activities in MasteringNutrition.

UPDATED Focus Figures

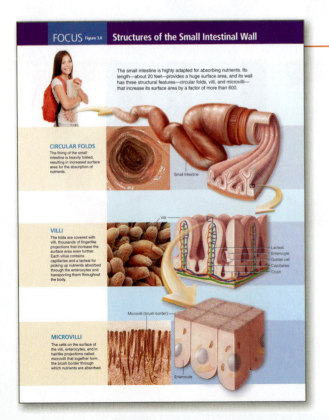

These colorful, full-page figures teach students key concepts in nutrition through bold, clear, and detailed visual presentations. These dynamic figures also have corresponding tutorials in MasteringNutrition. New topics for the Third Edition include the nutrition facts panel, diabetes, and energy balance.

Focus Figures include introductory text that explains how the figure is central to concepts that students will cover throughout the text.

- Students get clear directions via text and stepped-out art that guide the eye through complex processes, breaking them down into manageable pieces that are easy to teach and understand.

- Focus Figures provide dynamic illustrations—often paired with photographs—that make topics come alive.

- Full-page format enables micro-to-macro levels of explanation for complex topics.

Health Connection

Portion Distortion

LO 2.7 Compare the terms "portion" and "serving size" and summarize the health benefits of controlling your portions.

Portion distortion, or perceiving larger portions of food as appropriate sizes, may be contributing to obesity. These larger-than-recommended portion sizes, which are viewed as typical by Americans today, add kilocalories to our diets and may contribute to weight gain.

Portion versus Serving Size: What's the Difference?

The USDA defines a portion as the amount of food eaten at one sitting. In contrast, a serving size (a term that's only used on nutrient labels) is a standard amount of food for which the nutrient composition is presented. We can illustrate the difference with a food that people often pile on their plates, such as spaghetti. A generous helping of cooked spaghetti that spills over the edge of a plate is probably equal to about 3 cups.

serving size A recommended portion of food that is used as a standard reference on food labels.

According to MyPlate, a standard serving size of pasta is ½ cup. A portion of 3 cups of cooked pasta is therefore six servings, which contains more than 600 kilocalories!

Just what size is a small drink? Is it 6 fluid ounces or more? How much is 3 ounces? Unfortunately, many of us frequently underestimate the portion sizes we put on our plates or in our glasses and therefore overconsume foods during snacks and mealtimes.[30,31] One easy way to tell if you are helping yourself to too much of a food is to use a visual that represents a standard **serving size** of the food, such as a cup of vegetables, three ounces of meat, or 1 tablespoon of salad dressing. Having a food scale available is not always possible. Instead, use an everyday item that you always have with you—your hand—to visualize the correct portion sizes (**Figure 2.13**). This provides an easy way to approximate how much you are consuming.

How Have Portion Sizes Changed?

If your great-grandmother treated herself to a Hershey's chocolate bar when it was first introduced, at the beginning

of the last century, she would have paid a small amount of money for about 0.6 ounce of chocolate. Today the same milk chocolate bar is sold in 0.75-, 1.6-, 2.6-, 4.0-, 7.0-, and 8.0-ounce weights. When McDonald's first introduced french fries in 1954, the standard serving weighed 2.4 ounces. Although a small 2.4-ounce size is still on the menu, you can also choose the medium french fries weighing 5.3 ounces or the large at 6.3 ounces. Twenty years ago, a cup of coffee was 8 ounces and just 45 kilocalories with added milk and sugar. Today, consumers enjoy 16-ounce lattes on their way to work, to the tune of 350 kilocalories.[32] Portion sizes have changed across the menu, from french fries to coffee. **Table 2.12** illustrates several foods that people commonly consume in oversized portions.

The restaurant industry has appealed to Americans' interest in getting more food for less money with larger portion sizes at relatively low costs. Americans eat out more often than they did in the past, and are offered a wide variety of inexpensive choices sold in larger-than-normal portion sizes that often exceed the standards defined by the federal government.[33] And most people are

The typical portion of pasta (left) is much often larger than the recommended serving size (right).

A woman's palm is the size of approximately 3 ounces of cooked meat, chicken, or fish

The "O" made by a woman's thumb and forefinger is the size of about 1 tablespoon of vegetable oil.

A woman's fist is the size of about 1 cup (a man's fist is the size of about 2 cups)

The tip of the finger is about 1 teaspoon of margarine

▲ **Figure 2.13 What's a Portion Size? Eat with Your Hands!**
Your hands can help you estimate the appropriate portion size of foods.

TABLE 2.12	Comparison of Portion Sizes of Common Foods		
Food	**Typical Portion**	**Recommended Serving Size**	**FDA Label**
Cooked pasta	2.9 cups	0.5 cup	1.0 cup
French fries	5.3 oz	3.0 oz	2.5 oz
Bagel	4.4 oz	1.0 oz	2.0 oz
Coffee	12.0 fl oz	6.0 fl oz	6.0 fl oz
Cookie, chocolate chip	4.0 oz	0.5 oz	1.1 oz

Source: Adapted from L. R. Young and M. Nestle. 2003. "Expanding Portion Sizes in the U.S. Marketplace: Implications for Nutrition Counseling." *Journal of the American Dietetic Association* 103:231–234.

unaware of the changes in their portion sizes. Though getting more food for the money may be beneficial on the wallet, the health costs may be higher than Americans realize.

In addition to restaurant and packaged foods, home-cooked meals have also bulked up over the past few decades. If you were to measure your grandmother's favorite dinner plates, they would likely be much smaller, about 9 inches in diameter, than the plates in your cupboard, which probably measure closer

to 11.5 inches across. The bigger the plate, the more food you are likely to put on it. Further, your perception of what a normal serving size is changes as the portions on your plate become bigger. Thus, a large plate covered with pasta appears to be normal, whereas the ½ cup of pasta suggested by the MyPlate guide seems small.

Another adverse result of oversized portions is that the larger the portion, the less we are able to estimate kilocalorie intake. For example, eating potato

chips directly from the bag, rather than taking a handful out of the bag and only eating that portion, will likely mean consuming significantly more kilocalories.

Health Effects of Increased Portion Size

Eating larger portions of certain foods, such as foods high in sugar and fat, not only alters the daily kilocalorie intake but can also decrease the amount of nutrients you consume overall. For example, eating larger portions of red meat as an entree will increase the total fat, saturated fat, and cholesterol you ingest. Instead, if the entree portion is limited and the plate is filled with healthier portions of vegetables, fruits, and whole grains at each meal, the result is an increase in the overall content of vitamins, minerals, and dietary fiber content in the meal in addition to a lower intake of total kilocalories. Research has shown that even slight changes in the portion sizes of typical foods can lead to increased energy intake and weight gain.[34,35] As body weight increases, the risk of developing chronic disease including cardiovascular disease, diabetes, joint problems, and some cancers also increases.

Knowing the Kilocalorie Content of Foods May Not Influence Portion Size

Restaurants can play a major role in helping consumers reduce their energy intake.[36] Labeling takeout or restaurant menus with kilocalorie content is aimed at reducing the portion sizes you choose. But is it working? It appears that there seems to be a disconnect between knowing the amount of kilocalories you're eating, and the portion size of the foods you eat. Recently reported studies show that posting the kilocalorie content of your favorite large blueberry muffin has little impact on your behavior.[37]

Continuous Learning **Before**, **During** & **After** Class with **MasteringNutrition**™ with MyDietAnalysis

Mastering is the most effective and widely used online homework, tutorial, and assessment system for the sciences. MasteringNutrition with MyDietAnalysis includes content specific to introductory nutrition courses, delivering self-paced tutorials that focus on your course objectives, provides individualized coaching, and responds to each student's progress.

BEFORE CLASS

Dynamic Study Modules and Pre-Class Assignments provide students with a preview of what's to come.

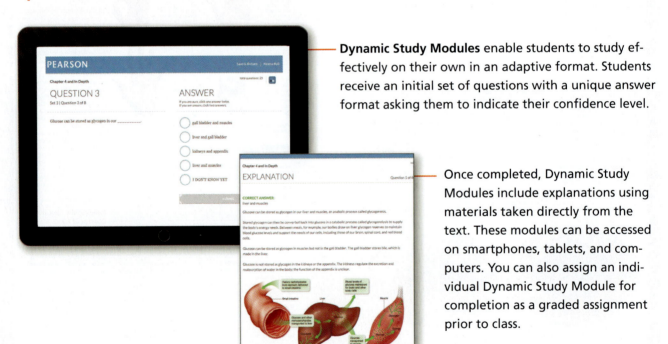

Dynamic Study Modules enable students to study effectively on their own in an adaptive format. Students receive an initial set of questions with a unique answer format asking them to indicate their confidence level.

Once completed, Dynamic Study Modules include explanations using materials taken directly from the text. These modules can be accessed on smartphones, tablets, and computers. You can also assign an individual Dynamic Study Module for completion as a graded assignment prior to class.

Mastering offers Pre-Lecture Quiz Questions that are easy to customize and assign.

Reading Questions ensure that students complete the assigned reading before class and stay on track with reading assignments. Reading Questions are 100% mobile ready and can be completed by students on mobile devices.

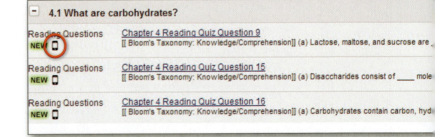

DURING CLASS

Learning Catalytics™ and Engaging Media

What has professors and students so excited? Learning Catalytics, a "bring your own device" student engagement, assessment, and classroom intelligence system, allows students to use their smartphone, tablet, or laptop to respond to questions in class. With Learning Catalytics, you can:

- Assess students in real-time using open-ended question formats to uncover student misconceptions and adjust lectures accordingly.

- Automatically create groups for peer instruction based on student response patterns, optimizing discussion productivity.

My students are so busy and engaged answering Learning Catalytics questions during lecture that they don't have time for Facebook.

Declan De Paor
Old Dominion University

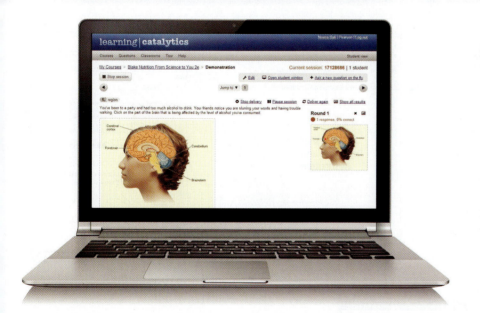

Engaging In-class Media

Instructors can also incorporate dynamic media from the **Teaching Toolkit DVD** into lecture and build class discussions and activities around Nutrition Animations, *ABC News* Lecture Launchers, and more. For more information, please see the last page of this walkthrough.

MasteringNutrition™

AFTER CLASS

Easy-to-Assign, Customizable, and Automatically Graded Assignments

The breadth and depth of content available to you to assign in Mastering is unparalleled, allowing you to quickly and easily assign homework to reinforce key concepts.

Focus Figure Coaching Activities

Coaching activities guide students through key nutrition concepts with interactive mini-lessons that provide hints and feedback.

Nutrition Animations

Animations built specifically for nutrition help students master tough topics with assessment and feedback.

ABC News Videos

25 *ABC News* videos with assessment and feedback help nutrition come to life and show how it's related to the real world.

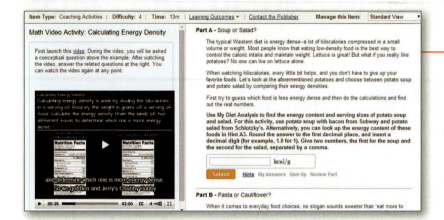

Math Video Activities

These interactive activities walk students through important calculations and provide hands-on practice with wrong-answer feedback to help students understand and apply the material.

NutriTool Build-A-Meal Activities

These unique activities allow students to combine and experiment with different food options and learn first-hand how to build healthier meals.

MasteringNutrition also Includes Access to MyDietAnalysis

MyDietAnalysis is now available as a single sign on to MasteringNutrition. For smartphone users, a new mobile website version of MyDietAnalysis is available. Students can track their diet and activity intake accurately, anytime and anywhere, from their mobile device.

Learning Outcomes

All of the MasteringNutrition assignable content is tagged to book content and to Bloom's Taxonomy. You also have the ability to add your own outcomes, helping you track student performance against your learning outcomes. against the specified learning outcomes and share those results quickly and easily by exporting to a spreadsheet.

Everything You Need to Teach **In One Place**

Teaching Toolkit DVD for *Nutrition: From Science to You*

The Teaching Toolkit DVD provides everything that you need to prep for your course and deliver a dynamic lecture in one convenient place. These valuable resources are included on three disks:

DISK 1
Robust Media Assets for Each Chapter

- *25 ABC News* Lecture Launcher videos
- Practical Nutrition Tip videos
- Nutrition Animations
- PowerPoint Lecture Outlines
- Media Link PowerPoint slides for easy importing of videos and animations
- PowerPoint clicker questions and Jeopardy-style quiz show questions
- Files for all illustrations and tables and selected photos from the text

DISK 2
Comprehensive Test Bank

- Test Bank in Word and RTF formats
- Computerized Test Bank, which includes all of the questions from the test bank in a format that allows you to easily and intuitively build exams and quizzes

DISK 3
Additional Innovative Supplements for Instructors and Students

For Instructors
- Instructor's Resource Support Manual
- Introduction to Mastering Nutrition
- Introductory video for Learning Catalytics

For Students
- *Eat Right! Healthy Eating in College and Beyond*
- *Food Composition Table*

User's Quick Guide for *Nutrition: From Science to You*

This easy-to-use printed supplement accompanies the Teaching Toolkit and offers easy instructions for both experienced and new faculty members to get started with rich Toolkit content, how to access assignments within MasteringNutrition, and how to "flip" the classroom with Learning Catalytics.

THIRD EDITION

NUTRITION

FROM SCIENCE TO YOU

Joan Salge Blake
BOSTON UNIVERSITY

Kathy D. Munoz
HUMBOLDT STATE
UNIVERSITY

Stella Volpe
DREXEL UNIVERSITY

Contributions by Barbara J. Rolls
PENNSYLVANIA STATE UNIVERSITY

PEARSON

Executive Editor: Sandra Lindelof
Senior Acquisitions Editor: Michelle Cadden
Director of Development: Barbara Yien
Program Manager: Susan Malloy
Development Editors: Kari Hopperstead, Claire Alexander
Art Editor: Kelly Murphy
Media Producers: Nicole Tache, Chelsea Logan
Editorial Assistant: Leah Sherwood
Text Permissions Project Manager: Timothy Nicholls
Text Permissions Specialist: Elizabeth Kincaid
Project Manager – Team Lead: Nancy Tabor
Project Manager: Mel Valentin

Production Management: S4Carlisle Publishing Services
Copyeditor: Anna Reynolds Trabucco
Compositor: S4Carlisle Publishing Services
Design Manager: Derek Bacchus
Interior Designer: Gary Hespenheide
Cover Designer: Gary Hespenheide
Illustrator: Precision Graphics
Photo Permissions Management: PreMedia Global
Photo Researchers: Steve Merland, Kristin Piljay
Senior Procurement Specialist: Stacey Weinberger
Executive Marketing Manager: Neena Bali

Cover Photo Credit: Radius Images/Corbis.

Library of Congress Cataloging-in-Publication Data
Blake, Joan Salge.
    Nutrition: from science to you/Joan Salge Blake, Kathy D. Munoz,
and Stella Volpe. — Third edition.
        pages cm
    Includes bibliographical references and index.
    ISBN 978-0-321-99549-0 (alk. paper) — ISBN 0-321-99549-X (alk. paper) 1. Nutrition—
Textbooks. I. Munoz, Kathy D., 1951– II. Volpe, Stella, 1963– III. Title.
    RA784.B553 2015
    613.2—dc23
                                                                    2014039209

ISBN 10: 0-321-99549-X; ISBN 13: 978-0-321-99549-0 (Student Edition)
ISBN 10: 0-13-399298-5; ISBN 13: 978-0-13-399298-4 (Instructor's Review Copy)
1 2 3 4 5 6 7 8 9 10—V003—17 16 15 14

Manufactured in the United States of America.

Brief Contents

Contents

4
Carbohydrates   111

5
Lipids   159

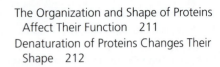

Special Features

Chemistry Boost

EXAMINING THE EVIDENCE

Nutrition in Practice

Self-Assessment

SPOTLIGHT

TABLE TIPS

FITNESS TIPS

About the Authors

Joan Salge Blake, MS, RD, LDN
Boston University

Joan Salge Blake is a Clinical Associate Professor and Dietetics Internship Director at Boston University's Sargent College of Health and Rehabilitation Sciences. She teaches both graduate and undergraduate nutrition courses. She received her MS from Boston University.

Joan is a member of the Academy of Nutrition and Dietetics (formerly the American Dietetic Association) and the Massachusetts Dietetic Association (MDA). She has been a presenter and Presiding Officer at both the AND Annual Meeting and the MDA Annual Convention and is a guest lecturer at both the Boston University Goldman School of Dental Medicine and the Boston University School of Medicine. She was previously named MDA's "Young Dietitian of the Year" and is the past Director of Education and Nominating Committee Chairperson for the MDA. She currently serves on the MDA board. Joan has received the Whitney Powers Excellence in Teaching award from Boston University and the Annie Galbraith Outstanding Dietitian award from the Massachusetts Dietetic Association.

In addition to teaching and writing, Joan has a private practice specializing in weight management and lifestyle changes. Joan is often asked to translate complex nutritional issues in popular terms. As an AND National Media Spokesperson she has conducted over 850 media interviews, and is a contributor of nutrition articles to a variety of magazines and news outlets.

Kathy D. Munoz, EdD, RDN
Humboldt State University

Kathy D. Munoz is a professor emerita and professor of nutrition in the Department of Kinesiology and Recreation Administration at Humboldt State University. She teaches undergraduate introductory nutrition, exercise nutrition, and weight management courses, and teaching preparation in higher education courses in the Department of Education. She received her EdD from the University of Southern California in curriculum design and an MS in Foods and Nutrition with a minor in exercise physiology from Oregon State University.

Kathy is a member of the Academy of Nutrition and Dietetics and the California Dietetic Association. Her professional memberships include Dietitians in Integrative and Functional Medicine (DIFM), Sports, Cardiovascular, and Wellness Nutrition (SCAN), and Weight Management (WM).

Kathy has published articles in *Research Quarterly for Exercise and Sport, Children's Health Care,* the *Journal of Nutrition Education,* and the *International Journal of Sport Nutrition and Exercise,* and has co-authored a series of nutrition and physical activity curriculum guides for elementary teachers. Kathy has also been recognized for her research in, and development of curriculum for, asynchronous learning.

Stella L. Volpe, PhD, RD, LDN, FACSM
Drexel University

Dr. Stella Lucia Volpe is Professor and Chair of the Department of Nutrition Sciences at Drexel University. She is also Co-Director of their newly established Center for Integrated Nutrition and Performance. Stella is Chair of the President's Council for Fitness, Sports and Nutrition. Stella is a nutritionist and exercise physiologist who has built a program of research focusing on three interrelated areas that traverse the lifespan: (1) obesity and diabetes prevention via mineral supplementation, (2) weight management through diet, exercise, and educational programs, and (3) environmental change leading to weight management. She is presently conducting a randomized controlled trial on the effect of magnesium supplementation on the prevention of metabolic syndrome. Stella has also become interested in studying the effects of the human–animal interaction on weight loss and health in children and older adults.

Prior to beginning her faculty appointment at Drexel University, Stella was on the faculty of the University of Pennsylvania, and previous to that, she was on the faculty at the University of Massachusetts, Amherst. Stella is both a Certified Clinical Exercise Specialist (American College of Sports Medicine [ACSM]), and a Registered Dietitian Nutritionist. She is a Fellow of the ACSM. Stella is a competitive athlete in field hockey, rowing, and ice hockey. She enjoys being active with her family, which includes her German Shepherd dogs, Sasha and Bear.

Preface

Why We Wrote *Nutrition: From Science to You*

We wrote *Nutrition: From Science to You* to provide you with a solid foundation about nutrition and how it affects *you* and your nutritional needs, concerns, and questions.

Between the three of us, we have more than 55 years of experience teaching college-level nutrition. We've conducted and published research, studied the literature, and listened to and watched our students learn the science. We've taken copious notes regarding students' questions, interests, concerns, and misunderstandings, both in and outside the classroom. These years of experience have culminated in a textbook that we believe translates the latest nutrition science into a readable format to provide you with information that you can easily incorporate into your life and the lives of others.

As a college student, you are exposed to a steady stream of nutrition and health information from the media, your family and friends, and the Internet. Although you may think Google has the answer to your nutrition questions, we have seen students frequently fall victim to misinformation found on the Web. We designed *Nutrition: From Science to You* to be as user friendly as possible, and packed exclusively with sound nutrition information. The text goes beyond basic nutrition science and provides realistic advice and strategies to help you apply what you learn in your own life. The text is written to meet *your* nutritional concerns and answer *your* questions.

Remember, nutrition matters to *you!* What you eat today and tomorrow will affect you and your body for years to come. Just as important, what you learn about nutrition today will enable you to make a positive effect on the lives of others from now on.

New to This Edition

- **10 New Focus Figures** teach key concepts in nutrition. These full-page figures explore targeted and integrated topic areas through visual information displays that are bold, clear, and detailed. These figures also have corresponding coaching activities in MasteringNutrition.
- **Learning Outcomes** are now used to structure the chapter: each main heading is accompanied by its own learning outcome; **The Take-Home Message** at the end of each main section repeats the learning outcome number before a brief summation of the key points; and the **Visual Chapter Summary** is organized by learning outcome number and contains key images and concepts. This strong pedagogical structure throughout the chapter promotes comprehension and facilitates study and review.
- **Health Connections** now appear in each chapter directly before the Visual Chapter Summary. These sections, which are tied to learning outcomes, highlight diseases and disorders in which nutrition plays a major role, as well as nutritional practices that offer unique health benefits.

- **Content has been updated throughout** to be consistent with new guidelines, data, research, and trends.
- **MasteringNutrition™,** the online homework, tutorial, and assessment system, delivers self-paced tutorials and activities that provide individualized coaching, focus on your course objectives, and are responsive to your personal progress. The Mastering system is the most effective and widely used online homework, tutorial, and assessment system for the sciences. It helps instructors maximize class time with customizable, easy-to-assign, and automatically graded assessments that motivate students to learn outside of class and arrive prepared for lectures. MasteringNutrition for the third edition includes new Focus Figure Coaching Activities, updated NutriTools Coaching Activities, and much more. Learn more at www.masteringhealthandnutrition.com.
- **MyDietAnalysis mobile website** is now available, so you can track your diet and activity intake accurately, anytime, and anywhere from your mobile device. Learn more at www.mydietanalysis.com.

Other Key Features

- **Examining the Evidence** features look at the latest research on hot topics in nutrition today. These features guide you to making better, informed choices in your personal nutrition, while also demonstrating the ways nutrition professionals are constantly expanding and refining our understanding of nutritional science.
- **Nutrition in Practice case studies** draw upon Joan Salge Blake's experience as a dietitian working with actual clients. They encourage critical thinking and emphasize the applicability of the content to your own life and future career.
- **Exploring Micronutrients** within Chapters 9, 10, 12, and 13 are self-contained sections that incorporate photos, illustrations, and text to present each vitamin and mineral. Each micronutrient is discussed using the same categories (forms, absorption and transport, functions, daily needs, food sources, and toxicity and deficiency symptoms) for a consistent and easy-to-study format.
- **Chemistry Boosts** review chemistry concepts within the context in which you need to know them.
- **Calculation Corners** walk through mathematical equations used in the chapter and give you practice working the equations themselves. These features also have corresponding math video activities in MasteringNutrition, which you can be accessed via smartphone by scanning QR codes.
- **True or False?** pretests open each chapter with 10 true/false statements that help you realize that the things you think you know about nutrition aren't always accurate. Answers are given at the end of the chapter.
- **Table Tips** give practical ideas for incorporating adequate amounts of each nutrient into your diet using widely available foods.
- **Self-Assessments** throughout the book ask you to think about your own diet and behaviors and how well you are meeting your various nutrient needs.

Chapter-by-Chapter Updates

Nutrition research and applications continue to expand our understanding of this advancing and dynamic science. To keep pace, we've reorganized the content, and visually improved the figures and tables to enrich student learning in each chapter in the 3rd edition of *Nutrition: From Science to You.*

Chapter 1: What Is Nutrition?

- Learning Outcomes tie into major headings, The Take-Home Messages, and Visual Chapter Summaries.
- Updated statistics on such key topics as the obesity epidemic, consumption trends, the quality of the American diet, leading causes of death in the United States.
- Moved content on meeting nutrition needs into its own section with Learning Outcome and The Take-Home Message.
- Created a new Health Connection on *Finding Credible Nutrition Information.*

Chapter 2: Tools for Healthy Eating

- Learning outcomes are highlighted to match the major headings, the Take-Home Message, and visual chapter summaries.
- Added a new Focus Figure 2.3, *Dietary Reference Intakes.*
- Created a new Focus Figure 2.10, *The Nutrition Facts Panel,* to describe the newest proposed food label changes.
- Developed a new Health Connection, with accompanying Learning Outcome and The Take-Home Message, on *Portion Distortion* to provide guidance on how to recognize healthy portion sizes to reduce the risk of weight gain.

Chapter 3: Digestion, Absorption, and Transport

- Learning Outcomes tie into major headings, The Take-Home Messages, and Visual Chapter Summary sections.
- Added a new Figure 3.12 summarizing the actions of digestive hormones.
- Added a new Figure 3.13 on how the cardiovascular and lymphatic systems transport nutrients.
- Added a new Figure 3.16 on the effects celiac disease has on the wall of the small intestine.
- Consolidated coverage of celiac disease and other digestive disorders into a new Health Connection with accompanying Learning Outcome and The Take-Home Message.

Chapter 4: Carbohydrates

- Learning Outcomes tie into major headings, The Take-Home Messages, and Visual Chapter Summaries.
- Created a new Figure 4.9 on absorption and storage of monosaccharides.
- Added a discussion of hypoglycemia to the section on regulating blood glucose.
- Added a new Focus Figure 4.23, *Diabetes,* showing the mechanisms involved in both type 1 and type 2 diabetes.
- Revised all carbohydrate food source diagrams to feature new foods.
- Added a discussion of glycemic index and glycemic load to the section on best food sources of carbohydrates.
- Created a new Examining the Evidence feature, *Do Sugar-Sweetened Beverages Cause Obesity?*
- Updated coverage of sugar substitutes.
- Relocated Health Connection on diabetes and included Learning Outcome and The Take-Home Message.

Chapter 5: Lipids

- Learning Outcomes tie into major headings, The Take-Home Messages, and Visual Chapter Summaries.
- Revised headings to clarify when the discussion covers lipids in general or triglycerides specifically.
- Revised the Focus Figure 5.16, *Lipid Digestion and Absorption.*
- Created a new Figure 5.15, *Lipoproteins,* to illustrate the both the size and compositions differences between the lipoproteins.
- Created a new Figure 5.18 on the metabolism of linoleic acid and alpha-linolenic acid.
- Moved both Figure 5.19 on the production of bile from cholesterol and Figure 5.20 on the phospholipid bilayer to the section discussing the roles of phospholipids and cholesterol in the body.
- Revised all lipid food source diagrams to feature new foods.
- Updated the research on the Mediterranean Diet in a new Spotlight box and added a new figure of the latest Healthy Mediterranean Diet Pyramid.
- Added a new Examining the Evidence feature, *Is Coconut Oil the Next Superfood?*
- Updated the Health Connection on heart disease and added a Learning Outcome and The Take-Home Message.
- Created a new Focus Figure 5.25, *Atherosclerosis.*

Chapter 6: Proteins

- Learning Outcomes tie into major headings, The Take-Home Messages, and Visual Chapter Summaries.
- Revised Figure 6.1 on the structural differences between carbohydrates, proteins, and fats.
- Revised Figure 6.2 on the organization and shape of proteins.
- Modified Focus Figure 6.6 on the digestion and absorption of protein.
- Revised Focus Figure 6.7 on protein synthesis.
- Modified Figure 6.9 on deamination and transamination.
- Moved coverage of amino acid score, PDCAAS, biological value, protein quality to the section discussing food sources of protein.
- Updated the statistics and references in the Examining the Evidence feature, *Does Soy Reduce the Risk of Disease?*
- Revised all protein food source diagrams to feature new foods.
- Expanded the Health Connection on vegetarian diets, with accompanying Learning Outcome and The Take-Home Message, to include benefits and potential risks of vegetarian diets.
- Added Figure 6.20, *MyVeganPlate.*

Chapter 7: Alcohol

- Learning Outcomes tie into major headings, The Take-Home Messages, and Visual Chapter Summaries.
- Reorganized the order of the topics presented and updated latest statistics and research.
- Moved content on reasons for drinking into its own section with Learning Outcome and The Take-Home Message.
- Moved content on short-term effects of alcohol into its own section with Learning Outcome and The Take-Home Message.
- Expanded the coverage of the negative impact of alcohol consumption, including the statistics on depression.

- Moved *Figure 1, How Red Wine May Affect the Risk of Cardiovascular Disease* to the Examining the Evidence, *Does Moderate Alcohol Consumption Provide Health Benefits?*
- Expanded the information on the moderate consumption of alcohol to emphasize the age-related benefits not seen in younger adults.
- Expanded the content on alcohol abuse and alcoholism in the Health Connection, with accompanying Learning Outcome and The Take-Home Message, and updated statistics on the prevalence of different types of alcohol abuse.

Chapter 8: Energy Metabolism

- Learning Outcomes tie into major headings, The Take-Home Messages, and Visual Chapter Summaries.
- Modified references to high-energy electrons and hydrogen ions throughout the chapter.
- Created a new figure for the Chemistry Boost box that illustrates oxidation-reduction reactions.
- Revised Figure 8.5, *The Metabolic Fate of Food.*
- Created a new Table 8.2, *Glucogenic and Ketogenic Amino Acids*
- Revised Figure 8.11, *Fatty Acids Are Oxidized for Energy.*
- Revised Figure 8.13, *The Electron Transport Chain.*
- Revised explanation of electron transport chain and oxidative phosphorylation.
- Revised Figure 8.18, *The Metabolism of Alcohol.*
- Created a new Figure 8.19 to illustrate galactosemia.
- Expanded the Health Connection, with accompanying Learning Outcome and The Take-Home Message, on inborn errors of metabolism.

Chapter 9: Fat-Soluble Vitamins

- Learning Outcomes tie into major headings, The Take-Home Messages, and Visual Chapter Summaries.
- For each fat-soluble vitamin, included the Learning Outcome at the beginning of the section, and added a new The Take-Home Message at the end.
- Revised all fat-soluble vitamin food source diagrams to feature new foods.
- Created a new Focus Figure 9.8, *Retinal and Its Role in Vision.*
- Revised Table 9.4 on the function, daily needs, food sources, toxicity, and deficiency of each fat-soluble vitamin.
- Moved the Nutrition in Practice on vitamin D deficiency to fall within the vitamin D section.
- Created a new Health Connection, with accompanying Learning Outcome and The Take-Home Message, on the role of vitamin supplements in good health.
- Added a new Figure 9.27 on dietary supplement labels.

Chapter 10: Water-Soluble Vitamins

- Learning Outcomes tie into major headings, The Take-Home Messages, and Visual Chapter Summaries.
- Revised Figure 10.1, *Digesting and Absorbing Water-Soluble Vitamins.*
- Moved Figure 10.3 on the functions of B vitamins in energy metabolism to the section discussing the primary functions of water-soluble vitamins.
- Revised Table 10.1 on the function, daily needs, food sources, toxicity, deficiency, and active form of each water-soluble vitamin.
- For each water-soluble vitamin, included the Learning Outcome at the beginning of the section, and added a new The Take-Home Message at the end.

- Revised all water-soluble vitamin food source diagrams to feature new foods.
- Revised Figure 10.16, *Pantothenic Acid and Energy Metabolism.*
- Revised Figure 10.20, *Vitamin B_6 Assists in Transamination.*
- Revised Figure 10.23, *The Digestion of Folate*
- Added new Figure 10.28 on the absorption of vitamin B_{12}, including the reactions of vitamin B_{12} with the R protein and intrinsic factor in the gastrointestinal tract.
- Revised discussion of how folate deficiency may mask vitamin B_{12} deficiency.
- Updated the information in the Examining the Evidence feature on vitamin C and the common cold.
- Added a new Health Connection, with accompanying Learning Outcome and The Take-Home Message, on the role of a healthy diet and lifestyle in cancer risk.

Chapter 11: Water

- Learning Outcomes tie into major headings, The Take-Home Messages, and Visual Chapter Summaries.
- Revised Figure 11.1, *The Composition of the Body.*
- Revised Figure 11.5, *Sources of Body Water and Routes of Excretion.*
- Updated the Examining the Evidence feature on bottled water to include the most recent research.
- Updated coverage of the health effects of too much or too little water with the latest research and moved into a new Health Connection, with accompanying Learning Outcome and The Take-Home Message,
- Added a new Focus Figure 11.12, *Fluid Balance during Exercise.*

Chapter 12: Major Minerals

- Learning Outcomes tie into major headings, The Take-Home Messages, and Visual Chapter Summaries.
- Revised Table 12.2 on the function, daily needs, food sources, toxicity, and deficiency, of each major mineral.
- For each major mineral, included the Learning Outcome at the beginning of the section, and added a new The Take-Home Message at the end.
- Revised all major mineral food source diagrams to feature new foods.
- Revised Figure 12.4, *Sodium Helps Transport Some Nutrients.*
- Revised Figure 12.8 to illustrate the size of a kidney stone.
- Created a new Focus Figure 12.11 on the hormonal regulation of blood calcium levels.
- Revised and updated the content on bone mass and osteoporosis in the Health Connection, with accompanying Learning Outcome and The Take-Home Message.

Chapter 13: Trace Minerals

- Learning Outcomes tie into major headings, The Take-Home Messages, and Visual Chapter Summaries.
- Revised Table 13.1 on the function, daily needs, food sources, toxicity, deficiency, and interaction of each trace mineral.
- For each trace mineral, included the Learning Outcome at the beginning of the section, and added a new The Take-Home Message at the end.
- Revised all trace mineral food source diagrams to feature new foods.
- Expanded the Health Connection, with accompanying Learning Outcome and The Take-Home Message, to include the causes, symptoms, testing, and treatment for both microcytic and macrocytic anemia.

- Revised Figure 13.18 compares healthy red blood cells to microcytic and macrocytic red blood cells affected by anemia.

Chapter 14: Energy Balance and Body Composition

- Learning Outcomes tie into major headings, The Take-Home Messages, and Visual Chapter Summaries.
- Added a new Focus Figure 14.1 describing energy balance, negative energy balance, and positive energy balance.
- Expanded discussion of the health risks associated with underweight and overweight.
- Added Table 14.6 defining the terms underweight, overweight, and obesity classified by BMI.
- Added Table 14.7 listing different methods of classifying obesity in adults.
- Created a new Health Connection, with accompanying Learning Outcome and The Take-Home Message, on disordered eating using updated content previously located in Chapter 15.
- Added Table 14.8 presenting the diagnostic criteria for classifying eating disorders.
- Added Table 14.9 explaining the warning signs associated with eating disorders.
- Added a Self-Assessment feature, *Are You At Risk for an Eating Disorder?*

Chapter 15: Weight Management

- Learning Outcomes tie into major headings, The Take-Home Messages, and Visual Chapter Summaries.
- Updated all statistics about the prevalence of overweight and obesity.
- Added new information on weight bias and discrimination and the classification of obesity as a disease by the AMA.
- Created a new Figure 15.1 describing the cost of treating obesity in America.
- Created a new Focus Figure 15.2 on hormonal regulation of hunger and satiety.
- Created a new Figure 14.4 illustrating lipoprotein lipase activity in lean, overweight, and obese adults.
- Included a new section on the role of nutrigenomics and epigenetics in obesity and weight management.
- Created a new Figure 15.5 on the structure of an epigenome.
- Added a discussion of decreased physical activity due to the prevalence of the automobile.
- Added a new Examining the Evidence feature on carbohydrates and their role in obesity.
- Expanded the discussion on low-energy-density foods as they relate to weight management.
- Added a new Examining the Evidence feature on microbiomes and their possible link to obesity.
- Added a new Examining the Evidence feature on whether anaerobic or aerobic exercise is the most effective for weight loss.
- Revised and updated the content on obesity medications and bariatric surgery in the Health Connection feature, with accompanying Learning Outcome and The Take-Home Message.

Chapter 16: Nutrition and Fitness

- Learning Outcomes tie into major headings, The Take-Home Messages, and Visual Chapter Summaries.
- Added a new Focus Figure 16.5 on energy sources that fuel different levels of activity.

- Added a new Table 16.3 on the timing of foods and amount of macronutrients needed to improve exercise performance.
- Added a new Nutrition in Practice on an athlete, which introduces the student to the process of nutrition counseling and dietetics in a real-world setting.
- Revised the Spotlight feature on the female athlete triad with the latest diagnostic terminology.
- Created a new Health Connection, with accompanying Learning Outcome and The Take-Home Message, on the role of various dietary supplements in exercise performance and fitness.
- Added discussion of the potential risks and benefits of bicarbonate loading and amino acid supplementation.

Chapter 17: Life Cycle Nutrition: Pregnancy through Infancy

- Learning Outcomes tie into major headings, The Take-Home Messages, and Visual Chapter Summaries.
- Revised coverage of fetal health risks associated with pregnancy in overweight or underweight women with latest research.
- Revised coverage of fetal health risks associated with drug use during pregnancy.
- Revised discussion of goals for weight gain during pregnancy.
- Revised discussions of iron and vitamin D needs during pregnancy to emphasize the value of supplementation for most women.
- Revised Figure 17.8, *The Letdown Response.*
- Revised coverage of the relationship between breast-feeding and risk of developing food allergies with latest research.
- Updated discussion of feeding infants juice with the latest recommendations from the AAP.
- Updated the Health Connection on food allergies and added a Learning Outcome and The Take-Home Message.

Chapter 18: Life Cycle Nutrition: Toddlers through Adolescence

- Learning Outcomes tie into major headings, The Take-Home Messages, and Visual Chapter Summaries.
- Updated discussion of young children's iron needs.
- Revised Figure 18.3 on the USDA's SuperTracker website.
- Revised coverage of the National School Lunch Program.
- Added discussion of the School Breakfast Program.
- Added a section on determining childhood overweight and obesity.
- Updated Figure 18.4, *Increase in Overweight among U.S. Children and Adolescents.*
- Updated and expanded section on the factors contributing to overweight and obesity in children to include discussions of sugary beverages, genetics, family environment, targeting marketing, and peer influence.
- Updated the Examining the Evidence feature, *Does Sugar Cause Behavior Problems in Children?*
- Updated coverage of eating disorders in adolescents with latest research.
- Updated and expanded Health Connection, with accompanying Learning Outcome and The Take-Home Message, on health effects of childhood obesity to include risks of CVD and psychological problems, as well as approaches to obesity reduction and management.

Chapter 19: Life Cycle Nutrition: Older Adults

- Learning Outcomes tie into major headings, The Take-Home Messages, and Visual Chapter Summaries.
- Updated discussion of lifestyle factors that contribute to the leading causes of death in older Americans.
- Revised discussion of changes in body composition during aging.
- Created a new Table 19.1 on the recommended dietary changes for older adults.
- Updated the Examining the Evidence feature, *Does Kilocalorie Restriction Extend Life?*.
- Updated discussion of older adults' potential benefit from supplements with latest research.
- Revised coverage of Alzheimer's disease.
- Added a new Health Connection, with accompanying Learning Outcome and The Take-Home Message, on hypertension.

Chapter 20: Food Safety, Technology, and Availability

- Learning Outcomes tie into major headings, The Take-Home Messages, and Visual Chapter Summaries.
- Revised chapter opening section.
- Updated statistics throughout chapter.
- Revised Figure 20.1, *Bioaccumulation of Toxins*.
- Revised Figure 20.3 on cross-contamination.
- Updated Table 20.2, *Safe Food Temperatures*.
- Revised Table 20.3, *Agencies that Oversee the Food Supply*.
- Revised Figure 20.7, *The Farm-to-Table Continuum*.
- Moved coverage of label terms for animal foods to the section on the use of hormones and antibiotics.
- Updated and relocated discussion of organic food production.
- New Figure 20.13 of a sustainable systems framework.
- Updated coverage of genetically engineered food in a new Health Connection, with accompanying Learning Outcome and The Take-Home Message.

Chapter 21: Global Nutrition and Malnutrition

- Learning Outcomes tie into major headings, The Take-Home Messages, and Visual Chapter Summaries.
- Revised focus of chapter to address hunger as well as other forms of malnutrition, including overnutrition.
- Added a new section defining hunger, malnutrition, undernutrition, and overnutrition.
- Updated statistics about the prevalence of hunger and food insecurity in the United States and worldwide.
- Updated Figure 21.1, *Hunger in the United States*.
- Created new Figure 21.2 on world population growth.
- Added a new section on food deserts in the United States.
- Created a new Figure 21.3 showing food insecurity worldwide.
- Added new sections on food waste and nutrition transition to the discussion of malnutrition worldwide.
- Added new section on malnutrition in overweight and obese individuals.
- Created new Table 21.2, *Food Assistance Programs in the United States*.
- Added a new section on global programs addressing issues related to food and water supply.
- Revised discussion of health effects of chronic hunger in a new Health Connection, with accompanying Learning Outcome and The Take-Home Message.

Supplements

MasteringNutrition™ with MyDietAnalysis with eText 2.0

www.masteringnutrition.pearson.com or www.pearsonmylabandmastering.com

The MasteringNutrition with MyDietAnalysis online homework, tutorial, and assessment system delivers self-paced tutorials that provide individualized coaching, focus on your course objectives, and are responsive to each student's progress. Set up your course in 15 minutes with proven, assignable, and automatically graded nutrition activities that reinforce your course's learning outcomes.

- **NEW Visual Chapter Summary Coaching Activities** review the main ideas of the chapter while incorporating engaging assessments.
- **Focus Figure Coaching Activities** guide students through key nutrition concepts with interactive mini-lessons.
- **MyDietAnalysis Case Study Activities** provide students with hands-on diet analysis practice that can also be automatically graded.
- **Reading Quizzes** (20 questions per chapter) ensure that students have completed the assigned reading before class.
- **25 *ABC News* Videos** with quizzing bring nutrition to life and spark discussion on current hot topics in the nutrition field. They include multiple-choice questions that provide wrong-answer feedback to redirect students to the correct answer.
- **40 Nutrition Animations Activities** explain big-picture concepts that help students learn the hardest topics in nutrition. These animations have questions that provide wrong-answer feedback that address students' common misconceptions.
- **Math Video Coaching Activities,** accessible via QR codes throughout the book, provide hands-on practice of important nutrition-related calculations.
- **Mobile-ready NutriTools Coaching Activities** allow students to combine and experiment with different food options and learn firsthand how to build healthier meals.
- **MP3 Chapter Summary** relate to chapter content and come with multiple-choice questions that provide wrong-answer feedback.
- **Access to *Get Ready for Nutrition*** gives students extra math and chemistry study assistance.
- **The Study Area** is broken down into learning areas and includes videos, animations, MP3s, and much more.

MyDietAnalysis Premium Website

www.mydietanalysis.com

MyDietAnalysis was developed by the nutrition database experts at ESHA Research, Inc. and is tailored for use in college nutrition courses. MyDietAnalysis is available as a single sign-on to MasteringNutrition.

- View a classwide nutritional average. MyDietAnalysis will allow you to see a nutritional profile of your entire class, enabling you to base your lecture on your students' needs.
- Video help with associated quizzes covers the topics students struggle with most.
- For online users, a new mobile website version of MyDietAnalysis is available.

Learning Catalytics

Learning Catalytics is a "bring your own device" student engagement, assessment, and classroom intelligence system that allows students to use their smartphones, tablets, or laptops to respond to questions in class. With Learning Catalytics, you can assess students in real-time using open ended question formats to uncover student misconceptions and adjust lecture accordingly and automatically create groups for peer instruction based on student response patterns, to improve discussion productivity.

Teaching Toolkit DVD

This valuable teaching resource offers everything you need to create lecture presentations and course materials, including JPEG and PowerPoint* files of all the art, tables, and selected photos from the text, and "stepped-out" art for selected figures from the text, as well as animations, all in one place.

The IR-DVD also includes:

- PowerPoint lecture outlines with links to Nutrition Animations and *ABC News* Lecture Launcher Videos
- Media Link PowerPoint slides for easy importing of videos and animations
- PowerPoint slides with a Jeopardy-type quiz show
- Questions for Classroom Response Systems (CRS) in PowerPoint format, allowing you to import the questions into your own CRS
- Instructor's Resource and Support Manual
- Test Bank (Microsoft* Word, RTF, and PDF files) and Computerized Test Bank
- Introduction to Mastering Nutrition
- Introductory video for Learning Catalytics
- *East Right! Healthy Eating in College and Beyond*
- *Food Composition Table*

Acknowledgments

It takes a village, and then some, when it comes to writing a dynamic textbook. *Nutrition: From Science to You* is no exception. We personally want to extend our gratitude to all of those who passionately shared their expertise and support to make *Nutrition: From Science to You* better than we could have envisioned.

Beginning with the energetic staff at Pearson, we would like to thank Sandy Lindelof, who helped make our vision for this textbook into a reality. Kari Hopperstead's on-the-mark developmental editing improved *Nutrition: From Science to You* and made it more enjoyable to read. Crackerjack media producers Nicole Tache and Chelsea Logan worked diligently to create the best media supplements for *Nutrition: From Science to You*. Thanks also to editorial assistant Leah Sherwood for all of her behind-the-scenes work.

A very special thanks to Mel Valentin, project manager, and Mary Tindle, production coordinator at S4Carlisle Publishing Services, for all of their hard work shepherding this book through to publication. Our humble appreciation also goes to Kelly Murphy, art development editor, for developing our stunning new Focus Figures; to Stephen Merland and Kristin Piljay for obtaining the most vivid and unique photos available; to Gary Hespenheide, whose design made the text, art, and photos all come alive; and to design manager Derek Bacchus.

Marketing takes energy, and that's exactly what marketing manager Neena Bali and her team generate nonstop. The many instructors who reviewed the first and second editions, as well as those who reviewed and class-tested early versions of this book, are listed on the following pages. We are grateful to all of them for helping in the development of *Nutrition: From Science to You*.

The village also included loyal contributors who lent their expertise to specific chapters. They are: Elizabeth Ward who revised the three "life cycle" chapters; Heidi Wengreen at Utah State University, who overhauled and expanded the food safety, technology, and availability chapter; and Claire Alexander, who updated the global nutrition and malnutrition chapter.

We especially want to acknowledge the thoughtful contributions from Barbara J. Rolls at Pennsylvania State University. Dr. Rolls, author of over 250 scientific articles and six books, including *Thirst, The Volumetrics Weight-Control Plan: Feel Full on Fewer Calories, The Volumetrics Eating Plan,* and *The Ultimate Volumetrics Diet,* carefully reviewed Chapter 15, Weight Management and Disordered Eating and the "What Nutrition-Related Issues May Affect School-Aged Children?" section of Chapter 18, Life Cycle Nutrition: Toddlers through Adolescence. We appreciate her careful review and recommendations.

Lastly, an endless thanks to our colleagues, friends, and especially our families. Joan would like to "thank my family, Adam, Brendan, and Craig for their love and support when I was working more than I should have been." Kathy sends a special thanks to "my husband Rich and our children Heather, Wes, and Ryan for keeping me sane and grounded, and my Dad and sister Vicki for their steadfast support." Stella would like to acknowledge "my husband, Gary Snyder, for his constant support; and our wonderful dogs, Sasha and Bear, for always making me smile! And to my Mom and Dad, who both instilled in me a wonderful relationship with food, especially home grown and homemade food."

Reviewers

First Edition

Janet Anderson
Utah State University

Sandra Baker
University of Delaware

Gita Bangera
Bellevue College

Lisa Blackman
Tarrant County College, Northwest

Jeanne Boone
Palm Beach State College

John Capeheart
University of Houston-Downtown

Susan Chou
American River College

Nicole Clark
Indiana University of Pennsylvania

Susan Cooper
Montana State University-Great Falls College of Technology

Jessica Coppola
Sacramento City College

Lynn Monahan Couch
West Chester University of Pennsylvania

Wendy Cunningham
California State University, Sacramento

Jeannette Davidson
Bradley University

Holly Dieken
The University of Tennessee at Chattanooga

Johanna Donnenfield
Scottsdale Community College

Roberta Durschlag
Boston University

Brenda Eissenstat
The Pennsylvania State University

Sheryl L. Fuller-Espie
Cabrini College

Eugene J. Fenster
Metropolitan Community College, Longview

Alyce D. Fly
Indiana University

Sara Folta
Tufts University

Betty Forbes
West Virginia University

Sue Fredstrom
Minnesota State University, Mankato

Teresa Fung
Simmons College

Susan Gaumont
Chandler-Gilbert Community College

Jill Golden
Orange Coast College

Gloria Gonzalez
Pensacola State College

Donna Handley
The University of Rhode Island

William Helferich
University of Illinois at Urbana-Champaign

Catherine Howard
Texarkana College

Karen Israel
Anne Arundel Community College

Seema Jejurikar
Bellevue College

Jayanthi Kandiah
Ball State University

Vicki Kloosterhouse
Oakland Community College

Allen Knehans
The University of Oklahoma

Kathy Knight
The University of Mississippi

Shui-Ming Kuo
University at Buffalo

Robert D. Lee
Central Michigan University

Sharon Lemons
Tarrant County College, Northwest

Darlene Levinson
Oakland Community College

Rose Martin
Iowa State University

Mary Martinez
Central New Mexico Community College

George F. McNeil
Fort Hays State University

Monica Meadows
The University of Texas at Austin

Kathleen Melanson
The University of Rhode Island

Mithia Mukutmoni
Sierra College

Pat Munn
Metropolitan Community College, Longview

Megan Murphy
Southwest Tennessee Community College

Dan Neisner
Walla Walla Community College

Corin Nishimura
Leeward Community College

Anna Page
Johnson County Community College

Jill Patterson
The Pennsylvania State University

Janet Peterson
Linfield College

Gwendolyn Pla
Howard University

Roseanne Poole
Tallahassee Community College

Linda Pope
Southwest Tennessee Community College

Elizabeth Quintana
West Virginia University

Denise Russo
Cabrillo College

Kevin Schalinske
Iowa State University

Diana Spillman
Miami University

Sherry Stewart
Navarro College

Leeann Sticker
Northwestern State University

Susan Swadener
California Polytechnic State University, San Luis Obispo

Janelle Walter
Baylor University

Sandy Walz
West Chester University of Pennsylvania

Daryl Wane
Pasco-Hernando Community College

Garrison Wilkes
University of Massachusetts-Boston

Jessie Yearwood
El Centro College

Gloria Young
Virginia State University

Maureen Zimmerman
Mesa Community College

Second Edition

Ellen Brennan
San Antonio College

Wendy Buchan
California State University, Sacramento

Nicole A. Clark
Indiana University of Pennsylvania

Mary Dean Coleman-Kelly
The Pennsylvania State University

Eugene J. Fenster
*Metropolitan Community College,
Longview*

Karen Friedman-Kester
Harrisburg Area Community College

Amy Frith
Ithaca College

Susan Edgar Helm
Pepperdine University

Shanil Juma
Texas Woman's University

Allen Knehans
*The University of Oklahoma Health
Sciences Center*

Julia L. Lapp
Ithaca College

John Radcliffe
Texas Woman's University

Nancy L. Shearer
Cape Cod Community College

Eric Vlahov
The University of Tampa

Heidi Wengreen
Utah State University

Third Edition

Julie Albrecht
University of Nebraska Lincoln

Sandra Brown
University of Delaware

Donna M. Cain
Collin County Community College

Jana Gonsalves
American River College

Cindy Hudson
Hinds Community College

Ruth Anne McGinley
Harrisburg Area Community College

Judith Myhand
Louisiana State University

Rebecca Orr
Collin County Community College

John Radcliffe
Texas Woman's University

Jacqueline Vernarelli
Fairfield University

Stanley Wilfong
Baylor University

Class Testers

Janet Anderson
Utah State University

Jeanne Boone
Palm Beach State College

Jessica Coppola
Sacramento City College

Robert Cullen
Illinois State University

Gloria Gonzales
Pensacola State College

Jill Goode-Englett
University of North Alabama

Debra Head
University of Central Arkansas

Lenka Humenikova-Shriver
Oklahoma State University

Allen Knehans
The University of Oklahoma

Janet Levin
Pensacola State College

Darlene Levinson
Oakland Community College

Anna Miller
De Anza College

Vijaya Narayanan
Florida International University

Anna Page
Johnson County Community College

Nancy Parkinson
Miami University

Renee Romig
Western Iowa Tech Community College

Janet Sass
*Northern Virginia Community College,
Annandale*

Susan Swadener
*California Polytechnic State University,
San Luis Obispo*

Janelle Walter
Baylor University

Suzy Weems
Baylor University

Jennifer Zimmerman
Tallahassee Community College

I am nothing without my ABCs. Thanks.

—*Joan Salge Blake*

I dedicate this to my family for their love and support that sustained me through the development of this book. And to my students, both present and past, for whom this book was written.

—*Kathy D. Munoz*

I would like to dedicate this book to my Mom, Felicetta Volpe, and my Dad, Antonio Volpe (in memory).

—*Stella Lucia Volpe*

1 What Is Nutrition?

Learning Outcomes

After reading this chapter, you will be able to:

1.1 Discuss the factors that drive our food choices.

1.2 Define the term nutrition and identify the essential nutrients.

1.3 Explain the primary roles of essential nutrients found in food.

1.4 Describe the best dietary approach to meet your nutrient needs.

1.5 Summarize how a healthy diet improves health.

1.6 Summarize the ABCD method used to assess the nutrient status of individuals and populations.

1.7 Discuss the current nutritional state of the average American diet.

1.8 Describe the scientific method that leads to reliable and accurate nutrition information.

1.9 Explain how to identify reliable nutrition information and how to recognize misinformation.

True or False?

1. Food choices are driven primarily by flavor. **T/F**
2. Nutrition is the study of dietary supplements. **T/F**
3. Carbohydrates provide our main source of energy. **T/F**
4. Alcohol is a nutrient. **T/F**
5. Taking a dietary supplement is the only way to meet your nutrient needs. **T/F**
6. The most effective method of nutritional assessment is to ask a client to write down what he's eaten in the last 24 hours. **T/F**
7. The number of obese Americans is lower than it was 5 years ago. **T/F**
8. Eliminating all fat from the diet will reduce your risk of developing heart disease. **T/F**
9. Cancer is the leading cause of death in the United States. **T/F**
10. You can get good nutrition advice from anyone who calls himself a nutritionist. **T/F**

See page 33 for the answers.

During the course of a day, we make over 200 decisions about food, from when to eat, how much to eat, and what to eat, to how the food is prepared, and even what size plate to use.[1] You make these decisions for reasons you may not even be aware of. If your dietary advice comes from media sound bites, you may receive conflicting information. Yesterday's news flash announced that eating more protein would help you fight a bulging waist. Last week's headline boldly announced you should minimize *trans* fats in your diet to avoid cardiovascular disease. This morning, the TV news lead was a health report advising you to consume more whole grains to live longer, but to cut back on sodium to avoid hypertension.

It can be frustrating to hear dietary advice that seems to change daily, but this barrage of nutrition news illustrates the progress nutritional scientists are making toward understanding what we eat and how it affects our health. Today's research validates what nutrition professionals have known for decades: Nutrition plays an invaluable role in your health.

In addition to exploring the factors that affect food choice, this chapter will introduce you to the study of nutrition. Let's begin with the basic concepts of why and what you eat, why a healthy diet is important to your well-being, and how you can identify credible sources of nutrition information.

What Drives Our Food Choices?

LO 1.1 Discuss the factors that drive our food choices.

Have you ever considered what drives your food choices? Or are you on autopilot as you stand in line at the sub shop and squint at yet another menu board? Do you enjoy some foods and eat them often, while avoiding others with a vengeance? You obviously need food to survive, but beyond your basic instinct to eat are many other factors that affect your food choices. These factors include taste and enjoyment; culture and environment; social life and trends; nutrition knowledge; advertising; time, convenience, and cost; and habits and emotion (**Figure 1.1**).

Taste and Enjoyment

Research confirms that when it comes to making food choices, taste is the most important consideration.[2,3] This shouldn't be too much of a surprise, considering there are more than 10,000 taste buds in the mouth. These taste buds tell you that chocolate cheesecake is sweet, fresh lemon juice is sour, and a pretzel is salty. This preference for sweet, salty, or creamy foods begins during infancy, may be influenced by our genes,[4] and changes as we age.[5]

We have a taste for fat, which may also be genetically linked.[6] When fat is combined with sugar, such as in a sugar-laden doughnut, our taste for that food is even stronger.[7]

Texture also affects our likelihood of enjoying foods. We enjoy a flaky piecrust but dislike one that is tough; we prefer crunchy apples to mealy ones, and creamy rather than lumpy soups. Almost 30 percent of adults dislike

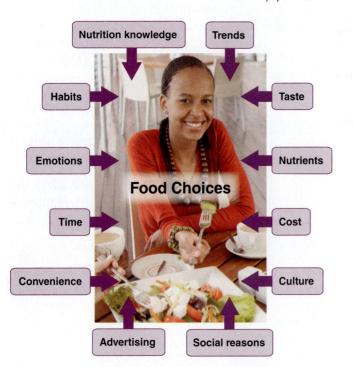

Nutrition knowledge

Trends

Habits

Taste

Emotions

Nutrients

Food Choices

Time

Cost

Convenience

Culture

Advertising

Social reasons

▲ **Figure 1.1 Many Factors Influence Your Food Choices**

slippery foods, such as oysters and okra.[8] Researchers have suggested that these preferences for sweetness, high fat, and specific textures begin early in life and this makes them resistant to change.[9]

Culture and Environment

Enjoying food is not just a physiological sensation. Other factors, such as our culture and the environment, also play a role in which foods we eat.[10] If you were a student in Mexico, you may regularly feast on corn tortillas and tamales, as corn is a staple of Mexican cuisines. In India, meals commonly include lentils and other legumes with rice and vegetables, whereas Native Americans often enjoy stews of mutton (sheep), corn, vegetables, and berries. And, in Asian countries, rice likely would be front and center on your plate.

Roughly one in three Americans is of Hispanic, Native American, Asian, or African descent. Cultural food preferences often influence food choices.

The environment in which its people live significantly influences a culture's cuisine. This includes the climate and soil conditions as well as the native plants and animals, and the distance people live from rivers, lakes, or the sea. Foods that are available and accessible are more likely to be regularly consumed than foods that are scarce. For example, native Alaskans feast on fish because it is plentiful, but eat less fresh produce, which is difficult to grow locally. For most Americans, eating only locally available foods is less of an issue today than in the past, due to global food distribution networks. However, the tendency persists for some food items.

Our food environment—the variety of food choices available, the size and shape of plates and glassware, the packaging of foods, and the types and amounts of food that are visible—has a strong influence on what and how much we consume. We eat more food when the serving plates are larger, or drink less when beverages are served in taller glassware. Environmental cues also affect eating patterns. You are more likely to linger over a meal when the light is dimmed,[11] or quickly finish your meal when you are standing rather than sitting. Physical cues, such as a friend's empty appetizer plate covered with disposed-of cocktail sticks, may signal you to eat more.

Social Life and Trends

Every year on the fourth Thursday in November, over 85 percent of Americans gather with family and friends to consume close to 736 million pounds of turkey as they celebrate Thanksgiving.[12] A person is likely to eat more on Thanksgiving than on any other Thursday, and this is partly because of the number of people eating with them. Eating dinner with others has been shown to increase the size of the meal by over 40 percent, and the more people present at the meal, the more you'll eat.[13]

Eating is an important way to bond with others. Sharing a meal with family or friends stimulates conversation, creates traditions, and expands our food experiences. Although eating a quick meal in the campus cafeteria may not be the best choice for healthy food options, it will allow you to socialize with classmates.

For many people, activities such as watching a football game with fellow fans or going to a movie with friends often involve particular foods. More pizzas are sold on Super Bowl Sunday than on any other day of the year.[14] Movie theater owners bank on their patrons buying popcorn, candy, and beverages at the concession stand before heading in to watch the film, and moviegoers are more likely to buy these snacks if they're with a group of friends.[15]

Eating junk food while watching sports or attending a sporting event sometimes seems like an American way of life.

The USDA certifies that foods labeled "organic" are grown without the use of pesticides, herbicides, or chemical fertilizers.

Food choices are also affected by popular trends. For instance, home cooks in the 1950s bought bags of "newfangled" frozen vegetables in order to provide healthy meals in less time. A few decades later, vegetables went upscale and consumers bought them as part of ready-to-heat stir-fry mixes. Today, shoppers pay a premium for bags of fresh veggies, like carrots, that have been prewashed and peeled, sliced, or diced, and they pay even more of a premium if the food is labeled "organic." In 2011 alone, Americans spent more than $29 billion on organic foods.[16] Consumers also ate more plant-based products, especially from locally grown farmers' markets, and ate more foods with added benefits, such as eggs with more omega-3 fatty acids or calcium-fortified orange juice, and gluten-free foods.[17] Now most markets provide dozens of choices in flavored and enhanced bottled teas, a popular beverage for many college students. As food manufacturers pour more money into research and development, who knows what tomorrow's trendy food item will be?

Nutrition Knowledge

Individuals may choose certain foods because they perceive them as being healthy, or avoid other foods that are associated with weight gain or loss. For example, Americans consume more vegetables and fruits to control blood pressure and prevent colon cancer. At the same time, Americans worry about fried eggs causing heart disease and butter-laden pastries or sugar-sweetened beverages leading to obesity. The latest research suggests that consumers are paying more attention to nutrition labels when purchasing foods now than in 2011.[18]

Your current state of health can influence your perception of foods. For example, if you are overweight, you are more likely to be aware of the kilocalorie content of foods and avoid foods that are high in fat and sugar.[19] This can have a positive effect on health as long as body image concerns don't become extreme or cause disordered eating patterns.

The more aware you are of the effects of food choices on health, the more likely you are to make an effort to improve your eating habits, even when dining out.[20] If you believe that low-sodium foods decrease blood pressure or eating Greek yogurt with active cultures improves your digestion, you are more likely to choose these foods.

Advertising

Manufacturers spend $10 billion to $15 billion annually on food advertising, over $700 million of which is spent to market breakfast cereals, candy, and gum. Another $500 million is spent to advertise carbonated soft drinks.[21] You probably saw at least a few processed food ads as you surfed online, watched TV, or drove to campus today. In comparison, when was the last time you saw an advertisement for broccoli?

Food companies spend these large sums on advertising for one reason: They work, especially on young people.[22] American children view up to 40,000 television commercials annually. On Saturday morning, more than half of the between-cartoon ads are for foods. Of these, over 40 percent are for items such as candy, soft drinks, chips, and sugary breakfast cereals.

In contrast, commercials for fruits and vegetables are rare, which is unfortunate, because healthy foods can be successfully marketed. When the dairy industry

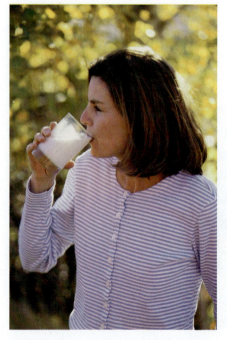

Rates of milk consumption increased after the *Got Milk?* advertising campaign.

noted a decline in milk consumption among Americans in 1994, it launched the *Got Milk?* ad campaign, which featured celebrities wearing milk mustaches. This campaign strove to make drinking milk sexy and it worked. Milk sales increased by nearly 1.5 billion pounds: the equivalent of about 45 pounds of milk sold for each advertising dollar spent.[23]

Time, Convenience, and Cost

When it comes to making a meal, time is often at a premium. Americans, especially working women with families, spend less than 30 minutes preparing a meal, including cleanup.[24] Consequently, supermarkets offer more prepared and partially prepared foods. If chicken is on the menu tonight, you can buy it uncooked at the meat counter in the supermarket, or you can go to the deli and buy it hot off the rotisserie, cooked and stuffed with bread crumbs, or grilled with teriyaki sauce. Rice or pasta side dishes and cooked vegetables are also available to complete the meal.

Convenience has also become more of a factor in food selection. Foods that are easily accessible to you are more likely to be eaten. Decades ago, the most convenient way to get a hot cup of coffee was to brew it at home. Today, Americans are more likely to get their latte or half-caff from one of the 17,000 coffee shops, carts, and kiosks across the United States.[25]

For reasons related to both time and convenience, people eat out more often today than they did a few decades ago. In the 1970s, Americans spent about 33 percent of their household food budget on eating out, compared with over 49 percent today.[26] Because cost is often an issue when considering where to eat out, most meals consumed away from home are fast food, which is often cheaper and quicker than more nutritious meals. Though cheap fast food may be easy on the pocketbook, it is taking its toll on the health of Americans. Epidemiological research suggests that low-cost, high-kilocalorie diets, such as those that incorporate lots of burgers, fries, tacos, and soft drinks, increase the risk of obesity, especially among those at lower socioeconomic levels.[27]

The good news is that cheaper food doesn't have to always mean fast food, and when healthy foods are offered at lower prices, people do buy them. More Americans are opting for boxes of fresh fruits and vegetables or meal kits delivered directly to their door. They may eat home-cooked meals more often because of this than before. However, the healthy kits are more expensive than preparing from scratch, but may be cheaper than ordering takeout or eating at a restaurant.[28]

Researchers have found that lowering the cost of fresh fruits, vegetables, and lower-fat snacks improves the consumption of these nutritious foods.[29] Results were consistent across various food types and populations. These studies demonstrate that price reductions are an effective strategy to increase the purchase of more-healthful foods.

Habits and Emotions

Your daily routine and habits often affect both when you eat and what you eat. For example, if you routinely start your day with a bowl of cereal and a glass of orange juice, you're not alone. Ready-to-eat cereals are the number-one breakfast food choice among Americans, and citrus juice is their top juice in the morning.[30] Many individuals habitually snack when watching television or sitting at the computer.[31]

For some individuals, emotions can sometimes drive food choice: feeling happy or sad can trigger eating. In some cases, appetite is suppressed during periods of sadness or depression. For many, food is used as an emotional crutch during times of stress, depression, or joy.

Although brown rice is a healthy whole-grain addition to any meal, it generally takes almost an hour to cook. For time-strapped consumers, food manufacturers have developed brown rice that cooks in 10 minutes, and a precooked, microwavable variety that reheats in less than 2 minutes.

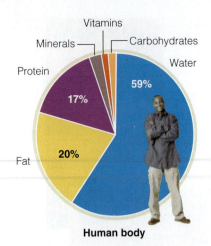

Human body

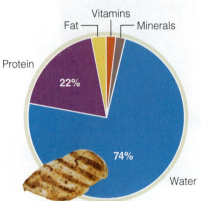

Chicken breast

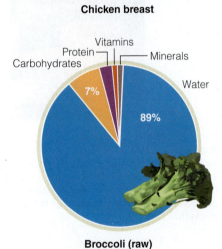

Broccoli (raw)

▲ **Figure 1.2 Nutrients in Foods and in the Body**
Water is the most abundant nutrient found in foods and in the body. Carbohydrates, fats, protein, vitamins, and minerals make up the rest. Note that foods also contain nonnutritive compounds, such as phytochemicals and fiber.

nutrition The science that studies how nutrients and compounds in foods nourish the body and affect body functions and overall health.

nutrients Compounds in foods that sustain body processes. There are six classes of nutrients: carbohydrates, fats (lipids), proteins, vitamins, minerals, and water.

LO 1.1: THE TAKE-HOME MESSAGE Taste and enjoyment are the primary reasons people prefer certain foods. A food's availability makes it more easily become part of a culture, and many foods can be regularly eaten out of habit. Advertising, food trends, limited time, convenience, emotions, and the perception that foods are healthy or unhealthy also influence food choices.

What Is Nutrition?

LO 1.2 Define the term nutrition and identify the essential nutrients.

The science of **nutrition** is the study of food and the nutrients we need to sustain life and reproduce. It examines the way food nourishes the body and affects health. Since its inception, the science of nutrition has explored how food is digested, absorbed, transported, metabolized, and used or stored in the body. Nutritional scientists study how much we need of each nutrient, the factors that influence our needs, and what happens if we don't consume enough. As with any science, nutrition is not stagnant. The more we discover about the relationship between nutrition and well-being, the greater the impact will be on long-term health.

Nutrients Are Essential Compounds in Food

The body is one large organism made up of millions of cells that grow, age, reproduce, and die, all without your noticing. You slough off millions of skin cells when you towel off after a shower, yet your skin isn't noticeably thinner today than it was last week. Your body replaces skin cells at a rate fast enough to keep you covered, and it manufactures new cells using the same nutrients found in a variety of foods. As cells die, **nutrients** from food provide the building blocks to replace them. Nutrients also provide the energy we need to perform all body functions and processes, from maintaining heart beat to playing tennis.

There are six categories of nutrients found in foods and in the body: carbohydrates, lipids (fats), protein, vitamins, minerals, and water. Foods also often contain nonnutrient compounds, such as phytochemicals or zoochemicals, nondigestible fiber, and other chemicals added by food manufacturers to enhance color, flavor, or texture, or extend shelf life.

Plant foods are made up of about 10 percent carbohydrates, fats, proteins, vitamins, and minerals (**Figure 1.2**). The rest is typically water, and plant foods contain more water (about 90 percent) than do animal foods (about 70 percent). Animal foods are comprised of about 30 percent protein, lipids, vitamins, and minerals. One unique quality of animal foods, with the exception of dairy products, is that they do not contain any carbohydrates by the time we consume them.

A healthy human body is about 60 percent water. The other 40 percent is made up of protein and fat, as well as a small amount of stored carbohydrates, minerals in the bone, and small amounts of vitamins. Thus, the old saying is true: *we are what we eat*, from the carbohydrates in broccoli to the proteins in meat; the six biochemical ingredients needed to sustain life are all provided by the foods in our diets.

Most Nutrients Are Organic

Carbohydrates, proteins, lipids, and vitamins are the most complex of the six classes of nutrients. These nutrients are **organic** because their chemical structures contain carbon. Organic nutrients also contain the elements hydrogen and oxygen, and in the case of proteins and some vitamins, nitrogen is also part of the molecule (**Figure 1.3**).

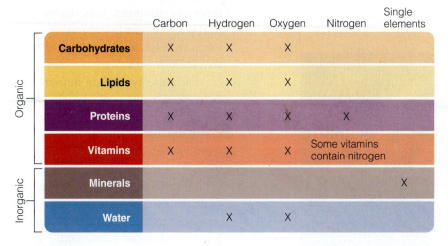

	Carbon	Hydrogen	Oxygen	Nitrogen	Single elements
Organic					
Carbohydrates	X	X	X		
Lipids	X	X	X		
Proteins	X	X	X	X	
Vitamins	X	X	X	Some vitamins contain nitrogen	
Inorganic					
Minerals					X
Water		X	X		

▲ Figure 1.3 The Chemical Composition of the Six Classifications of Nutrients in Food
Each nutrient contains a unique combination of chemical elements.

Minerals are the least complex of the nutrients and are **inorganic** because their chemical structure does not include carbon. Each mineral is an individual element, and its atoms are exactly the same whether found in food or in the body. For instance, the structure of zinc found in lean meats and nuts is the same as that found in a cell membrane or a hair follicle. Water, a three-atom molecule comprised of hydrogen and oxygen, is also inorganic.

Most Nutrients Are Essential

In general, nutrients are **essential** and must come from foods, because either they cannot be made in the body, or they cannot be made in sufficient amounts to meet the body's needs. A few **nonessential nutrients** can be made in sufficient quantities in the body. An example of this is vitamin D, which is synthesized in the skin upon exposure to sunlight. Under some circumstances, *nonessential* nutrients can become *essential*. We refer to these nutrients as *conditionally essential*. In the case of vitamin D, if you are not exposed to enough sunlight, you will not be able to synthesize an adequate amount of the vitamin. You must then obtain vitamin D from foods.

Some Nutrients Provide Energy

All creatures need energy in order to function, and humans are no exception. **Energy** is defined as the capacity to do work and provides a source of heat. The body derives chemical energy from certain nutrients in foods, which store energy in their chemical bonds. During digestion and metabolism, the bonds are broken, and the energy is released. This chemical energy released when the foods are digested can be converted into **adenosine triphosphate (ATP)**, a form of energy the body can use. Carbohydrates, lipids (fats), and proteins are defined as the **energy-yielding nutrients** because they contribute energy to the body. Alcohol, although not a nutrient, also provides energy.

Energy in foods is measured in kilocalories. A **kilocalorie** is the term used by scientists to quantify the amount of energy found in a food. The term kilocalorie (*kilo* = 1,000) is defined as the amount of energy needed to raise the temperature of one kilogram of water 1 degree Celsius. A kilocalorie is not the same as a *calorie* (with a lowercase "c"), which is a much smaller unit of measurement. (In fact, a "calorie" is so small that one slice of bread contains about 63,000 calories.) One kilocalorie is equal to 1,000 calories.

To add to the confusion, the term Calorie (with an uppercase "C") is used on nutrition labels to express the energy content of foods and is often used in science

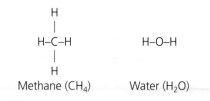

Carbohydrates
4 kcal/g

Fats
9 kcal/g

Protein
4 kcal/g

Alcohol
7 kcal/g

▲ **Figure 1.4 Nutrients and Alcohol Provide Kilocalories to Fuel the Body**
Carbohydrates, fats, protein, and alcohol provide energy, or kilocalories.

textbooks to mean kilocalories. This textbook will refer to the units of energy found in foods as kilocalories, abbreviated kcalories or kcals.

Each energy-yielding nutrient provides a set number of kilocalories per gram. Thus the number of kilocalories in one serving of a given food can be determined based on the amount (weight, in grams) of carbohydrates, protein, and fat in the food. Carbohydrates and protein provide 4 kilocalories per gram; so, for example, a food that contains 5 grams of carbohydrate and 3 grams of protein would have 32 kilocalories ([5 × 4] + [3 × 4] = 32). Fats yield 9 kilocalories per gram, more than twice the number of kilocalories in either carbohydrates or protein. Alcohol contains 7 kilocalories per gram, which must be taken into account when calculating the energy of alcohol-containing foods and beverages (**Figure 1.4**).

Calculation Corner

Calculating Kilocalories in a Meal

Suppose you ate an entire bag of potato chips and drank a 16-ounce cola while you studied for an exam. Together these two items contain 144 grams of carbohydrate (in the cola and chips), 12 grams of protein (from the chips), and 60 grams of fat (also in the chips). How many kilocalories did you consume?

(a) To calculate the total kilocalories in this snack, multiply the total grams of each energy nutrient times the number of kilocalories per gram of that nutrient. Remember, a gram of carbohydrate and protein each contain 4 kilocalories and a gram of fat contains 9 kilocalories.

(144 g × 4 kcals/g) + (12 g × 4 kcals/g) + (60 g × 9 kcals/g) = 1,164 kcals
576 kcals + 48 kcals + 540 kcals = 1,164 kcals

In one sitting, you consumed more than 1,100 kilocalories, which for some people may be more than half of the amount they need to meet their daily energy requirement. If behaviors like this become habits, they can quickly result in weight gain.

(b) Another useful measure for assessing the nutritional quality of the snack is the percentage of fat, protein, and/or carbohydrate found in the food (you will learn in later chapters that there are ranges for each nutrient that are considered part of a healthy diet). For example, what percent of kilocalories in the chips and soda is from fat? To answer this question, divide the fat kilocalories by the total kilocalories in the food and multiply by 100:

(540 kcals ÷ 1,164 kcals) × 100 = 46% fat

Almost half of the kilocalories in this snack are from fat. Do you think this is likely to be a desirable proportion?

For practice, complete the same calculations for carbohydrate and protein.

Scan this QR code with your mobile device to access practice math activities. You can also access the activities in **Mastering**Nutrition™.

Covalent Bonds

A chemical reaction unites two atoms by creating a covalent bond to form a new molecule. This covalent bond is formed when atoms share their electrons, as in the case of water. The oxygen atoms require two additional electrons and the hydrogen atoms need one electron to be stable. When these three atoms combine, the oxygen shares one electron with each of the hydrogen atoms and the hydrogen atoms share one electron with the oxygen atom. The atoms are held together because of their affinity to share each other's electrons. The covalent bond that is formed is strong and difficult to break. Trapped within the bonds is stored energy that is released when the bonds are broken.

Use the Calculation Corner to determine the number of kilocalories in a potato-chip-and-cola snack.

Energy in foods and in the body is trapped within the bonds that keep the molecules together. When the bonds are broken during the process of metabolism, a significant amount of energy, including some heat, is released. The energy can then be used to digest and absorb the meal, contract muscles, fuel the heart, and synthesize new cells, as well as other functions.

People's energy needs vary according to their age, gender, and activity level. Males generally need more energy because they weigh more, and have more muscle mass (which requires more kilocalories to function) and less body fat. A younger person requires more energy than an older adult because he is still growing and is therefore synthesizing more new tissue. Physically active individuals require more energy than sedentary people to fuel their activities and meet their body's basic energy needs.

Energy that is not used to fuel the body will be stored, predominantly as fat, for later use. If you regularly consume more kilocalories than you expend, you will accumulate stored fat in adipose tissue and gain weight. The opposite is also true. Eating fewer kilocalories than the body needs will result in the breakdown of stored energy and weight loss.

LO 1.2: THE TAKE-HOME MESSAGE Nutrition is the science of how the nutrients and compounds in foods nourish the body, and how the body uses nutrients to manufacture and replace cells, and produce energy. Carbohydrates, lipids, proteins, and vitamins are organic nutrients composed of the chemical elements carbon, hydrogen, oxygen, and sometimes nitrogen. Minerals and water are inorganic because they don't contain carbon. Energy in foods is measured in kilocalories. The energy-yielding nutrients—carbohydrates (4 kilocalories per gram), lipids (9 kilocalories per gram), and proteins (4 kilocalories per gram)—provide fuel to be used by the body or stored for future use. Alcohol (7 kilocalories per gram) is not a nutrient but does provide energy.

What Are the Primary Roles of the Individual Nutrients?

LO 1.3 Explain the primary roles of essential nutrients found in food.

Individual nutrients supply energy, regulate metabolism, and provide structure (Table 1.1). Some nutrients, including carbohydrates, lipids, proteins, and water, are called **macronutrients** (*macro* means large) because they are needed in much larger amounts to support normal functioning. Vitamins and minerals, though equally important to health, are considered **micronutrients** (*micro* means small) because they are required in smaller amounts to perform their key roles. We introduce each of the six classifications of nutrients briefly in this chapter; they are discussed in much greater detail later in the textbook.

Carbohydrates Are the Primary Energy Source

All forms of carbohydrates are composed of carbon (*carbo*-), hydrogen, and oxygen (*hydrate* means water). Carbohydrates supply the simple sugar, glucose, which is the primary source of energy for several body cell types, including red blood cells and brain cells.

Carbohydrates are found in most foods. Breads, cereals, legumes, nuts, fruits, vegetables, and dairy products are all rich in carbohydrates. The only foods that do not provide significant amounts of carbohydrates are animal products other than dairy, such as eggs, meat, poultry, and fish. (Chapter 4 covers carbohydrates in detail.)

Lipids Also Provide Energy

The term *lipid* refers to a diverse group of organic compounds including fats (also called triglycerides), oils, phospholipids, and sterols that are insoluble in water. These nutrients contain the same chemical elements as carbohydrates, including carbon, hydrogen, and oxygen. The difference is that lipids are much more concentrated than carbohydrates and contain less oxygen and water.

Triglycerides make up the majority of the lipids we eat and are found in margarine, butter, oils, and animal products. Triglycerides are an important energy source for the body, especially during rest and sleep. The body stores excess energy as triglycerides in the adipose tissue beneath the skin, which insulates the body and cushions the organs. (Chapter 5 presents more information on lipids.)

Carbohydrates are found in a variety of foods, including breads, grains, and pasta.

macronutrients Organic nutrients, including the energy-containing carbohydrates, lipids, and proteins, and water that the body needs in large amounts.

micronutrients Essential nutrients the body needs in smaller amounts: vitamins and minerals.

TABLE 1.1	Functions of the Major Nutrients by Type			
	Nutrient	**Provides Energy**	**Participates in Growth, Maintenance, Support, or Structure**	**Regulates Body Processes**
Macronutrients	Carbohydrates	Yes	No	No
	Protein	Yes	Yes	Yes
	Fats	Yes	Yes	Yes
	Water	No	Yes	Yes
Micronutrients	Vitamins	No	Yes	Yes
	Minerals	No	Yes	Yes

Proteins Provide the Building Blocks for Tissue Synthesis

Proteins contribute the basic building blocks, known as amino acids, to synthesize, grow, and maintain tissues in the body. The tissues in muscles, bones, and skin are primarily made up of protein. Proteins also participate as neurotransmitters in the complex communication network between the brain and the rest of the body, and they play a role in the immune system and as **enzymes** that catalyze chemical reactions.

Proteins are similar in composition to carbohydrates and lipids in that they contain carbon, hydrogen, and oxygen. But proteins are unique in that they all contain the element nitrogen, and some also contain sulfur. Proteins can be used for energy but are usually not the primary energy source.

Protein is found in a variety of foods, including meats, dairy products, and legumes such as soy, nuts, and seeds. Whole grains, vegetables, and some fruits contain smaller amounts of protein. (Chapter 6 covers protein in detail.)

Meats and dairy products are excellent sources of protein. Plant products, such as nuts, seeds, and legumes, also provide protein to the diet.

Vitamins and Minerals Play Vital Roles in Metabolism

Vitamins and minerals do not provide energy, but they are involved in numerous key functions in the body. They are essential to help regulate metabolism, for example, and without them we would be unable to use carbohydrates, fats, and proteins for energy or to sustain numerous chemical reactions. A deficiency of vitamins and minerals can cause a cascade of ill health effects ranging from fatigue to stunted growth, weak bones, and organ damage. The metabolic fate of carbohydrates, protein, and fats in the body depends on consuming enough vitamins and minerals in the daily diet.

Vitamins

Many vitamins function as **coenzymes,** that is, they help enzymes catalyze reactions in the body. For example, the B vitamin thiamin attaches to and assists an enzyme involved in carbohydrate metabolism. Vitamins also activate enzymes that participate in building bone and muscle, energy production, fighting infections, and maintaining healthy nerves and vision.

There are 13 known vitamins, and each has a unique chemical structure. They are grouped into two classifications according to their **solubility,** which affects how they are absorbed, stored, and excreted. **Water-soluble vitamins,** which include vitamin C and the eight B-complex vitamins, are easily absorbed and excreted by the body, and need to be consumed daily. The **fat-soluble vitamins,** A, D, E, and K, are stored in the liver and other organs and thus don't need to be consumed on a daily basis. (Vitamins are described in Chapters 9 and 10.)

A wide variety of fruits and vegetables are abundant sources of water-soluble vitamins.

enzymes Proteins in living cells that act as catalysts and control chemical reactions.

coenzymes Substances, such as vitamins or minerals, that facilitate the activity of enzymes.

solubility The ability to dissolve into another substance.

water-soluble vitamins Vitamins that dissolve in water; they generally cannot be stored in the body and must be consumed daily.

fat-soluble vitamins Vitamins that dissolve in fat and can be stored in the body.

major minerals Minerals found in the body in amounts greater than 5 grams; also referred to as macrominerals.

Minerals

Minerals are inorganic substances that assist in body processes and are essential to the structure of hard tissues, such as bone, and soft tissues, including the red blood cells. Minerals such as calcium and phosphorus work with protein-containing hormones and enzymes to maintain and strengthen teeth and bones. A deficiency of any of the minerals can cause disease symptoms. Falling short of daily iron needs, for example, can cause fatigue and impair your immunity.

Minerals are classified by the amount needed in the diet and total content found in the body. **Major minerals** are needed in amounts of at least 100 milligrams per day, and are found in amounts of at least 5 grams in the body. Calcium and magnesium are two examples of major minerals. In addition to the structure of bones and teeth, some major minerals help maintain fluid balance, participate in energy production, and participate in muscle contractions. (Details on each individual major mineral are discussed in Chapter 12.)

Trace minerals are needed in amounts of less than 100 milligrams per day and are found in amounts of less than 5 grams in the body. Iron and zinc are two examples of trace minerals. Among other functions, trace minerals transport oxygen and carbon dioxide, participate in cell growth and development, control the metabolic rate, and play a role as antioxidants. (Chapter 13 provides more specific detail on the role of these trace minerals.)

Water Is Critical for Numerous Functions

Some of the essential roles of water in the body probably seem obvious, as it makes up the majority of all body fluids, including digestive secretions, blood, urine, and perspiration. Less obvious is the fact that water is part of every cell in the body, from muscle and bone cells to brain and nerve cells. Water is also vital to several key body functions. It is essential during metabolism, for example, because it provides the medium in which metabolic reactions take place. Water functions in digestion and absorption, and as a transport medium that delivers nutrients and oxygen to the cells and excretes waste products through the urine. Water helps maintain body temperature and acts as a lubricant for the joints, eyes, mouth, and intestinal tract. It surrounds vital organs and cushions them from injury. Because the body can't store water, it must be replenished every day to maintain hydration. (The role of water in the body is discussed in detail in Chapter 11.)

> **LO 1.3: THE TAKE-HOME MESSAGE** The six classes of essential nutrients, carbohydrates, lipids (fats), protein, vitamins, minerals, and water, each have specific roles in the body. Carbohydrates, fats, and protein provide energy, while vitamins, minerals, and water are needed to use the energy-producing nutrients and for various body processes.

How Can You Be Sure to Meet Your Nutrient Needs?

LO 1.4 Describe the best dietary approach to meet your nutrient needs.

There is no question that you need all six classes of nutrients to function properly. A chronic deficiency of even one nutrient will impact the body's ability to function in the short term. Over time, chronic deficiencies, excesses, and imbalances will affect long-term health.

Is there an advantage to consuming the essential nutrients through food rather than taking them as supplements? Is there more to a healthy diet than just meeting your basic nutrient needs?

The Best Approach to Meet Nutrient Needs Is a Well-Balanced Diet

Most credible nutrition experts will tell you that the best way to maintain nutritional health is to eat a variety of whole foods, including whole grains, fruits, vegetables, lean meats, and low-fat dairy. Among the reasons for this recommendation is that many foods provide a variety of nutrients. For example, low-fat milk is high

Healthy eating is a way of life.

trace minerals Minerals found in the body in amounts less than 5 grams; also referred to as microminerals.

in carbohydrates and protein, and provides a small amount of fat. Milk is also a good source of the vitamins A, D, and riboflavin, as well as the minerals potassium and calcium, and is approximately 90 percent water by weight.

Whole foods and a well-balanced diet will also provide other dietary compounds, including phytochemicals, zoochemicals, and fiber, which have been shown to help fight many diseases. Further, whole foods almost always contain more than one beneficial compound.

Improving Health through Functional Foods, Phytochemicals, and Zoochemicals

Americans have been consuming **functional foods** to improve their health since the late 1920s, when iodine was first added to salt. Today's functional foods include whole foods such as oatmeal, genetically modified foods that are developed to have a higher nutrient content, and foods that contain or have been fortified with **phytochemicals** and **zoochemicals.**

Phytochemicals are nonnutritive plant chemicals found in foods that reduce your risk of developing certain diseases. At least 900 different phytochemicals have been identified in foods and more are likely to be discovered. For example, lutein is found in spinach, lycopene is found in tomatoes, and anthocyanins are found in dark purple grapes. The disease-fighting properties of phytochemicals may be due to more than the compounds themselves. It is the interactions between the phytochemicals and fiber, nutrients, or other unknown substances in the food itself that provide the health benefits. These compounds can't be extracted from foods and put in a pill and still produce the same positive health effects. Foods with phytochemicals added, such as phytosterols added to margarine, have the same appearance and taste as your favorites but provide added health benefits.

Zoochemicals are naturally occurring chemicals found in animal foods that have health-enhancing properties such as strong antioxidant benefits.[32] Examples include lutein and zeaxanthin found in egg yolks, which may protect against macular degeneration or the formation of cataracts. Omega-3 fatty acids from fish, added to butter substitutes and eggs, may improve heart health and reduce inflammation, protecting us against heart disease, cancer, and a decline in cognitive function.

Some Nutrient Needs Can Be Met with a Supplement

Some individuals with diet restrictions or higher nutrient needs may benefit from taking a supplement if they cannot meet their nutrient requirements through whole foods alone. For example, someone who is lactose intolerant (has difficulty digesting milk products) has to meet his or her calcium needs from sources other than dairy products. A calcium-fortified food, such as orange juice, or a calcium supplement would be an option for such an individual. Pregnant women should take an iron supplement because their increased need for this mineral is unlikely to be met through a healthy diet alone.

Note that a well-balanced diet and dietary supplements aren't mutually exclusive. In some situations, the use of enriched and fortified foods can be partnered with dietary supplements as the best nutritional strategy for good health.

> **LO 1.4: THE TAKE-HOME MESSAGE** A well-balanced diet is the best way to meet all nutrient needs and also provide a variety of compounds that may help prevent chronic diseases. People who cannot meet their nutrient needs through food alone may benefit from taking a supplement or consuming functional foods high in phytochemicals and zoochemicals to reduce the risk of developing certain diseases.

functional foods Foods that may provide additional health benefits beyond the basic nutrient value.

phytochemicals Nonnutritive plant compounds, found in fruits and vegetables, that may play a role in fighting chronic diseases.

zoochemicals Nonnutritive animal compounds that play a role in fighting chronic diseases.

How Can You Use Diet to Improve Your Health?

LO 1.5 Summarize how a healthy diet improves health.

A healthy diet has long been associated with improving overall health. Good nutrition reduces the risk of four of the top ten leading causes of death in the United States, including the top two—heart disease and cancer—as well as stroke and diabetes (Table 1.2). Nutrition also plays an important role in preventing other diseases and conditions that can impede one's lifestyle. A healthy diet, for example, can keep bones strong and reduce the risk of developing osteoporosis. Eating well will also improve body weight, which in turn will reduce the risk of developing obesity, diabetes mellitus, and high blood pressure. A healthy diet maximizes nutrient-dense whole foods, has a moderate intake of lean meats and low-fat dairy, and minimizes processed foods.

The relationship between food and health has changed drastically over several centuries as people have realized the beneficial effects of foods. For example, in the 1600s it was discovered that citrus juice prevents scurvy; the British Navy supplied sailors with limes, and the term "limey" for a British sailor was born. During the 1700s, scientists recognized the value of what we eat in treating disease, so that by the early 1900s the concept of *essential nutrients* had been widely accepted. By the late nineteenth century, nutrition was becoming more quantitative, addressing the question of how much of each nutrient is required as well as accepting that individuals vary in their nutrient requirements. Nutrition epidemiology had been developed by the end of the twentieth century, and the advent of dietary surveys conducted by the government was used to further the science. Nutrition in the twenty-first century has evolved to developing new functional foods and nutraceuticals, and designing diets for longevity rather than just for preventing chronic disease. The completion of the Human Genome Project in 2003 has enabled nutritionists and researchers to actively examine the synergistic effects of nutrition and genetics. These efforts may eventually result in more personalized gene-driven diet plans.

TABLE 1.2	Leading Causes of Death in the United States
Disease/Cause of Death	**Nutrition Related**
1. **Heart Disease**	X
2. **Cancer**	X
3. Respiratory Diseases	
4. **Stroke**	X
5. Accidents	
6. Alzheimer's Disease	
7. **Diabetes**	X
8. Kidney Disease	
9. Influenza and Pneumonia	
10. Suicide	

Source: Centers for Disease Control. 2013. *National Vital Statistics Reports.* 62 (6): 1–97. Available at www.cdc.gov.

Genetics and Nutrition Combine to Impact Health Risks

Most chronic diseases stem from the interplay between our genetic makeup, our environment, and our diet (**Figure 1.5**). Each one of us carries a unique combination of genes that were transferred from our parents. These genes are responsible for what we look like, our metabolism, and our susceptibility to disease. Some of our genes have variations in their codes, which make us more susceptible to diseases including cancer, cardiovascular disease, and diabetes, whereas other gene variants enhance our ability to resist chronic disease. Variants alone don't cause the disease; instead they increase the risk that the disease will develop given a conducive environment.

The interactions between genes and your environment are complex. Scientific advances point to a variety of mechanisms in which the environment and genes interact to increase or decrease your risk of disease. While you can't change the genetic cards you are dealt, you can change your environment or the way you play the game.

Research suggests that the nutrients we eat attach to proteins that bind to DNA or to the cell surface. This reaction either increases or decreases **gene expression,** producing greater or smaller amounts of proteins, which in turn affects body function. For example, if your genetic makeup includes a gene variant that responds to salt, the gene expression results in a higher blood pressure when exposed to a high-salt diet. When you reduce dietary salt, blood pressure drops. Individuals without these gene variants who develop hypertension would not benefit from a low-salt diet and must rely on other means, including medications, to reduce high blood pressure.

The area of research that studies the relationship between gene expression, nutrition, and health, called **nutritional genomics,** may have far-reaching effects on health and disease. Until this new science emerged, nutrition research and the study of genetics contributed separately to the body of knowledge about chronic disease. Studied together, these two fields help us understand the interaction between genes and nutrients, and whether the genes are responding to the nutrients we eat (nutrigenetics), or whether the nutrients themselves influence genetic expression (nutrigenomics).

Recent advances in nutritional genomics have already yielded potential clinical applications. For example, research has shown that chronic inflammation can be reduced with certain bioactive compounds found in food, including resveratrol in the skin of red grapes,[33] theaflavins in tea, omega-3 fatty acids in flaxseed and fish, and lactones in chicory (a coffee substitute).[34] Adding foods to the diet that contain these compounds may regulate the gene expression that causes inflammation.

Nutritional genomics may have tremendous potential to provide personalized dietary recommendations based on an individual's genetic makeup. Ultimately, future Registered Dietitian Nutritionists may be able to use this information to recommend diet modifications that are specific to a patient's DNA.

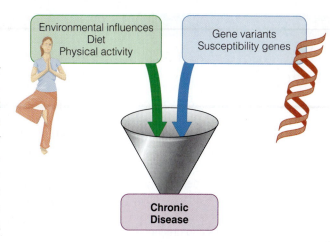

▲ **Figure 1.5 Chronic Disease Is a Mixture of Genetic Influences and Our Environment**

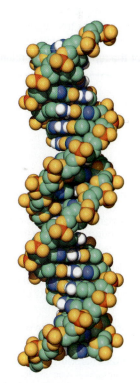

The study of nutritional genomics may one day allow individuals to tailor their diets based on their DNA.

LO 1.5: THE TAKE-HOME MESSAGE Eating a well-balanced diet that includes a mixture of the six classifications of nutrients is the best way to stay healthy and reduce the risk of developing four of the top ten leading causes of death in the United States, including heart disease, cancer, stroke, and diabetes. A healthy diet may modify the way your genetic makeup and the environment interact to increase or decrease your risk of disease.

gene expression The processing of genetic information to create a specific protein.

nutritional genomics A field of study of the relationship between genes, gene expression, and nutrition.

How Healthy Is Your Family Tree?

You inherited your DNA from your parents, so the extent to which DNA affects health is largely hereditary. Does your family have a history of heart disease, diabetes, or obesity? What about other chronic diseases or conditions? Before you learn about the role that healthy eating plays in preventing chronic diseases, ask your parents and grandparents about your family's health history. If there are certain diseases or conditions that run in your family, you'll want to pay particular attention to these as you learn more throughout this book.

An easy way to gather information about your family's health history is by visiting My Family Health Portrait at http://familyhistory.hhs.gov. The site generates a family tree report according to the medical history you enter. Save a copy of the report for future reference.

malnourished A condition that results when the body does not receive the right amount of essential nutrients to maintain health; overnourished and undernourished are forms of malnutrition.

undernourished A condition in which the individual lacks sufficient energy or is deficient in quality or quantity of essential nutrients.

overnourished The condition of having consumed excess energy or nutrients.

Registered Dietitian Nutritionist (RDN) A health professional who is a food and nutrition expert; RDNs obtain a college degree in nutrition from an Academy of Nutrition and Dietetics–accredited program, and pass a national exam to become a Registered Dietitian Nutritionist.

acute Describes a sudden onset of symptoms or disease.

chronic Describes a symptom or condition that lasts over a long period of time.

malabsorption A problem associated with the lack of absorption of nutrients through the intestinal tract.

How Do We Assess Nutritional Status?

LO 1.6 Summarize the ABCD method used to assess the nutrient status of individuals and populations.

How do you know if you are eating enough of the essential nutrients? A person's *state of nutrition* is usually described as either healthy or **malnourished.** Someone who lacks a specific nutrient, or isn't consuming enough energy, is **undernourished,** which means that person is at risk of losing too much weight or developing a disease related to a nutrient deficiency. In contrast, an individual who overconsumes a particular nutrient, or eats too many kilocalories, is described as being **overnourished.** This person runs the risk of becoming overweight, developing diseases such as diabetes or heart disease, and potentially accumulating toxic amounts of a specific nutrient in the body.

A variety of methods are used to assess both under- and overnutrition of individuals. No one measurement is sufficient to determine malnutrition, and thus a combination of tools is used (see **Table 1.3**). If you suspect you may not be meeting all of your nutrient needs, or that you are suffering from a nutrition-related disease or condition, turn to a nutrition professional, such as a **Registered Dietitian Nutritionist (RDN),** to determine your current nutrition status. An RDN or nurse will conduct a complete assessment to find out if you are getting too much, too little, or the right amount of a nutrient.

Use the ABCD Method to Assess the Nutritional Status of Individuals

Part of evaluating a person's current nutrition status is to look at that person's health history, including any experiences with **acute** or **chronic** illness, and diagnostic procedures, therapies, or treatments that may increase nutrient needs or induce **malabsorption.** Does the patient have a family history of diabetes or heart disease? Has the patient been overweight or underweight in the past?

Registered Dietitian Nutritionists use a number of specialized methods to assess the nutrition status of individuals, including dietary intake assessments, collecting anthropometric data, conducting physical exams, and collecting laboratory data.

TABLE 1.3	The ABCDs of Nutrition Assessment	
Type of Assessment	**Measurements**	**What They Determine**
Anthropometric	Height Weight Body mass index Waist-to-hip ratio Waist circumference	Growth, obesity, changes in weight, and risk of developing chronic diseases such as diabetes and heart disease
Biochemical	Blood, urine, and feces	Protein, mineral, and vitamin status and disease
Clinical	Observe hair, fingernails, skin, lips, mouth, muscles, joints, overall appearance	Signs of deficiencies and excesses of nutrients
Dietary Intake	Diet history Diet record Food frequency questionnaire 24-hour dietary recall	Usual nutrient intake, and deficiencies or excesses of various nutrients

Assessing Dietary Intake through Questionnaires and Interviews

Questioning an individual about his or her dietary intake and diet history is an important aspect of a nutrition assessment. A detailed diet history is conducted by a skilled researcher who knows just what types of questions to ask to help a patient remember not only current food intake but food intake in the past.

Two tools used to collect dietary intake data are questionnaires and interviews. Food frequency questionnaires (FFQs) and food records can be used to gather information about how often a specific food or category of food is eaten. A nutrition interview can reveal data about lifestyle habits, such as how many meals are eaten daily, where they are eaten, and who prepares them.

One of the easiest ways to determine an individual's intake of nutrients is to use the *food frequency questionnaire* (FFQ). This form of assessment provides evidence of consumption patterns over time. For example, if you wanted to determine the usual calcium intake over time of an older woman with osteoporosis, an FFQ could be used to indicate the number of servings "per day, per week, and per month," as well as whether she "seldom" or "never" consumes milk, cheese, or yogurt. The FFQ is a reasonably reliable, accurate, and inexpensive method to assess usual intake.[35]

This assessment tool is not as helpful in assessing the actual grams consumed of a nutrient, nor does it always accurately reveal usual intake. For that information, a food record or 24-hour dietary recall usually provides a better picture.[36]

A *food record* is simply a diary of what foods and beverages are eaten, how much, and when they are eaten over a defined period of time. Food records are often kept for three to seven days and are considered by some to be one of the best methods for collecting diet information. There are drawbacks to this method. The accuracy depends on the individual's skill and commitment to keeping a valid record. Many people start out strong and then lose interest or simply forget to record the food. Or, they might alter their usual food intake to avoid feeling embarrassed about what they eat.

Food records can be kept in written form, such as a journal, or with an electronic diet analysis program. There are also new handheld devices being tested that may help improve the accuracy, ease, and evaluation of recording dietary intake.[37]

The FFQ or a diet record should be selected based on the specific information the assessor needs to know, such as iron intake over time and how much iron the individual eats daily, as well as the assessor's ability to complete the instrument accurately. The information obtained from these tools is then compared with current dietary standards, which we discuss in the next chapter.

The *24-hour dietary recall* method is a quick assessment conducted by a trained interviewer who asks a patient to recall all the food and drink, including snacks, eaten the previous day. This tool relies on the skills of the interviewer and the individual's ability to remember what he ate and drank the day before. Because dietary intake varies from one day to the next, one 24-hour period may not provide an accurate estimate of typical intake.

A handwritten food diary can be a useful tool for assessing nutritional status.

Collecting Anthropometric Data

Data about body size or body composition is also called *anthropometric data*. In adults, this usually means height, weight, **body mass index (BMI),** waist-to-hip ratios, and waist circumference. For children, growth charts have been developed that compare height to weight, as well as how a child's height and weight compare with others of the same age. All of these measurements are easily obtained with a scale and tape measure.

The BMI is a measure of weight relative to height, and waist circumference measures abdominal fat. Body composition measurements can provide data on an individual's lean body tissue and the percent body fat, depending on the tool

body mass index (BMI) A measurement calculated using the metric formula of weight in kilograms divided by height in meters squared; used to determine whether an individual is underweight, at a healthy weight, or overweight or obese.

used. These measurements can be assessed with specialized equipment, such as skin calipers, or more expensive equipment, such as the Bod Pod. (We discuss these measurements in greater detail in Chapter 14.)

Data collected from anthropometric measurements is then compared with reference standards. Patterns and trends become evident when more than one measurement is taken over time and compared with the initial values. By combining the results of the BMI and waist circumference with other information gathered during the nutrition assessment, an individual's risk of developing diseases associated with obesity, such as diabetes and heart disease, can be determined.

Conducting a Physical Examination

A person who is malnourished will exhibit physical symptoms as the body adjusts to the lack or overaccumulation of nutrients. Therefore, several parts of the body can be inspected during a clinical exam for evidence of poor nutrition. Observing the hair, skin, eyes, fingernails, tongue, and lips of an individual can provide clues that point to under- or overnutrition. For example, cracks at the corners of the mouth can be evidence of B vitamin deficiencies, while small pinpoint hemorrhages on the skin may reflect a deficiency of vitamin C. Observations of physical symptoms should be followed up by more direct measurements, including laboratory assessments.

Collecting Biochemical Data

Laboratory tests based on body fluids, including blood and urine, can be important indicators of nutritional status, but they are also influenced by nonnutritional factors. Biochemical tests assess nutritional status by measuring the nutrient levels in body fluids, how fast a nutrient is excreted through the urine, and the metabolic by-products of various nutrients found in urine. For example, low levels of albumin (a blood protein) in the serum reflect protein deficiency; low hemoglobin levels in the blood indicate iron-deficiency anemia; and a high fasting blood sugar level may suggest diabetes.

Surveys Are Used to Assess the Nutritional Status of a Population Group

Assessing the nutritional status of an individual in a clinical setting is one thing, but how do we determine the nutritional status of a population? What percentage of Americans is meeting the dietary recommendations for healthy eating? To find out, we collect dietary intake information on a large scale. Such information allows researchers to determine the adequacy of the current recommendations for different population groups, to evaluate and develop food assistance programs, and to assess risk.

Assessing groups of people involves gathering the same type of information used to evaluate individuals, usually through the use of surveys.

Conduct or Review National Surveys

Numerous national surveys have been developed by a variety of federal agencies to assess the health and nutritional status of Americans. These surveys, such as the National Health and Nutrition Examination Survey (NHANES), collect and publish reliable data that has been used to develop the current dietary recommendations.

The National Health and Nutrition Examination Survey (NHANES) is a series of surveys established to determine the nutritional status of Americans of all ages and to monitor their risk behaviors over time. The intake of carbohydrates, lipids, protein, vitamins, minerals, and fiber has been collected using a 24-hour recall method and reported in the document *What We Eat In America*.

The Framingham Heart Study, which coined the term "risk factors," had a major impact on the dietary intake of Americans. This study used surveys to collect longitudinal data on two generations and more than 10,000 participants to establish the current recommendations for cardiovascular disease. For instance, once the connection between blood cholesterol levels and heart disease was revealed, the common bacon-and-eggs breakfast eaten by most Americans in 1948 was replaced with whole grains and low-fat dairy.

> **LO 1.6: THE TAKE-HOME MESSAGE** An individual's nutritional status is assessed by gathering information from health history, dietary record, and anthropometric, clinical, and biochemical (laboratory) data. When the information from several tools is viewed together, a comprehensive picture of the individual's nutritional status can be determined. The National Health and Nutrition Examination Survey (NHANES) is used to determine the nutritional status of a large population. The Framingham Heart Study provided the foundation for the current dietary recommendations for heart health.

How Healthy Is the Average American Diet?

LO 1.7 Discuss the current nutritional state of the average American diet.

The food supply in the United States provides an array of nutritious choices to meet the dietary needs of Americans. Fresh fruits and vegetables, whole grains, lean meats, fish, and poultry are easily accessible and affordable through local grocery stores and farmers' markets. With such an abundance of healthy foods to choose from, are Americans adopting healthy diets?

The Quality of the American Diet Needs Improvement

In general, Americans eat too much added sugar, sodium, and saturated fat, and too little fiber and some vitamins and minerals. Our low fiber intake is partly due to inadequate consumption of fruits and vegetables and overconsumption of refined grains.[38] While dietary fiber intakes are below recommended levels, added sugars account for almost 16 percent of America's daily kilocalories. This is largely due to Americans' love of soft drinks, other sugary beverages, and sweets and treats.[39]

The fat intake of most Americans ranges at the high end of the recommendation, at about 33 percent. The American diet contains too much saturated fat, but most Americans don't exceed the recommended dietary cholesterol intake limit of 300 milligrams per day.[40]

American men meet their recommendations for most vitamins and minerals, but women fall short of many nutrients—iron, for example. Americans in general eat too much sodium, but not enough vitamin D, potassium, and calcium.[41] In an attempt to balance their poor choice in foods, 50 percent of Americans take at least one vitamin or mineral supplement per day.[42]

The lack of a healthy diet may be due to *where* we eat. Today, many Americans eat their meals away from home.[43] Some of us eat in the car, or buy prepared foods from the supermarket or takeout meals. When we eat at home, it's often in front of the television or the computer screen. Research reports that meals eaten while watching television are usually lower in fruits and vegetables and higher in fat and soft drinks. Families are improving their patterns of eating together. Eighty-six

2012

Prevalence of self-reported obesity

▢ 15%–<20%	▉ 30%–<35%
▢ 20%–<25%	▉ ≥35%
▢ 25%–<30%	

▲ **Figure 1.6 Obesity Trends among U.S. Adults**
Over the past few decades, rates of overweight and obesity have risen significantly in the United States.

Source: Centers for Disease Control. 2013. "Prevalence of Self-Reported Obesity among U.S. Adults." Available at www.cdc.gov.

overweight For adults, having a BMI greater than 24.9.

obesity For adults, having a BMI greater than 29.9.

Healthy People 2020 A set of disease prevention and health promotion objectives for Americans to meet during the second decade of the twenty-first century.

percent of Americans eat dinner with all or most of their family at least twice a week and only 14 percent report never eating together with family.[44]

The majority of Americans understand the positive benefits of eating breakfast but only 34 percent actually take the time to eat it.[45] Breakfast provides about 18 percent of the fiber and energy, and 25 percent of the vitamins A and C, folate, calcium, and iron that we need to consume each day.

Rates of Overweight and Obesity in Americans Are Too High

As people take in more kilocalories than they burn, usually due to sedentary lifestyles, they create a recipe for poor health. This is reflected in the high rates of **overweight** and **obesity** in the United States (see **Figure 1.6**). Over 35 percent of American adults are obese regardless of their gender, age, race, ethnicity, socioeconomic status, education level, or geographical region.[46] These rates are too high, and reducing them is a top priority.

Along with the weight gain have come higher rates of type 2 diabetes, particularly among children, and increased rates of heart disease, cancer, and stroke.

Healthy People 2020 Provide Health Objectives for Americans

The U.S. Surgeon General has issued calls for a nationwide health improvement program since 1979. The latest edition of this report, *Healthy People 2020,* contains a set of health objectives for the nation to achieve over the second decade of the twenty-first century.[47]

There are more than 35 topic areas in *Healthy People 2020,* ranging from ensuring that Americans have adequate access to health services to improvements in their diet and physical activity. Objectives are developed within each topic area. For example, research indicates that Americans' body weights are increasing rather than decreasing. Thus, "Nutrition and Weight Status" is one topic area. Its goal is to promote health and reduce chronic diseases associated with diet and weight. There are numerous objectives developed within this topic area that, if fulfilled, will help Americans improve their diet and reduce their weight. **Table 1.4** lists a few objectives in this topic area.

As you can see from the table, consuming adequate amounts of fruits and vegetables is beneficial to managing one's weight. Americans should increase their intake of both of these food sources to help them improve their nutrition and weight status.

TABLE 1.4 *Healthy People 2020* Nutrition and Weight Status Objectives

Objectives	Target for Americans (%)	Status of Americans (%)
Increase the proportion of adults who are at a healthy weight	33.9	30.8
Reduce the proportion of adults who are obese	30.5	33.9
Reduce the proportion of children and adolescents aged 2 to 19 who are considered obese	14.5	16.1
Increase the contribution of fruits to diets of the population aged 2 years and older	0.9 cups/1,000 kcals	0.5 cups/1,000 kcals
Increase the variety and contribution of vegetables to the diets of the population aged 2 years and older	1.1 cups/1,000 kcals	0.8 cups/1,000 kcals

Source: United States Department of Health and Human Services. 2013. *Healthy People 2020.* Available at www.HealthyPeople.gov. Accessed January 2014.

What Is Credible Nutrition Research?

LO 1.8 Describe the scientific method that leads to reliable and accurate nutrition information.

If you Google the word *nutrition*, you will get a list of about 103,000,000 entries in 0.25 second. Obviously, the world is full of nutrition information at our fingertips. But is it credible?

Anyone who has attempted to lose weight can probably tell you how hard it is to keep up with the latest diet advice—because it seems to keep changing. In the 1970s, waist watchers were told that carbohydrates were the bane of their existence and that a protein-rich, low-carbohydrate diet was the name of the game when it came to shrinking their waistline. A decade later, avoiding fat was the key to winning the battle of the bulge. By 2000, carbohydrates were being ousted again, and protein-rich diets were back in vogue. But recently protein-heavy diets seem to be less popular and high-carbohydrate diets are once again becoming the way to fight weight gain. So . . . are you frustrated yet?

Nutrition-related stories often lead in newspapers and magazines and on websites.

Whereas diet trends and popular wisdom seem to change frequently, basic scientific knowledge about nutrition does not. Results from individual studies are often deemed newsworthy and publicized in the media, but the results of one report do not radically change expert opinion. Only when multiple affirming research studies have been conducted is a **consensus** reached about nutrition advice. News of the results of one study is just that: news. In contrast, advice from an authoritative health organization or committee, such as the American Heart Association or the Dietary Guidelines Committee, which is based on a consensus of research information, is sound information that can be trusted for the long term.

Sound Nutrition Research Begins with the Scientific Method

Sound research studies begin with a process called the **scientific method.** Scientists observe something in the natural world, ask questions, and propose an explanation (or **hypothesis**) based on their observations. They then test their hypothesis to determine if their idea is correct. There are many steps in the scientific method and many adjustments are made along the way before a scientist has gained enough information to draw a conclusion about his or her hypothesis. In fact, the entire process can take years to complete.

Let's walk through a nutrition-related study in which scientists used the scientific method to study rickets (**Figure 1.7**). Rickets is a disease in children in which

consensus Agreed-upon conclusion of a group of experts based on a collection of information.

scientific method A process used by scientists to gather and test information for the sake of generating sound research findings.

hypothesis An idea or explanation proposed by scientists based on observations or known facts.

peer-reviewed journal A journal in which scientists publish research findings, after the findings have gone through a rigorous review process by other scientists.

laboratory experiment A scientific experiment conducted in a laboratory. Some laboratory experiments involve animals.

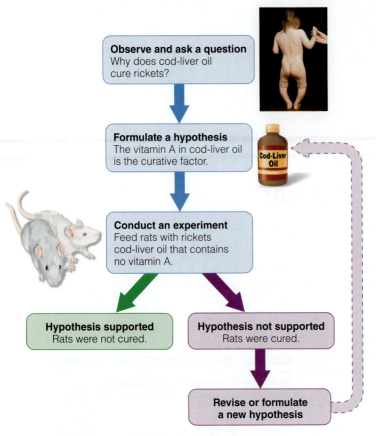

Observe and ask a question
Why does cod-liver oil cure rickets?

Formulate a hypothesis
The vitamin A in cod-liver oil is the curative factor.

Conduct an experiment
Feed rats with rickets cod-liver oil that contains no vitamin A.

Hypothesis supported
Rats were not cured.

Hypothesis not supported
Rats were cured.

Revise or formulate a new hypothesis

▲ **Figure 1.7 Steps of the Scientific Method**
The scientific method is used to conduct credible research in nutrition and other scientific fields.

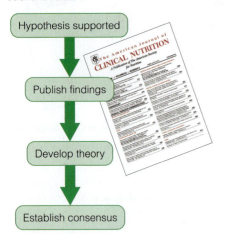

Hypothesis supported

Publish findings

Develop theory

Establish consensus

▲ **Figure 1.8 A Hypothesis Can Lead to a Scientific Consensus**
When a hypothesis is supported by research, the results are published in peer-reviewed journals. Once a theory has been developed and supported by subsequent experiments, a consensus is reached in the scientific community.

observational research Research that involves systematically observing subjects to see if there is a relationship to certain outcomes.

epidemiological research Research that studies the variables that influence health in a population; it is often observational.

the leg bones are so weakened that they cannot hold up the child's body weight. The legs bow as a result. In the early 1800s, parents often used cod-liver oil to treat rickets because it seemed to provide a miraculous cure.

Scientists noticed the cod-liver oil curing phenomenon and asked themselves why it cured rickets. In making note of the fact that cod-liver oil had an effect on rickets, and in asking why this was the case, these scientists were using the first step in the scientific method: observing and asking questions.

The second step of the scientific method is to formulate a hypothesis. Because cod-liver oil is very rich in vitamin A, scientists initially thought that this vitamin was the curative factor. To confirm this, scientists proceeded to the third step, which was to conduct an experiment.

The scientists altered the cod-liver oil to destroy its vitamin A. The altered oil was given to rats that had been fed a diet that caused rickets. Surprisingly, the rats were still cured of rickets. This disproved the scientists' original hypothesis that vitamin A was the curative factor. They then needed to modify their hypothesis, as it was obvious that there was something else in the cod-liver oil that cured rickets. They next hypothesized that it was the vitamin D that cured the rats, and conducted another experiment to confirm this hypothesis, which it did.

What good would it be to make such an important discovery if other scientists couldn't find out about it? Fortunately, scientists today share their findings by summarizing and submitting their research to a **peer-reviewed journal** (**Figure 1.8**). Other scientists (peers) review the researchers' findings to make sure that they are sound. If so, the research study is published in the journal. After that, it may be picked up by the popular press and relayed to the rest of the population. If the relationship between vitamin D and rickets were discovered today, it would probably be the lead story on CNN.

As more and more studies confirmed that vitamin D could cure and prevent rickets, a theory developed. By the 1920s, researchers knew with great certainty that vitamin D prevents rickets, and that a deficiency of vitamin D can cause deformed bones in children. Because of this, there is a consensus among health professionals as to the importance of vitamin D in the diets of children.

Research Studies and Experiments Confirm Hypotheses

Scientists can use different types of experiments to test a hypothesis. A **laboratory experiment** is done within the confines of a lab setting, such as the rickets experiments with rats. Research conducted with humans is usually observational or experimental.

Observational research involves exploring factors in two or more groups of subjects to see if there is a relationship to a certain disease or health outcome. One type of observational research is **epidemiological research,** which looks at health and disease in populations of people. For example, scientists may notice that there is a higher incidence of rickets among children who live in Norway than among children who live in Australia. Through their observations, they may find a relationship between the lack of sun exposure in Norway and the high incidence of rickets there compared with sunny Australia. However, the scientists can't rule out that the difference in the incidence of rickets in these two populations may also be due to other factors in the subjects' diet or lifestyle. This type of research does not answer the question of whether one factor directly causes another.

Experimental research involves at least two groups of subjects. One group, the **experimental group,** is given a treatment, and another group, the **control group,** isn't. When scientists hypothesized that vitamin D cured rickets, they would have randomly assigned children with rickets to one of two groups (**Figure 1.9**). The scientists would have given the experimental group a vitamin D supplement but would have given the control group a **placebo,** which looked just like the vitamin D supplement but contained only sugar. If neither of the two groups of subjects knew which pill they received, then the subjects were "blind" to the treatment. If the scientists who gave the placebo and the vitamin D supplement also didn't know which group received which treatment, the experiment would be called a **double-blind placebo-controlled study.** The scientists would also have to make sure that the variables were the same or controlled for both groups during the experiment.

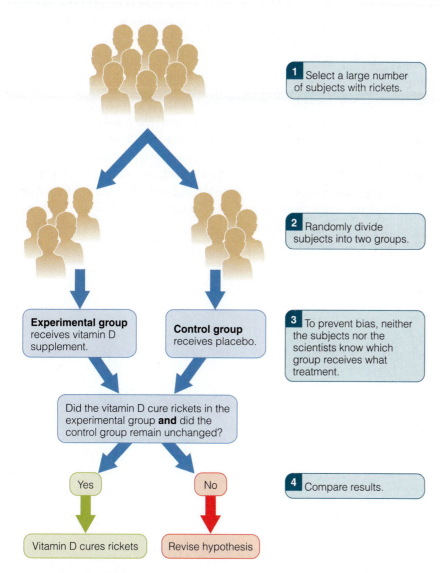

1 Select a large number of subjects with rickets.

2 Randomly divide subjects into two groups.

Experimental group receives vitamin D supplement.

Control group receives placebo.

3 To prevent bias, neither the subjects nor the scientists know which group receives what treatment.

Did the vitamin D cure rickets in the experimental group **and** did the control group remain unchanged?

Yes

No

4 Compare results.

Vitamin D cures rickets

Revise hypothesis

▲ **Figure 1.9 Controlled Scientific Experiments**
Scientists use experimental research to test hypotheses.

experimental research Research involving at least two groups of subjects receiving different treatments.

experimental group In experimental research, the group of participants given a specific treatment, such as a drug, as part of the study.

control group In experimental research, the group that does not receive the treatment but may be given a placebo instead; used as a standard for comparison.

placebo An inactive substance, such as a sugar pill, administered to a control group during an experiment.

double-blind placebo-controlled study An experimental study in which neither the researchers nor the subjects in the study are aware of who is receiving the treatment or the placebo.

For example, they couldn't let the control group go outside in the sunshine and at the same time keep the experimental group of subjects inside, since sunlight is known to allow humans to synthesize vitamin D. The exposure to the sunshine would change the outcome of the experiment.

A double-blind placebo-controlled study is considered the "gold standard" of research because all of the variables are the same and controlled for the groups of subjects, and neither the subjects nor the researcher are biased toward one group.

In any scientific research, sample sizes must be large enough to ensure that differences found in the study are due to the treatment rather than to chance. Studying an entire population is usually impossible, because the population is too large, the study would be too expensive or time-consuming, or all members of the population do not want to participate. This was the case with the vitamin D and rickets study mentioned earlier. It would be virtually impossible to measure all children with rickets. Instead, a sample of children with rickets was used and a statistical comparison was done to estimate the effects on the population. Generally, the larger the sample size, the more confident the researchers are that the data reflects reliable differences that would most likely be seen in the population.

The beauty of science is that one discovery builds on another. Though this may seem frustrating when the findings of one research study contradict the results of another from just a few months before, conflicting findings actually help scientists formulate new questions. Though many hypotheses fail along the way, a great many discoveries are also made.

> **LO 1.8: THE TAKE-HOME MESSAGE** Sound nutrition advice is based on years of research using the scientific method. Several methods can be used to conduct nutrition research, including laboratory experiments (on animals), experimental research (on humans), and observational, particularly epidemiological, research. Double-blind placebo-controlled studies mean that neither the subjects nor the researchers are aware of who is receiving treatment, and such studies are therefore considered the gold standard of experimental research. Findings from observational and epidemiological research are only considered valid if the study was conducted with an adequate sample size of subjects.

How Can You Find and Recognize Credible Nutrition Information?

LO 1.9 Explain how to identify reliable nutrition information and how to recognize misinformation.

If you need legal advice, you seek the expertise of an attorney. If you need knee surgery, you go to an orthopedic surgeon. Where do you go for nutrition advice?

Seek Information from the Nutrition Experts

Who is a credible expert with training in the field of nutrition? Different health professionals have varying levels of nutrition training, but by far, the professional with the most nutrition training is the Registered Dietitian Nutritionist (RDN). An RDN has completed at least a bachelor's degree from a university or college accredited by the Academy of Nutrition and Dietetics (AND) and has passed the national exam administered by the credentialing body of the AND. The Academy of Nutrition and Dietetics is the largest professional organization in the United States, with a membership of almost 67,000 nutrition experts. RDNs must maintain registration with the national organization and participate in continuing professional education to remain current in the fast-changing world of nutrition, medicine, and health.

RDNs are trained to administer **medical nutrition therapy** and work with patients to make dietary changes that can help prevent diseases such as heart disease, diabetes, stroke, and obesity. Many physicians, based on the diagnoses of their patients, refer them to RDNs for nutrition advice and guidance. RDNs must participate in continuing professional education in order to remain current in the fast-changing world of nutrition, medicine, and health and to maintain their registration. RDNs work in hospitals and other health care facilities, private practice, universities, medical schools, professional athletic teams, food companies, and other nutrition-related businesses.

Some individuals other than RDNs, including those with advanced degrees in nutrition, can also provide credible nutrition information. Some physicians have taken a nutrition course in medical school and gone on to get a master of science in public health (MPH), which involves some nutrition courses, or an MS in nutrition at an accredited university or college.

Some **public health nutritionists** may have an undergraduate degree in nutrition but didn't complete a supervised practice, so are not eligible to take the Academy of Nutrition and Dietetics exam. These individuals can work in the government organizing community outreach nutrition programs, such as programs for the elderly.

In order to protect the health of the public, over 40 states currently license nutrition professionals. A person who meets these qualifications is a **licensed dietitian nutritionist (LDN)** and so will have the letters "LDN" after his or her name. Because RDNs have completed the rigorous standards set forth by the Academy of Nutrition and Dietetics, they automatically meet the criteria for LDN and often will have both "RDN" and "LDN" after their names.

Be careful when taking nutrition advice from a trainer at the gym or the person who works at the local health food store. Whereas some of these people may be credible, many are not, and thus, less likely to give you information based on solid scientific evidence. Anyone who calls himself or herself a **nutritionist** may have taken few or no accredited courses in nutrition.

Beware of Quackery

Whereas credible nutrition experts can provide highly useful nutrition guidance, people of questionable credentials often dole out misinformation, usually for the sake of turning a profit. These skilled salespeople specialize in health **quackery,** or fraud, introducing health

medical nutrition therapy The integration of nutrition counseling and dietary changes, based on individual medical and health needs, to treat a patient's medical condition.

public health nutritionists Individuals who may have an undergraduate degree in nutrition but who are not Registered Dietitian Nutritionists.

licensed dietitian nutritionist (LDN) An individual who has met specified educational and experience criteria deemed by a state licensing board necessary to be considered an expert in the field of nutrition. An RDN would meet all the qualifications to be an LDN.

nutritionist A generic term with no recognized legal or professional meaning. Some people may call themselves a nutritionist without having any credible training in nutrition.

quackery The promotion and selling of health products and services of questionable validity. A quack is a person who promotes these products and services in order to make money.

fears and then trying to sell services and products to allay these newly created fears. Part of their sales pitch is to make unrealistic promises and guarantees.

To avoid falling for one of their shady schemes, there are certain "red flags" that should alert and warn you to be leery of infomercials, magazine ads, mail-order catalogs, and websites that try to convince you that:

- There is a quick fix for what ails you.
- Their product is all natural and miraculously cures.
- One product does it all.
- You can lose a lot of weight in a short amount of time and without dieting or exercising.
- The product contains a secret ingredient.
- The product shrinks tumors.
- There is no risk, as there is a money-back guarantee. (Good luck getting your money back!)

Evaluate Nutrition News with a Critical Eye

In your lifetime, you will read thousands of newspaper and website headlines, as well as watch and listen to countless television and radio reports reporting sensational headlines about nutrition. Dramatic headlines are designed to grab your attention, but they can be misleading. Whether they're delivered via a magazine or newspaper, TV, or online, these headlines should always be considered with a critical eye.

The media are routinely bombarded by press releases sent from medical journals, food companies, organizations, and universities about research being conducted and/or conferences being sponsored by these institutions. These releases are sent for one reason: to gain publicity. Reputable news organizations that report these findings will seek out independent experts in the field to weigh in on the research and, just as importantly, explain how these findings relate to the public. Even with

this added context, there's often much detail that's left out of the story. Here are some questions to consider when hearing or reading about a new study, finding, or claim in the mainstream media:

- **Was the Research Finding Published in a Peer-Reviewed Journal?** You can be confident that studies published in a peer-reviewed journal have been thoroughly reviewed by experts in this area of research. In most cases, if there are flaws in the study, the study does not get published. If the research isn't published in a peer-reviewed journal, you have no way of knowing if the study was conducted in an appropriate manner and whether the findings are accurate. A study about the possible virtues of chocolate in fighting heart disease that is published in the *New England Journal of Medicine* has more credibility than a similar article published in a baking magazine.
- **Was the Study Done Using Animals or Humans?** Experiments with animals are often used to study how a particular substance affects a health outcome. But if the study is conducted in rats, it doesn't necessarily mean that the substance will have the same effect if consumed by humans. This doesn't mean that animal studies are frivolous. They are important stepping stones to designing and conducting similar experiments involving humans.
- **Do the Study Participants Resemble Me?** When you read or hear about studies involving humans, you should always find out more information about the individuals who took part in the research. For example, were the people in the chocolate studies college-aged subjects or older

individuals with heart disease and high blood pressure? If older adults were studied, then would these findings be of any benefit to young adults who don't have high blood pressure or heart disease?

- **Is This the First Time I've Heard about This?** A single study in a specific area of research is a lonely entity in the scientific world. Is this the first study regarding the health benefits of chocolate? If the media article doesn't confirm that other studies have also supported these findings, this one study may be the *only* study of its kind. Wait until you hear that these research findings have been confirmed by a reputable health organization, such as the American Heart Association, before considering making any changes in your diet. Reputable organizations will only change their advice based on a consensus of research findings.

Know How to Evaluate Nutrition Information on the Internet

Many people turn to various websites when they have a question about health or nutrition. In fact, approximately 60 percent of American adult Internet users, have surfed millions of websites looking for health and medical information.[48] Remember that anyone with computer skills can put up a slick website, and there are many that promote misleading or false information.

To help evaluate the validity of websites, the National Institutes of Health (NIH) has developed ten questions to consider:[49]

1. **Who Runs the Site?** Credible websites are willing to show their credentials. For example, the National Center for Complementary and Alternative Medicine (www.nccam .nih.gov) provides information about its association with the NIH and its extensive ongoing research and educational programs.

When surfing the Internet for nutrition information, look for a credible, reliable site with up-to-date information.

2. Who Pays for the Site? Running a website is expensive, and finding out who's paying for a particular site will tell you something about the reliability of its content. Websites sponsored by the government (with URLs ending in .gov), a nonprofit organization (ending in .org), or an academic institution (.edu) are more reliable than many commercial websites (.com or .net). Some commercial websites, such as WebMD, carry articles that can be reliable if credible health professionals write them, but other websites may be promoting information to suit a company's own purposes. For example, if the funding source for the website is a vitamin and mineral supplement company, are all the articles geared toward supporting the use of supplements? Does the website have advertisers and do their products influence the content of the website?

3. What Is the Purpose of the Site? After you answer the first two questions, look for the "About This Site" link. This will help you understand the website's purpose. For example, at www.nutrition.gov, the purpose is to "provide easy access to the best food and nutrition information across the federal government." This website doesn't exist to sell anything, but to help you find reliable information.

4. Where Does the Information Come From? You should always know who wrote what you are reading. Is the author a qualified nutrition expert or did she or he interview qualified individuals? If the site obtained information from another source, was that source cited?

5. What Is the Basis for the Information? Is the article's information based on medical facts and figures that have references? For example, any medical news items released on the American Heart Association website (www.heart.org/HEARTORG) will include the medical journal from which the information came.

6. How Is the Information Selected? Check to see if the website has an editorial board of medical and health experts and if qualified individuals review or write the content before it is released.

7. How Current Is the Information? Once a website is on the Internet, it will stay there until someone removes it. Consequently, the health information that you read may not be the most up to date. Check the date; if it is over a year old, check to see if it has been updated.

8. How Does the Site Choose Links to Other Sites? Some medical sites don't like to link to other sites, as they don't have control over other sites' credibility and content. Others do link, if they are confident that these sites meet their criteria. Don't assume that the link is credible.

9. What Information Is Collected about the Viewer and Why? Websites track the pages consumers visit to analyze popular topics. Sometimes they elicit personal information such as gender, age, and health concerns, which can then be sold to interested companies. Credible sites should state their privacy policy and if they will or will not give or sell this information to other sources.

10. How Does the Site Manage Interactions with Visitors? Contact information of the website's owners should be listed in case readers have any concerns or questions that they want answered. If the site has a chat room or ongoing discussion group, how is it moderated? Read the discussion group dialogue before you jump in.

When obtaining information from the Internet, carefully peruse the site to make sure that it is credible and contains up-to-date information, and that its content isn't influenced by those who fund and support the website.

LO 1.9: THE TAKE-HOME MESSAGE
Credible nutrition information is obtained from trained nutritional professionals including Registered Dietitian Nutritionists or other valid experts. These professionals have the education and experience to provide reliable nutrition information to achieve an overall healthy diet. Use a critical eye when considering health and nutrition headlines in the media, and be careful when obtaining nutrition information from the Internet. Peruse the website to make sure it is credible, contains up-to-date information, and its content is not influenced by those that fund and support the website.

Visual Chapter Summary

LO 1.1 Many Factors Drive Your Food Choices

Food choices are influenced by personal taste, culture and environment, social life and trends, nutrition knowledge, advertising, time, convenience, and cost. People often eat out of habit, in response to emotions, and, of course, because food is delicious.

LO 1.2 Nutrition Is the Science of Food

Nutrition is the science that studies how the nutrients in food nourish the body, manufacture and replace cells, and produce energy. There are six categories of nutrients: carbohydrates, lipids, proteins, vitamins, minerals, and water. Carbohydrates, lipids, proteins, and vitamins contain carbon and are classified as organic. Minerals and water are inorganic because they do not contain carbon. Carbohydrates and proteins each contain 4 kilocalories per gram, while fats contain 9 kilocalories per gram. Alcohol, though not a nutrient, also contains energy at 7 kilocalories per gram.

		Carbon	Hydrogen	Oxygen	Nitrogen	Single elements
Organic	**Carbohydrates**	X	X	X		
	Lipids	X	X	X		
	Proteins	X	X	X	X	
	Vitamins	X	X	X	Some vitamins contain nitrogen	
Inorganic	**Minerals**					X
	Water		X	X		

LO 1.3 Individual Nutrients Have Primary Roles in the Body

Carbohydrates, fats (lipids), and proteins provide energy in the form of kilocalories. Carbohydrates are the body's preferred source of energy. Fats insulate the body and cushion internal organs. The primary role of dietary protein is to build and maintain body tissues. Protein also acts as enzymes that catalyze chemical reactions. Vitamins and minerals do not provide energy but are necessary to properly metabolize carbohydrates, fats, and protein. Many vitamins aid enzymes in the body. Water bathes the inside and outside of the cells, helps maintain body temperature, acts as a lubricant and protective cushion, and delivers nutrients and oxygen to the cells.

LO 1.4 Eating a Balanced Diet Is the Best Approach to Meet Your Nutrient Needs

A well-balanced diet that helps prevent chronic diseases includes whole foods and functional foods that have been fortified with phytochemicals, zoo-chemicals, and fiber. In some situations, the use of enriched and fortified foods can be combined with dietary supplements for good health.

LO 1.5 A Healthy Diet Can Reduce the Risk of Chronic Disease

Nutrition plays an important role in preventing many of the leading causes of death in the United States, including heart disease, cancer, stroke, and type 2 diabetes. Interactions between nutrition and disease are explored in the science of nutritional genomics, which studies how diet may modify the way genes work and how genetic makeup affects nutrient requirements.

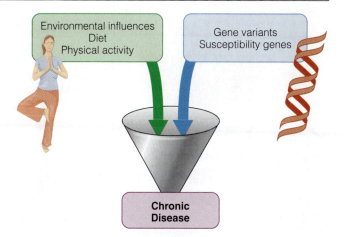

LO 1.6 We Assess Nutritional Status Using the ABCD Method

Reliable nutrition information can be obtained from Registered Dietitian Nutritionists, licensed nutritionists, or professionals with advanced degrees in nutrition. Nutrient assessment methods for individuals include assessing health history, collecting anthropometric and biochemical laboratory data, clinical observation, and dietary intake surveys. The nutritional status of population groups is determined by national surveys and studies, including the National Health and Nutrition Examination Survey (NHANES) and the Framingham Heart Study.

LO 1.7 The Current State of the American Diet Needs Improvement

Most Americans are not meeting all their nutrient needs without exceeding their kilocalorie requirements. The average American diet is high in added sugar, sodium, and saturated fat, but low in vitamin D, calcium, and potassium. In addition, the rates of overweight and obesity among Americans are too high.

2012

Prevalence of self-reported obesity

15%–<20%	30%–<35%
20%–<25%	≥35%
25%–<30%	

LO 1.8 The Scientific Method of Research Provides Credible Nutrition Information

Sound nutrition information is the result of numerous scientific studies that are based on the scientific method and that are reviewed by the medical and scientific community. Nutrition research is conducted through laboratory experiments, experimental research, and observational and epidemiological studies. Findings are presented in peer-reviewed journals.

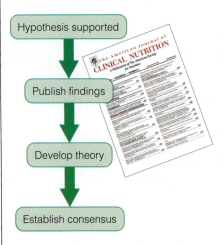

Hypothesis supported

↓

Publish findings

↓

Develop theory

↓

Establish consensus

LO 1.9 Reliable Nutrition Information Comes from Credible Sources

Nutrition advice should come from credible sources including Registered Dietitian Nutritionists who have the education and training to provide reliable and accurate information. Individuals who call themselves nutritionists may or may not have a credible nutrition education. Use critical thinking to evaluate media headlines and product claims relating to health and nutrition. When looking for nutrition and health information on the Internet, seek out the sites of credible organizations that provide up-to-date information from reliable sources.

Terms to Know

- nutrition
- nutrients
- organic
- inorganic
- essential nutrients
- nonessential nutrients
- energy
- adenosine triphosphate (ATP)
- energy-yielding nutrients
- kilocalorie
- macronutrients
- micronutrients
- enzymes
- coenzymes
- solubility
- water-soluble vitamins
- fat-soluble vitamins
- major minerals
- trace minerals
- functional foods
- phytochemicals
- zoochemicals
- gene expression
- nutritional genomics
- malnourished
- undernourished
- overnourished
- Registered Dietitian Nutritionist (RDN)
- acute
- chronic
- malabsorption
- body mass index (BMI)
- overweight
- obesity
- Healthy People 2020
- consensus
- scientific method
- hypothesis
- peer-reviewed journal
- laboratory experiment
- observational research
- epidemiological research
- experimental research
- experimental group
- control group
- placebo
- double-blind placebo-controlled study
- medical nutrition therapy
- public health nutritionists
- licensed dietitian nutritionist (LDN)
- nutritionist
- quackery

MasteringNutrition™

To hear an MP3 Chapter Review, scan here or visit the Study Area in MasteringNutrition.

Check Your Understanding

1. Megan picks up a sandwich at the campus food truck after class every day before dashing off to her part-time job. Which of the following most likely drives Megan's food choice?
   a. her ethnic background
   b. her busy schedule
   c. her emotions
   d. her limited budget

2. Nutrition is
   a. the study of genes, how they function in the body, and the environment.
   b. the study of how the body functions.
   c. the study of nutrients and compounds in foods that nourish and affect body functions and health.
   d. the study of hormones and how they function in the body.

3. Which of the following roles do nutrients perform in the body?
   a. Nutrients provide energy.
   b. Nutrients provide structure for bone, muscle, and other tissues.
   c. Nutrients facilitate metabolism.
   d. Nutrients perform all of the above functions.

4. Minerals are considered an organic nutrient because they contain the element carbon.
   a. true
   b. false

5. A slice of whole-wheat bread contains 1 gram of fat, 18 grams of carbohydrate, and 4 grams of protein. How many kilocalories does it contain?
   a. 65 kilocalories
   b. 72 kilocalories
   c. 89 kilocalories
   d. 97 kilocalories

6. Dietary supplements are necessary to meet your nutrient needs.
   a. true
   b. false

7. Which of the ABCD methods would an RDN use first to determine if you are overweight?
   a. anthropometric
   b. biochemical
   c. clinical
   d. dietary intake

8. The current state of the American diet is reflected in the _____ percent of adult Americans who are considered obese.
   a. 35
   b. 45
   c. 55
   d. 65

9. Changing your diet alone can reduce your risk of chronic disease.
   a. true
   b. false

10. The first step in the scientific method is to
    a. make observations and ask questions.
    b. form a hypothesis.
    c. do an experiment.
    d. develop a theory.

Answers

1. (b) While food choices are influenced by many factors, including ethnic background, emotions, and costs, in Megan's case her limited time for food preparation and/or shopping influences her food choices.

2. (c) Nutrition is the science related to how nutrients are used in the body and how they affect health. The study of genes is called genomics. Physiology is the study of how the body functions. The study of hormones is called endocrinology.

3. (d) Nutrients help perform numerous vital body functions. Carbohydrates, protein, and fats provide energy in the form of kilocalories; protein and some minerals help build body tissues; and several vitamins and minerals are essential during metabolic processes.

4. (b) Minerals are actually inorganic nutrients because they do not contain carbon. Nutrients that do contain carbon, including protein, carbohydrates, lipids, and vitamins, are classified as organic.

5. (d) A slice of bread contains 97 kilocalories: (18 g × 4 kcal) + (4 g × 4 kcal) + (1 g × 9 kcal).

6. (b) False. Dietary supplements can be beneficial for individuals with diet restrictions or higher nutrient needs, but they are not essential. Consuming a diet rich in a variety of whole foods is the best way to achieve a healthy, well-balanced diet.

7. (a) An RDN would begin with anthropometric measurements such as using height and weight to determine BMI and assess body weight. Biochemical measurements use blood, urine, and feces tests, and clinical tools are observations of your hair, skin, muscles, and overall appearance to assess signs of deficiencies or excess nutrients. Dietary intake records diet history, or uses a survey, food frequency questionnaire, or diet record to assess nutrient intake.

8. (a) Over 35 percent of American adults are considered obese.

9. (b) False. Risk factors for chronic disease are usually a cluster of factors. For example, obesity is usually a combination of overeating and lack of physical activity.

10. (a) The scientific method begins with scientists observing and asking questions. They then formulate a hypothesis and test it using an experiment to confirm their hypothesis. After many experiments that confirm their hypothesis, a theory is developed.

Answers to True or False?

1. **True.** Taste is the strongest motivating factor for choosing foods. However, numerous other factors, including culture, social setting, health, advertising, habit, emotion, time, cost, and convenience, also play a role in food choice.

2. **False.** Nutrition is the science related to how nutrients are used in the body and how they affect health.

3. **True.** Carbohydrates are the primary source of energy to the body.
4. **False.** Whereas alcohol does provide kilocalories, eliminating it from the diet would not result in malnutrition. Therefore, alcohol is not a nutrient.
5. **False.** There is no replacement for whole foods in a healthy diet. A supplement can augment a healthy diet, but it can't replace it to meet your nutrient needs.
6. **False.** The 24-hour diet record is one tool for gathering information about the quality of an individual's diet, but it doesn't reveal a complete picture. Long-term food records, interviews, and anthropometric data are additional tools that can help a dietitian assess an individual's eating habits.
7. **False.** The rate of obesity in American adults shows little sign of declining. In 2012, more than 35 percent of adult Americans were considered obese.
8. **False.** Reducing all fat from your diet would result in nutrient deficiencies and do little to reduce your risk of heart disease. Chronic disease such as heart disease is often the result of a cluster of risk factors including diet, exercise, and tobacco use.
9. **False.** Heart disease is the leading cause of death among Americans. The good news is that your diet can play an important role in preventing it.
10. **False.** There is no standard for or legal definition of the word "nutritionist," so it does not convey expert status. In fact, anyone can call himself or herself a nutritionist.

Web Resources

Examples of reliable nutrition and health websites include:

- Agricultural Research Service: www.ars.usda.gov
- American Cancer Society: www.cancer.org
- American College of Sports Medicine: www.acsm.org
- Academy of Nutrition and Dietetics: www.eatright.org
- American Medical Association: www.ama-assn.org
- Center for Science in the Public Interest: www.cspinet.org
- Centers for Disease Control and Prevention: www.cdc.gov
- Food and Drug Administration: www.fda.gov
- Food and Nutrition Information Center: www.nal.usda.gov/fnic
- National Institutes of Health: www.nih.gov
- NHANES Surveys: www.cdc.gov/nchs/nhanes.htm
- Shape Up America!: www.shapeup.org
- Tufts University Health and Nutrition Newsletter: www.healthletter.tufts.edu
- Nutrition.gov: www.nutrition.gov
- Vegetarian Resource Group: www.vrg.org

References

1. Ogden, J., N. Coop, C. Cousins, R. Crump, L. Field, S. Hughes, and N. Woodger. 2013. Distraction, the Desire to Eat, and Food Intake. Towards an Expanded Model of Mindless Eating. *Appetite* 62:119–126.
2. Freeland-Graves, J., and S. Nitzke. 2013. Position Paper of the Academy of Nutrition and Dietetics: Total Diet Approach to Healthy Eating. *Journal of the Academy of Nutrition and Dietetics* 113:307–317.
3. Block, J. P., M. W. Gillman, S. K. Linakis, and R. E. Goldman. 2013. "If It Tastes Good, I'm Drinking It": Qualitative Study of Beverage Consumption among College Students. *Journal of Adolescent Health* 52:702e–706e.
4. Freeland-Graves, J. 2013.
5. Freeland-Graves, J. 2013.
6. Degrace-Passilly, P., and P. Besnarad. 2012. CD36 and Taste of Fat. *Current Opinion in Clinical Nutrition and Metabolic Care* 15(2):107–111.
7. Drewnowski, A., and E. Almiron-Roig. 2010. Human Perceptions and Preferences for Fat-Rich Foods. In J. P. Montmayeur and J. le Coutre, editors, *Fat Detection: Taste, Texture, and Post-Ingestive Effects*. Boca Raton (FL): CRC Press, Chapter 11.
8. Drewnowski, A. 1997. Taste Preferences and Food Intake. *Annual Review of Nutrition* 17:237–253.
9. Cooke, L. J., and J. Wardle. 2005. Age and Gender Differences in Children's Food Preferences. *British Journal of Nutrition* 93:741–746.
10. Sneider, P., and H. F. Te Molder. 2005. Disputing Taste: Food Pleasure as an Achievement in Interaction. *Appetite* 45:51–61.
11. Wansink, B., C. R. Payne, and M. Shimizu. 2010. "Is This a Meal or Snack?" Situational Cues that Drive Perceptions. *Appetite* 54:214–216.
12. National Turkey Foundation. 2011. *Turkey Facts and Trivia*. Available at www.eatturkey.com. Accessed January 2014.
13. Freeland-Graves, J. 2013.
14. National Restaurant Association. 2011. *Pizza Is King of Super Bowl Takeout*. Available at www.restaurant.org. Accessed January 2014.
15. New York Post. 2012. *Regal Revenue Up Mainly on Concession Sales*. Available at http://nypost.com. Accessed January 2014.
16. Organic Trade Association. 2011. *2011 Organic Industry Survey*. Available at www.ota.com. Accessed January 2014.
17. Food Processing. 2012. *Gluten-Free: Friend or Foe?* Available at www.foodprocessing.com. Accessed January 2014.
18. Prevention. 2012. *Shoppers Are Paying More Attention to Nutrition: Increasing Interest in Healthy Labeling and Private Brands*. Available at www.fmi.org. Accessed January 2014.
19. Forwood, S. E., A. Ahern, G. J. Hollands, P. C. Fletcher, and T. M. Marteau. 2013. Underestimating Calorie Content When Healthy Foods Are Present: An Averaging Effect or a Reference-Dependent Anchoring Effect? *PLoS ONE* 8(8):e71475. Accessed January 2014.
20. Barzegari, A., M. Ebrahimi, M. Azizi, and K. Ranjbar. 2011. A Study of Nutrition Knowledge, Attitudes and Food Habits of College Students. *World Applied Sciences Journal* 15(7):1012–1017.
21. McKee, S. 2012. A Marketer's Homage to the Soda Can. *Bloomberg Business Week*. Available at www.businessweek.com. Accessed January 2014.
22. Bernhardt, A. M., C. Wiling, A. M. Adachi-Mejia, E. Bergamini, J. Marjinissen, and J. D. Sargent. 2013. How Television Fast Food Marketing Aimed at Children Compares with Adult Advertisements. Robert Wood Johnson Foundation. Available at www.rwjf.org. Accessed January 2014.
23. Blisard, N. 1999. Advertising and How We Eat: The Case of Dairy Products. In *America's Eating Habits: Changes and Consequences*. Edited by Economic Research Service.
24. Freeland-Graves, J. 2013.
25. Specialty Coffee Association. 2012. *Specialty Coffee in the USA 2008–2009*. Available at www.scaa.org. Accessed January 2014.
26. U.S. Department of Agriculture. 2013. *Food Expenditures. Table 3*. Available at www.ers.usda.gov. Accessed January 2014.
27. Poti, J. M., K. J. Duffey, and B. M. Popkin. 2013. The Association of Fast Food Consumption with Poor Dietary Outcomes and Obesity Among Children: Is It the Fast Food or the Remainder of the Diet? *American Journal of Clinical Nutrition* 99(1):162–171.
28. The Dallas Morning News. 2013. *New Trend in Groceries by Web: Meal Kits Delivered to Your Door*. Available at www.dallasnews.com. Accessed January 2014.
29. Andreyeva, T., M. W. Long, and K. D. Brownell. 2010. The Impact of Food Prices on Consumption: A Systematic Review of Research on the Price Elasticity of Demand for Food. *American Journal of Public Health* 100(2):216–222.

30. Mintel International Group. 2012. *Breakfast Foods-US*; Mintel International Group. 2012. *Fruit Juice and Juice Drinks-US*. Available at www.reports.mintel.com. Accessed January 2014.

31. Maddison, R., L. Foley, C. N. Mhurchu, Y. Jiang, A. Jull, H. Prapavessis, M. Hohepa, and A. Rodgers. 2011. Effects of Active Video Games on Body Composition: A Randomized Controlled Trial. *American Journal of Clinical Nutrition* 94:156–163.

32. Remi, M. L. 2013. Free Radical Scavenging Properties Like Beta-Carotene, Lutein, Lycopene, Catachins, Cryptoxanthins, Zoochemicals and Various Indoles and Flavonoids. *Journal of Medical Pharmaceuticals and Allied Sciences* 4:62–67.

33. Bo, S., G. Ciccone, A. Castiglione, R. Gambino, F. DeMichieli, P. Villois, M. Durazzo, P. Cavallo-Perin, and M. Cassader. 2013. Anti-Inflammatory and Antioxidant Effects of Resveratrol in Healthy Smokers. A Randomized, Double-Blind, Placebo-Controlled, Cross-Over Trial. *Current Medicinal Chemistry* 20(10):1323–1331.

34. Danthir, V., N. R. Burns, T. Nettelbeck, C. Wilson, and G. Wittert. 2011. The Older People, Omega-3, and Cognitive Health (EPOCH) Trial Design and Methodology: A Randomised, Double-Blind, Controlled Trial Investigating the Effect of Long-Chain Omega-3 Fatty Acids on Cognitive Ageing and Well-being in Cognitively Healthy Older Adults. *Nutrition Journal* 10:117. Available at www.nutritionj.com. Accessed January 2014.

35. Tayyem, R. F., S. S. Abu-Mweis, H. A. Bawadi, L. Agraib, and K. Bani-Hani. 2013. Validation of a Food Frequency Questionnaire to Assess Macronutrient and Micronutrient Intake among Jordanians. *Journal of the Academy of Nutrition and Dietetics* S2212–2672(13):01374–01379.

36. Eaton, D. K., E. O. Olsen, N. D. Brener, K. S. Scanlon, S. A. Kim, Z. Demissie, and A. L. Yaroch. 2013. A Comparison of Fruit and Vegetable Intake Estimates from Three Survey Question Sets to Estimates from 24-Hour Dietary Recall Interviews. *Journal of the Academy of Nutrition and Dietetics* 113(9):1165–1174.

37. Illner, A-K., H. Freisling, H. Boeing, I. Huybrechts, S. P. Crispim, and N. Slimani. 2012. Review and Evaluation of Innovative Technologies for Measuring Diet in Nutritional Epidemiology. *International Journal of Epidemiology* 41(4):1187–1203.

38. U.S. Department of Agriculture, Agricultural Research Service. 2012. *Nutrient Intakes from Food: Mean Amounts Consumed per Individual, by Gender and Age, What We Eat in America, NHANES 2009–2010*. Available at www.ars.usda.gov. Accessed January 2014.

39. Ibid.

40. U.S. Department of Agriculture, Agricultural Research Service. 2012.

41. Ibid.

42. Bailey, R. L., V. L. Fulgoni, D. R. Keast, and J. T. Dwyer. 2012. Examination of Vitamin Intakes among U.S. Adults by Dietary Supplement Use. *Journal of the Academy of Nutrition and Dietetics* 112(5):657–663.

43. Todd, J., L. Mancino, and B. Lin. 2010. *The Impact of Food Away from Home on Adult Diet Quality, ERR-90, U. S. Department of Agriculture, Economic Service*. Available at http://uhs.berkeley.edu. Accessed January 2014.

44. Larson, N., R. MacLehose, J. A. Fulkerson, J. M. Berge, M. Story, and D. Neumark-Sztainer. 2013. Eating Breakfast and Dinner Together as a Family: Associations with Sociodemographic Characteristics and Implications for Diet Quality and Weight Status. *Journal of the Academy of Nutrition and Dietetics* 113:1601–1609.

45. Kellogg's. 2011. *Kellogg Reveals Results of Monumental Breakfast Survey*. Available at http://newsroom.kelloggcompany.com. Accessed January 2014.

46. Centers for Disease Control. 2013. *Adult Obesity Facts*. Available at www.cdc.gov. Accessed January 2014.

47. U.S. Department of Health and Preventative Services. Updated 2013. *Healthy People 2020*. Available at www.healthypeople.gov. Accessed January 2014.

48. Fox, S., and M. Duggan. 2013. *Health Online 2013. Pew Research Center's Internet and American Life Project*. Available at www.pewinternet.org. Accessed January 2014.

49. National Center for Complementary and Alternative Medicine. Updated 2013. *10 Things to Know about Evaluating Medical Resources on the Web*. Available at www.nccam.nih.gov. Accessed January 2014.

2 Tools for Healthy Eating

Learning Outcomes

After reading this chapter, you will be able to:

2.1 Describe the key principles of healthy eating.

2.2 Distinguish between the Dietary Reference Intake terms EAR, AI, RDA, UL, and AMDR.

2.3 Describe the recommendations included in the *Dietary Guidelines for Americans*.

2.4 Explain the concept of the MyPlate food guidance system, including the food groups and typical foods represented.

2.5 Describe how the exchange system can be used as a guide to plan a balanced diet.

2.6 Identify the required components of a food label and Nutrition Facts panel.

2.7 Compare the terms "portion" and "serving size" and summarize the health benefits of controlling your portions.

True or False?

1. Having a balanced diet means eating the same number of servings from each food group. **T/F**

2. There isn't any risk in overconsuming the essential nutrients in your diet. **T/F**

3. The current Dietary Reference Intakes for vitamins and minerals are set at the amount you should consume daily to maintain good health. **T/F**.

4. If you follow the advice in the *Dietary Guidelines for Americans* you can reduce your risk of dying from chronic diseases such as heart disease, high blood pressure, and diabetes mellitus. **T/F**

5. According to the USDA MyPlate food guide, there are five basic food groups. **T/F**

6. Healthy oils are an important food group in MyPlate. **T/F**

7. Exchange lists are similar to MyPlate except the foods are based on the carbohydrate, protein, fat, and kilocalorie contents. **T/F**

8. A nutrient claim on a food label tells you how healthy that nutrient is in the food. **T/F**

9. All packaged foods must contain a food label. **T/F**

10. A portion of food is defined as a standard serving size. **T/F**

See page 72 for the answers.

Many Americans believe that to eat a healthful diet means giving up their favorite foods. Nothing could be farther from the truth! With a little planning, you can still occasionally eat almost any food even if it contains added sugars and fat and is high in kilocalories. All it takes are the right tools to balance those higher kilocalorie foods with more nutritious choices each day.

The good news is that a number of tools are available to help you achieve a healthful, balanced eating plan. In this chapter we will learn how to use these tools in a positive, consistent manner that over time will lead to better eating habits while still enjoying those comfort foods. Let's begin with a discussion on what is healthy eating.

A meal that contains foods from every food group is part of a balanced, healthy diet.

balance The diet principle of providing the correct proportion of nutrients to maintain health and prevent disease.

vary The diet principle of consuming a mixture of different food groups and foods within each group.

moderate The diet principle of providing reasonable but not excessive amounts of foods and nutrients.

nutrient density A measurement of the nutrients in a food compared with the kilocalorie content; nutrient-dense foods are high in nutrients and low in kilocalories.

energy density A measurement of the kilocalories in a food compared with the weight (grams) of the food.

undernutrition A state of inadequate nutrition whereby a person's nutrient and/or energy needs aren't met through the diet.

What Are the Key Principles of Healthy Eating?

LO 2.1 Describe the key principles of healthy eating.

Healthy eating means you need to **balance, vary,** and **moderate** your nutrient intake. As a student, you are probably familiar with these principles from other areas of your life. You balance your time between work, school, family, and friends. You engage in a variety of activities to avoid being bored, and enjoy each in moderation, as spending too much time on one activity (like working) will disrupt the amount of time you can spend on others (like studying or socializing). A chronic imbalance of any one of these activities will affect the others. If you regularly forgo sleep in order to work extra hours at a job, sleep deprivation will affect your ability to stay awake in class, which will hamper your studies. Your unbalanced life would soon become unhealthy and unhappy. Likewise, your eating pattern must be balanced, varied, and moderate in order to be healthy. In addition, a healthy diet includes foods that are high in **nutrient density** and low in **energy density.**

Healthy Eating Means Balance between Food Groups

A balanced diet includes healthy proportions of all nutrients and is adequate in energy. A diet that lacks balance can cause **undernutrition.** For instance, a student subsisting largely on bread, bagels, muffins, crackers, chips, and cookies might be eating too much carbohydrate and fat but too little protein, vitamins, and minerals. If the diet lacks a particular nutrient, such as protein, over time the body suffers from **malnutrition.** A meal that contains foods from the grain, vegetable, fruit, meat, and dairy groups, such as a lunch of a turkey-and-cheese sandwich with lettuce and tomato plus an apple, provides the proper proportion of foods from each of the food groups. This balancing act prevents **overnutrition** of a specific nutrient, such as fat,[1] or too many kilocalories, which can lead to overweight and obesity. Consuming adequate amounts of all essential nutrients is key to avoiding nutrient deficiencies, and, in many cases, chronic disease.

Healthy Eating Means Consuming a Variety of Foods

Choosing a variety of foods improves the quality of the diet because the more varied the food choices, the better the chance of consuming adequate amounts of all the essential nutrients.[2] Even within one food group, the nutrient composition of foods can vary dramatically. For example, while broccoli is a good source of folate, it has less than half the vitamin A of a carrot. Similarly, if the only fruit you eat is bananas, your diet would include an excellent source of potassium, but little vitamin C. Because no single food or food group contains everything you need to be healthy, you should choose a variety of foods from within each food group and among food groups each day to achieve a healthy diet. This is the basic principle of the *Fruits & Veggies—More Matters* campaign developed by the Produce for Better Health Foundation and the Centers for Disease Control and Prevention.[3] This campaign promotes eating a variety of colorful fruits and vegetables, which are rich in vitamins, minerals, fiber, and phytochemicals, each day to help reduce the risk of cancer and heart disease, and slow the effects of aging.

Choosing a variety of nutrient-dense foods you enjoy is a key to eating a healthy diet.

Healthy Eating Means Moderate Intake of All Foods

According to many Registered Dietitian Nutritionists, "there are no good or bad foods, just good or bad habits." What they mean is that all foods—even less nutritious foods—can be part of a healthy diet, as long as they are consumed in moderation. Foods such as sweets and fried or packaged snack foods should be eaten only in small amounts to avoid consuming too much sugar and fat. Eating too much of these foods can also mean taking in more energy than you need, potentially resulting in weight gain. Finally, these foods can displace more nutrient-rich choices, resulting in a diet that lacks essential nutrients. Even some healthy foods, such as nutrient-dense nuts, can be high in kilocalories and should be consumed in moderation. Healthy eating doesn't mean you can't enjoy your favorite foods. It simply means eating those foods in moderation by limiting the **portion** size and number of servings you eat.

Many people overestimate the appropriate portion sizes of foods. An entire body of research is devoted to studying factors that affect how much we put on our plates. The important point is that, in general, we tend to consume two or more portions of a given food at a given meal. See the Health Connection on pages 66–68 for examples of visuals you can use to estimate portion sizes.

Healthy Eating Includes Nutrient-Dense Foods

Healthy eating includes not only choosing foods based on these key principles of balance, moderation, and variety, but also choosing foods that are nutrient dense. Nutrient-dense foods are high in nutrients, such as vitamins and minerals, but low in energy (kilocalories). Nutrient-dense foods provide more nutrients per kilocalorie (and in each bite) than less nutrient-dense foods.[4] Fresh fruits and vegetables, for example, are nutrient dense because they are high in B vitamins, vitamin C, minerals such as calcium and magnesium, and fiber, while usually providing fewer than 60 kilocalories per serving.

Nutrient-dense foods are also low in fat and added sugars. To illustrate this concept, compare the nutrient density of two versions of the same food: a baked potato and potato chips (**Figure 2.1**). Although a medium baked potato and one ounce of potato chips have about the same number of kilocalories, the baked potato provides much higher amounts of vitamins and minerals than the deep-fried chips.

malnutrition The long-term outcome of consuming a diet that is either lacking in the essential nutrients or contains excess energy; an imbalance of nutrients in the diet.

overnutrition The state of consuming excess nutrients or energy.

portion The quantity of a food usually eaten at one sitting.

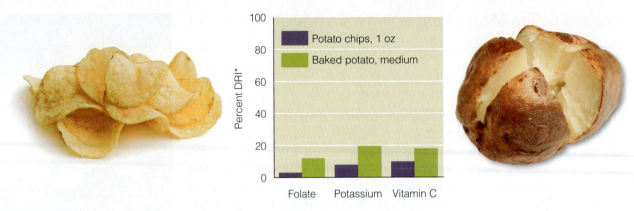

▲ Figure 2.1 Which Is the Healthier Way to Enjoy Potatoes?
Whereas one ounce of potato chips and one medium baked potato have similar amounts of kilocalories, their nutrient content is worlds apart. A baked potato contains more folate, potassium, and vitamin C, and fewer fat kilocalories, than its fried counterpart. The baked potato is therefore more nutrient dense than potato chips.

*Note: Based on the percentage of the DRI for 19-to-50-year-old males. All these percentages apply to females in the same age range, except for vitamin C. Females have lower vitamin C needs than males, so a baked potato provides over 20 percent of the DRI of this vitamin for women.

Though many foods, such as broccoli and carrots, are clearly nutrient dense, and other foods, such as potato chips and doughnuts, are clearly not, not all foods fit neatly into these two categories. Items such as dried fruits, nuts, peanut butter, and avocados are high in kilocalories, but they are also excellent sources of important nutrients, including polyunsaturated fatty acids, calcium, and iron. Other foods, such as whole milk or yogurt, contain the same nutrients, but higher amounts of fat and kilocalories than their nonfat or low-fat counterparts. These higher fat versions still provide significant amounts of calcium, riboflavin, vitamins A and D, and protein. Some foods, such as fruit-flavored yogurt and some fortified cereals, contain added sugars in addition to several essential nutrients. Do you think these foods can be considered nutrient dense?

In all of these scenarios, the answer is yes. Whereas nutrient dense usually means high in nutrients and low in energy, foods that are high in nutrients and high in energy can also be considered nutrient dense. The key is to be aware of the extra kilocalories and make up for them elsewhere in the diet. If you don't like skim milk and won't drink it, but do enjoy the taste of whole milk, then drinking whole milk is preferable to drinking non-calcium-containing beverages, such as soda. Just remember that unless you compensate for the extra kilocalories (by forgoing that nighttime cookie, for example), you may gain weight.

Healthy Eating Includes Low-Energy-Dense Foods

In contrast to nutrient density, energy density refers to foods that are high in energy but low in weight or volume, such as that potato chip. A serving of deep-fried chips weighs much less than a plain baked potato, but is considerably higher in fat and kilocalories. Therefore, the chip contains more energy per gram. A big, leafy green salad, on the other hand, is large in volume but low in energy density, due to its high water content.

Most high-fat foods are considered energy dense.[5] This is because fat has 9 kilocalories per gram and is thus 2.25 times more energy dense than either carbohydrates or protein at 4 kilocalories per gram. Individuals who choose low-energy-dense foods will generally have diets that are lower in fat and higher in nutrient content.

Eating a low-energy-dense diet can sometimes be the key to weight loss. Recent studies have found that leaner individuals ate more low-energy-dense foods and

TABLE 2.1   Bargain Shopping on an Energy Budget

Use the following guidelines when choosing energy-dense foods.

Foods	Energy Density	Are They an Energy Bargain?
Soups Fruits Vegetables	0.0 to 0.6 kcal/g	**Great Energy Bargain:** Eat as much of these low-energy-density foods as you want on a low-energy budget; however, take care that soups don't contain too much sodium, and are broth rather than cream based.
Starchy fruits and vegetables Lean meats Beans and legumes	0.6 to 1.5 kcal/g	**Good Energy Bargain:** Consume healthy portions of these foods on a low-energy budget.
Cheese Salad dressings Snack foods Desserts	1.5 to 4.0 kcal/g	**More Expensive Choices:** These foods should be chosen carefully and consumed in moderation.
Chocolates Deep-fat fried foods Nuts Chips Candy	4.0 to 9.0 kcal/g	**Very Expensive Choices:** These foods will blow your energy budget! Eat less of these foods and be aware of the portion size to avoid overconsuming kilocalories.

Source: Adapted from B. Rolls. 2012. *The Ultimate Volumetrics Diet: Smart, Simple, Science-Based Strategies for Losing Weight and Keeping It Off.* New York: HarperCollins.

fewer kilocalories, while consuming a greater volume of food, compared with their obese counterparts.[6] Eating low-density foods means larger portions for the same number of kilocalories.

Even modest changes in dietary intake may promote and help maintain weight loss[7] over time.[8] One reason for this may be improved satiety and appetite control.[9] Eating a larger volume of low-energy foods improves satiety and decreases hunger. In other words, low-energy foods will "fill you up before they fill you out."

If you are trying to maintain your current weight, or lose weight, you are probably on a limited energy budget and need to choose foods that are nutrient dense and low in kilocalories. Use the guide in **Table 2.1** to help stretch your energy budget while consuming the most nutrient-dense foods.

Many Resources Are Available for Planning a Healthy Diet

Do you think all this advice for planning a healthy diet is hard to keep straight? If so, you're not alone. Fortunately, there are several tools that can help you avoid both under- and overnutrition, including:

- The Dietary Reference Intakes (DRIs), which provide recommendations regarding your nutrient needs
- The *Dietary Guidelines for Americans*, which provide broad dietary and lifestyle advice
- MyPlate, part of the ChooseMyPlate.gov Web-based initiative, which is designed to help you eat healthfully and implement the recommendations in the DRIs and the advice in the *Dietary Guidelines*
- The exchange system, which groups foods according to their macronutrient content, thus making it easier to plan meals
- The Nutrition Facts panel on food labels, which contains the Daily Values, and which can help you decide which foods to buy

TABLE TIPS

Tips for an Adequate, Balanced, Varied, and Moderate Diet

Keep healthy snacks such as whole-grain crackers in your dorm room and combine them with protein-rich peanut butter or low-fat yogurt.

Pop a snack-pack size of *light* microwave popcorn for a portion-controlled whole-grain snack while you study.

Adopt a multicolor code to guide your food choices. Add tomato slices and a low-fat cheese slice to your whole-grain sandwich and carrots to your tossed green salad to ensure that your choices are adequate and varied.

Pack your own snack-sized portions of dried fruit, trail mix, whole-wheat crackers, baby carrots, or salt-free pretzels to carry in your backpack. Snack-sized bags of nuts and seeds are a nutritious way to help you avoid the vending machine and eat smaller, more moderate portions.

Keep your sweets to no more than about 100 kilocalories a day.

▶ **Figure 2.2 Dietary Recommendations and Implementation Tools**
The *Dietary Guidelines for Americans* serve as the basis for several tools that guide Americans in choosing healthy diets.

Together, these tools help you plan a balanced, moderate, and varied diet that meets your nutrient and health needs (**Figure 2.2**). **Table 2.2** provides a comparison of these tools, and the following text sections discuss each in more detail.

Let's look at each of these tools, beginning with the DRIs.

LO 2.1: THE TAKE-HOME MESSAGE Healthy eating emphasizes consuming the right amount of food from a variety of food groups to provide an adequate intake of nutrients and a moderate level of energy. Choosing nutrient-dense and low-energy-dense foods ensures a diet high in nutrient content and low enough in energy to prevent weight gain. Reference values, guidelines, and tools have been developed to help individuals make healthy choices.

What Are the Dietary Reference Intakes?

LO 2.2 Distinguish between the Dietary Reference Intake terms EAR, AI, RDA, UL, and AMDR.

The **Dietary Reference Intakes (DRIs)** are specific reference values for each nutrient issued by the Food and Nutrition Board (FNB) of the National Academy of Sciences' Institute of Medicine. The DRIs are the specific amounts of each nutrient that one needs to consume to maintain good health, prevent chronic diseases, and avoid unhealthy excesses.[10] The Institute of Medicine periodically organizes committees of U.S. and Canadian scientists and health experts to update these recommendations based on the latest scientific research. Since the 1940s, the DRIs have been updated ten times.

In the 1990s, nutrition researchers identified expanded roles for many nutrients. Though nutrient deficiencies were still an important issue, research suggested that higher amounts of some nutrients could play a role in disease prevention. Also, as consumers began using more dietary supplements and fortified foods, committee members grew concerned that excessive consumption of some nutrients might be as unhealthy

Dietary Reference Intakes (DRIs) Reference values for nutrients developed by the Food and Nutrition Board of the Institute of Medicine, used to plan and evaluate the diets of healthy people in the United States and Canada. It includes the Estimated Average Requirement (EAR), the Recommended Dietary Allowance (RDA), the Adequate Intake (AI), and the Tolerable Upper Intake Level (UL).

TABLE 2.2   Putting It All Together: Tools for Healthy Eating

	DRIs	Dietary Guidelines for Americans, 2010	MyPlate	Nutrition Facts Panel	Exchange Lists for Healthy Eating
What Are They?	Specific reference values for each nutrient by age and gender	Reflect the most current nutrition and physical activity recommendations for good health	A representational icon that depicts five food groups using the familiar mealtime visual of a place setting	Contains important nutrition information to be used to compare food products	Lists that are organized into food groups by their carbohydrate, protein, fat, and kilocalorie contents
How Do They Guide You in Healthy Eating?	DRIs provide recommendations to prevent malnutrition and chronic diseases for each nutrient. The upper level is designed to prevent overnutrition or toxicity.	The Dietary Guidelines emphasize healthy food choices, maintaining healthy weight, and physical activity. Guidelines for types of foods, moderate alcohol intake, and food safety are also included.	MyPlate is the focal point for the Web-based ChooseMyPlate .gov initiative, which provides information to build a healthy diet based on the Dietary Guidelines for Americans, 2010.	You can use the Nutrition Facts panel to compare the nutrient density of foods.	It's easy to plan healthy menus with a variety of foods. The exchanges are based on specific food portion sizes plus various fat levels in foods.
What Are They Made Up Of?	EARs, RDAs, AIs, ULs, and AMDRs	Divided into nine categories: 1. Adequate nutrients 2. Weight management 3. Physical activity 4. Food groups 5. Fats 6. Carbohydrates 7. Sodium and potassium 8. Alcoholic beverages 9. Food safety	Recommendations are made for physical activity as well as five food groups, plus oils: 1. Vegetables 2. Fruits 3. Grains 4. Protein 5. Dairy 6. Oils	Information is presented about: - Serving size - Servings per package - Total kilocalories and kilocalories from fat - Macronutrients - Vitamins and minerals - % Daily Values	Exchange lists consist of six food groups: 1. Starch 2. Meat 3. Vegetables 4. Fruit 5. Milk 6. Fat

as, or even more dangerous than, not consuming enough. Hence the Food and Nutrition Board (FNB) convened a variety of committees between 1997 and 2004 to take on the enormous task of reviewing the research on vitamins, minerals, carbohydrates, fats, protein, water, and other substances such as fiber, and developing the current DRI reference values for all the nutrients. As research evolves, changes are made in the DRIs.

The DRIs Suggest an Intake Level for Each Nutrient

Individuals have different **nutrient requirements** during different life stages, such as during pregnancy or older age. A teenager may need more of a specific nutrient than a 55-year-old (and vice versa) and women need more of certain nutrients during pregnancy and lactation. Men and women vary in some of their nutrient requirements due to the physiological differences of their bodies.[11]

The DRIs Encompass Several Reference Values

The DRIs cover five reference values: the Estimated Average Requirement (EAR), the Recommended Dietary Allowance (RDA), the Adequate Intake (AI), the

nutrient requirements The amounts of specific nutrients needed to prevent malnutrition or deficiency; reflected in the DRIs.

Tolerable Upper Intake Level (UL), and the Acceptable Macronutrient Distribution Range (AMDR) (**Focus Figure 2.3**). Each of these values is unique, and serves a different need in planning a healthy diet. Only three of these values, the RDA or AI (not both), the AMDR, and the UL, are used to assess whether your diet is meeting your nutrient needs.

The EAR is the starting point in the process of determining the other values. Let's look at how the values are determined.

Estimated Average Requirements

The DRI committee members begin by reviewing a variety of research studies to determine the **Estimated Average Requirement (EAR)** for a nutrient. They may look at studies that investigate the consequences of eating a diet too low in the nutrient and the associated side effects or physical changes that develop, as well as how much of the nutrient should be consumed to correct the deficiency. They may also review studies that measure the amount a healthy individual absorbs, stores, and maintains daily. Additionally, they look at research studies that address the role the nutrient plays in reducing the risk of associated chronic diseases, such as heart disease. After a thorough review process, the EAR for the nutrient is determined.

The EAR is the average amount of a nutrient projected to meet the needs of 50 percent of healthy Americans by age and gender.[12] The EAR is a good starting point to determine the amount of a nutrient an individual should consume daily for good health. As you can see from Figure 2.3, if a nutrient's requirements were set using the EAR, 50 percent of the individuals would need more and 50 percent would need less than this amount to meet their needs.

An EAR for each nutrient is established based on a measurement that indicates whether an individual is at risk of a deficiency. For example, to determine the EAR for iron for a 19-year-old female, scientists measure hemoglobin concentrations in the blood. The measurement differs from nutrient to nutrient. If there aren't enough studies or collected data to develop an appropriate measurement for a nutrient, an EAR or requirement for that nutrient is not established. Once the EAR has been set for each nutrient, the Recommended Dietary Allowances (RDAs) can be calculated.

Recommended Dietary Allowances

The **Recommended Dietary Allowance (RDA)** is based on the EAR, but it is set higher. It represents the amount for each nutrient that should meet the needs of nearly all (97 to 98 percent) of the individuals in a specific gender and age group. Let's use iron to illustrate the relationship between the EAR and the RDA. After careful review of the latest research on iron metabolism, the EAR for iron was set at 6 milligrams per day for both men and women over all age groups.[13] The amount is increased to an RDA of 18 milligrams per day to cover the needs 97 to 98 percent of females aged 19 to 30. For 19- to 30-year-old males, the RDA for iron is 8 milligrams daily. The RDA for each nutrient according to age and gender is presented in the front of the textbook.

Although the RDA is a valuable reference for healthy eating, researchers have not established RDAs for all nutrients. If there is insufficient evidence to determine an EAR for a nutrient, the RDA can't be calculated. When this is the case, such as with calcium, an Adequate Intake (AI) can provide an alternative guideline.

Adequate Intakes

Adequate Intake (AI) is a formal reference value that is estimated based on the judgment of the members of the FNB, according to the latest research. The AI is the next best scientific estimate of the amount of a nutrient that groups of similar individuals should consume to maintain good health.

There are several differences between the RDAs and the AIs. First, the RDAs are based on EARs, whereas the AIs are set without having established an estimated

Estimated Average Requirement (EAR) The average daily amount of a nutrient needed by 50 percent of the individuals in a similar age and gender group.

Recommended Dietary Allowance (RDA) The recommended daily amount of a nutrient that meets the needs of nearly all individuals (97 to 98 percent) in a similar age and gender group. The RDA is set higher than the EAR.

Adequate Intake (AI) The *approximate* daily amount of a nutrient that is sufficient to meet the needs of similar individuals within a population group. The Food and Nutrition Board uses AIs for nutrients that do not have enough scientific evidence to calculate an RDA.

Dietary Reference Intakes

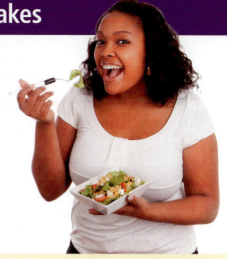

Dietary Reference Intakes (DRIs) are specific reference values for each nutrient issued by the United States National Academy of Sciences, Institute of Medicine. They identify the amounts of each nutrient that one needs to consume to maintain good health.

DRIs FOR MOST NUTRIENTS

EAR The Estimated Average Requirement (EAR) is the average daily intake level estimated to meet the needs of half the people in a certain group. Scientists use it to calculate the RDA.

RDA The Recommended Dietary Allowance (RDA) is the average daily intake level estimated to meet the needs of nearly all people in a certain group. Aim for this amount!

AI The Adequate Intake (AI) is the average daily intake level assumed to be adequate. It is used when an EAR cannot be determined. Aim for this amount if there is no RDA!

UL The Tolerable Upper Intake Level (UL) is the highest average daily intake level likely to pose no health risks. Do not exceed this amount on a daily basis!

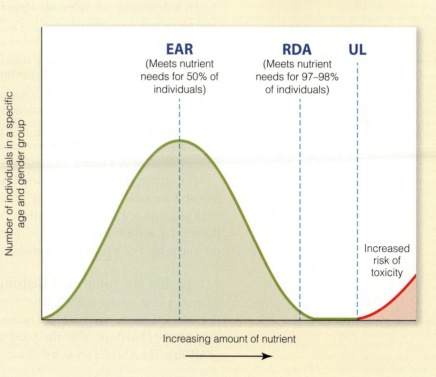

EAR (Meets nutrient needs for 50% of individuals)

RDA (Meets nutrient needs for 97–98% of individuals)

UL

Number of individuals in a specific age and gender group

Increased risk of toxicity

Increasing amount of nutrient

DRIs RELATED TO ENERGY

AMDR The Acceptable Macronutrient Distribution Range (AMDR) is the recommended range of carbohydrate, fat, and protein intake expressed as a percentage of total energy.

EER The Estimated Energy Requirement (EER) is the average daily energy intake predicted to meet the needs of healthy adults.

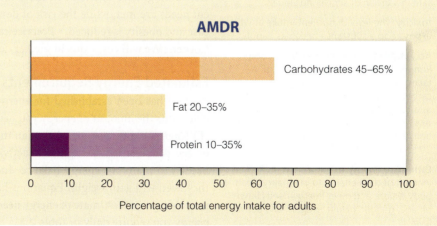

AMDR

Carbohydrates 45–65%

Fat 20–35%

Protein 10–35%

Percentage of total energy intake for adults

average requirement. If a nutrient has an AI, then more research must be done to accurately set an RDA. Second, the RDAs should cover the needs of 97 to 98 percent of the population, but the AIs do not estimate how many people will be covered because the EAR is not available. However, if you consume an amount equal to the AIs you will likely exceed the EARs or RDAs. Finally, for infants, AIs are the only estimations for nutrients to evaluate dietary adequacy. This is because conducting the types of studies necessary to determine more specific information would be unethical.

The nutrients with AIs are noted in the DRI tables in the front of your textbook and include some vitamins and minerals, such as biotin, pantothenic acid, and vitamins D and K, and the minerals calcium and potassium.

Tolerable Upper Intake Level

Because consuming too much of some nutrients can lead to harmful side effects, the FNB developed the **Tolerable Upper Intake Level (UL).** The tolerable upper intake level is not a recommended intake. It refers to the highest amount of a nutrient that is unlikely to cause harm if consumed daily. The higher the consumption above the UL, the higher the risk of **toxicity.** These reference values became necessary because of individuals' increased interest in consuming dietary supplements and fortified foods in pursuit of supposed health benefits. For example, the U.S. Poison Centers report more than 60,000 annual cases of vitamin toxicity from dietary supplements.[14] Unfortunately, many Americans believe that vitamin supplements are safe in any dose but that consuming too much of other nutrients, such as fat or cholesterol, can have a deleterious effect.

Not all nutrients have UL values. This doesn't mean that high intakes of those nutrients are safe, however. Because there aren't any known benefits for a healthy adult to consume a higher amount than the UL, people should aim to consume less than the UL and avoid the risk of health problems. The UL for selected nutrients according to age and gender is presented in the front of the textbook.

Acceptable Macronutrient Distribution Ranges

To ensure that intake of the energy nutrients is adequate and proportionate to physiological needs, recommended ranges of carbohydrates, fats, and proteins have been developed and are called the **Acceptable Macronutrient Distribution Ranges (AMDRs).** The AMDRs are as follows:

- Carbohydrates should comprise 45 to 65 percent of your daily kilocalories
- Fat should comprise 20 to 35 percent of your daily kilocalories
- Proteins should comprise 10 to 35 percent of your daily kilocalories

Consuming these nutrients in these ranges will ensure that kilocalorie and nutrient needs are met, while the risk of developing chronic diseases such as heart disease and obesity is reduced.[15] Practice calculating the AMDR using the Calculation Corner. (We will cover this in greater detail in Chapter 14.)

Estimated Energy Requirements

No DRI has been established for energy (kilocalorie) intake. The method used to determine the amount of energy you need, or your **Estimated Energy Requirement (EER),** uses a different approach than the RDAs or AIs. The EER is calculated based on age, gender, height, weight, and activity level, and indicates the amount of energy needed to maintain energy balance. Individuals who consume more energy than they need will gain weight. Equations have been designed for males and females to provide a general estimate of energy needs. You can find the approximate amount of energy you require daily in **Table 2.3.**

Tolerable Upper Intake Level (UL) The maximum daily amount of a nutrient considered safe in a group of similar individuals.

toxicity The level of nutrient intake at which exposure to a substance becomes harmful.

Acceptable Macronutrient Distribution Ranges (AMDRs) A healthy range of intakes for the energy-containing nutrients—carbohydrates, proteins, and fats—expressed as a percentage of total daily energy. The AMDRs for adults are 45 to 65 percent carbohydrates, 10 to 35 percent protein, and 20 to 35 percent fat.

Estimated Energy Requirement (EER) The amount of daily energy to maintain a healthy body weight and meet energy needs based on age, gender, height, weight, and activity level.

TABLE 2.3 How Many Kilocalories Do You Need Daily?

The amount of kilocalories needed daily to maintain a healthy weight is based upon age, gender, and activity level.*

	Males				Females		
Age	Sedentary	Moderately Active	Active	Age	Sedentary	Moderately Active	Active
16–18	2,400	2,800	3,200	18	1,800	2,000	2,400
19–20	2,600	2,800	3,000	19–20	2,000	2,200	2,400
21–25	2,400	2,800	3,000	21–25	2,000	2,200	2,400
26–30	2,400	2,600	3,000	26–30	1,800	2,000	2,400
31–35	2,400	2,600	3,000	31–35	1,800	2,000	2,200
36–40	2,400	2,600	2,800	36–40	1,800	2,000	2,200
41–45	2,200	2,600	2,800	41–45	1,800	2,000	2,200
46–50	2,200	2,400	2,800	46–50	1,800	2,000	2,200

Note: *These kilocalorie levels are based on the Institute of Medicine's Estimated Energy Requirements from the *Dietary Reference Intakes: Macronutrients Report,* 2002. Sedentary: Partaking in less than 30 minutes a day of moderate physical activity in addition to daily activities. Moderately Active: Partaking in at least 30 minutes and up to 60 minutes a day of moderate physical activity in addition to daily activities. Active: Partaking in 60 or more minutes a day of moderate physical activity in addition to daily activities.

Source: U.S. Department of Agriculture. 2011. *Dietary Guidelines for Americans, 2010.* Available at www.health.gov/dietaryguidelines.

 ## Calculation Corner

Calculating AMDR

Use the following scenario to calculate the AMDR for carbohydrate and fat:

Suppose a woman needs 2,150 kcal per day to maintain her current healthy weight.

The AMDR for carbohydrate is 45 to 65 percent of total daily kilocalories. To determine the number of kilocalories she needs to obtain daily from carbohydrate, we run the following equations:

2,150 kcal $\times$ 45 percent carbohydrates = 2,150 $\times$ 0.45 = 968 kcal
2,150 kcal $\times$ 65 percent carbohydrates = 2,150 $\times$ 0.65 = 1,398 kcal

Thus, of the 2,150 kcal the woman eats each day, 968 to 1,398 kcal should be from carbohydrates.

The AMDR for fat is 20 to 35 percent of daily kilocalories. Therefore:

2,150 kcal $\times$ 20 percent fats = 2,150 $\times$ 0.20 = 430 kcal
2,150 kcal $\times$ 35 percent fats = 2,150 $\times$ 0.35 = 753 kcal

Of the 2,150 kcal the woman eats each day, 430 to 753 kcal should be from fat.

Can you calculate the AMDR for your daily intake of kilocalories?

Scan this QR code with your mobile device to access practice math activities. You can also access the activities in **Mastering**Nutrition™.

You Can Use the DRIs to Plan a Quality Diet

You can use the DRIs to make healthy food choices and plan a quality diet. To meet your needs, your goal should be to achieve the RDA or the AI of all nutrients, but not exceed the UL. **Table 2.4** summarizes how to use the DRIs to plan a quality diet. (You will also find the DRIs for all nutrients on the inside front cover of this textbook.)

Each chapter in this textbook will further explain what each nutrient is, why it is important, how much (based on the DRIs) you need to consume, and how to get enough, without consuming too much, in your diet.

TABLE 2.4	The Do's and Don'ts of the DRIs
Reference Value	**When Planning Your Diet**
Estimated Average Requirement (EAR)	**Don't** use this amount.
Recommended Dietary Allowance (RDA)	**Do** aim for this amount!
Adequate Intake (AI)	**Do** aim for this amount if an RDA isn't available.
Tolerable Upper Intake Level (UL)	**Don't** exceed this amount on a daily basis.
Acceptable Macronutrient Distribution Range (AMDR)	**Do** follow these guidelines regarding the percentage of carbohydrates, protein, and fat in the diet.

Source: Adapted from the Subcommittee on Interpretation and Uses of Dietary Reference Intakes and the Standing Committee on the Scientific Evaluation of Dietary Reference Intakes, Institute of Medicine and Food and Nutrition Board. 2003. *Dietary Reference Intakes: Applications in Dietary Planning.* National Academics Press. Reprinted with permission.

LO 2.2: THE TAKE-HOME MESSAGE The Dietary Reference Intakes (DRIs) are specific reference values that help individuals determine daily nutrient needs to maintain good health, prevent chronic diseases, and avoid unhealthy excesses. The reference values include the EAR, RDA, AI, UL, and AMDR. The EER can help determine the appropriate amount of energy needed to maintain a healthy body weight given one's age, gender, height, weight, and activity levels. You should try to meet your RDA or AI and consume below the UL for each nutrient daily while maintaining sufficient energy intake.

The *Dietary Guidelines* encourage consumption of a variety of fruits and vegetables.

Dietary Guidelines for Americans Guidelines published every five years by the Department of Health and Human Services and the United States Department of Agriculture that provide dietary and lifestyle advice to healthy individuals aged 2 and older to maintain good health and prevent chronic diseases. They are the basis for the federal food and nutrition education programs.

What Are the *Dietary Guidelines for Americans*?

LO 2.3 Describe the recommendations included in the *Dietary Guidelines for Americans.*

Whereas the DRIs were released to prevent undernutrition, the *Dietary Guidelines for Americans* were developed out of concern over the incidence of overnutrition among Americans. By the 1970s, research had shown that Americans' overconsumption of foods rich in fat, saturated fat, cholesterol, and sodium was increasing their risk for chronic diseases such as heart disease and stroke.[16] In 1977, the U.S. government released the *Dietary Goals for Americans,* which were designed to improve the nutritional quality of Americans' diets and to try to reduce the incidence of overnutrition and its associated health problems.[17]

Amid controversy over the scientific validity of the goals, the government asked scientists to lend credence to the goals and provide dietary guidance. Their work culminated in the 1980 *Dietary Guidelines for Americans,* which emphasized eating a variety of foods to obtain a nutritionally well-balanced daily diet. Since 1990, the U.S. Department of Agriculture (USDA) and the Department of Health and Human Services (DHHS) have been mandated by law to update the guidelines every five years. The guidelines serve as one governmental voice to shape all federally funded nutrition programs in areas such as research and labeling, and to educate and guide consumers about healthy diet and lifestyle choices.[18]

The *Dietary Guidelines for Americans* reflect the most current nutrition and lifestyle advice for good health. They are designed to help individuals aged 2 and over improve the quality and content of their diet and lifestyle to lower their risk of chronic diseases and conditions, such as high blood pressure, high blood cholesterol levels, diabetes mellitus, heart disease, certain cancers, and osteoporosis.

The most recent guidelines are different from previous reports, as they address the obesity epidemic that is occurring among Americans.[19] **Table 2.5** provides an overview of the current major goals, along with helpful dietary and lifestyle recommendations.

LO 2.3: THE TAKE-HOME MESSAGE The *Dietary Guidelines* consist of key recommendations and lifestyle advice designed to help Americans lead a healthy lifestyle. They are updated every five years.

TABLE 2.5 The *Dietary Guidelines for Americans* at a Glance

Balance Kilocalories to Manage Weight	■ Prevent and/or reduce overweight and obesity through improved eating and physical activity behaviors. ■ Control total kilocalorie intake to manage body weight. For people who are overweight or obese, this will mean consuming fewer kilocalories from foods and beverages. ■ Increase physical activity and reduce time spent in sedentary behaviors. ■ Maintain appropriate kilocalorie balance during each stage of life—childhood, adolescence, adulthood, pregnancy and breast-feeding, and older age.
Reduce These Foods and Food Components	■ Reduce daily sodium intake to less than 2,300 mg and further reduce intake to 1,500 mg among persons who are 51 and older and those of any age who are African-American or have hypertension, diabetes, or chronic kidney disease. The 1,500-mg recommendation applies to about half of the U.S. population, including children, and the majority of adults. ■ Consume less than 10 percent of kilocalories from saturated fatty acids by replacing them with mono-unsaturated and polyunsaturated fatty acids. ■ Consume less than 300 mg per day of dietary cholesterol. ■ Keep *trans* fatty acid consumption as low as possible by limiting foods that contain synthetic sources of *trans* fats, such as partially hydrogenated oils, and by limiting other solid fats. ■ Reduce the intake of kilocalories from solid fats and added sugars. ■ Limit the consumption of foods that contain refined grains, especially refined grain foods that contain solid fats, added sugars, and sodium. ■ If alcohol is consumed, it should be consumed in moderation—up to 1 drink per day for women and 2 drinks per day for men—and only by adults of legal drinking age.
Increase These Foods and Nutrients	■ Increase vegetable and fruit intake. ■ Eat a variety of vegetables, especially dark green and red and orange vegetables and beans and peas. ■ Consume at least half of all grains as whole grains. Increase whole-grain intake by replacing refined grains with whole grains. ■ Increase intake of fat-free or low-fat milk and milk products, such as milk, yogurt, cheese, or fortified soy beverages. ■ Choose a variety of protein foods, which include seafood, lean meat and poultry, eggs, beans and peas, soy products, and unsalted nuts and seeds. ■ Increase the amount and variety of seafood consumed by choosing seafood in place of some meat and poultry. ■ Replace protein foods that are higher in solid fats with choices that are lower in solid fats and kilocalories and/or are sources of oils. ■ Use oils to replace solid fats where possible. ■ Choose foods that provide more potassium, dietary fiber, calcium, and vitamin D, which are nutrients of concern in American diets. These foods include vegetables, fruits, whole grains, and milk and milk products.
Build Healthy Eating Patterns	■ Select an eating pattern that meets nutrient needs over time at an appropriate kilocalorie level. ■ Account for all foods and beverages consumed and assess how they fit within a total healthy eating pattern. ■ Follow food safety recommendations when preparing and eating foods to reduce the risk of foodborne illnesses.

Source: Report of the Dietary Guidelines Advisory Committee on the *Dietary Guidelines for Americans, 2010.* Available at www.cnpp.usda.gov. Accessed January 2014.

What Is the MyPlate Food Guidance System?

LO 2.4 Explain the concept of the MyPlate food guidance system, including the food groups and typical foods represented.

Illustrated graphics called **food guidance systems** are often used to summarize guidelines for healthy eating. **MyPlate** is the most recent food guidance system developed by the USDA for Americans. Released in 2011, MyPlate is a tool that reflects the recommendations in the *Dietary Guidelines for Americans, 2010*. Its online component, ChooseMyPlate.gov, is a Web-based communication and education initiative that provides information, tips, and tools to help people build a healthier diet based on the latest nutrition and health recommendations from the Dietary Guidelines Advisory Committee Report and the DRIs. The website also contains an interactive food guidance system, based on the USDA Food Patterns, which provides personalized food plans based on the latest nutrition and health recommendations.

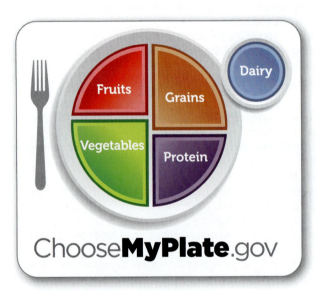

▲ **Figure 2.4 Anatomy of MyPlate**
The MyPlate icon reinforces important concepts of meal planning, healthful choices, proportionality, and moderation to be used in planning a healthful diet.
Source: U.S. Department of Agriculture. 2011. ChooseMyPlate.gov.

food guidance systems Visual diagrams that provide a variety of food recommendations to help a person create a well-balanced diet.

MyPlate A food guidance system that illustrates the recommendations in the *Dietary Guidelines for Americans* and the Dietary Reference Intakes (DRIs) nutrient goals.

proportionality The relationship of one entity to another. Vegetables and fruits should be consumed in a higher proportion than dairy and protein foods in the diet.

MyPlate Emphasizes Changes in Diet

MyPlate shows five food groups in relative proportion using the familiar mealtime visual of a place setting. It serves as an icon to remind consumers to eat healthfully. In addition, the tool MyPlate and the supporting information at ChooseMyPlate.gov promote proportionality, moderation, variety, and personalization. As you can see in **Figure 2.4**, MyPlate shows a place setting split into sections, with each colored section representing one of five food groups: fruits, vegetables, grains, protein, and dairy. Whereas oils are an important part of a healthy diet, they are not represented on the plate, as they are not considered a food group.

You can now easily see **proportionality** in how these food groups should dominate your diet. The MyPlate logo divides a plate into four sections for fruits, vegetables, grains, and proteins, with a fifth section for fat-free or low-fat dairy. Half of your plate should be devoted to waist- and heart-friendly vegetables and fruits, with a smaller portion for grains (at least half of which should be whole grains) and lean protein foods such as fish, skinless poultry, lean meats, dried beans, and peas. The blue circle next to the plate is a visual reminder to make sure that fat-free and low-fat dairy foods such as milk should not be forgotten at mealtimes. Shifting the food proportionality on your plate can have a dramatic effect on your kilocalorie intake and thus on your weight. Devoting at least half of the surface of the plate to low-kilocalorie fruits and vegetables should crowd out higher kilocalorie grains and protein food choices. Take the Self-Assessment to see how well-proportioned your diet is.

Several important nutrition messages at ChooseMyPlate.gov are based on three general areas of recommendation from the current *Dietary Guidelines*:

1. Balance kilocalories
   - Enjoy your food, but eat less.
   - Avoid oversized portions.
2. Increase the following foods
   - Make half your plate fruits and vegetables.
   - Make at least half your grains whole grains.
   - Switch to fat-free or low-fat (1%) milk.

Does Your Diet Have Proportionality?

Answer "yes" or "no" to the following questions:

1. Are grains the main food choice at all your meals?

   Yes ☐   No ☐

2. Do you often forget to eat vegetables?

   Yes ☐   No ☐

3. Do you typically eat fewer than three pieces of fruit daily?

   Yes ☐   No ☐

4. Do you often have fewer than three cups of milk daily?

   Yes ☐   No ☐

5. Is the portion of meat, chicken, or fish the largest item on your dinner plate?

   Yes ☐   No ☐

Answer

If you answered "yes" to three or more of these questions, it is very likely that your diet lacks proportionality. You can use the information in this chapter to help improve the proportionality of your diet.

3. Reduce the following foods
   - Compare sodium in foods like soup, bread, and frozen meals—and choose the foods with lower numbers.
   - Drink water instead of sugary drinks.

These messages emphasize not only that you should balance your kilocalories daily to better manage your weight but also that you should choose mostly nutrient-dense foods from each food group.

Individuals who choose high-nutrient-dense and low-energy-dense foods will generally have diets that are lower in solid fats and added sugars and higher in nutrient content. **Figure 2.5** helps you compare some nutrient-dense food choices with less healthy food choices in each food group. As you look at the figure, notice which foods are, by contrast, energy dense.

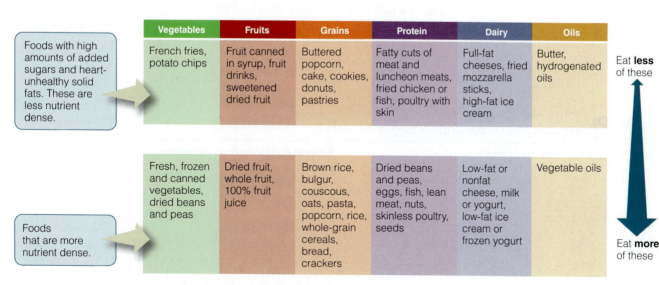

	Vegetables	Fruits	Grains	Protein	Dairy	Oils
Foods with high amounts of added sugars and heart-unhealthy solid fats. These are less nutrient dense.	French fries, potato chips	Fruit canned in syrup, fruit drinks, sweetened dried fruit	Buttered popcorn, cake, cookies, donuts, pastries	Fatty cuts of meat and luncheon meats, fried chicken or fish, poultry with skin	Full-fat cheeses, fried mozzarella sticks, high-fat ice cream	Butter, hydrogenated oils	Eat **less** of these
Foods that are more nutrient dense.	Fresh, frozen and canned vegetables, dried beans and peas	Dried fruit, whole fruit, 100% fruit juice	Brown rice, bulgur, couscous, oats, pasta, popcorn, rice, whole-grain cereals, bread, crackers	Dried beans and peas, eggs, fish, lean meat, nuts, skinless poultry, seeds	Low-fat or nonfat cheese, milk or yogurt, low-fat ice cream or frozen yogurt	Vegetable oils	Eat **more** of these

▲ **Figure 2.5 Nutrient-Dense Food Choices**
Choose nutrient-dense foods more often to build a well-balanced diet.

▶ **Figure 2.6** **Mix Up Your Choices within Each Food Group**

Source: USDA Consumer Brochure. 2005. *Finding Your Way to a Healthier You*. Based on the *Dietary Guidelines for Americans*.

Focus on fruits. Eat a variety of fruits—whether fresh, frozen, canned, or dried—rather than fruit juice for most of your fruit choices. For a 2,000-calorie diet, you will need 2 cups of fruit each day (for example, 1 small banana, 1 large orange, and ¼ cup of dried apricots or peaches).

Vary your veggies. Eat more dark green veggies, such as broccoli, kale, and other dark leafy greens; orange veggies, such as carrots, sweet potatoes, pumpkin, and winter squash; and beans and peas, such as pinto beans, kidney beans, black beans, garbanzo beans, split peas, and lentils.

Get your calcium-rich foods. Get 3 cups of low-fat or fat-free milk—or an equivalent amount of low-fat yogurt and/or low-fat cheese (1½ ounces of cheese equals 1 cup of milk)—every day. For kids aged 2 to 8, it's 2 cups of milk. If you don't or can't consume milk, choose lactose-free milk products and/or calcium-fortified foods and beverages.

Make half your grains whole. Eat at least 3 ounces of whole-grain cereals, breads, crackers, rice, or pasta every day. One ounce is about 1 slice of bread, 1 cup of breakfast cereal, or ½ cup of cooked rice or pasta. Look to see that grains such as wheat, rice, oats, or corn are referred to as "whole" in the list of ingredients.

Go lean with protein. Choose lean meats and poultry. Bake it, broil it, or grill it. And vary your protein choices—with more fish, beans, peas, nuts, and seeds.

Know the limits on fats, salt, and sugars. Read the Nutrition Facts label on foods. Look for foods low in saturated fats and *trans* fats. Choose and prepare foods and beverages with little salt (sodium) and/or added sugars (caloric sweeteners).

Eating a variety of foods among and within the food groups highlighted in MyPlate will increase your chances of consuming all 40 of the nutrients your body needs. Because no single food or food group provides all the nutrients, a varied diet of nutrient-dense foods is the savviest strategy. **Figure 2.6** provides tips on how to choose a variety of foods from each food group.

Lastly, physical activity is an important component in the successful implementation of a weight loss or weight management program. Being physically active (see **Table 2.6**) helps you stay fit and reduce your risk of chronic diseases such as heart disease and cancer. Advice regarding physical activity can be found at ChooseMyPlate.gov.

TABLE 2.6 What Is Moderate and Vigorous Activity?	
Examples of Moderate Activities (Expend 3.5 to 7 Kilocalories per Minute):	**Examples of Vigorous Activities (Expend More Than 7 Kilocalories per Minute):**
■ Brisk walking	■ Jogging or running
■ Bicycling 5 to 9 mph	■ Bicycling more than 10 mph
■ Shooting hoops	■ Playing competitive sports like basketball, soccer, or lacrosse
■ Using free weights	■ Rowing on a machine vigorously
■ Yoga	■ Karate, judo, or tae kwon do
■ Walking a dog	■ Jumping rope

Source: Adapted from the Centers for Disease Control and Prevention. 2011. *Physical Activity for a Healthy Weight*. Available at www.cdc.gov. Accessed February 2012.

How to Use MyPlate

You now know to eat a variety of nutrient-dense foods to be healthy, and that MyPlate helps you select a diverse group of foods, but you may be wondering how much from each food group a person should be eating. The ChooseMyPlate.gov interactive website will give you the exact numbers of servings to eat from each food group based on your daily kilocalorie needs. If you cannot go to the website, you can obtain similar information by using Tables 2.3 and 2.7 in this chapter. Table 2.7 will tell you the quantity from each food group you should consume to healthfully obtain the daily kilocalories you need.

For a moderately active female who needs 2,000 kilocalories daily, a healthy daily diet would consist of the following:

- 6 servings from the grains group
- 2 ½ cups of dark green, orange, starchy, and other vegetables, and some legumes
- 2 cups of fruits
- 3 cups of fat-free or low-fat milk and yogurt
- 5 ½ ounces of lean meat, poultry, and fish, or the equivalent in meat alternatives such as beans
- 6 teaspoons of vegetable oils

The kilocalorie levels and distribution of food groups in daily food plans are calculated using the leanest food choices with no added sugar. If all food selections are low in fat and added sugar, this menu will provide a total of about 1,740 kilocalories (Figure 2.7). If you pour whole milk (high in fat) over your sweetened cereal (added sugar) instead of using skim milk (fat free) to drench your shredded wheat (no added sugar), the extra fat and sugar kilocalories add up quickly to reach 2,000 kilocalories (Table 2.8).

260 kilocalories (added fats and sugars)

1,740 kilocalories (lean foods without added sugars)

2,000 total daily kilocalories

▲ **Figure 2.7 How Solid Fats and Added Sugars Fit into a Balanced Diet**
If you select mostly nutrient-dense, lean foods that contain few solid fats and added sugars, you may have leftover kilocalories to "spend" on extra helpings or a sweet dessert.

TABLE 2.7	How Much Should You Eat from Each Food Group?

The following are suggested amounts to consume daily from each of the basic food groups and the oils based on daily kilocalorie needs. Remember that most food choices should be fat free or low fat and contain little added sugar.

Kilocalorie Level	Grains (oz eq)	Vegetables (cups)	Fruits (cups)	Oils (tsp)	Dairy (cups)	Protein (oz eq)
1,400	5	1.5	1.5	4	2	4
1,600	5	2	1.5	5	3	5
1,800	6	2.5	1.5	5	3	5
2,000	6	2.5	2	6	3	5.5
2,200	7	3	2	6	3	6
2,400	8	3	2	7	3	6.5
2,600	9	3.5	2	8	3	6.5
2,800	10	3.5	2.5	8	3	7

Note: *Grains:* Includes all foods made with wheat, rice, oats, cornmeal, or barley, such as bread, pasta, oatmeal, breakfast cereals, tortillas, and grits. In general, 1 slice of bread, 1 cup of ready-to-eat cereal, or ½ cup of cooked rice, pasta, or cooked cereal is considered 1 ounce equivalent (oz eq) from the grains group. *At least half of all grains consumed should be whole grains such as whole-wheat bread, oats, or brown rice.*
Vegetables: Includes all fresh, frozen, canned, and dried vegetables, and vegetable juices. In general, 1 cup of raw or cooked vegetables or vegetable juice, or 2 cups of raw leafy greens, is considered 1 cup from the vegetable group.
Fruits: Includes all fresh, frozen, canned, and dried fruits, and fruit juices. In general, 1 cup of fruit or 100% fruit juice, or ½ cup of dried fruit, is considered 1 cup from the fruit group.
Oils: Includes vegetable oils such as canola, corn, olive, soybean, and sunflower oil, fatty fish, nuts, avocados, mayonnaise, salad dressings made with oils, and soft margarine.
Dairy: Includes all fat-free and low-fat milk, yogurt, and cheese. In general, 1 cup of milk or yogurt, 1½ ounces of natural cheese, or 2 ounces of processed cheese is considered 1 cup from the dairy group.
Proteins: In general, 1 ounce of lean meat, poultry, or fish, 1 egg, 1 tablespoon peanut butter, ¼ cup cooked dry beans, or ½ ounce of nuts or seeds is considered 1 ounce equivalent (oz eq) from the protein group.

Source: U.S. Department of Agriculture. 2011. Available at www.ChooseMyPlate.gov.

TABLE 2.8 Choose Right

As you can see, your daily food plan can include solid fats and added sugars, depending on food choices.

Choosing . . .	Over . . .	Will Cost You
Whole milk (1 cup)	Fat-free milk (1 cup)	65 kilocalories
Roasted chicken thigh with skin (3 oz)	Roasted chicken breast, skinless (3 oz)	70 kilocalories
Glazed doughnut, (3¾" diameter)	English muffin (one muffin)	165 kilocalories
French fries (one medium order)	Baked potato (one medium)	299 kilocalories
Regular soda (one can, 12 fl oz)	Diet soda (one can, 12 fl oz)	150 kilocalories

Source: Adapted from the U.S. Department of Agriculture, MyPlate. "Empty Calories: How Do I Count the Empty Calories I Eat?" 2011. Available at www.ChooseMyPlate.gov.

Figure 2.8 shows how servings from the various food groups can create well-balanced meals and snacks throughout the day. Although this particular menu is balanced and the foods are nutrient dense, it is unlikely that every day will be this ideal. Fortunately, nutrient needs are averaged over time. If an individual eats insufficient servings of one food group or a specific nutrient one day, he or she can

▼Figure 2.8 **A Healthy Daily Food Plan**
A variety of foods from each food group creates a well-balanced diet.

Breakfast

Vegetables	Fruits	Grains	Protein	Dairy	Oils
	Banana, 1 small; Orange juice, 1 cup	Bran flakes, 1 cup; Whole-wheat English muffin, ½		Fat-free milk, 1 cup	Soft margarine, 1 tsp

Lunch

Vegetables	Fruits	Grains	Protein	Dairy	Oils
Diced celery, 1 tbs; Romaine lettuce, ½ cup; Tomatoes, 2 slices	Pear, 1 medium	Whole-wheat bread, 2 slices	Tuna (packed in water), 2.5 oz	Fat-free milk, 1 cup	Mayonnaise, 2 tsp

Dinner

Vegetables	Fruits	Grains	Protein	Dairy	Oils
Baked sweet potato, 1 large; Peas and onions, ½ cup; Leafy green salad, 1 cup		Dinner rolls, 2 1 oz each	Roasted chicken breast (boneless and skinless), 3 oz		Soft margarine, 1 tsp; Sunflower oil, 3 tsp

Snack

Vegetables	Fruits	Grains	Protein	Dairy	Oils
	Dried apricots, ¼ cup			Low-fat vanilla yogurt, 1 cup	

make up for it the next day. For example, if you did not eat enough fruit one day, but did eat an extra serving of grains, you could adjust your diet the next day by cutting back on your grain servings and adding an extra serving of fruit.

Should you worry about *when* you eat? Read more about the time of day you should eat in Examining the Evidence: Does the Time of Day You Eat Impact Your Health? on pages 56–57.

> **LO 2.4: THE TAKE-HOME MESSAGE** MyPlate depicts the five food groups using the familiar mealtime visual of a place setting. It is part of the USDA's Web-based initiative at ChooseMyPlate.gov, providing information, a food guidance system, and a personalized daily food plan to help you build a healthy diet based on the *Dietary Guidelines for Americans*. Try to consume nutrient-dense foods—fruits, vegetables, whole grains, and lean dairy and protein foods—but limit energy-dense foods, which provide kilocalories from solid fats and added sugars but little nutrition. Daily physical activity is encouraged to better manage your weight and health.

What Is the Exchange System?

LO 2.5 Describe how the exchange system can be used as a guide to plan a balanced diet.

The **exchange lists** for meal planning were designed in 1950 to give people with diabetes a structured, balanced eating plan. The lists are still in use today. Unlike some of the other dietary guides, the exchange lists group foods according to their carbohydrate, protein, and fat composition and provide specific portion sizes for each food. In addition, each food in the group has a similar amount of kilocalories.

There are six food groups in the exchange lists: starch, fruit, milk, vegetable, meat, and fat. You might be surprised to find some foods located in unexpected places. For example, in MyPlate, cheese is in the milk group because of its calcium content. In the exchange system, cheese is in the meat group because it has less carbohydrate than milk or yogurt but contains levels of protein and fat similar to those found in chicken or meat. Potatoes are not found in the vegetable list, but in the starch list; bacon is considered a fat exchange because it contains more fat than protein; and peanut butter is found in both the high-fat meat list and the fat list because it is high in both protein and fat.

Using the exchange lists is a convenient method for designing a flexible meal plan that controls proportions of carbohydrate, protein, and fat intake. Because of their similar macronutrient composition, foods within each group can be exchanged or swapped with each other. **Table 2.9** presents the number of food group choices in healthy, balanced diets of different kilocalorie levels that consist of fifty-five percent carbohydrate, twenty percent protein, and twenty-five percent fat. For example, using these percentages of macronutrients, a daily menu that contains approximately 1,800 kilocalories would include nine starch, four fruit, two low-fat milk, five nonstarchy vegetable, five

exchange lists A diet-planning tool that groups foods together based on their carbohydrate, protein, and fat content. One food on the list can be exchanged for another food on the same list.

| TABLE 2.9 | Number of Exchanges per Food Group per Day by Kilocalorie Intake |

Food Group	1,500 kcal	1,800 kcal	2,000 kcal	2,200 kcal	2,400 kcal
Starch	8	9	10	11	12
Fruit	3	4	4	4	5
Milk, low fat	2	2	3	3	3
Nonstarchy vegetables	4	5	6	6	7
Meat and meat substitutes, lean	3	5	5	6	7
Fat	5	6	6	7	7

Does the Time of Day You Eat Impact Your Health?

We are all creatures of habit. Some of these habits, such as the time of day we eat, can either enhance or detract from overall health. Do you typically eat breakfast? Do you often snack after dinner or late at night? Do you overload on high-fat or fried foods, or drink a lot of alcohol, when you go out on the weekends? The choice to skip breakfast, eat later in the day, or overeat on the weekend can impact your nutrient intake, appetite, and body weight.

Eating Breakfast Means More Energy and Fewer Kilocalories throughout the Day

You probably know that grabbing a latte on the way to your morning class is not a healthy breakfast, but do you understand how such a habit impacts your overall

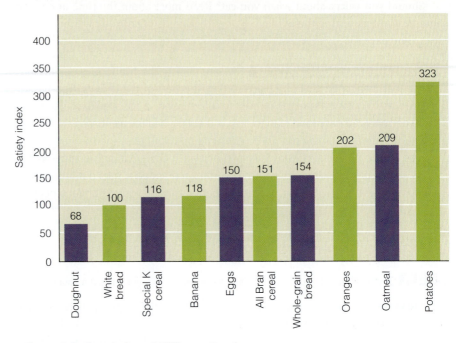

▲ Figure 2 **Satiety Index of Different Foods**
Subjects were asked to rate their feelings of hunger every 15 minutes for 2 hours after eating 240-kilocalorie portions of specific foods. All foods were compared with white bread, which scored a satiety index of 100.

Source: Data from S. H. Holt, J. C. Miller, P. Petocz, and E. Farmakalidis. 1995. "A Satiety Index of Common Foods." *European Journal of Clinical Nutrition* 49:675–690.

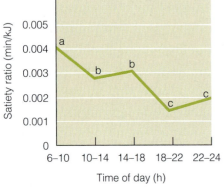

▲ Figure 1 **Satiety Ratios Based on Time between Meals and Energy Content**
Satiety ratios were calculated during five 4-hour periods of the day reported in 7-day diet diaries and were calculated as the duration of the after-meal interval divided by the meal size in kJ.* To be considered a meal, there had to be at least 15 minutes from the preceding or following meal. Meal **(a)** contained 15 minutes and 209 kJ; **(b)** 45 minutes and 209 kJ or **(b)** 45 minutes and 418 kJ; and **(c)** 45 minutes and 837 kJ or **(c)** 90 minutes and 209 kJ. Values are means, $n = 867$; pooled SEM = 0.00007. Means without a common letter differ; $p < 0.05$.

*Note: The International System uses kilojoules (kJ) to define energy in foods. One kilocalorie equals 4.184 joules.

Source: Data from J. M. de Castro. 2003. "The Time of Day of Food Intake Influences Overall Intake in Humans." *Journal of Nutrition* 134:104–111.

nutrient intake? For one thing, skipping breakfast may affect the total number of kilocalories you consume the rest of the day. Dr. John de Castro evaluated the timing of food intake in 867 people over a seven-day period and found that people who ate a larger proportion of food earlier in the day had a significantly lower intake of total kilocalories (**Figure 1**).[1] In other words, if you eat breakfast, you are more likely to eat less by the end of the day than if you skip this important meal.

The reduction in total kilocalories when you eat breakfast may be due to the size of the meal and how satisfied you feel. Most of us eat smaller meals at breakfast and more food at lunch and dinner. We also appear to spend less time eating breakfast than other meals. In Dr. de Castro's study, both of these factors affected satiety. Satiety ratios, or the time between meals based on the size of the previous meal, decreased over the day from breakfast through late-evening snacks.[2] Thus, a more substantial breakfast is more satiating than the evening meal.

One reason breakfast may be more satiating involves the types of foods consumed. Holt and colleagues investigated the effects of a high-fat breakfast versus a high-carbohydrate meal on the amount of snacking reported later in the day (**Figure 2**).[3] If the breakfast included higher fiber foods, such as cereal, and a good protein source, the subjects ate less later in the day. Breakfast foods including potatoes, eggs, and high-fiber cereals ranked higher than doughnuts or white bread for satiety.

What if you skip breakfast? Not only will you eat more during the day, chances are you will choose less-nutrient-dense foods. Those who eat breakfast, lunch, and dinner tend to have higher calcium and iron intakes than individuals who skip breakfast.[4, 5]

Eating breakfast may also be a good strategy for weight control. Several studies have reported higher BMIs and body weight in subjects who don't consistently eat breakfast compared with their breakfast-eating counterparts.[6] In addition, eating breakfast helps maintain weight loss.[7]

Eating More during Evenings and Weekends Can Lead to Overconsumption of Kilocalories

Do you eat after 7:00 p.m.? Most young adults do, especially during the weekend.[8] For most students, eating schedules are influenced by hunger, pressures from work and school, convenience, and social habits. Recent studies suggest that the craving for late night carbohydrate snacks is related to your circadian rhythms.[9] Regardless of why you eat at various times, the timing of your meals can affect body weight, the level of hormones in the blood, body temperature, and blood pressure. Because eating later is less satisfying, you are likely to eat more food, and hence consume more kilocalories, particularly from carbohydrates, fat, and alcohol, in the evening hours.

Though there is no current evidence that eating later in the day increases BMI or the risk of obesity,[10] timing of meals may impact changes in body composition during a weight-loss program. In a controlled metabolic ward study, overweight women who ate the bulk of their kilocalories in the morning hours had a slightly greater weight loss than when the bulk of the kilocalories was consumed later in the day. However, when they ate more of their kilocalories later in the day, they retained more lean muscle mass.[11] More research is needed before any strong conclusions can be drawn from these results.

Weekend eating patterns can also influence overall dietary intake. Haines reports that people in their study ate an average of 82 kilocalories more per day on Friday, Saturday, and Sunday compared with weekdays. These increases in kilocalories were mostly due to an increase in fat (approximately 0.7 percent) and alcohol (1.4 percent); carbohydrates decreased by 1.6 percent.[12] Over time, this increase in kilocalorie intake may lead to weight gain.

Recommendations

Based on the current research on eating and time of day, it is recommended that you:

- Start your day with a nutrient-dense breakfast as part of a healthy eating pattern. Many breakfast foods, such as dry whole-grain cereals, fresh fruit, or whole-grain toast or bagels with low-fat cream cheese, can be eaten on the go. You'll have more energy and will most likely eat fewer total kilocalories by the end of the day.
- Choose breakfast foods that are more satisfying to improve your appetite control throughout the day. Enjoy foods such as whole-grain cereals and whole fruits, which are higher in fiber, protein, and water, and lower in fat and sugar.
- Control kilocalorie intake on nights and weekends. Monitor your weekend eating habits to maintain a consistent balance of carbohydrates, fats, and proteins and to reduce alcohol consumption.

References

1. J. M. de Castro. 2003. "The Time of Day of Food Intake Influences Overall Intake in Humans." *Journal of Nutrition* 134:104–111.
2. Ibid.
3. S. H. Holt, J. C. Miller, P. Petocz, and E. Farmakalidis. 1995. "A Satiety Index of Common Foods." *European Journal of Clinical Nutrition* 49:675–690.
4. J. M. Kerver, E. Yang, S. Obayashi, L. Bianchi, and W. Song. 2006. "Meal and Snack Patterns Are Associated with Dietary Intake of Energy and Nutrients in U.S. Adults." *Journal of the American Dietetic Association* 106:46–54.
5. T. W. Boon, R. Zedek, and Z. M. Kasi. 2012. "Association between Snacking Patterns, Energy and Nutrient Intakes, and Body Mass Index among School Adolescents in Kuala Lumpur." *American Journal of Food and Nutrition* 2(3):69–77.
6. Center for Nutrition Policy and Promotion. 2011. "Breakfast Consumption, Body Weight, and Nutrient Intake: A Review of the Evidence." Available at www.cnpp.usda.gov/Publications/NutritionInsights/Insight45.pdf. Accessed January 2014.
7. Ibid.
8. R. H. Striegel-Moore, D. L. Franko, D. Thompson, S. Affenito, and H. C. Kraemer. 2006. "Night Eating: Prevalence and Demographic Correlates." *Obesity* 14:139–147.
9. Frank A. J. L. Scheer, Christopher J. Morris, and Steven A. Shea. 2013. "The Internal Circadian Clock Increases Hunger and Appetite in the Evening Independent of Food Intake and Other Behaviors." *Obesity* 21(3): 421 DOI: 10.1002/oby.20351.
10. N. K. A. Stockman, T. C. Schenkel, J. N. Brown, and A. Duncan. 2005. "Comparison of Energy and Nutrient Intakes among Meals and Snacks of Adolescent Males." *Preventive Medicine* 41:203–210.
11. N. L. Keim, M. D. Van Loan, W. F. Horn, T. F. Barbieri, and P. L. Mayclin. 1997. "Weight Loss Is Greater with Consumption of Large Morning Meals and Fat-Free Mass Is Preserved with Large Evening Meals in Women on a Controlled Weight Reduction Program." *Journal of Nutrition* 127:75–82.
12. P. S. Haines, M. Y. Hama, D. K. Guilkey, and B. M. Popkin. 2003. "Weekend Eating in the United States Is Linked with Greater Energy, Fat, and Alcohol Intake." *Obesity Research* 11:945–949.

lean meat or meat substitute, and six fat choices. As you can see from the table, the higher the kilocalorie intake, the greater the number of choices from the exchange lists that are allowed. For complete exchange lists for meal planning, see Appendix C.

> **LO 2.5: THE TAKE-HOME MESSAGE** The exchange system is a convenient tool for creating meal plans based on the macronutrient content and total kilocalories of foods. The plan contains six food groups: starch, fruit, milk, vegetables, meat, and fat. Foods within each group can be exchanged or swapped to add variety to meals and snacks.

What Information Is on the Food Label?

LO 2.6 Identify the required components of a food label and Nutrition Facts panel.

Do you pay close attention to the food labels of items you purchase at the supermarket? The information on labels can be tremendously useful when it comes to planning a healthy diet.

Food Labels Are Strictly Regulated by the FDA

To help consumers make informed food choices, the Food and Drug Administration (FDA) regulates the labeling of all packaged foods in the United States. Since the 1930s, the FDA has mandated that every packaged food (**Figure 2.9**) be labeled with:

- The name of the food
- The net weight, which is the weight of the food in the package, excluding the weight of the package or packing material
- The name and address of the manufacturer or distributor
- A list of ingredients in descending order by weight, with the heaviest item listed first

New labeling laws have been enacted to further benefit the consumer.[20] In 1990, the Nutrition Labeling and Education Act (NLEA) began mandating that labels

▶ **Figure 2.9 Labeling Requirements Mandated by the FDA**

The **Nutrition Facts panel** lists standardized serving sizes and specific nutrients, and shows how a serving of the food fits into a healthy diet by stating its contribution to the percentage of the Daily Value for each nutrient.

The **name** of the product must be displayed on the front label.

The **ingredients** must be listed in descending order by weight. Whole-grain wheat is the predominant ingredient in this cereal.

The **net weight** of the food in the box is located at the bottom of the package.

include uniform nutrition information, serving sizes, and specific criteria for health claims. Additional requirements for food labels have since been passed to require that labels now also show:

- Nutrition information, which lists total kilocalories, kilocalories from fat, total fat, saturated fat, *trans* fats, cholesterol, sodium, total carbohydrate, dietary fiber, sugars, vitamin A, vitamin C, calcium, and iron
- Serving sizes that are uniform among similar products, which allows for easier comparison shopping
- An indication of how a serving of the food fits into an overall daily diet
- Uniform definitions for descriptive label terms such as "light" and "fat free"
- Health claims that are accurate and science based, if made about the food or one of its nutrients
- The presence of any of eight common allergens that might be present in the food, including milk, eggs, fish, shellfish, tree nuts (cashews, walnuts, almonds, etc.), peanuts, wheat, and soybeans

Whereas raw fruits and vegetables and fresh fish typically don't have a label, these foods fall under the FDA's voluntary, point-of-purchase nutrition information program. Under the guidelines of this program, at least 60 percent of a nationwide sample of grocery stores must post the nutrition information of the most commonly eaten fruits, vegetables, and fish near where the foods are sold. The FDA surveys a sample of nationwide grocery stores every two years. The latest findings show that over 70 percent of stores surveyed are in compliance with the program.[21]

Although a similar voluntary program was in place for meat and poultry, the USDA (which regulates meat and poultry) now requires food labels in grocery stores on meat and poultry to indicate in which country the animal was born, raised, and slaughtered, called the country-of-origin labeling, or COOL.[22, 23]

The Nutrition Facts Panel Indicates Nutrient Values

One area of the food label in particular, the **Nutrition Facts panel,** provides a nutritional snapshot of the food inside a package. As mentioned earlier, by law the panel must list amounts of specific nutrients. If an additional nutrient such as vitamin E or vitamin B_{12} has been added, or if the product makes a claim about a nutrient, then that nutrient must also be listed. Other nutrients, such as additional vitamins and minerals, can be voluntarily listed by the manufacturer. The majority of packaged foods contain this nutrition information.

Very few foods are exempt from carrying a Nutrition Facts panel on the label. Such foods include plain coffee and tea; some spices, flavorings, and other foods that don't provide a significant amount of nutrients; deli items, bakery foods, and other ready-to-eat foods that are prepared and sold in retail establishments; restaurant meals; and foods produced by small businesses (companies that have total sales of less than $500,000).[24]

We can use **Figure 2.10** to walk through a sample Nutrition Facts panel for a box of macaroni and cheese. At the top of the panel is the serving size. By law, the serving size must be listed both by weight in grams and in common household measures, such as cups and ounces. Because serving sizes are standardized among similar food products, consumers can compare one brand of macaroni and cheese with a different brand to assess which one better meets their needs.

The rest of the information on the panel is based on the listed serving size (in this case, one cup) of the food. For example, if you ate two servings (two cups) of this macaroni and cheese, which is the number of servings in the entire box, you would double the nutrient information on the label to calculate the kilocalories as well as the fat and other nutrients. The servings per container are particularly useful for portion control.

Nutrition Facts panel The area on the food label that provides a list of specific nutrients obtained in one serving of the food.

Source: U.S. Food and Drug Administration. 2012. *Understanding and Using the Nutrition Facts Label*. Available at www.fda.gov. Accessed January 2014.

The U.S. Food and Drug Administration (FDA) is proposing new changes to the 20-year-old nutrition labels on packaged foods. The changes to the nutrition label provide information to help compare products and make healthy food choices.

Current Label

GRANOLA

Nutrition Facts
Serving Size 2/3 cup (55g)
Servings Per Container About 8

Amount Per Serving		
Calories 230	Calories from Fat 72	
		% Daily Value*
Total Fat 8g		**12%**
Saturated Fat 1g		**5%**
Trans Fat 0g		
Cholesterol 0mg		**0%**
Sodium 160mg		**7%**
Total Carbohydrates 37g		**12%**
Dietary Fiber 4g		**16%**
Sugars 1g		
Protein 3g		
Vitamin A		10%
Vitamin C		8%
Calcium		20%
Iron		45%

* Percent Daily Values are based on a 2,000 calorie diet. Your daily value may be higher or lower depending on your calorie needs.

		Calories:	2,000	2,500
Total Fat	Less than		65g	80g
Sat Fat	Less than		20g	25g
Cholesterol	Less than		300mg	300mg
Sodium	Less than		2,400mg	2,400mg
Total Carbohydrate			300g	375g
Dietary Fiber			25g	30g

SERVINGS
- Serving sizes are standardized, making comparison shopping easier.

NEW
- Servings and serving sizes are larger and bolder.
- "Amount per serving" will be changed to "Amount per (serving size)" such as "Amount per cup."

CALORIES
- Calories per serving and the number of servings in the package are listed.

NEW
- Calories are larger to stand out more.
- "Calories from fat" is removed.

DAILY VALUES
- Daily Values are general reference values based on a 2,000 calorie diet.
- The %DV can tell you if a food is high or low in a nutrient or dietary substance.

NEW
- Daily Values are listed first.
- The meaning of the Daily Values will be explained in a new detailed footnote.

ADDED SUGARS
NEW
- Added sugars are listed.

VITAMINS & MINERALS
- Vitamin A, vitamin C, calcium, and iron are required.
- Other vitamins and minerals are voluntary.

NEW
- Vitamin D and potassium are required, in addition to calcium and iron.
- Vitamins A and C are voluntary.
- Actual amounts of each nutrient are listed as well as the %DV.

Proposed New Label

GRANOLA

Nutrition Facts
8 servings per container
Serving size   2/3 cup (55g)

Amount per 2/3 cup
Calories 230

% DV*	
12%	**Total Fat** 8g
5%	**Saturated Fat** 1g
	Trans Fat 0g
0%	**Cholesterol** 0mg
7%	**Sodium** 160mg
12%	**Total Carbs** 37g
14%	Dietary Fiber 4g
	Sugars 1g
	Added Sugars 0g
	Protein 3g
10%	**Vitamin D** 2mcg
20%	**Calcium** 260mg
45%	**Iron** 8mg
5%	**Potassium** 235mg

* Footnote on Daily Values (DV) and calories reference to be inserted here.

Below the serving size is listed the kilocalories per serving. The kilocalories from fat listing gives you an idea of what proportion of the food's kilocalories comes from fat. In this box of macaroni and cheese, 110 out of a total of 250 kilocalories—that is, nearly half—are from fat.

Next are the nutrients that should be limited or added to the diet. Americans typically eat too much fat, including saturated fat, *trans* fat, and cholesterol, and too much sodium. In contrast, they tend to fall short in dietary fiber, vitamins A and C, and iron. These are on the label to remind consumers to make sure to eat foods rich in these substances. The Nutrition Facts panel can be your best shopping guide when identifying and choosing foods that are low in the nutrients you want to limit (like saturated fat) and high in the nutrients that you need to eat in higher amounts (like fiber).

Are you wondering what determines if a food contains a "high" or "low" amount of a specific nutrient? That's where the Daily Values come into play.

The Daily Values Help You Compare Packaged Foods

The **Daily Values (DVs),** listed on the Nutrition Facts panel, are general reference levels for the nutrients listed on the food label. The DVs give a general idea of how the nutrients in the food fit into the overall diet. The DVs are based on older reference levels and are not as current as the DRIs. For example, whereas the DRIs recommend an upper level of dietary sodium of no more than 2,300 milligrams daily, the DVs use less than 2,400 milligrams as the reference level.

There are no DVs listed on the label for *trans* fat, sugars, and protein. For *trans* fat and sugars there isn't enough information available to set reference values for these nutrients. Although there are reference values for protein, consuming adequate amounts of protein isn't a health concern for most Americans over age 4, so listing the percent of the DV for this nutrient isn't warranted on the label. The DV for protein will only be listed if the product, such as a jar of baby food, is being marketed for children under the age of 4, or if a claim is made about the food, such as that it is "high in protein."[25]

The DVs on the food label are based on a 2,000-kilocalorie diet. Individuals who need more or fewer than 2,000 kilocalories daily may have DV values that are higher or lower than those listed on the Nutrition Facts panel.

If a serving provides 20 percent or more of the DV for a given nutrient, it is considered high in that nutrient. A serving of the macaroni and cheese (refer again to Figure 2.10) is high in sodium, potassium, and calcium. If a serving provides 5 percent or less of the DV for a nutrient, it is considered low in that nutrient. A serving of macaroni and cheese provides little fiber, vitamin A, vitamin C, or iron.

Lastly, depending on the size of the food package, there may be a footnote at the bottom of the label. This provides a summary of the DVs for a 2,000-kilocalorie diet as well as a 2,500-kilocalorie diet. This area of the panel is something of a "cheat sheet" when you are shopping so that you don't have to memorize the values. As you can see from the footnote, you should try to keep your sodium intake to less than 2,400 milligrams daily. Because you know that this macaroni and cheese is high in sodium, providing 470 milligrams, or 20 percent of the DV, you should try to keep the sodium in your remaining food choices during the day to less than 2,000 milligrams.

The Nutrition Facts panel on the side or back of the package can help you make healthier food choices, and some foods carry claims on their front labels that may also influence your decision to buy.

Label Claims Can Reveal Potential Health Benefits

In the 1980s, the Kellogg Company ran an ad campaign for its fiber-rich All Bran cereal reminding the public of the National Cancer Institute's recommendation to eat low-fat, high-fiber foods, fresh fruits, and vegetables to maintain a healthy weight. According to the FDA, sales of high-fiber cereals increased over 35 percent

Daily Values (DVs) Reference values developed by the Food and Drug Administration and used on nutrition labels to describe the amount of a nutrient provided in one serving of the food.

nutrient content claims Claims on the food label that describe the level or amount of a nutrient in the food. Terms such as *free, high, reduced,* or *lite* are examples of nutrient content claims.

health claims Claims on food labels that describe a relationship between a food, food component, dietary ingredient, or dietary supplement and a disease or health-related condition.

structure/function claims Claims on the label that describe the role of a nutrient or dietary compound that is proposed to influence the structure or function of the human body. For example, "Calcium builds strong bones" is a structure/function claim.

within a year.[26] Manufacturers realized that putting nutrition and health claims on labels was effective in influencing consumer purchases. Supermarket shelves were soon crowded with products boasting various claims.

The FDA mandates that all claims on labels follow strict guidelines. Currently, the FDA allows the use of three types of claims on food products: (1) **nutrient content claims,** (2) **health claims,** and (3) **structure/function claims.** All foods displaying these claims on the label must meet specified criteria.

Nutrient Content Claims

A food product can make a claim about the amount of a nutrient it contains (or doesn't contain) by using descriptive terms such as *free* (fat-free yogurt), *high* (high-fiber crackers), *low* (low saturated fat cereal), *reduced* (reduced-sodium soup), and *extra lean* (extra lean ground beef) as long as it meets the strict criteria designated by the FDA. These terms can help identify at a glance the food items that best meet your needs. For instance, if you want to decrease or limit the amount of sodium in your diet, you could look for low-sodium claims on labels.

Look at the labels of the canned soups in **Figure 2.11**. Note that the "low-sodium" version of the chicken soup cannot contain more than 140 milligrams of sodium per serving. In contrast, the soup with the term "less sodium" on the label contains

▼ **Figure 2.11 Soup's On!** Nutrient claims on the food label must conform to strict criteria.

a Because this can of chicken noodle soup displays the "low sodium" nutrient claim, it can't provide more than 140 milligrams of sodium in a serving.

b This can of soup has more than 25 percent less sodium than the classic version, so the term "less" can be displayed on its label.

c The classic variety of chicken noodle soup has the most sodium per serving.

450 milligrams of sodium per serving, which is at least 25 percent less sodium than the regular variety. The can of classic chicken soup contains almost 900 milligrams for a serving, which is likely the same or even more sodium than the average American consumes at dinner. Table 2.10 provides some of the most common nutrient claims on food labels, and the specific criteria that each claim must meet as mandated by the FDA.

Health Claims

Suppose you are sitting at your kitchen table eating a bowl of Cheerios in skim milk, and staring at the cereal box. You notice a claim on the front of box that states: "The soluble fiber in Cheerios, as part of a heart-healthy diet, can help lower your cholesterol." Do you recognize this as a health claim that links Cheerios with better heart health?

A health claim must contain two important components: (1) a food or a dietary compound, such as fiber, and (2) a corresponding disease or health-related condition that is associated with the substance.[27] In the Cheerios example, the soluble fiber (the dietary compound) that naturally occurs in oats has been shown to lower blood cholesterol levels (the corresponding health-related condition), which can help reduce the risk of heart disease.

TABLE 2.10   What Does That Labeling Term Mean?

Nutrient	Free	Low	Reduced/Less	Light
Kilocalories	<5 kilocalories (kcal) per serving	<40 kcal per serving	At least 25% fewer kcal per serving	If the food contains 50% or more of its kcal from fat, then the fat must be reduced
Fat	<0.5 grams (g) per serving	<3 g per serving	At least 25% less fat per serving	Same as above
Saturated fat	<0.5 g per serving	<1 g per serving	At least 25% less saturated fat per serving	N/A
Cholesterol	<2 milligrams (mg) per serving	<20 mg per serving	At least 25% less cholesterol per serving	N/A
Sodium	<5 mg per serving	<140 mg per serving	At least 25% less sodium per serving	If the sodium is reduced by at least 50% per serving
Sugars	<0.5 g	N/A	At least 25% less sugar per serving	N/A

Other Labeling Terms

Term	Definition
"High," "Rich in," or "Excellent source of"	The food contains 20% or more of the DV of the nutrient in a serving. Can be used to describe protein, vitamins, minerals, fiber, or potassium.
"Good source of"	A serving of the food provides 10–19% of the DV of the nutrient. Can be used to describe protein, vitamins, minerals, fiber, or potassium.
"More," "Added," "Extra," or "Plus"	A serving of the food provides 10% of the DV. Can only be used to describe vitamins, minerals, protein, fiber, and potassium.
"Lean"	Can be used on seafood and meat that contains less than 10 g of fat, 4.5 g or less of saturated fat, and less than 95 mg of cholesterol per serving.
"Extra lean"	Can be used on seafood and meat that contains less than 5 g of fat, less than 2 g of saturated fat, and less than 95 mg of cholesterol per serving.
"Healthy"	Low in fat and saturated fat; limited in cholesterol content; sodium content can't exceed 360 mg for individual foods or 480 for meal-type foods; contains 10% of the DV of one or more of vitamins A and C, iron, calcium, protein, or fiber.

Note: N/A = not applicable.

There are three types of health claims: (1) authorized health claims, (2) health claims based on authoritative statements, and (3) qualified health claims. The differences between them lie in the amount of supporting research and agreement among scientists about the strength of the relationship between the food or dietary ingredient and the disease or condition. See **Table 2.11** for a definition and examples of each type of health claim.

TABLE 2.11	Sorting Out Label Claims	
Type of Claim	**Definition**	**Examples**
Authorized health claims (well established)	Claims are based on a well-established relationship between the food or compound and the health benefit. Food manufacturers must submit a petition to the FDA and provide the scientific research that backs up the claim. If there is significant agreement in the supporting research and a consensus among numerous scientists and experts in the field that there is a relationship between the food or dietary ingredient and the disease or health condition, the FDA will allow an authorized health claim. Specified wording must be used.	The FDA has approved 12 authorized health claims. 1. Calcium and osteoporosis 2. Sodium and hypertension 3. Dietary fat and cancer 4. Dietary saturated fat and cholesterol and risk of coronary heart disease 5. Fiber-containing grain products, fruits, and vegetables and cancer 6. Fruits, vegetables, and grain products that contain fiber, particularly soluble fiber, and the risk of coronary heart disease 7. Fruits and vegetables and cancer 8. Folate and neural tube defects 9. Dietary sugar, alcohol, and dental caries 10. Soluble fiber from certain foods and risk of coronary heart disease 11. Soy protein and risk of coronary heart disease 12. Plant sterol/stanol esters and risk of coronary heart disease
Health claims based on authoritative statements (well established)	Claims based on statements made by a U.S. government agency, such as the Centers for Disease Control and Prevention (CDC) and the National Institutes of Health (NIH). If the FDA approves a claim submitted by the manufacturer, the wording of the claim must include "may," as in "whole grains may help reduce the risk of heart disease," to illustrate that other factors in addition to the food or dietary ingredient may play a role in the disease or condition. This type of health claim can only be used on food and cannot be used on dietary supplements.	■ Whole-grain foods and risk of heart disease and certain cancers ■ Potassium and the risk of high blood pressure
Qualified health claims (less well established)	Claims based on evidence that is still emerging. However, the current evidence to support the claim is greater than the evidence suggesting that the claim isn't valid. These claims are allowed in order to expedite the communication of potential beneficial health information to the public. They must be accompanied by the statement "the evidence to support the claim is limited or not conclusive" or "some scientific evidence suggests. . . ." Many experts, including the Academy of Nutrition and Dietetics, don't support this type of health claim, as it is based on emerging evidence. Qualified health claims can be used on dietary supplements if approved by the FDA.	■ Selenium and cancer ■ Antioxidant vitamins and cancer ■ Nuts and heart disease ■ Omega-3 fatty acids and coronary heart disease ■ B vitamins and vascular disease ■ Monounsaturated fatty acids from olive oil and coronary heart disease

Structure/Function Claims

The last type of label claim is the structure/function claim, which describes how a nutrient or dietary compound affects the structure or function of the human body (**Figure 2.12**).[28] The claims "calcium (nutrient) builds strong bones (body structure)" and "fiber (dietary compound) maintains bowel regularity (body function)" are examples of structure/function claims. Structure/function claims cannot state that the nutrient or dietary compound can be used to treat a disease or a condition.[29] These claims can be made on both foods and dietary supplements. Unlike the health claims, structure/function claims don't need to be preapproved by the FDA. They do need to be truthful and not misleading, but the manufacturer is responsible for making sure that the claims are accurate.

Structure/function claims can be a source of confusion. Shoppers can easily fall into the trap of assuming that one brand of a product with a structure/function claim on its label is superior to another product without the claim. For instance, a yogurt that says "Calcium builds strong bones" on its label may be identical to another yogurt without the flashy label claim. The consumer has to recognize the difference between claims that are supported by a significant amount of solid research and approved by the FDA, and structure/function claims that don't need prior approval for use.

Dietary supplements that use structure/function claims must display a disclaimer on the label stating that the FDA did not evaluate the claim and that the dietary supplement is not intended to "diagnose, treat, cure or prevent any disease." Manufacturers of foods bearing structure/function claims do not have to display this disclaimer on the label.

Although keeping the types of health claims and the structure/function claims straight can be challenging, here's one way to remember them: Authorized health claims and health claims based on authoritative statements are the strongest, as they are based on years of accumulated research or an authoritative statement. Qualified health claims are made on potentially healthful foods or dietary ingredients but because the evidence is still emerging, the claim has to be "qualified" as such. All health claims provide information on how the food or dietary ingredient can help reduce your risk of a condition or a disease.

Structure/function claims are the weakest claims, as they are just statements or facts about the role the nutrient or dietary ingredient plays in the body. They can't claim how the food or dietary ingredient lowers the risk of developing a chronic disease such as heart disease or cancer. In general, label claims with less established scientific evidence behind them have the weakest wording.

Cheerios uses an authorized health claim stating that soluble fiber reduces the risk of heart disease.

▲ **Figure 2.12 A Structure/Function Label Claim**
A structure/function claim describes how a nutrient or substance, such as the antioxidants that have been added to this cereal, support a function in the body, such as the immune system.

LO 2.6: THE TAKE-HOME MESSAGE The FDA regulates the labeling on all packaged foods. Every food label must contain the name of the food, its net weight, the name and address of the manufacturer or distributor, a list of ingredients, and standardized nutrition information. The FDA allows and regulates the use of nutrient content claims, health claims, and structure/function claims on food labels. Any foods or dietary supplements displaying these label claims must meet specified criteria and the claims must be truthful.

Portion Distortion

LO 2.7 Compare the terms "portion" and "serving size" and summarize the health benefits of controlling your portions.

Portion distortion, or perceiving larger portions of food as appropriate sizes, may be contributing to obesity. These larger-than-recommended portion sizes, which are viewed as typical by Americans today, add kilocalories to our diets and may contribute to weight gain.

Portion versus Serving Size: What's the Difference?

The USDA defines a portion as the amount of food eaten at one sitting. In contrast, a serving size (a term that's only used on nutrient labels) is a standard amount of food for which the nutrient composition is presented. We can illustrate the difference with a food that people often pile on their plates, such as spaghetti. A generous helping of cooked spaghetti that spills over the edge of a plate is probably equal to about 3 cups.

serving size A recommended portion of food that is used as a standard reference on food labels.

According to MyPlate, a standard serving size of pasta is ½ cup. A portion of 3 cups of cooked pasta is therefore six servings, which contains more than 600 kilocalories!

Just what size is a small drink? Is it 6 fluid ounces or more? How much is 3 ounces? Unfortunately, many of us frequently underestimate the portion sizes we put on our plates or in our glasses and therefore overconsume foods during snacks and mealtimes.[30,31] One easy way to tell if you are helping yourself to too much of a food is to use a visual that represents a standard **serving size** of the food, such as a cup of vegetables, three ounces of meat, or 1 tablespoon of salad dressing. Having a food scale available is not always possible. Instead, use an everyday item that you always have with you—your hand—to visualize the correct portion sizes (**Figure 2.13**). This provides an easy way to approximate how much you are consuming.

How Have Portion Sizes Changed?

If your great-grandmother treated herself to a Hershey's chocolate bar when it was first introduced, at the beginning

of the last century, she would have paid a small amount of money for about 0.6 ounce of chocolate. Today the same milk chocolate bar is sold in 0.75-, 1.6-, 2.6-, 4.0-, 7.0-, and 8.0-ounce weights. When McDonald's first introduced french fries in 1954, the standard serving weighed 2.4 ounces. Although a small 2.4-ounce size is still on the menu, you can also choose the medium french fries weighing 5.3 ounces or the large at 6.3 ounces. Twenty years ago, a cup of coffee was 8 ounces and just 45 kilocalories with added milk and sugar. Today, consumers enjoy 16-ounce lattes on their way to work, to the tune of 350 kilocalories.[32] Portion sizes have changed across the menu, from french fries to coffee. **Table 2.12** illustrates several foods that people commonly consume in oversized portions.

The restaurant industry has appealed to Americans' interest in getting more food for less money with larger portion sizes at relatively low costs. Americans eat out more often than they did in the past, and are offered a wide variety of inexpensive choices sold in larger-than-normal portion sizes that often exceed the standards defined by the federal government.[33] And most people are

The typical portion of pasta (left) is much often larger than the recommended serving size (right).

A woman's palm is the size of approximately 3 ounces of cooked meat, chicken, or fish

a

The "O" made by a woman's thumb and forefinger is the size of about 1 tablespoon of vegetable oil.

c

A woman's fist is the size of about 1 cup (a man's fist is the size of about 2 cups)

b

The tip of the finger is about 1 teaspoon of margarine

d

▲ **Figure 2.13 What's a Portion Size? Eat with Your Hands!**
Your hands can help you estimate the appropriate portion size of foods.

TABLE 2.12 Comparison of Portion Sizes of Common Foods

Food	Typical Portion	Recommended Serving Size	FDA Label
Cooked pasta	2.9 cups	0.5 cup	1.0 cup
French fries	5.3 oz	3.0 oz	2.5 oz
Bagel	4.4 oz	1.0 oz	2.0 oz
Coffee	12.0 fl oz	6.0 fl oz	6.0 fl oz
Cookie, chocolate chip	4.0 oz	0.5 oz	1.1 oz

Source: Adapted from L. R. Young and M. Nestle. 2003. "Expanding Portion Sizes in the U.S. Marketplace: Implications for Nutrition Counseling." *Journal of the American Dietetic Association* 103:231–234.

chips directly from the bag, rather than taking a handful out of the bag and only eating that portion, will likely mean consuming significantly more kilocalories.

Health Effects of Increased Portion Size

Eating larger portions of certain foods, such as foods high in sugar and fat, not only alters the daily kilocalorie intake but can also decrease the amount of nutrients you consume overall. For example, eating larger portions of red meat as an entree will increase the total fat, saturated fat, and cholesterol you ingest. Instead, if the entrée portion is limited and the plate is filled with healthier portions of vegetables, fruits, and whole grains at each meal, the result is an increase in the overall content of vitamins, minerals, and dietary fiber content in the meal in addition to a lower intake of total kilocalories. Research has shown that even slight changes in the portion sizes of typical foods can lead to increased energy intake and weight gain.[34,35] As body weight increases, the risk of developing chronic disease including cardiovascular disease, diabetes, joint problems, and some cancers also increases.

Knowing the Kilocalorie Content of Foods May Not Influence Portion Size

Restaurants can play a major role in helping consumers reduce their energy intake.[36] Labeling takeout or restaurant menus with kilocalorie content is aimed at reducing the portion sizes you choose. But is it working? It appears that there seems to be a disconnect between knowing the amount of kilocalories you're eating, and the portion size of the foods you eat. Recently reported studies show that posting the kilocalorie content of your favorite large blueberry muffin has little impact on your behavior.[37]

unaware of the changes in their portion sizes. Though getting more food for the money may be beneficial on the wallet, the health costs may be higher than Americans realize.

In addition to restaurant and packaged foods, home-cooked meals have also bulked up over the past few decades. If you were to measure your grandmother's favorite dinner plates, they would likely be much smaller, about 9 inches in diameter, than the plates in your cupboard, which probably measure closer

to 11.5 inches across. The bigger the plate, the more food you are likely to put on it. Further, your perception of what a normal serving size is changes as the portions on your plate become bigger. Thus, a large plate covered with pasta appears to be normal, whereas the ½ cup of pasta suggested by the MyPlate guide seems small.

Another adverse result of oversized portions is that the larger the portion, the less we are able to estimate kilocalorie intake. For example, eating potato

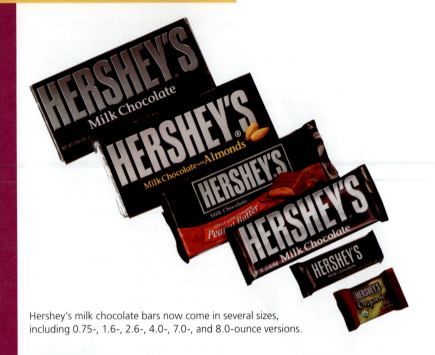

Hershey's milk chocolate bars now come in several sizes, including 0.75-, 1.6-, 2.6-, 4.0-, 7.0-, and 8.0-ounce versions.

TABLE 2.13	Controlling Portion Sizes
When You Are	**Do This**
At Home	■ Measure your food until you develop an "eye" for correct portion sizes, and check your measurements now and then to make sure they haven't crept up. ■ Use smaller plates so portions appear larger. ■ Plate your food at the counter before sitting down at the table or in front of the television. ■ Store leftover foods in portion-controlled containers. ■ Don't eat snacks directly from the box or bag; measure a portion first, then eat only that amount. ■ Cook smaller quantities of food so you don't pick at the leftovers. ■ Keep tempting foods, such as high-sugar or -kilocalorie foods, out of sight.
Eating Out	■ Ask for half orders when available. ■ Order an appetizer as your entrée. ■ Don't be compelled to "clean your plate"; stop eating when you're full and take the rest home.
Buying Groceries	■ Divide a package of snacks into individual portion sizes and consume only one portion at any one sitting. ■ Be aware of the number of servings in a package; read the labels. ■ Buy foods that are already divided into portion sizes, such as 1 oz sliced cheese or lunch meat. ■ Avoid "mini" sizes of crackers, cookies, etc.; just because they're small doesn't mean you can eat the whole box!

Tips for Controlling Portion Size

According to recent studies, adults have distorted views of what a correct portion size should be.[38] To reduce overconsumption of fat and kilocalories, and therefore the likelihood for an unhealthy body weight, consumers need to recognize healthy portion sizes, which are based on serving sizes. Steps that can help reduce oversized portions include buying smaller or single-portion packages of foods, or dividing larger packages into individual portion sizes. In restaurants, order one meal to share with your companion, or split the food in half and take the other half home. In your cupboard, replace larger glasses and plates with smaller versions. Table 2.13 provides further tips for controlling your portion sizes at home and elsewhere.

LO 2.7: THE TAKE-HOME MESSAGE

A portion size is defined as the amount of food eaten at one sitting, versus the term serving size, which is the standard amount of food for nutrient comparison used on nutrient labels. Portion sizes have continued to increase, leading to weight gain. The risk of developing chronic diseases including cardiovascular disease, diabetes, joint problems, and even some cancers increases as body weight increases. Measure your foods until you recognize a healthy portion size, use smaller glasses and plates, divide larger packages of food into individual portion sizes, and share meals when eating out to control weight gain.

Visual Chapter Summary

LO 2.1 Healthy Eating Is Based on Five Key Principles

Healthy eating involves the key principles of balance, variety, moderation, and consuming nutrient-dense and low-energy-dense foods. Foods should be nutrient dense to provide adequate nutrition, but low in energy density to prevent unwanted weight gain.

LO 2.2 Dietary Reference Intakes Are Reference Values for Each Nutrient

The Dietary Reference Intakes (DRIs) are specific reference values, based on age and gender, that express the quantities of the essential nutrients needed daily. The DRIs are designed to prevent nutrient deficiencies, maintain good health, prevent chronic diseases, and avoid unhealthy excesses. The DRIs consist of the Estimated Average Requirement, Recommended Dietary Allowance, Adequate Intake, Tolerable Upper Intake Level, and the Acceptable Macronutrient Distribution Ranges. The EER indicates how much energy an individual needs based on age, gender, and activity level.

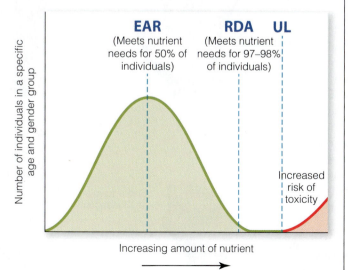

LO 2.3 Dietary Guidelines for Americans Are Recommendations to Lower Risk of Disease

The *Dietary Guidelines for Americans* give the current nutrition and physical activity recommendations for healthy Americans aged 2 and older. These guidelines can help improve the diet and lower the risk of chronic diseases and conditions such as diabetes mellitus, heart disease, certain cancers, osteoporosis, obesity, high blood pressure, and high blood cholesterol levels.

Lo 2.4 MyPlate Is a Food Guidance System Comprised of Five Food Groups

MyPlate is the USDA's latest food guidance system. It visually represents many of the recommendations in the *Dietary Guidelines for Americans, 2010* and helps plan a diet to meet the daily DRIs for the essential nutrients. There are five food groups: fruits, vegetables, grains, protein, and dairy. Oils are not shown on MyPlate because they are not a food group.

Lo 2.6 The Required Components of Food Labels Provide Nutrient Content Information

The FDA regulates all packaged food labels. The Nutrition Facts panel must list the serving size of the food and the corresponding amount of kilocalories, fat, saturated fat, *trans* fat, cholesterol, sodium, sugars, protein, vitamins A and C, calcium, and iron. The Daily Values are reference levels of intakes for the nutrients listed on the food label.

A food product label can carry a nutrient content claim using descriptive terms such as *free*, *high*, *low*, *reduced*, and *extra lean*, as long as it meets the strict criteria for each item designated by the FDA. A health claim must contain a food compound or a dietary ingredient and an associated disease or health-related condition. Structure/function claims describe how a food or dietary compound affects the structure or function of the body.

GRANOLA

Nutrition Facts
8 servings per container

	Serving size	2/3 cup (55g)

Amount per 2/3 cup

Calories   **230**

% DV*		
12%	**Total Fat** 8g	
5%	**Saturated Fat** 1g	
	Trans **Fat** 0g	
0%	**Cholesterol** 0mg	
7%	**Sodium** 160mg	
12%	**Total Carbs** 37g	
14%	**Dietary Fiber** 4g	
	Sugars 1g	
	Added Sugars 0g	
	Protein 3g	
10%	**Vitamin D** 2mcg	
20%	**Calcium** 260mg	
45%	**Iron** 8mg	
5%	**Potassium** 235mg	

* Footnote on Daily Values (DV) and calories reference to be inserted here.

Lo 2.5 The Exchange System Is Based on the Macronutrient Content of Foods

Exchange lists group foods according to their carbohydrate, protein, fat, and kilocalorie content while providing specific portion sizes. Using the exchange lists for meal planning is a convenient method for developing flexible meal plans.

Lo 2.7 Controlling Portion Size Can Contribute to Weight Maintenance and Disease Prevention

A portion size is the amount of food eaten at one sitting, regardless of the standard serving size printed on nutrient labels. Larger portion sizes, even slight changes, can lead to increased energy intake and weight gain. Over time weight gain can increase your risk for cardiovascular disease, diabetes, joint problems, and cancer. Learn to recognize a healthy portion size, use smaller plates and glassware, and divide large portions into individual portions to improve healthy eating and prevent weight gain.

Size equivalent of 3 ounces of meat

Size equivalent of 1 tablespoon

Size equivalent of 1 cup

Size equivalent of 1 teaspoon

Terms to Know

- balance
- vary
- moderate
- nutrient density
- energy density
- undernutrition
- malnutrition
- overnutrition
- portion
- Dietary Reference Intakes (DRIs)

- nutrient requirements
- Estimated Average Requirement (EAR)
- Recommended Dietary Allowance (RDA)
- Adequate Intake (AI)
- Tolerable Upper Intake Level (UL)
- toxicity
- Acceptable Macronutrient Distribution Ranges (AMDRs)
- Estimated Energy Requirement (EER)
- *Dietary Guidelines for Americans*

- food guidance systems
- MyPlate
- proportionality
- exchange lists
- Nutrition Facts panel
- Daily Values (DVs)
- nutrient content claims
- health claims
- structure/function claims
- serving size

MasteringNutrition™

To hear an MP3 Chapter Review, scan here or visit the Study Area in MasteringNutrition

Check Your Understanding

1. Nutrient-dense foods
   a. contain an equal balance of carbohydrates, proteins, and fats.
   b. are high in nutrients and lower in kilocalories.
   c. have a nutrition label.
   d. have greater weight than volume.
2. Which of the following foods is the most nutrient dense?
   a. an orange ice pop
   b. an orange
   c. orange-flavored drink
   d. orange sherbet
3. The Dietary Reference Intakes (DRIs) are reference values for nutrients and are designed to
   a. only prevent a nutritional deficiency.
   b. provide a general range of nutrient needs.
   c. prevent nutritional deficiencies by meeting nutrient needs and prevent the consumption of excessive and dangerous amounts of nutrients.
   d. apply only to infants and children.
4. An Estimated Average Requirement (EAR) is
   a. the estimated amount of a nutrient that should be consumed daily to be healthy.
   b. the amount of a nutrient that meets the average needs of 50 percent of individuals in a specific age and gender group.

   c. the maximum safe amount of a nutrient that should be consumed daily.
   d. the amount of a nutrient that meets the needs of 99 percent of the population.
5. The *Dietary Guidelines for Americans, 2010* recommend that you
   a. maintain a kilocalorie balance over time and sustain a healthy body weight.
   b. stop smoking and walk daily.
   c. sleep eight hours a night and jog every other day.
   d. maintain a kilocalorie balance over time and stop smoking.
6. Which of the following are the food groups in MyPlate?
   a. grains, vegetables, dairy, sweets, and protein
   b. grains, fruits, alcohol, sweets, and proteins
   c. grains, vegetables, fruits, dairy, and protein
   d. grains, vegetables, oils, dairy, and proteins
7. The exchange system places foods in groups based on their carbohydrate, fat, and protein content.
   a. true
   b. false
8. By law, which of the following MUST be listed on the food label?
   a. kilocalories, fat, and potassium
   b. fat, saturated fat, and vitamin E
   c. kilocalories, fat, and saturated fat
   d. kilocalories, sodium, and vitamin D
9. A yogurt that states that a serving provides 30 percent of the Daily Value (DV) contains a _____ amount of calcium.
   a. high
   b. medium

   c. low
   d. negligible
10. The bran cereal you ate for breakfast carries a "high fiber" claim on its label. This is an example of
    a. a nutrient claim.
    b. a structure claim.
    c. a health claim.
    d. a function claim.

Answers

1. (b) Nutrient-dense foods are high in nutrients, such as vitamins and minerals, but low in energy (kilocalories).
2. (b) Though an orange ice pop or orange sherbet may be a refreshing treat on a hot day, the orange is by far the most nutrient-dense food among these choices. The orange-flavored drink is a sugary drink.
3. (c) The DRIs recommend the amount of nutrients needed to prevent deficiencies, maintain good health, and avoid toxicity.
4. (b) The EAR is the amount of a nutrient that would meet the needs of half of the individuals in a specific age and gender group. The EAR is used to obtain the Recommended Dietary Allowance (RDA), which is the amount of a nutrient that should be consumed daily to maintain good health. The Tolerable Upper Intake Level (UL) is the maximum amount of a nutrient that can be consumed on a regular basis that is unlikely to cause harm.
5. (a) The *Dietary Guidelines for Americans* recommend that you balance kilocalorie intake over time

and sustain a healthy body weight. Walking or jogging are wonderful ways to be physically active. Though the *Dietary Guidelines* do not specifically address stopping smoking, this is a habit worth kicking. Sleeping eight hours a night isn't mentioned in the *Dietary Guidelines* but is another beneficial lifestyle habit.

6. (c) Grains, vegetables, fruits, dairy, and protein are the five basic food groups in MyPlate. Sweets and alcohol are not food groups and should be limited in the diet.

7. (a) True. The exchange system lists the foods in groupings according to their carbohydrate, protein, and fat composition and provides specific portion sizes for each food.

8. (c) The Nutrition Facts panel on the package must indicate the amounts of kilocalories, fat, and saturated fat per serving. Vitamins E and D do not have to be listed unless they have been added to the food and/ or the product makes a claim about them on the label.

9. (a) If you consume 20 percent or more of the Daily Value for a nutrient, it is considered "high" in that nutrient. If the label states that a serving contains 5 percent or less of the Daily Value, it is considered "low" in that nutrient.

10. (a) This high-fiber cereal boasts a nutrient claim and is helping you meet your daily fiber needs.

Answers to True or False?

1. **False.** Eating a balanced diet means not eating too much of any one food.
2. **False.** Because consuming too much of some essential nutrients can be harmful, the Tolerable Upper Intake Level (UL) of the DRIs was established for many nutrients.
3. **True.** The Dietary Reference Intakes are specific reference values for each nutrient according to age, gender, and life stage. Their main focus is to maintain good health and reduce the risk of developing chronic diseases and avoid unhealthy excesses.

4. **True.** These *Dietary Guidelines for Americans* are the latest recommendations for nutrition and physical activity for healthy Americans over the age of 2.

5. **True.** The five food groups that make up the MyPlate recommendations are grains, vegetables, fruits, dairy, and protein.

6. **False.** Oils are not considered a food group but you should add some daily for good health.

7. **True.** Exchange lists allow you to swap foods within each food group while still controlling the amount of carbohydrate, protein, fat, and kilocalories you ingest.

8. **False.** A nutrient claim uses descriptive terms to make a claim about the amount of a nutrient a serving of the food contains (or doesn't contain). Specific terms approved by the FDA must be used.

9. **True.** The FDA requires a food label on all packaged food items with specific information required.

10. **False.** A portion of food is the amount of food you choose to eat. A standard serving size is defined by the USDA as a standard amount used on food labels.

Web Resources

- For more tips and resources for MyPlate, visit www.ChooseMyPlate.gov
- For details on the *Dietary Guidelines for Americans, 2010,* visit www.cnpp .usda.gov/DietaryGuidelines.htm
- For more on food labels, visit www.fda.gov

References

1. Freeland-Graves, J. H., and S. Nitzke. 2013. Position of the Academy of Nutrition and Dietetics: Total Diet Approach to Healthy Eating. *Journal of the Academy of Nutrition and Dietetics.* 113(2):307–317.
2. Ibid.
3. Produce for Better Health Foundation. 2012. *Fruits and Vegetables—More Matters.* Available at www.fruitsandveggiesmorematters .org. Accessed January 2014.
4. Azadbakht, L., F. Haghighatdoost, and A. Esmaillzadeh. 2012. Dietary Energy Density is Inversely Associated with the Diet Quality Indices among Iranian Young Adults. *Journal of Nutritional Science and Vitaminology* 58(1):29–35.
5. Jaworowska, A., T. Blackham, I. G. Davies, and L. Stevenson. 2013. Nutritional Challenges and Health Implications of Takeaway and Fast Food. *Nutrition Reviews* 71(5):310–318.
6. Hill, B. R., B. J. Rolls, L. S. Roe, M. J. De Souza, and N. I. Williams. 2013. Ghrelin and Peptide YY Increase with Weight Loss during a 12-Month Intervention to Reduce Dietary Energy Density in Obese Women. *Peptides* 49:138–144.
7. Ledikwe, J. H., B. J. Rolls, H. Smiciklas-Wright, D. C. Mitchell, J. D. Ard, C. Champagne, N. Karanja, et al. 2007. Reductions in Dietary Energy Density Are Associated with Weight Loss in Overweight and Obese Participants in the PREMIER Trial. *American Journal of Clinical Nutrition* 85:1212–1221.
8. Lau, D. C., and H. Teoh. 2013. Benefits of Modest Weight Loss on the Management of Type 2 Diabetes Mellitus. *Canadian Journal of Diabetes* 37(2):128–134.
9. Williams, R. A., L. S. Roe, and B. J. Rolls. 2013. Comparison of Three Methods to Reduce Energy Density. Effects on Energy Density Intake. *Appetite* 66:75–83.
10. Institute of Medicine. 2003. Dietary Reference Intakes: Applications in Dietary Planning. Washington, DC: The National Academies Press. Updated 2013. Available at http://fnic.nal.usda.gov. Accessed January 2014.
11. Ibid.
12. Ibid.
13. Ibid.
14. American Association of Poison Control Centers' National Poison Data System. 2012. *Annual Reports.* Available at www.aapcc.org. Accessed January 2014.
15. U.S. Department of Agriculture. 2011. *Dietary Guidance.* Available at http://fnic .nal.usda.gov. Accessed January 2014.
16. Farazo, E. 1999. *America's Eating Habits: Changes and Consequences.* Updated 2012. Available at www.ers.usda.gov. Accessed January 2014.
17. Lee, P. R. 1978. Nutrition Policy: From Neglect and Uncertainty to Debate and Action. *Journal of the American Dietetic Association* 72:581–588.
18. Report of the DGAC on the *Dietary Guidelines for Americans, 2010.* 2013. Available at www.cnpp.usda.gov. Accessed January 2014.
19. U.S. Department of Agriculture. 2011. *Dietary Guidelines for Americans, 2010.* Available at www.cnpp.usda.gov. Accessed January 2014.
20. Food and Drug Adminstration. Revised 2013. *A Food Labeling Guide.* Available at www.fda.gov. Accessed January 2014.
21. Ibid.
22. Food and Drug Administration. 2013. *Nutrition Information for Raw Fruits, Vegetables

and Fish. Available at www.fda.gov. Accessed January 2014.

23. USDA Food Safety and Inspection Service. 2013. *Country of Origin Labeling for Meat and Chicken.* Available at www.fsis.usda.gov. Accessed January 2014.

24. Food and Drug Administration. 2011. *Food Labeling and Nutrition.* Available at www .fda.gov. Accessed February 2012.

25. Center for Food Safety and Applied Nutrition. 2012. *How to Understand and Use the Nutrition Facts Label.* Available at www.fda .gov. Accessed January 2014.

26. Kurtzweil, P. 1998. Staking a Claim to Good Health. *FDA Consumer.* Available at www.fda.gov. Accessed January 2014.

27. U.S. Food and Drug Administration. 2014. *A Food Labeling Guide* Available at www.fda .gov. Accessed January 2014.

28. Academy of Nutrition and Dietetics. 2013. Position of the Academy of Nutrition and Dietetics: Functional Foods. *Journal of the Academy of Nutrition and Dietetics* 113:1096–1103.

29. Institute of Food Technologists. 2005. *Expert Report on Functional Foods: Opportunities and Challenges, Executive Summary.* Available at www.ift.org. Accessed February 2012.

30. Almiron-Roig E., I. Solis-Trapala, J. Dodd, and S. A. Jebb. 2013. Estimating Food Portions. Influence of Unit Number, Meal Type and Energy Density. *Appetite* 71:95–103.

31. Just, D. R., and B. Wansink. 2013. One Man's Tall Is Another Man's Small: How the Framing of Portion Size Influences Food Choice. *Health Economics.* DOI:10.1002/hec.2949.

32. Smiciklas-Wright, H., D. C. Mitchell, S. Mickle, J. Goldman, and A. Cook. 2003. Foods Commonly Eaten in the United States, 1989–1991 and 1994–1996: Are Portion Sizes Changing? *Journal of the American Dietetic Association* 103:41–47.

33. Vermeer, W. M., E. Alting, I. H. M. Steenhuis, and J. C. Seidell. 2010. Value for Money or Making the Healthy Choice: The Impact of Proportional Pricing on Consumers' Portion Size Choices. *European Journal of Public Health* 20:65–69.

34. Urban, L. E., A. H. Lichtenstein, C. E. Gary, et al. 2013. The Energy Content of Restaurant Foods without Stated Calorie Information. *Journal of the American Medical Association Internal Medicine* 173(14):1292–1299.

35. Young, L. R., and M. Nestle. 2012. Reducing Portion Sizes to Prevent Obesity. *American Journal of Preventive Medicine* 43(5):565–568.

36. Stran, K. A., L. W. Turner, and L. Knol. 2013. Mandating Nutrient Menu Labeling in Restaurants: Potential Public Health Benefits. *Journal of the Arkansas Medical Society* 109(10):209–211.

37. Downs, J. S., J. Wisdom, B. Wansink, and G. Loewenstein. 2013. Supplementing Menu Laeling with Calorie Recommendations to Test for Facilitation Effects. *American Journal of Public Health* 103(9):1604–1609.

38. Barbara J. Rolls. 2010. Plenary Lecture 1: Dietary Strategies for the Prevention and Treatment of Obesity. *Proceedings of the Nutrition Society* 69:70–79.

3 Digestion, Absorption, and Transport

Learning Outcomes

After reading this chapter, you will be able to:

3.1 Describe the processes and organs involved in digestion.

3.2 Describe how food is propelled through the gastrointestinal tract.

3.3 Explain the role of enzymes and other secretions in chemical digestion.

3.4 Describe how digested nutrients are absorbed.

3.5 Explain how hormones and the nervous system regulate digestion.

3.6 Explain how absorbed nutrients are transported throughout the body.

3.7 Describe the most common digestive disorders.

True or False?

1. Saliva can alter the taste of food. **T**/**F**

2. Without mucus, the stomach would digest itself. **T**/**F**

3. The major function of bile is to emulsify fats. **T**/**F**

4. Acid reflux is caused by gas in the stomach. **T**/**F**

5. The primary function of the large intestine is to absorb water. **T**/**F**

6. Feces contain a high amount of bacteria. **T**/**F**

7. The lymphatic system transports all nutrients through the body once they've been absorbed. **T**/**F**

8. Hormones play an important role in digestion. **T**/**F**

9. Diarrhea is always caused by bacterial infection. **T**/**F**

10. Irritable bowel syndrome is caused by an allergy to gluten. **T**/**F**

See page 106 for the answers.

The digestion of food begins even before you take that first bite. Just the sight and smell of warm homemade apple pie stimulates the release of saliva in the mouth. The secretion of saliva and other digestive juices starts a cascade of events that prepares the body for digestion.

When digestion works properly, these complex processes go unnoticed. You consciously chew and swallow the pie, but you don't feel the muscular contractions that propel it through the GI tract organs. Nor is it obvious when the pancreas and small intestine release secretions, or when the single molecules of nutrients are absorbed into the intestinal cell wall. Unless you feel the rumbling as your GI tract works, you are unconscious of the entire process until about 48 hours after eating, when the body is ready to eliminate waste through the rectum.

The body digests food *chemically*, by actions of digestive secretions such as enzymes, and *mechanically*, by the actions of the teeth and powerful muscular contractions of the GI tract. We will explore the processes of both **chemical digestion** and **mechanical digestion** in this chapter, and learn more about absorption and transport of digested nutrients, the organs involved, and the other biological mechanisms that regulate our bodies' processing of food and nutrients. We'll also discuss the causes and treatments of some common gastrointestinal conditions and disorders.

What Are the Processes and Organs Involved in Digestion?

LO 3.1 Describe the processes and organs involved in digestion.

For the nutrients in food to be absorbed, the bonds that link the nutrients together must be broken down in the **gastrointestinal (GI) tract** (digestive tract). **Digestion** is the process in which chemicals and mechanical processes break the bonds and reduce food into individual molecules. These small molecules move along the gastrointestinal tract by **propulsion** and pass through the wall of the small intestine by **absorption.** Once the nutrients are absorbed, the blood and lymph **transport** them through the cardiovascular and lymphatic systems to the liver and various tissues throughout the body. Those nutrients that aren't digested or absorbed are excreted as waste (feces) by **elimination. Focus Figure 3.1** illustrates the organs and processes of the digestive system.

The Organs of the GI Tract Process Food

The GI tract is a muscular tube, approximately 20 to 24 feet long in an adult, which extends from the mouth to the anus. Stretched vertically, the tube would be about as high as a two-story building. It provides a barrier between the food we eat (external) and our body cells (internal). This barrier regulates which nutrients enter the body based on need, and which nutrients pass through the GI tract unabsorbed.

The six organs that make up the digestive tract—the mouth, pharynx, esophagus, stomach, small intestine, and large intestine—contain numerous specialized cells and tissues involved in both chemical and mechanical digestive processes. Cells in the lining of the small intestine, for example, secrete enzymes, while specialized muscles of the stomach break up and propel food through the tract.

Various **sphincters** along the way allow food to pass from one organ to the next. These muscular rings act like one-way doors, allowing the mixture of food and digestive juices to flow into one organ but not back out.

chemical digestion Breaking down food through enzymatic reactions.

mechanical digestion Breaking down food by chewing, grinding, squeezing, and moving food through the GI tract by peristalsis and segmentation.

gastrointestinal (GI) tract A long tube comprised of the organs of the digestive tract. It extends from the mouth through the esophagus, stomach, and small and large intestines to the anus.

digestion A process that breaks down food into individual molecules small enough to be absorbed through the intestinal wall.

propulsion The process that moves food along the gastrointestinal tract during digestion.

absorption The process of moving nutrients from the GI tract into the circulatory system.

transport The process of moving absorbed nutrients throughout the body through the circulatory and lymph systems.

elimination Excretion of undigested and unabsorbed food through the feces.

sphincter A circular ring of muscle that opens and closes in response to nerve input.

The human digestive system consists of the organs of the gastrointestinal (GI) tract and associated accessory organs. The processing of food in the GI tract involves ingestion, mechanical digestion, chemical digestion, propulsion, absorption, and elimination.

ORGANS OF THE GI TRACT

MOUTH

Ingestion Food enters the GI tract via the mouth.

Mechanical digestion Mastication tears, shreds, and mixes food with saliva, forming a bolus.

Chemical digestion Salivary amylase begins carbohydrate breakdown.

PHARYNX AND ESOPHAGUS

Propulsion Swallowing and peristalsis move the bolus from mouth to stomach.

STOMACH

Mechanical digestion This process mixes and churns the bolus with acid, enzymes, and gastric fluid into a liquid called chyme.

Chemical digestion Pepsin begins digestion of proteins.

Absorption A few fat-soluble substances are absorbed through the stomach wall.

SMALL INTESTINE

Mechanical digestion and **Propulsion** Segmentation mixes chyme with digestive juices; peristaltic waves move it along the tract.

Chemical digestion Digestive enzymes from pancreas and brush border digest most classes of food.

Absorption Nutrients are absorbed into blood and lymph through enterocytes.

LARGE INTESTINE

Chemical digestion Some remaining food residues are digested by bacteria.

Absorption Salts, water, and some vitamins are reabsorbed.

Propulsion Compacts waste into feces.

RECTUM

Elimination Feces are temporarily stored before voluntary release through the anus.

ACCESSORY ORGANS

SALIVARY GLANDS
Produce saliva, a mixture of water, mucus, enzymes, and other chemicals

LIVER
Produces bile to digest fats

GALLBLADDER
Stores bile before release into the small intestine through the bile duct

PANCREAS
Produces digestive enzymes and bicarbonate ions that are released into the small intestine via the pancreatic duct

Whole foods must first be broken down into individual nutrients that can be used by the body's cells.

Digestion Begins in the Mouth

Both chemical digestion and mechanical digestion begin in the mouth. During **mastication**, the teeth, powered by strong jaw muscles, mechanically cut and grind food into smaller pieces as the tongue mixes it with **saliva**. Saliva dissolves small food particles, which allows them to react with the taste buds so we can savor food, and it moistens and binds food to lubricate it for comfortable swallowing and travel down the esophagus. Saliva also contains the enzyme amylase, which begins to break down carbohydrate. (You can taste this enzyme working when you eat a starch-containing food; as the enzyme breaks down starch into smaller pieces, or sugars, the flavor becomes sweeter. Remember this the next time you eat a cracker.)

Once food has been adequately chewed and moistened, the tongue rolls it into a **bolus**, and thrusts it into the **pharynx** to be swallowed. The pharynx is the gateway to the **esophagus**, as well as to the *trachea* (or windpipe, the tube that connects to the lungs). Normally, a flap of cartilage called the **epiglottis** closes off the trachea during swallowing, so that food doesn't accidentally "go down the wrong pipe" (see **Figure 3.2**). When the epiglottis doesn't work properly, food can get lodged in the trachea and potentially cause choking.

The esophagus has only one function—to transport food and fluids from the mouth to the stomach. As food passes through the pharynx, the **upper esophageal sphincter** opens, allowing the bolus to enter the esophagus. After swallowing, rhythmic muscular contractions, with the help of gravity, move the bolus toward the stomach. The esophagus narrows at the bottom (just above the stomach) and ends at the **lower esophageal sphincter (LES)** (**Figure 3.3**). Under normal conditions, when the bolus reaches the stomach, the LES relaxes and allows food to pass into the stomach. The stomach also relaxes to comfortably receive the bolus. After food enters the stomach, the LES closes to prevent the stomach contents from regurgitating backward into the esophagus.

mastication Chewing food.

saliva Secretion from the salivary glands that softens and lubricates food, and begins the chemical breakdown of starch.

bolus A soft mass of chewed food.

pharynx The area of the GI tract between the mouth and the esophagus; also called the throat.

esophagus Tube that connects the mouth to the stomach.

epiglottis Cartilage at the back of the tongue that closes off the trachea during swallowing.

upper esophageal sphincter The muscular ring located at the top of the esophagus.

lower esophageal sphincter (LES) The muscular ring located between the base of the esophagus and the stomach.

The Stomach Stores, Mixes, and Prepares Food for Digestion

The primary function of the **stomach** is to mix food with various gastric juices to chemically break it down into smaller and smaller pieces (**Figure 3.4**). The stomach lining includes four layers. The innermost layer contains **goblet cells** and **gastric pits** or ducts, which contain gastric glands that secrete a variety of critical digestive juices. Various other cells in the stomach lining, among them **parietal** (*puh-RIA-tl*) **cells**, **chief cells**, and mucous neck cells, secrete other gastric juices and mucus.

Mechanical digestion in the stomach occurs as the *longitudinal, circular*, and *diagonal* muscles that surround the organ forcefully push, churn, and mix the contents of the stomach with the gastric juices. These powerful muscles can also stretch to accommodate different volumes of food. Stomach capacity is a little less than a cup when it's empty but it can expand to hold up to 1 gallon (4 liters).[1] For several hours, food is continuously churned and mixed in the stomach.

By the time the mixture reaches the lower portion of the stomach it is a semi-liquid mass called **chyme**, which contains digestive secretions plus the original food. As the chyme accumulates near the pyloric sphincter, between the stomach and the small intestine, the sphincter relaxes and the chyme gradually enters the small intestine. You eat much faster than you can digest and absorb food, so the stomach also acts as a holding tank for chyme until it can be released into the small intestine. The numerous folds of the stomach lining, which stretch out after a large meal, make it an ideal site for temporarily storing chyme. Approximately 1 to 5 milliliters (1 teaspoon) of chyme is released into the small intestine every 30 seconds.[2] The pyloric sphincter prevents chyme from exiting the stomach too soon, and blocks the intestinal contents from returning to the stomach.

Most Digestion Occurs in the Small Intestine

As chyme passes through the pyloric sphincter, it enters the long, coiled **small intestine.** This organ consists of three segments—the duodenum, jejunum, and ileum—and extends from the pyloric sphincter to the ileocecal valve at the

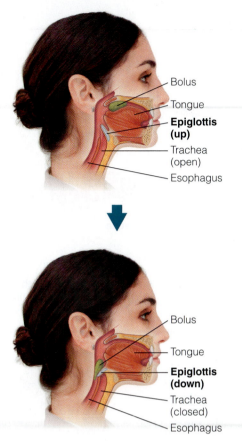

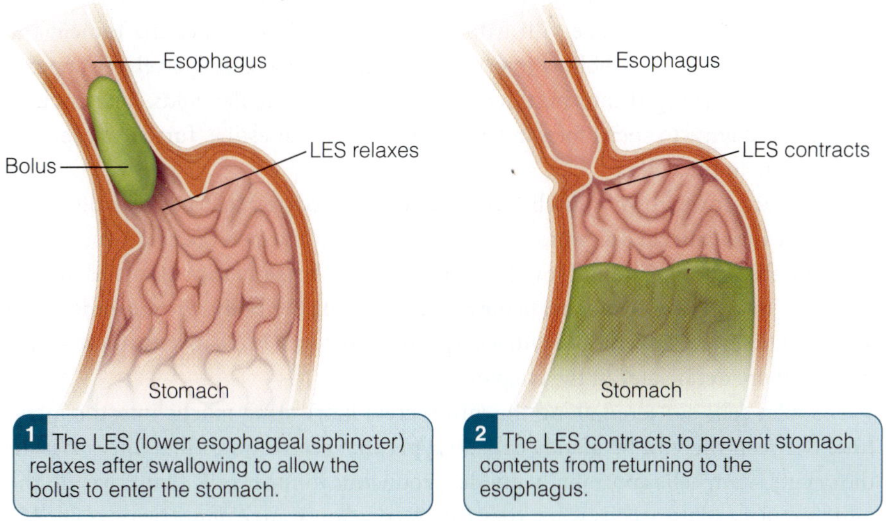

▲ Figure 3.2 **The Role of the Epiglottis**
The epiglottis prevents food from entering the trachea during swallowing.

▲ Figure 3.3 **Sphincters at Work**
Sphincters control the passage of food by contracting or relaxing.

1 The LES (lower esophageal sphincter) relaxes after swallowing to allow the bolus to enter the stomach.

2 The LES contracts to prevent stomach contents from returning to the esophagus.

stomach A J-shaped muscular organ that mixes and churns food with digestive juices and acid to form chyme.

goblet cells Cells throughout the GI tract that secrete mucus.

gastric pits Indentations or small pits in the stomach lining where the gastric glands are located; gastric glands produce gastric juices.

parietal cells Specialized cells in the stomach that secrete the gastric juices hydrochloric acid and intrinsic factor.

chief cells Specialized cells in the stomach that secrete an inactive protein-digesting enzyme called pepsinogen.

chyme The semiliquid, partially digested food mass that leaves the stomach and enters the small intestine.

small intestine The long coiled chamber that is the major site of food digestion and nutrient absorption.

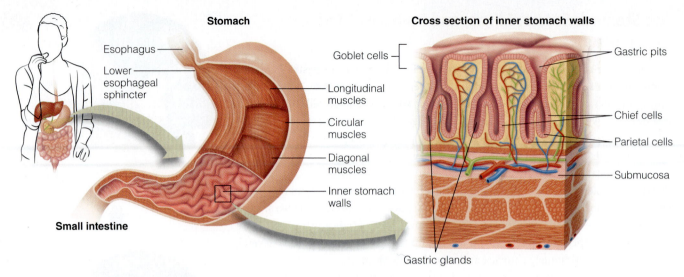

Stomach

Esophagus

Lower esophageal sphincter

Longitudinal muscles

Circular muscles

Diagonal muscles

Inner stomach walls

Small intestine

Cross section of inner stomach walls

Goblet cells

Gastric pits

Chief cells

Parietal cells

Submucosa

Gastric glands

▲ **Figure 3.4 Anatomy of the Stomach**
The cross section of the stomach illustrates the gastric cells that secrete digestive juices.

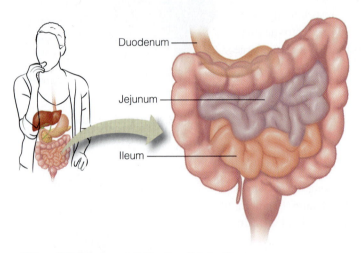

Duodenum

Jejunum

Ileum

▲ **Figure 3.5 Anatomy of the Small Intestine**
The small intestine is highly adapted for absorbing nutrients. Its length—about 20 feet—provides a huge surface area, and its wall has three structural features—circular folds, villi, and microvilli—that increase its surface area by a factor of more than 600.

villi Small, fingerlike projections that line the interior of the small intestine.

lumen The channel or inside space of a vessel such as the intestine or artery.

enterocytes Absorptive epithelial cells that line the walls of the small intestine.

microvilli Tiny projections on the villi in the small intestine.

crypts Glands at the base of the villi; they contain stem cells that manufacture young cells to replace the cells of the villi when they die.

beginning of the large intestine (**Figure 3.5**). The first segment, the duodenum, is approximately 10 inches long. The second, the jejunum, measures about 8 feet long, and the third, the ileum, is about 12 feet long. The "small" in "small intestine" refers to its diameter (about 1 inch), not its extended length.

As in the stomach, both mechanical and chemical digestion occur in the small intestine. Muscular contractions squeeze chyme forward while digestive secretions from the pancreas, gallbladder, and intestinal lining chemically break down the nutrients.

Numerous fingerlike projections, called **villi**, line the small intestine. They increase the surface area to maximize absorption and they help mix the partially digested chyme with intestinal secretions (**Focus Figure 3.6**). Each villus contains capillaries and lymphatic vessels called *lacteals* that pick up digested nutrients during absorption. The villi extend about 1 millimeter into the **lumen**, the hollow interior of the intestine, creating a velvety appearance, and are arranged into hundreds of overlapping, circular folds. The circular folds cause chyme to spiral forward through the small intestine, further increasing its exposure to the villi.

Villi are covered by epithelial cells called **enterocytes** that have smaller projections called **microvilli**, which provide additional surface area and maximize nutrient absorption. The microvilli, also called the *brush border*, trap and absorb nutrients into the cells to be transported throughout the body. Brush border cells also secrete several enzymes that digest specific nutrients. We'll discuss these secretions in more detail later in the chapter.

Goblet cells scattered along the villi secrete lubricating mucus into the intestine. Between the villi lie glands called **crypts** that secrete intestinal juice. Within the crypts, stem cells continually divide, producing younger cells that travel up the villi to replace mature cells when they die. A constant source of nutrients is needed to replace these cells and maintain a healthy absorptive surface. Without the proper nutrients, the villi deteriorate and flatten, resulting in malabsorption.

Structures of the Small Intestinal Wall

The small intestine is highly adapted for absorbing nutrients. Its length—about 20 feet—provides a huge surface area, and its wall has three structural features—circular folds, villi, and microvilli—that increase its surface area by a factor of more than 600.

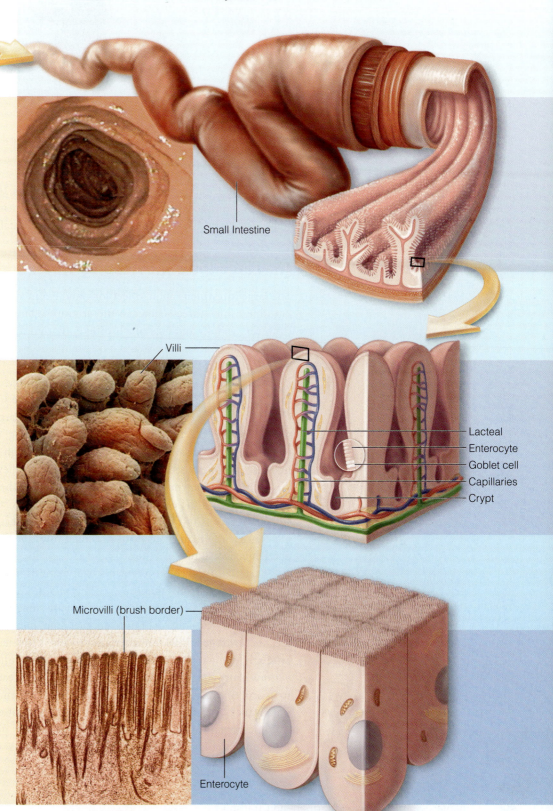

CIRCULAR FOLDS

The lining of the small intestine is heavily folded, resulting in increased surface area for the absorption of nutrients.

Small Intestine

VILLI

The folds are covered with villi, thousands of fingerlike projections that increase the surface area even further. Each villus contains capillaries and a lacteal for picking up nutrients absorbed through the enterocytes and transporting them throughout the body.

Villi

Lacteal
Enterocyte
Goblet cell
Capillaries
Crypt

MICROVILLI

The cells on the surface of the villi, enterocytes, end in hairlike projections called microvilli that together form the brush border through which nutrients are absorbed.

Microvilli (brush border)

Enterocyte

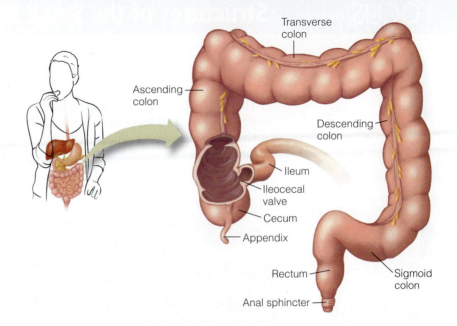

▶ **Figure 3.7 Anatomy of the Large Intestine**
By the time chyme reaches the large intestine, most of its nutrients have been absorbed. However, water and some electrolytes are absorbed in the colon. The final waste products of digestion pass out of the body through the anus.

Depending on the amount and type of food eaten, the contact time in the small intestine is between 3 and 10 hours. Usually, by the time you sit down to dinner, your breakfast is just about reaching the end of the small intestine.

The Large Intestine Absorbs Water and Some Nutrients

The **large intestine** is about 5 feet long and 2.5 inches in diameter. Like the small intestine, it has three segments: the cecum, colon, and rectum (see **Figure 3.7**). However, it looks and acts much differently than the small intestine in that it is much shorter, does not have villi or microvilli, does not produce digestive enzymes, and is not tightly coiled.

The **cecum** (*SEE-kum*) marks the beginning of the large intestine. Chyme from the small intestine passes through the **ileocecal valve** into the cecum before entering the colon. The **colon** is the largest portion of the large intestine, and it is further subdivided into the ascending, transverse, descending, and sigmoid regions. These regions are relatively long and straight. Note that though the terms "colon" and "large intestine" are often used interchangeably, technically they're not the same thing.

By the time chyme enters the large intestine, the majority of the nutrients, except water and the electrolytes sodium, potassium, and chloride, have been absorbed. The cells of the large intestine absorb water and these electrolytes much more efficiently than the cells of the small intestine. The large intestine also produces mucus that protects the cells and acts as a lubricant for fecal matter.

Bacteria in the colon produce some vitamins, including vitamin K, thiamin, riboflavin, biotin, and vitamin B_{12}. Only biotin and vitamin K can be absorbed in the colon, however. Bacteria also **ferment** some of the undigested and unabsorbed dietary carbohydrates into simpler compounds, methane gas, carbon dioxide, and hydrogen. This fermentation process is the major source of intestinal gas. Similarly, some of the colon's bacteria break down undigested fiber and produce various short-chain fatty acids. Amino acids that reach the colon are converted to hydrogen, sulfide, some fatty acids, and other chemical compounds. Given the importance of bacteria in the healthy functioning of the colon, foods containing live microorganisms, called probiotics, have become popular in recent years. The Examining the Evidence feature evaluates the claims of health benefits associated with probiotic consumption.

large intestine The lowest portion of the GI tract, where water and electrolytes are absorbed and waste is eliminated.

cecum A pouch at the beginning of the large intestine that receives waste from the small intestine.

ileocecal valve The sphincter that separates the small intestine from the large intestine.

colon Another name for the large intestine.

ferment To metabolize sugar into carbon dioxide and other gases.

About 1 liter of fluid material, consisting of water, undigested or unabsorbed food particles, indigestible residue, and electrolytes, passes into the colon each day. Gradually, the material is reduced to about 200 grams of brown fecal matter (also called **stool**, or feces). Stool consists of the undigested food residue, as well as sloughed-off cells from the GI tract, and a large quantity of bacteria. The brown color is due to unabsorbed iron mixing with a yellowish-orange substance called bilirubin. The greater the iron content, the darker the feces. The intestinal matter passes through the colon within 12 to 70 hours, depending on a person's age, health, diet, and fiber intake.

Stool is propelled through the large intestine until it reaches the final 8-inch portion called the **rectum**. The **anus** is connected to the rectum and controlled by two sphincters: an internal and an external sphincter. Under normal conditions, the anal sphincters are closed. When stool distends the rectum, the action stimulates stretch receptors that in turn stimulate the internal anal sphincters to relax, allowing the stool to enter the anal canal. This causes nerve impulses of the rectum to communicate with the rectum's muscles, resulting in defecation. The final stage of defecation is under voluntary control and influenced by age, diet, prescription medicines, health, and abdominal muscle tone.

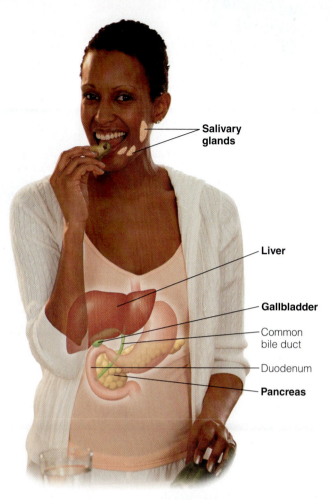

Salivary glands

Liver

Gallbladder

Common bile duct

Duodenum

Pancreas

▲ Figure 3.8 **The Accessory Organs**
The salivary glands, liver, gallbladder, and pancreas produce digestive secretions that flow into the duodenum through various ducts.

The Accessory Organs Secrete Digestive Juices

The salivary glands, liver, gallbladder, and pancreas are considered accessory organs because food does not pass through them during digestion (**Figure 3.8**). These organs are still key to the digestive process, however. They contribute digestive secretions such as saliva, bile, and enzymes that help with breakdown and transport of nutrients.

The **salivary glands**, located beneath the jaw and under and behind the tongue, produce about 1 quart of saliva per day.[3] Saliva helps dissolve small food particles and allows you to comfortably swallow dry food. In addition to water, saliva contains electrolytes, a few enzymes, and mucus. The mucus helps lubricate the food, helps it stick together, and protects the inside of the mouth.

Weighing in at about three pounds, the **liver** is the largest organ in the body. It is located just beneath the rib cage, and functions as a major player in the digestion, absorption, and transport of nutrients. The liver plays an essential role in carbohydrate metabolism, produces proteins, and manufactures bile salts used to digest fats. The bile produced by the liver is secreted into the gallbladder for storage. The liver is also the site for alcohol metabolism and removes and degrades toxins and excess hormones from the circulation.

The **gallbladder** is located beneath the right side of the liver. This pear-shaped organ receives bile from the liver through the common hepatic duct, concentrates it, and secretes bile into the small intestine through the common bile duct.

The **pancreas** is a flat organ about 10 to 15 centimeters long that hides behind the stomach and snugly fits in the bend of the duodenum. The function of the pancreas is both *endocrine* (*endo* = inside) and *exocrine* (*exo* = outside). As an endocrine organ, the pancreas releases hormones to maintain blood glucose levels. As an exocrine organ, the pancreas produces and secretes digestive enzymes into the small intestine.

stool Waste produced in the large intestine; also called *feces*.

rectum Final 8-inch portion of the large intestine.

anus The opening of the rectum, or end of the GI tract.

salivary glands Cluster of glands located underneath and behind the tongue that release saliva in response to the sight, smell, and taste of food.

liver The largest organ in the body, located in the upper abdomen. This organ aids digestion by secreting bile.

gallbladder A pear-shaped organ located behind the liver. The gallbladder stores bile produced by the liver and secretes the bile through the common bile duct into the small intestine.

pancreas A large gland located behind the stomach that releases digestive enzymes after a meal. The pancreas also secretes the hormones insulin and glucagon, which control blood glucose.

Do Probiotics Improve Your Intestinal Health?

If you are like most people, the thought of eating food that contains live bugs is not very appealing. But did you know that consuming certain live microorganisms may improve your overall health? This is probably the reason that consumer attraction for foods that contain live microorganisms, called **probiotics** (*pro* = for, *bios* = life), has taken off in the United States. Sales of probiotic supplements and foods increased to almost $2 billion in 2011 and are projected to reach $31 billion by 2015.[1] What are probiotics and why are Americans clamoring to buy them?

What Are Probiotics?

Probiotics are defined as "live microorganisms, which when administered in adequate amounts, confer a health benefit on the host."[2] These live bacteria are similar to the more than 10 trillion microflora that colonize your colon. Medications, stress, diet, and illness can disrupt the balance of friendly microflora, and probiotics may bring them back into balance.

How Do Probiotics Work to Improve Health?

Probiotics function in the same way the native bacteria in your GI tract do—they

probiotics Live microorganisms, which, when administered in adequate amounts, confer a health benefit on the host.

produce organic acids that inhibit disease-causing bacteria from growing. The friendly bacteria compete with these pathogens for nutrients and receptor sites, keeping the population of harmful bacteria in check.

Specific strains of bacteria have different effects on our health.

- Several strains of probiotics, including *L. rhamnosus GG* and *Saccharomyces boulardii lyo,* may reduce diarrhea and constipation.[3]
- *Bifidobacterium lactis* DN-173 010, *Lactobacillus casei* reduces the transit time of chyme through the

GI tract.[4] This results in fewer bouts of constipation.
- *Galacto-Oligosaccharide* RP-G28 may alleviate lactose intolerance symptoms, including cramping and bloating, although studies are not conclusive.[5]
- *Lactobacillus reuteri* shows promise in the prevention of food allergy.[6]
- *Lactobacillus gasseri* PA 16/8, *Bifidobacterium longum* SP 07/3, and *B. bifidum* MF 20/5 have been shown to shorten duration of the common cold and reduce the severity of the symptoms.[7]

LO 3.1: THE TAKE-HOME MESSAGE Digestion takes place in the GI tract. Chemicals break the molecular bonds in food so that nutrients can be absorbed and transported throughout the body. Saliva mixes with and moistens food in the mouth, making it easier to swallow. Once a bolus of food mixes with gastric juices in the stomach, it becomes chyme. Maximum digestion and absorption occur in the small intestine. Undigested residue enters the large intestine, where water is removed from the chyme as it is prepared for elimination. Eventually, the remnants of digestion reach the anus and exit the body in the feces. The liver, gallbladder, and pancreas are important accessory organs. The liver produces bile and the gallbladder concentrates and stores it. The pancreas produces enzymes and hormones.

Beneficial Bacteria

If You Have This Problem	Try This Probiotic	Found in These Foods and Dietary Supplements
Diarrhea	■ *Lactobacillus reuteri* 55730 ■ *Saccharomyces boulardii* yeast	■ BioGai tablets, drops, and lozenges ■ Florastor dietary supplement
Constipation	■ *Bifidobacterium animalis* DN-173 010	■ Dannon Activia yogurt
Irritable bowel syndrome and overall digestion problems	■ *Bifidobacterium infantis* 35624	■ Align supplement
Poor immune system	■ *Bifidobacterium lactis* Bb-12 ■ *Lactobacillus casei* Shirota ■ *Lactobacillus casei* DN-114 001	■ Yo-Plus Yogurt ■ Yakult fermented dairy drink ■ Dannon's DanActive dairy drink
Vaginal infections	■ *Lactobacillus rhamnosus* GR-1 combined with *Lactobacillus reuteri*	■ Fem Dophilus dietary supplement

■ *Lactobacillus reuteri* ATCC 55730 has been shown to reduce colic in infants.[8]

Where Do We Find Probiotics?

Probiotics are found in foods, such as fermented dairy and soy products, and in dietary supplements, and are known by a variety of names (see the table). Read the label carefully to learn the strain of the bacteria used, when the product expires, the suggested serving size, and how to store the product to make sure the bacteria are still alive when you eat it. A serving should contain at least one billion CFUs (a measure of live bacteria called colony-forming units) to provide the level of probiotics found to deliver health benefits.

Although there is a great deal we don't know about probiotics and the impact on our health, research does suggest that probiotics in the daily diet help maintain a healthy digestive system.

References

1. J. Townsend. 2011. *Probiotics Sales Proliferate at a Stunning Rate in 2011.* Available at http://newhope360.com. Accessed January 2014.
2. M. Kechagia, D. Basoulis, S. Konstantopoulou, D. Dimitriadi, K. Gyftopoulou, N. Skarmoutsou, and E. M. Fakiri. 2013. "Health Benefits of Probiotics: A Review." *ISRN Nutrition*, Article ID 481651, 7 pages. doi:10.5402/2013/481651. Accessed January 2014.
3. M. L. Ritchie and T. N. Romanuk. 2012. "A Meta-Analysis of Probiotic Efficacy for Gastrointestinal Diseases." *PLoS ONE* 7(4): e34938. doi:10.1371/journal.pone.0034938.
4. Ibid.
5. D. A. Savaiano, A. J. Ritter, T. R. Klaenhammer, G. M. James, A. T. Longcore, J. R. Chandler, W. A. Walker, and H. L. Foyt. 2013. "Improving Lactose Digestion and Symptoms of Lactose Intolerance with a Novel Galacto-Oligosaccharide (RP-G28): A Randomized, Double-Blind Clinical Trial." *Nutrition Journal* 12:160 doi:10.1186/1475-2891-12-160.
6. B. W. Ritz. 2011. *Probiotics for the Prevention of Childhood Eczema.* Available at http://naturalmedicinejournal.com. Accessed February 2014.
7. L. Swanson. 2013. *Probiotics in the Regulation of Cold and Flu.* Available at http://probiotics101.probacto.com. Accessed February 2014.
8. J. Anabrees, F. Indrio, B. Paes, and K. AlFaleh. 2013. "Probiotics for Infantile Colic: A Systematic Review." *BMC Pediatrics* 13:186 doi:10.1186/1471-2431-13-186.

How Is Food Propelled through the GI Tract?

LO 3.2 Describe how food is propelled through the gastrointestinal tract.

Wavelike movements of the muscles throughout the GI tract propel food and liquid forward. The two primary types of contractions, called **peristalsis** and **segmentation**, depend upon coordination between the muscles, nerves, and hormones in the digestive tract (**Figure 3.9**). As food moves down the GI tract, the muscles help mechanically digest the food by mixing and pushing it at just the right pace through each organ.

peristalsis The forward, rhythmic motion that moves food through the digestive system. Peristalsis is a form of mechanical digestion because it influences motion, but it does not add chemical secretions.

segmentation Muscular contractions of the small intestine that move food back and forth, breaking the mixture into smaller and smaller pieces and combining it with digestive juices.

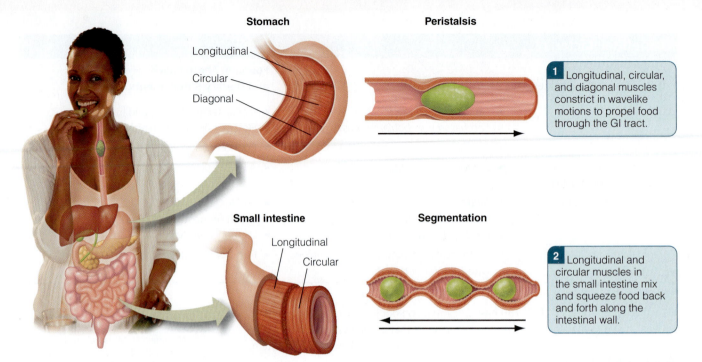

Stomach

Longitudinal
Circular
Diagonal

Peristalsis

1 Longitudinal, circular, and diagonal muscles constrict in wavelike motions to propel food through the GI tract.

Small intestine

Longitudinal
Circular

Segmentation

2 Longitudinal and circular muscles in the small intestine mix and squeeze food back and forth along the intestinal wall.

▲ Figure 3.9 **Peristalsis and Segmentation**

Peristalsis Squeezes Food Forward

The circular muscles that contract during peristalsis in the esophagus prevent food from moving backward. Repeated waves of contractions follow as the circular muscles relax and the longitudinal muscles constrict and push the food forward.

In the stomach, circular, longitudinal, and diagonal muscles move the food from the top of the stomach toward the pyloric sphincter at the base of the stomach. The waves of contractions in the stomach are slower than in other GI organs, as peristalsis mixes and churns the stomach contents with gastric juices until the food is liquefied.

Segmentation Shifts Food along the Intestinal Wall

As the partially digested food leaves the stomach, the second form of mechanical digestion, called segmentation, helps break down the mass of food into smaller pieces while mixing it with the chemical secretions of the intestine. Segmentation differs from peristalsis in that food is shifted (rather than squeezed) back and forth along the intestinal walls. This shifting action increases the time food is in contact with the surface of the small intestine, and moves food through the small intestine at a rate of 1 centimeter per minute.[4]

Segmentation contractions in the large intestine are much stronger and slower as the chyme moves through the colon, allowing for the maximum amount of water to be absorbed. Three or four times a day, these slow but powerful muscular contractions force the waste products toward the rectum. These contractions often occur shortly after eating and are stronger when the diet contains more fiber.

LO 3.2: THE TAKE-HOME MESSAGE Food is propelled through the GI tract by strong muscular contractions. Peristalsis in the esophagus, stomach, and small intestine squeezes the food and propels it forward, while segmentation in the small and large intestines shifts food back and forth along the intestinal walls, moving it further down the intestinal tract.

How Is Food Chemically Digested?

LO 3.3 Explain the role of enzymes and other secretions in chemical digestion.

While food travels through the organs of the GI tract during digestion, specific chemicals break down the food into nutrients. How do these chemicals work? Chemical digestion is accomplished with the aid of digestive enzymes and other substances. The chemicals generally complete their activities by the time the food reaches the large intestine.

Enzymes Drive the Process of Digestion

Enzymes are proteins that catalyze or speed up **hydrolysis** (*hydro* = water, *lysis* = break), the chemical reaction that uses water to split the bonds of all digestible carbohydrates, fats, proteins, and alcohol. Hydrolysis produces single molecules small enough to be absorbed by the intestines. During hydrolysis, the hydroxyl (OH) group from water joins one of the molecules, while the hydrogen ion (H) joins the other molecule, forming two new molecules. This is illustrated in the Chemistry Boost. Enzymes aren't changed in the reaction and can thus be used over and over again.

In order for enzymes to catalyze hydrolytic reactions, three conditions must be present.

1. The compatible enzyme and nutrient are both present.
2. The pH of the surrounding environment falls in the correct range.
3. The temperature of the environment is optimal.

Enzymes Are Specific in Their Action

First, enzymes are compatible only with a specific compound or nutrient, referred to as a **substrate**. Each enzyme has a binding site that only fits certain substrates, much like a key fits a specific lock. When the substrate binds to the active site of the enzyme, the bond is hydrolyzed. This reaction is illustrated in **Figure 3.10**.

Chemistry Boost

Hydrolysis

Most food molecules are digested by the process known as hydrolysis, in which the addition of water and a specific enzyme breaks down the corresponding molecule. In the figure below, a molecule of sucrose (sugar) is digested by the enzyme sucrase when it breaks the bond with the addition of water by adding a hydroxyl group (OH) to form glucose and hydrogen (H) to form fructose.

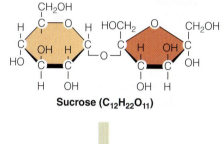

Sucrose ($C_{12}H_{22}O_{11}$)

Sucrase

H_2O

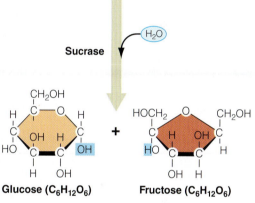

Glucose ($C_6H_{12}O_6$) + **Fructose ($C_6H_{12}O_6$)**

Once food enters the mouth, enzymes begin to chemically break the bonds that bind the nutrients.

enzymes Substances, mostly proteins, that increase the rate of chemical changes or catalyze chemical reactions; also called biological catalysts.

hydrolysis A chemical reaction that breaks the bond between two molecules with water. A hydroxyl group is added to one molecule and a hydrogen ion is added to the other molecule.

substrate A substance or compound that is altered by an enzyme.

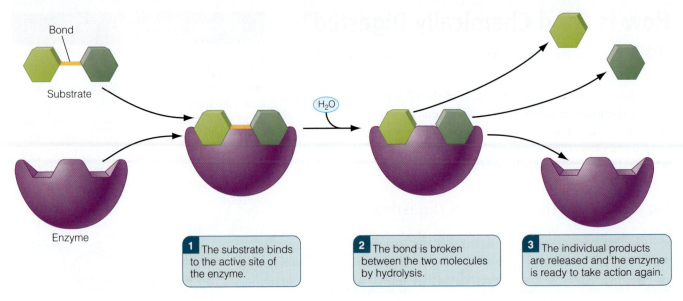

1	The substrate binds to the active site of the enzyme.
2	The bond is broken between the two molecules by hydrolysis.
3	The individual products are released and the enzyme is ready to take action again.

▲ **Figure 3.10 An Enzyme in Action**
Enzymes increase the rate of digestion without altering their shape.

Enzymes are often named according to the type of substrate they act upon, plus the suffix *-ase*. So, sucr*ase* hydrolyzes the sugar sucrose, and malt*ase* hydrolyzes maltose. Some enzymes, such as the protein enzyme pepsin, were named before this new nomenclature was developed and don't follow these naming rules.

Enzymes and pH Range

Second, enzymes are the most active and efficient when the fluid environment falls within a certain **pH** range, a range of acidity or alkalinity (see the Chemistry Boost). When the pH falls outside of that range, the activity of the enzyme is decreased or even halted. For example, saliva has a pH of about 6.4, which is optimal for the starch-digesting enzymes in the mouth. When the bolus containing the salivary enzymes reaches the stomach, where the pH is closer to 1, the salivary enzyme activity is stopped. However, another enzyme, pepsin, becomes activated in this acidic environment. As chyme continues to travel through the GI tract, various organs secrete digestive juices that produce the optimal range of pH for the enzymes to function.

Enzymes and Temperature

Third, as temperature falls below optimal levels, enzyme activity slows. If the temperature becomes too high, the enzyme is inactivated. In the body, the optimal temperature for enzymatic activity is 98.6°F (35.7°C), which is considered normal body temperature. Temperature also controls enzyme activity in foods. Cooling food in a refrigerator or freezing it in a freezer slows down enzymes, and cooking food completely inactivates any enzymes it contains.

Digestive enzymes are secreted all along the GI tract, but most are produced in the pancreas. The pancreas secretes digestive enzymes into the duodenum through the pancreatic duct. The last of the digestive enzymes is released by the brush border of the small intestine. **Table 3.1** summarizes the digestive enzymes, the organs that secrete them, and their actions.

Other Secretions Essential for Digestion

Enzymes and other essential compounds are often contained in fluids that are secreted throughout the digestion process. These secretions, including saliva, the gastric juices, bile, and bicarbonate ions, provide optimal conditions for digestion to occur.

pH A measure of the acidity or alkalinity of a solution.

pH Scale

Acids and bases describe the chemical properties of a substance. Acidity level is expressed using a pH scale that measures the hydrogen ion concentration. The range of a pH scale is 0 to 14, with 7 considered a neutral pH. A solution that has a pH lower than 7 is considered acidic (0 is the most acidic); one higher than 7 is basic (14 is the most basic).

The lower the number on the pH scale, the greater the concentration of hydrogen ions (H^+) in a solution. The more H^+ in a solution, the stronger the acid. For example, the acidic gastric juice, with a pH of 1, has a higher concentration of H^+ and is considered highly acidic compared with pancreatic juice, which has a pH of 8.

Basic compounds contain more hydroxide ions (OH^-) and have a low concentration of H^+. The more OH^- in a solution, the stronger the base. For example, sodium hydroxide has a pH of 1, whereas bile, which is more basic, has a pH of 9.

Each pH unit below 7 is ten times more acidic than the next pH unit. For example, tomato juice, a pH of 4, contains 10 times more H^+ than coffee, with a pH of 5, and 100 times more H^+ than saliva, with a pH of 6. Each pH unit above 7 is ten times more basic than the next pH unit.

Low concentration of hydrogen ions

Basic

pH neutral

Acidic

High concentration of hydrogen ions

pH of Common Substances

- 14 — Concentrated lye
- 13 — Oven cleaner
- 12 — Chlorine bleach
- 11 — Household ammonia
- 10 — Toothpaste
- 9 — Baking soda
  - **Bile**
- 8 — **Pancreatic juice**
  - Blood
- 7 — Water
- 6 — **Saliva**
  - Urine
- 5 — Coffee
- 4 — Tomato juice
- 3 — Orange juice
  - Soda
- 2 — Lemon juice
- 1 — **Gastric juice**
- 0 — Battery acid

TABLE 3.1　Digestive Enzymes and Their Actions

Organ or Gland	Enzyme	Action	Nutrient
Salivary glands	Salivary amylase	Begins the digestion of starch	Carbohydrates
Stomach	Pepsinogen → Pepsin	Begins the hydrolysis of polypeptides	Protein
	Gastric lipase	Begins digestion of lipids	Lipids
Pancreas	Pancreatic amylase	Digests starch	Carbohydrates
	Trypsinogen → Trypsin	Catalyzes the hydrolysis of proteins in the small intestine to form smaller polypeptides	Protein
	Chymotrypsinogen → Chymotrypsin	Catalyzes the hydrolysis of proteins in the small intestine into polypeptides and amino acids	Protein
	Procarboxypeptidase → Carboxypeptidase	Hydrolyzes the carboxyl end of a peptide, releasing the last amino acid in the peptide chain	Protein
	Pancreatic lipase	Digests triglycerides	Lipids
Small Intestine	Sucrase	Digests sucrose	Carbohydrates
	Maltase	Digests maltose	Carbohydrates
	Lactase	Digests lactose	Carbohydrates
	Dipeptidase	Digests dipeptides	Protein
	Tripeptidase	Digests tripeptides	Protein
	Lipase	Digests monoglycerides	Lipids

Saliva

Saliva is 99 percent water and rich in **mucus**, electrolytes, salivary amylase, and antibacterial compounds. Saliva functions mostly as a lubricant, but it also helps protect teeth and sanitize the mouth. It contains an antiseptic enzyme called lysozyme, which destroys the cell membranes of oral bacteria. What's more, saliva contains bicarbonate, which neutralizes acids in food. This change in pH is essential for optimal enzyme activity of salivary amylase.

Gastric Juices

The gastric juices secreted by the stomach are produced by the specialized parietal and chief cells introduced earlier in the chapter. When food enters the stomach, the parietal cells produce **hydrochloric acid (HCl)** and a protein called *intrinsic factor* (which is important for the absorption of vitamin B_{12} in the ileum).

Hydrochloric acid is unique in that it can destroy the activity of some proteins while activating others. It is essential for digestion because of its ability to change the acidity of digestive fluids to a pH close to 1.5. This acidic pH denatures proteins, which means it inactivates the protein by uncoiling its strands. Once the protein is denatured, **proteases**, or protein-digesting enzymes, attack the bonds and hydrolyze the bonds into shorter chains. Denaturing applies to all proteins, including hormones, and to bacteria found in food, which are destroyed before they can be absorbed intact.

Hydrochloric acid can also activate proteins, such as pepsinogen, a protein-digesting enzyme secreted from the chief cells lining the gastric glands. In the presence of HCl, **pepsinogen** is converted to its active form, **pepsin**, which begins the digestion of protein. HCl also enhances the absorption of certain minerals, such as calcium. In addition to pepsinogen, the chief cells also secrete *gastric lipase*, which begins to digest fats, although this enzyme is not a particularly active digestive enzyme in adults.

mucus Secretion produced throughout the GI tract that moistens and lubricates food and protects membranes.

hydrochloric acid (HCl) A strong acid produced in the stomach that aids in digestion.

proteases A classification of enzymes that catalyze the hydrolysis of protein.

pepsinogen The inactive protease secreted by the chief cells in the stomach; this enzyme is converted to the active form called pepsin in the presence of HCl.

pepsin The active protease that begins the digestion of proteins in the stomach.

You might think that an acid as strong as HCl would "digest" the stomach itself, but mucus secreted by the goblet cells acts as a barrier between the HCl and the stomach lining, protecting the lining from irritation or damage. This slippery secretion is also produced in the mucous membranes lining the esophagus to lubricate food as it passes down the GI tract.

Bile

Bile, the yellowish-green substance synthesized in the liver, helps digest dietary fat. This dilute, alkaline liquid is stored in concentrated form—up to five times its original composition—in the gallbladder. Bile, which is comprised of water, bile salts, bile pigments, fat, and cholesterol, **emulsifies** fat by breaking down large fat globules into smaller globules, much like dishwashing detergent breaks up the grease in a frying pan. Emulsification increases the surface area of the fat globule. The increased surface raises the efficiency of fat digestion to more than 95 percent.

In addition to dietary fat, bile also increases the absorption of the fat-soluble vitamins A, D, E, and K. Because bile has an alkaline pH, it also helps neutralize excess HCl and exhibits antibacterial properties that destroy bacteria in food.

Unlike other digestive juices, bile can be reused. From the large intestine, bile is recycled back to the liver through **enterohepatic** (*entero* = intestine, *hepatic* = liver) **circulation**. This recycling allows bile to be reused up to 20 times.

Bicarbonate

Bicarbonate ions alter the pH of food at various points along the GI tract. The salivary glands produce enough bicarbonate to neutralize the food you eat and produce a favorable pH (between 6.5 and 7.5) for salivary enzymes to hydrolyze starch. The pancreas secretes bicarbonate ions that flow into the duodenum via the pancreatic duct. The bicarbonate helps neutralize chyme as it arrives in the small intestine. The alkaline pH (about 8) is critical to protect the cells lining the duodenum, which are not resistant to damage by HCl, and to provide a favorable pH for the pancreatic and brush border enzymes (sucrase, maltase, lactase).

Table 3.2 summarizes the important digestive compounds and the organs that secrete them.

bile A secretion produced in the liver and stored in the gallbladder. It is released through the common bile duct into the duodenum to digest dietary fat.

emulsify To break large fat globules into smaller droplets.

enterohepatic circulation The process of recycling bile from the large intestine back to the liver to be reused during fat digestion.

bicarbonate A negatively charged alkali ion produced from bicarbonate salts; during digestion, bicarbonate ions are released from the pancreas to neutralize HCl in the duodenum.

TABLE 3.2	Secretions of the GI Tract and Their Actions	
Secretion	**Secretion Pathway**	**Action(s)**
Saliva	Secreted by salivary glands into mouth	Moistens food, eases swallowing; contains the enzyme salivary amylase
Hydrochloric acid (HCl)	Secreted by parietal cells into stomach	Denatures protein; activates pepsinogen → pepsin
Intrinsic factor	Secreted by parietal cells into stomach	Needed for vitamin B_{12} absorption
Mucus	Secreted by gastric glands into stomach	Lubricates and coats the internal mucosa to protect it from chemical or mechanical damage
Intestinal juice	Secreted by the crypts into small intestine	Contains enzymes that digest carbohydrate, protein, and lipid
Mucus	Secreted by intestinal glands into small intestine	Protects the intestinal cells
Bile	Secreted by liver into gallbladder for storage; released from gallbladder into small intestine via common bile duct	Emulsifies large globules of lipid into smaller droplets
Bicarbonate ions	Secreted by pancreas through the pancreatic duct into the small intestine	Raise pH and neutralize stomach acid

How Are Digested Nutrients Absorbed?

LO 3.4 Describe how digested nutrients are absorbed.

Digestion is the key to breaking down food. Absorption is the key to using food once it's digested. Some absorption occurs in the stomach and large intestine, but the small intestine absorbs most nutrients via special cells lining its wall. Nutrients that are digested by the time they reach the duodenum are absorbed quickly. Nutrients that need more time to be disassembled are absorbed lower in the GI tract. The body is remarkably efficient when it comes to absorbing nutrients. Under normal conditions, you digest and absorb 92 to 97 percent of the nutrients in food.

Nutrients Are Absorbed through the Small Intestinal Lining

The remarkable surface area of the folds and crevices of the small intestine lining allows for continuous, efficient absorption of virtually all digested nutrients. The villi are covered with mature enterocytes—cells that absorb digested nutrients. These cells live only a few days before they are sloughed off and digested themselves.

Nutrients move across cell membranes in the small intestine via one of four mechanisms: passive diffusion, facilitated diffusion, active transport, or endocytosis. **Figure 3.11** illustrates these four processes.

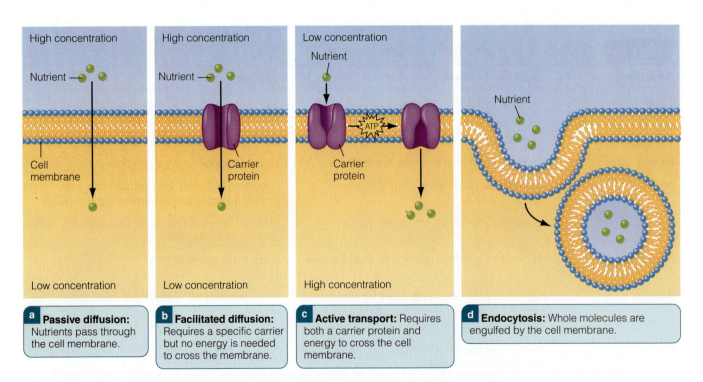

a **Passive diffusion:** Nutrients pass through the cell membrane.

b **Facilitated diffusion:** Requires a specific carrier but no energy is needed to cross the membrane.

c **Active transport:** Requires both a carrier protein and energy to cross the cell membrane.

d **Endocytosis:** Whole molecules are engulfed by the cell membrane.

▲ **Figure 3.11 Four Methods of Nutrient Absorption in the Small Intestine**

Passive Diffusion

Passive diffusion is a process in which nutrients are absorbed due to a concentration gradient. When the concentration of a nutrient is greater in the GI tract than inside the enterocyte, the nutrient is forced across the cell membrane. Thus, the nutrient moves from a high concentration to a low concentration. This simple process requires neither energy nor a special carrier molecule. Water, small lipids, a few minerals, and vitamin C are examples of nutrients absorbed via passive diffusion.

Facilitated Diffusion

Enterocytes have a lipid layer that is impermeable to most nutrients. Thus, most nutrients require an alternate route for absorption: facilitated diffusion. In **facilitated diffusion**, nutrients are helped across the membrane by specific carrier proteins. This form of absorption is similar to passive diffusion in that it does not require energy and transport is from a higher to a lower concentration. Fructose is an example of a nutrient that needs a carrier to move across a membrane.

Active Transport

In **active transport**, a carrier molecule and energy in the form of ATP shuttle nutrients across the cell membrane from a low to a high concentration. This transport mechanism allows absorption of nutrients even when the concentration outside the absorptive cell is lower than inside the cell. Glucose and amino acids are examples of nutrients absorbed by active transport.

Endocytosis

Endocytosis occurs when a cell forms a *vesicle* to surround and engulf a nutrient. Once inside the vesicle, the nutrient is dissolved in water; endocytosis is often referred to as "cell drinking." This type of absorption allows whole proteins, such as an immunoglobulin from breast milk, to be absorbed intact.

Fluid Absorption Occurs in the Large Intestine

By the time chyme enters the large intestine, the majority of the nutrients have been absorbed. The large intestine absorbs water and salts that remain in the chyme before it reaches the rectum for excretion. The same mechanisms used to absorb water and salts in the small intestine are also used in the large intestine. Water is absorbed via passive diffusion and sodium is absorbed via active transport.

> **LO 3.4: THE TAKE-HOME MESSAGE** The brush border of the small intestine is the major site of absorption for digested nutrients. Water and salts not absorbed in the small intestine are absorbed in the large intestine. Nutrients are absorbed by passive diffusion, facilitated diffusion, active transport, or endocytosis.

How Do Hormones and the Nervous System Regulate Digestion?

LO 3.5 Explain how hormones and the nervous system regulate digestion.

Each of us eats and drinks without worrying too much about what we are consuming. We don't have to worry about distributing nutrients to our cells because our body systems do the work for us. The endocrine and nervous systems work together to control and coordinate digestion, absorption, and excretion of waste products.

The endocrine glands in the GI tract are scattered throughout the lining of the stomach and the small intestine. These specialized cells secrete hormones when a stimulus is present and stop secreting the hormones when the stimulus is gone.

TABLE TIPS

Improve Your Digestion

Eat and drink slowly and thoroughly chew your food. This will reduce the amount of air taken in, and may reduce the need for belching later on.

Drink plenty of fluids and add more fiber to increase the bulk of feces and prevent constipation.

Include probiotic bacteria such as *Lactobacillus acidophilus* and *Bifidobacterium bifidum*, found in yogurt, kefir, kimchi, and sauerkraut, in your diet because they may help to maintain the health of the intestinal tract.

Practice mindful eating. Savor the flavor of food and enjoy every bite to allow the brain time to receive signals from digestive hormones that you are becoming full. This reduces overeating and improves portion control.

Identify foods that cause irritation or sensitivities. Reduce or eliminate these foods if necessary to improve digestion.

passive diffusion The process of absorbing nutrients freely across the cell membrane.

facilitated diffusion The process of absorbing nutrients with the help of a carrier molecule.

active transport The process of absorbing nutrients with the help of a carrier molecule and energy expenditure.

endocytosis A type of active transport in which the cell membrane forms an indentation, engulfing the substance to be absorbed.

For example, when the food you eat reaches your stomach, endocrine glands release gastric hormones to signal the rest of the GI tract to prepare for digestion. When food is not present, these hormones are not released. The pancreas also secretes hormones that participate in digestion.

Digestion is also controlled by the enteric nervous system. The enteric nervous system is a network of nerve fibers that innervate the GI tract, pancreas, and gallbladder. These nerves monitor the contractions of your stomach when you eat and the secretions of the cells of the GI tract.

Let's take a closer look at how these two systems communicate and ultimately control the digestive process.

Hormones in the GI Tract Regulate Digestion

Hormones secreted throughout the GI tract regulate digestion by controlling the release of gastric and pancreatic secretions, peristalsis, and enzyme activity. **Enterogastrones**, for example, are produced and secreted by the cells lining the stomach and small intestine. These hormones, including gastrin, secretin, cholecystokinin, and gastric inhibitory peptide (GIP), have a powerful influence on gastrointestinal motility (the pace of digestion), stomach emptying, gallbladder contraction, intestinal absorption, and even hunger.

The release of hormones is stimulated by the type of food passing through the digestive tract. For example, when a protein-containing bolus passes through the lower esophageal sphincter (LES), the hormone **gastrin** is secreted from the stomach. This hormone causes the release of gastric secretions that contain gastric lipase and stimulates the secretion of HCl. Gastrin also increases gastric motility and emptying, and increases the tone of the LES.

The duodenum releases **secretin** when the acidic chyme passes through the pyloric sphincter. The release of secretin in turn stimulates the pancreas to send bicarbonate ions through the pancreatic duct to neutralize the acid.

At the same time that secretin is stimulating the release of bicarbonate ions, the intestinal wall secretes another hormone, **cholecystokinin (CCK)**, (*koli-sis-te-KI-nin*) as partially digested protein and fat enter the duodenum. This powerful hormone stimulates the pancreas to release lipase and the gallbladder to contract and release bile, while it slows down gastric motility and contributes to meal satisfaction.

Gastric inhibitory peptide (GIP) also inhibits gastric motility and stomach secretions. This allows time for the digestive process to proceed in the duodenum before it receives more chyme.

This synchronized effort by the GI tract hormones ensures the efficiency of digestion and maintains homeostasis in the body. Refer to **Table 3.3** for a summary of the individual hormones, the tissues that secrete them, and their actions.

The Nervous System Communicates with the GI Tract

The main role of the nervous system in digestion is to tell you when to eat and drink, and when to stop. The brain, with the help of hormones, communicates and interprets the message of hunger and encourages you to seek food. Receptors within the walls of the GI tract organs respond to changes in the cells and communicate these changes to the brain.

Nervous System Receptors

Two types of nerves are involved in communicating and interpreting these changes: extrinsic and intrinsic nerves. The extrinsic nerves originate in the brain or the spinal cord; the intrinsic nerves are woven into the linings of the esophagus, stomach, and the small and large intestines. These nerves communicate changes in the GI tract, which, in turn, affect motility and the release or inhibition of digestive juices.

enterogastrones A group of GI tract hormones, produced in the stomach and small intestine, that controls gastric motility and secretions.

gastrin A hormone released from the stomach that stimulates the release of acid.

secretin A hormone secreted from the duodenum that stimulates the stomach to release pepsin, the liver to make bile, and the pancreas to release digestive juices.

cholecystokinin (CCK) A hormone released by the duodenum that stimulates the gallbladder to release bile.

gastric inhibitory peptide (GIP) A hormone produced by the small intestine that slows the release of chyme from the stomach.

TABLE 3.3	Hormones of the GI Tract and Their Actions			
Organ	**Hormone**	**Stimulus**	**Secreted from**	**Action(s)**
Stomach	Ghrelin	Empty stomach	Gastric cells	Stimulates gastric motility; stimulates hunger
	Gastrin	Food in the stomach	Gastric cells	Stimulates parietal cells to release HCl
Small Intestine	Secretin	Acidic chyme in duodenum	Duodenum	Stimulates the pancreas to release bicarbonate ions
	Cholecystokinin (CCK)	Fats and proteins in duodenum	Duodenum	Stimulates the gallbladder to secrete bile and the pancreas to secrete bicarbonate ions and enzymes
	Gastric inhibitory peptide (GIP)	Nutrients in the small intestine	Duodenum	Stimulates secretions from the intestines and pancreas; inhibits stomach motility
	Peptide YY	Nutrients in the small intestine	Ileum	Slows stomach motility

Imagine that you walk by a bakery and smell freshly baked bread. The extrinsic nerves signal to the GI tract what you smelled, and the intrinsic nerves interpret this signal and respond by stimulating the release of digestive juices. If you haven't eaten in the past few hours, the fact that your stomach is empty is communicated from the intrinsic nerves back to your brain. The result is a feeling of hunger.

Hormones That Communicate with the Brain

Hormones, such as **ghrelin** and **peptide YY**, work together with the extrinsic and intrinsic nerves to communicate feelings of hunger or fullness (see **Figure 3.12**). Ghrelin, which is referred to as the "hormone of hunger," is released from the gastric cells when the stomach is empty. Peptide YY signals the brain when you have eaten or are full.

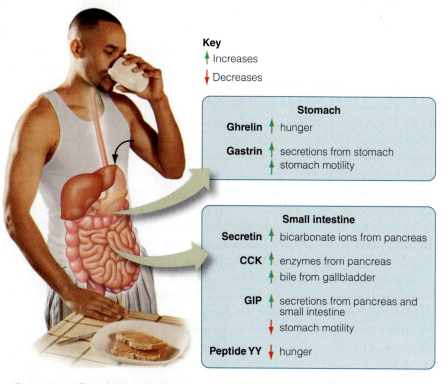

Key
↑ Increases
↓ Decreases

Stomach
Ghrelin ↑ hunger
Gastrin ↑ secretions from stomach
↑ stomach motility

Small intestine
Secretin ↑ bicarbonate ions from pancreas
CCK ↑ enzymes from pancreas
↑ bile from gallbladder
GIP ↑ secretions from pancreas and small intestine
↓ stomach motility
Peptide YY ↓ hunger

▲ **Figure 3.12 Digestive Hormones**
Digestive hormones from the stomach and small intestine control and coordinate digestive processes and hunger.

ghrelin A hormone produced in the stomach that stimulates hunger.

peptide YY A hormone produced in the small intestine that reduces hunger.

After you eat that warm piece of fresh bread, the receptor cells lining the gastrointestinal tract stretch, and the L cells located in the crypts of the small intestine respond by releasing the hormone peptide YY.[5] This hormone travels through the circulation to the brain and signals that you've eaten.

In addition, the extrinsic nerves excite the muscles stimulating peristalsis, pushing the food and digestive juices through the GI tract. Once the stomach has emptied, the release of hormones and digestive juices ceases and the process begins again.

LO 3.5: THE TAKE-HOME MESSAGE The enterogastrones gastrin, secretin, cholecystokinin, and gastric inhibitory peptide regulate digestion by stimulating or inhibiting the release of secretions from the stomach, small intestine, pancreas, and gallbladder. They also influence gastric motility, which controls the pace of digestion. Extrinsic and intrinsic nerves communicate and interpret changes in the GI tract, which affects gastric motility, the release or inhibition of digestive juices, and hunger. Two hormones, ghrelin and peptide YY, communicate with the nervous system to help you decide when to eat and when to stop eating.

How Are Nutrients Transported throughout the Body?

LO 3.6 Explain how absorbed nutrients are transported throughout the body.

Once the nutrients have been absorbed through the lining of the small intestine, they are carried off either through the bloodstream or the lymphatic system to other parts of the body (**Figure 3.13**). These two transportation systems consist of varying levels of pathways that deliver nutrients to, and pick up waste products from, cells in a simple route that begins with the heart.

The Cardiovascular System Distributes Nutrients through Blood

The blood is the body's primary transport system, shuttling oxygen, nutrients, hormones, and waste products throughout the body. The heart pumps blood through this closed system of vessels through the entire body and back to the heart.

The heart is divided into four chambers: two upper atria and two lower ventricles. The oxygen-poor blood the heart receives from the body flows into the right atrium, through the right ventricle, and into the lungs, where it is replenished with oxygen. The oxygen-rich blood flows from the lungs to the left atrium and then into the left ventricle. As the left ventricle contracts, blood is pumped through the aorta and arteries to the capillaries, where it exchanges a variety of substances, including water, glucose, and amino acids, with the cells. These substances picked up by the blood are eventually returned via the veins as the blood completes its route. Carbon dioxide produced during metabolism is one example of a substance that is picked up from the cells, taken to the lungs, and expelled.

During digestion the blood travels through the arteries to the capillaries lining the intestinal tract. Water-soluble nutrients, including carbohydrates, amino acids, and water-soluble vitamins, cross the intestinal wall into the capillaries and travel via the **hepatic portal vein** to the liver. The portal vein branches out into capillaries supplying all the liver cells with nutrient-rich blood. Blood leaves the liver and continues on its journey through the **hepatic vein** back to the heart. Thus, the liver plays a key role in nutrition—it is the first organ to receive water-soluble nutrients absorbed through the intestines via the hepatic portal vein.

hepatic portal vein A large vein that connects the intestinal tract to the liver and transports newly absorbed nutrients.

hepatic vein The vein that carries the blood received from the hepatic portal vein away from the liver.

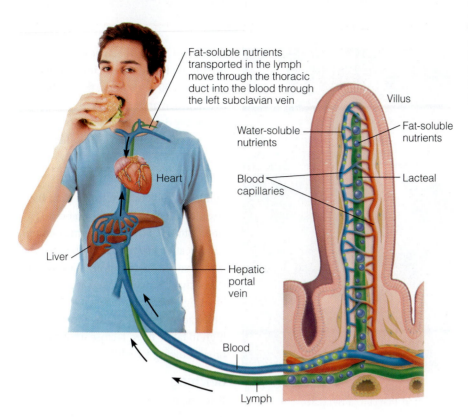

Fat-soluble nutrients transported in the lymph move through the thoracic duct into the blood through the left subclavian vein

Villus

Water-soluble nutrients

Fat-soluble nutrients

Heart

Blood capillaries

Lacteal

Liver

Hepatic portal vein

Blood

Lymph

The Lymphatic System Distributes Some Nutrients through the Lymph

The **lymphatic system** is a complex network of capillaries, small vessels, valves, nodes, and ducts that transport fat-soluble nutrients throughout the body. Lacteals in the villi collect fat-soluble vitamins, long-chain fatty acids, and some proteins too large to be transported via the capillaries. The vessels of the lymph system are different from those of the circulatory system. The cells of the lymph capillary overlap one another, allowing the contents of the lymph vessels to seep out under pressure and circulate between the cells. The fat-soluble nutrients are transported from the lymph capillaries through the lymphatic vessels and eventually arrive at the thoracic duct. At the junction of the thoracic duct is a valve that allows the lymph fluid to flow into the subclavian vein, where it finally enters the blood. The nutrients can then be circulated by the blood to be picked up and used by cells.

The Excretory System Eliminates Waste

After the cells have gleaned the nutrients and other useful metabolic components they need from the blood, their waste must be eliminated through the excretory system. For instance, cells break down proteins, which creates nitrogen-containing waste, such as urea. The kidneys filter the blood, allowing these waste products to be concentrated in the urine and excreted.

LO 3.6: THE TAKE-HOME MESSAGE The cardiovascular and lymphatic systems transport absorbed nutrients throughout the body and deliver them to cells. Water-soluble nutrients, including carbohydrate, proteins (amino acids), and the water-soluble vitamins, are transported via the cardiovascular system; fat-soluble nutrients, including the fat-soluble vitamins and long-chain fatty acids, are transported via the lymphatic system. The excretory system filters the blood and eliminates waste.

lymphatic system A system of interconnected spaces and vessels between the tissues and organs that contains lymph and circulates fat-soluble nutrients throughout the body.

What Are Some Common Digestive Disorders?

LO 3.7 Describe the most common digestive disorders.

Sometimes the digestive system gets "off track" and the resulting symptoms can quickly catch your attention. Some of the problems are minor, like occasional heartburn or indigestion; other problems such as ulcers or colon cancer are very serious and require medical treatment.

Esophageal Problems

Several minor esophageal problems can lead to annoying symptoms such as belching, hiccups, burning sensations, or uncomfortable feelings of fullness. More serious esophageal problems include cancer, obstruction from tumors, faulty nerve impulses, severe inflammation, abnormal sphincter function, and even death.

Gastroesophageal Reflux Disease (GERD)

One of the most common problems involving the esophagus is the burning sensation in the middle of the chest known as *heartburn* (also called indigestion or acid reflux). About 60 million Americans experience heartburn once a month; about 15 million report daily heartburn. Collectively, this adds up to millions of people experiencing heartburn symptoms.[6]

Heartburn generally occurs when the lower esophageal sphincter (LES) doesn't close properly, and HCl from the stomach flows back into the esophagus and irritates its lining. Chronic heartburn and the reflux of stomach acids are

gastroesophageal reflux disease (GERD) The backward flow of stomach contents into the esophagus due to improper functioning of the LES, resulting in heartburn.

gastroenteritis Inflammation of the lining of the stomach and intestines; also known as stomach flu.

Being overweight and eating certain foods are two factors that can cause GERD.

typical symptoms of **gastroesophageal reflux disease (GERD)**.

A weak lower esophageal sphincter is often the culprit in acid reflux, because it sometimes permits this backflow of stomach fluids into the esophagus. Certain foods, including chocolate, fried or fatty foods, coffee, soda, onions, and garlic, seem to be associated with this condition.[7] Lifestyle factors also play a role. For example, smoking cigarettes, drinking alcohol, wearing tight-fitting clothes, being overweight or obese, eating large evening meals, and reclining after eating tend to cause or worsen the condition.

If dietary changes and behavior modification are insufficient to relieve heartburn, over-the-counter antacids or prescription drugs may help. In rare circumstances, surgical intervention is required to treat severe, unrelenting heartburn.

Esophageal Cancer

Esophageal cancer is another medical condition that has serious consequences. According to the National Cancer Institute, esophageal cancer is one of the most common cancers of the digestive tract, and the seventh leading cause of cancer-related deaths worldwide. In

the United States, this type of cancer is typically found among individuals older than 50 years, men, those who live in urban areas, long-term smokers, and heavy drinkers. Treatments include surgery, radiation, and chemotherapy.[8]

Disorders of the Stomach

Stomach problems can range from the trivial, such as belching or an occasional stomachache, to life-threatening complications such as bleeding ulcers or stomach cancer. Common causes of stomachache include overeating, gastric bloating, or eating too fast. Other possible causes include eating foods that are high in fat or fiber, lactose intolerance, or swallowing air while eating.

Belching

Belching is usually caused by swallowing air. The air may distend the stomach, and then be expelled up through the esophagus and out through the mouth, to relieve abdominal discomfort. Swallowing large amounts of air (called *aerophagia*) is most often due to eating or drinking too fast, consuming carbonated beverages, or anxiety. However, aerophagia can occur without any act of swallowing, such as during chewing gum or smoking.

Stomach Flu and Foodborne Illness

A stomachache can be due to a number of causes, including stomach flu or foodborne illness. Despite its name, stomach flu, or **gastroenteritis**, is not caused by the influenza virus but rather by a variety of viruses (the most common being the rotavirus) that cause an inflammation of the stomach or intestines. Stomach flu symptoms include nausea, vomiting, diarrhea, and abdominal cramping. Sometimes the problem requires medical intervention, but usually rest, oral rehydration therapy, and a soft-food diet will help with the symptoms of this type of illness.

Foodborne illnesses are usually contracted by eating food or drinking fluid that is contaminated with a pathogenic microbe such as the bacteria campylobacter, salmonella, or *E. coli*, or a calicivirus (also known as the Norwalk and Norwalk-like viruses). Symptoms such as vomiting, abdominal cramps, diarrhea, and fever occur when enough of the pathogen has been ingested to trigger the body's immune response. Most foodborne illnesses are self-limiting and require oral rehydration therapy and rest. More severe foodborne infections may require medical intervention. (You will read more about specific foodborne illnesses in Chapter 20.)

Ulcers

An **ulcer** is a sore or erosion in the lining of the lower region of the stomach or the upper part of the duodenum (**Figure 3.14**). Ulcers are named according to their location, such as gastric ulcers, duodenal ulcers, and esophageal ulcers. Whereas spicy foods and stress were once thought to cause most ulcers, researchers have since discovered that a bacterium, *Helicobacter pylori*, is often involved. The use of anti-inflammatory drugs, such as aspirin, ibuprofen, naproxen, and ketoprofen, may also cause or aggravate ulcers. These pain relievers inhibit the hormonelike substances that protect the stomach lining from HCl, which results in bleeding and ulceration. Nicotine increases the production of HCl, which increases the risk of developing an ulcer and slows the healing process of ulcers that have already developed. Both excess consumption of alcohol and stress can contribute to ulcer formations, although these factors may not be directly involved.

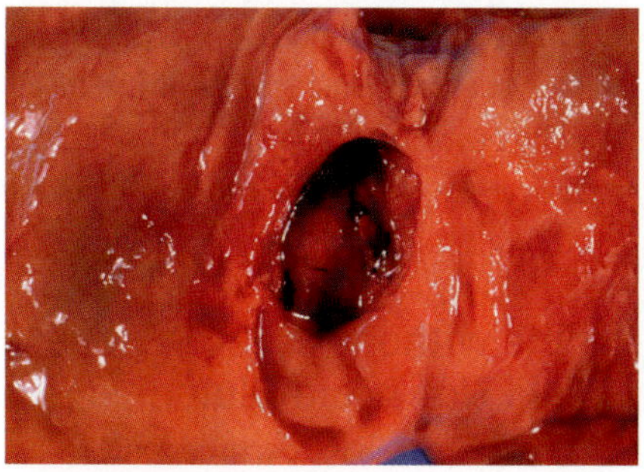

Burning pain is the most common symptom of an ulcer, along with vomiting, fatigue, bleeding, and general weakness. Medical treatments may consist of prescription drugs and dietary recommendations, such as limiting alcohol and caffeine-containing beverages, and/or restricting spices and acidic foods. Surgery is necessary only when an ulcer does not respond to drug treatment. Left untreated, ulcers can result in internal bleeding and perforation of the stomach or intestinal lining, causing peritonitis, or infection of the abdominal cavity. Scar tissue can also form in the GI tract, obstructing food and causing vomiting and weight loss. People who have ulcers caused by *H. pylori* have a greater risk of developing stomach cancer.

Gallbladder Disease

The incidence of gallbladder disease is high in the United States, especially in women and older Americans. Obesity is one of the major risk factors, and this risk is even greater following rapid weight loss.[9]

One common problem of an unhealthy gallbladder is the presence of **gallstones** (**Figure 3.15**). Most people with gallstones have abnormally thick bile, and the bile is high in cholesterol and low in bile acids. Over time, the high-cholesterol bile forms crystals, then sludge, and finally gallstones. Some individuals with gallstones experience no pain or mild pain. Others have severe pain accompanied by fever, nausea, vomiting, cramps, and obstruction of the bile duct.

Medical treatment for gallstones may involve surgery to remove the gallbladder, prescription medicine to dissolve the stones, shock-wave therapy (a type of ultrasound treatment) to break them up, or a combination of therapies. If surgery is required to remove the gallbladder, patients typically recover quickly. After gallbladder removal surgery, the anatomy of the biliary tract adapts. The liver continues to produce the bile and secretes it directly into the duodenum.

Celiac Disease

One of the more serious malabsorption conditions to occur in the small intestine is **celiac disease**. In a healthy small intestine, millions of villi and microvilli efficiently absorb nutrients from food. In celiac disease, the lining of the small intestine flattens out, and it can no longer absorb nutrients (**Figure 3.16**). The flattening is caused by an abnormal reaction to the protein gluten, found in wheat, rye, and barley.

Celiac disease is a genetic, autoimmune disease that causes a person's own immune system to damage the small intestines when gluten from wheat and other grains is consumed. Note that celiac disease is not the same thing as gluten intolerance, which does not involve the immune system or damage the wall of the small intestine. However, individuals with gluten intolerance can experience similar symptoms such as stomachaches, diarrhea, bloating, and tiredness if gluten is consumed.

Celiac disease is most common among genetically susceptible people of European descent. The most recent estimates suggest that 1 in 133 people (less than 1 percent) have been diagnosed with celiac disease in

ulcer A sore or erosion of the stomach or intestinal lining.

gallstones Stones formed from cholesterol in the gallbladder or bile duct.

celiac disease Genetic disease that causes damage to the small intestine when gluten-containing foods are eaten.

▲ **Figure 3.14 Ulcer**
An ulcer is created when the mucosal lining of the GI tract erodes.

▲ **Figure 3.15 Gallstones**
The size and composition of gallstones vary.

What Are Some Common Digestive Disorders? **99**

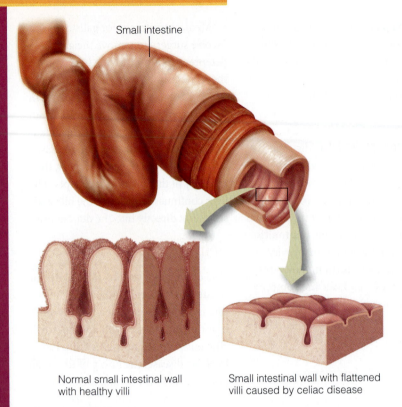

Small intestine

Normal small intestinal wall
with healthy villi

Small intestinal wall with flattened
villi caused by celiac disease

▲ **Figure 3.16 Celiac Disease**
Popcorn is a gluten free snack that people with celiac disease can safely enjoy.

Rice noodles are a good gluten-free substitute
for pasta.

the United States. When an individual has celiac disease, the incidence among close family members is estimated to be as high as 4.5 percent.[10] Because of this genetic link, celiac disease is classified as a lifelong disorder.

The symptoms for celiac disease vary. Classic celiac symptoms include reoccurring abdominal bloating, cramping, diarrhea, gas, fatty and foul-smelling stools, weight loss, anemia, fatigue, bone or joint pain, and even a painful skin rash called dermatitis herpetiformis. Some people develop the symptoms of celiac disease in infancy or childhood. Others develop it later in life, after being misdiagnosed with irritable bowel syndrome or various food intolerances.

Depending on the length of time between symptom development and diagnosis, the complications from celiac disease can be serious. Celiac patients have an increased incidence of osteoporosis from poor calcium absorption, diminished growth because of nutrient malabsorption, and even seizures due to inadequate folate absorption. Celiac

disease also increases the risk of developing certain types of cancer, including esophageal cancer and melanoma.[11]

Diagnosis and Treatment of Celiac Disease

In the past, diagnosing celiac disease was sometimes difficult because it resembles other similar malabsorption diseases. The contemporary method of diagnosis begins with a simple blood test measuring gluten-reactive T cells.[12] If the test proves positive, the next step is a tissue biopsy of the small intestine to confirm the diagnosis.[13, 14]

The only treatment for celiac disease is a strict, lifelong gluten-free diet.[15] This should stop the symptoms from progressing, allow the intestine to heal, and prevent further damage. The symptoms often improve within a few days after beginning the gluten-free diet. If the diet is followed faithfully, the absorption area of the intestinal tract often returns to normal status within three to six months.

Adhering to a gluten-free diet, which means avoiding all gluten-containing

foods, can be challenging. All breads, pasta, cereals, and other wheat-containing foods must be eliminated. Gluten-free foods such as meat, milk, eggs, fruit, and vegetables are permissible. Rice, potatoes, corn, and beans, as well as grains such as quinoa, amaranth, and millet, do not contain gluten and are also acceptable. The Academy of Nutrition and Dietetics maintains a comprehensive list of foods allowed on a gluten-free diet on its website, www.eatright.org.[16]

Until recently, oats had been considered a forbidden food for celiac patients. Recent studies suggest that moderate amounts of gluten-free oats, up to about ¼ cup of dry oats daily, may be safe for adults and children with celiac disease.[17] Concerns about adding oats to the gluten-free diet are related to the possibility that oats may be contaminated with hidden sources of gluten. Such concerns can be allayed by purchasing oats from companies that advertise gluten-free products and avoiding oats sold in bulk bins.

People without Celiac Disease Should Not Avoid Gluten

Gluten-free diets have become somewhat of a fad. The number of individuals consuming a gluten-free diet is fueling a market of gluten-free products reportedly

Eat Gluten Free

Be a label reader to avoid products that contain all forms of wheat, barley, rye, triticale, or their hybrids.

Substitute whole-wheat bread with gluten-free whole grains, such as quinoa, buckwheat, amaranth, sorghum, and millet.

If you like a hot cereal for breakfast, try teff, a nutritious cereal grain from Ethiopia with a nutty, chewy texture.

Avoid packaged foods that contain modified food starch, dextrin, malt, or malt syrup, as they may be sources of gluten-containing grains.

Enjoy coffee, tea, sodas, fruit juices, and even fermented or distilled beverages, such as wine, sake, and distilled spirits on a gluten-free diet. But avoid coffee flavorings or creamers.

Look for either the GFCO or CSA Seal of Recognition marks on labels to assure the product is gluten free.

Maintain a high fiber intake by incorporating gluten-free fresh fruits, vegetables, beans, peas, and lentils in your diet.

Consume calcium-rich dairy or calcium-fortified gluten-free products, such as orange juice, soy products, or nonmilk beverages made from rice or nuts.

Snack on gluten-free nuts, fruits, popcorn, raisins, rice cakes, and fruit smoothies.

Enjoy homemade meals to control gluten intake and eat a variety of nutrient-dense foods.

as high as $4.2 billion in 2012 and that is expected to rise to $6.6 billion by 2017.[18] There are currently more people following a gluten-free diet than there are diagnosed with celiac disease.[19] Is this healthy?

Going gluten free is not necessarily healthier when it means eliminating many common, nutritious foods. Gluten itself doesn't provide any nutritional benefits, but the foods that contain gluten do. These foods are rich in dietary fiber, vitamins, and minerals. Many gluten-free products are made with refined, unenriched gluten-free grains low in essential nutrients, high in fat and kilocalories, and expensive.[20]

Gluten itself may provide some health benefits for individuals without celiac disease or gluten sensitivity. Recent studies have shown gluten-rich foods may improve blood lipids, control blood pressure, and boost the immune system.[21] For this reason, there are no real benefits to eating a gluten-free diet if you are not gluten sensitive, have not been diagnosed with celiac disease, or do not have other autoimmune disorders.

Other Intestinal Disorders

Disorders of the intestines can occur anywhere along the length of the small and large intestines. Common, temporary problems can include gassiness, diarrhea, or constipation. Both diarrhea and constipation can be indicative of small- and large-intestine problems that involve nutrient malabsorption, which can cause severe health consequences. Celiac disease, gastroenteritis, duodenal ulcers, intestinal enzyme deficiencies, irritable bowel syndrome, ulcerative colitis, Crohn's disease, and colon cancer are examples of serious intestinal disorders. The symptoms of these diseases vary, but they include abdominal pain, nausea, vomiting, bloating, loss of appetite, diarrhea, anxiety, weight loss, and fatigue. The prevalence of some of these disorders may be increasing or it could be that these disorders are now being more readily recognized and documented.

Flatulence

Flatulence is an uncomfortable and sometimes embarrassing (but normal) condition that results from the formation of intestinal gas. Intestinal gas is produced for a variety of reasons, and most adults release it 10 to 20 times a day.

Eating too fast, or drinking beverages with added air such as beer or carbonated beverages, can result in the intake of incidental air that makes its way through the digestive tract. Foods like beans, lentils, and other legumes can lead to gas production because they contain indigestible carbohydrates that are fermented by intestinal bacteria. The bacteria produce the gas as a by-product. Lack of exercise and smoking have also been identified as culprits in flatulence.

The gas (or *flatus*) is a mixture of carbon dioxide, hydrogen, nitrogen, oxygen, and methane. The offending odor comes from gases that contain sulfur, chiefly hydrogen sulfide and methylmercaptan. Foods high in fiber and starches tend to produce more intestinal gas. Using products such as Beano or eating smaller meals will help reduce the amount of gas produced.

Diarrhea and Constipation

Two of the most common intestinal disorders are diarrhea and constipation. **Diarrhea** is the passage of watery, loose stools more than three times a day. Acute diarrhea lasts for up to two days and is usually the result of bacterial, viral, or parasitic infection. The infection results in the enterocytes becoming inflamed and secreting, rather than absorbing, fluid into the GI tract. The result is that food and fluids pass too quickly through the colon and out through the rectum.

Diarrhea can be potentially serious because of the loss of fluids and electrolytes. Whereas brief episodes of diarrhea may be a sign of infection or an adverse reaction to a specific food, medication, or other compound (such as the sugar substitute sorbitol), chronic diarrhea may be a sign of irritable bowel syndrome (see below) or colitis, two conditions that require medical treatment and must be diagnosed by a health care provider.

flatulence Production of excessive gas in the stomach or the intestines.

diarrhea The abnormally frequent passage of watery stools.

Diarrhea is generally treated with fluid and electrolyte replacement. Diarrhea that lasts for an extended period of time can lead to malabsorption of additional nutrients, which can in turn lead to malnutrition. Left untreated, diarrhea can lead to dehydration and potentially even death. The condition can be particularly dangerous for children and the elderly, who are more susceptible to dehydration.

Constipation is caused by excessively slow movements of the undigested residue through the colon, and is often due to insufficient fiber or water intake. Ignoring or putting off the need to defecate can also result in more absorption of water from fecal matter in the large intestine, leading to harder, drier stools. Stress, inactivity, cessation of smoking, or various illnesses can also lead to constipation.[22, 23]

Because fiber attracts water, adds bulk to stool in the colon, and stimulates peristalsis, constipation is often treated with a high-fiber, high-liquid diet. Daily exercise, establishing eating and resting routines, and using over-the-counter stool softeners are usually recommended to treat this condition without the use of laxatives or enemas.

If constipation persists, laxatives can provide some relief, but should be used sparingly. A variety of laxatives can be purchased over the counter, including bulk-forming laxatives, stool softeners, and stimulants. Bulk-forming or stool-softening laxatives trigger peristalsis by drawing water into the GI tract, which increases the bulk of the feces and stretches the circular muscles in the

constipation The infrequent passage of dry, hardened stools.

hemorrhoid Swelling in the veins of the rectum and anus.

irritable bowel syndrome (IBS) An intestinal disorder resulting in abdominal discomfort, pain, diarrhea, constipation, and bloating; the cause is unknown.

ulcerative colitis A chronic inflammation of the colon or large intestine that results in ulcers forming in the lining of the colon.

Crohn's disease A form of ulcerative colitis in which ulcers form throughout the GI tract and not just in the colon.

Constipation can be prevented with a diet higher in fiber and fluid, and daily exercise.

intestine. Stimulant laxatives, such as Ex-lax or Senokot, are the harshest form of laxative and work by irritating the lining of the GI tract to stimulate peristalsis. Because laxatives can cause dehydration, salt imbalances, and laxative dependency, they should not be used routinely unless a physician supervises.

One harmful and unnecessary practice is colonic cleansing, which involves an enema to draw water or other fluids out of the large intestine through the anus and rectum. The practice can interfere with the absorption of fat-soluble vitamins, and can be dangerous if the equipment used to administer the enema isn't sanitized, or if the bowel is perforated when the rubber tube is inserted. Other problems may result from electrolyte and water imbalance, and dependency.

Hemorrhoids

The term **hemorrhoid** refers to a condition in which pressure in the veins in the rectum and anus causes swelling and inflammation similar to varicose veins in the legs. The walls of the veins dilate, become thin, and bleed. Though the exact cause of hemorrhoids is not known, there are contributing factors that result in pressure

buildup within the veins. These factors include straining to pass dry stools, pregnancy, constant constipation or diarrhea, and aging. Whatever the cause, the result is that the walls of the veins dilate, become thin, and bleed. As the pressure builds, the vessels protrude. The presence of hemorrhoids may not be noticed until they begin to bleed (following a bowel movement), itch, or become painful.

The most common treatment for hemorrhoids is the same as for constipation: Increase dietary fiber and fluid intake. Other symptoms, including itching and pain, can be relieved with over-the-counter creams, ice packs to relieve swelling, and soaking in a warm bath. In severe cases of hemorrhoids, surgery may be necessary.

Irritable Bowel Syndrome (IBS)

Irritable bowel syndrome (IBS) is a general term used to describe changes in colon rhythm, not an actual disease. It causes a great deal of discomfort for the estimated 30 million North Americans who have it.[24] People with IBS do not have tissue damage, inflammation, or immunologic involvement of the colon. They do, however, overrespond to colon stimuli. This results in alternating patterns of diarrhea, constipation, and abdominal pain. The exact cause of IBS is unknown, but low-fiber diets, stress, consumption of foods that trigger the symptoms (such as alcohol, chocolate, and dairy products), and intestinal motility disorders are all suspected factors. Medical management includes increasing dietary fiber, managing stress, and occasional use of prescription drugs.

Ulcerative Colitis and Crohn's Disease

Ulcerative colitis is a chronic inflammation of the large intestine that results in ulcers in the lining of the colon. This disorder of the large intestine usually begins between the ages of 15 and 30, occurs in both men and women, and tends to run in families, especially in Caucasians and people of Jewish descent. **Crohn's disease** is similar to ulcerative colitis except that the ulcers can occur throughout the gastrointestinal tract, from the mouth to the anus, not just in the colon.

The cause of ulcerative colitis and Crohn's disease is not known and there is no cure. Physical examinations, laboratory tests, and a colonoscopy are often used to distinguish between the two conditions. Treatment includes drug therapy; in severe cases, surgery may be required.

Colon Cancer

Colon cancer is one of the leading forms of cancer and the third leading cause of cancer death.[25] Fortunately, colon cancer is one of the most curable forms of cancer, if it is detected in the early stages.

Colon cancer often begins with polyps on the lining of the colon (**Figure 3.17**). They vary in size from that of a small

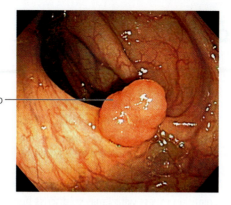

Polyp

▲ **Figure 3.17 Colon Polyp**
Polyps on the lining of the colon can be one of the first signs of colon cancer.

pea to that of a mushroom or plum. The good news is that polyps are often small and benign, and they can be removed surgically. If the polyps are not removed, or if they develop into cancerous tumors, colon cancer can be difficult to cure.

Individuals diagnosed with colon cancer may require radiation therapy, chemotherapy, and surgery to remove part or all of the colon. After surgery, patients are given dietary advice regarding the foods that would be the most comfortable to eat. Survival rates vary depending on the individual's age, health, treatment response, and stage of cancer diagnosis.

LO 3.7: THE TAKE-HOME MESSAGE
Gastrointestinal diseases and digestive disorders include conditions from the esophagus to the anus. Some disorders, such as ulcers, GERD, celiac disease, irritable bowel syndrome, ulcerative colitis, Crohn's disease, and colon or esophageal cancer are more serious and may result in nutrient malabsorption and/or malnutrition. Less serious conditions, like constipation, diarrhea, hemorrhoids, heartburn, and stomach flu, are temporary. **Table 3.4** summarizes the common digestive disorders.

TABLE 3.4	Common Digestive Disorders			
Site	**Disorder**	**Symptoms**	**Cause**	**Treatment**
Esophagus	GERD	Heartburn, nausea, and belching	Reflux of HCl into esophagus	Lifestyle changes including diet, exercise, and smoking cessation
Stomach	Gastroenteritis	Flulike symptoms	Virus or bacteria; irritation of the stomach lining	Soft-food diet and fluid
	Peptic ulcer	Abdominal pain, vomiting, bleeding, and general weakness	Drugs, alcohol, or *H. pylori* bacteria	Drug therapy and limiting alcohol, caffeine, and acidic foods
Gallbladder	Gallstones	Cramps, nausea, fever, vomiting	Bile high in cholesterol; obesity; rapid weight loss	Surgery and drug therapy
Small Intestine	Celiac disease	Malabsorption	Error of gluten metabolism	Gluten-free diet
Large Intestine	Diarrhea	Frequent loose, watery stools	Contaminated water or food; stress; excessive fiber intake	Water and electrolyte replacement
	Constipation	Cramping, bloating	Insufficient water and fiber intake; inactivity	High fiber, high fluid intake; exercise
	Irritable bowel syndrome (IBS)	Diarrhea, constipation, and abdominal pain	Unknown cause(s); stress worsens the condition	Self-management with increased dietary fiber, stress relief, good sleep habits
	Ulcerative colitis	Abdominal pain and bleeding	Unknown cause	Drug therapy
	Crohn's disease	Abdominal pain and bleeding	Unknown cause	Drug therapy
	Colon cancer	Often none detectable	Multiple causes (genetics, various colon diseases, smoking, dietary carcinogens)	Surgery, radiation, and chemotherapy

Nutrition in Practice: Emily

College senior Emily doesn't eat breakfast before her 10 a.m. nutrition class because she knows she's likely to feel uncomfortably full and bloated after. Lately, Emily has had frequent bouts of abdominal pain that are only relieved by a bowel movement, followed by several loose, watery stools. Her symptoms are worse when she eats large meals, and right before a midterm exam or a paper is due. For a few weeks at the beginning of the semester, her symptoms had subsided, and she actually became constipated. But lately, the abdominal pains and diarrhea returned and appear to be getting worse. She is experiencing difficulty falling asleep at night, which is causing her to become tired by midday. She decides to visit the campus health center.

After meeting with the doctor at the health center, Emily is told that she has irritable bowel syndrome (IBS) and is referred to the campus's Registered Dietitian Nutritionist for an appointment. The dietitian meets with Emily to discuss her diet and lifestyle habits.

Emily's Stats:
- Age: 21
- Height: 5 feet 4 inches
- Weight: 125 lbs
- Symptoms: Frequent bouts of abdominal pain; loose, watery stool

Emily's Food Log

Food/Beverage	Time Consumed	Hunger Rating*	Location	Feelings/Symptoms
Latte with whole milk, 24 oz	7:30 a.m.	1	Walking to class	Anxious about midterms
Pepperoni pizza, 3 slices	12 noon	5	Campus dining hall	Tired
Large cola	1 p.m.	1	Library	Some diarrhea
Energy drink, 12 oz	3 p.m.	1	Walking to dorm	Tired
Clam chowder	6 p.m.	2	In dorm	Stressed, stomach cramps; feeling bloated

*Hunger Rating (1–5): 1 = not hungry; 5 = super-hungry.

Critical Thinking Questions

1. What aspect of Emily's lifestyle may be contributing to her IBS symptoms?
2. What foods/beverages could be contributing to Emily's bouts of diarrhea and why?
3. How could exercise help Emily with her IBS?

Dietitian's Observation and Plan for Emily:

- Exercise 30 minutes daily to release stress, which is a trigger for IBS.
- Slowly reduce the caffeine (coffee, energy drinks) in her diet. Caffeine can increase jitteriness (anxiety), cause a spastic colon (diarrhea), and interfere with the ability to fall asleep (fatigue).
- Get 8 hours of sleep each night.
- Avoid large meals. Eat three smaller meals and two small snacks throughout the day.

Three weeks later, Emily visits the dietitian again and reports that she has reduced her caffeine intake by eliminating her daily energy drinks. She is walking every day and is sleeping better at night. Her symptoms have subsided somewhat, but she is experiencing more constipation than diarrhea. A dietary analysis of Emily's food intake reveals she is eating less than 30 percent of the recommended intake for fiber. The dietitian works with Emily to add fiber-rich whole grains, fruits, and vegetables along with adequate fluids to her diet to alleviate the constipation.

Visual Chapter Summary

LO 3.1 The Process of Digestion Takes Place in the GI Tract, Helped by the Accessory Organs

Digestion is the process of breaking down whole food into absorbable nutrients. Digestion takes place in the GI tract, a long tube comprised of the mouth, pharynx, esophagus, stomach, small intestine, and large intestine. Several sphincters control entry and exit of food and chyme through the various organs of the GI tract. Accessory organs, including the liver, gallbladder, and pancreas, secrete bile, hormones, and enzymes that help regulate and facilitate digestion.

The small intestine is the primary organ for the absorption of digested nutrients. The large intestine absorbs water and electrolytes before pushing waste through the colon and out of the body via the rectum.

Bile produced in the liver helps digest fat. The liver is the first organ to receive, process, and store absorbed nutrients. The pancreas and gallbladder are two other accessory organs that provide digestive fluids to the GI tract.

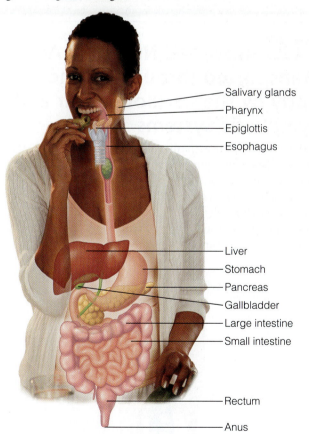

- Salivary glands
- Pharynx
- Epiglottis
- Esophagus
- Liver
- Stomach
- Pancreas
- Gallbladder
- Large intestine
- Small intestine
- Rectum
- Anus

LO 3.2 Peristalsis and Segmentation Propel Food through the Gastrointestinal Tract

Food is propelled along the gastrointestinal tract by peristalsis and segmentation. Peristalsis moves food through the stomach and intestines by rhythmic contractions of longitudinal and circular muscles. Segmentation squeezes the mass of food into smaller pieces while mixing it with the chemical secretions of the intestine. Muscular contractions in the large intestine facilitate the absorption of water from the feces by compacting the mass and pushing it toward the rectum for excretion.

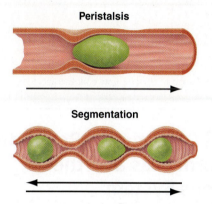

Peristalsis

Segmentation

LO 3.3 Enzymes and Other Secretions Chemically Digest Food

Chemical digestion involves mixing food with enzymes that break the bonds by adding water through hydrolysis. HCl also denatures protein and activates pepsinogen to initiate protein digestion. Bile from the gallbladder emulsifies large fat globules into smaller pieces to improve enzymatic action. Digestion is completed by the brush border enzymes maltase, sucrase, and lactase, and the proteases, breaking nutrients down into single molecules that can be absorbed into the small intestine lining.

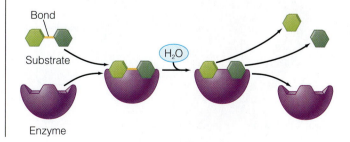

Bond

Substrate

H_2O

Enzyme

LO 3.4 Digested Nutrients Are Absorbed Primarily through the Small Intestine

Digested nutrients pass through the brush border of the small intestinal wall via passive diffusion, facilitated diffusion, active transport, or endocytosis. The water and salts not absorbed in the small intestine are absorbed in the large intestine.

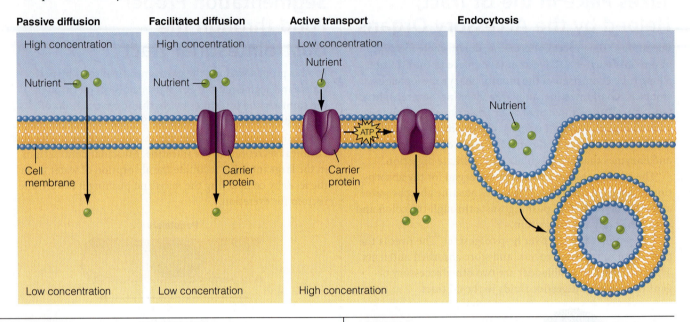

Passive diffusion
High concentration
Nutrient
Cell membrane
Low concentration

Facilitated diffusion
High concentration
Nutrient
Carrier protein
Low concentration

Active transport
Low concentration
Nutrient
Carrier protein
ATP
High concentration

Endocytosis
Nutrient

LO 3.5 Digestion Is Regulated by Hormones and the Nervous System

Hormones, including gastrin, secretin, cholecystokinin, and gastric inhibitory peptide, are chemical messengers secreted from the GI tract that direct enzymes and the release of digestive secretions during digestion. The nervous system communicates signals of hunger and thirst.

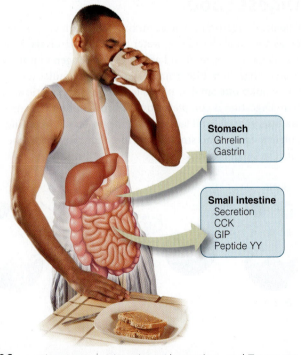

Stomach
Ghrelin
Gastrin

Small intestine
Secretion
CCK
GIP
Peptide YY

LO 3.6 Absorbed Nutrients Are Transported throughout the Body by the Cardiovascular and Lymphatic Systems

Body systems other than the digestive system are involved in the body's digestion, absorption, and transport of nutrients. The cardiovascular system distributes water-soluble nutrients throughout the body and carries carbon dioxide and other waste products to be excreted through the lungs and the kidneys. The lymphatic system transports fat-soluble vitamins from the GI tract through the lymphatic system and into the cardiovascular system.

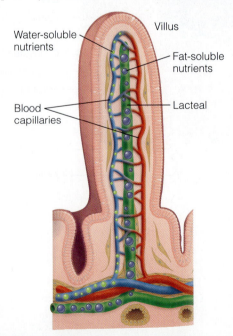

Water-soluble nutrients
Villus
Fat-soluble nutrients
Blood capillaries
Lacteal

LO 3.7 Digestive Disorders Can Result in Malabsorption and Malnutrition

Several digestive disorders can result in malabsorption and malnutrition, including celiac disease, irritable bowel syndrome, ulcers, ulcerative colitis, and Crohn's disease. Celiac disease is an autoimmune disorder that damages the villi of the small intestine due to gluten ingestion. Heartburn, constipation, diarrhea, and hemorrhoids are common, less serious digestive disorders. If left unchecked, even diarrhea can be potentially life-threatening.

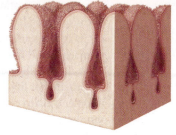

Normal small intestinal wall   Small intestinal wall with celiac disease

Terms to Know

- chemical digestion
- mechanical digestion
- gastrointestinal (GI) tract
- digestion
- propulsion
- absorption
- transport
- elimination
- sphincters
- mastication
- saliva
- bolus
- pharynx
- esophagus
- epiglottis
- upper esophageal sphincter
- lower esophageal sphincter (LES)
- stomach
- goblet cells
- gastric pits

- parietal cells
- chief cells
- chyme
- small intestine
- villi
- lumen
- enterocytes
- microvilli
- crypts
- large intestine
- cecum
- ileocecal valve
- colon
- ferment
- stool
- rectum
- anus
- salivary glands
- liver
- gallbladder
- pancreas

- probiotics
- peristalsis
- segmentation
- enzymes
- hydrolysis
- substrate
- pH
- mucus
- hydrochloric acid (HCl)
- proteases
- pepsinogen
- pepsin
- bile
- emulsify
- enterohepatic circulation
- bicarbonate
- passive diffusion
- facilitated diffusion
- active transport
- endocytosis
- enterogastrones

- gastrin
- secretin
- cholecystokinin (CCK)
- ghrelin
- peptide YY
- hepatic portal vein
- hepatic vein
- lymphatic system
- gastroesophageal reflux disease (GERD)
- gastroenteritis
- ulcer
- gallstones
- celiac disease
- flatulence
- diarrhea
- constipation
- hemorrhoid
- irritable bowel syndrome (IBS)
- ulcerative colitis
- Crohn's disease

MasteringNutrition™

To hear an MP3 Chapter Review, scan here or visit the Study Area in MasteringNutrition.

Check Your Understanding

1. _____ is defined as breaking apart food by mechanical and enzymatic means in the stomach and the small intestine.
   a. Absorption
   b. Transport
   c. Digestion
   d. Elimination

2. The protective tissue that covers the trachea during swallowing is the
   a. esophagus.
   b. tongue.
   c. pharynx.
   d. epiglottis.

3. Food is moved through the GI tract by rhythmic muscular waves called
   a. segmentation.
   b. peristalsis.
   c. bowel movement.
   d. mastication.

4. Which of the following secretions chemically breaks apart foods?
   a. bile
   b. bicarbonate ions
   c. cholecystokinin
   d. enzymes

5. What is the function of hydrochloric acid in the digestive process?
   a. activates pepsinogen to pepsin
   b. slows peristalsis
   c. neutralizes the pH in the stomach
   d. begins carbohydrate digestion

6. Which of the following is true regarding the small intestine?
   a. It is shorter than the large intestine.
   b. It is the major organ for digestion and absorption.

c. It has access to lymph tissue but not to the bloodstream.

d. It is composed of the ileum, duodenum, and jejunum, in that order.

7. The emulsifying agent that is produced by the liver is
   a. pepsin.
   b. gastrin.
   c. cholecystokinin.
   d. bile.

8. Glucose is absorbed by
   a. passive diffusion.
   b. facilitated diffusion.
   c. active transport.
   d. osmosis.

9. Which of the following transports fat-soluble nutrients to the blood?
   a. hepatic portal vein
   b. lymph vessels
   c. red blood cells
   d. the kidneys

10. Celiac disease is caused by a reaction to gluten found in which foods?
    a. citrus fruits
    b. wheat, barley, and rye
    c. legumes, nuts, and seeds
    d. milk, cheese, and yogurt

Answers

1. (c) Digestion is defined as the process of breaking apart food by mechanical and enzymatic means. Once food is digested it can be absorbed into the blood or lymphatic system to be transported to the cells. Any waste products are eliminated through urine and feces.

2. (d) The epiglottis covers the trachea. The esophagus is a tube that connects the mouth with the stomach. The tongue is a muscle that pushes food to the back of the mouth into the pharynx, a chamber that food passes through before being swallowed.

3. (b) Peristalsis is the process that moves food through the stomach and small intestine. Segmentation squeezes chyme back and forth along the intestinal walls. A bowel movement involves peristalsis moving feces through the large

intestine. Mastication is the process of chewing food.

4. (d) Enzymes secreted from the stomach, small intestine, and pancreas chemically break apart food. Bile emulsifies lipids. Bicarbonate ions neutralize acid. Cholecystokinin slows peristalsis.

5. (a) Hydrochloric acid produced in the stomach activates pepsinogen to pepsin, breaks down connective tissue in meat, and destroys some microorganisms. Cholecystokinin and gastric inhibitory hormones slow peristalsis. Bicarbonate ions neutralize pH in the duodenum. Amylase begins carbohydrate breakdown in the mouth.

6. (b) The small intestine is critical to digestion and absorption. With numerous villi and microvilli, it has a vast surface area to enhance absorption. It allows nutrients to pass into both blood and lymph. It consists of the duodenum, then the jejunum, and finally the ileum. It is much longer than the large intestine.

7. (d) The liver makes bile in a dilute, liquid form that is concentrated and stored in the gallbladder. Pepsin is the active form of a protease secreted by the chief cells in the stomach. Gastrin and cholecystokinin are GI tract hormones.

8. (c) Glucose and amino acids are absorbed by active transport.

9. (b) The fat-soluble nutrients are transported through the lymphatic vessels and eventually arrive at the thoracic duct, where they reach the blood. The hepatic portal vein transports water-soluble nutrients to the liver. Red blood cells transport oxygen. The kidneys filter the blood to remove and excrete waste into the urine.

10. (b) Wheat, barley, and rye contain gluten, which causes the symptoms associated with celiac disease. Fruits, vegetables, dairy foods, meat, nuts, legumes, and seeds are free of gluten and are safe to eat on a gluten-free diet.

Answers to True or False?

1. **True.** The enzyme salivary amylase, found in saliva, begins digesting carbohydrate during chewing; hence, starchy foods will begin to taste sweet as they are broken down.

2. **True.** The stomach secretes a powerful acid, HCl, that is critical to digestion. The acid is also strong enough to damage the stomach wall, so a thick layer of mucus protects it.

3. **True.** Bile emulsifies fat by breaking up the large globules into smaller fat droplets.

4. **False.** Acid reflux occurs when stomach contents pass back through the lower esophageal sphincter into the esophagus.

5. **True.** After food has been completely broken down and its nutrients absorbed in the small intestine, it passes into the large intestine, where water and electrolytes continue to be absorbed.

6. **True.** Fecal matter consists of 50 percent bacteria, while the rest is undigested food, water, and sloughed intestinal cells.

7. **False.** Lymph only transports fat-soluble components. Blood transports water-soluble materials.

8. **True.** Several hormones, including gastrin, secretin, cholecystokinin (CCK), and gastric inhibitory peptide help regulate digestion.

9. **False.** Though foodborne illness can cause diarrhea, the condition can also result from an adverse reaction to certain foods, medications, or other compounds.

10. **False.** The cause of irritable bowel syndrome is not known, but low-fiber diets, stress, consumption of irritating foods, and intestinal motility disorders are all suspected factors.

Web Resources

- To learn more about the various conditions related to digestion, absorption, and elimination, visit the Center for Digestive Health and Nutrition at www.gihealth.com
- Search the National Digestive Diseases Information Clearinghouse site for more information about various digestive diseases at http://digestive.niddk.nih.gov

References

1. Marieb, E. N., and K. Hoehn. 2012. *Human Anatomy and Physiology.* 9th ed. San Francisco: Benjamin Cummings.
2. Gropper, S. S., and J. L. Smith. 2012. *Advanced Nutrition and Human Metabolism.* 6th ed. Belmont, CA: Wadsworth Cengage Learning.
3. Marieb E. N., and K. Hoehn. 2012. *Human Anatomy and Physiology.* 9th ed. San Francisco: Benjamin Cummings.
4. Tortora, G. J., and B. H. Derrikson. 2011. *Principles of Anatomy and Physiology.* 13th ed. New York: Harper & Row Publishers.
5. Gunawardene, A. R., B. M. Corfe, and C. A. Staton. 2011. Classification and Functions of Enteroendocrine Cells of the Lower Gastrointestinal Tract. *International Journal of Experimental Pathology* 94(4):219–231.
6. Health Grades. 2013. *Prevalence and Incidence of Heartburn.* Available at www.rightdiagnosis.com. Accessed January 2014.
7. National Digestive Diseases Information Clearinghouse. *Gastroesophageal Reflux (GER) and Gastroesophageal Reflux Disease in Adults.* Available at http://digestive.niddk.nih.gov. Accessed January 2014.
8. National Cancer Institute. 2012. *Esophageal Cancer.* Available at www.cancer.gov. Accessed February 2014.
9. Weight Control Information Network. 2013. *Dieting and Gallstones.* Available at http://win.niddk.nih.gov. Accessed January 2014.
10. Rubio-Tapia, A., J. F. Ludvigsson, T. L. Brantner, J. A. Murray, and J. E. Everhart. 2012. The Prevalence of Celiac Disease in the United States. *American Journal of Gastroenterology* 107(10):1538–1544.
11. Pelkowski, T. D., and A. J. Viera. 2014. Celiac Disease: Diagnosis and Management. *American Family Physician* 89(2):99–105.
12. Guandalini, S., and A. Assiri. 2014. Celiac Disease: A Review. *Journal of the American Medical Association Pediatrics* doi: 10.1001/jamapediatrics.2013.3858.
13. Rubio-Tapia, A. 2012.
14. Pelkowski, T. D. 2014.
15. National Foundation for Celiac Awareness. 2011. *The Gluten Free Diet.* Available at www.celiaccentral.org. Accessed January 2014.
16. Academy of Nutrition and Dietetics. 2012. If You Have Celiac Disease: Grains & Plant Foods to Include on Your Grocery List. Available at www.eatright.org. Accessed February 2014.
17. Academy of Nutrition and Dietetics. 2011. Celiac Disease Toolkit. Available at www.eatright.org.
18. Packaged Facts. 2012. Gluten-Free Foods and Beverages in the US. 4th ed. [press release]. Available at www.packagedfacts.com. Accessed January 2014.
19. Gaesser, G. A., and S. S. Angadi. 2012. Gluten-Free Diet: Imprudent Dietary Advice for the General Population? *Journal of the Academy of Nutrition and Dietetics* 112(9):1330–1333.
20. Peregrin, T. 2013. Frequently Asked Questions of the Academy's Knowledge Center. *Journal of the Academy of Nutrition and Dietetics* 113(7): 887–891.
21. Gaesser, G. A. 2012.
22. Hajek, P., F. Gillison, and H. McRobbie. 2003. Stopping Smoking Can Cause Constipation. *Addiction.* 98:1563–1567.
23. Leung, L., T. Riutta, J. Kotecha, and W. Rosser. 2011. Chronic Constipation: An Evidence-Based Review. *Journal of the American Board of Family Medicine* 24(4): 436–451.
24. National Digestive Diseases Information Clearinghouse. 2013. *Irritable Bowel Syndrome.* Available at http://digestive.niddk.nih.gov. Accessed January 2014.
25. National Cancer Institute. 2012. *Colon and Rectal Cancer.* Available at www.cancer.gov. Accessed February 2014.

4 Carbohydrates

Learning Outcomes

After reading this chapter, you will be able to:

4.1 Describe the carbohydrates and how they are classified.

4.2 Explain the process of digesting and absorbing dietary carbohydrates.

4.3 List the functions of carbohydrates in the body.

4.4 Explain how the body maintains blood glucose levels.

4.5 Describe the role of fiber in promoting health.

4.6 Describe the guidelines for carbohydrate intake and list best food sources.

4.7 Describe the differences between natural sugars, added sugars, and alternative sweeteners used as sugar substitutes.

4.8 Describe the cause, symptoms, and treatment for different classifications of diabetes.

True or False?

1. Carbohydrates are the least important macronutrient. **T/F**
2. Most babies are born lactose intolerant. **T/F**
3. Carbohydrates are a main cause of obesity. **T/F**
4. Sugar causes hyperactivity in children. **T/F**
5. Whole grains are more nutrient dense than refined grains. **T/F**
6. Sugar causes tooth decay. **T/F**
7. Aspartame causes cancer in humans. **T/F**
8. Americans do not consume enough fiber. **T/F**
9. Soda and other sugar-sweetened beverages play a big role in Americans' rising rate of obesity. **T/F**
10. Obese individuals are more likely to develop type 2 diabetes. **T/F**

See page 156 for the answers.

C arbohydrates are essential macronutrients produced mainly in plants. These compounds, often referred to as *sugars*, can be as simple as a single sugar unit or as complex as a molecule containing 1,000 or more sugar units. Carbohydrates' main role in the body is to supply fuel, primarily in the form of glucose (*ose* = sugar), the predominant sugar in high-carbohydrate foods. Cells use glucose as the primary source of energy (ATP) to fuel the demands of the brain, red blood cells, and the nervous system. With such an important role in the body, it isn't surprising that foods high in carbohydrates are a big part of the diet, no matter what continent you live on.

Carbohydrate-rich foods, including rice, beans, fruits, tubers, and nuts, make up the foundation of diets the world over. These foods are staples in cuisines from Asia to Latin America and the United States to the Mediterranean. In Asia, rice accounts for 80 percent of people's daily kilocalories. In Latin America, flatbreads and fruits adorn most dinner plates. In the Mediterranean, grain-based pastas, breads, and couscous are plentiful, and here in the United States, many people consume the potato on a daily basis.[1]

In this chapter, you will learn about different types of carbohydrates and the functions they perform in the body. We will also discuss how we digest carbohydrates, how the body metabolizes glucose, and what happens when metabolic control fails, as in the disease diabetes mellitus. You will learn the role that certain types of carbohydrates can play in fighting obesity, heart disease, cancer, and diabetes. Finally, we will explore how to incorporate a rich balance of carbohydrates into your daily diet.

photosynthesis A process by which plants create carbohydrates using the energy from sunlight.

chlorophyll The green pigment in plants that absorbs energy from sunlight to begin the process of photosynthesis.

glucose The primary monosaccharide and primary energy source for the body.

simple carbohydrates Carbohydrates that consist of one sugar unit (monosaccharides) or two sugar units (disaccharides).

monosaccharide Simple sugar that consists of a single sugar unit. The three most common monosaccharides: glucose, fructose, and galactose.

disaccharide Simple sugar that consists of two sugar units combined. The three most common disaccharides: sucrose, lactose, and maltose.

oligosaccharides Three to ten units of monosaccharides combined.

complex carbohydrates A category of carbohydrates that contain many sugar units combined. Oligosaccharides and polysaccharides are complex carbohydrates.

polysaccharides Many sugar units combined. Starch, glycogen, and fiber are all polysaccharides.

starch The storage form of glucose in plants.

fiber Food components that humans cannot digest. Most are carbohydrates.

What Are Carbohydrates and How Are They Classified?

LO 4.1 Describe the carbohydrates and how they are classified.

Carbohydrates originate in plants during a process called **photosynthesis** (**Figure 4.1**). During photosynthesis, plants use the **chlorophyll** in their leaves to absorb the energy in sunlight. The absorbed energy splits water in the plant into its component parts of hydrogen and oxygen. The hydrogen joins with carbon dioxide that the plant has taken in from the air to form **glucose.** Thus, carbohydrates are literally hydrated carbons. Plants use the glucose they produce directly for energy, store it, or combine it with minerals from the soil to make other compounds, including protein and vitamins. We then eat the plants and digest, absorb, and utilize the glucose.

All carbohydrates consist of strings of sugar units bound together. We classify carbohydrates according to how many of these units are in the string. **Simple carbohydrates** consist of either a single sugar unit called a **monosaccharide** (*mono* = one, *saccharide* = sugar) or two units bonded together as a **disaccharide** (*di* = two). **Oligosaccharides** (*oligo* = a few) are slightly longer and contain three to ten units. **Complex carbohydrates** include more than ten and up to hundreds or thousands of connected units. Such **polysaccharides** (*poly* = many) include **starch** and **fiber.**

Monosaccharides Are Single Sugar Units

There are three nutritionally important monosaccharides: glucose, fructose, and galactose. Glucose is the most abundant monosaccharide in foods. Glucose is also the most abundant monosaccharide in the body. The brain in particular relies on glucose (also known as blood glucose or blood sugar) as its main source of ATP, as do the red blood cells and nerve cells.

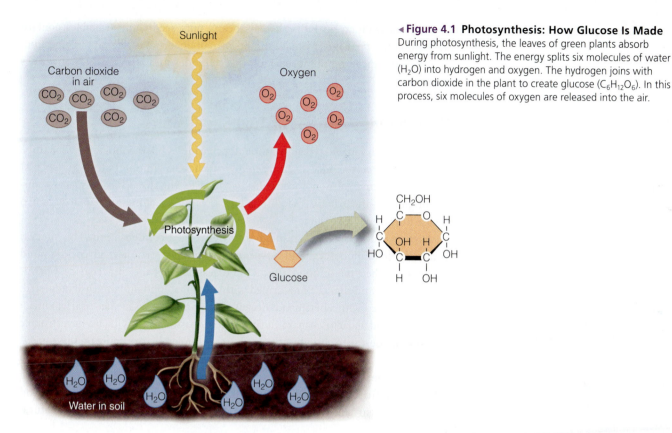

◀ **Figure 4.1 Photosynthesis: How Glucose Is Made**
During photosynthesis, the leaves of green plants absorb energy from sunlight. The energy splits six molecules of water (H_2O) into hydrogen and oxygen. The hydrogen joins with carbon dioxide in the plant to create glucose ($C_6H_{12}O_6$). In this process, six molecules of oxygen are released into the air.

While glucose is the most common, **fructose** and **galactose** are also found naturally in foods. All three simple sugars share the same molecular formula of six carbon atoms, twelve hydrogen atoms, and six oxygen atoms ($C_6H_{12}O_6$), referred to as a **hexose** (*hex* = six). The difference between the three monosaccharides lies in how their atoms are arranged (see **Figure 4.2**). Glucose and galactose are both six-sided ring structures that, at first glance, look identical to each other. Examine both structures carefully. The hydroxyl group (OH) and the hydrogen (H) of glucose are arranged in a specific way on the fourth carbon. Now look at the structure of galactose. You'll notice that the hydrogen (H) on the fourth carbon is shifted to the right side of the carbon, while the hydroxyl group (OH) is on the left. This slight rearrangement of atoms makes a difference in the way the body metabolizes and uses these two monosaccharides.

Fructose contains the same number of carbon, hydrogen, and oxygen atoms as glucose and galactose but its molecular structure is arranged as a five-sided, rather than a six-sided, ring. However, fructose is still classified as a hexose because it contains six carbons (notice the location of all six carbons on the fructose molecule in Figure 4.2). The sweetest of the natural sugars, fructose is found abundantly in fruits and is also known as fruit sugar. Fructose is part of high-fructose corn syrup, a sweetener commonly used by the food industry in soft drinks and fruit beverages.

Galactose is seldom found on its own in nature; it is most commonly bound with glucose as part of the disaccharide lactose found in milk and milk products.

Hexose sugars ($C_6H_{12}O_6$)

Glucose   Fructose   Galactose

▲ **Figure 4.2 The Structural Differences between Glucose, Fructose, and Galactose**
The three monosaccharides are shown in their linear form (as found in foods) and in the ring structure found in the body.

fructose The sweetest of all the monosaccharides; also known as fruit sugar or levulose.

galactose A monosaccharide that links with glucose to create the disaccharide found in dairy foods.

hexose A sugar that contains six carbons; glucose, galactose, and fructose are all hexoses.

What Are Carbohydrates and How Are They Classified?   **113**

Several plant products, including cereals, beans, nuts, seeds, and vegetables, contain slight amounts of galactose, but it is in the form of fiber that is resistant to digestion.

From the three monosaccharides, disaccharides and complex carbohydrates are created.

Disaccharides Consist of Two Sugar Units

A disaccharide is created when two monosaccharides are joined together. The three disaccharides, *sucrose, lactose,* and *maltose,* all have a common characteristic: At least one of their two monosaccharides is glucose. The disaccharide sucrose consists of glucose and fructose; lactose is glucose and galactose; and maltose is two glucose units linked together.

Disaccharides are joined through a process called **condensation.** This process chemically links monosaccharides with either an alpha or a beta **glycosidic bond** (**Figure 4.3**). The type of bond affects the digestibility of the disaccharide. For instance, sucrose and maltose are formed with an alpha bond and are easily digested. Lactose is formed with a beta bond. Because they lack the enzyme necessary to break the glucose and galactose apart during digestion, some individuals have trouble digesting lactose. (See Spotlight: What Is Lactose Intolerance for more on this topic.)

The white granulated sugar you add to coffee and the brown sugar you use to make cookie dough are examples of **sucrose** (brown sugar is made by adding molasses to refined sugar and is about 90 percent sucrose[2]). Sucrose is also found naturally in sugar cane and sugar beets and is the most commonly used natural sweetener.

condensation A chemical reaction in which two molecules combine to form a larger molecule, and water is released.

glycosidic bond A bond that forms when two sugar molecules are joined together during condensation.

sucrose A disaccharide composed of glucose and fructose; also known as table sugar.

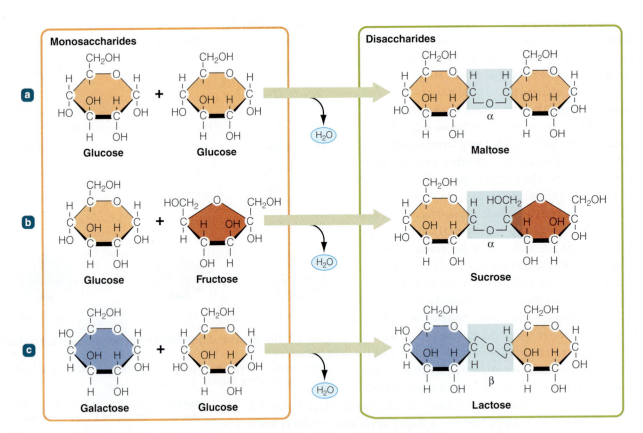

▲ **Figure 4.3 Condensation Reaction Links Monosaccharides to Form Disaccharides**
Through the process of condensation, monosaccharides join together to form disaccharides. **(a)** Two glucose units join together with an alpha bond to produce maltose. **(b)** The disaccharide sucrose is composed of a molecule of glucose linked to a molecule of fructose by an alpha bond. **(c)** The disaccharide lactose is composed of glucose and galactose. Lactose differs from sucrose and maltose in that the two monosaccharides are joined by a beta bond.

Lactose, or milk sugar, is present in milk and dairy products. Lactose is a particularly important carbohydrate in the diets of newborn infants because it is the first and only carbohydrate they consume in breast milk.

Maltose, or malt sugar, is the least common of the disaccharides and is formed during the digestion of starch. Manufacturers add maltose as a sweetener and to improve the shelf life of their products. This makes processed food the main source of maltose in our diets. Maltose is also formed during the fermentation of barley used to brew beer.

In general, simple carbohydrates are sweeter than complex carbohydrates (which we'll discuss next). Foods such as table sugar and fruit, which are high in fructose, are perceived as sweet compared with the carbohydrates found in starchy foods such as rice or bread. This perception is due to the structure of the molecule. The five-sided ring of fructose mixes with saliva and reacts with taste buds, signaling the brain that the food is sweet.

Some of us experience a stronger taste of sweetness than others do when we eat foods high in monosaccharides and disaccharides. For example, across all ethnic groups, females seem to crave sweetness more than males.[3, 4] This ability to taste sweetness may be influenced by age or by health conditions, or may have a genetic component.[5]

Oligosaccharides Have Few Sugar Units

Oligosaccharides are generally classified as complex carbohydrates. They are short chains of three to ten monosaccharides that are similar in length to simple carbohydrates. They are similar to polysaccharides in that they make up part of the plant cell walls, and, like fiber, most of the oligosaccharides we consume escape digestion.[6] Oligosaccharides are found in legumes, beans, cabbage, brussels sprouts, and broccoli.

Two common oligosaccharides are raffinose (**Figure 4.4**) and stachyose. Humans lack the enzyme necessary to break apart the bonds in oligosaccharides and they pass undigested into the large intestine, where the intestinal microflora digest and ferment them. This fermentation may result in bloating, discomfort, and flatulence (gas). Taking a product such as Beano, which contains enzymes that digest oligosaccharides, with a meal can reduce flatulence.[7]

Oligosaccharides are also present in human breast milk. Even though these carbohydrates aren't digested, they may stimulate the immune system and increase the amount of healthy intestinal microflora in newborn infants.[8]

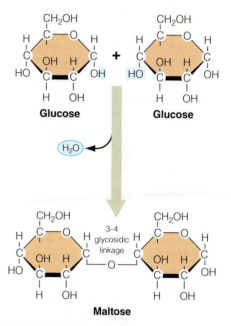

Beano helps reduce the production of gas in the large intestine.

lactose A disaccharide composed of glucose and galactose; also known as milk sugar.

maltose A disaccharide composed of two glucose units joined together.

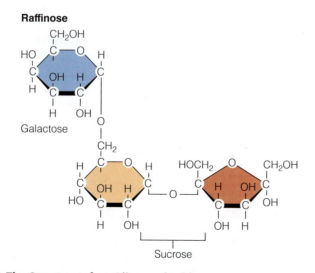

▲ **Figure 4.4 The Structure of an Oligosaccharide**
The oligosaccharide raffinose consists of galactose connected to sucrose.

What Is Lactose Intolerance?

Lactose intolerance is a digestive disorder with symptoms of bloating, flatulence, cramps and diarrhea. People who are lactose intolerant have a deficiency of the brush border enzyme lactase, and they cannot properly digest lactose, the principal carbohydrate found in dairy products. The undigested lactose can draw water into the digestive tract, causing diarrhea. Once the lactose reaches the colon, the bacteria in the colon ferment the sugar and produce various gases, and the resulting uncomfortable symptoms.[1]

As they age, many people develop **lactose maldigestion,** a reduction in the ability to digest lactose. In fact, as soon as a child stops nursing, his body makes less lactase. An estimated 33 percent of Americans, and 75 percent of adults around the world, have a decrease in lactose. Individuals of some specific ethnic origins, such as those from northern Europe, central Africa, and the Middle East, aren't as prone to developing lactose maldigestion. They appear to have a genetic predisposition to maintaining higher levels of lactase throughout their adult life.[2]

If you have lactose maldigestion, don't despair. You don't necessarily need to eliminate dairy foods from the diet. In fact, many people continue to consume milk, yogurt, and cheese without any problems or unpleasant side effects.[3] This is good news, as dairy products provide over 70 percent of the calcium in the

lactose intolerance When maldigestion of lactose results in symptoms such as nausea, cramps, bloating, flatulence, and diarrhea.

lactose maldigestion The inability to digest lactose due to low levels of the enzyme lactase.

diet, along with protein, potassium, and certain vitamins.[4]

However, people with lactose intolerance have varying thresholds for tolerating lactose-containing foods and beverages. These thresholds can be raised depending upon how much of a lactose-containing food one eats at a time. Consuming smaller amounts of dairy foods throughout the day can be better tolerated than having a large amount at one time. Eating lactose-containing foods with a meal or snack, rather than by themselves, can also influence how much can be tolerated.[5]

People respond differently to various dairy foods.[6] Whole milk tends to be tolerated better than skim milk. Cheese typically has less lactose than milk. This is especially true of hard, aged cheeses, as the amount of lactose remaining after the aging process is negligible. Yogurts that contain active cultures are better tolerated than skim or low-fat milk. Your own tolerance may depend on the brand you choose. For example, Greek yogurt is thicker than

regular yogurt because most of the lactose, which is in the liquid portion called *whey*, is strained out in processing. Avoid yogurts with added whey protein concentrate, which adds lactose. Or choose yogurt made with milk treated with lactase prior to processing. **Table 1** shows the amounts of lactose in some common dairy foods.

Consuming dairy foods regularly may improve lactose tolerance. The continuous exposure to undigested lactose promotes an acidic environment created by the fermenting of lactose by the bacteria in the colon, which inhibits further fermentation. Also, the constant presence of lactose in the colon perpetuates an increase in the growth of nongaseous bacteria and subsequent displacement of the gas-producing bacteria.[7]

Those who need to ingest dairy foods as part of a healthy calcium-rich diet can ingest lactose-reduced dairy products such as milk, cottage cheese, and ice cream, which are available in many supermarkets. Lactase pills or drops can also

The Polysaccharides Consist of Many Sugar Units

Complex carbohydrates, or polysaccharides, consist of long chains and branches of glucose linked together. Some polysaccharides, such as starch and **glycogen,** serve as storage forms of glucose in plants and animals, while dietary fiber provides structure in plant cells.

glycogen The storage form of glucose in animals, including humans.

Table 1 How Much Lactose Is in Your Foods?

Food	Amount	Lactose (grams)
Milk, whole, 1%, or skim	1 cup	11
Lactaid milk	1 cup	<1
Soy milk	1 cup	0
Ice cream	½ cup	6
Yogurt, plain, nonfat	6 oz	14
Greek yogurt	6 oz	6
Cottage cheese	½ cup	2
Provolone, Cheddar, or Parmesan cheese	1 oz	<1
Cream cheese	1 oz	1

Don't Forget These Hidden Sources of Lactose

Baked goods

Baking mixes for pancakes, biscuits, and cookies

Bread

Breakfast drinks

Candies

Cereals, processed

Instant potatoes

Lunch meats (other than kosher meats)

Margarine

Salad dressings

Soups

Adapted from J. Joneja, *The Health Professional's Guide to Food Allergies and Intolerances* (Chicago: The Academy of Nutrition and Dietetics, 2013).

TABLE TIPS

Improving Lactose Tolerance

To determine the amount of milk you can tolerate, start with less than one cup and gradually increase the serving size until symptoms develop.

Choose aged hard cheeses such as Cheddar, Colby, and Parmesan over softer cheeses.

Drink one serving of milk with lunch and have an ounce of cheese as an afternoon snack, rather than having the milk and the cheese at the same time.

Drink that cup of milk along with a meal or snack, rather than by itself.

Try reduced-lactose yogurt or cottage cheese.

3. Nicklas, T. A., L. Jahns, M. L. Bogle, D. N. Chester, M. Giovanni, D. M. Klurfeld, K. Laugero, et al. 2013. Barriers and Facilitators for Consumer Adherence to the *Dietary Guidelines for Americans*: The HEALTH Study. *Journal of the Academy of Nutrition and Dietetics* 113(10):1317–1331.
4. National Institutes of Health. 2013. *Calcium: Dietary Supplement Fact Sheet.* Available at http://ods.od.nih.gov.
5. Clerfeuille, E., M. Maillot, E. O. Verger, A. Lluch, et al. 2013. Dairy Products: How They Fit in Nutritionally Adequate Diets. *Journal of the Academy of Nutrition and Dietetics* 113(7):950–956.
6. Ibid.
7. Barrett, J. S., and P. R. Gibson. 2012. Fermentable Oligosaccharides, Disaccharides, Monosaccharides and Polyols (FODMAPs) and Nonallergic Food Intolerance: FODMAPs or Food Chemicals? *Therapeutic Advances in Gastroenterology* 5(4):261–268.
8. National Institute of Allergy and Infectious Diseases. 2012. *Food Allergy: Quick Facts.* Available at www.niaid.nih.gov. Accessed February 2014.

be used to break down lactose in foods before or while they are eaten. See the Table Tips for more ideas on improving your lactose tolerance.

Finally, note that lactose intolerance is not the same as having an allergy to milk. A milk allergy is a response by the immune system to one or more of the proteins in cow's milk. This condition typically affects only about 1 to 3 percent of children, and rarely occurs in adults.[8] (Food allergies are covered in Chapter 17.)

References

1. National Digestive Diseases Information Clearinghouse. 2012. *Lactose Intolerance.* Available at http://digestive.niddk.nih.gov. Accessed February 2014.
2. Ibid.

Starch

Plants store glucose in chains of starch. These chains can be hundreds or even thousands of glucose units long. Straight chains are called **amylose,** and the branched chains are called **amylopectin** (**Figure 4.5**). Although plants contain both forms of these polysaccharides, about 60 percent of most starches is usually amylopectin,

amylose A straight chain of polysaccharides found in starch.

amylopectin A branched chain of polysaccharides found in starch.

Amylose

Amylopectin

a Two types of starch are amylose (straight chain) and amylopectin (branched).

Starch

b Dietary fiber is a nondigestible food component found in the cell walls of plants. Most dietary fiber is in the form of cellulose, a straight chain of glucose units with a beta-glycosidic bond that humans lack the enzyme to digest.

Fiber

c Glycogen, the storage form of glucose in animals, including humans, is more branched than amylopectin.

Glycogen

with the remainder (about 40 percent) in the form of amylose. When we eat plant foods such as corn, rice, and potatoes, we consume the stored glucose.

Some starch is resistant to digestion. In beans, half of the starch is digestible and the remainder is in the form of **resistant starch.** The amylose in starch is more resistant to digestion than is the amylopectin. Linear chains of amylose are harder to break down during digestion because the molecules stack together into tight granules, which hinders the ability of enzymes to reach and break down the bonds. The branched-chain shape of amylopectin makes it impossible to compact and therefore allows for much easier digestion. Unripe bananas, cooked and chilled pasta, raw potatoes, baked beans, and plantains are examples of foods with high levels of resistant starch.[9]

Resistant starches are added to foods for health benefits.[10] Some researchers have reported that resistant starch may improve the health of the digestive tract by increasing bulk; improve glucose tolerance by lowering the glycemic impact on the blood and increasing insulin sensitivity;[11] and stimulate the growth of beneficial intestinal bacteria.[12]

Fiber

Most forms of dietary fiber are nondigestible polysaccharides and occur naturally as a structural component called **cellulose** in the cell walls of plants. Cellulose looks simple—just a straight string of glucose units (never branched like amylopectin) linked with beta-glycosidic bonds (**Figure 4.6**). When several strands stack together they give the plant cell its structure and shape, which contributes to the texture of fruits and vegetables. **Lignin,** which is also a type of dietary fiber, is not a carbohydrate but acts as an adhesive in cell walls.

As mentioned earlier, humans lack the digestive enzyme needed to break the beta form of the glycosidic bond, so for the most part, fiber cannot be digested, and passes through the intestines intact. This means that fiber does not provide energy

Plantains contain a fair amount of resistant starch.

resistant starch A type of starch that is not digested in the GI tract but has important health benefits in the large intestine.

cellulose A nondigestible polysaccharide found in plant cell walls.

lignin A noncarbohydrate form of dietary fiber that binds to cellulose fibers to harden and strengthen the cell walls of plants.

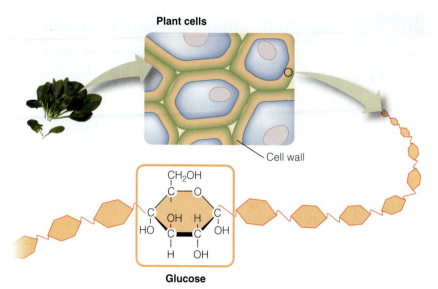

Plant cells

Cell wall

CH₂OH

Glucose

▸ **Figure 4.6 Plants Contain Cellulose**
Found in the cell walls of plants, cellulose is a polysaccharide composed of numerous glucose units linked together.

or kilocalories but it does add bulk. Fiber performs numerous key roles in the body: It helps maintain a healthy intestinal tract, reduces hunger, and is an essential component of a healthy diet.

Dietary fiber is sometimes classified according to its affinity for water. **Soluble fiber** dissolves in water, while **insoluble fiber** does not. Viscous, soluble fibers include pectins; beta-glucans; some gums, such as guar gum; and mucilages (for example, psyllium). Cellulose, lignin, and some hemicelluloses are considered insoluble, nonviscous fibers.[13] Soluble fibers are more easily fermented by intestinal bacteria. Fruits and vegetables that are rich in pectin and hemicellulose can be hydrolyzed by these bacteria to form carbon dioxide, methane, and some fatty acids. Insoluble fibers, including cellulose found in grains, are not easily fermented.

Soluble fibers may have numerous health benefits. The gels formed by soluble fibers slow gastric emptying and may delay the absorption of some nutrients, which helps to reduce serum cholesterol, improve appetite control, and normalize blood glucose levels.

Insoluble fibers may also have health benefits. In comparison with soluble fibers, less viscous, insoluble fibers increase the bulk of the stool. The greater stool weight stimulates peristalsis, which speeds up the movement of the feces through the intestinal tract. This increase in movement, called transit time, relieves constipation and keeps the gastrointestinal tract healthy. There are exceptions to these statements because not all soluble fibers reduce serum cholesterol, and constipation may be relieved by some soluble fiber. Ultimately, whether fiber is soluble is not as important as the overall dietary fiber intake, and the good news is that most plant foods contain both soluble and insoluble forms of dietary fiber (**Figure 4.7**). Animal products do not contain fiber.

Many compounds can be classified as both dietary fiber and functional fiber, depending on how they are used. **Functional fiber** is a type of fiber that has been extracted or isolated from a plant or manufactured by the food industry, and has been shown to have health benefits.[14] For example, psyllium, used in products such as Metamucil, is isolated from psyllium seed husks. Psyllium is high in soluble fiber and has been reported to reduce total cholesterol and LDL cholesterol. Synthetic or manufactured forms of functional fiber also include some forms of resistant starch. Together, dietary fiber and functional fiber contribute to the total fiber in the diet.

Cellulose: insoluble fiber

Pectin: soluble fiber

▴ **Figure 4.7 Most Plant Foods Contain Both Soluble and Insoluble Fibers**
The skin of an apple is high in cellulose and insoluble fiber, while the pulp is high in pectin, a soluble fiber.

soluble fiber A type of fiber that dissolves in water and is fermented by intestinal bacteria. Many soluble fibers are viscous and have thickening properties.

insoluble fiber A type of fiber that isn't dissolved in water or fermented by intestinal bacteria.

functional fiber The nondigestible polysaccharides that are added to foods because of a specific desired effect on human health.

TABLE 4.1	Forms of Dietary Fiber and Their Health Benefits	
Type	**Found in These Foods**	**Reduces the Risk of**
Insoluble Fiber		
▪ Cellulose ▪ Hemicellulose ▪ Lignins	Whole grains, whole-grain cereals, amaranth, bran, bulgur, couscous, oats, rice, quinoa, sorghum, fruit, vegetables, legumes	Constipation, diverticulosis, certain cancers, heart disease, obesity
Soluble Fiber		
▪ Pectin ▪ Beta-glucan ▪ Gums ▪ Psyllium	Citrus fruits, prunes, legumes, oats, barley, quinoa, teff, sorghum, flax seed, brussels sprouts, carrots	Constipation, heart disease, diabetes mellitus, obesity

Table 4.1 summarizes the various types of fiber, some of their sources, and some of their health benefits.

Glycogen

Whereas starch is the storage form of glucose in plants, glycogen is the storage form in animals, including humans. Molecules of glycogen are long, branched chains, similar to amylopectin, and are stored in muscle and in the liver. The branched structure enables the body to break glycogen down quickly and easily because there are so many sites where enzymes can attach. When blood glucose levels decrease, the liver breaks down the stored glycogen branches, one glucose molecule at a time, and releases the glucose into the blood. Muscle glycogen can similarly be broken down to glucose to provide energy for the muscle. Because it breaks down quickly after an animal dies, animal products do not contain glycogen. In other words, eating meat or poultry will not provide glycogen.

LO 4.1: THE TAKE-HOME MESSAGE Carbohydrates are found primarily in plant-based foods and are needed by the cells for energy. Glucose is the preferred source of energy in the body. Glucose is stored in plants in the form of starch and fiber. Simple carbohydrates include the monosaccharides glucose, fructose, and galactose, which combine to form the disaccharides sucrose, lactose, and maltose. Oligosaccharides contain three to ten glucose units and are part of cellulose in cell walls.

The complex carbohydrates starch, fiber, and glycogen are all polysaccharides. The total fiber in the diet is a combination of both soluble and insoluble dietary fiber and functional fiber added to foods. Viscous, soluble fiber has thickening properties, can be fermented by intestinal bacteria, and moves slowly through the intestinal tract. Insoluble fiber typically moves quickly through the digestive system, reducing constipation.

How Do We Digest and Absorb Carbohydrates?

LO 4.2 Explain the process of digesting and absorbing dietary carbohydrates.

Disaccharides and starch are digested into monosaccharides that can be easily absorbed through the walls of the small intestine. Fiber generally passes through the GI tract undigested. Let's follow the carbohydrates from a sandwich through the digestive process, as illustrated in **Focus Figure 4.8**.

Carbohydrate Digestion and Absorption

Carbohydrate digestion begins in the mouth and ends with the absorption of the monosaccharides glucose, fructose, and galactose in the small intestine.

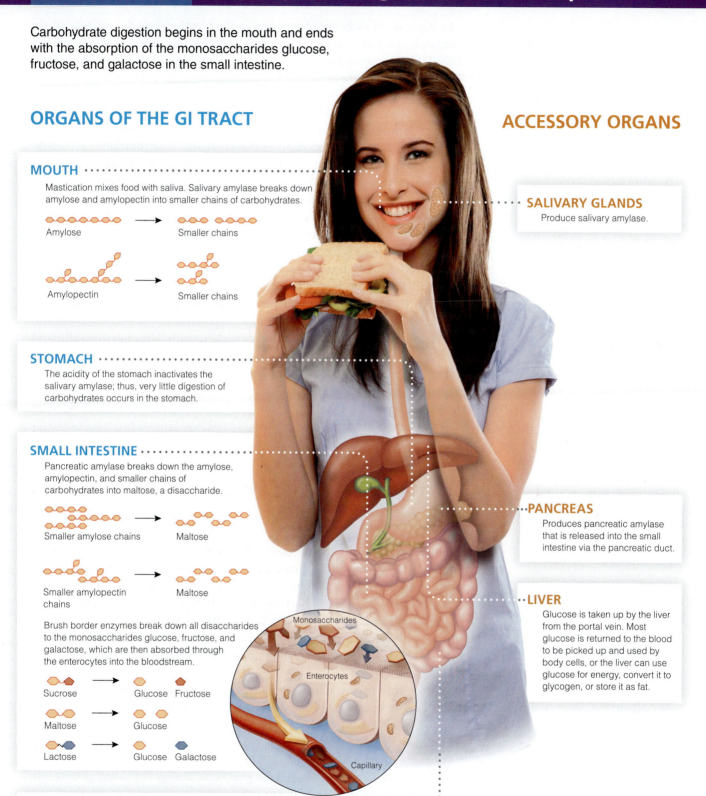

ORGANS OF THE GI TRACT

MOUTH

Mastication mixes food with saliva. Salivary amylase breaks down amylose and amylopectin into smaller chains of carbohydrates.

Amylose → Smaller chains

Amylopectin → Smaller chains

STOMACH

The acidity of the stomach inactivates the salivary amylase; thus, very little digestion of carbohydrates occurs in the stomach.

SMALL INTESTINE

Pancreatic amylase breaks down the amylose, amylopectin, and smaller chains of carbohydrates into maltose, a disaccharide.

Smaller amylose chains → Maltose

Smaller amylopectin chains → Maltose

Brush border enzymes break down all disaccharides to the monosaccharides glucose, fructose, and galactose, which are then absorbed through the enterocytes into the bloodstream.

Sucrose → Glucose Fructose

Maltose → Glucose

Lactose → Glucose Galactose

Monosaccharides

Enterocytes

Capillary

LARGE INTESTINE

Starches and simple sugars are broken down and absorbed in the small intestine; only fiber passes into the large intestine. Bacteria in the colon metabolize some of the fiber. The majority of fiber is eliminated in the stool.

ACCESSORY ORGANS

SALIVARY GLANDS

Produce salivary amylase.

PANCREAS

Produces pancreatic amylase that is released into the small intestine via the pancreatic duct.

LIVER

Glucose is taken up by the liver from the portal vein. Most glucose is returned to the blood to be picked up and used by body cells, or the liver can use glucose for energy, convert it to glycogen, or store it as fat.

Digestion of Carbohydrates Begins in the Mouth

The digestion of carbohydrates begins in the mouth, where the teeth grind the sandwich and mix it with saliva, which contains the enzyme **salivary amylase** (recall that *ase* = enzyme). The amylase begins breaking down some of the amylose and amylopectin in the bread into the disaccharide maltose. The disaccharides and fiber are not altered in the mouth.

This food mixture, which now contains starch and amylase, along with the maltose, lactose, sucrose, and fiber, travels down the esophagus to the stomach. The amylase continues to break down the starch until the hydrochloric acid in the stomach deactivates this enzyme. There are no carbohydrate-digesting enzymes in the stomach; thus, little to no carbohydrate digestion takes place there.

The arrival of polysaccharides in the small intestine signals the pancreas to release an enzyme called pancreatic amylase. The pancreatic amylase breaks down the remaining starch units from the bread into maltose.

The disaccharides maltose, lactose, and sucrose will need further dismantling by the brush border enzymes, including maltase, lactase, and sucrase, housed in the microvilli of the small intestine. These enzymes break down the disaccharides into monosaccharides, specifically glucose, fructose, and galactose. The monosaccharides are now ready to be absorbed into the blood.

By the time the remnants of the sandwich reach the large intestine, all starch and simple sugars have been broken down and absorbed, and only the fiber remains. The bacteria in the colon can metabolize some of the fiber, producing water, gas, and some short-chain fatty acids. The colon uses these short-chain fatty acids for energy. The majority of the fiber is eliminated from the body in the feces. Resistant starch can also be metabolized by intestinal bacteria or excreted in the feces.

Carbohydrates Are Absorbed as Monosaccharides

After carbohydrate digestion, the monosaccharides are absorbed into the intestinal cell mucosa. Glucose and galactose are absorbed by active transport, which requires energy and a carrier protein (**Figure 4.9**). The carrier that helps transport glucose and galactose into the enterocyte is sodium dependent. Once glucose and galactose are absorbed into the enterocyte, they diffuse into the capillaries and are transported through the portal vein to the liver. Fructose is absorbed by facilitated diffusion, requires no energy, and is slower to be absorbed than glucose or galactose. Fructose stays in the intestinal lining longer than glucose or galactose and for this reason, fructose does not raise the blood glucose levels as quickly as glucose.

The fate of the monosaccharides once they've reached the liver depends on an individual's metabolic needs. The liver uses galactose and fructose mostly for energy. They can also be converted into glucose before entering the blood to circulate throughout the body. Any surplus glucose that is not used immediately for energy is stored as glycogen.

The process of converting excess glucose to glycogen is called **glycogenesis** and occurs mostly in the liver and muscle cells. As you learned earlier in the chapter, the body can use this stored form of glucose when the diet lacks sufficient carbohydrate.

Once the glycogen stores are fully replenished and the diet contains sufficient kilocalories to meet energy needs, excess glucose is converted into glycerol and fatty acids. These two are combined into a triglyceride and stored in the adipocytes (fat cells).

salivary amylase A digestive enzyme that begins breaking down carbohydrate (starch) in the mouth; other important enzymes during carbohydrate digestion include pancreatic amylase, maltase, sucrase, and lactase.

glycogenesis The process of assembling excess glucose into glycogen in the liver and muscle cells.

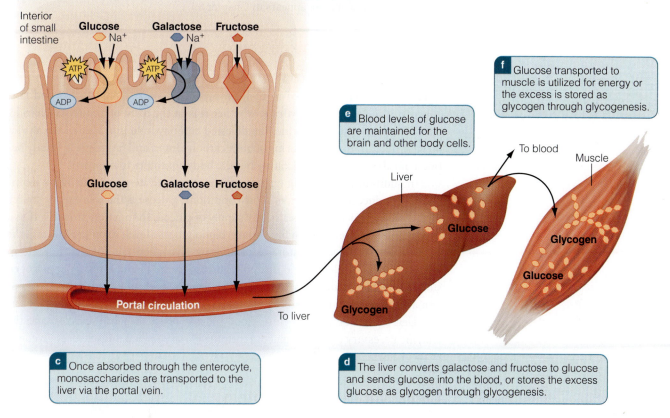

a Glucose and galactose are absorbed by active transport with sodium (Na⁺), ATP, and a carrier protein.

b Fructose is absorbed via facilitated diffusion and a carrier protein.

f Glucose transported to muscle is utilized for energy or the excess is stored as glycogen through glycogenesis.

e Blood levels of glucose are maintained for the brain and other body cells.

Interior of small intestine

Glucose Galactose Fructose
Na⁺   Na⁺

ATP   ATP

ADP   ADP

Glucose   Galactose Fructose

To blood

Muscle

Liver

Glucose

Glycogen

Glucose

Glycogen

Portal circulation

To liver

c Once absorbed through the enterocyte, monosaccharides are transported to the liver via the portal vein.

d The liver converts galactose and fructose to glucose and sends glucose into the blood, or stores the excess glucose as glycogen through glycogenesis.

▲ Figure 4.9 **Absorption and Storage of Monosaccharides**
Glucose and galactose are absorbed into the enterocyte using a different mechanism than fructose. Once transported to the liver, galactose and fructose are converted to glucose, then used for energy or used to raise blood glucose. Excess glucose is stored in the liver and muscle cells as glycogen. The liver glycogen can be used to supply the blood with glucose when the diet is deficient in carbohydrates. Muscle glycogen provides glucose to the muscle cell.

LO 4.2: THE TAKE-HOME MESSAGE Digestion of carbohydrates begins in the mouth, where salivary amylase breaks down starch. Most carbohydrate digestion occurs in the small intestine. Pancreatic and small intestinal enzymes break down the carbohydrates into disaccharides and then monosaccharides so that they can be absorbed. Glucose and galactose are actively absorbed with the help of a sodium-dependent carrier and ATP. Fructose is absorbed by facilitated diffusion. All the monosaccharides are converted to glucose in the liver to be used as energy, or stored as glycogen in the liver and muscle cells. When glycogen stores are full and energy needs have been met, excess glucose is converted to glycerol and fatty acids and stored as fat. Fiber travels to the colon undigested and most of it is eliminated from the body.

What Functions Do Carbohydrates Perform in the Body?

LO 4.3 List the functions of carbohydrates in the body.

Carbohydrates—primarily glucose—provides about half of the energy used by the muscles and other tissues; the rest of the energy you use each day comes mostly from fats. Glucose is the only source of energy used by the red blood cells and the primary fuel source for the brain. For this reason, carbohydrates are the most desirable source of energy for the body. This section briefly describes the overall functions of carbohydrates and the variety of health benefits they provide. (A complete discussion of the metabolism of glucose appears in Chapter 8.)

Carbohydrates Provide Energy and Maintain Blood Glucose Levels

Much of the energy we need to fuel our activities comes from glucose and fats. When you consume carbohydrate, whether it is in the form of a monosaccharide, disaccharide, or polysaccharide, the digested carbohydrate provides 4 kilocalories of energy per gram. Stored forms of both carbohydrates and fats come in handy between meals when you aren't eating but the body continues to need fuel.

In addition to providing energy, eating carbohydrate-rich foods helps maintain blood glucose levels. Under most conditions, glucose is the sole energy source for the brain, which requires a steady supply of glucose to function properly. If you haven't eaten for longer than four hours, blood glucose levels drop too low and the body will tap its glycogen stores by initiating **glycogenolysis** (*lysis* = loosening) to hydrolyze liver glycogen and supply glucose to the blood. Once liver glycogen stores are depleted, the body turns to other sources, such as amino acids from protein and glycerol found in stored fat, to maintain blood glucose. Note that muscle glycogen cannot be used to raise blood glucose levels, because muscles lack the enzyme necessary to release glucose into the blood. Instead, muscle uses glycogen to fuel its own energy needs.

Carbohydrates Spare Protein

Glucose is the body's preferred fuel source, and as long as there is adequate glucose in the blood, protein can be spared for its many other essential functions. In times of carbohydrate deprivation, however, the body turns to noncarbohydrate sources, particularly amino acids (the building blocks of protein, which we will discuss in Chapter 6), to generate glucose. The process of creating glucose from noncarbohydrate sources is called **gluconeogenesis** (*gluco* = sugar/sweet, *neo* = new, *genesis* = origin). Gluconeogenesis primarily occurs in the liver, but can also take place in the kidneys, because these are the only organs that contain the enzymes needed for this process. The kidney is not an active site of gluconeogenesis except after long periods of fasting.

The body does not store extra protein to provide fuel during times of deprivation. Instead, the body dismantles protein from the muscles and organs to generate the needed glucose. While gluconeogenesis can provide needed glucose to the blood, the use of muscle protein can have negative consequences for the body.

Carbohydrates Prevent Ketosis

After about 18 hours of fasting, liver glycogen is depleted and the body will begin to look for other sources, mostly stored fat, to meet the body's energy needs. The by-products of the incomplete breakdown of fat, called **ketone bodies,** are created and spill out into the blood. Most ketone bodies are acids and reduce the pH of the blood, making it slightly acidic. After about two days of fasting, the number of ketone bodies in the blood doubles, which results in an unhealthy state of **ketosis.** If left unchecked, ketosis can increase the acidity in your blood and lead to liver and kidney problems. Individuals who fast or follow strict, low-carbohydrate diets are often in ketosis.

glycogenolysis The hydrolysis of glycogen to release glucose.

gluconeogenesis The creation of glucose from noncarbohydrate sources, predominantly protein.

ketone bodies The by-products of the incomplete breakdown of fat.

ketosis The condition of increased ketone bodies in the blood.

How Do We Maintain Blood Glucose Levels?

LO 4.4 Explain how the body maintains blood glucose levels.

Blood glucose levels are not constant—they rise and fall depending on the body's energy needs. Blood glucose levels also change following a carbohydrate-heavy meal. How does the body regulate blood glucose levels, given these changes in metabolic needs and dietary intake? The answer is: hormones. In fact, two hormones in particular, **insulin** and **glucagon,** secreted from the pancreas, maintain blood glucose levels between 70 and 110 milligrams per deciliter (mg/dl) (**Focus Figure 4.10**). Other hormones, including epinephrine, norepinephrine, cortisol, and growth hormone, also assist in the process.

Insulin Regulates Glucose in the Blood

After eating a carbohydrate-heavy meal, the blood is flooded with glucose, which cannot be used by the cells until it crosses the cell membrane. The high blood glucose levels stimulate the release of insulin from the beta cells of the pancreas. Insulin helps glucose enter cells by attaching to specific receptor sites on the cell membrane, which stimulates an increase in the number of glucose transporters found on the membrane surface. These transporters unlock the cell membrane and transport glucose inside the cell. As soon as glucose enters the cell, insulin stimulates the enzymes that will convert glucose to ATP or store it as glycogen for later use. This role of stimulating the uptake of glucose by the cells is what makes insulin so integral to blood glucose regulation. However, note that liver, kidney, and brain cells can use glucose without the aid of insulin.

In addition to helping glucose enter cells, insulin also helps convert glucose to glycogen if the amount of glucose in the blood exceeds the body's immediate energy needs. It does this by stimulating glycogenesis in both the liver and the muscle, and by inhibiting the enzymes involved in glycogenolysis and gluconeogenesis. The body will store excess glucose as glycogen until it reaches its limit.

When glycogen stores are full, excess glucose may be converted into fatty acids in a process called **lipogenesis.** The method insulin uses to promote lipogenesis is similar to the way it promotes glycogenesis: by increasing the number of glucose receptors on the surface of the fat cell. Insulin also inhibits lipolysis (fat breakdown) by reducing the activity of the enzyme that hydrolyzes stored fat. The result of insulin's actions is that more fat is formed and fewer fatty acids are found in the blood.

insulin The hormone secreted from the beta cells of the pancreas that stimulates the uptake of glucose from the blood into the cells.

Glucagon Regulates Liver Glycogenolysis

Glucagon has the opposite effect of insulin on blood glucose levels: It stimulates release of glucose into the blood (see Focus Figure 4.10). The alpha cells of the pancreas release glucagon into the circulation when blood glucose levels are low—for example, following a protein-rich meal, or during a period of stress. The main

glucagon The hormone secreted from the alpha cells of the pancreas that stimulates glycogenolysis and gluconeogenesis to increase blood levels of glucose.

lipogenesis The process that converts excess glucose into fat for storage.

Hormones Regulate Blood Glucose

Our bodies regulate blood glucose levels within a fairly narrow range to provide adequate glucose to the brain and other cells. Insulin and glucagon are two hormones that play a key role in regulating blood glucose levels.

HIGH BLOOD GLUCOSE

1 **Insulin secretion:** When blood glucose levels increase after a meal, the pancreas secretes the hormone insulin from the beta cells into the bloodstream.

2 **Cellular uptake:** Insulin travels to the tissues where it alters the cell membranes to allow the transport of glucose into the cells by increasing the number of glucose transporters on the cell membrane.

3 **Glucose storage:** Insulin also stimulates the storage of glucose in body tissues. Glucose is stored as glycogen in the liver and muscles (glycogenesis), and is stored as triglycerides in adipose tissue (lipogenesis).

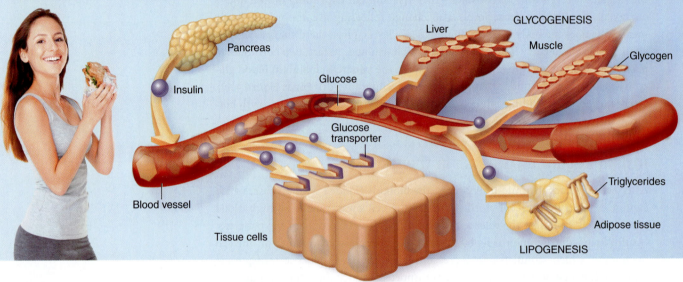

LOW BLOOD GLUCOSE

1 **Glucagon secretion:** When blood glucose levels are low, the pancreas secretes the hormone glucagon from the alpha cells into the bloodstream.

2 **Glycogenolysis:** Glucagon stimulates glycogenolysis in the liver to break down stored glycogen to glucose, which is released into the blood and transported to the cells for energy.

3 **Gluconeogenesis:** Glucagon also activates gluconeogenesis in the liver, stimulating the conversion of glucogenic amino acids to glucose.

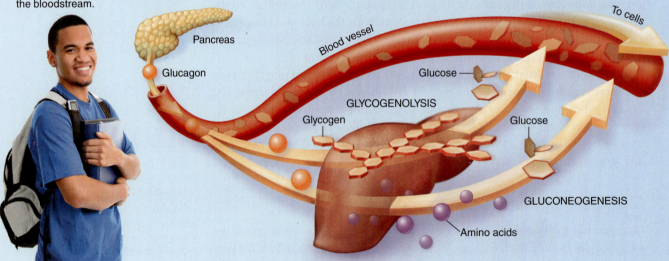

target organ of glucagon is the liver, where it promotes glycogenolysis to release a burst of glucose into the blood. Under the control of glucagon, liver glycogen stores will be depleted after 10 to 18 hours without sufficient dietary carbohydrate.

Glucagon stimulates glucose production by encouraging the uptake of amino acids by the liver. The carbon skeletons of the amino acids are then used to produce glucose through gluconeogenesis. Glucagon also promotes the conversion of lactic acid to glucose through the same process.

Four Other Hormones Help Regulate Glucose Metabolism

In addition to glucagon, other hormones can increase blood glucose levels. **Epinephrine** (also known as adrenaline) and **norepinephrine,** both secreted from the adrenal glands, act on the liver to stimulate glycogenolysis and gluconeogenesis to raise blood glucose. Epinephrine production can increase in the body during periods of emotional and physical stress, such as fear, excitement, and bleeding. For example, if a ferocious dog was chasing you down the street, your body would be pumping out epinephrine to help provide the fuel you need to run. For this reason, epinephrine is also referred to as the "fight-or-flight" hormone.

A low blood glucose level can trigger the release of both epinephrine and norephinephrine. In fact, some of the symptoms that you may experience when your blood glucose level dips too low, such as anxiety, rapid heart beat, turning pale, and shakiness, are caused by the release of both of these hormones.

Two other hormones—**cortisol** and **growth hormone**—also regulate glucose metabolism. Cortisol, often referred to as the stress hormone, stimulates gluconeogenesis and reduces the uptake of glucose by the muscle cells. Both of these actions increase blood glucose levels. Growth hormone has the opposite effect of insulin: It conserves glucose by stimulating fat breakdown for energy, reducing the uptake of glucose by the muscle cells, and increasing glucose production in the liver.

Hypoglycemia Results When Blood Glucose Drops below Normal

For most healthy individuals, when the blood glucose levels drop below normal, the pancreas stops releasing insulin until the blood glucose returns to normal. In some cases, too much insulin is released and causes a lower than normal blood glucose level called **hypoglycemia** (usually less than 70 mg/dl). Individuals who experience hypoglycemia may feel hungry, nervous, dizzy, light-headed, confused, weak, and shaky, and even begin to sweat. Eating or drinking carbohydrate-rich foods, such as hard candies, juice, or soda, will stimulate insulin release and quickly raise the blood glucose level to a normal range (see **Figure 4.11**).[15] More severe reactions to hypoglycemia can cause seizures, coma, and even death.

Though not common, some people may experience bouts of *reactive hypoglycemia* within four hours after a meal. The cause of reactive hypoglycemia is not known, but may relate to the type of food eaten and the timing of the food as it moves through the gastrointestinal tract. Some people may be overly sensitive to epinephrine, which is released when the blood glucose level begins to drop. The hormone glucagon may also play a role. Eating smaller, well-balanced meals throughout the day can help avoid reactive hypoglycemia.

Another type of hypoglycemia, called *fasting hypoglycemia*, can occur in the morning, after overnight fasting. It can also occur during long stretches between meals or after exercise. Some medications, illnesses, certain tumors, hormone imbalances, or drinking too much alcohol may cause this type of hypoglycemia.

epinephrine A hormone produced by the adrenal glands that signals the liver cells to release glucose; also referred to as the "fight-or-flight" hormone.

norepinephrine A hormone produced by the adrenal glands that stimulates glycogenolysis and gluconeogenesis.

cortisol A hormone produced by the adrenal cortex that stimulates gluconeogenesis and lipolysis.

growth hormone A hormone that regulates glucose metabolism by increasing glycogenolysis and lipolysis.

hypoglycemia A blood glucose level that drops to lower than 70 mg/dl.

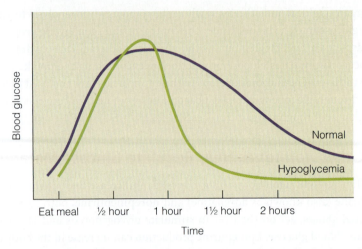

▲ **Figure 4.11 Change in Blood Glucose after Eating a High-Carbohydrate Meal**
An individual with hypoglycemia experiences a more rapid decline in blood glucose after a carbohydrate-rich meal.

LO 4.4: THE TAKE-HOME MESSAGE Blood glucose levels are maintained by two hormones, insulin and glucagon, both secreted from the pancreas. When blood glucose levels rise, insulin is released to stimulate the uptake of glucose by the body cells, including the muscle, lowering blood levels back to normal. When blood glucose levels fall below normal, glucagon is released to stimulate glycogenolysis of liver glycogen, raising blood glucose levels. Epinephrine, norepinephrine, cortisol, and growth hormone also raise blood glucose by stimulating either glycogenolysis or gluconeogenesis. Hypoglycemia or low blood sugar can result from hormone imbalances or the type of food eaten.

Why Is Dietary Fiber So Important for Promoting Health?

LO 4.5 Describe the role of fiber in promoting health.

Even though fiber passes through the GI tract undigested, it can have many powerful positive health effects in the body. As mentioned earlier, fiber has been shown to help prevent constipation and diverticulosis, as well as reduce the risk of obesity, heart disease, cancer, and diabetes.

Fiber Helps Prevent Constipation and Diverticulosis

Over 4 million Americans complain about being constipated, with pregnant women, children, and adults 65 years of age and older experiencing it more often than others.[16] Constipation is usually caused by sluggish muscle contractions in the colon that move stool along too slowly, causing excessive water absorption along the way. This can create hard, dry stools that are more difficult and painful to expel.

A diet plentiful in insoluble fibers such as bran, whole grains, and many fruits and vegetables contributes bulk to the feces, which stretches the circular muscles in the large intestine, thus reducing the transit time in the colon and decreasing the likelihood of constipation. Some soluble fibers, such as psyllium, can also relieve constipation; psyllium's water-attracting capability allows the stool to increase in bulk and form a gel-like, soft texture, which makes it easier to pass.

Dried fruits and nuts are excellent sources of fiber, though nuts can also contribute significantly to fat intake, and should be eaten in moderation.

Chronic constipation can lead to a disorder called **diverticulosis** (*osis* = condition), in which increased pressure in the colon causes weak spots along its wall to bulge out and form pouches called **diverticula** (see **Figure 4.12**). Infection of the diverticula, a condition known as **diverticulitis** (*itis* = inflammation), can lead to stomach pain, fever, nausea, vomiting, cramping, and chills. Approximately 50 percent of Americans aged 60 to 80 and the majority of individuals over 80 years of age have diverticulosis.[17] The best way to prevent both diverticulosis and diverticulitis is to eat a diet that is adequate in fiber.

Fiber Helps Prevent Heart Disease, Diabetes, and Cancer

A diet rich in fiber from whole grains, vegetables, and fruits is important to prevent or treat certain chronic diseases. Let's look at the role that fiber plays in reducing the risk of developing heart disease, diabetes, and cancer.

Heart Disease

Viscous, soluble fibers have been shown to help lower elevated blood cholesterol levels, which may decrease the risk of heart disease. Viscous fiber is believed to interfere with the reabsorption of bile acids in the intestines (**Figure 4.13**). Bile acids are contain cholesterol and are secreted into the intestine by the gallbladder to help with the digestion of fat. The bile acids are likely "grabbed" or sequestered by the fiber before the body can reabsorb them. They end up being excreted along with the fiber in the feces. The liver then removes cholesterol from the blood to replace the bile acids that were lost. Blood cholesterol levels are lowered as a result.

Slow-moving, viscous, soluble fibers may also reduce the rate at which fat and carbohydrates are absorbed from meals. Delayed absorption can lower the surge of fat in the blood after a meal, and may help improve sensitivity to the hormone insulin. Both high levels of fat in the blood and a decreased sensitivity to insulin are considered risk factors for heart disease.

While soluble fibers may decrease the risk for heart disease, insoluble fiber may also promote heart health. Several research studies have shown that cereal and grains, which contain insoluble fiber, may help to lower the risk of heart disease.[18]

Diabetes

Research studies involving both men and women have shown that a higher consumption of fiber from cereals helped reduce the risk of developing certain

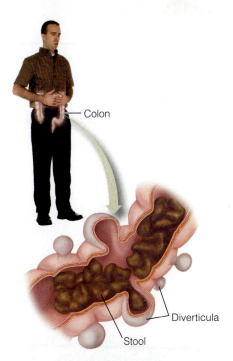

Colon

Diverticula

Stool

▲ **Figure 4.12 Diverticulosis**
Diverticulosis is a condition in which small pouches, or diverticula, bulge out along the colon. When stool gets trapped in these pouches, they can become inflamed, leading to diverticulitis.

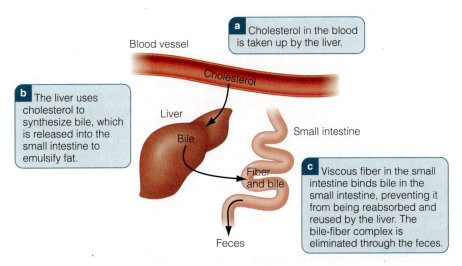

a Cholesterol in the blood is taken up by the liver.

Blood vessel

Cholesterol

b The liver uses cholesterol to synthesize bile, which is released into the small intestine to emulsify fat.

Liver

Bile

Small intestine

Fiber and bile

c Viscous fiber in the small intestine binds bile in the small intestine, preventing it from being reabsorbed and reused by the liver. The bile-fiber complex is eliminated through the feces.

Feces

▲ **Figure 4.13 Dietary Fiber Reduces Blood Cholesterol Levels**
Dietary fiber acts as a bile acid sequestrator, as it binds the bile in the intestinal tract and carries it out in the feces.

diverticulosis The existence of diverticula in the lining of the large intestine or colon.

diverticula Small bulges at weak spots in the colon wall.

diverticulitis Infection of the diverticula.

types of diabetes mellitus.[19] Viscous, soluble fibers have also been shown to help individuals who already have diabetes mellitus manage the condition. Viscous fibers slow the release of food from the stomach, and thus slow down the digestion and absorption of glucose. This could help avoid a large spike in blood glucose after eating and help individuals with diabetes improve the long-term control of their blood glucose level.[20] See Health Connection: What Is Diabetes? on pages 145–151 for a complete discussion of diabetes, its prevalence, control, and prevention.

Cancer

Fiber is thought to have many positive and protective effects in the fight against certain cancers. Fiber from cereals has been shown to help lower the risk of breast cancer.[21] This may be due to fiber's effect on reducing estrogen levels. Research suggests that fiber binds to the estrogen in bile and then eliminates the estrogen in the feces. This leads to lower estrogen levels in the blood. The evidence is not conclusive but it is promising.

Research also suggests that as fiber consumption increases, the incidence of colorectal cancer is reduced.[22, 23] This may be due to the increase in the bulk of stools, which can dilute cancer-promoting substances in the colon. Fiber helps keep things moving through the digestive tract so that potential cancer-promoting substances spend less time in contact with the intestinal lining. Fiber encourages the growth in the colon of friendly bacteria and their fermentation by-products, both of which may have cancer-fighting potential. Because an increased amount of bile acids in the colon is thought to be associated with colon and rectal cancer, fiber's ability to bind and excrete these acids is viewed as a cancer deterrent.[24]

Fiber Helps Prevent Obesity

A fiber-rich diet can be a key factor in the fight against obesity. High-fiber foods, such as whole grains, fruits, and vegetables, can help you feel fuller faster (recall the concept of *satiety* from Chapter 2), helping reduce overall caloric intake. Research studies have shown that obese men and women tend to consume lower amounts of dietary fiber daily than their leaner counterparts. This lends credence to the concept that fiber plays a role in weight management.[25, 26] Some weight-loss diets restrict carbohydrates, but these plans would work better if they *increased* high-fiber carbohydrates. Results of longitudinal studies in women suggest that the intake of dietary fiber, especially whole grains, is a useful dietary tool to control body weight.[27, 28] Similar effects have been observed in men.[29, 30]

A word of caution: Initially, a high-fiber diet can have negative side effects (flatulence and bloating). Consuming too much fiber may cause fluid imbalance or lead to mineral deficiencies by reducing the absorption and increasing the excretion of minerals such as iron and zinc, especially when the diet is low in these minerals or needs have temporarily increased, such as during pregnancy.[31, 32] Gradually increase the fiber in your diet, rather than suddenly adding large amounts. This will allow your body to adjust to the increased amount of fiber and minimize these side effects. See the Table Tips for some easy ways to gradually introduce more fiber into your diet.

> **LO 4.5: THE TAKE-HOME MESSAGE** A diet high in fiber has been found to have numerous health benefits, including reduced risk for constipation, diverticulosis, heart disease, obesity, diabetes, and certain cancers.

The abundant fiber found in beans and legumes will help provide bulk to stool and may help with weight management.

TABLE TIPS
Increasing Daily Fiber Intake

Choose whole-grain breakfast cereals such as shredded wheat, bran flakes, raisin bran, and oatmeal.

Enjoy a lunchtime sandwich made with a whole-wheat pita or 100% whole-grain bread.

Have two pieces of whole fresh fruit daily.

Layer lettuce, tomatoes, or other vegetables on sandwiches.

Include plenty of root vegetables, such as carrots, turnips, and potatoes, at lunch and dinner.

whole grains Grain foods that are made with the entire edible grain kernel: the bran, the endosperm, and the germ.

What Are the Recommendations for Carbohydrate Intake and What Are the Best Food Sources?

LO 4.6 Describe the guidelines for carbohydrate intake and list best food sources.

The body needs a minimum amount of carbohydrate daily to support brain and nerve function and to efficiently meet its energy needs. The latest Dietary Reference Intakes (DRIs) for carbohydrates recommend that adults and children consume a minimum of 130 grams of carbohydrate daily. This is based on the estimated minimum amount of glucose the brain needs to function efficiently. Though this may seem high, 130 grams is less than the amount found in the recommended daily servings for each food group in MyPlate, that is, six servings from the grain group, three servings each from the vegetable and dairy groups, and two servings from the fruit group.

In the United States, most adults consume well over the minimum DRI. Adult males consume, on average, over 300 grams of carbohydrates daily, whereas adult females eat over 200 grams daily.

The AMDR for carbohydrates is 45 to 65 percent of total daily kilocalories (see Chapter 2). Adults in the United States consume at least 50 percent of their kilocalories from carbohydrate-rich foods, so they are easily within this optimal range. Practice calculating the carbohydrate content of your diet in the Calculation Corner.

For fiber, the current DRIs recommend 14 grams of fiber for every 1,000 kilocalories consumed. The AI for fiber is 25 to 38 grams per day for adults, which is based on the amount needed to protect them from developing cardiovascular disease (see **Table 4.2**). Adults in the United States fall short of these recommendations and currently consume only about 12 to 18 grams per day. Thus, whereas most Americans consume an adequate amount of carbohydrate overall, they are getting less than the AI for dietary fiber, on average.

Whole Plant Foods and Dairy Products Are Good Sources of Carbohydrates

The DRIs indicate the minimum amount of carbohydrate that individuals should consume daily, but it's important to note that all carbohydrates are not created equal, and some carbohydrate-rich foods are nutritionally better than others. Whole, intact foods, including grains, fruits, vegetables, and beans, deliver vitamins, minerals, fiber, and a host of phytochemicals. Refined, high-carbohydrate foods lack these nutrients and contain considerably higher amounts of kilocalories than others, which can lead to weight gain. Eating high-sugar foods that don't contain many other nutrients will provide kilocalories but not much else. If the high-carbohydrate foods are high in saturated fat, they can also be unhealthy for the heart. Therefore, the best food choices for meeting carbohydrate requirements include a range of nutrient-dense, low-saturated-fat foods, with low to moderate amounts of simple carbohydrates and higher amounts of fiber and other complex carbohydrates.

Whole Grains

Whole grains (but not refined grains) are abundant in complex carbohydrates, including starch and dietary fiber, and they are an important staple in the diet. Moreover, whole grains are associated with a reduced risk of several chronic diseases.[33, 34] In view of these potential health benefits, MyPlate recommends three servings per day of whole grains. Currently, Americans are consuming less than one serving of grains per day, most of which are refined rather than whole grains.[35] Select whole-grain breads

Calculation Corner

Daily Carbohydrate Intake

(a) Adam needs to eat approximately 4,000 kilocalories (kcals) daily to maintain his current weight, given his age, gender, height, weight, and activity level. Calculate how many kcals of carbohydrate Adam should eat each day to meet the AMDR.

$$4,000 \text{ (kcals)} \times 0.45 = 1,800 \text{ (kcals)}$$
$$4,000 \text{ (kcals)} \times 0.65 = 2,600 \text{ (kcals)}$$

Answer: If Adam ate between 1,800 and 2,600 kilocalories of carbohydrate each day, he would meet the AMDR for carbohydrates.

(b) How many grams of carbohydrate should Adam eat to equal 45 to 65 percent of his total kilocalories?

$$1,800 \text{ kcals} \div 4 \text{ kcals/gram} = 450 \text{ grams}$$
$$2,600 \text{ kcals} \div 4 \text{ kcals/gram} = 650 \text{ grams}$$

Answer: Adam should eat between 450 and 650 grams of carbohydrate each day.

(c) Would this intake of carbohydrate meet the minimum suggested intake?

Answer: Yes; Adam needs a minimum of 130 grams of carbohydrate.

Scan this QR code with your mobile device to access practice math activities. You can also access the activities in MasteringNutrition™.

TABLE 4.2	What Are Your Fiber Needs?	
	Grams of Fiber Daily*	
	Males	*Females*
14 through 18 years old	38	26
19 through 50 years old	38	25
51 through 70+ years old	30	21
Pregnancy		28
Lactation		29

*Based on an Adequate Intake (AI) for fiber.

Data from Institute of Medicine, *Dietary Reference Intakes for Energy, Carbohydrate, Fiber, Fat, Fatty Acids, Cholesterol, Protein, and Amino Acids* (Washington, DC: The National Academies Press, 2005).

Choosing whole-grain rather than refined-grain products, such as quinoa, provides more nutrition, including fiber, per bite.

A kernel of wheat

a

Bran
• High fiber
• B vitamins
• Phytochemicals
• Minerals

Germ
• Vitamin E
• Healthy unsaturated fats
• Antioxidants
• Phytochemicals
• Minerals
• B vitamins

Endosperm
• Starch
• Protein
• B vitamins

b Whole kernel used

c Only endosperm used

d Only endosperm used

Whole-Wheat Flour

Enriched Wheat Flour

Folic acid, thiamin, niacin, riboflavin, and iron added

Wheat Flour (not enriched)

Missing ingredients:
• Folic acid

Missing ingredients:
• Bran (fiber)
• Phytochemicals
• Calcium
• Vitamin E
• Heart-healthy fats
• Antioxidants

Missing ingredients:
• Bran (fiber)
• Phytochemicals
• Calcium
• Vitamin E
• Heart-healthy fats
• Antioxidants
• Folic acid
• Thiamin
• Niacin
• Riboflavin
• Iron

▲ **Figure 4.14 From Wheat Kernel to Flour**
(a) The wheat grain kernel has three parts: bran, germ, and endosperm. **(b)** Whole-wheat flour is made using the entire grain kernel. It is not enriched. **(c)** Enriched wheat flour doesn't contain the bran and germ, so it is missing nutrients and phytochemicals. Some nutrients, including folic acid, thiamin, niacin, riboflavin, and iron, are added back to the flour during an enrichment process. **(d)** Wheat flour that is not enriched lacks not only the bran and germ, but also many nutrients and phytochemicals.

and cereals that have at least 2 to 3 grams of total fiber per serving, such as whole-wheat (or whole-grain) bread, bulgur, brown rice, and whole-grain pasta. Increase your dietary fiber intake with a variety of ancient whole grains including quinoa, teff, amaranth, and sorghum that all contain at least 6 grams of total fiber per serving.

What is a whole grain and why is it important? Before processing, a kernel of a grain, such as wheat or oats, includes three edible parts: the **bran**, the **endosperm**, and the **germ** (**Figure 4.14**). Whole-grain foods contain all three parts of the grain.

bran The indigestible outer shell of the grain kernel.

endosperm The starchy inner portion of a cereal grain.

germ The vitamin-rich embryo, or seed, of a grain.

The grain kernel in **refined grains,** such as are found in wheat or white bread and white rice, goes through a milling process that strips out the bran and germ, leaving only the endosperm of the kernel in the end product. As a result, some, though not all, of the B vitamins, iron, phytochemicals, and dietary fiber are removed. Refining also improves the digestibility of the carbohydrate in the endosperm, resulting in a more rapid rise in blood glucose and an increased demand for insulin.[36]

To restore some of the nutrition lost from refined grains, **enriched grains** have folic acid, thiamin, niacin, riboflavin, and iron added back after the milling process. This improves their nutritional quality somewhat, but the fiber and the phytochemicals are lost.

Whole grains are potential disease-fighting allies in the diet. As little as one serving of whole grains daily may help lower the risk of dying from heart disease[37] or cancer,[38] reduce the risk of stroke,[39] improve intestinal health,[40] and improve body weight.[41] Several research studies have also shown that the fiber in whole grains may help reduce the risk of diabetes.[42] Because whole grains are abundant with vitamins, minerals, fiber, and phytochemicals, it is uncertain which substances are the disease-fighting heroes or if some or all of them work in a complementary fashion to provide the protection. Try the suggestions in the Table Tips to increase your intake of tasty and nutritious whole grains.

Low-Fat and Fat-Free Dairy Products

Milk and milk products, including cheese and yogurt, contain 1 to 17 grams of lactose per serving. Choose low-fat or fat-free dairy products whenever possible, for the sake of heart health. The lactose content is the same regardless of the fat content.

Fruits and Vegetables

Whole fruits, 100 percent fruit juices, and vegetables are naturally good sources of both simple and complex carbohydrates. The flesh of fruit is also rich in simple sugars, including fructose and glucose. Though you can also get simple sugars from processed foods and sweets, the higher kilocalorie and lower nutrient levels in these foods make them a less healthy option. The skins of many fruits contain the fiber cellulose, so eating an unpeeled fruit is preferable to eating a peeled fruit. Another type of fiber, pectin, is found in the flesh of fruit, and makes up about 15 to 30 percent of the fiber in fruit. Fruit overall contains about 2 grams of dietary fiber per serving.

When selecting fruit, fresh or frozen versions will provide more nutrients than canned versions, which lose some vitamins and minerals during processing. If canned fruit is the only option, be sure the product is packed in fruit juice, rather than heavy syrup, to cut down on added sugar and kilocalories.

Vegetables contain abundant amounts of complex carbohydrates, including starch and fiber. In general, starchy vegetables, such as corn and potatoes, contain more carbohydrate per serving than nonstarchy vegetables like green beans or carrots (**Figure 4.15**). Overall, a serving of vegetables contains approximately 2 grams of soluble and insoluble fiber. As with fruit, many vegetable skins are an excellent source of fiber, so consuming edible skins whenever possible will also increase fiber intake.

Legumes, Nuts, and Seeds

Legumes, such as black beans and peas, are a rich source of starch and dietary fiber (**Figure 4.16**). Legumes provide an average of 4 grams of fiber per serving, about half of which is in the form of hemicellulose.

Nuts and seeds contain very little starch but are good sources of fiber. Nuts provide over 1 gram of fiber in a half ounce or small handful. A half ounce of nuts is about 15 peanuts, 7 walnut halves, or 24 shelled pistachios.

TABLE TIPS

Ways to Enjoy Whole Grains

Choose whole-grain cereal such as shredded wheat, bran flakes, raisin bran, or oatmeal in the morning.

Combine a 100% whole-wheat English muffin and low-fat Cheddar cheese for a hearty breakfast cheese melt.

Enjoy your lunchtime sandwich made with a whole-wheat pita or 100% whole-grain bread.

Try instant brown rice for a quick whole grain at dinner.

Snack on popcorn or 100% whole-wheat crackers for a high-fiber filler in the afternoon.

---

refined grains Grain foods that are made with only the endosperm of the kernel. The bran and germ have been removed during milling.

enriched grains Refined grain foods that have folic acid, thiamin, niacin, riboflavin, and iron added.

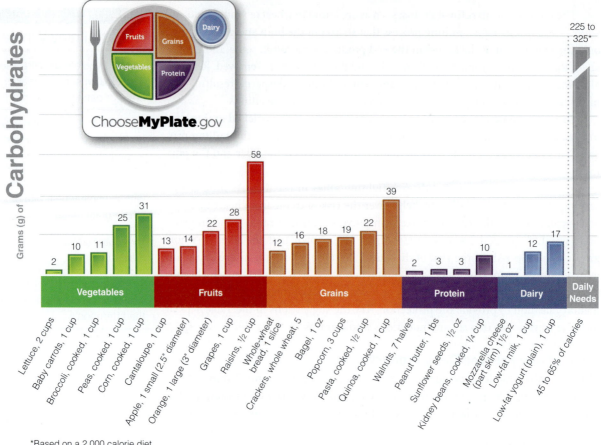

*Based on a 2,000 calorie diet

▲ **Figure 4.15 Food Sources of Carbohydrates**
Eating the minimum recommended servings from the grains, vegetables, fruits, and dairy groups will meet the need to consume 130 grams of carbohydrate daily.

▶ **Figure 4.16 Food Sources of Fiber**
Adults need to consume about 25 to 38 grams of fiber daily.

Source: Data from J. Anderson and S. Bridges. 1988. "Dietary Fiber Content of Selected Foods." *American Journal of Clinical Nutrition* 47: 440–447. USDA *National Nutrient Database for Standard Reference, Release 25*. Available at www.ars.usda.gov.

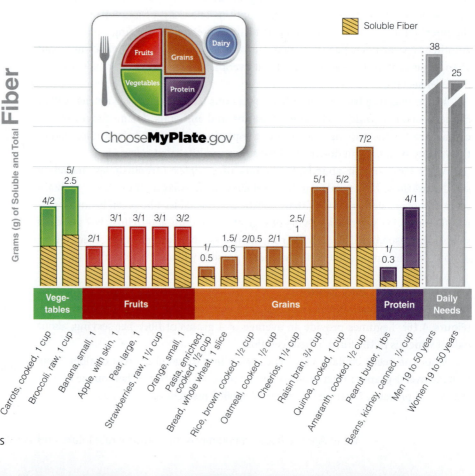

a

Nutrition Facts
Serving Size 1 cup (30.0g)

Amount Per Serving

Calories 120   Calories from Fat 9

	% Daily Value*
Total Fat 1.0g	2%
Saturated Fat 0.2g	1%
Trans Fat 0.0g	
Polyunsaturated Fat 0.2g	
Monounsaturated Fat 0.5g	
Cholesterol 0mg	0%
Sodium 190mg	8%
Total Carbohydrates 26.5g	9%
Dietary Fiber 1.2g	5%
Sugars 13.0g	
Protein 1.0g	
Vitamin A	0%
Vitamin C	10%
Calcium	10%
Iron	25%

* Based on a 2,000 calorie diet.

b

Nutrition Facts
Serving Size ½ cup (30g)
Servings Per Container about 15

Amount Per Serving	Fiber One Cereal	with ½ cup skim milk
Calories	60	100
Calories from Fat	10	10
	% Daily Value*	
Total Fat 1g	1%	2%
Saturated Fat 0g	0%	0%
Trans Fat 0g		
Polyunsaturated Fat 0g		
Monounsaturated Fat 0g		
Cholesterol 0mg	0%	1%
Sodium 105mg	4%	7%
Potassium 180mg	5%	11%
Total Carbohydrate 25g	8%	10%
Dietary Fiber 14g	57%	57%
Soluble Fiber 1g		
Sugars 0g		
Other Carbohydrates 11g		
Protein 2g		
Vitamin A	0%	
Vitamin C	10%	
Calcium	10%	
Iron	25%	

* Based on a 2,000 calorie diet.

◀ **Figure 4.17 Dietary Fiber Content of Breakfast Cereals**
Nutrition labels list total carbohydrates, dietary fiber, and sugars per serving. Compare the two breakfast cereal labels. Which cereal provides more than 50 percent of the DV for fiber in just one serving? Which cereal is higher in sugar content per serving?

Packaged Foods Can Be Good Sources of Carbohydrates

Packaged and processed foods, such as ready-to-eat cereals and baked crackers, can be good sources of starch and fiber, but can also contain high amounts of added sugar (which we'll discuss in depth later in this chapter), fat, kilocalories, and salt, and should generally be consumed in moderation. When selecting packaged foods, choose products that contain at least two grams of dietary fiber per serving, and be aware of the amounts of added sugar, fat, and total kilocalories. If you're buying snack items, aim for the baked, whole-grain crackers or low-fat pita bread rather than the box of cookies or doughnuts. The amount of total carbohydrates, including starch, dietary fiber, and sugars, in a packaged food is listed on the nutrition label (see **Figure 4.17**).

Glycemic Index and Glycemic Load Can Be Used for Meal Planning

The fat and fiber content of a food lowers the effect the carbohydrates have on blood glucose levels. This is often referred to as the glycemic index and may be beneficial for meal planning.

The terms **glycemic index (GI)** and **glycemic load (GL)** have been used to classify the effects of carbohydrate-containing foods on blood glucose and may be potentially helpful for those with diabetes. The GI refers to the measured upward rise, peak, and eventual fall of blood glucose following the consumption of a high-carbohydrate food. Some foods cause a sharp spike and rapid fall in blood glucose

glycemic index (GI) A rating scale of the likelihood of foods to increase the levels of blood glucose and insulin.

glycemic load (GL) The amount of carbohydrate in a food multiplied by the amount of the glycemic index of that food.

Foods	GI*
Rice, low amylose	126
Potato, baked	121
Cornflakes	119
Jelly beans	114
Green peas	107
Cheerios	106
Puffed wheat	105
Bagel, plain	103
White bread	100
Angel food cake	95
Ice cream	87
Bran muffin	85
Rice, long grain†	80
Brown rice	79
Oatmeal	79
Popcorn	79
Corn	78
Banana, overripe	74
Chocolate	70
Baked beans	69
Sponge cake	66
Pear, canned in juice	63
Custard	61
Spaghetti	59
Rice, long grain‡	58
Apple	52
Pear	47
Banana, underripe	43
Kidney beans	42
Whole milk	39
Peanuts	21

*GI = Glycemic Index

†Boiled for 25 minutes.

‡Boiled for 5 minutes.

▲ **Figure 4.18 The Glycemic Index of Commonly Eaten Foods**
The glycemic index is a ranking of foods that indicates their potential to raise insulin and glucose levels in the blood.

naturally occurring sugars Sugars such as fructose and lactose that are found naturally in foods.

added sugars Sugars that are added to processed foods and sweets.

empty calories Kilocalories that provide little nutrition, such as those found in candy.

levels; others cause less of a spike and a more gradual decline. The index ranks foods according to their effect on blood glucose levels compared with that of an equal amount of white bread or pure glucose (**Figure 4.18**).

A problem with using the GI is that it doesn't take into account the amount of carbohydrate consumed. For example, two slices of white bread usually weighs about 60 grams, which would be over 5 cups of puffed wheat cereal, an amount that is unlikely to be eaten in one sitting. The glycemic load (GL) adjusts the GI to take into account the amount of carbohydrate consumed in a typical serving of a food, and in the case of puffed wheat cereal, the normal portion size has a dramatically lower effect on blood glucose.

The usefulness of the GI for disease prevention or weight management is controversial. Research suggests that high–glycemic index foods do not raise blood glucose levels as rapidly as once believed. In fact, blood glucose levels peak at about the same level regardless of the source of the carbohydrate.[43] Following the dietary recommendations to increase the consumption of whole plant foods will result in an intake of lower GI and GL foods.

LO 4.6: THE TAKE-HOME MESSAGE Fresh fruits and vegetables, whole grains, legumes, and low-fat dairy products are the best food sources of carbohydrates. Whole grains, fruits, vegetables, legumes, nuts, and seeds are excellent sources of fiber. Packaged foods can be a good source of starch and fiber, but nutrition labels should be read carefully to avoid consuming too much added sugar, fat, or kilocalories. Foods with a low glycemic index and glycemic load may be useful for meal planning.

What Is the Difference between Natural Sugars, Added Sugars, and Sugar Substitutes?

LO 4.7 Describe the differences between natural sugars, added sugars, and alternative sweeteners used as sugar substitutes.

Finding the taste of sweet foods pleasurable is an innate response. You don't have to fight this taste for sweetness. A modest amount of sweet foods can easily be part of a well-balanced diet. However, some sources of sugar provide more nutrition than others.

Your taste buds can't distinguish between **naturally occurring sugars,** like the fructose and lactose found in fruit and dairy products, and **added sugars,** which are added by manufacturers to foods such as soda or candy. From a nutritional standpoint, however, there is a big difference between these sugar sources.

Foods with Natural Sugars Generally Provide More Nutrients for Fewer Kilocalories

Foods that contain naturally occurring sugar tend to be nutrient dense and thus provide more nutrition per serving. In contrast, foods that contain a lot of added sugar tend to provide high amounts of kilocalories but little else. The kilocalories in sugar-laden foods are often called **empty calories** because they provide so little nutrition.

Many fruits are among the most naturally sweet foods available. Just one bite into a ripe peach or navel orange will confirm that fruit can contain more than 15 percent sugar by weight. There are many nutritional advantages of satisfying a sweet tooth with fruit, such as a whole orange, rather than with sweets that have added sugar, such as a package of candy orange slices. Let's compare these two snacks (**Figure 4.19**).

For the 65 kilocalories in six slices of a navel orange, you get more than 100 percent of the daily value for vitamin C, and 3.5 grams of fiber, which is more than 10 percent of the amount of fiber that many adults should consume daily. These juicy slices of orange also provide fluid. In fact, *over 85 percent* of the weight of an orange is water. The hefty amounts of fiber and water make the orange a sweet snack that provides bulk. This bulk can increase satiety and reduce the likelihood that you'll need to eat a second or third orange to feel satisfied. Eating fruit not only meets the urge for something sweet but reduces the risk of overeating.

In contrast, for the 300 kilocalories found in six candy orange slices, you'll get about 19 teaspoons of added sugar and little else. Although the candy is quite energy dense, it provides no fiber and only negligible amounts of water, and it contains a concentrated amount of kilocalories in relationship to the volume of food in the serving. You wouldn't likely feel satiated after consuming six candy orange slices. To consume close to the 300 kilocalories found in the six pieces of candy, you would have to eat more than four oranges. It would be easier to overeat candy orange slices than fresh oranges.

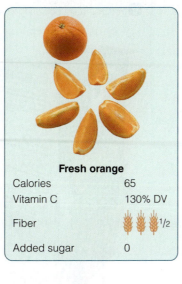

Fresh orange

Calories	65
Vitamin C	130% DV
Fiber	🌾🌾🌾½
Added sugar	0

Candy orange

Calories	300
Vitamin C	0% DV
Fiber	0
Added sugar	

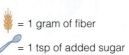
🌾 = 1 gram of fiber
🥄 = 1 tsp of added sugar

▲ **Figure 4.19 Slices of an Orange versus Orange Slices**
A fresh orange provides more nutrients for fewer kilocalories, and without any added sugars, compared with candy orange slices.

Added Sugars Are Used during Food Processing

Sugars are added to foods for many reasons. In baked goods, they can hold onto water, which helps keep the product moist, and they help turn pastries a golden brown color. Sugars function as preservatives and thickeners in foods such as sauces. Fermenting sugars in dough produce the carbon dioxide that makes yeast breads rise. And of course, sugars make foods taste sweet. In the last decade, Americans' consumption of soda has decreased but that of sugar-laden sports and energy drinks tripled from 4 percent to 12 percent.[44]

While sucrose and fructose are the most common added sugars in our foods, sugars can appear on the food label under numerous different names (see **Figure 4.20**). To find the amount and type of added sugars in a food, read the ingredients list. If added sugars appear first or second on the list, or if the product contains many varieties of added sugars, it is likely high in sugar. Note, for example, that the ingredient label from the box of low-fat chocolate chip granola bars lists added sugars ten different times!

The Nutrition Facts panel that is currently used on food labels doesn't distinguish between naturally occurring and added sugars. For example, the nutrition labels on a box of raisin bran and a carton of milk list 21 grams of sugars for raisin bran and 12 grams for low-fat milk. This can be misleading, as the grams of sugars listed for the raisin bran include both the amount of naturally occurring sugars from the raisins and the sugars added to sweeten the cereal. For the milk, the sugar listed on the Nutrition Facts panel is just the naturally occurring sugar, lactose. With the growing concern about the rising levels of added sugars in the diets of Americans, various health professionals and organizations have pressured the FDA to require that all *added* sugars be disclosed on the food label. A final decision by the FDA is pending.

a Sugar can be called a number of different names on ingredient lists and labels.

Corn sweetener   Corn syrup
Dextrose   Sucrose   Brown sugar
Fructose   Lactose   Honey   Syrup
High-fructose corn syrup
Fruit juice concentrate
Invert sugar   Raw sugar
Malt syrup   Maltose
Molasses

Ingredients: Granola (whole grain rolled oats, sugar, rice flour, whole grain rolled wheat, partially hydrogenated soybean and cottonseed oils* with TBHQ and citric acid added to preserve freshness and/or sunflower oil with natural tocopherol added to preserve freshness, whole wheat flour, molasses, sodium bicarbonate, soy lecithin, caramel color, barley malt, salt, nonfat dry milk), corn syrup, crisp rice (rice, sugar, salt, barley malt), semisweet chocolate chunks (sugar, chocolate liquor, cocoa butter, soy lecithin, vanillin [an artificial flavor]), sugar, corn syrup solids, glycerin, high fructose corn syrup, partially hydrogenated soybean and/or cottonseed oil*, sorbitol, fructose, calcium carbonate, natural and artificial flavors, salt, soy lecithin, molasses, water, BHT (a preservative), citric acid.

* Adds a dietarily insignificant amount of *trans* fat.

b You can also look on the Nutrition Facts panel to see the total grams of sugar.

Nutrition Facts
Serving Size 1 Bar (24g)
Servings Per Container 10

Amount Per Serving

Calories 90	Calories from Fat 20

	% Daily Value*
Total Fat 2g	3%
Saturated Fat 0.5g	3%
Trans Fat 0g	
Sodium 80mg	3%
Total Carbohydrate 19g	6%
Dietary Fiber 1g	3%
Sugars 7g	
Protein 1g	

Calcium	8%	•	Iron	4%

Not a significant source of Cholesterol, Vitamin A, Vitamin C

* Percent Daily Values are based on a 2,000 calorie diet. Your Daily Values may be higher or lower depending on your calorie needs:

	Calories:	2,000	2,500
Total Fat	Less than	65g	80g
Sat Fat	Less than	20g	25g
Cholesterol	Less than	300mg	300mg
Sodium	Less than	2,400mg	2,400mg
Total Carbohydrate		300g	375g
Dietary Fiber		25g	30g

▲ **Figure 4.20 Finding Added Sugars on the Label**
A food is likely to contain a large amount of sugar if added sugars appear first or second on the ingredients list and/or if there are many varieties of added sugars listed.

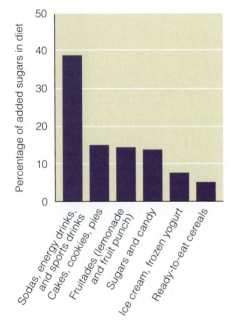

▲ **Figure 4.21 Where Are All the Added Sugars Coming From?**
Sodas, energy drinks, and sports drinks are collectively the number-one source of added sugars in the diets of Americans.
Source: *Dietary Guidelines for Americans, 2010.*

Americans don't eat the majority of the added sugars in their diets—they drink them (see **Figure 4.21**). The number-one source of added sugars in the United States is sweetened soft drinks, energy drinks, and sports drinks. Sugar-sweetened beverages have been implicated in many health-related problems, including obesity.[45] See Examining the Evidence: Do Sugar-Sweetened Beverages Cause Obesity? for more information on the relationship of body weight and the consumption of sugar-sweetened beverages. Review the Table Tips for ideas on ways to cut down your consumption of added sugars.

TABLE TIPS

Lowering Consumption of Added Sugars

Mix chocolate milk with an equal amount of regular low-fat milk.

Mix equal amounts of sweetened cereal with an unsweetened variety for a breakfast cereal with half the added sugar.

Drink water rather than soda or sweetened beverages throughout the day.

Buy sweets such as candy and cookies packaged in individual serving sizes rather than in large packages. The less you buy, the less you'll eat.

Mix an ounce of 100% fruit juice with 10 ounces of sparkling water for a no-sugar-added "fruit" drink.

Do Sugar-Sweetened Beverages Cause Obesity?

The evidence is overwhelming: the United States is becoming an obese nation. Recent estimates suggest that more than 66 million adult Americans and 12.5 million American children are obese.[1] Although there are many factors that contribute to this, health professionals note that this rise in obesity coincides with an increase in consumption of sugar-sweetened beverages, at least among children, who drink more sugary beverages than they do milk.[2] This observation has prompted some policy makers to propose new limits to soda purchases. To reverse this obesity epidemic, should the focus be placed squarely on sugar-sweetened beverages as the culprit?

Consumption of Sugar-Sweetened Beverages in the United States

Every day, 50 percent of Americans consume some form of sugary drinks equivalent to about one 12-ounce soda.[3] The top sugar-sweetened beverages reported include soda, fruit drinks, tea, coffee, energy and sports drinks, and flavored milks. Consuming one of any of these beverages adds about 180 additional kilocalories to a person's daily intake.[4] The larger the sweetened beverage, the more added sugars (see **Figure 1**). A classic (and rare) 8-ounce bottle of cola provides almost 7 teaspoons of added sugars. In today's vending machine, you are more likely to find a 12-ounce can or a 20-ounce bottle. Because people typically consume the entire can or bottle, regardless of its size, they consume more sugar.

The consumption patterns shown in **Table 1** suggest that males consume more of their total kilocalories per day from sugar-sweetened beverages than do females, and both genders reduce consumption of sugary beverages as they age.

The good news is that the overall consumption of sugar-sweetened soda is declining.[5] Yet while Americans are drinking fewer sodas, they have almost tripled their consumption of sugar-sweetened sports/energy drinks,[6] which makes sugar-sweetened beverages the single largest source of added sugar in the U.S. diet. Regardless of whether Americans are drinking more soda or sports or energy drinks, do these beverages contribute to our expanded waistlines?

The Theories of Sugar-Sweetened Drink Consumption and Weight Gain

A couple of theories have been proposed to explain the possible connection between weight gain and our consumption of sugar-sweetened beverages. One theory suggests that the additional

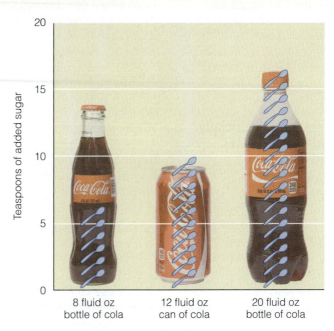

▲ **Figure 1 The Many Sizes of Soft Drinks**
A single soda can provide from 6 to 17 teaspoons of added sugars, depending upon the size of the container.

Table 1	Consumption Patterns of Sugar-Sweetened Beverages			
Gender	Age	Teaspoons*	Kilocalories**	% of Total Kcals per Day
Males	12–19	18.4	294	11.6
	20–39	18.1	289	10.3
	40–59	12.6	202	7.7
	>60	5.9	94	4.6
Females	12–19	12.1	194	10.5
	20–39	10.8	173	9.3
	40–59	7.7	123	6.9
	>60	3.8	60	4.0

*teaspoons of sugar consumed per day from sugar-sweetened beverages

**total kilocalories consumed per day from sugar-sweetened beverages

Adapted from P. E. Miller, et al. 2013. "Sugar-Sweetened Beverage Consumption in the U.S.: Novel Assessment Methodology." *American Journal of Preventive Medicine* 45(4):416–421.

kilocalories consumed in the sweetened beverages leads to excess overall kilocalorie intake and thus weight gain. The second theory is that sugar in liquid form increases our appetite, leading to an increased consumption of kilocalories from other foods. Research exploring both of these theories has yielded some interesting results.

Sugar-Sweetened, Artificially Sweetened Drinks, Water, and Weight Gain

There is evidence that adding kilocalories to your daily intake by drinking sugar-sweetened beverages adds body weight. For example, normal-weight adults who drank one additional 12-ounce sugar-sweetened beverage each day gained an average of one extra pound every four years compared with people who did not add an extra beverage.[7] This research suggests that simply ingesting additional kilocalories through sugar-sweetened beverages is enough to contribute to weight gain. What if we replaced sugar-sweetened drinks with artificially sweetened beverages without kilocalories?

In children at least, the research is promising. Results from the Double-Blind, Randomized Intervention Study in Kids (DRINK) suggests that when the sugar in the beverage was replaced with sucralose, healthy children lost weight, mostly due to loss of body fat.[8] Other studies contradict these results and report that artificially sweetened beverages, such as diet soda, result in weight gain, not weight loss. Data from a 10-year longitudinal study reported that adults who drank two or more diet sodas a day increased their waist size by six times more than those who did not drink diet sodas.[9] Another study found no effect on weight gain in individuals using sweetened cocoa versus sugar-free cocoa.[10] Thus, the relationship between sugar-sweetened beverages versus artificially sweetened beverages on weight gain is still unclear.

If the increase in kilocalories from sugary beverage consumption indeed causes weight gain, perhaps the best alternative is to switch from sugary drinks to kilocalorie-free water. It appears that adults gain less weight over time when they switch from sugar-sweetened beverages to water.[11] However, to add to the confusion, published reviews suggest that switching to plain water had no effect overall on body weight.[12]

Sugar-Sweetened Beverages May Impact Satiation

Perhaps the answer lies in the second theory, that consuming sugar-sweetened beverages increases appetite or results in feeling less satisfied. Most beverages are sweetened with high-fructose corn syrup or sucrose, and most people who sweeten their coffee or tea do so with table sugar (sucrose). What links sucrose and high-fructose corn syrup is that both sweeteners contain fructose. Some researchers have suggested that it is the fructose component of these sweeteners that may change our appetite-control mechanisms, resulting in less satiation and a greater intake of kilocalories from other foods.[13] This theory is based on earlier studies conducted with pure crystalline fructose, which reported that fructose ingestion resulted in a decrease in the hormones insulin and leptin.[14] Both of these hormones increase satiety. Whereas glucose stimulates insulin production, thus increasing satiety, fructose alone does not stimulate insulin production.

This is significant in that the release of insulin in turn stimulates the release of leptin, a hormone that decreases appetite.[15] These two hormones also suppress the release of ghrelin, another hormone that stimulates our appetite (see Chapter 15 for more information on hormones and satiety).[16] If insulin is reduced, as would be the case with pure fructose as a sweetener, then leptin is reduced and ghrelin is not suppressed, which leads to feeling hungry and eating

more kilocalories. The flaw in this theory is that we rarely consume pure fructose in our diet. This monosaccharide is consumed as part of the disaccharide sucrose or as high-fructose corn syrup, which is about 50 percent fructose and 50 percent glucose.[17]

If sugar-sweetened beverages do increase hunger, research subjects would report a decrease in satiety and an increase in kilocalorie intake compared with artificially sweetened drinks. A recent study showed that sugary beverages sweetened with either sucrose or high-fructose corn syrup versus artificially sweetened drinks had similar satiety ratings.[18] Not only were the satiety ratings the same, but the sugar-sweetened beverage did not increase the amount of food eaten later in the day when compared with an artificially sweetened beverage. This data would suggest that substituting sugar-sweetened beverages with artificially sweetened beverages isn't the answer to the obesity problem. However, the effect of drinking sugary beverages on increasing body weight has also been reported. Six hundred forty-one children were given either an 8-ounce sugar-sweetened beverage containing 104 kilocalories or an 8-ounce artificially sweetened beverage with zero kilocalories each day in school. After 18 months, the students who drank the sugar-sweetened beverage gained more weight and accumulated more body fat than did those who drank the artificially sweetened beverages.[19]

Not all beverages have to be sweetened with sucrose or artificial sweeteners. Using whey protein as a sweetener has shown some promise in reducing hunger and kilocalorie intake. A recent study tested this theory in normal-weight and overweight females.[20] Subjects were given beverages sweetened with glucose, whey protein, or whey protein plus glucose after an overnight fast. Their blood glucose and appetite were measured nine times for up to 2 hours following ingestion of the sweetened beverage. The kilocalorie intake was measured at a meal 3 hours after drinking the sweetened beverage. The results reported that the whey protein and whey protein plus glucose reduced the rise in blood glucose and reduced appetite and kilocalorie intake compared with glucose in both groups.

The Bottom Line: Do Sugar-Sweetened Beverages Cause Obesity?

Obesity is the result of a combination of factors, including total kilocalories consumed, genetics, and physical inactivity. Currently, whereas there are some well-designed double-blind studies, most of the studies are observational and of short duration. Based on the current type of studies available, there is no conclusive evidence that sugar-sweetened drinks *alone* contribute more to obesity than do other energy sources.

Although sugar-sweetened beverages may or may not be the main culprit in the dramatic rise in obesity, they play a significant role in Americans' overall increased caloric intake. A recent study reported that over a four-year period, weight gain in adults was mostly associated with the intake of potato chips, potatoes, sugar-sweetened beverages, red meat, and processed meats, in that order.[21] Weight gain was inversely related to the ingestion of vegetables, whole grains, fruits, nuts, and yogurt. Sugar-sweetened beverages, including soda, fruit drinks, flavored milks, sports/energy drinks, and sweetened tea or coffee, add unnecessary kilocalories and could be responsible for weight gain.[22] However, one single dietary factor is unlikely to be the sole cause of obesity. It is more likely a combination of increased energy intake from all foods and beverages, lack of physical activity, and genetics.

The DRI recommends reducing all refined sugars, whether in beverages or foods. The "eat less and exercise more" approach may be the best strategy for reversing the obesity epidemic in the United States, including drinking fewer sugar-sweetened beverages.

References

1. Centers for Disease Control. 2013. *Adult Obesity Facts*. Available at www.cdc.gov. Accessed February 2014.
2. T. Sherman. 2013. *Examining New York City's Proposed Ban on Sugar-Sweetened Fountain Drink Sizes Greater than 16 Ounces*. Available at https://blogs.commons.georgetown.edu. Accessed February 2014.
3. C. L. Ogden, B. K. Kit, M. D. Carroll, and S. Park. 2011. "Consumption of Sugar Drinks in the United States, 2005–2008." *NCHS Data Brief* 2011:1–8.
4. E. Han and L. M. Powell. 2013. "Consumption Patterns of Sugar-Sweetened Beverages in the United States." *Journal of the Academy of Nutrition and Dietetics* 113(1):43–53.
5. P. E. Miller, R. A. McKinnon, S. M. Krebs-Smith, et al. 2013. "Sugar-Sweetened Beverage Consumption in the U.S.: Novel Assessment Methodology." *American Journal of Preventive Medicine* 45(4):416–421.
6. Ibid.
7. D. Mozaffarian, T. Hao, E. B. Rimm, W. C. Willett, and F. B. Hu. 2011. "Changes in Diet and Lifestyle and Long-Term Weight Gain in Men and Women." *New England Journal of Medicine* 364(25):2392–2404.
8. J. C. de Ruyter, M. R. Olthof, J. C. Seidell, and M. B. Katan. 2012. "A Trial of Sugar-Free or Sugar-Sweetened Beverages and Body Weight in Children." *New England Journal of Medicine* 367:1397–1406.
9. S. P. Fowler, K. Williams, and H. P. Hazuda. 2011. "Diet Soft Drink Consumption is Associated with Increased Waist Circumference in the San Antonio Longitudinal Study of Aging." *Diabetes Pro*. Available at http://professional.diabetes.org. Accessed February 2014.
10. V. Y. Njike, Z. Faridi, K. Shuval, et al. 2011. "Effects of Sugar-Sweetened and Sugar-Free Cocoa on Endothelial Function in Overweight Adults." *International Journal of Cardiology* 149(1):83–88.
11. A. Pan, V. S. Malik, T. Hao, W. C. Willett, D. Mozaffarian, and F. B. Hu. 2013. "Changes in Water and Beverage Intake and Long-Term Weight Changes: Results from Three Prospective Cohort Studies." *International Journal of Obesity* 37(10):1378–1385.
12. R. Muckelbauer, G. Sarganas, A. Grüneis, and J. Müller-Nordhorn. 2013.

13. K. A. Page, O. Chan, J. Arora, R. Belfort-Deaguiar, J. Szuira, B. Roehmholdt, G. W. Cline, et al. 2013. "Effects of Fructose vs. Glucose on Regional Cerebral Blood Flow in Brain Regions Involved with Appetite and Reward Pathways." *Journal of the American Medical Association* 309(1):63–70.
14. G. A. Bray, S. J. Nielsen, and B. M. Popkin. 2004. "Consumption of High-Fructose Corn Syrup in Beverages May Play a Role in the Epidemic of Obesity." *American Journal of Clinical Nutrition* 79(4):537–543.
15. H. Schloegl, R. Percik, A. Horstmann, A. Villringer, and M. Stumvoll. 2011. "Peptide Hormones Regulating Appetite—Focus on Neuroimaging Studies in Humans." *Diabetes Metabolism Research and Reviews* 27(2):104–112.
16. Ibid.
17. J. M. Rippe. 2013. "The Metabolic and Endocrine Response and Health Implications of Consuming Sugar-Sweetened Beverages: Findings from Recent Randomized Controlled Trials." *Advanced Nutrition* 4:677–686.
18. J. C. de Ruyter, M. B. Katan, L. D. J. Kuijper, D. G. Liem, and M. R. Olthof. 2013. "The Effect of Sugar-Free versus Sugar-Sweetened Beverages on Satiety, Liking and Wanting: An 18-Month Randomized Double-Blind Trial in Children." *PLoS ONE* 8(10):e78039. doi:10.1371/journal.pone.0078039.
19. J. C. de Ruyter et al. 2012. "A Trial of Sugar-Free or Sugar-Sweetened Beverages and Body Weight in Children."
20. T. A. Zafar, C. Waslien, A. AlRaefaei, N. Alrashidi, and E. AlMahmoud. 2013. "Whey Protein–Sweetened Beverages Reduce Glycemic and Appetite Responses and Food Intake in Young Females." *Nutrition Research* 33(4):303–310.
21. D. Mozaffarian, et al. 2011. "Changes in Diet and Lifestyle and Long-Term Weight Gain in Men and Women."
22. F. B. Hu. 2013. "Resolved: There Is Sufficient Scientific Evidence that Decreasing Sugar-Sweetened Beverage Consumption Will Reduce the Prevalence of Obesity and Obesity-Related Diseases." *Obesity Review* 14(8):606–619.

"Association between Water Consumption and Body Weight Outcomes: A Systematic Review." *American Journal of Clinical Nutrition* 98:282–299.

Sugar Can Cause Dental Carries

Carbohydrates play a role in tooth decay. Sugars and starches contribute to **dental caries** because sugar is a readily available food source for the bacteria in the mouth. As the bacteria grow, they produce acids that erode the enamel of the teeth. The stickier the carbohydrate, the longer it is in contact with the teeth and the more opportunity there is for the bacteria to produce their damaging acids. Hence, hard candies that dissolve slowly in the mouth or dried fruits that can adhere to the teeth are potentially more harmful than foods that are quickly swallowed, such as whole fruits and vegetables. To avoid increased risk of dental caries, sugary snacks should be kept to a minimum, and whole fruits and raw vegetables should be chosen over candies or pastries as snacks.

Some foods may actually help reduce the risk of acid attacks on teeth. For example, chewing sugarless gum encourages the production of saliva and provides a postmeal bath for your teeth.

Sugar Substitutes Add Sweetness but Not Kilocalories

Because most people perceive eating too much sugar as unhealthy, food manufacturers often use artificially created **sugar substitutes** to provide the sweet taste of sugar for fewer kilocalories, and Americans' consumption of these products has increased steadily over the last two decades (see **Figure 4.22**). All sugar substitutes must be approved by the FDA and deemed safe for consumption before they are allowed in food products sold in the United States.

Several sugar substitutes are presently available to consumers, including polyols, saccharin, aspartame, acesulfame-K, sucralose, rebaudioside A, and neotame. Alitame and cyclamate are two other sugar substitutes that are not yet approved for use in the United States, but are on the horizon. Polyols don't promote dental caries, and they cause a slower rise in blood glucose than sugar. Saccharin, aspartame, acesulfame-K, sucralose, and neotame also don't promote dental caries and have the added advantage of not affecting blood glucose levels at all. These sugar substitutes are a plus for people with diabetes, who have a more challenging time managing their blood glucose levels. Additionally, all sugar substitutes are either

A variety of sugar substitutes are available to consumers.

dental caries Tooth decay.

sugar substitutes Alternatives to table sugar that sweeten foods for fewer kilocalories.

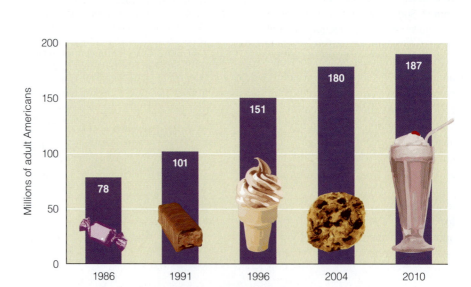

▲ **Figure 4.22 Growing Interest in Sugar-Free Foods and Beverages**
The use of sugar-free products has more than doubled since 1986.
Source: Calorie Control Council, "Trends and Statistics." Copyright © 2012 by Calorie Control Council. Reprinted with permission.

TABLE 4.3   Oh So Sweet!

Sweetener	Kilocalories/Gram	Trade Names	Sweetening Power	The Facts
Sucrose	4.0	Table sugar	—	Sweetens food, enhances flavor, tenderizes, and contributes browning properties to baked goods
Reduced-Kilocalorie Sweeteners				
Polyols (Sugar Alcohols)				
Sorbitol	2.6	Sorbitol	50% to 70% as sweet as sucrose	Found in foods such as sugarless chewing gum, jams, baked goods, and candy
Mannitol	1.6	Mannitol	50% to 70% as sweet as sucrose	Found in foods such as chewing gum, jams, and as a bulking agent in powdered foods. May cause diarrhea.
Xylitol	2.4	Xylitol	Equally sweet as sucrose	Found in foods such as chewing gum, candies; also in pharmaceuticals and hygiene products
Hydrogenated Starch Hydrolysates (HSH)	3.0	HSH	50% to 70% as sweet as sucrose	Found in confections and can be used as a bulking agent
Kilocalorie-Free Sweeteners				
Saccharin	0	Sweet'N Low	200% to 700% sweeter than sucrose	Retains its sweetening power at high temperatures such as baking
Aspartame	4.0*	NutraSweet, Equal	Approximately 200% sweeter than sucrose	Sweetening power is reduced at high temperatures such as baking. Can be added at end stages of recipes such as cooked puddings if removed from heat source. Individuals with PKU need to monitor all dietary sources of phenylalanine, including aspartame.
Acesulfame-K	0	Sunette	200% sweeter than sucrose	Retains its sweetening power at high temperatures
Sucralose	0	Splenda	600% sweeter than sucrose	Retains its sweetening power at high temperatures
Rebaudioside A	0	Truvia, Sun Crystals, PureVia	200% sweeter than sucrose	Retains its sweetening power at high temperatures
Tagalose	1.5	Naturlose	92% as sweet as sugar	Texture and taste similar to sucrose
Neotame	0	Neotame	7,000% to 13,000% sweeter than sucrose	Retains its sweetening power at high temperatures

*Because so little aspartame is needed to sweeten foods, it provides negligible kilocalories.

reduced in kilocalories or are kilocalorie free. See **Table 4.3** for a comparison of available sweeteners.

Saccharin

Consumers today often associate saccharin with the pink packets found on restaurant tables, but it's been in use for more than a century. In 1977, the FDA banned saccharin due to reports from the research community that it could cause bladder cancer in rats. Congress immediately implemented an 18-month moratorium on

Foods and beverages that contain aspartame must carry a label warning that phenylalanine is present.

this ban through the Saccharin Study and Labeling Act. This allowed the continued commercial use of saccharin, but required that any saccharin-containing products bear a warning label stating that saccharin was potentially hazardous to health as it caused cancer in laboratory animals.

In 2000, the National Toxicology Program (NTP) removed saccharin from the list of substances that could potentially cause cancer. After extensive review, the NTP determined that the observed bladder tumors in rats were actually from a mechanism that wasn't relevant to humans.[46] The lesson learned from this is that you can safely consume saccharin in moderation.

Aspartame

In 1965, a scientist named James Schlatter was conducting research on amino acids in his quest to find a treatment for ulcers. To pick up a piece of paper in his laboratory, he licked his finger—and stumbled upon a sweet-tasting compound.[47] It was the "lick" that was soon to be "tasted" around the world. Schlatter had just discovered aspartame, a substance that has become one of the most-used sugar substitutes in the world.

Aspartame is composed of two amino acids: a modified aspartic acid and phenylalanine. Enzymes in the digestive tract break down aspartame into its component parts and the amino acids are absorbed, providing 4 kilocalories per gram. Because aspartame is 200 times sweeter than sucrose, only a small amount is needed to sweeten a food.

In 1981, the FDA approved aspartame for use in tabletop sweeteners, such as Equal and NutraSweet, and to sweeten breakfast cereals, chewing gums, and carbonated beverages. The majority of the aspartame that is consumed in the United States is in soft drinks. In 1996, the FDA gave the food industry carte blanche to use aspartame in all types of foods and beverages. It is currently used as a sweetener in over 100 countries, and can now be found in over 6,000 foods, pharmaceuticals, and personal care products sold in the United States.

Aspartame has undergone continual, vigorous reviews to ensure that it is safe for human consumption. Despite its intense evaluation, aspartame has been, and still is, blamed for ailments ranging from headaches to Gulf War Syndrome. Major health organizations such as the Academy of Nutrition and Dietetics, the American Medical Association, and the American Diabetes Association all support aspartame's use by healthy adults, children, and pregnant women in moderation as part of a well-balanced diet.[48]

Individuals with a rare inherited disorder known as phenylketonuria (PKU) are unable to metabolize phenylalanine, one of the amino acids in aspartame, and must adhere to a special diet. Because of the seriousness of this disorder, the FDA mandates that all food products that contain phenylalanine carry a label declaring its content.

LO 4.7: THE TAKE-HOME MESSAGE Your taste buds can't distinguish between naturally occurring and added sugars. Foods with naturally occurring sugars, such as whole fruit, tend to provide more nutrition and satiation than empty-calorie sweets such as candy. Numerous names for sugar are found on food labels, and soft drinks are the number-one contributor of added sugars to Americans' diets. Millions of Americans consume reduced-kilocalorie or kilocalorie-free sugar substitutes. The FDA has approved polyols, saccharin, aspartame, acesulfame-K, sucralose, rebaudioside A, tagalose, and neotame to be used in a variety of foods. These sugar substitutes add sweetness to your food without the added kilocalories, do not promote dental caries, and can benefit those with diabetes who need to carefully manage their blood glucose.

What Is Diabetes?

LO 4.8 Describe the cause, symptoms, and treatment for different classifications of diabetes.

Diabetes mellitus, or *diabetes*, is a condition related to inadequate regulation of blood glucose. An estimated 25.8 million Americans—more than 8 percent of the population—have diabetes.[49] Of these individuals, 7 million have the disease, but don't know it yet. The incidence of adults being diagnosed with diabetes in the United States has more than doubled since the early 1990s. According to the CDC, if this trend continues, it is likely that one-third of Americans will develop diabetes in their lifetime, reducing their life expectancy, on average, by 10 to 15 years.[50]

The number of people who have diabetes is not only strikingly high; it's rising, particularly among children. Whereas the most prevalent form of diabetes, known as type 2, used to be common only in adults, in the last couple of decades there's been a steady increase among those under age 20. Approximately 215,000 people under the age of 20, or 0.26 percent, were diagnosed with diabetes in the year 2010.

Over 200,000 Americans die from diabetic complications annually, and diabetes is the seventh leading cause of death in the United States. Diabetes is not only a deadly disease, but also an extremely costly one. Disability insurance payments, time lost from employment, and the medical costs associated with diabetes cost more than $170 billion annually in the United States.[51, 52] This is an epidemic that is spiraling out of control.[53, 54]

Diabetes Types and Risk Factors

There are different types of diabetes, but they all result from the inability of the body to make or properly use the hormone insulin. Insulin directs glucose into the cells to be used as immediate energy or stored for later use. Diabetes develops when individuals either produce an inadequate amount of insulin and/or develop **insulin resistance,** such that their cells do not respond to the insulin when it arrives. In either case, the bloodstream is flooded with glucose that can't get into the cells. When this happens, the body shifts into fasting mode. The liver begins the process of breaking down its glycogen stores (glycogenolysis) and making glucose from noncarbohydrate sources (gluconeogenesis) in an attempt to provide glucose to the cells. This floods the blood with even more glucose. Eventually, the level of glucose builds up in the blood and some of it spills over into the urine.

At the same time, the body has called on its energy reserve—fat—to be used as fuel. The body needs glucose in order to thoroughly burn fat; otherwise, it makes ketone bodies. In poorly managed diabetes, when glucose is unable to get into the cells, acidic ketone bodies build up in the blood to dangerous levels, causing **ketoacidosis.** Diabetic ketoacidosis can cause nausea and confusion, and if left untreated, could result in coma or death. (Note: Ketoacidosis occurs when insulin is lacking in the body, and is different from the condition of ketosis, which can develop in individuals who are fasting or consuming a low-carbohydrate diet; unlike diabetic ketoacidosis, ketosis is not life-threatening.)

All forms of diabetes involve insulin and unregulated blood glucose levels. Some are due to insulin resistance and others are due to a lack of insulin production. Still another version occurs only during pregnancy, called gestational diabetes. The most prevalent types of diabetes are type 1 and type 2 (**Focus Figure 4.23**).

Type 1 Diabetes

Type 1 diabetes is considered an autoimmune disease and is the rarer of the two main forms.[55] This form of diabetes usually begins in childhood or the early adult years and is found in 5 percent of all diagnosed cases in the United States.[56] The immune

diabetes mellitus A medical condition whereby an individual either doesn't have enough insulin or is resistant to the insulin available, resulting in a rise in blood glucose levels. Diabetes mellitus is often called diabetes.

insulin resistance The inability of the cells to respond to insulin.

ketoacidosis The buildup of ketone bodies in the blood to dangerous levels, which can result in coma or death.

type 1 diabetes Autoimmune form of diabetes in which the pancreas does not produce insulin.

Supreme Court Justice Sonia Sotomayor has type 1 diabetes and maintains good control by injecting insulin, monitoring her blood glucose levels, and following a proper diet.

Diabetes is a chronic disease in which the body can no longer regulate glucose within normal limits, and blood glucose becomes dangerously high.

NORMAL

1 Liver releases glucose into bloodstream.

2 The cells of the pancreas release insulin into bloodstream.

3 Insulin stimulates uptake of glucose into cells.

4 As glucose is taken into interior of cells, less glucose remains in the bloodstream.

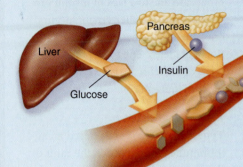

Pancreas

Liver

Insulin

Glucose

Insulin

Glucose transporter

Glucose

TYPE 1 DIABETES

1 Liver releases glucose into bloodstream.

2 The cells of the pancreas are damaged or destroyed. Little or no insulin is released into bloodstream.

3 In the absence of insulin, glucose is not taken up by cells.

4 High levels of glucose remain in the bloodstream.

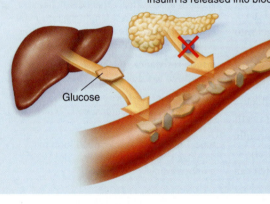

Glucose

TYPE 2 DIABETES

1 Liver releases glucose into bloodstream.

2 The cells of the pancreas release insulin into bloodstream.

3 Insulin is present, but cells fail to respond adequately. Progressively higher amounts of insulin must be produced to stimulate cells to uptake glucose.

4 High levels of glucose remain in the bloodstream.

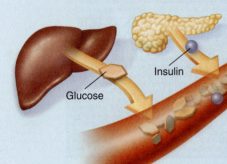

Insulin

Glucose

Insulin

system in people with type 1 diabetes destroys the insulin-producing cells in the pancreas. An obsessive, uncontrollable thirst, excessive urination, and a strong desire to eat are common symptoms associated with undiagnosed or untreated diabetes. Other common symptoms are constant blurred vision, hunger, weight loss, and fatigue, because the glucose can't get into the cells of the body. Once they have been diagnosed, individuals with type 1 diabetes must monitor their glucose levels and inject insulin every day in order to avoid these symptoms.

The hormone insulin is a protein and is digestible by the GI tract, so it can't be taken orally. Therefore, most individuals have to inject insulin directly into their fat or muscle tissue with a syringe.

Researchers are continually testing alternative, non-needle methods for those with diabetes to self-administer insulin. Insulin pens, insulin jet injectors, and insulin pumps are among the devices becoming available.

Type 2 Diabetes

Type 2 diabetes is more common than type 1, accounting for 90 to 95 percent of diagnoses of the disease. Being overweight increases the risk of developing type 2 diabetes.[57] People with type 2 diabetes initially produce insulin but have become insulin resistant. The insulin resistance prompts the pancreas to overproduce insulin in order to compensate. After several years of exhausting the insulin-producing cells in the pancreas, the

production of insulin may decrease to the point where a person with type 2 diabetes may have to take medication and/or inject insulin to manage his or her blood glucose level.

One of the major problems with type 2 diabetes is that this condition can go undiagnosed for some time. Some people may have symptoms such as fatigue, blurred vision, and increased thirst and urination; others may not have any symptoms at all. Consequently, diabetes can damage a person's vital organs without their being aware of it. Because of this, the American Diabetes Association (ADA) recommends that everyone 45 years of age and older

type 2 diabetes Form of diabetes characterized by insulin resistance.

Self-Assessment

Are You at Risk for Type 2 Diabetes?

Take the following quiz to assess if you are at risk for developing type 2 diabetes. Whereas this list contains the presently known risk factors for type 2 diabetes, there may be others. If you have questions or doubts, check with your doctor.

Do you have a body mass index (BMI) of 25 or higher*?

Yes ☐ **No** ☐

If you answered "no," you don't need to continue. If you answered "yes," continue.

1. Does your mom, dad, brother, or sister have diabetes?
   Yes ☐ **No** ☐

2. Do you typically exercise for less than 30 minutes daily?
   Yes ☐ **No** ☐

3. Are you of African-American, Alaskan Native, Native American, Asian-American, Hispanic, or Pacific Islander-American descent?
   Yes ☐ **No** ☐

4. Have you ever delivered a baby that weighed more than 9 pounds at birth?
   Yes ☐ **No** ☐

5. Have you ever had diabetes during pregnancy?
   Yes ☐ **No** ☐

6. Do you have a blood pressure of 140/90 millimeters of mercury (mmHg) or higher?
   Yes ☐ **No** ☐

7. Have you been told by your doctor that you have too much triglyceride (fat) in your blood (more than 250 mg/dl) or too little of the "good" HDL cholesterol (less than 35 mg/dl)?
   Yes ☐ **No** ☐

8. Have you ever had blood glucose test results that were higher than normal?
   Yes ☐ **No** ☐

9. Have you ever been told that you have vascular disease or problems with your blood vessels?
   Yes ☐ **No** ☐

10. Do you have metabolic syndrome**?
    Yes ☐ **No** ☐

Answers

If you are overweight and answered "yes" to any of the above 10 questions, you could benefit from speaking with your doctor.

*BMI is a measure of your weight in relationship to your height. See Chapter 14 for a chart to determine your BMI.

**Metabolic syndrome is a cluster of symptoms including elevated blood glucose and lipids, high blood pressure, and obesity. This disorder increases the risk of diabetes as well as of heart disease and stroke.

undergo testing for diabetes every three years. However, people who are overweight or obese, or who are genetically predisposed shouldn't wait until age 45 to be tested. Overweight children should be screened when they turn 10 years old and repeat the screening every two years. (See the Self-Assessment to determine whether you are at risk for type 2 diabetes.)

One predictor of type 2 diabetes is a disorder called metabolic syndrome, which is associated with insulin resistance. A cluster of symptoms found in cardiovascular disease, including elevated fasting blood glucose and blood lipids, high blood pressure, and obesity, characterizes this syndrome. The same risk factors of metabolic syndrome, such as eating a poor diet, obesity, and lack of exercise, are also risk factors for type 2 diabetes. In fact, a diagnosis of metabolic syndrome often precedes a diagnosis of type 2 diabetes.[58]

Prediabetes

A simple blood test at a physician's office can reveal if a person's blood glucose is higher than normal and whether he or she has **impaired glucose tolerance,** or *prediabetes*. The blood is typically drawn first thing in the morning after fasting overnight for 8 to 12 hours. A fasting blood glucose level of under 100 milligrams per deciliter (mg/dl) is considered "negative," and a fasting blood glucose of 126 mg/dl or higher is considered a "positive" test for diabetes (**Table 4.4**). A reading between

100 mg/dl and 126 mg/dl is classified as prediabetes. Individuals with prediabetes have a blood glucose level that is higher than it should be but not yet high enough to be classified as diabetic. About 79 million Americans over the age of 20 have prediabetes and are at a higher risk of developing not only diabetes, but also heart disease.[59] When a person is in this prediabetic state, damage may already be occurring to the heart and circulatory system. The approach to treating individuals with prediabetes is illustrated in the Nutrition in Practice on page 149.

Gestational Diabetes

Gestational diabetes is a form of diabetes that may develop during pregnancy in women who have not been diagnosed as diabetic prior to the pregnancy. The cause of gestational diabetes is the ineffectiveness of insulin, most likely due to the influence of pregnancy-related hormones.

Blood glucose levels are screened throughout the pregnancy in women diagnosed with gestational diabetes. If blood glucose levels are controlled through a healthy diet and physical activity, there is no detrimental effect on the mother or the fetus. Uncontrolled blood glucose levels can increase the risk of a larger newborn baby, and may require cesarean section rather than a natural birth.

The good news is that gestational diabetes is temporary. However, the risk of the mother developing type 2 diabetes later in life is increased.[60]

Diabetes Can Result in Long-Term Damage

Constant exposure to high blood glucose levels can damage vital organs over time. Diabetes, especially if it is poorly managed, increases the likelihood of a multitude of health effects such as nerve damage, leg and foot amputations, eye diseases, blindness, tooth loss, gum problems, kidney disease, and heart disease.[61]

Nerve damage occurs in an estimated 50 percent of individuals with diabetes, and the longer the person has diabetes, the greater the risk of damage.[62] Numbness in the toes, feet, legs, and hands, as well as changes in bowel, bladder, and sexual function are all signs of damage to nerves. This nerve damage can affect the ability to feel a change in temperature or pain in the legs and feet. A cut or sore on the foot could go unnoticed until it becomes infected. The poor blood circulation common in persons with diabetes can also make it harder for sores or infections to heal. Over time, an infection can infiltrate the bone, causing the need for an amputation.

Diabetes can also damage the tiny blood vessels in the retina of the eye, which can cause bleeding and cloudy vision, and eventually destroy the retina and cause blindness. A high blood glucose level can cause tooth and gum problems, including the loss of teeth, and damage to the kidneys. If the kidneys are damaged, protein can leak into the urine and, at the same time, cause a backup of wastes in the blood. Kidney failure could result.

impaired glucose tolerance A condition whereby a fasting blood glucose level is higher than normal, but not high enough to be classified as having diabetes mellitus. Also called *prediabetes*.

gestational diabetes Form of diabetes that may develop during pregnancy in women who were not previously diagnosed with diabetes.

TABLE 4.4	Interpreting Blood Glucose Levels
If a Fasting Blood Glucose Level Is	**It Means That the Level Is Considered**
<100 mg/dl	Normal
100 to 125 mg/dl	Prediabetic
126 mg/dl*	Diabetic

*There must be two "positive" tests, done on separate days, for an official diagnosis of diabetes.

Data from the American Diabetes Association. 2012. "Diagnosis and Classification of Diabetes Mellitus." *Diabetes Care* 35:S64–S71.

Nutrition in Practice: Brendan

Brendan is a math professor. His annual physical at the campus health center uncovered that his blood glucose levels classified him as having "prediabetes." According to his doctor, his blood glucose levels are higher than ideal but not high enough to be diagnosed as having full-fledged diabetes. Because his father and grandfather both developed diabetes later in their lives, the doctor explained that his family history and excess weight put Brendan at a higher risk for developing type 2 diabetes. Brendan's limited physical activity consists of parking his car in the faculty lot and walking less than one block to his office.

Brendan's doctor refers him to the campus Registered Dietitian Nutritionist for an appointment. Brendan is dreading meeting with the dietitian because as a bachelor, he doesn't enjoy cooking and is concerned that his diet of takeout foods, along with his sedentary lifestyle, is about to end. The dietitian meets with Brendan to discuss his diet and lifestyle habits and their effect on his blood glucose levels.

Brendan's Stats:
- Age: 45
- Height: 6 feet 1 inch
- Weight: 230 pounds
- BMI: 30
- Fasting Blood Glucose: 124 mg/dl

Brendan's Food Log

Food/Beverage	Time Consumed	Hunger Rating*	Location
Doughnut and coffee with cream	8:30 AM	2	Coffee shop
Hamburger, fries, and cola	1 PM	5	Fast-food eatery
Chocolate bar	4 PM	4	Vending machine in faculty lounge
Fried chicken, mashed potatoes, corn	6:30 PM	4	Picked up from supermarket takeout. Consumed at home.
Ice cream	9 PM	1	Home, watching TV

*Hunger Rating (1–5): 1 = not hungry; 5 = super hungry.

Critical Thinking Questions

1. How does Brendan's weight contribute to his elevated blood glucose levels?
2. What foods/beverages could be contributing to Brendan's weight and blood glucose levels and why?
3. How could increasing Brendan's daily physical activity improve his blood glucose levels and why?

Dietitian's Observation and Plan for Brendan:

- Discuss the need to lose weight. A weight loss of as little as 5 to 7 percent of a person's body weight can reduce the cells' resistance to insulin. This enables glucose to be taken up by the cells and improve his blood glucose levels.
- Increase his dietary fiber. Fiber has been shown to improve insulin sensitivity, or the use of insulin by the cells.
- Plan a well-balanced, kilocalorie-reducing diet that includes fruits, vegetables, whole grains, legumes, and low-fat dairy, along with some lean protein and healthy oils, to promote weight loss of approximately ½ to 1 pound weekly. Provide him with healthier choices when dining out and purchasing takeout foods.
- Increase physical activity to at least 2.5 hours weekly. Exercise improves the cells' sensitivity to insulin and lowers blood glucose levels.

Two weeks later, Brendan visits the dietitian again and is excited that he has lost 2 pounds. He is parking his car in a parking lot that is five blocks from his office so he walks more every day. A review of his food record shows that his diet is still too low in vegetables and fruit. The dietitian works with Brendan to increase his produce not only at meals but also as snacks. They also discuss ways that Brendan can walk during the day on campus to increase his daily physical activity.

Diabetes is a risk factor for heart disease. The excess amount of lipids often seen in the blood in poorly managed diabetes is likely an important factor in this increased risk. Fortunately, good nutrition habits play a key role in both the prevention and management of diabetes.[63]

Control Is Key

People with diabetes can manage the disease by keeping their blood glucose level under control. Some people with type 2 may be able to do this through diet and exercise alone. Others may also need to incorporate insulin injections or other medications. People with type 1 diabetes must inject insulin to control their blood glucose level. Maintaining a healthy level of blood glucose through these means, along with monitoring blood sugar levels and routinely visiting health care professionals, can slow the onset of some of the complications of diabetes. **Table 4.5** lists the dietary recommendations necessary to control blood glucose.

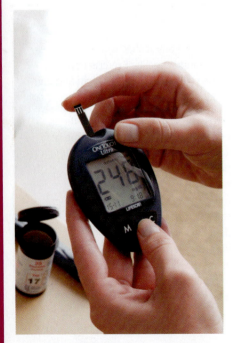

Individuals with diabetes must regularly monitor blood glucose levels using portable blood glucose monitors like this one.

TABLE 4.5 Dietary Recommendations for Diabetes

- Carbohydrate intake and monounsaturated fat together should provide 60 to 70 percent of total daily energy intake.
- Foods containing soluble fiber, such as oats and bran, should be part of a healthy plan to lower blood glucose and cholesterol.
- Dietary cholesterol should be less than 300 mg per day; if LDL cholesterol levels are high, dietary cholesterol should be lowered to not more than 200 mg per day.
- Saturated fat intake should be less than 10 percent of total daily energy intake or less than 7 percent if evidence of heart disease is present.
- Polyunsaturated fat should be less than 10 percent of total daily energy intake.
- Whole grains, fruits, vegetables, and low-fat milk should be consumed as part of a healthy diet.
- Sugars do not need to be eliminated but should be eaten in moderation as part of a healthy diet.
- Protein intake of 15 to 20 percent of total daily energy intake is sufficient if kidney function is normal.
- The total amount of carbohydrate in meals or snacks is more important than the source or type.
- Vitamin and mineral supplements are not necessary to prevent or treat diabetes.
- Moderate alcohol consumption (1 drink per day for adult women, and 2 drinks for adult men) is considered safe for people with diabetes.

Data from the American Diabetes Association. 2004. "Nutrition Principles and Recommendations in Diabetes." *Diabetes Care* 27:S36–S46.

The nutrition and lifestyle goals for individuals with type 1 or type 2 diabetes are the same: to minimize the complications of diabetes by adopting a healthy, well-balanced diet and participating in regular physical activity that maintains blood glucose levels in a normal or close-to-normal range.

Eat a Balanced Diet

Individuals diagnosed with diabetes should consume a combination of predominantly high-fiber carbohydrates from whole grains, fruits, and vegetables, along with low-fat milk, adequate amounts of lean protein, and unsaturated fats.[64] This diabetic diet translates into eating a moderate amount of foods that are rich in nutrients plus maintaining regular mealtimes.

The glycemic index can be a useful tool for diabetics to select carbohydrate foods; however, a less confusing approach to blood glucose control is to follow the current guidelines suggested by the American Diabetes Association (refer to Table 2) and using food exchange groups. As you may recall from Chapter 2, the exchange system organizes foods together by

their carbohydrate, fat, and protein content. One exchange has about the same amount of each macronutrient per serving, as well as the same effect on blood glucose, as all the foods listed in the same group. For example, you could trade ⅓ cup of pasta for one slice of whole-grain bread and ingest 15 grams of carbohydrate, 0–3 grams of protein, 0–1 gram of fat, and 80 kilocalories. See Appendix C for the lists of foods by exchange group.

Although sugar has a high glycemic index and was once thought of as a "diabetic no-no," it can now be part of a diabetic's diet. Research has found that eating sucrose doesn't cause a greater rise in a person's blood glucose level than starch does, so avoidance of sugar isn't necessary. However, because weight management is often a concern, especially for those with type 2 diabetes, there's little room for sweets and treats in a diabetic diet (or *anyone's* diet, for that matter).

Be sure to read food labels for the number of kilocalories from fat, fiber, and sugar content per serving. The nutrition facts panel also provides Daily Values (DV) to illustrate the percentage

Exercise improves the control of blood glucose.

of nutrients provided by one serving of the food. Remember that the DV is based on 2,000 kilocalories, which may be more than most diabetics need. Also, the servings on food labels may not be equivalent to the exchange lists. Diabetics may need to recalculate the grams of carbohydrate, protein, and fat to fit their personal meal plan.

Diabetics should not skip meals, especially if they are injecting insulin. Skipping a meal can lead to low blood glucose. The American Diabetic Association recommends diabetics eat three meals a day at regular intervals, and have both a midmorning and a midafternoon snack.

Be Physically Active

Exercise is important for everyone, but especially for diabetics. Exercise on a regular basis, even brisk walking, improves insulin sensitivity. During moderate exercise, muscles take up glucose at more than 20 times the normal rate when you're sedentary, which lowers blood glucose levels. Any exercise that raises your heart rate for a total of 30 minutes a day is key to maintaining healthy blood glucose. In addition to the effect on blood glucose, exercise also lowers blood pressure and blood lipids, burns kilocalories to help maintain a healthy body weight,[65] improves sleep, strengthens muscles and bones, including the cardiac muscle, and improves quality of life.

A change in exercise level may result in hypoglycemia, especially in type 1 diabetics.[66] Diabetics should check their blood glucose regularly during a workout, especially if the exercise lasts more than an hour. They should carry a small carbohydrate snack, such as fruit or fruit juice, in case blood glucose levels dip too low, and be sure to drink water before, during, and after exercise to prevent dehydration.

Preventing Type 2 Diabetes

When it comes to avoiding diabetes, a healthful diet and physical activity is the best game plan. A landmark study by the Diabetes Prevention Program of over 3,000 individuals with prediabetes showed that those who made changes in their lifestyle were 58 percent less likely to develop type 2 diabetes than those who did not make these changes.[67] Lifestyle changes, such as losing as little as 5 to 7 percent of your body weight, can reduce the cells' resistance to insulin. Simple steps, including exercising 150 minutes a week, eating a plant-based, heart-healthy diet, and meeting with a health professional for ongoing support and education, can lower your risk of developing type 2 diabetes and improve overall health.

LO 4.8: THE TAKE-HOME MESSAGE
Diabetes mellitus is a complex disorder in which an individual either does not produce enough insulin or is unable to use the insulin produced, causing the blood glucose level to rise. Type 1 diabetes is an autoimmune disorder in which the insulin-producing cells of the pancreas are destroyed. Type 2, the most common form, develops from insulin resistance, in which the body cells do not properly respond to the presence of insulin. Prediabetes can be a precursor to type 2 diabetes. Pregnancy hormones may cause gestational diabetes. In type 1 and type 2, hyperglycemia is the main characteristic. Persons with type 1 diabetes require insulin to manage their blood glucose; persons with other types of diabetes may be able to manage the condition through diet and lifestyle changes, or they may need insulin or other medications. Poorly managed diabetes increases the likelihood of nerve damage, leg and foot amputations, eye diseases, tooth loss, gum problems, kidney disease, and heart disease. Diabetes can also damage the retina of the eye, which can cause bleeding, cloudy vision, and eventually blindness. A moderate, well-balanced diet with regular mealtimes, exercise, and maintaining a healthy body weight are key to controlling blood glucose levels in both type 1 and type 2 diabetics.

Visual Chapter Summary

LO 4.1 Carbohydrates Are Nutrients with Different Classifications

Carbohydrates are energy nutrients composed of carbon, hydrogen, and oxygen that are predominant in plant-based foods.

Carbohydrates are divided into two categories: simple and complex carbohydrates. Simple carbohydrates, or sugars, include monosaccharides and disaccharides. Complex carbohydrates include oligosaccharides and polysaccharides.

The three nutritionally important monosaccharides are glucose, fructose, and galactose. Each monosaccharide is called a hexose ($C_6H_{12}O_6$). Monosaccharides linked together with a glycosidic bond form disaccharides, including sucrose, lactose, and maltose.

Oligosaccharides contain three to ten glucose units and are part of cellulose in plant cell walls. The polysaccharide glycogen is the storage form of glucose in animals. Starch and fiber are polysaccharides found in plants. Fiber can be classified as either soluble or insoluble.

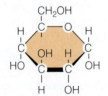

Glucose, a monosaccharide

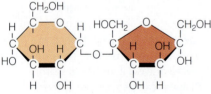

Sucrose, a disaccharide

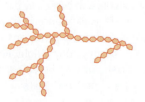

Starch, a polysaccharide

LO 4.2 Carbohydrates Are Digested and Absorbed in the Mouth and Small Intestine

Salivary amylase begins digestion of carbohydrates in the mouth, although most carbohydrate digestion occurs in the small intestine, facilitated by pancreatic amylase. Sucrose, maltose, and lactose are broken down into monosaccharides by small intestine enzymes. Glucose and galactose are absorbed into the enterocyte by active transport with the aid of sodium. Fructose is absorbed by facilitated diffusion. Once in the enterocyte, the monosaccharides are transported through the portal vein to the liver. There they can be used for energy, converted to glucose and stored as glycogen through glycogenesis, or sent into the blood for delivery to cells. Fiber is nondigestible; it travels through the colon and is eliminated.

Glucose, fructose, galactose (monosaccharides)

Enterocytes

Capillary

LO 4.3 Energy Is the Key Function of Carbohydrates

The body uses carbohydrates, specifically glucose, for energy. Surplus glucose is converted to glycogen by glycogenesis, and stored in the liver and muscle. Carbohydrates spare protein from being used for energy and prevent the rapid breakdown of triglycerides (lipolysis). When insufficient carbohydrates are consumed, blood glucose levels are maintained for a short time by liver glycogen through glycogenolysis, or glycerol and amino acids generate glucose through gluconeogenesis. Low-carbohydrate diets also result in ketosis from the incomplete breakdown of fat used to generate energy.

LO 4.4 Hormones Control Blood Glucose Levels

The pancreatic hormones insulin and glucagon maintain the amount of glucose in the blood at 70 to 110 mg/dl. Insulin directs glucose uptake by cells, which lowers the blood levels. Insulin also directs the storage of glucose as glycogen (glycogenesis) and fat (lipogenesis), both of which processes remove glucose from the blood and lower blood glucose levels. Glucagon breaks down glycogen, a process called glycogenolysis, to raise blood glucose levels. Glucagon also stimulates gluconeogenesis in the liver, which also releases glucose into the blood and raises blood glucose levels. Hypoglycemia, or low blood sugar, can occur in individuals with diabetes, especially if they are taking medication and/or insulin and are not eating properly. People without diabetes may also experience reactive hypoglycemia or fasting hypoglycemia, possibly due to overreactive hormones or a hormone imbalance. The symptoms include shakiness, dizziness, light-headedness, hunger, and perspiration.

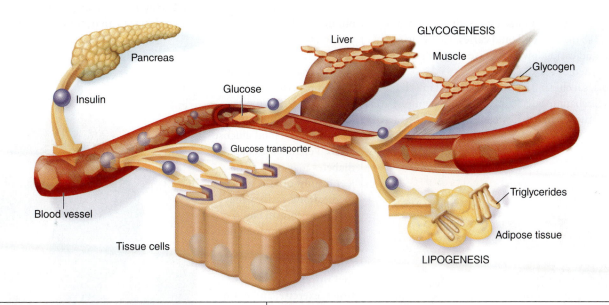

LO 4.5 Fiber Has Many Health-Promoting Benefits

Fiber may help lower the risk of developing constipation, diverticulosis, obesity, heart disease, cancer, and diabetes mellitus. Foods high in fiber can add to satiation. Viscous, soluble fibers help lower blood cholesterol levels. Insoluble fibers increase the bulk of the feces and reduce the risk of constipation and diverticulosis.

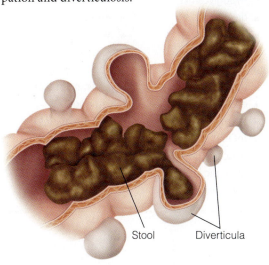

LO 4.6 Whole Plant Foods Are the Best Sources of Carbohydrates

The latest Dietary Reference Intakes (DRIs) for carbohydrates recommend that adults and children consume a minimum of 130 grams daily. The AMDR for carbohydrates is 45 to 65 percent of total daily kilocalories.

The DRI for fiber is 14 grams per 1,000 kilocalories per day. A range of 20 to 38 grams per day is considered adequate to reduce the risk of cardiovascular disease in adults. No UL is set for dietary fiber.

Simple carbohydrates are found naturally in fruits, vegetables, and dairy foods or in processed foods. Soft drinks are the major source of dietary added sugar. Complex carbohydrates are abundant in grains, whole fruits, and vegetables. Grains and potatoes provide starch, while fiber is found in whole grains, whole fruits, vegetables, legumes, nuts, and seeds.

The concept of glycemic index and glycemic load can be used to plan meals. Foods with a lower glycemic index and glycemic load may not raise blood glucose levels as quickly compared with foods that have a higher glycemic index or greater glycemic load.

LO 4.7 There Are Differences among Natural Sugars, Added Sugars, and Sugar Substitutes

Foods with naturally occurring sugars are more nutritious than foods with a lot of added sugar. A diet too high in added sugar may increase the level of body fat and decrease the level of "good" cholesterol in the blood.

Starch and sugary foods, especially sticky foods, can increase the risk of dental caries. Chewing sugarless gum and eating low-fat cheese may help reduce the risk of dental caries.

Polyols, saccharin, aspartame, acesulfame-K, sucralose, rebaudioside A, tagalose, and neotame are sugar substitutes currently deemed safe by the FDA.

LO 4.8 Diabetes Results in Elevated Blood Glucose Levels

Individuals develop diabetes because they aren't producing enough insulin (type 1 diabetes) and/or they have developed insulin resistance (type 2 diabetes). Type 1 diabetes is an autoimmune disease and is not as common as type 2 diabetes. In both cases, hyperglycemia is the main characteristic. Poorly managed diabetes increases the likelihood of nerve damage, leg and foot amputations, tooth loss, gum problems, kidney disease, and heart disease. Diabetes can also damage the retina of the eye, which can cause bleeding, cloudy vision, and eventually blindness. Hypoglycemia, or low blood sugar, can occur in individuals with diabetes, especially if they are taking medication and/or insulin and are not eating properly.

Persons with type 1 diabetes must inject insulin to control blood glucose levels. Persons with type 2 diabetes may need to inject insulin or take other medications, or they may be able to control blood glucose levels through diet and lifestyle changes. A moderate, well-balanced diet with regular mealtimes, exercise, and maintaining a healthy body weight are key to controlling blood glucose levels in both type 1 and type 2 diabetics.

Terms to Know

- photosynthesis
- chlorophyll
- glucose
- simple carbohydrates
- monosaccharide
- disaccharide
- oligosaccharides
- complex carbohydrates
- polysaccharides
- starch
- fiber
- fructose
- galactose

- hexose
- condensation
- glycosidic bond
- sucrose
- lactose
- maltose
- lactose intolerance
- lactose maldigestion
- glycogen
- amylose
- amylopectin
- resistant starch
- cellulose
- lignin

- soluble fiber
- insoluble fiber
- functional fiber
- salivary amylase
- glycogenesis
- glycogenolysis
- gluconeogenesis
- ketone bodies
- ketosis
- insulin
- glucagon
- lipogenesis
- epinephrine
- norepinephrine

- cortisol
- growth hormone
- hypoglycemia
- diverticulosis
- diverticula
- diverticulitis
- whole grains
- bran
- endosperm
- germ
- refined grains
- enriched grains
- glycemic index (GI)
- glycemic load (GL)

- naturally occurring sugars
- added sugars
- empty calories
- dental caries
- sugar substitutes
- diabetes mellitus
- insulin resistance
- ketoacidosis
- type 1 diabetes
- type 2 diabetes
- impaired glucose tolerance
- gestational diabetes

MasteringNutrition™

To hear an MP3 Chapter Review, scan here or visit the Study Area in MasteringNutrition.

Check Your Understanding

1. Sucrose is a
   a. monosaccharide.
   b. disaccharide.
   c. oligosaccharide.
   d. polysaccharide.
2. _____ is the storage form of glucose in animals, including humans.
   a. Glucagon
   b. Glycogen
   c. Gluconeogenesis
   d. Glucose
3. Three brush border enzymes that hydrolyze carbohydrates in the small intestine are
   a. insulin, glucagon, and cortisone.
   b. salivary amylase, salivary lipase, and gastric lipase.
   c. maltase, lactase, and sucrase.
   d. fiber, starch, and glycogen.
4. The hormone that directs the breakdown of glycogen is
   a. galactose.
   b. glucagon.
   c. insulin.
   d. cortisol.
5. The minimum amount of carbohydrates needed daily is
   a. 75 grams.
   b. 100 grams.
   c. 120 grams.
   d. 130 grams.
6. Which of the following can help someone who is lactose intolerant enjoy dairy products?
   a. drinking Lactaid milk
   b. having a milkshake for an afternoon snack
   c. eating a large bowl of ice cream before going to bed
   d. drinking milk on an empty stomach
7. Reducing consumption of which item would have the biggest impact on decreasing the amount of added sugars that Americans consume?
   a. watermelon
   b. candy
   c. soft drinks
   d. apples
8. Your blood cholesterol level is too high, so you would like to eat additional viscous, soluble high-fiber foods to help lower it. A good choice would be
   a. low-fat milk.
   b. chocolate chip cookies.
   c. hard-boiled eggs.
   d. oatmeal.
9. Which of the following can help reduce your risk of type 2 diabetes?
   a. avoiding sugar
   b. eating a high-fiber, plant-based diet
   c. playing computer games
   d. eating a high-fat diet
10. An individual who has PKU should not consume which of the following sugar substitutes?
    a. sucralose
    b. acesulfame-K
    c. aspartame
    d. neotame

Answers

1. (b) Sucrose contains the two monosaccharides glucose and fructose, and is therefore a disaccharide. Oligosaccharides and polysaccharides contain more than two sugar units.
2. (b) Glycogen is stored in the liver and muscles and provides a ready-to-use form of glucose for the body. Glucagon is the hormone that directs the release of glucose from the stored glycogen. Gluconeogenesis is the creation of glucose from noncarbohydrate sources.
3. (c) The enzymes maltase, lactase, and sucrase are located in the brush border of the small intestine and hydrolyze the disaccharides maltose, lactose, and sucrose, respectively. Insulin, glucagon, and cortisone are hormones, not enzymes. Salivary amylase is an enzyme in the saliva that begins digesting starch, a form of complex carbohydrate.
4. (b) When the blood glucose level drops too low, glucagon is released from the pancreas to direct the breakdown of glycogen in the liver, which provides glucose to the blood. Insulin is a hormone that directs the uptake of glucose by cells. Cortisol is a stress hormone that stimulates the production of glucose from amino acids. Galactose is a monosaccharide found in dairy foods.
5. (d) The DRI for carbohydrate is to consume at least 130 grams daily. This is the minimum amount needed to supply the glucose that the body, particularly the brain and red blood cells, must have to function effectively.
6. (a) Lactaid milk is pretreated to facilitate the breakdown of lactose in the milk. Having a milkshake for an afternoon snack, eating ice cream before going to bed, or drinking milk on an empty stomach are all ways to consume a fair amount of lactose at one time and increase the symptoms of lactose intolerance.
7. (c) Soft drinks are the number-one source of added sugars in the American diet, so reducing the intake of these sugary beverages would go a long way in reducing the amount of added sugars that Americans consume. Reducing the amount of candy would also help reduce the added sugars in the diet but not as much as soft drinks. Watermelon and apples contain only naturally occurring sugars.
8. (d) Oatmeal is rich in beta-glucan, a viscous fiber that can help lower cholesterol when eaten as part of a heart-healthy diet. Though nutrient dense, the hard-boiled eggs and milk do not contain fiber. Cookies won't help lower cholesterol.
9. (b) Eating a high-fiber, plant-based diet is the best approach, at present, to help reduce the risk of developing type 2 diabetes. If you want to prevent diabetes, getting regular exercise and not playing sedentary computer games or eating a high-fat diet are the healthiest approaches. Eating sugar doesn't cause diabetes.
10. (c) Individuals diagnosed with PKU, or phenylketonuria, should not consume aspartame because it contains the amino acid phenylalanine.

Answers to True or False?

1. **False.** All macronutrients are essential for health, including carbohydrate, which is vital for numerous body functions.
2. **False.** In fact, infants have higher amounts of lactase, the enzyme necessary for lactose digestion, due to their initial diet of breast milk. As people get older, however, their bodies produce less of this enzyme, which can result in the condition of lactose intolerance.
3. **False.** Kilocalories, not carbohydrates, are the main culprit behind most weight gain. In fact, some high-fiber carbohydrates can actually help people lose weight.
4. **False.** There is insufficient evidence to suggest that eating sugar causes hyperactivity or other behavioral problems in children.
5. **True.** Whole grains contain more fiber and nutrients than refined grains, which have had much of the grain kernel removed during processing.
6. **True.** Simple carbohydrates, especially added sugars, encourage the growth of acid-producing bacteria in the mouth, which in turn promote dental caries.
7. **False.** There is no scientific evidence to support claims that aspartame causes cancer or other health problems in humans.
8. **True.** The average American consumes about half the amount of fiber that's recommended daily.
9. **True.** Much of the added sugars and excess kilocalories in the American diet come from sodas and other sugary beverages. Consuming more kilocalories than are necessary to meet energy needs causes weight gain.
10. **True.** Being overweight or obese can increase one's chances of developing type 2 diabetes.

Web Resources

- For more on fiber, visit the American Heart Association at www.americanheart.org
- For more on diabetes, visit the FDA's Diabetes Information site at www.fda.gov/diabetes or the American Diabetes Association website at www.diabetes.org
- For more on lactose intolerance, visit the National Institute of Diabetes and Digestive and Kidney Diseases (NIDDK) at http://digestive.niddk.nih.gov

References

1. Oldways. 2013. *The Heritage Pyramids.* Available at http://oldwayspt.org. Accessed February 2014.
2. Lima, D. M., P. Fernandes, D. S. Nascimento, R. de Cassia, L. F. Ribeiro, and S. Aparecida de Assis. 2011. Fructose Syrup: A Biotechnology Asset. *Food Technology Biotechnol* 4(4):424–434.
3. Laeng, B., K. C. Berridge, and C. M. Butter. 1993. Pleasantness of a Sweet Taste During Hunger and Satiety: Effects of Gender and "Sweet Tooth." *Appetite* S21:247–254.
4. Zellner, D. A., A. Garriga-Trillo, E. Rohm, S. Centeno, and S. Parker. 1999. Food Liking and Craving: A Cross-Cultural Approach. *Appetite* 33:61–70.
5. Bachmanov, A. A., N. P. Bosak, W. B. Floriano, et al. 2011. Genetics of Sweet Taste Preferences. *Flavour and Fragrance Journal* 26(4):286–294.
6. Jeurink, P., B. van Esch, A. Rijnierse, J. Garssen, and L. Knippels. 2013. Mechanisms Underlying Immune Effects of Dietary Oligosaccharides. *American Journal of Clinical Nutrition* 98(2):572S–577S.
7. DiNardo, G., S. Oliva, F. Ferrari, S. Mallardo, G. Barbara, C. Cremon, M. Aloi, and S. Cucchiara. 2013. Efficacy and Tolerability of α-Galactosidase in Treating Gas-Related Symptoms in Children: A Randomized, Double-Blind, Placebo-Controlled Trial. *BMC Gastroenterology* doi:10.1186/1471-230X-13-142.
8. Lebrilla, L. 2012. Analysis and Role of Oligosaccharides in Milk. *BMB Reports* 45(8):442–451.
9. Landon, S., C. G. B. Colyer, and H. Salmon. 2012. The Resistant Starch Report. *Food Australia Supplement.* Available at www.foodaust.com.au/wp-content/.../04/Hi_Maize-supplement_web.pdf. Accessed February 2014.
10. Birt, D. F., T. Boylston, S. Hendrich, J. L. Jane, J. Hollis, L. Li, J. McClelland, et al. 2013. Resistant Starch: Promise for Improving Human Health. *Advanced Nutrition* 4(6):587–601.
11. Kwak, J. H., J. K. Paik, H. I. Kim, O. Y. Kim, D. Y. Shin, H. J. Kim, and J. H. Lee. 2012. Dietary Treatment with Rice Containing Resistant Starch Improves Markers of Endothelial Function with Reduction of Postprandial Blood Glucoses and Oxidative Stress in Patients with Prediabetes or Newly Diagnosed Type 2 Diabetes. *Atherosclerosis* 224(2):457–464.
12. Slizewska, K. 2013. The Citric Acid-Modified, Enzyme-Resistant Dextrin from Potato Starch as a Potential Prebiotic. *Acta Biochimica Polonica* 60(4):671–675.
13. Kay, R. 1982. Dietary Fiber. *Journal of Lipid Research* 23:221–242.
14. Hubner, F., and E. K. Arendt. 2013. Germination of Cereal Grains as a Way to Improve the Nutritional Value: A Review. *Critical Review of Food Science Nutrition* 53(8):853–861.
15. National Diabetes Information Clearinghouse. 2012. *Hypoglycemia.* Available at http://diabetes.niddk.nih.gov/dm/pubs/hypoglycemia/index.aspx. Accessed February 2014.
16. National Digestive Diseases Information Clearinghouse. 2013. *Constipation.* Available at http://digestive.niddk.nih.gov/ddiseases/pubs/constipation. Accessed February 2014.
17. National Digestive Diseases Information Clearinghouse. 2013. *Diverticulosis and Diverticulitis.* Available at http://digestive.niddk.nih.gov/ddiseases/pubs/diverticulosis/index.aspx. Accessed February 2014.
18. Tanaka, S., Y. Yoshimura, C. Kamada, S. Tanaka, et al. 2013. Intakes of Dietary Fiber, Vegetables, and Fruits and Incidence of Cardiovascular Disease in Japanese Patients with Type 2 Diabetes. *Diabetes Care* 36(12):3916–3922.
19. Cho, S. S., L. Qi, G. C. Fahey, and D. M. Klurfeld. 2013. Consumption of Cereal Fiber, Mixtures of Whole Grains and Bran, and Whole Grains and Risk Reduction in Type 2 Diabetes, Obesity, and Cardiovascular Disease. *American Journal of Clinical Nutrition* 98(2):594–619.
20. Silva, F. M., C. K. Kramer, J. C. de Almeida, T. Steemburgo, J. L. Gross, and M. J. Azevedo. 2013. Fiber Intake and Glycemic Control in Patients with Type 2 Diabetes Mellitus: A Systematic Review with Meta-Analysis of Randomized Controlled Trials. *Nutrition Reviews* 71(12):790–801.
21. Dong, J. Y., K. He, P. Wang, and L. Q. Qin. 2011. Dietary Fiber Intake and Risk of Breast Cancer: a Meta-Analysis of Prospective Cohort Studies. *American Journal of Clinical Nutrition* 94(3):900–905.
22. Ben, Q., Y. Sun, R. Chai, A. Qian, B. Xu, and Y. Yuan. 2013. Dietary Fiber Intake Reduces Risk for Colorectal Adenoma: A Meta-Analysis. *Gastroenterology* doi: 10.1053/j.gastro.2013.11.003.
23. Kyrø, C., A. Olsen, R. Landberg, et al. 2014. Plasma Alkylresorcinols, Biomarkers of Whole-Grain Wheat and Rye Intake, and Incidence of Colorectal Cancer. *Journal of the National Cancer Institute* 106(1):doi: 10.1093/jnci/djt352.
24. Henderson, A. J., C. A. Ollila, A. Kumar, et al. 2013. Chemopreventive Properties of Dietary Rice Bran: Current Status and Future Prospects. *Advanced Nutrition* 3(5):643–653.

25. Cho, S. S., et al. 2013. Consumption of Cereal Fiber.
26. Nicklas, T. A., L. Jahns, M. L. Bogle, D. N. Chester, M. Giovanni, D. M. Klurfeld, K. Laugero, et al. 2013. Barriers and Facilitators for Consumer Adherence to the *Dietary Guidelines for Americans*: The HEALTH Study. *Journal of the Academy of Nutrition and Dietetics* 113(10):1317–1331.
27. Ramage, S., A. Farmer, K. A. Eccles, and L. McCarga. 2014. Healthy Strategies for Successful Weight Loss and Weight Management: A Systematic Review. *Applied Physiology, Nutrition, and Metabolism* 39:1–20.
28. Giacco, R., J. Lappi, G. Costabile, M. Kolehmainen, et al. 2013. Effects of Rye and Whole Wheat versus Refined Cereal Foods on Metabolic Risk Factors: A Randomized Controlled Two-Centre Intervention Study. *Clinical Nutrition* 32(6):941–949.
29. Ramage, S. A., et al. 2014. Healthy Strategies for Successful Weight Loss and Weight Management.
30. Giacco, R., et al. 2013. Effects of Rye and Whole Wheat versus Refined Cereal Foods on Metabolic Risk Factors.
31. Foster, M., M. Karra, T. Picone, A. Chu, D. P. Hancock, P. Petocz, and S. Samman. 2012. Dietary Fiber Intake Increases the Risk of Zinc Deficiency in Healthy and Diabetic Women. *Biological Trace Element Research* 149(2):135–142.
32. Grosso, G., S. Buscemi, F. Galvano, A. Mistretta, et al. 2013. Mediterranean Diet and Cancer: Epidemiological Evidence and Mechanism of Selected Aspects. *BMC Surgery* 13: Supplement 2:S14.
33. Cho, S. S., et al. 2013. Consumption of Cereal Fiber.
34. Foroughi, M., M. Akhavanzanjani, Z. Maghsoudi, R. Ghiasvand, F. Khorvash, and G. Askari. 2013. Stroke and Nutrition: A Review of Studies. *International Journal of Preventive Medicine* 4(Suppl 2):S165–S179.
35. Nicklas, T. A., et al. 2013. Barriers and Facilitators for Consumer Adherence.
36. Giacco, R., et al. 2013. Effects of Rye and Whole Wheat.
37. Ibid.
38. Grosso, G., et al. 2013. Mediterranean Diet and Cancer.
39. Foroughi, M., et al. 2013. Stroke and Nutrition.
40. Ben, Q., et al. 2013. Dietary Fiber Intake.
41. Ramage, S., et al. 2014. Healthy Strategies for Successful Weight Loss.
42. Silva, F. M., et al. 2013. Fiber Intake and Glycemic Control.
43. Sluijs, I., J. W. J. Beulens, Y. T. van der Schouw, et al. 2013. Dietary Glycemic Index, Glycemic Load, and Digestible Carbohydrate Intake Are Not Associated with Risk of Type 2 Diabetes in Eight European Countries. *Journal of Nutrition* 143:93–99.
44. Han, E., and L. M. Powell. 2013. Consumption Patterns of Sugar-Sweetened Beverages in the United States. *Journal of the Academy of Nutrition and Dietetics* 113(1):43–53.
45. Hu, F. B. 2013. Resolved: There is Sufficient Scientific Evidence that Decreasing Sugar-Sweetened Beverage Consumption Will Reduce the Prevalence of Obesity and Obesity-Related Diseases. *Obesity Review* 14(8):606–619.
46. U.S. Department of Heath and Human Services. Public Health Service, National Toxicology Program. 2011. *Report on Carcinogens*. 12th ed. Available at http://ntp.niehs.nih.gov/ntp/roc/twelfth/roc12.pdf. Accessed February 2014.
47. Ajinomoto USA, Inc. 2006. *The History of Aspartame*. Available at www.aspartame.net. Accessed February 2014.
48. American Diabetes Association. 2014. *Low-Calorie Sweeteners*. Available at http://www.diabetes.org. Accessed February 2014.
49. Centers for Disease Control and Prevention. 2011. *2011 National Diabetes Fact Sheet*. Available at www.cdc.gov/diabetes/pubs/factsheet11.htm?loc=diabetes-statistics. Accessed February 2014.
50. Boyle, J., T. Thompson, E. Gregg, L. Barker, and D. Williamson. 2010. Projection of the Year 2050 Burden of Diabetes in the US Adult Population: Dynamic Modeling of Incidence, Mortality and Prediabetes Prevalence. *Population Health Metrics*. Available at www.pophealthmetrics.com/content/8/1/29. Accessed February 2014.
51. National Diabetes Information Clearinghouse. 2013. *Your Guide to Diabetes*. Available at http://diabetes.niddk.nih.gov. Accessed February 2014.
52. Centers for Disease Control and Prevention. 2013. *Diabetes Report Card 2012: National and State Profile of Diabetes and Its Complications*. Available at www.cdc.gov/diabetes/pubs/reportcard/diabetes-overview.htm. Accessed February 2014.
53. Centers for Disease Control and Prevention. 2011. *2011 National Diabetes Fact Sheet*.
54. Grundy, S. 2012. Prediabetes, Metabolic Syndrome, and Cardiovascular Disease. *Journal of the American College of Cardiology* 59(7):635–643.
55. Ibid.
56. National Diabetes Information Clearinghouse. 2013. *DCCT and EDIC: Diabetes Control and Complications Trial and Follow-Up Study (DCCT)*. Available at www.diabetes.niddk.nih.gov. Accessed February 2014.
57. Ibid.
58. Wheeler, M. L., S. A. Dunbar, L. M. Jaacks, W. Karmally, E. J. Mayer-Davis, J. Wylie-Rosett, and W. S. Yancy. 2012. Macronutrients, Food Groups, and Eating Patterns in the Management of Diabetes. A Systematic Review of the Literature, 2010. *Diabetes Care* 35:434–445.
59. Sluijs, I., et al. 2013. Dietary Glycemic Index.
60. Shah, B. R., L. L. Lipscombe, D. S. Feig, and J. M. Lowe. 2011. Missed Opportunities for Type 2 Diabetes Testing Following Gestational Diabetes: A Population-Based Cohort Study. *British Journal of Obstetrics and Gynecology* 118:1484–1490.
61. National Diabetes Information Clearinghouse. 2012. *Hypoglycemia*. Available at http://diabetes.niddk.nih.gov/dm/pubs/hypoglycemia/index.aspx. Accessed February 2014.
62. Abbot, C. A., R. A. Malik, E. R. van Ross, et al. 2011. Prevalence and Characteristics of Painful Diabetic Neuropathy in a Large Community-Based Diabetic Population in the U.K. *Diabetes Care* 34(10):2220–2224.
63. National Diabetes Information Clearinghouse. 2013. *Diabetes Prevention Program*. Available at http://diabetes.niddk.nih.gov/dm/pubs/preventionprogram. Accessed February 2014.
64. Wheeler, M. L., et al. 2012. Macronutrients, Food Groups, and Eating Patterns.
65. Green, A. J., K. M. Fox, and S. Grandy. 2011. Impact of Regular Exercise and Attempted Weight Loss on Quality of Life among Adults With and Without Type 2 Diabetes Mellitus. *Journal of Obesity* doi:10.1155/2011/172073.
66. Metcalf, K. M., A. Singhvi, E. Tsalikian, M. J. Tansey, M. B. Zimmerman, D. W. Esliger, and K. F. Janz. 2014. Effects of Moderate- to Vigorous-Intensity Physical Activity on Overnight and Next-Day Hypoglycemia in Active Adolescents with Type 1 Diabetes. *Diabetes Care* doi:10.2337/dc13-1973.
67. National Diabetes Information Clearinghouse. 2013. *Diabetes Prevention Program*.

5 Lipids

Learning Outcomes

After reading this chapter, you will be able to:

5.1 Define the term lipid and explain how lipids differ in their structure.

5.2 Describe how lipids are digested, absorbed, and transported in the body.

5.3 Describe the functions of lipids in the body.

5.4 Define the dietary recommendations for total fat, the essential fatty acids, cholesterol, and *trans* fat.

5.5 Identify the best, worst, and alternative food sources of the different types of fats, including the essential fatty acids, saturated fats, and *trans* fats.

5.6 Describe the development of atherosclerosis and heart disease, and explain how lifestyle factors can affect the risk of heart disease.

True or False?

1. Cholesterol should be consumed daily to meet the body's needs. **T/F**

2. A healthy diet is very low in fat. **T/F**

3. Only commercially made fried foods and snack items contain *trans* fats. **T/F**

4. Saturated fat is a major dietary factor for elevated blood cholesterol. **T/F**

5. Fat-free cookies tend to have half the kilocalories of full-fat varieties. **T/F**

6. A high level of HDL cholesterol in the blood is considered heart healthy. **T/F**

7. Butter is a healthier choice than margarine. **T/F**

8. Nuts are high in cholesterol. **T/F**

9. Taking fish oil supplements is the best way to consume adequate omega-3 fatty acids. **T/F**

10. Dietary LDL cholesterol is unhealthy for the heart. **T/F**

See page 203 for the answers.

When you go shopping, what is on your grocery list? If you're like many Americans, you probably have the best intentions of filling your grocery cart with low-fat, nonfat, or cholesterol-free items to eat a more healthful diet. Even just saying the words *fat* or *cholesterol* brings up negative images of foods that we should avoid. The truth is, a small amount of dietary fat is essential to the body.

In this chapter, we discuss the structure and functions of the different types of lipids, how they are handled in the body, and the amounts of each that should be consumed in a healthy diet. We also explore the role of high-fat foods in the development of cardiovascular disease and other health conditions.

What Are Lipids and How Do They Differ in Structure?

LO 5.1 Define the term lipid and explain how lipids differ in their structure.

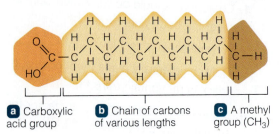

a Carboxylic acid group **b** Chain of carbons of various lengths **c** A methyl group (CH_3)

▲ **Figure 5.1 Chemical Structure of a Fatty Acid**
The basic chemical structure of a fatty acid is composed of three different parts.

lipid A category of carbon, hydrogen, and oxygen compounds that are insoluble in water.

triglycerides A type of lipid commonly found in foods and the body; also known as fat. Triglycerides consist of three fatty acids attached to a glycerol backbone.

phospholipids A category of lipids that consist of two fatty acids and a phosphorus group attached to a glycerol backbone. Lecithin is an example of a phospholipid found in food and in the body.

sterols A category of lipids that contains four connecting rings of carbon and hydrogen. Cholesterol is the most common sterol.

hydrophobic "Water fearing." In nutrition, the term refers to compounds that are not soluble in water.

fatty acid The most basic unit of triglycerides and phospholipids; fatty acids consist of carbon chains ranging from two to 80 carbons in length.

When you think of the word **lipid,** you may think it's a synonym for fat. But that's only partly correct. *Lipo* means *fatty,* and lipids actually refer to a category of compounds that includes **triglycerides** (*fats and oils*), **phospholipids,** and **sterols.** These compounds all contain carbon, oxygen, and hydrogen, and they are all **hydrophobic** (*hydro* = water, *phobic* = fearing). In other words, they don't dissolve in water. If you drop lipids like butter or olive oil into a glass of water, they rise to the top and sit on the water's surface. This repelling of water allows lipids to play a unique role in foods and in the body.

Whereas the popular press often portrays lipids as bad or unhealthy, the reality is that lipids serve several basic functions for maintaining health. In the body, lipids store and provide energy, provide insulation, help manufacture steroids and bile, and play a key role in transporting fat-soluble nutrients in the blood. They are also used to manufacture the major sex hormones, and one type of lipid is key to the structure of cell membranes.

We begin the discussion of lipids by introducing the chemical structure of fatty acids, the basic building blocks of most lipids, and continuing with triglycerides, phospholipids, and sterols.

Many Lipids Are Comprised of Fatty Acids

Triglycerides and phospholipids are built from a basic unit called a **fatty acid.** All fatty acids (**Figure 5.1**) are organic compounds that consist of chains of carbon and hydrogen atoms. The basic structure of every individual fatty acid has an acid group (called a carboxyl group, abbreviated as COOH) at one end, called the alpha end, and a methyl group (CH_3) on the other end, called the omega end. The carboxylic acid consists of a carbon atom attached with a double bond to an oxygen atom and single bonded to a hydroxyl group (OH).

The ratio of carbon and hydrogen to oxygen in the chain of a fatty acid accounts for the higher number of kilocalories in fat (9 kilocalories per gram) than in carbohydrates and proteins (4 kilocalories per gram). In short, a fatty acid takes fifty percent more oxygen per carbon atom to release energy. Thus, the fatty acid takes longer to oxidize but gives off more energy. We will cover this in more detail in Chapter 8.

There are over 20 different fatty acids. They vary in structure by the length of the carbon chain, degree of saturation, location of double bond, and shape.

Length of Fatty Acids

The carbon chains of most naturally occurring dietary fatty acids contain 4 to 24 carbons (usually in even numbers), with the most common fatty acids containing 12 to 24 carbons. If the fatty acid is two to four carbons long, it is a **short-chain fatty acid.** The fatty acid, butyric acid, contains four carbons (**Figure 5.2a**). Fatty acids with six to 10 carbons are called **medium-chain fatty acids,** and those with 12 or more carbons are called **long-chain fatty acids.** Long-chain fatty acids are the most common type of fatty acid found in foods.

The chain length of fatty acids is important because it affects the way we digest, absorb, and metabolize fatty acids. Long-chain fatty acids take longer to digest and absorb than do short- or medium-chain fatty acids. Shorter chain fatty acids are more water soluble than those fatty acids with more carbons. The length of the chain changes the way the body transports the fatty acids. We cover the details of fat digestion later in the chapter.

Saturation of Fatty Acids

The degree of saturation of a fatty acid refers to the presence or absence of a carbon-carbon double bond. Every carbon within the molecule has four bonds. The bonds between each carbon in the fatty acid chain can be either single or double bonds and the remaining bonds are attached to hydrogen atoms. The presence of a carbon-carbon double bond implies that the carbons are not *saturated* with hydrogens or have less than the number of hydrogens that are capable of bonding with each carbon. When each of the carbons in the carbon chain of a fatty acid are bound with two hydrogens, it is called a **saturated fatty acid**. In contrast, if the carbon chain has carbons that are not bound to two hydrogens so that there are one or more double bonds, the structure is called an **unsaturated fatty acid.**

Palmitic acid (Figure 5.2b) is an example of a saturated fatty acid, because all of its 14 carbons are bound with hydrogens with no double bonds to each other.

Chemistry Boost

Fatty Acid Notations

Fatty acids are frequently represented by two different methods of notation. The first method, the delta (Δ) system, is often used by chemists (see figure below). In this form, the first number indicates the number of carbons in the chain. The second number, after the colon, notes how many double bonds are in the molecule. The two superscript numbers indicate the location of the two double bonds from the carboxyl end of the fatty acid.

The second method, called the omega (ω) system, is similar to the delta system. This system uses either the symbol w or the letter *n* after the number of double bonds. This symbol notes the position of the first double bond from the omega (methyl) end of the fatty acid. In polyunsaturated fatty acids, double bonds are usually separated by three carbons. Using this notation makes it easy to locate the rest of the double bonds in a fatty acid molecule. With linoleic acid, the first double bond is located on carbon 6, followed by the second double bond on carbon 9.

Delta system describing linoleic acid:

$$18:2 \ \Delta^{9,12}$$

Omega system describing linoleic acid:

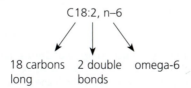

C18:2, n–6

18 carbons long | 2 double bonds | omega-6

---

short-chain fatty acid A fatty acid with a chain of two to four carbons.

medium-chain fatty acids Fatty acids with a chain of six to 10 carbons.

long-chain fatty acids Fatty acids with a chain of 12 carbons or more.

saturated fatty acid A fatty acid in which all of the carbons are bound with hydrogen.

unsaturated fatty acid A fatty acid in which there are one or more double bonds between carbons.

Due to their chemical properties, fats and oils don't dissolve in water.

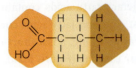
a Acetic acid (C2:0)

b Palmitic acid, a saturated fatty acid (C14:0)

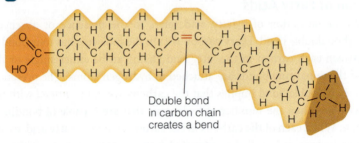
c Oleic acid, a monounsaturated fatty acid (C18:1)

Double bond in carbon chain creates a bend

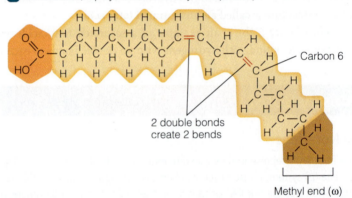
d Linoleic acid, a polyunsaturated fatty acid (C18:2)

Carbon 6

2 double bonds create 2 bends

Methyl end (ω)

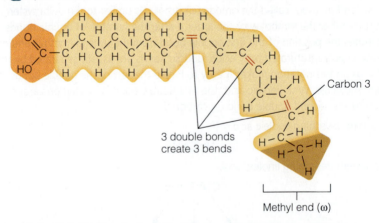
e Alpha-linolenic acid, a polyunsaturated, omega-3 fatty acid (C18:3)

Carbon 3

3 double bonds create 3 bends

Methyl end (ω)

▲ **Figure 5.2 Fatty Acids Vary by Length, Degree of Saturation, and Shape**
Fatty acids differ by the number of carbons in the chain, whether or not the chain contains any double bonds (the saturation of the fatty acid), and the shape of the carbon chains on either side of the double bonds.

monounsaturated fatty acid (MUFA)
A fatty acid that has one double bond.

polyunsaturated fatty acid (PUFA) A fatty acid with two or more double bonds.

oils Lipids that are liquid at room temperature.

rancidity The spoiling of lipids through oxidation.

hydrogenation Adding hydrogen to an unsaturated fatty acid to make it more saturated and solid at room temperature.

In contrast, two of the 18 carbons in oleic acid (Figure 5.2c) are paired with each other rather than hydrogen, forming one double bond. This lone double bond makes oleic acid a **monounsaturated fatty acid (MUFA)** (*mono* = one).

A **polyunsaturated fatty acid (PUFA)** (*poly* = many) contains two or more double bonds, and is less saturated with hydrogen. Linoleic acid, shown in Figure 5.2d, is an example of a polyunsaturated fatty acid.

The length of the fatty acid chain and the presence of double bonds between the carbons also determine the melting point of a fat, or the temperature at which it changes from a solid to a liquid (**Figure 5.3**). Double bonds cause a kink in the chain of the fatty acid, which prevents fatty acids from packing together tightly. Bends in the chain are due to double bonds and reduce the interaction between the molecules. This produces a fatty acid with a lower melting point. The lower melting points of shorter chain and unsaturated fatty acids mean they tend to be liquid at room temperature. Fats that are liquid at room temperature are called **oils.** The monounsaturated fatty acid oleic acid is found in olive oil, and the polyunsaturated fatty acids, linoleic acid and alpha-linolenic acid (Figure 5.2e), are found in soybean oil. In general, straight, long-chain saturated fatty acids have higher melting points than do unsaturated fatty acids. This is because the saturated fatty acids can stack closer together and interact with one another. An example is coconut or palm oils, which are solid at room temperature.

Stability of Fatty Acids

When exposed to oxygen, or *oxidized,* foods containing fatty acids may develop a bitter, pungent smell or taste, a condition called **rancidity.** The double bonds of an unsaturated fatty acid are the most reactive sites on the fatty acid chain. Notice in **Figure 5.4** that during the first step, a H^+ is extracted from the unstable fatty acid and forms a free radical. Oxygen then reacts with the unstable fatty acid, producing even more compounds in the chain reaction. At some point during this process, free radicals themselves combine to form compounds that eventually halt the reaction.

Because double bonds are less stable than single bonds, foods that contain unsaturated fatty acids become rancid faster than foods that contain saturated fatty acids. Similarly, polyunsaturated fatty acids are more susceptible to rancidity than monounsaturated fatty acids because they have more double bonds. Flax oil, which is rich in polyunsaturated fatty acids, is more susceptible to oxidation than corn oil, which contains more saturated and monounsaturated fatty acids. Saturated fatty acids have no double bonds, and are thus much less susceptible to oxidation.

Food manufacturers have tested various ways to reduce rancidity, including adding antioxidants to hinder the oxidation process. Antioxidants bond with the free radicals (more on antioxidants in Chapter 9), thereby preventing oxygen from attacking the double bonds. Vitamins such as C and E are natural antioxidants but lack the shelf life of synthetic antioxidants such as butylated hydroxyanisole (BHA) and butylated hydroxytoluene (BHT).

Limiting the food's exposure to oxygen, heat, and light can also reduce rancidity. Storing oils and fats in airtight containers, in a cool, dry, and dark location will lessen the formation of free radicals, which contribute to the rancidity of foods.

Another method used to stabilize unsaturated fatty acids is a process called **hydrogenation.** Hydrogenation involves heating oil and exposing it to hydrogen gas, which adds hydrogen to the carbons in the double bonds, making the fatty acids more saturated. This process gives crackers and snack foods a longer shelf life, improves the texture of pastries, and makes french fries crisper. Hydrogenation makes liquid oils become more solid at room temperature. It is less expensive and provides a "mouthfeel" like butter. We will discuss the use of hydrogenation in more detail later in the chapter.

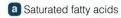
a Saturated fatty acids

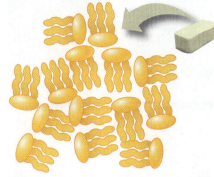
b Unsaturated fatty acids

▲ **Figure 5.3 Saturated and Unsaturated Fatty Acids Help Shape Foods**
The straight chains of saturated fatty acids pack tightly together and are solid at room temperature. The double bonds in unsaturated fatty acids cause kinks in their shape and prevent them from packing tightly together, so they tend to be liquid at room temperature.

▲ **Figure 5.4 Rancidity Reaction of a Fatty Acid**
When fatty acids become oxidized, the chemical structure is altered, creating the off smell and flavors characteristic of rancid food.

Margarine is made by hydrogenating vegetable oils to make them spreadable.

Location of the Double Bond

The location of the double bond in the fatty acid chain also affects the properties of a fatty acid (see Figure 5.2d and 5.2e). If the first double bond in a polyunsaturated fat is located between the third and fourth carbon from the methyl (or *omega*) end, it is referred to as an **omega-3 fatty acid.** If the first double bond is between carbons six and seven from the omega end, it is called an **omega-6 fatty acid.**

Linoleic acid is an omega-6 fatty acid. It has 18 carbons with two double bonds, the first of which is located on the sixth carbon from the omega end. **Alpha-linolenic acid** is an omega-3 fatty acid, and is the same length as the omega-6 (18 carbons) but has three double bonds, with the first double bond on carbon three from the omega end. These two fatty acids are called **essential fatty acids** because they must be obtained from foods.

Shape of Fatty Acids

Unsaturated fatty acids form two different shapes based on the position of the hydrogen atoms around the double bond. If the hydrogen atoms are on the same side of the double bond, as illustrated in **Figure 5.5**, the fatty acid has a *cis* configuration. If the hydrogen atoms are on opposite sides of the double bond, it is a *trans* configuration. Most double bonds in a fatty acid molecule are in the *cis* configuration. There are a few *trans* fatty acids found naturally in milk and meat, but most of the *trans* fatty acids are the result of food processing. This is important because the commercial *trans* fatty acids may change your blood lipids.

Triglycerides Are the Most Common Lipid

The most common lipid in both foods and the body is the triglyceride, commonly called *fat*. It makes up about 95 percent of the lipids found in food. A triglyceride molecule consists of three fatty acids connected to a **glycerol** (*glyc* = sweet, *ol* = alcohol) backbone made of three alcohol (OH) groups. Through a condensation reaction, a hydrogen from the glycerol bonds with the hydroxyl group (OH) of the fatty acid, and attaches the fatty acid to the glycerol (**Figure 5.6**). A molecule of water is released in the process for each fatty acid. A variety of fatty acids can bond with the same glycerol backbone, so a triglyceride usually contains a mixture of fatty acids. For example, canola oil is not just composed of polyunsaturated fatty acids; there are also small amounts of saturated and monounsaturated fats present.

omega-3 fatty acid A family of polyunsaturated fatty acids with the first double bond located at the third carbon from the omega end.

omega-6 fatty acid A family of polyunsaturated fatty acids with the first double bond located at the sixth carbon from the omega end.

linoleic acid A polyunsaturated essential fatty acid; part of the omega-6 fatty acid family.

alpha-linolenic acid A polyunsaturated essential fatty acid; part of the omega-3 fatty acid family.

essential fatty acids The two polyunsaturated fatty acids that the body cannot make and therefore must be eaten in foods: linoleic acid and alpha-linolenic acid.

cis The configuration of a fatty acid in which the carbon chains on each side of the double bond are on the same side.

trans The configuration of a fatty acid in which the carbon chains are on opposite sides of the double bond.

glycerol The three-carbon backbone of a triglyceride.

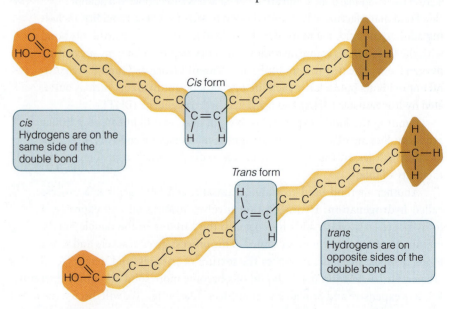

▲ Figure 5.5 The *Cis* and *Trans* Configurations of Unsaturated Fatty Acids

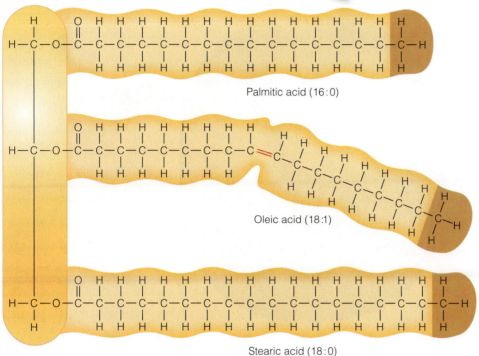

Glycerol backbone

Three fatty acids

Palmitic acid

Oleic acid

Stearic acid

A fat (triglyceride)

+ 3 H₂O
Water

Palmitic acid (16:0)

Oleic acid (18:1)

Stearic acid (18:0)

Triglycerides perform a variety of functions in food. They make pie crusts flaky and meat tender. Triglycerides can also preserve freshness, which makes them important in food processing.

In the body, triglycerides are carried through the blood and stored in the adipose tissue to provide a major source of available energy. Higher levels of triglycerides in the blood are a risk factor associated with heart disease. We cover this topic later in the chapter.

Phospholipids Differ from Triglycerides

Like triglycerides, phospholipids contain a glycerol backbone, but instead of three fatty acids, the glycerol is linked to two fatty acids, a phosphate group, and different nitrogen-containing compounds such as choline (**Figure 5.7**). The glycerol backbone and phosphorus group form a polar head, which means it attracts charged particles, such as water. The fatty acid–containing tail is nonpolar and therefore soluble with other nonpolar molecules, such as fats. In other words, one end of the phospholipid is hydrophilic (*philic* = loving) and the other end is hydrophobic.

One of the major phospholipids in the body is **lecithin,** also called phosphatidylcholine. Lecithin contains a **choline** group attached to the phosphate on the third carbon of the glycerol backbone. The fatty acids and the phosphate and

lecithin A phospholipid made in the body that is integral in the structure of cell membranes; also known as phosphatidylcholine.

choline A member of the B vitamin family that is a component of the phospholipid lecithin.

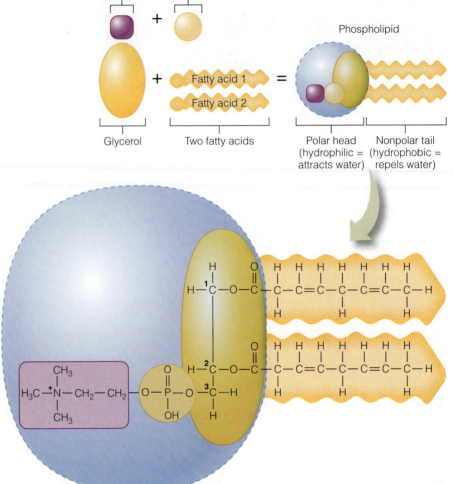

► **Figure 5.7 Structure of a Phospholipid**
Phospholipids, such as the lecithin shown here, are similar in structure to triglycerides, but they have only two fatty acids and a phosphate group connected to the glycerol backbone. This nitrogen-containing configuration allows phospholipids to be attracted to both water and fat.

Choline + Phosphate group

Glycerol + Two fatty acids (Fatty acid 1, Fatty acid 2) = Phospholipid

Polar head (hydrophilic = attracts water) — Nonpolar tail (hydrophobic = repels water)

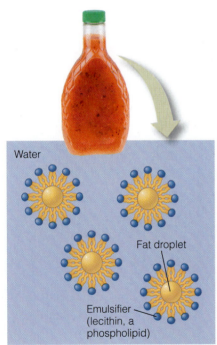

Water

Fat droplet

Emulsifier (lecithin, a phospholipid)

▲ **Figure 5.8 Keeping a Salad Dressing Blended**
Emulsifiers are often added to salad dressing to keep the oil part of the dressing blended in the watery solution. When a salad dressing does separate, it is usually because it doesn't contain an emulsifier.

choline give the phospholipid both fat-soluble and water-soluble properties, which allow it to shuttle other lipids across the cell membrane.

Because of its unique water- and fat-loving attributes, lecithin is used in many foods as an **emulsifier,** which helps keep incompatible substances, such as water and oil, mixed together. An emulsifier is sometimes added to commercially made salad dressings to prevent the fat from separating and rising to the top of the dressing (**Figure 5.8**). The emulsifier's nonpolar, fat-attracting tail surrounds the droplets of fat, which orients the polar, water-attracting head toward the watery solution of the dressing. This keeps the fat droplet suspended and allows the water and the oil to stay blended together.

Sterols Are More Complex than Triglycerides

Sterols are a much more complex molecule than phospholipids or triglycerides. They do not contain glycerol or fatty acids, but rather are composed mainly of four connecting rings of carbon and hydrogen (**Figure 5.9**). Unlike the other lipids, sterols do not provide energy.

The best-known sterol, **cholesterol,** is comprised of four carbon rings with a tail of carbons and hydrogens on one end and a hydroxyl group on the other end. The majority of sterols found in plants are **phytosterols** and **phytostanols,** which are similar in structure to cholesterol. Plant phytosterols have a double bond in the

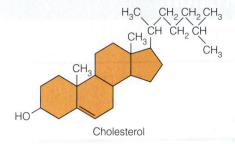

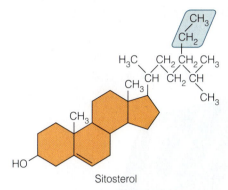

Cholesterol

Sitosterol

▲ Figure 5.9 **Structure of a Sterol**
Sterols have a carbon ring configuration with hydrogens and an oxygen attached. Cholesterol is the best-known sterol found in animal products. Sitosterol is a common sterol found in plants.

Lipid	Structure	Examples
Triglycerides	Glycerol — [fatty acids diagram] — Fatty acids	Saturated fat Unsaturated fat *Trans* fat
Phospholipids	Polar head — [diagram] — Fatty acids	Lecithin
Sterols	[sterol ring diagram] HO	Cholesterol
	[sterol ring diagram] HO	Sitosterol

▲ Figure 5.10 **Three Types of Lipids**
The three types of lipids vary in structure. Triglycerides and phospholipids are built from fatty acids, while sterols are composed of carbon rings.

sterol ring, such as campesterol, while phytostanols lack the double bond in the sterol ring (see Figure 5.9). Phytosterols may provide health benefits, as they inhibit the intestinal absorption of cholesterol.[1]

Figure 5.10 summarizes the three types of lipids.

> **LO 5.1: THE TAKE-HOME MESSAGE** Lipids are hydrophobic compounds made up of carbon, hydrogen, and oxygen. The three types of lipids are triglycerides, phospholipids, and sterols. Lipids provide and store energy for the body, transport fat-soluble nutrients, provide insulation, and are used to synthesize bile, sex hormones, and cell membranes. Fatty acids, which consist of a carbon and hydrogen chain, a carboxylic acid group, and a methyl group, are the basic structural units of triglycerides and phospholipids. Fatty acids differ in chain length, degree of saturation, and shape. Triglycerides consist of three fatty acids attached to a glycerol backbone by condensation reactions. Triglycerides are found in blood, stored in the adipose tissue, and are a major source of energy to the body. Phospholipids are made of two fatty acids and a phosphate and nitrogen-containing group attached to a glycerol backbone. Sterols are made up of four connected rings of carbon and hydrogen.

How Are Lipids Digested, Absorbed, and Transported in the Body?

LO 5.2 Describe how lipids are digested, absorbed, and transported in the body.

The lipids found in food are primarily in the form of fat (triglycerides) and, to a lesser extent, phospholipids and sterols. During the digestion of fat, the fatty acids are removed from the glycerol backbone by hydrolysis to form a combination of free fatty acids, glycerol, and monoglycerides (**Focus Figure 5.11**). This action is

emulsifier A compound that keeps two incompatible substances, such as oil and water, mixed together.

cholesterol A common sterol found only in animal products and made in the liver from saturated fatty acids.

phytosterols Naturally occurring sterols found in plants.

phytostanols A type of plant sterol similar in structure to cholesterol.

Most lipid digestion occurs in the small intestine with the aid of bile and lipase enzymes. The absorbed lipids are transported via chylomicrons into the lymphatic system.

ORGANS OF THE GI TRACT

MOUTH
Mastication begins the mechanical digestion of food. Solid fat melts with the warmth of the body. Lingual lipase in the saliva begins the chemical digestion of triglycerides.

STOMACH
Peristalsis mixes and churns the fat-containing food with gastric juices. Gastric lipase hydrolyzes some triglycerides, creating diglycerides and free fatty acids. In infants, lingual lipase also continues hydrolyzing triglycerides in the stomach.

SMALL INTESTINE
Bile secreted from the gallbladder through the common bile duct into the duodenum emulsifies fat into smaller globules.

Pancreatic lipase hydrolyzes triglycerides into monoglycerides, glycerol, and free fatty acids.

Phospholipases hydrolyze phospholipids.

The products of lipid hydrolysis are packaged into micelles for transport to enterocytes of the intestinal wall.

As they are absorbed into enterocytes, micelles separate into their component parts. Short-chain fatty acids enter the bloodstream directly. Long-chain fatty acids, cholesterol, phospholipids, and other remnants are repackaged into chylomicrons for transport into the lymphatic system.

LARGE INTESTINE
Any lipids not digested and absorbed in the small intestine bind to fiber and move into the large intestine to be eliminated in the feces.

ACCESSORY ORGANS

SALIVARY GLANDS
Produce saliva.

LIVER
Produces bile, which is stored in the gallbladder.

GALLBLADDER
Upon stimulation by CCK, releases bile into the duodenum through the common bile duct.

PANCREAS
Produces pancreatic lipase and phospholipases, which are secreted into the small intestine via the pancreatic duct.

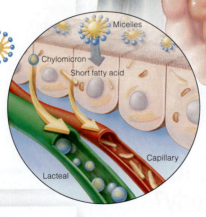

Micelles

Chylomicron

Short fatty acid

Capillary

Lacteal

accomplished by a group of enzymes called **lipases** (*-ase* = enzyme), which act on a specific site along the glycerol backbone. The digested fat is absorbed through the small intestine and transported by lipoproteins.

Triglyceride Digestion Begins in the Mouth and Stomach

The digestion of triglycerides begins in the mouth as the warmth of the body begins to melt it. As chewing continues and food mixes with saliva, lingual lipase (secreted from the glands located at the base of the tongue) begins to hydrolyze the medium-chain fatty acids. Lingual lipase, which plays only a minor role in adults, is structurally different from the other lipases found in the body, and it can hydrolyze fatty acids from any of the three carbons of the glycerol molecule. Lingual lipase travels with the bolus through the esophagus and into the stomach where it can function in the acid environment of the stomach before being deactivated.

The presence of the bolus as it enters the stomach stimulates the release of the hormone gastrin from the gastric pits lining the stomach. Gastrin in turn stimulates the release of gastric juices, rich in gastric lipase, from the chief cells. Fat mixes with the gastric lipase, and the enzyme hydrolyzes one fatty acid from the triglyceride, which produces a free fatty acid and a **diglyceride.**

Most Triglycerides Are Digested and Their Components Absorbed in the Small Intestine

The majority of triglyceride digestion occurs in the small intestine. When the triglyceride in chyme enters the duodenum, the hormone cholecystokinin (CCK) is secreted, which in turn stimulates the gallbladder to release bile through the bile duct into the duodenum. Just as oil can't disperse in water without the help of an emulsifier, the fat globules in chyme tend to cluster together rather than disperse in the watery digestive juices. Bile, the emulsifying greenish liquid made in the liver and stored in the gallbladder, begins to break up these fat globules. Hydrophobic portions of bile combine with the fat while hydrophilic portions attract the water in the digestive juices (**Figure 5.12**). This action reduces the fat globules to smaller droplets that are surrounded by bile and phospholipids, preventing the smaller droplets of fat from remerging. Reducing the size of the fat globules provides more surface area to expose the bonds so the enzyme pancreatic lipase can more easily hydrolyze the fat. The result is a smaller lipid complex called a **micelle,** which easily disperses throughout the fluids, with the hydrophilic head of phospholipids projecting into the intestinal juices surrounding a variety of lipids at the hydrophobic center of the complex.

Micelles also help transport the triglyceride remnants to the intestinal walls for absorption into the bloodstream. As pancreatic lipase continues to hydrolyze the triglyceride into two free fatty acids and a **monoglyceride,** these components are added to the micelle and transported inside the enterocyte.

Bile also emulsifies phospholipids during digestion. A group of enzymes called *phospholipases* hydrolyze phospholipids. These enzymes dismantle the phospholipids, producing two free fatty acids and the phospholipid remnant, which are part of the micelle complex transported through the intestinal wall.

Bile emulsifies sterols as well. Unlike triglycerides and phospholipids, however, sterols are not digested. Instead, they are absorbed intact in the center of the micelle through the intestinal wall.

If lipids are not digested and prepared for absorption in the small intestine, they bind to fiber and move into the large intestine, where they are eliminated in the feces. The large intestine does not have the enzymes necessary to digest lipids.

lipases A group of lipid-digesting enzymes.

diglyceride A remnant of fat digestion that consists of a glycerol with two attached fatty acids; also the form of fat used as an emulsifier in food production.

micelle Transport carrier in the small intestine that enables fatty acids and other compounds to be absorbed.

monoglyceride A remnant of fat digestion that consists of a glycerol with only one fatty acid attached to one of the three carbons.

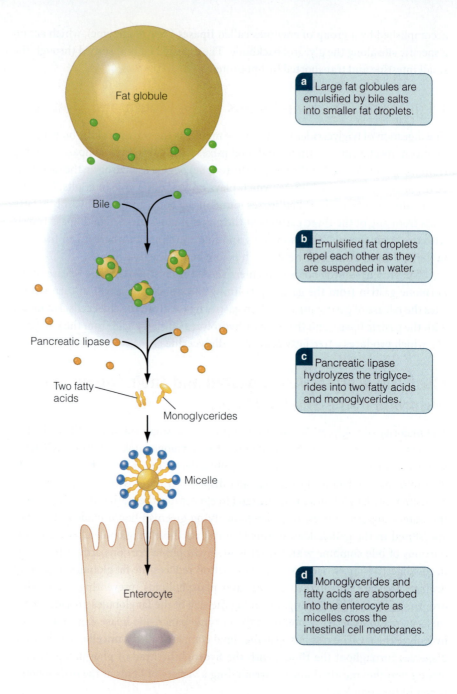

▶ Figure 5.12 Role of Bile in Emulsifying Fat
As fat globules enter the small intestine, bile breaks them apart into smaller globules called micelles.

Fat globule

Bile

a Large fat globules are emulsified by bile salts into smaller fat droplets.

b Emulsified fat droplets repel each other as they are suspended in water.

Pancreatic lipase

c Pancreatic lipase hydrolyzes the triglycerides into two fatty acids and monoglycerides.

Two fatty acids

Monoglycerides

Micelle

Enterocyte

d Monoglycerides and fatty acids are absorbed into the enterocyte as micelles cross the intestinal cell membranes.

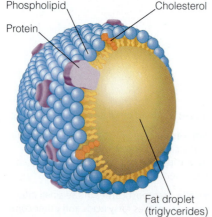

Phospholipid

Cholesterol

Protein

Fat droplet (triglycerides)

▲ Figure 5.13 Structure of a Chylomicron
A chylomicron contains a core of triglycerides and dietary lipids, surrounded by a coat of protein, phospholipids, and cholesterol.

Chylomicrons Facilitate Lipid Absorption

Micelles transport digested fats and phospholipids from the lumen of the GI tract into the enterocyte. Once inside, the different lipids are absorbed based on their structure. Glycerol and short- to medium-chain fatty acids pass into the bloodstream directly through the mucosa of the small intestine because they are more water soluble. They then enter the portal vein and go directly to the liver. Long-chain fatty acids and monoglycerides must be reassembled before they can pass into the bloodstream.

Inside the enterocyte, free long-chain fatty acids reattach to the monoglyceride to form a new triglyceride. These fats, together with carrier proteins and the other dietary lipids including phospholipids and cholesterol, are combined into a protein-containing transport carrier (or **lipoprotein**) called a **chylomicron** (**Figure 5.13**) and released into the tiny vessels of the lymph system called *lacteals* that contain **lymph fluid** (**Figure 5.14**).

Chylomicrons are too large to be absorbed directly into the bloodstream. They travel through the lymph system and enter the bloodstream when the lymph fluid joins the blood through the thoracic duct located next to the heart. As the

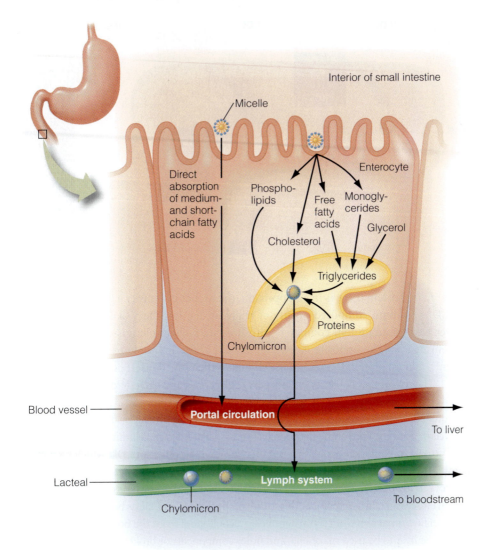

Interior of small intestine

Micelle

Enterocyte

Direct absorption of medium- and short-chain fatty acids

Phospho-lipids

Free fatty acids

Monogly-cerides

Glycerol

Cholesterol

Triglycerides

Proteins

Chylomicron

Blood vessel

Portal circulation

To liver

Lacteal

Lymph system

Chylomicron

To bloodstream

▲ **Figure 5.14 Absorption of Dietary Lipids**
Short- and medium-chain fatty acids are absorbed from the enterocytes directly into the bloodstream. Longer chain fatty acids, cholesterol, phospholipids, and other remnants are reassembled into chylomicrons and enter lymph before being routed into the bloodstream.

chylomicrons travel through the blood en route to the liver, they interact with the enzyme **lipoprotein lipase (LPL),** located in the walls of the capillaries. This enzyme hydrolyzes the triglycerides in the chylomicrons, separating the fatty acids from the glycerol backbone so they can be stored in the cells.

Fatty acids are used by muscles (including the heart) as energy, or stored as an energy reserve in the fat cells. After the fat is removed from the chylomicrons, the remnants of these lipoproteins travel to the liver to be dismantled.

Lipoproteins Transport Lipids

Chylomicrons are one form of lipoprotein, and they are made in the enterocytes to transport dietary lipids. The liver produces three other lipoproteins important to the transport of fat in the body: **very low-density lipoproteins (VLDLs)** formed from chylomicron remnants and lipids already present in the liver, **low-density lipoproteins (LDLs),** and **high-density lipoproteins (HDLs).** These lipoproteins are globular molecules comprised of a lipid center surrounded by a plasma membrane (refer again to the similarly shaped chylomicron in Figure 5.13).

The density of each lipoprotein determines how it functions. Density is determined by the amount of lipid and protein each lipoprotein contains (**Figure 5.15**).

lipoprotein Capsule-shaped transport carrier that enables fat and cholesterol to travel through the lymph and blood.

chylomicron A type of lipoprotein that carries digested fat and other lipids through the lymph system into the blood.

lymph fluid Fluid that circulates through the body in lymph vessels and eventually enters the bloodstream.

lipoprotein lipase (LPL) An enzyme that hydrolyzes triglycerides in lipoproteins into three fatty acids and glycerol.

very low-density lipoproteins (VLDLs) Lipoproteins that deliver fat made in the liver to the tissues. VLDL remnants are converted into LDLs.

low-density lipoproteins (LDLs) Lipoproteins that deposit cholesterol in the walls of the arteries. Because this can lead to heart disease, LDL is referred to as the "bad" cholesterol.

high-density lipoproteins (HDLs) Lipoproteins that remove cholesterol from the tissues and deliver it to the liver to be used as part of bile and/or to be excreted from the body. Because of this, HDL is known as the "good" cholesterol.

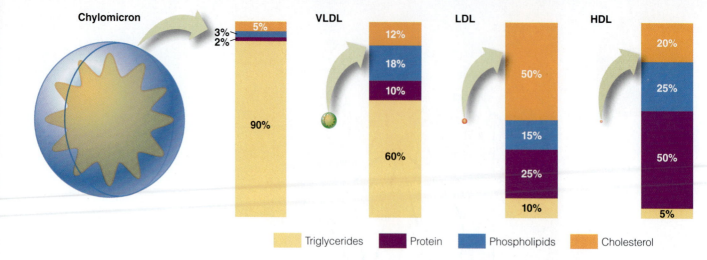

Chylomicron   VLDL   LDL   HDL

3% 2% 5%
90%

12%
18%
10%
60%

50%
15%
25%
10%

20%
25%
50%
5%

Triglycerides   Protein   Phospholipids   Cholesterol

▲ Figure 5.15 Lipoproteins
The ratio of protein to lipid determines the density of the lipoprotein (as well as its name). Chylomicrons are the largest of the lipoproteins and contain the least amount of protein.

The more protein there is in a lipoprotein, the higher its density. Chylomicrons and VLDLs are both composed mostly of triglycerides, but the VLDLs formed in the liver have more protein compared with lipid than chylomicrons do, which makes them denser. The opposite is true for HDLs. These lipoproteins are smaller and contain more protein than lipid, which makes them the densest of the lipoproteins.

The role of the VLDLs is to transport triglycerides and cholesterol from the liver to the cells, where they interact with lipoprotein lipase (**Focus Figure 5.16**). The enzyme lipoprotein lipase (LPL) resides on the surface of the cells and hydrolyzes the fatty acids and glycerol from the core of the lipoprotein. As fat is deposited in cells and tissues, the ratio of protein to lipid increases. What began as a VLDL becomes an LDL, which continues to transport triglycerides to the cells. The LDLs are often referred to as the "bad" cholesterol carriers because they deposit cholesterol in the walls of the arteries, which can lead to heart disease. To help remember this, think of the first "**L**" in **L**DL as being "**L**ousy."

The primary role of HDLs is to pick up cholesterol from the body cells and return it to the liver to be used make bile, and other components or broken down and excreted through the feces. In fact, approximately 25 percent of the cholesterol in blood is carried by HDLs back to the liver. Because of this function, HDLs are often referred to as the "good" cholesterol. An easy way to remember this is to think of the "**H**" in **H**DL as referring to "**H**ealthy." HDLs begin as high-density molecules, but as they pick up cholesterol from the cells, the percentage of lipid to protein changes and the density decreases. Thus, lipoproteins are constantly changing as they transport lipids throughout the body.

The level of LDL cholesterol relative to HDL cholesterol in the blood can be useful in determining the health of arteries. Essentially, the more HDL carriers in the blood, the harder the body is working to remove cholesterol from arterial cells and excrete it from the body. Higher levels of LDL carriers in the blood indicate that more fatty acids are being delivered to cells and deposited in the arterial walls, which may contribute to blockage.

LO 5.2: THE TAKE-HOME MESSAGE Most triglycerides are digested in the small intestine with the help of emulsifying bile and pancreatic lipase. Short- and medium-chain fatty acids are absorbed directly into the bloodstream. Longer chain fatty acids and other remnants of fat digestion are packaged as part of a chylomicron lipoprotein carrier, and then travel in the lymph before entering the bloodstream. Lipoproteins transport fat, cholesterol, and other lipids through the lymph and bloodstream. The VLDLs and LDLs deposit cholesterol in the cells and the arterial walls. HDL cholesterol carriers remove cholesterol from the arteries and deliver it to the liver to be used in the synthesis of bile and other compounds or excreted in the feces.

Dietary and endogenous lipids are transported in the body via several different lipoprotein compounds, such as chylomicrons, VLDLs, LDLs, and HDLs.

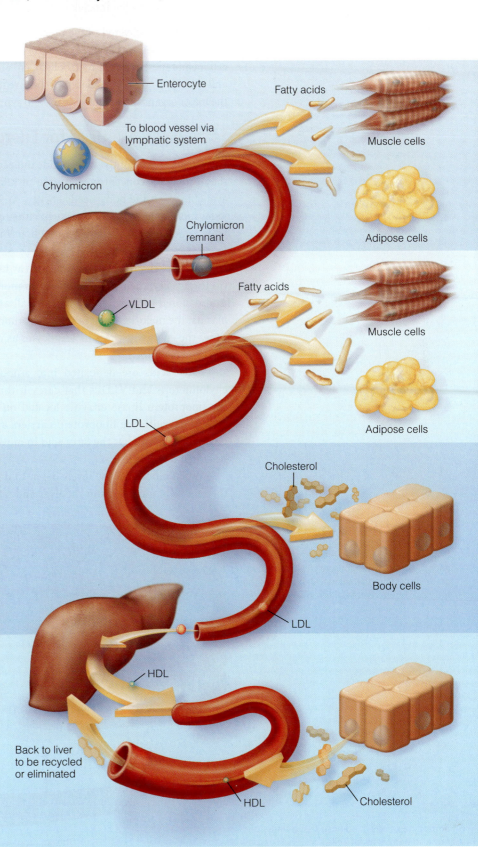

CHYLOMICRONS

Chylomicrons are formed in the enterocytes to transport lipids from a meal. Lipoprotein lipase, which is located on the surface of non-liver cells (mostly muscle and adipose cells), catalyzes the uptake of fatty acids into the cells through hydrolysis. The remaining chylomicron remnant is dismantled in the liver.

VLDLs

The liver produces VLDLs (very-low-density lipoproteins), which transport triglycerides to the cells. Lipoprotein lipase catalyzes the uptake of fatty acids into the cells, primarily those in muscle and adipose tissue, transforming VLDLs to LDLs (low-density lipoproteins).

LDLs

Low-density lipoproteins interact with receptor sites on body cells and release cholesterol into those cells. LDLs not taken up by cells degrade over time, releasing cholesterol that may then adhere to blood vessel walls.

HDLs

HDLs (high-density lipoproteins) produced by the liver circulate in the blood, picking up cholesterol from cells. The cholesterol is returned to the liver to be recycled or excreted, removing it from the bloodstream.

Enterocyte

Fatty acids

To blood vessel via lymphatic system

Muscle cells

Chylomicron

Chylomicron remnant

Adipose cells

Fatty acids

VLDL

Muscle cells

Adipose cells

LDL

Cholesterol

Body cells

LDL

HDL

Back to liver to be recycled or eliminated

HDL

Cholesterol

What Are the Functions of Lipids in the Body?

LO 5.3 Describe the functions of lipids in the body.

Once lipids are delivered to the tissues by lipoproteins, they serve several critical roles in the body. They are used as a source of energy, and to form body structures (including cell membranes), regulate metabolism, enhance the absorption of fat-soluble vitamins, and provide a layer of insulation to help regulate body temperature and help cushion the major organs; some lipids are used to synthesize hormones and bile.

Fatty Acids Are Used for Energy

Fatty acids as part of the triglyceride molecule are a powerful source of fuel because they provide a concentrated source of kilocalories, are easily stored, and readily available when the body needs energy. At 9 kilocalories per gram, dietary fat provides more than twice the energy of either carbohydrates or protein. In fact, dietary fat is a good source of energy throughout the day. The body has an *unlimited* ability to store excess energy as triglycerides in **adipocytes** (see **Figure 5.17**). These fat cells have the capacity to enlarge to as much as 1,000 times their original size. And if they fill to capacity, the body manufactures more adipocytes. Though some triglyceride is also stored in the muscle, and a small amount of fatty acids are found in blood plasma, the majority of fat is stored in adipose tissue. The body stores more than 60 times the energy reserves in adipocytes as it stores energy in both liver and muscle glycogen combined.

Fatty acids are deposited into adipose (and some muscle) cells from the chylomicrons and VLDLs that carry it through the blood. As mentioned earlier, the lipoprotein lipase enzyme located on the outside of adipocytes and muscle cells reacts with the lipoprotein carriers and cleaves the fatty acids from the triglyceride. This allows the fatty acid to move into the adipocyte and muscle cells to be stored for later use.

When blood glucose levels begin to decline, the hormone glucagon promotes the release of glucose from the liver and fatty acids from the triglyceride molecule

▶ **Figure 5.17 Adipocytes**
Excess triglycerides are stored in the adipocytes for later use. When the body needs energy, the enzyme lipoprotein lipase, located on the outside of the adipocyte, breaks off the fatty acids from the chylomicron or VLDL.

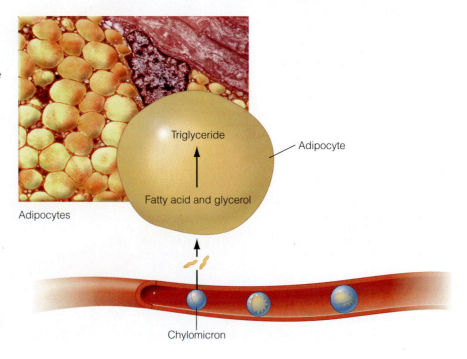

Adipocytes

Triglyceride

Adipocyte

Fatty acid and glycerol

Chylomicron

adipocytes Cells in adipose tissue that store fat; also known as fat cells.

stored in adipocytes to provide additional energy for the body. The heart, liver, and resting muscles prefer fatty acids as their fuel source, which spares glucose to be used by the central nervous system and red blood cells. The fatty acids stored in the adipocytes provide a backup source of energy between meals.

In a famine situation, some individuals could last months without eating, depending upon the extent of their triglyceride stores and the availability of adequate fluids. However, people can still die from starvation before their triglyceride stores are depleted if they do not consume some glucose. Stores of triglycerides alone cannot sustain life because glucose cannot be made from fatty acids or ketone bodies. Glycerol is the only part of the stored triglycerides that can be used for gluconeogenesis.

Dietary Fat Aids the Absorption of Lipid Compounds

Several essential nutrients, including the fat-soluble vitamins A, D, E, and K, as well as carotenoids, cholesterol, phospholipids, and other lipid compounds, require dietary fat in order to be absorbed. Twenty grams of dietary fat is needed daily to stimulate the formation of the chylomicrons that transport the fat-soluble vitamins. Consuming less than this amount may impede fat-soluble vitamin absorption.

Triglycerides Stored in Adipose Tissue Insulate the Body and Protect Vital Organs

The stored triglycerides located in the subcutaneous tissue, just under the skin, help to insulate the body and maintain body temperature, especially in cold temperatures. However, excess body fat may actually hinder temperature regulation in hot weather, as the excess layer of stored fat prevents heat from flowing to the skin for release.

Stored triglycerides also act as a protective cushion against trauma for the bones and vital organs, including the brain, liver, kidneys, and spinal cord. Stored triglycerides in the abdomen act like a fatty apron protecting the liver and stomach from injury. However, too much stored fat eliminates the protective benefits because of the accompanying increased risk of heart disease, hypertension, and diabetes.

Essential Fatty Acids Manufacture Eicosanoids and Maintain Cell Membranes

The essential fatty acids discussed earlier in the chapter, linoleic acid and alpha-linolenic acid, are needed as precursors to form other compounds in the body (**Figure 5.18**). For instance, linoleic acid can be elongated and desaturated to **arachidonic acid,** a 20-carbon, four-double-bond polyunsaturated fatty acid. Alpha-linolenic acid is desaturated into the omega-3 fatty acid **eicosapentaenoic acid (EPA)** and then elongated to a second omega-3 fatty acid, **docosahexaenoic acid (DHA)**. These omega-3 fatty acids can also be obtained by eating cold-water fish such as salmon, herring, tuna, and halibut. EPA and arachidonic acid are used to manufacture **eicosanoids,** which are hormonelike substances such as prostaglandins, thromboxanes, and leukotrienes. These compounds regulate the immune system, blood clotting, inflammation, and blood pressure.

Alpha-linolenic acid is also needed for the structure of healthy cell membranes, particularly in nerve tissues and the retina. A lack of this essential fatty acid in the diet can result in depression, impaired vision, and scaly skin.

The Liver Uses Cholesterol to Make Hormones, Bile, and Vitamin D

Cholesterol is also the precursor of some very important compounds. A key role of cholesterol is to serve as the starting material in the synthesis of steroid hormones,

arachidonic acid An omega-6 fatty acid formed from linoleic acid; it is used to synthesize the eicosanoids, including leukotrienes, prostaglandins, and thromboxanes.

eicosapentaenoic acid (EPA) and docosahexaenoic acid (DHA) EPA (C20:5n–3) and DHA (C22:6n–3) are omega-3 fatty acids that are synthesized in the body and found in cold-water fish. These compounds may be beneficial in reducing heart disease.

eicosanoids Hormonelike substances in the body. Prostaglandins, thromboxanes, and leukotrienes are all eicosanoids.

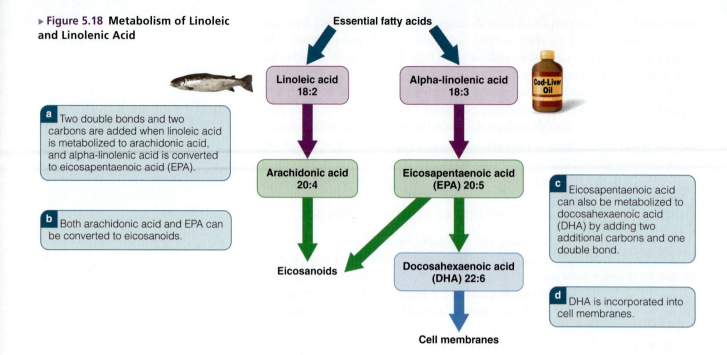

▶ **Figure 5.18 Metabolism of Linoleic and Linolenic Acid**

Essential fatty acids

Linoleic acid 18:2

Alpha-linolenic acid 18:3

Cod-Liver Oil

a Two double bonds and two carbons are added when linoleic acid is metabolized to arachidonic acid, and alpha-linolenic acid is converted to eicosapentaenoic acid (EPA).

Arachidonic acid 20:4

Eicosapentaenoic acid (EPA) 20:5

c Eicosapentaenoic acid can also be metabolized to docosahexaenoic acid (DHA) by adding two additional carbons and one double bond.

b Both arachidonic acid and EPA can be converted to eicosanoids.

Eicosanoids

Docosahexaenoic acid (DHA) 22:6

d DHA is incorporated into cell membranes.

Cell membranes

▶ **Figure 5.19 Bile Is Made from Cholesterol in the Liver**
Bile is made in the liver from cholesterol and stored in the gallbladder. It contains water, electrolytes, and a variety of *bile acids*. Cholic acid is one of the primary bile acids utilized for fat digestion.

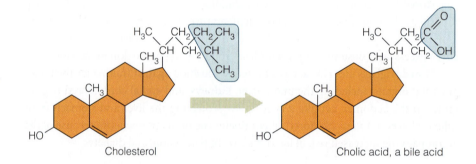

Cholesterol

Cholic acid, a bile acid

including the sex hormones estrogen and testosterone, and the adrenal corticoids such as cortisol and aldosterone. The liver uses cholesterol to manufacture bile (**Figure 5.19**), and a type of cholesterol in the skin is converted to a previtamin D by the ultraviolet rays of the sun.

Phospholipids and Cholesterol Make Up Cell Membranes

Phospholipids make up the phospholipid bilayer in cell membranes. Their hydrophilic polar heads are attracted to the watery fluids both outside and inside of the cells, and their hydrophobic tails line up with each other in the center, creating a phospholipid barrier that surrounds the cell (**Figure 5.20**). This structure of the cell membrane allows certain substances, such as water, to enter the cell but keeps others, like protein, from leaking out.

The body also uses cholesterol as a structural component in cell membranes by improving cell fluidity and firmness. In cell membranes, cholesterol is interwoven with phospholipids to provide integrity to the cells. The unique shape of cholesterol makes the outer surface of the cell membrane less soluble to very small molecules that could pass too easily across the cell membrane. Cholesterol helps keep phospholipids separate from each other so that the tails or fatty acid chains of the phospholipids don't crystallize. In this way, cholesterol improves cell fluidity.

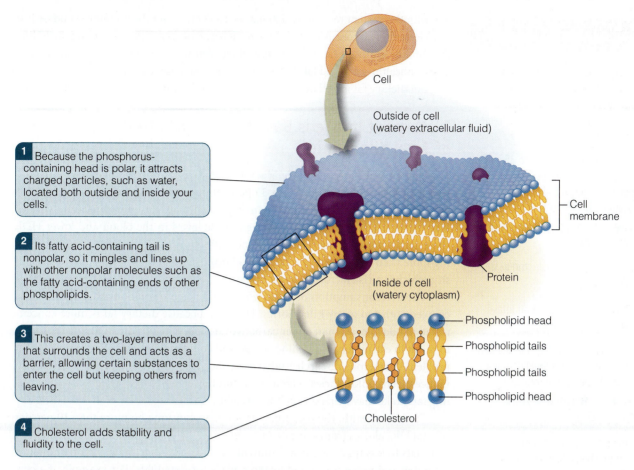

1 Because the phosphorus-containing head is polar, it attracts charged particles, such as water, located both outside and inside your cells.

2 Its fatty acid-containing tail is nonpolar, so it mingles and lines up with other nonpolar molecules such as the fatty acid-containing ends of other phospholipids.

3 This creates a two-layer membrane that surrounds the cell and acts as a barrier, allowing certain substances to enter the cell but keeping others from leaving.

4 Cholesterol adds stability and fluidity to the cell.

Cell

Outside of cell (watery extracellular fluid)

Cell membrane

Protein

Inside of cell (watery cytoplasm)

Phospholipid head

Phospholipid tails

Phospholipid tails

Phospholipid head

Cholesterol

▲ **Figure 5.20 The Role of Phospholipids and Cholesterol in Cell Membranes**
The two-layer cell membrane surrounding the cell is comprised of a polar head and nonpolar tail. Cholesterol keeps the phospholipids separate.

LO 5.3: THE TAKE-HOME MESSAGE Fatty acids are an energy-dense source of fuel for the body. Stored triglycerides cushion and protect bones, organs, and nerves, and help maintain body temperature. Dietary fat provides essential fatty acids and is needed for the absorption of fat-soluble vitamins and carotenoids. Essential fatty acids are precursors to arachidonic acid, EPA and DHA, which manufacture prostaglandins, thromboxanes, and leukotrienes, substances that regulate the immune system, blood clotting, inflammation, and blood pressure. Cholesterol is used to make sex hormones, bile, and vitamin D. Phospholipids and cholesterol are part of cell membranes.

What Are the Recommendations for Daily Intake of Triglycerides and Cholesterol?

LO 5.4 Define the dietary recommendations for total fat, the essential fatty acids, cholesterol, and *trans* fat.

Americans' fat consumption has gone up and down over the last century. In the 1930s, Americans were consuming about 34 percent of their kilocalories from fat; this number climbed to 42 percent in the mid-1960s. By 1984, fat consumption had declined to 36 percent of total kilocalories. The latest research indicates that our dietary fat intake is at 32 percent of total kilocalories.[2] However, while today's consumption levels are in

Calculation Corner

Calculating the AMDR for Fat

Approximately how many grams of total fat does an individual with a 2,000-kilocalorie energy requirement need to consume to meet the recommendations?

The AMDR recommends that 20 to 35 percent of daily kilocalories (kcal) come from fat, so the range for an individual who needs 2,000 kilocalories per day would be:

2,000 kcal × 0.20 (20%) = 400 kcal;
    9 kcal/g = 44 g

2,000 kcal × 0.35 (35%) = 700 kcal;
    9 kcal/g = 78 g

Answer: This person's range of fat intake should be 44 to 78 grams daily.

To find the maximum grams of saturated and *trans* fats that this person should consume daily, calculate 10 percent of total kcal:

2,000 kcal × 0.10 (10%) = 200 kcal;
    9 kcal/g = 22 g

Answer: The total amount of saturated fat and *trans* fat should be no more than 22 grams daily.

Scan this QR code with your mobile device to access practice math activities. You can also access the activities in MasteringNutrition™.

---

line with the current recommendations, we can't break out the hot fudge sundaes just yet. Measuring fat consumption as a percentage of total kilocalories, without including the absolute grams of fat, can be misleading. You will soon read that the amount of heart-unhealthy saturated fat that we are eating could use some adjusting.

But dietary fat is still essential for health. So how much should you consume?

Dietary Fat Intake Is Based on a Percentage of Total Kilocalories

The current AMDR (Acceptable Macronutrient Distribution Range) recommendation is to limit fat intake to 20 to 35 percent of daily kilocalories. For some individuals, a very low-fat diet of less than 20 percent that is also high in carbohydrates may increase LDL cholesterol and triglyceride levels in the blood and lower HDL cholesterol—which is not a healthy combination for the heart. For others, consuming more than 35 percent of total daily kilocalories from fat could perpetuate obesity, which is a risk factor for heart disease.

The overconsumption of dietary fat won't increase you body weight unless it's coupled with too many kilocalories. However, because dietary fat is more concentrated in kilocalories than either carbohydrates or protein, a diet high in fat is likely to result in eating too many kilocalories, and could make for a weight-management problem. Numerous research studies have shown that reducing dietary fat can also reduce dietary kilocalories, which can result in weight loss.[3] Consequently, controlling fat intake may help control body weight.

For heart health, the recommendation is to consume no more than 10 percent of total kilocalories from saturated fats (and ideally less than 7 percent) and to limit *trans* fats to less than 1 percent.[4] Individuals are encouraged to use more monounsaturated and polyunsaturated fats to replace saturated fats. For example, if a person consumes 30 percent of his total kilocalories as fat, about 6 percent should be derived from saturated fats, 1 percent or less from *trans* fat, about 10 percent from polyunsaturated fats, and 13 percent from monounsaturated fats. This is because monounsaturated fats are the best at lowering LDL cholesterol and either maintaining or slightly increasing HDL cholesterol.

When it comes to keeping track of fat intake, counting grams of fat in foods is a good strategy. **Table 5.1** provides a healthy range of recommended fat intake based on daily kilocalorie needs. (To figure out your approximate daily kilocalorie

---

How Much Fat Is in Your Diet?

Are you consuming too much fat, saturated fat, *trans* fat, or all three? Use a diet analysis program, the food tables in the appendix, or food labels to track your fat consumption for a day and fill out the food log below. How does your actual intake compare with the amount recommended for you in Table 5.1?

Food Log				
Meal	Food/Drink	Total Fat (g)	Saturated Fat (g)	*Trans* Fat (g)
Breakfast				
Snack				
Lunch				
Snack				
Dinner				
Snack				
Total				

TABLE 5.1 Capping Your Fat Intake

Daily Energy Needs (Kilocalories)	Maximum Recommended Amount of Daily Dietary Fat Intake	
	Fat (g) (20% to 35% of Total Kilocalories)	Saturated Fat and Trans Fat (g) (<10% of Total Kilocalories)
1,600	36–62	18
1,700	38–66	19
1,800	40–70	20
1,900	42–74	21
2,000	44–78	22
2,100	47–82	23
2,200	49–86	24
2,300	51–89	26
2,400	53–93	27
2,500	56–97	28
2,600	58–101	29
2,700	60–105	30
2,800	62–109	31

Sedentary women consume approximately 1,600 kilocalories daily. Teenage girls, active women, and many sedentary men need approximately 2,200 kilocalories daily. Teenage boys, many active men, and some very active women need about 2,800 kilocalories daily.

needs, see Chapter 2). Use the Self-Assessment to estimate how much total fat you currently consume daily.

Essential Fatty Acids Have Specific Recommendations

The only necessary dietary fats are the two essential fatty acids: linoleic acid and alpha-linolenic acid. The Adequate Intake (AI) of alpha-linolenic acid per day for men and women is 1.6 and 1.1 grams, respectively. The AI for linoleic acid is set much higher, at 17 grams per day for adult men and 12 grams per day for adult women.[5] Americans currently consume only about 0.1 to 0.2 grams of EPA and DHA in their daily diet.

The AMDR for linoleic acid is set at 5 to 10 percent of total kilocalories, while alpha-linolenic acid should make up 0.6 percent to 1.2 percent of total kilocalories. These recommended amounts are based on the estimated daily kilocalorie needs according to gender and age.

Based on randomized trials, the American Heart Association recommends that people diagnosed with heart disease consume about 1 gram of essential fatty acids each day. For those who have been diagnosed with **hypertriglyceridemia** (elevated blood triglycerides), 2 to 4 grams per day of EPA and DHA supplements may lower blood triglycerides.[6]

Dietary Cholesterol and Phospholipids Are Not Essential

Many people are confused about the merits of cholesterol. While high blood cholesterol has been proclaimed as unhealthy, cholesterol is the precursor in the synthesis of bile, hormones, and part of the cell membrane. But do we need to eat cholesterol to accomplish these tasks?

hypertriglyceridemia The presence of high levels of triglycerides in the blood. Defined as triglyceride levels between 400 and 1,000 milligrams per deciliter.

TABLE 5.2	How Much Cholesterol Is in Foods?	
		Cholesterol (mg)
Liver, 3 oz		324
Breakfast biscuit with egg and sausage, 1		290
Egg, 1 large		186
Shrimp, canned, 3 oz		147
Fast-food hamburger, large, double patty		122
Ice cream, soft serve, vanilla, ½ cup		78
Beef, ground, cooked, 3 oz		77
Salmon, cooked, 3 oz		74
Chicken or turkey, breast, cooked, 3 oz		72
Lobster, cooked, 3 oz		61
Turkey, light meat, cooked, 3 oz		59
Egg noodles, 1 cup		53
Butter, 1 tbs		31
Cheddar cheese, 1 oz		30
Frankfurter, beef, 1		24
Milk, whole, 1 cup		24
Cheddar cheese, low fat, 1 oz		6
Milk, skim, 1 cup		4

Data from USDA. 2014. *National Nutrient Database for Standard Reference, Release 26.* Available at www.ars .usda.gov. Accessed March 2014.

Eggs are an excellent source of protein, but egg yolks are high in dietary cholesterol.

The answer is no. Dietary cholesterol is not necessary because the liver synthesizes all that the body needs. The liver manufactures about 900 milligrams of cholesterol per day. This is three times greater than the 300 milligrams the average American consumes daily. However, if cholesterol is consumed, the body adjusts the amount it synthesizes. Normally, the total amount of cholesterol remains constant because the rate of cholesterol synthesis in the liver is under feedback control. When the dietary intake is high, liver synthesis is low; when intake is low, synthesis increases.

As mentioned earlier, dietary cholesterol should be limited to reduce the risk of developing cardiovascular disease. Healthy individuals over the age of 2 are advised to limit their dietary cholesterol to less than 300 milligrams (mg) daily, on average.[7] Adult males in the United States currently consume about 358 milligrams daily, whereas adult females take in slightly more than 237 milligrams of cholesterol daily, on average. **Table 5.2** lists a variety of foods and their cholesterol content. One diet that may reduce the risk of developing cardiovascular disease is the Mediterranean diet. For more on this diet, see the Spotlight feature, "The Mediterranean Diet: What Do People Living in the Mediterranean Do Differently?" on page 179.

Even though lecithin, the most common phospholipid in our diet, plays an important role in the body, it does not need to be consumed in foods or in supplements. The liver is able to synthesize all phospholipids, including lecithin. In fact, dietary lecithin is digested in the GI tract, which means it does not reach the cell membranes intact.

Despite their frequent mention in the popular press, lecithin supplements, which are often marketed as a miracle solution for weight loss, fat metabolism, cardiovascular health, exercise performance, and arthritis relief, have not been scientifically proven to be effective in weight loss or improving health. In addition, the fatty acids present in dietary phospholipids (which, like all lipids, contain 9 kilocalories per gram) can add unwanted kilocalories.

LO 5.4: THE TAKE-HOME MESSAGE Dietary lipids, particularly the essential fatty acids, are key for a healthy diet, but intake of saturated fats, *trans* fats, and cholesterol should be limited. Dietary fat intake should range from 20 to 35 percent of total kilocalories. To meet essential fatty acid needs, 5 to 10 percent of total daily kilocalories should come from linoleic acid and 0.6 to 1.2 percent of total daily kilocalories should come from alpha-linolenic acid. Dietary intake of saturated fat should be limited to no more than 10 percent of total fat consumption, and less than 1 percent of fat consumption should be from *trans* fats. Dietary cholesterol should be limited to less than 300 milligrams per day. Cholesterol and phospholipids are both made in the body and are not considered essential nutrients.

What Are the Best, Worst, and Alternative Food Sources for Fat?

LO 5.5 Identify the best, worst, and alternative food sources of the different types of fats, including the essential fatty acids, saturated fats, and *trans* fats.

Eating foods that contain unsaturated fats (which also contain essential fatty acids) is better for health than eating foods high in saturated fat, cholesterol, and/or *trans* fat. So, which foods contain the healthier fats?

The Best Food Sources Are Low in Saturated Fat

Unsaturated fats are abundant in vegetable oils, such as soybean, corn, and canola oils, as well as in soybeans, walnuts, flaxseeds, and wheat germ. These foods are also all good

The Mediterranean Diet: What Do People Living in the Mediterranean Do Differently?

The Mediterranean diet doesn't refer to the diet of a specific country but to the dietary patterns found in several areas of the Mediterranean region, specifically Crete (a Greek island), other areas of Greece, and southern Italy, circa 1960. Researchers were first drawn to these areas in the early 1990s because the adults living there had very low rates of chronic diseases, such as heart disease and cancer, and a very long life expectancy. For example, the natives of Greece had a rate of heart disease that was 90 percent lower than that of Americans at that time.[1] Ironically, the people in Crete, in particular, were less educated and affluent, and less likely to obtain good medical care than were Americans, so their health successes could not be explained by education level, financial status, or a superior health care system.

Early research found that compared with the diets of affluent Americans, the Cretans' diet was dramatically lower in foods from animal sources, such as meat, eggs, and dairy products, and higher in monounsaturated fats (mostly from olive oil and olives) and inexpensive grains, fruits, and vegetables.[2] In 2000, a study in Greece showed that greater adherence to a traditional Mediterranean diet was associated with greater longevity.[3] In another study, individuals who had experienced a heart attack, and then adopted a Mediterranean-style diet, had a 50 to 70 percent lower risk of recurrent heart disease compared with those following a more classic low-saturated-fat, low-cholesterol diet.[4, 5]

The latest research continues to support the health benefits of a Mediterranean-style diet, not just in high-risk populations, but also in young, working adults. Numerous studies indicate that adopting a Mediterranean-style diet lowers cardiovascular risk factors, including a decrease in LDL cholesterol and an increase in HDL cholesterol, lowered high blood pressure,[6] and lowered the risk of peripheral artery disease.[7] People who follow the Mediterranean diet are more likely to live longer,[8] have lower blood glucose, reduce their abdominal fat, and reduce inflammation.[9]

The newly updated Mediterranean Diet Pyramid (**Figure 1**) was designed to reflect these dietary patterns and lifestyle habits.[10] Let's look more closely at this pyramid, the dietary and lifestyle changes that augment it, and some potential changes that you could make in your diet and lifestyle to reap similar benefits.

Mediterranean Lifestyle

First, notice that there are no portion recommendations in the Mediterranean diet pyramid. This purposeful omission portrays the relative importance and frequency of each group of foods as it contributes to the whole diet, rather than to a strict diet plan. It was designed to include recommendations for every main meal, as well as daily and weekly guidelines that provide an overview of healthy food choices rather than dictate rigid amounts from each food group.[11]

Next, note that physical activity is front and center, at the base of this pyramid, reflecting the foundation for the Mediterranean way of life. In addition to exercise, Mediterranean citizens traditionally enjoyed other lifestyle habits that have been known to promote good mental and physical health. They had a supportive community of family and friends, long relaxing family meals, and afternoon siestas (naps). Exercising daily, resting, and relaxing with family and friends is good health advice for all, no matter what food plan you follow.

A Diet of Well-Seasoned Plant Foods, Olive Oil, Fish, and Dairy

Plant-based foods such as whole grains, fruits, vegetables, legumes, and nuts are the focus of the Mediterranean diet. In fact, more than 60 percent of the recommended calories are supplied by these high-fiber, nutritionally dense plant foods. In traditional Mediterranean-style eating, a combination of plant foods, such as vegetables and legumes combined with couscous or pasta, is the focus of the meal. Fruit can be served as dessert. Spices, herbs, garlic, and onions add flavor to foods while reducing the need for salt.

More than 75 percent of the fat in the Mediterranean Diet Pyramid is supplied by olives and olive oil. As previously discussed, vegetable oils are low in saturated fat, and olive oil in particular is high in monounsaturated fat. Two servings of heart-healthy meals featuring fish and seafood should be enjoyed weekly.

Nonfat milk and yogurt, and low- or reduced-fat cheeses can be enjoyed on a daily basis when eating

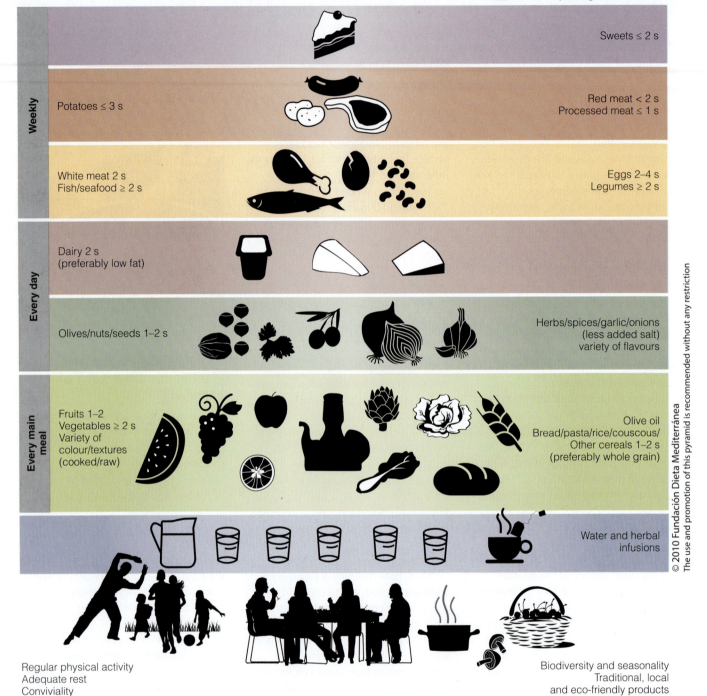

Serving size based on frugality and local habits

Wine in moderation and respecting social beliefs

Sweets ≤ 2 s

Weekly

Potatoes ≤ 3 s

Red meat < 2 s
Processed meat ≤ 1 s

White meat 2 s
Fish/seafood ≥ 2 s

Eggs 2–4 s
Legumes ≥ 2 s

Every day

Dairy 2 s
(preferably low fat)

Olives/nuts/seeds 1–2 s

Herbs/spices/garlic/onions
(less added salt)
variety of flavours

Every main meal

Fruits 1–2
Vegetables ≥ 2 s
Variety of
colour/textures
(cooked/raw)

Olive oil
Bread/pasta/rice/couscous/
Other cereals 1–2 s
(preferably whole grain)

Water and herbal
infusions

Regular physical activity
Adequate rest
Conviviality

Biodiversity and seasonality
Traditional, local
and eco-friendly products
Culinary activities

s = Serving

© 2010 Fundación Dieta Mediterránea
The use and promotion of this pyramid is recommended without any restriction

▲ **Figure 1** **The Healthy Mediterranean Diet Pyramid**
A plant-based diet with minimal amounts of high-saturated-fat, high-sugar foods, coupled with daily physical activity, reflects the healthy habits of the Mediterranean lifestyle.

Source: Fundacion Dieta Mediterranea. 2010. *Mediterranean Diet Pyramid Today: Science and Cultural Updates.* Available at http://dietamediterranea.com/en

a Mediterranean-style diet. A small amount of grated Parmesan cheese sprinkled over vegetables and a grain-based meal can provide a distinct Mediterranean flavor.

Occasional Poultry, Eggs, and Meat

Foods from animal sources are limited in the Mediterranean diet. The Mediterranean Diet Pyramid relegates red meat consumption to less than 2 servings weekly. No more than two to four servings of eggs should be eaten weekly and poultry should be limited to about two servings per week.

Sweets, Water, and Wine

Historically, sweets were more prevalent during the holidays and fruit was the standard daily dessert. Consequently, the Mediterranean Diet Pyramid recommends that consumption of honey- or sugar-based sweets remain modest or less than two servings per week. Water is recommended daily. Though the pyramid depicts wine on a daily basis, it is actually considered optional and based on personal preferences, family and medical history, and social situations.

Sustainability of the Mediterranean Diet

The Mediterranean diet is a perfect example of a food plan that is sustainable. This concept is not based on specific foods but rather the social, economic, and environmental issues that influence the food choices and health outcomes of following a specific food plan. This symbiotic approach to eating and lifestyle combines the old food ways of the Mediterranean with the environmentally conscious style that includes nutrition, health benefits, locally grown foods, and culture into a sustainable, healthy cuisine.[12]

How Does the Mediterranean Diet Pyramid Compare with MyPlate?

There are many similarities between the Mediterranean Diet Pyramid and MyPlate. Both emphasize the importance of regular physical activity, and both encourage a plant-based diet rich in whole grains, fruits, and vegetables, and daily consumption of dairy products. Mediterranean-style eating encourages the use of olive oil, a fat source that is rich in heart-healthy, unsaturated fat, and fish and seafood. Vegetable oils are also encouraged on MyPlate, but more modestly. Whereas poultry, eggs, and meat are recommended more modestly in the Mediterranean Diet Pyramid than in MyPlate, both advise minimizing intake of sweets. Both tools can be used as a foundation for a healthy diet.

References

1. E. Helsing. 1995. Traditional Diets and Disease Patterns of the Mediterranean, circa 1960. *American Journal of Clinical Nutrition* 61:1329S–1337S.
2. Ibid.
3. P. Kris-Etherton, R. H. Eckel, B. V. Howard, S. St. Jeor, and T. L. Bazzarre. 2001. Lyon Diet Heart Study: Benefits of a Mediterranean-Style, National Cholesterol Education Program/American Heart Association Step I Dietary Pattern on Cardiovascular Disease. *Circulation* 103:1823–1825.
4. A. N. Trichopoulou, T. Costacou, C. Bamia, and D. Trichopoulos. 2003. Adherence to a Mediterranean Diet and Survival in a Greek Population. *New England Journal of Medicine* 348:2599–2608.
5. M. de Loregil, P. Salen, J. L. Martin, I. Monjaud, J. Delaye, and N. Mamelle. 1999. Mediterranean Diet, Traditional Risk Factors, and the Rate of Cardiovascular Complications After Myocardial Infarction: Final Report of the Lyon Diet Heart Study. *Circulation* 99:779–785.
6. J. Yang A. Farioli, M. Korre, and S. N. Kales. 2014. Modified Mediterranean Diet Score and Cardiovascular Risk in a North American Working Population. *PLoS ONE* 9(2): e87539. doi:10.1371/journal.pone.0087539.
7. M. Ruiz-Canela, R. Estruch, D. Corella, J. Salas-Salvadó, and M. A. Martínez-González. 2014. Association of Mediterranean Diet with Peripheral Artery Disease. *Journal of the American Medical Association* 311(4):415–417.
8. M. Guasch-Ferré, M. Bulló, M. A. Martínez-González, E. Ros, D. Corella, R. Estruch, M. Fitó, et al. 2013. Frequency of Nut Consumption and Mortality Risk in the PREDIMED Nutrition Intervention Trial. *BMC Medicine* 11:164 DOI: 10.1186/1741-7015-11-164.
9. Sara Tulipani, Rafael Llorach, Olga Jáuregui, Patricia López-Uriarte, Mar Garcia-Aloy, Mònica Bullo, Jordi Salas-Salvadó, and Cristina Andrés-Lacueva. 2011. Metabolomics Unveils Urinary Changes in Subjects with Metabolic Syndrome Following 12-Week Nut Consumption. *Journal of Proteome Research* DOI: 10.1021/pr200514h.
10. A. Bach-Faig, E. M. Berry, D. Lairon, J. Reguant, A. Trichopoulou, S. Dernini, F. X. Medina, et al. 2011. Mediterranean Diet Pyramid Today. Science and Cultural Updates. *Public Health Nutrition* 14(12A): 2274–2284.
11. Ibid.
12. B. Burlingame and S. Dernini. 2011. Sustainable Diets: the Mediterranean Diet as an Example. *Public Health Nutrition* 14(12A): 2285–2287.

▶ Figure 5.21 Food Sources
of the Essential Fatty Acids
Many oils and nuts are good sources of the two
essential fatty acids.

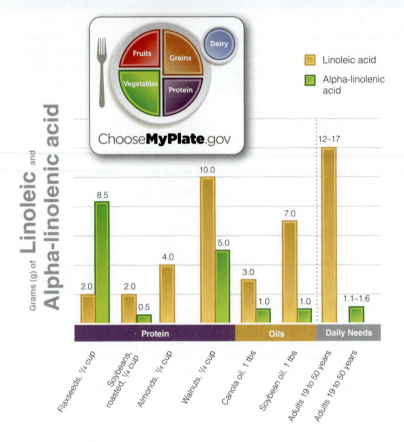

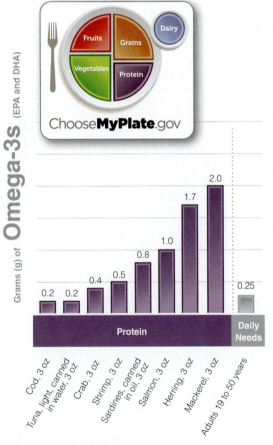

▲ Figure 5.22 Food Sources of Omega-3 Fatty Acids
Several types of fish, particularly fatty fish, are high in the
heart-healthy omega-3 fatty acids.

sources of linoleic acid. Walnuts, flaxseeds, and canola oil also contain alpha-linolenic acid. **Figure 5.21** lists examples of foods that are excellent sources of unsaturated fats and essential fatty acids.

Fish are generally good sources of omega-3 fatty acids, and all fish contain EPA and DHA, with fatty fish being especially rich sources (**Figure 5.22**). Cod-liver oil is abundant in EPA and DHA but it is also very high in vitamin A, which can be detrimental. Eating fish, rather than taking cod-liver oil, is a safer way to obtain EPA and DHA, and has been shown to improve heart health.[8]

Individuals are sometimes hesitant to consume fish due to a concern about mercury levels. Although all fish and shellfish contain a trace of mercury, the levels of mercury are not considered a health risk for most people.

Foods high in saturated fat should be limited in the diet. Most saturated fat comes from animal foods, such as fatty cuts of meat, whole-milk dairy products (including cheese, butter, and ice cream), and the skin on poultry. Certain vegetable oils, such as coconut, palm, and palm kernel oils, are also very high in saturated fat. These tropical oils are sometimes found in candies, commercially made baked goods, and gourmet ice cream. Reading the ingredient label on food packages is the best way to check for these oils. Read more on the use of coconut oil in Examining the Evidence: Is Coconut Oil the Next Superfood? on page 184.

While it's important to limit saturated fat in the diet, it's impossible to eliminate it entirely. All fats and oils contain a variety of fatty acids, some of which are bound to be saturated. Avoiding all fat-containing foods, or eliminating all oils during cooking, could lead to the unnecessary exclusion of healthy foods, such as soybean and canola oils, lean meats, fish, poultry, and low-fat dairy foods.

The result may be an inadequate intake of important nutrients such as essential fatty acids, fat-soluble vitamins, protein, and calcium. A better strategy is to consume lower fat versions of these foods, so you obtain the healthy nutrients while avoiding unnecessary, unhealthy fats. **Figure 5.23** helps compare high-fat and lower fat versions of several commonly eaten foods.

In the supermarket, read the Nutrition Facts panel to help you choose foods that are low in fat. The nutrition label of packaged foods can be used to compare the

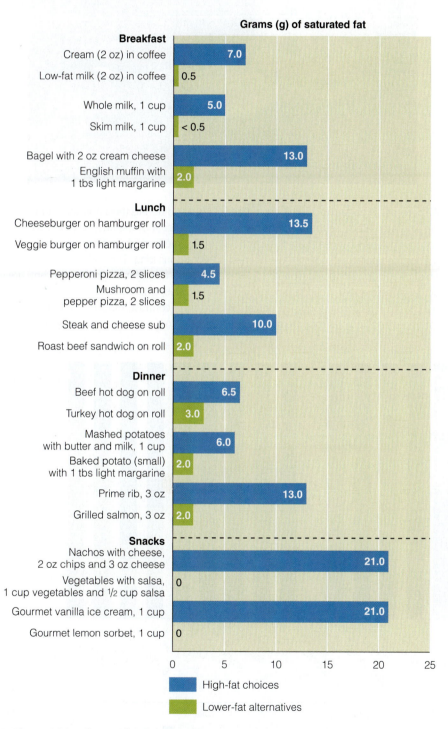

Grams (g) of saturated fat

Breakfast
Cream (2 oz) in coffee — 7.0 (High-fat)
Low-fat milk (2 oz) in coffee — 0.5 (Lower-fat)

Whole milk, 1 cup — 5.0 (High-fat)
Skim milk, 1 cup — < 0.5 (Lower-fat)

Bagel with 2 oz cream cheese — 13.0 (High-fat)
English muffin with 1 tbs light margarine — 2.0 (Lower-fat)

Lunch
Cheeseburger on hamburger roll — 13.5 (High-fat)
Veggie burger on hamburger roll — 1.5 (Lower-fat)

Pepperoni pizza, 2 slices — 4.5 (High-fat)
Mushroom and pepper pizza, 2 slices — 1.5 (Lower-fat)

Steak and cheese sub — 10.0 (High-fat)
Roast beef sandwich on roll — 2.0 (Lower-fat)

Dinner
Beef hot dog on roll — 6.5 (High-fat)
Turkey hot dog on roll — 3.0 (Lower-fat)

Mashed potatoes with butter and milk, 1 cup — 6.0 (High-fat)
Baked potato (small) with 1 tbs light margarine — 2.0 (Lower-fat)

Prime rib, 3 oz — 13.0 (High-fat)
Grilled salmon, 3 oz — 2.0 (Lower-fat)

Snacks
Nachos with cheese, 2 oz chips and 3 oz cheese — 21.0 (High-fat)
Vegetables with salsa, 1 cup vegetables and ½ cup salsa — 0 (Lower-fat)

Gourmet vanilla ice cream, 1 cup — 21.0 (High-fat)
Gourmet lemon sorbet, 1 cup — 0 (Lower-fat)

(x-axis: 0, 5, 10, 15, 20, 25)

■ High-fat choices
■ Lower-fat alternatives

▲ **Figure 5.23 Where's the Saturated Fat in Foods?**
Choosing less-saturated-fat versions of foods can dramatically lower the amount of saturated fat consumed in the diet.

Is Coconut Oil the Next Superfood?

If you're an avid label reader you've probably noticed coconut oil on the ingredients list of milk, spreads, and yogurt, or even seen the jars filled with a solid milky-white fat on the grocery shelves. Once thought of as an unhealthy, saturated fat, coconut oil is making a comeback, and is being touted as a healthy alternative to other oils.

Coconut oil used in movie theater popcorn, coffee creamers, and some candy is made from dried coconut that is treated to yield the refined oil used in these foods. Today's "virgin" coconut oil found on grocery store shelves is extracted from the meat of the coconut, which is heated, and the fat that rises to the top is skimmed off, much like cream is separated from milk. Regardless of the process used to produce coconut oil, the composition is still the same.[1]

The Composition of Coconut Oil

The difference between coconut oil and other more commonly used vegetable oils is their saturation and the chain length of the fatty acids (see **Figure 1**). About 87 percent of the fatty acids in coconut oil are saturated. Because the fatty acids in coconut oil are mostly saturated, it is solid at room temperature and isn't as susceptible to rancidity.[2] In fact, coconut oil is actually classified as a solid fat and not an oil. Olive oil, in comparison, is 15 percent saturated and liquid at room temperature.

In addition to the saturation point, sixty percent of the fatty acids in coconut oil are medium-chain fatty acids 6 to 10 carbons long. The majority of these medium-chain fatty acids (45 percent) are lauric acid, a 12-carbon-long chain of fatty acids. In contrast, most of the fatty acids in other oils are long-chain fatty acids

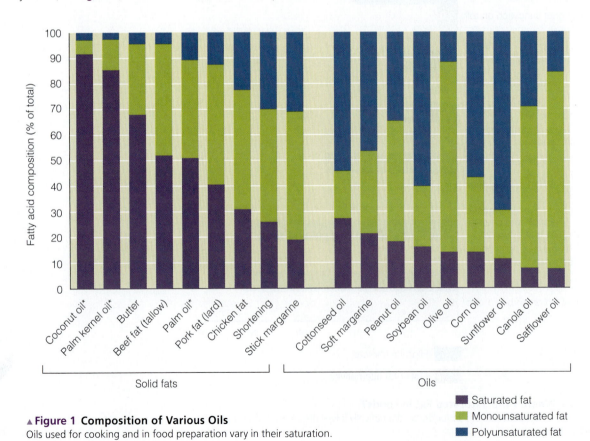

▲ **Figure 1 Composition of Various Oils**
Oils used for cooking and in food preparation vary in their saturation.

■ Saturated fat
■ Monounsaturated fat
■ Polyunsaturated fat

Table 1 — Saturated Fatty Acid Composition of Common Vegetable Oils

Oil	Caprylic C8:0	Capric C10:0	Lauric C12:0	Myristic C14:0	Palmitic C16:0	Linoleic C18:0
Coconut oil	1.0	0.8	6.1	2.3	1.1	0.4
Olive oil	0	0	0	0	11.2	1.9
Soybean oil	0	0	0	0	10.4	4.4
Canola oil	0	0	0	0	4.4	6.8
Corn oil	0	0	0	0	10.6	1.8
Flaxseed oil	0	0	0	0.1	5.1	3.4

*Adapted from the "Position Statement of the Academy of Nutrition and Dietetics: Dietary Fatty Acids for Healthy Adults." 2014. *Journal of the Academy of Nutrition and Dietetics* 114: 136–153.

between 12 to 18 fatty acids in length. For example, soybean oil is 100 percent long-chain fatty acids. The chain length is what gives coconut oil its advantage over other oils in food processing. Its high concentration of lauric acid makes coconut oil highly resistant to oxidation at high heats, which makes it a good choice for frying (see **Table 1**).

Possible Health Benefits of Coconut Oil

Coconut oil does not contain any polyunsaturated essential fatty acids, but it is rich in vitamin E and a variety of phytochemicals.[3] Does coconut oil's composition provide unique health benefits beyond those nutrients?

In spite of its high concentration of saturated fatty acids, there is anecdotal evidence that coconut oil may provide some health benefits, including reducing the risk of heart disease, improving weight loss, curing Alzheimer's, or protecting against infections.[4]

The original research supporting this idea came from studies indicating an absence of heart disease in individuals who live in the Polynesian islands, where most of the fat consumed is from coconuts.[5] There have been a number of reports in animal models about the heart-healthy benefits of coconut oil.[6] But well-controlled studies on the effects of coconut oil in humans are hard to find.

One such study reported the results of comparing LDL and HDL cholesterol blood levels in young adults fed 20 percent of their total kilocalories from either coconut oil or olive oil for five weeks.[7] A high LDL cholesterol level combined with a low HDL

cholesterol level seems to increase risk of heart disease. Both LDL cholesterol and HDL cholesterol were higher with coconut oil than olive oil. Olive oil appeared to have a neutral effect on both LDL cholesterol and HDL cholesterol. In other research, the plasma fatty acid concentration was changed with coconut oil versus sunflower oil, but the amount of plaque buildup in the arteries was not different.[8] And in yet another study, coconut oil increased HDL cholesterol and lowered the LDL:HDL ratio, while soybean oil increased both the total blood cholesterol and LDL cholesterol and decreased HDL cholesterol.[9]

This study also indicated that coconut oil may have an effect on weight loss: Using coconut oil versus soybean oil did result in a significantly reduced waist circumference in overweight women.[10] Does this mean that coconut oil may melt the pounds away? If so, how? The answer may lie in the way the body absorbs medium-chain fatty acids compared with long-chain fatty acids. Long-chain fatty acids are absorbed as part of chylomicrons, which deposit fatty acids in the adipose tissue en route to the liver. However, medium-chain fatty acids are absorbed directly into the bloodstream and not transported through the lymphatic system, as are long-chain fatty acids. Medium-chain fatty acids are used directly by the liver for energy, and not stored in the adipose tissue. A six-week pilot study reported that obese males significantly reduced their waist circumference after consuming coconut oil for four weeks.[11] One theory was that these subjects felt more satisfied after eating coconut oil and because they were less hungry, they consumed fewer kilocalories.

However, the effect of medium-chain fatty acids on satiety has not been supported by the current research. The change most likely is not due to the satiety effects of coconut oil in humans.[12] In short, there is insufficient evidence provided by well-controlled studies in humans to recommend switching to coconut oil for weight loss.

Similarly, there is no scientific evidence that switching to coconut oil prevents or improves cognitive function in Alzheimer's patients. In Alzheimer's disease, the brain loses its ability to utilize glucose for energy and switches to ketone bodies to provide fuel.[13] The medium-chain fatty acids in coconut oil are metabolized to ketone bodies but not at the level sufficient to provide fuel for the brain. Research testing coconut oil powder in patients with mild to moderate Alzheimer's found no significant changes compared with a placebo powder.[14] Research continues, however, to study if there are any benefits of using coconut oil to prevent or slow the progression of Alzheimer's disease.

The Bottom Line

Health professionals are divided over whether to recommend replacing heart-healthy polyunsaturated vegetable oils with coconut oil. There is a larger body of evidence in humans that monounsaturated and polyunsaturated fatty acids lower LDL cholesterol blood levels, a significant factor in heart disease risk. There is very little human research showing that coconut oil is more beneficial for heart health, weight loss, or Alzheimer's. The American Heart Association guidelines include reducing your saturated fat intake to less than 7 percent of your total kilocalories.[15] At this point, there is insufficient research to advise against these recommendations, so coconut oil, with its high saturated fat content, may not be the most healthful addition to your diet.

References

1. Tropical Traditions. 2013. *What Is Virgin Coconut Oil?* Available from www.tropicaltraditions.com. Accessed February 2014.
2. F. Hamam. 2013. "Specialty Lipids in Health and Disease." *Food and Nutrition Sciences* 4:63–70.
3. A. M. Marina, Y. B. Man, S. A. Nazimah, and I. Amin. 2009. "Antioxidant Capacity and Phenolic Acids of Virgin Coconut Oil."

International Journal of Food Science and Nutrition 60(Suppl 2):114–123.

4. Jackie Newgent. 2013. Coconut Oil: What Is It All About? Available at www.eatright.org. Accessed February 2014.

5. S. Lindeberg and B. Lundh. 1993. "Apparent Absence of Stroke and Ischaemic Heart Disease in a Traditional Melanesian Island: A Clinical Study in Kitava." Journal of Internal Medicine 233:269–275.

6. A. Vysakh, M. Ratheesh, T. P. Rajmohanan, C. Pramod, S. Premlal, K. B. Girish, and P. Sibi. 2014. "Polyphenolics Isolated from Virgin Coconut Oil Inhibits Adjuvant Induced Arthritis in Rats through Antioxidant and Anti-inflammatory Action." International Immunopharmacology 20(1):124–130.

7. P. T. Voon, T. K. Ng, V. K. Lee, and K. Nesaretnam. 2011. "Diets High in Palmitic Acid (16J), Lauric and Myristic Acids (12:0 + 14:0) or Oleic Acid (18:1) Do Not Alter Postprandial or Fasting Plasma Homocysteine and Inflammatory Markers in Healthy Malaysian Adults." American Journal of Clinical Nutrition 94(6):1451–1457.

8. S. Palazhy, P. Kamath, P. C. Rajesh, K. Vaidyanathan, S. K. Nair, and D. M. Vasudevan. 2012. "Composition of Plasma and Atheromatous Plaque among Coronary Artery Disease Subjects Consuming Coconut Oil or Sunflower Oil as the Cooking Medium." Journal of the American College of Nutrition 31(6): 392–396.

9. M. L. Assunção, H. S. Ferreira, A. F. dos Santos, C. R. Cabral, Jr., and T. M. Florêncio. 2009. "Effects of Dietary Coconut Oil on the Biochemical and Anthropometric Profiles of Women Presenting Abdominal Obesity." Lipids 44(7):593–601.

10. Ibid.

11. K. M. Liau, Y. Y. Lee, C. K. Chen, and A. H. Rasool. 2011. "An Open-Label Pilot Study to Assess the Efficacy and Safety of Virgin Coconut Oil in Reducing Visceral Adiposity." ISRN Pharmacology 2011:949686. doi: 10.5402/2011/949686.

12. S. D. Poppitt, C. M. Strik, A. K. MacGibbon, B. H. McArdle, S. C. Budgett, and A. T. McGill. 2010. "Fatty Acid Chain Length, Postprandial Satiety and Food Intake in Lean Men." Physiological Behavior 101(1):161–167.

13. S. T. Henderson, J. L. Vogel, L. J. Barr, F. Garvin, J. J. Jones, and L. C. Costantini. 2009. "Study of the Ketogenic Agent AC-1201 in Mild to Moderate Alzheimer's Disease: A Randomized, Double-Blind, Placebo-Controlled, Multicenter Trial." Nutrition and Metabolism doi:10.1186/1743-7075-6-31.

14. Ibid.

15. American Heart Association. 2014. Fats and Oils: AHA Recommendations. Available at www.heart.org. Accessed February 2014.

amount of total fat, the type of fat, and the calories from fat per serving of a food, as illustrated in **Figure 5.24**. Scan the ingredient list to make sure the product has little or no partially hydrogenated oil.

Reduce Foods That Contain *Trans* Fat and Cholesterol

At one time, saturated fats from animal sources, like lard, and highly saturated tropical plant oils, like coconut and palm oils, were staples in home cooking and commercial food preparation. These saturated fats worked well in commercial products because they provided a rich, flaky texture to baked goods and were more resistant to rancidity than the unsaturated fats found in oils. Later, the technique of hydrogenation of oils and the use of *trans* fat performed a similar function without adding cholesterol to the diet.

Foods with *Trans* Fats

Hydrogenated fats came into widespread commercial use when saturated fat fell out of favor in the 1980s. Research had confirmed that saturated fat played a role in increased risk of heart disease, so food manufacturers reformulated many of their products to contain less saturated fat. The easiest solution was to replace the saturated fat with hydrogenated fats. During the hydrogenation process, some of the unstable *cis* fatty acids are converted to *trans* fatty acids, increasing the level of **trans fat** found in processed foods. Everything from cookies, cakes, and crackers to fried chips and doughnuts used hydrogenated fats to maintain their texture and shelf life. Hydrogenated oils were also frequently used for frying at fast-food restaurants. Today, most fast-food companies seek alternatives to hydrogenated fats to reduce the level of *trans* fats in their products.

Despite the fact that the health effects of *trans* fats are now well known—research shows that *trans* fats raise LDL cholesterol levels and lower HDL cholesterol in the blood—these fats are still found in many foods. Processed foods, including commercially prepared baked goods, margarines, fried potatoes, snacks, shortenings, and salad dressings, are often major sources. About 15 to 20 percent of the *trans* fatty acids in the diet are naturally occurring in meat and dairy products. Ground beef, for

▼ Figure 5.24 **Read Food Labels to Lower Saturated and *Trans* Fat Intake**

a Butter is a rich source of saturated fatty acids and cholesterol. One tablespoon of butter contains over 7 grams of saturated fat.

b Margarine doesn't contain cholesterol but it may contain *trans* fat formed during hydrogenation of vegetable oils.

c Use liquid fats over solid fats on your food and in cooking. The more liquid a fat is at room temperature, the less saturated fat and *trans* fat it contains.

example, contains approximately one gram of *trans* fats per 100 grams (3.5 ounces) of beef, while butterfat has double that amount.[9] Even some plant products contain small amounts of *trans* fatty acids. Pomegranates are low in fat but almost 70 percent of the fat they do contain is a *trans* fatty acid called punicic acid.[10] (However, pomegranates are still considered a healthy fruit.) *Trans* fat currently provides an estimated 2.5 percent of the daily kilocalories in the diets of American adults. Of this amount, about 25 percent of them are coming from cakes, cookies, pies, and snacks such as chips.[11]

Research has suggested that *trans* fats pose a greater risk for heart health than saturated fat because they raise LDL cholesterol levels and lower HDL cholesterol in the blood. Whether naturally occurring *trans* fats have the same heart-unhealthy effects as do those that are created through hydrogenation has yet to be determined. The bottom line is that *trans* fats should be kept as low as possible in the diet.

Trans Fats on Food Labels

To make consumers more aware of *trans* fat, in 2006 the FDA mandated that most foods, and even some dietary supplements such as energy bars, list the grams of *trans* fats per serving.[12] Because of this labeling requirement, many food manufacturers reformulated their products to remove or reduce the amount of *trans* fats made with hydrogenation. In 2013, the FDA proposed a ban on the use of partially hydrogenated oils in foods to reduce the consumption of *trans* fat in the diets of Americans. Reducing the amount of food sources of solid fats in your diet will help reduce the consumption of both saturated fats and *trans* fats.

Pomegranates, while low in total fat, contain the *trans* fatty acid punicic acid.

What Are the Best, Worst, and Alternative Food Sources for Fat? **189**

Cholesterol and Plant Sterols

Most of the dietary cholesterol we consume comes from animal products, such as meat, chicken, fish, shellfish, eggs, and dairy products. Some plants also produce cholesterol as part of the cell walls and oils in their leaves.[13] However, the quantity of cholesterol in plants is so small when it is expressed as a percent of the total lipid content (about 5 milligrams per 100 grams in plants, versus as much as 500 milligrams per 100 grams in foods from animal sources) that plant oils are considered cholesterol free. Thus the main lipid in plant fats and oils is a triglyceride.

Phytosterols (which lower LDL cholesterol levels by competing with cholesterol for absorption in the intestinal tract) and stanols occur naturally in soybean oil, many fruits, vegetables, legumes, sesame seeds, nuts, cereals, and other plant foods.[14] In addition, food manufacturers fortify foods such as margarine with plant sterols and stanols to help lower blood cholesterol.

Fat Substitutes Lower Fat in Foods

If you enjoy the taste and texture of creamy foods but don't want the extra fat, you're not alone. A research survey found that over 160 million Americans (79 percent of the adult population) chose lower fat foods and beverages. Respondents cited their health as the major reason they were actively shopping for these foods.[15] To meet this demand, food manufacturers introduced more than 1,000 reduced-fat or low-fat products, from margarine to potato chips, each year during the 1990s.[16] Today, with few exceptions, almost any high-fat food on the grocery store shelves will be sitting next to its lower fat counterpart. The keys to these products' lower fat content are **fat substitutes.**

Foods made with fat substitutes aren't kilocalorie free.

Fat substitutes are designed to provide all the creamy properties of fat but with fewer kilocalories and total fat grams. Because fat has more than double the kilocalories per gram of carbohydrates or protein, fat substitutes have the potential to reduce kilocalories from fat by more than 50 percent without sacrificing taste and texture.

Carbohydrate-, Protein-, or Fat-Based Fat Substitutes

No single fat substitute works in all foods and with all cooking preparations, so several types of fat substitutes have been developed. Depending on their primary ingredient, fat substitutes fall into three categories: (1) carbohydrate-based substitutes, (2) protein-based substitutes, and (3) fat-based substitutes. **Table 5.3** lists all three types of fat substitutes and their uses in foods.

- **Carbohydrate-Based Substitutes** The majority of fat substitutes are carbohydrate based and use plant polysaccharides such as fiber, starches, gums, and cellulose to help retain moisture and provide a fatlike texture.[17] For example, low-fat muffins might have fiber added to them to help retain the moisture that is lost when fat is reduced. Carbohydrate-based substitutes have been used for years and work well under heat preparations other than frying.
- **Protein-Based Substitutes** Protein-based fat substitutes are created from the protein in eggs and milk. The protein is heated and broken down into microscopic balls that tumble over each other during chewing, providing a creamy feel in the mouth that's similar to fat. Protein-based substitutes break down under high temperatures and lose their creamy properties, which makes them unsuitable for frying and baking.[18]
- **Fat-Based Substitutes** Fat-based substitutes are fats that have been modified to either provide the physical attributes of fat for fewer kilocalories than regular fat or to interfere with the absorption of fat.[19] Mono- and

trans **fat** Substance that contains mostly *trans* fatty acids, a result of hydrogenating an unsaturated fatty acid, causing a reconfiguring of some of its double bonds. A small amount of *trans* fatty acid occurs naturally in foods from animal sources.

fat substitutes Substances that replace added fat in foods; they provide the creamy properties of fat for fewer kilocalories and total fat grams.

TABLE 5.3	The Lighter Side of Fat: Fat Substitutes			
Name (Trade Names)	Kilocalories per Gram	Properties		Used For
Carbohydrate Based				
Fibers from grains (Betatrim)	1–4	Gelling, thickener		Baked goods, meats, spreads
Fibers, cellulose (Cellulose gel)	0	Water retention, texture, mouthfeel		Sauces, dairy products, frozen desserts, salad dressings
Gums	0	Thickener, texture, mouthfeel, water retention		Salad dressings, processed meats
Polydextrose (Litesse)	1	Water retention, adds bulk		Baked goods, dairy products, salad dressings, cookies, and gum
Modified food starch (Sta-Slim)	1–4	Thickener, gelling, texture		Processed meats, salad dressings, frostings, fillings, frozen desserts
Protein Based				
Microparticulated protein (Simplesse)	1–4	Mouthfeel		Dairy products, salad dressings, spreads
Fat Based				
Mono- or diglycerides (Dur-Lo)	9*	Mouthfeel, moisture retention		Baked goods
Short-chain fatty acids (Salatrim)	5	Mouthfeel		Confections, baked goods
Olestra (Olean)	0	Mouthfeel		Savory snacks

*Less of this fat substitute is needed to create the same effect as fat, so the kilocalories are reduced in foods using this product.

Data from R. D. Mattes. 1998. "Fat Replacers." *Journal of the American Dietetic Association* 98:463–468; J. Wylie-Rosett. 2002. "Fat Substitutes and Health: An Advisory from the Nutrition Committee of the American Heart Association." *Circulation* 105:2800–2804.

diglycerides are used as emulsifiers in products such as baked goods and icings to provide moistness and mouthfeel. These emulsifiers are used with water to replace part of the fat in bakery goods and ice creams. Though these remnants of fat have the same amount of kilocalories per gram as fat, less of them are needed to create the same effect, so the total amount of kilocalories and fat is reduced.

One fat substitute, olestra (also known as Olean), approved in 1996 by the FDA, is a mixture of sucrose and long-chain fatty acids. Unlike fat, which contains three fatty acids connected to a glycerol backbone, olestra contains six to eight fatty acids connected to sucrose. The enzymes that normally break apart fatty acids from their glycerol backbones during digestion cannot hydrolyze the fatty acids in olestra. Instead, olestra moves through the GI tract unabsorbed. Thus, this fat substitute has zero kilocalories. Because olestra travels through the gastrointestinal tract untouched, there was concern that it may cause stomach cramps and loose bowels. Though there have been anecdotal reports of individuals experiencing diarrhea and cramps after eating olestra-containing foods, controlled research studies don't support these side effects.[20] Olestra is very heat stable, so it can be used in baked and fried foods.

Reduced-Fat Products

Despite their intended purpose, the use of fat substitutes doesn't seem to curb Americans' kilocalorie intake or help with weight management. One explanation for this may be that individuals feel a false sense of entitlement when eating low-fat and fat-free foods, and thus overeat. Research indicates that people who snack on olestra-containing products may be reducing their overall fat intake, but not their intake of total kilocalories.[21] As with sugar substitutes, consumers should recognize that using reduced-fat or fat-free products does not mean they can eat unlimited amounts of those foods. The foods still contain kilocalories, and overconsuming kilocalories leads to weight gain.

LO 5.5: THE TAKE-HOME MESSAGE Lean meat and poultry, fish, low-fat or nonfat dairy products, and limited amounts of nuts and cheese are the best food sources to obtain the essential fatty acids and limit saturated and *trans* fats. Commercially prepared baked goods and snack items are high in kilocalories, saturated fat, and *trans* fats, and should be consumed rarely. Vegetable oils should be used in place of butter. *Trans* fats are found in many commercially prepared foods and currently must be listed on the food label. The FDA has proposed banning all *trans* fats from prepared foods. Cholesterol is found mostly in animal products, while plant products, such as vegetable oils, nuts, legumes, whole grains, fruits, and vegetables, contain mostly phytosterols. Fat substitutes can be carbohydrate based, protein based, or fat based. Reduced-fat or fat-free foods still contain kilocalories and should be eaten in limited amounts.

What Is Heart Disease and What Factors Increase Risk?

LO 5.6 Describe the development of atherosclerosis and heart disease, and explain how lifestyle factors can affect the risk of heart disease.

Cardiovascular disease (CVD) is a term that encompasses several disorders affecting the heart, including problems with heart valves, heart beat irregularities, and infections. The most common type of heart disease, and the type we focus on in this chapter, is *coronary heart disease*, which affects the blood vessels that serve the heart muscle, and can lead to a heart attack.

Heart disease has been the number-one killer of adults in the United States since 1918. While the death rate from cardiovascular disease dropped by 31 percent between 2000 and 2010, one

in three Americans still dies of heart disease every 40 seconds.[22]

Heart Disease Begins with Atherosclerosis

Heart disease develops when the coronary arteries, the large blood vessels that lead to the heart, accumulate substances such as fat and cholesterol along their walls. As the artery narrows, blood flow is impeded, and less oxygen and nutrients are delivered to the heart. If the heart doesn't receive enough oxygen, chest pains can result. Narrowed arteries increase the likelihood that a blood clot can get caught and block the vessel, leading to a **heart attack.** If the artery leads to the brain, a **stroke** can occur.

The exact cause of the narrowed arteries, known as **atherosclerosis** (*athero* = porridge, *sclera* = hardening, *sis* = condition), is unknown, but researchers believe it begins with an injury to the lining of the arteries. Just as with a cut finger or sprained ankle, the injury

results in inflammation. Inflamed arterial walls may develop weak areas that can rupture easily, increasing the risk of blood clots and a heart attack. High blood levels of cholesterol and fat, high blood pressure, and smoking likely contribute to this damage.

Over time, LDLs and other lipid substances infiltrate the injured artery wall. The LDLs that accumulate become oxidized by reacting with free radicals and metal ions such as iron and attract macrophages (white blood cells), which

cardiovascular disease (CVD) A general term for diseases of the heart and blood vessels.

heart attack Permanent damage to the heart muscle that results from a sudden lack of oxygen-rich blood; also called a myocardial infarction (MI).

stroke A condition caused by a lack of oxygen to the brain that could result in paralysis and possibly death.

atherosclerosis Narrowing of the coronary arteries due to buildup of debris along the artery walls.

TABLE 5.4 Risk Factors for Heart Disease

Uncontrollable Risk Factors	Controllable Risk Factors	Emerging Risk Factors
■ Age ■ Gender ■ Family history of heart disease ■ Type 1 diabetes mellitus	■ Type 2 diabetes mellitus ■ High blood pressure ■ Smoking ■ Physical activity ■ Excess body weight ■ Low HDL blood cholesterol ■ High LDL blood cholesterol	■ Blood levels of C-reactive protein ■ High amount of homocysteine ■ Presence of *Chlamydia pneumoniae* in the blood ■ Lp(a) protein ■ Metabolic syndrome

become enlarged with cholesterol-laden LDLs and develop into foam cells. The foam cells stick to the walls of the artery and build up, along with platelets (fragments of cells in the blood) and other substances, into **plaque.** The plaque narrows the passageway of the artery (see **Focus Figure 5.25**).

Risk Factors for Heart Disease

The known risk factors for heart disease are listed in **Table 5.4.** Some of these risk factors you can control; others you cannot.

Uncontrollable and Emerging Risk Factors

Blood cholesterol, along with the risk of a heart attack, tends to rise with age until

plaque The hardened buildup of cholesterol-laden foam cells, platelets, cellular waste products, and calcium in the arteries that results in atherosclerosis.

C-reactive protein (CRP) A protein found in the blood that is released from the cells during inflammation; used as a marker for the presence of atherosclerosis.

Lp(a) protein A lipoprotein containing LDL cholesterol found in the blood; this lipoprotein has been correlated to increased risk of heart disease.

hypertension High blood pressure; defined as a systolic blood pressure higher than 140 mm Hg and/or a diastolic blood pressure greater than 90 mm Hg.

normal blood pressure A systolic blood pressure less than 120 mm Hg (the top number) and a diastolic blood pressure less than 80 mm Hg (the bottom number). Referred to as 120/80.

it stabilizes around age 65. Gender also plays a role. Up until menopause (usually around age 50), women tend to have a lower blood cholesterol level than men and a reduced risk of heart disease. After menopause, the blood cholesterol level in women tends to catch up and even surpass that of men of the same age.[23]

Genetics can also be a risk factor for heart disease, as high LDL cholesterol levels are partly determined by genes and can run in families.[24] An individual whose father or brother had early signs of heart disease before age 55, or whose mother or sister had them before age 65, is at a greater risk. This may be due to a genetic defect in the LDL receptor that regulates the amount of LDL cholesterol in the blood. Family members who have this defective gene have elevated LDL levels in the blood, which may produce premature atherosclerosis.[25]

Some individuals have normal levels of LDL cholesterol in their blood, yet still develop heart disease, which points to other factors that must be affecting their heart health. These other potential risk factors are referred to as *emerging risk factors.* These include high blood levels of **C-reactive protein (CRP),** which is produced when there is inflammation.[26] Because of the critical link between inflammation and heart disease, measuring CRP levels can assist in predicting the risk of heart attacks. Another blood marker associated with atherosclerosis is a high amount of the amino acid *homocysteine.*[27] High levels of this amino acid

may injure the arteries, decrease their flexibility, and increase the likelihood of blood clots. The presence of *Chlamydia pneumoniae,* a bacterium that can cause pneumonia and respiratory infections, in the blood may also damage or inflame the vessel walls.[28] Lastly, another lipoprotein, **Lp(a) protein,** is being investigated for its role in causing excessive blood clotting and exacerbating inflammation.[29] And metabolic syndrome refers to a cluster of risk factors that puts some people at risk for heart disease regardless of their level of LDL cholesterol. The culprit behind this syndrome appears to be the resistance of the cells in the body to insulin.[30]

Controllable Risk Factors

Because high HDL cholesterol can help protect against heart disease, having an HDL level of less than 40 milligrams per deciliter (mg/dl) increases risk. In contrast, having a high level of HDL cholesterol, 60 mg/dl or higher, is considered a negative risk factor. In other words, there is so much of this good cholesterol helping to protect against heart disease that it counteracts another risk factor on the list. While genetics plays a large role in determining blood cholesterol levels, diet is also a factor.

Blood pressure (the force of blood against the walls of the arteries) can affect the risk of heart disease. Chronic high blood pressure, or **hypertension,** can damage the arteries and begin the progression of atherosclerosis. A **normal blood pressure** is considered less than 120 millimeters mercury (Hg) for the systolic pressure (the top number in the blood pressure reading) and less than 80 millimeters Hg for the diastolic pressure (the bottom number). A blood pressure reading of 140/90 or higher is considered hypertension.

Chronic high blood pressure thickens the arteries and causes them to become stiff and less flexible, which may initiate injury to the arterial walls and accelerate plaque buildup. Chronic high blood pressure also causes the heart to work harder than normal and can lead to an

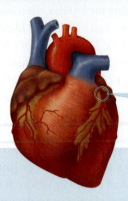

Plaque accumulation within coronary arteries narrows their interior and impedes the flow of oxygen-rich blood to the heart.

HEALTHY ARTERY

Blood flows unobstructed through a normal, healthy artery.

ARTERIAL INJURY

The artery's lining is injured, attracting immune cells, and prompting inflammation.

LIPIDS ACCUMULATE IN WALL

Lipids, particularly cholesterol-containing LDLs, seep beneath the wall lining. The LDLs become oxidized. Immune cells, attracted to the site, engulf the oxidized LDLs and are transformed into foam cells.

FATTY STREAK

The foam cells accumulate to form a fatty streak, which releases more toxic and inflammatory chemicals.

PLAQUE FORMATION

The foam cells, along with platelets, calcium, protein fibers, and other substances, form thick deposits of plaque, stiffening and narrowing the artery. Blood flow through the artery is reduced or obstructed.

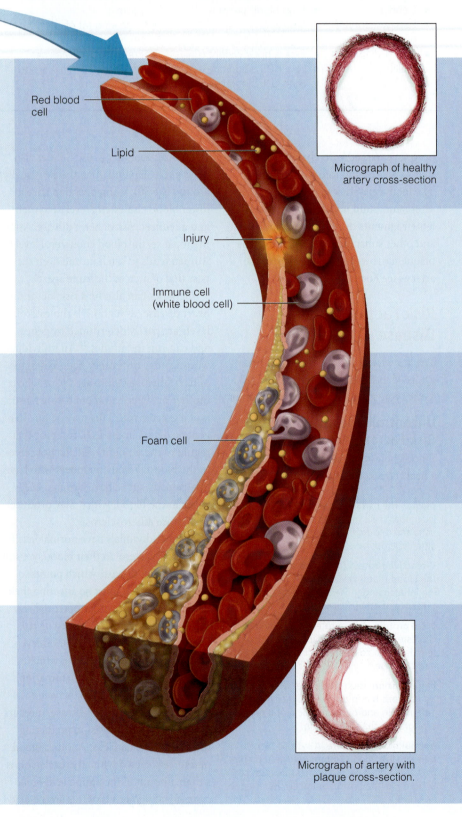

Red blood cell

Lipid

Micrograph of healthy artery cross-section

Injury

Immune cell (white blood cell)

Foam cell

Micrograph of artery with plaque cross-section.

enlarged heart. (Chapter 12 contains a detailed discussion of hypertension and how a healthy diet can help lower high blood pressure.)

Diabetes is a significant risk factor for heart disease; an estimated 75 percent of adults with diabetes die due to heart disease and stroke. It's not surprising, then, that controlling diabetes can help dramatically lower the risk of heart disease. Though the less common form of diabetes, type 1, is not preventable, the more prevalent form, type 2 diabetes, can be managed, and possibly even prevented, through diet, exercise, and other lifestyle changes.

Smoking damages the walls of the arteries and accelerates atherosclerosis. In fact, women smokers are two to six times more likely to have a heart attack than female nonsmokers.[31] Male smokers also increase their risk for heart disease.

Lowering Your Risk of Heart Disease

The primary risk factor for heart disease is elevated blood lipids, especially the LDL cholesterol level.[32] Starting at age 20, individuals should have their blood tested at least once every five years to obtain a **blood lipid profile.** This profile includes tests for total cholesterol, HDL cholesterol, LDL cholesterol, and triglycerides. Often the profile will also include the cholesterol-to-HDL ratio or a risk score calculated from the lipid measurements, age, gender, and other risk factors.[33] **Table 5.5** indicates the optimal blood levels for total cholesterol, LDL cholesterol, and HDL cholesterol.

The best way to impact blood levels of these lipids is through diet, exercise, and other lifestyle factors as described in the Nutrition in Practice.

Consume Less Saturated and *Trans* Fat and Moderate Cholesterol Intake

The ideal dietary pattern to reduce your risk of heart disease is one that lowers

TABLE 5.5	What Blood Cholesterol Levels* Indicate
If Total Cholesterol Level Is (mg/dl)	*That Is Considered*
< 200	Desirable
200–239	Borderline high
≥ 240	High
If LDL Cholesterol Level Is (mg/dl)	*That Is Considered*
< 100	Optimal
100–129	Near or above optimal
130–159	Borderline high
160–189	High
≥ 190	Very high
If HDL Cholesterol Is (mg/dl)	*That Is Considered*
> 60	Desirable
40–60	Adequate
< 40	Low

*All lipoprotein levels are measured in milligrams of cholesterol per deciliter of blood (mg/dl).

Data from National Cholesterol Education Program. 2001. "Detection, Evaluation, and Treatment of High Blood Cholesterol in Adults (Adult Treatment Panel III)." National Institutes of Health Publication No. 01-3290.

LDL cholesterol and raises HDL cholesterol simultaneously. In general, blood levels of LDL cholesterol increase on a high-saturated-fat and high-*trans*-fat diet, not a high-cholesterol diet.[34]

The Impact of Saturated Fatty Acids

It may not be just the total saturated fat intake that raises LDL cholesterol. The type of saturated fatty acid may have a greater influence. Saturated fatty acids such as myristic acid, found in butterfat, may decrease LDL cholesterol when substituted for other saturated fatty acids such as palmitic acid, which raises LDL cholesterol.[35] The same is true for stearic acid, which is good news for chocolate lovers.[36] Though the cocoa butter in chocolate is high in saturated fatty acids, the predominant fat is stearic acid, which neither raises nor lowers LDL cholesterol. Keep in mind that chocolate is still high in kilocalories and shouldn't be consumed in excessive amounts. Reducing saturated fat intake overall, regardless of the type of fatty acid in the molecule, will

reduce LDL cholesterol and the risk of heart disease.

The Impact of *Trans* Fats

Per kilocalorie, *trans* fats appear to increase the risk of heart disease more than any other nutrient.[37] Controlled studies have shown that a diet containing *trans* fats raises levels of LDL cholesterol, lowers HDL cholesterol, and increases the ratio of total cholesterol to HDL cholesterol. These fats also increase the blood levels of triglycerides and inflammation along the arterial wall.[38]

The best grocery list for lowering blood cholesterol levels includes foods that are low in saturated fats, *trans* fats, and cholesterol. Specifically, lean meats, fruits and vegetables, whole grains, fish, shellfish, and fat-free dairy products are healthy choices. Processed foods, such as snacks and bakery items that contain *trans* fats plus saturated fats, increase the risk of heart disease and therefore should

blood lipid profile A measurement of blood lipids used to assess cardiovascular risk.

Flaxseeds and flaxseed oil are low in saturated fat.

be consumed in moderation or avoided entirely.

Eat More Fish and Plant Foods

The American Heart Association (AHA) encourages Americans to increase their fish and plant-based foods consumption as part of a heart-healthy diet. This dietary pattern increases omega-3 fatty acids, reduces saturated fat and LDL cholesterol, and adds soluble dietary fiber and heart-healthy phytochemicals.

Fish and Other Seafood

In general, seafood contains an abundance of healthy fats. It's true that some shellfish, such as shrimp, are high in cholesterol, but they are very low in saturated fat and contain some heart-healthy omega-3 fatty acids. Lobster has less than one-third the amount of cholesterol of shrimp and is very low in total fat.

The American Heart Association (AHA) recommends consuming at least two servings of fish (especially fatty fish) per week to obtain omega-3 fatty acids. These recommendations should be met with baked, poached, or broiled fish. Fried fish that is commercially prepared tends to have few omega-3 fatty acids and is often fried in unhealthy fat. The

TABLE TIPS

Easy Ways to Add Fish to the Diet

Flake canned salmon over a lunch or dinner salad.

Add tuna to cooked pasta and vegetables and toss with a light salad dressing for a quick pasta salad meal.

Order baked, broiled, or grilled fish when dining out.

Try a shrimp cocktail for added omega-3 fatty acids.

Table Tips provide a few quick ways to add fish to your diet.

Though consuming some omega-3 fatty acids is good, more may not be better. Because EPA and DHA interfere with blood clotting, consuming more than 3 grams, which typically only happens by taking supplements, could raise both blood glucose and LDL cholesterol levels, increase the risk of excessive bleeding, and cause other related problems such as hemorrhagic stroke (*hemo* = blood, *rhagic* = ruptured flow) in certain people.[39] Because of these potential adverse side effects, omega-3 fatty acid supplements (fish oil supplements) should only be consumed with the advice and guidance of a doctor. Eating one gram of EPA and

DHA daily from fish may provide some protection against heart disease without any known adverse side effects.[40]

Plant Foods

In addition to fish, the AHA also recommends consuming plant-based foods such as walnuts, flaxseeds, and soybean and canola oils, which are all high in alpha-linolenic acid.

Eating more plant foods high in viscous, soluble fiber may be one of the easiest ways to decrease LDL cholesterol levels and lower risk of stroke.[41] While the DRI for fiber ranges from 20 to 38 grams daily, consuming about half of this amount, or 10 to 25 grams, can help decrease high LDL cholesterol levels. Increasing the soy in your diet may lessen your risk of heart disease by lowering blood pressure.[42]

Plant foods are not only cholesterol free but they also contain phytosterols, which are plant sterols similar to cholesterol that are found in the plant's cell membranes. Plant sterols can help lower LDL cholesterol levels by competing with cholesterol for absorption in the intestinal tract. With less cholesterol being absorbed, there will be less in the blood. Plant sterols occur naturally in soybean oil, many fruits, vegetables, legumes, sesame seeds, nuts, cereals, and other plant foods. Consuming 2 grams of plant sterols per day lowers LDL cholesterol levels by 10 percent

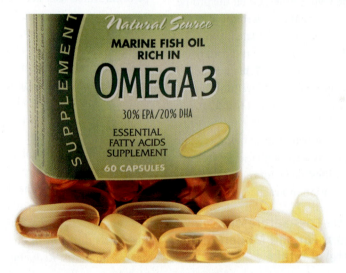

Although fish oil supplements contain omega-3 fatty acids, excessive amounts can be unhealthy for some individuals.

Though high in kilocalories, nuts are an excellent source of antioxidants, have zero cholesterol, and are low in saturated fat.

Benecol, a margarine made with plant sterols, may reduce LDL cholesterol levels in the blood.

and may cut heart disease risk up to 15 percent.[43] Products such as margarines, yogurt, cream cheese spreads, cereals, fruit juices, and soft-gel tablets that contain plant sterols are now available.

Antioxidants and Phytochemicals

You might think that a substance that begins with the prefix "anti" couldn't be good for you. However, a diet rich in plants contains antioxidants and phytochemicals that protect tissues from oxidative damage (for more explanation on antioxidants, see Chapter 9). These potent chemicals neutralize free radicals that are formed during oxidative metabolism, stimulate your immune system to repair tissue damage, and reduce the risk of heart disease.[44]

Nuts are one type of food that is rich in antioxidants and fiber and can have a positive effect on LDL cholesterol levels. A diet with 20 percent of kilocalories from walnuts lowered LDL cholesterol by a little over 15 percent in healthy men.[45] In women, those who ate one ounce of nuts at least five times a week had a 35 percent reduction in the risk of heart disease compared with women who rarely ate nuts.[46] The only downside to nuts is that they are high in kilocalories. A mere ounce of nuts can contribute a hefty 160 to 200 kilocalories to your diet. The Table Tips provide ideas on how to enjoy a modest amount of nuts in your diet.

Other plant substances may provide an extra boost to heart health. Garlic has been found in some studies to reduce high blood cholesterol levels by inhibiting cholesterol synthesis in the body, decreasing the clustering of platelets, interfering with blood clotting, and helping to lower blood pressure. Black and green tea are high in **flavonoids,** phytochemicals similar to antioxidants that are believed to prevent LDL cholesterol from becoming oxidized in the body. Drinking tea is associated with

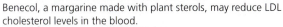

TABLE TIPS

Nuts about Nuts?

Toss some nuts into a mealtime salad. Use less oil or salad dressing and more nonfat vinegar to adjust for the added kilocalories.

Swap nuts for meat, like chicken or beef, in meals such as stir-fries. A third of a cup of nuts is equal in protein to an ounce of red meat or chicken.

Add a tablespoon of nuts to morning cereal, and use skim rather than reduced-fat milk to offset some of the extra kilocalories.

Add a tablespoon of chopped nuts to an afternoon yogurt.

Add a handful of peanuts to air-popped popcorn for a snack.

a lower incidence of dying from heart disease.[47] Green tea is particularly high in catechins, which are antioxidants and may also reduce total and LDL cholesterol.[48]

When it comes to reducing the risk of heart disease, the whole diet may be greater than the sum of its parts. Consume a diet low in saturated fat and cholesterol, and high in soluble fiber, soy protein, plant sterols, and nuts to lower total cholesterol and LDL cholesterol. The Table Tips summarize several eating tips for a heart-healthy diet.

Get Plenty of Exercise, Manage Your Weight, and Quit Smoking

Regular exercise is one way to help lower LDL cholesterol, raise HDL cholesterol, reduce hypertension and insulin resistance, and lose weight.[49] A review of over 50 studies involving more than 4,500 people found that exercise training for more than 12 weeks increased HDL cholesterol levels by about 4.5 percent. Currently, the AHA recommends that healthy individuals partake in 30 minutes or more of moderate exercise on most days, if not every day. This amount of

flavonoids Phytochemicals found in fruits, vegetables, tea, nuts, and seeds that have antioxidant properties and neutralize free radicals.

TABLE 5.6	To Decrease Excess LDL Cholesterol	
Dietary Changes		**Lifestyle Changes**
■ Consume less saturated fat ■ Consume less *trans* fats ■ Consume less dietary cholesterol ■ Consume more soluble fiber–rich foods ■ Consume a more plant-based diet		■ Lose excess body weight ■ Exercise more

physical activity is considered sufficient to help reduce the risk of heart disease, but exercising longer than 30 minutes or at higher intensity could offer greater protection, especially when it comes to maintaining a healthy body weight.[50] Sedentary individuals should "move" and sedentary,

overweight individuals should "move and lose" to lower their risk of heart disease. Table 5.6 summarizes the diet and lifestyle changes that can help lower LDL cholesterol levels and risk for heart disease.

In addition to regular exercise and losing excess weight, quit smoking. Smoking damages the walls of the arteries and accelerates atherosclerosis. In fact, individuals who smoke are three times more likely to have a heart attack than nonsmokers.[51]

A Word about the Protective Effects of Red Wine and Alcohol

Some studies have shown that drinking alcohol in moderate amounts (1 serving for females, 2 servings for males daily) can reduce the risk of heart disease.[52] The heart-protective action of alcohol may occur through three different mechanisms. Alcohol can increase the level of the heart-protective HDL cholesterol. In fact, approximately 50 percent of alcohol's heart-protective effect is probably due to this positive effect on HDL cholesterol. Other studies have suggested that alcohol may decrease blood clotting

by affecting the coagulation of platelets or by helping the blood to break up clots.[53] Still other research has suggested that the antioxidants in wine as well as in dark beer also contribute to the heart-protective aspects of alcohol.[54]

However, the health benefits of alcohol have only been shown to occur in middle-aged individuals and the problems associated with overconsumption far outweigh the health benefits of moderate consumption. In fact, individuals who consume three or more drinks per day *increase* their risk of dying prematurely.[55] (We will talk more about alcohol in Chapter 7.)

LO 5.6: THE TAKE-HOME MESSAGE

Heart disease is primarily caused by atherosclerosis, the narrowing of the arteries due to a buildup of plaque. Uncontrollable risk factors for heart disease include age, gender, and genetics; controllable risk factors include high LDL blood cholesterol, low HDL blood cholesterol, high blood pressure, excess body weight, inactivity, type 2 diabetes, and smoking. Limiting saturated fat, cholesterol, and *trans* fat, and increasing fish consumption, as well as consuming antioxidant-rich fruits, vegetables, whole grains, and nuts, are associated with a reduction in the risk of heart disease. Regular exercise and maintaining a healthy body weight can also help lower LDL cholesterol levels and raise HDL cholesterol levels. If you currently smoke, quit, because smoking damages the walls of the arteries. Drinking a moderate amount of alcohol may help reduce the risk of heart disease in middle-aged and older adults.

Nutrition in Practice: Adam

Adam, a 20-year-old junior in finance, returned from spring break with a laboratory report from his doctor's office that showed that his blood cholesterol levels were too high. The note on the report stated that he should meet with a Registered Dietitian Nutritionist to see if he could change his diet to lower his levels. Both his mom and dad have high blood cholesterol, so Adam wasn't shocked by his own results. Because he has an unlimited meal plan at college, his mom suggested that he set up an appointment with the campus dietitian for nutrition counseling and advice about what to eat at the dining hall.

Adam's Stats:
- Age: 20
- Height: 5 feet 11 inches
- Weight: 170 pounds
- BMI: 23.7
- Total Cholesterol: 240 mg/dl
- LDL Cholesterol: 185 mg/dl
- HDL Cholesterol: < 40 mg/dl

Adam's Food Log

Food/Beverage	Time Consumed	Hunger Rating*	Location
3-egg omelet with cheese Wheat toast w/butter OJ	9:30 AM	5	In dining hall
Ham and cheese sandwich Potato chips Whole milk	1:30 PM	3	In dining hall
Oreos and whole milk	3 PM	4	Studying in dorm room
Steak, mashed potatoes, peas	6:30 PM	4	In dining hall
Pretzels	11 PM	4	In dorm room

*Hunger Rating (1–5): 1 = not hungry; 5 = super hungry.

Critical Thinking Questions
1. How could Adam's food and beverage choices potentially contribute to his high blood cholesterol level?
2. What foods could be added to Adam's diet that may help lower his cholesterol?
3. What lifestyle changes could Adam make to possibly increase his HDL cholesterol?

Dietitian's Observation and Plan for Adam:
- Discuss the need to reduce saturated fat to less than 10 percent of total kilocalories and dietary cholesterol to less than 300 milligrams (mg) per day.

Use egg whites or an egg substitute when ordering an omelet, switch from whole to 2% milk, replace butter with tub margarine, and use reduced-fat Cheddar cheese instead of full-fat cheese. Order a turkey sandwich at lunch and skinless poultry or fish more often at dinner. Try to consume at least two fish meals weekly.
- Increase dietary fiber, especially soluble fiber. Try to have a soup or salad with meals and add beans from the salad bar. Add a piece of fruit to breakfast and snacks.
- Increase physical activity to at least 2.5 hours weekly. Exercise may help increase the HDL cholesterol.

Three weeks later, Adam visits the dietitian again. He has made the switch from whole milk to 2% milk and butter to margarine, added the soup and salad to his meals, and is walking on the treadmill at the gym. A review of his food record shows that his saturated fat is a little over 10 percent of his total calorie intake but his dietary cholesterol is less than 300 mg. He is having difficulty eating two fish meals weekly and eating fruit. The dietitian suggests that Adam consume tuna fish sandwiches at lunch at least twice a week and switch to 1% milk to decrease his saturated fat intake. She also recommends that he take a couple of pieces of fruit from the dining hall for a high-fiber evening snack.

Visual Chapter Summary

LO 5.1 Lipids Are Organic Water-Insoluble Compounds That Vary in Structure

Lipids refer to a category of carbon, oxygen, and hydrogen compounds that don't dissolve in water. There are three types of lipids: triglycerides, phospholipids, and sterols. Triglycerides and phospholipids are built from a fatty acid, which consist of a chain of carbon and hydrogen atoms with an acid group (COOH) at the alpha end and a methyl group (CH₃) at the omega end.

Short-chain fatty acids contain fewer than six carbons; medium-chain fatty acids have six to 10 carbons; and long-chain fatty acids have 12 or more carbons. A saturated fatty acid has all of its carbons bound with hydrogen. An unsaturated fatty acid that has one double bond is called a monounsaturated fatty acid. A polyunsaturated fatty acid contains two or more double bonds. If the first double bond is located between the third and fourth carbon from the omega end it is called an omega-3 fatty acid. The first double bond for an omega-6 fatty acid is between carbons six and seven from the omega end.

Unsaturated fatty acids have either a *cis* (hydrogen atoms are on the same side of the double bond) or a *trans* configuration (one hydrogen atom is on the opposite side of the double bond). Phospholipids are made of two fatty acids and a phosphate-containing group attached to a glycerol backbone. Sterols do not contain glycerol or fatty acids but are composed of four connecting rings of carbon and hydrogen.

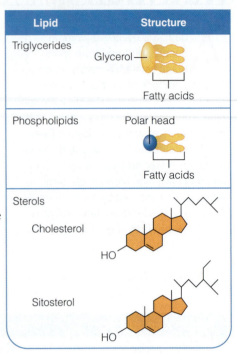

Lipid	Structure
Triglycerides	Glycerol — Fatty acids
Phospholipids	Polar head — Fatty acids
Sterols — Cholesterol	HO
Sitosterol	HO

LO 5.2 Lipids Are Digested and Absorbed in the Small Intestine and Transported by Lipoproteins

Most fat digestion occurs in the small intestine. Fat globules are emulsified by bile before pancreatic lipase hydrolyzes the fatty acids, producing two free fatty acids and a monoglyceride. Sterols are absorbed intact. Phospholipids are hydrolyzed by phospholipases.

Glycerol and short- and medium-chain fatty acids enter the portal vein and go directly to the liver. Free long-chain fatty acids reattach to the glycerol molecule to reform a triglyceride in the enterocyte. These fats are combined into a chylomicron with other dietary lipids and released into the lymph fluid.

Chylomicrons transport dietary fat to the cells. Very low-density lipoproteins (VLDLs) and low-density lipoproteins (LDLs) carry lipids from the liver to the cells. High-density lipoproteins (HDLs) pick up cholesterol from the body cells and return it to the liver.

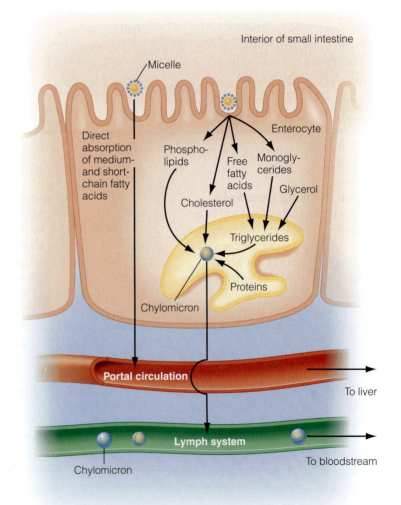

LO 5.3 Lipids Plays Many Key Roles in the Body

Lipids provide essential fatty acids, enhance the absorption of the fat-soluble vitamins, provide a layer of insulation, and cushion the major organs. Essential fatty acids are needed for healthy cell membranes and to produce hormonelike compounds that regulate the immune system and blood clotting, reduce inflammation, and control blood pressure. Fat is also an important source of energy, providing 9 kilocalories per gram.

Phospholipids and cholesterol make up the cell membranes. Cholesterol is also a precursor for vitamin D, bile, and sex hormones such as estrogen and testosterone.

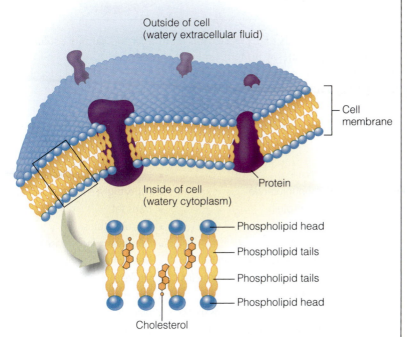

Outside of cell (watery extracellular fluid)

Cell membrane

Inside of cell (watery cytoplasm)

Protein

Phospholipid head
Phospholipid tails
Phospholipid tails
Phospholipid head

Cholesterol

LO 5.4 Moderate Consumption of Dietary Fat Is Essential for Health

The AMDR recommendation is for 20 to 35 percent of the daily kilocalories to come from fat, no more than 10 percent from saturated fat and less than 1 percent from *trans* fats. A minimum of 5 to 10 percent of the total kilocalories should come from linoleic acid and 0.6 to 1.2 percent from alpha-linolenic acid.

Men aged 19 to 50 need 17 grams and women need 12 grams of linoleic acid daily. Men aged 14 to 70 need 1.6 grams and women need 1.1 grams of alpha-linolenic acid daily.

Healthy individuals over the age of 2 are advised to limit their dietary cholesterol to under 300 milligrams daily. Cholesterol and phospholipids are both made in the body and are not considered essential nutrients.

LO 5.5 The Best Food Sources of Fat Contain Unsaturated Fats and Essential Fatty Acids

Unsaturated fats are abundant in vegetable oils, soybeans, walnuts, flaxseeds, and wheat germ, and these are also all good sources of linoleic acid. Walnuts, flaxseeds, and canola oil are good sources of alpha-linolenic acid.

Most saturated fat comes from animal foods such as fatty cuts of meat, whole-milk dairy products, butter, ice cream, and the skin of poultry. Certain vegetable oils, such as coconut, palm, and palm kernel oils, are very high in saturated fat and are often found in candies, commercially made baked goods, and gourmet ice cream. *Trans* fats are mostly found in processed foods, and must be listed on the food label. The FDA has proposed to ban *trans* fats from commercially prepared foods. Dietary cholesterol is found only in foods from animal sources such as egg yolks, meats, and whole-fat dairy. Fat substitutes can be carbohydrate based, protein based, or fat based. Reduced-fat or fat-free foods still contain kilocalories and should be eaten in limited amounts.

LO 5.6 A Heart-Healthy Diet and Lifestyle Changes Can Reduce Risk of Heart Disease

Atherosclerosis, the narrowing of arteries due to plaque buildup, is a primary cause of cardiovascular disease, including coronary heart disease. Consuming too much dietary fat can lead to high blood cholesterol levels, which can precipitate atherosclerosis. The goal is to lower the LDL level to less than 100 milligrams per deciliter (mg/dl) and raise the HDL level to greater than 40 mg/dl.

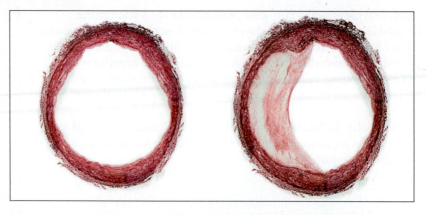

To lower LDL cholesterol, eat a well-balanced plant-based diet that contains lean meats and dairy foods with moderate amounts of heart-healthy unsaturated fat; limit commercially prepared baked goods, snack items, and fried foods to decrease *trans* fat intake; and eat more soluble fiber–containing foods such as oats, legumes, psyllium-containing cereal, soy protein, and plant sterols.

Regular exercise and maintaining a healthy weight can also help lower LDL cholesterol levels and raise HDL cholesterol levels. If you currently smoke, it is vital to quit because smoking damages the walls of the arteries. Drinking a moderate amount of alcohol may help reduce the risk of heart disease in middle-aged and older adults.

Terms to Know

- lipid
- triglycerides
- phospholipids
- sterols
- hydrophobic
- fatty acid
- short-chain fatty acid
- medium-chain fatty acid
- long-chain fatty acid
- saturated fatty acid
- unsaturated fatty acid
- monounsaturated fatty acid
- polyunsaturated fatty acid
- oils
- rancidity
- hydrogenation

- omega-3 fatty acid
- omega-6 fatty acid
- linoleic acid
- alpha-linolenic acid
- essential fatty acids
- *cis*
- *trans*
- glycerol
- lecithin
- choline
- emulsifier
- cholesterol
- phytosterols
- phytostanols
- lipases
- diglyceride

- micelle
- monoglyceride
- lipoprotein
- chylomicron
- lymph fluid
- lipoprotein lipase (LPL)
- very low-density lipoproteins (VLDLs)
- low-density lipoproteins (LDLs)
- high-density lipoproteins (HDLs)
- adipocytes
- arachidonic acid
- eicosapentaenoic acid (EPA) and docosahexaenoic acid (DHA)

- eicosanoids
- hypertriglyceridemia
- *trans* fat
- fat substitutes
- cardiovascular disease (CVD)
- heart attack
- stroke
- atherosclerosis
- plaque
- C-reactive protein (CRP)
- Lp(a) protein
- hypertension
- normal blood pressure
- blood lipid profile
- flavonoids

MasteringNutrition™

To hear an MP3 Chapter Review, scan here or visit the Study Area in MasteringNutrition.

Check Your Understanding

1. Which statement best describes the characteristics of a polyunsaturated fatty acid?

a. They are solid at room temperature.
b. They are higher in kilocalorie content than a saturated fatty acid.
c. They tend to be liquid at room temperature.
d. They are more stable than saturated fatty acids and resist oxidation.

2. Fatty acids are classified by
a. the number of carbons in the fatty acid chain.
b. the number of double bonds in the fatty acid chain.

c. the shape of the fatty acid chain.
d. all of the above.

3. The type of lipoprotein that carries absorbed dietary fat and other lipids through the lymph system is called
a. Lp(a) protein.
b. a VLDL.
c. an LDL.
d. a chylomicron.

4. Arachidonic acid and docosahexaenoic acid (DHA) are
a. used to manufacture hormonelike substances called eicosanoids.

b. stored as part of the subcutaneous tissue needed to insulate the body.

c. the main fatty acids used to manufacture bile in the liver.

d. used by the body to manufacture the essential fatty acids linoleic acid and alpha-linolenic acid.

5. The AMDR for dietary fat is
   a. 8 to 10 percent of daily kilocalories.
   b. 20 to 35 percent of daily kilocalories.
   c. 40 to 45 percent of daily kilocalories.
   d. under 300 milligrams to 500 milligrams daily.

6. At least two fish meals should be consumed weekly to obtain the heart-healthy omega-3 fatty acids. Examples of heart-healthy fish meals include
   a. a tuna fish sandwich and a Burger King fish sandwich.
   b. boiled or grilled shrimp and grilled salmon.
   c. fish and chips and flounder.
   d. fried fish sticks and steamed lobster.

7. Which of the following foods does not contain dietary cholesterol?
   a. steak
   b. chicken
   c. low-fat milk
   d. peanut butter

8. Which of the following foods are good sources of the essential fatty acids linoleic acid and alpha-linolenic acid?
   a. flaxseeds
   b. cheese
   c. butter
   d. oranges

9. The major dietary component that raises LDL cholesterol is
   a. viscous soluble fiber.
   b. dietary cholesterol.
   c. saturated fat.
   d. plant sterols.

10. To raise the level of HDL cholesterol,
    a. increase the viscous, soluble fiber in the diet.
    b. increase exercise.
    c. maintain a healthy body weight.
    d. do all of the above.

Answers

1. (c) The double bonds in polyunsaturated fatty acids prevent them from packing together tightly. This causes them to be liquid at room temperature, not solid. The double bonds are less stable and more easily oxidized compared with saturated fatty acids. All fatty acids, regardless of type, have 9 kilocalories per gram.

2. (d) The number of carbons in the chain determine whether a fatty acid is short chain, medium chain, or long chain. Fatty acids are either saturated or unsaturated, depending on the presence of double bonds, and they have either a *cis* or a *trans* shape, or configuration.

3. (d) Chylomicrons are capsule-shaped carriers that enable insoluble fat as well as cholesterol and phospholipids to travel through the watery lymph system to the bloodstream. Lp(a) protein contains cholesterol and is correlated with an increased risk for heart disease. VLDLs and LDLs are lipoproteins that transport fat and other lipids through the blood.

4. (a) Arachidonic acid and docosahexaenoic acid (DHA) are used to manufacture eicosanoids such as prostaglandins, thromboxanes, and leukotrienes, not to be stored in subcutaneous tissue, or used to synthesize cholesterol. These two compounds are made from the essential fatty acids linoleic acid and alpha-linolenic acid.

5. (b) The AMDR for daily fat intake is 20 to 35 percent of total daily kilocalories. Saturated fat and *trans* fat intake should be less than 10 percent of daily kilocalories and dietary cholesterol should be kept under 300 milligrams daily.

6. (b) While tuna fish is a wonderful way to enjoy fish at lunch, the commercially prepared fried fish sandwich, fish and chips, and fish sticks have little of the heart-healthy omega-3 fatty acids. Boiled shrimp and grilled salmon are much healthier ways to enjoy fish.

7. (d) Because plant sources are not a significant source of dietary cholesterol, peanut butter, which is made from peanuts and vegetable oils, is free of dietary cholesterol.

8. (a) Flaxseeds are a good source of essential fatty acids.

9. (c) Whereas dietary cholesterol raises LDL cholesterol, saturated fat is the bigger culprit behind elevated LDL cholesterol in the blood. Viscous, soluble fiber, such as psyllium, as well as plant sterols can help lower LDL cholesterol.

10. (b) Increasing exercise can help increase the HDL cholesterol level. Increasing soluble fiber intake and maintaining a healthy body weight can help lower the LDL cholesterol level but does not affect the level of HDL cholesterol.

Answers to True or False?

1. **False.** While the body *does* need cholesterol for important functions, it can be synthesized in the liver in sufficient amounts. Thus, consuming dietary cholesterol is not necessary.

2. **False.** Whereas too much dietary fat may cause weight gain, eating too little isn't healthy, either. A diet low in fat but high in added sugars may increase the level of triglycerides in the blood.

3. **False.** Though the majority of *trans* fats are made from hydrogenated oils that are found in commercially prepared, processed foods, *trans* fats also occur naturally in foods such as meat and dairy products.

4. **True.** A diet high in saturated fat can raise blood cholesterol.

5. **False.** Fat-free foods often have added carbohydrates, which add back kilocalories. The savings in fat kilocalories is usually not much of a savings in total kilocalories.

6. **True.** High levels of HDL cholesterol can help reduce the risk of heart disease.

7. **False.** Although stick margarines can contain heart-unhealthy *trans* fats, butter has more total cholesterol-raising fats than margarine, and so is ultimately less healthy.

8. **False.** Because nuts are plant foods, they do not contain cholesterol but are rich sources of essential fatty acids.

9. **False.** Consuming too much fish oil can be unhealthy. The best source of omega-3 fatty acids is fresh fish.
10. **False.** LDL cholesterol is a lipoprotein carrier found in the blood and is not found in foods.

Web Resources

To learn more about lipids and health, visit
- National Cholesterol Education Program at www.nhlbi.nih.gov
- EPA Fish Advisories at www.epa.gov
- American Heart Association at www.americanheart.org
- EFA Education at http://efaeducation.nih.gov
- National Heart, Lung, and Blood Institute at www.nhlbi.nih.gov
- Centers for Disease Control and Prevention, Physical Activity, Energize Your Life! at www.cdc.gov
- Heart Healthy Women at www.hearthealthywomen.org
- WebMD Heart Health Center at www.webmd.com
- Lipid Corner for the Lipid Research Division of ASBMB at www.asbmb.org
- MEDLINE Plus Health Information at www.nlm.nih.gov/medlineplus
- Seafood Watch at www.seafoodwatch.org

References

1. MacKay, D. S., and P. J. H. Jones. 2011. Phytosterols in Human Nutrition: Type, Formulation, Delivery, and Physiological Function. *European Journal of Lipid Science and Technology* 113:1427–1432.
2. Lin, B., and R. Morrison. 2012. *Food and Nutrient Intake Data: Taking a Look at the Nutritional Quality of Foods Eaten at Home and Away From Home.* Available at www.ers.usda.gov. Accessed February 2014.
3. Ibid.
4. Institute of Medicine. 2006. *Dietary Reference Intakes: The Essential Guide to Nutrient Requirements.* Washington, DC: The National Academies Press.
5. Ibid.
6. Schuchardt, J. P., I. Schneider, H. Meyer, J. Neubronner, C. von Schacky, and A. Hahn. 2011. Incorporation of EPA and DHA into Plasma Phospholipids in Response to Different Omega-3 Fatty Acid Formulations—A Comparative Bioavailability Study of Fish Oil vs. Krill Oil. *Lipids in Health and Disease* 10:145.
7. Asghari, G., S. Sheikholeslami, P. Mirmiran, A. Chary, M. Hedayati, A. Shafiee, and F. Azizi. 2012. Effect of Pomegranate Seed Oil on Serum TNF-α Level in Dyslipidemic Patients. *International Journal of Food Science in Nutrition* 63(3):368–371.
8. Schuchardt. J. P., et al. 2011. Incorporation of EPA and DHA into Plasma Phospholipids.
9. Aroa, A., J. M. Antoineb, L. Pizzoferratoc, O. Reykdald, and G. van Poppel. 1998. *Trans*-Fatty Acids in Dairy and Meat Products from 14 European Countries: The TRANSFAIR Study. *Journal of Food Composition and Analysis* 11:150–160.
10. Asghari, G., et al. 2012. Effect of Pomegranate Seed Oil on Serum TNF-α Level.
11. Kris-Etherton, P. M., M. Lefere, and B. D. Flickinger. 2012. *Trans*-Fatty Acid Intakes and Food Sources in the U.S. Population: NHANES 1999–2002. *Lipids* 47(10):931–940.
12. Food and Drug Administration. 2011. Trans Fat Now Listed with Saturated Fat and Cholesterol on the Nutrition Facts Label. Available at www.fda.gov. Accessed February 2014.
13. Behrman, E. J., and V. Gopalan. 2005. Cholesterol and Plants. *Journal of Chemical Education* 82:1791–1793.
14. Law, M. 2000. Plant Sterol and Stanol Margarines and Health. *British Medical Journal* 320:861–864.
15. Calorie Control Council. 2014. *Fat Replacers.* Available at www.caloriecontrol.org. Accessed February 2014.
16. Ibid.
17. Wylie-Rosett, J. 2002. Fat Substitutes and Health: An Advisory from the Nutrition Committee of the American Heart Association. *Circulation* 105:2800–2804.
18. Calorie Control Council. 2014. *Fat Replacers.*
19. Ibid.
20. Patterson, R. E., A. R. Kristal, J. C. Peters, M. L. Neuhouser, C. L. Rock, L. J. Cheskin, D. Neumark-Sztainer, and M. D. Thornquist. 2000. Changes in Diet, Weight, and Serum Lipid Levels Associated with Olestra Consumption. *Archives of Internal Medicine* 160:2600–2604.
21. Kris-Etherton, P. M., et al. 2012. *Trans* Fatty Acid Intakes and Food Sources.
22. American Heart Association. 2014. *Heart Disease and Stroke Statistics—2014 Update.* Available at www.myamericanheart.org. Accessed February 2014.
23. National Heart, Lung, and Blood Institute. 2005. *High Blood Cholesterol: What You Need to Know.* NIH Publication No. 01-3290. Available at www.nhlbi.nih.gov. Accessed February 2014.
24. Goldstein, J. L., and M. S. Brown. 1987. Regulation of Low-Density Lipoprotein Receptors: Implications for Pathogenesis and Therapy of Hypercholesterolemia and Atherosclerosis. *Circulation* 76:504–507.
25. Ibid.
26. Windgassen, E. B., L. Funtowicz, T. N. Lunsford, et al. 2011. C-Reactive Protein and High-Sensitivity C-Reactive Protein: An Update for Clinicians. *Postgraduate Medicine* 123:114–119.
27. Tehlivets, O. 2011. Homocysteine as a Risk Factor for Atherosclerosis: Is Its Conversion to S-Adenosyl-L-Homocysteine the Key to Deregulated Lipid Metabolism? *Journal of Lipids* doi:10.1155/2011/702853.
28. Joshi, R., B. Khandelwal, D. Joshi, and O. P. Gupta. 2013. *Chlamydophila pneumoniae* Infection and Cardiovascular Disease. *North American Journal of Medicine* 5(3):169–181.
29. Tsimikas, S., and J. L. Hall. 2012. Lipoprotein(a) as a Potential Causal Genetic Risk Factor of Cardiovascular Disease: A Rationale for Increased Efforts to Understand Its Pathophysiology and Develop Targeted Therapies. *Journal of the American College of Cardiology* 60(8):716–721.
30. American Heart Association. 2012. *High Blood Pressure and Metabolic Syndrome.* Available at www.heart.org. Accessed February 2014.
31. Howe, M., A. Leidal, D. Montgomery, and E. Jackson. 2011. Role of Cigarette Smoking and Gender in Acute Coronary Syndrome Events. *American Journal of Cardiology* 108(10):1382–1386.
32. American Heart Association. 2013. *Why Cholesterol Matters.* Available at www.heart.org. Accessed February 2014.
33. Ibid.
34. Siri-Tarino, P. W., Q. Sun, F. B. Hu, and R. M. Krauss. 2010. Meta-Analysis of Prospective Cohort Studies Evaluating the Association of Saturated Fat with Cardiovascular Disease. *American Journal of Clinical Nutrition* 91:535–546.
35. Hunter, J. E., J. Zhang, and P. M. Kris-Etherton. 2010. Cardiovascular Disease Risk of Dietary Stearic Acid Compared with *Trans*, Other Saturated, and Unsaturated Fatty Acids: A Systematic Review. *American Journal of Clinical Nutrition* 91(1):46–63.
36. Ibid.
37. American Heart Association. 2014. Trans *Fats.* Available at www.heart.org. Accessed February 2014.
38. Brouwer, I. A., A. J. Wanders, and M. B. Katan. 2013. *Trans* Fatty Acids and Cardiovascular Health: Research Completed? *European Journal of Clinical Nutrition* 67:541–547.
39. Mozaffarian, D. R., N. Lemaitre, I. B. King, X. Song, H. Huang, F. M. Sacks, E. B. Rimm, et al. 2013. Plasma Phospholipid Long-Chain ω-3 Fatty Acids and Total and Cause-Specific Mortality in Older Adults: A Cohort Study. *Annals of Internal Medicine* 158(7):515–525.
40. American Heart Association. 2014. *Fish and Omega-3 Fatty Acids.* Available at www.heart.org. Accessed February 2014.
41. American Heart Association. 2013. *Eating More Fiber May Lower Risk of First-Time Stroke.* Available at http://newsroom.heart.org. Accessed February 2014.
42. Steinberg, F. M., M. J. Murray, R. D. Lewis, et al. 2011. Clinical Outcomes of a 2-y Soy Isoflavone Supplementation in Menopausal Women. *American Journal of Clinical Nutrition* 93(2):356–367. DOI: 10.3945/ajcn.110.008359.

43. Gylling, H., J. Plat, S. Turley, et al. 2014. Plant Sterols and Plant Stanols in the Management of Dyslipidaemia and Prevention of Cardiovascular Disease. *Atherosclerosis* 232(2):346–360.

44. Shaghaghi, A. M., S. S. Abumweis, and P. J. Jones. 2013. Cholesterol-lowering Efficacy of Plant Sterols/stanols Provided in Capsule and Tablet Formats: Results of a Systematic Review and Meta-analysis. *Journal of the Academy of Nutrition and Dietetics* 113(11):1494–1503.

45. Wu, L., K. Piotrowski, T. Rau, et al. 2013. Walnut-Enriched Diet Reduces Fasting Non-HDL Cholesterol and Apolipoprotein B in Healthy Caucasian Subjects: A Randomized Controlled Cross-Over Clinical Trial. *Metabolism* doi: 10.1016/j.metabol.2013.11.005.

46. Eilat-Adar, S., T. Sinai, C. Yosefy, and Y. Kenkin. 2013. Nutritional

Recommendations for Cardiovascular Disease Prevention. *Nutrients* 5(9):3646–3683.

47. de Koning Gans, J., Y. Uiterwaal, J. van der Schouw, D. Boer, W. Verschuren, and J. Beulen. 2012. Tea and Coffee Consumption and Cardiovascular Morbidity and Mortality. *Arteriosclerosis, Thrombosis, and Vascular Biology* 30:1665–1671.

48. Kim, A., A. Chiu, M. Barone, D. Avino, F. Wang, and C. Coleman. 2011. Green Tea Catechins Decrease Total and Low-Density Lipoprotein Cholesterol. A Systematic Review and Meta-Analysis. *Journal of the American Dietetic Association* 111:1720–1729.

49. Brekke, H. K., F. Bertz, K. M. Rasmussen, et al. 2014. Diet and Exercise Interventions Among Overweight and Obese Lactating Women: Randomized Trial of Effects on Cardiovascular Risk Factors. *PLoS One*

9(2):e88250. doi: 10.1371/journal .pone.0088250.

50. Ibid.

51. American Heart Association. 2011. *Why Quit Smoking?* Available at www.heart.org. Accessed February 2014.

52. American Heart Association. 2011. *Alcoholic Beverages and Cardiovascular Disease.* Available at www.heart.org. Accessed February 2014.

53. Ibid.

54. Ibid.

55. Zaridze, D., S. Lewington, D. Phil, A. Boroda, G. Scelo, et al. 2014. Alcohol and Mortality in Russia: Prospective Observational Study of 151,000 Adults. *The Lancet* doi: 10.1016/S0140-6736(13)62247-3.

6 Proteins

Learning Outcomes

After reading this chapter, you will be able to:

6.1 Describe protein, its basic structure and shape, and the classification of amino acids.

6.2 Identify the key steps in digesting proteins and absorbing amino acids.

6.3 Explain the metabolism of amino acids and the role of the amino acid pool.

6.4 Describe the functions of proteins in the body.

6.5 Calculate the daily amount of protein recommended based on the Dietary Reference Intakes.

6.6 Describe the best food sources of protein and the methods available to determine protein quality.

6.7 Explain the health consequences of consuming too little or too much protein.

6.8 Describe the benefits and risks of a vegetarian diet.

True or False?

1. Proteins are chemically different from carbohydrates or lipids because they contain nitrogen. **T/F**

2. Proteins are made up of 20 essential amino acids. **T/F**

3. The first step in the chemical digestion of protein occurs in the mouth with the enzyme pepsin. **T/F**

4. Hydrochloric acid denatures protein in the stomach. **T/F**

5. The body can use protein as a source of glucose. **T/F**

6. The primary function of protein is to provide energy to the cells. **T/F**

7. Growing children are in a state of negative nitrogen balance. **T/F**

8. Animal products are a good source of incomplete protein. **T/F**

9. Eating too much protein is associated with high blood cholesterol levels. **T/F**

10. Consuming a diet inadequate in protein may lead to a disease called kwashiorkor. **T/F**

See page 246 for the answers.

Proteins are the predominant structural and functional materials in every cell. In fact, protein alone makes up 50 percent of your body's dry weight. Proteins do most of the work of the cell and facilitate movement in bones and muscles. Your protein-rich muscles enable you to swim, jog, walk, and hold your head up so you can read this chapter. Without adequate protein, your body couldn't replace the skin cells that slough off when you shower or produce sufficient antibodies to fight off infections. Your hair and fingernails wouldn't grow and you wouldn't be able to digest your food.

In this chapter we discuss the structure and roles of proteins and how they are digested, absorbed, and metabolized in the body. We also cover the health risks associated with consuming too much or too little protein and the pros and cons of different eating patterns, including vegetarian diets.

Protein-rich muscles enable you to perform daily activities.

What Are Proteins?

LO 6.1 Describe protein, its basic structure and shape, and the classification of amino acids.

Proteins are found in each cell in the body. These diverse molecules play a role in virtually every cellular activity, from building, repairing, and maintaining cells to storage, transport, and use of the foods you eat.

Many enzymes and some hormones, which control essential metabolic processes, are made of proteins. They direct how fast the body burns kilocalories, how quickly the heart beats, and possibly your attraction to another person.[1] In fact, proteins are involved in all of the body's functions, and without them, you wouldn't survive.[2]

Proteins Differ Structurally from Carbohydrates and Lipids

In Chapters 4 and 5, you learned that dietary carbohydrates are chains of glucose units, while most dietary lipids contain fatty acids (see **Figure 6.1**). Proteins are also made of chains, but in this case the units (or building blocks) are called **amino acids.** These proteins are synthesized based on the individual's unique DNA.

Macronutrients	Composed of	Example
Carbohydrates	Monosaccharides	Polysaccharide — Glucose units
Lipids	Fatty acids	Triglyceride — Fatty acids
Proteins	Amino acids	Peptide — Amino acids

▲ **Figure 6.1 Structural Differences between Carbohydrates, Lipids, and Proteins** Carbohydrates, some lipids, and proteins are similar in their chainlike structures. The main difference is that proteins contain nitrogen, and carbohydrates and lipids do not. Carbohydrates are composed of glucose chains; triglycerides and phospholipids contain fatty acids and proteins are made of chains of amino acids.

proteins Large molecules, made up of chains of amino acids, found in all living cells; the sequence of amino acids is determined by the DNA.

amino acids The building blocks of protein. There are 20 amino acids composed of carbon, hydrogen, oxygen, and nitrogen.

Unlike dietary carbohydrates and triglycerides, excess dietary protein cannot be stored in the body.

Chemically, the structure of protein is similar to carbohydrates and lipids in that all three nutrients contain atoms of carbon (C), hydrogen (H), and oxygen (O). Protein is unique, however, because 16 percent of each protein molecule is nitrogen (N), found in the amine groups of the amino acids. In fact, protein is the only food component that provides the nitrogen the body needs for important processes, such as the synthesis of neurotransmitters. Some proteins also contain the mineral sulfur (S), which is not found in either carbohydrates or lipids.

The Building Blocks of Proteins Are Amino Acids

All proteins in the body consist of a unique combination of up to 20 different amino acids and are classified according to the number of amino acids in the chain. Proteins typically contain between 100 and 10,000 amino acids in a sequence. For instance, the protein that forms the hemoglobin in red blood cells consists of 574 amino acids. In contrast, collagen, a protein found in connective tissue, contains approximately 1,000 amino acids.

Amino acids are like numeric digits: Their specific sequence determines a specific function of the protein. Consider that telephone numbers, Social Security numbers, and bank PIN numbers are all made up of the same digits (0 to 9) arranged in different sequences of varying lengths. Each of these numbers has a specific purpose. Similarly, amino acids can be linked together to make unique sequences of varying lengths, giving each protein a specific function.

As illustrated in **Figure 6.2**, each amino acid contains a central carbon (C) surrounded by a **carboxyl** or **acid group** (COOH), which is why it is called an amino "acid"; an **amine group** (NH₂) that contains the nitrogen; a hydrogen atom; and a distinctive **side chain** also referred to as the R group. All amino acids contain the same five parts, and the side chain makes each amino acid unique.

Side chains can be as simple as a single hydrogen atom, as in the amino acid glycine, or they can be as complex as the ring structure in phenylalanine. Though each side chain is distinct, some have similar properties. For example, some side chains cause their amino acids to be basic, such as those found in arginine and histidine, while others, such as the side chain in aspartic acid, cause their amino acid to be acidic. Two amino acid side chains contain sulfur, methionine and cysteine, and some side chains are branched, as in the case of leucine, isoleucine, and valine.

Side chains influence the function of each amino acid, whether the body can make the amino acid, and the metabolic pathway the amino acid follows after absorption. Side chains also influence the shape of the protein due to their interactions with each other. Some side chains are attracted to other side chains; some are neutral; and some repel each other, causing the protein to be either linear or globular in shape. It is the shape of the protein that determines its function in the body. Therefore, anything that alters the attractions between the side chains will alter the protein's shape and thus its function.

Any amino acid chain that contains fewer than 50 amino acids is called a **peptide,** connected with a **peptide bond.** If a chain consists of two joined amino acids it is called a **dipeptide;** three joined amino acids form a **tripeptide;** more than 10 amino acids joined together is called a **polypeptide.** A polypeptide chain that contains more than 50 amino acids is called a protein.

Peptide Bonds

Peptide bonds link amino acids into unique chains. These bonds are formed when the carbon from the acid group (COOH) of one amino acid joins with the nitrogen atom from the amine group (NH₂) of another amino acid by a condensation reaction (**Figure 6.3**), releasing a molecule of water. In contrast, peptide bonds are broken by hydrolysis, which is particularly important during digestion. In this process,

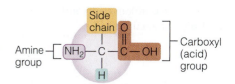

a **Amino acid structure.** All amino acids contain a central carbon surrounded by a side chain, carboxylic acid (COOH), a hydrogen, and an amine group (NH₂).

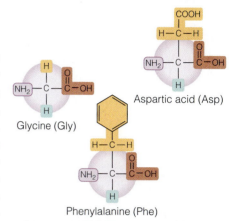

Aspartic acid (Asp)

Glycine (Gly)

Phenylalanine (Phe)

b **Different amino acids with their unique side chains.** A unique side chain (shown in yellow) distinguishes the various amino acids.

▲ Figure 6.2 **The Anatomy of an Amino Acid**

carboxyl or **acid group** The organic group attached to an amino acid that is composed of one carbon, one hydrogen, and two oxygen atoms (COOH).

amine group The nitrogen-containing part (NH₂) connected to the central carbon of an amino acid.

side chain The part of an amino acid that provides its unique qualities; also referred to as the R group.

peptide A chain of amino acids.

peptide bonds The bonds that connect amino acids, created when the acid group of one amino acid is joined with the nitrogen-containing amine group of another amino acid through condensation.

dipeptide A chain of two amino acids joined together by a peptide bond.

tripeptide A chain of three amino acids joined together by peptide bonds.

polypeptide A chain consisting of ten or more amino acids joined together by peptide bonds.

a A peptide bond forms by condensation when the acid group (COOH) and amine group of two different amino acids join and release a molecule of water.

b When peptide bonds are broken by hydrolysis, the hydroxyl group (OH) and hydrogen (H) from water are added.

a molecule of water is used to split the bond, adding the hydroxyl (OH) group to one amino acid and hydrogen to the other.

Essential, Nonessential, and Conditional Amino Acids

Nine of the 20 amino acids that the body uses to make protein are classified as **essential** amino acids. It is *essential* that the diet provide them because these amino acids either cannot be made by the body or cannot be made in sufficient quantities to sustain the body's needs.

The remaining 11 amino acids are considered **nonessential** because the body can make them. It is not essential to consume them. **Table 6.1** lists the 20 known, nutritionally important amino acids by their classification.

TABLE 6.1	The Mighty Twenty	
Essential Amino Acids	**Nonessential Amino Acids (Conditionally Essential[b] Amino Acids in Italics)**	
Histidine (His)[a]	Alanine (Ala)	
Isoleucine (Ile)	*Arginine (Arg)*	
Leucine (Leu)	Asparagine (Asn)	
Lysine (Lys)	Aspartic acid (Asp)	
Methionine (Met)	*Cysteine (Cys)*	
Phenylalanine (Phe)	Glutamic acid (Glu)	
Threonine (Thr)	*Glutamine (Gln)*	
Tryptophan (Trp)	*Glycine (Gly)*	
Valine (Val)	*Proline (Pro)*	
	Serine (Ser)	
	Tyrosine (Tyr)	

[a] Histidine was once thought to be essential only for infants. It is now known that small amounts are also needed for adults.
[b] These amino acids can be "conditionally essential" if there are either inadequate precursors or inadequate enzymes available to create these in the body.

essential [amino acids] The nine amino acids that the body cannot synthesize; they must be obtained through dietary sources.

nonessential [amino acids] The 11 amino acids the body can synthesize and that therefore do not need to be consumed in the diet.

Some nonessential amino acids may become **conditionally essential** if the body cannot make them because of illness, or because the body lacks the necessary precursors or enzymes. In such situations, the amino acid involved is considered essential and must be consumed. An example of this is when premature infants are not able to make enough of the enzymes needed to synthesize arginine, they need to get this amino acid in their diet.

The Organization and Shape of Proteins Affect Their Function

Each protein is composed of hundreds to thousands of amino acids linked in a specific order, the length and pattern determined by your genes. Every protein has four different levels of structure: primary, secondary, tertiary, and quaternary; each level must be correct in order for the protein to function (**Figure 6.4**).

The **primary structure** is the order of amino acids and the length of the polypeptide chain. The amino acids are held together by peptide bonds in a sequence that is

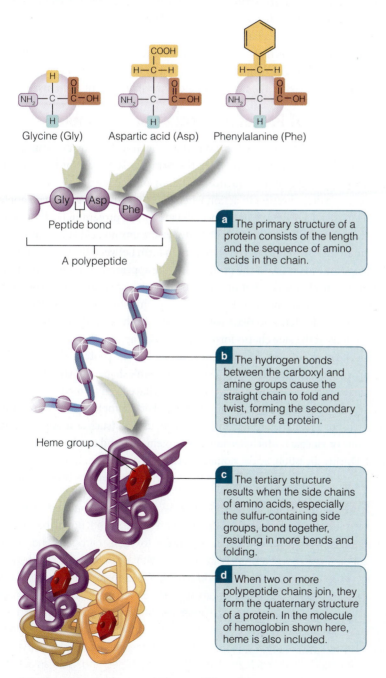

Glycine (Gly)   Aspartic acid (Asp)   Phenylalanine (Phe)

Peptide bond

A polypeptide

a The primary structure of a protein consists of the length and the sequence of amino acids in the chain.

b The hydrogen bonds between the carboxyl and amine groups cause the straight chain to fold and twist, forming the secondary structure of a protein.

Heme group

c The tertiary structure results when the side chains of amino acids, especially the sulfur-containing side groups, bond together, resulting in more bends and folding.

d When two or more polypeptide chains join, they form the quaternary structure of a protein. In the molecule of hemoglobin shown here, heme is also included.

▲ Figure 6.4 **The Organization and Shape of Proteins**

conditionally essential [amino acids] Those nonessential amino acids, such as tyrosine and glycine, that become essential (and must be consumed in the diet) when the body cannot make them.

primary structure The first stage of protein synthesis after transcription when the amino acids have been linked together with peptide bonds to form a simple linear chain.

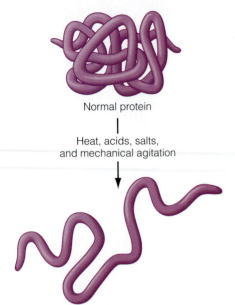

Normal protein

|
Heat, acids, salts,
and mechanical agitation
↓

Denatured protein

▲ **Figure 6.5 Denaturing a Protein**
A protein can be denatured, or unfolded, by exposure to heat, acids, or salts or by mechanical agitation. Any change in a protein's shape will alter its function.

Whipping egg whites denatures the protein.

secondary structure The geometric shape of a protein caused by the hydrogen ions of amino acids linking together with the amine group, causing the straight chain to fold and twist.

tertiary structure The third-level shape of a protein; occurs when the side chains of the amino acids, most often containing sulfur, form bridges, causing the protein to form even stronger bonds than in the secondary structure; these bonds form loops, bends, and folds in the molecule.

quaternary structure The fourth geometric pattern of a protein; formed when two or more polypeptide chains cluster together, forming a final rod-like or ball-like structure.

denature To alter a protein's shape, either its secondary, tertiary, or quaternary structure, which prevents its function; the chains of amino acids remain linked together by peptide bonds.

unique to that protein. A change in just one amino acid in the sequence results in a dramatic change in the shape of the protein and, therefore, its function, in the same way that a telephone number with digits out of order or missing will no longer work.

Once the sequence is formed, the amino acids either attract and form bonds with one another or repel each other. This formation of hydrogen bonds between the amino acids creates the **secondary structure.** The hydrogen bonds between the carboxyl and amine groups cause the straight chain to fold, twist, and coil.

In addition, side chains can be attracted to (*hydrophilic*) or repelled by (*hydrophobic*) water in the cells, which affects how they interact with their environment. This is especially true for sulfur-containing side chains. The hydrophobic side chains cluster together on the inside and combine to form a globular shape called the **tertiary structure,** while the hydrophilic side chains assemble on the outside of the protein and interact with the watery portion of blood and other body fluids.

Finally, the **quaternary structure** of a protein forms when two or more polypeptide chains bond together with a hydrogen bond or there is a reaction between the sulfur-containing side chains of the amino acids methionine and cysteine. A good example of a quaternary structure of a protein is hemoglobin (Figure 6.4d). The iron-containing heme groups shown in red in the illustration assist in binding oxygen and are not part of the normal quaternary structure of proteins.

Denaturation of Proteins Changes Their Shape

Heat, acids, bases, salts, or mechanical agitation can unfold, or **denature,** proteins (**Figure 6.5**). Denaturation doesn't alter the primary structure of the protein (the amino acids stay in the same sequence), but does change the shape.

You can see denaturation in action when you cook an egg. When you apply heat to a raw egg, such as by frying it, the heat denatures the protein in both the yolk and the egg white. Heat disrupts the bonds between the amino acid side chains, causing the protein in the egg to uncoil. New bonds then form between the side chains, changing the shape and structure of the protein, and the appearance and texture of the egg.

Similarly, mechanical agitation, such as beating egg whites when you prepare a meringue, can denature protein. Beating an egg white uncoils the protein, allowing the hydrophilic side chains to react with the water in the egg white, while the hydrophobic portions of the side chains form new bonds, trapping the air from the beating. The stiffer the peaks of egg white, the more denatured the protein. Whether you cook an egg, or whip egg whites, the change in the protein's shape and structure is permanent because new bonds between the amino acids have been formed.

Salts and acids can also denature proteins. For example, when you marinate a chicken breast or a steak before cooking, you might use salt (such as in soy sauce) or acid (such as wine or vinegar), which denatures its protein. The end result is juicier, more tender meat. During digestion, acidic stomach juices help denature and untangle proteins to reveal the peptide bonds. This allows digestive enzymes to break the bonds apart.

LO 6.1: THE TAKE-HOME MESSAGE Proteins are chains of amino acids linked together with peptide bonds by condensation and broken down by hydrolysis. Amino acids, which contain carbon, hydrogen, oxygen, nitrogen, and, in some cases, sulfur, are comprised of a central carbon with a carboxyl group, a hydrogen, a nitrogen-containing amine group, and a unique side chain. There are 20 different side chains and therefore 20 unique amino acids. Eleven are classified as nonessential and nine are classified as essential. Under certain circumstances, some nonessential amino acids become essential. The attractions and interactions between the side chains cause the protein to fold into a precise three-dimensional shape that determines its function. Heat, mechanical agitation, acids, bases, and salts can denature a protein and alter its shape and function.

What Are the Key Steps in Digesting and Absorbing Protein?

LO 6.2 Identify the key steps in digesting proteins and absorbing amino acids.

When you eat a peanut butter sandwich, what happens to the protein in the peanut butter and the whole-wheat bread after it has been chewed and swallowed? How do proteins in food become body proteins?

Even before you eat the sandwich, the sight and smell of the food stimulates the mouth to produce saliva and the stomach to produce gastric juices to prepare for digestion.

Protein Digestion Begins in the Stomach

The peanut butter sandwich is prepared for digestion in the mouth, where teeth tear and shred the food, breaking the sandwich into smaller pieces while mixing it with saliva (**Focus Figure 6.6**). This mechanical digestion helps make the food easy to swallow, and is the only digestion of protein that takes place in the mouth. No chemical or enzymatic digestion of proteins occurs in the mouth.

After you eat a meal, the hormone **gastrin** directs the release of hydrochloric acid (HCl) from the parietal cells in the stomach wall. At the same time, gastrin directs the release of **pepsinogen,** an inactive protein enzyme, from the chief cells. Once the bolus enters the stomach, HCl begins to denature the protein strands. HCl also converts the pepsinogen to an active enzyme called **pepsin,** which begins breaking the polypeptides into shorter chains by hydrolysis. The strands are then propelled into the small intestine as part of the chyme.

Table 6.2 provides a complete list of enzymes that participate in protein digestion.

Protein Digestion Continues in the Small Intestine

When the protein-rich chyme reaches the small intestine, the intestinal cells release the hormone cholecystokinin into the blood. This hormone stimulates the pancreas to secrete **proteases,** which are protein-digesting enzymes including trypsin, chymotrypsin, and carboxypeptidase, through the pancreatic duct into the small intestine. Trypsin and chymotrypsin continue to break apart the peptide bonds in the center of the polypeptide chain, resulting in smaller and smaller peptide chains. The enzyme carboxypeptidase breaks apart the first peptide bond closest to the carboxylic end of

gastrin A stomach hormone released after eating a meal that stimulates the release of hydrochloric acid.

pepsinogen The inactive precursor of pepsin; pepsinogen is stored in the gastric cells and is converted to pepsin by hydrochloric acid.

pepsin An enzyme in the stomach that begins the digestion of dietary protein.

proteases Protein-digesting enzymes that can break the peptide bonds linking amino acids together.

TABLE 6.2	Enzymes Involved in Protein Digestion	
Digestive Enzyme	**Where Released**	**Purpose**
Pepsinogen	From chief cells in the stomach (activated to pepsin by HCl)	Breaks apart polypeptides into shorter polypeptide chains
Trypsin	From pancreas into small intestine	Breaks apart peptide bonds
Chymotrypsin	From pancreas into small intestine	Breaks apart peptide bonds
Carboxypeptidase	From pancreas into small intestine	Breaks free one amino acid at a time from the carboxyl end of a peptide chain
Aminopeptidase	Brush border of the small intestine	Breaks free the end amino acids from tri- and dipeptides into single amino acids
Tripeptidase	Brush border of the small intestine	Breaks tripeptides into single amino acids
Dipeptidase	Brush border of the small intestine	Breaks dipeptides into single amino acids

Protein Digestion and Absorption

Protein digestion begins in the stomach with the aid of hydrochloric acid (HCl) and the enzyme pepsin. Proteases continue the digestion in the small intestine, releasing single amino acids to be absorbed into the portal vein for delivery to the liver.

ORGANS OF THE GI TRACT

ACCESSORY ORGANS

MOUTH

Mechanical digestion of protein begins with chewing, tearing, and mixing food with salivary juices to form a bolus.

STOMACH

Hydrochloric acid denatures protein and activates pepsinogen to form pepsin.

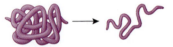

Pepsin breaks the polypeptide chain into smaller polypeptides.

PANCREAS

Produces proteases that are released into the small intestine via the pancreatic duct.

LIVER

Uses some amino acids to make new proteins or converts them to glucose. Most amino acids pass through the liver and return to the blood to be picked up and used by body cells.

SMALL INTESTINE

Proteases continue to cleave peptide bonds, resulting in dipeptides, tripeptides, and single amino acids.

Tripeptidases and dipeptidases on the surface of the enterocytes finish the digestion to yield single amino acids, which can then be absorbed into the bloodstream and travel through the portal vein to the liver.

Amino acids

Enterocytes

Capillary

the chain. What started out in the peanut butter as a very large protein molecule has now been reduced to tripeptides and dipeptides. Dipeptidases and tripeptidases help break down the smaller peptide chains into single amino acids.

Amino Acids Are Absorbed in the Small Intestine

Amino acids are absorbed into the cells of the small intestine. The single amino acids pool inside the enterocytes, where they can be used for energy, used to synthesize new compounds, or until they exit the cell, and are transported via the portal vein to the liver. After reaching the liver, amino acids can be used to synthesize new proteins, or can be converted to ATP, glucose, or fat. When other cells need them, the liver releases amino acids into the bloodstream and they are transported throughout the body.

Almost all dietary proteins are digested, absorbed, and transported via the portal vein as single amino acids. However, there are some circumstances when whole proteins are absorbed intact, such as in the absorption of antibodies from breast milk or in the case of food allergies.[3]

LO 6.2: THE TAKE-HOME MESSAGE Chemical digestion of protein begins in the stomach. Gastrin stimulates the release of HCl from the parietal cells and the inactive enzyme pepsinogen from the chief cells. HCl denatures the protein and converts pepsinogen to pepsin, which breaks polypeptides into shorter chains. Cholecystokinin from the duodenum stimulates release of trypsinogen, carboxypeptidase, and chymotrypsinogen from the pancreas. These proteases hydrolyze the shorter chains into tripeptides and dipeptides. Dipeptidases and tripeptidases hydrolyze the tripeptides and dipeptides into single amino acids that are absorbed through the enterocytes via the portal vein to the liver. Absorbed amino acids are used to synthesize new proteins, or are converted to nonessential amino acids, energy, glucose, or fat.

How Are Amino Acids Metabolized?

LO 6.3 Explain the metabolism of amino acids and the role of the amino acid pool.

How the liver metabolizes newly absorbed amino acids depends on the needs of the body. For example, amino acids might be used to replace old proteins or synthesize new ones or, if necessary, they may be used as an energy source. If an individual is not eating sufficient carbohydrates, amino acids can be converted to glucose through a process called gluconeogenesis. However, most amino acids travel back out to the blood to be picked up and used by cells.

Amino Acid Pools Supply the Body's Ongoing Needs for Protein Synthesis

Proteins don't last indefinitely. The daily wear and tear on the body causes the breakdown of hundreds of grams of proteins each day. For example, the protein-rich cells in the skin are constantly sloughed off, and proteins help create a new layer of outer skin every 25 to 45 days.[4] Because red blood cells have a short life span—only about 120 days—new red blood cells must be continually regenerated. The cells that line the inner surfaces of the organs, such as the lungs and intestines, are recycled and replaced every three to five days, thanks to protein synthesis.

In addition to regular maintenance, extra protein is sometimes needed for emergency repairs. Protein is essential in healing, and a person with extensive wounds, such as severe burns, may have dietary protein needs that are more than triple his or her normal needs.

Amino acid pool

Protein turnover:
Proteins are constantly made and broken down, releasing their amino acids into the amino acid pool or using the amino acids for protein synthesis and other important compounds such as niacin and serotonin.

Gluconeogenesis:
Amino acids can be used to make glucose when glucose is limited.

Energy production:
Amino acids can be used for energy when the diet is deficient in kilocalories.

Fat cells:
Amino acids can be converted to fatty acids and stored as a triglyceride in the adipose tissue when kilocalorie intake is sufficient.

▲ **Figure 6.7 Metabolic Fate of Amino Acids**
Once in the amino acid pool, most amino acids are used for protein synthesis. Under certain conditions, amino acids can be used for gluco-neogenesis or energy production, or converted to fatty acids and stored in fat cells.

amino acid pools Limited supplies of amino acids that accumulate in the blood and cells; amino acids are pulled from the pools and used to build new proteins.

protein turnover The continual process of degrading and synthesizing protein.

gene The basic biological unit in a segment of DNA that contributes to the function of a specific protein.

transcription The first stage in protein synthesis, in which the DNA sequence is copied from the gene and transferred to messenger RNA.

messenger RNA (mRNA) A type of RNA that copies the genetic information from the DNA and carries it from the nucleus to the ribosomes in the cell.

translation The second phase of protein synthesis; the process of converting the information in mRNA to an amino acid sequence in the ribosomes.

ribosomes Organelles found in the cytosol that read the mRNA and build the protein in the proper sequence during elongation.

Newly absorbed amino acids collect in limited amounts in **amino acid pools** found in the blood and inside cells. When cellular proteins are degraded or broken down into their component parts, the resulting amino acids also enter the amino acid pools. The body can then use the amino acids in the pool to create proteins on demand. This process of degrading and synthesizing protein is called **protein turnover** (**Figure 6.7**). More than 200 grams of protein are turned over daily. The proteins in the intestines and liver—two tissue types with rapid degradation and resynthesis rates—account for as much as 50 percent of this turnover. Some of the amino acids in the pools are also used to synthesize nonprotein substances, including thyroid hormones and melanin, the pigment that gives color to dark skin and hair.

Protein Synthesis Is Regulated by Your Genes

The body is made up of over 100,000 different proteins. When the body is ready to build new or repair old proteins, the cells receive a signal to begin the process of protein synthesis. This signal is communicated to a cell receptor by hormones, cell-to-cell contact, or neurotransmitters. Cells can "turn on" and "turn off " protein synthesis as needed, similar to controlling the light in a room with an electrical switch.

The exact code to create specific proteins is stored in your **genes** located within the cell's DNA. Because the DNA cannot leave the nucleus of the cell and protein is synthesized outside the nucleus in the cytoplasm, the code must be copied, translated, and reproduced to build the exact sequence of amino acids described in the code. Let's walk through the two steps of the process of protein synthesis (**Focus Figure 6.8**).

1. **Transcription.** The first step in making a new polypeptide chain is to transcribe (or copy) the information contained in the DNA. The information contained in the DNA includes the sequence and number of amino acids in the chain and how to assemble the protein, similar to written instructions you follow when putting together a new bookshelf. The DNA transcribes the instructions by replicating a segment or piece of itself, forming a new molecule called **messenger RNA (mRNA).**

2. **Translation.** Once the code has been transcribed from DNA to mRNA, the new mRNA detaches from the DNA, leaves the nucleus, and enters the cytoplasm to transfer this information to the **ribosomes.** This is the second phase of the process, called translation. During this stage, the ribosome moves along the mRNA, reading or translating the instructions. The sequence of the amino

Protein Synthesis

Protein synthesis is the process by which the DNA code within a cell's nucleus is transcribed and translated to produce specific proteins.

Cell

Nucleus

1 In the nucleus, DNA unwinds to allow a copy of the code, called messenger RNA (mRNA) to be made. This process is called **transcription**.

2 The mRNA leaves the nucleus and travels to the cytosol.

3 Once the mRNA reaches the cytosol, it binds to a ribosome.

4 **Translation** is initiated as the ribosome moves along the mRNA, reading the code. Transfer RNA (tRNA) brings specific amino acids to the ribosome based on the code.

5 The process of **elongation** occurs as translation continues. The ribosome builds a chain of amino acids (the protein) in the proper sequence, based on the code in the mRNA.

6 Translation and elongation are terminated when all the appropriate amino acids are added and the protein is complete. The protein is released from the ribosome.

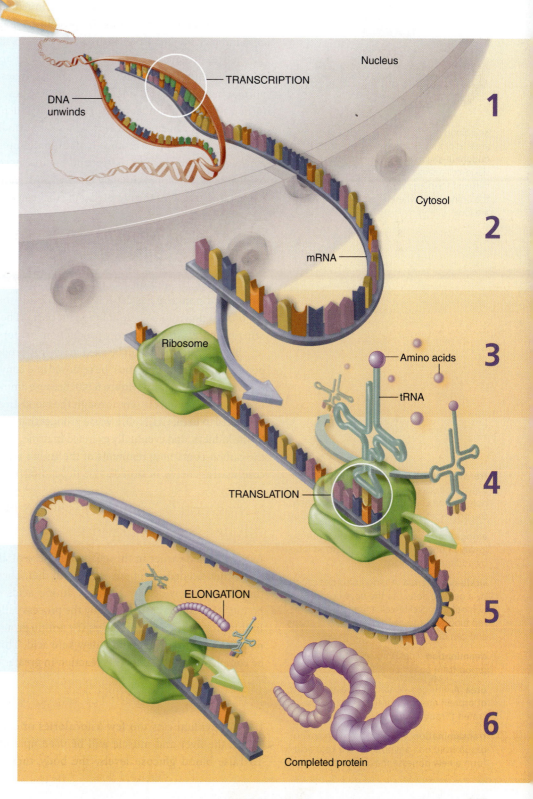

Nucleus

TRANSCRIPTION

DNA unwinds

1

Cytosol

2

mRNA

Ribosome

3

Amino acids

tRNA

TRANSLATION

4

ELONGATION

5

6

Completed protein

Red blood cells with normal hemoglobin are smooth and round, like the three red doughnut-shaped cells. A person with sickle-cell anemia has red blood cells that are stiff and form a sickle (half-moon) shape, like the orange cell, when blood oxygen levels are low.

acids recorded in the mRNA is communicated to a second type of RNA called **transfer RNA (tRNA).** Based on the pattern copied from the DNA, tRNA collects and transports the amino acids to the ribosomes to build the polypeptide chain in the proper sequence. There is a unique tRNA for each of the 20 different amino acids. This gathering and building step is called **elongation,** and continues until the sequence has been completed and a new protein is released.

When the sequence of amino acids is incorrect, abnormalities occur and medical conditions can result. One such condition is **sickle-cell anemia.** The most common inherited blood disorder in the United States, sickle-cell anemia is caused by the abnormal formation of the protein hemoglobin. The displacement of just *one* amino acid, glutamine, with another amino acid, valine, in polypeptide chains of hemoglobin causes the chains to stick to one another and form crescent-shaped structures rather than the normal globular ones. Whereas red blood cells with normal hemoglobin are smooth and round, those with this mutation are stiff and form a sickle shape under certain conditions, such as after vigorous exercise, when oxygen levels in the blood are low. These abnormal sickle cells are easily destroyed, which can lead to anemia, and they can build up in blood vessels, causing painful blockages and damage to tissues and organs. According to the National Institutes of Health (NIH), approximately one in 12 African-Americans and one in 100 Hispanics are carriers of the mutated gene that causes the disease.[5]

Deamination Removes the Amine Group from Amino Acids

What happens if amino acids in the pool aren't used for protein synthesis? As the amino acid pool reaches capacity, amino acids that are not used to build proteins are broken down into their component parts. These component parts are used for other purposes, such as energy production, or stored in another form.

Before amino acids can be used for energy production or converted to other compounds, the amine group must be removed and converted to ammonia (NH_3) in a process called **deamination** (**Figure 6.9a**). Because ammonia in high amounts can be toxic to cells, the ammonia is sent through the bloodstream to the liver, where it is quickly converted to **urea,** CH_4N_2O, a waste product that is released into the blood, filtered out by the kidneys, and eventually excreted in urine. Once the nitrogen has been removed, the carbon-containing remnants of the amino acids are eventually converted to glucose, used as energy, or stored as fat, depending on the needs of the body.

Nonessential Amino Acids Are Synthesized through Transamination

As you learned earlier in this chapter, nonessential amino acids can be made in the body when needed or not present in your diet. These amino acids can be made from the nitrogen provided by essential amino acids or ammonia, and another compound referred to as a *keto acid* by the process called **transamination** (Figure 6.9b). In this process, the liver transfers the amino group to the keto acid, creating a new, nonessential amino acid and a new keto acid. This reaction requires vitamin B_6 to be complete. We'll discuss this reaction in greater detail in Chapter 8.

Protein Can Be Used for Gluconeogenesis

If an individual eats too few kilocalories or carbohydrates, the stores of glycogen in the liver and muscle will be used up and blood glucose levels will drop. To raise blood glucose levels, the body turns to specific amino acids called

transfer RNA (tRNA) A type of RNA that transfers a specific amino acid to a growing polypeptide chain in the ribosomes during the processes of translation and elongation.

elongation The phase of protein synthesis in which the polypeptide chain grows longer by adding amino acids.

sickle-cell anemia A blood disorder caused by a genetic defect in the development of hemoglobin. Sickle-cell anemia causes the red blood cells to distort into a sickle shape and can damage organs and tissues.

deamination The removal of the amine group from an amino acid.

urea A nitrogen-containing waste product of protein metabolism that is mainly excreted through the urine via the kidneys.

transamination The transfer of an amino group from one amino acid to a keto acid to form a new nonessential amino acid.

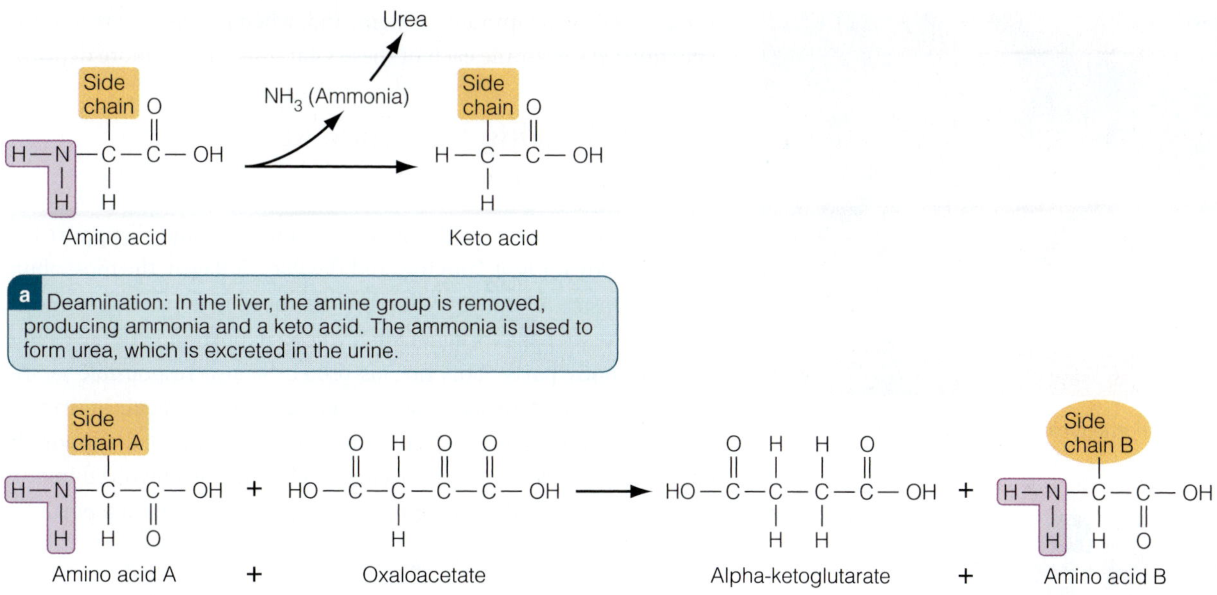

a Deamination: In the liver, the amine group is removed, producing ammonia and a keto acid. The ammonia is used to form urea, which is excreted in the urine.

b Transamination: An amine group from an essential amino acid is transferred to a keto acid, producing a nonessential amino acid and a new keto acid.

▲ Figure 6.9 **Deamination and Transamination**

glucogenic amino acids. These amino acids are converted to glucose through the process of **gluconeogenesis,** the creation (*genesis*) of glucose (*gluco*) from new (*neo*) compounds other than carbohydrates. (Remember that the brain and nervous system need glucose to function properly.)

Excess Protein Is Converted to Body Fat

If you add too much water to a swimming pool, the excess overflows. The same is true of an amino acid pool. When the diet contains sufficient carbohydrates, and protein intake exceeds requirements, the amino acid pool becomes saturated. The "overflow" amino acids are deaminated, and the remaining carbon remnants are converted to fatty acids and stored as triglycerides in adipose tissue.

LO 6.3: THE TAKE-HOME MESSAGE During digestion food, proteins are broken down into amino acids with the help of gastric juices, enzymes in the stomach and small intestine, and enzymes from the pancreas and small intestinal lining. A limited supply of amino acids exists in the amino acid pools, which act as a reservoir for protein synthesis. Surplus amino acids are deaminated, with the carbon-containing remnants used for glucose or energy, or stored as fat, depending on the body's needs. The nitrogen in the amine groups is eventually converted to the waste product urea and excreted in urine. Nonessential amino acids are synthesized through transamination.

What Is the Function of Protein in the Body?

LO 6.4 Describe the functions of protein in the body.

Proteins play many important roles in the body, from providing structural and mechanical support and maintaining body tissues to functioning as enzymes and hormones and helping maintain acid-base and fluid balance. They also transport

glucogenic amino acids Amino acids that can be used to form glucose through gluconeogenesis.

gluconeogenesis The formation of glucose from noncarbohydrate sources such as glucogenic amino acids, pyruvate, lactate, and glycerol.

Proteins play an important role in keeping skin healthy and nails strong.

nutrients, assist the immune system, and, when necessary, are a source of energy. Let's examine each of these vital functions in more depth.

Proteins Provide Structural Support and Enable Movement

Proteins provide much of the structural and mechanical support that keeps the body upright, moving, and flexible. Collagen, the most abundant protein in the body, is found in all connective tissues, including the bones, tendons, and ligaments, which support and connect joints and other body parts. This fibrous protein is also responsible for the skin's elasticity and forms the scar tissue necessary to repair injuries.

The proteins actin and myosin provide mechanical support by contracting muscles during movement. They are also involved in nonmuscle movement when cells divide during mitosis or chemicals are transported in the nerve cells.

Proteins Act as Catalysts

When the body requires a reaction to take place promptly, such as breaking down carbohydrates after a meal, it calls upon enzymes, biological **catalysts** that speed up reactions. Most enzymes are proteins, although to be activated, some may also need a coenzyme, such as a vitamin. Without enzymes, reactions would occur so slowly that you couldn't survive.

Each of the thousands of enzymes in the body catalyzes a specific reaction. Some enzymes, such as digestive enzymes, are **catabolic** enzymes: They break compounds apart. The enzyme lactase is needed to break down the milk sugar lactose (Chapter 4). Other enzymes are **anabolic,** and build substances. For example, the anabolic enzyme glycogen synthetase converts excess glucose units one by one into a chain of glycogen that is then stored. Enzymes aren't changed, damaged, or used up in the process of speeding up a particular reaction. Thus, an enzyme is available to catalyze additional reactions. **Figure 6.10** shows how an enzyme joins two compounds, yet isn't changed in the process.

Proteins Act as Chemical Messengers

While enzymes expedite reactions, **hormones** are messengers that regulate the actions carried out in the cells. Hormones direct or alter reactions, often by turning on or shutting off enzymes. Although many hormones are proteins (amino acid based), some hormones, such as steroids, are made from cholesterol (refer to Chapter 5). Hormones are released from tissues and organs and travel to target cells in another part of the body to direct an activity. There are over 70 trillion cells in the body, and all of these cells interact with at least one of over 50 known hormones.[6]

Consider an example of one peptide hormone in action. Under certain situations, such as dehydration, blood levels of salt (referred to as solutes) can become highly concentrated. Receptors in the blood vessels sense the change in concentration, and signal the hypothalamus to synthesize and release antidiuretic hormone (ADH) into the blood, a hormone that limits urine production. ADH travels to the kidneys and directs them to reabsorb more water, which, in turn, causes the kidneys to produce less urine, thus raising the blood volume and lowering the solute concentration. Once the blood concentration of solutes returns to normal, ADH levels are reduced.

1 A compound approaches a specific enzyme.

Compound Enzyme

2 The compound binds to the enzyme.

3 The enzyme changes shape.

Products

4 Two products are released and the enzyme is available for another reaction.

▲ Figure 6.10 **An Enzyme in Action**
Enzymes speed up reactions in the body, yet they aren't changed, damaged, or used up in the process.

catalysts Substances that aid and speed up reactions without being changed, damaged, or used up in the process.

catabolic An energy-releasing process that breaks larger molecules into smaller parts.

anabolic An energy-requiring process in which smaller molecules are combined to form larger molecules.

hormones Molecules, usually protein- or lipid-based, that initiate or direct specific actions from one organ to another. Insulin, glucagon, ADH, and estrogen are examples of hormones in the body.

Proteins Help Regulate Fluid Balance

The body is made up predominantly of water, which is distributed both outside (extracellular) and inside (intracellular) the cells. Fluid can generally flow easily in and out of cells. However, proteins are too large to move across the cell membranes and thus stay either within the cells or outside in the extracellular fluid. Normally, blood pressure forces the nutrient- and oxygen-rich fluids out of capillaries and into the spaces between the cells (called interstitial spaces). But protein remains in the blood, especially the protein **albumin.** As fluid is forced out of the blood, the concentration of albumin increases, which draws fluid from the interstitial spaces back into the blood by osmosis. Hence, protein plays an important role in moving fluids and keeping water dispersed evenly inside and outside of cells, which helps maintain a state of **fluid balance.** (Note: Sodium, and other minerals discussed in Chapter 12, also play a major role in fluid balance.)

When fewer proteins are available to draw the fluid from between the cells back into the bloodstream, as during severe malnutrition, a fluid imbalance results. The interstitial spaces between the cells become bloated and the body tissue swells, a condition known as **edema (Figure 6.11).**

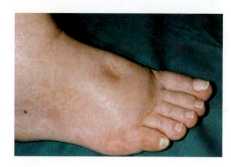

▲ **Figure 6.11 Edema**
Inadequate protein in the blood can cause edema.

Proteins Help Regulate Acid-Base Balance

Proteins can alter the **pH** of the body fluids. Normally, the blood has a pH of about 7.4. Even a small change in the pH of the blood in either direction can be harmful or even fatal. With a blood pH below 7.35, a condition called **acidosis** sets in, which can result in a coma. A blood pH above 7.45, known as **alkalosis,** can result in convulsions.

Proteins act as **buffers** and minimize the changes in acid-base levels by picking up hydrogen ions in the blood or donating hydrogen ions to the blood. Should the blood become too basic (contain too few hydrogen ions), the carboxyl groups of amino acids lower the pH of the blood by donating hydrogen ions; if blood becomes too acidic (too many hydrogen ions), the amine groups bind the excess hydrogen ions and restore the pH to an optimal level. This dual buffering role helps maintain the acid-base balance in the cells and the blood.

Proteins Transport Substances throughout the Body

Transport proteins shuttle oxygen, waste products, lipids, some vitamins, sodium and potassium and other substances through the blood and across cell membranes. For example, hemoglobin is a transport protein that carries oxygen to cells from the lungs; hemoglobin also picks up carbon dioxide for delivery to the lungs to be exhaled. Lipoproteins are another example; they transport fat-soluble nutrients through the bloodstream (Chapter 5).

Some nutrients, such as vitamin A, are fat soluble, and need assistance to move through the water-based blood. Once in the blood, vitamin A attaches to the protein albumin for transport to the liver and other cells.

Other nutrients, such as essential minerals—for example, iron and zinc—have specialized transport proteins whose sole function is to escort them across the enterocytes to their intended locations.

Transport proteins in cell membranes form a channel that allows substances such as sodium and potassium to pass in and out of cells (**Figure 6.12**). Without these membrane proteins, cells would be unable to maintain an optimal concentration of nutrients or remove waste from the cell. Substances that are not fat soluble or that are too big to pass through the cell membrane also have to enter the cell through a protein channel. If your diet is deficient in essential amino acids, fewer

albumin A protein produced in the liver and found in the blood that helps maintain fluid balance.

fluid balance The difference between the amount of water taken into the body and the amount of water excreted.

edema The accumulation of excess water in the spaces surrounding the cells, which causes swelling of the body tissue.

pH A measurement of the concentration of hydrogen ions in body fluids.

acidosis A condition in which the blood pH is too low, generally due to excessive hydrogen ions.

alkalosis A condition in which the blood pH is too low due to a low concentration of hydrogen ions.

buffers Substances that help maintain the proper pH in a solution by accepting or donating hydrogen ions.

transport proteins Proteins that carry other substances, mainly nutrients, through the blood to various organs and tissues. Proteins can also act as channels through which some substances enter your cells.

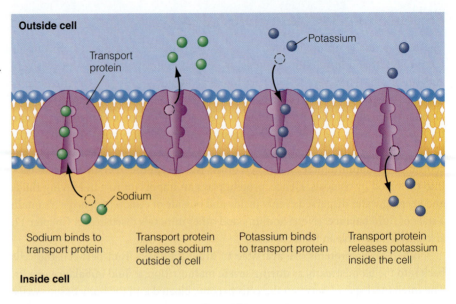

Outside cell

Transport
protein

Potassium

Sodium

| Sodium binds to transport protein | Transport protein releases sodium outside of cell | Potassium binds to transport protein | Transport protein releases potassium inside the cell |

Inside cell

▲ **Figure 6.12 Proteins as Transport Channels**
Transport proteins form a channel through which substances such as sodium and potassium can move from one side of the cell membrane to the other.

transport proteins are produced, causing an unhealthy balance of nutrients inside and outside of the cell membrane.

Proteins Contribute to a Healthy Immune System

The immune system protects the body from pathogens. Once pathogens, including bacteria and viruses, enter the cells, they can multiply rapidly, eventually causing illness. An army of specialized protein "soldiers," called **antibodies,** work quickly to eliminate these potentially harmful substances before they have a chance to multiply.

Once the body knows how to create antibodies against a specific foreign substance, such as a particular virus, it stores that information and the body has **immunity** to that pathogen. The next time the invader enters the body, the body can respond very quickly (producing up to 2,000 precise antibodies per second!) to fight it.

Sometimes, the body incorrectly perceives a nonthreatening substance, such as a protein, as an intruder and attacks it. This perceived invader is called an **allergen.** Food allergens are proteins that are resistant to being broken down during cooking or digestion. Individuals who react to these allergens are diagnosed with food allergies.

Proteins Can Provide Energy

Because proteins provide 4 kilocalories per gram, they can be used as an energy source. After amino acids are deaminated, the remaining carbon remnants can enter the energy cycle to produce ATP. (We'll cover this process in depth when we talk about metabolism in Chapter 8.)

However, the last thing you want to do is use this valuable nutrient, which plays so many important roles in the body, as a regular source of fuel, because carbohydrates and fats are far better suited to providing energy. When the diet contains adequate amounts of kilocalories from carbohydrates and fat, proteins are spared and used for their more important roles. For optimal health, individuals need to eat enough protein daily to meet the body's needs, and enough carbohydrates and fats to prevent protein from being used as energy.

Specialized proteins called antibodies (the white cell in the photo) protect the body from the disease-causing bacteria and viruses shown in yellow.

antibodies Proteins that bind to and neutralize pathogens as part of the body's immune response.

immunity The state of having built up antibodies to a particular pathogen so that pathogen enter the body, it is destroyed by the antibodies.

allergen A substance, such as wheat protein, that causes an allergic reaction.

TABLE 6.3 The Many Roles of Proteins

Role of Protein	How It Works
Structural and mechanical support and maintenance	Proteins are the body's building materials, providing strength and flexibility to tissues, tendons, ligaments, muscles, organs, bones, nails, hair, and skin. Proteins are also needed for the ongoing maintenance of the body.
Enzymes and hormones	Proteins are needed to make most enzymes that speed up reactions in the body and many hormones that direct specific activities, such as regulating blood glucose levels.
Fluid balance	Proteins play a major role in ensuring that body fluids are evenly dispersed in the blood and inside and outside cells.
Acid-base balance	Proteins act as buffers to help keep the pH of body fluids within a tight range. A drop in pH will cause body fluids to become too acidic, whereas a rise in pH can make them too basic.
Transport	Proteins shuttle substances such as oxygen, waste products, and nutrients (such as sodium and potassium) through the blood and into and out of cells.
Antibodies and the immune response	Proteins create specialized antibodies that attack pathogens that may cause illness.
Energy	Because proteins provide 4 kilocalories per gram, they can be used as fuel or energy.
Satiety	Protein increases satiety, which can help control appetite and weight.

Table 6.3 summarizes the many structural and functional roles proteins play in the body.

Protein Improves Satiety and Appetite Control

In addition to the structural and functional roles protein plays in the body, protein also improves satiety after a meal more than either carbohydrate or fat.[7] Eating a meal that contains a good source of protein will leave you more satisfied than will a high-carbohydrate meal with the same number of kilocalories. The satiety following a high-protein meal may be due to dietary protein suppressing the release of ghrelin.[8] Recall that ghrelin, which is produced in the stomach, stimulates the hypothalamus to sense hunger. Including protein in each meal helps to control appetite, which in turn can help maintain a healthy weight.

LO 6.4: THE TAKE-HOME MESSAGE Proteins play many important roles in the body: (1) the synthesis, repair, and maintenance of structural tissues, (2) helping facilitate muscular contraction, (3) catalyzing reactions as enzymes, (4) acting as hormones, (5) maintaining fluid balance, (6) maintaining acid-base equilibrium, (7) transporting nutrients throughout the body, (8) providing antibodies for a strong immune system, (9) providing energy when kilocalorie intake doesn't meet daily energy needs, and (10) promoting satiety and appetite control.

How Much Protein Do You Need Daily?

LO 6.5 Calculate the daily amount of protein recommended based on the Dietary Reference Intakes.

Healthy, nonpregnant adults should consume enough dietary protein to replace the amount they use each day. However, pregnant women, people recovering from surgery or an injury, and growing children need more protein to supply the necessary amino acids and nitrogen to build new tissue. **Nitrogen balance** studies are often used to determine how much protein individuals need to replace or build new tissue.

nitrogen balance The difference between nitrogen intake and nitrogen excretion.

Nitrogen Balance

(a) Using the fact that protein is 16 percent nitrogen, a common factor of 6.25 is used to calculate how much nitrogen is in a given amount of food (100/16 = 6.25).

We analyzed the food and beverages from a meal and found that it contained 73 grams (g) of protein. Divide this by 6.25 to determine the nitrogen content of the meal:

$$\text{Nitrogen} = \frac{73 \text{ g protein}}{6.25 \text{ g nitrogen}} = 11.6 \text{ g of nitrogen}$$

(b) Now calculate the amount of nitrogen lost from the body. First, nitrogen is lost in the urine as urea nitrogen, and in other nitrogen sources that are not part of the urea molecule. Because it's difficult to account for the non-urea sources directly, a factor of 0.2 grams × urinary urea nitrogen (UUN) is used to determine these losses. In this example, let's assume we analyzed the urine and found 8 grams of UUN. The total nitrogen lost in the urine would be calculated as follows:

$$8 \text{ g UUN} + (0.2 \times 8 \text{ g UUN}) = 9.6 \text{ g nitrogen lost}$$

(c) Next, we must account for nitrogen lost through other means, including hair, skin, and feces—approximately 2 grams per day. Add this to the equation.

$$8 \text{ g UUN} + (0.2 \times 8 \text{ g UUN}) + 2 \text{ g} = 11.6 \text{ g nitrogen lost}$$

(d) Now let's put it all together with the equation:

$$\text{Nitrogen balance} = \text{nitrogen in} - \text{nitrogen out}$$

$$\text{Nitrogen balance} = (73 \text{ g protein}/6.25) - (8 \text{ g UUN} + [0.2 \times 8 \text{ g UUN}] + 2 \text{ g})$$
$$= 0 \text{ g of nitrogen}$$

The calculation for nitrogen balance can be useful to dietitians as well as researchers to determine protein requirements.

Scan this QR code with your mobile device to access practice math activities. You can also access the activities in **Mastering**Nutrition™.

Healthy Adults Should Be in Nitrogen Balance

A person's protein requirement can be estimated by using what we know about the structure of an amino acid. We know that 16 percent of every dietary protein molecule is nitrogen. And we know that the body retains this nitrogen during protein synthesis. It follows that we can assess a person's protein status by checking their nitrogen balance—measuring the amount of nitrogen they consume and subtracting the amount of nitrogen they excrete, mostly as urea. The goal is to achieve nitrogen balance. See the Calculation Corner for an example of the calculation done to assess nitrogen balance.

Once we know the amount of nitrogen consumed, we can compare that to the amount of nitrogen excreted to determine if an individual is in nitrogen balance. If the nitrogen intake from dietary protein is equivalent to the amount of nitrogen excreted as urea in the urine, then a person is in nitrogen balance. Healthy, non-pregnant adults are typically in nitrogen balance.

A body that retains more nitrogen than it excretes is in positive nitrogen balance. Rapidly growing babies, children, or teenagers are all in positive nitrogen balance. This is because their bodies excrete less nitrogen than they take in to incorporate into new tissues as they grow, build muscles, and expand the supply of red blood cells. When a woman is pregnant, she, too, is in positive nitrogen balance because she is building a robust baby.

An individual is in negative nitrogen balance when nitrogen losses are greater than nitrogen intake, such as immediately following surgery, when fighting an

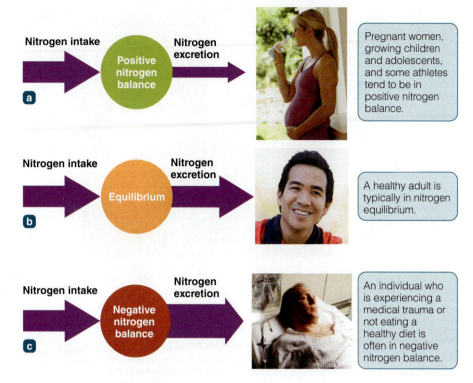

Figure 6.13 legend content:

Nitrogen intake → **Positive nitrogen balance** → Nitrogen excretion

Pregnant women, growing children and adolescents, and some athletes tend to be in positive nitrogen balance.

a

Nitrogen intake → **Equilibrium** → Nitrogen excretion

A healthy adult is typically in nitrogen equilibrium.

b

Nitrogen intake → **Negative nitrogen balance** → Nitrogen excretion

An individual who is experiencing a medical trauma or not eating a healthy diet is often in negative nitrogen balance.

c

▲ **Figure 6.13 Nitrogen Balance and Imbalance**

infection, or when experiencing severe emotional trauma. These situations all increase the body's need for both kilocalories and protein. If the kilocalories and protein in the diet are inadequate to cover these increased demands, then proteins from tissues are broken down to meet the body's needs. **Figure 6.13** lists some of the situations that lead to nitrogen balance or imbalance in the body.

You Can Determine Your Own Protein Needs

The RDA for protein has been established to provide adequate amounts of essential amino acids and nitrogen. This ensures the body will have the materials necessary to make the nonessential amino acids and body proteins necessary to meet daily needs.

There are two ways to determine protein intake in the diet. It can be measured as grams of protein eaten per day or as a percentage of total kilocalories.

The RDA for Protein

The Recommended Dietary Allowances (RDAs) for the essential amino acids are illustrated in **Figure 6.14**. As you can see, the RDA per day for each of the nine essential amino acids is based on grams per kilogram of body weight.

The current RDA for protein is based on the age and weight of healthy individuals. Adults older than 19 years of age should consume 0.8 grams of protein for each kilogram of body weight. For individuals under the age of 19, the RDA is somewhat higher (see the tables in the front cover of this textbook).

In the United States, men aged 20 and older consume, on average, more than 100 grams of protein daily, and women on average consume more than 70 grams. In general, Americans are meeting, and even exceeding, their dietary protein needs. Follow the steps in the Calculation Corner to calculate your RDA for protein.

Adequate Protein

Total protein intake in the diet is also measured as a percentage of total kilocalories. The latest recommendation, based on data from numerous nitrogen balance studies, is

Calculation Corner

Protein Requirements

(a) To calculate protein requirements, the first step is to convert body weight in pounds to kilograms. The conversion factor is 2.2. For example, an adult who weighs 176 pounds (lb) would weigh 80 kilograms (kg):

$$176 \text{ lb} \div 2.2 = 80 \text{ kg}$$

(b) Next, multiply weight in kilograms × 0.8 grams of protein. In this example, a healthy adult who weighs 80 kg should consume 64 grams (g) of protein per day.

$$80 \text{ kg} \times 0.8 \text{ g} = 64 \text{ g protein}$$

(c) How much protein should a healthy adult who weighs 130 pounds consume each day?

Data from Institute of Medicine, National Academy of Science. 2002. *Dietary Reference Intakes for Energy, Carbohydrate, Fiber, Fat, Fatty Acids, Cholesterol, Protein, and Amino Acids* (Washington, DC: The National Academies Press).

Scan this QR code with your mobile device to access practice math activities. You can also access the activities in **Mastering**Nutrition™.

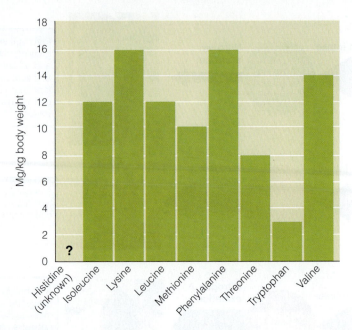

▲ **Figure 6.14 RDAs for Essential Amino Acids**
Recommended Dietary Allowances for the nine essential amino acids based on body weight.
Data from Institute of Medicine. 2005. *Dietary Reference Intakes for Energy, Carbohydrate, Fiber, Fat, Fatty Acids, Cholesterol, Protein, and Amino Acids.* (Washington, DC: National Academies Press).

to consume from 10 to 35 percent of total daily kilocalories from protein. Currently, adults in the United States consume about 15 percent of their daily kilocalories from protein, which falls within this range.

Even though many Americans are consuming more protein than they need, their percentage of daily kilocalories contributed by protein (15 percent) falls within the recommended range (10 to 35 percent). This is because Americans are consuming an abundant amount of kilocalories from carbohydrates and fats, which lowers the percentage of the total kilocalories coming from protein.

An overweight individual's protein needs are not much greater than those of a normal-weight person of similar height because the RDA for dietary protein is based on a person's need to maintain protein-dependent tissues, like lean muscle and organs, and to perform protein-dependent body functions. Because most overweight people carry most of their extra body weight as fat, not muscle, they do not need to consume significantly more protein than normal-weight people.

The American College of Sports Medicine, the Academy of Nutrition and Dietetics, and other experts have advocated an increase of 50 to 100 percent more protein for competitive athletes participating in endurance exercise (marathon runners) or resistance exercise (weight lifters) to meet their needs.[9, 10] However, due to their active lifestyles, athletes typically have a higher intake of food and thus already consume higher amounts of both kilocalories and protein.

LO 6.5: THE TAKE-HOME MESSAGE When protein intake equals the amount of nitrogen excreted, a healthy body is in nitrogen balance. Nitrogen balance studies suggest adults should consume 0.8 gram of protein for each kilogram of body weight. In the United States, men typically consume more than 100 grams of protein daily, and women more than 70 grams—in both cases, far more than is needed. Adequate protein intake to achieve nitrogen balance is between 10 to 35 percent of total daily kilocalories.

What Are the Best Food Sources of Protein?

LO 6.6 Describe the best food sources of protein and the methods available to determine protein quality.

The content of protein varies in foods commonly consumed in the United States and other developed countries. Although fruits are an excellent dietary choice, most contain one gram or less of protein per serving. Other foods, especially animal products, can contribute substantial amounts of protein to the diet.

Not All Protein Is Created Equal

A high-quality protein is digestible, contains all the essential amino acids, and provides a sufficient quantity of protein to be used to synthesize the nonessential amino acids and support the body's requirements for growth and maintenance. Thus, while it is important to eat enough protein, the quality of protein also matters.

The quality of the protein is determined by two factors: your body's ability to digest the protein and the types and amounts of amino acids that the protein contains. If a single essential amino acid is in low supply in the diet and thus in the amino acid pool, the ability to synthesize proteins will be limited.

Which protein is best? Several methods have been used to yield chemical scores to answer this question. These methods include the amino acid score, protein digestibility corrected amino acid score, and biological value.

Amino Acid Score

The quality of a food protein refers to its amino acid profile compared with a standard or reference protein. For example, egg white protein is used as a standard because it is known to have a balance of all of the essential amino acids needed to support growth. Other food proteins are compared with egg protein using an **amino acid score.** The Calculation Corner provides an example of how to calculate this score for peanut butter using the information shown in **Table 6.4**.

TABLE 6.4	Amino Acid Scores for Peanut Butter		
Essential Amino Acid	Peanut Butter (mg/g)	Egg Protein (mg/g)	Amino Acid Score
Histidine	30	22	1.36
Isoleucine	40	54	0.74
Leucine	77	86	0.90
Lysine	39	70	0.56
Methionine plus cysteine	24	57	0.42
Phenylalanine plus tyrosine	108	93	1.16
Threonine	30	47	0.64
Tryptophan	12	17	0.71
Valine	46	66	0.71

Data from Institute of Medicine. 2002 *Dietary Reference Intakes for Energy, Carbohydrate, Fiber, Fat, Fatty Acids, Cholesterol, Protein, and Amino Acids* (Washington, DC: National Academies Press).

amino acid score The composition of essential amino acids in a protein compared with a standard, usually egg protein.

Amino Acid Score

The formula used to calculate the amino acid score for any food is:

$$\text{Amino acid score} = \frac{\text{essential amino acid for protein (mg/g)}}{\text{essential amino acid for standard (mg/g)}}$$

We can use peanut butter to illustrate this calculation. Table 6.4 shows the essential amino acid content for peanut butter in column two. The third column shows the essential amino acid content for egg protein, which is most often used as the standard for this calculation. As you read across the table to column four, you can see the amino acid score. This means that peanut butter contains 136 percent of the histidine that egg protein does. This is how you calculate the amino acid score. Begin with histidine and divide the amount of histidine in peanut butter by the amount found in egg protein:

$$30 \text{ mg/g} \div 22 \text{ mg/g} = 1.36$$

You continue the calculation for each of the amino acids. Each of the nine essential amino acid scores is calculated individually and presented in column four in Table 6.4. Now calculate the entire food of peanut butter compared with egg protein using the total mg/g for each as follows:

$$406 \text{ mg/g peanut butter} \div 674 \text{ mg/g egg protein} = 0.60 \text{ or } 60\%$$

This amino acid score means that overall, peanut butter contains 60 percent of the essential amino acids that egg protein does.

The essential amino acid that has the lowest score is called the **limiting amino acid.** In the case of peanut butter, the limiting amino acid is methionine, with a score of 0.42. This score means that peanut butter contains 42 percent of the methionine found in egg protein.

The amino acid score is one method for comparing food proteins and their essential amino acid composition. Though it is a useful method of comparison, it doesn't take into consideration how protein is digested.

Protein Digestibility Corrected Amino Acid Score (PDCAAS)

The **protein digestibility corrected amino acid score (PDCAAS)** combines the chemical score with the digestibility of a food protein to give a more accurate indication of quality. This is important because only amino acids that are digested and absorbed can contribute to the amino acid pool and be used to build and maintain body proteins. An example of the PDCAAS calculation for peanut butter is presented in the Calculation Corner.

The digestibility of proteins varies, depending on their source. In general, animal proteins are more digestible than plant proteins. Some plant proteins, especially when consumed raw, are protected by the plant's cell walls and cannot be broken down by the enzymes in the intestinal tract, whereas 90 to 99 percent of the proteins from animal sources (cheese and other dairy foods, meat, poultry, and eggs) are digestible. Raw plant proteins, such as in oatmeal (86 percent digestible) and soybeans (78 percent digestible), are generally only 70 to 90 percent digestible.[11]

Milk protein, which is easily digested and meets essential amino acid requirements, has a PDCAAS of 1.00. In comparison, kidney beans garner a PDCAAS of 0.68, and wheat has a score of only 0.40. If your only dietary source of protein is

limiting amino acid An essential amino acid that is in the shortest supply, relative to the body's needs, in an incomplete protein.

protein digestibility corrected amino acid score (PDCAAS) A score measured as a percentage that takes into account both digestibility and amino acid score and provides a good indication of the quality of a protein.

PDCAAS

The digestibility of a food has a major impact on the protein quality. This calculation, called the Protein Digestibility Corrected Amino Acid Score (PDCAAS), compares the amino acid content of a food with the amino acid requirement for humans and then corrects for digestibility. This is how the calculation works:

1. First you need to know the amino acid score of the food. For this calculation you use the lowest amino acid score. From Table 6.4 you see that the lowest amino acid score for peanut butter is methionine plus cysteine, or 0.42.

2. Next, to determine the PDCAAS for peanut butter, multiply the score for its lowest limiting amino acid (0.42) by the protein digestibility of peanut butter (95%):

$$\text{PDCAAS for peanut butter} = 0.42 \times 0.95 = 0.40$$

In other words, because the protein in peanut butter is not completely digested, the amino acid score for methionine plus cysteine has been corrected from 0.42 to 0.40.

These calculations are used by the Food and Drug Administration to determine the Daily Values represented on food labels. For example, one serving (2 tbs) of peanut butter contains 8 grams (g) of protein. To calculate the % Daily Value, this number is multiplied by the PDCAAS:

$$8 \text{ g} \times 0.40 = 3.2$$

Next, divide this by 50 grams, which is the recommended intake of protein for adults used on the label:

$$3.2 \div 50 \text{ g} = 0.064 \text{ or } 6.4\%$$

In this example, a serving of peanut butter would represent 6.4 percent of the Daily Value for protein.

---

biological value The percentage of absorbed amino acids that are efficiently used to synthesize proteins.

▼ **Figure 6.15 Protein on Nutrition Labels**
Protein is listed on nutrition labels in grams and as a percentage of the daily value if the manufacturer makes a health claim.

wheat, you are not meeting your essential amino acid needs. However, when wheat is combined with another protein source, such as peanut butter, the protein quality of the meal is improved.

The PDCAAS is used by the Food and Drug Administration to calculate the % Daily Value of protein used on food labels. Manufacturers use 50 grams of protein as the standard to calculate the % Daily Value for a serving of a food for adults and children 4 or more years of age. As you can see in **Figure 6.15**, the serving of low-fat milk contains 21 percent of the daily value, or 10.5 grams of protein (0.21 × 50 grams = 10.5 grams), which the manufacturer has rounded up to 11 grams. Not all labels are required to list the % Daily Value for protein. It is only required on a label if a protein claim is made for the product.

Biological Value

The **biological value** of a protein refers to how quickly the nitrogen from the absorbed protein can be synthesized into body protein. If the food contains all nine essential amino acids, the synthesis can proceed quickly. But if even one essential amino acid is missing, protein synthesis halts, the unfinished protein is deaminated, and the amino acids are used to make glucose, used as energy, or stored as fat (refer again to Figure 6.7).

To calculate biological value, the amount of nitrogen retained by the body is divided by the amount consumed. Egg protein has a

Does Soy Reduce the Risk of Disease?

Soy consumption in the United States, in foods ranging from soy milk to soy burgers, has been increasing in recent decades. From 1996 to 2011, the market for soy products grew from $1 billion to over $5 billion.[1] According to a survey conducted by the United Soybean Board, 80 percent of U.S. consumers perceive soy foods as being healthy.[2]

The popularity of soy foods is increasing among many age groups and ethnic groups, including baby boomers, who are more interested in good health and longevity than was their parents' generation; Asian populations in the United States looking for traditional soy-based foods; and young adults with an increasing interest in vegetarian diets.[3]

Soy is a high-quality protein source that is low in saturated fat and that contains **isoflavones,** which are naturally occurring phytoestrogens (*phyto* = plant). These plant **estrogens** have a chemical structure similar to human estrogen, a female sex hormone. Though they are considered weak estrogens (they have less than a thousandth the potential activity of estrogen), they may interfere with or mimic some of estrogen's activities in certain cells in the body.[4] Though isoflavones can also be found in other plant foods, such as grains, vegetables, and legumes, soybeans contain the largest amount found in food.

Soy and Your Health

Epidemiological studies, which look at health and disease in populations, have suggested that isoflavones may reduce the risk of chronic diseases, including heart disease and certain cancers. Observational studies suggest that isoflavones may help relieve menopausal symptoms, although a well-designed, double-blind study reported no benefit.[5] At the same time, because isoflavones act as weak estrogens in the body, some concern exists that they may have a harmful impact on diseases such as breast cancer. Several new reports

isoflavones Naturally occurring phytoestrogens, or weak plant estrogens, that function in a similar fashion to the hormone estrogen in the human body.

estrogens The hormones responsible for female sex characteristics.

have found no link between breast cancer prognosis and soy isoflavones.[6]

Eating soy protein as part of a heart-healthy diet may reduce the risk of heart disease by lowering cholesterol levels. Research suggests that soy protein can lower LDL cholesterol and raise HDL cholesterol levels.[7] Soy protein may also help lower blood pressure, a risk factor for heart disease.[8]

Some studies have suggested that isoflavones may also reduce the risk of certain cancers, such as breast cancer.[9] The isoflavones in soy may help reduce the risk of cancer, as these weak estrogens may have anticancer functions in the body.[10] For example, isoflavones compete with the hormone estrogen for its binding site on specific cells. Because estrogen may increase the risk of breast cancer, inhibiting or blocking the actions of estrogen may help reduce the risk.[11]

Timing may be an important part of the preventive role that soy plays in breast cancer. A study of Chinese women revealed that those who ate the most soy during their adolescent years had a reduced risk of breast cancer in adulthood.[12] Early exposure to soy foods may be protective by stimulating the growth of cells in the breast, enhancing the rate at which the glands mature, and altering the tissues in a beneficial way.

There was some concern that once the isoflavones are bound to the estrogen receptors, they can initiate the production of cancer cells, which can *raise* the risk of breast cancer. However, research supports the safety of soy isoflavones when consumed as soy and soy products.[13] According to the American Cancer Society, women with breast cancer should consume a healthy, plant-based diet with only moderate amounts of soy foods and should avoid

Soy meat analogs, such as hot dogs, sausages, burgers, and cold cuts, are made using soy.

soy-containing pills, powders, and supplements with high levels of isoflavones.[14]

Soy can be an inexpensive, heart-healthy protein source that may also help lower your LDL cholesterol and blood pressure, raise HDL cholesterol, and reduce your risk of certain cancers.

References

1. Soyfoods Association of North America. 2012. *Sales and Trends.* Available at www.soyfoods.org. Accessed February 2014.
2. United Soybean Board. 2012. *Consumer Attitudes About Nutrition: Insights into Nutrition, Health, and Soyfoods.* Available at www.soyconnection.com. Accessed February 2014.
3. Ibid.
4. H. Fritz, D. Seely, G. Flower, B. Skidmore, R. Fernandes, S. Vadeboncoeur, D. Kennedy, et al. 2013. "Soy, Red Clover, and Isoflavones and Breast Cancer: A Systematic Review." *PLoS One* 8(11):e81968. doi: 10.1371/journal.pone.0081968.
5. S. Levis, N. Strickman-Stein, P. Ganjei-Azar, P. Xu, D. R. Doerge, and J. Krischer. 2011. "Soy Isoflavones in the Prevention of Menopausal Bone Loss and Menopausal Symptoms: A Randomized Double-Blind Trial." *Archives of Internal Medicine* 171(15):1363–1369.
6. B. J. Caan, L. Natarajan, B. Parker, E. B. Gold, C. Thomson, V. Newman, C. L. Rock, et al. 2011. "Soy Food Consumption and Breast Cancer Prognosis." *Cancer Epidemiology Biomarkers Prevention* 20(5):854–858.
7. M. R. Wofford, C. M. Rebholz, K. Reynolds, J. Chen, C.-S. Chen, and L. Myers. 2012. "Effect of Soy and Milk Protein Supplementation on Serum Lipid Levels: A Randomized Controlled Trial." *European Journal of Clinical Nutrition* 66:419–425.
8. J. He, M. Wofford, K. Reynolds, J. Chen, C. Chen, L. Myers, et al. 2011. "Effect of Dietary Protein Supplementation on Blood Pressure: A Randomized Controlled Trial." *Circulation* 124:589–595.
9. H. Fritz, et al. 2013. "Soy, Red Clover, and Isoflavones and Breast Cancer: A Systematic Review."
10. American Institute of Cancer Research. 2013. *Foods that Fight Cancer.* Available at www.aicr.org. Accessed February 2014.
11. Ibid.
12. H. Fritz, et al. 2013. "Soy, Red Clover, and Isoflavones and Breast Cancer: A Systematic Review."
13. American Cancer Society. 2013. *Soybeans.* Available at www.cancer.org. Accessed February 2014.
14. American Institute of Cancer Research. 2013. *Foods that Fight Cancer.*

biological value of 100, which means that 100 percent of consumed nitrogen in egg protein is absorbed and retained for use by the body.

Complementary and Complete Proteins

Protein from animal products is considered a high-quality, **complete protein** based on higher chemical scores and nitrogen balance studies. Complete proteins provide all nine of the essential amino acids, along with some of the 11 nonessential amino acids. Plant proteins are considered to be **incomplete protein** because plants are deficient in one or more essential amino acids. Two exceptions to this generalization are gelatin and soy. Gelatin, an animal protein, is not a complete protein because it is missing the amino acid tryptophan. Soy, a plant protein, has an amino acid profile that resembles the protein needs in the body, making it a complete protein by itself. Examining the Evidence: Does Soy Reduce the Risk of Disease? discusses a variety of soy products to incorporate into a vegetarian diet to improve the quality of your meals.

Does this mean that plant proteins are of less value in the diet? Absolutely not. When incomplete proteins are eaten with modest amounts of animal proteins or soy, or combined with other plant proteins that are rich in the incomplete protein's limiting amino acids, the incomplete protein is *complemented*. In other words, its amino acid profile is upgraded to a complete protein. For example, when rice, which is low in lysine but high in methionine, is combined with beans, which provide a sufficient source of lysine, they complement each other and provide all nine essential amino acids. In addition, adding a small amount of cheese or meat to a plant protein, such as in macaroni and cheese or a shrimp stir-fry, provides the amino acid that is limited in the plant food.

Complementary proteins do not need to be consumed at the same meal to improve the quality of the protein source. As long as the foods are consumed in the same day, all the essential amino acids will be provided to meet your biological needs. Vegetarian diets can contain a sufficient quality as well as quantity of protein in carefully planned meals. Read more on this topic in the Health Connection on page 240.

Eggs, Meat, Soy, and Dairy Contain Significant Amounts of Protein

Protein is particularly abundant in dairy foods, meat, fish, poultry, and meat alternatives such as dried beans, peanut butter, nuts, and soy (**Figure 6.16**). A 3-ounce serving of cooked meat, poultry, or fish provides 21 to 25 grams of protein, or about 7 grams per ounce. A serving size of 3 ounces, which is about the size of a deck of cards, is plenty of protein for one meal. Grains and vegetables are less robust protein sources, providing about 3 to 4 grams per serving, but as part of a varied, balanced diet, they can contribute significantly to daily needs.

Eating a wide variety of foods is the best approach to meeting protein needs. A diet that consists of the recommended servings from the five food groups based on 1,600 kilocalories (which is far less than most adults consume daily) will supply an adequate amount of protein for adult women and most adult men. In fact, many people have met their daily protein needs before they even sit down to dinner.

Most People Don't Need Protein Supplements

Some of the most popular supplements in the United States are protein and amino acids, often marketed especially to athletes (see Spotlight: Protein Supplements).

Egg protein has a biological value of 100, the highest quality protein in the diet.

Chickpeas are short of the limiting amino acid methionine. The addition of sesame seed paste, which has an abundance of methionine, completes the protein. Add garlic and lemon as seasonings for a *completely* delicious hummus.

complete protein A protein that provides all the essential amino acids, along with some nonessential amino acids. Soy protein and protein from animal sources are complete proteins.

incomplete protein A protein that is low in one or more of the essential amino acids. Proteins from plant sources tend to be incomplete.

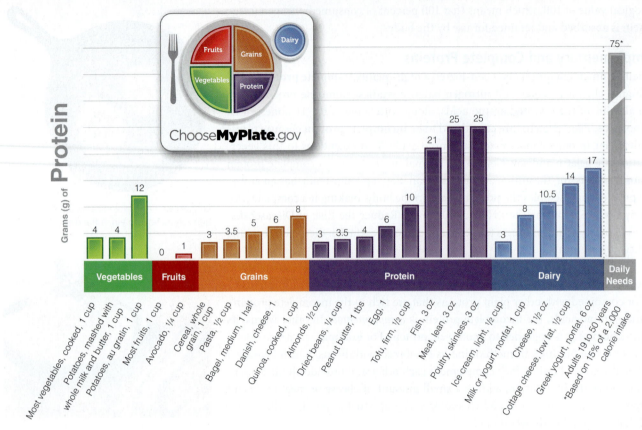

▲ Figure 6.16 Food Sources of Protein
Food choices from the meat, poultry, fish, meat alternative, and dairy groups are the most abundant sources of dietary protein. Grains and vegetables provide less protein per serving, but as part of a varied, balanced diet can contribute to daily needs.

Data from *USDA National Nutrient Database for Standard Reference.* 2011. Available at www.nal.usda.gov/fnic. Accessed February 2014.

Physically active people may take protein supplements as an ergogenic aid to increase muscle size and strength, and endurance performance. While the debate on the benefits of protein supplements (especially four amino acids with a branched side chain, referred to as *branched-chain amino acids,* or *BCAAs*) continues, you don't need to supplement your diet with protein. The DRIs for protein are based on healthy food choices and do not recommend additional protein in the form of supplementation. (We'll discuss protein and sport performance in greater detail in Chapter 16.)

LO 6.6: THE TAKE-HOME MESSAGE Protein quality is determined by the digestibility of protein and the amino acid profile, which includes the types and amounts of amino acids it contains. Protein from animal foods is more digestible than plant proteins. Biological value is the amount of nitrogen in the protein that is absorbed and retained for use by the body. A complete protein, found in animal foods and soy, provides a complete set of essential amino acids and some nonessential amino acids. Plant proteins can be complemented with protein from other plant sources or animal food sources to improve their protein quality. Meat, fish, poultry, and meat alternatives such as dried beans, peanut butter, nuts, and soy are particularly abundant in protein. Dairy products and some vegetables are also good sources.

Protein Supplements

The sale of protein supplements has skyrocketed over the last decade, fueling an industry that now generates almost two billion dollars annually.[1] These products are enticing. They promise to give you an energy boost, help shed those unwanted pounds, build muscle, fight aging, and cure a host of health problems. With very few exceptions, purchasing and consuming these products is, at best, a waste of money, and at worst, exposure to potentially harmful heavy metals.

Protein supplement manufacturers use phrases such as "scientifically proven," "nutritious and time-saving snack or meal replacement," and "look years younger" as a promise to consumers. Unfortunately, dietary supplements do not go through rigorous testing for quality or efficacy. So how do you know if these supplements contain what they say they contain, do what they say they do, and are safe? Is more protein always better?

Protein Shakes and Powder

Most protein shakes and powders use whey (concentrates, isolates, and hydrolysates), soy, or occasionally rice protein as a key ingredient. The amount of protein their label claims they contain ranges from 10 to 40 grams of protein per serving, along with added vitamins and minerals. Muscle Milk® lists 25 grams of protein per serving and suggests 3 servings per day for a total of 75 grams of protein. This amounts to almost 100 percent of the RDA for protein for a male weighing 176 pounds (RDA = 80 grams per day). This does not account for the other foods consumed during the day.

Do these products actually contain what is listed on the label? Based on research conducted by ConsumerLab .com, twenty protein supplements tested did contain what the label claimed, but two products were contaminated with lead (6 to 19 mcg per day) and one product contained an additional 4 grams of sugar not accounted for on the label.[2] Other labs report arsenic, cadmium, lead, and mercury in fifteen tested samples.[3] Chronic ingestion of these toxic metals can cause severe health consequences, including kidney and pulmonary damage, anemia, and osteoporosis. Exposure is avoidable because most consumers more than meet their daily protein requirements by choosing whole foods.

Protein intake does enhance muscle synthesis.[4] But athletes consume enough protein for muscle growth and repair in an average mixed diet. Whey protein used in protein supplements is abundant in milk and dairy products, including Greek yogurt.[5] Additional protein not used for protein synthesis is either burned for energy or stored as fat. In fact, excessive amounts of protein can be unhealthy and produce undesirable results.

The key to increasing muscle weight is a well-designed strength-training program combined with additional calories from all three macronutrients. These calories allow dietary protein to be used for muscle synthesis instead of energy. Another important key is timing. Research suggests that ingestion of protein with carbohydrate before and immediately after a workout improves muscle synthesis.[6] A glass of nonfat milk, rather than a protein supplement, before and after a workout will provide both key amino acids and the carbohydrate to stimulate muscle growth.

Protein shakes and powders are also marketed as meal replacers. Dieters might lose weight using a high-protein meal replacer, but the same results can be obtained with a kilocalorie-controlled meal of whole foods, without the risk and the added expense. When it comes to losing weight, it's the total kilocalories that count.

There are instances where protein shakes and supplements may be a nutritionally sound approach. Older adults, who may have limited appetites and be less likely to consume adequate nutrients in foods, may benefit from ingesting a protein shake every day. However, these products should be used to *supplement* their meals, not replace them.

Amino Acid Supplements

Amino acid supplements, including those containing individual amino acids such as tryptophan and lysine, are marketed as remedies for a range of health issues, including pain, depression, insomnia, and certain infections. These supplements contain single amino acids often in amounts or combinations not found naturally in foods. Consuming single amino acids in unnatural doses can compete with other amino acids for absorption, possibly resulting in a deficiency of other amino acids. Furthermore, overconsuming specific amino acids can lead to side effects such as nausea, lightheadedness, vomiting, and drowsiness.

Protein Bars and Energy Bars

The sales of protein bars and energy bars have fueled an industry that now generates over a billion dollars annually. There are bars advertised for women, bars for men, bars for the elderly, and junior bars for children. When they emerged in the 1980s, these bars were marketed as a portable snack or a quick meal in a cellophane wrapper to help athletes stay fueled for long-distance or endurance outings.

As you learned from the previous two chapters, all foods provide kilocalories and therefore energy. Whether your kilocalories come from a balanced meal or a "balanced bar," your body will either use them for fuel or store them as body fat if they are not immediately needed. You also just learned that you can meet your daily protein needs by making wise food choices. Given this knowledge, what advantage, if any, do you think protein supplements provide?

If convenience and portability are the main attractions of protein bars, then consider another convenient and portable food, the peanut butter sandwich. It can be made in a snap, and since it doesn't have to be refrigerated, it can travel anywhere.

From a price standpoint, a peanut butter sandwich is a bargain compared with bars that cost more than $2.50 each, or ten times as much as the sandwich. While the kilocalories and protein content of the sandwich are similar to that in many bars, the saturated fat and sugar contents are not. Some bars provide up to 7 grams of saturated fat, which is about one-third of the daily upper limit recommended for many adults. In contrast, the sandwich contains less saturated fat than the bars pictured here. Because these bars can contain up to 7 teaspoons of sugar, which

supplies up to 50 percent of the kilocalories in the bar, much of the "energy" is simply sugar. The bars with the most sugar tend to have the least amount of fiber. Ironically, most consumers need more fiber in their diet. Because the peanut butter sandwich has lower amounts of sugar and a higher amount of fiber than almost all of the bars, it's actually the healthier food choice.

References

1. Euromonitor International. 2012. Moo-ve Over Milk: Plant Alternatives Primed to Benefit from Protein Supplement Demand. Available at http://blog.euromonitor.com. Accessed February 2014.
2. Consumer Lab.com. 2012. *Tests of Protein Powders and Shakes Contain Some Lead Contamination but No Melamine.* Available from www.consumerlab.com. Accessed February 2014.
3. Consumer Reports Magazine. 2010. Alert! You Don't Need the Extra Protein or the Heavy Metals Our Tests Found. *Consumer Reports* 75:24.
4. R. J. Maughan and S. M. Shirreffs. 2012. "Nutrition for Sports Performance: Issues and Opportunities." *Proceedings of the Nutrition Society* 71:112–119.
5. S. Graf, S. Egert, and M. Heer. 2011. "Effects of Whey Protein Supplements on Metabolism: Evidence from Human Intervention Studies." *Current Opinion in Clinical Nutrition and Metabolic Care* 14:569–580.
6. M. Spillane, N. Schwarz, S. Leddy, T. Correa, M. Minter, V. Longoria, and D. S. Willoughby. 2011. "Effects of 28 Days of Resistance Exercise while Consuming Commercially Available Pre- and Post-Workout Supplements, NO-Shotgun® and NO- Synthesize®, on Body Composition, Muscle Strength and Mass, Markers of Protein Synthesis, and Clinical Safety Markers in Males. *Nutrition & Metabolism* 8:78.

What Happens If You Eat Too Much or Too Little Protein?

LO 6.7 Explain the health consequences of consuming too little or too much protein.

Protein is essential to health and normal body function, and eating either too much or too little can be unhealthy. Most people in industrialized nations consume more than enough protein, while people from less developed countries may struggle to meet even the minimum requirements. Let's look at what happens to the human body when it gets too much or too little protein.

Eating Too Much Protein May Mean Too Much Heart-Unhealthy Fat and Weaker Bones

A diet high in protein has long been proposed to increase risk of heart disease, kidney stones, osteoporosis, and some types of cancer in normal, healthy people. Recent research provides some reassurance that eating too much protein (0.8 to 2.0 g/kg per day) may not be as bad as we once thought.[12] However, consuming too much protein, to the point where it replaces other essential nutrients, also leads to an unbalanced diet.

Heart Disease

Recent research reports that the type of protein is more important in reducing the risk of heart disease than the quantity.[13] A diet low in red meat that contains nuts, low-fat dairy, poultry, or fish lessens the risk for heart disease compared with a diet high in red meat and high-fat dairy. A high-red-meat diet may mean overloading on heart-unhealthy saturated fat (see **Figure 6.17**). Even lean meats and skinless poultry, which contain less saturated fat than some other cuts of meat, are not saturated fat free. A diet high in saturated fat can raise LDL ("bad") cholesterol levels in the blood, whereas

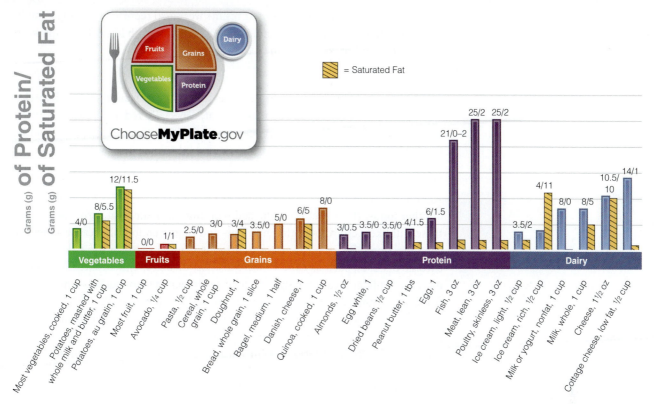

Grams (g) **of Protein/**
Grams (g) **of Saturated Fat**

= Saturated Fat

Vegetables: 4/0, 8/5.5, 12/11.5
Fruits: 0/0, 1/1
Grains: 2.5/0, 3/0, 3/4, 3.5/0, 5/0, 6/5, 8/0
Protein: 3/0.5, 3.5/0, 3.5/0, 4/1.5, 6/1.5, 21/0–2, 25/2, 25/2
Dairy: 3.5/2, 4/11, 8/0, 8/5, 10.5/10, 14/1

Most vegetables, cooked, 1 cup
Potatoes, mashed with whole milk and butter, 1 cup
Potatoes, au gratin, 1 cup
Most fruit, 1 cup
Avocado, 1/4 cup
Pasta, 1/2 cup
Cereal, whole grain, 1 cup
Doughnut, 1
Bread, whole grain, 1 slice
Bagel, medium, 1 half
Danish, cheese, 1
Quinoa, cooked, 1 cup
Almonds, 1/2 oz
Egg white, 1
Dried beans, 1/2 cup
Peanut butter, 1 tbs
Egg, 1
Fish, 3 oz
Meat, lean, 3 oz
Poultry, skinless, 3 oz
Ice cream, light, 1/2 cup
Ice cream, rich, 1/2 cup
Milk or yogurt, nonfat, 1 cup
Milk, whole, 1 cup
Cheese, 1 1/2 oz
Cottage cheese, low fat, 1/2 cup

▲ **Figure 6.17 Where's the Protein and Saturated Fat in Foods?**
Though many foods, in particular dairy foods and meats, can provide a hefty amount of protein, they can also provide a large amount of saturated fat. Choose nonfat and low-fat dairy foods, lean cuts of meat, and skinless poultry to avoid overloading on saturated fat.

lowering the saturated fat may lower the risk of heart disease. While the overall effect of high protein intake on heart disease is still not clear, it is clear that eating a variety of plant proteins low in saturated fat and cholesterol is the best heart-healthy approach.

Kidney Stones

A high-protein diet may increase the risk of kidney stones. Eating a diet high in animal protein and low in carbohydrate lowers the pH of the urine, which raises the risk of developing kidney stones, especially in people who are more susceptible to the condition.[14] This change in pH may be due to higher levels of oxalates in the urine from oxalic acid; oxalic acid combines with other compounds, including calcium, to form kidney stones. The impact of protein on the change in pH may be the type of protein, not the amount of protein, consumed. A diet that contains plenty of fluid, a lower protein intake (not greater than 0.8 g/kg), and a balance of fruits and vegetables may be beneficial, especially for people who already have kidney disease.

Osteoporosis

Though still controversial, past studies have shown that bones lose calcium when a person's diet is too high in protein. The loss seems to occur because calcium is removed from bone to neutralize the acid generated when specific amino acids are broken down. In fact, in a study of individuals on a low-carbohydrate, high-protein diet, researchers observed a 50 percent loss of calcium in the subjects' urine.[15] The calcium loss was not observed when these individuals were on a lower-protein diet, so the researchers concluded that it was due to the buffering effect.

More recent research suggests a more positive effect of high protein intake on bone health as long as dietary calcium is sufficient.[16, 17] In fact, a higher dietary protein intake, especially if it is coming from foods such as low-fat milk, yogurt, and cheese, can add calcium to the diet.[18] Unfortunately, many American adults are falling short of their recommended calcium intake, and if their diets are also high in protein, the combination may not be healthy for their bones.

Eating too little protein can also lead to loss of bone mass. A study of more than 900 elderly men and women showed that higher protein consumption was associated with denser bone.[19] Similar results were also reported in younger adults. When it comes to our bones, too much protein coupled with low calcium intake, or too little protein intake, can both be unhealthy.[20]

Cancer

The relationship between high-protein diets and cancer is another less-than-clear association. Although large amounts of meat, especially red and processed meats, may increase the risk for colon cancer, research doesn't support a connection between high amounts of total protein and increased colon cancer risk.[21]

Displacing Other Nutrients

An important health concern surrounding a high-protein diet is the displacement of other foods. If the diet is overloaded with high-protein meat, fish, and poultry, these will likely crowd out other nutrient- and fiber-rich foods. Because a diet that contains ample fiber and nutrient-rich foods can help reduce the risk of several chronic diseases, such as cancer, heart disease, diabetes, and stroke, filling up on meat and milk at meals and snacks could shortchange foods such as whole grains, fruits, and vegetables, which contain disease-fighting compounds.

Whereas many individuals have the luxury of worrying about consuming too much protein, others are desperately trying to meet their daily needs. Let's look at the serious health implications of chronically eating too little dietary protein.

Eating Too Little Protein Can Lead to Protein-Energy Malnutrition

Every day, 842 million people, or one in eight (many of them children), around the world don't have access to enough food.[22] These children's diets are inadequate in either protein or energy or both, a condition known as **protein-energy malnutrition (PEM).** When kilocalories and protein are inadequate, dietary protein is used for energy rather than for its other roles in the body. Moreover, other important nutrients, such as vitamins and minerals, also tend to be in short supply, which further compounds PEM.

Many factors can lead to PEM, including poverty, poor food quality, insufficient food intake, unsanitary living conditions (causing diarrhea and infection), ignorance regarding the proper feeding of children, and the cessation of breastfeeding in the first few months of age.[23] Because infants and children are growing, they have higher nutritional needs for their size than adults. They are also dependent on others to provide them with food. For these reasons, PEM is more frequently seen in infants and children than in adults.

Because protein is needed for so many functions in the body, it isn't surprising that chronic protein deficiency can lead to numerous health problems. Without adequate dietary protein, cells lining the gastrointestinal tract aren't sufficiently replaced as they're sloughed off. The inability to regenerate these cells inhibits digestive function. Absorption of the little amount of food that may be available is reduced, and bacteria that normally stay in the intestines can get into the blood and poison it, causing septicemia. Malnourished individuals frequently have a compromised immune system, which can make fighting even a minor infection, such as a respiratory infection or diarrhea, impossible. Malnourished children have died after exposure to measles as well as after bouts of diarrhea.[24, 25]

Though deficiencies of kilocalories and protein often occur simultaneously, sometimes one may be more prevalent than the other. A severe deficiency of protein is called **kwashiorkor,** whereas a severe deficiency of kilocalories is called **marasmus.** A condition that is caused by a chronic deficiency of both kilocalories and protein is called marasmic kwashiorkor.

protein-energy malnutrition (PEM) A lack of sufficient dietary protein and/or kilocalories.

kwashiorkor A state of PEM where there is a severe deficiency of dietary protein.

marasmus A state of PEM where there is a severe deficiency of kilocalories, which perpetuates wasting; also called starvation.

Kwashiorkor

Kwashiorkor was first observed in the 1930s in tribes in Ghana (a republic of West Africa) when frequently a firstborn child became sick following the birth of a new sibling. Typically, the newborn displaced the first child from receiving their mother's nutritionally balanced breast milk. The first child was then relegated to an inadequate and unbalanced diet high in carbohydrate-rich grains but severely deficient in protein. This sets the stage for serious medical complications.

A classic symptom of severe kwashiorkor is edema in the legs, feet, and stomach (see **Figure 6.18**). Because protein plays an important role in maintaining fluid balance in the blood and around the cells, a protein deficiency can cause fluid to accumulate in the spaces surrounding the cells, causing swelling. The body wastes away as the muscle proteins are broken down to generate the amino acids needed to synthesize other proteins. Consequently, muscle tone and strength diminish. Those with kwashiorkor may have skin that is dry and peeling. Rashes or lesions can also develop. Their hair is often brittle and can be easily pulled out. Children with kwashiorkor often appear pale, sad, and apathetic, and cry easily. They are prone to infections, rapid heart beats, excess fluid in the lungs, pneumonia, septicemia, and water and electrolyte imbalances—all of which can be deadly.

Marasmus and Marasmic Kwashiorkor

The bloating seen in kwashiorkor is the opposite of the frail, emaciated appearance of marasmus (**Figure 6.19**). Because they are not consuming enough kilocalories, marasmic individuals literally look as though they are starving. They are often not even at 60 percent of their desirable body weight. Marasmic children's bodies use all available kilocalories to stay alive; thus, growth is interrupted. Such children are weakened and appear apathetic. Many can't stand without support. They look old beyond their years, as the loss of fat in their face—one of the last places that the body loses fat during starvation—diminishes their childlike appearance. Their hair is thin and dry and lacks the sheen found in healthy children. Their body temperature and blood pressure are both low, and they are prone to dehydration, infections, and unnecessary blood clotting.

Individuals with marasmic kwashiorkor have the worst of both conditions. They often have edema in their legs and arms, yet have a "skin and bones" appearance in other parts of the body. When these individuals are provided with medical and nutritional treatment, such as receiving adequate protein, the edema subsides and their clinical symptoms more closely resemble that of a person with marasmus.

Appropriate medical care and treatment can dramatically reduce the 22 to 40 percent mortality rate seen among children with severe PEM worldwide.[26] The treatment for PEM should be carefully and slowly implemented using a three-step approach. The first step addresses the life-threatening factors, such as severe dehydration and fluid imbalances, using electrolyte solutions. The second step is to restore the individual's depleted tissues by gradually providing nutritionally dense kilocalories and high-quality protein. The third step involves transitioning the person to solid foods and introducing physical activity.

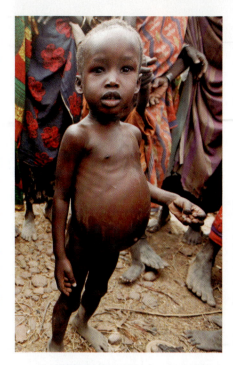

▲ **Figure 6.18 Kwashiorkor**
The edema in this child's belly is a classic sign of kwashiorkor.

▲ **Figure 6.19 Marasmus**
The emaciated appearance of this child is a symptom of marasmus.

LO 6.7: THE TAKE-HOME MESSAGE A high-protein diet may play a role in increasing the risk of heart disease, kidney problems, and calcium loss from bone. Consuming too much protein from animal sources can increase the amount of saturated fat in the diet. Too many protein-rich foods can displace whole grains, fruits, and vegetables, which have been shown to help reduce many chronic diseases. A low-protein diet has also been shown to lead to loss of bone mass. PEM is caused by an inadequate amount of protein, kilocalories, or both in the diet. A severe deficiency of protein is called kwashiorkor; a deficiency of kilocalories is called marasmus.

What Is a Vegetarian Diet?

LO 6.8 Describe the benefits and risks of a vegetarian diet.

For many people, being a **vegetarian** is a lifestyle choice made for a particular reason. Whereas some vegetarians avoid foods from animal sources for ethical, religious, or environmental reasons, others choose a vegetarian lifestyle for health reasons.[27] An estimated 5 percent of Americans consider themselves vegetarians.[28] There are several types of vegetarians and associated ranges of acceptable foods. See **Table 6.5** for a description of different vegetarian diets and the foods associated with each.

Because vegetarians avoid meat, which is high in complete protein, they need to be sure to get adequate protein from other food sources. Vegetarians can meet their daily protein needs by consuming a varied plant-based diet that contains meat alternatives such as soy, dried beans and other legumes, and nuts. Vegetarians who consume some animal products, such as milk, eggs, and/or fish, can use these foods to help meet their protein needs.

In the United States, the vegetarian food market continues to grow as manufacturers accommodate increased consumer demand with an array of new vegetarian products each year.[29] Many sit-down restaurants offer vegetarian entrées on their menus, and even some fast-food restaurants now offer veggie burgers. University food services are increasingly making vegetarian options available to meet growing student demand.

vegetarian A person who avoids eating animal foods. Some vegetarians only avoid meat, fish, and poultry, while others (vegans) avoid all animal products, including milk, eggs, and cheese.

Beans add protein, antioxidants, and a variety of minerals to a healthful plant-based diet.

Vegetarian Diets Carry Potential Benefits

A plant-based vegetarian diet can be rich in high-fiber whole grains, vegetables, fruits, legumes, and nuts, and naturally lower in saturated fat and cholesterol-containing foods. These qualities are fundamental for reducing the risk of heart disease, high blood pressure, diabetes, cancer, stroke, and obesity, assuming the diet is not limited or unbalanced in nutrients.

Vegetarian food staples such as soy, nuts, and soluble fiber–rich foods including beans and oats have all been shown to reduce blood cholesterol levels. Research collected from numerous studies has shown that deaths from heart disease are about 29 percent lower among vegetarians than among nonvegetarians.[30]

Vegetarians also tend to have lower blood pressure. The incidence of high blood pressure has been shown to be over two times higher in nonvegetarians.[31]

TABLE 6.5	The Many Types of Vegetarians	
Type	**Eats**	**Avoids**
Lacto-vegetarian	Grains, vegetables, fruits, legumes, seeds, nuts, dairy foods	Meat, fish, poultry, and eggs
Lacto-ovo-vegetarian	Grains, vegetables, fruits, legumes, seeds, nuts, dairy foods, eggs	Meat, fish, and poultry
Ovo-vegetarian	Grains, vegetables, fruits, legumes, seeds, nuts, eggs	Meat, fish, poultry, dairy foods
Vegan	Grains, vegetables, fruits, legumes, seeds, nuts	Any animal foods (meat, fish, poultry, dairy foods, eggs)
Semivegetarian	A vegetarian diet that occasionally includes meat, fish, and poultry	Meat, fish, and poultry on occasion

High blood pressure is a risk factor not only for heart disease, but also for stroke.

Because you know from Chapter 4 that a plant-based diet can help reduce the risk of type 2 diabetes; you shouldn't be surprised to learn that vegetarians tend to have a lower risk of diabetes. Diabetes mellitus is also a risk for heart disease. For those with diabetes, the predominance of foods rich in fiber and low in saturated fat and cholesterol in a vegetarian diet can help them manage the disease.[32]

Vegetarian diets have been shown to lower cancer rates compared with the general population. The latest World Cancer Research Fund Report advocates a plant-based diet that is high in nutrients and dietary fiber yet low in energy-dense foods (highly processed foods with added sugars and fat, as well as sugary beverages) to reduce the risk for cancer.[33]

Also, a plant-based diet that contains mostly fiber-rich whole grains and low-kilocalorie, nutrient-dense vegetables and fruits tends to be one that "fills you up before it fills you out," which means that you are likely to eat fewer overall kilocalories. Consequently, eating the plant-based foods of a vegetarian diet can be a healthy and satisfying strategy for fighting the battle against obesity.

Vegetarian Diets Carry Potential Risks

The biggest risk of a vegetarian diet is underconsuming certain nutrients, such as protein, or certain vitamins and minerals. Vegetarian foods contain protein, but the amount per serving is lower than that found in animal sources. For example, 100 grams, or a serving, of kidney beans contains 7 grams of protein, whereas 100 grams of cooked chicken breast, or the size of a medium boneless chicken breast, contains 17 grams. Most plant foods also do not contain complete protein. A vegetarian's protein needs can be met by consuming a *variety* of plant foods. A combination of protein-rich soy foods, legumes, nuts, or seeds should be eaten daily.

A vegetarian diet combines a variety of plant foods with fortified foods or supplements rich in vitamin B$_{12}$.

The form of iron in plants is not as easily absorbed as the form of iron in meat, milk, and poultry. Also, phytate in grains and rice, and polyphenols in tea and coffee, can inhibit iron absorption. The iron needs of vegetarians are about 1.5 times higher than those of nonvegetarians. Consuming iron-fortified cereals, enriched grains, pasta, wheat germ, and nuts and seeds can improve iron intake in vegetarians.

Consuming animal protein enhances the absorption of zinc. Following a vegetarian diet means that you lose out on this benefit and are more likely to develop a zinc deficiency. Phytates found in grains and rice also binds zinc, making it less bioavailable. A vegan's zinc needs may be as much as 50 percent higher than a nonvegetarian's. A diet rich in soybeans, fortified soy burgers, legumes, nuts, and seeds will increase the zinc content of the diet.

Calcium is abundant in low-fat dairy foods such as nonfat or low-fat milk, yogurt, and cheese. If you follow a lactovegetarian diet, these foods would be in adequate amounts to meet your calcium needs; however, if you follow a vegan diet, you may have more difficulty meeting your calcium needs.

Calcium-fortified soymilk and orange juice as well as tofu can provide about the same amount of calcium per serving as is found in dairy foods. Adding calcium-rich vegetables including bok choy, broccoli, kale, collard greens, and okra will enhance calcium intake.

Vitamin A and vitamin D may be low in a vegetarian diet. Preformed vitamin A is found only in animal foods. However, vegetarians can meet their needs by consuming the vitamin A precursor beta-carotene found in vegetables such as carrots and spinach. Some vegetarians will need to consume vitamin D–fortified milk or soy products to ingest sufficient vitamin D. Egg yolk, vitamin D–fortified soymilk and yogurt, and ready-to-eat cereals, in addition to a vitamin supplement, will add sufficient vitamin D to the diet.

Vitamin B$_{12}$ is also a concern in vegetarian diets because it is only found in animal foods.[34] If the vegetarian diet contains eggs and dairy products, the diet may contain some vitamin B$_{12}$. If the diet plan is strictly vegan, alternative foods should be included. Plant foods that are fermented or sprouted may contain a little vitamin B$_{12}$ but the amount is not consistent or dependable. Foods fortified with vitamin B$_{12}$ such

TABLE 6.6	Suggested Servings for a Healthy Vegetarian Diet		
Food Group	**Number of Servings**	**Serving Size**	**Calcium-Rich Foods (8 servings daily)**
Grains	6	Bread, 1 slice Cooked grain or cereal, ½ cup Ready-to-eat cereal, 1 oz	Whole-wheat bread, 1 slice Calcium-fortified cereal, 1 oz
Legumes, nuts, and other protein-rich foods	5	Cooked beans, peas, or lentils, ½ cup Tofu or tempeh, ½ cup Nut or seed butter, 2 tbs Nuts ¼ cup Meat analog, 1 oz Egg, 1	Cow's milk or yogurt, ½ cup Calcium-fortified soy milk, ½ cup Cheese ¾ oz
Vegetables	4	Cooked vegetables, ½ cup Raw vegetables, 1 cup Vegetable juice, ½ cup	Bok choy, collards, broccoli, Chinese cabbage, kale, mustard greens, or okra; 1 cup cooked or 2 cups raw Calcium-fortified tomato juice, ½ cup
Fruits	2	Medium fruit, 1 Cut-up or cooked fruit, ½ cup Fruit juice, ½ cup Dried fruit, ¼ cup	Calcium-fortified fruit juice, ½ cup Figs, 5
Fats	2	Oil, 1 tsp Soft margarine, 1 tsp Mayonnaise, 1 tsp	

Adapted from V. Messina, V. Melina, and A. R. Mangels. 2003. "A New Food Guide for North American Vegetarians," *Journal of the American Dietetic Association* 103:771–775.

as cereals, fortified soy products, nutritional yeast, and yeast extracts should be incorporated into the menu. Vitamin B_{12} supplements can also be used, or vitamin B_{12} intramuscular injections from a physician will prevent vitamin B_{12} deficiencies.

If your vegetarian diet doesn't include fish, you may not be consuming enough of the essential omega-3 fatty acid called alpha-linolenic acid. Fish, especially fatty fish such as salmon and sardines, are an excellent source of omega-3 fatty acids. Walnuts, flaxseed and flaxseed oil, and soybean and canola oil are other good vegetarian food sources to increase the omega-3 content of the diet.

Planning a Healthy Vegetarian Diet

To avoid nutrient deficiencies, vegetarians must consume adequate amounts of a wide variety of foods. Monitor those nutrients found in abundance in animal foods, including protein, iron, zinc, calcium, vitamin D, vitamin B_{12}, vitamin A, and omega-3 fatty acids. A vitamin and mineral supplement may be necessary. The tips in **Table 6.6** and **Figure 6.20** can help vegetarians

easily incorporate these nutrients into their diet. Analyze the dietary habits of Erinn, a college sophomore who has recently become a vegan, in the Nutrition in Practice on page 237.

LO 6.8: THE TAKE-HOME MESSAGE
Vegetarian diets can be a healthy eating style that may reduce the risk of some chronic diseases. Some vegetarians abstain from all animal foods, while others may eat eggs and dairy products in limited amounts. A balanced vegetarian diet may reduce the risk of heart disease, high blood pressure, diabetes, cancer, stroke, and obesity. All vegetarians must take care in planning a varied diet that meets their nutrient needs, especially for protein, iron, zinc, calcium, vitamin A, vitamin D, vitamin B_{12}, and omega-3 fatty acids.

▲ **Figure 6.20 My Vegan Plate**
Source: The Vegetarian Resource Group, www.vrg.org.

Nutrition in Practice: Erinn

After much reading about vegetarian diets, Erinn, a college sophomore, decided that she wanted to become a vegan. Unfortunately, after two months of following a vegan diet, she has lost 5 pounds, and her clothes are beginning to look "baggy." She also notices that she seems to always be hungry between meals. Although she eats tons of fruits, vegetables, and grains, she is finding it a challenge to add protein-rich, vegan choices at her lunch and dinner. She has a micro-fridge in her dorm room, so she eats breakfast in her room. Her lunch and dinner are eaten in the campus dining hall. Erinn decides to seek the advice of the campus dietitian.

Erinn's Stats:
- Age: 19
- Height: 5 feet 4 inches
- Weight: 115 pounds
- BMI: 19.7

Erinn's Food Log

Food/Beverage	Time Consumed	Hunger Rating*	Location
Whole-wheat bread with jelly Clementine	8 AM	5	In dorm room
Salad bar salad: lettuce, tomato, carrots, peppers, and cucumbers with oil and red wine vinegar along with pita bread. Diet soda.	12:30 PM	5	In dining hall
Apple	3 PM	5	Studying in dorm room
Pasta with broccoli. Diet soda.	6:30 PM	5	In dining hall

*Hunger Rating (1–5): 1 = not hungry; 5 = super hungry.

Critical Thinking Questions

1. Why do you think Erinn is so hungry between meals?
2. What foods could be added to Erinn's diet to increase her protein intake?
3. Based on her food log, which other food group is she falling short of?

Dietitian's Observation and Plan for Erinn:

- Discuss the need to add vegan protein sources at each meal to meet her daily needs. Add peanut butter to morning toast. Order a soy burger along with her salad bar lunch. Add tofu and beans to all dinners.
- Need to consume a vegan equivalent of dairy foods. Add a soy yogurt at breakfast and replace diet soda with soy milk at lunch and dinner.

A month later, Erinn returns for a follow-up visit with the dietitian. By incorporating all of the dietitian's suggestions, she has gained 1.5 pounds!

A review of her food record shows that she is meeting her daily protein needs. However, she is still hungry late in the afternoon. The dietitian recommends that Erinn consume some nuts with her afternoon snack to increase her satiety.

Visual Chapter Summary

LO 6.1 Proteins Are Made of Amino Acids Linked with a Peptide Bond

Proteins are made up of 20 amino acids, 11 nonessential and nine essential. Nonessential amino acids can be made in the body, but the essential amino acids must be consumed in the diet. A third category, conditionally essential, contains those amino acids that under certain conditions must be supplied by food.

Amino acids are composed of carbon, hydrogen, oxygen, nitrogen, and, in some cases, sulfur. Every amino acid contains a central carbon, an acid group (COOH), an amine group (NH_2), a single hydrogen, and a unique side chain. The side chain varies for each amino acid and gives each its distinguishing qualities.

Amino acids are joined together by peptide bonds through condensation. Two amino acids joined together form a dipeptide, three amino acids form a tripeptide, and a polypeptide consists of many amino acids joined together. The unique sequence of amino acids in the chain is the primary structure of a protein. The

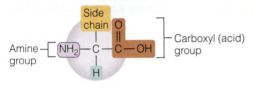

formation of hydrogen bonds between the carboxyl and amine groups of the amino acids creates the secondary structure, which causes the straight chain to fold, twist, and coil. The hydrophobic side chains cluster together on the inside and combine to form a globular shape called the tertiary structure. The quaternary structure of a protein forms when two or more polypeptide chains bond together through hydrogen bonding. Heat, acids, bases, salts, or mechanical agitation denature proteins. The primary structure doesn't change but the shape of the protein does.

LO 6.2 Protein Digestion Occurs in the Stomach and Small Intestine

The chemical digestion of protein begins in the stomach. Gastrin stimulates the release of HCl from the parietal cells and the inactive enzyme pepsinogen from the chief cells. HCl denatures the protein and converts pepsinogen to pepsin, which breaks polypeptides into shorter chains. Cholecystokinin from the duodenum stimulates trypsinogen, carboxypeptidase, and chymotrypsinogen from the pancreas. These proteases hydrolyze the shorter chains into tripeptides and dipeptides. Dipeptidases and tripeptidases hydrolyze the tripeptides and dipeptides into single amino acids that are absorbed through the enterocytes via the portal vein to the liver. Absorbed amino acids are used to synthesize new proteins, or are converted to energy, glucose, or fat and stored in the adipose tissue.

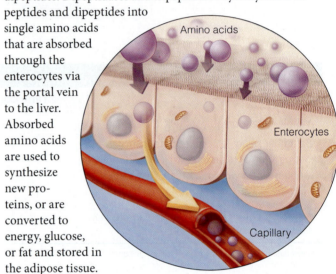

LO 6.3 The Metabolism of Protein Is Based on the Body's Needs

Amino acids located in the amino acid pools throughout the body can be used to synthesize new proteins when needed, or excess amino acids can be deaminated and then transformed into ATP, or converted to glucose or fatty acids. When other cells need to be replenished, the amino acids are released into the bloodstream and transported throughout the body. Transamination is used to synthesize nonessential amino acids.

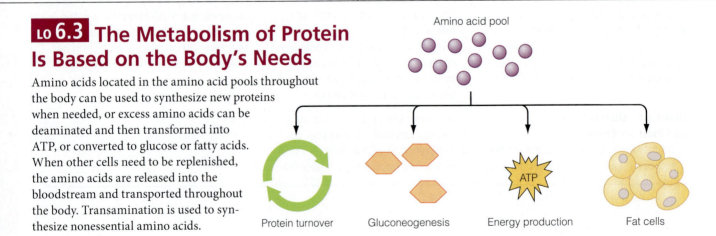

LO 6.4 Protein Plays Key Roles in the Body

Proteins provide structural and mechanical support and help maintain body tissues. Proteins are used to build specialized molecules called enzymes that act as a catalyst in metabolic reactions. Most hormones that stimulate activity in the tissues and cells are made from protein. Proteins help maintain fluid and acid-base balance, transport substances throughout the body, and act as channels in membranes. Antibodies and other proteins assist the immune response. Proteins also provide energy, improve satiety, and help control appetite.

LO 6.5 Protein Needs Are Based on the Dietary Reference Intakes and Determined by Nitrogen Balance Studies

For a healthy adult, the amount of dietary protein consumed every day should equal the amount of protein used. Nitrogen balance studies suggest that adults over the age of 18 need 0.80 gram per kilogram of body weight daily. Men typically consume more than 100 grams of protein daily, and women more than 70 grams—in both cases, far more than is needed. Adequate protein intake to achieve nitrogen balance is between 10 to 35 percent of total daily kilocalories.

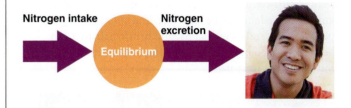

LO 6.6 Protein Foods Are Evaluated by Their Digestibility, Amino Acid Score, and Essential Amino Acid Content

Protein quality is determined by the body's ability to digest the protein and the essential or nonessential amino acids that the protein contains, called the chemical, or amino acid, score. A protein's digestibility and its amino acid score are combined to yield a protein digestibility corrected amino acid score (PDCAAS). The essential amino acid with the lowest score is called the limiting amino acid. Proteins with a higher PDCAAS are of higher quality. A complete protein, found in animal foods and soy, provides a complete set of the essential amino acids. Plant proteins are typically incomplete, as they are missing or low in one or more of the essential amino acids. Combining nonmeat protein sources can provide high-quality protein and is particularly important for vegetarians. The best food sources of proteins are found in animal products and include eggs, lean meats, and low-fat or fat-free dairy products. Plant proteins such as soy, grains, and vegetables also supply substantial protein to the diet. Most people consume more than enough protein each day and thus protein supplements are not necessary.

LO 6.7 Too Much or Too Little Protein Is Linked to Health Problems

A diet too high in protein is linked to health problems such as cardiovascular disease, kidney stones, osteoporosis, and some types of cancer. An excess of protein-rich foods can displace whole grains, fruits, and vegetables in the diet. Eating too little protein can also compromise bone health.

Diets that are inadequate in protein, kilocalories, or both lead to protein-energy malnutrition (PEM), also called marasmus and kwashiorkor. Marasmus is a disease caused by insufficient intake of kilocalories. Kwashiorkor occurs when a person consumes sufficient kilocalories but not sufficient protein. Symptoms of severe kwashiorkor include edema in the legs, feet, and stomach, dry and peeling skin, rashes or lesions, and brittle hair that can be easily pulled out. PEM can be improved with proper nutrition and treatment.

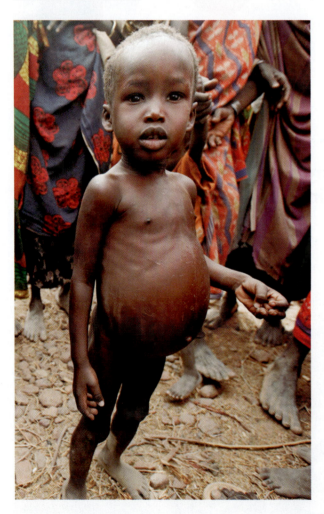

LO 6.8 Vegetarian Diets Can Reduce the Risk of Certain Diseases

Healthy vegetarian diets can reduce the risk of heart disease, high blood pressure, diabetes, cancer, stroke, and obesity. All vegetarians must take care to eat a varied diet that meets all of their nutrient needs, especially for protein, iron, zinc, calcium, vitamin D, vitamin B_{12}, vitamin A, and omega-3 fatty acids.

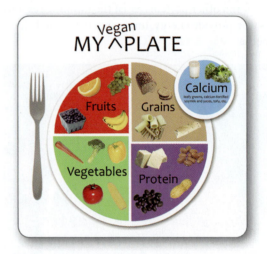

Terms to Know

- proteins
- amino acids
- carboxyl or acid group
- amine group
- side chain
- peptide
- peptide bonds
- dipeptide
- tripeptide
- polypeptide
- essential amino acid
- nonessential amino acid
- conditionally essential amino acid
- primary structure
- secondary structure
- tertiary structure
- quaternary structure
- denature
- gastrin

- pepsinogen
- pepsin
- proteases
- amino acid pools
- protein turnover
- genes
- transcription
- messenger RNA (mRNA)
- translation
- ribosomes
- transfer RNA (tRNA)
- elongation
- sickle-cell anemia
- deamination
- urea
- transamination
- glucogenic amino acids
- gluconeogenesis
- catalysts
- catabolic

- anabolic
- hormones
- albumin
- fluid balance
- edema
- pH
- acidosis
- alkalosis
- buffers
- transport proteins
- antibodies
- immunity
- allergen
- nitrogen balance
- amino acid score
- limiting amino acid
- protein digestibility corrected amino acid score (PDCAAS)
- biological value
- isoflavones
- estrogens
- complete protein
- incomplete protein
- protein-energy malnutrition (PEM)
- kwashiorkor
- marasmus
- vegetarian

MasteringNutrition™

To hear an MP3 Chapter Review, scan here or visit the Study Area in MasteringNutrition.

Check Your Understanding

1. Proteins differ from carbohydrates and lipids because
   a. they contain carbon-carbon bonds.
   b. they contain nitrogen.
   c. they contain carbon, hydrogen, and oxygen.
   d. they have a longer chain length.
2. Which of the following nonessential amino acids can also be considered a conditional amino acid?
   a. alanine
   b. serine
   c. glutamic acid
   d. proline
3. The enzyme that begins the chemical digestion of protein in the stomach is
   a. carboxypeptidase.
   b. pepsin.
   c. ADH.
   d. ghrelin.
4. Gluconeogenesis is stimulated when
   a. the diet is high in carbohydrate.
   b. the diet is high in fat.
   c. the diet is low in protein.
   d. the diet is low in carbohydrate.
5. Which of the following will *not* denature a protein?
   a. grilling a chicken breast
   b. frying an egg
   c. marinating a steak in red wine
   d. refrigerating milk

6. Before an excess amino acid can be used for energy or stored as fat, it must first be
   a. deaminated.
   b. digested.
   c. denatured.
   d. deactivated.
7. Proteins play important roles in the body, but do not
   a. regulate fluid balance.
   b. contract muscles.
   c. act as chemical messengers.
   d. constitute part of bile used to emulsify fat.
8. Protein is found abundantly in
   a. fruits.
   b. milk, eggs, meat, and beans.
   c. vegetables and whole grains.
   d. oils and sugars.
9. Which of the following is a source of complete protein?
   a. kidney beans
   b. peanut butter
   c. soy milk
   d. pasta
10. Kwashiorkor is a type of PEM that develops when
   a. there is a severe deficiency of protein in the diet but an adequate amount of kilocalories.
   b. there are inadequate amounts of both protein and kilocalories in the diet.
   c. there is inadequate amount of animal protein in the diet.
   d. there are adequate amounts of both protein and kilocalories in the diet.

Answers

1. (b) Proteins differ from carbohydrates because they contain nitrogen found in the amine group. All three macronutrients contain carbon, hydrogen, and oxygen. The chains of glucose units or fatty acids vary in lengths similar to proteins.
2. (d) Proline can be a conditional amino acid under certain conditions.
3. (b) Pepsin is the active form of the enzyme that begins protein digestion. Carboxypeptidase and ADH are other digestive enzymes. Ghrelin is a hormone that stimulates appetite.
4. (d) If an individual does not eat an adequate amount of carbohydrates, the body can break down proteins to create glucose.
5. (d) Refrigeration does not alter the bonds between the amino acid side chains and therefore does not denature proteins. Heat (from frying or grilling) and acids (from marinating) will denature proteins.
6. (a) Before amino acids can be converted to glucose or fatty acids, or enter the energy cycle, the amine group must first be removed through deamination. Denaturing is the process of unfolding or changing the shape of proteins.
7. (d) The body needs adequate amounts of protein to maintain fluid balance, to provide structural and mechanical support when contracting muscles, and as hormones, which act as chemical messengers. Protein is not part of bile used to emulsify fat.
8. (b) Animal foods and some plant-based proteins, such as beans, are protein rich. There is some protein in vegetables, but little in fruits. Oils and sugars do not contain protein.

9. (c) Soy foods provide all the essential amino acids, and thus are a source of complete protein. Kidney beans, peanut butter, and pasta are missing adequate amounts of the essential amino acids and are considered incomplete proteins.

10. (a) Kwashiorkor occurs when protein is deficient in the diet even though kilocalories may be adequate. Marasmus occurs when kilocalories are inadequate in a person's diet. Protein from animal sources is not necessary because people can meet their protein needs from a combination of plant proteins. There doesn't need to be a balance between animal and plant proteins.

Answers to True or False?

1. **True.** Proteins are the only macronutrients that contain nitrogen.
2. **False.** Of the 20 amino acids that make up protein, nine are considered essential and 11 are nonessential.
3. **False.** Chemical digestion of protein begins in the stomach with the enzyme pepsin, which is secreted by the chief cells lining the stomach.
4. **True.** When proteins arrive in the stomach, hydrochloric acid uncoils them, revealing the peptide bonds that connect the amino acids.
5. **True.** Amino acids can be converted to glucose through gluconeogenesis.
6. **False.** The primary function of protein is to build new tissues and repair proteins that have been degraded or sloughed off in the body.
7. **False.** Growing children are in a state of positive nitrogen balance, which means that more nitrogen is being retained by the body than excreted in the urine.
8. **False.** Animal proteins are considered complete proteins because they contain all nine essential amino acids.
9. **False.** Protein itself doesn't raise blood cholesterol levels. It depends on the type of protein food you consume.
10. **True.** A diet that is inadequate in protein results in kwashiorkor, characterized by edema and body wasting.

Web Resources

- For information on specific genetic disorders, including those that affect protein use in the body, visit the National Human Genome Research Institute at www.nhgri.nih.gov
- For more information on protein bars and supplements, visit the Center for Science in the Public Interest at www.cspinet.org
- For more information on vegetarian diets, visit the Vegetarian Resource Group at www.vrg.org

References

1. Marieb, E. N., and K. Hoehn. 2013. *Human Anatomy and Physiology.* 9th ed. San Francisco: Benjamin Cummings.
2. Ibid.
3. Stevens, B. R. 1992. Amino Acid Transport in the Intestine. In *Mammalian Amino Acid Transport: Mechanisms and Control.* M. S. Kilberg and D. Haussinger, eds. New York: Plenum.
4. Marieb. 2013. *Human Anatomy and Physiology.*
5. National Human Genome Research Institute. 2011. *Learning About Sickle-Cell Disease.* Available at www.genome.gov. Accessed February 2014.
6. Berg, J. M., J. L. Tymoczko, and L. Stryer. 2013. *Biochemistry.* 7th ed. New York: W. H. Freeman and Company.
7. Abou-Samra, R., L. Keersmaekers, D. Brienza, R. Mukherjee, and K. Macé. 2011. Effect of Different Protein Sources on Satiation and Short-Term Satiety When Consumed as a Starter. *Nutrition Journal* 10:139–148.
8. Sedlackova, D., J. Kopeckova, H. Papezova, V. Hainer, H. Kvasnicklova, M. Hill, and J. Nedvidkova. 2012. Comparison of a High-Carbohydrate and High-Protein Breakfast Effect on Plasma Ghrelin, Obestatin, NPY and PYY Levels in Women with Anorexia and Bulimia Nervosa. *Nutrition and Metabolism* 9:52–61.
9. Breen, L., and S. M. Phillips (2012). Nutrient Interaction for Optimal Protein Anabolism in Resistance Exercise. *Current Opininion in Clinical Nutrrition and Metabolic Care* 15:226–232.
10. Beelen, M., A. Zorenc, B. Pennings, J. M. Senden, H. Kuipers, and L. J. van Loon. (2011b). Impact of Protein Coingestion on Muscle Protein Synthesis during Continuous Endurance Type Exercise. *American Journal of Physiology* 300:E945–E954.
11. Stipanek, M., and M. A. Caudill. 2013. *Biochemical, Physiological, and Molecular Aspects of Human Nutrition.* 3rd ed. St. Louis: Elsevier Sanders.
12. Aldrich, N. D., C. Perry, W. Thomas, S. K. Raatz, and M. Reicks. 2013. Perceived Importance of Dietary Protein to Prevent Weight Gain: A National Survey among Midlife Women. *Journal of Nutrition Education and Behavior* 45(3):213–221.
13. Clifton, P. M. 2011. Protein and Coronary Heart Disease: The Role of Different Protein Sources. *Current Atherosclerosis Report* 13:493–498.
14. National Kidney and Urologic Diseases Information Clearinghouse (NKUDIC). 2013. *Diet for Kidney Stone Prevention.* Available at http://kidney.niddk.nih.gov. Accessed February 2014.
15. Allen, L. H., E. A. Oddoye, and S. Margen. 1979. Protein-Induced Calciuria: A Longer-Term Study. *American Journal of Clinical Nutrition* 32:741–749.
16. Thorpe, M. P., and E. M. Evans. 2011. Dietary Protein and Bone Health: Harmonizing Conflicting Theories. *Nutrition Reviews* 69(4):215–230.
17. Bonjour, J. P. 2011. Protein Intake and Bone Health. *International Journal of Vitamin Nutrition Research* 81:134–142.
18. Jesudason, D., C. Nordin, J. Keogh, and P. Clifton. 2013. Comparison of Two Weight-Loss Diets of Different Protein Content on Bone Health: A Randomized Trial. *American Journal of Clinical Nutrition* 98(5):1343–1352.
19. Bonjour. 2011. Protein Intake and Bone Health.
20. Cao, J. J., S. M. Pasiakos, L. M. Margolis, E. R. Sauter, L. D. Whigham, J. P. McClung, A. J. Young, and G. F. Combs, Jr. 2014. Calcium Homeostasis and Bone Metabolic Responses to High-Protein Diets during Energy Deficit in Healthy Young Adults: A Randomized Controlled Trial. *American Journal of Clinical Nutrition* 99(2):400–407.
21. Egeberg, R., A. Olsen, J. Christensen, J. Halkjaer, M. U. Jakobsen, K. Overvad, and A. Tjønneland. 2014. Associations between Red Meat and Risks for Colon and Rectal Cancer Depend on the Type of Red Meat Consumed. *Journal of Nutrition* 143(4):464–472.
22. Food and Agriculture Organization of the United Nations. 2013. *The State of Food Insecurity in the World, 2013.* Available at www.fao.org. Accessed April 2014.
23. World Health Organization. 2012. *WHO Global Database on Child Growth and Malnutrition Introduction.* Available at www.who.int. Accessed February 2014.

24. Denno, D. M. 2013. Child Health Part 2: Interventions to Combat the Major Childhood Killers. *Global Health Education Consortium.* Available at www.cugh.org. Accessed February 2014.

25. de Onis, M., M. Blossner, E. Borghi, A. Frongillo, and R. Morris. 2004. Estimates of Global Prevalance of Childhood Underweight in 1990 and 2015. *Journal of the American Medical Association* 291:2600–2606.

26. Agozie, C. U., N. S. Ibeziako, C. I. Ndiokwelu, C. M. Uzoka, and C. A. Nwafor. 2012. Under-Five Protein Energy Malnutrition Admitted at the University of Nigeria Teaching Hospital, Enugu: A 10-Year Retrospective Review. *Nutrition Journal* 11:43–50.

27. Nordin, S., M. Boyle, and T. Kemmer. 2013. Position of the Academy of Nutrition and Dietetics: Nutrition Security in Developing Nations: Sustainable Food, Water, and Health. *Journal of the Academy of Nutrition and Dietetics* 113:581–595.

28. Gallup Wellbeing. 2012. *Gallup's July 9–12 Consumption Habits Survey.* Available at www.gallup.com. Accessed February 2014.

29. Ginsberg, C. 2011. *The Market for Vegetarian Foods.* Available at www.vrg.org. Accessed February 2014.

30. Huang, T., B. Yang, J. Zheng, G. Li, M. L. Wahlqvist, and D. Li. 2012. Cardiovascular Disease Mortality and Cancer Incidence in Vegetarians: A Meta-Analysis and Systematic Review. *Annals of Nutrition and Metabolism* 60(4):233–240.

31. Yokoyama, Y., K. Nishimura, N. D. Barnard, et al. 2013. Vegetarian Diets and Blood Pressure: A Meta-Analysis. *Journal of the American Medical Association Internal Medicine* doi:10.1001/jamainternmed.2013.14547.

32. Tonstad, S., K. Stewart, K. Oda, M. Batech, R. P. Herring, and G. E. Fraser. 2013. Vegetarian Diets and Incidence of Diabetes in the Adventist Health Study-2. *Nutrition, Metabolism, and Cardiovascular Diseases* 23(4):292–299.

33. Collins, K., and S. Palmer. 2013. *Eating Patterns to Lower Cancer Risk: More Than One Route to a Plant-Based Diet.* Available at www.aicr.org. Accessed February 2014.

34. Pawlak, R., S. J. Parrott, S. Raj, D. Cullum-Dugan, and D. Lucus. 2013. How Prevalent is Vitamin B_{12} Deficiency among Vegetarians? *Nutrition Reviews* 71(2):110–117.

7 Alcohol

Learning Outcomes

After reading this chapter, you will be able to:

7.1 Describe the sources of alcohol and how alcohol is made.

7.2 Explain why people drink alcohol, and define a standard drink.

7.3 Explain how alcohol is absorbed and metabolized, and how it circulates throughout the body.

7.4 Describe the short-term effects of alcohol consumption on the body.

7.5 Describe the long-term effects of chronic alcohol consumption on the body.

7.6 Summarize the methods used to diagnose and treat alcohol abuse and alcoholism.

True or False?

1. Alcohol is an essential nutrient. **T/F**
2. A shot of whiskey contains more alcohol than a can of beer. **T/F**
3. Red wine contains phytochemicals that are beneficial for the heart. **T/F**
4. Women feel the effects of alcohol sooner than men. **T/F**
5. The body can metabolize three alcoholic beverages per hour. **T/F**
6. The best way to cure a hangover is to drink a Bloody Mary. **T/F**
7. Alcohol provides 7 kilocalories per gram. **T/F** .
8. Drinking too much alcohol can lead to malnutrition. **T/F**
9. Moderate drinking means consuming six or more drinks once a week. **T/F**
10. Alcoholism can be cured through counseling. **T/F**

See page 277 for the answers.

Alcohol is not classified as an essential nutrient because your body doesn't need alcohol to survive. But alcohol does contain kilocalories. In fact, alcohol contributes more energy per gram than either carbohydrates or protein. For example, a 12-ounce beer contains almost as much energy as a Hershey's chocolate candy bar; it contributes more kilocalories than two large hard-boiled eggs. For this reason, we cover alcohol following the chapters on the three classifications of macronutrients.

Alcohol not only adds kilocalories to the diet but it can put a dent in your budget. Ounce for ounce, alcohol can cost 100 times more than bottled water. It's legally sold in the United States, but supposedly off-limits to those who aren't adults, even though teenagers often feel under social pressure to consume it. Some medical reports say that in moderation, alcohol can provide health benefits, at least in older adults, while others tell you that drinking too much alcohol can be fatal.

Understanding alcohol warrants a more detailed look. In this chapter, we discuss how the body handles alcohol, its positive and negative health effects, and how to tell if you or someone you know has become an alcohol abuser. We begin with the basic definition of alcohol.

What Is Alcohol and How Is It Made?

LO 7.1 Describe the sources of alcohol and how alcohol is made.

What is the first image that comes to mind when you hear the word **alcohol?** Do you envision a bottle of beer, a glass of wine, or a stiff martini? While they aren't alcohol by themselves, these beverages all contain a form of alcohol called *ethyl alcohol,* or **ethanol.**

Ethanol (C_2H_5OH) is one of a group of organic compounds called alcohols, in which one or more hydroxyl (OH) groups are attached to the carbon atoms in place of hydrogen atoms (see **Figure 7.1**). In Chapter 5, we covered another type of alcohol, *glycerol,* which is found in food and the body as part of the triglyceride molecule. The difference between glycerol and ethanol is that glycerol has three hydroxyl groups (one attached to each of the three carbons that make up the glycerol backbone), while ethanol contains only one hydroxyl group.

Two other alcohol compounds, methanol (CH_3OH), used in antifreeze, and isopropanol (C_3H_7OH), used in rubbing alcohol, are both poisonous when ingested. Ethanol is considered safe for consumption, but it is not harmless; consuming excessive amounts of ethanol can be toxic, even lethal.

Alcohol compounds tend to be soluble in water because the OH is polar and attracts water. Ethanol is also a lipid solvent, which means it can dissolve lipids,

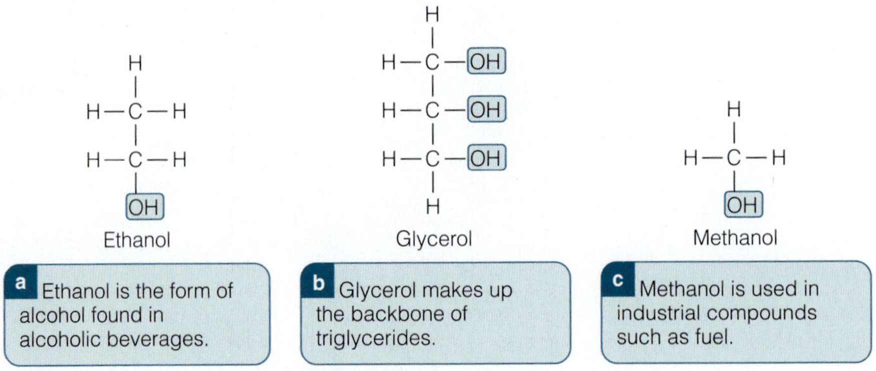

alcohol A class of organic compounds that contain one or more hydroxyl groups attached to carbons. Examples include ethanol, glycerol, and methanol. Ethanol is often referred to as "alcohol."

ethanol The type of alcohol, specifically *ethyl alcohol* (C_2H_5OH), found in alcoholic beverages such as wine, beer, and liquor.

a Ethanol is the form of alcohol found in alcoholic beverages.

Ethanol

b Glycerol makes up the backbone of triglycerides.

Glycerol

c Methanol is used in industrial compounds such as fuel.

Methanol

▲ **Figure 7.1 Structure of Three Alcohols**

including those that make up cell membranes. Although ethanol is the scientific name for the alcohol found in consumable beverages, we also use the more common term "alcohol" throughout the chapter.

From Sugar to Alcohol

Ethanol is made when yeasts **ferment** the natural sugars in grains (glucose and maltose) and fruits (fructose and glucose). Yeasts are single-celled organisms that metabolize glucose into ethanol and carbon dioxide (see the Chemistry Boost). Yeast is used in the production of all alcoholic beverages at some point in the fermentation process.

The most common form of yeast used to make alcohol, brewer's yeast, can tolerate up to about 5 percent alcohol. Beyond this level of alcohol, the yeast dies. Wine yeast is still active in 12 percent alcohol and some cultured strains of yeast can tolerate up to 21 percent alcohol. Depending on the type of yeast that is used, the fermentation reaction stops once the alcohol content reaches 11 to 14 percent because the level of alcohol becomes toxic to the yeast and the yeast itself dies. The carbon dioxide formed during fermentation bubbles through the liquid and evaporates, leaving an alcohol-containing beverage.

Wine is made by fermenting the sugars glucose and fructose in grapes and other fruits. The characteristics of wines—whether the wine is spicy, zesty, acidic,

⬡ Chemistry Boost

Fermentation

The process of fermentation involves converting glucose ($C_6H_{12}O_6$) into alcohol (CH_3CH_2OH) and carbon dioxide gas (CO_2). The basic reaction of fermentation happens within the yeast as shown below.

$$C_6H_{12}O_6 \rightarrow 2\ (CH_3CH_2OH) + 2\ (CO_2) + 2\ ATP$$

Glucose → Ethyl alcohol + Carbon dioxide gas + Energy

Fermentation begins with glucose, the main energy source for yeast. The enzymes in the yeast convert the glucose first to pyruvate, which generates energy in the form of ATP. Once pyruvate is formed, the enzymes in the yeast convert it to acetaldehyde and carbon dioxide. In the final step of ethyl alcohol production, acetaldehyde is converted into ethanol. The hydrogen needed to convert the acetaldehyde to ethanol is provided by the coenzyme form of the B vitamin niacin NADH + H^+.

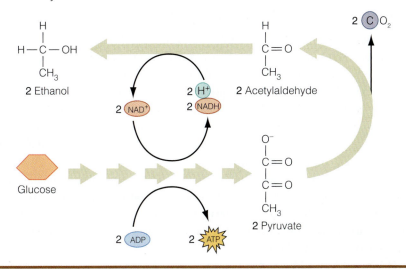

ferment (fermentation) The process by which yeast converts sugars in grains or fruits into ethanol and carbon dioxide.

Beer is made when yeast converts the glucose in grain to ethyl alcohol and carbon dioxide gas.

or sweet—vary depending on the types of grapes or fruit that are used, where they are grown, and the climate.

Malted cereal grains, such as barley, are used to make beer. In malting, the barley partially germinates, releasing enzymes that hydrolyze the starch in the endosperm into smaller sugar molecules, or maltose. The brewer stops germination before the plant uses all the sugars. The brewing process hydrolyzes maltose further into glucose, which then undergoes fermentation. The carbon dioxide is captured and used to carbonate the brew. The basic ingredients added to beer include hops for flavor, sugar, water, and different types of yeast, which account for the varying types of beer.

Like beer and wine, liquors begin with the fermentation of sugars from an initial food item. Vodka begins with potatoes or grains, rum begins with molasses or sugarcane juice, and tequila begins with the blue agave plant. After fermentation, the alcoholic liquids undergo **distillation:** the liquid is heated, causing the ethanol to vaporize. The vapor is collected, cooled, and condensed into a concentrated beverage called *liquor* (or, more accurately, distilled spirits). The alcohol content of these beverages is indicated by its **proof,** a number that reflects twice the alcohol content in the beverage. For example, 80 proof vodka contains 40 percent alcohol.

LO 7.1: THE TAKE-HOME MESSAGE Ethanol is the type of alcohol consumed in alcoholic beverages. It is an organic chemical produced by the fermentation of sugars by yeast, as in beer or wine, or by distillation, as with distilled spirits. Alcohol provides kilocalories but very little nutritional value. It is not a nutrient because your body doesn't need it to survive.

Why Do People Drink Alcohol and What Is Considered a Standard Drink?

LO 7.2 Explain why people drink alcohol, and define a standard drink.

Alcohol is a drug that alters your conscious mind. Within minutes of sipping an alcoholic beverage, a person feels more relaxed. After a few more sips, a mild, pleasant euphoria sets in and inhibitions begin to loosen. By the end of the first or second drink, a person often feels more outgoing, happy, and social. This initial effect may be just one reason people seek out and continue to drink alcohol.[1]

People Drink to Relax, Celebrate, and Socialize

People around the world drink alcohol in many different forms and for many different reasons. The Japanese drink sake (rice wine) during tea and Shinto ceremonies, while Irish pub patrons consume dark beer to celebrate their favorite sport. Russians enjoy vodka and the French appreciate wine to relax and for pleasure. Wine is part of many religious traditions, including the Catholic Mass and the Jewish Sabbath, and in some cultures, it's the beverage of choice during the main meal of the day. For parts of human history, wine and beer were safer to drink than water, which was often contaminated with disease-causing microbes.

In the United States, more than half of adults consume at least one alcoholic beverage per month.[2] Americans drink alcohol for many of the same reasons people in other parts of the world do: to relax, celebrate, and socialize. For college-aged students, alcohol is sometimes used to enhance their social experiences as they transition to young adulthood.[3]

Having a drink with another person also symbolizes social bonding.[4] When it comes to mingling with others or celebrating a special occasion, whether it's with

distillation The evaporation and then collection of a liquid by condensation. Liquors are made using distillation.

proof A measure of the amount of ethanol contained in alcoholic beverages.

friends, coworkers, or even strangers, pubs and parties are common gathering spots, and alcoholic drinks are commonly served. This is considered **social drinking,** which is defined as drinking patterns that are considered acceptable by society. Social drinking is not the same as moderate drinking (see the next section), as consuming too much alcohol, even in socially acceptable situations, can be harmful, even if it is only done on the weekends. Later in this chapter we discuss binge drinking, which often occurs in social settings.

Some researchers believe that advertising influences alcohol consumption. One need only drive down a major highway or turn on the television to see billboards and commercials for a beer or liquor brand. In some media, including popular magazines like *Rolling Stone* and *Sports Illustrated,* alcohol ads can outnumber non–alcohol ads by almost three to one.[5] Some studies have shown that advertisements for alcoholic beverages are associated with an increase of drinking among adolescents.[6] Many ads tend to emphasize sexual and social stereotypes. When targeted to underage drinkers, this type of message has been shown to increase adolescents' desire to emulate those portrayed in the advertisements.[7] **Figure 7.2** shows a typical alcohol advertisement that may appear in a magazine. These ads should be viewed with caution, as the messages in them are often misleading and in some cases blatantly false.

Moderate Drinking Is Measured in Terms of a Standard Drink

It is not whether you choose to drink alcohol that is of concern, but how much you drink. **Moderate drinking** is considered the amount of alcohol that puts the individual and others at the lowest risk of alcohol-related problems. Moderation is defined in the latest *Dietary Guidelines for Americans* as up to one drink per day for women and up to two drinks a day for men. In order to be a moderate drinker, an individual must limit both the size of drinks and the frequency of drinking.

A standard drink, whether it's in a 12-ounce bottle of beer, a shot of liquor, or a 5-ounce glass of wine, contains about ½ ounce of alcohol (**Figure 7.3**). Sometimes, the drinks ordered at a local bar or restaurant appear to be a standard size, but are actually larger than that. If an 8-ounce wine glass gets filled to the brim, or if a mug of beer is the size of a pitcher, an individual can consume multiple standard drinks in one glass or mug (**Figure 7.4**). Mixed drinks also often contain more than one standard drink. A rum and coke, for example, could provide the equivalent of over 2 ½ alcoholic drinks.

▲ Figure 7.2 **Alcohol Advertisements Target Young Adults**
Alcohol advertisements often portray people who drink as happy, successful, attractive, and popular.

▲ Figure 7.3 **What Is a Standard Drink?**
One standard drink of beer, liquor, or wine contains about ½ ounce of alcohol.

| 12 oz (1 drink) | 16 oz (1⅓ drink) | 5 oz (1 drink) | 8 oz (1½ drink) |

▲ Figure 7.4 **Size Does Matter**
Depending on the size, one drink may actually be the equivalent of 1½ to more than two standard drinks.

social drinking Moderate drinking of alcoholic beverages in social settings within safe limits.

moderate drinking According to the *Dietary Guidelines for Americans,* up to one drink per day for women and up to two drinks a day for men.

Why Do People Drink Alcohol and What Is Considered a Standard Drink?   **253**

Another very important point about drinking in moderation is that abstaining from alcohol for six days and then drinking 10 beers on the seventh day does not count as moderate drinking. There isn't any "banking" allowed when it comes to alcohol; drinking excessive quantities in a short amount of time is *binge drinking* (which we'll discuss in more detail later in the chapter).

LO 7.2: THE TAKE-HOME MESSAGE People drink alcohol to relax, celebrate, socialize, and to feel more "adult." The *Dietary Guidelines for Americans* emphasize moderation for those who choose to drink alcohol, defined as up to one drink a day for women and two drinks a day for men. One drink contains ½ ounce of alcohol. Drinking excessive amounts of alcohol in a short time is binge drinking.

How Is Alcohol Absorbed, Circulated, and Metabolized in the Body?

LO 7.3 Explain how alcohol is absorbed and metabolized, and how it circulates throughout the body.

The body treats alcohol differently from any other substance. Unlike carbohydrates and fats, the body cannot store alcohol. Because alcohol is a toxin that can stimulate pathological changes in the liver and brain, the body quickly works to metabolize and eliminate it.

Alcohol Is Absorbed in the Stomach and Small Intestine

Alcohol doesn't require digestion, so it can be absorbed by simple diffusion through the gastric mucosa into the bloodstream. About 20 percent of alcohol is absorbed through the stomach, while the majority is absorbed through the duodenum of the small intestine. As soon as alcohol enters the blood, it travels through the body and is distributed throughout the watery tissues (**Figure 7.5**). This means that it quickly reaches the brain. Many factors, including the amount of food in the stomach, gender, age, ethnicity, and the amount of alcohol consumed, affect how quickly alcohol is absorbed.[8]

Food in the Stomach Affects Alcohol Absorption

One factor controlling the rate at which the stomach empties is the amount and type of food in the stomach. If a swallow of beer chases a cheeseburger and fries, the alcohol takes longer to leave the stomach and enter the small intestine than if the beer were consumed on an empty stomach. This is partly due to the fact that a partially full or full stomach is more likely to keep the alcohol away from the stomach wall, thereby reducing the amount that diffuses through the gastric lining. Fat- and carbohydrate-containing foods have additional effects. Fat slows down peristalsis, which slows the departure of food from the stomach, and carbohydrates slow the absorption of alcohol through the stomach lining.[9]

Here lies the logic behind not drinking alcohol on an empty stomach. Without food in the stomach, alcohol has greater opportunity to react with and diffuse through the gastric cells and be absorbed into the blood. In fact, a study showed that an alcoholic drink consumed after a meal was absorbed about three times more slowly than if it had been consumed on an empty stomach.[10]

Keep in mind, however, that while a full stomach delays the arrival of alcohol in the small intestine, the alcohol will still eventually arrive there. If a person drinks several glasses of beer with dinner, the alcohol will be absorbed once the stomach starts emptying.

Eating food while drinking alcohol affects the rate at which the alcohol is absorbed.

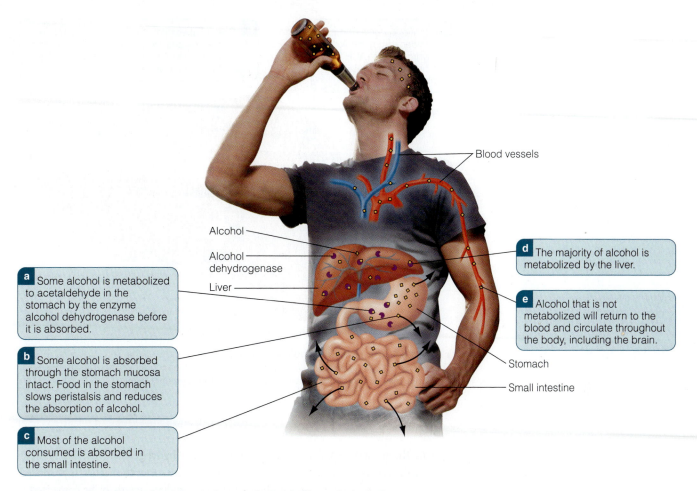

Alcohol

Alcohol
dehydrogenase

Liver

Blood vessels

Stomach

Small intestine

a Some alcohol is metabolized to acetaldehyde in the stomach by the enzyme alcohol dehydrogenase before it is absorbed.

b Some alcohol is absorbed through the stomach mucosa intact. Food in the stomach slows peristalsis and reduces the absorption of alcohol.

c Most of the alcohol consumed is absorbed in the small intestine.

d The majority of alcohol is metabolized by the liver.

e Alcohol that is not metabolized will return to the blood and circulate throughout the body, including the brain.

▲ **Figure 7.5 The Absorption, Circulation, and Metabolism of Alcohol**

Alcohol Is Metabolized in the Stomach and the Liver

The stomach gets the first pass at metabolizing alcohol before it is absorbed into the bloodstream. The rate at which alcohol is metabolized in the stomach is affected by how quickly the stomach empties into the duodenum. The longer alcohol lingers in the stomach, the more time the enzyme **alcohol dehydrogenase (ADH),** which is secreted by the gastric cells, has to metabolize it,[11] and the less alcohol directly enters the blood and eventually reaches the brain.

The liver, however, is the main site for alcohol metabolism. The liver can metabolize a limited amount of alcohol every hour, and the amount depends on body mass and liver size.

There are two pathways that metabolize alcohol in the liver. The majority of alcohol is metabolized by the same enzyme secreted by the gastric cells, alcohol dehydrogenase (ADH). This is the same enzyme secreted by the gastric cells when alcohol is metabolized in the stomach. The second system of enzyme pathways is known as the MEOS, or microsomal ethanol oxidizing system, which uses niacin in the form of NADPH.

The Alcohol Dehydrogenase (ADH) Pathway

The initial pathway to oxidize alcohol is an anaerobic, two-step enzyme process in the cytosol, or fluid portion of the cell. The enzyme ADH with the help of NAD^+ converts ethanol to **acetaldehyde** by removing two hydrogen atoms (**Figure 7.6**).

alcohol dehydrogenase (ADH) One of the alcohol-metabolizing enzymes, found in the stomach and the liver, that converts ethanol to acetaldehyde.

acetaldehyde One of the first compounds produced in the metabolism of ethanol. Eventually, acetaldehyde is converted to carbon dioxide and water and excreted.

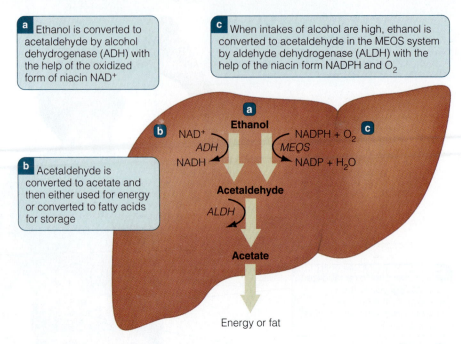

a
Ethanol

b NAD^+ $NADPH + O_2$ **c**
ADH   *MEOS*
NADH $NADP + H_2O$

Acetaldehyde

ALDH

Acetate

Energy or fat

▲**Figure 7.6 The Liver Metabolizes Alcohol**
The liver rapidly breaks down ethanol to acetyl CoA through either the alcohol dehydrogenase (ADH) pathway or using the microsomal enzyme oxidizing system (MEOS).

During the second step, the enzyme **acetaldehyde dehydrogenase (ALDH)** removes more hydrogen atoms from acetaldehyde to form acetate. Once the acetate is produced, it can continue through the metabolic pathways to produce energy or be converted to a fatty acid and stored as body fat in the adipocytes. (See Chapter 8 for more details on the metabolic pathways for alcohol.)

The Microsomal Ethanol Oxidizing System (MEOS)

When an individual consumes too much alcohol, the ADH enzymes become overwhelmed and can't keep up with the need to oxidize ethanol into acetaldehyde. Under these circumstances, a second major enzyme system in the liver that usually metabolizes drugs—the **microsomal ethanol oxidizing system (MEOS)**—takes over. Chronic alcohol abuse increases the number of these enzymes, which in turn increases the rate of alcohol that can be metabolized. As a result of the increase in liver enzymes in the MEOS, there is a small increase in the ability of the liver to metabolize alcohol, so that a larger dose of alcohol is needed to achieve the same effects. The more alcohol you drink, the more active the MEOS becomes, which can result in **alcohol tolerance.** However, because the MEOS usually metabolizes drugs (and other compounds foreign to cells), using it to metabolize alcohol may interfere with the body's ability to metabolize drugs. Alcohol takes precedence over drugs, so consuming drugs and alcohol together can result in the drugs building up to lethal levels while waiting for the MEOS to metabolize them.

The difference between the MEOS and the ADH pathway is that the MEOS takes place in the **microsomes** of the cell rather than the cytosol, the fluid inside the cell. The reactions in these small vesicles use oxygen (aerobic) and produce water as a by-product; use a different form of the B vitamin niacin, NADPH, rather than NAD^+; and consume energy rather than produce it to convert ethanol to acetaldehyde.

acetaldehyde dehydrogenase (ALDH) An alcohol-metabolizing enzyme found in the liver that converts acetaldehyde to acetate.

microsomal ethanol oxidizing system (MEOS) The second major enzyme system in the liver that metabolizes alcohol.

alcohol tolerance When the body adjusts to long-term alcohol use by becoming less sensitive to the alcohol. More alcohol needs to be consumed in order to get the same euphoric effect.

microsomes Small vesicles in the cytoplasm of liver cells where oxidative metabolism of alcohol takes place.

Alcohol Circulates in the Blood

If the liver cannot metabolize alcohol as fast as it is consumed, some of the alcohol remains in the blood, and is continually circulated in the fluid portions of the body. Though the liver eventually metabolizes 95 percent of the alcohol that is consumed, the other 5 percent is excreted intact either through the lungs, the skin in perspiration, and/or the kidneys through the urine. The amount of alcohol expelled through the lungs correlates with the amount of alcohol in the blood. For this reason, a Breathalyzer test can be used by police officers if they suspect that a person has consumed too much alcohol.

The **blood alcohol concentration (BAC)** is the amount of alcohol in the blood measured in grams of alcohol per deciliter, usually expressed as a percentage (**Table 7.1**). Because alcohol infiltrates the brain, as the BAC increases so does the level of mental impairment and intoxication.

A Breathalyzer is used to measure a person's blood alcohol concentration (BAC).

TABLE 7.1	Blood Alcohol Concentration Tables					

For Women
Body Weight in Pounds

Drinks Per Hour	100	120	140	160	180	200
1	0.05	0.04	0.03	0.03	0.03	0.02
2	0.09	0.08	0.07	0.06	0.05	0.05
3	0.14	0.11	0.10	0.09	0.08	0.07
4	0.18	0.15	0.13	0.11	0.10	0.09
5	0.23	0.19	0.16	0.14	0.13	0.11
6	0.27	0.23	0.19	0.17	0.15	0.14
7	0.32	0.27	0.23	0.20	0.18	0.16
8	0.36	0.30	0.26	0.23	0.20	0.18
9	0.41	0.34	0.29	0.26	0.23	0.20
10	0.45	0.38	0.32	0.28	0.25	0.23

For Men
Body Weight in Pounds

Drinks Per Hour	100	120	140	160	180	200
1	0.04	0.03	0.03	0.02	0.02	0.02
2	0.08	0.06	0.05	0.05	0.04	0.04
3	0.11	0.09	0.08	0.07	0.06	0.06
4	0.15	0.12	0.11	0.09	0.08	0.08
5	0.19	0.16	0.13	0.12	0.11	0.09
6	0.23	0.19	0.16	0.14	0.13	0.11
7	0.26	0.22	0.19	0.16	0.15	0.13
8	0.30	0.25	0.21	0.19	0.17	0.15
9	0.34	0.28	0.24	0.21	0.19	0.17
10	0.38	0.31	0.27	0.23	0.21	0.19

Notes: Shaded area indicates the condition of being mentally and physically impaired; the definition of legal intoxication.

Blood alcohol concentrations are expressed as percent, meaning grams of alcohol per 10 milliliters (per deciliter) of blood.

Source: Tables are adapted from those of the Pennsylvania Liquor Control Board, Harrisburg, PA.

blood alcohol concentration (BAC) The amount of alcohol in the blood. BAC is measured in grams of alcohol per deciliter of blood, usually expressed as a percentage.

Estimate Blood Alcohol Concentration

The current BAC estimation calculators are based on the original equation developed by Widmark 80 years ago.[1] The estimation of BAC takes into account the amount of alcohol in a drink, the individual's metabolism rate of alcohol, the amount of body water (recall that males have more body water than females), and the time since alcohol was consumed and metabolized. In the equation below, use 7.5 for the gender constant for males and 9.0 for the gender constant for females. Body weight is in pounds (lbs), and 0.017 g/dl per hour is the average rate of alcohol metabolism.[2]

$$BAC = [(\text{\# of standard drinks} \div 2) \times (\text{gender constant} \div \text{body weight})] - (0.017 \times \text{hours})$$

Example #1: Calculate Mark's BAC if he weighs 175 lbs and drank three regular 12-ounce beers in 2 hours.

Mark's estimate of BAC:
$$= [(3 \div 2) \times (7.5 \div 175)] - (0.017 \times 2)$$
$$= [(1.5 \times 0.04)] - (0.03)$$
$$= 0.06 - 0.03$$
$$= 0.03$$

Does Mark's BAC indicate he would be legally impaired?

Example 2: Calculate Ruby's percent BAC if she weighs 120 lbs and drank three regular 12-ounce beers in 2 hours.

Ruby's estimate of BAC:
$$= [(3 \div 2) \times (9.0 \div 120)] - (0.017 \times 2)$$
$$= [(1.5 \times 0.075)] - (0.034)$$
$$= 0.11 - 0.034$$
$$= 0.08$$

Does Ruby's estimate of BAC indicate she would be legally impaired?

References

1. Widmark, E. M. P. 1932. *Principles and Applications of Medicolegal Alcohol Determination*, translated into English by R. C. Baselt, Department of Pathology, University of California, Davis, 1981, p. 163.
2. Hustad, J. T. P., and K. B. Carey. 2005. Using Calculations to Estimate Blood Alcohol Concentrations for Naturally Occurring Drinking Episodes: A Validity Study. *Journal of Studies on Alcohol* 66:130–138.

Scan this QR code with your mobile device to access practice math activities. You can also access the activities in MasteringNutrition™.

Gender, Genetics, and Ethnicity Affect Blood Alcohol Levels

When females consume the same amount of alcohol as men, they have a higher alcohol concentration in the blood, even when the difference in body size is taken into account. This is because women have about 20 to 30 percent less alcohol dehydrogenase (ADH) secreted from their gastric mucosa than men, so more ethanol enters the blood through a female's gastric lining. In essence, every alcoholic beverage that a male consumes is equivalent to about 1⅓ alcoholic beverages for a woman.

In addition to a reduced first-pass metabolism of alcohol in the stomach, women also have less muscle mass, and thus less body water, than men (recall that fat tissue has less water than muscle). Because alcohol mixes in water, muscular individuals are able to distribute more of the alcohol throughout their bodies than those who have more fat tissue and, consequently, less body water. So even if a woman is the same height and weight as a man, the female, drinking the same amount of alcohol, will have a higher concentration of alcohol in her blood than the male.

Because of these two factors—less gastric ADH and less body water in which to distribute the ingested alcohol—women feel alcohol's narcotic effects sooner than men. Women take note: Females can't keep up, drink for drink, with their male friends.

Genetics and ethnicity may also influence the effects of alcohol. There are several genes that code for ADH activity. These genes can have polymorphic changes that affect how quickly ADH metabolizes alcohol. People who carry the genetic polymorphisms may be at greater risk of feeling the effects of alcohol than those whose genes are not polymorphic.[12] Some ethnic groups, such as Asians, also have lower ADH activity levels and feel the effects of alcohol much sooner than Caucasians.[13]

LO 7.3: THE TAKE-HOME MESSAGE Alcohol is absorbed in the stomach and small intestine. Some alcohol is metabolized in the stomach by the enzyme alcohol dehydrogenase before it can be absorbed through the gastric mucosa. Alcohol is mainly metabolized in the liver by two enzyme systems. The initial pathway is controlled by alcohol dehydrogenase. This anaerobic pathway converts ethanol to acetate. The MEOS system kicks into play when too much alcohol is consumed and overwhelms alcohol dehydrogenase. Both enzyme pathways use the B vitamin niacin. Alcohol circulates in the blood until the liver metabolizes it. The blood alcohol concentration (BAC) is the amount of alcohol in the blood expressed as a percentage. A person's gender, genetics, ethnicity, and the amount of food and alcohol consumed affect the rate of absorption and metabolism in the body.

What Are the Immediate and Short-Term Effects of Alcohol Consumption on the Body?

LO 7.4 Describe the short-term effects of alcohol consumption on the body.

Alcohol can have many harmful effects on the body and the brain, caused mostly by the products of metabolism: acetaldehyde and acids. The more alcohol consumed, the more acetaldehyde is formed. These effects can be acute and short term, occurring while an individual is intoxicated, or they can occur within 72 hours following intoxication.

Alcohol is a toxin, and the body works quickly to eliminate it to avoid damage. Drinking in moderation allows the body time to eliminate the alcohol and to repair itself. Moderate drinkers probably will not experience short-term physiological consequences. In contrast, drinking in excess can have quick, dangerous physiological consequences, and also often puts personal safety at risk. However, even at low doses, alcohol can impair judgment and coordination.

Alcohol Affects the Brain

Alcohol is considered a *drug* because of its effects on the central nervous system and other systems of the body. Although many people think alcohol is a stimulant, because it has the effect of lowering inhibitions, it is actually a *depressant* of the central nervous system, which means it slows communication between neurons. The brain is part of the central nervous system and is very sensitive to alcohol, which can easily cross the blood–brain barrier. The depressant effect of alcohol on the brain is also what slows down a person's reaction time to stimuli (such as an oncoming car on the road) after drinking.

The more alcohol consumed, the more areas of the brain are affected. Look at **Figure 7.7** to see how increasing alcohol levels impact specific areas of the brain.

The area of the brain affected by alcohol first is the cerebral cortex, where you process information received from your senses, including sight, smell, and hearing. When alcohol reaches this part of the brain, individuals become more talkative and less inhibited, and have more confidence. The ability to think clearly or make good judgments is reduced. The higher the BAC, the more noticeable the effects.

The hippocampus, which is buried deep inside the forebrain and is responsible for memory, is affected next. Alcohol prevents short-term memories from becoming long-term memories and may result in "blacking out." Even a small amount of alcohol can make you forget what you were doing (or learning) while drinking. The hippocampus also controls emotions. As alcohol intake is increased, feelings such as sadness, aggressiveness, and withdrawal become exaggerated.

The cerebellum controls your balance and movements such as walking and talking. The more alcohol consumed, the more difficult it is to control body movements and speech. The result is the inability to stand, walk in a straight line, or speak clearly.

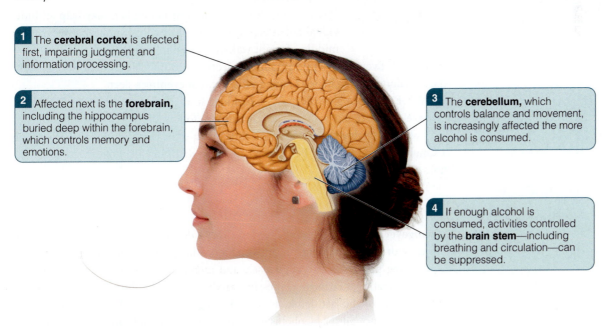

1 The **cerebral cortex** is affected first, impairing judgment and information processing.

2 Affected next is the **forebrain,** including the hippocampus buried deep within the forebrain, which controls memory and emotions.

3 The **cerebellum,** which controls balance and movement, is increasingly affected the more alcohol is consumed.

4 If enough alcohol is consumed, activities controlled by the **brain stem**—including breathing and circulation—can be suppressed.

▲ Figure 7.7 **The Brain and Alcohol**
As more alcohol is consumed, additional areas of the brain are affected. The cerebral cortex is affected first, followed by the forebrain, cerebellum, and brain stem. The greater the alcohol intake, the greater the physical and behavioral changes in the body.

If enough alcohol has been consumed, the activities of the brain stem, which controls breathing and circulation, can be suppressed, impairing breathing and heart rate and ultimately causing death. A particular area at the top of the brain stem, called the *reticular activating system* (RAS), controls whether an individual is awake or asleep. Excessive quantities of alcohol can shut down the RAS, causing unconsciousness. This reaction to excessive alcohol may be a beneficial mechanism that prevents drinking to the point that breathing and heart rate shut down.

Alcohol Poisoning

Drinking to excess without stopping, even when you feel the effects of alcohol, can result in alcohol poisoning even before you pass out. Alcohol in the stomach and intestines is still being absorbed into the bloodstream, raising BAC even after you've stopped drinking. Alcohol poisoning results when the BAC is so high that basic physiological functions, including breathing, heart rate, and the gag reflex, which prevents choking, are depressed. Alcohol irritates the stomach and can cause vomiting. Because the gag reflex is depressed, an unconscious person can choke on the vomit, leading to asphyxiation, which can result in death. Even if an individual survives alcohol poisoning, he or she can still experience lingering problems.

Drinking and driving can be deadly.

Unintentional Injuries

Deaths and injuries from car accidents, falls, assaults, and other non–chronic-disease-related events are not uncommon when an individual is intoxicated. Each year nearly 600,000 students between the ages of 18 and 24 are unintentionally injured because of drinking, and close to 700,000 are hit or assaulted by another intoxicated student.[14] Numerous instances of sexual abuse, unsafe sex, suicide attempts, drunk driving, and property damage also occur due to the influence of alcohol.[15] More than 1,800 students die each year as a result of drinking alcohol.[16]

Sleep Disruption

Having a drink within an hour before bed may help an individual fall asleep sooner, but it disrupts the sleep cycle, causes middle-of-night wakefulness, and makes returning to sleep a challenge.[17] Even a moderate amount of alcohol consumed at dinner or even late in the afternoon during happy hour can disrupt that evening's sleep.

After a poor night's sleep, it's a bad idea to drink alcohol the next day. Studies have shown that a night of sleep disruption followed by even small amounts of alcohol the next day reduces reaction time and alertness in individuals performing a simulated driving test.[18] Being tired and then drinking alcohol exacerbates alcohol's sedating effect.[19]

Alcohol Causes Hangovers

A **hangover** is the body's way of saying, "Don't do that to me again." After a bout of heavy drinking, individuals can experience hangover symptoms ranging from a pounding headache, fatigue, nausea, and increased thirst to a rapid heart beat, tremors, sweating, dizziness, depression, anxiety, and irritability. A hangover begins within hours of the last drink, as the BAC begins to drop. The symptoms appear in full force once all the alcohol is gone from the blood, and can linger for up to an additional 24 hours.[20] In other words, a few hours of excessive alcohol consumption on a Saturday night can not only ruin an entire Sunday, but even disrupt part of Monday morning.

hangover A collective term for the unpleasant symptoms, such as a headache and dizziness, that occur after drinking an excessive amount of alcohol; many of the symptoms are caused by high levels of acetaldehyde in the blood.

Alcohol causes the symptoms of a hangover in several ways. Acetaldehyde, the intermediate by-product of alcohol metabolism, is mildly toxic. In large enough amounts, acetaldehyde causes nausea, headache, fatigue, and irritability, all the symptoms of a hangover. But this is not the only cause of hangovers. Alcohol is also a diuretic, so it can cause dehydration, and thus, electrolyte imbalances. It inhibits the release of antidiuretic hormone from the pituitary gland, which in turn causes the kidneys to excrete water, as well as electrolytes, into the urine. Vomiting and sweating during or after excessive drinking contributes further to dehydration and electrolyte loss. Dehydration also increases thirst and can cause feelings of lightheadedness, dizziness, and weakness. Increased acid production in the stomach and secretions from the pancreas and intestines can cause stomach pain, nausea, and vomiting.

Staying hydrated by drinking water between alcoholic beverages can help you avoid the effects of a hangover.

Lastly, alcoholic beverages often contain compounds called **congeners.** Congeners include tannins found in wine or acetaldehyde formed during the metabolism of alcohol. Congeners can be produced during the fermentation process or be added during production of alcoholic beverages. This enhances their taste and appearance but may contribute to hangover symptoms. The greatest amounts of congeners are found in red wine and darker liquors such as tequila, brandy, or bourbon. Bourbon has more than forty times the quantity of congeners that vodka does. Combining alcoholic beverages that contain different levels of congeners can cause severe hangover symptoms. Drinking beer, which is carbonated, along with liquor that contains congeners speeds up the absorption of the alcohol, which gives the body less time to eliminate the congeners.

Forget the old wives' tale of consuming an alcoholic beverage to "cure" a hangover. Drinking more alcohol, even if it is mixed with tomato or orange juice, during a hangover only prolongs the recovery time. Nor do caffeine, hot showers, and long walks improve the symptoms. The only cure for a hangover is time.

Whereas aspirin and other nonsteroidal anti-inflammatory medications, such as ibuprofen, can ease a headache, these medications can also contribute to stomachache and nausea. Taking acetaminophen (Tylenol) during and after alcohol consumption, when the alcohol is being metabolized, has been shown to intensify this pain reliever's toxicity to the liver and may cause liver damage in some cases.[21] The best strategy for dealing with a hangover is to avoid it by limiting the amount of alcohol consumed.

> **LO 7.4: THE TAKE-HOME MESSAGE** Alcohol is a central nervous system depressant. Because the brain is sensitive to the effects of alcohol, alcohol affects brain function and behavior. Excessive drinking can cause alcohol poisoning and asphyxiation, leading to death. Alcohol can also result in unintentional injuries, disrupt your sleep, and cause hangovers.

What Are the Long-Term Effects of Alcohol Consumption on the Body?

LO 7.5 Describe the long-term effects of chronic alcohol consumption on the body.

The long-term effects of alcohol consumption are not completely understood. However, data suggests that alcohol abuse may result in malnutrition, affect metabolism and hormones, and increase the risk of developing depression, cardiovascular disease, and some cancers. **Figure 7.8** summarizes the many harmful effects of excessive drinking. The health consequences associated with abuse of and dependence upon alcohol are explored in Health Connection: What Are Alcohol Abuse and Alcoholism? on page 267.

congeners Fermentation by-products or additives in alcohol that may contribute to hangover symptoms.

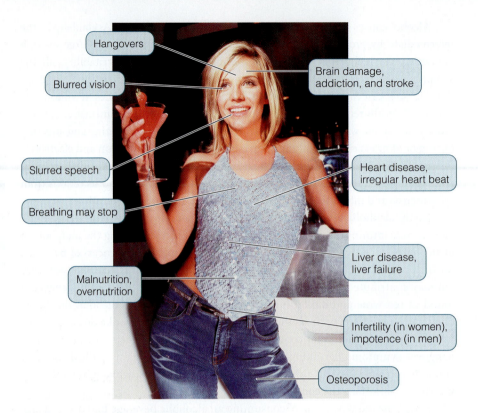

Hangovers

Blurred vision

Slurred speech

Breathing may stop

Malnutrition, overnutrition

Brain damage, addiction, and stroke

Heart disease, irregular heart beat

Liver disease, liver failure

Infertility (in women), impotence (in men)

Osteoporosis

▲ **Figure 7.8 Effects of Alcohol on the Body**
Consuming more than a moderate amount of alcohol leads to both short-term and long-term adverse health effects.

Alcohol Can Interfere with Digestion, Absorption, and Nutrition

Even if an individual consumes a healthy diet while consuming too much alcohol, the alcohol can interfere with the digestion and absorption of nutrients consumed. Individuals who drink heavily tend to eat poorly, and a major concern is that alcohol's effects on the digestion of food and use of nutrients may shift a mildly malnourished person toward severe malnutrition.

Impaired Digestion, Absorption, and Nutrient Metabolism

Chronic consumption of alcohol can lead to an inflamed esophagus, which reduces the effectiveness of the lower esophageal sphincter in contracting and preventing stomach acids from refluxing back into the esophagus. The more alcohol consumed, the more acid that can reflux and damage the lining of the esophagus.

Alcohol can inhibit chemical digestion of food by decreasing secretion of digestive enzymes from the pancreas, thereby inhibiting the breakdown of nutrients into usable molecules, for instance dietary triglycerides.[22] Because alcohol interferes with fat digestion, it also impairs the absorption and transport of fat-soluble vitamins. Alcohol also impairs nutrient absorption by damaging the cells lining the stomach and intestines and disabling transport of some nutrients into the blood. Nutritional deficiencies themselves may lead to further absorption problems. For example, folate deficiency alters the cells lining the small intestine, which in turn impairs absorption of water and other essential nutrients such as glucose, sodium, and vitamins, including vitamin B_{12}.[23] Heavy drinkers also have increased incidences of **gastritis** (*gastr* = stomach, *itis* = inflammation) and stomach ulcers,[24] which can impact digestion. Chronic consumption of alcohol can also cause pancreatitis, a painful inflammation of the pancreas, and reduce its ability to function properly.[25]

gastritis Inflammation of the lining in the stomach.

Malnutrition, Wernicke-Korsakoff Syndrome, and Weight Gain

Individuals who consume more than 30 percent of their daily kilocalories from alcohol over the long term often have some form of malnutrition. Their diets tend to be low in protein, fiber, vitamins A, C, D, riboflavin, and thiamin, and the minerals calcium and iron.[26] Because alcohol provides very little nutritional value, people who drink large amounts fuel their energy needs with alcohol rather than healthful energy sources. They cut nutritious foods from the diet, which means they can fall short of meeting their specific nutrient needs, and **primary malnutrition** may occur.

Excessive alcohol consumption can also interfere with nutrient metabolism even after the nutrients have been absorbed, resulting in **secondary malnutrition.** Alcohol can alter nutrient transport, storage, and excretion of a variety of nutrients, including protein, zinc, and magnesium, and the B vitamins thiamin, folate, and B_{12}, as well as the fat-soluble vitamins A, D, E, and K. Decreased liver stores of vitamins such as vitamin A, and increased excretion of nutrients such as fat in the feces, indicate impaired use of nutrients by alcoholics.

Alcoholism is the number-one cause of **Wernicke-Korsakoff syndrome,** a condition that includes mental confusion and uncontrolled muscle movement.[27] This syndrome is due to a thiamin deficiency that affects brain function, including memory loss. Thiamin helps the brain convert glucose to energy. When the levels of thiamin in the body fall too low, the brain can't generate enough energy to function. Alcoholics are at risk for thiamin deficiency because their diet is often poor in thiamin content and because chronic alcoholism reduces the absorption of thiamin and may reduce the activation of thiamin. While the actual mechanism by which Wernicke-Korsakoff syndrome manifests is unclear, the severe lack of thiamin may destroy brain cells and cause bleeding in the brain and scar tissue buildup.[28]

At 7 kilocalories per gram, alcohol provides almost as much energy as fat (9 kilocalories per gram) and more than either carbohydrates or protein (4 kilocalories per gram). On top of that, mixed drinks almost always contain more kilocalories than just those from the alcohol (**Table 7.2**). For example, a rum and coke contains the kilocalories from both the rum and the coke; the added coke almost triples the calories of the rum alone. In many mixed drinks, depending on the mixers and other ingredients, the kilocalorie count can approach that of a meal. The popular mudslide, for example, made with vodka, Irish cream, coffee liqueur, ice cream, and cream, should be ordered from the dessert menu and served with a spoon. If high-kilocalorie "bar foods" are consumed with the drinks, the kilocalories can add up rapidly (**Figure 7.9**).

Consistently adding extra kilocalories from alcoholic beverages—or any food or beverage source—to a diet that is already meeting daily energy needs will cause weight gain. However, epidemiological data from the National Health and Nutrition Examination Survey (NHANES) reported that alcohol consumption did not increase obesity.[29] In fact, in a 10-year follow-up study, people who consumed alcohol did not gain weight but rather had more stable weight than those who didn't drink alcohol.[30] Even consuming as much as two drinks or more a day did not appear to increase the risk of weight gain. However, other studies have reported weight gain, at least in college freshman males, associated with a higher intake of alcohol and kilocalories from other foods.[31] At this point, there is no clear relationship between drinking alcohol and an expanding waistline. Other factors, not just alcohol, may also be responsible for the weight gain.[32]

Interaction with Hormones

When individuals who overindulge in alcohol don't eat enough while they are drinking, their body's glucose stores can become depleted, and their blood glucose levels can fall. Typically, the hormones insulin and glucagon would automatically be

primary malnutrition A state of being malnourished due to poor diet, consuming either too much or too little of a nutrient or energy..

secondary malnutrition A state of being malnourished due to interference with nutrient absorption or metabolism.

Wernicke-Korsakoff syndrome A severe brain disorder associated with chronic excessive alcohol consumption; symptoms include vision changes, loss of muscle coordination, and loss of memory; the cause is a thiamin deficiency.

TABLE 7.2	Kilocalories in Selected Alcoholic Drinks

Beer

Serving size: 12 oz

Alcohol serving: 1

Kilocalories per drink: 150

Light beer

Serving size: 12 oz

Alcohol serving: 1

Kilocalories per drink: 110

Mudslide

Serving size: 12 oz

Alcohol servings: 4

Kilocalories per drink: 820

Distilled spirits (whiskey, vodka, gin, rum)

Serving size: 1.5 oz

Alcohol serving: 1

Kilocalories per drink: 100

Bloody Mary

Serving size: 5.5 oz

Alcohol serving: 1

Kilocalories per drink: 97

Red or white wine

Serving size: 5 oz

Alcohol serving: 1

Kilocalories per drink: 100–105

Margarita

Serving size: 6.3 oz

Alcohol servings: 3

Kilocalories per drink: 327

Cosmopolitan

Serving size: 2.5 oz

Alcohol servings: 1.7

Kilocalories per drink: 131

Rum and Coke

Serving size: 12 oz

Alcohol servings: 2.7

Kilocalories per drink: 361

Note: Alcohol servings are per beverage.

Source: Data from U.S. Department of Agriculture. 2010. *Dietary Guidelines for Americans, 2010*. Available at www.health.gov. Accessed March 2014.

Dinner 1

5 12-oz beers

1,719 total kilocalories

8 BBQ chicken wings

1 handful Goldfish crackers

1 large serving nachos with cheese

Total fat (g)	**51**
Saturated fat (g)	**16**
Cholesterol (mg)	**154**

Dinner 2

724 total kilocalories

2 oz whole-wheat dinner roll
4 tsp soft margarine

1 cup fat-free milk

4 oz grilled chicken breast
3/4 cup mashed potatoes
1 1/2 cups steamed carrots

28	Total fat (g)
8	Saturated fat (g)
89	Cholesterol (mg)

▲ **Figure 7.9 Too Much Alcohol Costs Good Nutrition**
A dinner of several alcoholic beverages and bar foods not only adds kilocalories, fat, and saturated fat to the diet, but displaces healthier foods that would provide better nutrition.

released to control blood glucose, but chronic alcohol consumption reduces insulin sensitivity and can result in hyperglycemia. Acute alcohol consumption, such as when binge drinking, has the opposite effect. In this case, insulin secretion is over-stimulated and can cause hypoglycemia. Because the brain needs glucose to function properly, a low blood glucose level can contribute to the feelings of fatigue, weakness, mood changes, irritability, and anxiety often experienced during a hangover.[33]

Alcohol can interfere with other hormones in addition to those that regulate blood glucose levels. Alcohol negatively affects parathyroid hormone and other bone-strengthening hormones, which can increase the risk of osteoporosis.[34] Alcohol can also increase estrogen levels in women, which may increase the risk of breast cancer.[35] Drinking alcohol can affect reproductive hormones and is associated with both male[36] and female sexual dysfunction and infertility.[37]

Alcohol Can Cause Liver Disease

The liver bears the brunt of the impact of overconsumption of alcohol, so it's not surprising that individuals who drink in excess over a long period of time are likely to develop **alcoholic liver disease,** a condition that kills more than 12,000 people each year.[38] The disease develops in three stages, although some stages can occur simultaneously.

Stage 1: The first stage is **fatty liver** (**Figure 7.10**), which can result from just a weekend or a few days of excessive drinking. Because alcohol metabolism takes top priority in the liver, the metabolism of other nutrients, including fats, takes a back seat to metabolizing alcohol.[39] The metabolic reactions of alcohol cause a buildup of the coenzymes NADH and NADP, which disrupts the breakdown of fatty acids for energy. Fatty acids that are not metabolized accumulate in the liver cells, resulting in fatty liver. The liver tries to reduce this accumulation of fatty acids by transporting them away from the liver into the blood. The result is *hyperlipidemia*—an excess of lipids in the blood, which contributes to atherosclerosis (see Chapter 5).

alcoholic liver disease A degenerative liver condition that occurs in three stages: (1) fatty liver, (2) alcoholic hepatitis, and (3) cirrhosis.

fatty liver Stage 1 of alcoholic liver disease, in which fat begins to build up in the liver cells.

▲ **Figure 7.10** **The Progression of Alcoholic Liver Disease**

As fat accumulates in the liver, the liver's ability to perform vital functions is impaired. For example, the liver can't make bile for fat digestion, produce proteins needed for blood clotting, or remove dangerous toxins from the blood. In addition, the hydrogen ions created during the conversion of ethanol to acetaldehyde and acetaldehyde to acetate lower the pH, making the liver more acidic. The good news is that at this stage a fatty liver can reverse itself *if* the alcohol consumption is stopped.

Stage 2: If the drinking doesn't stop, the second stage of liver disease, **alcoholic hepatitis,** can develop. In alcoholic hepatitis, the various by-products of alcohol metabolism, such as acetaldehyde and free radicals, irritate the liver. Acetaldehyde inhibits liver function, while free radicals damage cells by reacting with their proteins, lipids, and DNA. Nausea, vomiting, fever, jaundice, and loss of appetite are signs of alcoholic hepatitis. Chronic, excessive amounts of alcohol may also impair the immune system, which can contribute to liver damage and increase the susceptibility to infectious diseases.

Heavy drinking can also cause the increased passage of destructive **endotoxins,** found in the cell walls of bacteria that live in your intestines, into the blood. Once an endotoxin arrives in the liver, it stimulates the release of substances called **cytokines** that further damage healthy liver cells. Studies have reported that alcoholics have elevated levels of endotoxins in their blood, which may lead to further liver damage and eventually alcoholic hepatitis.[40]

Alcoholic hepatitis can last for years before progressing to the most serious stage of liver disease. If someone is diagnosed with alcoholic hepatitis, alcohol use must cease to reverse this condition or, in more advanced cases, prevent it from progressing to cirrhosis.

Stage 3: As many as 70 percent of individuals with alcoholic hepatitis develop **cirrhosis,** the final stage of alcoholic liver disease.[41] Cirrhosis occurs with continued bouts of heavy drinking, as chronic inflammation further injures and kills the liver cells and causes more scarring. The scar tissue prevents the liver from performing critical metabolic roles, such as filtering toxins and waste products in the blood and out of the body. If toxins and waste products build up, it can lead to mental confusion, nausea, tremors or shakiness, and even coma.

alcoholic hepatitis Stage 2 of alcoholic liver disease, in which the liver becomes inflamed.

endotoxins Damaging products produced by intestinal bacteria that travel in the blood to the liver and initiate the release of cytokines.

cytokines Substances that damage liver cells and lead to scarring.

cirrhosis Stage 3 of alcoholic liver disease, in which liver cells die and are replaced by scar tissue.

By the time scar tissue develops, the liver is permanently damaged, and only a liver transplant will cure the condition. Cirrhosis is the second leading cause of the need for liver transplants in the United States; liver damage due to hepatitis C virus is the most common reason. The survival rate for those with cirrhosis is grim: More than 50 percent of individuals with the condition die within four years.[42]

Alcohol and Depression

Have you ever thought about having a beer or glass of wine after failing an exam or getting in an argument? As you learned earlier in the chapter, moderate alcohol consumption can calm the brain. While an occasional beer or glass of wine may relax you, research suggests that using alcohol to deal with problems may be a sign of alcohol abuse.[43]

Alcohol use, especially excessive alcohol consumption, may result in depression. This theory has been reported mainly from observational studies in which the more alcohol consumed, the greater the depression. For example, one study reported that 43 percent of patients who were classified as alcoholics were clinically depressed. But when these patients were abstinent, only six percent remained depressed after four weeks.[44]

Whether alcohol consumption causes depression, or you drink because you're depressed is still unclear. Some researchers report that the relationship between alcohol ingestion and depression is probably explained by other factors, such as your genetic makeup, rather than the alcohol itself.[45] It is the variation of your genes that may put you at risk of developing depression with greater alcohol consumption. These researchers also concluded that a glass of wine or beer once in a while might actually reduce the risk of developing depression.[46] But you may want to reconsider that drink if you're using alcohol to cope with everyday stresses.

Alcohol and Cardiovascular Disease

Alcohol has both favorable and adverse effects on the risks associated with cardiovascular disease (CVD). Higher intakes of alcohol (more than three drinks per day) can increase the risk of developing or dying from cardiovascular disease.[47] Studies have reported that alcohol may stimulate the synthesis of cholesterol in the liver, which increases blood lipids such as cholesterol.[48]

Drinking more than two drinks a day is considered an important determinant of hypertension. The Nurses' Health Study reported that adult women between 30 and 55 years of age who drank more than 20 grams of alcohol per day (about two drinks) had an increase in hypertension.[49] In fact, compared with nondrinkers, both men and women drinking six to eight drinks in one day had increased systolic blood pressure of more than 9 mm Hg, and their diastolic blood pressure went up more than 5 mm Hg.[50]

Excessive amounts of alcohol can trigger a **cardiac arrhythmia,** which likely plays a role in the sudden deaths of some alcoholics.[51] In addition, alcohol can cause **cardiac myopathy,** a condition in which the heart enlarges and becomes weak, thin, and unable to pump blood effectively throughout the body. Excessive drinking plus a poor diet can result in heart failure over time.

Moderate alcohol intake (up to three drinks a day) may have the opposite effect and lower CVD risk by increasing the levels of HDL cholesterol, decreasing LDL cholesterol and lipoprotein(a), and/or reducing clot formations in both men and women.[52] For more information on the possible health benefits of moderate alcohol intake, see the Examining the Evidence feature on page 264.

Alcohol Contributes to Cancer Risk

In addition to the damaging effects of alcohol on the liver, heart, esophagus, and pancreas, alcohol consumption contributes to the risk of developing cancers, including cancers of the mouth, esophagus, liver, colon or rectum, and breast. Cancer

cardiac arrhythmia A disturbance in the beating and rhythm of the heart; can be caused by excessive alcohol consumption.

cardiac myopathy Condition in which the heart becomes thin and weak and is unable to pump blood throughout the body; also called disease of the heart muscle.

Does Moderate Alcohol Consumption Provide Health Benefits?

The popular press is notorious for publishing frequent reports on the health benefits of alcohol. Consumers, however, need to proceed with caution. The benefits from drinking moderate amounts of alcohol are not endorsed by the medical community because most, but not all, of the evidence supporting the beneficial effects is epidemiological in nature.[1] Epidemiological evidence does not prove cause and effect but shows a pattern of health effects when moderate alcohol is consumed. In addition, alcohol consumption is not endorsed because of the potential risks associated with drinking in excess.

Are the benefits due to the natural compounds found in certain types of alcoholic beverages? Wine contains the same polyphenol, resveratrol, that is found in grapes and purple grape juice. Large amounts of resveratrol and other polyphenols are found in the skins of the grape, and the bark, leaves, and twigs of the grapevine. When red wine is produced, the grape skins and other parts of the plant are included in the fermentation process. This is in contrast to white wine, which is fermented without the skins. Liquor, such as tequila or whiskey, is distilled, which removes the polyphenols. Resveratrol and the other polyphenols in red wine are powerful antioxidants that neutralize free radicals and are associated with reduced risk for heart disease and cancer.

Though its nutrient content is still negligible, beer contains more protein and B vitamins (B_6 and folate) than wine, and a similar amount of antioxidants.[2] The type of flavonoid differs, however, because beer is made from barley and hops and wine is made mostly from grapes. Beer also contains more kilocalories and carbohydrates than wine.

While beer and wine contain healthful compounds, is alcohol in general beneficial for health?

Alcohol May Reduce Cardiovascular Risk in Older Adults

Since the 1990s, researchers have explored the possible relationship between wine consumption and heart disease. They have been trying to get to the bottom of the "French Paradox." The French, even though they eat as much saturated fat as Americans, still have lower rates of heart disease.[3] They also drink more red wine than Americans do, which is thought to be the differentiating factor. However, the French also consume fewer *trans* fats and have a less stressful lifestyle and better-developed social networks, which can also contribute to their impressively lower risk of heart disease.[4]

Scientists report that drinking moderate amounts of alcohol, especially red wine, appears to reduce the incidence of heart disease (see **Figure 1**). The lowest risk for heart disease is reported to be associated with drinking one to two drinks, or 12.5 to 25 grams of alcohol, per day as compared to zero or more than two drinks per day.[5] This may be due to the effect that a moderate intake of red wine has on lowering hypertension. The greatest benefit in reducing blood pressure was seen with one 5-ounce glass per day for females and two glasses per day for men.[6] At higher intakes, blood pressure increases, and the larger the dose, the higher the blood pressure. Moderate intakes of red wine also may lower LDL cholesterol and raise HDL cholesterol, reduce the stickiness of platelets, which lowers the chance of blood clots, and reduce inflammation.[7] These benefits are not linear, however, but rather J shaped. A J-shaped relationship means that low to moderate amounts of alcohol may reduce cardiovascular risk, but higher intakes actually increase risk.

Age may play a factor in the health benefits of alcohol. Until recently, it was believed that people who gain health benefits from moderate alcohol consumption were women aged 55 and older

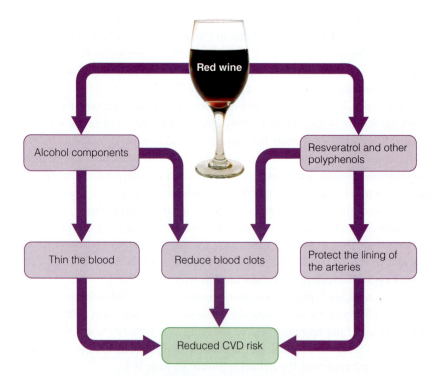

▲ **Figure 1 How Red Wine May Affect the Risk of Cardiovascular Disease**
Red wine contains phenolic compounds that appear to be beneficial by reducing LDL oxidation; the alcohol itself affects the risk of CVD by thinning the blood.
Adapted from S. D. Wollin and P. J. H. Jones. 2001. "Alcohol, Red Wine and Cardiovascular Disease." *Journal of Nutrition* 131:1401–1404.

and men aged 45 and older, but another study suggests that women as young as 45 may also benefit.[8] For people younger than 45, no beneficial effects have been found.[9] In fact, drinking heavily in college may lead to heart disease later in life.[10]

Moderate Consumption May Reduce the Risk of Diabetes and Metabolic Syndrome

In studies involving individuals with diabetes, moderate alcohol intake has been shown to increase insulin sensitivity,[11] and does not appear to adversely affect glycemic control, at least in type 2 diabetes. However, these studies do not prove cause and effect. People with diabetes who consume alcohol should limit consumption to one (for women) or two (for men) drinks per day and be sure to drink alcohol with a meal to reduce the risk of hypoglycemia. For those who have been diagnosed with type 1 diabetes, alcohol ingestion of greater than three drinks per day may actually reduce blood glucose levels into dangerously low levels or hypoglycemia.[12]

Alcohol consumption and its effects on metabolic syndrome are related to the amount of alcohol consumed. An analysis of more than 28,000 participants reported that light alcohol intake of less than 10 grams of alcohol per day, or the amount in about 4.5 ounces of wine, was significantly related to a lower risk for metabolic syndrome.[13] Heavy drinking (greater than 35 grams of alcohol per day) increased the risk.

Moderate Consumption Is Associated with Longevity

Older moderate drinkers appear to live longer. In fact, the lowest death rate from any cause has been reported in those who drink one to two drinks per day.[14] Meta-analysis research that reviewed 34 studies and over a million older adults from countries around the world reported that one to two drinks per day for women and two to four drinks per day for men increased life expectancy by two years when compared with mortality risk for

those who don't drink at all.[15] The other side of the spectrum tells a different story. Alcohol abuse is the leading risk factor for premature death.[16]

The type of alcoholic beverage that increases longevity is still unclear. Although not all health professionals agree, the results in the meta-analysis suggest that living longer is more closely related to wine than liquor.[17] This may be due to the fact that the health benefits of wine have been studied the most. Convincing evidence suggests that red wine and beer may both have some health benefits. For example, when red and white wine, beer, and liquor were compared, red wine and dark-colored beer showed the most health protection. Liquor, on the other hand, did not.[18] Liquor or spirits, but not wine or beer, appear to relate more to cirrhosis, heart disease, and head and neck cancer mortality.[19] Researchers suggested this was probably because liquor is distilled, thus it does not contain polyphenols, which appear to be the compounds in alcoholic beverages that contribute to the reduction of cardiovascular risk.

The bottom line is, if you don't drink alcohol, don't start. If you do consume

alcohol, regardless of whether it is beer, wine, or distilled liquor, be sure to drink no more than one drink per day if you are a female and no more than two drinks per day if you are a male.

References

1. E. K. Howie, X. Sui, D. Lee, S. P. Hooker, J. R. Hebert, and S. N. Blair. 2011. "Alcohol Consumption and Risk of All-Cause and Cardiovascular Disease Mortality in Men." *Journal of Aging Research* doi:10.4061/2011/805062.
2. B. Hansel, R. Roussel, V. Diguet, et al. 2013. "Relationships between Consumption of Alcoholic Beverages and Healthy Foods: The French Supermarket Cohort of 196,000 Subjects." *European Journal of Preventive Cardiology* doi: 10.1177/2047487313506829.
3. S. Vendrame. 2013. "The French Paradox: Was It Really the Wine?" *American Society for Nutrition.* Available at www.nutrition .org. Accessed March 2014.
4. Ibid.
5. D. E. King, A. G. Mainous, and M. E. Geesey. 2008. "Adopting Moderate Alcohol Consumption in Middle Age: Subsequent Cardiovascular Events." *American Journal of Medicine* 121:201–206.
6. J. Chick, 1998. "Alcohol, Health, and the Heart: Implications for Clinicians." *Alcohol and Alcoholism* 33:576–591.
7. A. E. Barden, K. D. Croft, L. J. Beilin, M. Phillips, T. Ledowski, and I. B. Puddey. 2013. "Acute Effects of Red Wine on Cytochrome P450 Eicosanoids and Blood Pressure in Men." *Journal of Hypertension* 31(11):2195–2202.
8. King, et al. 2008. "Adopting Moderate Alcohol Consumption."
9. Ibid.
10. R. A. Vogel. 2013. "Binge Drinking and Vascular Function: A Sober Look at the Data." *Journal of the American College of Cardiology* 62(3):208–209.
11. M. L. Wheeler, M. J. Franz, and J. C. Froehlich. 2004. "Alcohol Consumption and Type 2 Diabetes." *DOC News* 1:7.
12. K. Desjardins, A. S. Brazeau, I. Strychar, and R. Rabasa-Lhoret. 2013. "Are Bedtime Nutritional Strategies Effective in Preventing Nocturnal Hypoglycaemia in Patients with Type 1 Diabetes?" *Diabetes Obesity Metabolism* doi:10.1111/dom.12232.
13. K. Sun, M. Ren, D. Liu, C. Wang, C. Yang, and L. Yan. 2013. "Alcohol Consumption and Risk of Metabolic Syndrome: A Meta-Analysis of Prospective Studies." *Clinical Nutrition* doi:10.1016/j.clnu.2013.10.003.
14. L. Baglietto, D. R. English, J. L. Hopper, J. Powles, and G. G. Giles. 2006. "Average Volume of Alcohol Consumed, Type of Beverage, Drinking Pattern and the Risk of Death from All Causes." *Alcohol and Alcoholism* 46:664–671.
15. Ibid.
16. J. H. O'Keefe, S. K. Bhatti, A. Bajwa, J. J. Dinicolantonio, and C. J. Lavie. 2014. "Alcohol and Cardiovascular Health: The Dose Makes the Poison . . . or the Remedy." *Mayo Clinical Proceedings* 89(3):382–393.
17. L. Baglietoo, et al. 2006. "Average Volume of Alcohol Consumed."
18. L. B. Mann and J. D. Folts. 2004. "Effects of Ethanol and Other Constituents of Alcoholic Beverages on Coronary Heart Disease: A Review." *Pathophysiology* 10:105–112.
19. W. C. Kerr and Y. Ye. 2011. "Beverage-Specific Mortality Relationships in U.S. Population Data." *Contemporary Drug Problems* 38(4):561–578.

of the mouth is six times greater in people who drink alcohol. Individuals who smoke while drinking alcohol increase their chances of developing esophageal cancer, as well as mouth and throat cancer, as the alcohol exacerbates the cancer-causing effects of cigarettes.[53] Alcohol is the primary cause of liver cancer, which is often preceded by cirrhosis of the liver.[54] Breast cancer studies have shown a relationship to alcohol intake.[55] The more alcohol consumed, the greater the risk. A meta-analysis suggests that there is a link between drinking more than one alcoholic beverage a day and colorectal cancer.[56]

How alcohol contributes to cancer is not well understood, but it probably relates to the toxic effects of acetaldehyde.[57] Research is currently being conducted to test whether or not folate supplements may reduce cancer risk in those who consume alcohol.

Alcohol Can Put a Pregnancy at Risk

When a pregnant woman drinks, she is never drinking alone—her fetus becomes her drinking partner. Alcohol easily crosses the placenta and enters the bloodstream of the fetus through the umbilical cord. Because the baby is developing, the alcohol isn't metabolized in its underdeveloped organs as quickly as in the mother's body. This results in the baby's BAC becoming higher and staying higher longer than the mother's, potentially causing serious damage to its central nervous system, particularly the brain. Because researchers do not fully understand when alcohol ingestion might be safe, zero alcohol ingestion during pregnancy is the only safe approach to ensure zero risk for the fetus.

Ultimately, a child exposed to alcohol in utero may be born with **fetal alcohol syndrome (FAS)** and exhibit numerous debilitating symptoms, including facial abnormalities such as eyes with very small openings and thin upper lips (**Figure 7.11**). They may not physically grow as normally as other children their age, and they are likely to have mental and behavioral difficulties, such as reduced attention span and memory, and learning disabilities.[58]

FAS is the most common and preventable cause of mental retardation and birth defects in the United States.[59] Children with FAS often have problems in school and in interacting socially with others, poor coordination, low IQ, and problems with everyday living. Approximately 4 million infants each year in the United States experience prenatal exposure to alcohol, and an estimated 12,000 babies are born with FAS.[60]

fetal alcohol syndrome (FAS) The most severe of the fetal alcohol spectrum disorders (FASDs); children with FAS display physical, mental, and behavioral abnormalities.

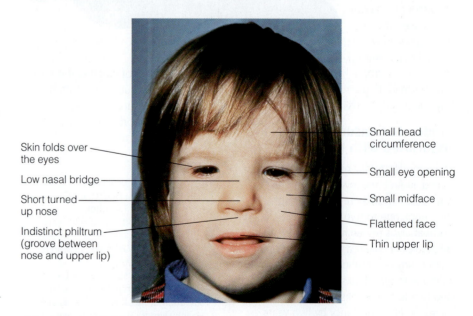

Skin folds over the eyes

Low nasal bridge

Short turned up nose

Indistinct philtrum (groove between nose and upper lip)

Small head circumference

Small eye opening

Small midface

Flattened face

Thin upper lip

▲ Figure 7.11 Fetal Alcohol Syndrome
Children born with fetal alcohol syndrome often have facial abnormalities.

Recently a newer term, **fetal alcohol spectrum disorders (FASDs),** which includes FAS, has been adopted by major health organizations to describe a wide range of conditions that can occur in children exposed to alcohol in utero.[61] Not all children exposed to alcohol during pregnancy experience *all* of the physical, mental, and behavioral abnormalities seen in FAS, which is the severe end of the FASDs. However, no matter the degree of abnormalities, FASDs are permanent. The only proven, safe amount of alcohol a pregnant woman can consume is *none*. Women should avoid alcohol if they think they are, or could become, pregnant.

> **LO 7.5: THE TAKE-HOME MESSAGE** Long-term consequences of excessive alcohol consumption can include damage to the digestive organs, heart, and liver; malnutrition and weight gain; hormone imbalances; increased risk of cancer and heart disease, depression, and irreversible damage to a developing fetus during pregnancy. Individuals with alcoholic liver disease can experience a fatty liver and deterioration of the liver that develops into alcohol-related hepatitis and cirrhosis.

fetal alcohol spectrum disorders (FASDs) A range of conditions that can occur in children who are exposed to alcohol in utero.

What Are Alcohol Abuse and Alcoholism?

LO 7.6 Summarize the methods used to diagnose and treat alcohol abuse and alcoholism.

When people choose not to drink alcohol responsibly, they often end up abusing alcohol or suffering from a full-blown addiction. **Alcohol abuse** begins when a person allows alcohol to interfere with his or her life. He may have to call in sick to work or school due to a hangover, or she may have blank spots in her memory due to intoxication. At the extreme end of the spectrum is the disease of **alcoholism.** By the time a person is addicted to alcohol, he or she is no longer in control of drinking habits and is at serious risk of suffering long-term health damage. Approximately 17 percent of regular drinkers either abuse or are addicted to alcohol.[62]

Forms of Alcohol Abuse

When people continue to consume alcohol even though the behavior has created social, legal, and/or health problems for them, they are abusing alcohol. These problems can include binge drinking, driving while under the influence of alcohol, and underage drinking.

Binge Drinking

Binge drinking occurs when a male consumes five or more drinks and when a woman consumes four or more drinks in about two hours.[63]

Binge drinkers, the incidence of which is highest in individuals 18 to 24 years of age, report binge drinking more than four times per month and consuming 7.9 drinks each time they binge.[64] College students who binge drink are more likely to miss classes, have hangovers, and experience unintentional injuries such as falling, motor vehicle accidents, and drowning, and may even die (see **Figure 7.12**).[65] Research also indicates that binge drinkers engage in more unplanned sexual activity and fail to use safe-sex strategies more frequently than non–binge drinkers.[66] Sexual aggression and assaults on campus increase when drinking enters the picture. Alcohol is involved with over 70 percent of the reported rapes of women on college campuses;[67] victims are often too drunk to consent to or refuse the actions of the other person.

Binge drinking is associated with many health problems, such as hypertension, heart attack, sexually transmitted infection, suicide, homicide, and child abuse. Binge drinking can also cause **blackouts,** which are periods of time that a person cannot remember, even though he or she may have been conscious. A research study of over 700 college students found that more than half of them had blacked out from alcohol consumption at least once in their lives, and many found out after the fact that they had taken part in activities such as vandalism, unprotected sex, and driving a motor vehicle during the blackout period.[68]

Binge drinking can lead to **alcohol poisoning,** as alcohol depresses the

alcohol abuse Continuing to consume alcohol even though the behavior has created social, legal, and/or health problems.

alcoholism A chronic disease characterized by craving for and elevated tolerance to alcohol, inability to control alcohol intake, and dependency on alcohol to prevent withdrawal symptoms; also referred to as *alcohol dependence.*

binge drinking The consumption of five or more alcoholic drinks by men, or four or more drinks by women, in about two hours.

blackouts Periods of time when an intoxicated person cannot recall part or all of an event.

alcohol poisoning When the BAC rises to the point that a person's central nervous system is affected and his or her breathing and heart rate are interrupted.

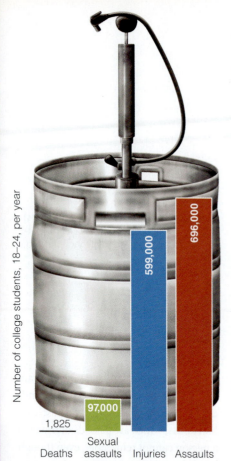

▲ **Figure 7.12 Consequences of College Binge Drinking**
Alcohol use by college students results in numerous assaults, injuries, and deaths each year.
National Institute on Alcohol Abuse and Alcoholism, based on information from R. Hingson, et al. 2005. "Magnitude of Alcohol-Related Mortality and Morbidity Among U.S. College Students Ages 18–24: Changes from 1998 to 2001." *Annual Review of Public Health* 26: 259–279.

nerves involved in numerous actions in the body, such as breathing and heart rate. The stomach and intestine continue to absorb alcohol and the BAC continues to rise even after an individual passes out.

Drinking and Driving

In the United States in 2010, more than 10,000 people died in automobile accidents that involved an alcohol-impaired driver.[69] Driving in the United States with a BAC of 0.08 or higher is illegal (some states in the United States have set their legal limit even lower), but the level of alcohol in the blood doesn't need to get that high to impair driving. Even the lowest level of BAC, the level that occurs after one alcoholic beverage, impairs alertness, judgment, and coordination (see Table 7.3).

Underage Drinking

The average age of the first drink for Americans from 12 to 20 years of age is 14.[70] By the time they graduate from high school, over 30 percent of teenagers are binge drinking at least once a month. Underage drinking not only increases the risk of violence, injuries, and other health risks as discussed earlier, but alcohol consumption at this age can also interfere with brain development and lead to permanent cognitive and memory damage in teenagers.

TABLE 7.3	Progressive Effects of Alcohol		
Blood Alcohol Concentration	**Changes in Feelings and Personality**	**Brain Regions Affected**	**Impaired Functions (continuum)**
0.01–0.05	Relaxation, sense of well-being, loss of inhibition	Cerebral cortex	Alertness; judgment
0.06–0.10	Pleasure, numbing of feelings, nausea, sleepiness, emotional arousal	Cerebral cortex and forebrain	Coordination (especially fine motor skills); visual tracking
0.11–0.20	Mood swings, anger, sadness, mania	Cerebral cortex, forebrain, and cerebellum	Reasoning and depth perception; appropriate social behavior
0.21–0.30	Aggression, reduced sensations, depression, stupor	Cerebral cortex, forebrain, cerebellum, and brain stem	Speech; balance; temperature regulation
0.31–0.40	Unconsciousness, coma, death possible	Entire brain	Bladder control; breathing
0.41 and greater	Death		Heart rate

Source: National Institute on Alcohol Abuse and Alcoholism. 2003. *Understanding Alcohol: Investigations into Biology and Behavior.* Available at http://science.education.nih.gov. Accessed March 2014.

There is another danger in consuming alcohol at a young age. The earlier a person starts drinking, the higher the chances that alcohol will become a problem later in life. A person who starts drinking at age 15 is four times more likely to suffer from alcoholism than an individual who doesn't start drinking until age 20.[71]

Drinking games can result in extreme intoxication.

Alcoholism Is a Disease

A person who suffers from alcoholism exhibits four classic symptoms of the disease; he or she:

1. Craves alcohol
2. Has developed a higher tolerance for it
3. Can't control or limit his or her intake once drinking starts
4. Has developed a dependency on alcohol—if the person stops drinking, withdrawal symptoms begin

An alcoholic's craving, loss of control, and physical dependence distinguishes him or her as an "alcoholic" rather than a person who abuses alcohol but doesn't have these three other characteristics.

A family history of alcoholism—for example, you may have a father and grandfather who both died of cirrhosis due to alcoholism and a brother who drinks heavily—puts a person at a higher than average risk for alcoholism. Research has shown that approximately 50 percent of the risk for alcoholism is determined genetically.[72] However, this genetic risk alone does not mean that an individual is destined to become an alcoholic. A person's risk for alcoholism is also influenced by his or her environment. Home life, the drinking habits of family and friends, social pressures, and access to alcohol all impact whether a person develops the disease. If a person's roommate and friends drink heavily, and he or she works part-time as a bartender, that person is more likely to develop alcoholism. If she chooses to surround herself with acquaintances and a lifestyle that don't focus on alcohol, she can reduce her risk of following in her grandfather's, father's, and brother's footsteps.

There is no cure for alcoholism. However, it can be treated using a combined physical and psychological approach. The physical symptoms, such as the severe craving for alcohol, can be treated with medication that helps reduce the craving. Psychologically, self-help therapies and support groups can be invaluable to an alcoholic on the road to recovery. Because alcoholics can't limit their consumption once they start drinking, reducing the amount of alcohol consumed will not work for them. To recover successfully, they must eliminate alcohol entirely from their lives.

Self-Assessment

Red Flags for Alcohol Abuse

Complete the following self-assessment to see if you may be at increased risk for alcohol abuse.

1. Do you fail to fulfill major work, school, or home responsibilities because of your consumption of alcohol?

Yes ☐ **No** ☐

2. Do you drink in situations that are potentially dangerous, such as while driving a car or operating heavy machinery?

Yes ☐ **No** ☐

3. Do you experience repeated alcohol-related legal problems, such as being arrested for driving while intoxicated?

Yes ☐ **No** ☐

4. Do you have relationship problems that are caused or made worse by alcohol?

Yes ☐ **No** ☐

5. Do you try to hide your alcohol consumption from family or friends because you know they will tell you to stop?

Yes ☐ **No** ☐

Answers

If you answered "yes" to any of these questions, you should speak with your health care provider. You may benefit from an alcohol abstinence program, or other guidance.

Adapted from Recovery Through Support.Com. 2010. Available at www.recoverythroughsupport.com. Accessed May 2014.

LO 7.6: THE TAKE-HOME MESSAGE

Individuals who abuse alcohol by binge drinking, drinking and driving, and underage drinking are putting themselves and others at risk of injuries, violence, and even death. Alcoholism is a disease that can't be cured, but it can be treated with medical help and psychological support. People who are addicted to alcohol need to abstain from drinking it entirely.

Visual Chapter Summary

LO 7.1 Alcohol Is Produced by Fermentation of Sugars

Ethanol is the type of alcohol in alcoholic beverages. In beer and wine production, alcohol is produced by the fermentation of sugars by yeast. In liquor, distillation is used to concentrate the alcohol produced by fermentation. Alcohol is not a nutrient, having very little nutritional value, but it does provide kilocalories.

```
        H
        |
    H — C — H
        |
    H — C — H
        |
       [OH]
      Ethanol
```

LO 7.2 People Drink Alcohol to Relax, Celebrate, and Socialize

Alcohol produces an initial euphoric, pleasurable state of mind. Adults drink alcohol to relax, celebrate, and socialize. A standard drink (1/2 ounce of alcohol) is equal to 12 ounces of beer, 5 ounces of wine, or 1.5 ounces of liquor. For adults who choose to drink, moderate alcohol consumption is up to one drink daily for women and up to two drinks daily for men.

LO 7.3 Alcohol Is Absorbed in the Stomach and Small Intestine, Metabolized in the Stomach and Liver, and Circulated by the Blood

Some alcohol is absorbed into the bloodstream directly in the stomach, but most alcohol is absorbed in the small intestine. Alcohol mixes with water and is distributed in the watery tissues of the body. Some of the alcohol remains in the blood and is continually circulated in the fluid portions of the body until it is finally metabolized. The amount of alcohol in a person's blood is called blood alcohol content, or BAC, and is stated as a percentage of the weight of alcohol per volume of blood. A person's gender, age, ethnicity, the amount of food in the stomach, and the quantity of alcohol consumed affect the rate of absorption and metabolism in the body. Some alcohol in the blood is lost in the breath and urine.

Some alcohol is metabolized in the stomach before it is absorbed. However, most of the alcohol is metabolized in the liver by the enzymes alcohol dehydrogenase (ADH) and acetaldehyde dehydrogenase (ALDH). The microsomal ethanol oxidizing system (MEOS) is a secondary pathway that takes over when the ADH pathway is overwhelmed. MEOS is also the primary pathway for drugs and pharmaceuticals, but alcohol takes precedence over these substances.

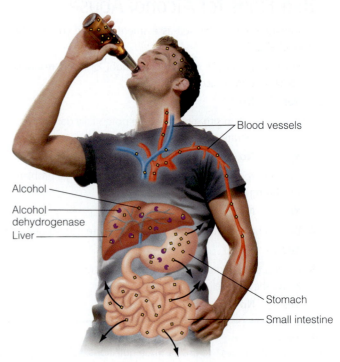

Blood vessels

Alcohol

Alcohol dehydrogenase

Liver

Stomach

Small intestine

LO 7.4 Alcohol Has Immediate and Short-Term Effects on the Body

Alcohol is a central nervous system depressant. The brain's cerebral cortex, forebrain, cerebellum, and brain stem are sensitive to the effects of alcohol, and, depending on the amount consumed, alcohol can cause numerous mental, behavioral, and physical changes in the body. Alertness, judgment, and coordination are initially affected. Higher BACs can cause impaired vision, speech, reasoning, and balance. Alcohol poisoning (usually at a BAC of 0.30 or higher) can result in impaired breathing and heart rate, and can ultimately lead to death. Alcohol can lead to unintentional injuries, disrupted sleep, and hangovers.

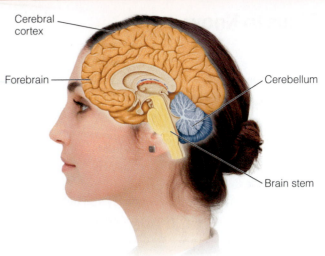

Cerebral cortex

Forebrain

Cerebellum

Brain stem

LO 7.5 Excessive Alcohol Consumption Can Result in Damage to the Body and Offspring

Excess alcohol can interfere with digestion, absorption, and hormone function. Alcohol can contribute to excess kilocalorie intake and displace healthier food choices from the diet. Chronically consuming excessive amounts of alcohol can harm the digestive organs, heart, and liver, can lead to heart disease and cancer, and may increase the risk of depression in genetically predisposed individuals. Alcohol can put a fetus at risk for fetal alcohol spectrum disorders.

The liver is damaged from excess alcohol consumption. The three stages of alcoholic liver disease are fatty liver, alcoholic hepatitis, and cirrhosis.

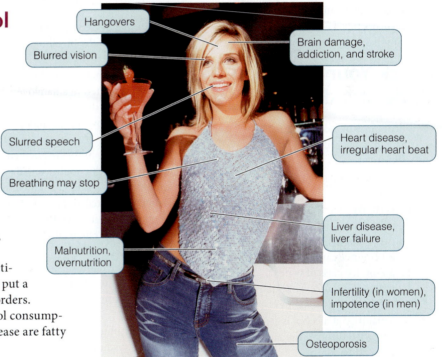

Hangovers

Blurred vision

Slurred speech

Breathing may stop

Brain damage, addiction, and stroke

Heart disease, irregular heart beat

Liver disease, liver failure

Malnutrition, overnutrition

Infertility (in women), impotence (in men)

Osteoporosis

LO 7.6 Alcohol Abuse and Alcoholism Negatively Affect One's Life and Health

Alcohol abuse, such as binge drinking, underage drinking, and drinking and driving, occurs when people continue to consume alcohol even though this behavior negatively affects their lives. Individuals who binge drink are at risk for blackouts and alcohol poisoning. Alcoholism is a disease characterized by four symptoms: a craving for alcohol, a higher tolerance for alcohol, the inability to control or limit its intake, and a physical dependence on it. Though alcoholism can't be cured, it can be treated with medical and psychological support.

Terms to Know

- alcohol
- ethanol
- fermentation
- distillation
- proof
- social drinking
- moderate drinking
- alcohol dehydrogenase (ADH)
- acetaldehyde
- acetaldehyde dehydrogenase (ALDH)
- microsomal ethanol oxidizing system (MEOS)
- alcohol tolerance
- microsomes
- blood alcohol concentration (BAC)
- hangover
- congeners
- gastritis
- primary malnutrition
- secondary malnutrition
- Wernicke-Korsakoff syndrome
- alcoholic liver disease
- fatty liver
- alcoholic hepatitis
- endotoxins
- cytokines
- cirrhosis
- cardiac arrhythmia
- cardiac myopathy
- fetal alcohol syndrome (FAS)
- fetal alcohol spectrum disorders (FASDs)
- alcohol abuse
- alcoholism
- binge drinking
- blackouts
- alcohol poisoning

MasteringNutrition™

Build your knowledge—and confidence!— in the Study Area of MasteringNutrition with a variety of study tools.

Check Your Understanding

1. Alcohol, also known as ethanol, is made by the process known as
   a. distillation.
   b. fermentation.
   c. malting.
   d. germination.
2. Which of the following is *not* considered a standard drink?
   a. a 12-ounce can of beer
   b. a 7-ounce glass of wine
   c. a shot (1.5 ounces) of liquor
   d. a 5-ounce glass of wine
3. The majority of alcohol is
   a. absorbed through the mucosa lining the mouth.
   b. absorbed slowly on an empty stomach.
   c. absorbed mainly through the small intestine into the blood.
   d. absorbed directly into the liver through the lymph system.
4. _____ is the enzyme that begins metabolizing alcohol in the liver and the stomach.
   a. Sucrase
   b. Insulin
   c. Alcohol dehydrogenase (ADH)
   d. Ethanol

5. MEOS is
   a. the enzyme system found in the liver that metabolizes alcohol and drugs.
   b. an intermediate compound formed during the metabolism of alcohol.
   c. the chemical that causes the symptoms related to a hangover.
   d. a form of liver disease.
6. Which of the following statements is true?
   a. All areas of the brain are affected equally even when only a small amount of alcohol is consumed.
   b. Drinking an excessive amount of alcohol can shut down the reticular activating system (RAS) in the brain that controls consciousness.
   c. The more alcohol you consume, the greater the effect on the forebrain that controls walking and talking.
   d. Alcohol stimulates the central nervous system.
7. Which of the following factors affect(s) your rate of alcohol absorption and metabolism?
   a. whether you're male or female
   b. the place where you are drinking
   c. the time of day you drink
   d. the individuals you are drinking with
8. The four characteristics of alcoholism are (1) a craving for alcohol, (2) the development of a higher tolerance for alcohol, (3) the inability to control or limit the intake of alcohol, and (4) _____.

a. the inability to keep a stable job
b. the inability to maintain social relationships
c. the tendency to become violent
d. the development of a dependency on alcohol

9. The first stage of alcoholic liver disease is
   a. malnutrition.
   b. a fatty liver.
   c. cirrhosis.
   d. alcoholic hepatitis.
10. Drinking four to five alcoholic beverages on one occasion in a span of two hours is called
    a. alcoholism.
    b. drunk driving.
    c. a blackout.
    d. binge drinking.

Answers

1. (b) Alcohol found in alcoholic beverages is made by fermentation of natural sugars in grains such as glucose and maltose and fruit sugar or fructose by yeast. After fermentation, liquors go through a distillation process, which concentrates the beverage. Beer is made by germinating cereal grains to convert starch into sugar, referred to as malting. The sugar is then fermented by yeast to make beer.
2. (b) Five ounces of wine is considered a standard drink, so a 7-ounce glass of wine is the equivalent of almost 1.5 drinks.

3. (c) Most alcohol is absorbed through the small intestine into the blood, where it is taken up by the liver and metabolized. Some alcohol is also absorbed through the stomach on an empty stomach, but absorption is reduced after eating. Alcohol is water-soluble and therefore is not absorbed through the lymph system. Alcohol is not absorbed through the mouth.

4. (c) ADH is the enzyme in the stomach and the liver that begins metabolizing alcohol. Sucrase is an enzyme that breaks down the sugar sucrose. Insulin is a hormone, not an enzyme; it regulates blood glucose levels. Ethanol is the chemical name for the form of alcohol found in alcoholic beverages.

5. (a) The term MEOS (microsomal ethanol oxidizing system) refers to a set of enzymes found in the liver that oxidize ethanol when the consumption is greater than the ADH enzymes can handle. This system also oxidizes drugs. The MEOS does not refer to an intermediate compound, or a compound that causes the symptoms of a hangover.

6. (b) Excessive alcohol can shut down the reticular activating system in the brain, causing unconsciousness. The more alcohol you consume, the more areas of the brain are affected. Alcohol affects the cerebellum, which controls walking, while the forebrain controls behavior. Alcohol is a depressant, not a stimulant.

7. (a) Your gender will affect the rate of absorption and the metabolism of alcohol. Women have less alcohol dehydrogenase in their stomachs, which means they metabolize less alcohol in the stomach and more alcohol will be absorbed into the blood. They also have less body water, so the concentration of alcohol in their systems is higher. The time of day and the place where you drink do not have any effect on the absorption and metabolism of alcohol. Your drinking partners also won't alter the absorption or metabolism of alcohol. Of course,

they could influence the *amount* of alcohol you drink.

8. (d) The last characteristic of alcoholism is the development of a dependency on alcohol, such that withdrawal causes symptoms in the body. Although alcoholism can have financial consequences (such as job instability), interfere with personal relationships, and increase the risk of violence, not all individuals with alcoholism have these experiences.

9. (b) The first stage of alcoholic liver disease is a fatty liver. Alcoholic hepatitis is the second stage, followed by cirrhosis. Some people who have alcoholic liver disease are also malnourished.

10. (d) Consuming that much alcohol in a very short time is considered binge drinking. Binge drinking can lead to alcoholism. Individuals who binge drink may experience blackouts or may drive while drunk.

Answers to True or False?

1. **False.** Although alcohol provides kilocalories, the body does not need it to function and it is therefore not an essential nutrient.

2. **False.** A straight shot of liquor may look and taste more potent than a can of beer, but they contain the same amount of alcohol.

3. **True.** Red wine does contain heart-healthy phytochemical compounds.

4. **True.** Women have less body water and less of the enzyme that metabolizes alcohol in the stomach; they therefore respond more quickly to the narcotic effects of alcohol than do men.

5. **False.** In general, the body can only metabolize about one drink per 1½ hours.

6. **False.** Drinking more alcohol isn't going to take away the ill effects of a hangover. The only cure for a hangover is time.

7. **True.** However, not all alcoholic beverages contain equal amounts of kilocalories. In fact, some mixed

drinks can contain almost as many kilocalories as a meal.

8. **True.** Overconsumption of alcohol can lead to displacement of more nutritious foods, and diminish the body's ability to absorb or use some essential nutrients.

9. **False.** Moderate drinking is defined as up to one drink per day for women and up to two drinks per day for men. Drinking several alcoholic beverages in one sitting is binge drinking, not moderate drinking.

10. **False.** Although counseling is an important component of alcoholism recovery, there is no cure for alcoholism.

Web Resources

- For research-based information about alcohol abuse and binge drinking among college students, visit www.collegedrinkingprevention.gov
- For more information about alcohol and your health, visit the National Institute on Alcohol Abuse and Alcoholism (NIAAA) at www.niaaa.nih.gov
- For more information about alcohol consumption and its consequences, visit the National Center for Chronic Disease Prevention and Health Promotion, Alcohol and Public Health, at www.cdc.gov/alcohol/index.htm
- For an overview of the risks and benefits of alcohol, visit The Harvard School of Public Health, The Nutrition Source, *Alcohol: Balancing Risks and Benefits* at www.hsph.harvard.edu

References

1. Holmes, A., P. J. Fitzgerald, K. P. MacPherson, L. DeBrouse, et al. 2012. Chronic Alcohol Remodels Prefrontal Neurons and Disrupts NMDAR-Mediated Fear Extinction Encoding. *Nature Neuroscience* doi: 10.1038/nn.3204.
2. Centers for Disease Control and Prevention. 2011. *Alcohol Use and Health.* Available at www.cdc.gov. Accessed March 2014.

3. Boynton Health Service. 2012. *2012 College Student Health Survey Report.* Available at www.bhs.umn.edu. Accessed March 2014.

4. Association for Psychological Science. 2012. *Moderate Doses of Alcohol Increase Social Bonding in Groups.* Available at www.psychologicalscience.org. Accessed March 2014.

5. Centers for Disease Control. 2013. *Youth Exposure to Alcohol Advertising on Television—25 Markets, United States 2010.* Available at www.cdc.gov. Accessed March 2014.

6. Ross, C. S., J. Ostroff, and D. H. Jernigan. 2014. Evidence of Underage Targeting of Alcohol Advertising on Television in the United States: Lessons from the Lockyer v. Reynolds Decisions. *Journal of Public Health Policy* 35(1):105–118.

7. Grenard, J. L., C. W. Dent, and A. W. Stacy. 2013. Exposure to Alcohol Advertisements and Teenage Alcohol-Related Problems. *Pediatrics* 131(2):e369–e379.

8. National Institute on Alcohol Abuse and Alcoholism. 2007. *Alcohol Metabolism: An Update.* Available at http://pubs.niaaa.nih.gov. Accessed March 2014.

9. Finnigan, F., R. Hammersley, and K. Millar. 1998. Effects of Meal Composition on Blood Alcohol Level, Psychomotor Performance and Subjective State after Ingestion of Alcohol. *Appetite* 31:361–375.

10. Jones, A. W., and K. A. Jonsson. 1994. Food-Induced Lowering of Blood-Ethanol Profiles and Increased Rate of Elimination Immediately After a Meal. *Journal of Forensic Sciences* 39:1084–1093.

11. Oneta, C., U. Simanowski, M. Martinez, A. Allali-Hassani, X. Pares, N. Homann, C. Conradt, et al. 1998. First-Pass Metabolism of Ethanol Is Strikingly Influenced by the Speed of Gastric Emptying. *Gut* 43:612–619.

12. Enoch, M. A. 2013. Genetic Influences on Response to Alcohol and Response to Pharmacotherapies for Alcoholism. *Pharmacological Biochemical Behavior* doi:10.1016/j.pbb.2013.11.001.

13. Duranceaux, N. C. E., M. A. Schuckit, S. E. Luczak, M. Y. Eng, L. G. Carr, and T. L. Wall. 2008. Ethnic Differences in Level of Response to Alcohol between Chinese Americans and Korean Americans. *Journal of Studies on Alcohol and Drugs* 69:227–234.

14. College Drinking—Changing the Culture. 2013. *Snapshot of High-Risk College Drinking Consequences.* Available at www.collegedrinkingprevention.gov. Accessed March 2014.

15. Ibid.

16. Quinn, P. D., and K. Fromme. 2011. Alcohol Use and Related Problems among College Students and Their Non-College Peers: The Competing Roles of Their Personality and Peer Influence. *Journal of Studies on Alcohol and Drugs* 72:622–632.

17. Ebrahim, I. O., C. M. Shapiro, A. J. Williams, and P. B. Fenwick. 2013. Alcohol and Sleep I: Effects on Normal Sleep. *Alcoholism: Clinical & Experimental Research* 37(4):539–540.

18. Roehrs, T., D. Beare, F. Zorick, and T. Roth. 1994. Sleepiness and Ethanol Effects on Simulated Driving. *Alcoholism: Clinical and Experimental Research* 18:154–158.

19. Ebrahim et al., 2013. Alcohol and Sleep.

20. Roehrs, et al. 1994. Sleepiness and Ethanol Effects on Simulated Driving.

21. Swift, R. S., and D. Davidson. 1998. Alcohol Hangover: Mechanisms and Mediators. *Alcohol Health and Research World* 22:54–60.

22. Nikkola, J. 2013. Abstinence After First Acute Alcohol-Associated Pancreatitis Protects Against Recurrent Pancreatitis and Minimizes the Risk of Pancreatic Dysfunction. *Alcohol and Alcoholism* 49(4):483–486.

23. Lieber, C. S. 2000. Alcohol: Its Metabolism and Interaction with Nutrients. *Annual Review of Nutrition* 20:394–430.

24. Nikkola. 2013. Abstinence After First Acute Alcohol-Associated Pancreatitis.

25. Ibid.

26. Lewis, M. J. 2011. Alcohol and Nutrient Intake. Mechanisms of Reinforcement and Dependence. *Physiology and Behavior* 104(1):138–142.

27. Sullivan, E., and A. Pfefferbaum. 2009. Neuroimaging of the Wernicke-Korsakoff Syndrome. *Alcohol and Alcoholism* 44(2):155–165.

28. Ibid.

29. National Obesity Observatory. 2012. *Obesity and Alcohol: An Overview.* Available at www.noo.org.uk. Accessed March 2014.

30. Sayon-Orea, C., M. A. Martinez-Gonzalez, and M. Bes-Ratrollo. 2011. Alcohol Consumption and Body Weight: A Systemic Review. *Nutrition Reviews* 69(8):419–432.

31. Ibid.

32. National Institute on Alcohol Abuse and Alcoholism. 2007. *State of the Science Report on the Effects of Moderate Drinking.* Available at http://pubs.niaaa.nih.gov. Accessed March 2014.

33. National Institute on Alcohol Abuse and Alcoholism. 1998. *Alcohol Alert: Alcohol and Hormones.* Available at http://pubs.niaaa.nih.gov. Accessed March 2014.

34. Garcia-Sanchez, A., J. L. Gonzalez-Calvin, A. Diez-Ruiz, J. L. Casals, F. Gallego-Rojo, and D. S. Vatierra. 1995. Effect of Acute Alcohol Ingestion on Mineral Metabolism and Osteoblastic Function. *Alcohol* 30:449–453.

35. Seitz, H. K., C. Pelucchi, V. Bagnardi, and C. LaVecchia. 2012. Epidemiology and Pathophysiology of Alcohol and Breast Cancer: Update 2012. *Alcohol and Alcoholism* 47(3):204–212.

36. Gordon, G. C., K. Altman, K., A. L. Southren, A.L., E. Rubin, and C. S. Lieber. 1976. The Effects of Alcohol (Ethanol) Administration on Sex Hormone Metabolism in Normal Men. *New England Journal of Medicine* 295:793–797.

37. Mello, N. K., J. H. Mendelson, and S. K. Teoh. 1993. An Overview of the Effects of Alcohol on Neuroendocrine Function in Women. In: Zakhari, S., ed. *Alcohol and the Endocrine System.* National Institute on Alcohol Abuse and Alcoholism Research Monograph No. 23. NIH Pub. No 93-3533. Bethesda, MD: National Institutes of Health, pp. 139–170.

38. National Institute on Alcohol Abuse and Alcoholism. 2000. *Alcohol and the Liver: Research Update.* Available at http://pubs.niaaa.nih.gov. Accessed March 2014.

39. Ibid.

40. Kawaratani, H., T. Tsujimoto, A. Douhara, et al. 2013. The Effect of Inflammatory Cytokines in Alcoholic Liver Disease. *Mediators of Inflammation* doi: 10.1155/2013/495156.

41. Pinzani, M., M. Rosselli, and M. Zuckermann. 2011. Liver Cirrhosis. Best Practice and Research. *Clinical Gastroenterology* 25(2):281–290.

42. National Institute on Alcohol Abuse and Alcoholism. 2000. *Alcohol and the Liver: Research Update.*

43. Kenney, S. R., A. Lac, J. W. Labrie, J. F. Hummer, and A. Pham. 2013. Mental Health, Sleep Quality, Drinking Motives, and Alcohol-Related Consequences: A Path-Analytic Model. *Journal of Studies on Alcohol and Drugs* 74(6):841–851.

44. Gjestad, R., J. Franck, K. A. Hagtvet, and B. Haver. 2011. Level and Change in Alcohol Consumption, Depression and Dysfunctional Attitudes among Females Treated for Alcohol Addiction. *Alcohol and Alcoholism* 46(3):292–300.

45. Almeida, O. P., G. J. Hankey, B. B. Yeap, J. Golledge, and L. Flicker. 2013. The Triangular Association of ADH1B Genetic Polymorphism, Alcohol Consumption and the Risk of Depression in Older Men. *Molecular Psychiatry* doi:10.1038/mp.2013.117.

46. Ibid.

47. Matsumoto, C., M. D. Miedema, P. Ofman, J. M. Gaziano, and H. D. Sesso. 2014. An Expanding Knowledge of the Mechanisms and Effects of Alcohol Consumption on Cardiovascular Disease. *Journal of Cardiopulmonary Rehabilitation and Prevention* doi: 10.1097/HCR.0000000000000042.

48. Visiolia, F., S. Montia, C. Colomboa, and C. Gallia. 1998. Ethanol Enhances Cholesterol Synthesis and Secretion in Human Hepatomal Cells. *Alcohol* 15:299–303.

49. Witteman, J. C., W. C. Willett, and M. J. Stampfer. 1990. Relation of Moderate Alcohol Consumption and Risk of Systemic Hypertension in Women. *American Journal of Cardiology* 65:633–637.

50. Ibid.

51. Rosenqvist, M. 1998. Alcohol and Cardiac Arrhythmias. *Alcoholism: Clinical and Experimental Research* 22:318s–322s.

52. Barden, A. E., K. D. Croft, L. J. Beilin, M. Phillips, T. Ledowski, and I. B. Puddey. 2013. Acute Effects of Red Wine on Cytochrome P450 Eicosanoids and Blood Pressure in Men. *Journal of Hypertension* 31(11):2195–2202.

53. American Cancer Society. 2014. *Alcohol Use and Cancer.* Available at www.cancer.org. Accessed March 2014.

54. Turati, F., C. Galeone, M. Rota, C. Pelucchi, E. Negri, V. Bagnardi, G. Corrao, et al. 2014. Alcohol and Liver Cancer: A Systematic Review and Meta-Analysis of Prospective Studies. *Annals of Oncology* doi:10.1093/annonc/mdu020.

55. Scoccianti, C., B. Lauby-Secretan, P.Y. Bello, V. Chajes, and I. Romieu. 2014. Female Breast Cancer and Alcohol Consumption: A Review of the Literature. *American Journal of Preventative Medicine* 46(3 Supplement 1):S16–S25.

56. Fedirko, V., I. Tramacere, V. Bagnardi, M. Rota, L. Scotti, F. Islami, E. Negri, et al. 2011. Alcohol Drinking and Colorectal Cancer Risk: An Overall and Dose-Response Meta-Analysis of Published Studies. *Annals of Oncology* 22(9):1958–1972.

57. Ibid.

58. Jones, K., and D. Smith. 1973. Recognition of the Fetal Alcohol Syndrome in Early Infancy. *The Lancet* 2:999–1001.

59. Centers for Disease Control. 2012. *Data and Statistics.* Available at www.cdc.gov. Accessed March 2014.

60. Ibid.

61. Ibid.

62. National Institute on Alcohol Abuse and Alcoholism. 2006. *National Epidemiologic Survey on Alcohol and Related Conditions: Selected Findings.* Available at http://pubs.niaaa.nih.gov. Accessed March 2014.

63. National Institute on Alcohol Abuse and Alcoholism. 2004. National Institute of Alcohol Abuse and Alcoholism Council Approves Definition of Binge Drinking. *NIAAA Newsletter.* Available at http://pubs.niaaa.nih.gov. Accessed March 2014.

64. Centers for Disease Control and Prevention. 2012. *Vital Signs: Binge Drinking Prevalence, Frequency, and Intensity Among Adults— United States, 2010.* Available at www.cdc.gov. Accessed March 2014.

65. World Health Organization. 2009. *Alcohol and Injuries.* Available at www.who.int. Accessed March 2014.

66. Simone, J. 2010. *Binge Drinking and Risky Sex among College Students.* Available at www.wine-economics.org. Accessed March 2014.

67. Center for Women Students. 2012. *Know the Facts. Sexual Assault and Rape.* Available at http://studentaffairs.psu.edu. Accessed March 2014.

68. Mundt, M. P., L. I. Zakletskaia, D. D. Brown, and M. F. Fleming. 2012. Alcohol-Induced Memory Blackouts as an Indicator of Injury Risk among College Drinkers. *Injury Prevention* 18(1):44–49.

69. Centers for Disease Control. 2013. *Impaired Driving: Get the Facts.* Available at www.cdc.gov. Accessed March 2014.

70. Chen, C. M., H. Yi, and V. B. Faden. 2011. *Trends in Underage Drinking in the United States, 1991–2009. Surveillance Report #91.* National Institute on Alcohol Abuse and Alcoholism. Available at http://pubs.niaaa.nih.gov. Accessed March 2014.

71. Ibid.

72. Villafuerte, S., M. M. Heitzeg, S. Foley, W.-Y. Wendy Yau, K. Majczenko, I.-K. Zubieta, R. A. Zucker, and M. Burmeister. 2011. Impulsiveness and Insula Activation during Reward Anticipation Are Associated with Genetic Variants in GABRA2 in a Family Sample Enriched for Alcoholism. *Molecular Psychiatry* DOI: 10.1038/mp.2011.33.

8 Energy Metabolism

Learning Outcomes

After reading this chapter, you will be able to:

8.1 Define metabolism and provide examples of anabolic and catabolic reactions and the hormones that regulate these reactions.

8.2 Explain the role of adenosine triphosphate (ATP) as an energy source for cells.

8.3 Compare and contrast the major metabolic pathways that carbohydrates, fatty acids, glycerol, and amino acids follow to produce ATP.

8.4 Explain how metabolism changes during the absorptive, postabsorptive, and starvation stages of food intake.

8.5 Describe the metabolism of alcohol.

8.6 Describe the causes, diagnosis, symptoms, and dietary treatments of the most common genetic disorders of metabolism.

True or False?

1. Metabolism takes place within cells. **T**/**F**

2. The body prefers to use carbohydrates for fuel because very little energy is needed to break them down during metabolism. **T**/**F**

3. Fructose is preferable to glucose as an energy source. **T**/**F**

4. Lactate buildup during exercise causes a burning sensation in the legs. **T**/**F**

5. Excess dietary protein is stored in the muscle and therefore increases muscle size. **T**/**F**

6. Fat is the main fuel used during high-intensity energy metabolism. **T**/**F**

7. Alcohol is converted to blood glucose during metabolism. **T**/**F**

8. B vitamins provide energy. **T**/**F**

9. Kilocalories consumed after 7:00 p.m. are automatically stored as fat and contribute to weight gain. **T**/**F**

10. Children with inborn errors of metabolism outgrow such disorders when they reach puberty. **T**/**F**

See page 313 for the answers.

Every second of every day, your cells produce a steady supply of energy from the foods you eat. There are hundreds of complex chemical reactions needed to transform energy-yielding macronutrients in food to a form of energy the cells can use. The cells then adjust to times when you feed and times when you aren't eating to provide a continuous, uninterrupted source of energy.

Energy is defined as the capacity to perform work. When you eat, the energy held within the bonds of the energy-yielding nutrients is converted through a series of reactions to mechanical energy to move muscles, heat to warm you, electrical energy to conduct nerve impulses, or stored as chemical energy. Understanding these intricate energy-transforming reactions is an important aspect of the study of nutrition. This may seem a little daunting as you begin to study these processes, but remember that the process is not unlike assembling a jigsaw puzzle. Once the first pieces are in place, the larger picture begins to take shape and the later pieces are easier to understand.

In this chapter we discuss the chemical reactions within the pathways and how the individual nutrients—the pieces—flow into this larger metabolic puzzle. We discuss how the body adapts to the day-to-day changes in dietary intake and what happens when metabolic processes fail to work properly.

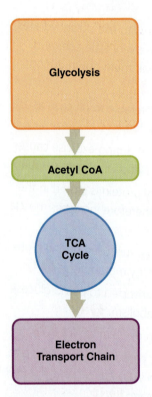

▲ **Figure 8.1 The Stages of Metabolism**
The chemical reactions of energy metabolism include glycolysis, the intermediate reaction of pyruvate to acetyl CoA, the TCA cycle, and the electron transport chain.

metabolism The sum of all chemical reactions in the body.

metabolic pathway A sequence of reactions that convert compounds from one form to another.

anaerobic A reaction that does not require oxygen.

aerobic A reaction that requires oxygen.

What Is Metabolism?

LO 8.1 Define metabolism and provide examples of anabolic and catabolic reactions and the hormones that regulate these reactions.

How does a kilocalorie from food transform into the energy required to throw a baseball, open a door, or think through a math equation? The answer can be summed up in one word: **metabolism.**

Metabolism is the sum of all the chemical reactions that take place within the 10 trillion cells in the body. These chemical reactions follow **metabolic pathway** in which the product of one reaction is the starting substance for the next reaction. This chapter focuses on the metabolic pathways involved with ATP production, beginning with *glycolysis*, and following the chemical reactions through the completion of the *electron transport chain*. **Figure 8.1** illustrates the main stages in which food is transformed into metabolic by-products and ATP.

Each of the chemical reactions within these pathways produces a change in energy as a new bond is formed or old bonds are broken. For example, when glucose is stored as glycogen, new bonds form, which requires energy, whereas when glycogen is broken down to yield glucose, energy is released. The energy that is produced when the bonds are broken result from **anaerobic** (without oxygen) or **aerobic** (with oxygen) reactions, depending on the fuel that is available and the amount of oxygen present within the cell.

Because the body constantly needs energy, metabolism never stops. The major energy nutrient, glucose, fuels metabolism from the first stage through the final stage, much like electricity flowing through wires. Other macronutrients—fatty acids and amino acids—contribute to metabolism as they are transformed into different substrates along the pathway. These metabolic processes continue to adapt and shift, whether you're in the middle of a meal or fasting during sleep, to maintain a continual source of energy for the cells.

Metabolism Takes Place within Cells

The chemical reactions involved in energy production and storage take place within the body's cells. Even though different cells perform different metabolic functions,

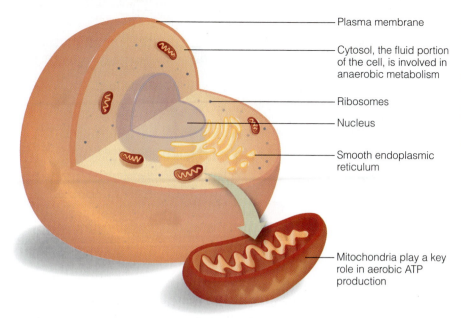

- Plasma membrane
- Cytosol, the fluid portion of the cell, is involved in anaerobic metabolism
- Ribosomes
- Nucleus
- Smooth endoplasmic reticulum
- Mitochondria play a key role in aerobic ATP production

◄ **Figure 8.2 Metabolism Takes Place within Cells**
The mitochondrion is a metabolically active organelle located in the cytoplasm of a cell. Other cell structures involved in metabolism include the cytosol, where glycolysis takes place; the ribosomes, which help manufacture proteins; and the smooth endoplasmic reticulum, which produces lipids used by the organelles.

their structure is similar (**Figure 8.2**). All cells have an outer envelope, called the *plasma membrane*, which holds in the cell's contents, and several specialized internal structures, called *organelles*. The organelles shown in Figure 8.2 include the ribosomes, nucleus, endoplasmic reticulum, and the mitochondria.

One particular organelle, the **mitochondrion** (plural: mitochondria), is referred to as the powerhouse of the cell. The mitochondria generate most of the cell's energy through aerobic metabolism. Almost all body cells contain mitochondria. The exception is the red blood cells, which produce energy anaerobically in the **cytosol,** or fluid portion of the cell.

Other organelles also participate in metabolism. The ribosomes, for example, help to manufacture proteins (as you learned in Chapter 6) and the smooth endoplasmic reticulum produces lipids used by the other organelles.

The Liver Plays a Central Role in Metabolism

The most metabolically active organ in the body is the liver. Once nutrients have been absorbed, the liver is the first organ to metabolize, store, or send them through the blood to other tissues. In previous chapters you learned that the proteins, carbohydrates, and fats in foods are digested and absorbed as amino acids, monosaccharides, glycerol, and fatty acids, respectively. The liver, along with other cells in the body, splits these nutrients into different molecules through a series of chemical reactions to produce energy or to synthesize new compounds—for instance, converting essential amino acids into nonessential amino acids. The liver also stores some of these nutrients—glycogen, for example—to use in the future.

Metabolism Is a Series of Chemical Reactions

Metabolic reactions within each pathway can be as simple as only two to three chemical reactions, or they can be much more complex and require many more reactions to complete each pathway.

Anabolic Reactions

As mentioned earlier in the chapter, chemical reactions involved in metabolism either absorb energy for the reaction or they produce energy (**Figure 8.3**).

Metabolism allows the body to convert energy from foods into energy needed for physical activity.

mitochondrion A cellular organelle that releases energy from carbohydrates, proteins, and fats to make ATP; *pl.* mitochondria.

cytosol The fluid portion of the cell where anaerobic metabolism takes place.

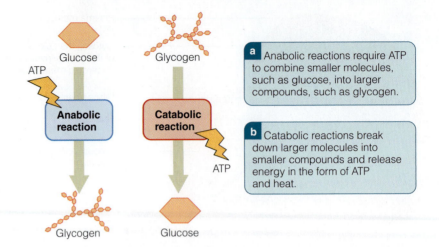

Glucose   Glycogen

ATP

a Anabolic reactions require ATP to combine smaller molecules, such as glucose, into larger compounds, such as glycogen.

Anabolic reaction   **Catabolic reaction**

b Catabolic reactions break down larger molecules into smaller compounds and release energy in the form of ATP and heat.

ATP

Glycogen   Glucose

Anabolic reactions generally use or absorb energy to combine simpler molecules into larger, more complex ones. For example, single amino acids join to form proteins; excess glucose molecules combine in a branched-chain structure to form glycogen; and excess fatty acids attach to glycerol molecules to make triglycerides.

Catabolic Reactions

Catabolic reactions are the opposite of anabolic processes: They provide the energy or ATP to fuel anabolic reactions. Catabolic processes break down large molecules into simple structures that can be used for energy, recycled for their individual parts, or excreted. For example, larger glycogen molecules can be hydrolyzed to yield smaller molecules of glucose, and triglycerides are disassembled to yield fatty acids and glycerol. The smaller glucose, fatty acid, and glycerol molecules are then broken down through the stages of energy metabolism to produce ATP. In both catabolic and anabolic reactions, some of the energy is released as heat.

Enzymes and Hormones Regulate Metabolism

Enzymes and their assistant coenzymes enable the chemical reactions of metabolism to occur at fast enough rates to maintain normal body function. Nearly every metabolic reaction requires a specific enzyme to catalyze the reaction and, in some cases, a coenzyme, or helper, that is often a vitamin, assists the enzyme. For example, the B vitamin niacin in its coenzyme form NAD^+ and riboflavin in its coenzyme form FAD assist enzymes by accepting or donating electrons and hydrogen ions produced during oxidation-reduction reactions (see the Chemistry Boost).

Anabolic and catabolic reactions can also be regulated by hormones. When the endocrine system detects a change in the concentration of nutrients, such as when blood glucose levels rise, hormones are released that influence whether enzymes are activated or deactivated to regulate the metabolic pathways. For instance, the hormone insulin lowers blood glucose levels by allowing the movement of glucose into the cells. Further, within the cells, insulin controls the metabolic fate of glucose. Three other hormones, namely glucagon, epinephrine, and cortisol, can also influence metabolism and result in an increase in blood glucose by stimulating glycogenolysis. **Table 8.1** outlines the major hormones controlling anabolic and catabolic reactions.

anabolic reactions Metabolic reactions that combine smaller compounds into larger molecules.

catabolic reactions Metabolic reactions that break large compounds into smaller molecules.

TABLE 8.1	The Major Hormones That Control Metabolism				
Hormone	Produced by	Type of Reaction	Control of Protein Metabolism	Control of Carbohydrate Metabolism	Control of Fat Metabolism
Insulin	Pancreas	Anabolic	Stimulates protein synthesis	Stimulates glycogen synthesis	No effect
Glucagon	Pancreas	Catabolic	Stimulates protein degradation	Stimulates glycogenolysis	Stimulates lipolysis
Epinephrine	Adrenal glands	Catabolic	No effect	Stimulates glycogenolysis	Stimulates lipolysis
Cortisol	Adrenal glands	Catabolic	Stimulates protein degradation	Stimulates gluconeogenesis	No effect

Chemistry Boost

Oxidation-Reduction Reactions

We obtain energy during metabolism by oxidation-reduction reactions (also called redox reactions), which involve the transfer of electrons. Oxidation reactions involve the loss of an electron, while reduction reactions gain an electron. These reactions happen in sets: When an oxidation reaction occurs and one molecule loses an electron, another molecule is reduced and gains an electron.

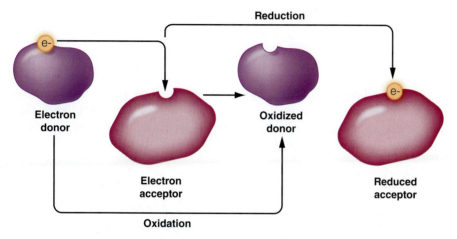

During glycolysis, glucose is oxidized to pyruvate and the coenzyme form of the B vitamin niacin (NAD^+) is reduced to NADH.

LO 8.1: THE TAKE-HOME MESSAGE Metabolism is the sum of all metabolic processes that occur in cells. Most of these reactions take place within the mitochondria. Metabolic processes use energy to build new substances through anabolic reactions or produce energy by breaking molecules apart through catabolic reactions. Enzymes catalyze the reactions involved in metabolism along with the aid of coenzymes, and hormones, including insulin, glucagon, epinephrine, and cortisol.

How Does ATP Fuel Metabolism?

LO 8.2 Explain the role of adenosine triphosphate (ATP) as an energy source for cells.

All body actions require energy, whether you're running a marathon or lying in bed. Further, the more strenuous the action, the more energy the body requires. For example, your body burns more energy to lift a 50-pound bag of dog food than to lift a 5-pound bag of flour. You know by now that the source of fuel for all this energy is food.

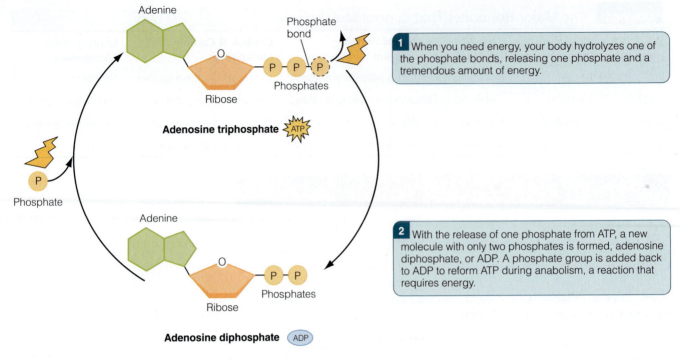

1 When you need energy, your body hydrolyzes one of the phosphate bonds, releasing one phosphate and a tremendous amount of energy.

2 With the release of one phosphate from ATP, a new molecule with only two phosphates is formed, adenosine diphosphate, or ADP. A phosphate group is added back to ADP to reform ATP during anabolism, a reaction that requires energy.

Adenine

Phosphate bond

Phosphate

Phosphates

Ribose

Adenosine triphosphate ATP

Adenine

Phosphates

Ribose

Adenosine diphosphate ADP

▲ **Figure 8.4 ATP to ADP**
The high-energy molecule adenosine triphosphate (ATP) releases energy to be used by the cells when the phosphate bond is broken, producing adenosine diphosphate (ADP).

However, before your body can use the energy in the cereal, fruit, and toast you ate for breakfast, it must first disassemble the macronutrients, break them into smaller compounds, and transfer their energy into the high-energy molecule **adenosine triphosphate,** or **ATP.**

Adenosine Triphosphate Is the Cell's Energy Source

ATP is the only source of energy that cells can use directly for work. The process of disassembling food to create ATP actually requires some ATP to convert the food into energy and more ATP. (In other words, you have to "spend" ATP to make ATP.) The cells then use that ATP to fuel other metabolic processes.

ATP is made of adenine (a nitrogen-containing compound), ribose (a five-carbon sugar), and three phosphate groups (which contain phosphorus and oxygen). The energy is stored in the bonds that connect the phosphate groups to each other.

As **Figure 8.4** illustrates, when you need energy, one of the bonds connecting the phosphate groups is hydrolyzed, which releases one phosphate *plus* a tremendous amount of energy. The new molecule that is formed is called **adenosine diphosphate,** or **ADP.**

At any given moment, cells only have 3 to 5 seconds' worth of ATP available for immediate use. Therefore, the body must continually produce ATP to provide a constant supply of energy.

ATP Can Be Regenerated from ADP and Creatine Phosphate

Regenerating ATP from ADP requires a source of phosphate. As illustrated in Figure 8.4, the phosphate produced from the initial breakdown of ATP is one source. Another source of phosphate is **creatine phosphate,** also called phosphocreatine, or **PCr.** PCr is a high-energy compound formed in muscle cells when creatine (an amino acid structure found in foods and produced in the body) combines with phosphate.

adenosine triphosphate (ATP) A high-energy molecule composed of adenine, ribose, and three phosphate molecules; cells use this to fuel all biological processes.

adenosine diphosphate (ADP) A nucleotide composed of adenine, ribose, and two phosphate molecules; it is formed when one phosphate molecule is removed from ATP.

creatine phosphate (PCr) A compound that provides a reserve of phosphate to regenerate ADP to ATP.

This phosphate can be released from creatine phosphate and added to ADP to form ATP. In addition, when the phosphate bond is broken, energy is released, which provides the fuel needed to restore ATP. These two sources of phosphate, ATP and PCr, can provide enough ATP to sustain a sprint for about 10 seconds. (See Chapter 16's Chemistry Boost on page 594 for further discussion of creatine phosphate).

As the available ATP dwindles and creatine phosphate in the muscle cell is exhausted, the body relies on anaerobic and aerobic metabolism to produce the needed ATP. Anaerobic metabolism produces more ATP per minute than aerobic metabolism, but it is very limited in its use (it only provides about 1 to 1.5 minutes of maximal activity). Activities that primarily involve anaerobic metabolism are high-intensity, short-duration activities such as sprinting or heavy weight lifting. When the demand for ATP is greater than the rate at which metabolism can produce it, the activity slows down or stops completely. This is one reason why individuals who lift weights have to rest between sets; it gives the body time to form more ATP to be used for the next set of lifts. Aerobic metabolism produces less ATP per minute than anaerobic metabolism, but it can continue indefinitely. Low-intensity, long-duration activities, such as walking or slow jogging, primarily involve aerobic metabolism.

The transformations that convert energy stored in carbohydrate, protein, and fat into ATP are tightly integrated and somewhat complex. To learn this material, we break down these integrated processes by stages.

LO 8.2: THE TAKE-HOME MESSAGE ATP is the energy source cells use to fuel metabolic reactions. No ATP is stored, thus ATP must be regenerated from ADP and phosphate (which can be donated by creatine phosphate), or produced during anaerobic or aerobic metabolism.

How Do the Macronutrients Provide ATP?

LO 8.3 Compare and contrast the major metabolic pathways that carbohydrates, fatty acids, glycerol, and amino acids follow to produce ATP.

All three macronutrients—carbohydrates, proteins, and fats—fuel the production of ATP by entering the metabolic pathway at some point in the stages of metabolism. Their metabolic fate is determined by the chemical reactions within each metabolic pathway (**Figure 8.5**).

Carbohydrates are unique in that they are oxidized anaerobically in **glycolysis** (stage 1) and the intermediate stage of converting **pyruvate** to **acetyl CoA** (stage 2), and also aerobically in the **tricarboxylic acid (TCA) cycle** (stage 3) to release electrons and hydrogen ions to generate ATP in the **electron transport chain** (stage 4). Fatty acids from triglycerides are only oxidized aerobically, which is slower than anaerobic metabolism in producing ATP. The fatty acids are split from the glycerol backbone before they are metabolized and converted to acetyl CoA, while glycerol enters metabolism through glycolysis.

When amino acids from proteins are needed for energy, they are converted to substrates in the first three stages, depending on the structure of their side groups. The glucogenic amino acids can be transformed to substrates in glycolysis or into glucose through gluconeogenesis when carbohydrate intake is low. Other amino acids can be converted to acetyl CoA and intermediate substrates in the TCA cycle.

Regardless of the stage in which energy nutrients enter metabolism, they eventually all converge at acetyl CoA. Let's take a closer look at each stage.

glycolysis The breakdown of glucose; for each molecule of glucose, two molecules of pyruvate and two ATP molecules are produced.

pyruvate A three-carbon molecule formed from the oxidation of glucose during glycolysis.

acetyl CoA A two-carbon compound formed when pantothenic acid combines with acetate.

tricarboxylic acid cycle (TCA) A cycle of aerobic chemical reactions in the mitochondria that oxidize glucose, amino acids, and fatty acids, producing hydrogen ions to be used in the electron transport chain, some ATP, and by-products carbon dioxide and water.

electron transport chain The final stage of energy metabolism. NADH or FADH$_2$ transports high-energy electrons from glycolysis and the TCA cycle to the cytochromes in the electron transport chain, resulting in the formation of ATP and water.

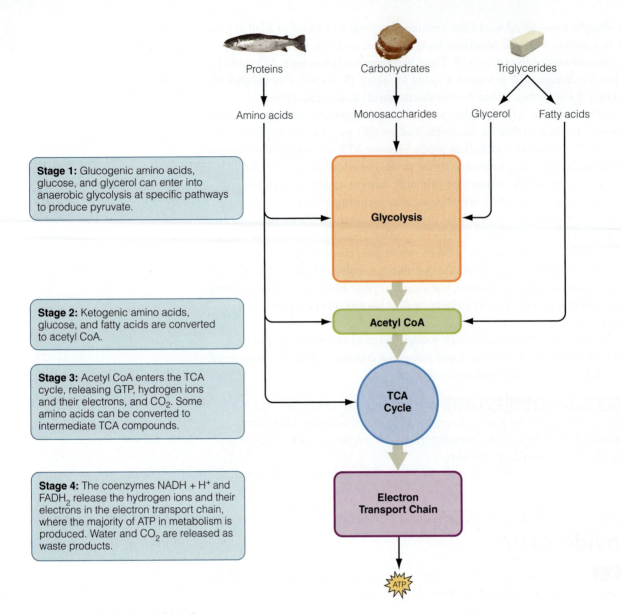

Stage 1: Glucogenic amino acids, glucose, and glycerol can enter into anaerobic glycolysis at specific pathways to produce pyruvate.

Stage 2: Ketogenic amino acids, glucose, and fatty acids are converted to acetyl CoA.

Stage 3: Acetyl CoA enters the TCA cycle, releasing GTP, hydrogen ions and their electrons, and CO_2. Some amino acids can be converted to intermediate TCA compounds.

Stage 4: The coenzymes NADH + H$^+$ and FADH$_2$ release the hydrogen ions and their electrons in the electron transport chain, where the majority of ATP in metabolism is produced. Water and CO_2 are released as waste products.

Proteins → Amino acids
Carbohydrates → Monosaccharides
Triglycerides → Glycerol, Fatty acids

Glycolysis

Acetyl CoA

TCA Cycle

Electron Transport Chain

ATP

▲ **Figure 8.5 The Metabolic Fate of Food**
After the energy-containing nutrients have been absorbed through the small intestine, they can enter a metabolic pathway and be converted to energy, or be stored as fat for later use.

Glycolysis Transforms Glucose to Pyruvate

The first step in forming ATP from glucose begins with glycolysis (*glyco* = glucose, *lysis* = break apart), the universal pathway for glucose oxidation. Glucose metabolism is an essential energy source for all cells and particularly the brain and red blood cells. As you follow the metabolic pathway, illustrated in **Figure 8.6**, track the carbons through the process from beginning to end.

Notice that glucose is now depicted as a row of 6 carbons, rather than a six-sided ring structure as shown in Chapter 4. This representation makes it easier to see the movement of carbon during metabolism.

Glycolysis is a ten-step anaerobic catabolic pathway that takes place in the cytosol of the cells. It begins with one six-carbon glucose molecule and ends with two three-carbon molecules of pyruvate and a net of two molecules of ATP. The initial step absorbs or uses ATP. In this reaction, a phosphate is transferred from ATP to the sixth carbon of glucose as the glucose enters the cell, forming glucose 6-phosphate and ADP. Once glucose 6-phosphate is formed, it continues through

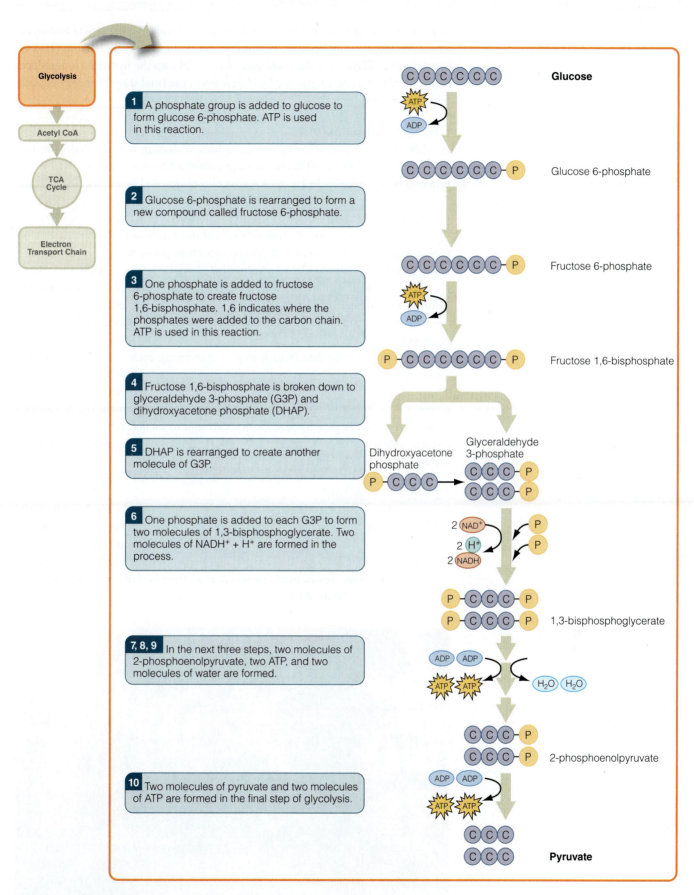

Glycolysis

1 A phosphate group is added to glucose to form glucose 6-phosphate. ATP is used in this reaction.

2 Glucose 6-phosphate is rearranged to form a new compound called fructose 6-phosphate.

3 One phosphate is added to fructose 6-phosphate to create fructose 1,6-bisphosphate. 1,6 indicates where the phosphates were added to the carbon chain. ATP is used in this reaction.

4 Fructose 1,6-bisphosphate is broken down to glyceraldehyde 3-phosphate (G3P) and dihydroxyacetone phosphate (DHAP).

5 DHAP is rearranged to create another molecule of G3P.

6 One phosphate is added to each G3P to form two molecules of 1,3-bisphosphoglycerate. Two molecules of $NADH^+ + H^+$ are formed in the process.

7, 8, 9 In the next three steps, two molecules of 2-phosphoenolpyruvate, two ATP, and two molecules of water are formed.

10 Two molecules of pyruvate and two molecules of ATP are formed in the final step of glycolysis.

Glucose

Glucose 6-phosphate

Fructose 6-phosphate

Fructose 1,6-bisphosphate

Dihydroxyacetone phosphate

Glyceraldehyde 3-phosphate

1,3-bisphosphoglycerate

2-phosphoenolpyruvate

Pyruvate

▲ Figure 8.6 Glycolysis
Glycolysis is a ten-step process that takes place in the cytosol of the cell; it converts glucose to pyruvate.

nine more reactions until the anaerobic stage of glycolysis is complete and pyruvate is created. In addition to ATP, glycolysis also generates hydrogen ions (H^+). As you can see in Figure 8.6, the coenzyme NAD^+ picks up the hydrogen ion, reduces NAD^+ to NADH, and carries the hydrogen ion to the final stage of energy production, the electron transport chain.

Fructose and Galactose

In addition to glucose, other monosaccharides, including fructose and galactose, can be used to produce ATP, but they are converted to substrates in glycolysis at different points. In muscle, fructose is first phosphorylated before it enters glycolysis as fructose 6-phosphate (see step 3 in Figure 8.6). In the liver, however, fructose passes through a more complex conversion before it becomes a substrate in glycolysis. Fructose is first phosphorylated to form fructose 1-phosphate, which is then split into glyceraldehyde and dihydroxyacetone phosphate (DHAP), and then enters glycolysis as glyceraldehyde 3-phosphate (see steps 4 and 5 in Figure 8.6).

Galactose is also metabolized in the liver and must be converted to glucose before it can enter glycolysis. The first step is to add a phosphate to galactose to produce galactose 1-phosphate. After four more metabolic steps, galactose enters glycolysis as glucose 6-phosphate (see step 1 in Figure 8.6).

A specific enzyme directs each step of converting each monosaccharide into an intermediate substrate in glycolysis. Although rare, deficiencies in any of these enzymes due to genetic mutations have a debilitating effect on metabolism. For example, a deficiency in the enzyme that converts galactose into glucose results in a condition known as galactosemia, which can lead to mental retardation and liver damage unless dietary intake of galactose is controlled. We discuss genetic errors of metabolism in more detail at the end of this chapter.

Pyruvate to Lactate

Pyruvate sits at the junction between several significant pathways in energy metabolism. It is the end product for anaerobic glycolysis and the beginning molecule for gluconeogenesis. It can be converted to acetyl CoA and enter the TCA cycle, or provide the basis for long-chain fatty acids to be stored in the adipose tissue as a triglyceride. In other words, pyruvate serves as an intermediate substrate that helps balance the energy needs of the cells.

Strenuous exercise can cause a buildup of hydrogen ions in the muscle.

Most people associate the term lactate with muscle, even though the metabolic conversion of pyruvate to lactate happens in any human cell. For this discussion we use the muscle cell as an example.

When mitochondria lack sufficient oxygen (anaerobic metabolism), such as during intense exercise, pyruvate is reduced to **lactate** to prevent the buildup of hydrogen ions in the cell (**Figure 8.7**). In some situations, such as during strenuous exercise, lactate is not produced fast enough to keep up with the production of hydrogen ions. Under these conditions the hydrogen ions build up, which reduces the pH in the muscle cell, making the cell more acidic. Contrary to popular belief, it is the buildup of hydrogen ions, not lactate, that produces the uncomfortable "burning" sensation in the muscles after exercise.

Lactate diffuses out of the cell into the blood, where it is transferred to the liver. Once in the liver cells, enzymes convert the lactate back to pyruvate, which is then transformed by gluconeogenesis into glucose through the **Cori cycle** (**Figure 8.8**) and released back into the blood as glucose. The glucose is picked up by the muscle to begin glycolysis over again. This gluconeogenic mechanism occurs mainly in the liver and to a lesser extent in the kidneys. The muscles do not contain the necessary gluconeogenic enzymes to catalyze the conversion of lactate to glucose.

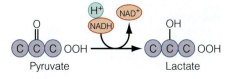

▲ **Figure 8.7 The Conversion of Pyruvate to Lactate**
Pyruvate is reduced to lactate during anaerobic metabolism and NADH is oxidized to NAD$^+$ that can be used in glycolysis.

lactate A three-carbon compound generated from pyruvate when mitochondria lack sufficient oxygen.

Cori cycle The metabolic pathway in the liver that regenerates glucose from lactate released from the muscle.

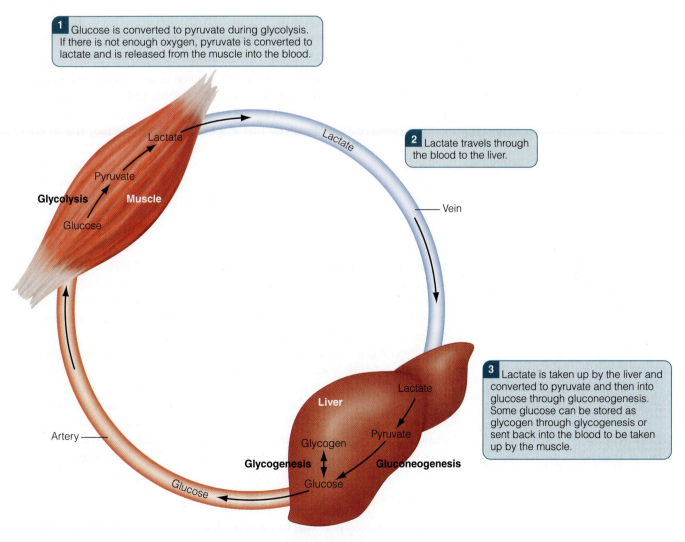

1 Glucose is converted to pyruvate during glycolysis. If there is not enough oxygen, pyruvate is converted to lactate and is released from the muscle into the blood.

2 Lactate travels through the blood to the liver.

3 Lactate is taken up by the liver and converted to pyruvate and then into glucose through gluconeogenesis. Some glucose can be stored as glycogen through glycogenesis or sent back into the blood to be taken up by the muscle.

▲ **Figure 8.8 The Cori Cycle Is a Metabolic Pathway between the Muscle and Liver**
The Cori cycle in the liver regenerates glucose from lactate released from the muscle.

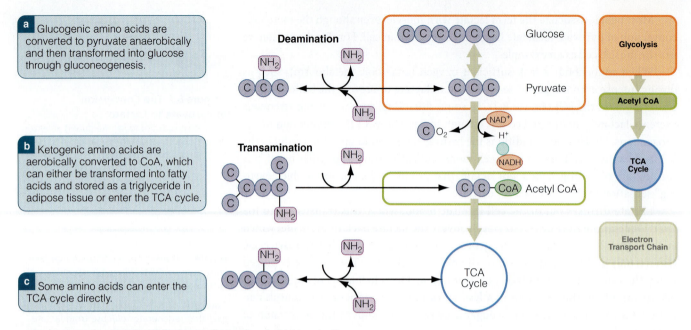

a Glucogenic amino acids are converted to pyruvate anaerobically and then transformed into glucose through gluconeogenesis.

b Ketogenic amino acids are aerobically converted to CoA, which can either be transformed into fatty acids and stored as a triglyceride in adipose tissue or enter the TCA cycle.

c Some amino acids can enter the TCA cycle directly.

▲ **Figure 8.9** **Glucogenic and Ketogenic Amino Acid Metabolism**

Glucogenic Amino Acids to Pyruvate

Eighteen out of twenty amino acids are considered glucogenic because they can produce glucose—that is, they can be transformed into pyruvate and other TCA cycle intermediates that enter gluconeogenesis. Six of these amino acids—alanine, serine, glycine, threonine, tryptophan, and cysteine—enter the metabolic pathway at pyruvate.[1] The pyruvate formed can be converted to glucose, through gluconeogenesis, and enter glycolysis to produce ATP through the later stages of metabolism. Or the pyruvate can be transported into the mitochondria and transformed into acetyl CoA. The other twelve glucogenic amino acids enter the metabolic pathway at points along the TCA cycle. Glucogenic amino acids, which come from food or the breakdown of proteins in muscle, are a major source of blood glucose when the diet is lacking in carbohydrate. These conversions are shown in **Figure 8.9**. **Table 8.2** lists the glucogenic amino acids.

Glycerol to Pyruvate

Dietary fat (triglycerides) is a more concentrated source of kilocalories and yields about six times more energy than either carbohydrates or proteins. Both glycerol and fatty acids can be used for fuel, but only the glycerol portion of the triglyceride is glucogenic and thus able to contribute to blood glucose levels. As an energy source, glycerol produces very little energy compared with glucose, amino acids, or fatty acids.

Glycerol can enter the main pathway at two distinct points. First, glycerol can be taken up by the liver cells and converted to glucose via gluconeogenesis. The first step in this pathway uses ATP to phosphorylate (add a phosphate group to) the three-carbon glycerol into DHAP (dihydroxyacetone phosphate), one of the intermediate substrates in glycolysis. Once glycerol is converted to DHAP it can be changed into glucose in one direction or it can follow a different series of chemical reactions to produce pyruvate, depending on the body's need for glucose.

Pyruvate Is Transformed into Acetyl CoA

At the end of glycolysis, what began as one six-carbon molecule of glucose has produced two three-carbon molecules of pyruvate, a net of two ATP, two coenzyme molecules in the form of NADH, two hydrogen ions (which enter the electron

TABLE 8.2 Glucogenic and Ketogenic Amino Acids

Glucogenic Amino Acids	Ketogenic Amino Acids	Amino Acids That Are Both Glucogenic and Ketogenic
Alanine	Leucine	Isoleucine
Arginine	Lysine	Phenylalanine
Asparagine		Tryptophan
Aspartate		Tyrosine
Cysteine		
Glutamate		
Glutamine		
Glycine		
Proline		
Serine		
Histidine		
Methionine		
Threonine		
Valine		

Adapted from J. M. Berg, J. L. Tymoczko, and L. Stryer. 2012. *Biochemistry*. 7th ed. (New York: W. H. Freeman).

transport chain), and two molecules of water. Now let's continue down the metabolic pathway with the newly formed pyruvate as it is transformed into acetyl CoA.

Acetyl CoA is often called the "gateway" molecule for aerobic metabolism because all energy-producing nutrients—glucose, amino acids, fatty acids, glycerol, even alcohol—are usually transformed to acetyl CoA before entering the TCA cycle. Until this point along the metabolic pathway, energy is produced anaerobically. When cells contain an ample supply of oxygen, pyruvate now continues down the aerobic energy pathway to create acetyl CoA. In the presence of oxygen, the two molecules of pyruvate formed during glycolysis cross the outer mitochondrial membrane and enter the mitochondria, where they each lose a carbon. Coenzyme A (which contains the B vitamin pantothenic acid) attaches to the remaining two carbons from each pyruvate molecule to form acetyl CoA. Thus a three-carbon pyruvate molecule is changed into a two-carbon acetyl CoA. The third carbon combines with oxygen to form carbon dioxide, and is expelled through the lungs as waste. This stage is illustrated in **Figure 8.10**.

Walking or low-intensity exercise uses mostly fatty acids and glucose to produce ATP through aerobic metabolism.

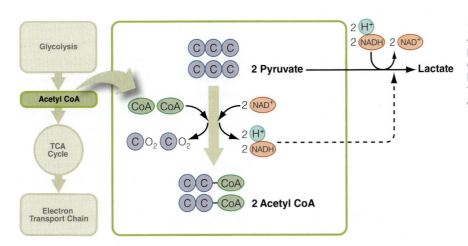

◄ **Figure 8.10 The Fate of Pyruvate**
At the end of glycolysis, two molecules of pyruvate are formed for every molecule of glucose. These three-carbon molecules can be converted to acetyl CoA and enter the TCA cycle or be transformed into lactate, which diffuses out of the cell into the blood.

How Do the Macronutrients Provide ATP? **293**

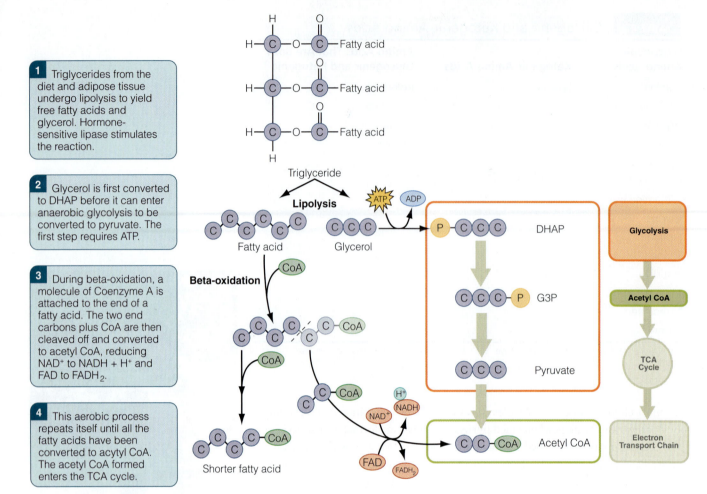

1 Triglycerides from the diet and adipose tissue undergo lipolysis to yield free fatty acids and glycerol. Hormone-sensitive lipase stimulates the reaction.

2 Glycerol is first converted to DHAP before it can enter anaerobic glycolysis to be converted to pyruvate. The first step requires ATP.

3 During beta-oxidation, a molecule of Coenzyme A is attached to the end of a fatty acid. The two end carbons plus CoA are then cleaved off and converted to acetyl CoA, reducing NAD^+ to $NADH + H^+$ and FAD to $FADH_2$.

4 This aerobic process repeats itself until all the fatty acids have been converted to acytyl CoA. The acetyl CoA formed enters the TCA cycle.

▲ **Figure 8.11 Fatty Acids Are Oxidized for Energy**
Stored triglycerides can be used for energy after the fatty acids are first hydrolyzed from the glycerol backbone.

Once acetyl CoA is formed it can continue down the pathway to enter the TCA cycle if ATP is scarce. If there is sufficient ATP to meet the body's needs, the acetyl CoA is transported out of the mitochondria and into the cytosol to be converted into a fatty acid. The newly formed fatty acids can be stored as fat through lipogenesis. Thus, energy needs determine whether acetyl CoA enters the TCA cycle (stage 3), where hydrogen ions are produced for use by the electron transport chain (stage 4).

Fatty Acids to Acetyl CoA

Before they can be used for energy, fatty acids are hydrolyzed from triglycerides by lipolysis (*lipo* = fat, *lysis* = break apart). **Figure 8.11** illustrates this process. An enzyme called **hormone-sensitive lipase** in the adipose tissue catalyzes the reaction. The activity of this enzyme is stimulated by the hormone glucagon when blood glucose levels are low (as when the diet is low in carbohydrate or kilocalories), or by the adrenal hormones epinephrine or cortisol when an individual is under stress. The free fatty acids are released into the blood and taken up by various tissues, including the muscle and the liver.

Just as you put on a coat to prepare to step outside on a cold day, fatty acids are "prepared" or activated before they cross into the mitochondria. In this step, which uses ATP, coenzyme A joins the carboxylic end of the fatty acid chain. The resulting long-chain fatty acetyl CoA can then cross the mitochondrial membrane with the help of a carrier molecule.

hormone-sensitive lipase The enzyme that catalyzes lipolysis of triglycerides.

The fatty acid is disassembled inside the mitochondrion by a series of chemical reactions called **beta-oxidation.** During beta-oxidation the fatty acid is taken apart two carbon fragments at a time, beginning at the carboxyl end of the molecule. The two-carbon fragments are joined with a molecule of CoA and converted to acetyl CoA. This process continues, forming a new acetyl CoA and a shorter fatty acid chain, until all of the carbons have been oxidized.

As each pair of carbons is cleaved from the fatty acid chain, hydrogen ions and electrons are released and picked up by two coenzymes, NAD^+ and FAD, forming $NADH + H^+$ and $FADH_2$. These coenzymes unload the electrons they carry in the electron transport chain.

Fatty acids are considered **ketogenic** (*keto* = ketone, *genic* = forming), not *glucogenic*, which means fatty acids can be used to produce ketone bodies, which are used as backup fuel for the brain and nerve functions when glucose is limited. (We discuss ketogenesis later in the chapter.) There is no metabolic pathway to convert fatty acids to glucose.

Amino Acids to Acetyl CoA

Recall that earlier in the chapter you learned that 18 of the 20 amino acids are considered glucogenic. The other two amino acids, leucine and lysine, are considered strictly ketogenic (refer to Figure 8.9b and Table 8.2), while four of the glucogenic amino acids, isoleucine, tryptophan, phenylalanine, and tyrosine, can also be ketogenic.[2]

Leucine and lysine first undergo transamination with the TCA acid **alpha-ketoglutarate** accepting the amino group that is transferred (review Chapter 6 on the transamination reaction). After several more steps, leucine and lysine are ultimately converted to acetyl CoA. Both amino acids are considered ketogenic because once they have been transformed into acetyl CoA they can be converted into a fatty acid or acetoacetate and then into ketone bodies, depending on cellular needs.

Isoleucine and tryptophan are converted to acetyl CoA using the same pathway as leucine. Phenylalanine and tyrosine are transformed into acetoacetyl CoA first before they are converted to acetyl CoA.

Remember that acetyl CoA cannot be used to make glucose, so once these amino acids are transformed, they are committed to continue through the energy pathway, to be converted to fatty acids and stored as a triglyceride in the adipocyte, or to undergo ketogenesis.

Tricarboxylic Acid (TCA) Cycle Releases High-Energy Electrons and Hydrogen Ions

The tricarboxylic acid (TCA) cycle, also known as the citric acid cycle or the Kreb's cycle, the third stage for energy metabolism and results in the oxidation of acetyl CoA (**Figure 8.12**) and occurs in the mitochondria. Up to this point, the macronutrients have followed different pathways, and entered the energy pathway at different points; now, they have all arrived at acetyl CoA. Recall that fuel molecules are carbon-containing compounds that can be oxidized or lose electrons. During each turn of the TCA cycle, high-energy electrons and hydrogen ions are released and gathered up by NAD^+, forming $NADH + H^+$, and FAD, forming $FADH_2$. These electron carriers release the electrons in the electron transport chain. Hydrogen ions released in the TCA cycle drive the production of ATP in the electron transport chain.

One molecule of acetyl CoA enters the cycle at a time. The first step is to remove the CoA and combine the two remaining carbons with a four-carbon molecule called **oxaloacetate.** Together, oxaloacetate and acetyl CoA form a new six-carbon compound called citrate. The cycle continues with seven more reactions, ending with oxaloacetate

beta-oxidation A series of metabolic reactions in which fatty acids are oxidized to acetyl CoA; also called *fatty acid oxidation.*

ketogenic Describing molecules that can be transformed into ketone bodies.

alpha-ketoglutarate A compound that participates in the formation of nonessential amino acids during transamination.

oxaloacetate The starting molecule for the TCA cycle.

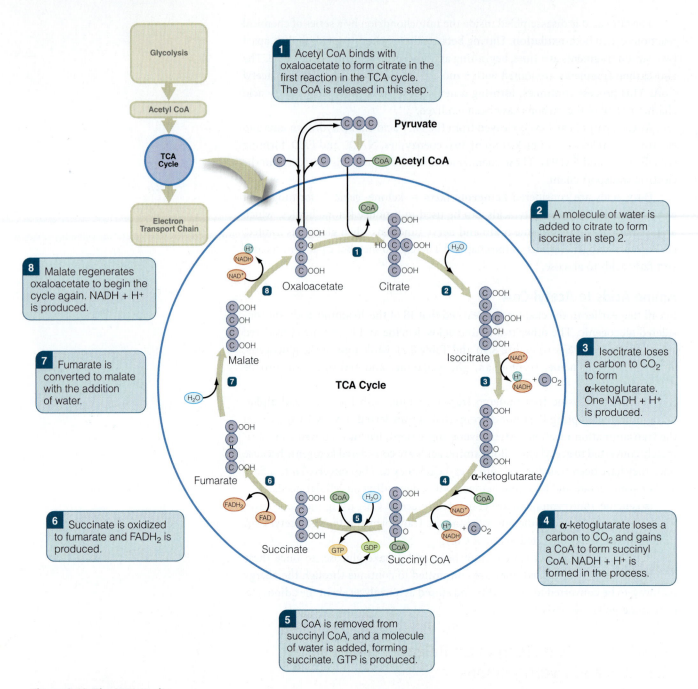

▲ Figure 8.12 The TCA Cycle
(**1**) The TCA cycle begins with oxaloacetate combining with acetyl CoA to form citrate. (**2–8**) The cycle continues through seven more steps, changing the molecules and releasing hydrogen atoms. Pyruvate can provide some oxaloacetate as a starting molecule for the cycle.

as the last molecule formed at the end of every turn of the TCA cycle. This brings us back to the beginning of the cycle. You'll notice as you track the carbons in Figure 8.12 that for every acetyl CoA that enters the TCA cycle, two carbons are lost as CO_2.

In addition to the two carbons lost as CO_2, three NADH + H$^+$ and one FADH$_2$ are produced during each turn of the TCA cycle. For example, in the third step of the cycle, high-energy electrons are grabbed by the coenzyme carrier NAD$^+$. In the succeeding steps of the cycle, three more coenzymes are reduced, NADH in step 4 and step 8, and FADH$_2$ in step 6. In total, for each turn of the TCA cycle, four coenzymes are reduced, along with the formation of carbon dioxide.

Also notice in step 5, a molecule called *guanosine triphosphate (GTP)* is generated. This energy molecule is readily converted to ATP.

The Electron Transport Chain and Oxidative Phosphorylation Produce the Majority of ATP

The electron transport chain is comprised of a series of protein complexes located in the inner mitochondrial membrane that function as electron carriers. The high-energy electrons delivered to the electron transport chain by NADH + H$^+$ and FADH$_2$ are passed from one protein complex to the next until they reach oxygen.

As the electrons are passed along the chain, the hydrogen ions are pumped out of the mitochondrial matrix into the intermembrane space. The hydrogen ions accumulate, creating a high concentration gradient that forces them back across the mitochondrial membrane into the matrix through the protein complex ATP synthase. This enzyme uses the energy generated by the concentration gradient to add a phosphate to ADP, forming ATP through the process called **oxidative phosphorylation.** At the same time, oxygen accepts the electrons and combines with the hydrogen ions to form water. The ATP produced flows into the cytoplasm to be used by the body.

The majority of the ATP you use every day for energy, growth, and maintenance is generated during this final stage of energy metabolism. This step is illustrated in **Figure 8.13**.

oxidative phosphorylation The metabolic pathway in the mitochondria in which ATP is formed using energy from the oxidation-reduction reactions in the electron transport chain.

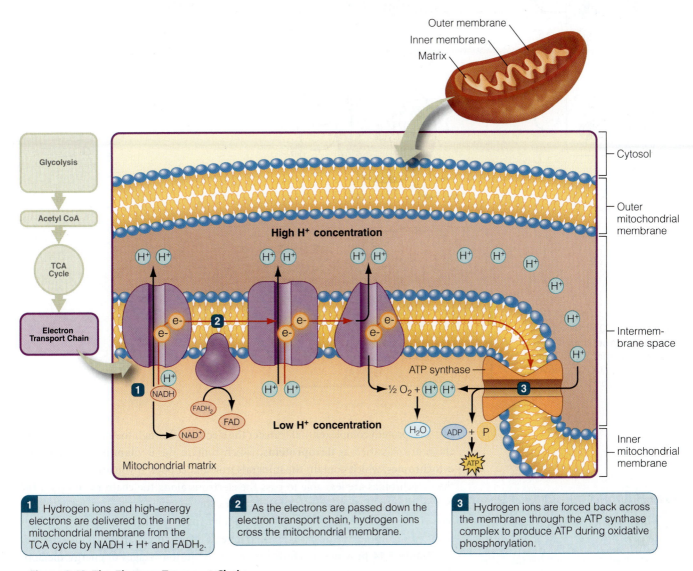

1. Hydrogen ions and high-energy electrons are delivered to the inner mitochondrial membrane from the TCA cycle by NADH + H$^+$ and FADH$_2$.

2. As the electrons are passed down the electron transport chain, hydrogen ions cross the mitochondrial membrane.

3. Hydrogen ions are forced back across the membrane through the ATP synthase complex to produce ATP during oxidative phosphorylation.

▲ **Figure 8.13 The Electron Transport Chain**

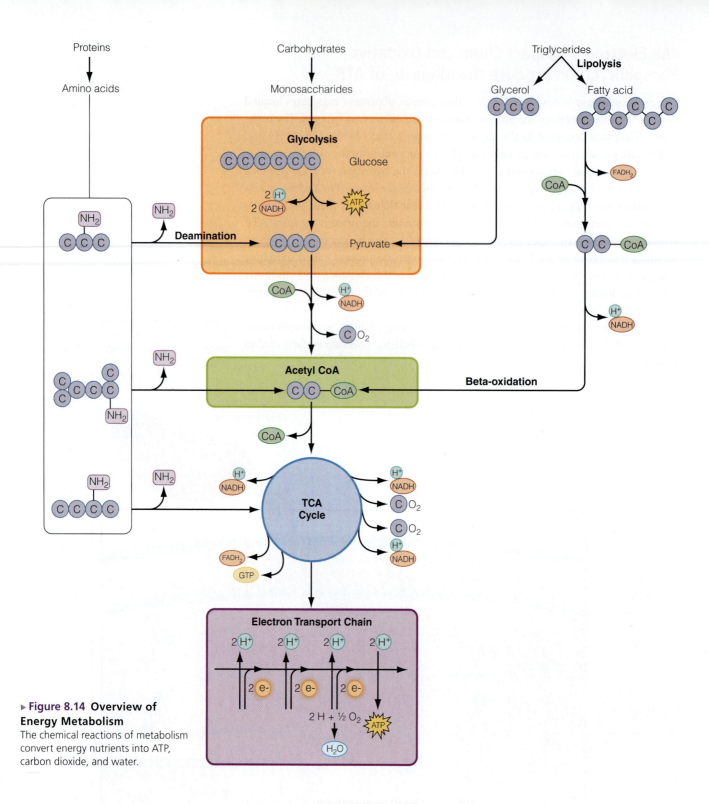

Proteins

Amino acids

Carbohydrates

Monosaccharides

Triglycerides

Lipolysis

Glycerol   Fatty acid

Glycolysis

Glucose

$2\ H^+$
$2\ NADH$ ATP

Deamination

Pyruvate

CoA   FADH$_2$

CoA

H^+
NADH

CoA H^+
NADH

$C\ O_2$

Acetyl CoA

CoA   **Beta-oxidation**

CoA

H^+
NADH H^+
NADH

TCA Cycle

$C\ O_2$
$C\ O_2$

FADH$_2$
GTP H^+
NADH

Electron Transport Chain

$2\ H^+$ $2\ H^+$ $2\ H^+$ $2\ H^+$

$2\ e-$ $2\ e-$ $2\ e-$

$2\ H + \frac{1}{2}\ O_2$ ATP

H_2O

▶ **Figure 8.14 Overview of Energy Metabolism**
The chemical reactions of metabolism convert energy nutrients into ATP, carbon dioxide, and water.

The protein complexes that transfer the electrons through the electron transport chain are classified as **flavoproteins,** which contain the B vitamin riboflavin, and **cytochromes,** which contain the minerals iron and copper. If you are iron deficient, the cytochromes are less able to pass the electrons along the chain to complete the production of ATP. This is one of the reasons someone with inadequate iron intake feels tired or fatigued. This illustrates the point that though vitamins and minerals do not provide energy, they are essential for energy production in the body.

Figure 8.14 provides a detailed overview of all four stages of energy metabolism. Look at the figure closely and check your understanding; can you describe

flavoproteins Protein complexes that move electrons down the electron transport chain; they contain the B vitamin riboflavin.

cytochromes Protein complexes that move electrons down the electron transport chain; they contain the minerals iron and copper.

			Can Be Used in	Excess Can
TABLE 8.3 Role of Individual Nutrients and Alcohol in Energy Metabolism				
Nutrient	**Produces ATP?**	**Can Produce Glucose?**	**Transamination (To Produce Amino Acids)?**	**Be Stored as Fat?**
Glucose	Yes	Yes	Yes	Yes
Amino acid	Yes	Yes	Yes	Yes
Fatty acid	Yes	No	No	Yes
Glycerol	Yes	Yes	Yes	Yes
Alcohol	Yes	No	No	Yes

what's happening in each stage? **Table 8.3** summarizes the role of individual nutrients in producing ATP, glycogen, nonessential amino acids, and fat.

LO 8.3: THE TAKE-HOME MESSAGE The metabolism of the macronutrients and tissues involved during various metabolic pathways is summarized in **Table 8.4**. Carbohydrates provide energy to cells through glycolysis, a ten-step conversion pathway that yields two molecules of pyruvate, a net of two ATP, two coenzymes, two hydrogen ions, and two molecules of water. Pyruvate is reduced to lactate during anaerobic metabolism, or converted to acetyl CoA during aerobic metabolism. Glycerol can produce energy by entering glycolysis or form glucose through gluconeogenesis and thus help maintain blood glucose levels. Fatty acids are ketogenic and cannot be used to form glucose. Fatty acids are broken down into two-carbon fragments and converted into acetyl CoA through beta-oxidation. Amino acids can be used to produce energy and glucose or converted to fatty acids and stored as triglycerides. All of the energy nutrients come together in the gateway molecule acetyl CoA. Once acetyl CoA is formed, it combines with oxaloacetate to form citrate in the first step of the TCA cycle. One turn of the TCA cycle produces two coenzymes, one molecule of CO_2, and a small amount of energy in the form of guanosine triphosphate (GTP, the equivalent of a molecule of ATP). The electrons generated are carried by coenzymes to the electron transport chain, where they are passed along the chain by protein complexes. During this process, the hydrogen ions are used to form ATP during oxidative phosphorylation and join with oxygen to make water.

How Does Metabolism Change during the Absorptive and Postabsorptive States?

LO 8.4 Explain how metabolism changes during the absorptive, postabsorptive, and starvation stages of food intake.

After eating a meal, once food has been digested and absorbed, the amino acids, monoglycerides, and triglycerides are available to be used by the body. We refer to this as the **absorptive state,** or that period within four hours following a meal in which anabolic processes exceed catabolic processes. During the absorptive state, the body uses glucose as the primary source of energy (see the Table Tips on Important Advice for Maintaining Energy Levels). Later, when you need energy during sleep, between meals, or when you're too busy to eat, your body uses the glucose

TABLE TIPS

Important Advice for Maintaining Energy Levels

Eat breakfast! It's the most important meal and improves energy levels throughout the day.

Don't skip meals; instead, be sure to eat at least three meals and one to two small snacks throughout the day.

Be sure each meal includes a combination of protein, carbohydrates, and some fat.

Enjoy carbohydrate-rich foods such as whole-grain crackers, baby carrots, grapes, string cheese, or nuts as snacks when you need a pick-me-up between meals.

Drink plenty of fluid, especially water, so you're sure to stay hydrated.

absorptive state The period after you eat when the stomach and small intestine are full and anabolic reactions exceed catabolic reactions.

TABLE 8.4   Summary of Metabolic Processes in the Cells

Metabolic Pathway	Nutrient(s) Involved in the Pathway	Description of the Pathway	Major Tissues Involved	Type of Pathway
Glycolysis	Carbohydrates	Metabolism of glucose to produce pyruvate and two ATP	All cells	Catabolic and anabolic
Glycogenesis	Carbohydrates	Producing glycogen from excess glucose	Muscle and liver	Anabolic
Glycogenolysis	Carbohydrates	Breakdown of glycogen to glucose	Muscle and liver	Catabolic
Gluconeogenesis	Noncarbohydrates, including glucogenic amino acids, glycerol, pyruvate, and lactate	Producing glucose from noncarbohydrate sources	Liver and kidneys	Anabolic
Beta-oxidation	Fatty acids	Fatty acid oxidation to acetyl CoA	Liver and muscle	Catabolic
Lipolysis	Fatty acids	Breakdown of triglycerides to yield fatty acids and glycerol	Adipose tissue and liver	Catabolic
Lipogenesis	Fatty acids	Synthesis of fatty acids and triglycerides	Adipose tissue and liver	Anabolic
Ketogenesis	Fatty acids and ketogenic amino acids	The conversion of fatty acids and ketogenic amino acids to acetyl CoA and to ketone bodies	Liver	Catabolic
Transamination	Amino acids	Formation of nonessential amino acids produced by transferring an amine group from one amino acid to an alpha-keto acid	Liver	Catabolic and anabolic
TCA cycle	All nutrients	Oxidation of acetyl CoA to produce high-energy electrons, hydrogen ions, carbon dioxide, and GTP	All cells (except RBCs)	Catabolic and anabolic
Electron transport chain and oxidative phosphorylation	All nutrients	Formation of ATP is generated from the energy released in glycolysis and the TCA cycle and delivered by NADH + H^+ and $FADH_2$. Process requires oxygen, which is reduced to water.	All cells (except RBCs)	Catabolic and anabolic

stored as glycogen, and the fatty acids and glycerol stored in triglycerides, for fuel. This is referred to as the **postabsorptive state,** or the period of time usually more than four hours after eating, such as during the late afternoon or overnight. Both the absorptive and postabsorptive states are regulated by hormones.

During the Absorptive State, Metabolism Favors Energy Storage

Metabolism adjusts to either provide energy for immediate use or store it for later, depending on your energy needs and intake. In the normal process of eating, if you consume more kilocalories than you require for your immediate energy needs, your metabolism favors anabolic reactions for the sake of storing the excess kilocalories for later use. For instance, if you eat excess protein, the excess is converted to fatty acids and stored as a triglyceride. If you overconsume carbohydrates, the anabolic reactions include converting the excess carbohydrates to glycogen. Once the glycogen stores are full, carbohydrates are converted to fatty acids.

Take a close look at **Focus Figure 8.15**, which illustrates the anabolic and catabolic pathways of the absorptive state.

postabsorptive state The period when you haven't eaten for more than four hours and the stomach and intestines are empty. Energy needs are met by the breakdown of stores.

Metabolism during the Absorptive State

The absorptive (fed) state is generally an anabolic state: After digestion, absorption, and transport in the body, the end products of digestion can be synthesized into important biological compounds, used for energy, or converted to storage forms of energy.

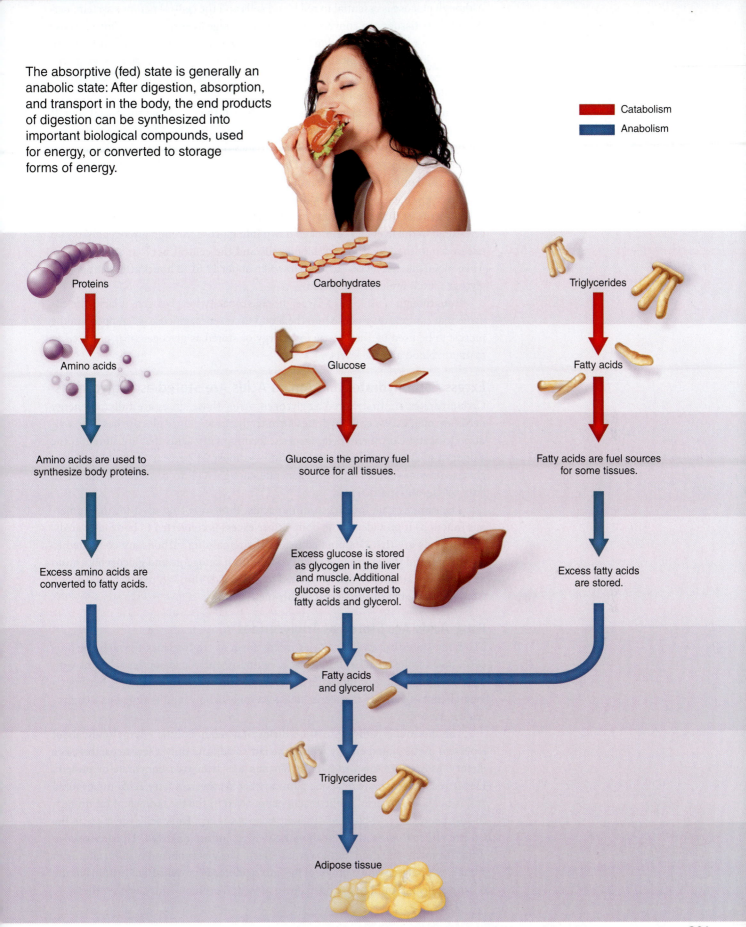

Catabolism
Anabolism

Proteins

Carbohydrates

Triglycerides

Amino acids

Glucose

Fatty acids

Amino acids are used to synthesize body proteins.

Glucose is the primary fuel source for all tissues.

Fatty acids are fuel sources for some tissues.

Excess amino acids are converted to fatty acids.

Excess glucose is stored as glycogen in the liver and muscle. Additional glucose is converted to fatty acids and glycerol.

Excess fatty acids are stored.

Fatty acids and glycerol

Triglycerides

Adipose tissue

Carbohydrates Are Stored as Glycogen

Although glucose is essential to red blood cells and the central nervous system, neither of these tissues can convert glucose to its storage forms, and both burn glucose readily. The red blood cells don't have mitochondria, which means that they can only use glucose anaerobically. The nervous system can't store glucose as glycogen, nor can it convert excess glucose to fat. Only the liver and muscles can convert excess glucose to glycogen for storage.

Remember that dietary glucose arrives first at the liver from the portal vein. If glucose levels are high in the liver, glucose can be converted to glycogen through glycogenesis, or it can circulate to other tissues. Enzymes in muscle cells can also convert excess glucose to glycogen. The body has a limited ability to store glycogen, however, and only about 1 percent of body weight is in the form of glycogen.

Liver glycogen plays an important role in maintaining glucose homeostasis. When intake of dietary carbohydrate is low, blood glucose levels drop. The glycogen stored in the liver can be broken down into glucose through glycogenolysis and released into the blood for red blood cells and the central nervous system to use when blood glucose levels are low. However, about 12 to 18 hours after eating, liver glycogen levels are nearly depleted.

Even though muscle has a larger storage capacity for glycogen, it lacks the enzyme that can release glucose into the blood. In essence, glucose is "trapped" in the muscle to be used by the muscle for energy or stored as glycogen; it is not used to maintain blood glucose levels.

Excess Carbohydrates and Amino Acids Are Stored as Triglycerides

Carbohydrates are first stored as glycogen. After those stores are full and energy needs are met, excess carbohydrates form triglycerides. Once glucose has been oxidized to acetyl CoA it enters lipogenesis, forming fatty acids that are stored in the adipocytes. This conversion is very costly—almost 25 percent of the kilocalories glucose provides must be used to generate enough ATP to convert the glucose to fatty acids—and inefficient.

The same is true for excess amino acids. Protein is first used for the numerous functions it provides to the body before excess is converted to body fatty acids. Amino acids are first deaminated before the remaining carbons are converted to acetyl CoA and then formed into fatty acids. Both ketogenic and glucogenic amino acids can be catabolized and converted to fatty acids through pyruvate and acetyl CoA pathways, but the process is highly inefficient.

Fatty Acids Are Stored as Triglycerides

The body stores excess kilocalories in any form as triglycerides through the process known as lipogenesis, or fatty acid synthesis. Fatty acid synthesis begins with the two-carbon gateway molecule acetyl CoA. This molecule eventually becomes a long-chain fatty acid that attaches to a glycerol backbone and is stored as a triglyceride in fat cells.

The metabolic pathway to store dietary fat requires little energy (only about 5 percent of the stored energy within the fatty acid) and only a few steps; therefore dietary fat is easier to store as body fat than are dietary carbohydrate or protein. Lipogenesis is a separate anabolic pathway that synthesizes fatty acids to be stored and is not just a reversal of the reactions involved in the breakdown of fat. In fact, the two processes take place in different parts of the cell. Fatty acids are made in the cytosol rather than in the mitochondria, where fats are oxidized. Lipogenesis also differs from fat oxidation in the way it's affected by glucagon and insulin. Glucagon stimulates lipolysis, which provides the fatty acids for beta-oxidation. Insulin has the opposite effect: It inhibits the breakdown of fat and promotes fatty acid synthesis.

During the Postabsorptive State, Metabolism Favors Energy Production

Many Americans consume more than enough kilocalories to meet their energy demands, which is reflected in the current obesity crisis. But what happens when the opposite is true? That is, you're too busy to consume enough food, or you choose not to eat? Regardless of the reason, when you do not consume enough kilocalories to meet your energy needs, your body turns to stored energy to fuel itself. During this postabsorptive state—usually more than four hours after eating—the stomach and small intestine are empty and the need for energy is met from stored energy.

Take a look at **Focus Figure 8.16**, which illustrates the metabolic pathways that are active during the postabsorptive state.

Stores Are Depleted during Fasting

Whereas glycogen stores supply energy during short periods of fasting, such as overnight or between meals, the body adapts differently if you go more than 18 hours without consuming carbohydrates. Initially, the body maintains blood glucose levels by tapping into liver glycogen through glycogenolysis. At the same time, an increase in lipolysis provides fatty acids for energy, thus reducing the use of glucose by the cell. In addition, once liver glycogen has been depleted, gluconeogenesis is initiated, using amino acids, glycerol, pyruvate, and lactate to meet the body's glucose needs.

Fat reserves are broken down faster as fasting continues. The brain has quickly used up the glycogen reserves from the liver and must switch to an alternative source of energy—ketone bodies—derived from the fatty acids. A severe, prolonged fast, or starvation, depletes fat reserves and begins to break down muscle tissue to provide energy.

Ketogenesis Generates Energy during Prolonged Fasting

When deprived of carbohydrates, the body depends less and less on glucose, and resorts to using ketone bodies instead. **Ketogenesis** (the formation of ketone bodies, illustrated in **Figure 8.17**) occurs when there is an excess buildup of acetyl CoA. Acetyl CoA accumulates because it is not being metabolized in the TCA cycle due to a reduced supply of oxaloacetate (which comes from pyruvate and, ultimately, glucose).

Ketogenesis reaches peak levels after an individual has fasted or consumed a limited-carbohydrate diet for three days. By the fourth day of a fast, the ketone bodies are providing almost half of the fuel used by the mitochondria.[3] The presence of ketone bodies is referred to as ketosis (described in Chapter 4). As you continue to fast, your brain switches from glucose to ketone bodies for fuel to reduce the drain on blood glucose. Eventually, about 30 percent of the brain's energy comes from ketone bodies, with the rest provided by blood glucose.

Ketogenesis is a normal metabolic response to fasting, and ketosis is not life-threatening. The kidneys reabsorb ketone bodies to be used by other tissues for energy or excrete excess ketone bodies in the urine to maintain a balanced pH under normal conditions. There can be consequences, however, when ketosis advances to **ketoacidosis.** This condition can occur in individuals with untreated type 1 diabetes mellitus because of the lack of usable insulin, which lowers glucose availability to the cells. When ketone bodies accumulate, the blood pH drops. The body responds by increasing breathing to excrete more CO_2, which increases the pH. If the level of ketone bodies surpasses the kidneys' ability to reabsorb them, they spill into the urine. Severe diabetic ketoacidosis can lead to impaired heart activity, coma, and even death.

ketogenesis The formation of ketone bodies from excess acetyl CoA.

ketoacidosis A form of metabolic acidosis, or pH imbalance due to excess acid, that occurs when excess ketone bodies are present in the blood; most often seen in individuals with untreated type I diabetes.

Metabolism during the Postabsorptive State

The postabsorptive (fasting) state is generally a catabolic state: After a period of fasting, when the body glycogen stores are reduced, the body increases its use of stored fatty acids.

- 🟥 Catabolism
- 🟦 Anabolism
- 🟪 Nutrient Transport

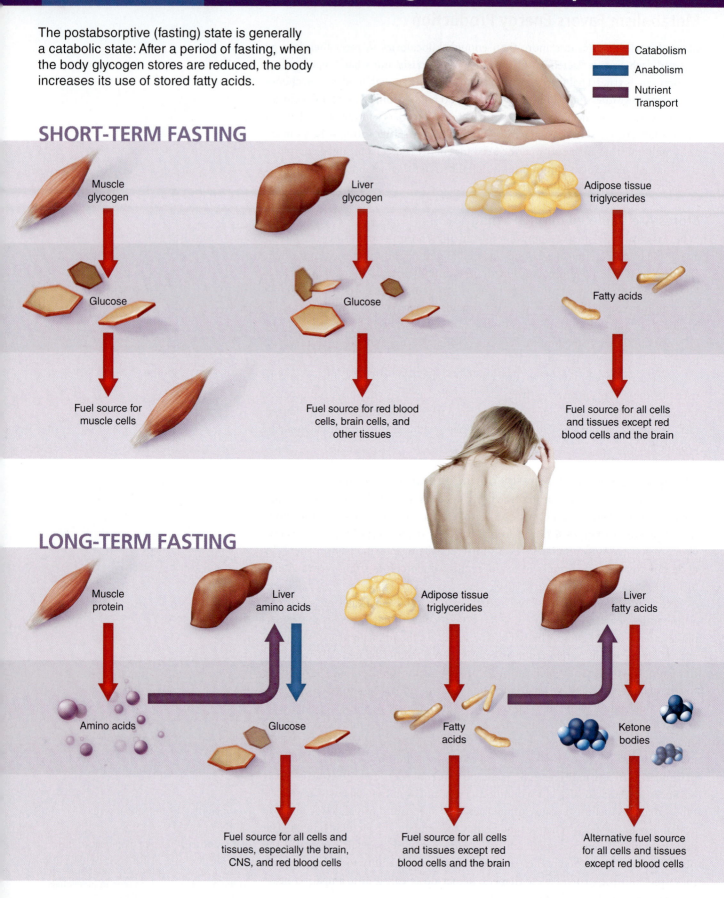

SHORT-TERM FASTING

Muscle glycogen → Glucose → Fuel source for muscle cells

Liver glycogen → Glucose → Fuel source for red blood cells, brain cells, and other tissues

Adipose tissue triglycerides → Fatty acids → Fuel source for all cells and tissues except red blood cells and the brain

LONG-TERM FASTING

Muscle protein / Liver amino acids → Amino acids → Glucose → Fuel source for all cells and tissues, especially the brain, CNS, and red blood cells

Adipose tissue triglycerides → Fatty acids → Fuel source for all cells and tissues except red blood cells and the brain

Liver fatty acids → Ketone bodies → Alternative fuel source for all cells and tissues except red blood cells

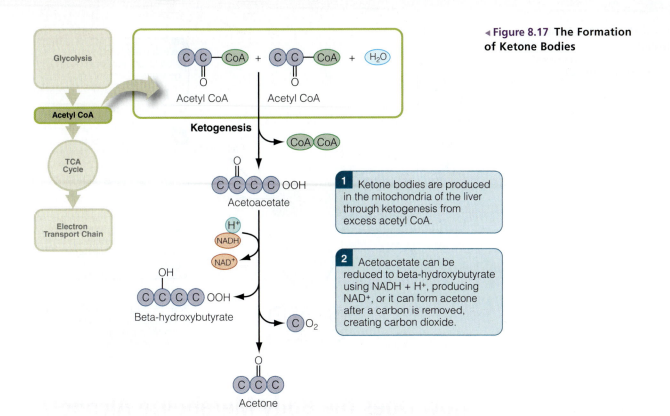

◂ Figure 8.17 The Formation of Ketone Bodies

Glycolysis

Acetyl CoA

TCA Cycle

Electron Transport Chain

Ketogenesis

Acetyl CoA + Acetyl CoA + H_2O

Acetoacetate

H^+
NADH
NAD^+

Beta-hydroxybutyrate

C O_2

Acetone

1 Ketone bodies are produced in the mitochondria of the liver through ketogenesis from excess acetyl CoA.

2 Acetoacetate can be reduced to beta-hydroxybutyrate using NADH + H^+, producing NAD^+, or it can form acetone after a carbon is removed, creating carbon dioxide.

LO 8.4: THE TAKE-HOME MESSAGE The differences in metabolism between the absorptive, or feeding, state and the postabsorptive, or fasting, state are listed in Table 8.5. During the absorptive state, anabolic reactions are favored. Carbohydrates are first used for ATP synthesis with excess stored as glycogen or triglycerides in the adipose tissue. Excess amino acids and dietary fat are also converted to triglycerides and stored. During the postabsorptive state, metabolism shifts to favor catabolic reactions. Fat is broken down to fatty acids to be used for ATP synthesis, while liver glycogen, glycerol, and glucogenic amino acids are used to maintain blood glucose levels. As fasting continues, glycogen stores are depleted, and muscle is broken down to provide amino acids for energy and gluconeogenesis. A lack of sufficient glucose in the blood can lead to excess breakdown of fat and the synthesis of ketone bodies, which can be used by the brain and muscles for energy. If ketogenesis is prolonged, ketoacidosis can lead to serious conditions, including death.

TABLE 8.5 Metabolism during Feeding and Fasting

	Feeding: Metabolism Following a Meal in the Absorptive State	Fasting: Metabolism Following a Meal in the Postabsorptive State	If Fasting Continues after Liver and Muscle Glycogen Stores Are Depleted
Proteins	Amino acids are used for protein synthesis or stored as a triglyceride in the adipose tissue		Amino acids are used for gluconeogenesis or catabolized for energy
Carbohydrates	Glucose is used for energy or stored as glycogen in the liver or muscle	Liver and muscle glycogen is broken down to provide glucose for energy	
Triglycerides	Fatty acids and glycerol are stored as a triglyceride in the adipose tissue	Triglycerides in adipose tissue are broken down to glycerol and fatty acids to be used for energy metabolism	Fatty acids are used to produce ketone bodies and oxidized for energy

◀ **Figure 8.18 The Metabolism of Alcohol**
The liver is the main organ involved in the metabolism of alcohol.

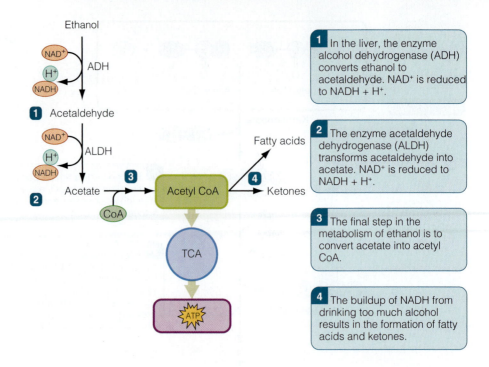

Ethanol

1 Acetaldehyde

2 Acetate

3 Acetyl CoA

Fatty acids

Ketones

CoA

TCA

ATP

1 In the liver, the enzyme alcohol dehydrogenase (ADH) converts ethanol to acetaldehyde. NAD⁺ is reduced to NADH + H⁺.

2 The enzyme acetaldehyde dehydrogenase (ALDH) transforms acetaldehyde into acetate. NAD⁺ is reduced to NADH + H⁺.

3 The final step in the metabolism of ethanol is to convert acetate into acetyl CoA.

4 The buildup of NADH from drinking too much alcohol results in the formation of fatty acids and ketones.

How Does the Body Metabolize Alcohol?

LO 8.5 Describe the metabolism of alcohol.

Despite the fact that alcohol (ethanol) contains kilocalories, it adds no nutritional value to the diet, has no function in the human body, and is therefore not an essential nutrient. However, alcohol can be a significant source of energy. In fact, alcohol contains almost twice the amount of energy (7 kilocalories per gram) of an equal amount of carbohydrate or protein (4 kilocalories per gram).

Alcohol is also different from carbohydrates, proteins, and fats because it doesn't have to be digested before the body absorbs it. Rather, some of the alcohol consumed is metabolized in the stomach while the rest is absorbed directly through the stomach mucosa and small intestine lining. This means that alcohol makes its way into the blood soon after it's ingested. Through the blood, alcohol is transported to the liver, where it is metabolized.

The body can easily metabolize about half an ounce of alcohol, the amount in a standard drink, in an hour and a half; however, when more than this amount is consumed in that period of time, the excess alcohol circulates throughout the body until the liver enzymes can break it down.

The Enzymes That Metabolize Ethanol

Alcohol is metabolized through three distinct pathways. The primary pathway involves the oxidation of ethanol by the enzyme alcohol dehydrogenase (ADH) (described in Chapter 7), which is found in both the stomach and the liver. The liver contains enough ADH to metabolize alcohol efficiently. As you can see in **Figure 8.18**, as soon as the capillaries deliver the alcohol to the liver cells, it is converted to acetaldehyde. In this reaction, ADH removes hydrogen ions from alcohol, which are picked up by the coenzyme NAD⁺. More hydrogens are removed as acetaldehyde is quickly changed to acetate by a similar enzyme called **acetaldehyde dehydrogenase (ALDH).** The final step converts acetate to acetyl CoA. The acetyl CoA can then either be used to produce energy in the TCA cycle if needed, or be transformed into fatty acids and stored as a triglyceride in the adipocyte.

The alternative pathway in the liver that can oxidize alcohol is the **microsomal ethanol oxidizing system (MEOS).** This system is not as significant as ADH for small

acetaldehyde dehydrogenase (ALDH) The enzyme that converts acetaldehyde to acetate; this is the second step in oxidizing ethanol in the liver.

microsomal ethanol oxidizing system (MEOS) The second metabolic pathway for oxidizing ethanol, used at higher intakes of alcohol; it also participates in metabolizing drugs.

amounts of alcohol, but becomes more important with the chronic consumption of alcohol. This liver system also metabolizes many prescription and over-the-counter medications. If you drink alcohol while taking certain medications, the liver metabolizes the alcohol first, which causes the effects of the drugs to be felt over a longer period of time. This is the reason drugs and alcohol should never be taken together.

Not all alcohol is metabolized in the liver or stomach. A third metabolic pathway for alcohol takes place in the brain, where alcohol is oxidized to acetaldehyde by the enzyme catalase.[4] This pathway may be responsible for some of the psychological effects people experience, such as reduced inhibitions, when they consume alcohol.

Excess Alcohol Is Stored as Fat

Fat metabolism shifts after you drink alcohol. When alcohol is consumed, fewer fatty acids are used for energy. At the same time, the excess kilocalories in alcohol are metabolized and stored as fatty acids in the adipose tissue and liver. In chronic alcoholics, excess fatty deposits in the liver can result in cirrhosis (see the discussion of this dangerous condition in Chapter 7). Note that fat can begin to accumulate in the liver after a single bout of binge drinking.[5]

> **LO 8.5: THE TAKE-HOME MESSAGE** Alcohol is primarily absorbed and metabolized in the liver by two enzyme systems. The most efficient enzyme system is alcohol dehydrogenase (ADH) and acetaldehyde dehydrogenase (ALDH), which convert the ethanol to acetaldehyde in the initial stages of metabolism, and ultimately to acetyl CoA. The MEOS system, which is used with chronic consumption of alcohol, also metabolizes drugs. A third system is found in the brain and metabolizes alcohol to acetaldehyde. Alcohol is not stored, but the excess kilocalories from alcohol not used for ATP production are converted to fatty acids and stored as a triglyceride.

Health Connection

What Are Genetic Disorders of Metabolism?

LO 8.6 Describe the causes, diagnosis, symptoms, and dietary treatments of the most common genetic disorders of metabolism.

Healthy individuals are born with gene coding for all the enzymes they need to control metabolism and function properly. However, some people inherit a genetic defect in one or more genes that code for the enzymes that control a specific metabolic pathway. Of the hundreds of genes that have been identified as causing disease in humans, more than 95 percent of them are due to a single, dysfunctional gene referred to as *monogenic*.[6] These monogenic disorders are fairly rare, especially relative to other diseases such as diabetes or heart disease that are much more common.

The lack of the appropriate enzyme prevents one substrate from being converted to another. The result is a buildup of abnormal by-products that can be toxic. Though genetic disorders cannot be cured, they can be controlled through careful dietary treatment.

As you learned in Chapter 1, the science of nutrigenomics has been used for decades to manage gene–diet interactions and decrease gene expression to prevent further complications. Some genes, called *susceptibility* genes, are very sensitive to diet.

Each genetic disorder presented here is named for either the enzyme that is dysfunctional or a symptom that is caused by the disorder. Some of these disorders are monogenic, such as phenylketonuria, while others involve more than one gene, such as maple syrup urine disease. Some of the most common genetic disorders involving protein and carbohydrate metabolism are presented in Table 8.6.

Phenylketonuria (PKU)

A simple blood test at birth can detect **phenylketonuria (PKU),** a rare monogenic disorder that causes serious health problems if untreated. Classic PKU is the most severe form of the genetic disorder, resulting in behavior problems and

phenylketonuria (PKU) A genetic disorder characterized by the inability to metabolize the essential amino acid phenylalanine.

TABLE 8.6	Five Genetic Disorders in Metabolism			
Disorder	Incidence	Enzyme That Is Lacking	Examples of Acceptable Foods	Examples of Foods to Avoid
Phenylketonuria	1:15,000	Phenylalanine hydroxylase	Fruits, vegetables, breads, cereals, special formulas	Meat, chicken, fish, eggs, dairy, nuts, legumes
Maple syrup urine disease	1:185,000	Branched-chain alpha-keto acid dehydrogenase	Foods low in branched-chain amino acids, fruits, vegetables, breads, cereals, specialized formulas	Meats, eggs, dairy, nuts, legumes
Homocystinuria	1:300,000	Cystathionine beta-synthase	Fruits, vegetables, special formulas	Meats, eggs, dairy
Galactosemia	1:60,000	Galactose 1-phosphate uridyltransferase	Fruits, vegetables, breads, cereals, eggs, meats	Milk, cheese, milk chocolate, organ meats, legumes, hydrolyzed protein made from milk, casein, fermented soy products
Glycogen Storage Disease	1:50,000	Glucose 6-phosphatase	Corn starch and continuous overnight feeds	Milk, cheese, fruits

mental retardation before the child's first birthday. The mild to moderate conditions of PKU have a lower risk of mental retardation that can be prevented by following a prescribed, controlled diet.

Individuals with phenylketonuria (PKU) lack the enzyme *phenylalanine hydroxylase* that converts the essential amino acid phenylalanine to the nonessential amino acid tyrosine (see table). Under these conditions, phenylalanine accumulates in the blood, a condition called **hyperphenylalanemia.** Phenylketonuria can be easily diagnosed with a heel stick to analyze the blood of newborns shortly after birth. If the initial tests are positive for PKU, further blood and urine tests are completed to confirm the diagnosis. The treatment for PKU is a controlled-phenylalanine diet designed to maintain blood levels of phenylalanine and provide sufficient tyrosine, energy, and protein to grow and

hyperphenylalanemia Elevated levels of blood phenylalanine due to a lack of the enzyme phenylalanine hydroxylase.

maple syrup urine disease (MSUD) A genetic disorder characterized by the inability to metabolize branched-chain amino acids; symptoms include a maple syrup smell in the urine.

homocystinuria A genetic disorder characterized by the inability to metabolize the essential amino acid methionine.

develop normally. Individuals with PKU must avoid high-protein foods and eliminate any products containing aspartame (the sugar substitute found in NutraSweet), which contains phenylalanine, from their diet. Individuals must follow the diet strictly through adolescence and generally throughout their entire life.

Many diet sodas contain phenylalanine, a major ingredient in the artificial sweetener aspartame, also called Equal or NutraSweet.

Maple Syrup Urine Disease

Another protein-related disorder is **maple syrup urine disease (MSUD).** The disorder results from the mutations of four different genes that provide the instructions for making proteins from the branched-chain amino acids leucine, isoleucine, and valine. The mutated genes eliminate or reduce the ability to metabolize these four amino acids. The result is a buildup of the amino acids and their by-products in the blood. Excessive levels of these four amino acids in the blood are toxic to several organs, including the brain. Babies with MSUD appear normal at birth but begin to show signs of the

disease, such as a maple syrup smell to their urine (hence the name), within a few weeks. If left untreated, the condition can result in seizures, coma, and even death.[7] The prescribed diet includes specially designed formulas and avoidance of foods such as beef, chicken, fish, eggs, nuts, and legumes, which are high in the three affected amino acids.[8] Unfortunately, such a restrictive diet often means the child subsists solely on specially designed formulas or medically created foods.

Homocystinuria

Homocystinuria is an inherited monogenic disorder that occurs when the enzyme cystathionine beta-synthase that converts homocysteine to

Infants with genetic orders such as maple syrup urine disease require special formulas and medically designed foods to meet their nutritional needs.

cystathionine is lacking or not working properly.[9] Homocystinuria is an autosomal recessive disorder, which means both parents have to be a carrier of the defective gene for their offspring to be affected.

A diet rich in the essential amino acid methionine adds to the buildup of homocysteine because methionine is converted to homocysteine during metabolism. The prescribed treatment is a diet low in methionine, along with a supplement of B vitamins, including folate, vitamin B_6, and vitamin B_{12}, which are often low in individuals with homocystinuria. The low-methionine diet must be followed for life. Homocysteine and certain amino acids, such as methionine,

building up in the blood can result in dislocation of the lens in the eye, nearsightedness, and blood clots in the veins and arteries.[10] In adults, the high rate of blood clots and atherosclerosis, especially in the carotid artery, could cause premature cardiovascular disease.[11]

Galactosemia

The genetic disorder **galactosemia** results in the inability to convert galactose to glucose due to the lack of the enzyme galactose 1-phosphate uridyltransferase (also called GALT; see **Figure 8.19**). The result is a buildup of galactose in the blood, which can damage several different organs in the body if left untreated, including the liver, brain, kidneys, and eyes.[12]

Infants with galactosemia develop diarrhea and vomiting within a few days of drinking milk or formula containing lactose. They will show signs of irritability, failure to grow, lethargy, and poor sucking response to feeding. Untreated babies may develop mental retardation or die from liver disease.[13]

The treatment focuses mainly on restricting dietary lactose and galactose, which means avoiding milk and all dairy products, and products that contain milk

chocolate, whey protein or whey solids, casein, and dry milk solids, all of which may contain galactose.

Glycogen Storage Disease

Glycogen storage disease is a genetic disorder that disrupts glycogenolysis in the liver. The gene mutation causes a deficiency of the enzyme glucose 6-phosphatase, the enzyme that converts liver glycogen to glucose. If glycogen is trapped in the liver, the body is unable to maintain normal blood glucose levels between meals. Babies with glycogen storage disease can have hypoglycemia, which can lead to seizures. They can also develop high levels of lactic acid in the blood, high levels of uric acid in the urine, and excess amounts of lipids in the blood, or hyperlipidemia.[14]

To treat glycogen storage disease, foods that contain sucrose, lactose, galactose, and fructose are restricted because these carbohydrates are often stored as glycogen in the liver. Individuals diagnosed with glycogen storage disease follow the dietary recommendations for life.

LO 8.6: THE TAKE-HOME MESSAGE
Genetic disorders are formed from an inherited genetic defect in one or more genes that code for the enzymes that control metabolic processes. The metabolic process is disrupted when the enzyme for protein or carbohydrate metabolism is lacking. For infants with some genetic disorders, formulas are used to control the amount of specific nutrients consumed, such as with maple syrup urine disease. Other dietary restrictions, such as a diet low in the amino acids methionine, isoleucine, leucine, and lysine, or the sugars sucrose, lactose, glucose, and galactose, are necessary to treat the disorders.

galactosemia The genetic disorder characterized by high levels of galactose in the blood due to the inability to convert galactose to glucose.

glycogen storage disease A genetic disorder characterized by the inability to break down glycogen due to the lack of glucose 6-phosphatase.

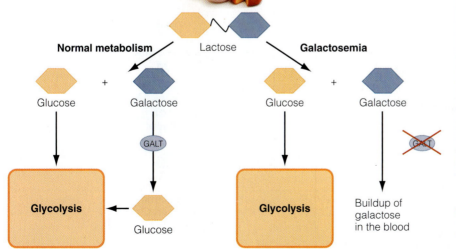

▲ **Figure 8.19 Metabolic Disruption of Galactose Metabolism in Galactosemia**
The lack of the enzyme galactose-1-phosphate uridyltransferase, or GALT, blocks the conversion of galactose to glucose. Galactose builds up in the blood and can cause serious complications.

Visual Chapter Summary

LO 8.1 Metabolism Is the Sum of All Chemical Reactions in the Body

Metabolism is the term given to all chemical reactions in the cells. The mitochondria are the organelles within the cells that generate most of the cell's ATP through aerobic metabolism. Metabolism balances anabolic reactions that create large molecules from smaller parts, such as glucose to glycogen, with catabolic reactions that break apart large molecules, such as triglycerides to glycerol and fatty acids, to produce ATP. Carbon dioxide and water will be the final products of fat catabolism. These reactions are turned on and off by enzymes and coenzymes and are stimulated by hormones.

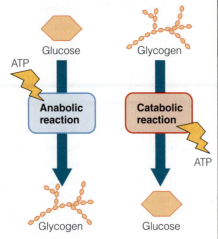

Glucose — ATP — **Anabolic reaction** — Glycogen

Glycogen — **Catabolic reaction** — ATP — Glucose

LO 8.2 ATP Is the Energy Source That Fuels Metabolism

Adenosine triphosphate, or ATP, is the energy source cells use to fuel metabolic reactions. ATP is not stored and must be regenerated. Energy is released when a phosphate bond is broken, producing adenosine diphosphate, or ADP. This energy is used to fuel anabolic reactions. ATP is regenerated from ADP plus a phosphate molecule, which can be donated from creatine phosphate.

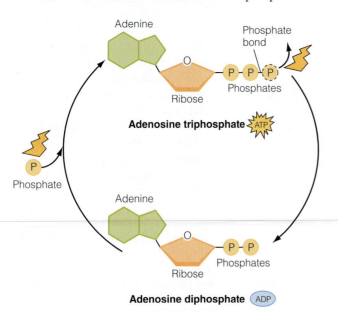

Adenine

Phosphate bond

O

Ribose

P P P Phosphates

Adenosine triphosphate ATP

Phosphate P

Adenine

O

Ribose

P P Phosphates

Adenosine diphosphate ADP

LO 8.3 Carbohydrates, Triglycerides, and Amino Acids Follow Metabolic Pathways

Glucose, the main monosaccharide in metabolism, is oxidized in the cytosol through glycolysis to form pyruvate. If there is sufficient oxygen in the cell, pyruvate continues down the pathway to acetyl CoA and enters the TCA cycle.

Triglycerides are hydrolyzed to glycerol and fatty acids. Glycerol enters the metabolic pathway through glycolysis, while fatty acids undergo beta-oxidation to form acetyl CoA.

Deaminated amino acids can be oxidized in the TCA cycle. Glucogenic amino acids can be transformed into pyruvate and participate in gluconeogenesis. Ketogenic amino acids are converted to acetyl CoA and are either oxidized in the TCA cycle or turned into fatty acids and stored as triglycerides.

The TCA cycle, which occurs in the mitochondria, begins with acetyl CoA. Its products include hydrogen atoms and electrons that are transferred to the electron transport chain and ultimately to ATP synthase, where the majority of ATP is generated through oxidative phosphorylation.

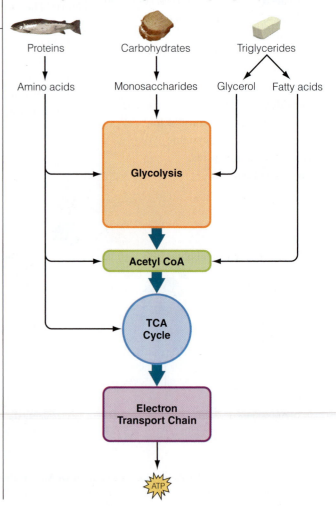

Proteins — Carbohydrates — Triglycerides

Amino acids — Monosaccharides — Glycerol — Fatty acids

Glycolysis

Acetyl CoA

TCA Cycle

Electron Transport Chain

ATP

LO 8.4 Metabolism Switches between Anabolic Processes and Catabolic Processes during the Absorptive State, Postabsorptive State, and Starvation

During the absorptive state, excess kilocalories stimulate fat synthesis and are stored as triglycerides. Excess carbohydrates can also be stored as glycogen.

Fasting during the postabsorptive state shifts the metabolism to catabolic reactions to maintain energy balance. The body uses stored glycogen and fatty acids from stored triglycerides in the early stages of fasting. As fasting continues, the body increases the breakdown of fats for energy and conversion to ketone bodies, which can be used by the brain and muscle. Blood glucose levels are maintained using amino acids, pyruvate, lactate, and glycerol as precursors in gluconeogenesis.

LO 8.6 Genetic Disorders Can Disrupt Metabolism

Genetic disorders of metabolism can disrupt one or more metabolic processes, due to the lack of an enzyme involved in either protein or carbohydrate metabolism. Serious metabolic consequences can occur if dietary treatment is not followed. For infants with some genetic disorders, formulas are used to control the amount of specific nutrients consumed, such as with maple syrup urine disease.

LO 8.5 The Liver Metabolizes Alcohol

Alcohol is metabolized in the liver to acetyl CoA by the enzyme system ADH. The acetyl CoA enters the TCA cycle to produce ATP. When an excess of alcohol builds up, the acetyl CoA is converted to fatty acids and can be stored as a triglyceride in the liver or sent out into the blood. The consumption of excess alcohol can result in the buildup of stored fat in the liver, leading to a condition called cirrhosis.

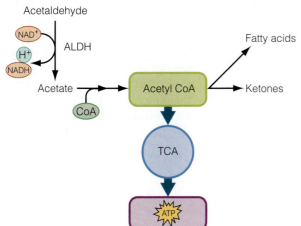

Terms to Know

- mitochondrion
- cytosol
- anabolic reactions
- catabolic reactions
- adenosine diphosphate (ADP)
- creatine phosphate (PCr)
- glycolysis
- pyruvate
- acetyl CoA
- tricarboxylic acid (TCA) cycle
- electron transport chain
- lactate
- Cori cycle
- beta-oxidation
- alpha-ketoglutarate
- oxaloacetate
- oxidative phosphorylation
- flavoproteins
- cytochromes
- absorptive state
- postabsorptive state
- ketogenesis
- ketoacidosis
- acetaldehyde dehydrogenase
- microsomal ethanol oxidizing system (MEOS)
- phenylketonuria (PKU)
- hyperphenylalanemia
- maple syrup urine disease (MSUD)
- homocystinuria
- galactosemia
- glycogen storage disease
- metabolism
- metabolic pathway
- anaerobic
- aerobic
- adenosine triphosphate (ATP)
- hormone-sensitive lipase
- ketogenic

Check Your Understanding

1. Metabolism is defined as
   a. the breakdown of large compounds into smaller particles.
   b. the synthesis of new compounds.
   c. the sum of all chemical reactions in the body.
   d. the storage of fat in the adipocyte.
2. Glycolysis is a metabolic pathway that breaks down glucose for energy. This is an example of a(n)
   a. anabolic reaction.
   b. catabolic reaction.
   c. redox reaction.
   d. glucogenic reaction.
3. Your metabolism is regulated by
   a. hormones such as insulin and glucagon.
   b. hydroxylase activity.
   c. the amount of creatine phosphate in your cells.
   d. all of the above.
4. The energy molecule that fuels metabolism is
   a. adenosine diphosphate.
   b. adenosine triphosphate.
   c. creatine phosphate.
   d. acetyl CoA.
5. The first stage in using glucose for energy metabolism is called
   a. beta-oxidation.
   b. the Cori cycle.
   c. glycolysis.
   d. the electron transport chain.
6. The compounds that can be used for gluconeogenesis include
   a. fatty acids.
   b. lactate.
   c. ketogenic amino acids.
   d. acetaldehyde.

7. Fatty acids cannot be used for gluconeogenesis because
   a. they lack sufficient carbons to form glucose.
   b. they are converted to acetyl CoA, which can't reform pyruvate.
   c. they are converted to oxaloacetate, which can't reform pyruvate.
   d. they enter the TCA cycle through citrate.
8. If your diet contains excess protein, the excess amino acids are
   a. deaminated and then converted to ATP or fatty acids.
   b. stored as glycogen in the liver.
   c. stored as protein in the muscle.
   d. excreted in the urine.
9. Ketogenic amino acids can be converted into glucose.
   a. true
   b. false
10. Homocystinuria is a genetic disorder caused by
    a. a buildup of galactose.
    b. a lack of the enzyme cystathionine beta-synthase.
    c. the inability to break down glycogen.
    d. a deficiency in the amino acid methionine.

Answers

1. (c) Metabolism is defined as the sum of all chemical reactions in the body. This includes anabolic reactions that build larger compounds from smaller molecules, catabolic reactions that break molecules apart, or lipogenesis—storing fat in the adipocyte.
2. (b) Catabolic reactions are those that break apart larger molecules into smaller molecules. Anabolic reactions are the opposite and build larger molecules from smaller molecules. Redox reactions, or oxidation-reduction reactions, involve the transfer of electrons, and glucogenic reactions produce glucose.

3. (a) Metabolism is controlled by hormones, which are released in response to changes in ATP and enzyme activity.
4. (b) Adenosine triphosphate (ATP) is a high-energy molecule that, when hydrolyzed to adenosine disphosphate (ADP), provides energy to cells. ATP can be reformed by adding an inorganic phosphate to ADP donated from the initial reaction, or from creatine phosphate (PCr).
5. (c) Glycolysis is the first stage of carbohydrate metabolism. Eventually, the hydrogen atoms and electrons generated from glycolysis are carried to the electron transport chain. Beta-oxidation is the metabolic pathway used to convert fatty acids to acetyl CoA. At the end of glycolysis, pyruvate can be converted to lactate, which is converted into glucose through the Cori cycle in the liver.
6. (b) Lactate can be transformed into glucose through gluconeogenesis. Fatty acids, ketogenic amino acids, and acetaldehyde are not gluconeogenic substrates.
7. (b) Fatty acids contain sufficient carbons but they are converted to acetyl CoA, which is not able to form the pyruvate needed for gluconeogenesis.
8. (a) Because we can't store excess amino acids as protein, we have to either use them for ATP synthesis or convert them to fatty acids and store them as a triglyceride.
9. (b) Ketogenic amino acids are converted to acetyl CoA or acetoacetate, which are precursors to fatty acids or ketone bodies. Ketogenic amino acids cannot be converted to glucose.
10. (b) Homocystinuria is caused by the lack or impaired function of the enzyme cystathionine beta-synthase that converts homocysteine to cystathionine. Homocysteine and certain amino acids, such as methionine,

build up in the blood. Controlling methionine intake is essential to reducing the buildup of homocysteine. A buildup of galactose is called galactosemia and glycogen storage disease results in the inability to break down stored glycogen.

Answers to True or False?

1. **True.** All chemical reactions involved in metabolism take place within the mitochondria or the cytosol of cells.
2. **True.** The body metabolizes carbohydrates mostly as glucose through glycolysis, which produces more energy in the form of ATP than it uses, compared with amino acid and fatty acid metabolism.
3. **False.** Most fructose is converted to glucose before entering the metabolic pathway.
4. **False.** A burning sensation in muscles during strenuous exercise is caused by the reduction in pH due to the buildup of hydrogen ions, not the buildup of lactate.
5. **False.** Once protein and energy needs have been met, excess amino acids are converted to fatty acids through acetyl CoA and stored as triglycerides in adipocytes. Thus excess intake of dietary protein will not result in larger muscle.
6. **False.** Fatty acids are oxidized in the TCA cycle when cells contain sufficient oxygen. Under the anaerobic conditions of high-intensity exercise, a larger percentage of glucose, rather than fatty acids, is used for energy production.
7. **False.** During alcohol metabolism in the liver, ethanol is converted to acetyl CoA, which either enters the TCA cycle or is transformed into fatty acids. Acetyl CoA cannot be used to produce glucose.
8. **False.** Vitamins and minerals in foods do not provide energy. However, the B vitamins niacin and riboflavin are essential for energy production because of their roles as coenzymes during metabolism. As coenzymes, they accept hydrogen atoms and electrons produced during glycolysis and the TCA cycle, which are in turn used by the electron transport chain to produce energy.
9. **False.** Regardless of what time of day you eat, an excess of total kilocalories favors anabolic metabolism, which means you store the excess kilocalories as body fat or glycogen. If you consume fewer kilocalories than you need each day for metabolism, catabolic reactions are favored, resulting in a breakdown of triglycerides.
10. **False.** Inborn errors of metabolism are the result of a genetic mutation that causes a specific metabolic enzyme to be either missing or produced in inadequate amounts. The gene is not repaired during puberty, and the disorders cannot be outgrown.

Web Resources

- For general information on genetic disorders, visit the National Human Genome Research Institute at www.nhgri.nih.gov
- For more information on phenylketonuria, visit the National PKU Alliance at www.npkua.org
- For more information on galactosemia, visit the Galactosemia Foundation at http://galactosemia.org
- For more information from a peer-reviewed online journal, visit *Nutrition and Metabolism* at www.nutritionandmetabolism.com

References

1. Berg, J. M., J. L. Tymoczko, and L. Stryer. 2012. *Biochemistry.* 7th ed. New York: W. H. Freeman.
2. Gropper, S. S., and J. L. Smith. 2013. *Advanced Nutrition and Human Metabolism.* 6th ed. Belmont, CA: Wadsworth—Cengage Learning.
3. Ibid.
4. Zimatkin, S. M., and A. L. Buben. 2007. Ethanol Oxidation in the Living Brain. *Alcohol and Alcoholism* 42:529–532.
5. Berg, et al. 2012. *Biochemistry.*
6. National Human Genome Research Institute. 2012. *What Are Genetic Disorders?* Available at www.genome.gov. Accessed March 2014.
7. Genetics Home Reference. 2013. *Maple Syrup Urine Disease.* Available at http://ghr.nlm.nih.gov. Accessed March 2014.
8. Ibid.
9. Picker, J. L., and H. L. Levy. 2011. Homocystinuria Caused by Cystathionine Beta-Synthase Deficiency. *Gene Reviews.* Available at www.ncbi.nlm.nih.gov. Accessed March 2014.
10. National Institutes of Health. 2014. *Homocystinuria.* Available at www.nlm.nih.gov. Accessed March 2014.
11. Ibid.
12. American Liver Foundation. 2011. *Galactosemia.* Available at www.liverfoundation.org. Accessed March 2014.
13. Ibid.
14. Genetics Home Reference. 2013. *Glycogen Storage Disease Type 1.* Available at http://ghr.nlm.nih.gov. Accessed March 2014.

9 Fat-Soluble Vitamins

Learning Outcomes

After reading this chapter, you will be able to:

9.1 Explain the characteristics of vitamins, and classify vitamins according to their solubility.

9.2 Compare and contrast the absorption and storage of fat-soluble and water-soluble vitamins.

9.3 Define the term "antioxidant" and explain which vitamins perform this function.

9.4 Describe the best sources of vitamins and the factors that affect the vitamin content of foods.

9.5 Describe the functions, recommended intakes, food sources, and the deficiency and toxicity effects of vitamin A.

9.6 Describe the functions, recommended intakes, food sources, and the deficiency and toxicity effects of vitamin D.

9.7 Describe the functions, recommended intakes, food sources, and the deficiency and toxicity effects of vitamin E.

9.8 Describe the functions, recommended intakes, food sources, and the deficiency and toxicity effects of vitamin K.

9.9 Explain the role of dietary supplements in maintaining a healthy diet.

True or False?

1. Vitamins provide the body with energy. **T**/**F**

2. Fat-soluble vitamins are found in fatty foods. **T**/**F**

3. Taking vitamin supplements is *never* harmful. **T**/**F**

4. Most people can meet their vitamin needs through food, so supplements are unnecessary. **T**/**F**

5. Steaming is the best cooking method to retain the vitamins in vegetables. **T**/**F**

6. Carrots, winter squash, and broccoli are good sources of vitamin A. **T**/**F**

7. The body makes vitamin D with the help of sunlight. **T**/**F**

8. Vitamin K is an anticoagulant. **T**/**F**

9. Vitamin E helps keep bones strong. **T**/**F**

10. Antioxidants are a magic pill that will prevent aging. **T**/**F**

See page 355 for the answers.

Vitamins remained nameless and undiscovered substances until the early part of the twentieth century, when scientists sought substances to cure diseases such as beriberi, scurvy, and rickets. These may sound like the names of rock bands, but they are actually devastating diseases caused by deficiencies of thiamin (for beriberi), vitamin C (for scurvy), and vitamin D (for rickets). Throughout the twentieth century, scientists discovered the vitamins that cured these and other diseases. By the 1940s, the U.S. government mandated the addition of specific vitamins to grains and milk to improve the nation's health.

In the latter part of the twentieth century, improved diets meant that vitamin deficiencies were less of an issue for most Americans. Scientists shifted their focus from using vitamins to cure disease to using them to prevent disease. Today, researchers seek to find out how vitamins affect and prevent everything from birth defects to heart disease and cancer.

In this chapter, we begin with an overview of vitamins, followed by a discussion of differences between the fat-soluble and water-soluble vitamins. We then cover the four fat-soluble vitamins in detail, including their functions, recommended intakes, food sources, and the deficiency and toxicity effects. (We cover water-soluble vitamins in Chapter 10.)

What Are Vitamins?

LO 9.1 Explain the characteristics of vitamins, and classify vitamins according to their solubility.

Vitamins are tasteless organic compounds the body requires in small amounts for normal metabolic functions. Vitamins act as coenzymes to help regulate metabolism; assist the body to convert the energy in fat, carbohydrates, and protein into ATP; and promote growth and reproduction. Vitamins do not provide energy themselves, but a deficiency of any vitamin can cause a lack of energy and other serious health problems.

Vitamins Were Discovered about One Hundred Years Ago

During the eighteenth century alone, an estimated 2 million sailors died of scurvy, the deficiency disease caused by a lack of vitamin C. The mottled skin and spongy gums that are symptomatic of the disease frequently occurred among men on long sea voyages, during which supplies of fresh foods would be depleted before the end of the trip. Eventually, the acid in citrus fruit was recognized as a curative factor, and British sailors came to be known as "Limeys" because of the British Navy's policy of issuing lime juice on board its ships to prevent scurvy. What they didn't recognize was that the citrus fruit provides vitamin C, which is the vitamin needed to ward off scurvy.

In the early part of the twentieth century, scientists searching for substances to cure diseases such as beriberi and rickets[1] eventually identified thiamin as the curative vitamin for beriberi, and vitamin D as the cure for rickets. As they associated additional vitamins with other diseases and conditions, scientists realized their value in promoting public health.

As each new vitamin was discovered, it was given a temporary name until its structure was isolated. Researchers started at the beginning of the alphabet with vitamins A, B, C, D, E, and K. The letters F, G, and H were dropped once those substances were found not to be needed to support life.

This nomenclature changed after vitamin B was found to have more than one chemical compound, and chemists began adding a subscript number to each newly isolated structure. Together, these vitamins became known as the B complex, with

vitamins Thirteen essential, organic micronutrients that are needed by the body for normal functions, such as regulating metabolism and assisting in energy production, growth, reproduction, and overall health.

individual vitamins labeled B_1, B_2, and so forth. While vitamins B_6 and B_{12} still retain their numeric names, most of the B vitamins are now better known by their scientific names, such as thiamin (for B_1) and riboflavin (for B_2).

There Are Criteria for Classifying Vitamins

Vitamins are unique nutrients in that they are not alike in their chemical structure nor do they have similar functions. Whereas, as you learned from earlier chapters, amino acids each have a basic structure but differ in their side groups, this is not the case with vitamins. How, then, are vitamins classified?

An organic, non-energy-providing nutrient is classified as a vitamin when it cannot be synthesized in ample amounts in the body. For instance, vitamin K and two of the B vitamins (niacin and biotin) can be made in the body, but not in amounts sufficient to meet the body's metabolic needs, so they must also be consumed in the diet. A second requirement for a compound to be called a vitamin is that a chronic deficiency of the compound is likely to cause physical symptoms, from fatigue or confusion to scaly skin or blindness. The symptoms are likely to disappear once the vitamin has been sufficiently restored to the diet and absorbed into the body, provided the deficiency has not caused permanent damage.

Based on these criteria, 13 compounds are classified as vitamins. Choline, recognized by some to be a new vitamin, is not included here. The vitamins are further organized according to their solubility. There are four fat-soluble (hydrophobic) vitamins: A, D, E, and K, and nine water-soluble (hydrophilic) vitamins, including the B vitamin complex and vitamin C (see **Figure 9.1**). The distinction in solubility is important because it influences how the body digests, absorbs, transports, stores, and excretes these essential nutrients.

All Vitamins Are Organic, but Differ in Structure and Function

All vitamins are organic because they contain carbon. Vitamins also contain hydrogen and oxygen and, in some cases, nitrogen, cobalt, or sulfur. The chemical structure of each vitamin is unique. That is, unlike proteins, which consist of and vary by chains of amino acids, vitamins are singular units. There are no bonds for the body to hydrolyze during digestion, and vitamins are absorbed intact into the intestinal wall.

Vitamins perform numerous essential functions in the body. Some, including thiamin, riboflavin, and niacin, participate in releasing energy from the macronutrients. Vitamin D helps regulate bone metabolism, while vitamins E and C donate or accept electrons as antioxidants. Several vitamins play more than one role in metabolism. **Table 9.1** illustrates the variety of functions vitamins play in maintaining health.

Provitamins Can Be Converted to Active Vitamins by the Body

Provitamins are substances found in foods that are not in a form directly usable by the body, but that can be converted into an active form once they are absorbed. The most well-known example of this is beta-carotene, which is split into two molecules of vitamin A in the small intestinal cell wall or in the liver cells. Vitamins found in foods that are already in the active form, called **preformed vitamins,** do not undergo conversion.

Overconsumption of Some Vitamins Can Be Toxic

Vitamin **toxicity,** or **hypervitaminosis,** results when a person ingests more of a vitamin than the body needs, to the point where tissues become saturated. The

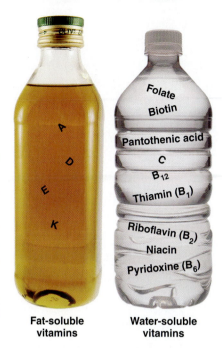

▲ **Figure 9.1 Categorizing the Vitamins: Fat Soluble and Water Soluble**
A vitamin is either fat soluble or water soluble, depending on how it is absorbed and handled in the body. Fat-soluble vitamins need dietary fat to be properly absorbed, while water-soluble vitamins are absorbed with water.

provitamin A vitamin precursor that is converted to a vitamin in the body.

preformed vitamins Vitamins found in food.

toxicity The accumulation of a substance to a harmful level.

hypervitaminosis A condition resulting from the presence of excessive amounts of vitamins in the body; also referred to as *vitamin toxicity.*

TABLE 9.1

TABLE 9.1 The Many Roles of Vitamins in Maintaining Health

Metabolic Function	Vitamins That Play a Role
Antioxidants	Vitamin C, vitamin E, beta-carotene
Blood clotting and red blood cell synthesis	Folate, vitamin B_6, vitamin B_{12}, vitamin K
Bone health	Vitamin A, vitamin C, vitamin D, vitamin K
Energy production	Biotin, niacin (B_3), pantothenic acid, riboflavin (B_2), thiamin (B_1), vitamin B_6, vitamin B_{12}
Growth and reproduction	Vitamin A, vitamin D
Immune function	Vitamin A, vitamin C, vitamin D
Protein metabolism and synthesis	Folate, vitamin B_6, vitamin B_{12}, vitamin C

excess vitamin can damage cells, sometimes permanently. Vitamin toxicity does not occur by eating a normal balanced diet. While rare, vitamin toxicity can result when individuals consume **megadose** levels of vitamin supplements, usually in the false belief that "more is better." Many individuals, for example, overload on vitamin C tablets to ward off a cold, despite the fact that there is no evidence that vitamin C prevents the common cold, and they may suffer unpleasant side effects, including diarrhea. In general, water-soluble vitamins do not cause toxicity because the excess is excreted in the urine. Some water-soluble vitamins, such as vitamin B_6, and the fat-soluble vitamins, A D, and E, which are stored, can be toxic in megadose amounts.

To prevent excessive intake, the Dietary Reference Intakes include a tolerable upper intake level for most vitamins. Even though sufficient evidence to establish a UL is lacking for some vitamins, there still may be risks in taking them in megadose amounts.

LO 9.1: THE TAKE-HOME MESSAGE Vitamins are essential nutrients needed in small amounts for growth, reproduction, and overall good health. All vitamins are either fat soluble or water soluble. Provitamins are converted to their active form before they can be directly used in the body. Most water-soluble vitamins are not toxic. Vitamins A, D, and E can be toxic if taken in megadose amounts.

How Do Vitamins Differ in Their Absorption and Storage?

LO 9.2 Compare and contrast the absorption and storage of fat-soluble and water-soluble vitamins.

All vitamins are absorbed in the small intestine, but they differ in their bioavailability from foods. Also, fat-soluble vitamins are absorbed differently from water-soluble vitamins. Let's take a closer look at these differences.

Vitamins Differ in Bioavailability

Not all of the vitamins consumed in foods are completely absorbed. The **bioavailability** of individual vitamins varies according to several factors, including the amount of the vitamin in the food; whether the food is cooked, raw, or refined;

megadose An amount of a vitamin or mineral that's at least 10 times the amount recommended in the DRI.

bioavailability The degree to which a nutrient is absorbed from foods and used in the body.

how efficiently the food is digested and absorbed; the individual's nutritional status and general health; and whether or not the vitamin is natural or synthetic. In general, if the body needs more of a certain vitamin, a greater percentage is absorbed. For example, a young child or pregnant woman absorbs a higher percentage of ingested vitamins than does a nonpregnant adult.

The bioavailability of vitamins differs based on their solubility and the type of food. Fat-soluble vitamins are usually less bioavailable than water-soluble vitamins because fat-soluble vitamins require bile and the formation of a micelle in order to be absorbed. Vitamins in plant foods are typically less bioavailable than those in animal foods because plant fiber can trap vitamins.

Fat-Soluble Vitamins Are Stored after They Are Absorbed

Fat-soluble vitamins are often attached to food components, usually protein, in foods. To be absorbed, the vitamin must be released from the protein with the help of pepsin and hydrochloric acid (refer to Chapter 3). The freed fat-soluble vitamins are then ready to be absorbed, primarily in the duodenum (**Figure 9.2**). They are packaged with fatty acids and bile in micelles that transport them close to the intestinal mucosa. Once there, the fat-soluble vitamins travel through the cells in the intestinal wall, and are repackaged with fat and other lipids into chylomicrons. The vitamins then travel through the lymph system before they enter the bloodstream. Note that absorption of fat-soluble vitamins can be compromised in the absence of adequate fatty acids or bile. This is why having some fat in the diet is absolutely necessary to avoid fat-soluble vitamin deficiencies.

Fat-soluble vitamins are stored in the body and used as needed when dietary intake falls short of the body's needs. The liver is the main storage depot for vitamin A and to a lesser extent vitamins K and E, whereas vitamin D is mainly stored in fat and muscle tissues. Because they are stored in the body, large quantities of some of the fat-soluble vitamins, particularly A, can build up to the point of toxicity, causing harmful symptoms and conditions.

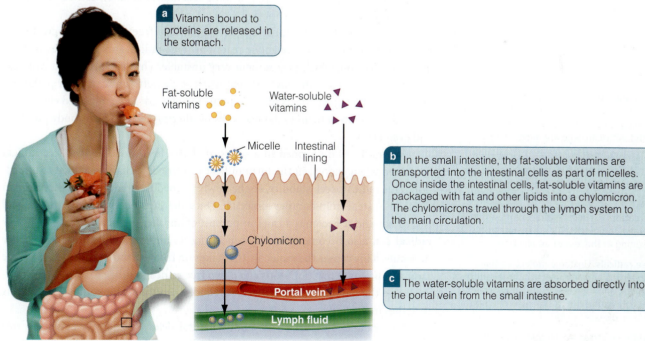

a Vitamins bound to proteins are released in the stomach.

Fat-soluble vitamins

Water-soluble vitamins

Micelle

Intestinal lining

Chylomicron

b In the small intestine, the fat-soluble vitamins are transported into the intestinal cells as part of micelles. Once inside the intestinal cells, fat-soluble vitamins are packaged with fat and other lipids into a chylomicron. The chylomicrons travel through the lymph system to the main circulation.

c The water-soluble vitamins are absorbed directly into the portal vein from the small intestine.

Portal vein

Lymph fluid

▲ Figure 9.2 **Digesting and Absorbing Vitamins**

Water-Soluble Vitamins Are Not Stored after Absorption

Water-soluble vitamins are absorbed with water and enter the bloodstream directly from the small intestine. Most water-soluble vitamins are absorbed in the duodenum and jejunum, although vitamin B_{12} is absorbed in the ileum. Water-soluble vitamins are not stored in the body, and excess amounts are excreted, so it's important to consume adequate amounts of them every day. Note that even though most water-soluble vitamins aren't stored, dietary excesses can still be harmful.

> **LO 9.2: THE TAKE-HOME MESSAGE** Bioavailability of individual vitamins varies based on the amount of the vitamin in the food, whether the food is cooked, raw, or refined, the digestibility of the food, an individual's nutrition status, and whether the vitamin is in natural or synthetic form. Fat-soluble vitamins—A, D, E, and K—are not as bioavailable as water-soluble vitamins. They need dietary fat to be absorbed and are stored in the body. Because they are stored, overconsumption of fat-soluble vitamins can be toxic. The water-soluble B and C vitamins are absorbed with water. Excess water-soluble vitamins are excreted through the urine, and generally aren't stored.

What Are Antioxidants?

LO 9.3 Define the term "antioxidant" and explain which vitamins perform this function.

Antioxidants (*anti* = against, *oxidants* = oxidizing agents) are a group of compounds that include vitamins E and C, the mineral selenium, **flavonoids** (colorful pigments found in fruits and vegetables), and carotenoids (such as beta-carotene, zeaxanthin, lutein, and lycopene). Just as their name implies, antioxidants counteract the **oxidation** that takes place in cells. Recall that oxidation reactions are essential chemical reactions that are part of metabolism, such as energy production (discussed in Chapter 8). However, in some reactions, oxidation can be damaging, such as when free radicals are formed.

During oxidation, harmful oxygen-containing **free radicals** are created as by-products of the body's metabolic reactions. Free radicals are molecules with an unpaired electron, which makes them very unstable. They can also result from exposure to chemicals in the environment (such as cigarette smoke and air pollution) or from the damaging effects of the sun's ultraviolet rays. The unpaired electron in free radicals enables them to damage cells by altering cell structure, body proteins, and even DNA.[2]

Free radicals are formed in a series of chain reactions. The first free radical is formed when energy, in the form of heat or ultraviolet light, is added to a reaction. Free radicals seek stability, so the newly formed free radical will search for an electron to steal from another molecule. Once the theft occurs, a new free radical is created, and it becomes a thief in pursuit of another molecule to attack. A free radical can also become stable by depositing its unpaired electron onto another molecule. This causes the molecule that takes on the electron to become a new free radical. The chain reaction stops when two free radicals collide to form a new molecule and the number of free radicals is reduced. **Figure 9.3** illustrates free radicals in action in the body.

Antioxidants are part of the body's natural defense system to neutralize free radicals and stop them from damaging cells. If free radicals accumulate faster than the body can neutralize them, causing **oxidative stress,** their damaging effects can

antioxidants Substances that neutralize harmful oxygen-containing free radicals that can cause cell damage. Vitamins A, C, and E and beta-carotene are antioxidants.

flavonoids Food pigments that act as antioxidants and may help reduce the risk of chronic diseases; flavonoids are found in many fruits, vegetables, tea, and wine.

oxidation A chemical reaction in which oxygen combines with other substances, resulting in the loss of an electron.

free radicals Unstable molecules that contain an unpaired electron; free radicals can damage the cells of the body and possibly contribute to the increased risk of chronic diseases.

oxidative stress A condition whereby free radicals are being produced in the body faster than they are neutralized.

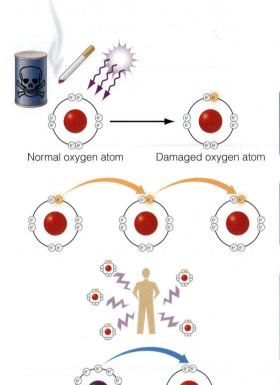

Normal oxygen atom   Damaged oxygen atom

Antioxidant   Repaired oxygen molecule

a Normal reactions in the body, and stressors such as chemicals in the environment, smoking, and ultraviolet light create free radicals.

b Free radicals have an unpaired electron that seeks an electron from another compound, causing a chain reaction of oxidation.

c Free radicals lead to oxidative stress. This accelerates the aging process and increases the risk of heart disease, cancer, diabetes, arthritis, macular degeneration, Parkinson's disease, and Alzheimer's disease.

d Antioxidants, such as vitamin E, neutralize free radicals by "lending" an electron to stabilize damaged atoms.

▲ **Figure 9.3** **Antioxidants Neutralize Free Radicals**

a Normal vision and the ability to clearly see the world around you is often taken for granted.

b People with age-related macular degeneration (AMD) have difficulty seeing things directly in front of them.

c Cataracts cause vision to become cloudy.

▲ **Figure 9.4** **Normal and Impaired Vision**

Source: National Institutes of Health, National Eye Institute.

contribute to various chronic diseases and conditions, including heart disease, cancer, aging, diabetes mellitus, arthritis, Parkinson's disease, and Alzheimer's disease.[3]

Free radicals can also damage eyes, contributing to **age-related macular degeneration (AMD)** and cataracts. AMD affects over 1.8 million Americans[4] and results from damage to the macula, a tiny area of the eye that is needed for central vision (the ability to see things that are directly in front of you). The macula is shown in the eye illustrated in the vitamin A section on page 330. AMD can make activities such as reading, driving, and watching television impossible (**Figure 9.4**). AMD is the most common cause of permanent impairment for reading and other activities requiring close-up vision in Americans 60 years of age and older.[5] In the early stages of AMD, there are few symptoms or vision loss. As the disease progresses, images become blurred, or a dark, empty area can appear in the center of your vision. Colors can also become less vivid as AMD progresses. While there is no cure for AMD, there are certain vitamins and minerals that may reduce the risk of developing AMD or improve vision in those who already have AMD. A number of well-designed studies have indicated that vitamin A, beta-carotene, vitamin C, and vitamin E, along with the minerals zinc and copper, may be effective in reducing the risk of AMD as well as the loss of vision in individuals with advanced stages of AMD.[6]

Some studies have also suggested that specific antioxidants—namely vitamins C and E and the carotenoids lutein and zeaxanthin—may help lower the risk of cataracts.[7] A **cataract** is a common eye condition among older adults in which the lens of the eye becomes cloudy, resulting in blurred vision, as shown in Figure 9.4c. More than 20 million Americans over the age of 40 (17.5 percent)

age-related macular degeneration (AMD) A disease that affects the macula of the retina, causing blurry vision and, potentially, blindness.

cataract A common eye disorder that occurs when the lens of the eye becomes cloudy.

have cataracts in at least one or both eyes.[8] The National Eye Institute recommends consuming antioxidant- and carotenoid-rich vegetables and fruits, such as citrus fruits, broccoli, and dark green leafy vegetables, for the health of the eyes.[9]

The antioxidants carotenoids and flavonoids are part of a larger group of **phytochemicals** (*phyto* = plant), naturally occurring plant compounds that have many beneficial functions in the body, such as acting as antioxidants, stimulating the immune system, and interacting with hormones that may help prevent certain cancers.[10, 11] Some phytochemicals, including carotenoids, are also responsible for the vibrant colors of many fruits and vegetables. **Table 9.2** emphasizes the importance of consuming a colorful diet so as to take in an abundance of phytochemicals.

The big question that remains is if antioxidant *supplements* provide the same health protection as antioxidants consumed in foods. Studies are currently under way exploring the role of antioxidant supplements in fighting disease. At this time, the American Heart Association, National Cancer Institute, and United States Preventive Services Task Force do not advocate taking supplements to reduce the risk of specific diseases, but encourage eating a phytochemical- and antioxidant-rich, well-balanced diet.[12, 13]

> **LO 9.3: THE TAKE-HOME MESSAGE** Antioxidants, such as vitamins E and C, the mineral selenium, flavonoids, and carotenoids, help counteract the damaging effects of oxygen-containing molecules called free radicals. If free radicals accumulate faster than the body can neutralize them, the damaging effects of oxidative stress can contribute to chronic diseases and conditions. Fruits, vegetables, and whole grains are excellent sources of antioxidants and other phytochemicals.

phytochemicals Naturally occurring substances in fruits, vegetables, and whole grains that protect against certain chronic diseases.

TABLE 9.2 The Phytochemical Color Guide

The National Cancer Institute recommends eating a variety of colorful fruits and vegetables daily to provide your body with valuable vitamins, minerals, fiber, and disease-fighting phytochemicals. Whole grains also have phytochemicals and have been added to this list.

Color	Phytochemical	Found in
Red	Anthocyanins	Apples, beets, cabbage, cherries, cranberries, red cabbage, red onions, red beans
Yellow/ Orange	Beta-carotene	Apricots, butternut squash, cantaloupe, carrots, mangoes, peaches, pumpkin, sweet potatoes
	Flavonoids	Apricots, clementines, grapefruits, lemons, papaya, pears, pineapple, yellow raisins
White	Alliums/allicin	Chives, garlic, leeks, onions, scallions
Green	Lutein, zeaxanthin	Broccoli, collard greens, honeydew melon, kale, kiwi, lettuce, mustard greens, peas, spinach
	Indoles	Arugula, broccoli, bok choy, brussels sprouts, cabbage, cauliflower, kale, Swiss chard, turnips
Blue/Purple	Anthocyanins	Blackberries, black currants, elderberries, purple grapes
	Phenolics	Eggplant, plums, prunes, raisins
Brown	Beta-glucan, lignans, phenols, plant sterols, phytoestrogens, saponins, tocotrienols	Barley, brown rice, oats, oatmeal, whole grains, whole-grain cereals, whole wheat

Source: Adapted from Fruits & Veggies—More Matters. 2012. Available at www.fruitsandveggiesmorematters.org.

What's the Best Source of Vitamins?

LO 9.4 Describe the best sources of vitamins and the factors that affect the vitamin content of foods.

Eating whole foods, including fruits, vegetables, and whole grains, remains the best way to meet vitamin needs: They provide more than just vitamins because they are also rich in disease-fighting phytochemicals, antioxidants, and fiber. The *Dietary Guidelines for Americans* recommends eating a wide variety of foods from each food group, with ample amounts of vitamin-rich fruits, vegetables, whole grains, and dairy foods. **Figure 9.5** illustrates each food group and the vitamins it contributes to the diet.

Table 9.3 shows the estimated intake for each nutrient that a 2,000-kilocalorie diet based on the *Dietary Guidelines* provides. As shown in the table, vitamins D and E are the only nutrients in which Americans typically fall short. Add some margarine on toast, a few nuts to yogurt, and a little salad dressing on a dinner salad to increase overall intake of both vitamins D and E. Refer to the Table Tips for vitamin D (on page 342) and vitamin E (on page 344) for more suggestions.

Vitamins Can Be Destroyed during Cooking or Storage

How you prepare and store fresh foods once you obtain them can affect their nutritional content. Water-soluble vitamins can be destroyed by exposure to air, ultraviolet (UV) light, water, changes in pH, or heat. In fact, vegetables and fruits begin to lose their vitamins almost immediately after being harvested, and some preparation and storage methods can accelerate vitamin loss. Though the fat-soluble vitamins tend to be more stable than water-soluble vitamins, some food preparation techniques can cause the loss of these vitamins as well.

Exposure to Oxygen

Air—or, more specifically, exposure to oxygen—can destroy the water-soluble vitamins and the fat-soluble vitamins A, E, and K. Thus, fresh vegetables and fruits should be stored in airtight, covered containers and used soon after being purchased.

◄ **Figure 9.5 Vitamins Found Widely in the Food Groups**
Eating a wide variety of foods from all food groups ensures that you meet your vitamin needs.

Vegetables	Fruits	Grains	Protein	Dairy
Folate	Folate	Folic acid	Niacin	Riboflavin
Vitamin A	Vitamin C	Niacin	Thiamin	Vitamin A
Vitamin C	Vitamin A	Vitamin B_6	Vitamin B_6	Vitamin B_{12}
Vitamin E		Vitamin B_{12} (if fortified)	Vitamin B_{12}	Vitamin D
Vitamin K		Riboflavin		
		Thiamin		

TABLE 9.3

TABLE 9.3 | Meeting the Dietary Reference Intakes with Healthy Food Choices

Nutrient	Estimated Vitamin Intake Based on 2,000 Kilocalories*	Institute of Medicine Recommendations, Nutrient RDA/AI
Vitamin A, μg RAE	851	700–900
Vitamin D, IU	258	600
Vitamin E, mg	8.3	15.0
Vitamin K, μg	140	90–120
Thiamin, mg	1.8	1.1–1.2
Riboflavin, mg	2.2	1.1–1.3
Niacin, mg	23.0	14.0–16.0
Vitamin B_6, mg	2.3	1.3–1.7
Vitamin B_{12}, μg	6.5	2.4
Folate, μg	628	400
Vitamin C, mg	126	75–90
Choline, mg	340	425–550

*The highest intake level for young adult men or women is stated.

RDA = Recommended Dietary Allowance; AI = Adequate Intakes; RAE = retinol activity equivalents; mg = milligrams; μg = micrograms.

Data from U.S. Department of Agriculture. 2010. *Report of the Dietary Guidelines Advisory Committee on the Dietary Guidelines for Americans, 2010.* Available at www.cnpp.usda.gov; Food and Nutrition Board, Institute of Medicine, National Academies. *Dietary Reference Intakes Series.* Available at www.iom.edu. Accessed March 2014.

TABLE TIPS

Preserve Your Vitamins!

Cook vegetables in a small amount of already boiling water—not cold water brought to a boil. Use any leftover cooking liquid as a soup or gravy base.

Don't rinse rice before cooking it or pasta after cooking it. You'll wash away water-soluble vitamins.

Microwave or stir-fry vegetables instead of boiling or frying them. These methods reduce the amount of time vegetables are exposed to heat and therefore the amount of vitamins that are lost.

Store produce in a refrigerator and eat it soon after purchasing.

Cut vegetables and fruits in larger pieces to reduce the surface area exposed to oxygen. Prepare vegetables close to the time that they are going to be cooked and/or served.

Source: Adapted from U.S. Department of Agriculture Food and Nutrition Services. 2002. *Chapter 5, Quality Meals in Building Blocks for Fun and Healthy Meals—A Menu Planner for the Child and Adult Care Food Program.* USDA Team Nutrition Resources. Available at www.fns.usda.gov/tn/Resources/buildingblocks.html. Accessed March 2014.

Exposure to Light

Light, especially ultraviolet light (UV), can destroy vitamins. Foods stored in glass containers, such as milk or grains, or sun-dried fruits and vegetables, can lose vitamins. For example, up to 80 percent of the riboflavin content of milk in glass containers can be destroyed by UV light.[14] For this reason, milk is sold in opaque containers. The traditional methods of sun-drying fruits and vegetables destroy susceptible vitamins such as beta-carotene and vitamin C. However, new advances in solar drying have shown some promise.[15]

Exposure to Water

Water-soluble vitamins leach out of foods when soaked or cooked in liquids, so cooking foods in as little water as possible is recommended.[16] Water should be boiling before vegetables are added even if you use a steamer basket. Some enzymes naturally found in the food oxidize specific vitamins, changing them to forms that are not metabolically active. Boiling water inactivates these enzymes. For instance, potatoes are a good source of vitamin C but they also contain an enzyme, ascorbic oxidase, that changes the chemical structure of vitamin C to an inactive form. Potatoes added to boiling water retain more vitamin C than if they are added to cold water and brought to a boil.

Changes in pH

Changes in pH can destroy some vitamins, especially thiamin and vitamin C. Most vitamins are stable in acid, but adding ingredients such as baking soda to foods increases the pH and destroys pH-sensitive vitamins. For instance, adding baking soda to shorten the cooking time of beans or other legumes destroys the thiamin content.

Exposure to Heat

Heat, especially prolonged heat from cooking, also destroys water-soluble vitamins, especially vitamin C. Because they are exposed to less heat, vegetables cooked by microwaving, steaming, or stir-frying can have approximately one-and-a-half times more vitamin C after cooking than if they were boiled, which involves longer heat exposure.[17] Whereas heat reduces the vitamin content of foods, cooler temperatures help preserve them. For this reason, produce should be stored in the refrigerator rather than on a counter or in a pantry. A package of fresh spinach left at room temperature loses over half of its folate, a B vitamin, after four days. Refrigeration delays that loss to eight days.[18] See the Table Tips for more ways to preserve the vitamins in foods.

Cooking foods in the microwave allows for a shorter cooking time, which means fewer vitamins are lost.

Some Foods Are Fortified with Vitamins

When you pour a glass of orange juice, you know that you are getting a significant intake of vitamin C. However, depending on the brand of orange juice, you may also be meeting the recommendations for vitamin E and vitamin D—two nutrients that are not naturally found in oranges. This is due to the process called fortification. **Fortified foods** are becoming more popular with the American consumer. For example, sales of foods fortified with one popular nutrient, omega-3 fatty acids, approached $4 billion in 2010.[19]

Food fortification is the addition of nutrients by manufacturers to enhance the nutrient quality of the food and to prevent or correct dietary deficiencies. Vitamins and minerals are the most commonly used nutrients in fortified foods, but fiber, amino acids, essential fatty acids, and other bioactive ingredients are also sometimes added. Based on current Food and Drug Administration (FDA) regulations, all 13 vitamins and 20 minerals can be added to foods.[20]

Enrichment of foods is a form of fortification. Foods that are enriched, such as rice, bread, flour, pasta, and other refined grains, have levels of nutrients added that may bring the nutritional value closer to its state before the grain was processed. Four water-soluble B vitamins (thiamin, riboflavin, niacin, and folate) and the mineral iron are required by law to be added to refined grains.

Fortified Foods Can Help Ensure Adequate Intake for Some Individuals

Fortified foods can be a valuable option for individuals whose diet falls short of some nutrients. For instance, an adult on a very low-kilocalorie diet may not be getting adequate vitamins and minerals from food and would benefit from fortified cereals. Strict vegans or individuals who are lactose intolerant and do not consume dairy products would benefit from drinking vitamin D– and calcium-fortified soy milk. Older adults who are inactive and thus have lower kilocalorie needs may choose fortified foods to add vitamin E to their limited dietary selections. Women in their childbearing years may look to folic acid–fortified cereals to help them meet their daily needs for this B vitamin.

Fortified Foods Can Contribute to Health Risks

Because overconsumption of a vitamin or mineral can result in nutrient toxicity, individuals who consume high amounts of some fortified foods may be at risk for health problems. If a heavily fortified food, like some cereals, snack bars, and beverages, claims to contain "100% of the vitamins needed daily," then eating several servings of the food or a combination of several fortified foods is similar to taking several multivitamin supplements. Individuals are more likely to overconsume vitamins from fortified foods than from whole foods.

Fortified foods can also do a disservice in the diet if they displace other vitamin- and mineral-rich foods. For example, a sugary orange drink that has

fortified foods Foods with added vitamins and minerals; fortified foods often contain nutrients that are not naturally present in the food or that are in higher amounts than the food contains naturally.

▶ Figure 9.6 **The Nutritional Value of Juices versus Fruit Drinks**
While both of these beverages are a good source of vitamin C, they are worlds apart in nutrient content. Pure orange juice **(a)** is also an excellent source of the mineral potassium and doesn't contain any added sugar. Orange drink **(b)** is basically sugar water fortified with vitamin C. A glass of it contains the equivalent of 8 teaspoons of added sugar.

a 100% pure orange juice, no sugar added

Added sugar = 0

b Orange drink, sugar added

Added sugar =

= 1 tsp of added sugar

vitamin C added to it should not replace vitamin C–rich orange juice. The beverages may have the same vitamin C content, but the orange-flavored drink doesn't provide the nutrients and phytochemicals that the juice does. As you can see in **Figure 9.6**, the orange drink is basically orange-flavored water sweetened heavily with added sugar and fortified with vitamin C. Even though the sugar content is similar for each beverage, the orange-flavored drink is sweetened with corn syrup, whereas the pure orange juice is sweetened naturally with sugars found in the orange.

Now that we've discussed the general characteristics of vitamins, let's survey the individual fat-soluble vitamins presented in **Table 9.4**. Before we begin, take the Self-Assessment to see if your diet is rich in foods that contain these important nutrients.

LO 9.4: THE TAKE-HOME MESSAGE A well-balanced diet rich in whole foods that provides adequate kilocalories can meet many individuals' daily vitamin needs. Proper handling, storage, and cooking of fresh foods can retain vitamins. Vitamins in foods can be destroyed or lost by exposure to air, water, UV light, changes in pH, and heat. Fortified foods can add nutrients to a low-kilocalorie diet. Fortified foods can also contribute to overconsumption of individual nutrients and may lead to toxicity.

TABLE 9.4 Functions, Daily Needs, Food Sources, and Symptoms of Toxicity and Deficiency of the Fat-Soluble Vitamins

Fat-Soluble Vitamin	Metabolic Function	Daily Needs (19 years +)	Food Sources	Toxicity Symptoms/UL	Deficiency Symptoms
Vitamin A	Vision, protein synthesis, growth, immune function, bone health	Males: 900 μg RAE/day Females: 700 μg RAE/day	▪ Beef liver ▪ Fortified dairy products	Compromised bone health; birth defects during pregnancy UL: 3,000 μg/day	Night blindness, xerophthalmia, keratinization
Beta-carotenes			▪ Sweet potatoes ▪ Carrots ▪ Squash		
Vitamin D	Calcium balance, bone health, cell differentiation, immune system	Males and females: 15 μg/day	▪ Fatty fish such as salmon, tuna, sardines ▪ Fortified foods, such as dairy products, orange juice, and cereals	Hypercalcemia UL: 100 μg/day	Rickets and osteomalacia
Vitamin E	Antioxidant, health of cell membranes, heart health	Males and females: 15 mg alpha-tocopherol/day	▪ Vegetable and seed oils ▪ Nuts, seeds ▪ Fortified cereals ▪ Green leafy vegetables	Nerve problems, muscle weakness, and uncontrolled movement of body parts UL: 1,000 mg/day	Hemolysis of RBCs
Vitamin K	Carboxylation, blood clotting, and bone health	Males: 120 μg/day Females: 90 μg/day	▪ Green leafy vegetables ▪ Soybeans ▪ Canola and soybean oils ▪ Beef liver	None known UL: none established	Excessive bleeding

Self-Assessment

Are You Getting Enough Fat-Soluble Vitamins in Your Diet?

Take this brief self-assessment to see if your diet contains enough food sources of the four fat-soluble vitamins.

1. Do you eat at least 1 cup of deep yellow or orange vegetables, such as carrots and sweet potatoes, or dark green vegetables, such as spinach, every day?

   Yes ☐ **No** ☐

2. Do you consume at least 2 glasses (8 ounces each) of milk daily?

   Yes ☐ **No** ☐

3. Do you eat a tablespoon of vegetable oil, such as corn or olive oil, daily? (Tip: Salad dressings, unless they are fat free, count!)

   Yes ☐ **No** ☐

4. Do you eat at least 1 cup of leafy green vegetables in your salad and/or put lettuce in your sandwich every day?

   Yes ☐ **No** ☐

Answers

If you answered yes to all four questions, your diet is close to meeting your fat-soluble vitamin needs! If you answered no to any one of the questions, your diet needs some fine-tuning. Deep orange and dark green vegetables are excellent sources of vitamin A, and milk is an excellent choice for vitamin D. Adding small amounts of vegetable oils to a vitamin K–rich leafy green salad improves the vitamin E content.

Exploring **Vitamin A**

LO 9.5 Describe the functions, recommended intakes, food sources, and the deficiency and toxicity effects of vitamin A.

What Is Vitamin A?

The term vitamin A refers to a family of fat-soluble **retinoids** that include **retinol, retinal,** and **retinoic acid** (**Figure 9.7**). These compounds are similar in their chemical structure. They each contain a ring with a polyunsaturated hydrocarbon chain. Attached at the end of the hydrocarbon chain is either an alcohol group

(retinol), an aldehyde group (retinal), or an acid group (retinoic acid). Whereas retinol, retinal, and retinoic acid all participate in essential functions in the body, retinol, the alcohol form, is the most usable. In foods, vitamin A is found as retinol or as a **retinyl ester,** which has an ester group attached at the fatty acid tail. The body also stores vitamin A as a retinyl ester in the liver. Retinol can be reversibly converted to retinal, the

Form found in animal foods and stored in body

Retinyl ester

Form found in plants

Beta-carotene

Splits into
2 retinal

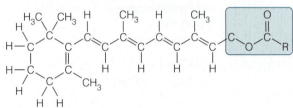

Retinol (alcohol form)
• Reproduction

Retinal (aldehyde form)
• Vision

▲ **Figure 9.7 The Conversion of the Three Vitamin A Compounds**
Retinyl esters, found in foods and the form of vitamin A stored in the liver, are converted to retinol (alcohol). Retinol can be transformed to retinal (aldehyde) and then to retinoic acid. Beta-carotene is split during digestion to yield two molecules of retinal.

Retinoic acid
• Regulates growth

aldehyde form. Retinal can be transformed into the acidic form called retinoic acid, but the process is irreversible. Retinoids are preformed vitamin A, which means they are in a form that the body can use immediately without first being activated. Preformed sources of vitamin A are found primarily in animal foods.

On the right side of Figure 9.7 is the structure of one of the family of provitamin A compounds called **carotenoids.** The provitamin A compounds found in plants are precursors to retinol in the body. Three such compounds— **beta-carotene** (β-carotene), beta-cryptoxanthin (β-cryptoxanthin), and alpha-carotene (α-carotene)—are the most common carotenoids, the yellow-red pigments that give carrots, butternut squash, and cantaloupe their vibrant, deep orange color. For vegans, these carotenoids are the only dietary source of vitamin A. Almost 25 to 35 percent of the dietary vitamin A consumed by adults in the United States comes from carotenoids, especially beta-carotene.[21]

Vitamin A Absorption and Transport

All forms of preformed vitamin A are absorbed by active transport in the small intestine with the help of bile salts and micelles. The rate of absorption of preformed vitamin A is high, ranging from 70 to 90 percent as long as the diet contains some fat. Beta-carotene, in contrast, is absorbed via passive diffusion at a much lower rate of 5 percent to up to 60 percent.[22] Fat in the diet enhances the absorption of vitamin A, but diarrhea or an infection in the GI tract reduces vitamin A absorption. Beta-carotene absorption is reduced with high fiber intakes and improved when foods are cooked. For example, the amount of beta-carotene absorbed from cooked carrots is much higher than that from raw carrots.

Most forms of vitamin A are packaged as chylomicrons along with other dietary lipids, and absorbed into the lymph fluid. Retinoic acid doesn't need a chylomicron, but rather is attached to a protein called albumin and absorbed into the portal vein. Carotenes are converted to vitamin A in the intestine before absorption.

Vitamin A is stored in the liver until needed by the body. Retinol binding protein transports the retinol from storage through the bloodstream to the receptor sites located on the cells.

Vitamin A is difficult to excrete from the body. When the liver becomes saturated with vitamin A, some is excreted through the bile to prevent toxicity.

Metabolic Functions of Vitamin A

Each form of retinoid plays a specific role in the body. Retinal (the aldehyde form) participates in vision. The hormonelike action of retinoic acid (the acid form) is essential for growth and development of cells, including bone development. Retinol (the alcohol form) supports reproduction and a healthy immune system. In addition to these critical roles, vitamin A may help prevent cancer.

retinoids The term used to describe the family of preformed vitamin A compounds.

retinol The alcohol form of preformed vitamin A.

retinal The aldehyde form of preformed vitamin A.

retinoic acid The acid form of preformed vitamin A.

retinyl ester The ester form of preformed vitamin A found in foods and stored in the body.

carotenoids The family of provitamin compounds that includes beta-carotene. Also a group of yellow, red, and orange pigments found in plants; three of them are precursors to vitamin A. The body stores carotenoids in the liver and in fat cells.

beta-carotene One of the provitamin A carotenoids.

continued

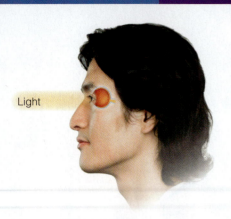

Light

Vitamin A is a component of two light-sensitive proteins, rhodopsin and iodopsin, that are essential for vision. Here we examine rhodopsin's role in vision. Although the breakdown of iodopsin is similar, rhodopsin is more sensitive to light than iodopsin and is more likely to become bleached.

EYE STRUCTURE

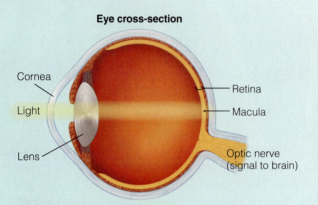

Eye cross-section

Cornea
Light
Lens
Retina
Macula
Optic nerve (signal to brain)

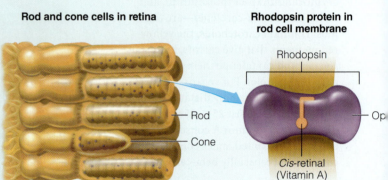

Rod and cone cells in retina

Rod
Cone

Rhodopsin protein in rod cell membrane

Rhodopsin
Op
Cis-retinal (Vitamin A)

1 After light enters your eye through the cornea, it travels to the back of your eye to the macula, which is located in the retina. The macula allows you to see fine details and things that are straight in front of you.

2 Inside the retina are two types of light-absorbing cells, rods and cones. Rods are responsible for black-and-white vision and contain the protein rhodopsin. Cones are responsible for color vision and contain the protein iodopsin. Both proteins contain vitamin A in the form of cis-retinal.

EFFECT OF LIGHT ON RHODOPSIN

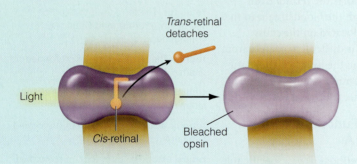

Trans-retinal detaches
Light
Cis-retinal
Bleached opsin

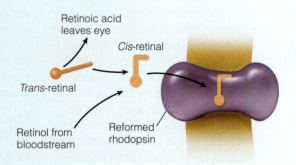

Retinoic acid leaves eye
Cis-retinal
Trans-retinal
Retinol from bloodstream
Reformed rhodopsin

1 As light interacts with rhodopsin, it transforms the cis-retinal to trans-retinal, separating it from the protein opsin. This process, called bleaching, causes a cascade of events that transmits visual messages through the optic nerve to the brain.

2 Trans-retinal is converted back to cis-retinal and binds with opsin to reform rhodopsin, regenerating the eye's light-absorbing capabilities. Some trans-retinal is irreversibly converted to retinoic acid and leaves the eye tissue. Retinol from the blood is converted to retinal to replenish what is lost.

Vitamin A in Vision

One of the most well-known functions of vitamin A is the role it plays in vision. Light that passes into the eyes and hits the retina is translated into visual images with the help of two vitamin A–dependent proteins, **rhodopsin** and **iodopsin.** These proteins are found in the tips of light-absorbing cells in the retina called **rods** and **cones,** respectively. Rhodopsin, which contains *cis*-retinal (the aldehyde form of vitamin A), absorbs the light entering the rods. The light changes the shape of *cis*-retinal to *trans*-retinal, detaching it from the protein opsin. This change in shape is referred to as **bleaching.** When rhodopsin is bleached, it transmits a signal through the optic nerve to the part of the brain involved in vision.

After rhodopsin is bleached, most of the *trans*-retinal returns to its *cis* shape. This form is now able to bind with opsin, which regenerates rhodopsin and the eye's light-absorbing capabilities. This reaction is illustrated in **Focus Figure 9.8**.

Walking into a dark building after being in the sun without sunglasses may require taking time to adjust to the dimmer light. This adjustment period occurs because the reformation of *trans*- to *cis*-retinal takes time. Fortunately, there is a pool of vitamin A in the retina to help with this conversion.

In order for vitamin A to participate in the visual cycle, it must first be metabolized in the retina. Retinol attaches to **retinol binding protein (RBP)** and is transported through the blood to the eye. Once inside the retina, retinol is converted to retinal before moving into the photoreceptor cells of the rods.

Vitamin A in Protein Synthesis and Cell Differentiation

Vitamin A is important for keeping the epithelial cells moist and structurally sound. **Epithelial cells** in the skin protect the body from damage from the sun. The epithelial cells that line the lungs, nose, eyes, and urinary tract are round, moist, secrete a thick mucus, and are lined with microscopic hairlike structures called cilia. The mucus coats the cells and protects them from bacteria and viruses that can infiltrate the body and cause infection. In the respiratory

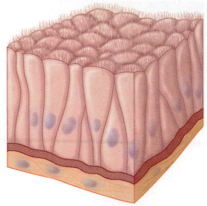

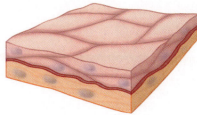

a Healthy epithelial cells are rounded, moist, and contain mucus-secreting cells and cilia lining the surface.

b A vitamin A deficiency can lead to unhealthy epithelial cells that are flat, hard, lacking cilia, and unable to produce mucus.

▲ **Figure 9.9 Healthy and Vitamin A–Deficient Epithelial Cells**

tract, the cilia sweep away dust and germs trapped in the mucus. Vitamin A deficiency can cause these cells to become flattened, hard, and unable to produce mucus (**Figure 9.9**). Vitamin A also works with the immune system to create white blood cells (*lymphocytes*) and antibodies that fight foreign invaders should they enter the bloodstream.

Vitamin A stimulates **cell division** and **cell differentiation** of the epithelial cells as they grow and develop. Retinoic acid prompts gene expression, a process that uses genetic information to make the proteins needed to begin cell division. As cells divide and cluster together, changes occur that cause them to become different from their initiating cells. This differentiation determines what cells become in the body. For immature skin cells to differentiate into mature skin cells, for example, vitamin A acts as a signal to turn on the genes to create the proteins needed to make healthy skin.

This role of vitamin A is one reason dermatologists prescribe retinoid-containing medications, such as Retin-A or tretinoin, to treat acne (**Figure 9.10**). Retin-A is a topical medication that works by enhancing the turnover of skin cells and inhibiting the formation of acne.[23] Accutane, or isotretinoin, is a medication taken orally that manipulates cell differentiation through gene expression of acne-producing cells to alter their development in the skin.[24]

Vitamin A in Growth and Reproduction

In addition to its role in cell differentiation, vitamin A plays several critical roles in growth and reproduction. Both retinol and retinoic acid participate in growth, although the mechanism is still unknown. What is known is that without vitamin A, embryonic and fetal development is impaired, especially in the development of the limbs, heart, eyes, and ears.[25]

rhodopsin A compound found in the rods of the eye that is needed for night vision. It is comprised of *cis*-retinal and the protein opsin.

iodopsin The compound found in the cones of the eye that is needed for color vision.

rods Light-absorbing cells responsible for black-and-white vision and night vision.

cones Light-absorbing cells responsible for color vision.

bleaching When light enters the eye and interacts with rhodopsin, splitting it into *trans*-retinal and opsin.

retinol binding protein (RBP) A protein made in the liver that transports retinol through the blood to the cells.

epithelial cells Cells that line the cavities in the body and cover flat surfaces such as the skin.

cell division The process of dividing one cell into two separate cells with the same genetic material.

cell differentiation The process of a less specialized immature cell becoming a specialized mature cell.

continued

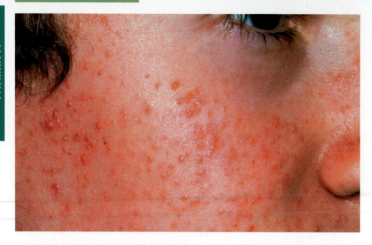

▲ **Figure 9.10** Vitamin A Derivatives Can Help Treat Acne

Children fail to grow when their diets lack vitamin A, but when either retinol or retinoic acid are given, growth is enhanced.

Retinol, but not retinoic acid, is essential for reproduction. Normal levels of retinol are required for sperm production in males and normal menstrual cycles in females.

Vitamin A and Bone Health

All three forms of vitamin A may help regulate the cells involved in bone growth. Too much vitamin A stimulates bone resorption—breaking down bone—and inhibits bone formation, which can negatively affect healthy bones and may be a risk factor for developing osteoporosis.[26] Both excessive intake and insufficient intake of vitamin A have negative impacts on bone density. Research reports that retinol intakes of less than 510 μg RAE (1,700 IU) and more than 2,030 μg RAE (6,700 IU) per day may increase fracture risk (beta-carotene has no effect).[27] A diet closer to 600 to 850 μg RAE (2,000 to 2,800 IU) per day of vitamin A is most likely to improve the bone mineral density of elderly men and women.[28]

Carotenoids as Antioxidants

Provitamin A compounds are able to quench free radical reactions and

retinol activity equivalents (RAE) The unit of measure used to describe the total amount of all forms of preformed vitamin A and provitamin A carotenoids in food.

international units (IU) A system of measurement of a biologically active ingredient such as a vitamin that produces a certain effect.

The carotenoid lycopene, found in tomatoes and tomato products, functions as an antioxidant in the body.

protect cells from damage. Lycopene, which is the form of carotenoid that gives red tomatoes their dark red color, is especially effective in quenching free radicals. Two other carotenoids, lutein and zeaxanthin (found in corn and dark green leafy vegetables), protect the eyes from free radical damage.[29]

Daily Needs for Vitamin A

The Recommended Dietary Allowance (RDA) for vitamin A is based on maintaining sufficient storage of the vitamin in the liver. Vitamin A in foods

and supplements can be measured in two ways: in micrograms (μg) of **retinol activity equivalents (RAE)** and in **international units (IU).**

Because retinol is the most usable form of vitamin A and because provitamin A carotenoids can be converted to retinol, the preferred way to measure vitamin A in foods is to include all forms as RAE. However, some vitamin supplements and food labels show the older measure, IU, on their products. (Note: 1 μg RAE is the equivalent of 3.3 IU.) The Calculation Corner provides more detail on the conversion from IU to micrograms RAE.

Adult females need 700 μg RAE (2,310 IU) of vitamin A daily, whereas adult males need 900 μg RAE (3,000 IU) daily. This is the average amount needed to maintain adequate stores in the body.[30] A daily recommendation for beta-carotene hasn't been established, but the Institute of Medicine suggests consuming 3 to 6 milligrams of beta-carotene every day from foods.[31] This can easily be obtained by consuming five or more servings of fruits and vegetables. This amount of beta-carotene also provides about 50 percent of the recommended vitamin A intake. Hence, eating beta-carotene-rich foods adds not only antioxidants to the diet, but also vitamin A.

Vegetarians who eat no animal foods, including vitamin A–rich milk and eggs, need to be especially conscientious about eating carotenoids and beta-carotene-rich foods to meet their daily vitamin A needs.

Food Sources of Vitamin A

Milk, cereals, cheese, egg yolks, and organ meats (such as liver) are the most popular sources of preformed vitamin A in the U.S. diet. Liver is especially abundant in vitamin A but can cause toxicity if consumed too often. For example, 1 ounce of beef liver contains 2 milligrams of retinol, or more than 100 percent of the RDA of vitamin A for adults.

Carrots, spinach, and sweet potatoes are American favorites for provitamin A carotenoids, including beta-carotene. Similar to vitamin A and other fat-soluble vitamins, carotenoids are absorbed more efficiently when fat is

Calculation Corner

Converting International Units for Vitamin A

International units (IU) are a system of measurement of the biologic activity or potency of a substance, such as a vitamin, that produces a particular effect. Because each vitamin differs in potency per milligram, the conversion factors from IU to milligrams also differ.

(a) Vitamin A is measured in retinol activity equivalents, or RAE. Use the following conversion factors to determine the micrograms retinol activity equivalents (μg RAE) found in 1 IU:

> 1 IU retinol is the biological equivalent of 0.3 μg retinol or 0.3 μg RAE or 0.6 μg beta-carotene

Example: A vitamin supplement contains 25,000 IU of retinol. How many μg RAE does it contain?

Answer: 0.3 μg $\times$ 25,000 IU = 7,500 μg RAE

(b) The requirements for vitamin A are expressed as RAE. To determine the amount of RAE in micrograms in a meal, you have to convert the various forms of vitamin A equivalents. For example:

> 1 μg RAE = 1 μg retinol and 12 μg beta-carotene.

The first step is to divide the amount of beta-carotene by 12 to convert to RAE. Next, add that number to the preformed vitamin A in the meal.

Example: If a meal contains 500 μg retinol and 1,800 μg beta-carotene, how many μg RAE does the meal contain?

Answer: 500 μg retinol + (1,800 μg beta-carotene $\div$ 12) = 650 μg RAE

---

present in the GI tract. Adding as little as 1 tablespoon of vegetable oil to the diet daily can increase the absorption of carotenoids by as much as 25 percent.[32]

Figure 9.11 shows the vitamin A content in μg RAE, and includes both retinoid- and carotenoid-rich sources.

Vitamin A Toxicity

Vitamin A toxicity is caused by ingesting too much preformed vitamin A, not carotenoids. Consuming more than 15,000 μg of preformed vitamin A at one time or over a short period of time can lead to nausea, vomiting, headaches, dizziness, and blurred vision. Overconsumption of preformed vitamin A is usually due to taking supplements and is less likely to occur from

overeating vitamin A in foods. Vitamin A supplements do not improve acne. Only specially formulated vitamin A–containing drugs such as Retin-A or Accutane are effective for preventing

and treating acne. Because 90 percent of vitamin A is stored in the liver, chronic daily consumption of more than 30,000 micrograms of preformed vitamin A (more than 300 times the RDA for adults) can lead to **hypervitaminosis A** (*hyper* = over, *osis* = condition), an extremely serious condition in which the liver accumulates toxic levels of vitamin A. Hypervitaminosis A can lead to deterioration and scarring of the liver and even death. To prevent toxicity, the tolerable upper intake level (UL) of preformed vitamin A for adults has been set at 3,000 μg (10,000 IU) daily.[33]

Higher intake of preformed vitamin A during pregnancy, particularly in the first trimester, can cause birth defects in the face and skull and damage the child's central nervous system. All women of childbearing age who are using retinoids for acne or other skin conditions should take the proper steps to avoid becoming pregnant.[34]

Vitamin A and Osteoporosis

While vitamin A is needed for bone health, some research suggests that consuming too much may lead to **osteoporosis,** which in turn increases the risk of fractures. Osteoporosis-related hip fractures appear to be prevalent in Swedes and Norwegians, who tend to have high consumption of vitamin A–rich cod-liver oil and specialty dairy products that have been heavily fortified with vitamin A.[35]

Additional studies involving both women and men have shown similar associations between high vitamin A intake and increased risk of fractures. As little as 1,500 micrograms (3,000 IU) of retinol, which is slightly more than twice the RDA recommended for women, can be unhealthy for bones.[36] This amount can be quickly reached when taking a supplement and eating a diet rich in vitamin A–fortified foods. The Daily Value (DV) for vitamin A used in the Nutrition Facts panel on food labels is 5,000 IU.

hypervitaminosis A The serious condition in which the liver accumulates toxic levels of vitamin A.

osteoporosis A condition in which bones become brittle and porous, making them fragile due to depletion of calcium and bone proteins.

continued

Vitamin A continued

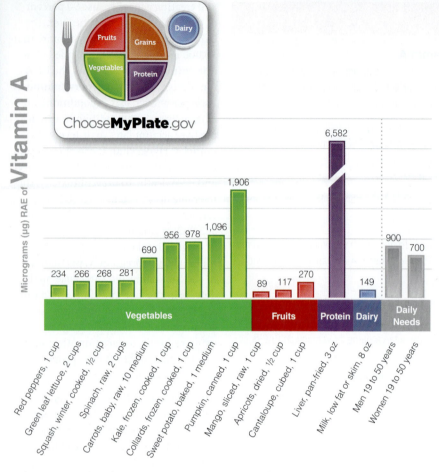

Microgoms (µg) RAE of Vitamin A

Red peppers, 1 cup	234
Green leaf lettuce, 2 cups	266
Squash, winter, cooked, ½ cup	268
Spinach, raw, 2 cups	281
Carrots, baby, raw, 10 medium	690
Kale, frozen, cooked, 1 cup	956
Collards, frozen, cooked, 1 cup	978
Sweet potato, baked, 1 medium	1,096
Pumpkin, canned, 1 cup	1,906
Mango, sliced, raw, 1 cup	89
Apricots, dried, ½ cup	117
Cantaloupe, cubed, 1 cup	270
Liver, pan-fried, 3 oz	6,582
Milk, low fat or skim, 8 oz	149
Men 19 to 50 years	900
Women 19 to 50 years	700

Categories: Vegetables, Fruits, Protein, Dairy, Daily Needs

▲ **Figure 9.11 Vitamin A Content in Selected Foods**

Recall from Chapter 2 that the DVs used on food labels are based on older recommendations, not the current recommended intakes. Consuming a serving of a food that provides a large percentage of the DV for vitamin A may mean consuming more than the upper limit.

Overconsuming Carotenoids

The upper levels apply only to preformed vitamin A from foods, fortified foods, and supplements. Provitamin A carotenoids in foods are not toxic and do not pose serious health problems. The body has a built-in safeguard to prevent provitamin A carotenoids from contributing to vitamin A toxicity, birth defects, or bone damage. If individuals consume more carotenoids than necessary to meet vitamin A needs, the body decreases their conversion to retinol. Extra

carotenodermia The presence of excess carotene in the blood, resulting in an orange color to the skin due to excessive intake of carrots or other carotene-rich vegetables.

amounts of carotenoids are stored in the liver and in the subcutaneous fat.

Eating too many carotenoids can, however, cause the nonthreatening

condition **carotenodermia** (*carotene* = carotene, *dermia* = skin), which results in orange-tinged skin, particularly in the palms of the hands and soles of the feet (**Figure 9.12**). Because these areas are cushioned with fat, they become more concentrated with the pigments and more visibly orange in color (right hand in photo). Cutting back on carotenoid-rich foods reverses carotenodermia.

Overconsuming Beta-Carotene Supplements

Although a diet abundant in carotenoid-rich foods is not dangerous, carotenoid supplements may be. In a study of adult male smokers, those who consumed beta-carotene supplements were shown to have significantly higher rates of lung cancer than those who didn't take the supplements.[37] While some earlier studies suggested alcohol may contribute to the effects of beta-carotene supplements on lung cancer risk, more recent research shows consistent evidence that beta-carotene supplements alone increase a smoker's risk of lung cancer and mortality.[38]

Vitamin A Deficiency

Vitamin A deficiency is uncommon in the United States but is a serious problem in developing countries. Signs of vitamin A deficiency, such as vision problems and increased infections, begin to develop after the liver stores of vitamin A are depleted.

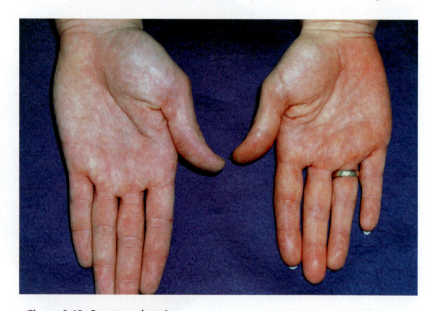

▲ **Figure 9.12 Carotenodermia**
The hand on the right exhibits the orange-tinged skin characteristic of carotenodermia.

Score an A

Dunk baby carrots in a tablespoon of low-fat ranch dressing for a healthy snack.

Keep dried apricots in your backpack for a sweet treat.

Add baby spinach to a lunchtime salad.

Bake sweet potatoes rather than white potatoes at dinner.

Buy frozen mango chunks for a ready-to-thaw beta-carotene-rich addition to cottage cheese or yogurt.

Vitamin A and Blindness

If the diet is deficient in vitamin A, an insufficient pool of retinal in the retina can result in **night blindness,** or the inability to see in the dark. Individuals with night blindness have difficulty seeing at dusk, because they can't adjust from daylight to dark, and may not be able to drive a car during this time of the day. If diagnosed early, night blindness can be reversed by taking vitamin A.

A prolonged vitamin A deficiency can lead to complete blindness. A severe deficiency of vitamin A results in dryness and permanent damage to the cornea, a condition called **xerophthalmia** (*xero* = dry, *ophthalm* = eye). Up to 10 million children, mostly in developing countries, suffer from xerophthalmia annually, and as many as 500,000 of these children go blind every year because they don't consume enough vitamin A.[39] Vitamin A deficiency is the number-one cause of preventable blindness in children.[40]

Vitamin A and Immunity

Keratinization of the epithelial tissues throughout the body occurs with vitamin A deficiency. The epithelial cells secrete keratin, which creates a hard, dry epithelial cell. Such a cell is unable to secrete the protective layer of mucus. Without mucus, the cells are unable to function properly, and they become susceptible to infection, especially in the nasal passages and the urinary and respiratory tracts. Keratinization also occurs in the skin.

night blindness The inability to see in dim light or at night due to a deficiency of retinal in the retina.

xerophthalmia Permanent damage to the cornea causing blindness due to a prolonged vitamin A deficiency.

keratinization The accumulation of the protein keratin in epithelial cells, forming hard, dry cells unable to secrete mucus due to vitamin A deficiency.

LO 9.5: THE TAKE-HOME MESSAGE

Vitamin A refers to a family of retinoids, which are essential for cell growth and development, reproduction, and a healthy immune system. Retinol is the most usable form of vitamin A in the body; retinal is essential for eye health and vision and retinoic acid regulates growth. Retinyl ester is found in foods and the form of vitamin A stored in the liver. Vitamin A is not excreted. Three carotenoids, including beta-carotene, are provitamins that must be converted to vitamin A to be used in the body. Most of the preformed dietary vitamin A, measured as retinol activity equvialents (RAE), is absorbed. Preformed vitamin A is found in milk, cereals, cheese, egg yolks, and organ meats, especially liver. Provitamin A is found in carrots, spinach, and sweet potatoes. Vitamin A deficiencies can result in vision problems and increased infections. Toxic amounts of vitamin A can compromise bone health and lead to birth defects during pregnancy.

Exploring Vitamin D

LO 9.6 Describe the functions, recommended intakes, food sources, and the deficiency and toxicity effects of vitamin D.

What Is Vitamin D?

Vitamin D (**calciferol**) is called the "sunshine vitamin" because it is derived from the reaction between ultraviolet (UV) rays and a form of cholesterol found in the skin. Exposure to sunlight can synthesize up to 100 percent of the vitamin D the body needs.[41] For this reason, vitamin D is often considered a conditionally essential nutrient. However, it still fits the criteria of a vitamin because a deficiency of this compound can cause symptoms that are cured once adequate intake is restored. Because of its function, vitamin D is also considered a **prohormone,** an inactive precursor, that is activated inside the body. Vitamin D is found in two forms. **Cholecalciferol** or **vitamin D₃** is the form produced in the skin and found in animal foods. **Ergocalciferol** or **vitamin D₂** is found in plants and dietary supplements.

Ergocalciferol and cholecalciferol differ chemically in the structure of their side chains, as illustrated in **Figure 9.13**.

calciferol The family of vitamin D compounds.

prohormone A physiologically inactive precursor to a hormone.

cholecalciferol (vitamin D₃) The form of vitamin D found in animal foods, supplements, and formed from precalciferol in the skin. This is the form absorbed from the skin into the blood.

ergocalciferol (vitamin D₂) The form of vitamin D found in plants and dietary supplements.

continued

Form found in plant foods

**Form found in animal foods
and made by the body**

Vitamin D$_2$ (ergocalciferol)

Vitamin D$_3$ (cholecalciferol)

▲ **Figure 9.13 The Chemical Structure of Vitamin D**
Vitamin D is found in the ergocalciferol (vitamin D$_2$) form in plants and the cholecalciferol (vitamin D$_3$) form in animal foods.

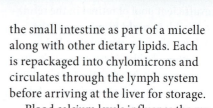

Ergocalciferol or D$_2$ contains a double bond in the side chain between carbons 22 and 23 and a methyl group on carbon 24. Cholecalciferol or D$_3$ has a single bond in the place of the double bond and two hydrogens on carbon 24. Even though their structures are different, they both have the same function in the body.

7-dehydrocholesterol (provitamin D$_3$) The compound in the skin that is converted to precalciferol by UV light from the sun; synthesized in the liver from cholesterol.

previtamin D$_3$ (precalciferol) The compound that is formed from 7-dehydrocholesterol when sunlight hits the skin.

vitamin D$_3$ binding protein (DBP) A protein made in the liver that transports vitamin D through the blood to the cells.

25-hydroxycholecalciferol The compound formed in the liver by adding a hydroxyl group to the 25th carbon of cholecalciferol.

1,25-dihydroxycholecalciferol The active form of vitamin D, also called calcitriol, that is formed in the kidney by adding a second hydroxyl group on the first carbon to 25-dihydroxycholecalciferol.

calcitriol The active form of vitamin D, also referred to as 1,25-dihydroxycholecalciferol.

parathyroid hormone (PTH) The hormone secreted from the parathyroid glands that activates vitamin D formation in the kidney.

Vitamin D Metabolism

Whether from food or sunlight, vitamin D is obtained in an inactive form. In the skin, a compound called **7-dehydrocholesterol** or **provitamin D$_3$** (which is made in the liver from cholesterol) is converted to **previtamin D$_3$** or **precalciferol** when UV rays hit the skin (see **Figure 9.14**). Precalciferol is changed to cholecalciferol, which slowly diffuses from the skin into the blood attached to a protein called **vitamin D$_3$ binding protein (DBP).** Cholecalciferol is then taken up by the liver to begin the activation process.

Once cholecalciferol reaches the liver, a two-step activation process begins. First, liver enzymes add a hydroxyl group on the twenty-fifth carbon of cholecalciferol, forming **25-hydroxycholecalciferol** (see step 3 in Figure 9.12). This newly formed compound circulates in the blood transported by DBP. In the kidneys a second hydroxyl group is added on the first carbon, forming **1,25-dihydroxycholecalciferol.** This is the active form of vitamin D, also called **calcitriol** (see step 4 in Figure 9.14), that leaves the kidney and enters the cells.

Vitamin D$_2$ and vitamin D$_3$ consumed in the diet are absorbed into the small intestine as part of a micelle along with other dietary lipids. Each is repackaged into chylomicrons and circulates through the lymph system before arriving at the liver for storage.

Blood calcium levels influence the metabolism of vitamin D (see **Figure 9.15**). When blood calcium levels drop, **parathyroid hormone (PTH)** is secreted from the parathyroid gland and travels to the kidney to activate vitamin D or 25-hydroxycholecalciferol. This boost in the levels of active vitamin D enhances the intestinal absorption of calcium, increases the amount of calcium reabsorbed through the kidneys, and mobilizes calcium from the bone. The result is that blood calcium levels return to normal.

Metabolic Functions of Vitamin D

Vitamin D regulates two important bone minerals, calcium and phosphorus. Vitamin D also participates in several other functions, including cell differentiation, stimulation of the immune system, blood pressure regulation, and insulin secretion.

The Role of Vitamin D in Bone Growth

Calcitriol functions as a hormone to stimulate the absorption of calcium and phosphorus in the intestinal tract. It also functions to maintain a healthy ratio of

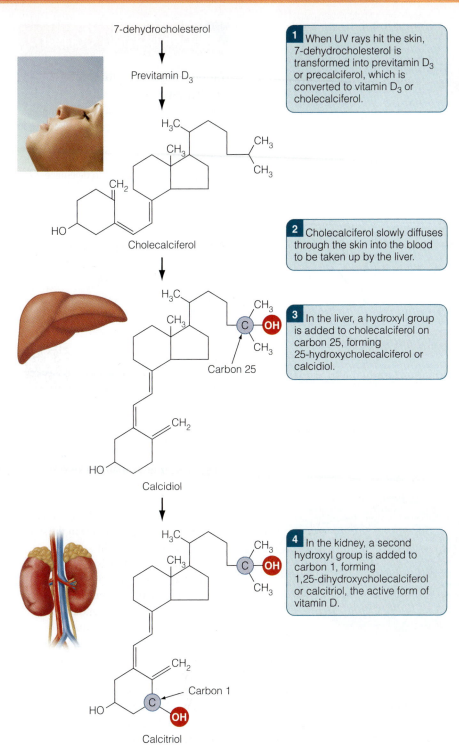

1 When UV rays hit the skin, 7-dehydrocholesterol is transformed into previtamin D₃ or precalciferol, which is converted to vitamin D₃ or cholecalciferol.

2 Cholecalciferol slowly diffuses through the skin into the blood to be taken up by the liver.

3 In the liver, a hydroxyl group is added to cholecalciferol on carbon 25, forming 25-hydroxycholecalciferol or calcidiol.

4 In the kidney, a second hydroxyl group is added to carbon 1, forming 1,25-dihydroxycholecalciferol or calcitriol, the active form of vitamin D.

▲ **Figure 9.14 The Metabolism of Vitamin D**

calcium and phosphorus levels in the blood, which promotes uptake of these two minerals in the bone. As calcium levels in the blood rise, more calcium is deposited in the bone. Vitamin D controls the interaction between *osteoblasts* and *osteoclasts,* the specialized bone cells involved in remodeling bone.

Because of its role in regulating calcium and phosphorus, vitamin D helps to build and maintain bone mass.

Vitamin D Helps Regulate the Growth of Cells

Research studies have shown that the incidence of breast, colon, and prostate cancers is greater among individuals living in sun-poor areas of the world than among those living in sunny regions.[42] Vitamin D helps regulate the growth and differentiation of certain cells. Researchers speculate that a deficiency of vitamin D in the body may reduce the proliferation of healthy cells and allow cancer cells to flourish.[43]

Vitamin D May Regulate the Immune System

The active form of vitamin D may reduce the risk of developing certain autoimmune disorders, such as inflammatory bowel syndrome (which is not the same thing as irritable bowel syndrome). Most cells in the immune system, such as T cells and macrophages, have a receptor for vitamin D. The role of vitamin D in immune system function is still not understood, but some researchers suggest that it may affect the function of the immune system and inhibit the development of autoimmunity.[44]

Vitamin D may also help reduce the risk of type 1 diabetes mellitus by up to 50 percent in adults.[45] Type 1 diabetes mellitus is an autoimmune disease in which the insulin-producing cells of the pancreas are attacked and destroyed by the body's own immune system. A large prospective study of military personnel reported that the risk of developing type 1 diabetes mellitus was highest when blood levels of 25-hydroxycholecalciferol fell below 20 percent of normal.[46] But no change in risk was noted above 20 percent of normal. The researchers proposed that low levels of 25-hydroxycholecalciferol may contribute to the autoimmune process. Although not an autoimmune disorder, similar results have been reported in individuals who have been diagnosed with type 2 diabetes mellitus, they also have low blood levels of vitamin D.[47] One study revealed that insulin resistance, or the inability of the cells to use insulin in the blood, was more pronounced in people with low levels of vitamin D in the blood, perhaps due to a genetic polymorphism.[48]

Vitamin D May Help Regulate Blood Pressure

Vitamin D reduces hypertension by acting on the gene that regulates the
continued

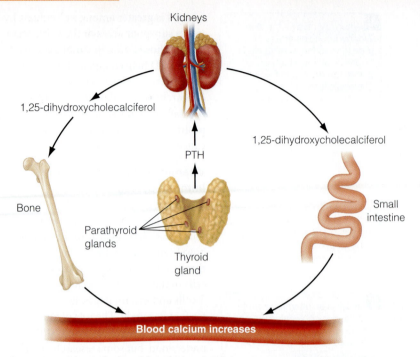

Kidneys

1,25-dihydroxycholecalciferol

PTH

1,25-dihydroxycholecalciferol

Bone

Parathyroid glands

Thyroid gland

Small intestine

Blood calcium increases

▲ **Figure 9.15 The Relationship of Blood Calcium to Parathyroid Hormone and Vitamin D**
Low blood levels of calcium stimulate the parathyroid glands to release parathyroid hormone (PTH). PTH stimulates the kidneys to increase the amount of active vitamin D, which in turn increases calcium absorption from the intestines, stimulates the reabsorption of calcium through the kidneys, and releases calcium from the bone. These actions help raise blood calcium back to normal levels.

Calculation Corner

Converting International Units for Vitamin D

Vitamin D content in dietary supplements and fortified foods is often listed in international units (IU), while vitamin D found in food is measured in μg cholecalciferol. Use the following conversion factor to determine the μg cholecalciferol in 1 IU.

1 IU of cholecalciferol is equivalent to 0.025 μg cholecalciferol

Example: A vitamin supplement contains 1,000 IU of cholecalciferol. How many μg cholecalciferol does it contain?

Answer: 0.025 μg cholecalciferol × 1,000 IU = 25 μg cholecalciferol

Scan this QR code with your mobile device to access practice math activities. You can also access the activities in **Mastering**Nutrition™.

renin-angiotensin system, the system that helps regulate blood pressure.[49] Vitamin D appears to reduce the activity of this gene, which results in less renin being produced. Renin is an enzyme that activates angiotensin which helps balance sodium and potassium levels in the blood, which affects blood pressure (we discuss the relationship of renin to hypertension in Chapter 11). In addition, blood pressure readings tend to be higher during the winter, when people are exposed to less sunlight, than in the summer. People with mild hypertension may be able to lower their blood pressure by spending a little time in the sun.

Daily Needs for Vitamin D

Not everyone can rely on the sun to meet his or her daily vitamin D needs. There are a number of limiting factors that influence vitamin D synthesis from sun: melanin content of the skin,

whether it is cloudy or smoggy, and use of sunscreen. There is new positive evidence, however, that even during the winter months sun exposure is strong enough to synthesize adequate vitamin D in the skin.[50]

Individuals with darker skin, such as African-Americans, have a higher amount of the skin pigment melanin, which reduces vitamin D production from sunlight. To derive the same amount of vitamin D as people with less melanin, these individuals need a longer period of sun exposure. A cloudy day can reduce the synthesis of vitamin D by 50 percent, and by 60 percent if it is smoggy or you sit in the shade.[51] And the use of sunscreen

can block the body's ability to synthesize vitamin D by more than 95 percent.[52] Because of these variables involving sun exposure, daily vitamin D needs are based on the amount in foods and are not based on the synthesis of vitamin D in the skin from exposure to sunlight.

The RDA for adults is 15 to 20 micrograms (600 to 800 IU) of vitamin D daily, depending on your age. These recommendations are listed in both micrograms and international units.[53] Learn how to convert micrograms to IUs in the Calculation Corner.

The RDA for children has been set at 15 micrograms (600 IU) of vitamin D per day for children aged 1 to 13. This is an increase in vitamin D from 5 micrograms due to newly reported research suggesting that the previous RDA was too low. Vitamin D supplementation as high as 2,500 IUs is safe for children aged 1 to 3 and up to 3,000 IUs for children 4 to 8 years old.[54]

When reading labels to assess the amount of vitamin D in foods, keep in mind that the Daily Value (DV) on the Nutrition Facts panel is set at 400 IU, a recommendation based on the older

RDA for vitamin D. This means that the amount of vitamin D in a serving of a packaged food does not reflect the new, higher recommendations for children and adults.[55]

Food Sources of Vitamin D

One of the easiest ways to get vitamin D from food is to drink fortified milk, which provides 100 IU, or 2.5 micrograms, of vitamin D per 8 fluid ounces. Other than fortified milk, breakfast cereals, yogurt, and fatty fish (such as sardines and salmon), very few foods provide ample amounts of vitamin D (see **Figure 9.16**). With this scarcity of naturally occurring food sources, it isn't surprising that many Americans are not meeting their daily vitamin D needs.[56]

Vitamin D Toxicity

The tolerable upper limit (UL) for vitamin D has been set at 100 micrograms (4,000 IU) for individuals nine years or older. This upper limit is over six times higher than the recommended daily amount. Consuming too much vitamin D can cause loss of appetite, nausea, vomiting, and constipation.

As with the other fat-soluble vitamins, excess amounts of vitamin D are stored in the adipocytes, and an accumulation can reach toxic levels, causing **hypervitaminosis D.** This condition causes overabsorption of calcium from the intestines as well as calcium loss from bones. When both of these symptoms occur, blood calcium levels can become dangerously high.

A chronically high amount of calcium in the blood, or **hypercalcemia** (*hyper* = over, *calc* = calcium, *emia* = blood), can cause damaging calcium deposits in the tissues of the kidneys, lungs, blood vessels, and heart. Excess vitamin D can also affect the nervous system and cause severe depression.[57]

Hypervitaminosis D rarely occurs as a result of consuming too much vitamin D from foods, even fortified foods. The only exception is fish oils, specifically cod-liver oil, which provides 34 micrograms (1,360 IU) of vitamin D per tablespoon. Luckily, the less-than-pleasant taste of cod-liver oil is a safeguard against overconsumption. A more likely culprit behind hypervitaminosis D is the overuse of vitamin D supplements.

Sun worshippers don't have to worry about hypervitaminosis D from the sun (although they should be concerned about the risk of skin cancer). Overexposing the skin to UV rays eventually destroys the inactive form of vitamin D in the skin, causing the body to shut down production of vitamin D. It is estimated that about 10 to 20 minutes of sun exposure two to three times per week is sufficient to obtain adequate vitamin D.[58]

Vitamin D Deficiency

Vitamin D deficiencies are increasing worldwide, most likely due to individuals' misunderstanding of the critical role of sunshine as a source of vitamin D. **Rickets** is one of the consequences of a lack of sunshine and insufficient dietary intake of vitamin D in children (**Figure 9.17**). The bones of children with rickets aren't adequately mineralized with calcium and phosphorus, and this causes them to weaken. Because of their "soft bones," these children cannot hold up their own body weight, and develop bowed legs.[59] Babies with rickets also

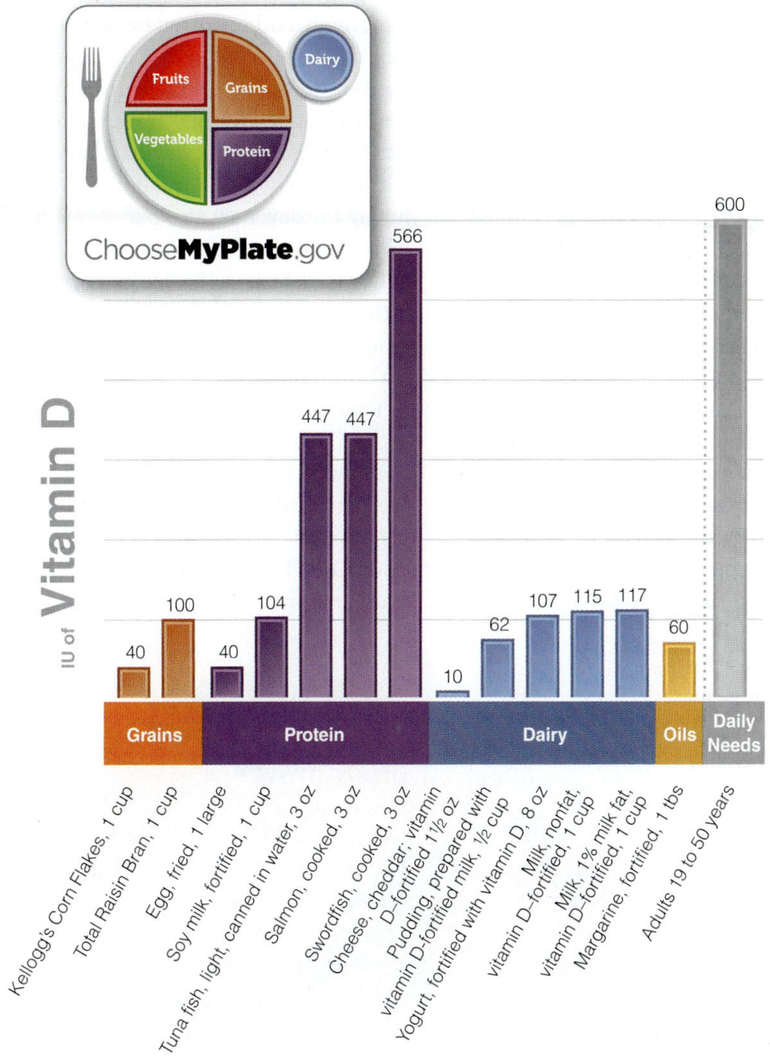

▲ Figure 9.16 **Vitamin D Content in Selected Foods**

hypervitaminosis D A condition resulting from excessive amounts of vitamin D in the body.

hypercalcemia A chronically high amount of calcium in the blood.

rickets A vitamin D deficiency in children resulting in soft bones.

continued

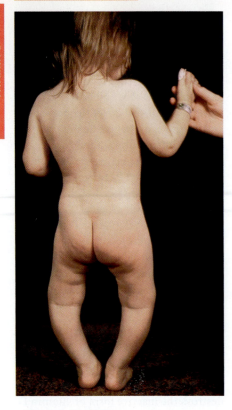

▲ **Figure 9.17 Rickets**
Rickets can cause bowed legs in children.

have a delayed closure of the anterior fontanel or "soft spot" in the skull.[60, 61]

Since fortification of milk with vitamin D began in the 1930s, rickets has been considered a rare disease among children in the United States. However, the disease has resurfaced as a public health concern. In the late 1990s, a review of hospital records in Georgia suggested that as many as five out of every 1 million children between 6 months and 5 years of age in that state were hospitalized with vitamin D–related rickets.[62] Similarly, more than 20 percent of over 300 adolescents at a Boston-based hospital clinic in 2004 were reported to be deficient in vitamin D.[63] Whether the increase in rickets is due to a rise in the incidence of rickets or an increased awareness is not clear. The majority of cases of rickets in the United States have been African-American infants who were solely breast-fed. In Canada,

osteomalacia The adult equivalent of rickets, causing muscle and bone weakness, and pain.

the incidence of rickets was reported as 2.9 per 100,000 infants, almost all of whom were breast-fed.[64] Because the vitamin D content of breast milk is affected by the vitamin D status of the mother, the American Academy of Pediatrics recommends that all breast-fed infants receive a supplement of 10 micrograms (400 IU) per day until they are also consuming 32 ounces of vitamin D–fortified formula or whole milk daily.[65]

The *Dietary Guidelines for Americans, 2010* and the Academy of Pediatrics recommends that all children 2 years and older drink low-fat milk to promote bone health. A National Health and Nutrition Examination Survey (NHANES) of children 2 to 19 years of age conducted from 2007 to 2008 reported that an average of 70 percent of children are drinking milk daily, most of which was 2 percent milk.[66] Children should be encouraged to drink low-fat milk to lower kilocaloric intake but at the same time consume a good source of vitamin D and calcium.

Increased concern over skin cancer may be a factor in the rise of rickets among American children. Skin cancer is the most common form of cancer in the United States, and childhood sun exposure appears to increase the risk of skin cancer in later years.[67] Because of this, organizations such as the Centers for Disease Control and the American Cancer Society have run campaigns that recommend limiting exposure to ultraviolet light. People are encouraged to use sunscreen, wear protective clothing when outdoors,

Most milk sold in the United States today has been fortified with vitamin D.

and minimize activities in the sun. The American Academy of Pediatrics also recommends that infants younger than 6 months not be exposed to direct sunlight. With less exposure to UV light, many children aren't able to synthesize vitamin D in adequate amounts to meet their needs, thereby increasing their risk of developing rickets. The increased use of child day-care facilities, which may limit outdoor activities during the day, may also play a role in this increased prevalence of rickets.

Osteomalacia is the adult equivalent of rickets and can cause muscle and bone weakness and pain. The bones can't mineralize properly because there isn't enough calcium and phosphorus available in the blood. Although there may be adequate amounts of these minerals in the diet, the deficiency of vitamin D hampers their absorption. Explore the Nutrition in Practice on page 341. How can Abby

Nutrition in Practice: Abby

Abby's mom is a cosmetologist, so she knows the effect of sunlight exposure and its impact on the aging of skin. Even though she grew up in Wisconsin, her mother lathered her up with a sunscreen with SPF of 30 every day before leaving for school or going outside to play, and always dressed her in hats and light cotton, long-sleeved shirts and pants in the summer. To Abby, putting on sunscreen and covering her skin from hat to toe before leaving the house is as routine as brushing her teeth.

For her college admission, Abby needed to get a complete physical. When taking a family history, the doctor uncovered that her mom has osteomalacia. When the doctor got her blood laboratory report back, he called Abby to tell her that her blood level of vitamin D was on the low side of normal and suggested she visit a dietitian.

Abby's Stats:
☐ Age: 17
☐ Height: 5 feet 5 inches
☐ Weight: 128 pounds

Abby's Food Log

Food/Beverage	Time Consumed	Hunger Rating*	Location
Nothing	6 AM	3	
Bagel with cream cheese	9:30 AM	5	High school cafeteria
Turkey and Swiss cheese sandwich, chips, cola	12:30 PM	5	High school cafeteria
Cheese and crackers	3:30 PM	3	Kitchen
Pizza, 2 slices	6:30 PM	4	With friends in a restaurant

*Hunger Rating (1–5): 1 = not hungry; 5 = super hungry.

Critical Thinking Questions
1. What symptoms might Abby expect to have if her levels of vitamin D continue to decline?
2. Why does Abby's avoidance of sunlight increase her potential deficiency of vitamin D?
3. Based on her food record, why do you think that she is deficient in vitamin D?

Dietitian's Observation and Plan for Abby:
☐ Discuss the need to add vitamin D–fortified foods to her diet to meet her daily needs. Explain why cheese is a good source of calcium, but it does not contain vitamin D.
☐ Abby agrees to eat cereal with skim milk for breakfast prior to leaving for school, having a vitamin D–fortified yogurt as a daily afternoon snack, and to consume a large glass of skim milk with dinner.

A month later, Abby returns to the dietitian. Because she often eats dinner with her friends at the local pizzeria, she is having a difficult time routinely having a glass of milk with dinner. The dietitian recommends that Abby consume a glass of milk or a mug of hot cocoa made with milk daily when she gets home in the evening.

continued

TABLE TIPS

Ways to Get Vitamin D

Use vitamin D–fortified low-fat milk, not cream, in hot or iced coffee.

Buy vitamin D–fortified low-fat yogurts and have one daily as a snack. Top it with a vitamin D–fortified cereal for another boost of D.

Start the morning with vitamin D–fortified cereal and low-fat or skim milk.

Flake canned salmon over a lunchtime salad.

Make instant hot cocoa with hot milk rather than water.

Drink vitamin D–fortified orange juice with breakfast.

improve her vitamin D intake to reverse osteomalacia?

Vitamin D deficiency and its subsequent effect on decreased calcium absorption can lead to osteoporosis, a condition in which the bones can mineralize properly, but there isn't enough calcium in the diet to maximize the bone density or mass.

Muscle weakness and pain is also associated with low levels of serum vitamin D concentrations. One study found that a vitamin D supplement of 20 micrograms (800 IU) per day plus calcium was more effective in increasing muscle strength and reducing the number of falls reported by elderly women than just calcium alone.[68]

LO 9.6: THE TAKE-HOME MESSAGE

Vitamin D can be made in the skin from exposure to ultraviolet rays from the sun. The active form of vitamin D is calcitriol. Vitamin D regulates blood calcium, enhances the absorption of calcium and phosphorus from the small intestine, and maintains healthy bones. It may also help regulate blood pressure and the immune system, and it may prevent diabetes and some cancers. Milk and fortified yogurts are excellent food sources of vitamin D. A deficiency of vitamin D can cause rickets in children and osteomalacia in adults. Hypervitaminosis D can result in hypercalcemia, affect the nervous system, and cause severe depression.

VITAMIN E

Exploring Vitamin E

LO 9.7 Describe the functions, recommended intakes, food sources, and the deficiency and toxicity effects of vitamin E.

What Is Vitamin E?

There are eight different forms of naturally occurring vitamin E, but one form, **alpha-tocopherol (α-tocopherol)**, is most active in the body with a side

alpha-tocopherol (α-tocopherol) The most active form of vitamin E in the body.

chain of saturated carbons (**Figure 9.18**). The synthetic form of vitamin E found in dietary supplements is only half as active as the natural form. Alpha-tocopherol is the only form of vitamin E that is reflected in the Dietary Reference Intakes.

Vitamin E Absorption and Transport

Vitamin E is absorbed with the aid of bile salts and micelles into the cells of the small intestinal lining. Once

absorbed, vitamin E is transported as part of chylomicrons through the lymph fluid into the blood, where it eventually arrives at the liver. Some researchers have suggested that vitamin E is transported through the cells of the small intestine attached to a protein, but so far a transport protein has not been discovered. More than 90 percent of the vitamin E is stored in the adipose tissue. Excess vitamin E is excreted through the bile, urine, feces, and the pores in the skin.

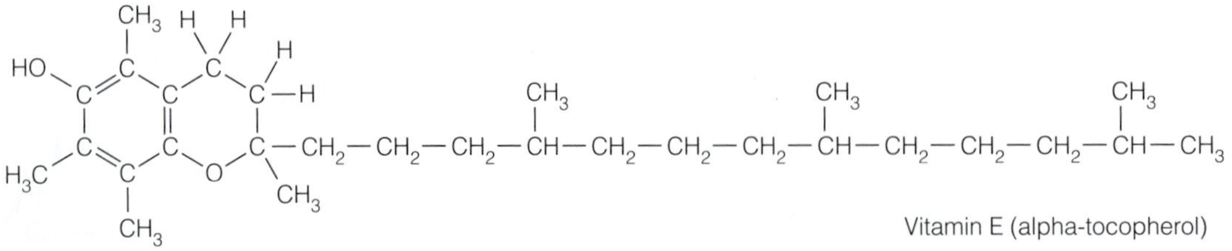

Vitamin E (alpha-tocopherol)

▲ **Figure 9.18 The Structure of Alpha-Tocopherol**
There are eight different types of vitamin E compounds (or tocopherols), but alpha-tocopherol is the most active and is the form reflected in the Dietary Reference Intakes.

Metabolic Functions of Vitamin E

Vitamin E is sometimes referred to as the vitamin in search of a disease to cure. For almost 40 years after its discovery, scientists searched unsuccessfully for a curative role for vitamin E. They now have shifted their focus and begun valuing the vitamin's importance as an effective antioxidant and in maintaining healthy cell membranes. Vitamin E also plays an important function in blood clotting. The role of vitamin E in preventing cardiovascular disease is still unclear. Even though vitamin E was thought to show promise in preventing other diseases such as cancer or cataracts, researchers have not been able to provide conclusive evidence supporting this.

Vitamin E as an Antioxidant

Vitamin E's nutritional claim to fame is its role as a powerful antioxidant, particularly in cell membranes. Recall from Chapter 5 that phospholipids are critical components of cell membranes. Many phospholipids contain unsaturated fatty acids, which are vulnerable to the damaging effects of free radicals. Vitamin E is unique in its ability to neutralize free radicals before they can harm cell membranes (see **Figure 9.19**). The hydrogen ions in vitamin E quickly react with the free radical and stop the chain reaction. In doing so, vitamin E is altered and loses its antioxidant abilities.

Oxidation of the LDL cholesterol carrier in the blood is also harmful, as it contributes to the buildup of artery-clogging plaque. Antioxidants, including vitamin E, help protect the LDL cholesterol carrier from being oxidized and reduce the risk of atherosclerosis in the arteries.[69]

Vitamin E as an Anticoagulant

Vitamin E is an anticoagulant (*anti* = against, *coagulant* = causes clotting), which means that it inhibits platelets from unnecessarily clumping together and creating a damaging clot in the bloodstream. Vitamin E also lessens the stickiness of the cells that line the lymph and blood vessels. This reduces plaque buildup that clogs the passageways, reducing the risk of heart attack or stroke. Although this function clearly helps maintain the health of the cardiovascular system, studies are still under

Calculation Corner

Converting International Units for Vitamin E

Vitamin E content in dietary supplements and fortified foods is often listed in international units (IU), while vitamin E found naturally in food is measured in milligrams of alpha-tocopherol (mg α-tocopherol). Use the following conversion factors to determine the alpha-tocopherol equivalents in mg α-tocopherol found in 1 IU.

> 1 IU of alpha-tocopherol is equivalent to 0.67 mg alpha-tocopherol

> 1 IU of alpha-tocopherol is equivalent to 0.45 mg of synthetic alpha-tocopherol

Example: A vitamin supplement contains 400 IU of alpha-tocopherol. How many mg α-tocopherol does it contain?

Answer: 0.67 mg × 400 IU = 268 mg α-tocopherol

or

0.45 mg × 400 IU = 180 mg α-tocopherol (synthetic α-tocopherol)

way to assess if the long-term use of vitamin E supplements could play a protective role against heart disease.

Daily Needs of Vitamin E

Adults should consume 15 milligrams (22.4 IU) of vitamin E daily (see the Calculation Corner to learn how to convert vitamin E in milligrams to international units) as an Adequate Intake (AI). Because alpha-tocopherol is the most active form of vitamin E in the body, vitamin E requirements are presented in alpha-tocopherol equivalents. Researchers speculate that healthy Americans are not consuming adequate amounts of vitamin E.[70]

Food Sources of Vitamin E

Vegetable oils (and foods that contain them), avocados, nuts, and seeds are good food sources of vitamin E. The *Dietary Guidelines for Americans* specifically recommend consuming vegetable

continued

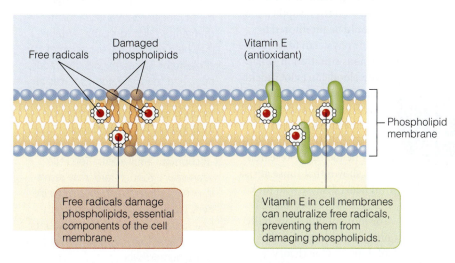

Free radicals

Damaged phospholipids

Vitamin E (antioxidant)

Phospholipid membrane

Free radicals damage phospholipids, essential components of the cell membrane.

Vitamin E in cell membranes can neutralize free radicals, preventing them from damaging phospholipids.

▲ **Figure 9.19** **Vitamin E as an Antioxidant in Cell Membranes**

Vitamin E

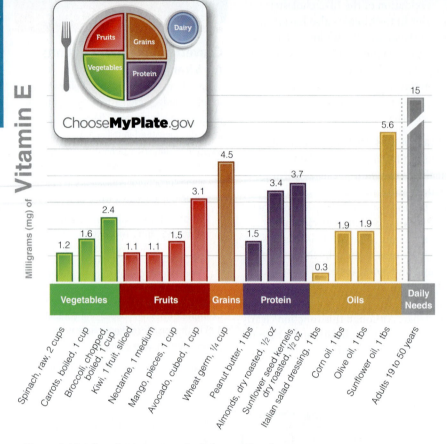

Milligrams (mg) of Vitamin E

ChooseMyPlate.gov

Vegetables	1.2	1.6	2.4
Fruits	1.1	1.1	1.5	3.1
Grains	4.5
Protein	1.5	3.4	3.7	0.3
Oils	1.9	1.9	5.6
Daily Needs	15

Spinach, raw, 2 cups
Carrots, boiled, 1 cup
Broccoli, chopped, boiled, 1 cup
Kiwi, 1 fruit, sliced
Nectarine, 1 medium
Mango, pieces, 1 cup
Avocado, cubed, 1 cup
Wheat germ, 1/4 cup
Peanut butter, 1 tbs
Almonds, dry roasted, 1/2 oz
Sunflower seed kernels, dry roasted, 1/2 oz
Italian salad dressing, 1 tbs
Corn oil, 1 tbs
Olive oil, 1 tbs
Sunflower oil, 1 tbs
Adults 19 to 50 years

▲ **Figure 9.20 Vitamin E Content in Selected Foods**

oils daily to meet vitamin E needs. Some green leafy vegetables and fortified cereals can also contribute to daily needs (see **Figure 9.20**).

Vitamin E Toxicity

There isn't any known risk of consuming too much vitamin E from natural food sources. However, overconsumption of the synthetic form that is found in supplements and/or fortified foods could pose risks.

Because vitamin E can act as an anticoagulant and interfere with blood clotting, excess amounts in the body increase the risk of **hemorrhage.** To prevent hemorrhage, the upper limit from

hemorrhage Excessive bleeding or loss of blood.

A Good Source of Natural Vitamin E

A Cholesterol Free Food

100% Pure

Mazola
CORN OIL

48 FL. OZ. (1-1/2 QT.) 1.42 L

supplements and/or fortified foods is 1,000 milligrams for adults. This applies only to healthy individuals consuming adequate amounts of vitamin K. (Vitamin K also plays a role in blood clotting.) Individuals taking anticoagulant medication and vitamin E supplements should be monitored by their physician to avoid the serious situation in which the blood can't clot quickly enough to stop the bleeding from a wound.

The upper level of 1,000 milligrams may actually be too high. Research has shown that those at risk of heart disease who took 265 milligrams (400 IU) or more of vitamin E daily for at least one year had an overall higher risk of dying.[71] One theory is that too much vitamin E may disrupt

the balance of other antioxidants in the body, causing more harm than good.

Vitamin E Deficiency

Though rare, a chronic vitamin E deficiency can cause nerve problems, muscle weakness, and uncontrolled movement of body parts. Because vitamin E is an antioxidant and is found in the membranes of red blood cells, a deficiency can also increase the susceptibility of cell membranes to damage by free radicals. Individuals who can't absorb fat properly may fall short of their vitamin E needs.

LO 9.7: THE TAKE-HOME MESSAGE

There are several forms of naturally occurring vitamin E but alpha-tocopherol is the most active form in the body. Vitamin E is transported via the chylomicron and stored in the adipose tissue. Vitamin E is an antioxidant that protects the cells' membranes and an anticoagulant that inhibits clot formation. Vitamin E may help prevent the oxidation of LDL cholesterol. Vegetable oils, avocados, nuts, and seeds are good sources of vitamin E. Green leafy vegetables and fortified cereals also contribute to daily intake. The recommended intake for vitamin E is presented in alpha-tocopherol equivalents. Too little vitamin E, although rare, may result in nerve problems and muscle weakness, and increase susceptibility to free radical damage. Excess amounts of vitamin E from supplements may cause hemorrhage.

Exploring **Vitamin K**

LO 9.8 Describe the functions, recommended intakes, food sources, and the deficiency and toxicity effects of vitamin K.

What Is Vitamin K?

Vitamin K is found naturally in two forms. Some plants manufacture **phylloquinone,** or **vitamin K_1.** Phylloquinone, shown in **Figure 9.21**, has a long chain of carbons with methyl groups attached at every fourth carbon. This is the primary source of vitamin K in the diet. In animals, bacteria that reside naturally in the colon synthesize **menaquinone,** also referred to as **vitamin K_2.** A third form of vitamin K, called **menadione,** or **vitamin K_3,** is synthetic and formulated for use in animal feed and vitamin supplements.

Vitamin K Absorption and Transport

About 80 percent of dietary vitamin K is absorbed, mostly in the jejunum. In contrast, only 10 percent of the vitamin K produced by bacteria in the large intestine is absorbed. Both forms of vitamin K are incorporated into chylomicrons and transported to the liver, where they are stored for future use. When the diet is deficient in vitamin K, the storage forms are transported by the lipoproteins VLDL, LDL, and HDL. Excess vitamin K is excreted, mostly bound to bile. It can also be eliminated through the urine once its been degraded by the liver. Vitamin K is stored in small amounts, mostly in the liver.

Metabolic Functions of Vitamin K

Vitamin K is so named because of its role in *koagulation*, the Danish word for **coagulation,** or blood clotting.[72] It also functions as a cofactor in several key roles in the body, and is essential for strengthening the bones.

Vitamin K Promotes Blood Clotting

A series of reactions, referred to as a cascade, must happen before the blood coagulates and forms a blood clot (**Figure 9.22**). At step seven in the cascade, a carboxyl group is added to a protein, which enables the protein to bind calcium ions. The reaction, called **carboxylation** (see the Chemistry Boost for an illustration), is catalyzed by a

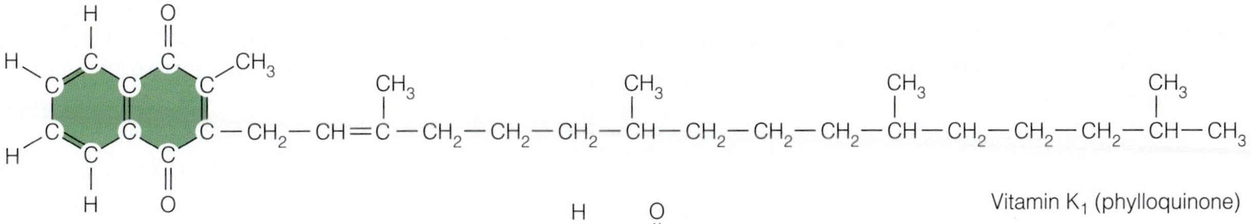

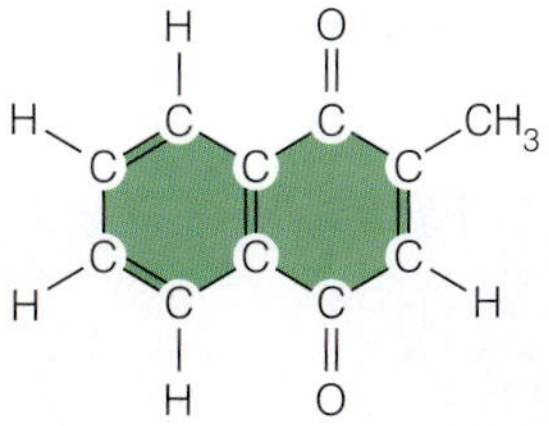

Vitamin K_1 (phylloquinone)

Vitamin K_3 (menadione)

▲ **Figure 9.21 The Structure of Vitamin K**
Vitamin K occurs naturally in plants as phylloquinone. Menadione is the synthetic form of vitamin K.

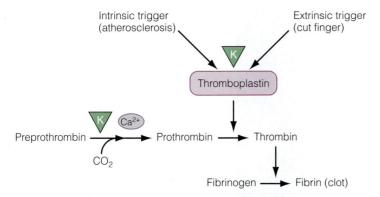

▲ **Figure 9.22 The Role of Vitamin K in Blood Clotting**
Vitamin K is a coenzyme involved in carboxylation reactions of several proteins during blood clotting.

phylloquinone (vitamin K_1) The form of vitamin K found in plants.

menaquinone (vitamin K_2) The form of vitamin K produced by bacteria in the colon.

menadione (vitamin K_3) The synthetic form of vitamin K used in animal feed and dietary supplements.

coagulation The process of blood clotting.

carboxylation The chemical reaction in which a carboxyl group is added to a molecule.

continued

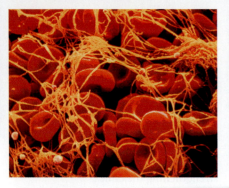

▲ Figure 9.23 **Blood Clot** (SEM, magnified 1,900×)

▲ Figure 9.24 **Bone Matrix** (colored SEM, magnified 2,000×).

carboxylase enzyme that is dependent on vitamin K as a coenzyme. Four of these vitamin K–dependent proteins are known as **clotting factors:** II (prothrombin), VII, IX, and X. Once calcium is bound to the clotting factors, the clotting process continues with the conversion of prothrombin to thrombin. Thrombin converts fibrinogen to fibrin, which holds together red blood cells to form the actual blood clot (**Figure 9.23**). As soon as vitamin K has completed its role in activating the carboxylase enzyme, it is released and the enzyme must be activated again. Without vitamin K, a simple nick or cut could quickly result in hemorrhage.

Anticoagulants (anticlotting medications) such as Coumadin (also known as **warfarin**) decrease vitamin K activity, resulting in thinner blood. Severe liver disease also results in lower blood levels of the vitamin K–dependent clotting factors and increases the risk of hemorrhage.

Vitamin K Promotes Strong Bones
Vitamin K participates in the carboxylation of other proteins. Two of these proteins are essential components in bone formation: *osteocalcin* and *matrix Gla protein*. Osteocalcin is a type of Gla protein secreted by bone-forming osteoblasts. Matrix Gla protein is found

in the bone matrix (**Figure 9.24**), blood vessels, and cartilage. The carboxylation of osteocalcin and matrix Gla protein is necessary for calcium ions to bind to the bone matrix, which strengthens the bone and improves bone mass.[73] Matrix Gla protein may also provide protection against atherosclerosis.[74]

Daily Needs for Vitamin K

Currently, the amount of vitamin K made from bacteria in the intestinal tract that contributes to meeting daily needs is not known. Because of this, it is hard to determine an Estimated

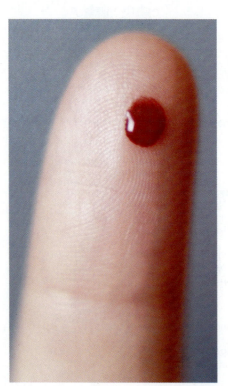

Average Requirement (EAR), so an Adequate Intake (AI) is reported instead. Therefore, the AI for dietary vitamin K is based on the average amount consumed by healthy Americans.[75] Adult women need 90 micrograms (1,000 IU) of vitamin K per day, and men need 120 micrograms (1,300 IU) daily.

Food Sources of Vitamin K

To meet vitamin K needs, think green. Green vegetables like broccoli, asparagus, spinach, salad greens, brussels sprouts, and green cabbage are all rich in vitamin K. Vegetable oils and margarine are the second largest source of vitamin K in the diet (see **Figure 9.25**). A green salad with oil-and-vinegar dressing at lunch and three-quarters of a cup of broccoli at dinner will meet an individual's vitamin K needs for the entire day.

Vitamin K Toxicity and Deficiency

There are no known adverse effects of consuming too much vitamin K from foods or supplements, so an upper intake level hasn't been set for healthy people.

Individuals taking anticoagulant medications such as Coumadin need to maintain a consistent intake of vitamin K. This medication decreases the activity of vitamin K and prolongs the time it takes

clotting factors Substances involved in the process of blood clotting, such as prothrombin and fibrinogen.

warfarin An anticoagulant drug given to prevent blood from clotting.

Chemistry Boost

Carboxylation Reactions
Carboxylation is a chemical reaction that occurs when a carboxyl group (COOH) is added to a protein, such as during the blood-clotting reaction. As illustrated, the glutamic acid molecule is converted to carboxyglutamic acid with the aid of vitamin K. The carboxyl group in this illustration is shown as COO^-.

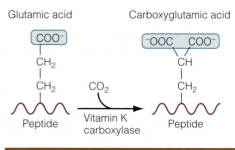

Glutamic acid → Carboxyglutamic acid

COO^- ... ^-OOC COO^-

CH_2 ... CH

CH_2 ... CH_2

CO_2 / Vitamin K carboxylase

Peptide ... Peptide

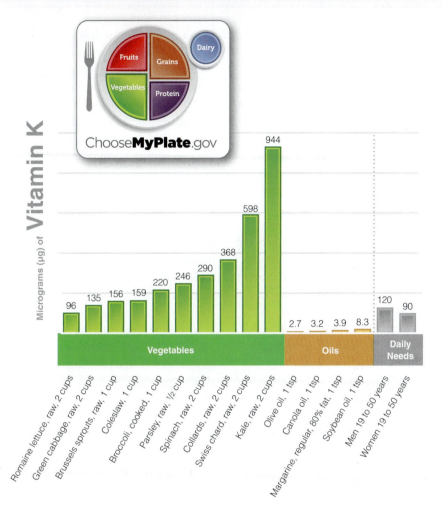

Microgram (μg) of **Vitamin K**

ChooseMyPlate.gov

Fruits | Grains | Dairy | Vegetables | Protein

944

598

368

290

246

220

156 | 159

135

96

2.7 | 3.2 | 3.9 | 8.3

120 | 90

Vegetables | **Oils** | **Daily Needs**

Romaine lettuce, raw, 2 cups
Green cabbage, raw, 2 cups
Brussels sprouts, raw, 1 cup
Coleslaw, 1 cup
Broccoli, cooked, 1 cup
Parsley, raw, ½ cup
Spinach, raw, 2 cups
Collards, raw, 2 cups
Swiss chard, raw, 2 cups
Kale, raw, 2 cups
Olive oil, 1 tsp
Canola oil, 1 tsp
Margarine, regular, 80% fat, 1 tsp
Soybean oil, 1 tsp
Men 19 to 50 years
Women 19 to 50 years

▲ **Figure 9.25 Vitamin K Content in Selected Foods**

Getting Your Ks

Have a green salad daily.

Cook with soybean oil.

Add shredded green cabbage to salad, or top a salad with a scoop of coleslaw.

Add a small amount of margarine to steamed spinach. Both provide some vitamin K.

Dunk raw broccoli florets in salad dressing for two sources of vitamin K.

for blood to clot. If individuals taking Coumadin suddenly increase the vitamin K in their diets, the vitamin can override the effect of the drug, enabling the blood to clot too quickly. In contrast, a sudden decline in dietary vitamin K can enhance the effectiveness of the drug and increase the risk of bleeding.[76]

Babies are born with low levels of vitamin K in their bodies. This is because little vitamin K passes through the placenta and newborns have sterile intestinal tracts with few bacteria to produce vitamin K. In addition, breast milk is low in vitamin K. For this reason, newborns are routinely given vitamin K soon after birth, either as an injection or by mouth, to enable blood clotting until the bacteria in the intestinal tract can begin to produce vitamin K.[77]

A vitamin K deficiency severe enough to affect blood clotting is extremely rare in healthy individuals.[78] People with conditions such as gallbladder disease, which reduces the absorption of fat and fat-soluble vitamins in the intestinal tract, may be at risk for not meeting their vitamin K needs.

Though the exact mechanism is unknown, a chronic dietary deficiency of vitamin K may be a factor in increased hip fractures in older men and women. A diet rich in phylloquinone (vitamin K_1) has been shown to improve bone mineral content in older women.[79]

LO 9.8: THE TAKE-HOME MESSAGE

Vitamin K is found in plants as phylloquinone and as menaquinone in the colon manufactured by bacteria. Vitamin K functions as a carboxylation coenzyme in blood clotting and bone formation. Leafy greens, vegetable oils, and margarine are good dietary sources of vitamin K. While there are no known toxicity problems for vitamin K, a deficiency may result in hemorrhage and bone fractures. Individuals taking anticoagulant medications such as Coumadin should monitor their vitamin K intake.

Are Vitamin Supplements Necessary for Good Health?

LO 9.9 Explain the role of dietary supplements in maintaining a healthy diet.

Sales of dietary supplements in the United States have increased markedly in the last several decades. More than 30 percent of Americans spent over $12 billion in 2012 on dietary supplements as single vitamins or minerals, or in the most popular form of a multivitamin and mineral combination.[80] One in three Americans reports taking a multivitamin and mineral supplement daily.[81] To encourage supplement use, manufacturers are developing new chewable forms, including chocolate, gummies, and soft gels alongside the pills, powders, and liquids. Are vitamin supplements worth the money? Are they harmful or essential to be healthy?

Some of the most popular forms of vitamin supplements sold today are in chewable, candylike forms.

Vitamin Supplements and Aging

The aging population appears to be one of the forces driving this increase in the use of supplements: Older people may use vitamin supplements in an attempt to mitigate ongoing medical issues or prevent chronic diseases,[82] especially cardiovascular disease, cancer, and cognitive decline in later years.

A staggering number of studies have examined the association between ingesting specific individual vitamins or combinations of vitamins to prevent cardiovascular disease and cancer, including the antioxidant vitamins A, C, E, beta-carotene, and folic acid. A recent review found that any single vitamin or combination of vitamins had no benefit in preventing cardiovascular disease or cancer. In the case of beta-carotene and vitamin E supplements, the risks outweighed any benefits. The researchers concluded that ingesting beta-carotene in supplement form might increase the risk of developing cancer in people who smoke. Vitamin E supplements do not impact the risk of developing cardiovascular disease or cancer,[83] nor did a daily multivitamin prevent heart attacks, stroke, or death from a cardiovascular event even after 10 years of supplementation.[84]

In addition to cardiovascular disease and cancer, middle-aged Americans are fearful that as they age, cognitive decline will rob them of their independence and quality of life. Does a daily multivitamin supplement help maintain mental sharpness and prevent cognitive decline? The research says no. The cognitive decline in men over a 13-year study found no benefit of taking a multivitamin supplement on four different cognitive tests.[85] Researchers suggest that the results could be due to the fact that the subjects were already too well nourished to benefit from a daily supplement.

While the idea that a multivitamin pill daily can ward off cardiovascular disease, cancer, and even cognitive decline is appealing, it's best to save your money. The current research doesn't support dietary supplements as a cure for aging or to prevent the chronic diseases that accompany aging.

Vitamin Supplements Are Not a Substitute for Healthy Eating

Consumers often choose supplements because they are unwilling to improve

Unlike synthetic supplements, whole fruits and vegetables contain fiber and phytochemicals that provide health benefits beyond those of the vitamin content.

their diets. However, supplements should never be used to replace a healthy diet. The Academy of Nutrition and Dietetics maintains that an unhealthy diet of nonnutritious foods cannot be transformed into a healthy diet by simply ingesting a daily supplement. There is little scientific evidence to promote the use of dietary supplements in place of eating a healthy, balanced diet. Remember that disease-fighting phytochemicals, fiber, and other substances that the body needs are all missing from a bottle of supplements.

Further, supplement use may have adverse side effects. In fact, supplement use, not food, is responsible for most of the reported problems associated with vitamin toxicity. Any individual who is considering taking supplements should consult a credible source of nutrition information, such as a Registered Dietitian Nutritionist, before purchasing or consuming supplements.

Supplements May Be Helpful for Some Individuals

Whereas many healthy individuals do not need to consume supplements, some supplements are useful for people who cannot meet their nutrient needs through a regular, varied diet. Others may have been advised by their physician to consume supplements to correct a vitamin or mineral deficiency.

Among those who may benefit from taking a dietary supplement are:[86]

- Women of childbearing age who may become pregnant, as they need to consume adequate synthetic folic acid (a B vitamin) to prevent certain birth defects
- Pregnant and lactating women who can't meet their increased nutrient needs with foods
- Older individuals, who need adequate amounts of synthetic vitamin B_{12}
- Individuals who do not drink enough milk and/or do not have

adequate sun exposure to meet their vitamin D needs
- Individuals on low-kilocalorie diets that limit the amount of vitamins and minerals they can consume through food
- Strict vegetarians, who have limited dietary options for vitamins D and B_{12} and other nutrients
- Individuals with food allergies or lactose intolerance that limit food choices
- Individuals who abuse alcohol, have medical conditions such as intestinal disorders, or are taking medications that may increase their need for certain vitamins
- Individuals who are food insecure and those who are eliminating food groups from their diet
- Infants who are breast-fed should receive 400 IU of vitamin D daily unless they are also consuming at least 1 quart of vitamin D–fortified formula daily. Children aged 1 and older should receive 400 IU of vitamin D daily if they consume less than 1 quart of milk per day. Adolescents who consume less than 400 IU of vitamin D daily from their diet would also benefit from a supplement.

Supplements can interact or interfere with certain medications, so individuals should consult a doctor before consuming a supplement if they are taking prescription medications.

Supplements Are Not Regulated Like Drugs

Another factor to keep in mind regarding the use of dietary supplements (including vitamins, minerals, and herbs) is that the FDA does not stringently regulate them. In fact, the individuals most responsible for regulating these substances are their manufacturers. Unlike drugs, dietary supplements—unless they contain a

▲ **Figure 9.26** The U.S. Pharmocopeia Verified Mark
Source: Registered trademark of The United States Pharmacopeial Convention. Used with Permission.

new ingredient—do not need approval from the FDA before they can be marketed to the public, and the FDA cannot remove a supplement from the marketplace unless it has been shown to be unsafe or harmful to the consumer.[87]

An option exists to help consumers choose among dietary supplements. **The United States Pharmacopeial Convention (USP)** is a nonprofit organization that sets standards for dietary supplements.[88] Though it does *not* endorse or validate health claims that the supplement manufacturers make, it sets standards for the identity, strength, quality, and purity of dietary supplements. Supplement manufacturers can voluntarily submit their products to the USP's staff of scientists for review. USP verifies supplements through a comprehensive testing and evaluation process and awards its USP Verified Mark (**Figure 9.26**) only after rigorous facility audits, product documentation reviews, and product testing have been completed and approved.

For individuals who choose to use supplements, the best place to start when picking a supplement is to carefully read the label. The FDA does have strict guidelines for the information that must appear on any supplement label. For example, the term "high potency" can only be used if at least two-thirds of the nutrients in the

The United States Pharmacopeial Convention (USP) A nonprofit organization that sets quality standards for dietary supplements.

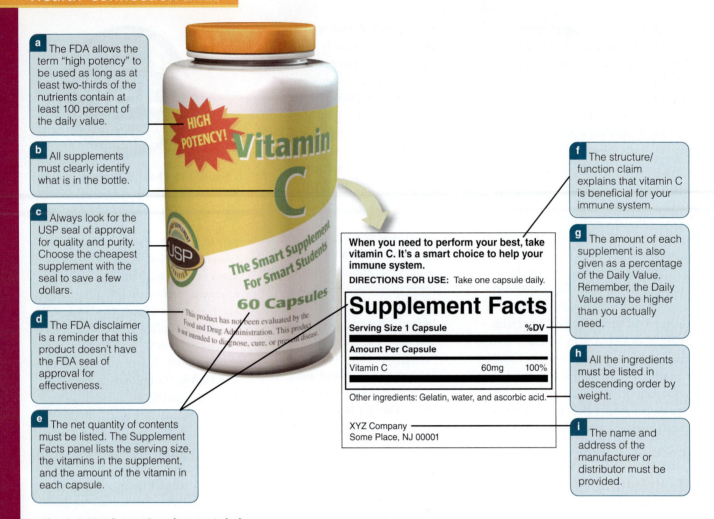

a The FDA allows the term "high potency" to be used as long as at least two-thirds of the nutrients contain at least 100 percent of the daily value.

b All supplements must clearly identify what is in the bottle.

c Always look for the USP seal of approval for quality and purity. Choose the cheapest supplement with the seal to save a few dollars.

d The FDA disclaimer is a reminder that this product doesn't have the FDA seal of approval for effectiveness.

e The net quantity of contents must be listed. The Supplement Facts panel lists the serving size, the vitamins in the supplement, and the amount of the vitamin in each capsule.

f The structure/function claim explains that vitamin C is beneficial for your immune system.

g The amount of each supplement is also given as a percentage of the Daily Value. Remember, the Daily Value may be higher than you actually need.

h All the ingredients must be listed in descending order by weight.

i The name and address of the manufacturer or distributor must be provided.

When you need to perform your best, take vitamin C. It's a smart choice to help your immune system.
DIRECTIONS FOR USE: Take one capsule daily.

Supplement Facts
Serving Size 1 Capsule   %DV

Amount Per Capsule

Vitamin C   60mg   100%

Other ingredients: Gelatin, water, and ascorbic acid.

XYZ Company
Some Place, NJ 00001

▲ **Figure 9.27 Dietary Supplement Labels**
The FDA has strict guidelines for the information that must appear on any supplement label.

supplement contain at least 100 percent of the daily value. The label must also clearly identify the contents of the bottle. While a supplement may have the USP seal of approval for quality and purity, it doesn't have the FDA's approval, even if it makes a claim. Supplements must contain a panel that lists the serving size, the number of capsules or tablets in the bottle, the amount of the vitamin in each capsule, and the percentage of the daily value (**Figure 9.27**). All the ingredients must also be listed.

LO 9.9: THE TAKE-HOME MESSAGE   The ingestion of a daily multivitamin supplement is on the rise in the United States, especially among older adults. The research doesn't support dietary supplements as a cure for aging or the chronic diseases that accompany aging, including cardiovascular disease, cancer, or cognitive decline. A well-balanced diet that provides adequate kilocalories can meet most individuals' daily vitamin needs without a vitamin supplement. A vitamin supplement is an option for individuals unable to meet their daily vitamin needs. The FDA does not strictly regulate vitamin supplements. Each supplement bottle contains a label and if the U.S. Pharmacopoeia (USP) has tested the supplement to determine if it meets the criteria for purity and accuracy, it will carry the USP seal. Consumers should seek guidance from a qualified health professional before taking a dietary supplement.

Visual Chapter Summary

LO 9.1 Vitamins Are Essential Organic Compounds

Vitamins are essential, organic compounds the body requires in small amounts for normal metabolic functions. There are 13 different vitamins found naturally in foods, added to foods through fortification, or concentrated in dietary supplements. These 13 vitamins are classified as either water soluble or fat soluble. The water-soluble vitamins include the B-complex vitamins and vitamin C. The fat-soluble vitamins are vitamins A, D, E, and K. Provitamins, such as the carotenoids, are converted to their active form before they can be directly used in the body. Most water-soluble vitamins are not toxic except vitamin B_6. Vitamins A, D, and E can be toxic if taken in megadose amounts.

LO 9.2 Vitamins Differ in Their Absorption and Storage

Bioavailability of individual vitamins varies based on the amount of the vitamin in the food, whether the food is cooked, raw, or refined, the food's digestibility, an individual's nutrition status, and whether the vitamin is a natural or synthetic form. Vitamins are often attached to proteins in food and must be released in the stomach to be absorbed. Once freed, fat-soluble vitamins are transported as part of micelles and absorbed through the lymph system as part of chylomicrons. Fat-soluble vitamins are stored in the body and need fat to be absorbed. Water-soluble vitamins are absorbed with water and typically aren't stored in the body for extended periods. Fat-soluble vitamins are less bioavailable than water-soluble vitamins.

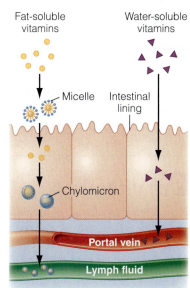

Fat-soluble vitamins — Water-soluble vitamins — Micelle — Intestinal lining — Chylomicron — Portal vein — Lymph fluid

Fat-soluble vitamins
A D E K

Water-soluble vitamins
Folate
Biotin
Pantothenic acid
C
B_{12}
Thiamin (B_1)
Riboflavin (B_2)
Niacin
Pyridoxine (B_6)

Fat-soluble vitamins — Water-soluble vitamins

LO 9.3 Antioxidants Suppress Free Radicals

Antioxidants, such as vitamins E and C and beta-carotene, neutralize harmful oxygen-containing molecules called free radicals that can damage cells by giving them an electron. Free radicals can contribute to chronic diseases such as cancer and heart disease and accelerate the aging process. Diets abundant in antioxidant-rich fruits, vegetables, and whole grains are associated with a lower incidence of many diseases. Carotenoids and flavonoids that give fruits and vegetables their vivid colors are referred to as phytochemicals and have antioxidant properties.

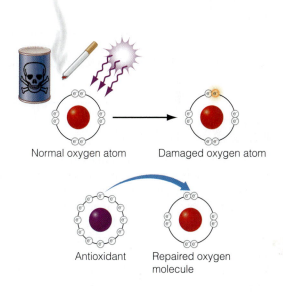

Normal oxygen atom — Damaged oxygen atom — Antioxidant — Repaired oxygen molecule

LO 9.4 Vitamins Are Found in Every Food Group

Whole foods, including fruits, vegetables, whole grains, legumes, dairy foods, and meats, provide phytochemicals, antioxidants, and fiber in addition to vitamins. Food handling and preparation techniques such as exposure to air, water, UV light, changes in pH, and heat can cause the loss of vitamins. Fortified foods

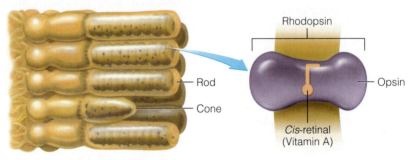

Vegetables	Fruits	Grains	Protein	Dairy
Folate	Folate	Folic acid	Niacin	Riboflavin
Vitamin A	Vitamin C	Niacin	Thiamin	Vitamin A
Vitamin C	Vitamin A	Vitamin B_6	Vitamin B_6	Vitamin B_{12}
Vitamin E		Vitamin B_{12} (if fortified)	Vitamin B_{12}	Vitamin D
Vitamin K		Riboflavin		
		Thiamin		

and vitamin supplements can help individuals with inadequate diets meet their nutrient needs. However, there are health risks associated with the overconsumption of vitamins in fortified foods.

LO 9.5 Vitamin A

Vitamin A refers to a family of retinoids, which include retinol, retinal, and retinoic acid. Retinol is most usable in the body. Retinal is essential for eye health and vision. The retinoids are also essential for cell growth and development, reproduction, and a healthy immune system. Three carotenoids, alpha-carotene, beta-carotene, and beta-cryptoxanthin, are provitamins that can be converted to vitamin A in the body; beta-carotene is the most commonly consumed. Vitamin A is stored in the liver until needed, and is not easily excreted from the body.

Most of the dietary, preformed vitamin A consumed (70 to 90 percent) is absorbed; absorption occurs via active transport in the small intestine. Beta-carotene is absorbed at a much lower rate. Vitamin A in foods is measured in retinol activity equivalents (RAE). Preformed vitamin A is found in milk, cereals, cheese, egg yolks, and organ meats, especially liver. Provitamin A sources include carrots, spinach, and sweet potatoes.

Vitamin A deficiencies can result in vision problems and increased infections. Toxic amounts of vitamin A can compromise bone health and can lead to birth defects during pregnancy.

Rod and cone cells in retina

LO 9.6 Vitamin D

Although vitamin D (the "sunshine vitamin") can be made in the body with the help of ultraviolet rays from the sun, some individuals are not exposed to enough sunlight to meet their needs. The active form of vitamin D, called calcitriol, regulates blood calcium, enhances the absorption of calcium and phosphorus from the small intestine, and maintains healthy bones. It may also help regulate blood pressure and the immune system, and it may help prevent diabetes and some cancers.

Milk and fortified yogurts are excellent food sources of vitamin D. A deficiency of vitamin D can cause rickets in children and osteomalacia in adults. Hypervitaminosis D can result in hypercalcemia, affect the nervous system, and cause severe depression.

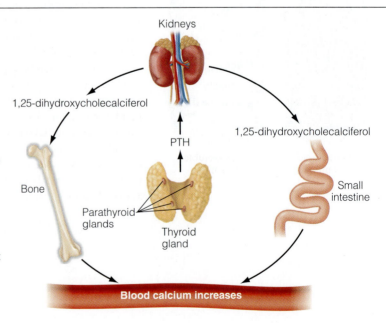

LO 9.7 Vitamin E

Alpha-tocopherol is the most active form of vitamin E in the body. Vitamin E is an antioxidant that protects the cells' membranes. It plays an important role as an anticoagulant and may help prevent the oxidation of LDL cholesterol.

Vegetable oils, avocados, nuts, and seeds are good sources of vitamin E. Green leafy vegetables and fortified cereals also contribute to daily intake. The recommended intake for vitamin E is presented in alpha-tocopherol equivalents.

Vitamin E deficiencies, although rare, may result in nerve problems, muscle weakness, and increased susceptibility to free radical damage. Excess amounts of vitamin E from supplements may cause hemorrhage.

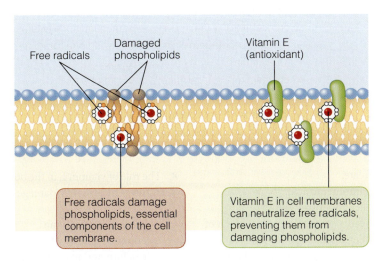

Free radicals damage phospholipids, essential components of the cell membrane.

Vitamin E in cell membranes can neutralize free radicals, preventing them from damaging phospholipids.

LO 9.8 Vitamin K

Vitamin K is a fat-soluble vitamin found naturally as phylloquinone in plants, and as menaquinone (manufactured by bacteria) in the colons of animals. Menadione is the synthetic form of vitamin K used in vitamin supplements. Vitamin K is a coenzyme for the carboxylation of factors involved in blood clotting and two proteins involved in bone formation. Dietary sources include leafy greens, vegetable oils, and margarine. A deficiency of vitamin K may result in hemorrhage and bone fractures. Individuals taking anticoagulant medications need to carefully monitor their vitamin K intake. There are no known toxicity problems.

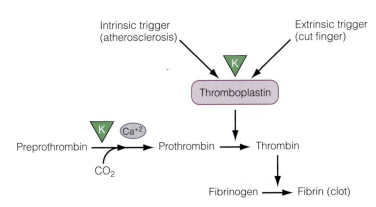

LO 9.9 Vitamin Supplements Are Not a Substitute for Healthy Eating

Individuals often take daily vitamin supplements to prevent chronic disease without scientific research that supports their use. Vitamin supplements should never replace a healthy diet. A vitamin supplement is an option for individuals unable to meet their daily vitamin needs, such as during pregnancy, lactation, solely breast-fed infants, older individuals, strict vegetarians, people with allergies, or people who are on strict weight-loss diets or who eliminate certain food groups.

Vitamin supplement standards are not strictly enforced by the FDA. Each vitamin supplement bottle carries a nutrition label consumers can use to compare products. The U.S. Pharmacopoeia (USP) seal on a supplement label indicates that the supplement has been tested and meets the criteria for purity and accuracy. It does not ensure safety. Consumers should seek guidance from a qualified health professional before taking a dietary supplement.

Terms to Know

- vitamins
- provitamins
- preformed vitamins
- toxicity
- hypervitaminosis
- megadose
- bioavailability
- antioxidants
- flavonoids
- oxidation
- free radicals
- oxidative stress
- age-related macular degeneration (AMD)
- cataract
- phytochemicals
- fortified foods
- retinoids
- retinol
- retinal
- retinoic acid
- retinyl ester
- carotenoids
- beta-carotene
- rhodopsin
- iodopsin
- rods
- cones
- bleaching
- retinol binding protein (RBP)
- epithelial cells
- cell division
- cell differentiation
- retinol activity equivalents (RAE)
- international units (IU)
- hypervitaminosis A
- osteoporosis
- carotenodermia
- night blindness
- xeropthalmia
- keratinization
- calciferol
- prohormone
- cholecalciferol (vitamin D$_3$)
- ergocalciferol (vitamin D$_2$)
- 7-dehydrocholesterol (provitamin D$_3$)
- previtamin D$_3$ (precalciferol)
- vitamin D$_3$ binding protein (DBP)
- 25-hydroxycholecalciferol
- 1,25-dihydroxycholecaliciferol
- calcitriol
- parathyroid hormone (PTH)
- hypervitaminosis D
- hypercalcemia
- rickets
- osteomalacia
- alpha-tocopherol (α-tocopherol)
- hemorrhage
- phylloquinone (vitamin K$_1$)
- menaquinone (vitamin K$_2$)
- menadione (vitamin K$_3$)
- coagulation
- carboxylation
- clotting factors
- warfarin
- U.S. Pharmacopoeia (USP)

MasteringNutrition™

Scan this QR code with your mobile device to access practice math activities. You can also access the activities in MasteringNutrition™.

Check Your Understanding

1. Vitamins are
   a. essential nutrients needed in large amounts to prevent disease.
   b. classified as either water-soluble or fat-soluble nutrients.
   c. defined as inorganic nutrients.
   d. easily made by the body from leftover glucose.
2. Vitamins can be destroyed by
   a. cold.
   b. ultraviolet light.
   c. acid pH.
   d. cooking in a microwave.
3. An individual who does not produce enough bile will have difficulty absorbing
   a. thiamin (B$_1$).
   b. vitamin A.

4. folate.
   d. pantothenic acid.
4. A megadose of a vitamin
   a. occurs when you eat too much of one particular food.
   b. is necessary to prevent a variety of diseases.
   c. is defined as 10 times the RDA.
   d. is safe because all vitamins are easily excreted from the body.
5. Which of the following are considered antioxidants?
   a. vitamin E and beta-carotene
   b. vitamin D and vitamin K
   c. vitamin E and vitamin K
   d. vitamin A and vitamin D
6. The most usable form of vitamin A in the body is
   a. retinol.
   b. retinal.
   c. retinoic acid.
   d. retinoids.
7. Vitamin D
   a. is not toxic if consumed in amounts greater than the RDA.
   b. is made in the skin from 1,25-dihydroxyvitamin D$_3$ and ultraviolet light.
   c. is found in whole milk, but not in skim milk.
   d. is found in fruits.

8. The role of vitamin E in the body is to
   a. prevent oxidative damage to cell membranes.
   b. serve as a coenzyme.
   c. enhance the absorption of calcium and phosphorus.
   d. participate in blood clotting.
9. Vitamin K is necessary for the synthesis of
   a. glycogen.
   b. rhodopsin.
   c. prothrombin.
   d. cholecalciferol.
10. Which of the following statements is NOT true regarding the USP seal on the vitamin supplement label?
    a. The dietary supplement contains the amount of the substance that is stated on the label.
    b. The dietary supplement is good quality.
    c. The dietary supplement is free of any contaminants.
    d. The dietary supplement meets your daily needs for that vitamin.

Answers

1. (b) Vitamins are classified by their solubility, as either fat-soluble or water-soluble nutrients. They are organic nutrients needed in small amounts in the diet because the body cannot synthesize sufficient amounts to maintain health.

2. (b) Some vitamins, especially vitamin B_{12}, are destroyed by exposure to ultraviolet light, heat (such as during cooking), and when prepared in an alkaline pH (adding baking soda, for example). Cold temperatures do not destroy vitamins. Microwave cooking increases the retention of vitamins compared to steaming or boiling.

3. (b) Fat-soluble vitamins such as vitamin A are absorbed along with dietary fat, which requires bile for the process. Thiamin, folate, and pantothenic acid are water-soluble vitamins and do not need bile for absorption.

4. (c) A megadose of a vitamin is defined as 10 times or more of the RDA. Megadose levels can only be achieved by taking a supplement and can be harmful even if the vitamin is water soluble.

5. (a) Both vitamin E and beta-carotene function as antioxidants in the body. Vitamins A, D, and K perform other essential functions, but are not antioxidants.

6. (a) Retinol is the most usable form of vitamin A in the body. Retinoids include all three forms of preformed vitamin A: retinol, retinal, and retinoic acid.

7. (b) Vitamin D is a fat-soluble vitamin stored in the liver. It can be toxic if ingested in supplemental form in amounts greater than the RDA. The active form of vitamin D is 1,25-dihydroxyvitamin D_3 and 7-dehydrocholesterol is the compound in the skin that is converted to vitamin D from sunlight. Both whole and skim milk are usually fortified with vitamin D but fruits do not contain vitamin D.

8. (a) Vitamin E functions as an antioxidant to prevent oxidative damage to cell membranes. Water-soluble vitamins usually serve as coenzymes, active vitamin D enhances the absorption of calcium and phosphorus, and vitamin K participates in blood clotting.

9. (c) Vitamin K is necessary for the synthesis of prothrombin, a protein that is involved in blood clotting. Rhodopsin is formed with retinal (vitamin A), and cholecalciferol is the active form of vitamin D in the body. Glycogen is the stored form of glucose found in muscles and liver.

10. (d) Manufacturers of dietary supplements can voluntarily have their products tested for the strength, quality, and purity of the supplement. It does not confirm that it will meet your daily need for the vitamin.

Answers to True or False?

1. **False.** Although vitamins perform numerous essential functions in the body, they do not provide energy. Only the macronutrients (carbohydrates, protein, and fat) and alcohol provide kilocalories.

2. **True.** Fat-soluble vitamins are often found in foods that contain fat. For example, vitamin E is found in vegetable oils and vitamin A is found in egg yolks. However, some fat-soluble vitamins are also found in fortified foods that are low in fat, such as fortified cereals.

3. **False.** Overconsumption of vitamin supplements can result in intakes above the tolerable upper limits. Such high intakes can in turn lead to harmful toxicity symptoms.

4. **True.** Healthy individuals can meet their vitamin requirements by consuming an adequate, balanced diet. However, some individuals, such as those with a specific vitamin deficiency, strict vegans, or those with dietary restrictions, may benefit from taking a vitamin supplement.

5. **False.** Cooking foods in a microwave helps retain more vitamins because of the reduced cooking time and exposure to heat. Foods prepared in a microwave oven also require very little cooking water; this prevents leaching of water-soluble vitamins.

6. **True.** Deep orange vegetables and some green vegetables are good sources of the vitamin A precursor beta-carotene, which is converted to vitamin A in the body.

7. **True.** In the skin is a compound called 7-dehydrocholesterol, which is converted to a previtamin D form when the ultraviolet rays of the sun alter its structure.

8. **False.** Vitamin K actually helps blood clot, as it participates in the synthesis of several proteins involved in the blood-clotting cascade.

9. **False.** The main role of vitamin E is as an antioxidant that helps protect cell membranes. However, the fat-soluble vitamins D and K are involved in bone health.

10. **False.** Antioxidants serve several beneficial functions in the body, but there is no magic pill for aging.

Web Resources

- To learn more about the importance of fruits and vegetables to vitamin intake, visit www.fruitsandveggiesmorematters.org
- To learn more about the role of alternative therapies and dietary supplements in health and disease prevention, visit www.complementarynutrition.org
- To find out the latest recommendations for vitamins, visit http://ods.od.nih.gov

References

1. Rosenfeld, L. 1997. Vitamine-Vitamin. The Early Years of Discovery. *Clinical Chemistry* 43:680–685.
2. Droge, W. 2002. Free Radicals in the Physiological Control of Cell Function. *Physiology Review* 82:47–95.
3. Fiedor, J., and K. Burda. 2014. Potential Role of Carotenoids as Antioxidants in Human Health and Disease. *Nutrients* 6(2):466–488.
4. Centers for Disease Control and Prevention. 2013. *Common Eye Disorders*. Available at www.cdc.gov. Accessed March 2014.
5. Parmeggiani, F., M. R. Romano, C. Costagliola, F. Semeraro, C. Incorvaia, S. D'Angelo, P. Perri, et al. 2012. Mechanism of Inflammation in Age-Related Macular Degeneration. *Mediators of Inflammation* doi: 10.1155/2012/546786.
6. Schleicher, M., K. Weikel, C. Garber, and A. Taylor. 2013. Diminishing Risk for Age-Related Macular Degeneration with Nutrition: A Current View. *Nutrients* 5(7):2405–2456.
7. American Optometric Association. 2014. *Cataract*. Available at www.aoa.org. Accessed March 2014.
8. Centers for Disease Control and Prevention. 2013. *Common Eye Disorders*.
9. National Eye Institute. 2011. *Are These High Levels of Antioxidants and Zinc Right for You?* Available at www.nei.nih.gov. Accessed March 2014.
10. Craig, W. J. 1997. Phytochemicals: Guardians of Our Health. *Journal of the American Dietetic Association* 97:S199–S204.
11. Bilecova-Rabajdova, M., A. Birkova, P. Urban, K. Gregova, E. Durovcova, and M. Marekova. 2013. Naturally Occuring Substances and Their Role in Chemo-Protective Effects. *Central Europe Journal of Public Health* 21(4):213–219.
12. Ruiz-Canela, M., and M. A. Martinez-Gonzalez. 2014. Lifestyle and Dietary Risk Factors for Peripheral Artery Disease. *Circulation Journal* 78(3):553–559.
13. U.S. Department of Agriculture, U. S. Department of Health and Human Services. 2010. *Dietary Guidelines for Americans, 2010*. 7th ed. Washington, DC: U.S. Government Printing Office.
14. Ross, A. C., B. Cabellero, R. J. Cousins, K. L. Tucker, and T. R. Ziegler. 2014. *Modern Nutrition in Health and Disease*. 11th ed. Philadelphia: Lippincott Williams & Wilkins.
15. Santos, P. H. S., and M. A. Silva. 2008. Retention of Vitamin C in Drying Processes of Fruits and Vegetables—A Review. *Drying Technology—An International Journal* 26:1421–1437.
16. Lee, S. K., and A. A. Kader. 2000. Preharvest and Postharvest Factors Influencing Vitamin C Content of Horticultural Crops. *Postharvest Biology and Technology* 20:207–220.
17. Hwang, I. G., Y. J. Shin, S. Lee, J. Lee, and S. M. Yoo. 2012. Effects of Different Cooking Methods on the Antioxidant Properties of Red Pepper (*Capsicum annuum L.*). *Preventive Nutrition and Food Science* 17(4):286–292.
18. Pandrangi, S., and L. E. LaBorde. 2004. Retention of Folate, Carotenoid and Other Quality Characteristics in Commercially Packaged Fresh Spinach. *Journal of Food Science* 69:C702–C707.
19. Packaged Facts Project. 2011. *Omega-3 Ingredient Market to Grow 40% by 2015*. Available at www.packagedfacts.com. Accessed March 2014.
20. *Principles for Nutrition Labeling and Fortification*. Washington, DC: The National Academies Press.
21. National Institutes of Health. 2013. *Vitamin A Fact Sheet for Health Professionals*. Available at http://ods.od.nih.gov. Accessed March 2014.
22. Gropper, S. S., and J. L. Smith. 2014. *Advanced Nutrition and Metabolism*. 6th ed. Belmont, CA: Wadsworth—Cengage Learning.
23. Kircik, L. H. 2014. Evaluating Tretinoin Formulations in the Treatment of Acne. *Journal of Drugs in Dermatology* 13(4):466–470.
24. Rasi, A., E. Behrangi, M. Rohaninasab, and Z. M. Nahad. 2014. Efficacy of Fixed Daily 20 mg of Isotretinoin in Moderate to Severe Scar-Prone Acne. *Advanced Biomedical Research* doi: 10.4103/2277-9175.129693.
25. Institute of Medicine, Food and Nutrition Board. 2001. *Dietary Reference Intakes: Vitamin A, Vitamin K, Arsenic, Boron, Chromium, Copper, Iodine, Iron, Manganese, Molybdenum, Nickel, Silicon, Vanadium, and Zinc*. Washington, DC: The National Academies Press.
26. Tanumihardjo, A. S. 2013. Vitamin A and Bone Health: The Balancing Act. *Journal of Clinical Densitometry* 16(4):414–419.
27. Lind, T., A. Sundqvist, L. Hu, G. Pejler, G. Andersson, A. Jacobson, and H. Melhus. 2013. Vitamin A Is a Negative Regulator of Osteoblast Mineralization. *PloS One* 8(12):e82388. doi:10.1371/journal.pone.0092388.
28. Promislow, J. H., D. Goodman-Guren, D. J. Slymen, and E. Barrett-Connor. 2002. Retinol Intake and Bone Mineral Density in the Elderly: The Rancho Bernardo Study. *Journal of Bone Mineral Research* 17:1359–1362.
29. Ross, et al. 2014. *Modern Nutrition*.
30. Institute of Medicine, Food and Nutrition Board. 2001. *Dietary Reference Intakes: Vitamin A, Vitamin K, Arsenic, Boron, Chromium, Copper, Iodine, Iron, Manganese, Molybdenum, Nickel, Silicon, Vanadium, and Zinc*.
31. Ibid.
32. Brown, M. J., M. G Ferruzzi, M. L. Nguyen, D. A. Cooper, A. L. Eldridge, S. J. Swartz, and W. S. White. 2004. Carotenoid Bioavailability Is Higher from Salads Ingested with Full-Fat than with Fat-Reduced Salad Dressings as Measured with Electrochemical Detection 1'2'3. *American Journal of Clinical Nutrition* 80:396–403.
33. Institute of Medicine, Food and Nutrition Board. 2001. *Dietary Reference Intakes: Vitamin A, Vitamin K, Arsenic, Boron, Chromium, Copper, Iodine, Iron, Manganese, Molybdenum, Nickel, Silicon, Vanadium, and Zinc*.
34. Ibid.
35. Brinkley, N., and D. Krueger. 2000. Hypervitaminosis A and Bone. *Nutrition Reviews* 58:138–144.
36. Feskanich, D. 2002. Vitamin A Intake and Hip Fractures among Postmenopausal Women. *Journal of the American Medical Association* 287:47–54.
37. Bjelakovic, G., D. Nikolova, L. L. Gluud, R. G. Simonetti, and C. Gluud. 2007. Mortality in Randomized Trials of Antioxidant Supplements for Primary and Secondary Prevention: Systematic Review and Meta-Analysis. *JAMA* 297(8):842–857.
38. Virtamo, J., P. R. Tayor, J. Kontto, S. Männistö, M. Utriainen, S. T. Weinstein, J. Huttunen, and D. Albanes. 2014. Effects of α-Tocopherol and β-Carotene Supplementation on Cancer Incidence and Mortality: 18-Year Postintervention Follow-Up of the Alpha-Tocopherol, Beta-Carotene Cancer Prevention Study. *International Journal of Cancer* 135(1):178–185.
39. Sommer, A. 2014. Preventing Blindness and Saving Lives: The Centenary of Vitamin A. *Journal of the American Medical Association Ophthalmology* 132(1):115–117.
40. Jones, G. 2014. Vitamin D. In A. C. Ross, et al., eds. *Modern Nutrition in Health and Disease*. 11th ed. Philadelphia: Lippincott Williams & Wilkins.
41. Autier, P., M. Boniol, C. Pizot, and P. Mullie. 2014. Vitamin D Status and Ill Health. *Lancet Diabetes Endocrinology* 2(1):76–89.
42. Holick, M. F. 2013. Vitamin D, Sunlight, and Cancer Connection. *Anticancer Agents in Medicinal Chemistry* 13(1):70–82.
43. Ibid.
44. Aranow, C. 2011. Vitamin D and the Immune System. *Journal of Investigative Medicine* 59(6):881–886.
45. Munger, K. L., L. I. Levin, J. Massa, R. Horst, T. Orban, and A. Ascherio. 2013. Preclinical Serum 25-Hydroxyvitamin D Levels and Risk of Type 1 Diabetes in a Cohort of U.S. Military Personnel. *American Journal of Epidemiology* doi:10.1093/aje/kws243.
46. Ibid.
47. Chih-Chien, S., L. Min-Tser, L. Kuo-Cheng, and W. Chia-Chao. 2012. Role of Vitamin D in Insulin Resistance. *Journal of Biomedical Biotechnology* doi: 10.1155/2012/634195.

48. Stadlmayr, A., E. Aigner, U. Huber-Schönauer, D. Niederseer, et al. 2014. Relations of Vitamin D Status, Gender and Type 2 Diabetes in Middle-Aged Caucasians. *Acta Diabetologica* doi.10.1007/s00592-014-0596-9.

49. Min, B. 2013. Effects of Vitamin D on Blood Pressure and Endothelial Function. *Korean Journal of Physiology and Pharmacology* 17(5):385–392.

50. National Institutes of Health. 2011. *Vitamin D Fact Sheet for Health Professionals.* Available at http://ods.od.nih.gov. Accessed March 2014.

51. Ibid.

52. Ibid.

53. Institute of Medicine, Food and Nutrition Board. 2010. *Dietary Reference Intakes for Calcium and Vitamin D.* Washington, DC: The National Academies Press.

54. Ibid.

55. Ibid.

56. Ibid.

57. Parker, G., and H. Brotchie. 2011. 'D' for Depression: Any Role for Vitamin D? *Acta Psychiatrica Scandinavica* 124(4):243–249.

58. Byrne, S. N. 2014. How Much Sunlight Is Enough? *Photochemical and Photobiological Sciences* 13:840–852.

59. Pettifor, J. M., and A. Prentice. 2011. The Role of Vitamin D in Paediatric Bone Health. *Best Practice & Research Clinical Endocrinology & Metabolism* 25(4):573–784.

60. Prentice, A. 2013. Nutritional Rickets Around the World. *The Journal of Steroid Biochemistry and Molecular Biology* 136:201–206.

61. Thacher, T. D., P. R. Fischer, P. J. Tebben, R. J. Singh, S. S. Cha., J. A. Maxon, and B. P. Yawn. 2013. Increasing Incidence of Nutritional Rickets: A Population-Based Study in Olmsted County, Minnesota. *Mayo Clinic Proceedings* 88(2):176–183.

62. Centers for Disease Control and Prevention. 2001. Severe Malnutrition among Young Children—Georgia, January 1997–1999. *Morbidity and Mortality Weekly Report.* Available at www.cdc.gov. Accessed April 2014.

63. Gordon, C. M., K. C. DePeter, H. A. Feldman, E. Grace, and S. J. Emans. 2004. Prevalence of Vitamin D Deficiency among Healthy Adolescents. *Archives of Pediatric and Adolescent Medicine* 158:531–537.

64. Ward, L. M., I. Gaboury, M. Ladhani, and S. Zlotkin. 2007. Vitamin D–Deficiency Rickets among Children in Canada. *Canadian Medical Association Journal* 177:161–166.

65. Gallos, S., K. Comeau, C. Vanstone, S. Agellon, et al. 2013. Effect of Different Dosages of Oral Vitamin D Supplementation on Vitamin D Status in Healthy, Breastfed Infants: A Randomized Trial. *Journal of the American Medical Association* 309(17):1785–1792.

66. Kit, B. K., M. D. Carroll, and C. L. Ogden. 2011. *Low-Fat Milk Consumption among Children and Adolescents in the United States, 2007–2008.* Available at www.cdc.gov. Accessed March 2014.

67. Centers for Disease Control and Prevention. 2013. *Skin Cancer Statistics.* Available at www.cdc.gov. Accessed March 2014.

68. Marantes, I., S. J. Achenbach, E. J. Atkinson, S. Khosla, L. J. Melton III, and S. Amin. Is Vitamin D a Determinant of Muscle Mass and Strength? *Journal of Bone Mineral Research* 26(12):2860–2870.

69. National Institutes of Health, Office of Dietary Supplements. 2013. *Vitamin E.* Available at http://ods.od.nih.gov. Accessed March 2014.

70. Ibid.

71. Miller, E. R., R. Pastor-Barriso, D. Dalal, R. A. Riemersma, L. J. Appel, and E. Vitamin E Supplementation May Increase All-Cause Mortality. *Annals of Internal Medicine* 142:37–46.

72. Almquist, H. J. 1975. The History of Vitamin K. *The American Journal of Clinical Nutrition* 28:656–659.

73. Hamidi, M. S., O. Gajic-Veljanoski, and A. M. Cheung. 2013. Vitamin K and Bone Health. *Journal of Clinical Densitometry* 16(4):409–413.

74. Shea, M. K., and R. M., Holden. 2012. Vitamin K Status and Vascular Calcification: Evidence from Observational and Clinical Studies. *Advances in Nutrition* 3:158–165.

75. Institute of Medicine. 2006. *Dietary Reference Intakes: The Essential Guide to Nutrient Requirements.* Washington, DC: The National Academies Press.

76. National Institutes of Health. 2003. *Coumadin and Vitamin K.* Available at http://ods.od.nih.gov. Accessed March 2014.

77. Lippi, G., and M. Franchini. 2011. Vitamin K in Neonates: Facts and Myths. *Blood Transfusion* 9(1): 4–9.

78. Institute of Medicine. 2006. *Dietary Reference Intakes: The Essential Guide to Nutrient Requirements.*

79. Booth, S. L., L. Martini, J. W. Peterson, E. Saltzman, G. E. Dallal, and R. J. Wood. 2003. Dietary Phylloquinone Depletion and Repletion in Older Women. *Journal of Nutrition* 133:2565–2569.

80. Gahche, J., R. Bailey, B. V. Hughes, E. Yetley, J. Dwyer, et al. 2011. *Dietary Supplement Use among U.S. Adults Has Increased Since NHANES III (1988–1994).* NCHS Data Brief. Available at www.cdc.gov. Accessed March 2014.

81. Nutrition Business Journal. 2012. NBJ's Supplement Business Report 2012. Penton Media, Inc.

82. National Institutes of Health, Office of Dietary Supplements. 2013. *Multivitamin/Mineral Supplements.* Available at http://ods.od.nih.gov. Accessed March 2014.

83. Moyer, V. A. 2014. Vitamin, Mineral, and Multivitamin Supplements for the Primary Prevention of Cardiovascular Disease and Cancer: U.S. Preventive Services Task Force Recommendation Statement. *Annuals of Internal Medicine* doi:10.7326/M14-0198.

84. Sesso, H. D., W. G. Christen, V. Bubes, J. P. Smith, J. MacFadyen, M. Schvartz, J. E. Manson, et al. 2012. Multivitamins in the Prevention of Cardiovascular Disease in Men: The Physicians' Health Study II Randomized Controlled Trial. *Journal of the American Medical Association* 308(17):1751–1760.

85. Grodstein, F., J. O'Brien, J. H. Kang, R. Dushkes, N. R. Cook, O. Okereke, J. E. Manson, et al. 2013. Long-Term Multivitamin Supplementation and Cognitive Function in Men: A Randomized Trial. *Annuals of Internal Medicine* 159(12):806–814.

86. Marra, M., and A. Boyar. 2009. Position of the American Dietetic Association: Nutrient Supplementation. *Journal of the American Dietetic Association* 109:2073–2085.

87. Van Lacck, R. 2014. *Foods and Dietary Supplements.* Available at www.fdalawblog.net. Accessed March 2014.

88. United States Pharmacopoeia. 2014. *USP Verified Dietary Supplements.* Available at www.usp.org. Accessed March 2014.

10 Water-Soluble Vitamins

Learning Outcomes

After reading this chapter, you will be able to:

10.1 Describe the function of water-soluble vitamins.

10.2 Describe the functions, recommended intakes, food sources, and the toxicity and deficiency effects of thiamin.

10.3 Describe the functions, recommended intakes, food sources, and the toxicity and deficiency effects of riboflavin.

10.4 Describe the functions, recommended intakes, food sources, and the toxicity and deficiency effects of niacin.

10.5 Describe the functions, recommended intakes, food sources, and the toxicity and deficiency effects of pantothenic acid.

10.6 Describe the functions, recommended intakes, food sources, and the toxicity and deficiency effects of biotin.

10.7 Describe the functions, recommended intakes, food sources, and the toxicity and deficiency effects of vitamin B_6.

10.8 Describe the functions, recommended intakes, food sources, and the toxicity and deficiency effects of folate.

10.9 Describe the functions, recommended intakes, food sources, and the toxicity and deficiency effects of vitamin B_{12}.

10.10 Describe the functions, recommended intakes, food sources, and the toxicity and deficiency effects of vitamin C.

10.11 Describe the functions of compounds that have vitamin-like biological roles but are not classified as vitamins.

10.12 Explain the role that a healthy diet and lifestyle plays in cancer risk and progression.

True or False?

1. All water-soluble vitamins are destroyed during cooking. **T/F**

2. Biotin and pantothenic acid are lesser known versions of vitamin C. **T/F**

3. The primary role of the B vitamins is to provide energy. **T/F**

4. The body can make plenty of niacin from the amino acid tryptophan. **T/F**

5. Consuming too much vitamin B_6 can cause nerve damage. **T/F**

6. Older adults are likely to absorb less vitamin B_{12} than younger adults. **T/F**

7. Folate reduces the risk of certain birth defects. **T/F**

8. It is difficult to obtain enough pantothenic acid from foods. **T/F**

9. Eating raw egg whites inhibits the absorption of biotin. **T/F**

10. Taking vitamin C supplements prevents the common cold. **T/F**

See page 401 for the answers.

In the previous chapter you learned that the four fat-soluble vitamins, A, D, E, and K, are vital to health. These tiny nutrients function to stimulate growth, keep bones strong, maintain sharp vision, clot blood, and protect cells from free radical damage. This chapter describes the nine water-soluble vitamins, the roles they play in the body, the best food sources, how much you need on a daily basis, and the risks associated with consuming excessive or insufficient amounts. We'll also look at how these vitamins work together to facilitate metabolism and other body processes.

What Are Water-Soluble Vitamins?

LO 10.1 Describe the function of water-soluble vitamins.

There are nine water-soluble vitamins: eight of them are B-complex vitamins and the ninth is vitamin C. When initially discovered in the early 1900s, the "water-soluble B" was thought to be one vitamin. After years of research, it became apparent that this was not a single substance but rather many vitamins—thiamin, riboflavin, niacin, vitamin B_6, folate, vitamin B_{12}, pantothenic acid, and biotin—known collectively as the B vitamins.

Water-soluble vitamins are different from fat-soluble vitamins in that they dissolve in water, are generally not stored in the body, and are often excreted through the urine. Most water-soluble vitamins are also not toxic, though there are exceptions when megadose levels are ingested.

Many water-soluble vitamins leach into water or are easily destroyed by heat, light, pH, or oxidation. Folate deteriorates during cooking; vitamin B_{12} and riboflavin are destroyed by ultraviolet light; thiamin, or B_1, is easily damaged in an alkaline pH, and vitamin C oxidizes when exposed to air and heat. All of the water-soluble vitamins leach when foods are soaked in water.

In general, all the water-soluble vitamins are absorbed, transported, and stored in the same way. In foods, water-soluble vitamins are usually attached to proteins and require hydrolysis during digestion to free the vitamin for absorption (**Figure 10.1**). Once digestion has released the vitamins, they pass through the small intestine by passive

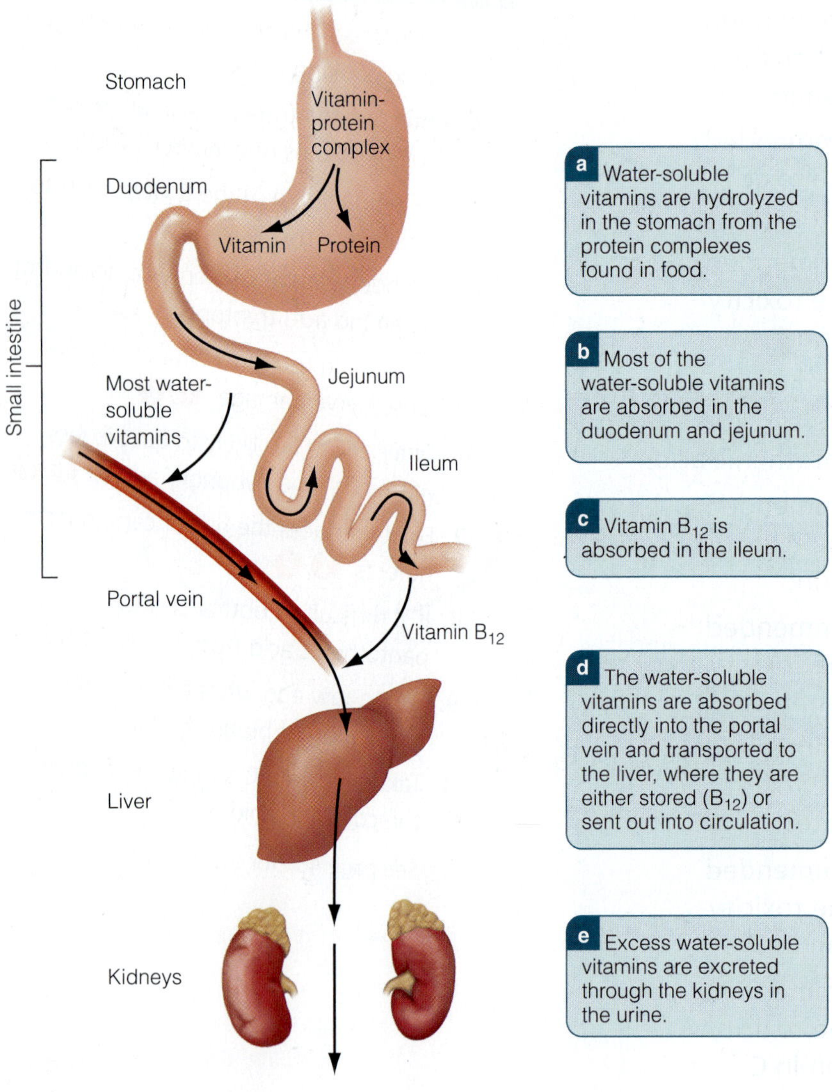

a Water-soluble vitamins are hydrolyzed in the stomach from the protein complexes found in food.

b Most of the water-soluble vitamins are absorbed in the duodenum and jejunum.

c Vitamin B_{12} is absorbed in the ileum.

d The water-soluble vitamins are absorbed directly into the portal vein and transported to the liver, where they are either stored (B_{12}) or sent out into circulation.

e Excess water-soluble vitamins are excreted through the kidneys in the urine.

Stomach — Vitamin-protein complex — Vitamin — Protein

Duodenum

Small intestine

Most water-soluble vitamins

Jejunum

Ileum

Portal vein

Vitamin B_{12}

Liver

Kidneys

▲ Figure 10.1 Digesting and Absorbing Water-Soluble Vitamins

diffusion when the diet contains large amounts and by active transport when intakes are low. The absorbed vitamins are then transported through the portal vein to the liver.

The Primary Functions of Water-Soluble Vitamins

Vitamins don't provide kilocalories, and thus aren't a source of energy. The B vitamins do share a role in energy production as **coenzymes** that unlock energy captured in the energy nutrients. Water-soluble vitamins are also involved in blood formation, maintaining a healthy nervous system, and, in the case of vitamin C, act as antioxidants in the body.

The B Vitamins Act as Coenzymes in Many Metabolic Processes

As coenzymes, vitamins bind to the active site of an enzyme to catalyze the enzyme either to build new compounds or break compounds apart (**Figure 10.2**). In fact, activating enzymes in energy production is the primary function of most water-soluble vitamins. The B vitamins, thiamin, riboflavin, niacin, pantothenic acid, biotin, and vitamin B_6, form key coenzymes that assist enzymes to breakdown carbohydrates, proteins, and fats to ATP. Thiamin activates an enzyme that removes a carbon from pyruvate during glycolysis. Vitamin B_6 acts as a coenzyme in all transamination reactions. Folate and vitamin B_{12} also assist enzymes in producing energy, but in a lesser role. Without the B vitamins, energy production would come to a halt. **Figure 10.3** summarizes their individual roles in energy metabolism.

Water-Soluble Vitamins in Other Critical Roles

The function of the water-soluble vitamins doesn't end with the B vitamins' roles as coenzymes. Vitamin C acts as an antioxidant and helps neutralize free radicals. Thiamin and vitamin B_{12} are necessary for nerve function, and niacin participates in protein synthesis. Folate and vitamin B_{12} function as coenzymes in the formation of red blood cells, a process called **hemopoiesis,** and the replenishment of cells.

We will cover each water-soluble vitamin in more detail. **Table 10.1** summarizes the nine water-soluble vitamins, their active coenzyme forms, major functions in the body, major food sources, and the toxicity and deficiency symptoms and diseases that result when the vitamins are consumed in inadequate amounts. Complete the Self-Assessment to see if you are consuming foods that are rich in the B vitamins and vitamin C.

LO 10.1: THE TAKE-HOME MESSAGE There are nine water-soluble vitamins: eight B-complex vitamins and vitamin C. All water-soluble vitamins dissolve in water, are absorbed from the small intestine and transported through the portal vein to the liver. They are generally not stored in the body, and are excreted through the urine. Water-soluble vitamins can be lost or destroyed by exposure to air, light, and heat. Most B-complex vitamins function as coenzymes in energy production. Some B vitamins are also involved in nerve health, blood formation, protein synthesis, and heart health. Vitamin C is needed for collagen synthesis and acts as an antioxidant.

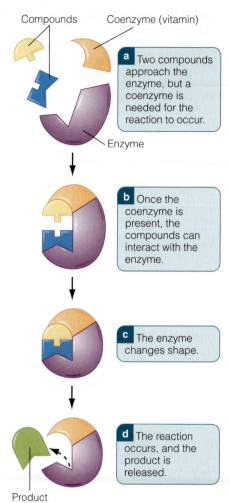

a Two compounds approach the enzyme, but a coenzyme is needed for the reaction to occur.

Compounds   Coenzyme (vitamin)

Enzyme

b Once the coenzyme is present, the compounds can interact with the enzyme.

c The enzyme changes shape.

d The reaction occurs, and the product is released.

Product

▲ **Figure 10.2 B Vitamins Function as Coenzymes**

coenzymes Organic substances, often vitamins, that bind to an enzyme to facilitate enzyme activity; unlike enzymes, coenzymes can be altered by the chemical reaction.

hemopoiesis The formation of red blood cells.

Legend: TPP = thiamin pyrophosphate

NAD = nicotinamide adenine dinucleotide (niacin)

NADP = nicotinamide adenine dinucleotide phosphate (niacin)

FAD = flavin adenine dinucleotide (riboflavin)

FMN = flavin mononucleotide (riboflavin)

PLP = pyridoxal phosphate (B_6)

CoA = coenzyme A (pantothenic acid)

Biotin = biotin

B_{12} = vitamin B_{12}

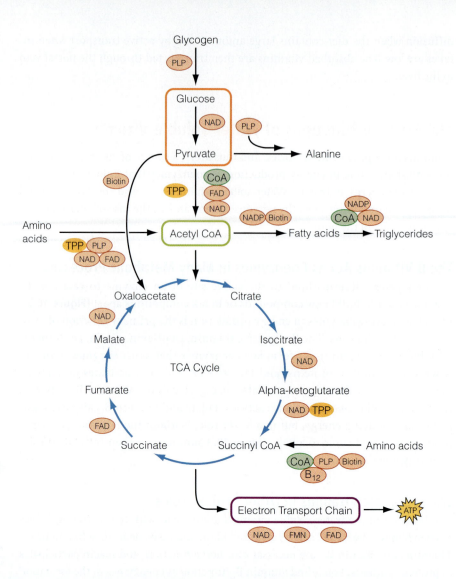

TABLE 10.1	Food Sources, Functions, Symptoms of Deficiencies and Toxicity, and the Recommended Intakes of the Water-Soluble Vitamins					
Vitamin	**Metabolic Function**	**Daily Needs (19 years +)**	**Food Sources**	**Toxicity Symptoms/UL**	**Deficiency/ Disease Symptoms**	**Coenzyme Form**
Thiamin (B_1)	Coenzyme in: • Carbohydrate metabolism • BCAA metabolism	Males: 1.2 mg/day Females: 1.1 mg/day	Pork, enriched and fortified foods, whole grains	None known	Beriberi; characterized by nerve damage	TPP
Riboflavin (B_2)	Coenzyme in oxidation-reduction reactions • Energy metabolism • Fat metabolism	Males: 1.3 mg/day Females: 1.1 mg/day	Milk, enriched and fortified foods, whole grains	None known	Ariboflavinosis; characterized by inflammation of the mouth and tongue	FAD, FMN
Niacin (B_3)	Coenzyme in oxidation-reduction reactions • Energy metabolism • Fat metabolism • DNA	Males: 16 mg/day Females: 14 mg/day	Lean meats, enriched and fortified grains and cereals	Flushing, blurred vision, liver dysfunction, and glucose intolerance UL: 35 mg/day	Pellagra; characterized by dermatitis, diarrhea, and dementia	NAD, NADP

Vitamin	Metabolic Function	Daily Needs (19 years +)	Food Sources	Toxicity Symptoms/UL	Deficiency/ Disease Symptoms	Coenzyme Form
Pantothenic Acid	Part of coenzyme A used in energy metabolism	Males and females: 5 mg/day	Widespread in foods, including whole-grain cereals, nuts and legumes, peanut butter, meat, milk, and eggs	None known	Symptoms include fatigue, nausea, vomiting, numbness, muscle cramps, and difficulty walking	Coenzyme A
Biotin	■ Energy metabolism ■ Fat synthesis ■ Glycogenesis ■ Amino acid metabolism	Males and females: 30 μg/day	Peanuts, yeast, egg yolks, grains, liver and other organ meats, and fish; also produced by bacteria in the GI tract	None known	Symptoms include dermatitis, conjunctivitis, depression, and hair loss	Biotin
Vitamin B_6	■ Protein metabolism ■ Homocysteine metabolism ■ Glycogenolysis	Males and females: 1.3 mg/day	Fortified cereals, meat, fish, poultry, many vegetables and fruits, nuts, peanut butter, and other legumes	Sore tongue, dermatitis, depression, confusion, irritability, headaches, and nerve damage UL: 100 mg/day	Microcytic hypochromic anemia; characterized by fatigue, paleness of skin, shortness of breath, dizziness, and lack of appetite	PLP
Folate	■ DNA and red blood cell formation ■ Homocysteine metabolism	Males and females: 400 μg/day Pregnant women and women of childbearing age who may become pregnant: 600 μg/day	Dark green leafy vegetables, enriched pasta, rice, breads and cereals, legumes	Masks vitamin B_{12} deficiency UL: 1,000 μg/day	Macrocytic anemia; characterized by fatigue, headache, glossitis, and GI tract symptoms such as diarrhea	THF
Vitamin B_{12}	■ Synthesis of new cells, especially red blood cells ■ Health of nerve tissue ■ Activates folate ■ Catabolism of amino acids and fatty acids in energy metabolism	Males and females: 2.4 μg/day	Animal products, including lean meats, fish, poultry, eggs, and cheese, and fortified foods	None known	Pernicious anemia; characterized by fatigue, glossitis, and nerve damage as indicated by tingling and numbness in the hands and feet	Methylco-balamin
Vitamin C	■ Collagen formation ■ Antioxidant ■ Iron absorption ■ Immune system	Males: 90 mg/day Females: 75 mg/day	Citrus fruit, tomatoes, peppers, potatoes, broccoli, and cantaloupe	Nausea, diarrhea, fatigue, insomnia UL: 2,000 mg/day	Scurvy; characterized by bleeding gums, pinpoint hemorrhages, joint pain	Ascorbic acid

Are You Getting Enough Water-Soluble Vitamins in Your Diet?

Take this brief self-assessment to see if your diet is rich in the water-soluble B vitamins and vitamin C.

1. Do you consume at least ½ cup of enriched rice or pasta daily?
   Yes ☐ **No** ☐

2. Do you eat at least 1 cup of a fortified, ready-to-eat cereal or hot cereal every day?
   Yes ☐ **No** ☐

3. Do you have at least one slice of bread, a bagel, or a muffin daily?
   Yes ☐ **No** ☐

4. Do you enjoy a citrus fruit or fruit juice, such as an orange, a grapefruit, or orange juice every day?
   Yes ☐ **No** ☐

5. Do you have at least one cup of vegetables throughout your day?
   Yes ☐ **No** ☐

Answer

If you answered "yes" to all of these questions, you are eating a healthy diet with abundant vitamin B and vitamin C! Rice, pasta, cereals, and bread and bread products are all excellent sources of B vitamins, and citrus fruits are rich in vitamin C. In fact, all vegetables can contribute to meeting daily vitamin C needs. If you answered "no" more often than "yes," read on to learn how to add more Bs and C to your diet.

Exploring **Thiamin (Vitamin B₁)**

THIAMIN

LO 10.2 Describe the functions, recommended intakes, food sources, and the toxicity and deficiency effects of thiamin.

What Is Thiamin (B₁)?

Thiamin, or vitamin B₁, was the first B vitamin to be discovered. The thiamin molecule (**Figure 10.4**) contains an amine ring, which includes nitrogen, and a thiazole ring that contains sulfur.

thiamin pyrophosphate (TPP) The coenzyme form of thiamin with two phosphate groups as part of the molecule.

Dietary forms of thiamin are converted to the active coenzyme form, **thiamin pyrophosphate (TPP),** in the body by adding two phosphate groups to the molecule.

Thiamin is one of the vitamins that are sensitive to changes in pH. The practice of using baking soda during cooking (to cook beans faster, for example) destroys thiamin and its ability to function. The basic solution breaks the bond between the rings and the central carbon. Using more acid-based foods, such as tomatoes, when cooking thiamin-rich foods protects the vitamin from destruction.

Thiamin is absorbed in the small intestine, mostly in the jejunum, primarily by passive diffusion. At lower intakes, thiamin is absorbed by active transport. It is transported through the blood and excreted through the urine.

Metabolic Functions of Thiamin

Thiamin participates in the production of ATP in several different reactions, most of which involve carbohydrates. The coenzyme TPP activates an enzyme (called a *decarboxylase*) that removes a carbon from pyruvate (a three-carbon molecule) to form acetyl

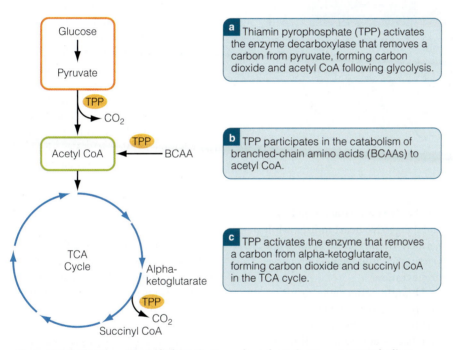

a Thiamin is composed of a nitrogen containing amine ring and a thiazole ring that contains sulfur.

Amine   Thiazole

Thiamin

b The active form of thiamin called thiamin pyrophosphate (TPP) has two phosphate groups added to thiamin.

Phosphate groups

Thiamin pyrophosphate

▲ **Figure 10.4 The Structures of Thiamin and Thiamin Pyrophosphate**

Glucose

Pyruvate

TPP

CO_2

Acetyl CoA ◄— BCAA

TCA Cycle

Alpha-ketoglutarate

TPP

CO_2

Succinyl CoA

a Thiamin pyrophosphate (TPP) activates the enzyme decarboxylase that removes a carbon from pyruvate, forming carbon dioxide and acetyl CoA following glycolysis.

b TPP participates in the catabolism of branched-chain amino acids (BCAAs) to acetyl CoA.

c TPP activates the enzyme that removes a carbon from alpha-ketoglutarate, forming carbon dioxide and succinyl CoA in the TCA cycle.

▲ **Figure 10.5 The Function of Thiamin Pyrophosphate in Energy Metabolism**

CoA (a two-carbon molecule) and carbon dioxide (**Figure 10.5**). A similar TPP-dependent enzyme converts alpha-ketoglutarate (a five-carbon molecule) to succinyl CoA (a four-carbon molecule) in the TCA cycle.

Thiamin pyrophosphate is also essential for protein metabolism. Thiamin assists in converting three branched-chain amino acids—leucine, isoleucine, and valine—into acetyl CoA to enter the TCA cycle. Without thiamin, energy production from glucose and amino acids would be impossible.

Thiamin is also used to synthesize sugars called pentoses that are needed as the starting material for DNA and RNA. This same pathway forms NADPH, a form of niacin needed for fat synthesis.

In addition, thiamin plays a nonco-enzyme role in the functioning of the nervous system. Although the actual mechanism is unclear, thiamin may participate in the manufacture of specific chemicals involved in conducting nerve signals.

Daily Needs for Thiamin

The RDA for thiamin for adults is 1.1 milligrams for women and 1.2 milligrams for men. Currently, adult American men consume close to 2 milligrams of thiamin daily, whereas women, on average, consume approximately 1.2 milligrams daily, so both groups are meeting their daily needs.[1] These requirements may be greater for those who ingest more kilocalories, especially from carbohydrates.

Food Sources of Thiamin

Thiamin enriched whole-grain foods, such as bread and bread products, ready-to-eat cereals, pasta, rice, and nuts, are the biggest contributors of thiamin in the American diet. Lean pork is the most nutrient-dense source of naturally occurring thiamin. A medium-sized bowl of thiamin-fortified ready-to-eat cereal in the morning and a sandwich at lunch will meet the daily thiamin requirement (see **Figure 10.6**).

continued

Thiamin

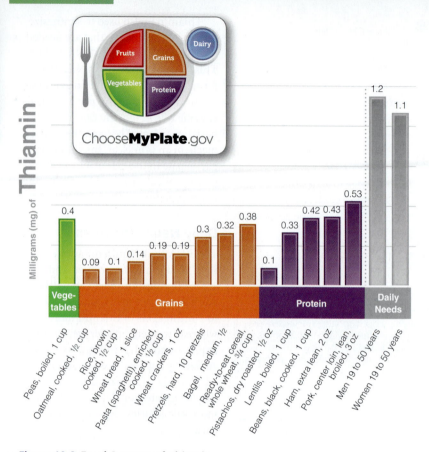

▲ Figure 10.6 Food Sources of Thiamin

TABLE TIPS
Thrive with Thiamin

Sprinkle cereal on yogurt.

Toss pasta with peas. Both foods boost thiamin intake.

Add cooked rice to soups.

Have a sandwich made with whole grains and lean meats.

Enjoy oatmeal for breakfast.

Americans, however, are not completely immune to thiamin deficiencies. Those who chronically abuse alcohol tend to eat poorly and thus lack thiamin. Chronic alcohol consumption also interferes with the absorption of the small amounts of thiamin that may be in the diet, accelerating its loss from the body and may lead to an advanced form of thiamin deficiency called Wernicke-Korsakoff syndrome (see Chapter 7). Wernicke-Korsakoff syndrome is a progressively damaging brain disorder that can cause mental confusion and memory loss, difficulty seeing clearly, low blood pressure, uncontrolled movement of the arms and legs, and even coma. Although some of these symptoms can be reversed after the person is medically treated with thiamin, some of the memory loss may be permanent.[2]

Thiamin Toxicity and Deficiency

There are no known toxicity symptoms from consuming too much thiamin. For this reason no tolerable upper level has been set.

The disease that occurs in humans≈who are deficient in thiamin is **beriberi.** General symptoms of beriberi include loss of appetite, weight loss, memory loss, confusion, muscle weakness, and **peripheral neuropathy.**

beriberi The thiamin deficiency that results in weakness; the name translates to "I can not."

peripheral neuropathy Damage to the peripheral nerves causing pain, numbness, and tingling in the feet and hands, and muscle weakness.

Wet beriberi is characterized by edema and congestive heart failure, while *dry* beriberi victims show signs of muscle wasting without edema and nerve degeneration.

Thiamin deficiencies result from insufficient dietary intake, malabsorption, alcoholism, or prolonged diarrhea. A deficiency of thiamin can also occur when there is an increased need and insufficient thiamin is consumed, such as during pregnancy and lactation.

In the United States, refined grains are enriched with thiamin, so instances of beriberi are rare. Individuals, who rely heavily on refined grains that are not enriched, are more susceptible to a thiamin deficiency and to the symptoms associated with beriberi.

LO 10.2: THE TAKE-HOME MESSAGE
Thiamin, found abundantly in lean pork and whole-grain foods, is necessary for energy metabolism and plays a role in nerve transmission. Adult females need 1.1 mg and males need 1.2 mg per day of thiamin. There is no known toxicity for thiamin. A thiamin deficiency leads to beriberi.

Exploring Riboflavin (Vitamin B₂)

LO 10.3 Describe the functions, recommended intakes, food sources, and the toxicity and deficiency effects of riboflavin.

What Is Riboflavin (B₂)?

Riboflavin, also known as vitamin B_2, is a water-soluble compound composed of a side chain and a ring structure. The structures of riboflavin and its two coenzyme forms are illustrated in **Figure 10.7**. **Flavin mononucleotide (FMN)** is composed of three rings plus a sugar alcohol, shown as a straight chain in Figure 10.7. Attached is one phosphate group. **Flavin adenine dinucleotide (FAD)** combines

FMN plus an additional phosphate group, an adenine and a five-carbon sugar, referred to as AMP. Both coenzyme forms are active in the body.

Riboflavin is fairly stable during cooking, but it degrades in the presence of ultraviolet light. Not so long ago, milk, a source of abundant riboflavin, made its way to a household not via the grocery store cooler, but by way of a daily visit from a milkman. At each delivery, the milkman placed the clear glass milk bottles inside a covered "milk box" outside the home to protect the light-sensitive riboflavin in the milk from being destroyed by sunlight. Today, some dairy farmers sell milk in glass bottles, touting the improved taste and environmental benefits of using reusable bottles rather than opaque plastic

containers. However, what they don't advertise is that the sunlight that reaches milk in glass containers destroys much of its riboflavin. In fact, in just 30 minutes, UV can destroy over 30 percent of the riboflavin in glass-bottled milk.[3] This is the reason that most milk is packaged in opaque bottles or cardboard containers.

Riboflavin is usually attached to proteins in food and must be released during digestion. Hydrochloric acid denatures the protein, which frees the riboflavin to be absorbed by active transport in the small intestine.

Metabolic Functions of Riboflavin

Riboflavin participates in energy metabolism mostly through oxidation-reduction reactions (see the Chemistry Boost on oxidation-reduction reactions). Both FMN and FAD are the main carriers of high-energy electrons generated in metabolic reactions. For example, in the conversion of carbohydrates and proteins into energy, high-energy electrons are transferred to FAD in the TCA cycle, which reduces it to $FADH_2$ (**Figure 10.8**). The $FADH_2$ transports the electrons to the electron transport chain to produce ATP. In addition to riboflavin's function

Riboflavin

a Riboflavin contains a 3-ring structure with a side chain attached.

Pyrophosphate

FMN

AMP

FAD

b The two active forms of riboflavin: FMN has one phosphate added to the riboflavin molecule. FAD has FMN plus an AMP molecule a second phosphate.

▲ **Figure 10.7 The Structures of Riboflavin and the Coenzyme Forms FAD and FMN**

flavin mononucleotide (FMN) A coenzyme form of riboflavin, which functions in the electron transport chain.

flavin adenine dinucleotide (FAD) A coenzyme form of riboflavin that functions as an electron carrier in energy metabolism.

continued

▶ Figure 10.8 The Role of FAD in the TCA Cycle

The riboflavin coenzyme FAD participates in the removal of hydrogen atoms from succinate to form fumarate and $FADH_2$ in the TCA cycle.

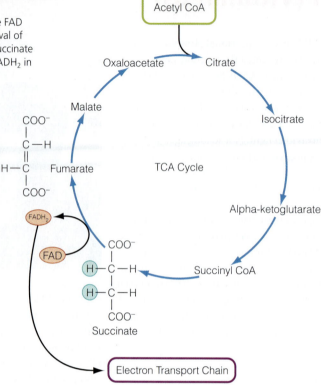

cereals and grains (see **Figure 10.9**). A breakfast of cereal and milk and a lunchtime pita sandwich and yogurt meets riboflavin needs for the day. For those individuals who follow a gluten-free diet, riboflavin needs can be met by consuming gluten-free grains such as quinoa, rice, or oats.

in converting carbohydrates, fats, and proteins into energy, it also participates as $FADH_2$ in beta-oxidation, which converts fatty acids into acetyl CoA. FAD is also involved in oxidation-reduction reactions that protect cells from oxidative stress.[4]

Riboflavin enhances the functions of other B vitamins, such as niacin, folate, and vitamin B_6. For instance, riboflavin as FAD helps convert folate to its active form and aids in the reaction that converts the amino acid tryptophan to niacin, and riboflavin as FMN is essential to convert vitamin B_6 to its coenzyme form.[5] Because riboflavin is involved in the metabolism of several other vitamins, a severe riboflavin deficiency may affect many enzyme systems.

Daily Needs for Riboflavin

The recommended daily intake of riboflavin for adult males is 1.3 milligrams and 1.1 milligrams for females. The average intake of riboflavin in the United States for adult males is about 2 milligrams per day, and adult females consume about 1.5 milligrams per day. This is well above the RDA.

Food Sources of Riboflavin

Milk and yogurt are the most popular sources of riboflavin in the diets of American adults, followed by enriched

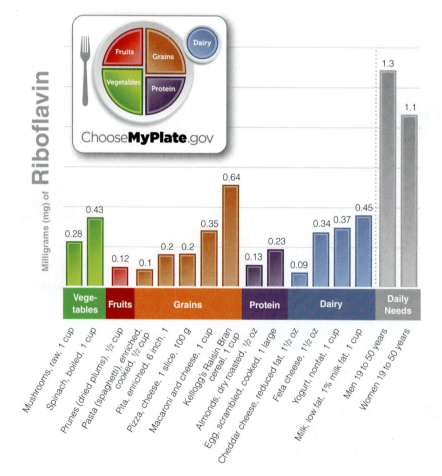

▲ Figure 10.9 Food Sources of Riboflavin

Chemistry Boost

Oxidation-Reduction Reactions

Oxidation-reduction reactions, also called redox reactions, are a family of chemical reactions in which electrons are transferred from one molecule to another for transport. The **oxidation reaction** and the **reduction reaction** always occur in pairs, and you can't have one without the other. In an redox reaction, an electron is lost from one molecule in an oxidation reaction and gained by another molecule in a reduction reaction.

FAD and FMN are major electron carriers in oxidation-reduction reactions during the TCA cycle. The oxidized form is FAD and the reduced form is $FADH_2$. The oxidation-reduction reaction is illustrated in the example below:

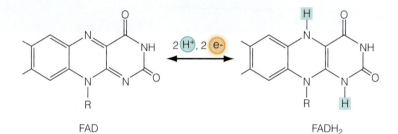

FAD $FADH_2$

During the TCA cycle, compounds release hydrogen ions and high-energy electrons during oxidation, which are grabbed by FAD to form $FADH_2$.

The reduced form ($FADH_2$) carries the electrons and hydrogen ions to the electron transport chain, where they are released and FAD is reformed to grab more hydrogen ions. The released hydrogen ions combine with oxygen to form water.

$$succinate + FAD \rightarrow fumarate + FADH_2$$

The oxidized form of flavin mononucleotide is FMN and the reduced form is $FMNH_2$. Other water-soluble vitamins such as niacin (NAD^+) and vitamin C also play important roles in oxidation-reduction reactions.

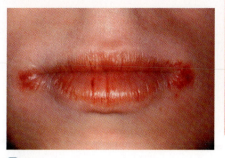

a Cheilosis

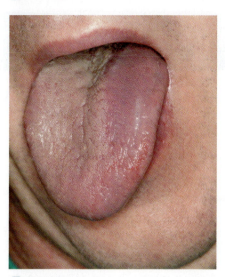

b Glossitis

▲ **Figure 10.10 The Symptoms of Ariboflavinosis**
The symptoms of a deficiency of many of the B vitamins (including ariboflavinosis) include (a) cheilosis and (b) glossitis.

Riboflavin Toxicity and Deficiency

The body tightly controls the metabolism of riboflavin depending on the riboflavin status of the individual. About 95 percent of riboflavin is absorbed, and excessive amounts are excreted in urine. In fact, because riboflavin is a bright yellow compound, consuming large amounts through supplements turns urine as yellow as a school bus. While this isn't dangerous to health, it isn't beneficial either. No tolerable upper level for riboflavin has been determined.

Ariboflavinosis is the name for riboflavin deficiency (**Figure 10.10**). The term covers a host of symptoms in which the cells in the tissues that line the throat, mouth, tongue, and lips become

TABLE TIPS

Raise Your Riboflavin

Have a glass of low-fat milk with meals.

A yogurt snack is a riboflavin snack.

Pizza is a good source of riboflavin.

Enriched pasta enriches the meal with riboflavin.

Macaroni and cheese provides a double source of riboflavin—the pasta and the cheese.

Spinach, almonds, Crimini mushrooms, asparagus, and eggs are gluten- and dairy-free sources of riboflavin.

inflamed or swollen. Symptoms include a sore throat, an irritated lining of the inside of the mouth (**stomatitis**), an inflamed tongue (**glossitis**) that may appear shiny and purplish red, and cracked or sore lips (**cheilosis**) with cracks at the

oxidation reaction A reaction in which an atom loses an electron.

reduction reaction A reaction in which an atom gains an electron.

ariboflavinosis A deficiency of riboflavin characterized by, stomatitis, glossitis, and cheilosis.

stomatitis Inflammation of the mucous lining of the mouth.

glossitis Inflammation of the tongue.

cheilosis A noninflammatory condition of the lips characterized by chapping and fissuring.

continued

Riboflavin continued

corners of the mouth. In older adults, a deficiency of riboflavin reduces the conversion of vitamin B_6 to its active form and is reversed when riboflavin supplements are given.[6] Riboflavin deficiencies also alter iron metabolism and the synthesis of hemoglobin.[7]

LO 10.3: THE TAKE-HOME MESSAGE

Riboflavin, or vitamin B_2, is stable in cooking but is degraded by ultraviolet light. Riboflavin participates in oxidation-reduction reactions. The RDA for adult males is 1.3 mg per day while females need 1.1 mg of riboflavin per day. Milk and yogurt are the most popular sources of riboflavin. Nondairy foods including leafy green vegetables, eggs, and almonds are also good sources of riboflavin. Excess amounts are excreted in urine and there are no known toxicity symptoms. A deficiency in riboflavin results in ariboflavinosis.

Exploring **Niacin (Vitamin B₃)**

LO 10.4 Describe the functions, recommended intakes, food sources, and the toxicity and deficiency effects of niacin.

nicotinic acid A form of niacin found in foods and sometimes prescribed to lower LDL cholesterol.

nicotinamide A form of niacin that is found in food and as a topical cream in treating acne.

nicotinamide adenine dinucleotide (NAD⁺) A coenzyme form of niacin that functions as an electron carrier and can be reduced to NADH during metabolism.

nicotinamide adenine dinucleotide phosphate (NADP⁺) A coenzyme form of niacin that functions as an electron carrier and can be reduced to NADPH during metabolism.

What Is Niacin (B₃)?

Niacin, or vitamin B_3, is the generic term for **nicotinic acid** and **nicotinamide** (not related to nicotine in tobacco), which are the two active forms of niacin derived from food (**Figure 10.11**). Both forms are converted to the active coenzymes **nicotinamide adenine dinucleotide (NAD⁺)** and **nicotinamide adenine dinucleotide phosphate (NADP⁺)** in the liver. These coenzymes play an essential role in energy metabolism.

Unlike some B vitamins, niacin is stable in foods and is not destroyed by heat or ultraviolet light. Because niacin is water soluble, it can leach if food is cooked or

soaked in water. The niacin found in plant foods, such as wheat or corn, is found complexed with proteins and is much less bioavailable than niacin from meat and dairy products. Niacin in corn, for example, is bound to a protein that is difficult to absorb. Soaking corn in alkaline lime water, as is done in some Meso-American cultures before using it to make tortillas, helps release the vitamin and improve its bioavailability.[8] This practice is not recommended, however, because the alkalinity increases the pH, which destroys the other B vitamins present in corn.

Most of the niacin in foods is absorbed by a sodium-dependent, carrier-mediated

a Two forms of niacin found in food.

b NAD⁺ is the active coenzyme form of niacin formed in the liver.

c The coenzyme NADP⁺ is similar to NAD⁺ but has a phosphate group in the place of a hydroxyl group.

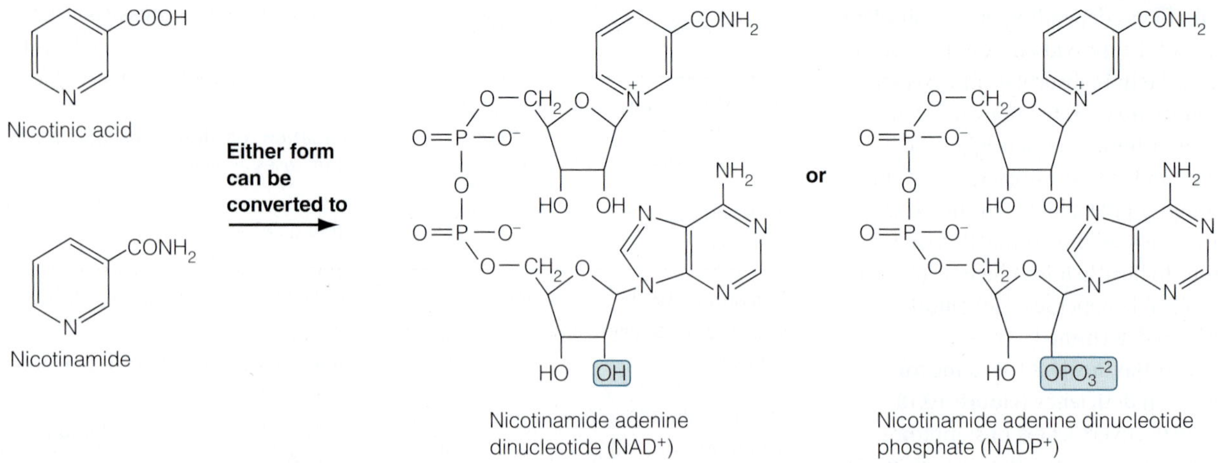

Nicotinic acid

Nicotinamide

Either form can be converted to →

Nicotinamide adenine dinucleotide (NAD⁺)

or

Nicotinamide adenine dinucleotide phosphate (NADP⁺)

▲ **Figure 10.11 The Structures of Niacin and Its Coenzyme Forms NAD⁺ and NADP⁺**

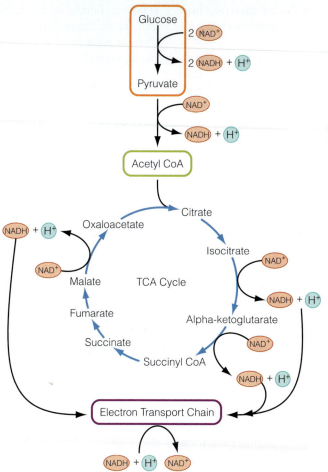

▲ **Figure 10.12 Niacin Functions as NAD⁺ in Energy Metabolism**
The coenzyme form of niacin, NAD⁺, participates in oxidation-reduction reactions in glycolysis, transporting H⁺ atoms to the electron transport chain.

to four grams per day often prescribed by a physician is more than 40 times the upper level of 35 milligrams per day for niacin. Individuals should *never* consume high amounts of niacin unless a physician monitors them.

Daily Needs for Niacin

While niacin is found in many foods, it can also be synthesized in the body from the amino acid tryptophan. For this reason, daily niacin needs are measured in **niacin equivalents (NE)**. It is estimated that 60 milligrams of tryptophan can be converted to 1 milligram of niacin or 1 milligram NE. This conversion depends on the B vitamins riboflavin and vitamin B₆, and the mineral iron.

facilitated diffusion in the small intestine. At high concentrations, such as when taking a niacin supplement, niacin is absorbed by passive diffusion. It circulates through the blood to the liver, where it is converted to NAD⁺ and NADP⁺.

Metabolic Functions of Niacin

NAD⁺ and NADP⁺ are key to the metabolism of glucose, protein, fat, and alcohol. These coenzymes both participate in oxidation-reduction reactions but have different roles in the cell. NAD⁺ functions mostly in oxidative reactions that are catabolic and produce energy (**Figure 10.12**). In fatty acid oxidation, for instance, NAD⁺ is reduced to NADH⁺, which carries electrons to the electron transport chain to produce ATP and water.

NADP⁺ acts mostly as a reducing agent. In reduction reactions, this coenzyme form of niacin can synthesize

compounds such as fat and cholesterol. Niacin also aids in vitamin C and folate metabolism.

Niacin is needed to keep skin cells healthy and the digestive system functioning properly. Niacin in the form of nicotinic acid (not nicotinamide) has been used since 1955 to lower the total amount of cholesterol in the blood, by lowering Lp(a) lipoprotein, the LDL cholesterol carrier. It can also lower high levels of fat (triglycerides) in the blood and simultaneously raise the level of the HDL cholesterol carrier.[9]

When nicotinic acid is used to treat high blood cholesterol, it is considered a pharmacological dose or drug. The two

niacin equivalents (NE) A measurement that reflects the amount of niacin and tryptophan in foods that can be used to synthesize niacin.

continued

Exploring Niacin (Vitamin B₃)   **371**

Calculation Corner

Niacin Equivalents

The recommendation for niacin is expressed in milligrams of niacin equivalents (mg NE) that reflect either the amount of preformed niacin in foods or the amount that can be formed from a food's content of the amino acid tryptophan.

Calculating milligrams NE from a meal can be completed by two different methods.

(a) If you know the amount of preformed niacin in milligrams (mg) and the amount of tryptophan in grams (g) in the meal, then use this formula to calculate the total amount of niacin equivalents in the meal:

$$(\text{tryptophan} \times 1{,}000 \div 60) + \text{preformed niacin} = \text{mg NE}$$

In this formula, the amount of tryptophan must be converted from grams to milligrams (tryptophan × 1,000) and then divided by 60 (60 mg of tryptophan can be converted into 1 mg of niacin). Then add the preformed niacin found in the meal for the total milligrams of niacin.

Example: A breakfast contains 0.02 g of tryptophan and 7.0 mg of preformed niacin. How many mg NE does the meal contain?

Answer: (0.02 g tryptophan × 1,000 ÷ 60) + 7.0 mg niacin = 7.3 mg NE

(b) If you only know the total amount of protein in the meal, but not the tryptophan content, you must estimate the amount of tryptophan. Total protein in a meal is approximately 1.1 percent tryptophan. This formula uses the 1.1 percentage to calculate mg NE:

$$(0.011 \times \text{g of protein}) \times 1{,}000 \div 60 + \text{preformed niacin} = \text{mg NE}$$

Example: A breakfast contains 8 g of protein and 3 mg of preformed niacin. How many mg NE does the meal contain?

Answer: (0.011 × 8 g protein) × 1,000 ÷ 60 + 3 mg preformed niacin = 4.5 mg NE

Scan this QR code with your mobile device to access practice math activities. You can also access the activities in **Mastering**Nutrition™.

The Calculation Corner illustrates how to calculate niacin equivalents from tryptophan.

The recommended daily amount of niacin for adults is 14 milligrams NE for women and 16 milligrams NE for men, an amount set to prevent the deficiency disease pellagra. American adults, on average, far exceed their daily niacin needs.[10]

Food Sources of Niacin

Niacin used by the body comes from two sources: preformed niacin found in food and niacin formed from excess amounts of the amino acid tryptophan. Preformed niacin is found in meat, fish, poultry, enriched whole-grain breads and bread products, and fortified cereals (see **Figure 10.13**). Protein-rich foods, particularly animal foods such as meat, are also good sources of tryptophan. However, if an individual is falling short of both dietary protein and niacin, the body first uses tryptophan to make protein, at the expense of niacin needs.[11]

Niacin Toxicity and Deficiency

As with most water-soluble vitamins, there isn't any known danger of consuming too much niacin from foods. However, overconsuming niacin (more than one gram per day) by taking supplements or eating too many overly fortified foods can cause flushing, a reddish coloring of the face, arms, and chest. Excess niacin can also cause nausea, heartburn, and vomiting, be toxic to the liver, and raise blood glucose levels. The upper level for niacin for adults is 35 milligrams. This upper level applies only to healthy individuals; it may be too high for those with certain medical conditions, such as diabetes mellitus and liver disease.[12]

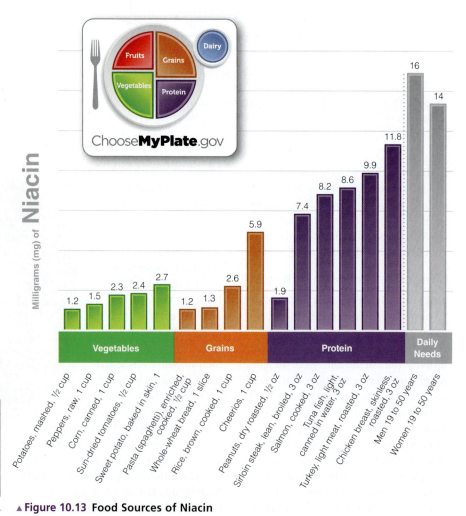

▲ Figure 10.13 **Food Sources of Niacin**

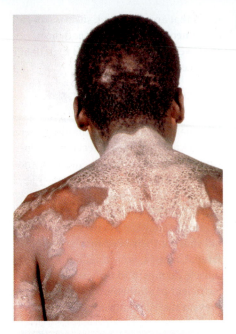

▲ **Figure 10.14 Pellagra Can Cause Dermatitis**

Too little niacin in the diet can result in the deficiency disease **pellagra** (**Figure 10.14**). In the early 1900s, pellagra was widespread

Need More Niacin?

Have a serving of enriched cereal in the morning.

Dip niacin-rich peppers in hummus.

Enjoy a lean chicken breast at dinner.

Snack on peanuts.

Put tuna fish flakes on salad.

among the poor living in the southern United States, where people relied on corn—which contains little available niacin and no tryptophan—as a dietary staple. The symptoms of pellagra—*dermatitis, dementia,* and *diarrhea*—led to its being known as the disease of the three Ds. A fourth D, *death,* was also often associated with the disease.

Once fortified cereal grains became available, pellagra disappeared as a widespread disease in the United States.

The niacin in fortified grains and protein-rich diets was later identified as the curative factor. Although no longer common in the United States, pellagra does occur among individuals who abuse alcohol and have a very poor diet.

LO 10.4: THE TAKE-HOME MESSAGE
Niacin functions in the catabolism and anabolism of carbohydrates, fats, and proteins in energy metabolism in oxidation-reduction reactions. The RDA for niacin is 16 NE for males and 14 NE for females. Niacin is found in a variety of foods, including meat, fish, poultry, fortified cereals, and enriched breads. There is no danger of consuming too much niacin, although overconsumption of niacin supplements can cause flushing. A deficiency of niacin results in pellagra.

pellagra A disease resulting from a deficiency of niacin or tryptophan.

Exploring **Pantothenic Acid**

LO 10.5 Describe the functions, recommended intakes, food sources, and the toxicity and deficiency effects of pantothenic acid.

What Is Pantothenic Acid?

Pantothenic acid makes up part of the compound *coenzyme A,* which also contains the amino acid cysteine, Coenzyme A combines with the two-carbon acetyl group to become *acetyl CoA,* the gateway molecule in energy metabolism (**Figure 10.15**). The small intestine absorbs this essential B vitamin by active transport when intake is low, and by passive diffusion at higher intakes. Once absorbed, pantothenic acid is circulated through the

blood to the liver. The vitamin itself is not stored, but high levels of acetyl CoA are found in the liver, kidney, adrenal glands, and brain.[13]

Metabolic Functions of Pantothenic Acid

As part of coenzyme A, pantothenic acid functions in numerous reactions that are essential to metabolism. Coenzyme A is needed in fat metabolism both for lipogenesis to synthesize fatty acids, and to convert them to energy through beta-oxidation. Pantothenic acid participates in the decarboxylation of pyruvate that produces acetyl CoA, the "gateway" molecule for aerobic metabolism (see **Figure 10.16**). Pantothenic

acid as coenzyme A also participates in protein metabolism by converting some amino acids to intermediate substrates in the TCA cycle and in the synthesis of cholesterol, steroid hormones, and the neurotransmitter acetylcholine.[14]

Daily Needs for Pantothenic Acid

The adequate intake (AI) for pantothenic acid has been set at 5 milligrams per day

continued

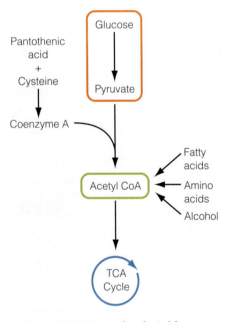

CH_3

$HO-CH_2-C-CH-C-NH-CH_2-CH_2-C-O^-$

$H_3C \quad OH \quad O \qquad O$

Pantothenic acid

↓ Is a component of

$CH_2-O-\overset{O}{\underset{O^-}{P}}-O-\overset{O}{\underset{O^-}{P}}-O-CH_2-\overset{CH_3}{\underset{H_3C}{C}}-CH-C-NH-CH_2-CH_2-C-NH-CH_2-CH_2-SH$

$OH \quad O \qquad O$

O — Adenine

H H

H — H

O — OH

$O=P-O^-$

O^-

Coenzyme A

▲ **Figure 10.15 The Structures of Pantothenic Acid and Coenzyme A**
Pantothenic acid is part of coenzyme A, which also contains the amino acid cysteine. Coenzyme A combines with the two-carbon acetyl group to become acetyl CoA, the gateway molecule for all energy nutrients to enter the TCA cycle during energy metabolism.

Pantothenic acid
+
Cysteine

↓

Coenzyme A

Glucose

↓

Pyruvate

Fatty acids

Acetyl CoA ← Amino acids

Alcohol

↓

TCA Cycle

▲ **Figure 10.16 Pantothenic Acid and Energy Metabolism**
As part of coenzyme A, pantothenic acid participates in energy metabolism through its role in forming acetyl CoA.

for both adult males and females. This recommendation is based on the amount needed to replace the amount excreted in the urine.

foods that are processed, such as frozen or canned vegetables, fish, and meat, are lower in pantothenic acid than their fresh counterparts.

Pantothenic Acid Toxicity and Deficiency

Like many of the other B vitamins, there are no known adverse effects from consuming too much pantothenic acid, and therefore no tolerable upper level has been established.

Although a pantothenic acid deficiency is rare, individuals who fall short of their need may experience fatigue, nausea, vomiting, numbness, muscle cramps, and difficulty walking. Sufficient pantothenic acid intakes can prevent these conditions.[15]

Food Sources of Pantothenic Acid

Pantothenic acid gets its name from the Greek word *pantothen*, which means "everywhere," because it is found in almost every food. The highest amounts are found in whole-grain cereals, nuts and legumes, peanut butter, meat, milk, and eggs. Pantothenic acid can be destroyed by heat, so refined grains and

TABLE TIPS

A Plethora of Pantothenic Acid

Sprinkle a tablespoon of brewer's yeast on cooked oatmeal in the morning.

Add colorful kale, avocado, and tomatoes to salad greens.

Enjoy a three-bean salad with the midday meal.

Include nuts and seeds, such as peanuts and sunflower seeds, among regular snack foods.

Substitute sweet potatoes for baked potatoes at dinner.

LO 10.5: THE TAKE-HOME MESSAGE
Pantothenic acid, found in whole-grain cereals, nuts and legumes, milk, meat, and eggs, makes up part of the molecule coenzyme A and participates in lipogenesis and beta-oxidation, in the conversion of pyruvate to acetyl CoA, and in converting some amino acids to substrates in the TCA cycle. The adequate intake (AI) for pantothenic acid is 5 mg. There are no known adverse affects from consuming too much pantothenic acid and deficiencies are rare.

Exploring **Biotin**

LO 10.6 Describe the functions, recommended intakes, food sources, and the toxicity and deficiency effects of biotin.

What Is Biotin?

In 1914, doctors discovered that adding raw egg white to a balanced diet resulted in dermatitis and hair loss, depression, and nausea. The condition, referred to as *egg white injury,* was caused by the binding of the vitamin biotin with **avidin,** a protein found in egg whites. Avidin can bind up to four molecules of biotin, which renders the vitamin unavailable for absorption. The problem only occurs when raw eggs are consumed, as cooking eggs denatures the avidin and prevents it from binding to biotin.

Biotin is made up of sulfur-containing double rings and a side chain (**Figure 10.17**). During digestion, the enzyme **biotinidase** releases biotin from food in the small intestine, allowing the free biotin to be absorbed by active transport. Once absorbed into the portal vein, biotin is taken up by the liver and stored in small amounts.

Metabolic Functions of Biotin

Biotin functions as a coenzyme for enzymes that add carbon dioxide to compounds involved in energy metabolism. As illustrated in **Figure 10.18**, biotin activates enzymes that synthesize fatty acids from acetate formed from acetyl CoA; it replenishes oxaloacetate

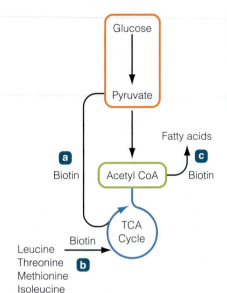

a Biotin helps add a CO_2 to pyruvate to form oxaloacetate, a compound in the TCA cycle. This is a key step in gluconeogenesis.

b Biotin helps break down leucine, threonine, methionine, and isoleucine to be used in the production of energy through the TCA cycle.

c Biotin plays a key role in synthesizing fatty acids from acetyl CoA.

▲ **Figure 10.18 The Role of Biotin as a Coenzyme in Energy Metabolism**

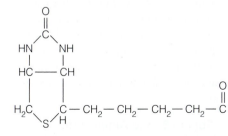

▲ **Figure 10.17 The Chemical Structure of Biotin**
A molecule of biotin contains both nitrogen and sulfur as part of its structure.

from pyruvate, which is important in the TCA cycle and in gluconeogenesis; it aids in the metabolism of the amino acid leucine; and helps convert some amino acids into compounds that can be used in the TCA cycle. Thus, without adequate biotin, energy metabolism would be impaired.

Biotin also plays a role in DNA replication and the transcription of genes. In fact, over 2,000 genes depend on biotin.[16] The exact mechanisms of biotin's role are still unclear.

Biotin plays a noncoenzyme role in cell development and growth. For this reason, some refer to biotin as the "beauty vitamin" because it helps maintain healthy hair and nails.

Daily Needs for Biotin

The adequate intake (AI) of biotin has been set at 30 micrograms per day for both adult males and females. However, compared with the other B vitamins, much less data is available on which to base the daily need for biotin. This is one reason that the Nutrition Facts panel used in food labeling lists the Daily Value for biotin at 300 micrograms, or ten times the AI. This is unusual because the Daily Value for most other water-soluble vitamins is much lower.

avidin A protein in raw egg whites that binds biotin.

biotinidase An enzyme in the small intestine that releases biotin from food to allow it to be absorbed.

continued

BIOTIN

Food Sources of Biotin

Even a small amount of peanuts (¼ cup) provides more than 60 percent of the daily requirement for biotin. Other biotin-rich food sources include yeast, egg yolks, whole grains, liver and other organ meats, and fish.

Biotin Toxicity and Deficiency

There is little evidence that consuming too much biotin can have toxic side effects, even at doses as high as 200 milligrams per day.[17] For this reason, a tolerable upper level has not been set.

Some biotin is synthesized by bacteria in the intestinal tract, which may be a reason deficiencies are rare. However, whether the biotin produced by bacteria is absorbed remains unknown.

Though deficiencies of biotin are rare, they can occur if an individual eats more than 12 raw eggs or egg whites per day over a prolonged period of time. Biotin deficiencies may also occur in patients receiving total nutrition intravenously when the GI tract is not functioning (such as after surgery) that lacks biotin. Other circumstances in which biotin may be lacking include conditions that impair absorption such as Crohn's disease or ulcerative colitis, and in some individuals with rare genetic disorders, such as a lack of biotinidase, the digestive enzyme that hydrolyzes biotin from protein.[18]

Symptoms of a biotin deficiency include dermatitis, especially around the eyes, nose, and mouth, conjunctivitis, hair loss, and alterations in the central nervous system resulting in lethargy, hallucinations, and depression.

TABLE TIPS
Boundless Biotin

Spread a tablespoon of peanut butter on whole-wheat toast at breakfast.

Add a chopped hard-boiled egg to a green salad for lunch.

Choose walnuts and almonds as a midmorning or midafternoon snack.

Mix fresh raspberries and strawberries with yogurt.

Bake salmon or halibut for a fresh fish dinner.

LO 10.6: THE TAKE-HOME MESSAGE
Biotin, found in peanuts, yeast, egg yolks, grains, fish, and liver, is active during energy metabolism, lipogenesis, gluconeogenesis, and the metabolism of amino acids. The AI for biotin is set at 30 micrograms. There is little evidence that excess biotin causes toxicity. Deficiencies of biotin are rare except when large amounts of raw eggs or egg whites are consumed.

Exploring Vitamin B₆

VITAMIN B₆

LO 10.7 Describe the functions, recommended intakes, food sources, and the toxicity and deficiency effects of vitamin B_6.

What Is Vitamin B₆?

Vitamin B_6 is a collective name for several related compounds, including **pyridoxine,** the major form found in

pyridoxine The alcohol form of vitamin B_6.

pyridoxal The aldehyde form of vitamin B_6.

pyridoxamine The amine form of vitamin B_6.

pyridoxal phosphate (PLP) The active coenzyme form of vitamin B_6.

plant foods and used in supplements and fortified foods.[19] Two other forms, **pyridoxal** and **pyridoxamine,** are found in animal food sources such as chicken and meat (**Figure 10.19**).

The bioavailability of vitamin B_6 is about 75 percent, and all forms are absorbed in the small intestine by passive diffusion. Once absorbed, the vitamin is attached to albumin and transported to the liver. The liver activates the vitamin by adding a phosphate group to form **pyridoxal phosphate (PLP).** This active form of B_6 is stored attached to enzymes in the muscle, and in smaller amounts in the liver, brain, kidneys, and spleen.

Metabolic Functions of Vitamin B₆

Vitamin B_6 acts as a coenzyme for more than 100 enzymes, most of which are enzymes involved in protein metabolism. Vitamin B_6 also is a key player in glucose metabolism and red blood cell synthesis, and it interacts with other nutrients, including riboflavin, niacin, and zinc.

Vitamin B₆ and Amino Acid Metabolism

Almost every amino acid needs PLP during its metabolism. For example, PLP is needed during transamination

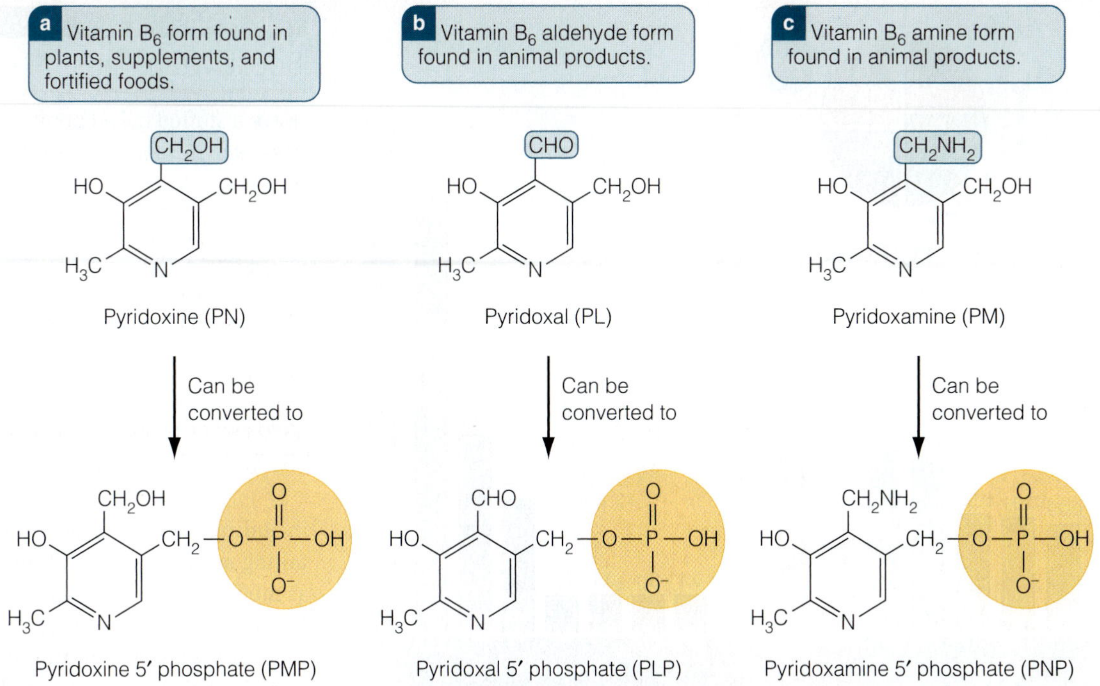

a Vitamin B$_6$ form found in plants, supplements, and fortified foods.

b Vitamin B$_6$ aldehyde form found in animal products.

c Vitamin B$_6$ amine form found in animal products.

▲ **Figure 10.19 The Structures of the Various Forms of Vitamin B$_6$**

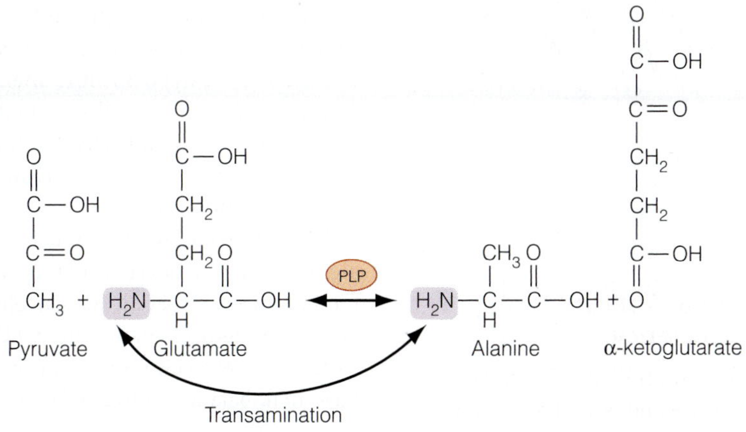

▲ **Figure 10.20 Vitamin B$_6$ Assists in Transamination**
PLP helps transfer an amine group to form a new amino acid.

to create nonessential amino acids (**Figure 10.20**). Because of this role, without vitamin B$_6$ all amino acids would become essential. Vitamin B$_6$ also helps convert the amino acid tryptophan to niacin.[20]

Vitamin B$_6$ and Carbohydrate Metabolism

Vitamin B$_6$ has a double role in the metabolism of carbohydrates. The PLP coenzyme participates in glycogenolysis in the muscle, thus enabling the body to tap into its glycogen stores for energy.

Its second role is to activate enzymes involved in gluconeogenesis to produce glucose from noncarbohydrate compounds.

Vitamin B$_6$ may also participate in fat metabolism, although the role is still unclear.

Other Functions of Vitamin B$_6$

Vitamin B$_6$ is needed to make the oxygen-carrying hemoglobin in the red blood cells and to keep the immune and nervous systems healthy.[21] Vitamin B$_6$ activates the enzyme responsible

for the first step in the synthesis of hemoglobin.

Recent research indicates that vitamin B$_6$, along with folate and vitamin B$_{12}$, may help reduce the risk of heart disease.[22]

Vitamin B$_6$ is routinely prescribed to reduce nausea and vomiting during pregnancy, although the mechanism is still uncertain. Some double-blind studies have reported that an intake of 30 milligrams of vitamin B$_6$ daily was helpful in reducing morning sickness; other studies have reported no benefit.[23]

Daily Needs for Vitamin B$_6$

Adult women need 1.3 to 1.5 milligrams and men need 1.3 to 1.7 milligrams of vitamin B$_6$ daily, depending on their age.

Food Sources of Vitamin B$_6$

Vitamin B$_6$ is found in a wide variety of foods, including fortified ready-to-eat cereals, meat, fish, poultry, many vegetables and fruits, nuts, peanut butter, and other legumes (see **Figure 10.21**). Because of the widespread availability of vitamin B$_6$, Americans on average easily meet their daily needs.

continued

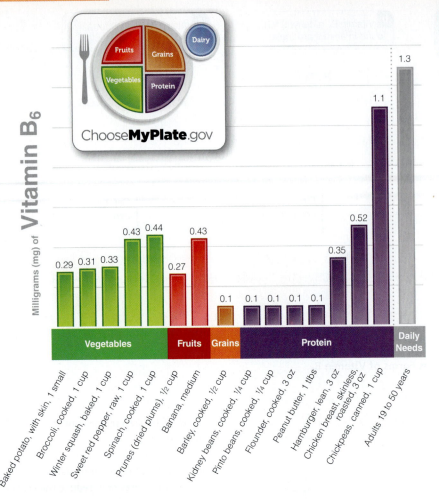

Milligrams (mg) of **Vitamin B₆**

ChooseMyPlate.gov

| Vegetables | | | | | | Fruits | Grains | | Protein | | | | | | Daily Needs |

0.29	Baked potato, with skin, 1 small
0.31	Broccoli, cooked, 1 cup
0.33	Winter squash, baked, 1 cup
0.43	Sweet red pepper, raw, 1 cup
0.44	Spinach, cooked, 1 cup
0.27	Prunes (dried plums), ½ cup
0.43	Banana, medium
0.1	Barley, cooked, ½ cup
0.1	Kidney beans, cooked, ¼ cup
0.1	Pinto beans, cooked, ¼ cup
0.1	Flounder, cooked, 3 oz
0.1	Peanut butter, 1 tlbs
0.35	Hamburger, lean, 3 oz
0.52	Chicken breast, skinless, roasted, 3 oz
1.1	Chickpeas, canned, 1 cup
1.3	Adults 19 to 50 years

▲ **Figure 10.21 Food Sources of Vitamin B₆**

microcytic hypochromic anemia A form of anemia in which red blood cells are small and pale in color due to lack of hemoglobin synthesis due to vitamin B₆ deficiency.

Vitamin B₆ Toxicity and Deficiency

Because vitamin B₆ attaches to enzymes in the muscle and other tissues, it remains in the body, and excess intake can be toxic. To protect against potential nerve damage, a tolerable upper limit of 100 milligrams per day has been set for adults over the age of 18.

Over the years, vitamin B₆ has been touted to aid a variety of ailments, including carpal tunnel syndrome and premenstrual syndrome (PMS), and individuals may take a supplement to try to relieve these conditions. However, research studies have failed to show any significant clinical benefit in taking vitamin B₆ supplements for either of these syndromes.[24]

Taking large amounts of vitamin B₆ through supplements may be associated with a variety of ill effects,

TABLE TIPS

Boost Vitamin B₆

Have a stuffed baked potato with steamed broccoli and grilled chicken for lunch.

Grab a banana for a midmorning snack.

Add cooked barley to soup.

Snack on prunes.

Add kidney beans to chili or salad.

including nerve damage. Individuals taking as little as 200 milligrams and as much as 6,000 milligrams of vitamin B₆ daily for two months experienced difficulty walking and tingling sensations in their legs and feet.[25] These symptoms subside once supplement consumption stops.

The telltale signs of a vitamin B₆ deficiency are a sore tongue, inflammation of the skin, depression, confusion, and **microcytic hypochromic anemia.** This type of anemia results in small (microcytic) red blood cells that look pale (hypochromic) in comparison with healthy red blood cells.

Those who consume too much alcohol are more likely to fall short of their vitamin B₆ needs. Not only does alcohol deplete the body of vitamin B₆, but those suffering from alcoholism are likely to have an unbalanced, unvaried diet.

LO 10.7: THE TAKE-HOME MESSAGE

Vitamin B₆, found in meat, fish, poultry, legumes, bananas, and fortified cereals, acts as a coenzyme for over 100 enzymes, most of which are involved in protein metabolism, glycogenolysis, and red blood cell synthesis. The RDA for vitamin B₆ is set at 1.3 to 1.5 mg for females and 1.3 to 1.7 mg for males depending on age. Excess vitamin B₆ in supplements may cause neurological damage. A deficiency of vitamin B₆ can result in microcytic hypochromic anemia, depression, and inflammation of the skin.

Exploring Folate

LO 10.8 Describe the functions, recommended intakes, food sources, and the toxicity and deficiency effects of folate.

What Is Folate?

The naturally occurring form of folate is found in many foods, while the synthetic form, **folic acid,** is added to foods and found in supplements. (Actually, a very small amount of folic acid can occur naturally in foods. But, for practical purposes, here folic acid refers to the synthetic variety.) Compared with folate, folic acid is a simpler molecule. It is also easier to absorb (more bioavailable) than the natural form, but once absorbed, both forms perform equally well. The synthetic form is more stable and not as easily destroyed as the natural form.[26]

There are three parts to the molecular structure of folate (**Figure 10.22**): *pteridine* (pronounced ter-e-deen), *para-aminobenzoic acid* or PABA, and at least one glutamate. Most folate found in foods is in **polyglutamate** form, which means it has at least three glutamate molecules. The synthetic folic acid is in a monoglutamate form.

Before folate can be absorbed, all but one of the glutamates must be removed from the side chain to form **monoglutamate** (one glutamate) during digestion (**Figure 10.23**). Folic acid is already in the monoglutamate form and thus doesn't need to go through digestion. Once inside the intestinal cell, both folate and folic acid are reduced to dihydrofolate and then further reduced by adding four hydrogen atoms (tetra) and a methyl group (CH_3) to the monoglutamate, creating **5-methyltetrahydrofolate (5-methyl THF).** This is the form of

folic acid The form of folate often used in vitamin supplements and fortification of foods.

polyglutamate A form of folate that naturally occurs in foods.

monoglutamate The form of folate absorbed through the cells of the small intestine.

5-methyltetrahydrofolate (5-methyl THF) The most active form of folate.

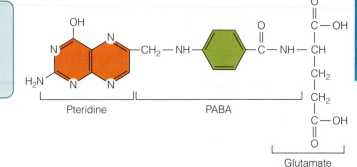

a Folate found in foods is composed of pteridine, PABA, and at least one glutamate molecule.

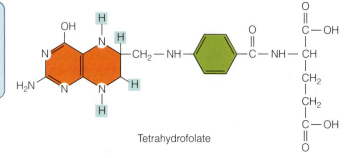

b Folate accepts four hydrogens to become tetrahydrofolate (THF), the active coenzyme form of folate.

Tetrahydrofolate

▲ **Figure 10.22** **The Structures of Folate and Its Coenzyme Form**

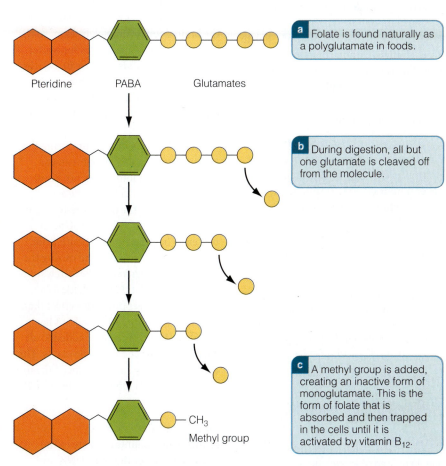

a Folate is found naturally as a polyglutamate in foods.

b During digestion, all but one glutamate is cleaved off from the molecule.

c A methyl group is added, creating an inactive form of monoglutamate. This is the form of folate that is absorbed and then trapped in the cells until it is activated by vitamin B_{12}.

▲ **Figure 10.23** **The Digestion of Folate**

continued

folate that is transported through the circulation to the liver. A small amount of folate is stored in the liver, but the majority is excreted in the urine.

Folate-rich foods can lose folate when exposed to heat and light, making raw foods more abundant in folate than cooked foods. Folic acid found in fortified foods is stable in heat but unstable in light. The bioavailability of folate can vary, and some foods, including beans, legumes, and cabbage, contain inhibitors of the enzymes that remove the glutamates during digestion. This reduces the absorption of folate.[27] Folic acid from supplements is almost all absorbed, especially on an empty stomach.[28]

Metabolic Functions of Folate

Vitamin B_{12} is needed to remove the methyl group from 5-methyl THF to form active tetrahydrofolate (THF). Without the interaction with vitamin B_{12}, folate would be trapped in the cell and unable to perform its functions (see Figure 10.29 on page 384). The active form of folate acts as a coenzyme in the transfer of single-carbon compounds, such as a methyl group (CH_3), to other compounds. Folate accepts single-carbon compounds on the pteridine ring of THF and then donates the single-carbon compounds to other structures. This function is necessary to form new compounds.

DNA and Amino Acid Synthesis

The transfer of single-carbon compounds is essential for the synthesis of several nonessential amino acids, such as converting homocysteine to methionine in DNA metabolism. To convert homocysteine to methionine, requires both 5-methyl folate and vitamin

neural tube defects Any major birth defect of the central nervous system, including the brain, caused by failure of the neural tube to properly close during fetal development.

anencephaly A neural tube defect that results in the absence of major parts of the brain and spinal cord.

spina bifida A serious birth defect in which the spinal cord is malformed and lacks the protective membrane coat.

dietary folate equivalents (DFE) A measurement used to express the amount of folate in a food or supplement.

B_{12}–dependent coenzymes. If the synthesis of DNA is disrupted, the body's ability to create and maintain new cells is impaired. For this reason, folate plays many important roles, from preventing birth defects to fighting cancer and heart disease. Folate also helps the body use amino acids and is needed to help red blood cells divide and increase in adequate numbers.

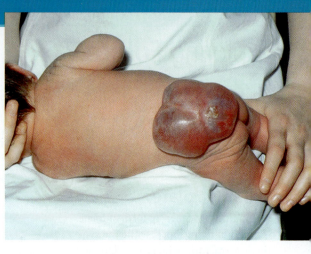
▲ **Figure 10.24 An Infant with Spina Bifida**

Neural Tube Development

Because of its participation in DNA synthesis, folate plays an extremely important role during pregnancy, particularly in the first few weeks after conception. Cells divide rapidly during fetal growth and development, and a folate deficiency during pregnancy can result in **neural tube defects.** The neural tube forms the baby's spine, brain, and skull. If the neural tube doesn't develop properly, two common birth defects, **anencephaly** and **spina bifida,** can occur. In anencephaly, the brain doesn't completely form, so the baby can't function and dies soon after birth. In spina bifida (**Figure 10.24**), the baby's spinal cord and backbone aren't properly developed, causing learning and physical disabilities, such as the inability to walk.[29]

Neural tube defects occur during the early stages of fetal development, at a point when the mother may not know she is pregnant. Increased folic acid consumption by the mother reduces the risk of these birth defects by 50 to 70 percent if begun at least a month prior to conception and continued during the early part of pregnancy.[30] Research studies to date suggest that synthetic folic acid has a stronger protective effect than food folate.[31] Since 1998, the FDA has mandated that folic acid be added to all enriched grains and cereal products. This enrichment program has reduced the incidence of neural tube defects by over 25 percent.[32]

Folate and Cancer Risk

Inadequate amounts of folate in the body can disrupt the cell's DNA and prevent repair, potentially triggering the

development of cancer.[33] In particular, folate has been shown to help reduce the risk of colon cancer. Studies show that men and women who are deficient in dietary folate have a higher risk of developing colon cancer.[34] Other studies report an association between diets low in folate and an increased risk of breast[35] and pancreatic cancers.[36]

Daily Needs for Folate

Synthetic folic acid is absorbed 1.7 times more efficiently than folate that is found naturally in foods.[37] Because of this, folate needs are measured in **dietary folate equivalents (DFE).** Most adults should consume 400 micrograms DFE of folate daily.

The Nutrition Facts panel on food labels doesn't make a distinction between folate and dietary folate equivalents. Some manufacturers use folate while others use folic acid, depending on the form used in the product. The Calculation Corner describes how to convert folic acid measurements on food labels to DFE.

Biotin enhances cell development, promoting the health of hair and nails.

Calculation Corner

Dietary Folate Equivalents

The RDA for folate is expressed in dietary folate equivalents (DFE) to account for the differences between the absorption of naturally occurring folate and the synthetic folate used in fortified foods and supplements. Folate found naturally in foods is only half as bioavailable as folate found in supplements or fortified foods. To adjust for this difference in bioavailability, one DFE is equal to 1 microgram (μg) of naturally occurring folate or 0.6 μg of folic acid. To convert the micrograms of folic acid found on a food label to DFE, multiply the amount listed on the label by the constant 1.7.

Example: A ready-to-eat cereal label shows that a serving contains 25 percent of the Daily Value for folate. The Daily Value uses 400 μg as the standard value. To find the folate in micrograms in a serving of cereal, multiply 400 μg × 0.25 = 100 μg of folate.

Next, multiply 100 μg of folate × 1.7 to determine the dietary folate equivalents:

Answer: 100 μg × 1.7 = 170 μg DFE
Remember, the RDA for folate is 400 μg DFE.

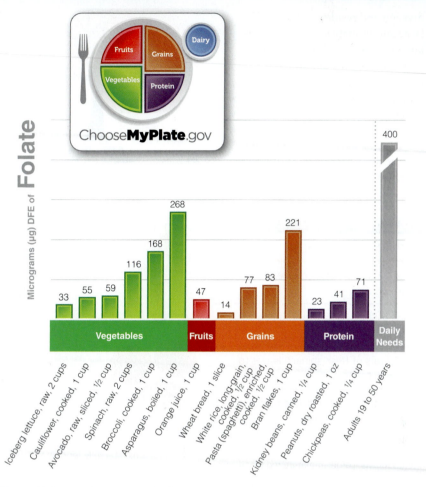

▲ Figure 10.25 **Food Sources of Folate**

Women who are planning to become pregnant should consume 400 micrograms of folic acid daily from fortified foods or supplements, along with a diet high in naturally occurring folate. Women with a family history of neural tube defects should, under the guidance of their physicians, take even larger amounts.[38] Because 50 percent of pregnancies in the United States are unplanned, any woman who may become pregnant is advised to follow these same recommendations.

Food Sources of Folate

Folic acid is required by law to be added to enriched cereals and grains, pastas, breads, rice, and flours. The best natural food sources of folate are dark green leafy vegetables such as spinach, broccoli, and asparagus. (This is easy to remember if you know that the term folate is derived from the Latin name

folium, or foliage). In addition, legumes (dried peas and beans), seeds, and liver are all good sources of this vitamin (see **Figure 10.25**).

Folate Toxicity and Deficiency

There is no danger in consuming excessive amounts of naturally occurring folate in foods. However, consuming too much folic acid, either through supplements or fortified foods, can be harmful for individuals who are deficient in vitamin B_{12}, because excessive folate masks the symptoms of B_{12} deficiency.

An upper level of 1,000 micrograms has been set for folic acid from enriched and fortified foods and supplements (not naturally occurring folate in foods) to safeguard those who may be unknowingly deficient in vitamin B_{12}. Over-the-counter prenatal vitamins can

contain as much as 800 micrograms of folic acid.

A folate deficiency interferes with normal red blood cell

continued

division and results in abnormally large and immature red blood cells known as **megaloblasts** (*megalo* = large). These cells develop into abnormally large red blood cells called **macrocytes,** which have a diminished oxygen-carrying capacity. Eventually, **macrocytic anemia** causes a person to feel tired, weak, and irritable and to experience shortness of breath. Because folate needs vitamin B_{12} to participate

TABLE TIPS
Fulfill Folate Needs

Have a bowl of fortified cereal in the morning.

Add chickpeas to a tossed green salad at lunch.

Add layers of fresh spinach leaves to your sandwich.

Have a handful of enriched crackers as a late-afternoon snack.

megaloblasts Large, immature red blood cells.

macrocytes Large cells such as a red blood cell.

macrocytic anemia A form of anemia characterized by large, immature red blood cells.

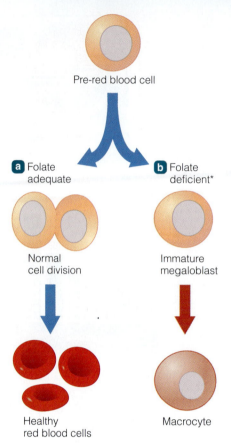

Pre-red blood cell

a Folate adequate

b Folate deficient*

Normal cell division

Immature megaloblast

Healthy red blood cells

Macrocyte

*A vitamin B_{12} deficiency can also cause the formation of macrocytes.

▲ **Figure 10.26 Altered Red Blood Cells with Folate Deficiency**
Folate is required for normal cell division. If the diet is deficient in folate, macrocytes are formed.

in cell division and produce healthy red blood cells, a deficiency of either vitamin can lead to macrocytic anemia (**Figure 10.26**).

LO 10.8: THE TAKE-HOME MESSAGE
Folate coenzymes function to accept and donate one-carbon compounds in a number of metabolic reactions, including DNA and amino acid synthesis. Adults need 400 micrograms DFE of folate per day. Folic acid is found in fortified foods such as enriched pasta, breads, and cereals, while foods including leafy green vegetables, asparagus, oranges, and rice contain folate. Consuming too much folic acid from supplements can obscure a vitamin B_{12} deficiency. Babies born to mothers who are deficient in folate have a higher risk of neural tube defects such as anencephaly and spina bifida. A deficiency of folate results in macrocytic anemia.

Exploring **Vitamin** B_{12}

VITAMIN B_{12}

LO 10.9 Describe the functions, recommended intakes, food sources, and the toxicity and deficiency effects of vitamin B_{12}.

What Is Vitamin B_{12}?

The family of compounds referred to as vitamin B_{12} is also called **cobalamin**

cobalamin The vitamin involved in energy metabolism and the conversion of homocysteine to methionine; another name for vitamin B_{12}.

because it contains the mineral cobalt. In **Figure 10.27**, two forms of vitamin B_{12} are illustrated: cyanocobalamin, the form of vitamin B_{12} found in foods, and methylcobalamin, the active form of vitamin B_{12}. Both forms contain cobalt (highlighted in orange in Figure 10.27), but cyanocobalamin also contains a cyanide,

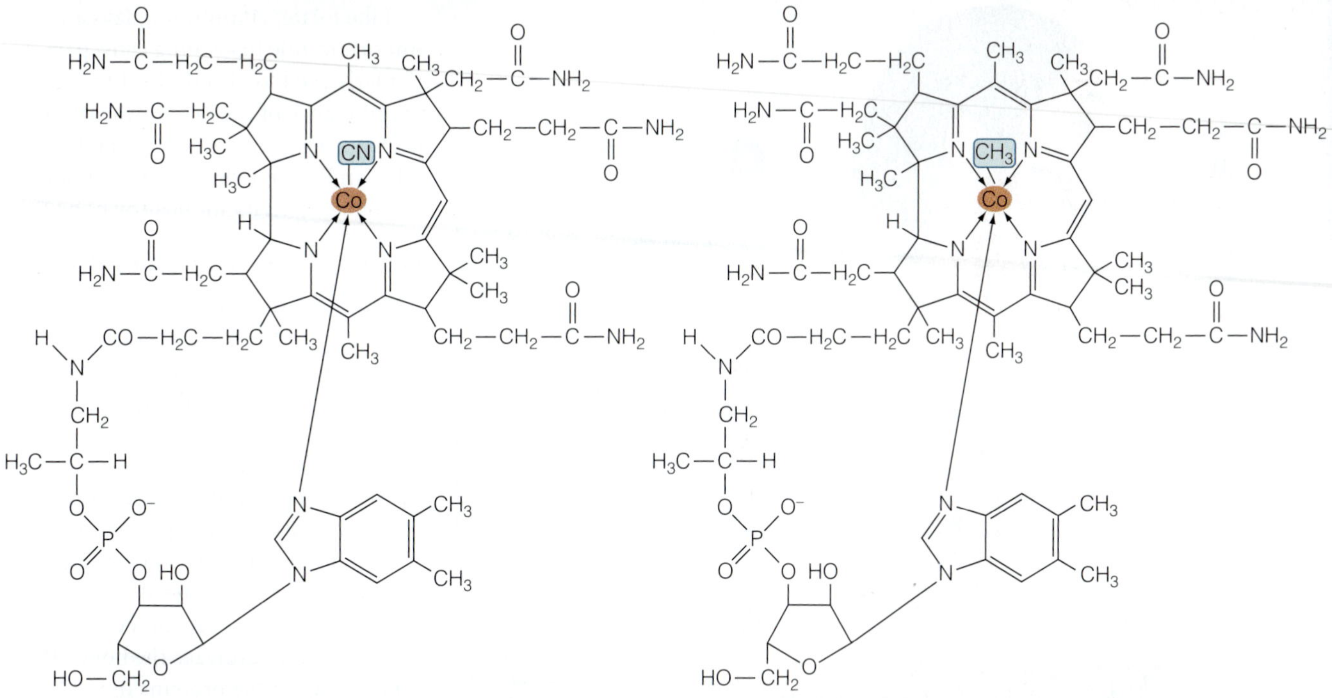

a **Cyanocobalamin** is the form of vitamin B_{12} found in foods. It contains an atom of cobalt and an atom of cyanide (shaded blue).

b **Methylcobalamin** is the active form of vitamin B_{12}. The cyanide has been replaced with a methyl group (shaded blue).

▲ **Figure 10.27 The Structure of Vitamin B_{12}**

illustrated as CN.[39] Methylcobalamin is similar in structure, except the cyanide is replaced with a methyl group.

In the stomach, vitamin B_{12} is released from food by the action of pepsin and hydrochloric acid during digestion, and then attaches to a transport protein secreted from the salivary glands called **R protein,** which carries vitamin B_{12} into the small intestine. Another type of protein called **intrinsic factor (IF)** is secreted from the parietal cells in the stomach (**Figure 10.28**) and travels in the chyme into the intestine. Pancreatic proteases hydrolyze the vitamin B_{12}–R protein complex, releasing vitamin B_{12} to bind with intrinsic factor. This newly formed complex travels to the ileum, where a specific receptor site recognizes the intrinsic factor and absorbs the vitamin B_{12}–IF complex by endocytosis into the cell. Inside the intestinal cell, IF is degraded, releasing B_{12} to bind to another protein carrier called **transcobalamin** for transport throughout the blood.

Vitamin B_{12} is stored mostly in the liver and excreted through the bile and the urine. Unlike the other water-soluble vitamins, the body stores plenty of vitamin B_{12}, so symptoms of a deficiency can take years to develop.[40]

Metabolic Functions of Vitamin B_{12}

Vitamin B_{12} functions as two coenzymes, **methylcobalamin** and **deoxyadenosylcobalamin.** Methylcobalamin is used to convert homocysteine to the amino acid methionine, which in turn provides the methyl group used in DNA and RNA synthesis. Without adequate vitamin B_{12}, homocysteine levels accumulate, which is considered a risk factor for cardiovascular disease, and DNA synthesis is slowed, causing macrocytic anemia.

The vitamin B_{12} coenzyme deoxyadenosylcobalamin helps form succinyl CoA during the TCA cycle. Thus, vitamin B_{12} plays an essential role in using nutrients for energy.

The relationship between vitamin B_{12} and folate is an important one to emphasize: Vitamin B_{12} activates folate and in turn becomes active itself (see **Figure 10.29**). Recall in the discussion on folate that for folate to be converted from the inactive 5-methyl THF, vitamin B_{12} must first cleave off the methyl group. The vitamin B_{12}-plus-methyl group is now active itself to convert homocysteine to methionine.

R protein The protein secreted from the salivary glands that binds vitamin B_{12} in the stomach and transports it into the small intestine during digestion.

intrinsic factor (IF) A glycoprotein secreted by the stomach that results in the absorption of vitamin B_{12}.

transcobalamin The protein that transports vitamin B_{12} in the blood.

methylcobalamin The coenzyme form of vitamin B_{12} that converts homocysteine to methionine.

deoxyadenosylcobalamin The coenzyme form of vitamin B_{12} that converts intermediate substances in the TCA cycle.

continued

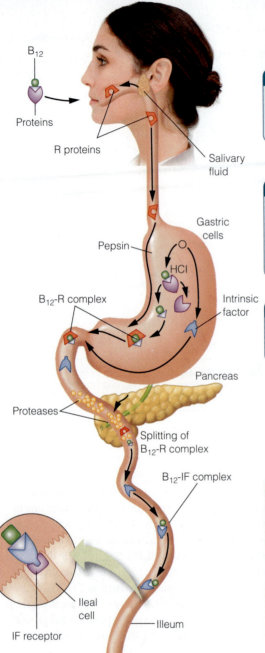

a The salivary glands produce R protein that will travel to the stomach and bind with vitamin B₁₂ there.

b Cells lining the stomach wall secrete HCl and pepsin, which release B₁₂ from proteins in the food, and intrinsic factor (IF), which travels with the chyme into the small intestine.

c After vitamin B₁₂ has been released from food proteins, it binds with R protein and moves into the small intestine.

d In the small intestine, pancreatic proteases release vitamin B₁₂ from the R protein. Vitamin B₁₂ then binds with IF and travels to the ileum.

e Intrinsic factors binds to a receptor site on an intestinal cell in the ileum and releases vitamin B₁₂ into the cell.

▲ **Figure 10.28 The Absorption of Vitamin B₁₂**

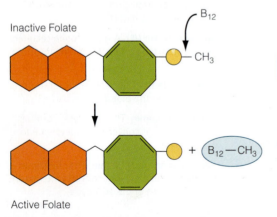

a Vitamin B₁₂ activates folate by removing the methyl group.

b Both folate and vitamin B₁₂ are now active and able to synthesize DNA.

Like folate, vitamin B₁₂ plays an important role in keeping cells, particularly red blood cells, healthy. The maintenance of the **myelin sheath** that protects nerve fibers also depends on vitamin B₁₂, and vitamin B₁₂ stimulates osteoblast activity for healthy bone.[41]

Daily Needs of Vitamin B₁₂

Adults need 2.4 micrograms of vitamin B₁₂ daily. Nonvegetarian American adults, on average, consume over 4 micrograms daily through animal foods.

The body's ability to absorb naturally occurring vitamin B₁₂ diminishes with age. This decline appears to be due to a reduction in hydrochloric acid in the stomach, which is needed to activate pepsinogen to pepsin. Pepsin is the enzyme that hydrolyzes the bonds that bind the B₁₂ to the proteins in food. If the bonds aren't broken, the vitamin can't be released. This condition, called **atrophic gastritis,** is experienced by up to 30 percent of individuals over the age of 50. Luckily, the synthetic form of vitamin B₁₂ used in fortified foods and supplements isn't bound to a protein and doesn't depend on hydrochloric acid secretions to be absorbed. Because the synthetic variety is a more reliable source, individuals over the age of 50 should meet their vitamin B₁₂ needs primarily from fortified foods or a supplement.

Hydrochloric acid is also important to keep an appropriate ratio of healthy bacteria to pathogenic bacteria in the intestine. With less acid present, the pathogenic bacteria normally found in the intestines aren't properly destroyed and so tend to overgrow. These abundant bacteria feed on unabsorbed vitamin B₁₂, diminishing the amount of the vitamin that may be available for absorption.

myelin sheath The tissue that surrounds and protects the nerves.

atrophic gastritis Chronic inflammation of the stomach.

◀ **Figure 10.29 Vitamin B₁₂ Activates Folate**

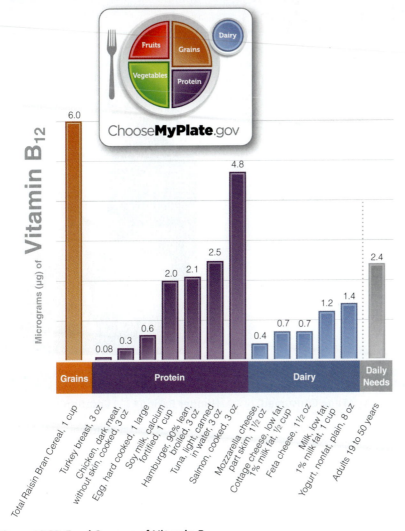

Vitamin B$_{12}$ is naturally found in animal products, but strict vegetarians can meet their daily needs by consuming fortified products, such as soy milk.

▲ Figure 10.30 Food Sources of Vitamin B$_{12}$

Food Sources of Vitamin B$_{12}$

Naturally occurring vitamin B$_{12}$ is found only in foods from animal sources, such as meat, fish, poultry, and dairy products. A varied diet that includes the minimum recommended servings of these food groups will easily meet daily needs (see **Figure 10.30**).

Using a microwave to cook vitamin B$_{12}$–rich foods may convert the active form of vitamin B$_{12}$ in the food to an inactive form, thus reducing the amount of the active vitamin by as much as 30 to 40 percent.[42] It appears that vitamin B$_{12}$ is the one exception when it comes to using a microwave to retain vitamins.

Synthetic vitamin B$_{12}$ is found in fortified soy milk and some ready-to-eat cereals, which are ideal sources for older adults and strict vegetarians who avoid all animal foods.

Vitamin B$_{12}$ Toxicity and Deficiency

At present, there are no known risks of consuming too much vitamin B$_{12}$ from foods, fortified foods, or supplements, and no upper level has been set. This may be due to reduced absorption of the vitamin at higher intakes. For healthy individuals, there is no known benefit from taking B$_{12}$ supplements if the diet provides adequate amounts of the vitamin.

Vitamin B$_{12}$ deficiency results from either a lack of intake, such as following a vegan diet without vitamin B$_{12}$ supplements, or malabsorption due to a lack of adequate HCl to begin breaking apart the vitamin B$_{12}$–protein complex in the stomach, insufficient intrinsic factor, or insufficient pancreatic enzymes to hydrolyze the B$_{12}$–R protein complex in the small intestine. Gastric bypass surgery, in which much of the stomach and duodenum are bypassed, limits the breakdown of vitamin B$_{12}$ and binding with intrinsic factor reducing the ability to absorb sufficient vitamin B$_{12}$.

The result of an inability to absorb vitamin B$_{12}$ causes **pernicious anemia** (*pernicious* = harmful). This form of anemia is due to a lack of sufficient intrinsic factor often caused by either gastritis or an autoimmune reaction in

pernicious anemia A form of anemia caused by a lack of intrinsic factor needed for absorption of vitamin B$_{12}$, forming large, immature red blood cells.

continued

Nutrition in Practice: Leland

Leland Yang has been a vegan for about 20 years. He feels that he has done a terrific job of sticking to his diet even though he travels monthly to corporate meetings across the United States. Lately, he has noticed a tingling in his legs. In fact, sometimes it feels as though his toes "fall asleep" as they became numb. Leland went to his doctor and described his symptoms. A tad perplexed, the doctor ordered blood tests for Leland and discovered that he is deficient in vitamin B$_{12}$, which is essential for a healthy nervous system. The doctor suggested that he speak with a dietitian.

Leland's Stats:

☐ Age: 52
☐ Height: 5 feet 10 inches
☐ Weight: 150 pounds

Leland's Food Log

Food/Beverage	Time Consumed	Hunger Rating*	Location
Whole-wheat bread with peanut butter, orange juice	6 AM	5	Kitchen
Handful of almonds	10 AM	3	Office
Hummus in a whole-wheat pita stuffed with lettuce and tomato, banana, soy yogurt, green tea	12:30 PM	5	Lunch room
Trail mix	3 PM	3	Office
Tofu stir-fry on brown rice, dinner roll with margarine, lemon sorbet, water	6:30 PM	4	In dining hall

*Hunger Rating (1–5): 1 = not hungry; 5 = super hungry.

Critical Thinking Questions

1. Why would a deficiency in vitamin B$_{12}$ cause Leland's symptoms?
2. Based on his food record, why do you think Leland is deficient in this specific vitamin?
3. What foods would Leland have to add to his diet to meet his daily need of this vitamin?

Dietitian's Observation and Plan for Leland:

☐ Discussed the need to add a synthetic source of vitamin B$_{12}$ to his diet in order to meet his daily needs as a vegan and because he is over the age of 50.
☐ Advised adding a serving of a whole-grain cereal that is fortified with 100% of the daily value for vitamin B$_{12}$, either at breakfast or as a snack along with his afternoon trail mix snack.
☐ Suggested taking a vitamin B$_{12}$ supplement.

Two weeks later, Leland returned for a follow-up visit with the dietitian. He is having difficulty obtaining a vitamin B$_{12}$–fortified cereal at hotels when he travels. The dietitian recommended that he take a vitamin B$_{12}$ supplement to make sure that he would be able to meet his vitamin B$_{12}$ need daily, as well as continue with a healthy, well-balanced diet.

which the body's immune system attacks the parietal cells.[43] Not surprisingly, pernicious anemia occurs in about 10 percent of individuals over the age of 60.[44] Regular injections of vitamin B₁₂ delivers the vitamin directly into the muscle and blood, bypassing the intestine.

The initial symptoms of pernicious anemia are the same as those seen in macrocytic anemia: fatigue and shortness of breath. Both forms of anemia due to a vitamin B₁₂ deficiency are characterized by immature and larger than normal red blood cells (macrocytic). Macrocytic anemia is also found with a deficiency of folate, as described earlier in the chapter. In the case of a vitamin B₁₂ deficiency, there is enough folate available for red blood cells to divide, but the folate is trapped as 5-methyl THF and can't be used properly and DNA synthesis slows down. In fact, in most cases of macrocytic anemia, the true cause is more likely a B₁₂ deficiency than a folate deficiency. If folate supplements are given, rather than vitamin B₁₂ supplements, the anemia may

clear up but the overabundance of folate masks the B₁₂ deficiency and allows other B₁₂ deficiency problems to continue. This delays a proper diagnosis and corrective therapy with vitamin B₁₂.

Because vitamin B₁₂ is also needed to protect nerve cells, including those in the brain and spine, one long-term consequence of a vitamin B₁₂ deficiency is

TABLE TIPS

Bolster Vitamin B₁₂

Enjoy heart-healthy fish at least twice a week.

Sprinkle steamed vegetables with reduced-fat shredded cheese.

Drink milk or fortified soy milk.

Try a cottage cheese-and-fruit snack in the afternoon.

Enjoy a grilled chicken breast on a bun for lunch.

nerve damage, indicated by tingling and numbness in the arms and legs and problems walking. If diagnosed early enough, these symptoms can be reversed with treatments of vitamin B₁₂. If the diagnosis is delayed, more dangerous, crippling, and irreversible nerve damage can occur.

Review the case of Leland, who was diagnosed with a vitamin B₁₂ deficiency, in the Nutrition in Practice feature on page 386.

LO 10.9: THE TAKE-HOME MESSAGE
Vitamin B₁₂, found only in animal products, fortified foods, and supplements, activates folate, maintains healthy red blood cells and the myelin sheath that surrounds nerves, and stimulates osteoblast activity. Adults need 2.4 micrograms of vitamin B₁₂ per day. There is no known toxicity of vitamin B₁₂ but a deficiency causes pernicious and macrocytic anemia, and nerve damage.

Exploring **Vitamin C**

LO 10.10 Describe the functions, recommended intakes, food sources, and the toxicity and deficiency effects of vitamin C.

What Is Vitamin C?

Vitamin C, also known as **ascorbic acid,** is probably more widely known to the public than any other vitamin. Whereas almost all other mammals can synthesize vitamin C, humans lack the necessary enzyme to convert glucose to vitamin C in the cells, and must rely on food to meet their daily needs.[45] The structure of vitamin C is similar to glucose in that it's a six-carbon molecule (**Figure 10.31**).

Vitamin C is absorbed all along the small intestine, mostly by active transport. Higher intakes are absorbed by simple diffusion in the stomach and small

intestine. As the intake of vitamin C increases, the amount absorbed decreases. In fact, the intestine absorbs less than 50 percent of vitamin C when the intake is one gram or greater, whereas almost

Ascorbic acid

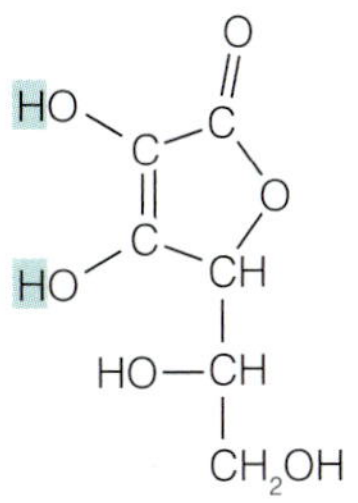

▲ **Figure 10.31 The Structure of Ascorbic Acid**
The hydrogen atoms of ascorbic acid are easily donated to free radicals.

98 percent is absorbed from intakes of less than 20 milligrams. Additionally, more vitamin C is excreted through the kidneys when intake is high.

Once absorbed into the portal vein, vitamin C is transported to the liver. The cells take up vitamin C assisted by glucose transport proteins. Vitamin C is not stored.

Metabolic Functions of Vitamin C

Vitamin C plays a complex role in most of the biological systems in the body. For instance, vitamin C is necessary for the synthesis of collagen and tyrosine. It also participates in neurotransmitter synthesis, as an antioxidant, and in the absorption of

ascorbic acid

iron. It differs from the B vitamins in that it does not act as a coenzyme; however, vitamin C does assist as a cofactor for enzymes in some reactions.

Vitamin C and Collagen Synthesis

Vitamin C participates in a number of hydroxylation reactions (adding OH groups). In particular, vitamin C enables hydroxylation reactions to make the fibrous protein **collagen,** the most abundant protein in the body. Collagen formation happens in several steps. First the three strands of collagen that contain the amino acids glycine and proline are assembled and twisted together to form a ropelike structure called *procollagen.* The rope is formed when hydroxyl groups are substituted for a hydrogen ion in the proline, forming hydroxyproline. Next, hydroxyl groups are substituted for the hydrogen ion in each lysine, forming hydroxylysine. The hydroxylation reaction is catalyzed by an iron-containing enzyme that must first be activated (**Figure 10.32**). Recall that enzymes must be restored or activated after they participate in a chemical reaction. In this case, the iron cofactor form of the enzyme that hydroxylates collagen must be reduced to

reactivate the enzyme. Vitamin C acts as the reducing agent, changing the iron (Fe^{+3}) cofactor back to its reduced form (Fe^{+2}). By donating the hydrogen to the inactive iron-enzyme complex, vitamin C is destroyed and can't be reused in the next reaction. Because collagen gives strength to connective tissue and acts as a glue that keeps cells together (including in the skin, bones, teeth, cartilage, tendons, and blood vessels),[46] a vitamin C–deficient diet affects the entire body.

Vitamin C as an Antioxidant

Like beta-carotene and vitamin E, vitamin C acts as an antioxidant that may help reduce the risk of chronic diseases such as heart disease and cancer. As you learned in Chapter 9, a free radical contains an unpaired electron. If the molecule is *oxidized* it has a positive charge when electrons are removed; a *reduced* molecule has a negative charge from an abundance of electrons. Vitamin C can donate or accept electrons to balance a free radical or change the charge in oxidation-reduction reactions.[47]

Vitamin C and Iron Absorption

Vitamin C enhances the absorption of nonheme iron. Plants and iron-fortified foods contain nonheme iron only, while meats, poultry, and fish contain both heme (found in red blood cells) and nonheme iron. When individuals consume vitamin C with foods that contain nonheme iron, it acts as a reducing agent, which improves the absorption of that form of iron.[48] This is also true for other minerals such as copper and chromium.

Vitamin C and the Immune System

Vitamin C helps maintain a healthy immune system by enabling the body to make white blood cells, like the ones shown in the photo. These blood cells fight infections, and this immune-boosting role has fostered the belief that high doses of vitamin C can cure the common cold. Examining the Evidence: Does Vitamin C Prevent the Common Cold? on page 390 takes a look at this theory.

Vitamin C and Stress

Vitamin C may reduce the body's response to stress, although the mechanism is unclear. When the body responds to a stressful situation, the

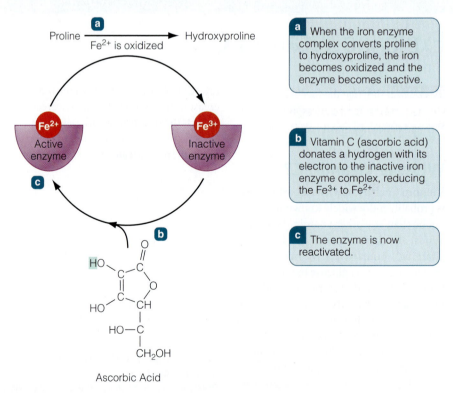

a When the iron enzyme complex converts proline to hydroxyproline, the iron becomes oxidized and the enzyme becomes inactive.

b Vitamin C (ascorbic acid) donates a hydrogen with its electron to the inactive iron enzyme complex, reducing the Fe^{3+} to Fe^{2+}.

c The enzyme is now reactivated.

Ascorbic Acid

collagen A protein found in connective tissue, including bones, teeth, skin, cartilage, and tendons.

▲ Figure 10.32 **The Role of Vitamin C in Collagen Formation**

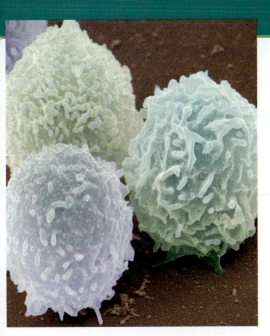

White blood cells

hypothalamus begins a cascade of reactions, starting with stimulating the pituitary gland to secrete stress hormones. In turn, the pituitary hormones direct the adrenal glands to synthesize and secrete cortisol into the blood. The cells of the adrenal glands contain high levels of vitamin C, which is released after cortisol during a response to stress.[49] The relationship between the stress response and vitamin C has prompted researchers to study the possibility of a link in humans, despite a lack of direct evidence for such a link.

Other Functions of Vitamin C

Vitamin C also participates in other important reactions in the body. Vitamin C donates an electron in the conversion of tryptophan and tyrosine to two neurotransmitters, serotonin and norepinephrine. Vitamin C is also essential in the synthesis of thyroxine (the hormone produced by the thyroid gland), converts cholesterol to bile, and helps break down histamine, the component behind the inflammation seen in many allergic reactions.[50]

Daily Needs for Vitamin C

Women need to consume 75 milligrams of vitamin C daily, and men need to consume 90 milligrams daily to meet their needs. Smoking accelerates the breakdown and elimination of vitamin C from the body, so all individuals who smoke need to consume an additional

35 milligrams of vitamin C every day to make up for these losses.[51]

Food Sources of Vitamin C

Americans meet about 90 percent of their vitamin C needs by consuming fruits and vegetables, with orange juice and grapefruit juice being the most popular sources in the diet. One serving of either juice just about meets an

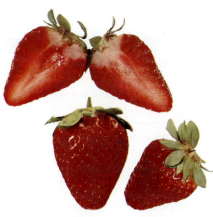

adult's daily needs. Tomatoes, peppers, potatoes, broccoli, oranges, and cantaloupe are also excellent sources (see **Figure 10.33**). Meats, dairy, grains, and legumes are considered poor sources of the vitamin.

Vitamin C Toxicity and Deficiency

Although excessive amounts of vitamin C aren't known to be toxic, consuming over 3,000 milligrams daily through the use of supplements has been shown to cause nausea, stomach cramps, and diarrhea. The upper level for vitamin C for adults is set at 2,000 milligrams. Too much vitamin C can also lead to the formation of kidney stones in individuals with a history of kidney disease or gout. In addition, vitamin C supplementation can result in false positives or false negatives in some medical tests.

Because vitamin C helps to absorb the form of iron found in plant foods, those with a rare disorder called

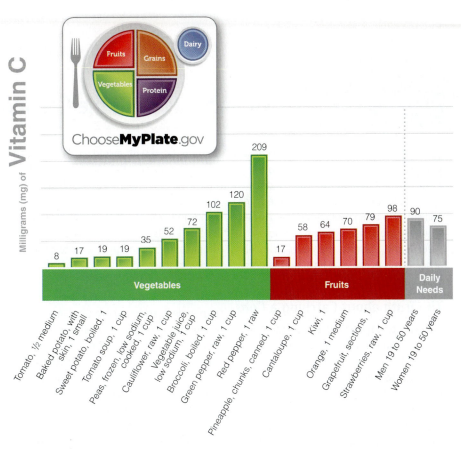

▲ **Figure 10.33 Foods Sources of Vitamin C**

continued

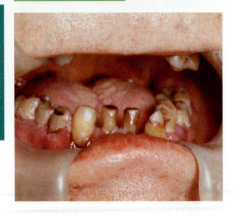

▲ **Figure 10.34 Gum Disease Can Result from Scurvy**

hemochromatosis, which causes the body to store too much iron, should avoid excessive amounts of vitamin C. Iron toxicity is extremely dangerous and can damage many organs, including the liver and heart.

hemochromatosis A blood disorder characterized by the retention of an excessive amount of iron.

scurvy A disease caused by a deficiency of vitamin C and characterized by bleeding gums and a skin rash.

For centuries, **scurvy,** the disease of vitamin C deficiency, was the affliction of sailors on long voyages. Without access to vitamin C–rich produce, sailors would develop the telltale symptoms: swollen and bleeding gums (**Figure 10.34**), a rough rash on the skin, coiled or curly arm hairs, and wounds that wouldn't heal. Most of these symptoms are related to vitamin C's role in collagen production.

TABLE TIPS

Juicy Ways to Get Vitamin C

Have at least one citrus fruit (such as an orange or grapefruit) daily.

Put sliced tomatoes on sandwiches.

Enjoy a fruit cup for dessert.

Drink low-sodium vegetable juice for an afternoon refresher.

Add strawberries to low-fat frozen yogurt.

Although rare, scurvy in the twenty-first century is associated with poverty, especially in young children.[52] Adult males are more susceptible than adult females, possibly due to lack of knowledge, lower intakes of fruits and vegetables, poor access to groceries, reclusiveness, or alcoholism.[53] Scurvy can be prevented by as little as 10 milligrams of vitamin C per day, or the amount found in a slice of a fresh orange.

LO 10.10: THE TAKE-HOME MESSAGE
Vitamin C, found in a variety of fruits and vegetables, assists in the formation of collagen, acts as an antioxidant, supports the immune system, and improves the absorption of non-heme iron. The RDA for vitamin C is 75 mg for women and 90 mg for men per day. Excessive amounts of vitamin C from supplements can cause intestinal discomfort. A deficiency of vitamin C results in scurvy.

EXAMINING THE EVIDENCE

Does Vitamin C Prevent the Common Cold?

More than 200 viruses can cause the common cold, and colds are the leading cause of doctor visits in the United States. Americans will suffer a billion colds this year alone.[1] Symptoms often last for up to two weeks, and students miss over 22 million school days every year battling the common cold.[2]

The Truth about Catching a Cold

Contrary to popular belief, you can't catch a cold from being outside without a coat or hat on a cold day. Rather, the only way to catch a cold is to come into contact with a cold virus. Contact can be direct, such as by hugging or shaking hands with someone who is carrying the virus, or indirect, such as by touching an object like a keyboard or telephone

contaminated with a cold virus. After you touch a contaminated object, the next time you touch your nose or rub your eyes, you transfer these germs from your hands into your body. You can also catch a cold virus by inhaling virus-carrying droplets from a cough or sneeze of someone with the cold.

The increased frequency of colds during the fall and winter is likely due to people spending more time indoors in the close quarters of classrooms, dorm rooms, and the workplace, which makes the sharing of germs easier. The low humidity of the winter air can also cause mucous membranes to be drier and more permeable to the invasion of these viruses. In addition, the most common cold viruses survive longer when the weather is colder and the humidity is low.

Vitamin C and the Common Cold

In the 1970s, a scientist named Linus Pauling theorized that consuming at least 1,000 milligrams of vitamin C daily would prevent the common cold.[3] Since that initial theory was published, there have been a number of double-blind studies to test whether vitamin C prevents the common cold or can be an effective treatment to reduce the duration and severity of the cold once the cold is contracted. A meta-analysis reported that supplementing with vitamin C did not affect the incidence of the common cold.[4] The same study did note that vitamin C supplements did reduce the duration of the cold. In special circumstances, such as marathon athletes using vitamin C prior to extreme exercise[5] or in people with other illnesses,[6] vitamin C supplementation may have some benefit in preventing upper respiratory infections, especially for people who have a low intake of dietary vitamin C or are under severe acute stress.

Other Cold Remedies: The Jury Is Still Out

Recently, other dietary substances, such as the herb echinacea and the mineral zinc, have emerged as popular treatment strategies for the common cold. Recent studies have shown that echinacea comes up short in preventing or affecting the duration or severity of a cold and may contribute to side effects such as a rash and intestinal discomfort.[7] The results of a recent review of studies testing echinacea found no benefit of using echinacea to either prevent or cure the common cold.[8]

Studies of zinc have also had mixed results. In a randomized, double-blind, placebo-controlled study, individuals who received 13 milligrams of zinc gluconate in lozenge form had fewer days of cold symptoms than the placebo group.[9] Similar results have been reported with zinc acetate.[10] A recent review reported that zinc lozenges, not pills or syrup, taken within 24 hours of the first sign of a cold, reduced the duration of the cold in otherwise healthy people.[11] Caution should be exercised, however, because chronic intake of zinc supplements can actually suppress the immune system.[12] We cover

zinc and its role in the immune system in the chapter on trace minerals.

What You Can Do

One of the best ways to reduce your chances of catching a cold is to wash your hands frequently with soap and water. This lowers the likelihood of transmitting germs from hands to mouth, nose, or eyes. One study found that children who washed their hands four times a day had over 20 percent fewer sick days from school than those who washed their hands less frequently.[13] When soap and water aren't available, gel sanitizers or disposable alcohol-containing hand wipes can be an effective alternative.[14] Covering the mouth and nose during coughing or sneezing and then immediately washing the hands helps prevent the spread of germs to other people and objects.

The Centers for Disease Control recommends the following steps to take if you do get a cold:[15]

- Get plenty of rest.
- Drink plenty of fluids. (Chicken soup and juices are considered fluids.)
- Gargle with warm salt water or use throat lozenges for a sore throat.
- Dab petroleum jelly on a raw nose to relieve irritation.
- Take aspirin* or acetaminophen (Tylenol) for headache or fever.

References

1. National Institute of Allergy and Infectious Diseases, National Institutes of Health. 2011. *The Common Cold.* Available at www.niaid.nih.gov. Accessed March 2014.
2. Centers for Disease Control. 2014. *Stopping Germs at Home, Work and School.* Available at www.cdc.gov. Accessed March 2014.
3. L. Pauling. 1971. "The Significance of the Evidence about Ascorbic Acid and the Common Cold." *Proceedings from the National Academy of Science* 68:2678–2681.
4. H. Hemilä and E. Chalker. 2013. "Vitamin C for Preventing and Treating the Common Cold." *Cochrane Database of Systematic Reviews* 1. Art. No.: CD000980. DOI: 10.1002/14651858.CD000980.pub4.
5. H. Hemilä. 2013. "Vitamin C May Alleviate Exercise-Induced Bronchoconstruction: A Meta-Analysis." *British Medical Journal* 3(6):e002416.
6. H. Hemliä. 2013. "Vitamin C and Common Cold-Induced Asthma: A Systematic Review and Statistical Analysis." *Allergy, Asthma, & Clinical Immunology* 9(1):46. doi: 10.1186/1710-1492-9-46.
7. R. B. Turner, R. Bauer, K. Woelkart, T. C. Haulsey, and D. Gangemie. 2005. "An Evaluation of *Echinacea angustifolia* in Experimental Rhinovirus Infections." *New England Journal of Medicine* 353:341–348.
8. M. Karsch-Volk, B. Barrett, D. Kiefer, R. Bauer, K. Ardjomand-Woelkart, and K. Linde. 2014. "Echinacea for Preventing and Treating the Common Cold." *Cochrane Database of Systematic Review* 2:CD000530.
9. S. B. Mossad, M. L. Macknin, S. V. Mendendorp, and P. Mason. 1996. "Zinc Gluconate Lozenges for Treating the Common Cold. A Randomized Double-Blind, Placebo-Controlled Study." *Annals of Internal Medicine* 125:81–88.
10. A. S. Prasad, F. W. Beck, B. Bao, D. Snell, and J. T. Fitzgerald. 2008. "Duration and Severity of Symptoms and Levels of Plasma Interleukin-1 Receptor Antagonist, Soluble Tumor Necrosis Factor Receptor, and Adhesion Molecules in Patients with Common Cold Treated with Zinc Acetate." *Journal of Infectious Disease* 197:795–802.
11. M. Singh and R. R. Das. 2013. "Zinc for the Common Cold." *Cochrane Database of Systematic Review* 6:CD001364.
12. Institute of Medicine. 2006. *Dietary Reference Intakes: The Essential Guide to Nutrient Requirements.* Washington, DC: The National Academies Press.
13. Education World. 2010. *School-Wide Handwashing Campaigns Cut Germs, Absenteeism.* Available at www.educationworld.com. Accessed March 2014.
14. National Institute of Allergy and Infectious Diseases, National Institutes of Health. 2011. *The Common Cold.*
15. Centers for Disease Control. 2014. *Stopping Germs at Home, Work and School.*

*The American Academy of Pediatrics recommends that children and teenagers avoid consuming aspirin or medicine containing aspirin when they have a viral illness, as it can lead to a rare but serious illness called Reye's syndrome which can cause brain damage or death.

What Are Other Vitamin-Like Compounds?

LO 10.11 Describe the functions of compounds that have vitamin-like biological roles but are not classified as vitamins.

Some compounds may not be classified as a vitamin by strict definition but are still essential to overall health. These compounds are often synthesized in adequate amounts in the body but may become essential in the diet under certain circumstances, such as during illness or chronic disease. The vitamin-like compounds include choline, carnitine, lipoic acid, and inositol.

Choline Helps Protect the Liver

Choline is a conditionally essential nutrient that the body needs for healthy cells and nerves. Choline is a nitrogen-containing compound that is often grouped with the family of B vitamins but by strict definition it is not classified as a vitamin. Although the body can synthesize choline from the amino acid methionine, it isn't able to synthesize enough of it to meet the body's needs.[54]

Choline serves a number of uses in the body. It is part of the phospholipid that makes up cell membranes; it functions in liver metabolism; it is a precursor for the neurotransmitter acetylcholine and thus participates in nerve transmission; it assists in the transport of lipids as part of the VLDL; and it plays a key role in fetal development.[55]

To be safe, the current recommendation of 425 milligrams for women and 550 milligrams for men is based on the amount of choline needed to guard against liver damage. Choline is so widely available in foods, especially milk, liver, eggs, and peanuts, that it is unlikely intake would ever fall short. However, too much choline from supplements can cause sweating and vomiting as well as hypotension (*hypo* = low), or low blood pressure and emit an unpleasant fishy odor as the body tries to get rid of the excess. The tolerable upper level (UL) of 3,500 milligrams for choline has been set to prevent blood pressure from dropping too low.

Carnitine, Lipoic Acid, and Inositol Are Needed for Overall Health

Carnitine, lipoic acid, and inositol, all vitamin-like substances, are needed for overall health and important body functions. Unlike choline, however, they are not essential nutrients because the body can synthesize them in adequate amounts without the need to consume them in foods. Deficiency symptoms are not known to occur in humans.

Carnitine (*carnus* = flesh), which is synthesized from the amino acids lysine and methionine, is needed to properly utilize fat. It is abundant in foods from animal sources, such as meat and dairy products. Although there is no research to support the claim, carnitine supplements are sometimes advertised to promote weight loss and help athletes improve their performance.[56]

Similar to many B vitamins, **lipoic acid** helps cells generate energy. In fact, when it was discovered, it was initially thought to be a vitamin.[57] The body synthesizes adequate amounts of lipoic acid from short-chain fatty acids and it is found in a variety of plant and animal foods. In addition to its role in energy metabolism, lipoic acid is also being studied for its potential role as an antioxidant that could help reduce the risk of certain chronic diseases, such as diabetes mellitus and cataracts.[58]

Lastly, **inositol** is needed to keep cell membranes healthy. As with the other important vitamin-like substances, healthy individuals can synthesize enough inositol

choline A vitamin-like substance that is a precursor for the neurotransmitter acetylcholine, which is essential for healthy nerves.

carnitine A vitamin-like substance used to transport fatty acids across the mitochondrial membrane to properly utilize fat.

lipoic acid A vitamin-like substance used in energy production; it may also act as an antioxidant.

inositol A water-soluble compound synthesized in the body that maintains healthy cell membranes.

from glucose or consume sufficient amounts in plant sources to meet their needs, so supplements are not necessary. Inositol can be ingested from plant sources, or synthesized from glucose.

> **LO 10.11: THE TAKE-HOME MESSAGE** Choline is an essential nutrient that is needed for the integrity of cell membranes, nerve transmission, lipid transport, and liver health. Carnitine, lipoic acid, and inositol are needed for important body functions and overall health, but are not essential nutrients because the body is able to synthesize them in sufficient amounts.

Health Connection

Do Vitamins and Antioxidants Reduce the Risk of Cancer?

LO 10.12 Explain the role that a healthy diet and lifestyle plays in cancer risk and progression.

The term **cancer** describes a group of more than 100 diseases characterized by uncontrolled growth and spread of abnormal cells.[59] The most common type for both men and women is lung cancer, with skin, breast, prostate, and colorectal cancers also occurring in large numbers. The types differ not only in where they occur in the body (see **Table 10.2**), but also in their causes, treatments, and prognoses. Carcinomas—cancers of epithelial cells that line the internal and external cavities of the body, including the glands—represent almost 80 to 90 percent of all cancers in adults. Sarcomas, or cancers of the

connective tissue, occur in bone and muscle. Lymphoma, including both Hodgkin's disease and non-Hodgkin's lymphoma, is the third most frequently diagnosed cancer in children. Leukemia differs from the other types of cancer in that it does not present as a tumor. It is an aggressive cancer of the white blood cells formed in the bone marrow.

Cancer is responsible for almost 25 percent of all deaths in the United States, making it the second leading cause of death, behind heart disease.[60] Even though the death rate from cancer has declined slightly since 2004, an estimated 580,350 Americans died of cancer in 2013, or 1,600 per day. About one-third of these cancer deaths in 2013 were related to overweight or obesity, physical inactivity, and poor diet.[61]

Carcinogenesis: The Cancer Process

Most cancers take years to develop, as abnormal cells need time to grow,

reproduce, and spread. The normal cell cycle is controlled by specific **protooncogenes,** which turn the cell replication cycle on and off, and suppressor genes, which stop any mutated cells from replicating. Cancer develops when a lack of control by these genes allows mutated cells to replicate, divide, and grow.

The process of cancer development, or **carcinogenesis,** generally occurs in three stages: initiation, promotion, and progression. Normally, cell damage is repaired before abnormal cells begin to accumulate or the cell dies before it proliferates, due to checkpoints along the various stages of cell division that help maintain the integrity of DNA. The initiation stage begins when a cell is exposed to a **carcinogen,** or cancer-causing agent, that damages the DNA (see **Figure 10.35**). **Cancer initiators** include a variety of environmental

cancer A general term for a large group of diseases characterized by uncontrolled growth and spread of abnormal cells.

protooncogenes Specialized genes that turn on and off cell division.

carcinogenesis The process of cancer development.

carcinogen Cancer-causing substance, including tobacco smoke, air and water pollution, ultraviolet radiation, and various chemicals.

cancer initiator A carcinogen that initiates the mutation in DNA; these mutations cause the cell to respond abnormally to physiological controls.

TABLE 10.2	Types of Cancer
Type of Cancer	**Description**
Carcinoma	Cancer of the epithelial cells; includes cancers of various glandular tissue, including breast, thyroid, and skin
Sarcoma	Cancer of connective tissue, such as bone or muscle
Leukemia	Cancer associated with the blood or blood-forming tissues
Lymphoma	Cancer of the lymph nodes or other lymph tissues

factors such as hormones, viruses, ultra-violet light, or smoke; or dietary factors such as alcohol, excess kilocalories, and excess dietary fat. This stage of cancer development is usually short lived because the damaged DNA is either repaired quickly or carcinogenesis progresses to the next stage, called cancer promotion.

Once the mutation is initiated, a **cancer promoter,** such as the hormone estrogen or alcohol, stimulates the damaged cells to divide and multiply in the promotion stage. As the mass of cells, or tumor, grows, it can disrupt surrounding tissues and even develop its own network of blood vessels to obtain nutrients.

Physical Activity, Obesity, and Cancer Risk

Maintaining a healthy weight throughout life may be one of the most important ways to protect against cancer. Among U.S. adults 50 years of age or older, it is estimated that twenty-five to thirty-three percent of all cancers are related to physical inactivity and obesity.[62] A healthy weight and physical activity reduce the risk of developing breast, colon, rectal, endometrial, esophageal, and kidney cancer.[63]

Routine physical activity reduces the risk of several types of cancer, in part by helping individuals maintain a healthy weight. The exercise does not have to be intense to be effective. In the California Teachers Study, women who participated in moderate exercise had a greater reduction in colon cancer risk than women who reported more strenuous physical activity.[64] The reason exercise reduces cancer risk is still not clear. However, the benefits may be due to a reduction in chronic inflammation, stimulating the immune system, or reducing obesity.[65]

cancer promoter A substance that induces a cell to divide and grow rapidly, and reduces the time that enzymes have to repair any damage or mutation; examples of cancer promoters are dietary fats, alcohol, and estrogen.

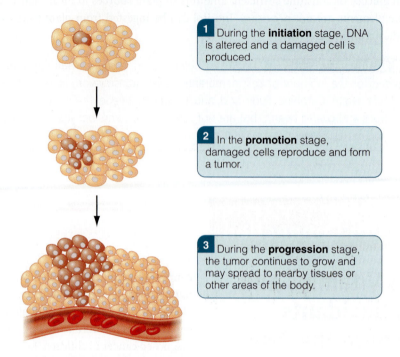

1 During the **initiation** stage, DNA is altered and a damaged cell is produced.

2 In the **promotion** stage, damaged cells reproduce and form a tumor.

3 During the **progression** stage, the tumor continues to grow and may spread to nearby tissues or other areas of the body.

▲ Figure 10.35 **The Stages of Carcinogenesis**

Overconsumption of energy-dense foods can increase risk of obesity and thus cancer risk. An energy-dense diet, especially one high in dietary fat, may contribute to obesity, especially in sedentary individuals. Dietary fat intake does not cause breast cancer, but weight gain later in life may.[66] Obesity increases the risk for thyroid, cervical, and prostate cancers.[67]

The Role of Diet in Cancer Risk and Progression

Dietary factors can influence the development of cancer cells at the initiation, promotion, and progression stages.

Foods That Can Lower Cancer Risk
Plant-based foods have a significant impact on reducing cancer risk.[68] Consumption of nonstarchy vegetables and fruits is associated with reductions

in lung, mouth and esophageal, stomach, and colon cancer.[69] Bladder cancer rates in men have been reduced with a higher intake of cruciferous vegetables, such as cauliflower, broccoli, and brussels sprouts; and eating more tomatoes may reduce the risk of developing prostate cancer.[70] These foods are high in phytochemicals, antioxidants, and dietary fiber, and low in energy density, all of which are likely to yield protective effects.

Some specific vitamins and minerals may help lower cancer risk. Retinoids (vitamin A), vitamin D, folate, and the mineral selenium help repair DNA in the initiation stage and can stop the development of cancer by inhibiting the progression of damaged cells (see **Figure 10.36**). Vitamins C and E and selenium may prevent cancer from spreading to nearby tissues. Omega-3

fatty acids may help to reduce cancer cell growth. Other nutrients, such as vitamin D, may inhibit the proliferation of cancer cells and stimulate cell differentiation.[71] This research is in the early stages, however, and no conclusive cause-and-effect evidence has been presented.

Waste products may contain cancer-promoting agents, and fiber helps dilute these waste products and quickly move them out of the body, reducing your exposure. Also, the healthy bacteria that live in the colon feast on the fiber, creating butyrate, a by-product that may also help in the fight against colorectal cancer. Fiber-containing fruits and vegetables are also low in kilocalories and high in bulk, so they improve satiety. Thus, a fiber-rich diet

can help individuals maintain a healthy body weight.

There is epidemiological evidence that some nutrients may retard the progress of cancer development, although the exact mechanism is still unknown.[72] These key nutrients, including the antioxidant vitamins A, C, and E, may protect DNA from the initial damage.

Foods That Can Raise Cancer Risk

Some foods may increase the risk of developing cancer. For example, red meat, especially when grilled, is associated with an increased risk of stomach, pancreatic, colon, and kidney cancer. When the saturated fat in meat hits a hot surface below the meat, such as a frying pan or charcoal grill, it forms benzopyrene, a probable carcinogen, which is absorbed back into the meat. Nitrates and nitrites, used as preservatives in processed meats, can be converted to another class of carcinogens known as nitrosamines. Evidence also suggests that excessive alcohol consumption increases liver, mouth, esophageal, breast, and colon cancer.[73]

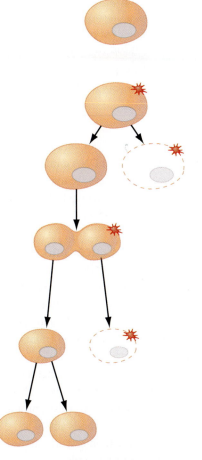

1. Hormones and growth factors stimulate the cell to grow. Nutrients are needed for parts of the cell to develop. Vitamin A can arrest the cell cycle at this time.

2. The cycle stops if DNA is damaged. The cell is either repaired or dies.

3. DNA is replicated. Folate is required at this step.

4. A second checkpoint stops the cell cycle if the DNA is damaged. The cell is either repaired or dies. DNA repair is stimulated by vitamin A, vitamin D, folate, and selenium.

5. A final checkpoint before the cell divides into two identical daughter cells ensures each daughter cell has the correct DNA.

▲ **Figure 10.36 Micronutrient Roles in Normal Cell Growth and Division**
Normally, damaged or mutated cells are repaired or die off to prevent them from producing more damaged cells. Various micronutrients are involved in different stages of the process.

TABLE 10.3	Recommendations for Reducing Cancer Risk
Recommendations	**Personal Health Goals**
Be as lean as possible within the normal range of body weight	■ Ensure that body weight through childhood and adolescent growth projects toward the lower end of the normal BMI range at age 21 ■ Maintain body weight within the normal range from age 21 ■ Avoid weight gain and increases in waist circumference throughout adulthood
Be physically active as part of everyday life	■ Be moderately physically active, equivalent to brisk walking, for at least 30 minutes every day ■ As fitness improves, aim for 60 minutes or more of moderate, or 30 minutes or more of vigorous, physical activity every day ■ Limit sedentary habits such as watching television
Limit consumption of energy-dense foods and avoid sugary drinks	■ Consume energy-dense foods sparingly ■ Avoid sugary drinks ■ Avoid fast foods, or consume only sparingly
Eat mostly foods of plant origin	■ Eat at least five portions/servings (at least 400 g or 14 oz) of a variety of fruits and nonstarchy vegetables every day ■ Eat relatively unprocessed cereals (grains) and/or legumes with every meal ■ Limit refined starch foods ■ People who consume starchy roots or tubers as staples need to also consume sufficient nonstarchy vegetables, fruits, and legumes
Limit intake of red meat and avoid processed meat	■ People who eat red meat should consume less than 500 g (18 oz) a week and avoid processed meats
Limit alcoholic drinks	■ If alcoholic drinks are consumed, limit consumption to no more than two drinks a day for men and one drink a day for women
Limit consumption of salt	■ Avoid salt-preserved, salted, or salty foods; preserve foods without using salt ■ Limit consumption of processed foods with added salt to ensure an intake of less than 6 g (2.4 g sodium) a day
Avoid moldy cereals (grains) or legumes	■ Do not eat moldy cereals (grains) or legumes
Aim to meet nutritional needs through diet alone	■ Dietary supplements are not recommended for cancer prevention

Dietary and Lifestyle Recommendations for Cancer Prevention

In 2007, a review of over 7,000 research studies and input from hundreds of scientists worldwide culminated in publication of a landmark report entitled *Food, Nutrition, Physical Activity, and the Prevention of Cancer: A Global Perspective.*[74] This report identified the nutritional and lifestyle factors that may modify the risk of developing cancer (see **Table 10.3**).

The best advice for reducing the risk of cancer is to consume a varied, healthy, plant-based diet, limit saturated fat and sugar intake, maintain a healthy weight, avoid tobacco, limit alcohol intake, and lead an active lifestyle. Because many cancers take years, if not decades, to develop after the initial DNA damage, the sooner healthy changes are made, the more likely they are to help individuals avoid cancer later in life.

The Future of Cancer and Nutrition Research

There are several promising areas of research that explore the relationship between nutrition and cancer. For example, consuming specific nutrients may turn on and off cancer genes[75] and promote healthy intestinal bacteria to favor a lower colon cancer risk.[76] The effects of new policies regarding promotion of energy-dense foods aimed at children, and fast-food restaurants, are also on the research agenda.

LO 10.12: THE TAKE-HOME MESSAGE
Cancer is a disease caused by the uncontrolled reproduction of damaged cells. Carcinogens, or cancer-causing substances, damage cells by altering their DNA. Genetic, environmental, and lifestyle factors all play a role in cancer risk, but lifestyle factors have the most influence. Dietary factors that reduce the risk for cancer include consumption of abundant amounts of fruits, vegetables, and whole grains; these provide antioxidants, phytochemicals, and fiber that may have a protective effect. Staying physically active and maintaining a healthy body weight are also key to reducing cancer risk.

Visual Chapter Summary

LO 10.1 Water-Soluble Vitamins Act as Coenzymes and Noncoenzymes in Metabolic Processes

Water-soluble vitamins are absorbed after hydrolysis releases them from protein complexes. When consumed in excess, most are excreted in the urine and not stored, with the exception of vitamin B_6 and vitamin B_{12}.

The B-complex vitamins thiamin, riboflavin, niacin, vitamin B_6, pantothenic acid, and biotin function as coenzymes in the conversion of carbohydrates, proteins, and fats to energy; in fatty acid, cholesterol, and protein synthesis; and in glycogenolysis and gluconeogenesis. Vitamins acting as coenzymes catalyze enzyme activity when they bind to the active site of an enzyme.

Folate and vitamin B_{12} form coenzymes that participate in the formation of red blood cells and in a lesser role in energy production. Vitamin C acts as an antioxidant to neutralize free radicals, and stimulates collagen synthesis.

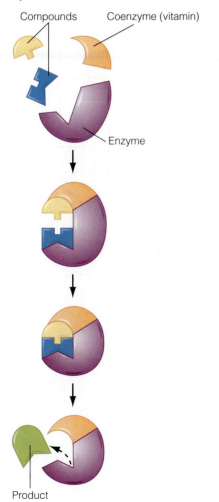

LO 10.2 Thiamin (B_1)

Thiamin in the active form of TPP functions in glycolysis and the TCA cycle. Thiamin also participates in nerve transmission. The best sources of thiamin are lean pork, enriched and whole-grain foods, ready-to-eat cereals, pasta, rice, and nuts. The thiamin RDA for adults is 1.1 milligrams for women and 1.2 milligrams for men. There are no known toxicity problems for thiamin. A deficiency of thiamin can result in beriberi. Chronic alcohol abuse can lead to an advanced form of thiamin deficiency called Wernicke-Korsakoff syndrome.

Thiamin pyrophosphate

Phosphate groups

LO 10.3 Riboflavin (B_2)

Riboflavin, or vitamin B_2, functions as two coenzymes, FMN and FAD, to transfer electrons in oxidation-reduction reactions. Riboflavin participates in the conversion of folate to its active form, vitamin B_6 to its coenzyme form, and the conversion of tryptophan to niacin. Milk and yogurt are the most popular sources of riboflavin. Nondairy foods including leafy green vegetables, eggs, and almonds are also good sources of riboflavin. Riboflavin is stable in cooking but is degraded in ultraviolet light. The riboflavin RDA for adults is 1.1 milligrams for women and 1.3 milligrams for men. Excess amounts are excreted in urine and there are no known toxicity symptoms. A deficiency in riboflavin results in ariboflavinosis.

FAD

$2H^+, 2e^-$

FADH$_2$

LO 10.4 Niacin (B₃)

Niacin, also called nicotinic acid and nicotin-amide, functions as the active coenzyme forms, nicotinamide adenine dinucleotide (NAD^+) and nicotinamide adenine dinucleotide phosphate ($NADP^+$). These two active coenzymes are involved in the catabolism of carbohydrates, fats, and proteins in energy metabolism, the synthesis of fats, maintenance of healthy skin, and promotion of a functional intestinal tract. Niacin is found in a variety of foods, including meat, fish, poultry, fortified cereals, and enriched breads. The niacin RDA for adults is 14 milligrams NE for women and 16 milligrams NE for men. There is no danger of consuming too much niacin, although overconsumption of niacin supplements can cause flushing. A deficiency of niacin results in pellagra.

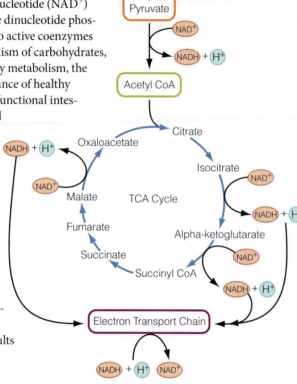

LO 10.6 Biotin

Biotin is a coenzyme for enzymes that add carbon dioxide to compounds during energy metabolism, and for enzymes that participate in lipogenesis, gluconeogenesis, and the metabolism of amino acids. Biotin also plays a role in DNA replication and transcription, and the transcription of genes. The adequate intake (AI) of biotin for both adult males and females is 30 micrograms. Biotin is found in peanuts, yeast, egg yolks, grains, fish, and liver. There is little evidence that excess biotin causes toxicity. Deficiencies of biotin are rare except when large amounts of raw eggs or egg whites are consumed. Avidin in raw egg whites binds biotin in the intestinal tract and prevents biotin from being absorbed. Some humans have a rare genetic disorder in which they lack the enzyme biotinidase, which breaks biotin away from protein in foods during digestion.

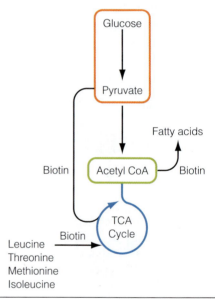

LO 10.5 Pantothenic Acid

Pantothenic acid makes up part of the molecule *coenzyme A* and participates in lipogenesis and beta-oxidation, in the conversion of pyruvate to acetyl CoA, and in converting some amino acids to substrates in the TCA cycle. The adequate intake (AI) of pantothenic acid for both adult males and adult females is set at 5 milligrams. Pantothenic acid is found in a number of foods, including whole-grain cereals, nuts and legumes, milk, meat, and eggs. There are no known adverse affects from consuming too much pantothenic acid and deficiencies are rare.

Pantothenic acid

Is a component of

Coenzyme A

Adenine

Lo 10.7 Vitamin B₆

Vitamin B₆, also known as pyridoxine, pyridoxal, and pyridoxamine, acts as a coenzyme for over 100 enzymes involved in protein metabolism, and red blood cell synthesis. Vitamin B₆ is also a key player in glycogenolysis and red blood cell synthesis, and interacts with other nutrients including riboflavin, niacin, and zinc. The active form of vitamin B₆ is pyridoxal phosphate (PLP). Vitamin B₆ is found in meat, fish, poultry, legumes, bananas, and fortified cereals. Adult women need 1.3 to 1.5 milligrams and adult men need 1.3 to 1.7 milligrams of B₆, depending on their age. In high supplement doses, PLP may cause neurological damage. The upper limit for adults is set at 100 milligrams per day. A deficiency of vitamin B₆ can result in microcytic hypochromic anemia, depression, and inflammation of the skin. Drinking too much alcohol can deplete the body of vitamin B₆.

Pyruvate   Glutamate   PLP   Alanine   α-ketoglutarate

Transamination

Lo 10.8 Folate

Folate is naturally found in foods, but is more easily absorbed as the synthetic form, folic acid, found mostly in fortified foods and supplements. The active form of folate is called tetrahydrofolate, or THF. Its role in metabolism is transferring single-carbon compounds, such as a methyl group, to other compounds. This function of folate is critical to DNA and amino acid synthesis, and cell division. Folate may also prevent some cancers, including colon cancer, by repairing DNA. Folate is found in fortified foods, leafy green vegetables, enriched pasta, rice, breads, and cereals. Adults should consume 400 micrograms DFE of folate daily. Consuming too much folate can obscure a vitamin B₁₂ deficiency. A deficiency of folate results in macrocytic anemia. Babies born to mothers who are deficient in folate have a higher risk of neural tube defects such as spina bifida.

Tetrahydrofolate

Lo 10.9 Vitamin B₁₂

Vitamin B₁₂ is a family of compounds also referred to as cobalamin. To be absorbed, vitamin B₁₂ requires the aid of R protein from the salivary glands and intrinsic factor from the parietal cells. It is transported through the blood attached to a protein carrier called transcobalamin. Vitamin B₁₂ functions as two different coenzymes involved in DNA and RNA synthesis, the conversion of homocysteine to methionine, and in utilizing fats and proteins for energy. Vitamin B₁₂ also activates folate by removing the methyl group from folate, which in turn activates vitamin B₁₂. Vitamin B₁₂ is found naturally in animal foods and the synthetic form is used in fortified soy milk and some cereals. Adults need 2.4 micrograms daily. There are no known toxicity risks of consuming too much vitamin B₁₂. A deficiency of vitamin B₁₂ causes pernicious anemia and macrocytic anemia. A prolonged vitamin B₁₂ deficiency can cause nerve damage.

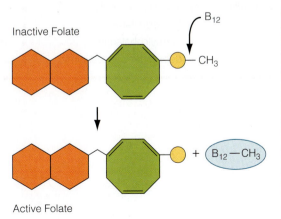

Inactive Folate

B₁₂

— CH₃

Active Folate

+ B₁₂—CH₃

Lo 10.10 Vitamin C

Vitamin C, also known as ascorbic acid, assists in the formation of collagen necessary for healthy bones, teeth, skin, and blood vessels. As an antioxidant, vitamin C reduces free radical damage and supports a healthy immune system. Vitamin C also improves the absorption of nonheme iron. Vitamin C is found in a wide variety of fruits and vegetables, including citrus fruits, tomatoes, potatoes, and broccoli. Adult women should ingest 75 milligrams and adult men need 90 milligrams of vitamin C daily. Smokers need to increase the daily intake by 35 mg. The tolerable upper limit is set at 2,000 milligrams per day. Vitamin C doesn't prevent the common cold but may reduce the duration of a cold in some people. A deficiency of vitamin C results in scurvy.

Ascorbic acid

LO 10.11 Other Vitamin-Like Compounds Are Not Essential

Choline is a conditionally essential nutrient that the body needs for healthy cells and nerves. Carnitine, lipoic acid, and inositol are vitamin-like compounds that are used for important body functions and overall health. They are not considered essential because they can be synthesized in sufficient amounts in the body.

LO 10.12 A Healthy Diet and Lifestyle May Reduce Cancer Risk

Cancer, the second leading cause of death in the United States, is a disease of uncontrolled abnormal cell reproduction. Cancer goes through three stages: initiation, promotion, and progression. Carcinogens, or cancer-causing substances, damage cells by altering their DNA. Genetic, environmental, and lifestyle factors all play a role in cancer risk, but lifestyle factors, including diet, have the most influence. Plant-based foods high in vitamin A, vitamin D, vitamin E, vitamin C, and folate reduce the risk of cancer, while red meat, especially when grilled or fried, can increase risk. Eating a varied, plant-based diet that limits saturated fat and sugar intake, avoiding tobacco, limiting alcohol intake, keeping physically active, and maintaining a healthy body weight may protect against cancer.

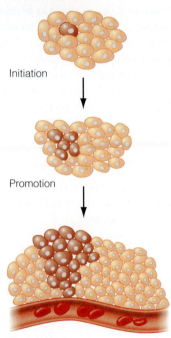

Initiation

Promotion

Progression

Terms to Know

- coenzymes
- hemopoiesis
- thiamin pyrophosphate (TPP)
- beriberi
- peripheral neuropathy
- flavin mononucleotide (FMN)
- flavin adenine dinucleotide (FAD)
- oxidation reaction
- reduction reaction
- ariboflavinosis
- stomatitis
- glossitis
- cheilosis
- nicotinic acid

- nicotinamide
- nicotinamide adenine dinucleotide (NAD$^+$)
- nicotinamide adenine dinucleotide phosphate (NADP$^+$)
- niacin equivalents (NE)
- pellagra
- avidin
- biotinidase
- pyridoxine
- pyridoxal
- pyridoxamine
- pyridoxal phosphate (PLP)
- microcytic hypochromic anemia
- folic acid

- polyglutamate
- monoglutamate
- 5-methyltetrahydrofolate (5-methyl THF)
- neural tube defects
- anencephaly
- spinal bifida
- dietary folate equivalents (DFE)
- megaloblasts
- macrocytes
- macrocytic anemia
- cobalamin
- R protein
- intrinsic factor (IF)
- transcobalamin
- methylcobalamin
- deoxyadenosylcobalamin

- myelin sheath
- atrophic gastritis
- pernicious anemia
- ascorbic acid
- collagen
- hemochromatosis
- scurvy
- choline
- carnitine
- lipoic acid
- inositol
- cancer
- protooncogenes
- carcinogenesis
- carcinogen
- cancer initiator
- cancer promoter

Check Your Understanding

1. The primary function of the B-complex vitamins is
   a. as a source of energy.
   b. as a coenzyme.
   c. as an antioxidant.
   d. to synthesize DNA.
2. The coenzyme that functions in the transfer of hydrogen atoms is
   a. pantothenic acid.
   b. vitamin B_6.
   c. riboflavin.
   d. biotin.
3. A deficiency of thiamin can cause
   a. rickets.
   b. beriberi.
   c. scurvy.
   d. osteomalacia.
4. Folic acid can reduce the risk of
   a. acne.
   b. neural tube defects.
   c. night blindness.
   d. pellagra.
5. The vitamin that is part of the structure of acetyl CoA is
   a. biotin.
   b. thiamin.
   c. pantothenic acid.
   d. niacin.
6. The body requires more of this water-soluble vitamin than any other.
   a. vitamin B_6
   b. niacin
   c. riboflavin
   d. vitamin B_{12}
7. The vitamin involved as a coenzyme in more than 100 enzymes, most of which are amino acid reactions, is
   a. riboflavin.
   b. pantothenic acid.
   c. vitamin B_6.
   d. biotin.
8. Vitamin B_{12} is essential for the health and function of
   a. nerve cells.
   b. epithelial cells.
   c. eye tissue.
   d. collagen.
9. A lack of intrinsic factor is associated with
   a. pernicious anemia.
   b. spina bifida.
   c. neural tube defects.
   d. microcytic hypochromic anemia.
10. You are enjoying a breakfast of raisin bran cereal in skim milk accompanied by a glass of orange juice. The vitamin C in the orange juice will enhance the absorption of
    a. the calcium in the milk.
    b. the vitamin D in fortified milk.
    c. the iron in the cereal.
    d. the fiber in the cereal.

Answers

1. (b) The primary function of the B-complex vitamins is to activate enzymes involved in a variety of chemical reactions. B-complex vitamins are not a source of energy but do act as coenzymes in energy metabolism. Unlike vitamin C, the B-complex vitamins are not antioxidants. Even though some of the B-complex vitamins are involved in DNA synthesis, it is not their primary function.
2. (c) Riboflavin, in the form of FAD and FMN, transfers hydrogen atoms during energy metabolism. Pantothenic acid is part of coenzyme A, which forms acetyl CoA; vitamin B_6 is a coenzyme for protein metabolism; and biotin is a coenzyme for carboxylase enzymes.
3. (b) A thiamin deficiency results in beriberi. Rickets and osteomalacia are caused by a lack of vitamin D and scurvy results from a vitamin C deficiency.
4. (b) Folic acid reduces the risk of birth defects such as neural tube defects. Vitamin A can reduce acne and night blindness, while niacin can prevent pellagra.
5. (c) Pantothenic acid is part of coenzyme A, which forms acetyl CoA. Biotin, thiamin, and niacin all function as coenzymes.
6. (b) The dietary requirement for niacin is 16 milligrams per day for males and 14 milligrams for females, compared with 1.3 milligrams of vitamin B_6 for males and females, 1.3 milligrams or 1.1 milligrams of riboflavin for males or females, respectively, and 2.4 micrograms per day of vitamin B_{12} for both genders.
7. (c) Vitamin B_6 activates more than 100 enzymes involved in protein metabolism. Riboflavin, pantothenic acid, and biotin are all involved in energy metabolism.
8. (a) Vitamin B_{12} is essential for the health and function of nerve cells. Vitamin A is essential for epithelial cells and eye tissue. Vitamin C participates in collagen formation.
9. (a) A lack of intrinsic factor causes the malabsorption of vitamin B_{12}, which results in pernicious anemia. Spina bifida and neural tube defects are the result of a folate deficiency. Microcytic hypochromic anemia is caused by a deficiency of vitamin B_6.
10. (c) Vitamin C will increase the absorption of iron in grain products and cereals but does not affect the absorption of calcium, vitamin D, or fiber.

Answers to True or False?

1. **False.** Some water-soluble vitamins, such as vitamin C and folate, are easily destroyed by heat while niacin and vitamin B_6, are stable in cooking. However, all water-soluble vitamins leach into water, so drier cooking methods help retain more of these vitamins.
2. **False.** Biotin and pantothenic acid are both B vitamins involved in energy production, not forms of vitamin C.
3. **False.** Vitamins do not provide energy. However, the B-complex vitamins are essential to energy production in that they are involved in numerous metabolic processes.

4. **False.** Niacin can be made from excess tryptophan, but the amount of niacin synthesized is insufficient to meet the body's needs.

5. **True.** Very large doses of vitamin B_6 (from as low as 500 milligrams) can cause sensory neuropathy, which causes pain, numbness, and tingling in the feet and hands.

6. **True.** Older adults may produce less hydrochloric acid and intrinsic factor than younger adults, which can hinder their ability to absorb adequate amounts of vitamin B_{12}.

7. **True.** Adequate folate intake before and during the early months of pregnancy can lower the risk of neural tube defects, including spina bifida and anencephaly.

8. **False.** A dietary deficiency of pantothenic acid is rare because this B vitamin is widespread throughout the food supply. Excellent sources include chicken, beef, egg yolk, and vegetables such as broccoli, tomatoes, and mushrooms.

9. **True.** The protein avidin, found in egg whites, can bind biotin and prevent it from being absorbed. Cooking the egg denatures the avidin and prevents this problem.

10. **False.** There is no clear evidence that vitamin C supplements prevent the common cold, though they may reduce the severity of cold symptoms in some people.

Web Resources

- To learn more about vitamin and mineral supplements, visit http://ods .od.nih.gov
- For tips on how to include more fruits and vegetables in your diet, visit www.cdc.gov/nccdphp/dnpao
- For more information on cooking with microwave ovens to preserve vitamins, visit www.foodscience .csiro.au/micwave1.htm

References

1. Institute of Medicine, Food and Nutrition Board. 1998. *Dietary Reference Intakes: Thiamin, Riboflavin, Niacin, Vitamin B_6, Folate, Vitamin B_{12}, Pantothenic Acid, Biotin, and Choline.* Washington, DC: The National Academies Press.

2. National Institute of Neurological Disorders and Stroke (NINDS). 2007. *NINDS Wernicke-Korsakoff Syndrome Information Page.* Available at www.ninds.nih.gov. Accessed March 2014.

3. Herreid, E. O., B. Ruskin, G. L. Clark, and T. B. Parks. 1952. Ascorbic Acid and Riboflavin Destruction and Flavor Development in Milk Exposed to the Sun in Amber, Clear, Paper, and Ruby Bottles. *Journal of Dairy Science* 35:772–778.

4. Institute of Medicine, Food and Nutrition Board. 1998. *Dietary Reference Intakes: Thiamin, Riboflavin, Niacin, Vitamin B_6, Folate, Vitamin B_{12}, Pantothenic Acid, Biotin, and Choline.*

5. McCormick, D. B. 1989. Two Interconnected B Vitamins: Riboflavin and Pyridoxine. *Physiology Review* 69:1170–1198.

6. Madigan, S. M., F. Tracy, H. McNulty, J. Eaton-Evans, J. Coulter, H. McCartney, and J. J. Strain. 1998. Riboflavin and Vitamin B_6 Intakes and Status and Biochemical Response to Riboflavin Supplementation in Free-Living Elderly People. *American Journal of Clinical Nutrition* 68:389–395.

7. Institute of Medicine. 2006. *Dietary Reference Intakes: The Essential Guide to Nutrient Requirements.* Washington, DC: The National Academies Press.

8. Squibb, R. L., J. E. Braham, G. Abboyave, and K. S. Scrimshaw. 1958. A Comparison of the Effect of Raw Corn and Tortillas (Lime-Treated Corn) with Niacin, Tryptophan or Beans on the Growth and Muscle Niacin of Rats. *Journal of Nutrition* 67:351–361.

9. Canner, P. L., K. G. Berge, N. K. Wenger, J. Stamler, L. Friedman, R. J. Prineas, and W. Friedewald. 1986. Fifteen-Year Mortality in Coronary Drug Project Patients: Long-Term Benefit with Niacin. *Journal of the American College of Cardiology* 8:1245–1255.

10. Institute of Medicine, Foods and Nutrition Board. 1998. *Dietary Reference Intakes: Thiamin, Riboflavin, Niacin, Vitamin B_6, Folate, Vitamin B_{12}, Pantothenic Acid, Biotin, and Choline.*

11. Kirkland, J. 2014. Niacin. In A. C. Ross, B. Caballero, R. J. Cousins, K. L. Tucker, and T. R. Ziegler, eds. *Modern Nutrition in Health and Disease.* 11th ed. Baltimore: Lippincott Williams & Wilkins.

12. Institute of Medicine, Food and Nutrition Board. 1998. *Dietary Reference Intakes: Thiamin, Riboflavin, Niacin, Vitamin B_6, Folate, Vitamin B_{12}, Pantothenic Acid, Biotin, and Choline.*

13. Trumbo, P. R. 2014. Pantothenic Acid. In A. C. Ross, B. Caballero, R. J. Cousins, K. L. Tucker, and T. R. Ziegler, eds. *Modern Nutrition in Health and Disease.* 11th ed. Baltimore: Lippincott Williams & Wilkins.

14. Tahiliani, A. G., and C. J. Beinlilch. 1991. Pantothenic Acid in Health and Disease. *Vitamins and Hormones* 46:165–228.

15. Glusman, M. 1947. The Syndrome of "Burning Feet" (Nutritional Melagia) as a Manifestation of Nutritional Deficiency. *American Journal of Medicine* 3:211–223.

16. Gropper, S. S., and J. L. Smith. 2013. *Advanced Nutrition and Human Metabolism.* 6th ed. Belmont, CA: Wadsworth, Cengage Learning.

17. Institute of Medicine. 2006. *Dietary Reference Intakes: The Essential Guide to Nutrient Requirements.*

18. U. S. National Library of Medicine. 2008. *Genetics Home Reference. Your Guide to Understanding Genetic Disorders.* Available at http://ghr.nlm.nih.gov Accessed March 2014.

19. Institute of Medicine, Food and Nutrition Board. 1998. *Dietary Reference Intakes: Thiamin, Riboflavin, Niacin, Vitamin B_6, Folate, Vitamin B_{12}, Pantothenic Acid, Biotin, and Choline.*

20. Da Silvia, V. R., A. D. Mackey, S. R. Davis, and J. F. Gregory III. 2014. Vitamin B_6. In A. C. Ross, B. Caballero, R. J. Cousins, K. L. Tucker, and T. R. Ziegler, eds. *Modern Nutrition in Health and Disease.* 11th ed. Baltimore: Lippincott Williams & Wilkins.

21. Ibid.

22. Qin, X., F. Fan, Y. Cui, F. Chen, et al. 2014. Folic Acid Supplementation with and without Vitamin B_6 and Revascularization Risk: A Meta-Analysis of Randomized Controlled Trials. *Clinical Nutrition* DOI:10.1016/j.clnu.2014.01.006.

23. Chittumma, P., K. Kaewkiattikun, and B. Wiriyasiriwach. 2007. Comparison of the Effectiveness of Ginger and Vitamin B_6 for Treatment of Nausea and Vomiting in Early Pregnancy: A Randomized Double-Blind Controlled Trial. *Journal of the Medical Association of Thailand* 90:15–20.

24. Chocano-Bedoya, P. O., J. E. Manson, S. E. Hankinson, W. C. Willett, et al. 2011. Dietary B Vitamin Intake and Incident Premenstrual Syndrome. *American Journal of Clinical Nutrition* 93(5):1080–1086.

25. Schaumburg, H., J. Kaplan, A. Windebran, N. Vick, S. Rasmus, D. Pleasure, and M. J. Brown. 1983. Sensory Neuropathy from Pyridoxine Abuse. *New England Journal of Medicine* 309:445–448.

26. Neuhouser, M. L., S. A. A. Beresford, D. E. Hickok, and E. R. Monsen. 1998. Absorption of Dietary and Supplemental Folate in Women with Prior Pregnancies with Neural Tube Defects and Controls. *Journal of the American College of Nutrition* 17:625–630.

27. Ibid.

28. Ross, A. C., B. Caballero, R. J. Cousins, K. L. Tucker, and T. R. Ziegler, eds. 2013. Water-Soluble Vitamins. In *Modern Nutrition in Health and Disease.* 11th ed. Baltimore: Lippincott Williams & Wilkins.

29. Centers for Disease Control and Prevention. 2014. *Folic Acid.* Available at www.cdc.gov. Accessed March 2014.

30. Ibid.

31. Mills, J. L., and C. Signore. 2004. Neural Tube Defect Rates before and after Food

Fortification with Folic Acid. *Birth Defects Research* 70(11):844–845.

32. Centers for Disease Control and Prevention. 2014. *Folic Acid*. Available at www.cdc.gov. Accessed March 2014.

33. Eussen, S. J., S. E. Vollset, J. Igland, et al. 2010. Plasma Folate, Related Genetic Variants, and Colorectal Cancer Risk in EPIC. *Cancer Epidemiology Biomarkers and Prevention* 19(5):1328–1340.

34. Nitter, M., B. Norgård, S. de Vogel, et al. 2014. Plasma Methionine, Choline, Betaine, and Dimethylglycine in Relation to Colorectal Cancer Risk in the European Prospective Investigation into Cancer and Nutrition (EPIC). *Annals of Oncology* DOI: 10.1093/annonc/mdu185.

35. Li, B., Y. Lu, L. Wang, and C. X. Zhang. 2014. Folate Intake and Breast Cancer Prognosis: A Meta-Analysis of Prospective Observational Studies. *European Journal of Cancer Prevention* doi: 10.1097/CEJ.0000000000000028.

36. Bao, Y., D. S. Michaud, D. Spiegelman, et al. 2011. Folate Intake and Risk of Pancreatic Cancer: Pooled Analysis of Prospective Cohort Studies. *Journal of the National Cancer Institute* 03(24):1840–1850.

37. Institute of Medicine, Food and Nutrition Board. 1998. *Dietary Reference Intakes: Thiamin, Riboflavin, Niacin, Vitamin B_6, Folate, Vitamin B_{12}, Pantothenic Acid, Biotin, and Choline.*

38. National Institutes of Health, Office of Dietary Supplements. 2012. *Dietary Supplement Fact Sheet: Folate*. Available at http://ods.od.nih.gov. Accessed March 2014.

39. National Institutes of Health, Office of Dietary Supplements. 2011. *Dietary Supplement Fact Sheet: Vitamin B_{12}*. Available at http://ods.od.nih.gov. Accessed March 2014.

40. Ibid.

41. Tucker, K. L., M. T. Hannan, P. F. Jacques, J. Selhub, I. Rosenberg, P. W. Wilson, and D. P. Kiel. 2005. Low Plasma Vitamin B_{12} Is Associated with Lower BMD: The Framingham Osteoporosis Study. *Journal of Bone Mineral Research* 20(1):152–158.

42. Watanabe, F., K. Abe, T. Fujita, M. Goto, M. Hiemori, and Y. Nakano. 1998. Effects of Microwave Heating on the Loss of Vitamin B_{12} in Foods. *Journal of Agricultural Food Chemistry* 46:206–210.

43. PubMed Health. 2012. Pernicious Anemia. Available at www.ncbi.nlm.nih.gov. Accessed April 2014.

44. Andrès, E., T. Vogel, L. Federici, J. Zimmer, E. Ciobanu, and G. Kaltenbach. 2008. Cobalamin Deficiency in Elderly Patients: A Personal View. *Current Gerontology and Geriatric Research* DOI: 10.1155/2008/848267.

45. Iqbal, L., A. Khan, and M. Khattak. 2004. Biological Significance of Ascorbic Acid (Vitamin C) in Human Health. *Pakistan Journal of Nutrition* 3:5–13.

46. Ibid.

47. Kubota, Y., H. Iso, C. Date, et al. 2011. Dietary Intakes of Antioxidant Vitamins and Mortality from Cardiovascular Disease: The Japan Collaborative Cohort Study (JACC) Study. *Stroke* 42(6):1665–1672.

48. Iqbal, et al. 2004. Biological Significance of Ascorbic Acid.

49. Padayatty, S., J. Doppman, R. Chang, Y. Wang, J. Gill, D. A. Papanicolaou, and M. Levine. 2007. Human Adrenal Glands Secrete Vitamin C in Response to Adrenocorticotropic Hormone. *American Journal of Clinical Nutrition* 86:145–149.

50. Iqbal, et al. 2004. Biological Significance of Ascorbic Acid.

51. Institute of Medicine, Food and Nutrition Board. 1998. *Dietary Reference Intakes: Thiamin, Riboflavin, Niacin, Vitamin B_6, Folate, Vitamin B_{12}, Pantothenic Acid, Biotin, and Choline.*

52. Hirschmann, J. V., and G. J. Raugi. 1999. Adult Scurvy. *Journal of the American Academy of Dermatology* 41:895–910.

53. English, J. 2013. *Vitamin C, Colds, and Acute Induced Scurvy*. Available at www.nutrition-review.org. Accessed March 2014.

54. Zeisel, S. H., K. A. Da Costa, P. D. Franklin, E. A. Alexander, J. T. Lamont, N. F. Sheard, and A. Beiser. 1991. Choline, an Essential Nutrient for Humans. *Federation of American Societies for Experimental Biology* 5:2093–2098.

55. Ziesel, S. H. 2014. Choline. In A. C. Ross, B. Caballero, R. J. Cousins, K. L. Tucker, and T. R. Ziegler, eds. *Modern Nutrition in Health and Disease*. 11th ed. Baltimore: Lippincott Williams & Wilkins.

56. National Institutes of Health, Office of Dietary Supplements. 2013. *Carnitine*. Available at http://ods.od.nih.gov. Accessed March 2014.

57. Packer, L., E. H. Witt, and H. J. Tritschler. 1994. Alpha-Lipoic Acid as a Biological Antioxidant. *Free Radical Biology and Medicine* 19:227–250.

58. Heinisch, B. B., M. Francesconi, F. Mittermayer, et al. 2010. Alpha-Lipoic Acid Improves Vascular Endothelial Function in Patients with Type 2 Diabetes: A Placebo-Controlled Randomized Trial. *European Journal of Clinical Investigation* 40(2):148–154.

59. World Cancer Research Fund. 2014. *Stopping Cancer before It Starts*. Available at www.wcrf.org. Accessed March 2014.

60. American Cancer Society. 2013. *Cancer Facts and Figures 2013*. Available at www.cancer.org. Accessed March 2014.

61. American Cancer Action Network. 2013. *Cancer Prevention and Early Detection Facts and Figures*. Available at www.cancer.org. Accessed March 2014.

62. Ibid.

63. Ibid.

64. Boyle, T., T. Keegle, F. Bull, J. Heyworth, and L. Fritsche. 2012. Physical Activity and Risks of Proximal and Distal Colon Cancers: A Systematic Review and Meta-Analysis. *Journal of the National Cancer Institute* 104(20):1548–1561.

65. Ibid.

66. Thompson, C. A. 2012. Diet and Breast Cancer: Understanding the Risks and Benefits. *Nutrition in Clinical Practice* 27(5):636–650.

67. National Cancer Institute. 2012. *Obesity and Cancer Risk*. Available at www.cancer.gov. Accessed March 2014.

68. Saxe, G. A., J. M. Major, L. Westerberg, S. Khandrika, and T. M. Downs. 2008. Biological Mediators of Effect of Diet and Stress Reduction on Prostate Cancer. *Integrative Cancer Therapy* 7:130–138.

69. Ibid.

70. Parsons, J. K., J. P. Pierce, L. Natarajan, et al. 2013. A Randomized Pilot Trial of Dietary Modification for the Chemoprevention of Noninvasive Bladder Cancer: The Dietary Intervention in Bladder Cancer Study. *Cancer Prevention Research* 6:971–978.

71. Gonzalo, S. 2013. Novel Roles of 1α,25(OH)2D3 on DNA Repair Provide New Strategies for Breast Cancer Treatment. *Journal of Steroid Biochemistry and Molecular Biology* doi: 10.1016/j.jsbmb.2013.09.009.

72. AIM-HIGH Investigators. 2011. The Role of Niacin in Raising High-Density Lipoprotein Cholesterol to Reduce Cardiovascular Events in Patients with Atherosclerotic Cardiovascular Disease and Optimally Treated Low-Density Lipoprotein Cholesterol: Rationale and Study Design. *American Heart Journal* 161(3):471–477.

73. Rehm, J., D. Baliunas, G. L. Borges, K. Graham, et al. 2010. The Relation between Different Dimensions of Alcohol Consumption and Burden of Disease: An Overview. *Addiction* 105(5):817–843.

74. World Cancer Research Fund. 2014. *Stopping Cancer before It Starts*.

75. Bouchard-Mercier, A., A. M. Paradis, I. Rudkowska, S. Lemieux, P. Couture, and M. C. Vohl. 2013. Associations between Dietary Patterns and Gene Expression Profiles of Healthy Men and Women: A Cross-Sectional Study. *Nutrition Journal* doi: 10.1186/1475-2891-12-24.

76. Underwood, M. A. 2014. Intestinal Dysbiosis: Novel Mechanisms by Which Gut Microbes Trigger and Prevent Disease. *Preventive Medicine* doi: 10.1016/j.ypmed.2014.05.010.

11 Water

Learning Outcomes

After reading this chapter, you will be able to:

11.1 Explain why water is essential to life.

11.2 Describe the various processes that maintain water balance in the body.

11.3 Describe the roles of water, sodium, hormones, and enzymes in the development of hypertension.

11.4 Describe the recommended daily intake for water consumption.

11.5 Explain the effects of diuretics, such as caffeine and alcohol, on the balance of body water.

11.6 Differentiate between dehydration and water intoxication, and describe the symptoms of each.

True or False?

1. The body can survive for weeks without food and water. **T/F**

2. A morning mug of coffee counts toward daily water needs. **T/F**

3. Daily consumption of at least 8 cups of water is essential for health. **T/F**

4. Drinking large amounts of water helps flush waste from the body. **T/F**

5. Drinking extra water leads to weight loss. **T/F**

6. Exercise often leads to dehydration. **T/F**

7. Sodium should be eliminated from the diet to prevent fluid retention. **T/F**

8. Eating bananas reduces hypertension. **T/F**

9. Drinking alcohol causes dehydration. **T/F**

10. Enhanced waters are healthier than plain water. **T/F**

See Page 430 for the answers.

veryone needs water to live. But exactly why is this the case, and how much water do you really need? In this chapter, we explore the essential functions that water plays in the body, as well as the mechanisms that keep fluids and other substances in a healthy balance. We also find out how to make sure that you are meeting your daily needs and, equally important, how to avoid consuming toxic amounts of water.

Why Is Water Essential to Life?

LO 11.1 Explain why water is essential to life.

Water (H_2O) is the most abundant substance in the body and, as such, is the most important. You could survive for weeks without food, but only for a few days without water.

The average healthy adult body is composed of about 45 to 75 percent water. The distribution of this water depends on an individual's age, gender, and the composition of fat and muscle in the body (**Figure 11.1**). Because lean muscle tissue is approximately 75 percent water, while fat tissue contains very little water (up to 20 percent), some individuals have less body water than others.[1] In general, males have a higher percentage of muscle mass and a lower percentage of fat tissue than females of the same age, and therefore males have more body water. For the same reason, muscular athletes have a higher percentage of body water than sedentary individuals. Body water also decreases with age. A newborn infant averages about 73 percent of body weight as water, while an older adult only has about 45 percent body water.[2]

Water is a polar molecule, which means it has an unbalanced charge from the positive charge on the hydrogen atoms and the negative charge on the oxygen atoms. This is possible because water, unlike carbon dioxide, is not linear but bent in shape (**Figure 11.2**). Its polarity allows water to attract other charged molecules and help maintain acid-base balance in the body.

polar Having a pair of equal and opposite charges; water is a polar molecule because oxygen has a negative charge and hydrogen has a positive charge.

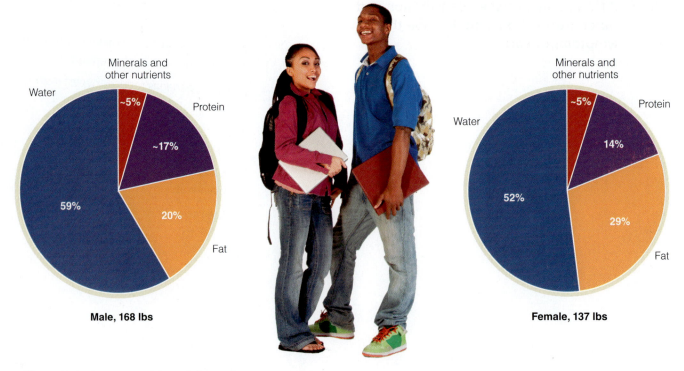

Male, 168 lbs

Female, 137 lbs

▲ **Figure 11.1 The Composition of the Body**
Water is the predominant body component for both men and women.

Water's polar quality enables it to play a role as a medium in which other substances can dissolve. As part of blood and other fluids, water transports nutrients, waste products, and other substances between cells and tissues. Water also helps maintain a constant body temperature; lubricates and protects joints and other areas; and enables chemical reactions, including those that provide the body with energy, and enables acid-base balance to take place within the cells. Without water, metabolism would grind to a halt.

Water Is a Universal Solvent and Transport Medium

Water is commonly known as a universal **solvent,** because it dissolves more substances than any other liquid. Its polarity allows it to attract charged particles into a solution, and dissolve a variety of other polar substances, including proteins, glucose, and some minerals. As illustrated in **Figure 11.3**, the positive and negative charges of water attract the positive and negative charges of table salt, called sodium chloride (Na^+Cl^-). The result is that salt dissolves in water. Compounds that are not polar, such as lipids, are not attracted to water and thus do not dissolve.

Water's function as a solvent is critically important in digestion and transport. For example, about 7,000 milliliters of watery gastric juices dissolve digested nutrients. Blood is made up of primarily water (about 83 percent) and red blood cells, and the water in blood allows it to transport oxygen, nutrients, white blood cells, and hormones to the cells. Water also helps transport waste products away from cells to be excreted in urine and stool.

Water Helps Maintain Body Temperature

Water is a heat buffer similar to the coolant fluid in a car. It absorbs heat from the body's internal core and carries it to the skin for release. Water works well as a coolant because it has a high **specific heat,** the amount of energy required to raise 1 gram of water 1 degree Celsius (1°C). Thus, with only a small rise in body temperature, water can absorb, hold onto, and release heat to return the body to a safe temperature.

If the body's core gets too hot, though, this cooling mechanism is not enough to maintain a safe temperature. A jog on a hot summer day, for example, can generate an enormous amount of internal heat and would likely tax the heat-absorbing capacity of the body's water. In this case, water transfers the heat to the skin to reduce the heat load. As the core temperature increases, the hypothalamus is triggered and dilates the blood vessels, increasing the flow of warmed blood to the skin's surface. At the same time, the rising skin temperature activates the three million sweat glands to release additional water and salts through the pores of the skin. The increasing heat

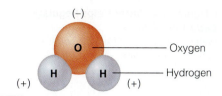

▲ **Figure 11.2 Water Is a Polar Molecule**
The oxygen atom of water has a partial negative charge and the hydrogen atoms have a partial positive charge, making the overall charge of a molecule unbalanced.

Water is vital for many body functions, but it is not stored in the body, so adequate amounts must be consumed daily.

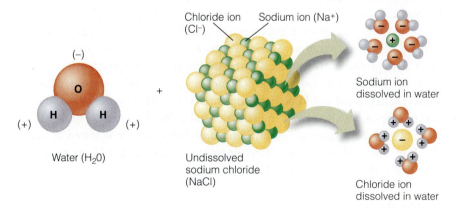

▲ **Figure 11.3 Water Is a Universal Solvent**
Water is a universal solvent that can dissolve salts such as sodium chloride (NaCl). The negatively charged Cl^- is attracted to the positive charge of the hydrogen ions (H^+) and the positive charge of Na^+ is attracted to the negative charge of oxygen (O^-). Thus, the water slowly dissolves the salt.

solvent A liquid in which substances dissolve to form a new solution. Water is called the universal solvent because it can dissolve a variety of substances, including minerals and glucose.

specific heat A measurement of the energy required to raise a gram of a substance, such as water, 1 degree Celsius.

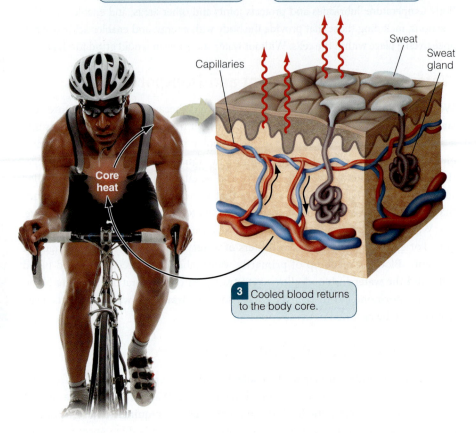

► **Figure 11.4 Water Helps Regulate Body Temperature**
Water transports heat from the body's core to the skin for release.

1 The water in blood carries heat to the capillaries at the skin surface.

2 The heat is released at the skin surface. Evaporation of sweat cools the skin.

Sweat

Sweat gland

Capillaries

Core heat

3 Cooled blood returns to the body core.

breaks apart the hydrogen bonds of the water, and transforms it from a liquid (*sweat*) to a vapor. Heat dissipates as the sweat evaporates from the surface of the skin, thus cooling the skin (**Figure 11.4**), leaving the salt behind. The cooled blood returns to the muscle. The water in sweat that drips off your body releases very little heat.

Water Is a Lubricant and a Protective Cushion, and Provides Structure to Muscle Cells

Water acts as a lubricant for joints and sensitive eye tissue. It lubricates and moistens food in the mouth as part of saliva, and is part of the mucus that lubricates the intestinal tract. Water is the main component of the fluid that bathes certain organs, including the brain. It thus acts as a cushion to protect organs from injury during a fall or other trauma. During pregnancy, a sac of watery amniotic fluid, which helps protect it from physical harm, surrounds a developing fetus.

Water also provides a structural component to cells, much like air in a balloon. Without water, a cell would be limp and shriveled. Athletes experience the structural features of water when the muscle feels full following a carbohydrate-loading diet. This is because glycogen is surrounded by water when it is stored in muscle cells. Every molecule of glucose within the glycogen structure has 2.7 grams of water associated with it, adding bulk and structure to the muscle cells.[3]

Water Participates in Hydrolysis and Condensation Reactions

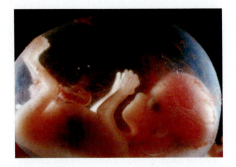

A developing fetus is cushioned in a sac of watery amniotic fluid to protect it from physical harm during pregnancy.

Water is essential for most chemical reactions in the body. During digestion water hydrolyzes the bonds that hold carbohydrate, protein, and fat molecules

Water and Acid-Base Balance

When water dissociates, it tends to break up into H^+ and OH^- (hydroxide) ions. One hydrogen atom breaks its bond with oxygen, leaves behind its electron, and becomes positively charged. (Recall that a positively charged hydrogen atom is called a hydrogen ion.) The other hydrogen remains attached to the oxygen molecule. Oxygen retains both of its original electrons and now has an extra electron from the hydrogen, which gives the molecule a negative charge. The OH^- molecule is called a hydroxide ion.

$$H_2O \leftrightarrow H^+ + OH^-$$

When a solution has more H^+ than OH^- ions, it is acidic. When the solution has more OH^- than H^+ ions, it is basic (refer to the pH scale in Chapter 3).

Water can regulate acid-base balance by forming or breaking down carbonic acid (H_2CO_3). This buffering action is reversible, as illustrated in the following two reactions:

(a) During exercise, carbon dioxide is produced as a by-product of energy metabolism. Carbon dioxide is a gas that quickly dissolves in water, forming carbonic acid (H_2CO_3). If the reaction continues, carbonic acid can be further reduced to hydrogen (H^+) and bicarbonate ions (HCO_3^-). The increase in H^+ results in a decrease in pH and makes the environment more acidic.

$$H_2O + CO_2 \rightarrow H_2CO_3 \rightarrow H^+ + HCO_3^-$$

(b) The reaction can be reversed and act as a buffer to neutralize excess hydrogen ions. In this reaction, H^+ ions formed during energy metabolism (recall from Chapter 8 that H^+ are formed during glycolysis and the TCA cycle) combine with bicarbonate (HCO_3^-) to form water and carbon dioxide. This increases the pH and makes the environment more alkaline.

$$H^+ + HCO_3^- \rightarrow H_2CO_3 \rightarrow H_2O + CO_2$$

together. For example, when sucrose is digested (refer to Chapter 4), hydrolysis adds a hydrogen ion to fructose and a hydroxyl group to glucose; then each monosaccharide is absorbed. When smaller molecules are combined through condensation, such as when excess glucose is stored as glycogen in the liver and muscle, the opposite occurs. In this case, a water molecule is released for every bond that is formed.

Water Plays a Role in Acid-Base Balance

Acid-base balance is essential to maintain homeostasis in the body. As you learned in Chapter 3, a normal pH in human blood ranges from 7.35 to 7.45, which reflects the amount of hydrogen ions present—more hydrogen ions means a lower, more acidic pH. Because water is polar, it can function to reduce or increase the pH levels by either breaking down or forming carbonic acid. In other words, water can act as either an acid or a base. These reactions are described in the Chemistry Boost.

LO 11.1: THE TAKE-HOME MESSAGE The body is 45 to 75 percent water. Muscle tissue has more water than fat tissue, therefore men have more body water than women and younger individuals have more body water than older individuals. Water is polar, interacts with other nutrients, serves as an acid-base buffer, transports oxygen and nutrients throughout the body, regulates body temperature, is a lubricant, adds structure to cells, participates in hydrolysis and condensation, and provides a protective cushion for the brain and other organs.

acid-base balance The mechanisms used to maintain body fluids close to a neutral pH so the body can function properly.

Food and beverages are a source of water for the body.

How Is Water Balance Maintained?

LO 11.2 Describe the various processes that maintain water balance in the body.

The amount of water in the fluid compartments in the body is tightly regulated. Maintaining fluid balance, or homeostasis, is necessary for normal reactions to take place within the cells. The body maintains this delicate balance by adapting to changes in water intake and water loss. When the amount of water consumed is equal to the amount excreted, the body is in **water balance.**

Sources of Body Water Include Beverages and Food

The first aspect of being in water balance is consuming enough water. The largest source of body water comes from beverages such as tap or bottled water, milk, juices, coffee, and soft drinks. An additional source of water comes from foods, especially from fruits and vegetables, which contain more water by weight than do grains or meats. Most foods contain some water.

In addition to the water ingested through beverages and foods, water is generated during metabolism, referred to as **metabolic water.** For example, condensation reactions, such as those that occur during energy metabolism, yield a small amount of water. One hundred grams of carbohydrate can yield almost 55 grams of metabolic water by the time it has been catabolized to ATP. In addition, the water that was joined with glucose during glycogenesis is later released when glycogen is hydrolyzed to produce glucose.

The intake of water from fluids, food, and metabolism contributes to the total average intake of 2,550 milliliters daily (about 2 quarts). **Figure 11.5** illustrates the sources of water in the body and the routes of excretion.

Water Is Excreted through the Kidneys, Large Intestine, Lungs, and Skin

To maintain water balance, water is excreted through urine and sweat, stool, and as water vapor through the lungs. The majority of fluid lost is through the kidneys, which produce approximately 1,500 milliliters of urine each day. The more water ingested, the more urine produced. The opposite is also true. The less water an adult consumes,

water balance A state of equilibrium when the intake of water equals the amount of water excreted.

metabolic water Water that is formed in the body as a result of metabolic reactions. Condensation reactions are an example of a chemical reaction that results in the production of water.

300 ml Metabolism

700 ml Food

1,500 ml Beverages

Water Intake

Water Output

100 ml Intestines (stool)

350 ml Lungs (breathing)

1,500 ml Kidneys (urine)

600 ml Skin (sweat)

2,550 ml

2,550 ml

▲ **Figure 11.5 Sources of Body Water and Routes of Excretion**
Most of the body's water comes from foods and beverages and a small amount is generated during metabolism. Water is lost from the body through the urine, stool, sweat, and exhaled breath. The amount of water consumed and generated is balanced with the amount excreted each day.

or if a greater amount of water is lost through other means such as through sweat, the less urine is produced. About 100 milliliters of water is also lost through intestinal fluids in the stool. This amount can vary depending on the dietary intake of plant fibers and whether an individual is experiencing diarrhea or vomiting. Excess water loss through diarrhea and vomiting can amount to as much as 1,500 to 5,000 milliliters and can result in dehydration. (We discuss dehydration in detail later in the chapter.)

Water that evaporates during exhalation and water lost through the skin as the body releases heat constitute **insensible water loss,** which takes place throughout the day, generally without being noticed. Exhaled air, which contains small water droplets, releases about 200 to 400 milliliters of water per day. This amount increases in an arid climate and with the heavier breathing that occurs during physical activity.[4]

Insensible water loss doesn't include the water lost in sweat. The amount of water lost during sweating varies greatly and depends upon many environmental factors, such as the temperature, humidity, wind, sun's intensity, clothing worn, and amount of physical activity. If you jump rope in the noontime sun on a summer day wearing a heavy coat, you could lose almost 2,000 to 3,000 milliliters of water per hour as sweat.[5] In contrast, you would lose only about 50 milliliters of water per hour as sweat if you sat under a shady tree on a dry, cool day wearing a light tee shirt and slacks.

Body Water Is Balanced between Fluid Compartments

Two-thirds of the body's fluids are located within cells; this is called **intracellular fluid (ICF).** The remaining one-third is located outside the cells, and is called **extracellular fluid (ECF).** This balance of body water between compartments is critical for optimal health of the cell. Each fluid contains specific components. ICF contains potassium, proteins, and various organic acids. ECF is primarily composed of sodium chloride and sodium bicarbonate solutions.

There are two types of ECF: interstitial fluid and intravascular fluid. **Interstitial fluid** bathes the outside of cells, but does not circulate throughout the body. **Intravascular fluid** is found in the blood and the lymph fluid, and circulates throughout the body. Interstitial fluid makes up about 75 percent of the ECF and acts as an area of exchange between the blood and the cells (**Figure 11.6**).

The fluids in the ECF and ICF are not static—they move between compartments easily. Water flows passively across cell membranes based on the concentration of dissolved minerals inside or outside the cell. A change in the concentration of these dissolved substances on either side of the cell membrane will cause a shift in water flow from a low concentration to a high concentration.

Electrolytes Participate in Fluid Balance

Some minerals act as **electrolytes** (*electro* = electricity, *lytes* = soluble), or charged ions that conduct electrical current. If they have a positive charge they are classified as **cations,** while negatively charged ions are called **anions.** Sodium (Na^+) and chloride (Cl^-) are the main electrolytes in the ECF, while potassium (K^+) and phosphate (HPO_4^{-2}) are the major ions in the ICF. Electrolytes help maintain water balance between compartments by "pulling" water into and out of blood and cells, a process referred to as **osmosis.**

Osmosis

Shifts in fluid from the ICF to the ECF are solely due to osmosis (*osmos* = pushing), a powerful factor influencing water balance between cell compartments. Electrolytes attract water. Water diffuses by osmosis through cell membranes, moving from a dilute or low concentration of electrolytes (also called *solutes*) on one side of the membrane to a high concentration of electrolytes on the other side of the membrane.

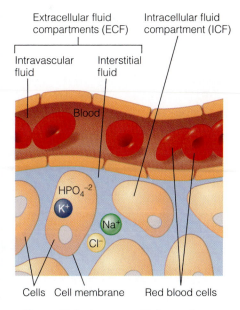

▲ **Figure 11.6 The Intracellular and Extracellular Fluid Compartments**
Water is a key component of the fluid both inside (intracellular) and outside (extracellullar) of cells. Potassium (K^+) is the major electrolyte found in the ICF and sodium (Na^+) is the major electrolyte located in the ECF.

insensible water loss The loss of body water that goes unnoticed, such as by exhalation during breathing and the evaporation of water through the skin.

intracellular fluid (ICF) The fluid found in the cytoplasm within the cells; it represents the largest fluid compartment in the body.

extracellular fluid (ECF) The water found outside the cell, including the intravascular fluid and the interstitial fluid.

interstitial fluid The fluid that surrounds cells. It is the main component of extracellular fluid.

intravascular fluid The fluid found inside the blood vessels and the lymph fluid.

electrolytes Ions such as sodium, potassium, chloride, and calcium in the blood and within the cells that are able to conduct electrical current when they are dissolved in body water.

cations Positively charged ions.

anions Negatively charged ions.

osmosis The diffusion of water or any solvent across semipermeable membranes from a weak concentration of solutes to a more concentrated solute.

▶ **Figure 11.7 Osmosis**

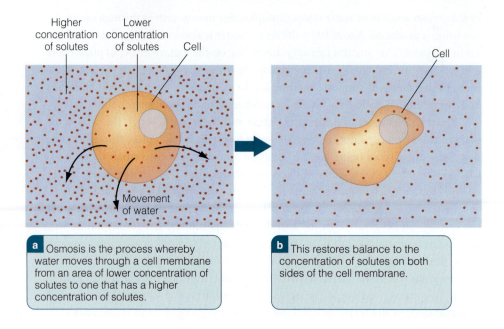

Higher concentration of solutes / Lower concentration of solutes / Cell

Cell

Movement of water

a Osmosis is the process whereby water moves through a cell membrane from an area of lower concentration of solutes to one that has a higher concentration of solutes.

b This restores balance to the concentration of solutes on both sides of the cell membrane.

Cell membranes are **selectively permeable,** which means they allow some substances, such as water, to pass freely while other substances, such as salts, are restricted.

The **osmolality,** or concentration of solutes in a solution, controls the directional flow of water. The difference between the osmolality (or number of solutes) on each side of the permeable membrane is called the **osmotic gradient.** As the osmolality on one side the membrane increases, the osmotic gradient increases, and water is drawn across the membrane to the solutes.

The membrane swells under the pressure of the increase in water, or **osmotic pressure.** This increase in osmotic pressure prevents water from flowing away from the concentrated side of the membrane until balance has been restored between the fluid compartments. For example, heavy sweating during work or exercise outdoors results in a greater loss of water than electrolytes from the blood (ECF) (sweat is 75 percent water), which increases the osmolality of the ECF and creates an osmotic gradient relative to the ICF. As the osmolality increases in the ECF, water is drawn from the ICF into the ECF, which increases the osmotic pressure in the ECF until balance is achieved. The opposite is also true. If you drink a large amount of water quickly, the water in the ECF dilutes the concentration of the solutes compared with the ICF and reduces the osmotic pressure in the ECF, allowing the flow of water from the ECF into the ICF. If the concentration of solutes to water is similar on either side of the membrane, water reaches equilibrium (**Figure 11.7**). Osmosis only affects the movement of water between compartments, not the electrolytes themselves. Electrolytes are moved between the two fluid compartments by the mechanism referred to as the sodium-potassium pump.

The Sodium-Potassium Pump

While the minerals sodium, potassium, phosphate, magnesium, calcium, and chloride all function as electrolytes in the body, sodium has the greatest effect on fluid balance. Sodium and potassium influence fluid balance through the action of the **sodium-potassium pump,** which is the mechanism that maintains the normal electrolyte concentrations within the cell (see **Figure 11.8**). Recall from Chapter 3 that the absorption of nutrients against a concentration gradient requires a carrier molecule and ATP for active transport. The sodium-potassium pump is a prime example of an active transport system in which an enzyme called Na^+-K^+ $ATPase$ acts as the carrier molecule to "pump" sodium ions out of, and potassium ions into, the ICF. Sodium is normally more concentrated in the ECF than the ICF, and sodium tends to leak into

selectively permeable Describes the feature of cell membranes that allows some substances to cross the membrane more easily than other substances.

osmolality A measurement of the concentration of solutes per kilogram of solvent in a solution.

osmotic gradient The difference in concentration between two solutions on each side of the permeable cell membrane.

osmotic pressure The pressure that prevents the solutes in a solution from drawing water across a semipermeable membrane.

sodium-potassium pump A protein located in the cell membrane that actively transports sodium out of the cell in exchange for potassium ions.

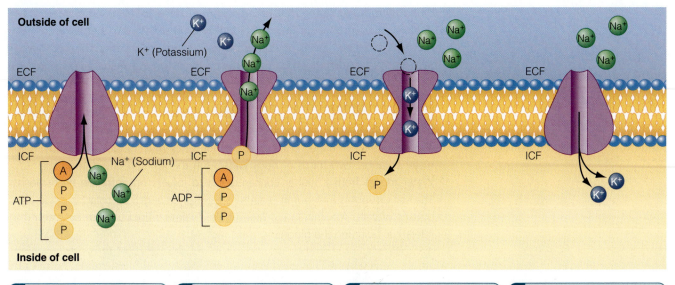

| 1 Inside the cell three Na⁺ ions and ATP bind to the surface of the protein channel of the sodium-potassium pump. | 2 The ATP is hydrolyzed into ADP and phosphate, providing the energy needed to change the shape of the protein. The change in shape forces the Na⁺ ions outside of the cell. A phosphate remains attached to the protein. | 3 Once the Na⁺ ions have been released, the pump binds two K⁺ ions in the ECF and releases the phosphate inside the cell. | 4 The pump changes back to its original shape and releases the two K⁺ ions inside the cell. The pump is then ready to go again. |

▲ **Figure 11.8 The Sodium-Potassium Pump**
The sodium-potassium pump is a protein in the cell membrane that transports sodium ions out of a cell while moving potassium ions inside the cell. This active transport of Na⁺ and K⁺ ions requires energy. For every three sodium ions pumped out of the cell, two potassium ions are transported into the cell.

the cell while potassium leaks out of the cell. As sodium enters the ICF, water diffuses across the cell membrane to follow the sodium ions. As water moves inside the cell, the cell swells, causing an increase in osmotic pressure. In healthy cells, to prevent the cell from bursting, the sodium-potassium pump transports three sodium (Na⁺) ions out of the cell and exchanges them for two potassium (K⁺) ions that move inside the cell. In other words, both Na⁺ and K⁺ ions are moving against their concentration gradients. The pump causes a net loss of ions, which creates an electrical and chemical gradient that drives water out of the cell, and reduces the swelling.

The sodium-potassium pump is found in every cell, but plays an especially important role in electrical conduction in nerve and muscle cells and in the absorption of nutrients. The transport of ions by the sodium-potassium pump creates an osmotic gradient, and changes the electrical charge that causes the nerve to transmit a signal or the muscle to contract. The sodium-potassium pump is also the driving force behind the absorption of as much as two liters of consumed fluid each day, plus the water secreted into the GI tract in gastric juices.

The sodium-potassium pump also drives the absorption of other nutrients, including glucose and amino acids. For example, as sodium ions move back inside the cell and across the cell membrane, they *drag* glucose along with them by binding to the same carrier protein. This allows glucose to move from a low concentration in the ECF to a higher concentration of glucose in the ICF. The sodium is then pumped back out of the cell to begin again.

Proteins Help Regulate Fluid Balance

Proteins in the ECF and ICF play a major role in keeping water dispersed evenly between the ECF and the ICF (refer to Chapter 6). This is especially true for the protein albumin. As the concentration of albumin rises in the blood, water is drawn out of the interstitial fluid into the blood by osmosis. If your diet is severely low in protein, the blood levels of albumin drop, causing an accumulation of water in the interstitial spaces and swelling of the body tissues. Adequate protein intake is essential to fluid balance.

> **LO 11.2: THE TAKE-HOME MESSAGE** When the amount of water consumed in foods and beverages, and produced as metabolic water, is equal to the amount excreted through urine, skin, sweat, stool, and water vapor, the body is in water balance. Two-thirds of body water is in the ICF and one-third in the ECF. Water moves from a higher concentration to lower concentration by osmosis. The sodium-potassium pump maintains electrolyte and fluid balance inside and outside of cells. Albumin in the blood helps maintain fluid balance between the interstitial fluid and the blood.

How Do Water and Sodium Affect Blood Pressure?

LO 11.3 Describe the roles of water, sodium, hormones, and enzymes in the development of hypertension.

If the body retains too much fluid, blood volume—and therefore blood pressure—is likely to rise. The kidneys play a key role in regulating blood volume, as well as electrolyte balance, through tightly controlled hormonal signals. Three hormones, including antidiuretic hormone (ADH, also called *vasopressin*), angiotensin, and aldosterone, plus an enzyme called renin, together orchestrate the retention and excretion of water and electrolytes based on blood volume (**Figure 11.9**).

ADH Helps Stimulate Fluid Intake and Reduce Urine Output

When blood volume drops, the hypothalamus detects a decrease in blood pressure and an increase in the concentration of electrolytes (osmolality). This stimulates the thirst mechanism and fluid intake. At the same time you begin to feel thirsty, the hypothalamus stimulates the pituitary gland to release **antidiuretic hormone (ADH).** ADH travels through the blood to the kidneys and stimulates the reabsorption of water, which reduces urine production. Together, the intake of water and the reduced urine output restore blood volume and return osmolality to normal levels.

Renin Helps the Body Reabsorb Water and Salts

The enzyme **renin,** secreted by the kidneys, is released when blood pressure falls or sodium concentration decreases. This enzyme splits off a protein called **angiotensin I** from the protein **angiotensinogen** produced by the liver and found in the blood. As the blood flows into the lungs, the angiotensin I is swiftly converted into **angiotensin II,** which has both short-term and long-term effects on blood pressure.

Angiotensin II is a powerful *vasoconstrictor* (*vaso* = vessel, *constrictor* = tightening) that narrows the blood vessels and raises blood pressure. This short-term reaction can prevent severe blood loss from hemorrhage or after an injury.

The long-term blood pressure control of angiotensin II relates to its action on the kidneys. First, it directly stimulates the kidneys to reabsorb water and electrolytes to increase blood volume and blood pressure. Secondly, angiotensin II

antidiuretic hormone (ADH) A hormone secreted by the pituitary gland when blood volumes are low; ADH reduces the amount of water excreted through the kidneys, constricts the blood vessels, and raises blood pressure; also known as vasopressin.

renin An enzyme secreted by the kidneys that participates in the renin-angiotensin system; renin increases blood volume, vasoconstriction of the blood vessels, and blood pressure.

angiotensin I and II The active protein in the blood that causes vasoconstriction in the blood vessels and triggers the release of aldosterone from the adrenal glands, which raises blood pressure.

angiotensinogen A precursor protein produced in the liver and found in the blood; it is converted to the active form called angiotensin.

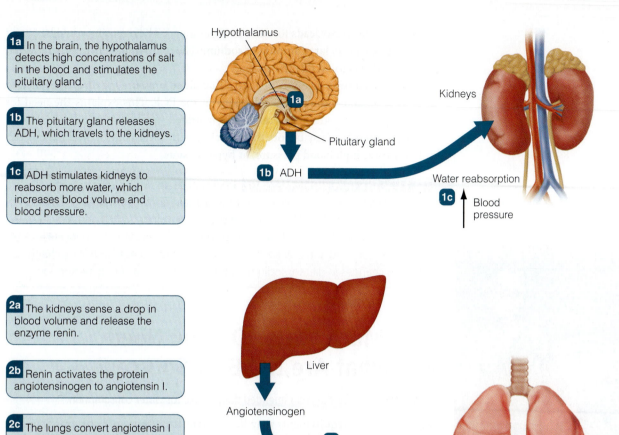

1a In the brain, the hypothalamus detects high concentrations of salt in the blood and stimulates the pituitary gland.

1b The pituitary gland releases ADH, which travels to the kidneys.

1c ADH stimulates kidneys to reabsorb more water, which increases blood volume and blood pressure.

Hypothalamus

Pituitary gland

1a

1b ADH

Kidneys

Water reabsorption

1c ↑ Blood pressure

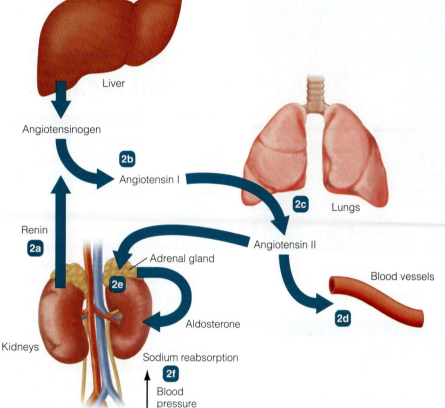

2a The kidneys sense a drop in blood volume and release the enzyme renin.

2b Renin activates the protein angiotensinogen to angiotensin I.

2c The lungs convert angiotensin I to angiotensin II.

2d Angiotensin II is a vasoconstrictor and causes the blood vessels to contract, which increases blood pressure.

2e Angiotensin II stimulates the adrenal glands to release aldosterone.

2f Aldosterone signals the kidneys to reabsorb more sodium, which increases blood volume and blood pressure.

Liver

Angiotensinogen

2b

Angiotensin I

2c Lungs

Angiotensin II

Renin

2a

Adrenal gland

2e

Aldosterone

Kidneys

Blood vessels

2d

Sodium reabsorption

2f

↑ Blood pressure

▲ **Figure 11.9 Blood Volume Regulates Blood Pressure**
Blood pressure is controlled by three hormones: antidiuretic hormone (ADH) secreted from the pituitary glands (1a–1c), angiotensin activated in the blood by renin (2a-2d), and aldosterone released from the adrenal glands (2e–2f).

stimulates the adrenal glands to release aldosterone. These long-term effects take hours or days to affect blood pressure.

Aldosterone Stimulates Sodium Reabsorption

The renin-angiotensin system adapts to changes in dietary sodium intake. If you consume very little sodium, osmolality drops in the ECF. Fluid automatically shifts from the blood to the interstitial fluid, causing a decrease in blood volume and blood pressure. Under these circumstances, angiotensin II would trigger the adrenal glands to release **aldosterone,** which signals the kidney to retain more

aldosterone A hormone secreted from the adrenal glands in response to reduced blood volume; aldosterone signals the kidneys to reabsorb sodium, which increases blood volume and blood pressure.

sodium; this indirectly leads to water being retained. The opposite would be true if you consumed a very large amount of sodium: The renin-angiotensin system would cause the kidneys to excrete the excess.

The mechanisms involved in controlling blood pressure are directly related to blood volume and sodium concentrations in the ECF. This explains the need for controlling dietary sodium and remaining hydrated, especially for individuals with high blood pressure. Any factors that interfere with these control mechanisms can lead to chronic high blood pressure, or hypertension.

LO 11.3: THE TAKE-HOME MESSAGE In response to changes in blood volume and osmolality, the body takes action to maintain homeostasis and return blood pressure to normal. The hormones antidiuretic hormone (ADH) and aldosterone direct the kidneys to reabsorb water and sodium. The enzyme renin increases sodium retention, and angiotensin II is a vasoconstrictor. These control mechanisms adjust to changes in dietary sodium and fluid intake to prevent hypertension.

How Much Water Do You Need and What Are the Best Sources?

LO 11.4 Describe the recommended daily intake for water consumption.

Your daily water requirements may be different from those of your grandparents, parents, siblings, and even the classmate sitting next to you. The amount of water a person needs depends on physical activity, diet, and environmental factors such as air temperature and humidity.

The current recommendation for daily water consumption is based on the reported total water intake (from both beverages and food) of healthy Americans.[6] Currently, healthy female adults consume the equivalent of 12 cups of water daily, whereas men consume the equivalent of 16 cups of water daily. About 80 percent of this intake is from beverages and the other 20 percent comes from foods. Therefore, adult women should ingest about 9 cups (~80 percent of 12 cups) and adult males approximately 13 cups (~80 percent of 16 cups) of beverages daily. People who are very active have higher water requirements because they lose more water by sweating. These beverage guidelines are illustrated in **Figure 11.10**.

If that sounds like a lot, keep in mind that a well-balanced, 2,200–kilocalorie diet that includes beverages at all meals and snacks provides about 12 cups of water.[7] Drinking bottled or tap water, milk, and juices throughout the day can help meet the body's needs. (Examining the Evidence: Is Bottled Water Healthier than Tap Water? discusses the differences and similarities between tap water and bottled water.)

Most foods can also contribute to daily water needs (see **Figure 11.11**). Fruits and vegetables, such as watermelon, grapes, and lettuce, which can be more than 70 percent water by weight, rank as the best food sources of water. Even grain products, like bagels and bread, provide some water.

LO 11.4: THE TAKE-HOME MESSAGE Daily water needs vary according to an individual's physical activity level, environment, and diet. Adult women should consume about 12 cups of water (9 cups from beverages; 3 cups from foods) daily, whereas adult men should consume about 16 cups (13 cups from beverages; 3 cups from foods) daily. Those who are very active need more water to avoid dehydration.

Physically active people and other individuals who lose a lot of water through sweating have higher water requirements.

TABLE TIPS

Bottoms Up

Drink low-fat or skim milk with each meal to help meet both calcium and fluid needs.

Freeze grapes for a juicy and refreshing snack.

Add a vegetable soup to lunch for a fluid-packed meal.

Spoon slightly thawed frozen strawberries onto low-fat vanilla ice cream for a cool sweet treat. Look for packaged berries in the frozen food section of the supermarket.

Add a slice of fresh lemon or lime to a glass of water to make it even more refreshing.

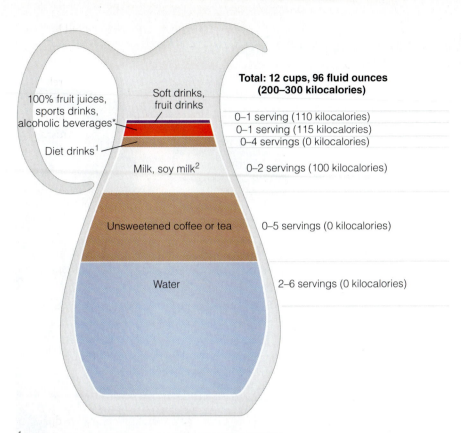

**Total: 12 cups, 96 fluid ounces
(200–300 kilocalories)**

100% fruit juices, sports drinks, alcoholic beverages*

Soft drinks, fruit drinks — 0–1 serving (110 kilocalories)

0–1 serving (115 kilocalories)

Diet drinks[1] — 0–4 servings (0 kilocalories)

Milk, soy milk[2] — 0–2 servings (100 kilocalories)

Unsweetened coffee or tea — 0–5 servings (0 kilocalories)

Water — 2–6 servings (0 kilocalories)

[1] Includes diet soft drinks and tea or coffee with sugar substitutes.
[2] Includes fat-free or 1% milk and unsweetened fortified soy milk.
* 0–2 servings of alcohol are okay for men.

◄ **Figure 11.10 Daily Beverage Recommendations**
The acceptable beverage patterns for an adult female on a 2,200-kilocalorie daily intake.
Source: B. M. Popkin, L. E. Armstrong, G. M. Bray, B. Caballero, B. Frei, and W. C. Willett. 2006. "A New Proposed Guidance System for Beverage Consumption in the United States." *American Journal of Clinical Nutrition* 83:529–542.

◄ **Figure 11.11 Water Content of Foods**
Source: A. Grandjean and S. Campbell, *Hydration: Fluids for Life* (Washington, DC: ILSI Press, 2004). Available at www.ilsi.org.

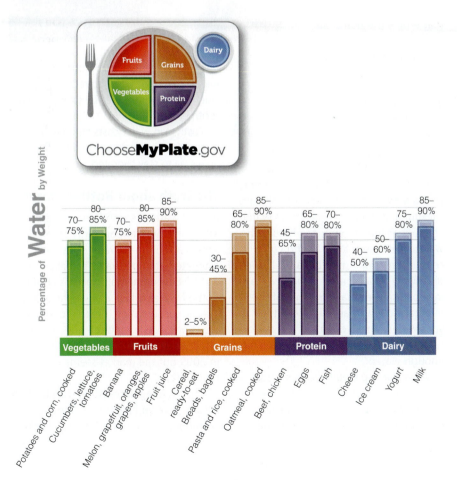

Percentage of **Water** by Weight

| Vegetables | | Fruits | | | Grains | | | Protein | | | Dairy | | | |

- Potatoes and corn, cooked: 70–75%
- Cucumbers, lettuce, tomatoes: 80–85%
- Banana: 70–75%
- Melon, grapefruit, oranges, grapes, apples: 80–85%
- Fruit juice: 85–90%
- Cereal, ready-to-eat: 2–5%
- Breads, bagels: 30–45%
- Pasta and rice, cooked: 65–80%
- Oatmeal, cooked: 85–90%
- Beef, chicken: 45–65%
- Eggs: 65–80%
- Fish: 70–80%
- Cheese: 40–50%
- Ice cream: 50–60%
- Yogurt: 75–80%
- Milk: 85–90%

ChooseMyPlate.gov

Is Bottled Water Healthier than Tap Water?

Do you carry and refill a reusable water bottle, or are you one of the many individuals who drink *only* commercially bottled water? If you buy your water already bottled, you're certainly not alone. But is bottled water really healthier than tap water?

Although many people drink bottled water in the belief that it is "pure," the reality is that drinking 100 percent *pure* water is unlikely. Both water from the tap and bottled water contain some impurities. However, this does not mean that the water is unsafe for most individuals to drink. (Note that individuals with a weakened immune system, such as those with HIV/AIDS, undergoing chemotherapy, and/or taking steroids, should speak with their health care provider about water consumption. These individuals may need to take precautions such as boiling their water—no matter the source—before consuming it.[1])

The sources of any water vary from faucet to faucet and bottle to bottle, making it virtually impossible to make a direct comparison. There are some basic points to understand about each type, though. Let's look at how tap and bottled water compare in terms of regulation, safety, and cost.

The Benefits of Tap Water

Tap water in the United States is clean, safe, and cheap. Most Americans obtain their drinking water from a community water system. The source of this municipal water can be underground wells or springs, rivers, lakes, or reservoirs. Regardless of the source, all municipal water is sent to a treatment plant where dirt and debris are filtered out, bacteria are killed, and other contaminants are removed. Hundreds of billions of dollars have been invested in these treatment systems to ensure that the public water is safe to drink.[2] The Environmental Protection Agency (EPA) oversees the safety of public drinking water with national standards

that set limits for more than 80 naturally occurring and man-made contaminants that may find their way into drinking water. Each year, the community water suppliers must provide an annual report about the quality and source of tap water. In fact, many of these regional reports can be accessed online at www.epa.gov. Even with these precautions, some individuals, who may not like the taste of their tap water or who have health concerns, use an in-home water treatment device to further filter their water. Filter devices can range from a less costly pitcher or device mounted on the kitchen faucet to a more costly, larger system that treats all the water that enters the home. Depending upon the device, it can filter contaminants such as bacteria, viruses, lead, nitrates, and pesticides. Whatever the device used, it is important that it be maintained regularly to ensure that it is working effectively.

You may have heard the terms "hard" or "soft" water used to describe tap water. The "hardness" refers to the amount of minerals—specifically, calcium and magnesium—in the water. The higher the amount, the harder the water. There aren't any health concerns from drinking hard water. In fact, there may be a benefit, as hard water may contribute small amounts of these minerals to your daily diet. Whether your water is hard or soft is less important than meeting your daily needs for enough water.

American tap water also has a positive impact on the nation's dental health. About two-thirds of Americans who drink from public systems are getting

fluoride in their water.[3] Fluoridation of water has been shown to reduce the incidence of dental caries by strengthening tooth enamel.[4]

Lastly, tap water costs less than a penny a gallon, making it a very affordable way to stay hydrated.

The Truth about Bottled Water

Bottled water is second only to carbonated soft drinks in popularity among Americans. Bottled water sales were estimated at more than $12 billion in 2011.[5] Environmental concerns about bottled water, which include increased energy consumption, greenhouse gas emissions, waste, and the environmental effect of water extraction, reduced sales in 2009 but the market seems to be rebounding.[6]

The FDA regulates bottled water that is sold through interstate commerce. Manufacturers must adhere to specific

TABLE 1 Sources of Bottled Water

Bottled water is labeled according to its source or how it is treated prior to bottling.

Mineral Water	Water that is derived from an underground source that contains a specific amount of naturally occurring minerals and trace elements. These minerals and elements cannot be added to the water after it has been bottled.
Spring Water	Water that is obtained from underground water that flows naturally to the surface. The water is collected at the spring, or at the site of a well purposefully drilled to obtain this water.
Sparkling Water	Spring water that has carbon dioxide gas added before it is bottled. Also called seltzer water or club soda. Note: This is technically considered a soft drink, not a bottled water. Sparkling water does not have to adhere to FDA regulations for bottled water.
Distilled Water	Water that has been boiled and processed to remove most, but not all, contaminants.
Flavored Water	Water that has a flavor such as lemon or lime added. It may also contain added sugars and kilocalories.
Vitamin Water	Water that has vitamins added to it. Such water may also contain added sugars and kilocalories.

Source: "Do You Know Where Your Bottled Water Comes From?" *Consumer Reports* (2012).

FDA regulations, such as standards of identity. In other words, if the label on the bottle states that it is "spring water," the manufacturer must derive the water from a very specific source (see **Table 1**).

Interestingly, some bottled water may actually come from a municipal water source. This bottled water must also adhere to a standard of quality set forth by the FDA, which specifies the maximum amount of contaminants that can be in the water for it still to be considered safe for consumption.[7] The FDA bases its standards for bottled water sold interstate on the EPA's standards for public drinking water. However, water that is bottled and sold within the same state is not regulated by the FDA.[8]

The price of bottled water can be hefty, ranging from $1 to $4 a gallon. An individual who spends $1.50 per bottle of water and buys one bottle daily would spend more than $10 per week and more than $40 per month buying bottled water. Over the course of an academic school year, that amounts to almost $400 for a beverage that you can get for free from a water fountain.

Finally, many bottled waters are not fluoridated, so relying on bottled water as a primary water source can shortchange your dental health.[9]

Another costly bottled beverage option is the newer 'designer' drinks such as vitamin waters and enhanced waters, discussed further in Spotlight: Enhanced Water: What Are We Really Drinking?

The Environmental Cost of Bottled Water

Almost 30 billion plastic bottles are sold each year in the United States, but only two out of every ten of these bottles are recycled:[10] The rest end up in landfills. Not only that, researchers estimate that the energy equivalent of more than 17 million barrels of oil are used to produce the plastic water bottles Americans use each year—enough energy to fuel a million cars for a year.[11]

Although refilling and reusing the bottles from bottled water may seem like an environmentally friendly and cost-effective idea, the practice is not advised. The plastic containers cannot withstand repeated washing and the plastic can actually break down, causing chemicals to leach into the water. Sturdier water bottles that are designed for reuse must be thoroughly cleaned with hot soapy water after each use to kill germs.

The bottom line is that both tap water and bottled water can be safe to drink, and the choice is likely to come down to personal preference, costs, and concern about environmental impacts. **Table 2** summarizes the similarities and differences between the two types of water.

TABLE 2 Bottled vs Tap Water: A Summary

	Bottled Water	Tap Water
Cost to Consumers	■ About $1.00–$4.00 per gallon	■ About $0.003 per gallon
Safety	■ Bottled water is generally safe. ■ Some bottled water is not tested for contaminants. ■ Only bottled water sold across state lines is regulated by the FDA. ■ Bottled water not sold across state lines is regulated by state and local guidelines.	■ Municipal water is regulated by EPA, state, and local regulations for contaminants. ■ EPA guidelines require that the public have access to water quality reports and that it be notified if water quality is outside established bounds.
Benefits to Consumers	■ The packaging of bottled water may make it more convenient than tap water. ■ Bottled water may taste better than tap water.	■ Tap water is available at the faucet. ■ Tap water often contains fluoride, which helps to prevent tooth decay. ■ Tap water doesn't contain any added sugars or kilocalories. ■ Much less energy is required to produce tap water, and much less waste is generated by using a cup or reusable container rather than disposable plastic bottles.

References

1. U. S. Environmental Protection Agency. 2012. *Basic Information about Regulated Drinking Water Contaminants and Indicators*. Available at http://water.epa.gov. Accessed March 2014.
2. H. Sheng. Body Fluids and Water Balance. In *Biochemical and Physiological Aspects of Human Nutrition*. 3rd ed. (Philadelphia: W. B. Saunders, 2013).
3. Institute of Medicine. *Dietary Reference Intakes: Water, Potassium, Sodium, Chloride, and Sulfate* (Washington, DC: The National Academies Press, 2004).
4. S. Shetty, M. N. Hedge, and T. P. Bopanna. 2014. Enamel Remineralization Assessement After Treatement with Three Different Remineralizing Agents Using Surface Microhardness: An In Vitro Study. *Journal of Conservative Dentistry* 17(1):49–52.
5. Mintel Reports. 2013. *Bottled Water—U.S.—March 2013*. Available at http://store.mintel.com. Accessed March 2014.
6. Beverage Marketing Corporation. 2011. *Bottled Water Recovers Somewhat from Recessionary Years, New Report from Beverage Marketing Corporation Shows*. Available at www.beveragemarketing.com. Accessed March 2014.
7. A. Grandjean and S. Campbell. 2004. *Hydration: Fluids for Life*. Available at www.ilsi.org. Accessed March 2014.
8. Ibid.
9. E. N. Marieb and K. Hoehn. *Human Anatomy and Physiology*. 9th ed. (San Francisco: Pearson/Benjamin Cummings, 2014).
10. Earth 911.com. 2012. *360: Recycling Plastic Bottles*. Available at http://earth911.com. Accessed March 2014.
11. The United States Conference of Mayors. 2008. *Supporting Municipal Water Systems*. Available at www.usmayors.org. Accessed March 2014.

Enhanced Water: What Are We Really Drinking?

Bottled water has become increasingly popular in the last few decades, but it seems to be losing ground to a new type of bottled beverage: enhanced waters, which often advertise health benefits beyond hydration.

The name "enhanced water" generally refers to any type of bottled water that has added ingredients to improve its taste and increase nutrient content. These beverages, which are sold under brand names such as Aquafina Alive, Propel, Fruit$_2$O, and Dasani Plus, have been fortified with vitamins, fiber, caffeine, herbs, protein, and sometimes even oxygen. Some contain as many kilocalories as a soft drink, or as much as 13 teaspoons of sugar, while others are similar in mineral content to a sports drink. Some enhanced waters are presented as energy boosters because they contain caffeine, while others, like Fruit$_2$O Relax, claim to calm and relax nerves. Still other products boast they improve mental acuity, elevate mood, or offer other functional benefits. **Table 1** compares some of the more popular brands.

Do enhanced waters provide any health benefits? In one study, when people without folate deficiency and normal homocysteine levels consumed mineral water fortified with folic acid, vitamins B$_6$, B$_{12}$, and D, and calcium, their folate status was enhanced and their homocysteine levels dropped.[1] Other results indicated that calcium used to fortify the enhanced water was bioavailable.[2] But that's not the whole picture.[3] Results reported from the Iowa Women's Health Study suggest that the use of multivitamin supplements, which include vitamins often found in enhanced waters, increased total mortality risk.[4] Whereas some results are promising, other results raise concerns.

Some enhanced waters can cost as much as $3.00 for a 20-ounce bottle that may provide 100 percent of one or more vitamins. A generic multivitamin pill costs approximately 10 cents a day for 100 percent or more of 13 vitamins and minerals. Thus, vitamin water costs about 30 times what a daily multivitamin does and provides fewer nutrients.

The bottom line is that the benefit of these enhanced waters in the diet is not clear, and it's much cheaper and more enjoyable to get vitamins and minerals from fruits and vegetables and balanced meals.

Table 1 The Nutrient Content of Enhanced Waters

Bottled Beverage	Serving Size	Kilocalories	Sweeteners	Added Nutrients
Dasani Plus	8 oz	0	Artificial sweeteners acesulfame potassium, sucralose	Guarana, ginseng, chromium, B vitamins
Fruit$_2$O Energy	8 oz	0	Acesulfame potassium, sucralose	Caffeine, B vitamins
Fruit$_2$O Relax	8 oz	0	Acesulfame potassium, sucralose	Chamomile, hibiscus, B vitamins
Propel Invigorating	8 oz	20	5 g sugar	Caffeine, B vitamins
Skinny Water	16.9 oz	10	None	Super CitriMax and ChromeMate, calcium
SoBe Life Water	8 oz	50	13 g sugar	Vitamin E, vitamin C, and B vitamins
Special K$_2$O Protein Water	16 oz	50	Acesulfame potassium, sucralose	Fiber, calcium, whey protein, niacin, vitamin B$_6$, vitamin B$_{12}$
Vitaminwater Defense	8 oz	50	13 g sugar	Zinc, four B vitamins, vitamin C, electrolytes
Vitaminwater Energy	8 oz	40	13 g sugar	Vitamins C, E, and A, B vitamins, caffeine, guarana, ginseng
Vitaminwater XXX	8 oz	50	13 g sugar	Vitamin C and B vitamins plus 50 mg of acai-blueberry-pomegranate extract

References

1. N. S. Tapola, H. M. Karvonen, L. K. Niskanen, and E. S. Karkkinen. 2004. "Mineral Water Fortified with Folic Acid, Vitamins B$_6$, B$_{12}$, D, and Calcium Improves Folate Status and Decreases Plasma Homocysteine Concentration in Men and Women." *European Journal of Clinical Nutrition* 58:376–385.

2. V. Coiro, G. Zanardi, J. G. Saccani, P. Rubino, G. Manfredi, and P. Chiodera. 2008. "High-Calcium Mineral Water as a Calcium Supplementing Measure for Post-Thyroidectomy Hypocalcemia." *Minerva Endocrinologica* 33:7–13.

3. Harvard School of Public Health. 2012. Enhanced Water *"Unequivocally Harmful to Health," Says HSPH Nutrition Expert.* Available at www.hsph.harvard.edu. Accessed March 2014.

4. J. Mursu, K. Robien, L. J. Harnack, K. Park, and D. R. Jacobs. 2011. "Less Is More: Dietary Supplements and Mortality Rates in Older Women. The Iowa Women's Health Study." *Archives of Internal Medicine* 171:1625–1633.

Do Diuretics Like Caffeine and Alcohol Affect Water Balance?

LO 11.5 Explain the effects of diuretics, such as caffeine and alcohol, on the balance of body water.

Beverages such as alcoholic drinks, regular coffee, and tea contribute significantly to total water intake, but alcohol and caffeine are also considered **diuretics,** and contribute to water loss. Overconsumption of some of these substances can upset fluid balance.

Caffeine Does Not Cause Significant Loss of Body Water

Caffeine is a mild diuretic that blocks the action of ADH in the kidneys. However, researchers have not been able to confirm that this mild diuretic actually results in dehydration. In fact, caffeine doesn't cause a significant loss of body water over the course of a day compared with noncaffeinated beverages. Individuals who routinely consume caffeinated beverages actually develop a tolerance for its diuretic effect and experience less water loss over time.[8] Although caffeine may have other detrimental effects on the body, such as jitteriness and insomnia, moderate intakes of caffeinated beverages don't appear to have a significant negative effect on hydration.

Alcohol Can Be Dehydrating

Similar to caffeine, alcohol interferes with water balance by inhibiting ADH, which can induce urination as quickly as 20 minutes after alcohol is consumed. Unlike caffeine, alcohol can be dehydrating. The water lost affects the concentrations of electrolytes in the body, especially potassium, which affects metabolism. This may be partly responsible for the thirst, lightheadedness, and dry mouth that are often part of a hangover. Older drinkers appear to overcome this suppression of ADH faster and resist dehydration better than do younger drinkers. Reducing the amount of alcohol consumed and drinking water after consuming alcohol can help prevent dehydration. (For more on alcohol, see Chapter 7.)

A cup of coffee gives you a "pick me up" without causing dehydration.

diuretics Substances that increase the production and secretion of urine; they are often used as antihypertensive drugs.

Diuretic Medications Can Help Treat Hypertension

Pharmaceutical diuretics are often prescribed as a first line of treatment for hypertension. These drugs promote diuresis (increased excretion of urine) by inhibiting the reabsorption of sodium. As you've already learned, if the kidney excretes more sodium, water loss also increases. This action reduces blood volume, which lowers blood pressure.

Some types of diuretics also increase potassium loss. This is because the increase in sodium loss from the ECF into the urine stimulates aldosterone and the sodium-potassium pump, which increases sodium reabsorption in exchange for potassium. This potassium loss raises the risk of **hypokalemia.** A small drop in potassium levels usually doesn't cause symptoms, but moderate to larger drops cause lower blood pressure, muscle weakness and cramps, and constipation. Patients taking diuretics are closely monitored by their doctors to prevent electrolyte imbalances. They are encouraged to eat potassium-rich foods such as bananas, peanut butter, and tomatoes. In some cases, potassium supplements may be prescribed.

> **LO 11.5: THE TAKE-HOME MESSAGE** Moderate caffeine intake does not affect fluid balance. Alcohol reduces the effects of ADH and can cause dehydration. Pharmaceutical diuretics are prescribed to reduce hypertension but may cause electrolyte imbalances.

hypokalemia A dangerously low level of blood potassium.

Health Connection

What Are the Effects of Too Much or Too Little Water?

LO 11.6 Differentiate between dehydration and water intoxication, and describe the symptoms of each.

Although water is an essential nutrient, it can also be harmful if consumed in excess. And, just as with other nutrients, consuming too little can lead to adverse symptoms and conditions.

Consuming Too Much Water Can Cause Hyponatremia

Water intoxication is rare because healthy individuals who consume a balanced diet simply produce more urine to eliminate excess water. However, drinking fluids too fast without adequate sodium replacement dilutes sodium and increases the rate of urine production. When too much water enters the cells, the tissues swell with the excess fluid and the concentration of sodium in the extracellular fluid drops, resulting in **hyponatremia** (*hypo* = under, *natrium* = sodium, *emia* = blood).

In April 2002, 28-year-old Cynthia Lucero was running the Boston Marathon. About five miles from the finish line, Lucero began to feel wobbly and mentioned to a friend that she felt dehydrated even though she had been consuming fluids throughout her run. She suddenly collapsed and was taken to a nearby hospital. She died the next day, due to swelling of the brain brought on by hyponatremia caused by overconsumption of fluids.[9] The condition doesn't just occur among endurance athletes. In January 2007, a woman named Jennifer Strange collapsed after competing in a California radio contest to see who could drink the most water without using the restroom. She was found dead in her home a few hours after completing the contest.

The cause of death for both of these individuals was swelling in the brain. Drinking too much fluid too quickly dilutes the electrolyte content, especially sodium, in the ECF. Recall that sodium is the main cation in the ECF. When the ECF is too dilute, hypnatremia results. This change in dilution in the ECF causes an increase in concentration of electrolytes in the ICF. Water rushes from the ECF into the ICF to balance the electrolyte concentration. When too much water enters the ICF, the tissues swell to the point of bursting. If the swelling occurs in the brain cells, it

water intoxication A potentially dangerous medical condition that results from drinking too much water too quickly, also known as *hyperhydration*; can lead to hyponatremia and possible death.

hyponatremia A dangerously low level of sodium in the blood that can result from water intoxication or a lack of sodium during heavy exercise.

Fluid Balance during Exercise

The health of our body's cells depends on maintaining the proper balance of fluids and electrolytes on both sides of the cell membrane, both at rest and during exercise. Let's examine how this balance can be altered under various conditions of exercise and fluid intake.

MODERATE EXERCISE

When you are appropriately hydrated, engaged in moderate exercise, and not too hot, the concentration of electrolytes is likely to be the same on both sides of cell membranes. You will be in fluid balance.

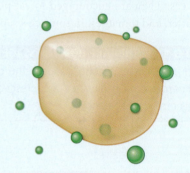

Concentration of electrolytes about equal inside and outside cell

STRENUOUS EXERCISE WITH RAPID AND HIGH WATER INTAKE

If a person drinks a great deal of water quickly during intense, prolonged exercise, the extracellular fluid becomes diluted. This results in the concentration of electrolytes being greater inside the cells, which causes water to enter the cells, making them swell. Drinking moderate amounts of water or sports drinks more slowly will replace lost fluids and restore fluid balance.

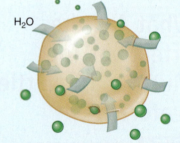

Lower concentration of electrolytes outside

H_2O

Higher concentration of electrolytes inside

STRENUOUS EXERCISE WITH INADEQUATE FLUID INTAKE

If a person does not consume adequate amounts of fluid during strenuous exercise of long duration, the concentration of electrolytes becomes greater outside the cells, drawing water away from the inside of the cells and making them shrink. Consuming sports drinks will replace lost fluids and electrolytes.

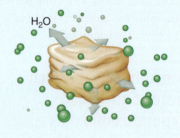

Higher concentration of electrolytes outside

H_2O

Lower concentration of electrolytes inside

may cause death unless water intake is restricted and a saline (salt) solution is given to achieve a balance between the ECF and the ICF (**Focus Figure 11.12**). Symptoms of water intoxication include fatigue, confusion, and disorientation.[10] Mistakenly treating these symptoms by consuming more fluids only makes matters worse. People who sweat, with a loss of both water and solutes, are advised to consume drinks that have added Na^+ instead of plain water to replenish both fluid and electrolytes.[11]

The seriousness of overhydration prompted the USA Track & Field Association to revise its hydration guidelines for long-distance and marathon runners to avoid hyponatremia.[12] Whereas older recommendations encouraged athletes to "stay ahead of thirst," the newer ones advise determining one's own rate of water loss and then replacing water at a 1:1 ratio during an endurance event. In addition, a small amount of sodium consumption is recommended when food consumption before or during prolonged activity is inadequate, physical activity lasts longer than four hours, and/or during initial days of hot weather.[13]

Consuming Too Little Water Is a Common Problem

While overhydration can have dire effects on the body, inadequate water intake, or **dehydration,** occurs much more frequently and can be just as harmful (see Figure 11.12). Dehydration can be the result of either not drinking enough water, strenuous exercise in the heat, or losing excessive amounts of water as a result of diarrhea, vomiting, high fever, or the use of diuretics. Dehydration can result from as little as a 2 percent loss of body water and can trigger a loss of short-term and long-term memory, lower attention span and cognition, and reduced ability to maintain core temperature. It can also increase the risk of urinary tract infections and fatigue.

For some populations, such as children, the elderly, and athletes, the consequences of dehydration can be severe. In the elderly, for example, dehydration has been misdiagnosed as dementia.[14] Even a 1 to 2 percent loss of body water can impair an athlete's cardiovascular and thermoregulatory response and reduce the athlete's capacity for exercise. See **Table 11.1** for common signs of dehydration.

The Thirst Mechanism Signals Dehydration

Have you ever been outside for a while on a hot day and noticed that your mouth was as dry as the Sahara Desert? The dry mouth is part of your **thirst mechanism.** Thirst, which is usually perceived after mild dehydration has begun, is often the first physical sign of dehydration. The resultant urge to drink plays an important role in preventing further dehydration and restoring water balance in the body.

Figure 11.13 illustrates the reactions that occur as part of the thirst mechanism. When fluid is lost from the ECF, reduced blood volume (called **hypovolemia;** *hypo* = reduced, *vol* = volume, *emia* = blood) can occur. Less circulating blood can lead to reduced blood pressure and, if severe enough, hypotension. The decrease in blood pressure signals the hypothalamus to stimulate thirst and fluid intake, and the pituitary gland to release ADH. Both actions result bring blood volume back to normal. If thirst is ignored and fluid is not replaced, hypovolemia and hypotension together can reduce cardiac output and impair digestion, and may cause fainting.

The dry mouth that makes you feel thirsty is also due in part to the increased concentration of electrolytes in the blood. As the concentration of electrolytes increases, less water is available to your salivary glands to make saliva, making your mouth feel dry. When you are dehydrated, water is depleted from the ECF and the ICF, but not necessarily in equal proportions. Initially, water loss is from the ECF, which becomes more concentrated in electrolytes. This increase in electrolyte concentration draws water from the ICF into the ECF in an attempt to maintain homeostasis and water balance. At this stage, the water balance in the ECF is maintained, but causes ICF dehydration. The loss of both fluid and electrolytes from the ICF causes the cell to *shrink* (see Figure 11.12), which is detected by the hypothalamus and triggers the renin-angiotensin system that stimulates thirst and an appetite for salt. Anti-diuretic hormone is also triggered to reduce the amount of water excreted excreted through the skin, lungs, and kidneys in an attempt to adapt to the change in fluid. These adaptations are important to reduce the effects on blood volume and the concentration of solutes, but they do not return fluid levels to normal. Fluids must be consumed to restore blood volume.

Just quenching thirst will not typically provide enough fluids to remedy dehydration. This isn't a concern for moderately active individuals eating a balanced

dehydration The excessive loss of body fluids; usually caused by lack of fluid intake, diarrhea, vomiting, or excessive sweating.

thirst mechanism A complex interaction between the brain and the hypothalamus triggered by a loss of body water; the interaction leads to a feeling of thirst.

hypovolemia Low blood volume.

TABLE 11.1	Signs of Dehydration	
Mild Dehydration	**Moderate Dehydration**	**Severe Dehydration**
Dry lips and mouth	Thirst	All signs of moderate dehydration
Thirst	Very dry mouth	
Inside of mouth slightly dry	Sunken eyes	Rapid and weak pulse
Low urine output; concentrated urine appears dark yellow	Sunken fontanelles (the soft spots on an infant's head)	Cold hands and feet
	Tenting (skin doesn't bounce back readily when pinched and lifted slightly)	Rapid breathing
		Blue lips
		Lethargic, comatose

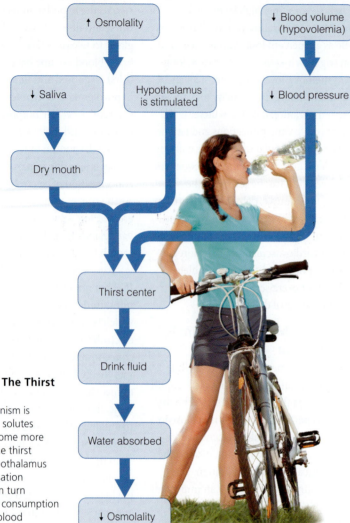

▶ **Figure 11.13 The Thirst Mechanism**
The thirst mechanism is stimulated when solutes in the blood become more concentrated. The thirst center in the hypothalamus stimulates a sensation of thirst, which in turn stimulates water consumption and returns the blood osmolality to normal.

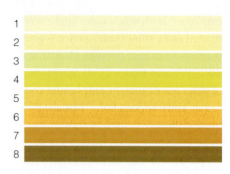

▲ **Figure 11.14 Urine Color Guide**
Clear or light yellow urine indicates adequate hydration. Dark urine (color 7 or darker) indicates dehydration and the need to consume more fluids.

dehydrated produce less urine due to the release of ADH. The urine that is produced is more concentrated, as it contains a higher proportion of compounds to the smaller volume of water. This causes the urine to be darker in color.[17] The National Athletic Trainers Association has created a chart to help individuals assess if they are drinking enough fluids to offset the amount of water lost through sweating (see **Figure 11.14**).[18] Individuals who are very physically active and who notice that the color of their urine darkens during the day, to the point where it resembles the shade of a yield sign or darker, likely need to increase their fluid intake. (Note: Other factors, such as consuming excessive amounts of the B vitamin riboflavin, and certain medications, can also affect the color of urine.)

diet, as fluids from beverages and food throughout the day will eventually restore water balance.[15] However, elderly people, and individuals who are very physically active or who have vigorous jobs, such as fire fighters, are at higher risk of dehydration if they don't take in enough fluid, or they lose body water copiously through sweating. These individuals need to take additional steps to ensure that they are properly hydrated.

Monitor Water Intake to Avoid Overhydration and Dehydration

One way to monitor hydration is the cornerstone method, which involves measuring body weight before and after long bouts of vigorous physical activity or labor and noting changes. If a person weighs less after an activity than before, the weight change is due to loss of body water, and that water must be replenished. The American College of Sports Medicine general recommends that for every pound of weight lost in water, 20-25 fluid ounces (about 2.5 to 4 cups) of water should be consumed.[16] Alternatively, if a weight gain is noted, overhydration is likely, and less fluid should be consumed before the next activity.

Urine color can also be used to assess hydration. Individuals who are

LO 11.6: THE TAKE-HOME MESSAGE
Excess water ingestion can result in water intoxication. Dehydration occurs when water consumed is less than water lost. If both excess water and solutes are lost, hypovolemia is the result. The thirst mechanism is stimulated by hypovolemia. To ensure proper hydration during exercise, monitor weight loss. For every pound of weight lost during exercise, drink at least two and a half cups of water to rehydrate. Clear or light colored urine signals hydration.

Visual Chapter Summary

LO 11.1 Water Is the Most Abundant Nutrient in the Body

Water (H₂O) is the most abundant substance in the body and makes up about 45 to 75 percent of body weight.

Water is a polar molecule, which makes it an excellent solvent. It is a key component of all body fluids, including blood, lymph, and the fluid inside and around cells, and is part of amniotic fluid. Water contributes to digestive juices and exports products through the intestinal cells; transports oxygen, nutrients, and hormones to the cells; and transports waste products to be excreted in urine and stool.

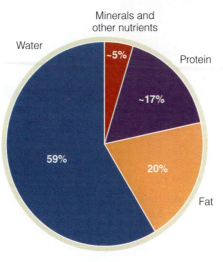

Male, 168 lbs

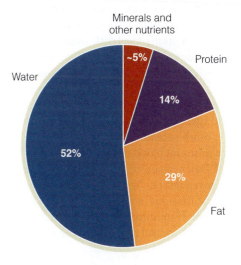

Female, 137 lbs

Water helps maintain body temperature, acts as a lubricant for joints and sensitive eye tissue, moistens food through the action of saliva, is part of mucus that lubricates the intestinal tract, and bathes organs, including the brain. Water is essential for most chemical reactions in the body.

LO 11.2 Water Balance Is Maintained through Ingestion and Excretion and between Fluid Compartments

Water balance is achieved when the amount of water consumed and produced by the body via food, beverages, and metabolism equals the amount excreted through the kidneys, skin, lungs, and feces. The majority of water intake comes from beverages (about 1,500 milliliters) and food (700 milliliters). Metabolic water produces about 300 milliliters per day. Water is lost through the urine (1,500 milliliters), the lungs as water vapor (350 milliliters), the feces (100 milliliters), and sweat (600 milliliters).

Two-thirds of body water is contained in the intracellular fluid found inside the cell, and one-third in the extracellular fluid compartments. Extracellular fluid is comprised of interstitial fluid, found immediately outside and between the cells, and intravascular fluid, found in blood and lymph. Osmosis and the sodium-potassium pump influence water balance between the ICF and the ECF. Albumin in the blood helps maintain fluid balance between the interstitial fluid and the blood.

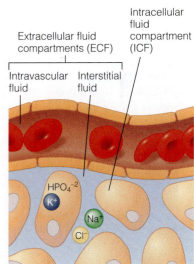

LO 11.3 Water, Sodium, and Hormones Affect Blood Pressure

The kidneys, hypothalamus, pituitary gland, lungs, adrenal glands, and liver all play a role in maintaining blood volume. The hypothalamus detects a drop in blood volume and signals the pituitary gland to release ADH, which increases the absorption of water through the kidneys. The kidneys also react to reduce blood volume by releasing the enzyme renin to convert a liver protein to angiotensin. This protein stimulates the adrenal gland to release the hormone aldosterone, which stimulates the kidneys to reabsorb sodium. The result is a return of blood volume and blood pressure to normal.

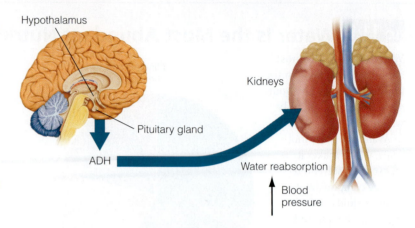

The mechanisms involved in blood pressure regulation directly relate to the sodium concentrations in the ECF. Low intakes of sodium decrease the osmolality in the ECF, which stimulates the renin-angiotensin system. If sodium intake is high, the renin-angiotensin system is reduced and the excess sodium is excreted. Any factors that alter this control mechanism can result in chronic hypertension.

LO 11.4 Daily Water Recommendations Are Based on Water Balance

The current daily water recommendations are based on the reported total water intake (from both beverages and food) of healthy Americans. Adult women should ingest about 9 cups (~80 percent of 12 total cups) of water, and adult males, approximately 13 cups (~80 percent of 16 total cups) of beverages daily. People who are very active and sweat a lot have higher water requirements. All foods contain some water. Cooked hot cereals and fruits and vegetables are robust sources of water.

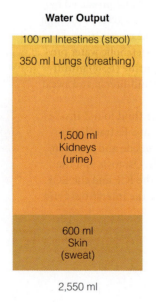

Water Intake

- 300 ml Metabolism
- 700 ml Food
- **1,500 ml Beverages**

2,550 ml

Water Output

- 100 ml Intestines (stool)
- 350 ml Lungs (breathing)
- 1,500 ml Kidneys (urine)
- 600 ml Skin (sweat)

2,550 ml

LO 11.5 Diuretics Can Cause Dehydration

Caffeinated beverages such as coffee, tea, and soft drinks contribute to daily water needs. Caffeine is a mild diuretic but doesn't cause a significant loss of body water compared with noncaffeinated beverages. Individuals who routinely consume caffeine develop a tolerance to its diuretic effect and experience less water loss over time. Alcohol interferes with water balance by inhibiting ADH.

Lo 11.6 Consuming Too Much or Too Little Water Can Be Dangerous

Consuming too much water, a condition called water intoxication, is rare but can be lethal. Drinking fluids too fast without adequate sodium replacement depletes sodium, increases urine production, and results in hyponatremia. This condition can cause fatigue, muscle weakness, confusion, convulsions, and even death.

Dehydration occurs when there is an insufficient amount of water in the body due to reduced fluid intake or to excessive loss due to diarrhea, vomiting, high fever, or the use of diuretics. Dehydration triggers short-term and long-term memory loss, lowers attention span and cognition, reduces the ability to maintain core temperature, and can increase the risk of urinary tract infections and fatigue.

Thirst is often the first sign of dehydration. When water is lost from the body, hypovolemia, or reduced blood volume, can result. The thirst mechanism, which is controlled by the hypothalamus and ADH, stimulates fluid consumption to return fluid levels to normal. Urine color can be used to monitor hydration.

Terms to Know
- polar
- solvent
- specific heat
- acid-base balance
- water balanec
- metabolic water
- insensible water loss
- intracellular fluid (ICF)
- extracellular fluid (ECF)
- interstitial fluid
- intravascular fluid
- electrolytes
- cations
- anions
- osmosis
- selectively permeable
- osmolality
- osmotic gradient
- osmotic pressure
- sodium-potassium pump
- antidiuretic hormone (ADH)
- renin
- angiotensin I and II
- angiotensinogen
- aldosterone
- diuretic
- hyponatremia
- water intoxication
- hypokalemia
- dehydration
- thirst mechanism
- hypovolemia

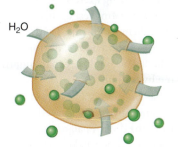

Lower concentration of electrolytes inside

H₂O

Higher concentration of electrolytes inside

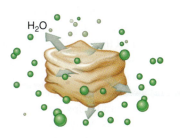

Higher concentration of electrolytes inside

H₂O

Lower concentration of electrolytes inside

MasteringNutrition™

To hear an MP3 chapter review, scan here or visit the Study Area in MasteringNutrition.

Check Your Understanding

1. Which of the following is a function that water performs in the body?
   a. provides energy to the muscles
   b. helps transport waste products for excretion
   c. acts as an antioxidant
   d. participates in the synthesis of proteins

2. Most of the excess body water is lost daily in
   a. exhaled water vapor.
   b. fecal matter.
   c. urine.
   d. sweat.

3. The sodium-potassium pump functions to pump
   a. sodium ions out of the cell and potassium ions into the cell.
   b. sodium ions into the cell and potassium ions out of the cell.
   c. sodium and potassium ions into the cell.
   d. sodium and potassium ions in both directions in and out of the cell.

4. Hypovolemia is the result of
   a. drinking too much water too quickly.
   b. hypernatremia.
   c. dehydration.
   d. drinking ice-cold water.

5. The fluid in the blood is an example of
   a. intracellular fluid.
   b. extracellular fluid.
   c. intravascular fluid.
   d. both b and c.

6. The hormone that signals the kidneys to reabsorb sodium is called
   a. antidiuretic hormone.
   b. aldosterone.
   c. angiotensin.
   d. renin.

7. The thirst mechanism is stimulated by
   a. an increase in blood volume.
   b. an increase in blood pressure.
   c. an increase in the concentration of solutes in the blood.
   d. a decrease in the concentration of solutes in the blood.
8. The purpose of sweating is to
   a. regulate body temperature.
   b. excrete waste products.
   c. excrete sodium ions.
   d. maintain potassium balance.
9. All bottled water is regulated by the FDA.
   a. True
   b. False
10. Hypokalemia is defined as
   a. low levels of sodium in the blood.
   b. low blood volume.
   c. high potassium levels in the blood.
   d. low levels of potassium in the blood.

Answers

1. (b) Water picks up waste products from cells and transports them to the kidneys to be excreted in the urine. Water participates in chemical reactions that provide energy but does not provide energy itself, nor does it act as an antioxidant or help synthesize proteins.
2. (c) The majority of fluid lost is through the kidneys, which produce approximately 1,500 milliliters of urine each day. Exhaled air and lung vapor excrete about 200 to 400 milliliters of water per day, and about 100 milliliters of water is lost through intestinal fluids in the stool. The amount of water lost through the skin as sweat varies depending on environmental temperatures and physical activity.
3. (a) The sodium-potassium pump pumps sodium ions out of the cell and potassium ions into the cell. This helps pull water into compartments to maintain fluid balance.
4. (c) Hypovolemia is the result of reduced blood volume usually due to dehydration or excessive blood loss. Drinking too much water too quickly can result in water intoxication. Hypernatremia, or excess levels of sodium in the blood, would increase blood volume rather than reduce blood volume. The temperature of the water affects absorption rates but doesn't cause hypovolemia.
5. (d) Extracellular fluid is the fluid outside the cell and includes the intravascular fluid, which is in the blood and the capillaries, and interstitial fluid, found between the cells. Intracellular fluid is located inside the cells.
6. (b) The hormone aldosterone signals the kidneys to reabsorb sodium. Antidiuretic hormone signals the kidneys to reabsorb water. Angiotensin is a vasoconstrictor and renin is an enzyme.
7. (c) The thirst mechanism is stimulated by an increase in the concentration of solutes in the blood. Consuming fluids dilutes the solute concentration, increases blood volume, and increases blood pressure, all of which decrease the sensation of thirst.
8. (a) Sweating releases heat from the body and helps regulate body temperature. Whereas sweat does contain waste products and sodium ions, excretion of these is not the main function of sweating.
9. (b) False. The FDA only regulates bottled water that is sold through interstate commerce. Bottled water that is produced and sold within the same state is not regulated by the FDA.
10. (d) Hypokalemia is a low level of potassium in the blood; hyperkalemia denotes high blood potassium levels. Hyponatremia refers to low levels of sodium in the blood, and hypovolemia means decreased blood volume.

Answers to True or False?

1. **False.** You may be able to survive weeks without food but you can't live for more than a few days without water.
2. **True.** Your morning cup of java does contribute to daily water needs, even though it may contain caffeine, a diuretic.
3. **True.** Depending on age, gender, and body composition, a minimum of eight glasses of water per day may be necessary to maintain a healthy level of body water. The recommended intake for adult women is 9 cups per day and 13 cups for men.
4. **False.** Water does transport waste products for excretion from the body, but drinking large amounts will not increase that function and may cause overhydration and hyponatremia, which is a dangerous condition.
5. **False.** Water participates in energy metabolism but does not directly contribute to weight loss.
6. **True.** It is easy to become dehydrated during exercise because of excess sweating, especially in warm, humid environments. Drinking plenty of fluid before, during, and after a workout is key to maintaining hydration.
7. **False.** Sodium is an essential nutrient and should never be eliminated from the diet. A balanced diet and adequate fluid intake prevent fluid retention.
8. **True.** Potassium-rich foods can play a role in reducing hypertension. Potassium works together with sodium to regulate fluid balance and reduce blood pressure.
9. **True.** Alcohol is a diuretic and excess consumption can cause dehydration.
10. **False.** Enhanced waters such as vitamin waters contain additional kilocalories. To improve fluid intake, plain water is just as healthy and much cheaper.

Web Resources

- For more information on high blood pressure, visit Your Guide to Lowering High Blood Pressure at www.nhlbi.nih.gov
- For more information on current research related to hydration during

exercise, visit the Gatorade Sports Science Institute at www.gssiweb.com
- For more information on FDA regulations and bottled water, visit www.fda.gov

References

1. Dunford, M., and J. A. Doyle. 2012. *Nutrition for Sport and Exercise*. 2nd ed. Belmont, CA: Wadsworth, Cengage Learning.
2. Marieb, E. N., and K. Hoehn. 2013. *Human Anatomy and Physiology*. 9th ed. San Francisco: Pearson/Benjamin Cummings.
3. McArdle, W. D., F. I. Katch, and V. L. Katch. 2009. *Sports and Exercise Nutrition*. 3rd ed. Baltimore: Lippincott Williams & Wilkins.
4. Passe, D., M. Horn, J. Stofan, C. Horswill, and R. Murray. 2007. Voluntary Dehydration in Runners Despite Favorable Conditions for Fluid Intake. *International Journal of Sport Nutrition and Exercise Metabolism* 17:284–295.
5. McArdle, et al. 2009. *Sports and Exercise Nutrition*.
6. Grandjean, A., and S. Campbell. 2004. *Hydration: Fluids for Life*. Available at www.ilsi.org. Accessed May 2012.
7. Institute of Medicine. 2004. *Dietary Reference Intakes: Water, Potassium, Sodium, Chloride, and Sulfate*. Washington, DC: The National Academies Press.
8. Killer, S. C., A. K. Blannin, and A. E. Jeukendrup. 2014. No Evidence of Dehydration with Moderate Daily Coffee Intake: A Counterbalanced Cross-Over Study in a Free-Living Population. *PLoS One* 9(1):e84154. doi: 10.1371/journal.pone.0084154.
9. Arnold, D. 2002. To the End, Marathon Was at Center of Student's Life. *The Boston Globe*. Available at www.remembercynthia.com. Accessed March 2014.
10. Grandjean, A. C., K. J. Reimers, and M. E. Buyckx. 2003. Hydration: Issues for the 21st Century. *Nutrition Reviews* 61:261–271.
11. Popkin, B. M., K. E. D'Anci, and I. H. Rosenburg. 2010. Water, Hydration, and Health. *Nutrition Reviews* 68(8):439–458.
12. Casa, D. J. 2003. *Proper Hydration for Distance Running—Identifying Individual Fluid Needs*. Available at www.usatf.org. Accessed June 2014.
13. Ibid.
14. Sentongo, T. A. 2004. The Use of Oral Rehydration Solutions in Children and Adults. *Gastroenterology Reports* 6:307–313.
15. Institute of Medicine. 2004. *Dietary Reference Intakes: Water, Potassium, Sodium, Chloride, and Sulfate*.
16. Sawka, M. N., L. M. Burke, E. R. Eichner, R. J. Maughan, S. J. Montain, and N. S. Stachenfield. 2007. American College of Sports Medicine Position Stand: Exercise and Fluid Replacement. *Medicine and Science in Sports & Exercise* 39:377–390.
17. Ibid.
18. Casa, D. J., L. E. Armstrong, S. K. Hillman, S. J. Montain, R. C. Reiff, B. S. E. Rich, W. O. Roberts, and J. A. Stone. 2000. National Athletic Trainers Association Position Statement: Fluid Replacement for Athletes. *Journal of Athletic Training* 35:212–224.

12 Major Minerals

Learning Outcomes

After reading this chapter, you will be able to:

12.1 Describe the differences between the major and trace minerals and the factors that affect their bioavailability, absorption, and retention.

12.2 List the functions, food sources, and the toxicity and deficiency symptoms associated with sodium.

12.3 List the functions, food sources, and the toxicity and deficiency symptoms associated with chloride.

12.4 List the functions, food sources, and the toxicity and deficiency symptoms associated with potassium.

12.5 List the functions, food sources, and the toxicity and deficiency symptoms associated with calcium.

12.6 List the functions, food sources, and the toxicity and deficiency symptoms associated with phosphorus.

12.7 List the functions, food sources, and the toxicity and deficiency symptoms associated with magnesium.

12.8 List the functions, food sources, and daily needs associated with sulfate.

12.9 Compare the roles of minerals in the development of healthy bone tissue and osteoporosis, and outline the factors that influence the risk of developing the disease.

True or False?

1. The very best way to ensure an adequate intake of minerals is to take supplements. **T/F**

2. Minerals are simpler molecules than vitamins. **T/F**

3. Hypertension is a preventable condition. **T/F**

4. Minerals are more bioavailable in plant foods than in animal foods. **T/F**

5. Eating more fruit can improve bone density. **T/F**

6. A diet rich in potassium can help lower blood pressure. **T/F**

7. Most dietary sodium comes from salt added to foods during cooking. **T/F**

8. A serving of milk provides about a third of an adult's daily calcium needs. **T/F**

9. Consuming too much phosphorus interferes with calcium absorption. **T/F**

10. Sulfate is not an essential nutrient. **T/F**

See page 465 for the answers.

What do a cast-iron skillet, the salt on an icy road, and the copper pipes used in plumbing all have in common? They contain one or more of the same minerals that play essential roles in the body.

In this chapter, we explore the roles that the major minerals play in the body. We discuss the average person's daily needs for each mineral and, equally important, how to avoid consuming toxic amounts. We cover the trace minerals in Chapter 13.

What Are Minerals?

LO 12.1 Describe the differences between the major and trace minerals and the factors that affect their bioavailability, absorption, and retention.

Like vitamins, **minerals** can be part of enyzmes to help chemical reactions take place in cells, work with the immune system, participate in muscle contraction, and keep the heart beating. In short, minerals are essential to overall health and well-being.

Minerals are classified into two groups. The **major minerals,** or *macrominerals,* are *major* because humans need to consume them in amounts greater than 100 milligrams per day (daily needs for some major minerals exceed 1,000 milligrams per day), and there are at least 5 grams of the mineral in the body (**Figure 12.1**). Calcium is considered a major mineral because adults need to consume at least 1,000 milligrams per day, and the body contains approximately 1,000 grams of calcium. The other major minerals are sodium, chloride, potassium, phosphorus, magnesium, and sulfur.

The second group, the **trace minerals,** or *microminerals,* are needed in amounts less than 20 milligrams per day, and the body contains less than 5 grams total. Iron is an example of a trace mineral; the average adult male needs about 8 milligrams per day and has a total of about 3 to 4 grams in his body. The other trace minerals are zinc, copper, selenium, chromium, iodide, manganese, molybdenum, and fluoride.

minerals Inorganic elements essential to the nutrition of humans.

major minerals Minerals needed in amounts greater than 100 milligrams per day. These include sodium, chloride, potassium, calcium, phosphorus, magnesium, and sulfur.

trace minerals Minerals needed in amounts less than 20 milligrams daily. These include iron, zinc, selenium, fluoride, chromium, copper, manganese, and molybdenum.

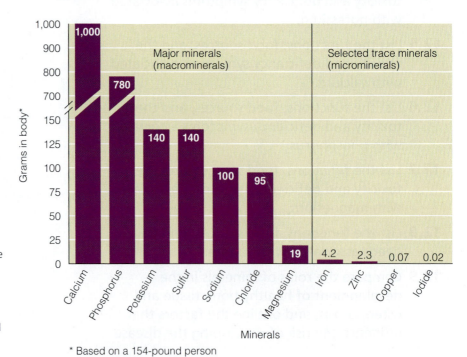

* Based on a 154-pound person

▲ Figure 12.1 **The Minerals in Your Body**
Major minerals are present in larger amounts than are trace minerals in the human body. However, all are equally important to health.

Minerals Are Inorganic Elements Needed by the Body

Minerals do not contain carbon, and are therefore classified as inorganic. Unlike vitamins, single elements of minerals contain only atoms of the same element, such as calcium (Ca), iron (Fe), or other essential minerals, in the form of inorganic salts, including sodium chloride, or NaCl (see **Figure 12.2**). Molecules of vitamins are more complex and contain other elements.

Minerals are also different from vitamins in that minerals are very stable in food; that is, they are not destroyed by heat, acid, oxygen, or ultraviolet light.[1] Most minerals are similar to water soluble vitamins and may leach out of foods.

When mineral salts dissolve in body water, they separate (or *dissociate*) into individually charged particles, or ions. Minerals found in the body are most often found as individual ions or as components of compounds such as hydroxyapatite or ATP.

Minerals differ from the macronutrients in that they remain intact during digestion and generally don't change their shape or structure when performing their biological functions. Thus, the potassium in bananas has the same ionic charge as the potassium inside muscle cells.

Minerals Vary in Their Bioavailability

Recall that the degree to which a nutrient is absorbed and ultimately available to be used in the body is called its **bioavailability.** The bioavailability of minerals is affected by several factors, including your nutritional status and the other contents in the GI tract. Nutritional status, or the amount of the mineral stored in the body, influences how much is absorbed. If you are deficient in a mineral, such as calcium, you absorb a greater percentage of that mineral from food. Similarly, if your body has an adequate amount of a mineral, it absorbs less of it from food. Because some minerals can be toxic in high amounts, this ability to adjust the amount absorbed helps prevent the body from accumulating harmful amounts.

Eating a meal that contains a food high in a particular mineral does not necessarily mean the body will absorb that mineral during digestion. Minerals often compete with each other for absorption in the GI tract. Some minerals, such as calcium, magnesium, iron, copper, and zinc, are absorbed in their ionic state. These minerals have the same ionic charge, so they vie for the same protein carriers during absorption. Too much of one mineral, such as calcium, Ca^{2+}, can cause a decrease in the absorption and metabolism of another mineral, such as magnesium, Mg^{2+}, leading to an imbalance.[2, 3] Thus, bioavailability of each mineral depends on the amount of both minerals in the intestinal tract at the time of absorption.[4] This is one reason why most people should avoid taking single-mineral supplements.

The bioavailability of minerals can also be reduced if the minerals are attached to **binders** such as oxalates (acids found in vegetables) or phytates (acids found in grains and legumes). The acid-mineral complex passes through the intestinal tract unabsorbed. Spinach, for example, is technically high in calcium, but the vegetable is actually a poor calcium source because its oxalates render most of the mineral unavailable for absorption. In fact, an individual absorbs only about one-tenth as much calcium from spinach as from milk.[5] In some cases, cooking a food, such as legumes that contain phytates, can help increase the bioavailability of its minerals by breaking the bonds between the minerals and the binders.[6]

Polyphenols in tea and coffee also bind and inhibit the body's absorption of minerals, such as iron, reducing bioavailability.[7] Juice, milk, or water are better choices for aiding mineral absorption than are coffee or tea.

a Na^+, an example of an inorganic nutrient

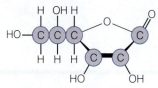

b Vitamin C, an example of an organic nutrient

▲ **Figure 12.2 The Structure of an Inorganic Versus an Organic Nutrient (a)** Minerals are inorganic, so their structure consists solely of the mineral itself, or in combination with another mineral. **(b)** Organic nutrients, including carbohydrates, proteins, lipids, and vitamins, contain carbon, hydrogen, and oxygen and sometimes nitrogen.

bioavailability The degree to which a nutrient is absorbed from foods and used in the body.

binders Compounds such as oxalates and phytates that bind to minerals in foods and reduce their bioavailability.

Oxalates found in spinach bind to calcium, reducing the amount of calcium the body is able to absorb.

Some nutrients improve the bioavailability of minerals. Vitamin C enhances the absorption of iron from plant foods. Animal protein from meat, fish, and poultry enhances zinc absorption, and vitamin D enhances calcium, phosphorus, and magnesium absorption. **Table 12.1** presents a summary of the factors that affect the bioavailability of minerals.

Minerals Serve Numerous Functions

Minerals play roles in fluid and electrolyte balance, they form blood cells (iron and copper), build healthy bones (calcium, phosphorus, magnesium, and fluoride), and maintain a healthy immune system (zinc).[8] Minerals can also be part of enzyme complexes, participate in energy metabolism, and play an invaluable role in structural growth.

The body maintains a tight control over mineral balance. Recall that the GI tract and the kidneys help to closely regulate water and electrolyte balance (Chapter 11). To maintain homeostasis, minerals found in the gastric juices and in sloughed-off intestinal cells are either excreted through the feces or reabsorbed through the large intestine. The kidneys respond to changing levels of minerals in the blood by filtering the blood through the tubules. The kidneys either excrete the excess minerals through the urine or reabsorb the minerals back into the blood when mineral needs are greater. For example, when sodium levels in the blood are low, the kidneys filter the sodium through the tubules and reabsorb the sodium back into the blood. Some potassium is excreted through the urine to balance positive ions in the body. These controls ensure that a sufficient amount of each mineral is available to perform normal muscle contraction, transmit nerve impulses, sustain heart function, and maintain healthy blood.

Minerals Help Maintain Fluid Balance

The electrically charged minerals are essential to balance fluid outside the cell (extracellular) with fluid inside the cell (intracellular), that is, to maintain fluid balance. The sodium and chloride located mainly outside of cells, and the potassium (with the help of calcium, phosphorus, magnesium, and sulfur) located mostly inside cells, all play key roles in maintaining fluid balance. Without these minerals, cells could swell and burst from taking in too much fluid, or shrink from dehydration.

Minerals Participate as Cofactors

Minerals are similar to many vitamins in that they can act as **cofactors** in important enzyme systems. Mineral cofactors may be loosely or tightly bound to an

cofactors Similar to a coenzyme, a substance that binds to an enzyme to help catalyze a reaction. The term cofactor generally refers to a metal ion, while a coenzyme is usually an organic molecule such as a vitamin.

TABLE 12.1	Factors That Affect the Bioavailability of Minerals
Factors That Increase Bioavailability	**Factors That Reduce Bioavailability**
Deficiency in a mineral increases absorption	Binders, such as oxalates found in some vegetables
Cooking increases the bioavailability of minerals in legumes	Phytates found in grains
Vitamin C increases the absorption of some minerals such as iron	Polyphenols in tea and coffee
Vitamin D increases the absorption of calcium, phosphorus, and magnesium	Supplementation of single minerals affects absorption of competing minerals

enzyme, and once a reaction is complete, the mineral is released. For example, the mineral selenium acts as a cofactor for the complex antioxidant enzyme system glutathione peroxidase. This system reduces free radical formation and repairs the damage already done by free radicals. Without the mineral selenium, glutathione peroxidase would be unable to convert free radicals to less harmful substances, and the effect would be oxidative tissue damage that could result in cardiovascular disease and cancer. Other metabolic processes such as energy metabolism, muscle contraction, and nerve transmission also require minerals as cofactors.

Minerals Make Up Bones and Teeth

The major minerals calcium, phosphorus, and magnesium, along with the trace mineral fluoride, make up the crystalline structure that gives strength to bones and teeth. In fact, **hydroxyapatite** crystals make up about 60 percent of bone mass. The hydroxyapatite minerals attach to the protein collagen during bone formation and accumulate during **mineralization.** Inadequate buildup of hydroxyapatite crystals during bone formation, or too much withdrawal of the minerals during adulthood, leads to weakened and brittle bones, similar to the way using too few bolts and girders during construction leads to an unsafe skyscraper.

Hydroxyapatite crystals in the outer layer of bone.

Minerals Can Be Toxic

Like some fat-soluble vitamins, minerals can be toxic if ingested in high amounts. However, mineral toxicity from an excess dietary intake is rare in healthy individuals because the amounts found in foods are not that high, and most Americans do not generally exceed the UL for minerals. Also, the body can adapt its absorption or excretion of many minerals according to its needs. In other words, the small intestine can reduce absorption of a particular mineral if the body already contains an adequate amount, and the kidneys can filter excess minerals from the blood and excrete them through the urine.

However, ingesting more than the UL of a mineral, such as by taking large amounts of supplements, may lead to illness and even death. Excessive levels of magnesium in the blood can result in heart problems or an inability to breathe,[9] while excessive amounts of calcium may cause nausea, vomiting, loss of appetite, increased urination, kidney toxicity, confusion, and irregular heart rhythm.[10] Although mineral toxicity is more likely to occur in individuals with certain conditions, such as acute or chronic kidney failure, even healthy people ingesting excessive amounts of minerals may experience unwanted side effects.

Though minerals have much in common with each other and work together to support numerous body functions, they are each important for individual reasons, and we explore these in greater detail. In the following pages, we discuss the metabolic functions, daily needs, food sources, and toxicity and deficiency symptoms for each of the major minerals. An overview of each of these major minerals is presented in **Table 12.2.**

LO 12.1: THE TAKE-HOME MESSAGE Major and trace minerals are inorganic nutrients classified based on the amount found in the body and the amount needed daily. The bioavailability of minerals varies based on nutrient status and whether the mineral is bound with other substances in food or ingested together. Minerals play a vital role in bone and blood health, fluid balance, as cofactors in energy metabolism and muscle contractions, and in nerve transmissions. Mineral toxicity is rare in healthy individuals but can occur by ingesting high doses of minerals through supplementation.

hydroxyapatite The crystalline salt structure that provides strength in bones and teeth. Calcium and phosphorus are the main minerals found in the structure.

mineralization The process of adding minerals, including calcium and phosphorus, to the collagen matrix in the bone, which makes the bone strong and rigid.

TABLE 12.2	Metabolic Function, Daily Needs, Food Sources, and Symptoms of Toxicity and Deficiency of the Major Minerals				
Major Mineral	**Metabolic Function**	**Daily Needs (19 years+)**	**Food Sources**	**Toxicity Symptoms/UL**	**Deficiency Symptoms**
Sodium (Na^+)	■ Major cation outside the cell ■ Regulates body water and blood pressure	1,500 mg/day	Processed foods, seaweed, table salt	■ Edema ■ Hypertension UL: 2,300 mg/day	■ Headache ■ Nausea and vomiting ■ Fatigue ■ Disorientation
Chloride (Cl^-)	■ Major anion out-side the cell ■ Part of HCl ■ Participates in acid-base balance	2,300 mg/day	Processed foods, seaweed, table salt, and rye	■ Vomiting UL: 3,600 mg/day	■ Rare that symptoms occur unless related to loss of sodium
Potassium (K^+)	■ Major cation inside the cell ■ Regulates body water and blood pressure	4,700 mg/day	Unprocessed foods, Fruits and vegetables, meat, dairy, and nuts	■ Irregular heart beat and heart damage UL: None established	■ Muscle weakness and cramps ■ Glucose intolerance ■ Irregular heart beat and paralysis
Calcium (Ca^{+2})	■ Formation of bones and teeth ■ Muscle contraction and relaxation ■ Blood clotting ■ Heart and nerve function	1,000 mg/day	Milk and dairy products, leafy greens, broccoli, salmon, sardines, legumes, calcium-fortified orange juice	■ Constipation ■ Impaired kidneys ■ Calcium deposits in tissues UL: 2,500 mg/day	■ Bone loss (osteoporosis) ■ Bone fractures
Phosphorus (PO_4^{-3})	■ Formation of bones and teeth ■ Part of DNA, RNA, coenzymes, and the ATP energy molecule ■ Transport of lipids ■ Acid-base balance	700 mg/day	Meat, fish, poultry, eggs, cereals	■ Decrease in bone mass ■ Calcium deposits in tissues UL: 4,000 mg/day	■ Muscle weakness ■ Bone pain
Magnesium (Mg^{+2})	■ Participates as a cofactor in many biochemical reactions including muscle contraction and nerve conduction	Women: 310 mg/day Men: 400 mg/day	Green leafy vegetables, whole grains, nuts, legumes, dairy, and fruits	■ Diarrhea, cramps, and nausea (from supplements, not food) UL: 350 mg/day (from supplements only; all adults)	■ Weakness and fatigue ■ Confusion and seizures ■ Depression ■ Irregular heart beats
Sulfate (SO_4^{-2})	■ Part of keratin found in hair and skin ■ Formation of collagen ■ Participates in acid-base balance and cellular respiration	None established	All protein-containing foods such as meat, fish, poultry, eggs, legumes, nuts, and dairy	■ May promote ulcerative colitis UL: None established	■ None known

Exploring Sodium

LO 12.2 List the functions, food sources, and the toxicity and deficiency symptoms associated with sodium.

What Is Sodium?

Sodium, in the form of sodium chloride or table salt (NaCl), has been part of our diet since the earliest recorded history when it was used to preserve and flavor food. In breads, sodium serves multiple functions beyond enhancing flavor: It is added to yeast breads to prevent the yeast from overexpanding the dough. It is also used to reduce the growth of bacteria and mold in many bread products and luncheon meats. Sodium chloride, or table salt, accounts for about 90 percent of the sodium you consume and approximately 40 percent of the weight of table salt is sodium. Thus, in 6 grams (1 teaspoon) of table salt, approximately 2.4 grams are sodium. Sodium in other forms, such as sodium phosphate, sodium carbonate, and sodium bicarbonate (baking soda), are food additives and preservatives that perform similar functions in other foods. Monosodium glutamate (MSG) is a form of sodium commonly added to Asian cuisines to intensify the flavor of foods.

In the body, **sodium (Na$^+$)** is a major electrolyte and cation found primarily in the blood and interstitial fluid surrounding the cells. It plays a key role in regulating blood volume and blood pressure. The rest of the body's sodium is located in bones, in nerve tissue, and in muscle tissue.

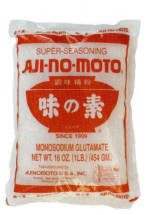

Absorption, Transport, and Excretion of Sodium

When you ingest table salt, fluid from the lining of the stomach breaks the bonds between the sodium and chloride ions and the ions mix with the digestive juices. Once the two ions dissociate they can both be absorbed.

Most sodium (95 to 100 percent) is absorbed throughout the small intestine, though a small amount (up to 5 percent) passes through the intestinal tract and is excreted in the feces. Once absorbed, sodium moves freely throughout the blood until it is filtered by the kidney and excreted through the urine.

The kidneys maintain the amount of sodium in the blood at a precise level. To maintain sodium balance, the amount eaten must equal the amount lost. If blood sodium levels drop, the hormone angiotensin II stimulates the adrenal glands to secrete the hormone aldosterone, which in turn stimulates the kidneys to reabsorb more sodium,

returning the blood levels to normal (see Chapter 11 to review this process). Likewise, when the blood levels of sodium are too high, angiotensin II is reduced and the adrenal glands stop releasing aldosterone, allowing the kidneys to excrete the excess sodium in the urine (**Figure 12.3**). The kidneys also reabsorb sodium in exchange for H$^+$ when the pH is too acidic, thereby restoring acid-base balance.

A small amount of sodium is also lost through daily perspiration. The amount of sodium lost through the skin depends upon the rate of sweating, the amount of sodium consumed (the more sodium in the diet, the higher the loss through sweat), and the intensity of heat in the environment. As you become more acclimated to environmental heat, you lose less sodium over time.

sodium (Na$^+$) The major cation in the extracellular fluid.

When Sodium Levels Are Low

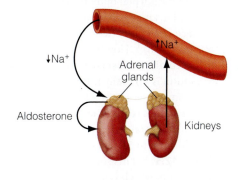

a When sodium levels in the blood are low, aldosterone is released from the adrenal glands, which triggers the kidneys to reabsorb sodium into the blood.

When Sodium Levels Are High

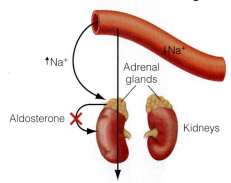

b When sodium levels in the blood are high, the adrenal glands stop secreting aldosterone, and the kidneys excrete the excess sodium through the urine. This lowers the levels of sodium in the blood.

▲ Figure 12.3 **Sodium Balance Is Maintained by the Kidneys**

continued

Metabolic Functions of Sodium

Sodium plays an important role in regulating fluid balance. In addition, sodium plays a role in transmission of nerve impulses, muscle contractions, and transport of nutrients.

Sodium Helps Regulate Fluid Balance

The volume of fluid in the extracellular compartment is determined by the amount of electrolytes, including sodium, that are present. Any shift in the electrolyte concentration in any fluid compartment affects the amount of fluid present.

As soon as dietary sodium is absorbed, it is quickly distributed throughout the circulation, increasing the concentration of Na^+ in the blood. This, in turn, stimulates the hypothalamus, which activates the thirst mechanism and triggers the release of ADH from the pituitary gland. The result is that you drink more water and excrete less urine, thereby helping to restore the balance between sodium and fluid in the body.

Sodium Transmits Nerve Impulses and Participates in Muscle Contraction

Sodium works with potassium to help transmit all nerve impulses, including those that signal muscles to contract. This mechanism is called the sodium-potassium pump (Chapter 11). Both sodium and potassium are cations, with sodium outside the cell and potassium inside the cell. When sodium is transported by the sodium-potassium pump through the membrane into a nerve cell, the cell becomes more positively charged, which triggers a signal along the nerves to the muscle cells. The muscle is then stimulated to contract.

Sodium Helps Transport Some Nutrients

As you learned in Chapter 11, sodium plays an important role in transporting nutrients across cell membranes as part of the sodium-potassium pump. As Na^+ flows down its concentration gradient attached to a protein carrier, it drags other

hypertension High blood pressure.

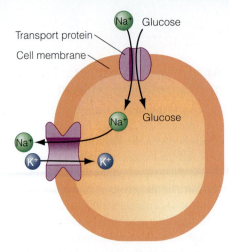

▲ **Figure 12.4 Sodium Helps Transport Some Nutrients**
A protein carrier on the cell membrane transports sodium (Na^+) along with other nutrients such as glucose inside the cell. Once inside the cell, Na^+ is pumped back out of the cell in exchange for K^+ through the sodium-potassium pump.

nutrients, such as glucose and some amino acids, along with it across the cell membrane and inside the cell (**Figure 12.4**).

Daily Needs for Sodium

The daily minimum amount of sodium needed for normal body function is 180 milligrams— about enough to cover the face of a penny (less than 1/16th of a teaspoon).[11] However, planning a balanced diet with such a small amount of sodium is virtually impossible, so the DRI committee set an AI recommendation at a more realistic level: 1,500 milligrams daily (about ¾ of a teaspoon) for adults up to 51 years of age (see **Figure 12.5**).[12] This sodium recommendation, which is about eight times the minimum amount needed, is set to accommodate a variety of foods from all the food groups so individuals can meet all their other nutrient needs. It also allows for increased needs of moderately active individuals, who lose more sodium in sweat, and those who are not

adjusted to the environmental temperature. Those who are very physically active or not acclimated to heat likely need to consume a higher amount of sodium. Americans currently consume more than double the recommended amount, or over 3,400 milligrams, of sodium (about 1½ teaspoons) daily, on average.[13]

Food Sources of Sodium

The vast majority of dietary sodium, a hefty 77 percent in American diets, comes from salt used in processed foods such as canned goods (particularly soups), cured meats, and frozen or packaged meals.[14] Comparing the amount of sodium in a fresh tomato (11 milligrams) to the amount found in a cup of canned tomatoes (355 milligrams) quickly illustrates just how much sodium is added by manufacturers during processing. Some sauces and condiments, such as soy sauce (900 milligrams/tablespoon) or ketchup (190 milligrams/tablespoon), also contribute hefty amounts of sodium.[15]

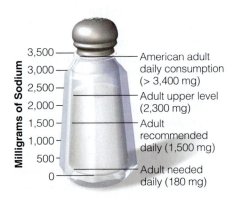

▲ **Figure 12.5 Recommended Intake of Sodium**

About 12 percent of Americans' sodium consumption is from eating foods that naturally contain sodium (see **Figure 12.6**). For example, rice rolls made with seaweed are naturally high in sodium (240 milligrams per serving) because of the high salt concentration in the seaweed. Another 5 percent of sodium intake is from salt that's added during cooking, and 6 percent is from salt used to season foods at the table.

Sodium

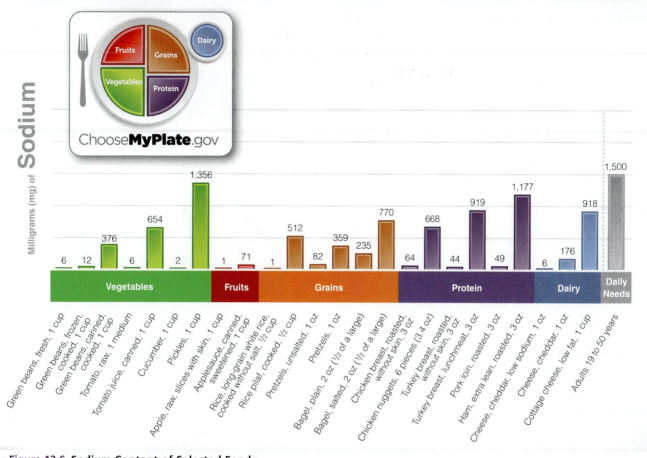

Milligrams (mg) of Sodium

Category	Food	mg
Vegetables	Green beans, fresh, 1 cup	6
	Green beans, frozen, cooked, 1 cup	12
	Green beans, canned, cooked, 1 cup	376
	Tomato, raw, 1 medium	6
	Tomato juice, canned, 1 cup	654
	Cucumber, 1 cup	2
	Pickles, 1 cup	1,356
Fruits	Apple, raw, slices with skin, 1 cup	1
	Applesauce, canned, sweetened, 1 cup	71
Grains	Rice, long-grain white rice, cooked without salt, ½ cup	1
	Rice pilaf, cooked, ½ cup	82
	Pretzels, unsalted, 1 oz	512
	Pretzels, 1 oz	359
	Bagel, plain, 2 oz (½ of a large)	235
	Bagel, salted, 2 oz (½ of a large)	770
Protein	Chicken breast, roasted, without skin, 3 oz	64
	Chicken nuggets, 6 pieces (3.4 oz)	668
	Turkey breast, roasted, without skin, 3 oz	44
	Turkey breast, lunchmeat, 3 oz	919
	Pork loin, roasted, 3 oz	49
	Ham, extra lean, roasted, 3 oz	1,177
Dairy	Cheese, cheddar, low sodium, 1 oz	6
	Cheese, cheddar, 1 oz	176
	Cottage cheese, low fat, 1 cup	918
Daily Needs	Adults 19 to 50 years	1,500

▲ Figure 12.6 **Sodium Content of Selected Foods**

Sodium Excess

Given that the body excretes excess dietary sodium, do you need to worry about eating too much? Yes. Researchers have established that there is a direct relationship between sodium intake from salt (sodium chloride), and elevated blood pressure (or **hypertension**), particularly in individuals who are *salt sensitive* or show a rise in blood pressure after eating salt.

Certain segments of the population are more likely to be salt sensitive, including elderly individuals, people with diabetes or chronic kidney disease, and African-Americans.[16] Whereas about 35 percent of Caucasians appear to be salt sensitive, African-Americans have a much higher rate of 75 percent. Overall, about 50 percent of individuals with hypertension are salt sensitive. However, in general, even if you are not salt sensitive, as a person's intake of sodium increases, so does his or her blood pressure,[17] and reducing dietary sodium may improve blood pressure.

High blood pressure increases the risk for heart disease, stroke, and kidney disease. Unfortunately, many Americans will develop hypertension sometime during their life. The upper level for sodium for adults is set at 2,300 milligrams, or about 1 teaspoon of table salt, in order to help reduce the risk. The current *Dietary Guidelines for Americans* also recommend that salt intake should be limited (see Chapter 2).

Hypernatremia

When the blood levels of sodium become too concentrated, not only is hypertension a concern, but a condition called **hypernatremia** (*hyper* = too much,

hypernatremia Excessive amounts of sodium in the blood.

continued

natrium = sodium, *emia* = blood) can also develop. The most common reason for hypernatremia is due to not replacing water that is lost due to vomiting or diarrhea, which causes blood levels of Na^+ to become too concentrated. This can also occur if too much Na^+ is ingested without sufficient water intake, such as athletes using salt tablets.

As the extracellular fluid becomes **hypertonic** (too concentrated in solutes), water moves from intracellular fluid to the extracellular fluid until a balance of concentrated ions to fluid is restored. Thus, changes in the concentration outside the cell affect the concentration of water inside the cell leading to dehydration. In addition, if the kidneys are functioning correctly, less fluid is excreted in the urine and the thirst mechanism is stimulated. Symptoms of hypernatremia include thirst, dry mouth, decreased urination, and lightheadedness.

Osteoporosis

Consuming too much sodium can also contribute to calcium-deficiency osteoporosis.[18, 19] In both human and animal studies, research has shown that sodium in the urine correlates to reduced reabsorption of calcium by the kidneys. This lack of reabsorption leads to greater calcium loss in the urine and may contribute to bone loss, especially in postmenopausal women.[20] Eating too much sodium can also contribute to fluid retention, weight gain, stomach ulcers, and stomach cancer.[21]

Reducing Sodium Intake

The DASH (Dietary Approaches to Stop Hypertension) diet plan and the Mediterranean diet have both been shown to reduce hypertension.[22] Both plans focus on consuming fruits, vegetables, low-fat or nonfat dairy products, lean meats, whole grains, and legumes.

Because the majority of sodium comes from sodium chloride in processed foods, and a fair amount comes from the salt that you add to your foods, cutting back on these two sources is the best way to lower dietary intake. One way to scale back sodium intake in processed foods is to read labels carefully. However, even this can be a challenge if you're not well versed in label terms.

"Low sodium," for instance, means there is less than 140 milligrams of sodium per serving, while "sodium free" means the product may contain up to 5 milligrams per serving. "Reduced sodium" means only that the sodium content of the "regular" version has been reduced by 25 percent, and "light in sodium" means it has been reduced by 50 percent. A regular version of a product like soy sauce may have 1,000 milligrams of sodium in 1 tablespoon, while 1 tablespoon of light soy sauce contains 500 milligrams, or 33 percent of the AI. Note that even though the product's sodium has been reduced, it is still considered high in sodium.

While reading nutrition labels is helpful in controlling sodium intake, the Daily Values are based on older reference values and are not as current as the DRIs. The Daily Value for sodium is based on 2,400 milligrams of sodium per day, which is higher than both the AI (1,500 milligrams) and the

UL (2,300 milligrams) for sodium. For example, the sodium content for a beef hot dog with a bun is approximately 1,400 milligrams, or 58 percent of the Daily Value. However, that one hot dog would satisfy the AI for sodium for the day. If you ate two hot dogs, your sodium intake would be 2,800 milligrams, which is greater than the UL. The FDA has proposed to reduce the Daily Value for sodium to 2,300 milligrams on the new labels.[23]

The best way to reduce sodium intake is to limit consumption of processed foods and bypass the saltshaker at the table. If you do purchase processed foods, buy only products labeled as "low sodium" or "sodium free." When cooking, season foods with a variety of herbs or other flavorings such as black pepper, Tabasco sauce, lemon juice, or a no-salt seasoning blend instead of salt.

TABLE TIPS

Shake the Salt Habit

Dilute canned soups by combining a can of regular vegetable soup and a can of low-sodium vegetable soup for soup with less sodium. Add cooked, frozen vegetables for an even healthier meal.

Limit deli meats to no more than 3 ounces on your sandwich, and pile on naturally low-sodium tomatoes, lettuce, cucumbers, and shredded cabbage.

Choose low-sodium dried fruits (apricots and raisins) and unsalted walnut pieces or almonds for a sweet or crunchy snack.

Skip salty french fries and enjoy a sodium-free baked potato instead.

Use olive oil and vinegar instead of salad dressing on your salad, or dilute regular salad dressing with an equal portion of vinegar to cut the sodium content.

---

hypertonic Having a high solute concentration.

Sodium Deficiency

Dietary sodium deficiency is rare in healthy individuals who consume a balanced diet. However, individuals who consume too much water in a short amount of time, such as marathon runners or military trainees, risk diluting sodium and other electrolytes in the excessive volume of body fluid (referred to as **hypotonic**), which can result in **hyponatremia** (*hypo* = under, *natrium* = sodium, *emia* = blood), a condition that can be fatal. Symptoms include headache, muscle weakness, fatigue, and seizures that can eventually lead to coma and death. Too little sodium can also result when excessive amounts of the mineral are lost through the kidneys, such as with the use of diuretics.[24]

LO 12.2: THE TAKE-HOME MESSAGE
Sodium functions in fluid balance between the blood and cells, transmits nerve impulses, participates in muscle contraction, and helps transport some nutrients across cell membranes. Adults need about 1,500 milligrams of sodium daily but consume more than double that amount, predominantly as sodium chloride. Processed foods are the major source of sodium in the diet. Excess sodium in the blood can cause hypertension, hypernatremia, and bone loss. Low sodium levels in the blood result in hyponatremia.

hypotonic Having a low solute concentration.

hyponatremia Abnormally low levels of sodium in the blood.

Exploring Chloride

LO 12.3 List the functions, food sources, and the toxicity and deficiency symptoms associated with chloride.

What Is Chloride?

Chloride (Cl⁻) is an anion almost always found bonded to sodium as sodium chloride in foods. Within the body, this major electrolyte is found mostly in the blood (approximately 88 percent), with the remainder (approximately 12 percent) found in the interstitial fluid and as part of hydrochloric acid in the stomach. Chloride is the ionic form of chlorine and should not be confused with the powerful disinfectant that is poisonous when inhaled or ingested.

When chloride is ingested as table salt (**Figure 12.7**), it dissociates in the stomach, mixes with the digestive juices, and is absorbed through the small intestine. Chloride is excreted through the urine, although small

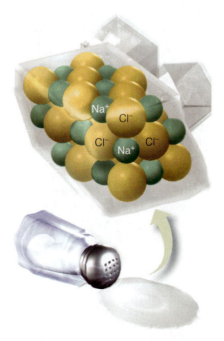

▲ Figure 12.7 **Sodium Chloride**
Sodium chloride, or table salt, is 60 percent chloride and 40 percent sodium.

amounts of chloride can be lost in the feces and through the skin.

Metabolic Functions of Chloride

The negative charge of Cl⁻ balances the positive charge of Na⁺ in the extracellular fluid to maintain fluid balance. Chloride assists in the removal of CO_2 from the blood, helping maintain a normal pH range, and participates in digestion as part of hydrochloric acid (HCl).

Daily Needs for Chloride

The AI for chloride is set at about 2,300 milligrams a day for adults aged 19 to 50. Americans in general consume well above this requirement. In fact, on average, Americans consume an estimated 3,400 milligrams to just over 7,000 milligrams of dietary chloride daily.[25]

chloride (Cl⁻) Major anion in the extracellular fluid.

continued

Food Sources of Chloride

Table salt accounts for almost all the chloride you ingest daily. Approximately 60 percent of the weight of table salt is chloride. Thus, in 6 grams (1 teaspoon) of table salt, approximately 3.6 grams are chloride. In addition to processed foods that contain sodium chloride, chloride is also found naturally in seaweed, tomatoes, olives, lettuce, celery, and rye. Chloride is also part of potassium chloride, the main ingredient in salt substitutes.

hyperchloremia Abnormally high level of chloride in the blood.

hypochloremia Abnormally low level of chloride in the blood.

Chloride Toxicity and Deficiency

Because sodium chloride is the major source of chloride in the diet, the upper level for adults for chloride is set at 3,600 milligrams to coincide with the upper level for sodium.[26]

Chloride toxicity is rare and produces no symptoms. However, athletes who become extremely dehydrated from prolonged sweating may experience **hyperchloremia,** or hyperconcentration of chloride in the blood. The best way to avoid this condition is to drink sufficient fluid and electrolytes when exercising in extreme heat.

Though chloride deficiency rarely occurs in healthy individuals, a serious bout of vomiting and/or diarrhea can cause excessive loss of chloride as part of hydrochloric acid. Some diuretics can cause an increase in chloride excretion in the urine, resulting in low chloride levels in the blood, or **hypochloremia.** The symptoms of hypochloremia include shallow breathing, muscle weakness, muscle spasms, and twitching.

LO 12.3: THE TAKE-HOME MESSAGE

Chloride helps maintains fluid balance, helps remove CO_2 from the blood, helps maintain pH balance, and participates in digestion as part of HCl in the stomach. Adults need 2,300 milligrams per day. Almost all the chloride ingested comes from sodium chloride (table salt). Chloride hyperchloremia, hyperchloridemia, and chloride deficiency, known as hypochloremia, are rare.

Exploring Potassium

LO 12.4 List the functions, food sources, and the toxicity and deficiency symptoms associated with potassium.

What Is Potassium?

Potassium (K^+) is the major cation found in the intracellular fluid (ICF). About 85 percent of consumed potassium is absorbed throughout the small intestine and colon. The kidney maintains potassium balance by excreting excess potassium through the urine and minor amounts through the sweat.

Potassium Balance in the Body

After it enters the blood, dietary potassium is quickly taken up into the cells. When there is excess potassium in the blood, the kidneys excrete more potassium in the urine. The kidneys control the level of potassium in the same way that they control sodium. When the blood levels of potassium are low, the kidneys reabsorb potassium and return the blood levels to normal. The difference between the maintenance of potassium and sodium blood levels is that the hormone aldosterone is stimulated when blood K^+ is high and Na^+ is low, resulting in potassium excretion and sodium reabsorption. In other words, the release of aldosterone causes potassium to be lost from the body, while sodium is retained.

Metabolic Functions of Potassium

Potassium is essential for cellular and electrical function of all cells, tissues, and organs in the human body. Together with other minerals, potassium participates in fluid and pH balance, conducts electrical impulses in the body (which helps maintain a regular heart beat), and plays a key role in skeletal and smooth muscle contraction, making it important for normal digestive and muscular function.

Potassium Helps Maintain Fluid Balance

Over 95 percent of the potassium in the body is found within cells. Together with sodium and chloride, potassium helps maintain fluid balance. Potassium is part of the sodium-potassium pump described in Chapter 11 in which three sodium ions are exchanged for two potassium ions to maintain proper electrolyte and fluid balance between the ECF and ICF. Water flows freely from the ECF to the ICF, depending on the concentration of electrolytes on either side of the cell membrane.

potassium (K^+) Main cation in the intracellular fluid.

Potassium Helps with Nerve Impulse Conduction and Muscle Contraction

As mentioned earlier, potassium, together with sodium, plays a key role in the contraction of muscles, including the heart, and the conduction of nerve impulses. Recall that potassium is exchanged for sodium in the sodium-potassium pump. This exchange generates an electrical current that travels as a wave along the muscle fibers triggering the muscle to contract.

Potassium Can Help Lower High Blood Pressure

A diet that is plentiful in potassium has been shown to help lower blood pressure, especially in salt-sensitive individuals who respond more intensely to sodium's blood pressure–raising capabilities. Potassium causes the kidneys to excrete excess sodium from the body, and keeping sodium levels low can help lower blood pressure. The DASH diet that was discussed earlier in relation to reducing high blood pressure is abundant in potassium-rich fruits and vegetables. Further, substituting potassium chloride for sodium chloride when seasoning foods during cooking or at the table has been found to reduce **systolic blood pressure.**[27]

Potassium Plays a Role in Bone Health and Reduces Kidney Stones

Because potassium acts as a buffer in the blood, it helps keep the bone-strengthening minerals calcium and phosphorus from being lost from the bones and kidneys. Numerous studies suggest that having plenty of potassium in the diet helps increase bone density, and thus bone strength.[28] Consuming potassium-rich foods may reduce the amount of calcium excreted and improve bone health.[29]

Potassium also may be beneficial in reducing kidney stones. Individuals with unusually high levels of calcium in the urine are at a higher risk of developing kidney stones. Increasing dietary potassium through fruits and vegetables or potassium supplements, such as potassium citrate, reduces the amount of calcium excreted in the urine. Potassium attaches to the calcium and prevents the formation of mineral crystals that can form kidney stones (**Figure 12.8**).[30]

Daily Needs for Potassium

An AI of 4,700 milligrams has been established for potassium for all adults. This amount is recommended to help those with sodium sensitivity reduce their risk of high blood pressure. This AI also lowers the risk of developing kidney stones and preserves bone health. A UL for potassium has not been established because there is no evidence that high levels of dietary potassium cause detrimental effects.

Because Americans fall short of their servings of fruits and vegetables, adult females consume only about 2,200 to 2,500 milligrams of potassium daily, and adult males consume only 3,300 to 3,400 milligrams daily.[31]

Food Sources of Potassium

Fruits and vegetables, especially bananas, watermelon, potatoes, leafy green vegetables, and sweet potatoes, are excellent sources of potassium. The *Dietary Guidelines for Americans* recommend consuming an abundance of fruits and vegetables to meet potassium needs. Seven servings, or about four cups, of fruit and vegetables is the minimum amount recommended daily for adults aged 19 and older. Lean meat, low-fat dairy products, and nuts are also good sources of potassium in the diet (see **Figure 12.9**).

Potassium Toxicity and Deficiency

There is little danger of consuming too much potassium from foods, and excess amounts are excreted in the urine. However, consuming too much potassium

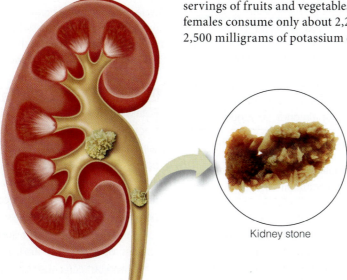

▲ **Figure 12.8 Kidney Stones**
A potassium-rich diet may reduce the risk of developing kidney stones.

Kidney stone

Most products marketed as salt substitutes contain potassium chloride.

systolic pressure The pressure within the arteries during a heart beat.

continued

Exploring Potassium **445**

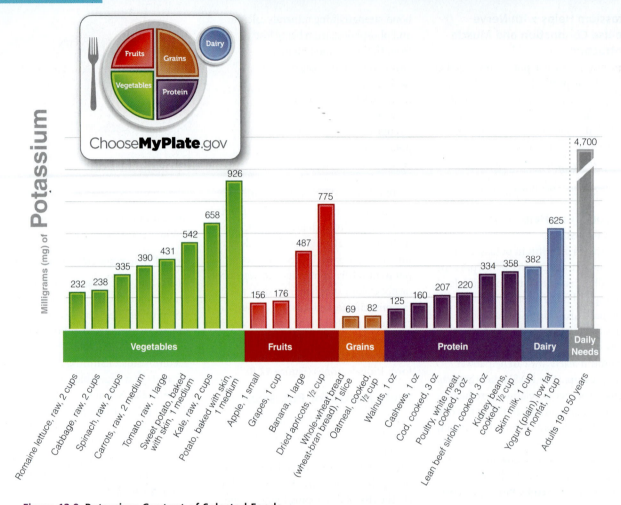

Milligrams (mg) of **Potassium**

ChooseMyPlate.gov

| Vegetables | Fruits | Grains | Protein | Dairy | Daily Needs |

- Romaine lettuce, raw, 2 cups — 232
- Cabbage, raw, 2 cups — 238
- Spinach, raw, 2 cups — 335
- Carrots, raw, 2 medium — 390
- Tomato, raw, 1 large — 431
- Sweet potato, baked with skin, 1 medium — 542
- Kale, raw, 2 cups — 658
- Potato, baked with skin, 1 medium — 926
- Apple, 1 small — 156
- Grapes, 1 cup — 176
- Banana, 1 large — 487
- Dried apricots, ½ cup — 775
- Whole-wheat bread (wheat-bran bread), 1 slice — 69
- Oatmeal, cooked, ½ cup — 82
- Walnuts, 1 oz — 125
- Cashews, 1 oz — 160
- Cod, cooked, 3 oz — 207
- Poultry, white meat, cooked 3 oz — 220
- Lean beef sirloin, cooked, 3 oz — 334
- Kidney beans, cooked, ½ cup — 358
- Skim milk, 1 cup — 382
- Yogurt (plain), low fat or nonfat, 1 cup — 625
- Adults 19 to 50 years — 4,700

▲ **Figure 12.9 Potassium Content of Selected Foods**

from supplements or salt substitutes can cause **hyperkalemia** (*kalemia* = potassium in blood) for some people. Hyperkalemia can cause an irregular heart beat, damage the heart, and even be life-threatening. The symptoms of hyperkalemia include nausea, fatigue, muscle weakness and tingling in feet and hands.

Those at a higher risk for hyperkalemia include individuals with impaired kidneys, such as people with type 1 diabetes mellitus, those with kidney disease, and individuals taking medications for heart disease or diuretics that cause the kidneys to block the excretion of potassium. These individuals may also need to consume less dietary potassium than the recommended daily amount as advised by their health care professional.

hyperkalemia Abnormally high levels of potassium in the blood.

hypokalemia Abnormally low levels of potassium in the blood.

TABLE TIPS

Potassium Pointers

Enjoy a 6-ounce glass of a citrus juice, such as orange or grapefruit, at breakfast to boost potassium intake.

Add leafy greens, such as spinach, to your lunchtime sandwich.

Add a spoonful of chopped nuts, such as walnuts or almonds, to yogurt.

Choose bean soup to go with a sandwich.

Bake a regular or sweet potato to increase potassium at dinner.

Deficiencies of dietary potassium, or **hypokalemia,** are rare. This may occur during bouts of vomiting and/or diarrhea, and has been observed in individuals who suffer with anorexia nervosa or bulimia nervosa. Hypokalemia can cause muscle weakness, cramps, glucose intolerance,

and, in severe situations, irregular heart beats and paralysis.[32] Even a moderately low intake of potassium, without developing hypokalemia, can increase the risk of developing high blood pressure, kidney stones, and loss of bone mass. Symptoms of hypokalemia include nausea, heart palpitations, weakness or tiredness, and fainting.

LO 12.4: THE TAKE-HOME MESSAGE
Potassium functions in muscle contraction and nerve conduction, maintains fluid and pH balance, preserves bone health, lowers blood pressure, and may prevent kidney stones. Adults need 4,700 milligrams of potassium per day. Fruits, vegetables, lean meats, low-fat dairy, and nuts are good food sources of potassium. Toxicity is rare from food but can cause hyperkalemia when taking supplements. Potassium deficiency, called hypokalemia, is rare.

Exploring Calcium

LO 12.5 List the functions, food sources, and the toxicity and deficiency symptoms associated with calcium.

What Is Calcium?

Calcium (Ca^{+2}) is one of the most abundant divalent (two positive charges) cations in nature. Calcium is also the most abundant mineral in the body. Over 99 percent of the body's calcium is in the bones and teeth.

Bioavailability and Absorption of Calcium

The bioavailability of calcium in various foods can be influenced by other food components. For example, vitamin D and lactose each improve the absorption of calcium, so vitamin D–fortified milk is a good source of absorbable calcium. Protein intake may also influence the absorption of calcium from a meal. Low protein intake reduces the amount of calcium absorbed through the intestines, and high protein intake may increase the amount of calcium excreted in the urine.[33, 34] On the other hand, oxalates and phytates found in foods that contain calcium, such as spinach (contains oxalates) or whole-wheat bread (contains phytates), reduce the bioavailability of calcium (**Figure 12.10**).[35]

A person who is deficient in calcium absorbs more of the mineral from foods than someone whose body has an adequate amount. However, the more calcium consumed at one time, the lower the rate of absorption. Therefore, consuming a calcium-containing food in smaller and more frequent portions, such as one 8-ounce glass of milk with breakfast and another with lunch, rather than a 16-ounce glass with dinner, increases the amount of calcium you absorb overall.

Hormones Regulate Calcium Balance

Hormones that respond to changes in blood calcium levels tightly control the amount of calcium in the body. When blood calcium levels are low (see **Focus Figure 12.11**), the parathyroid gland releases parathyroid hormone (PTH), which responds by stimulating the kidneys to convert more vitamin D to its active form, calcitriol. Together, calcitriol and PTH increase blood levels of calcium by increasing the amount of calcium absorbed through the intestinal tract, reducing the amount of calcium excreted through the kidneys, and releasing calcium from bone.

Another hormone, **calcitonin,** decreases blood calcium levels after a calcium-rich meal by stimulating the uptake of calcium into the bone. Calcitonin may also reduce the activation of vitamin D, thus reducing the amount of calcium absorbed through the small intestine. The action of calcitonin results in less calcium being absorbed, more calcium being deposited into the bone, and more calcium being excreted through the urine. The end result is normal levels of calcium in the blood and increased calcium levels in bones.[36]

Metabolic Functions of Calcium

Most people are probably aware that calcium is essential for building strong bones and teeth. But an optimal level of dietary intake of calcium is also essential for contracting muscles, sending and receiving nerve impulses, releasing hormones, blood clotting, and maintaining a normal heart beat. Calcium also helps lower blood pressure and may even reduce the risk of developing colon cancer, kidney stones, and obesity.

Calcium Helps Build Strong Bones and Teeth

Calcium is the primary mineral in the hydroxyapatite crystals that provide strength and structure to the bones and the enamel on teeth.[37]

The skeleton is made up of two types of bone (see **Figure 12.12**): **cortical bone,** which is the compact, dense bone that makes up the surface of bone tissue, and **trabecular bone,** which is the spongy interior portion. The trabecular bone has a high rate of turnover and is sensitive to changes in dietary calcium intake. It provides a reserve of calcium that can be used to raise blood levels when the diet is deficient in calcium.

Calcium Plays a Role in Muscles, Nerves, and Blood

The 1 percent of calcium that's not in the bones or teeth is in the extracellular fluid and in the intracellular components in the muscles and other tissues. When a muscle is stimulated by nerve impulses, calcium ions flow into the cell through a calcium channel and bind to proteins in the cell. This binding initiates a chain of events that results in the muscle contraction.

calcium (Ca^{2+}) One of the most abundant divalent cations found in nature and in the body.

calcitonin A hormone secreted by the thyroid gland that lowers blood calcium levels.

cortical bone The hard outer layer of bone.

trabecular bone The inner structure of bone, also known as spongy bone because of its appearance. This portion of bone is often lost in osteoporosis.

continued

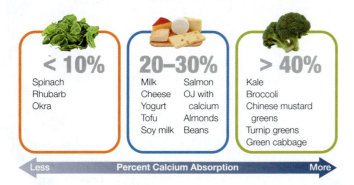

< 10%
Spinach
Rhubarb
Okra

20–30%
Milk   Salmon
Cheese   OJ with
Yogurt   calcium
Tofu   Almonds
Soy milk   Beans

> 40%
Kale
Broccoli
Chinese mustard
   greens
Turnip greens
Green cabbage

Less   **Percent Calcium Absorption**   More

▲ **Figure 12.10 Bioavailability of Calcium**

FOCUS Figure 12.11 — Hormones Maintain Calcium Homeostasis

Calcium homeostasis is tightly controlled to maintain a normal blood level of 8.5 to 11 mg per deciliter. Parathyroid hormone, calcitriol (activated vitamin D), and calcitonin are the three hormones involved in regulating blood calcium levels.

LOW BLOOD CALCIUM

When blood levels of calcuim fall below 8.5 mg/dl...

PTH and calcitriol increase reabsorption of calcium into the blood by the kidneys, decreasing its loss in urine.

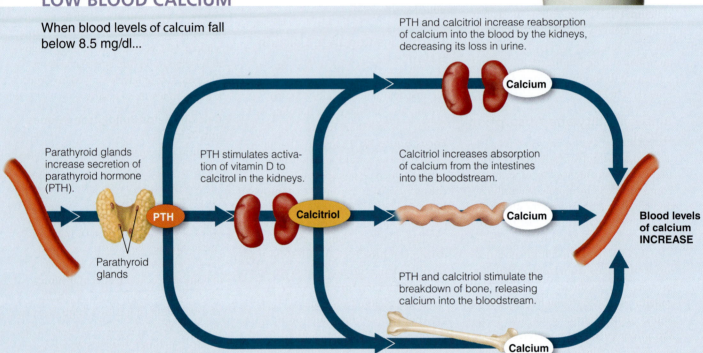

Parathyroid glands increase secretion of parathyroid hormone (PTH).

Parathyroid glands

PTH stimulates activation of vitamin D to calcitrol in the kidneys.

Calcitriol increases absorption of calcium from the intestines into the bloodstream.

PTH and calcitriol stimulate the breakdown of bone, releasing calcium into the bloodstream.

Blood levels of calcium INCREASE

HIGH BLOOD CALCIUM

When blood levels of calcium rise above 11 mg/dl...

Calcitonin reduces reabsorption of calcium by the kidneys, increasing its loss of urine.

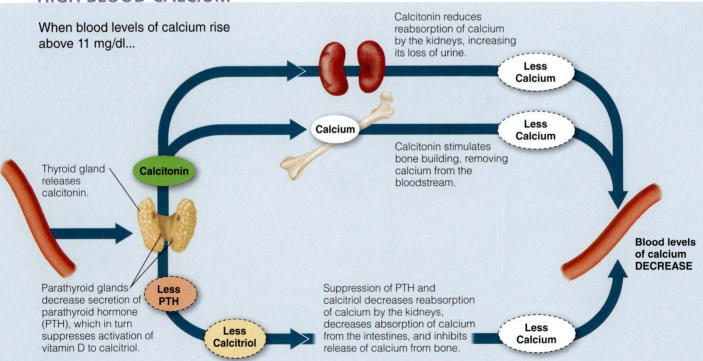

Thyroid gland releases calcitonin.

Calcitonin stimulates bone building, removing calcium from the bloodstream.

Parathyroid glands decrease secretion of parathyroid hormone (PTH), which in turn suppresses activation of vitamin D to calcitriol.

Suppression of PTH and calcitriol decreases reabsorption of calcium by the kidneys, decreases absorption of calcium from the intestines, and inhibits release of calcium from bone.

Blood levels of calcium DECREASE

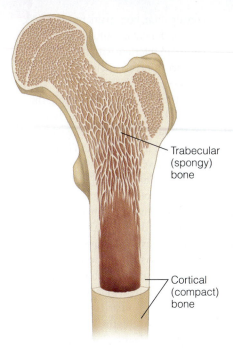

▲ **Figure 12.12 Trabecular and Cortical Bone**

Trabecular (spongy) bone

Cortical (compact) bone

Calcium in the blood stimulates the release of hormones, activates enzymes, and helps the nervous system transmit messages. For example, calcium stimulates the enzyme that breaks down glycogen to provide energy for muscles to contract. Blood calcium must be maintained at a constant level for the body to function properly.

Calcium is also needed to dilate and contract the blood vessels and help blood to clot. Calcium ions bind to the seven clotting factors that are vitamin K dependent, resulting in the formation of blood clots after an injury.

Calcium May Help Lower High Blood Pressure and Prevent Colon Cancer

Studies have shown that a heart-healthy diet rich in calcium, potassium, and magnesium can help lower blood pressure. The DASH diet contains three daily servings of low-fat dairy foods, the minimum amount recommended to obtain this protective effect.[38, 39]

A diet with plenty of calcium has also been shown to help reduce the risk of developing benign tumors in the colon that may eventually lead to cancer. Calcium may protect the lining of the colon from damaging bile acids and cancer-promoting substances.[40]

Calcium May Reduce the Risk of Kidney Stones

Calcium from food binds to oxalate in the intestinal tract and prevents calcium from entering the blood and pass through the urinary tract where it can form kidney stones. With fewer oxalates filtering through the kidneys, fewer stones are formed. Even though the majority of the more than 2 million kidney stones that Americans suffer every year consist mainly of calcium oxalate, dietary calcium is not the culprit. Although health professionals in the past often warned those who suffer with kidney stones to minimize their dietary calcium, this advice has since been reversed, as research has shown that a balanced diet, along with adequate (but not excessive) amounts of calcium, may actually reduce the risk of developing kidney stones.[41, 42]

Calcium May Reduce the Risk of Obesity

Some preliminary research suggests that low-calcium diets may trigger several responses that increase the risk for obesity, at least in those who are genetically predisposed to obesity.[43, 44] When calcium intake is inadequate, PTH is increased to reduce the amount of calcium lost through the urine. At the same time, the active form of vitamin D, calcitriol, increases in the body to enhance dietary calcium absorption. These hormone responses also cause a shift of calcium into fat cells, which stimulates fat production and storage. The opposite also appears to be true: When the diet is high in calcium, less PTH and calcitriol are produced, resulting in more calcium excreted in the urine to maintain calcium balance in the blood, less calcium stored in fat cells, and more fat being burned for energy. In addition, preliminary results suggest that high dietary calcium intake may increase the amount of fat excreted in the feces as well as increase core body temperature.[45] However, calcium is not a magic pill in the battle against obesity and clearly more research is needed to confirm this relationship.

Daily Needs for Calcium

The AI for calcium is 1,000 to 1,100 milligrams of calcium daily, depending on your age. Most Americans 20 years of age and older are consuming less than 800 milligrams of calcium daily.[46]

Food Sources of Calcium

Americans get the majority of their calcium from dairy products, with an average of 55 percent of their intake coming from these sources. An 8-ounce glass of nonfat milk, 1 cup of nonfat yogurt, or 1 ½ ounces of hard cheese each provides 300 milligrams of calcium. Three servings (or about 3 cups) of low-fat dairy foods will just about meet many adults' daily needs. Note that selecting low-fat and nonfat dairy products, such as skim milk and nonfat yogurt, is key to minimizing saturated fat intake.

continued

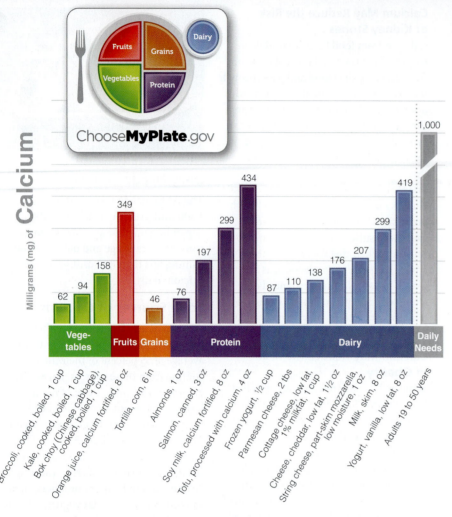

Calcium

Milligrams (mg) of

ChooseMyPlate.gov

62	Broccoli, cooked, boiled, 1 cup
94	Kale, cooked, boiled, 1 cup
158	Bok choy (Chinese cabbage), cooked, boiled, 1 cup
349	Orange juice, calcium fortified, 8 oz
46	Tortilla, corn, 6 in
76	Almonds, 1 oz
197	Salmon, canned, 3 oz
299	Soy milk, calcium fortified, 8 oz
434	Tofu, processed with calcium, 4 oz
87	Frozen yogurt, 1/2 cup
110	Parmesan cheese, 2 tbs
138	Cottage cheese, low fat, 1% milkfat, 1 cup
176	Cheese, cheddar, low fat, 1½ oz
207	String cheese, part-skim mozzarella, low moisture, 1 oz
299	Milk, skim, 8 oz
419	Yogurt, vanilla, low fat, 8 oz
1,000	Adults 19 to 50 years

Vege-tables | Fruits | Grains | Protein | Dairy | Daily Needs

▲ **Figure 12.13 Calcium Content of Selected Foods**

Dairy foods are not the only excellent source of calcium. Bok choy, broccoli, canned salmon with bones (the calcium is in the bones), and tofu that is processed with calcium can also add calcium to the diet. Calcium-fortified foods, such as juices and cereals, are also excellent sources (see Figure 12.13).

Calcium Toxicity and Deficiency

The upper limit for calcium is 2,500 milligrams daily to avoid **hypercalcemia,** or too much calcium in the blood, subsequent impaired kidneys, and calcium deposits in the body. Too much dietary calcium can also cause stomach upset, nausea,

hypercalcemia Abnormally high levels of calcium in the blood.

hypocalcemia Abnormally low levels of calcium in the blood.

constipation, bone pain, muscle weakness, and mental confusion. Excess calcium can interfere with the absorption of other minerals, such as iron, zinc, magnesium, and phosphorus.

If the diet is low in calcium, the mineral will be pulled from bone for the sake of maintaining a constant level in the blood. When blood calcium levels fall below normal, **hypocalcemia** results. A chronic deficiency of dietary calcium may not show any symptoms but can lead to less dense, weakened, and brittle bones (see **Figure 12.14**) and increased risk for osteoporosis, osteomalacia, rickets, and bone fractures. Acute calcium deficiencies can cause memory loss, muscle spasms, and numbness or tingling in your feet and hands. See Health Connection: What Is Osteoporosis? on page 457 for more about the importance of forming and maintaining healthy bone.

Ingesting Calcium Supplements

Some individuals, based on their diet, medical history, or both, are advised by their health care provider to take a calcium supplement. The calcium in these supplements is part of a compound, typically either calcium carbonate or calcium citrate. Calcium carbonate tends to be the least expensive and the most common form of calcium purchased. It is most effective when consumed with a meal, as the acidic juices in the stomach help with its absorption.[47] Calcium citrate can be taken any time throughout the day, as it doesn't need the help of acidic juices to be absorbed. Calcium citrate usually works best for those aged 50 and older who may produce less stomach acid as they age.[48]

Calcium from unrefined oyster shell, bone meal, or dolomite (a rock rich in calcium) may contain lead and other toxic metals. Supplements from these sources should state on the label that they are "purified" or carry the USP symbol to ensure purity.

Regardless of the form, all calcium, whether from supplements or from fortified or naturally occurring foods, should be consumed in doses of 500 milligrams or less, as this is

▲ **Figure 12.14 Normal and Abnormal Bone**
Healthy bone (left) vs. weakened bone (right).

the maximum that the body can absorb efficiently at one time. In other words, if a person has been advised to take 1,000 milligrams of calcium daily, 500 milligrams should be consumed in the morning and the other 500 milligrams in the afternoon or evening.[49] Because calcium can interfere with and reduce the absorption of iron, a calcium supplement shouldn't be taken at the same time of day as an iron supplement.

Calcium supplements can sometimes cause constipation and flatulence (gas), especially when taken in large amounts. Increasing the amount of fiber in the diet helps avoid these less-than-pleasurable side effects. As with any mineral supplement, be cautious about adding a calcium supplement to your diet if you are already consuming plenty of low-fat dairy foods and/or calcium-fortified foods.

TABLE TIPS

Calcium Counts

Use skim or low-fat milk on your morning cereal.

Spoon a few chunks of tofu onto a salad bar lunch for extra calcium.

Use low-fat pudding or yogurt to satisfy a sweet tooth.

Top calcium-rich pizza with more calcium from vegetables such as broccoli and raw leafy greens.

Spread nonfat or low-fat ricotta cheese on toast for a snack.

Drink calcium-fortified orange juice with your morning cereal.

LO 12.5: THE TAKE-HOME MESSAGE
Calcium provides strength and structure to bones and teeth, releases hormones, helps maintain a normal heart beat, and participates in muscle contraction and blood clotting and in sending and receiving nerve impulses. Calcium may reduce hypertension, and lower the risk of colon cancer, kidney stones, and obesity. The AI for calcium is 1,000 to 1,100 milligrams per day. Dairy products, green vegetables, canned salmon, tofu, and calcium-fortified foods are good sources of calcium. Toxicity of calcium is called hypercalcemia. Calcium deficiency or hypocalcemia can increase risk of osteoporosis and bone fractures.

Exploring **Phosphorus**

LO 12.6 List the functions, food sources, and the toxicity and deficiency symptoms associated with phosphorus.

What Is Phosphorus?

Phosphorus (PO_4^{-3}) is the second most abundant mineral in the body. The majority of phosphorus—about 85 percent—is found in bone tissue and teeth bound with calcium. The remainder is in the muscle, cell membranes, and intracellular fluids.

About 70 percent of the phosphorus in the diet is absorbed through the small intestine. Foods that contain the binder phytate reduce the absorption of phosphorus, whereas vitamin D enhances its absorption. Other minerals, including magnesium, calcium, and aluminum, decrease the absorption of phosphorus. These three minerals are often found in antacids and can be used to reduce high blood levels of phosphorus.[50]

Parathyroid hormone (PTH) controls phosphorus metabolism in a similar way it manages calcium metabolism. When blood levels of phosphorus are low, PTH stimulates the resorption of the mineral from the bone to raise blood levels. PTH

phosphorus (P) The second most abundant mineral in the body.

continued

helps store energy generated from the catabolism of carbohydrates, protein, and fat for later use. Phosphorus is also part of creatine phosphate, which is found in muscle. Creatine phosphate can provide phosphorus to ADP to form ATP when cells require more energy. Phosphorus is also a part of several coenzymes.

Phosphorus Acts as a Buffer and Is Part of the DNA and RNA of Every Cell

If the blood becomes too acidic or too basic, phosphorus can act as a buffer. Within the cells, phosphorus in the form of phosphate can bind excess hydrogen ions, thus increasing the pH. Blood pH must always stay within a very narrow range to prevent damage to tissues.

Another major function of phosphorus is that it is incorporated into the backbone of DNA and RNA molecules.

Daily Needs for Phosphorus

The RDA for adult males and females is 700 milligrams of phosphorus daily. Americans, on average, consume more than 1,000 milligrams of phosphorus daily.

Food Sources of Phosphorus

A balanced, varied diet easily provides an adequate amount of phosphorus (see **Figure 12.16**). Foods from animal sources such as meat, fish, poultry, and dairy products are excellent sources of phosphorus. Plant seeds such as beans, peas, nuts, and cereal grains contain phosphorus in the form of phytates, which are only about 50 percent bioavailable. Soft drinks and colas, which contain the additive phosphoric acid, are another common food source of phosphorus. However, these beverages should be limited in the diet due to their high refined sugar content.

Phosphorus Toxicity and Deficiency

Typically, consuming too much dietary phosphorus and its subsequent effect, **hyperphosphatemia,** is only an issue for individuals with kidney problems

also stimulates the kidneys to excrete phosphorus through the urine. Most phosphorus excess is excreted in the urine and the rest is lost in the feces.

Metabolic Functions of Phosphorus

Phosphorus plays a role in the health of bones and teeth. It also helps provide the structure for cell membranes, participates in metabolism, acts as an acid-base buffer, and is part of DNA and RNA.

Phosphorus Is Needed for Bones and Teeth and Is an Important Component of Cells

Together with calcium, phosphorus plays a key role in the formation of the crystalline structure called hydroxyapatite that gives bones and teeth their strength. There is about half as much total phosphorus in the bone as there is calcium.

Some of the body's phosphorus is found in the cells as part of phospholipids (see **Figure 12.15**), which give cell membranes their structure. Phospholipids act as a barrier to keep specific substances out of the cells while letting others in.

Phosphorus Is Needed during Metabolism

Phosphorus is part of the adenosine triphosphate (ATP) molecule and thus

hyperphosphatemia Abnormally high level of phosphorus in the blood.

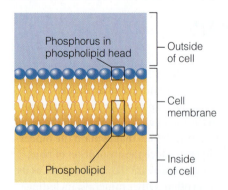

▲ **Figure 12.15 Phosphorus Forms Phospholipids**
Phosphorus makes up part of the phospholipids found in cell membranes.

Inside the figure:
Phosphorus in phospholipid head
Outside of cell
Cell membrane
Phospholipid
Inside of cell

TABLE TIPS

Balance Phosphorus with Calcium

Substitute sodas with refreshing lemonade to quench your thirst.

Blend together calcium-fortified orange juice and slightly thawed frozen strawberries for a refreshing smoothie.

Skip the butter and sprinkle chopped unsalted peanuts over calcium-rich steamed vegetables for a crunchy topping.

Dip raw broccoli florets into a nonfat sour cream–based dip for a snack.

Stir-fry chicken breast with calcium-rich vegetables for a balanced ratio of phosphorus to calcium.

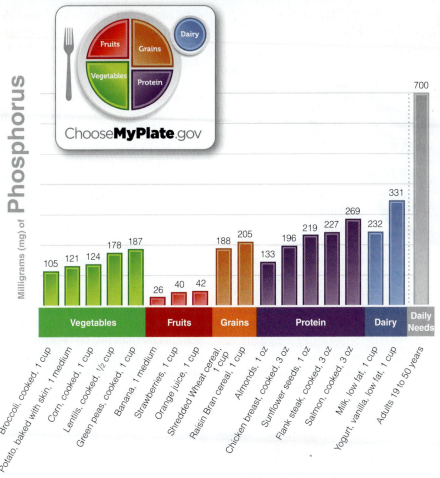

Milligrams (mg) of Phosphorus

Broccoli, cooked, 1 cup	105
Potato, baked with skin, 1 medium	121
Corn, cooked, 1 cup	124
Lentils, cooked, ½ cup	178
Green peas, cooked, 1 cup	187

Vegetables / Fruits / Grains / Protein / Dairy / Daily Needs

▲ **Figure 12.16 Phosphorus Content of Selected Foods**

the upper level for phosphorus has been set at 4,000 milligrams daily for adults aged 19 to 50 and 3,000 milligrams for those 50 years of age and older. Symptoms of hyperphosphatemia may include muscle cramps, tetany, and numbness or tingling in the feet and hands.

Too little phosphorus in the diet can cause dangerously low blood levels, a condition called **hypophosphatemia,** and result in muscle weakness, bone pain, rickets in children, confusion, and, at the extreme, death. Because phosphorus is so abundant in the diet, however, a deficiency is very rare. In fact, a person would have to be in a state of near starvation before experiencing a phosphorus deficiency.

> **LO 12.6: THE TAKE-HOME MESSAGE**
> Phosphorus is a structural component of bones and teeth, provides energy as part of the ATP molecule, acts as an acid-base buffer, and is part of DNA and RNA. Adults need 700 milligrams daily of phosphorus, which can be found in meat, fish, poultry, dairy, legumes, nuts, and cereal grains. Toxicity of phosphorus, hyperphosphatemia, occurs when the kidney can't excrete excess phosphorus. A dietary deficiency of phosphorus causes hypophosphatemia.

hypophosphatemia Abnormally low level of phosphorus in the blood.

who cannot excrete excess phosphorus. Consistently high phosphorus and low calcium intake can cause the loss of calcium from bones and a subsequent decrease in bone mass. Loss of bone mass increases the risk of osteoporosis. Hyperphosphatemia can also lead to depositing calcium (also known as calcification) in soft tissues such as the arteries and kidneys. To protect against this,

Exploring **Magnesium**

LO 12.7 List the functions, food sources, and the toxicity and deficiency symptoms associated with magnesium.

What Is Magnesium?

Magnesium (Mg⁺²) is the fourth most abundant cation in the body after calcium (Ca⁺²), potassium (K⁺), and sodium (Na⁺). About 60 percent of the body's magnesium is found in bones, 25 percent in muscle, and the remainder inside various other cells. A mere 1 percent is found in the blood—though, like blood calcium, this amount must be maintained at a constant level.

The bioavailability of magnesium in a typical diet is about fifty percent.

Diets that are high in fiber and whole grains, which are high in phytates, lower magnesium absorption.

The intestines and kidneys control the levels of magnesium in the body. When dietary intake is low, absorption of magnesium through the small

magnesium (Mg⁺²) A major divalent cation in the body.

continued

MAGNESIUM

intestine increases and the kidneys excrete less.

Metabolic Functions of Magnesium

Magnesium plays many roles in metabolism, including the synthesis of DNA, RNA, and protein. Magnesium also aids in the transmission of nerve impulses and has an impact on the health of muscles, bones, and the heart, and on blood sugar and blood pressure.

Magnesium Is Needed for Metabolism and to Maintain Healthy Muscles, Nerves, Bones, and Heart

Magnesium is associated with more than 300 enzymatic reactions in the body, including many associated with the metabolism of carbohydrates, proteins, and fats, and the phosphorylation of ADP to ATP.

Magnesium is used in the synthesis of DNA, RNA, and body proteins during the transcription, translation, and replication phases. Magnesium also plays a vital role in bone metabolism and cell membrane synthesis.

Magnesium helps muscles, including the heart muscle, and nerves to function properly. It is also needed to help maintain healthy bones and a regular heart beat.

Magnesium May Help Lower High Blood Pressure and Reduce the Risk of Diabetes Mellitus

Magnesium is another abundant mineral in the DASH diet, though the actual role of magnesium in blood pressure has not yet been identified.

Some studies suggest that a diet abundant in magnesium may help decrease the risk of type 2 diabetes.[51] Low blood levels of magnesium, which often occurs in individuals with type 2 diabetes, may impair the release of insulin, one of the hormones that regulate blood glucose. This may lead to elevated blood glucose levels in those with preexisting diabetes and those at risk for type 2 diabetes.[52]

Daily Needs for Magnesium

The RDA for adult females aged 19 and older ranges from 310 milligrams to 320 milligrams of magnesium, whereas men of the same age need 400 milligrams to 420 milligrams of magnesium daily.

Currently, many Americans fall short of the recommended intake of magnesium. Females consume only about 70 percent of their RDA, or about 220 milligrams daily, on average. Males consume approximately 320 milligrams daily, on average, or approximately 80 percent of the amount recommended. Because older adults tend to consume fewer calories, and thus less dietary magnesium, they are at an even higher risk of falling short of their needs.

Food Sources of Magnesium

The biggest contributors of magnesium in Americans' diets are green leafy vegetables, whole grains, nuts, legumes, and fruits. Milk, yogurt, meat, and eggs are also good sources (see **Figure 12.17**). A peanut butter sandwich on whole-wheat bread, along with a glass of low-fat milk and a banana, provides more than 200 milligrams, or about half of an adult's daily needs. Because the majority of the magnesium in bread products is in the bran and germ of the grain kernel, products made with refined grains such as white flour are poor magnesium sources. Finally, beverages such as coffee, tea, and cocoa also contain some magnesium.

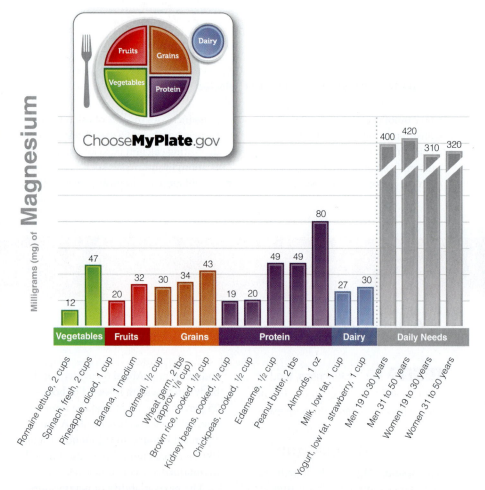

▲ Figure 12.17 **Magnesium Content of Selected Foods**

Magnesium Toxicity and Deficiency

There is no known risk in consuming too much magnesium from food sources. However, consuming large amounts from supplements has been shown to cause intestinal problems such as diarrhea, cramps, and nausea. In fact, some laxatives (such as milk of magnesia) contain magnesium because of its known cathartic effect. The upper level for magnesium from supplements, not foods, is set at 350 milligrams for adults. This level is to prevent diarrhea, the first symptom that typically arises when too much magnesium is consumed.

Even though many Americans don't meet their dietary magnesium needs, deficiencies are rare in healthy individuals because the kidneys compensate for low magnesium intake by excreting less of it. However, some medications may cause magnesium deficiency. Certain diuretics can cause the body to lose too much magnesium, and some antibiotics, such as tetracycline, can inhibit the absorption of magnesium, both of which can lead to a deficiency. Individuals with poorly controlled diabetes or who abuse alcohol can experience excessive losses of magnesium in the urine, which could also cause a deficiency. A severe magnesium deficiency can cause muscle weakness, seizures, fatigue, depression, and irregular heart beats.

LO 12.7: THE TAKE-HOME MESSAGE
Magnesium participates in metabolism; the synthesis of DNA, RNA, and proteins; and nerve transmission. Magnesium also impacts muscle, bones, heart function, blood pressure, and blood sugar. The RDA for magnesium for adult females ranges from 310 milligrams to 320 milligrams, whereas men need 400 milligrams to 420 milligrams of magnesium daily. Magnesium is abundant in leafy green vegetables, legumes, and beverages such as coffee and tea. Magnesium toxicity only occurs with supplements. Deficiencies of magnesium are rare.

Exploring Sulfate

LO 12.8 List the functions, food sources, and daily needs associated with sulfate.

What Is Sulfate?

Sulfate (SO_4^{2-}) is the oxidized form of the mineral sulfur that is found in plants and occurs naturally in drinking water.

In the body, sulfur is usually found as part of other compounds, mostly proteins. It is also part of two important B vitamins, thiamin and biotin.

Sulfate is absorbed throughout the GI tract, including the stomach, small intestine, and colon. About 80 percent of the sulfate you eat is absorbed, and the excess excreted in the urine. Sulfate is found in the body's tissues as part of keratin, especially in hair, skin, and nails.

Metabolic Functions of Sulfate

The amino acids methionine and cysteine both contain sulfur. These two

sulfate (SO_4) The oxidized form of the mineral sulfur.

continued

SULFATE

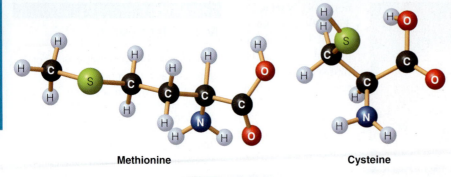

Methionine   **Cysteine**

▲ **Figure 12.18 Sulfate Is Part of Some Amino Acids**

amino acids are incorporated into body proteins and help give proteins their three-dimensional shape (**Figure 12.18**). This enables the proteins to perform effectively as enzymes and hormones and provide structure to the body.

Sulfur-based substances, called sulfites, are used as preservatives by food manufacturers. They help prevent food spoilage and discoloration in foods such as dried fruits. Sulfites occur naturally in wine due to the fermentation process, and are added to prevent oxidation. People who are sensitive to sulfites may experience headache, sneezing, swelling of the throat, or hives and should avoid sulfite-containing foods and beverages.

Daily Needs for Sulfate

There is insufficient data to determine an EAR, an RDA, an AI, or even a UL for sulfate. The amount of sulfate most Americans consume has been estimated from consumption data on the sulfur-containing amino acids.

Food Sources of Sulfate

About 65 percent of dietary sulfate comes from foods that contain methionine, cysteine, glutathione, and taurine. A varied diet that contains meat, poultry, fish, eggs, legumes, dairy foods, fruits, and vegetables provides good sources of sulfate.

Beverages including beer, wine, and some juices that are made from municipal water supplies also contain sulfate. As much as 1.3 grams of sulfate per day may come from drinking water due to contamination from groundwater, pipes, and harmless bacteria.[53] Some dietary supplements may also add to total sulfate intake. For example, chondroitin sulfate and glucosamine are popular supplements for osteoarthritis and joint problems.

Sulfate Toxicity and Deficiency

Although a UL has not been established, a possible link has been suggested between high levels of sulfate and ulcerative colitis. Bacteria in the colons of people with this condition appear to convert some of the sulfite-containing compounds into by-products that promote the disease.[54]

Most people eat sufficient protein to provide adequate amounts of sulfur-containing amino acids. There are no known toxicity or deficiency symptoms for sulfate.

LO 12.8: THE TAKE-HOME MESSAGE
Sulfur provides shape to proteins and is part of the vitamins thiamin and biotin, and part of some amino acids. There is insufficient data to establish an RDA, AI, or UL for sulfate. Sulfur is consumed in its oxidized form, sulfate, and is found in meat, poultry, fish, eggs, legumes, dairy foods, fruits, and vegetables, and also beer and wine. Excess sulfate may relate to ulcerative colitis. There are no known deficiencies symptoms for sulfate.

What Is Osteoporosis?

LO 12.9 Compare the roles of minerals in the development of healthy bone tissue and osteoporosis, and outline the factors that influence the risk of developing the disease.

If you are fortunate enough to have elders, such as grandparents, in your life, you may have heard them comment that they are "shrinking" as they age. Of course, they aren't really shrinking but they may be losing height as the tissues supporting their spine lose mass and elasticity and the joint capsules between the vertebrae of the spine lose their cushion of fluid.[55] This is normal, in many older adults; however, the vertebrae themselves lose mass and begin to collapse, so that it becomes more difficult for the spine to hold the weight of the head and upper body. This leads to a gradual curvature of the spine, which affects their posture[56] (see **Figure 12.19**).

The most effective way to prevent loss of mass and elasticity is to maintain strong, healthy bones with a high **bone mineral density (BMD).** BMD is the density of hydroxyapatite crystals within the trabecular bone and cortical bone.

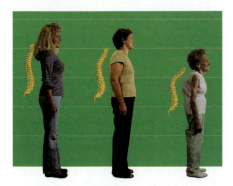

▲ **Figure 12.19 Deterioration of the Vertebrae**
Weakened bones in the vertebrae cause the spine to collapse over time, resulting in the "shrinking" effect experienced by some older adults.

Stronger bones have a higher density than weaker bone. Weak and brittle bones can lead to osteoporosis, one of the biggest physical problems experienced by older adults in the United States. Older adults with this condition experience a myriad of health problems, from bone breaks and fractures to reduced mobility and diminished quality of life. Unfortunately, by the time an older adult finds out he or she has osteoporosis, little can be done, because an individual's lifelong bone health is largely determined during childhood, adolescence, and early adulthood, when the person is accumulating peak bone mass. This means that, during your college years, you are building up the bone health you'll need for a healthy older age.

You can think of bone mass as being like a retirement account. The more you save when you are young and preserve throughout your adulthood, the more you will have for your later years. Conversely, if you don't save enough early in life, you may end up with little to fall back on when you need it. If children don't reach their maximum bone mass by young adulthood, they will not have adequate bone mass stored for their later years. If an adult doesn't have a healthy diet and lifestyle that includes regular exercise, he or she may experience accelerated bone loss after age 30.

Most Bone Growth Occurs Early in Life

Bones are dynamic, living tissues that are constantly being broken down and reformed. Specialized cells called osteoclasts work to remove older layers of bones, while osteoblasts continuously form new bone. Although this process occurs throughout the life span, the majority of bone growth and buildup of bone mass occurs during childhood, adolescence, and early adulthood, when the osteoblasts are more active than the osteoclasts. During these life stages, more bone mass is added than is lost in the body. Although growth of

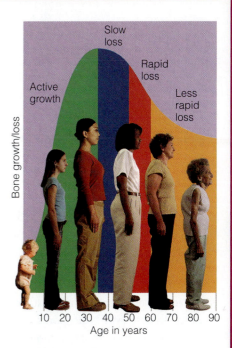

▲ **Figure 12.20 Change in Bone Mass As You Age**
In your early years, more bone is added than lost in your body. In their mid-30s, women begin to slowly lose bone mass until menopause, when the rate of loss is accelerated for several years. Bone loss continues after age 60 but at a slower rate.

bone length typically ceases during the teenage years, bone mass will continue to accumulate into the early years of young adulthood. The maximum bone mass an adult will accrue, referred to as **peak bone mass,** usually occurs when a person is in his or her 20s. Some additional bone mass can be added when an individual is in his or her 30s.

After peak bone mass is reached, the loss of bone mass begins to slowly exceed the rate at which new bone is added.[57] Starting in their mid-30s, women begin to slowly lose bone mass until menopause, when the rate of loss accelerates for several years (see **Figure 12.20**). Bone loss continues in women after age 60, but at a slower rate. Bone loss also occurs in men as they age.[58]

bone mineral density (BMD) The amount of minerals, in particular calcium, per volume in an individual's bone.

peak bone mass The genetically determined maximum amount of bone mass an individual can build up.

Osteoporosis Is a Disease of Progressive Bone Loss

As bones lose mineral mass they become porous and **osteoporosis** (*osteo* = bone, *porosis* = porous) can develop. There are two main classifications of osteoporosis. **Type I osteoporosis** is associated with a decrease in estrogen levels during menopause and is present in 5 to 20 percent of American women aged 50 to 75 years.[59] The lower levels of estrogen in a postmenopausal woman's body cause a reduction in bone mineral density. This, in turn, leads to weak and brittle bones. Type I osteoporosis is often associated with fractures of the spine, hip, wrist, or forearm. Because Type I osteoporosis is usually related to a drop in estrogen levels at menopause, it is more likely to occur in women than in men.

Type II osteoporosis, or age-related osteoporosis, occurs when the breakdown of bone outpaces the rebuilding of bone over time. Type II osteoporosis is mostly associated with leg and spinal fractures, and occurs in both men and women, although its more common in women. Note that older women can have both types of osteoporosis simultaneously.[60]

The weakened, fragile bones associated with both types of osteoporosis are prone to fractures. A minor stumble while walking can result in a fall that breaks a hip, ankle, or arm bone. Shopping, showering, and dressing, become challenges for many older people with osteoporosis.

Hip fractures can be devastating because they often render a person immobile,

osteoporosis A condition whereby the bones are less dense, increasing the risk of fractures.

Type I osteoporosis Osteoporosis that results from lowered estrogen levels women experience during menopause. This type of osteoporosis is characterized by rapid bone loss.

Type II osteoporosis Osteoporosis that occurs in both men and women; characterized by the slow loss of bone mass over time due to aging.

osteopenia A condition in which the bone mineral density is lower than normal but not low enough to be classified as osteoporosis.

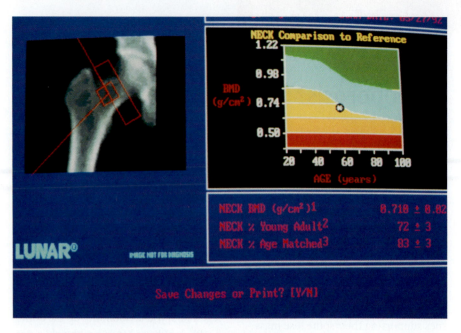

▲ **Figure 12.21 Dual-Energy X-Ray Absorptiometry**
A DEXA scan is the most accurate way to measure bone mineral density.

which quickly affects quality of life. Feelings of helplessness and depression often ensue. Up to two-thirds of all individuals with hip fractures are never able to regain the quality of life they had prior to the injury, and about 20 percent will die within a year due to complications from the injury.[61] By the year 2020, it is estimated that more than 61 million Americans will either have or be at risk for hip fractures due to osteoporosis, and even more will be at risk for fractures of other bones.[62]

Bone Density Can Be Measured by DEXA

Bone density tests for adults compare an individual's bone mineral density with that of a healthy 30-year-old. The most accurate tool is a dual-energy X-ray absorptiometry, or DEXA, test, which is a fast and easy test that uses two beams of low-energy X-ray radiation (see **Figure 12.21**). DEXA can measure bone loss of as little as 2 percent per year. In a DEXA scan, strong, dense bones allow less of the X-ray beam to pass through them. The amounts of each X-ray beam that are blocked by bone and soft tissue are compared with each other. The data from a DEXA is presented as a T-score, which is compared with the ideal or

peak bone mineral density of a healthy 30-year-old adult. A healthy normal bone will have a T-score of +1 to –1, whereas a low T-score between –1 and –2.5 indicates **osteopenia** (*penia* = poverty), signaling low bone mass. A very low score, less than –2.5, indicates osteoporosis.

Several Lifestyle Factors Influence Bone Mass

As with hypertension, diabetes, and other chronic conditions, there are choices you can make today to lessen your likelihood of experiencing weakened bones or osteoporosis in the future. Among the factors that matter most are diet, exercise, and the use of drugs (including nicotine) and alcohol.

The Role of Diet

Calcium intake during childhood and adolescence is strongly related to higher bone mineral density in older men and women. Adequate vitamin D intake is also important, as vitamin D promotes the absorption of calcium and is essential to attain peak bone mass.

Sufficient intake of the minerals magnesium and potassium has also been associated with increased bone health. One study found that the bone mineral density in the neck of the femur (or thigh bone) was higher in women who had consumed high amounts of fruit (a good source of both magnesium and potassium) in their childhood than in women who had consumed medium or low amounts.[63] Diets rich in vitamin K may reduce the risk of hip fractures, probably due to a reduction in bone turnover, although vitamin K doesn't appear to improve bone mineral density.[64] Consuming adequate levels of omega-3 fatty acids also has a positive effect in achieving peak bone mass.[65] The sodium-osteoporosis link is still unclear. A healthy diet that meets the current recommendations for calcium and sodium is adequate for the health and maintenance of bone.

One dietary habit that may have a negative impact on bone mineral density is the regular consumption of carbonated beverages. Several observational studies have shown a relationship between low bone mineral density and an increase in fracture rates in teenagers who consume higher amounts of soda and other carbonated beverages. In one study, the bone mineral density in the heels of females aged 12 to 15 was inversely related to the amount of carbonated beverages they consumed; however, no relationship was observed in boys the same age.[66] A similar study reported a relationship between carbonated beverage intake and risk of fracture.[67] However, this relationship has not been substantiated with experimental studies.[68] Researchers theorize that the correlation between carbonated beverage intake and poor bone health may have more to do with the displacement of milk in the diet than with the carbonated beverages themselves.

The role of protein in osteoporosis remains controversial. Protein positively correlates with an increase in bone density, but high protein intakes combined with lower intakes of calcium increase urinary calcium loss. It appears from the current research that protein should not be detrimental to bone density if both protein and calcium are present in the recommended levels.

Although food is the best source of nutrients to develop and maintain healthy bones, some individuals are advised to take a supplement by their health care provider. However, supplements that contain high doses of nutrients other than calcium have been shown to have adverse effects on bone health. For example, high doses of vitamin A supplements in the form of retinol can significantly increase the risk of hip fracture in older individuals.[69]

Taking high doses of vitamin C for bone health has produced mixed results. In some studies, vitamin C intakes of 100 milligrams to 125 milligrams have improved bone mineral density and reduced the risk of hip fractures in postmenopausal women.[70] However, higher intakes of vitamin C (greater than 2,000 milligrams) may increase the risk of fracture, as well as the risk of developing kidney stones, although more research is required to support these findings.

Exercise Improves Bone Mass

Weight-bearing exercises help maintain bone and increase bone mass. High-impact exercise, such as hiking or weight training, has been found to be an inexpensive, safe, and effective means to improve bone mineral density, prevent osteoporosis, and reduce the risk of falls and fractures. High-impact physical activity has been shown to increase the growth and the mineral content of the bones in girls and adolescent females.[71, 72] However, to achieve this benefit, the diet must also contain an adequate amount of calcium and kilocalories.

These same increases in bone mineral density are reported in premenopausal women over the age of 18 who have stopped growing in height but can still improve bone mineral density.[73] After menopause, the benefits of weight-bearing exercise show increases in not only bone mineral density but also overall muscle strength.[74] The muscle action of pulling on the bone stimulates the osteoblasts to build more bone.

Calcium supplements with vitamin D can be beneficial for people who do not consume adequate calcium in their diet.

Exercise only improves bone strength in the bones that are impacted by the exercise.[75] For example, weight training the lower body will not improve the upper arms or bones of the wrist, where many older women sustain fractures.

Intensity is also important to consider when choosing an exercise to improve bone mineral density. For example, moderate to high-intensity walking at a pace of more than 4 miles per hour increases the stress on the muscle and bone, relative to a leisurely stroll at about 2 miles per hour, and results in an increase in the bone mineral density of the hip.[76] Choose exercises that you enjoy but that provide the intensity required to improve both the mineral density of the bone and overall muscular strength.

Body Weight Impacts Bone Mass

Body weight also has an impact on achieving peak bone mass. Women who are slightly heavier than their normal-weight counterparts have higher bone mineral density, especially in the spine and the hip. However, when an individual loses weight, the effect may be detrimental to their bone. During moderate weight loss, bones appear to maintain mineral density, especially when there is adequate calcium in the diet.[77] However, when the weight loss is severe, such as in young women diagnosed with anorexia nervosa, the loss of bone mineral density is significant.[78] The key to maintaining

healthy bone mass appears to be losing weight slowly and eating adequate amounts of calcium and kilocalories.

The Effects of Smoking on Bone Mass

Bone mineral density is significantly reduced in people who smoke.[79]

Postmenopausal women who reportedly smoked prior to menopause were found to have significantly lower bone mineral density scores than women who never smoked.[80] Though the mechanism by which smoking has an impact on bone mineral density and fracture risk is not completely understood, several theories have been suggested. First, smokers have lower levels of parathyroid hormone and calcitriol, suggesting that more calcium is removed from the bone. Women who smoke also have lower body weights, which could account for less estrogen, less protective body fat (important during a fall), and reduced load on bones (load improves bone density). Regardless of the mechanism, the risk of fracture in smokers has been reported to be 35 percent higher compared with nonsmokers.[81] Similar effects of smoking have also been reported in men.[82] The good news is that stopping smoking causes bone mineral density to improve.[83]

The Impact of Alcohol on Bone Mass

Excessive alcohol intake has been associated with osteoporosis[84] and related fractures. This is due in part to the malnourishment often seen in chronic alcoholics, which may include insufficient calcium intake. In addition, alcohol may reduce vitamin D metabolism and alter osteoblast activity, thereby interfering with calcium absorption and bone formation, and produce a hormonal imbalance affecting parathyroid hormone, estrogen, and testosterone.

Not all research reports a negative relationship of alcohol to bone health. In a recent study of moderate drinkers, the results suggested that social drinking or moderate alcohol intake may have a positive impact on bone mineral density.[85] Researchers reported that alcohol intake of about 1 to 3 glasses of wine per day in elderly women correlated with higher bone mineral density. Two possible mechanisms have been proposed for the improved bone mineral density found with moderate alcohol consumption. First, calcitonin production may be stimulated, which has been shown to improve bone mineral density in the spine. Second, moderate alcohol intake may stimulate higher estrogen levels. More research is needed to clarify the impact of alcohol consumption on bone health.

Strategies to Prevent Osteoporosis

Osteoporosis is not inevitable as you age. To maintain a healthy bone mass and prevent fragile and brittle bones, eat a calcium and vitamin D rich diet, maintain a healthy body weight, participate in regular exercise, don't smoke and drink alcohol in moderation.

Complete the Self-Assessment "Estimating Your Calcium Intake" to see whether you ingest sufficient calcium to maintain healthy bone mass. What other factors may improve overall bone health? Apply the concepts of an adequate diet, healthy lifestyle, and exercise in the Nutrition in Practice to help Martha improve her bone density.

Self-Assessment

Estimating Your Calcium Intake

Complete the table below to estimate the total amount of calcium you consumed yesterday. How does your calcium intake compare to the AI of 1,000 mg per day? Are you meeting your calcium needs?

Product	Number of Servings	Calcium Content per Serving	Total Amount of Calcium (mg)
Milk, 8 oz		300 mg	
Fortified orange juice, 8 oz		300 mg	
Fortified cereals, snacks (no milk added)		100 mg	
Fortified cereal with 4 oz milk		250 mg	
Yogurt, 8 oz		400 mg	
Cheese, 1 oz		200 mg	
Legumes, 1 cup		225 mg	
Leafy green vegetables, 1 cup cooked (low-oxalate vegetables such as kale and collard greens)		185 mg	
Total mg calcium			

Adapted from the International Osteoporosis Foundation, 2014. www.iofbonehealth.org.

Nutrition in Practice: Martha

Martha is postmenopausal, so her doctor did a bone density scan at her last annual physical. Approximately two weeks after the test, the nurse practitioner (NP) called and told Martha that her T-score was "on the lower side." Martha was surprised to hear this, as she walks 4 miles daily and lifts weights three times a week, and considers herself in good shape. The NP recommended that Martha meet with a Registered Dietitian Nutritionist (RDN) to make sure that she was consuming adequate amounts of calcium in her diet. Martha is hesitant to talk to an RDN because she is afraid that the dietitian is going to ask her to take a calcium supplement. Martha will do *anything* to avoid swallowing pills. The NP convinces Martha to make an appointment with the RDN.

Martha's Stats
- Age: 54
- Height: 5 feet 5 inches
- Weight: 138 pounds
- BMI: 23

Martha's Food Log

Food/Beverage	Time Consumed	Hunger Rating*	Location
Banana (before her morning walk)	6 AM	4	Kitchen
Oatmeal made with water, orange juice, and tea with lemon and sugar	7:30 AM	5	Kitchen
Turkey sandwich with lettuce, small salad with Italian dressing, berries	12 PM	5	Employee's lunch room
Chicken, small baked potato, handful of broccoli	6:30 PM	5	Kitchen
½ pint of frozen yogurt	8 PM	3	Watching TV

*Hunger Rating (1-5): 1 = not hungry 5 = super hungry.

Critical Thinking Questions
1. How much calcium should Martha be consuming daily?
2. Based on her food log, approximately how much calcium is Martha consuming?
3. How can Martha add more calcium-rich foods at her meals and snacks to meet her daily needs?

Dietitian's Observation and Plan for Martha
- Discuss the need to consume at least 3 servings of low-fat dairy plus a serving of a calcium-fortified food to meet the 1,200 mg of calcium needed daily.
- Substitute a string cheese for the banana as a snack before her morning walk.
- Prepare the oatmeal with skim milk rather than water and switch to calcium-fortified orange juice in the morning.
- Remove an ounce of turkey from and add 1.5 ounces of low-fat Cheddar cheese to her lunchtime sandwich.
- Replace her evening snack with a blender smoothie that contains 8 ounces of yogurt, fruit, a splash of skim milk, and ice.

Two weeks later, Martha returns for a follow-up visit with the dietitian. She has made all of the changes that the RDN recommended but doesn't like the evening smoothie. She complains that the smoothie is "too watery." The RDN recommends that she use frozen berries rather than the fresh variety and eliminate the ice. Both of these changes will allow the smoothie to be cold and thick without it getting "too watery."

LO 12.9: THE TAKE-HOME MESSAGE Bone mineral density increases during childhood and adolescence, and peaks in early adulthood. Decreased bone mineral density during aging can lead to osteoporosis, a thinning of bones that increases the risk of fracture and injury. To improve and maintain bone mineral density, consume a diet adequate in calcium, magnesium, and potassium, the vitamins D and K, omega-3 fatty acids, and kilocalories. Maintain a healthy body weight, participate in weight-bearing exercise, don't smoke, and, if you drink alcohol, do so only in moderation.

Visual Chapter Summary

LO 12.1 Major and Trace Minerals Are Essential Inorganic Nutrients

Major and trace minerals are essential inorganic nutrients found in foods. Many become cofactors for enzymes. Minerals help maintain fluid and acid-base balance, play a role in energy metabolism, nerve transmission and muscle contractions, help strengthen bones, teeth, and the immune system, and are involved in growth. The major minerals include sodium, chloride, calcium, phosphorus, potassium, magnesium, and sulfur. The trace minerals include iron, zinc, copper, selenium, chromium, iodide, manganese, molybdenum, and fluoride.

Minerals are found in both plant and animal foods. They vary in their bioavailability due to binding agents, including phytates, found in grains, and oxalates, found in some vegetables. Mineral absorption can also be influenced by an individual's current mineral status, the amount of the mineral consumed at one time, and competition with other minerals that have the same ionic state in the GI tract. The kidney regulates mineral levels in the blood by excreting more or less of the mineral as needed, so mineral toxicity is generally rare except through ingesting high doses of supplements.

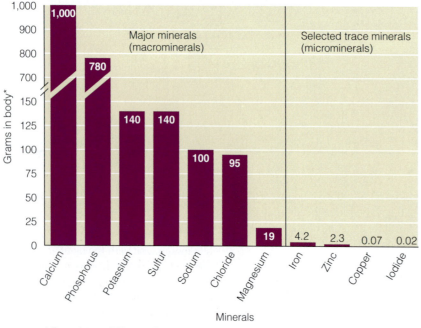

* Based on a 154-pound person

LO 12.2 Sodium

Sodium plays an important role in balancing the fluid between blood and cells, transmits nerve impulses, participates in muscle contraction, and transports some nutrients across cell membranes. Sodium also is used to preserve food and enhance food flavors. Adults need about 1,500 milligrams of sodium daily but consume more than double that amount, predominantly as sodium chloride (table salt). Processed foods are the major source of sodium in the diet. Too much sodium can cause hypertension, hypernatremia, and bone loss. Too little sodium results in hyponatremia. Symptoms of eating too much sodium include thirst, dry mouth, decreased urination, and lightheadedness. Symptoms of too little sodium include headache, muscle weakness, fatigue, and even seizures.

When Sodium Levels Are Low

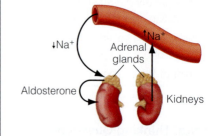

When Sodium Levels Are High

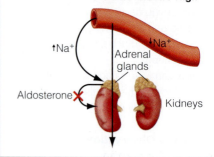

LO 12.3 Chloride

The anion chloride works with sodium to help maintain fluid balance. Chloride also assists in maintaining pH balance in the blood and is part of hydrochloric acid in the stomach. Adults need 2,300 milligrams per day. Table salt accounts for almost all the chloride you consume. Chloride toxicity is rare, and often goes unnoticed, but hyperchloremia can occur due to extreme dehydration. Deficiencies are also rare and are generally caused by extreme vomiting and diarrhea, resulting in hypochloremia. Symptoms of hypochloremia include shallow breathing, muscle weakness, spasms, and twitching.

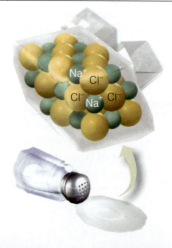

LO 12.4 Potassium

Potassium functions in muscle contraction and nerve impulse conduction; it can lower blood pressure, help maintain bone health, help maintain fluid balance, act as a blood buffer, and may prevent kidney stones. Adults need 4,700 milligrams of potassium per day. The current recommendations to increase fruits and vegetables in the diet will help meet potassium needs. Excess potassium from dietary supplements results in hyperkalemia, whereas a potassium deficiency causes hypokalemia. Hyperkalemia can cause an irregular heartbeat, nausea, fatigue, muscle weakness and tingling in feet and hands. Symptoms of hypokalemia are similar to hyperkalemia and include nausea, heart palpitations, weakness or tiredness, and fainting.

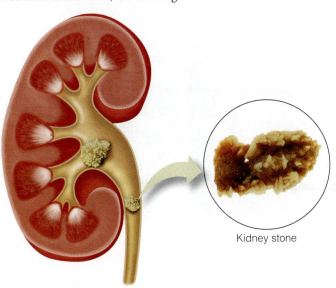

Kidney stone

LO 12.5 Calcium

Calcium, along with phosphorus, forms hydroxyapatite, which provides bones and teeth with strength and structure. Calcium also participates in muscle contraction, sending and receiving nerve impulses, releasing hormones, blood clotting, and maintaining a normal heart beat. It may also prevent colon cancer and reduce the risk of kidney stones. The AI for adults is 1,000 to 1,100 milligrams of calcium per day. Dairy foods can be a good source of both calcium and phosphorus. An excess of calcium causes hypercalcemia which may result in stomach upset, nausea, constipation, bone pain, muscle weakness, and mental confusion. Too much calcium can cause kidney stones or constipation. It may also interfere with the absorption of iron, zinc, magnesium, and phosphorus. A deficiency of calcium causes hypocalcemia and may not show any symptoms if the calcium levels are chronic. Acute calcium deficiencies can cause memory loss, muscle spasms, and numbness or tingling in your feet and hands. Calcium deficiency can lead to osteoporosis and bone fractures.

< 10%	20–30%		> 40%
Spinach	Milk	Salmon	Kale
Rhubarb	Cheese	OJ with	Broccoli
Okra	Yogurt	calcium	Chinese mustard
	Tofu	Almonds	greens
	Soy milk	Beans	Turnip greens
			Green cabbage

Less ← **Percent Calcium Absorption** → More

LO 12.6 Phosphorus

Phosphorus is a major component of bones and teeth and cell membranes. It functions as a component of ATP, as part of phospholipids, as an acid-base buffer, and as part of DNA and RNA. Phosphorus is abundant in meat, fish, poultry, and dairy products. The RDA for adults is 700 milligrams of phosphorus daily. Consuming too much phosphorus results in hyperphosphatemia, which can cause calcification of the soft tissues. Symptoms may include muscle cramps, tetany, and numbness or tingling. Too little phosphorus causes hypophosphatemia and results in symptoms such as muscle weakness, bone pain, and confusion. In children, rickets can develop.

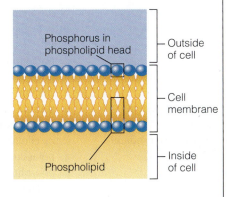

Phosphorus in phospholipid head

Outside of cell

Cell membrane

Phospholipid

Inside of cell

LO 12.7 Magnesium

Magnesium is part of more than 300 enzymes needed for metabolism, and to maintain healthy muscles, nerves, heart function, and bone structure. The RDA for adult females ranges from 310 milligrams to 320 milligrams of magnesium, whereas men need 400 milligrams to 420 milligrams of magnesium daily. Magnesium is abundant in leafy green vegetables, legumes, and beverages such as coffee and tea. Too much magnesium from taking supplements can cause intestinal problems such as diarrhea, cramps, and nausea. Deficiencies of magnesium are rare but the use of some medications can result in a magnesium deficiency and cause muscle weakness, seizures, fatigue, depression, and irregular heart beats.

LO 12.8 Sulfate

Sulfate is the oxidized form of the mineral sulfur. In the body, sulfate in the form of sulfur, provides shape to proteins and is part of the vitamins thiamin and biotin. Sulfur is part of some amino acids and is used as a preservative in processed foods. There is insufficient data to establish an RDA, AI, or UL for sulfate. The best food sources of sulfate are meats, chicken, and fish, and it can also be found in beverages such as beer and wine. Too much sulfate may relate to ulcerative colitis. There are no known deficiency symptoms of sulfate.

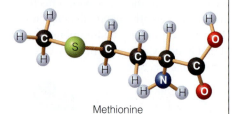

Methionine

LO 12.9 Mineral Intake Influences Bone Health

Osteoporosis is a progressive condition that results in weak, thin, frail bones that are prone to fracture. Bone growth and buildup of bone mass occurs during childhood, adolescence, and early adulthood, when the osteoblasts are more active than the osteoclasts and more bone mass is added than lost. Peak bone mass usually occurs in your 20s. Some additional bone mass can be added when an individual is in his or her 30s. The loss of bone mass begins in mid-30s and the loss continues to accelerate as we age. Diet and lifestyle factors such as a chronic deficiency of dietary calcium and/or vitamin D, excess alcohol consumption, and smoking also contribute to an increased risk of osteoporosis. Exercise can help prevent the loss of bone mass. Other strategies for preventing loss of bone mass include maintaining a healthy body weight, participating in weight-bearing exercise, not smoking, and drinking alcohol only in moderation, if at all.

Terms to Know

- minerals
- major minerals
- trace minerals
- bioavailability
- binders
- cofactors
- hydroxyapatite
- mineralization
- sodium (Na^+)
- hypertension
- hypernatremia
- hypertonic
- hypotonic
- hyponatremia
- chloride (Cl^-)
- hyperchloremia
- hypochloremia
- potassium (K^+)
- systolic pressure
- hyperkalemia
- hypokalemia
- calcium (Ca^{+2})
- calcitonin
- cortical bone
- trabecular bone
- hypercalcemia
- hypocalcemia
- phosphorus (P)
- hyperphosphatemia
- hypophosphatemia
- magnesium (Mg^{+2})
- sulfate (SO_4)\(PO_4^{-3})
- bone mineral density (BMD)
- peak bone mass
- osteoporosis
- Type I osteoporosis
- Type II osteoporosis
- osteopenia

MasteringNutrition™

To hear an MP3 chapter review, scan here or visit the Study Area in MasteringNutrition.

Check Your Understanding

1. The bioavailability of minerals is reduced by
   a. phytates.
   b. ascorbic acid.
   c. having a deficiency in the mineral.
   d. vitamin D.
2. In the body, minerals cannot
   a. help maintain fluid balance.
   b. be part of enzymes.
   c. work with the immune system.
   d. help absorb vitamin C.
3. The daily recommendation for sodium intake for adults up to age 51 is
   a. 3,400 milligrams.
   b. 2,300 milligrams.
   c. 1,500 milligrams.
   d. 180 milligrams.
4. Hypokalemia is due to a lack of sufficient _____ in the blood.
   a. potassium
   b. phosphorus
   c. calcium
   d. sodium
5. The major anion found in the extracellular fluid is
   a. potassium.
   b. phosphorus.
   c. sulfate.
   d. chloride.

6. Blood levels of calcium can be increased by
   a. increased excretion of calcium in the urine.
   b. increased absorption of calcium through the small intestine.
   c. increased secretion of PTH.
   d. high dietary intake of oxalates.
7. Phosphorus is necessary
   a. to maintain magnesium balance.
   b. to promote blood clotting.
   c. to provide energy as part of ATP.
   d. to transmit nerve impulses.
8. The majority of magnesium is in the
   a. blood.
   b. bones.
   c. muscle cells.
   d. extracellular fluid.
9. Which of the following minerals does not have an RDA, AI, or UL recommendation?
   a. sulfate
   b. magnesium
   c. calcium
   d. sodium
10. Fluid balance is maintained by which of the following minerals?
   a. magnesium and sulfur
   b. potassium and phosphorus
   c. calcium and chloride
   d. sodium and potassium

Answers

1. (a) The bioavailability of minerals is reduced by binders in food, including phytates found in grains.
2. (d) Although you need only small amounts of minerals in your diet, they play enormously important roles in the body, such as helping to maintain fluid balance, being part of enzymes, and working to keep the immune system healthy. Unfortunately, minerals can't help absorb vitamin C.
3. (c) The AI for sodium for adults up to 51 years of age is 1,500 milligrams. The upper level for sodium daily is 2,300 milligrams, whereas the absolute minimum is 180 milligrams per day.
4. (a) Hypokalemia is defined as a below-normal level of potassium in the blood. The term for low phosphorus levels in the blood is hypophosphatemia; hypocalcemia is a low level of calcium; hyponatremia is a low level of sodium in the blood.
5. (d) Chloride is the major anion in the extracellular fluid. Potassium is a major cation inside cells. Phosphorus is a major component of bones and teeth, and sulfate is the oxidized form of sulfur which helps give shape to proteins.
6. (b) Calcium blood levels can be raised by increasing the amount absorbed through the small intestine. Parathyroid hormone (PTH) lowers the level of calcium in the blood by stimulating the kidney to excrete more calcium in the urine. Dietary oxalates reduce the bioavailability of calcium.
7. (c) Phosphorus is a necessary mineral because it is part of the energy molecule ATP.
8. (b) More than half of the magnesium in the body is found in bone. Less than 1 percent is found in the extracellular fluid or the blood. Twenty-five percent of magnesium is found in the muscle.
9. (a) There is not enough data to determine an RDA, AI, or UL for sulfate. Calcium and sodium have established AIs, while magnesium has enough data for an RDA.
10. (d) Sodium and potassium are the major cations responsible for maintaining fluid balance. Magnesium, chloride, phosphorus, calcium, and sulfur play a variety of other key roles in the body.

Answers to True or False?

1. **False.** Consuming a diet rich in fruits, vegetables, lean meats, and low-fat dairy products provides ample intake of minerals without the need to take a supplement.
2. **True.** Minerals are single inorganic elements, often found in salt form or as electrically charged ions, whereas vitamins are complex molecules that contain carbon, hydrogen, oxygen, and, in some cases, nitrogen and sulfur.
3. **True.** For most people, following a diet rich in fruits and vegetables, moderating alcohol intake, and participating in aerobic exercise can reduce the risk of developing hypertension.
4. **False.** Both plant and animal products are bioavailable mineral sources.
5. **False.** Eating foods abundant in bioavailable calcium will improve bone density. Fruits are typically not high in calcium.
6. **True.** The DASH diet, which is high in potassium-rich fruits and vegetables, has been shown to lower blood pressure.
7. **False.** Most of the sodium Americans eat is from processed foods.
8. **True.** One serving of milk contains about 300 milligrams of calcium. The AI for adults aged 19 to 50 is 1,000 milligrams of calcium daily.
9. **True.** An excess of phosphorus may interfere with calcium absorption. However, if calcium intake is adequate, this will not cause a problem.
10. **False.** Sulfate plays a key role in shaping proteins and in the vitamins thiamin and biotin, and is essential to overall health. It is therefore an essential nutrient consumed in the oxidized form.

Web Resources

- For more on the DASH diet, visit DASH for Health at www.dashforhealth.com
- For more on osteoporosis, visit the National Osteoporosis Foundation at www.nof.org
- For more on high blood pressure, visit www.nhlbi.nih.gov

References

1. Adetuyi, O. F., and B. J. Stella. 2012. Effects of Different Traditional Cooking Methods on Nutrients and Mineral Bioavailability of Okra (*Abelmoschus esculentus*). *Journal of Agricultural Research and Development* 11(1):51–59.
2. Olivares, M., F. Pizarro, M. Ruz, and D. L. de Romana. 2012. Acute Inhibitions of Iron Bioavailability by Zinc: Studies in Humans. *Biometals* 25(4):657–664.

3. Espinoza, A., S. La Blanc, M. Olivares, F. Pizarro, M. Ruz, M. Arrendondo, and M. T. Nunez. 2012. Iron, Copper, and Zinc Transport: Inhibition of Divalent Metal Transporter 1 (DMT1) and Human Copper Transporter 1 (hCTR1) by shRNA. *Biological Trace Element Research* 146(2):281–286.

4. Olivares. 2012. Acute Inhibitions of Iron Bioavailability by Zinc: Studies in Humans.

5. Institute of Medicine. 2006. *Dietary Reference Intakes: The Essential Guide to Nutrient Requirements*. J. Otten, J. Hellwig, and L. Meyers, eds. Washington, DC: The National Academies Press.

6. Adetuyl. 2012. Effects of Different Traditional Cooking Methods on Nutrients and Mineral Bioavailability of Okra.

7. Hurrell, R., and I. Egli. 2010. Iron Bioavailability and Dietary Reference Values. *American Journal of Clinical Nutrition* 91(5):1461S–1467S.

8. Stipanuk, M. H., and M. A. Caudill. 2012. *Biochemical, Physiological, and Molecular Aspects of Human Nutrition*. 3rd ed. Philadelphia: W. B. Saunders.

9. Institute of Medicine. 2006. *Dietary Reference Intakes*.

10. Olivares. 2012. Acute Inhibitions of Iron Bioavailability by Zinc: Studies in Humans.

11. Stipanuk. 2012. *Biochemical, Physiological, and Molecular Aspects of Human Nutrition*.

12. Institute of Medicine. 2006. *Dietary Reference Intakes*.

13. Ibid.

14. Ibid.

15. Ibid.

16. Institute of Medicine. 2005. *Dietary Reference Intakes for Water, Potassium, Sodium, Chloride, and Sulfate*. Washington, DC: The National Academies Press.

17. American Heart Association. 2012. *About High Blood Pressure*. Available from www.americanheart.org. Accessed April 2014.

18. Jones, G., T. Beard, V. Parameswaran, T. Greenway, and R. von Witt. 1997. A Population-Based Study of the Relationship between Salt Intake, Bone Resorption, and Bone Mass. *European Journal of Clinical Nutrition* 51:561–565.

19. Moseley, K. F., C. M. Weaver, L. Appel, A. Sebastian, and D. E. Sellmeyer. 2013. Potassium Citrate Supplementation Results in Sustained Improvement in Calcium Balance in Older Men and Women. *Journal of Bone and Mineral Research* 28(3):497–504.

20. Matcovic, L., Ilich, J. Z., M. B. Andon, L. C. Hsieh, M. A. Tzagournis, B. J. Lagger, and P. K. Goel. 1995. Urinary Calcium, Sodium, and Bone Mass of Young Females. *American Journal of Clinical Nutrition* 62(2):417–425.

21. Tsugane, S., S. Sasazuki, M. Kobayashi, and S. Sasaki. 2004. Salt and Salted Food Intake and Subsequent Risk of Gastric Cancer among Middle-Aged Japanese Men and Women. *British Journal of Cancer* 90:128–134.

22. Toledo, E., F. B. Hu, R. Estruch, P. Buil-Cosiales, et al. 2013. Effect of the Mediterranean Diet on Blood Pressure in the PREDIMED Trial: Results from a Randomized Controlled Trial. *BMC Medicine* doi:10.1186/1741-7015-11-207.

23. Office of the Federal Register. 2014. Food Labeling: Revision of the Nutrition and Supplement Facts Label. Available at https://www.federalregister.gov/articles/2014/03/03/2014-04387/food-labeling-revision-of-the-nutrition-and-supplement-facts-labels. Accessed May 2014.

24. Institute of Medicine. 2006. *Dietary Reference Intakes*.

25. Frassetto, L. and I. Kohlstadt. 2011. Treatment and Prevention of Kidney Stones: An Update. *American Family Physician* 84(11):1234–1242.

26. Institute of Medicine. 2005. *Dietary Reference Intakes for Water, Potassium, Sodium, Chloride, and Sulfate*.

27. Zhou, B., H. L. Wang, W. L. Wang, X. M. Wu, L. Y. Fu, and J. P. Shi. 2013. Long-Term Effects of Salt Substitution on Blood Pressure in a Rural North Chinese Population. *Journal of Human Hypertension* 27(7):427–433.

28. Sacco, S. M., M. N. Horcajada, and E. Offord. 2013. Phytonutrients for Bone Health during Ageing. *British Journal of Clinical Pharmacology* 75(3):697–707.

29. Moseley. 2013. Potassium Citrate Supplementation Results in Sustained Improvement in Calcium Balance in Older Men and Women.

30. Curhan, G. C., W. C. Willett, E. B. Rimm, and M. J. Stampfer. 1993. A Prospective Study of Dietary Calcium and Other Nutrients and the Risk of Symptomatic Kidney Stones. *New England Journal of Medicine* 328:833–838.

31. Institute of Medicine. 2006. *Dietary Reference Intakes*.

32. Sheng, P. H. 2012. Body Fluids and Water Balance. In *Biochemical, Physiological, and Molecular Aspects of Human Nutrition*. Philadelphia: W. B. Saunders.

33. Kerstetter, J. E., K. O. O'Brien, and K. L. Insogna. 1998. Dietary Protein Affects Calcium Absorption. *American Journal of Clinical Nutrition* 68:859–865.

34. Bihuniak, J. D., R. R. Sullivan, C. A. Simpson, D. M. Casseria, T. B. Huedo-Medina, K. O. O'Brien, J. E. Kerstetter, and K. L. Insogna. 2014. Supplementing a Low-Protein Diet with Dibasic Amino Acids Increases Urinary Calcium Excretion in Young Women. *Journal of Nutrition* 144(3):282–288.

35. Weaver, C. M., R. P. Heaney, B. R. Martin, and M. L. Fitzsimmons. 1991. Human Calcium Absorption from Whole-Wheat Product. *Journal of Nutrition* 121:1769–1775.

36. Stipanuk. 2012. *Biochemical, Physiological, and Molecular Aspects of Human Nutrition*.

37. Ibid.

38. Da Silva, M. S., and I. Rudkoska. 2014. Dairy Products on Metabolic Health: Current Research and Clinical Implications. *Maturitas* 77(3):221–228.

39. Bertoia, M. L., E. W. Triche, D. S. Michaud, A. Baylin, et al. 2014. Mediterranean and Dietary Approaches to Stop Hypertension Dietary Patterns and Risk of Sudden Cardiac Death in Postmenopausal Women. *American Journal of Clinical Nutrition* 99(2):344–351.

40. Baron, J. A., M. Beach, J. S. Mandel, R. U. van Stolk, R. W. Haile, R. S. Sandler, R. Rothstein, et al. 1999. Calcium Supplements for the Prevention of Colorectal Adenomas. *New England Journal of Medicine* 340:101–107.

41. Manson, J. E., and S. S. Bassuk. 2014. Calcium Supplements: Do They Help or Harm? *Menopause* 21(1):106–108.

42. Alonso, D., E. Pieras, P. Piza, F. Grases, and R. M. Prieto. 2014. Effects of Short- and Long-Term Indapamide Treatments on Urinary Calcium Excretion in Patients with Calcium Oxalate Dihydrate Urinary Stone Disease: A Pilot Study. *Scandinavian Journal of Urology and Nephrology* 46(2):97–101.

43. Onakpoya, I. J., R. Perry, J. Zhang, and E. Ernst. 2011. Efficacy of Calcium Supplementation for Management of Overweight and Obesity: Systematic Review of Randomized Clinical Trials. *Nutrition Reviews* 69(6):335–343.

44. Larsen, S. C., L. Angquist, T. S. Ahluwalia, T. Skaaby, N. Roswall, A. Tjønneland, J. Halkjær, et al. 2014. Interaction between Genetic Predisposition to Obesity and Dietary Calcium in Relation to Subsequent Change in Body Weight and Waist Circumference. *American Journal of Clinical Nutrition* 99(4):957–965.

45. Boon, N., G. B. J. Hul, J. H. C. H. Stegen, W. E. M. Sluijsmans, C. Valle, D. Langin, N. Viguerie, and W. H. M. Saris. 2007. An Intervention Study of the Effects of Calcium Intake on Faecal Fat Excretion, Energy Metabolism, and Adipose Tissue mRNA Expression of Lipid Metabolism–Related Proteins. *International Journal of Obesity* 31:1704–1712.

46. Institute of Medicine. 2006. *Dietary Reference Intakes*.

47. Stipanuk. 2012. *Biochemical, Physiological, and Molecular Aspects of Human Nutrition*.

48. Straub, D. 2007. Calcium Supplementation in Clinical Practice: A Review of Forms, Doses, and Indications. *Nutrition in Clinical Practice: Official Publication of the American Society for Parenteral and Enteral Nutrition* 22:286–296.

49. Ibid.

50. Gropper, S. S., and J. L. Smith. 2013. *Advanced Nutrition and Human Metabolism*. 6th ed. Belmont, CA: Thomson Wadsworth.

51. Dong, J. Y., P. Xun, K. He, and L. Q. Qin. 2011. Magnesium Intake and Risk of Type 2 Diabetes: Meta-Analysis of Prospective Cohort Studies. *Diabetes Care* 34(9):2116–2122.

52. Sharma, A., S. Dabla, R. P. Agrawal, H. Barjatya, D. K. Kochar, and R. P. Kothari.

2007. Serum Magnesium: An Early Predictor of Course and Complications of Diabetes Mellitus. *Journal of the Indian Medical Association* 105:16–20.

53. Institute of Medicine. 2006. *Dietary Reference Intakes*.

54. Pitcher, M. C. L., E. R. Beatty, G. R. Gibson, and J. H. Cummings. 1996. Methionine Derivatives Diminish Sulphide Damage to Colonocytes—Implications for Ulcerative Colitis. *Gut* 39:77–81.

55. Forsmo, S., H. M. Hvam, M. L. Rea, S. E. Lilleeng, B. Schei, and A. Langhammer. 2007. Height Loss, Forearm Bone Density and Bone Loss in Menopausal Women: A 15-Year Prospective Study. The Nord-Trøndelag Health Study, Norway. *Osteoporosis International* 18:1261–1269.

56. National Institutes of Health. 2012 *Osteoporosis Overview*. Available at http://www.niams.nih.gov/Health_Info/Bone/Osteoporosis/overview.asp. Accessed April 2014.

57. Ibid.

58. Forsmo, S., H. M. Hvam, M. L. Rea, S. E. Lilleeng, B. Schei, and A. Langhammer. 2007. Height Loss, Forearm Bone Density and Bone Loss in Menopausal Women: A 15-Year Prospective Study. The Nord-Trøndelag Health Study, Norway. *Osteoporosis International* 18:1261–1269.

59. The ESHRE Capri Workshop Group. 2011. Perimenopause Risk Factors and Future Health. *Human Reproduction Update* DOI: 10.1093/humupd/dmr020.

60. Ibid.

61. National Osteoporosis Foundation. 2013 *Osteoporosis Report*. Available from www.nof.org. Accessed April 2014.

62. Ibid.

63. Sacco. 2013. Phytonutrients for Bone Health during Ageing.

64. Hamidi, M. S., O. Gajic-Veljanoski, and A. M. Cheung. 2013. Vitamin K and Bone Health. *Journal of Clinical Densitometry* 16(4):409–413.

65. Mangano, K., J. Kerstetter, A. Kenny, K. Insogna, and S. J. Walsh. 2014. An Investigation of the Association between Omega-3 FA and Bone Mineral Density among Older Adults: Results from the National Health and Nutrition Examination Survey Years 2005–2008. *Osteoporosis International* 25(3):1033–1041.

66. McGartland, C., P. J. Robson, L. Murray, G. Cran, M. J. Savage, D. Watkins, M. Rooney, and C. Boreham. 2003. Carbonated Soft Drink Consumption and Bone Mineral Density in Adolescence: The Northern Ireland Young Hearts Project. *Journal of Bone and Mineral Metabolism* 18:1563–1569.

67. Høstmark, A. T., A. J. Søgaard, K. Alvær, and H. E. Meyer. 2011. The Oslo Health Study: A Dietary Index Estimating Frequent Intake of Soft Drinks and Rare Intake of Fruit and Vegetables Is Negatively Associated with Bone Mineral Density. *Journal of Osteoporosis* doi: 10.4061/2011/102686.

68. Heaney, R. P. 2001. Carbonated Beverages and Urinary Calcium Excretion. *American Journal of Clinical Nutrition* 74:343–347.

69. Lind, T., A. Sundqvist, L. Hu, G. Pejler, G. Andersson, A. Jacobson, and H. Melhus. 2013. Vitamin A Is a Negative Regulator of Osteoblast Mineralization. *PLoS One* 8(12):e82388.

70. Ruiz-Ramos, M., L. A. Vargas, T. I. Fortoul Van der Goes, A. Cervantes-Sandoval, and V. M. Mendoza-Nunez. 2010. Supplementation of Ascorbic Aid and Alpha-tocoperhol is Useful to Preventing Bone Loss Linked to Oxidative Stress in Elderly. *Journal of Health Aging* 14(6):467–472.

71. Nichols, J. F., M. J. Rauh, M. T. Barrack, and H. S. Barkai. 2007. Bone Mineral Density in Female High School Athletes: Interactions of Menstrual Function and Type of Mechanical Loading. *Bone* 41:371–377.

72. Janz, K. F., J. M. Gilmore, S. M. Levy, E. M. Letuchy, T. L. Burns, and T. J. Beck. 2007. Physical Activity and Femoral Neck Bone Strength during Childhood: The Iowa Bone Development Study. *Bone* 41:216–222.

73. Aki, V., A. Vainionpaa, R. Korpelainen, J. Leppaluoto, and T. Jamsa. 2005. Effects of High-Impact Exercise on Bone Mineral Density: A Randomized Controlled Trial in Premenopausal Women. *Osteoporosis International* 16:191–197.

74. Engelke, K., W. Kemmler, D. Lauber, C. Beeskow, R. Pintag, and W. A. Kalender. 2006. Exercise Maintains Bone Density at Spine and Hip EFOPS: A 3-Year Longitudinal Study in Early Postmenopausal Women. *Osteoporosis International* 17:133–142.

75. Ducher, G., N. Tournaire, A. Meddahi-Pelle, C. L. Benhamou, and D. Courteix. 2006.

Short-Term and Long-Term Site-Specific Effects of Tennis Playing on Trabecular and Cortical Bone at the Distal Radius. *Journal of Bone and Mineral Metabolism* 24:484–490.

76. Gombos Császár, G., V. Bajsz, E. Sió, V. Steinhausz Tóth, B. Schmidt, L. Szekeres, and J. Kránicz. 2014. The Direct Effect of Specific Training and Walking on Bone Metabolic Markers in Young Adults with Peak Bone Mass. *Acta Physiologica Hungarica* 6:1–11.

77. Riedt, C. S., Y. Schlussel, N. von Thun, H. Ambia-Sobhan, T. Stahl, M. P. Field, R. M. Sherrell, and S. A. Shapses. 2007. Premenopausal Overweight Women Do Not Lose Bone during Moderate Weight Loss with Adequate or Higher Calcium Intake. *American Journal of Clinical Nutrition* 85:972–980.

78. Diamanti, A., C. Bizzarri, M. Gambarara, A. Calce, F. Montecchi, M. Cappa, G. Biaco, and M. Castro. 2007. Bone Mineral Density in Adolescent Girls with Early Onset of Anorexia Nervosa. *Clinical Nutrition* 26:329–334.

79. Emaus, N., T. Wilsgaard, and L. A. Ahmed. 2014. Impacts of Body Mass Index, Physical Activity, and Smoking on Femoral Bone Loss. The Tromsø Study. *Journal of Bone Mineral Research* doi: 10.1002/jbmr.2232.

80. Emaus, N., T. Wilsgaard, and L. A. Ahmed. 2014. Impacts of Body Mass Index, Physical Activity, and Smoking on Femoral Bone Loss. The Tromsø Study. *Journal of Bone Mineral Research* doi: 10.1002/jbmr.2232.

81. Baron, J. A., B. Y. Farahmand, E. Weiderpass, K. Michaellsson, A. Alberts, I. Persson, and S. Ljunghall. 2001. Cigarette Smoking, Alcohol Consumption, and Risk of Hip Fracture in Women. *Archives of Internal Medicine* 161:983–988.

82. Emaus. 2014. Impacts of Body Mass Index, Physical Activity, and Smoking on Femoral Bone Loss. The Tromsø Study.

83. Ibid.

84. Marrone, J. A., G. F. Maddalozzo, A. J. Branscum, K. Hardin, L. Cialdella-Kam, K. A. Phibrick, A. C. Breggia, et al. 2012. Moderate Alcohol Intake Lowers Biochemical Markers of Bone Turnover in Postmenopausal Women. 19(9):974–979.

85. Ibid.

13 Trace Minerals

Learning Outcomes

After reading this chapter, you will be able to:

13.1 Describe the characteristics and functions of trace minerals in the body.

13.2 Describe mechanisms of iron absorption and transport, key functions, recommended intakes, food sources, and toxicity and deficiency symptoms associated with iron.

13.3 Describe the key functions, recommended intakes, food sources, and toxicity and deficiency symptoms associated with copper.

13.4 Describe the key functions, recommended intakes, food sources, and toxicity and deficiency symptoms associated with zinc.

13.5 Describe the key functions, recommended intakes, food sources, and toxicity and deficiency symptoms associated with selenium.

13.6 Describe the key functions, recommended intakes, food sources, and toxicity and deficiency symptoms associated with fluoride.

13.7 Describe the key functions, recommended intakes, food sources, and toxicity and deficiency symptoms associated with chromium.

13.8 Describe the key functions, recommended intakes, food sources, and toxicity and deficiency symptoms associated with iodine.

13.9 Describe the key functions, recommended intakes, food sources, and toxicity and deficiency symptoms associated with molybdenum.

13.10 Describe the key functions, recommended intakes, food sources, and toxicity and deficiency symptoms associated with manganese.

13.11 Describe the potential roles, deficiency symptoms, food sources, and potential toxicity associated with arsenic, boron, nickel, silicon, and vanadium.

13.12 Explain the causes and treatments for the various nutrient-deficiency anemias.

True or False?

1. Trace minerals are called trace because food contains such small amounts. **T**/**F**

2. Meat is the primary source of iron in the American diet. **T**/**F**

3. Taking iron supplements can cause a copper deficiency. **T**/**F**

4. Zinc can cure the common cold. **T**/**F**

5. Consuming too much selenium can cause vomiting and diarrhea. **T**/**F**

6. Most bottled waters contain fluoride. **T**/**F**

7. Chromium can help weight lifters build bigger muscles. **T**/**F**

8. Iodized salt is the only reliable source of iodine. **T**/**F**

9. Cinnamon is a good source of manganese. **T**/**F**

10. Consuming leafy green vegetables ensures a diet rich in molybdenum. **T**/**F**

See page 505 for the answers.

There has been an eruption of new evidence in trace mineral research in the past decade. Science is now able to track the biochemical movement of these trace elements and is finding new links that connect a lack of these intriguing nutrients to disease. In this chapter, we'll examine the important functions and unique qualities of the trace minerals. We'll also discuss the amounts needed in the diet, the absorption and transport of each, and the best foods from which to obtain them.

What Are Trace Minerals and Why Do You Need Them?

LO 13.1 Describe the characteristics and functions of trace minerals in the body.

Iron, zinc, selenium, fluoride, chromium, copper, iodine, manganese, and molybdenum are known as the **trace minerals** (or microminerals). The human body needs them in much smaller amounts than it needs the major minerals. Collectively, less than 5 grams of trace minerals are found in the body,[1] and even though the daily dietary need for each is less than 20 milligrams, they are just as necessary for health as other nutrients are. **Table 13.1** outlines the trace minerals, their functions, food sources, and nutrient interactions that we will cover in this chapter.

Similar to the major minerals, trace minerals are found in both plant and animal foods, but the best food sources are whole grains, legumes, dairy, meat, and seafood. The trace mineral amount found in a given plant food depends partly on the mineral content in the soil in which the food was grown. In addition, processing removes trace minerals found in the bran and germ of grains. For this reason, whole grains contain more trace minerals than do refined grains. Trace minerals found in all foods are stable in cooking.

Bioavailability of Trace Minerals Can Vary

Like the major minerals, the bioavailability of trace minerals can vary according to an individual's nutritional status, other foods that are eaten, and the form of the mineral.

Trace minerals often compete with each other for absorption in the GI tract. Some trace minerals, such as iron, copper, and zinc, are absorbed in their ionic state. These minerals have the same ionic charge ($^{+2}$) and use the same protein carriers during absorption. Too much of one mineral, such as iron, Fe^{+2}, can cause a decrease in the absorption and metabolism of another mineral, for example, copper, Cu^{+2}, leading to an imbalance.[2] Thus, bioavailability of each mineral depends on the amount of both minerals in the intestinal tract at the time of absorption. This is one reason why most people should avoid taking single-mineral supplements. Some trace minerals, such as iron, are recycled in the body and can be used repeatedly.

Most Trace Minerals Function as Cofactors

Several trace minerals function as cofactors. This function is similar to that of coenzymes, in that trace minerals are part of an enzyme complex. The enzymes that trace minerals such as manganese and molybdenum attach to and activate are referred to as **metalloenzymes.**

trace minerals Minerals required in amounts smaller than 100 milligrams per day that are essential to health; also called microminerals.

metalloenzymes Active enzymes that contain one or more metal ions that are essential for their biological activity.

Trace Mineral	Metabolic Function	Daily Needs (19 years+)	Food Sources	Toxicity Symptoms/UL	Deficiency Symptoms	Interaction with Other Nutrients
Iron (Fe)	▪ Major component of hemoglobin and myoglobin; carries oxygen and carbon dioxide ▪ Part of cytochromes ▪ Enhances immune system	Women: 18 mg/day Men: 8 mg/day	Meat, fish, poultry, enriched and fortified breads and cereals	▪ Vomiting, nausea, diarrhea, constipation ▪ Organ damage, including the kidney and liver UL: 45 mg	▪ Fatigue ▪ Microcytic anemia ▪ Poor immune function ▪ Growth retardation in infants	▪ Zinc ▪ Calcium ▪ Ascorbic acid
Copper (Cu)	▪ A component of several metalloenzymes ▪ Enzymes involved in iron metabolism ▪ Connective tissue enzymes ▪ Antioxidant enzymes	900 μg/day	Cocoa, whole grains, legumes, and shellfish	▪ Vomiting, abdominal pain, nausea, diarrhea ▪ Liver damage UL: 10,000 μg	▪ Anemia ▪ Impaired immune function ▪ Impaired growth and development	▪ Zinc ▪ Iron
Zinc (Zn)	▪ Cofactor for several metalloenzymes ▪ DNA and RNA synthesis ▪ Part of the enzyme superoxide dismutase	Women: 8 mg/day Men: 11 mg/day	Seafood, meat, whole grains	▪ Nausea, vomiting, cramps, diarrhea ▪ Loss of appetite ▪ Headaches ▪ Impaired immune function UL: 40 mg	▪ Skin rash and hair loss ▪ Diarrhea ▪ Loss of taste and smell ▪ Depressed growth and development	▪ Iron ▪ Calcium and phosphorus ▪ Copper ▪ Folate ▪ Protein ▪ Phytates
Selenium (Se)	▪ A component of antioxidant enzymes	55 μg/day	Meat, seafood, fish, eggs, whole grains	▪ Brittle hair and nails ▪ Skin rash ▪ Garlic breath odor ▪ Fatigue ▪ Irritability UL: 400 μg	▪ Muscle weakness and pain ▪ May trigger Keshan disease	Unknown
Fluoride (F)	▪ Part of fluoroapatite, which makes teeth stronger ▪ Enhances bone formation	Women: 3 mg/day Men: 4 mg/day	Fluoridated water, tea, seaweed	▪ Fluorosis in teeth and skeletal fluorosis UL: 10 mg	▪ Increased susceptibility to dental caries	▪ Calcium
Chromium (Cr)	▪ Improves insulin response	Women: 20–25 μg/day Men: 30–35 μg/day	Pork, egg yolks, whole grains, nuts	▪ Unconfirmed toxicity effects Data insufficient to establish a UL	▪ Elevated post-meal blood glucose	▪ Vitamin C ▪ Phytates ▪ Simple sugars
Iodine (I)	▪ Component of the thyroid hormone thyroxine	150 μg/day	Iodized salt, seafood, dairy products	▪ Thyroiditis ▪ Goiter ▪ Hypothyroidism and hyperthyroidism UL: 1,100 μg	▪ Goiter ▪ Cretinism	Unknown
Molybdenum (Mo)	▪ Cofactor for a variety of metalloenzymes	45 μg/day	Legumes, nuts, leafy vegetables, dairy, cereals	Unknown in humans UL: 2,000 μg	Unknown in humans	Unknown
Manganese (Mn)	▪ Cofactor for metalloenyzmes involved in carbohydrate metabolism	Women: 1.8 mg/day Men: 2.3 mg/day	Beans, oats, nuts, tea	▪ Abnormal central nervous system effects UL: 11 mg	Unknown in humans	▪ Calcium ▪ Iron ▪ Phytates

The ingredients of this sandwich are good sources of trace minerals: The whole-wheat bread contributes zinc, copper, chromium, iodine, and manganese to your diet, while a few slices of low-fat turkey adds iron, zinc, and selenium. Top off your sandwich with manganese-rich leafy greens and cranberries packed with selenium to make this a meal brimming with a variety of essential trace minerals.

Other essential roles of trace minerals include helping hormones function; for example, iodine is a component of the thyroid hormone thyroxine. Trace minerals, including iron, maintain the health of red blood cells and some trace minerals, such as fluoride, are part of the structure of bones and teeth. Other trace minerals, including copper and selenium, are important components of antioxidant enzymes.

Trace Mineral Deficiencies and Toxicity Are Hard to Determine

Because trace minerals are found in short supply in the body, symptoms of deficiency are hard to identify, and deficiencies are often overlooked. This fact also makes it difficult to establish recommended intakes, including tolerable upper limits to prevent toxicity.

In this chapter we cover each individual trace mineral in detail, beginning with iron.

LO 13.1: THE TAKE-HOME MESSAGE Trace minerals are inorganic nutrients that the human body needs in small amounts. Their bioavailability is affected by the amount in the body, and whether the mineral competes with other substances for absorption. Trace minerals help enzymes and hormones function, maintain red blood cells, are part of the structure of bones and teeth, and act as cofactors.

Exploring Iron

LO 13.2 Describe mechanisms of iron absorption and transport, key functions, recommended intakes, food sources, and toxicity and deficiency symptoms associated with iron.

What Is Iron?

Iron (Fe) is the most abundant mineral on Earth, and the most abundant trace mineral in the body. A 130-pound female has over 2,300 milligrams (2.3 grams) of iron—about the weight of a dime—in her body, whereas a 165-pound male has 4,000 milligrams (4.0 grams)—slightly less than the weight of two dimes.[3] Iron deficiency is the most common nutrient deficiency around the world, and iron-deficiency anemia is common in women of childbearing age and children, particularly in the developing world, but also in the United States.

Heme and Nonheme Iron

Two forms of iron are found in foods: **heme iron** and **nonheme iron**. Heme iron is part of the proteins **hemoglobin** (in red blood cells) and **myoglobin** (in muscle cells), and part of cytochromes in the electron transport chain. It is therefore found in animal foods such as meat, poultry, and fish.

Nonheme iron is found in plant foods such as grains and vegetables and comprises more than 80 percent of the iron consumed in foods (100 percent for vegans). It is also the form of iron used to enrich breads and fortify cereals.

Iron Bioavailability

The bioavailability of iron is influenced by several factors, including the molecular form of the iron, iron status of the individual, and the types of food eaten at the same time. Iron is found in foods either as an oxidized form (Fe^{+3}) called **ferric iron** or nonheme iron, or the reduced form (Fe^{+2}) called **ferrous iron,** which is the heme form of iron.

Heme iron is two to three times more bioavailable than nonheme iron. Nonheme iron is often bound to acids, such as oxalates in leafy vegetables or polyphenols in tea and coffee, which makes it more difficult to absorb. A serving of cooked spinach, for example, contains approximately 6 milligrams of nonheme iron, but less than 1 percent is absorbed because of the oxalates in the spinach. The polyphenols in tea or coffee can reduce the absorption of nonheme iron in a meal by as much as 70 percent.[4]

There are ways in which nonheme iron bioavailability can be improved (see **Table 13.2**). For example, adding vitamin C to a meal that contains nonheme iron can enhance its rate of absorption. In the intestinal tract, vitamin C donates an electron to the ferric form, which reduces it to the more bioavailable ferrous form. As little as 25 milligrams of vitamin C— the amount in about one-quarter cup of orange juice—can double the amount of nonheme iron absorbed from a meal and 50 milligrams of vitamin C can increase the amount absorbed by about sixfold.

Another way to enhance nonheme iron absorption from foods is to eat meat, fish, or poultry at the same meal as the nonheme iron source; this is referred to as the MFP factor (**m**eat, **f**ish, and **p**oultry). The peptides in these animal-derived foods are thought to be the enhancing factors. The meat in a turkey sandwich helps enhance the absorption of the nonheme iron in whole-wheat bread.

Let's look more closely at the mechanisms that affect iron absorption.

Iron Absorption and Transport

The absorption-transport mechanism of iron (**Figure 13.1**) is tightly controlled, which helps regulate the amount of iron absorbed into the body and prevent iron toxicity. Once the iron is absorbed

---

Chemistry Boost

The Oxidation and Reduction of Iron

Iron can exist in two valence states: ferrous (Fe^{+2}) and ferric (Fe^{+3}). Ferric (Fe^{+3}) iron is *reduced* to ferrous (Fe^{+2}) iron, meaning it has gained electrons and has a more negative oxidation number ($^{+2}$ versus $^{+3}$). The opposite is true when ferrous iron is oxidized to ferric iron; it loses an electron and the oxidation number increases.

$$Fe^{+2} \leftrightarrow Fe^{+3} + e^-$$

Recall that:

When a substance is oxidized, it . . .	When a substance is reduced, it . . .
Loses electrons	Gains electrons
Has a more positive oxidation number	Attains a more negative oxidation number
Is the reducing agent	Is the oxidizing agent

---

heme iron Iron that is part of a heme group found in hemoglobin in the blood, myoglobin in muscles, and in the mitochondria as part of the cytochromes.

nonheme iron Iron that is not attached to heme.

hemoglobin The oxygen-carrying, heme-containing protein found in red blood cells.

myoglobin The oxygen-carrying, heme-containing protein found in muscle cells.

ferric iron The oxidized form of iron (Fe^{+3}).

ferrous iron The reduced form of iron (Fe^{+2}).

continued

TABLE 13.2 Factors That Influence Iron Absorption

Enhance Iron Absorption	Decrease Iron Absorption
■ Sufficient hydrochloric acid in the stomach ■ The form of iron in the food; heme iron is more easily absorbed than nonheme iron ■ Increased need for iron (blood loss, pregnancy, growth) ■ Vitamin C in the small intestine at the same time ■ Presence of MFP factor (meat, fish, poultry)	■ Phytates in cereal grains (dietary fiber) ■ Oxalates ■ Polyphenols (tea or coffee) ■ Reduced hydrochloric acid in stomach ■ Excess use of antacids ■ Excess minerals such as calcium, zinc, and magnesium

into the blood, only 1 to 2 grams is lost daily from the body except through blood loss.

ferritin A protein that stores iron in the intestine.

hemosiderin A protein that stores iron in the body.

Iron must cross two cell membranes in the small intestine, the brush border and the basolateral membrane, before it is absorbed into the portal vein. Heme iron crosses the brush border of the enterocyte attached to a protein carrier. Once inside the enterocyte, the enzyme *heme oxygenase* releases the ferrous iron

(Fe^{+2}) from hemoglobin.[5] If the body does not need the iron immediately, ferrous iron is oxidized to the ferric form and binds to the protein **ferritin,** which acts as a temporary storage form of iron in the intestine. Once ferritin becomes saturated with iron, additional iron can be attached to another protein called **hemosiderin** for storage. If not needed by the body, this iron remains stored until the intestinal cells are sloughed off and excreted through the feces.

Nonheme iron is absorbed less efficiently than heme iron. Nonheme iron must first be released during digestion and reduced to ferrous iron (Fe^{+2}) by stomach acids and pepsin to improve its absorption rate across the brush border. Both the ferrous (Fe^{+2}) and ferric (Fe^{+3}) forms of iron from nonheme sources are absorbed across the brush border attached to a transport protein. Nonheme iron is also affected by the alkaline environment

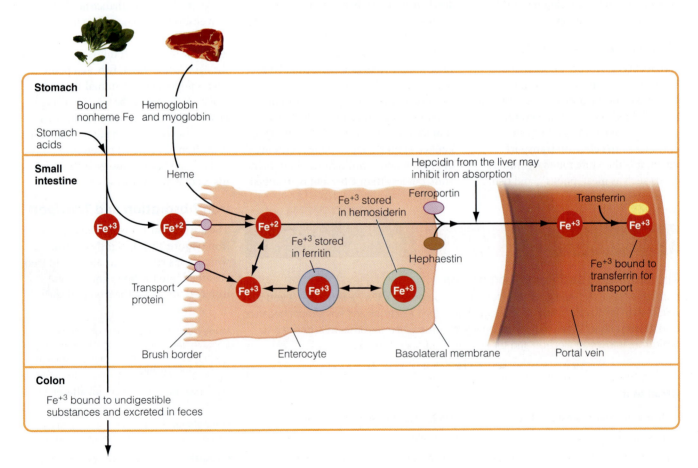

▲ **Figure 13.1 The Absorption and Transport of Iron**
Iron is absorbed into the enterocyte and attached to ferritin in the enterocyte. When the body requires iron, it is released from ferritin, attached to ferroportin, oxidized to ferric iron by hephaestin, and transported through the blood attached to transferrin. The liver hormone hepcidin controls the process.

of the small intestine, which renders it less soluble and thus less bioavailable. Similar to heme iron, once inside the enterocyte, nonheme iron is stored attached to ferritin until needed or excreted as intestinal cells are sloughed off. Any nonheme iron that remains bound to food or other compounds in the intestinal tract remains unabsorbed and is excreted in the feces.

When the body needs iron, the ferritin stored within the enterocyte releases the ferric (Fe^{+3}) iron, which is again reduced to the ferrous (Fe^{+2}) form. Ferrous iron attaches to **ferroportin,** a protein that transports the iron across the basolateral membrane into the portal vein. Once ferroportin crosses the basolateral membrane, it releases the ferrous iron (Fe^{+2}). Ferrous iron is once again oxidized to ferric iron (Fe^{+3}) by a copper-containing enzyme called **hephaestin** and attaches to a protein carrier in the blood called **transferrin,** which transports the iron throughout the body.[6]

Hormonal Regulation of Iron Absorption

A hormone produced by the liver called **hepcidin** controls iron absorption.[7] When iron stores are high, the liver produces more hepcidin, which inhibits ferroportin from transporting iron across the basolateral membrane—in a sense, trapping the iron in the enterocyte. When iron stores are low, hepcidin levels are decreased, which allows ferroportin to actively transport iron out of the enterocyte into the portal blood.

Stored Iron Affects Iron Absorption

Iron status influences the amount of ferritin produced in the intestinal tract. Thus, if the iron stores in the body are low, less ferritin is produced, to allow more iron to be absorbed directly into the bloodstream. In other words, the lower the stores, the greater the percentage of iron absorbed. If the body contains adequate iron stores, it absorbs an average of 14 to 18 percent of the iron consumed in the average mixed diet. When iron stores are high, the amount of iron absorbed can be as low as 5 percent of the iron consumed, because more ferritin is produced to block iron from absorption and to store the iron in the intestinal cells.

Iron Recycling

As a key component of blood, iron is highly valuable to the body and is treated accordingly. The amount of iron absorbed is not sufficient to meet the body's daily iron needs; therefore, approximately 95 percent of the iron in the body is recycled and reused.[8] In blood, the iron found in the heme portion of hemoglobin is broken down in the liver and spleen, with 20 to 25 milligrams of iron salvaged per day. This iron is then used for synthesizing new red blood cells in the bone marrow, incorporated into iron-containing enzymes, or stored as ferritin for use later. Very little iron is excreted or shed in hair, skin, and sloughed-off intestinal cells. In fact, most iron loss is due to bleeding.

Metabolic Functions of Iron

Iron plays a major role in a variety of key functions. It participates in oxidation-reduction reactions because of its ability to be changed from its ferrous (Fe^{+2}) to ferric (Fe^{+3}) forms and back again.

Hemoglobin and Myoglobin Transport Oxygen

Approximately two-thirds of the iron in the body is in hemoglobin and myoglobin (**Figure 13.2**). The heme in hemoglobin binds with oxygen from the lungs and transports it to the tissues for their use. Hemoglobin also picks up a small amount of carbon dioxide waste products from the cells and transports them back to the lungs to be exhaled.

Similarly, iron is part of the protein myoglobin that transports and stores oxygen in the muscles. Heme in myoglobin accepts oxygen from hemoglobin and transports it to the muscle and heart muscle cells. Myoglobin also transports the carbon dioxide produced in the muscle and heart muscle cells

ferroportin A protein found on the basolateral surface of the enterocyte that transports iron out of the enterocyte into the portal vein.

hephaestin A copper-containing enzyme that catalyzes the conversion of ferrous to ferric iron before attaching to transferrin for transport.

transferrin An iron-transporting protein.

hepcidin A hormone produced in the liver that regulates the absorption and transport of iron.

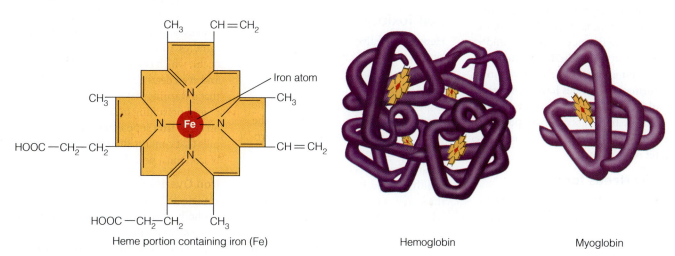

Heme portion containing iron (Fe)   Hemoglobin   Myoglobin

▲ **Figure 13.2 Iron-Containing Hemoglobin and Myoglobin**
Iron is part of the heme in hemoglobin and myoglobin.

continued

to hemoglobin in the blood for excretion. In other words, myoglobin in the muscle works with hemoglobin in the blood in the exchange of oxygen and carbon dioxide.

Iron Participates in Energy Metabolism

Iron performs as a cofactor in enzymes involved in energy metabolism. Recall from Chapter 8 that electrons produced during glycolysis and in the TCA cycle are delivered to the electron transport chain by nicotinamide adenine dinucleotide plus hydrogen and flavin adenine dinucleotide ($NADH^+ + H^+$ and $FADH_2$). Iron-containing cytochromes in the mitochondria carry the electrons to oxygen to eventually produce ATP, carbon dioxide, and water. Iron also participates in the conversion of citrate to isocitrate in the TCA cycle. In iron-deficiency anemia, both of these functions are diminished, which leads to fatigue.

Iron Is Important for Immune Function

Iron is necessary for the production of the lymphocytes and macrophages that help fight infection, and macrophages may store iron to prevent pathogens from using the mineral to multiply.[9] Iron is also a cofactor for several key enzymes involved in protecting cell membranes from free radical damage.

Iron Is Needed for Brain Function

In the brain, iron helps enzymes that are involved in the synthesis of neurotransmitters, including dopamine, epinephrine, norepinephrine, and serotonin, which send messages to the rest of the body.[10] A deficiency of iron in children can impact cognitive development and their ability to learn and retain information. Studies have shown that children with iron-deficiency anemia in their early years can have persistent, decreased cognitive ability during their later school years.[11]

Daily Needs for Iron

The current RDA for iron needed by adult females, ages 19 to 50, is 18 milligrams a day to cover the iron lost during

hemochromatosis A genetic disorder that causes the body to store excessive amounts of iron.

menstruation. After menopause, usually around age 50, a woman's daily iron needs drop to 8 milligrams because she is no longer losing blood monthly. Adult males need 8 milligrams of dietary iron daily. The recommendations for women and men take into account a typical American diet, which includes both heme and nonheme iron sources. Vegetarians may need to eat as much as 1.8 times the amount of iron as nonvegetarians. This is due to the lower bioavailability of iron from plant foods.[12]

Adult men consume more than twice their recommended iron needs—over 16 milligrams, on average, daily. Adult premenopausal women consume only about 70 percent of their daily need, or approximately 13 milligrams, on average. Postmenopausal women consume slightly over 12 milligrams of iron daily, so, like men, they are more than meeting their needs.

Food Sources of Iron

About half of Americans' dietary iron intake comes from iron-enriched bread and other grain foods such as cereals (see **Figure 13.3**).[13] Meat, fish, poultry, and egg yolks are rich sources of efficiently absorbed heme iron; however, this form of iron contributes 12 percent of the dietary needs of males and females.[14] Cooking foods in iron pans and skillets can also increase their nonheme iron content, as foods absorb iron from cookware.[15]

Iron Toxicity

Hepcidin, the liver hormone that circulates in the blood, controls iron balance and prevents iron toxicity. Hepcidin binds to ferroportin, the protein that exports iron out of the enterocyte, and prevents excess iron from entering the blood. The iron is stored in the enterocyte until the intestinal cells slough off and the iron is lost in the feces. In healthy people, hepcidin increases when the storage of iron is high, and decreases when iron storage is low.[16] When iron is overconsumed in supplements, this *mucosal block* is overwhelmed and too much iron is absorbed, causing iron toxicity. Consuming too much iron from

supplements can cause constipation, nausea, vomiting, and diarrhea. The upper level for iron for adults is set at 45 milligrams daily, as this level is slightly less than the amount known to cause

Cooking foods in a cast-iron skillet can increase the nonheme iron content of the food.

these intestinal symptoms. This upper level doesn't apply to, and is too high for, individuals with liver disease or other diseases that can affect iron stores in the body, such as certain genetic disorders.

Iron Poisoning in Children

In the United States the accidental consumption of supplements containing iron is the leading cause of poisoning deaths in children under age 6. Ingestion of as little as 200 milligrams has been shown to be fatal. Children who swallow iron supplements can experience symptoms such as nausea, vomiting, and diarrhea within minutes. Intestinal bleeding can also occur, which can lead to shock, coma, and even death. The FDA has mandated that a warning statement about the risk of iron poisoning in small children be put on every iron supplement label and that pills that contain 30 milligrams or more of iron must be individually wrapped.[17]

Iron Overload

Undetected excessive storing of iron in the body over several years is called *iron overload* and can damage a person's tissues and organs, including the heart, kidneys, liver, and nervous system. **Hemochromatosis,** a genetic disorder in which individuals absorb too much dietary iron, can cause iron overload. Though this condition is congenital, its symptoms often don't manifest until adulthood. If not diagnosed and treated early enough, organ damage can occur. Individuals with hemochromatosis need to avoid iron supplements throughout their lives, as well as large amounts of vitamin C supplements, which enhance iron absorption.

Other Effects of Iron Toxicity

Some studies suggest that iron can stimulate free radical production in the body, which can damage the arteries leading to the heart and may contribute to heart disease. It has also been suggested that iron's role in free radical production may increase the risk of cancer. Though this association is not definite, unless you are medically diagnosed with iron deficiency, it doesn't make any sense to consume excessive amounts of iron.

Iron Deficiency

If the diet is deficient in iron, body stores will be slowly depleted so as to keep blood hemoglobin in a normal range. Iron-deficiency anemia occurs when body stores are so depleted that blood hemoglobin levels decrease. Red blood cells contain less heme and become small and pale. This diminishes the delivery of oxygen through the body, causing fatigue and weakness. Individuals with iron-deficiency anemia are also more susceptible to and have a reduced ability to fight infections.[18] Health Connection: What Are Nutrient-Deficiency Anemias? provides more information on this deficiency.

Because of their increased iron needs, pregnant women, menstruating women and teenaged girls, especially those with heavy blood losses, and preterm or low birth weight infants, as well as older infants and toddlers, often don't meet their iron needs and are at risk of becoming deficient.[19]

The best way to prevent iron deficiency is through an iron-rich diet as described in Nutrition in Practice: Diane on page 478.

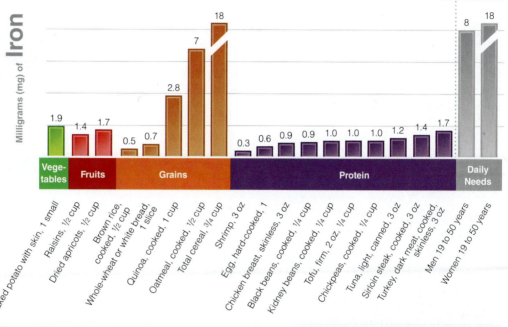

▲ **Figure 13.3 Food Sources of Iron**

TABLE TIPS
Enhance Your Iron Intake

Enjoy an iron-enriched whole-grain cereal along with a glass of vitamin C–rich orange juice to boost the nonheme iron absorption in cereal.

Add plenty of salsa (vitamin C) to bean burritos to enhance the absorption of the nonheme iron in both the beans and the flour tortilla.

Stuff a baked potato (nonheme iron, vitamin C) with shredded cooked chicken (heme iron) and broccoli (vitamin C) and top it with melted low-fat cheese for a quick and iron-rich dinner.

Eat a small box of raisins (nonheme iron) and a clementine or tangerine (vitamin C) as a sweet snack that's abundant in iron.

Add chickpeas (nonheme iron) to salad greens (vitamin C). Don't forget the tomato wedges for another source of iron-enhancing vitamin C.

continued

Nutrition in Practice: Diane

During her senior year at high school, Diane has been experiencing fainting spells, and according to her mother, she becomes short of breath prior to the faint. Diane's nails have become brittle, and she always seems to look "pale." At the pediatrician's office, the nurse drew some of Diane's blood and the doctor ordered a complete blood count (CBC) from the lab. The blood test revealed that she had iron-deficiency anemia. While the doctor recommended that Diane take an iron supplement, her mother wanted her to meet with a Registered Dietitian Nutritionist (RDN) to make sure that her diet contained iron-rich foods, especially since she will be leaving for college in a month.

Diane's Stats
- Age: 18
- Height: 5 feet 0 inches
- Weight: 98 pounds
- BMI: 19.1

Diane's Food Log

Food/Beverage	Time Consumed	Hunger Rating*	Location
Yogurt	7 AM	3	Kitchen
Candy bar	11:30 AM	5	High school
Cream cheese and jelly sandwich, milk	1:30 PM	5	High school cafeteria
Chocolate chip cookies and milk	4 PM	4	Kitchen, studying
Pork chop and rice	6:30 PM	5	Kitchen
Popcorn	10 PM	3	Bedroom, surfing Internet

*Hunger Rating (1–5): 1 = not hungry; 5 = super hungry.

Critical Thinking Questions

1. How much iron should Diane be consuming daily?
2. Based on her food log, how can Diane add more heme and nonheme iron–rich foods at her meals and snacks to meet her daily needs?
3. Which iron-rich food group is Diane likely falling short of in her diet?
4. What other foods can be added to her meals and snacks that would improve her body's absorption of nonheme iron?

Dietitian's Observation and Plan for Diane

- Discuss the difference between heme and nonheme iron in the diet.
- Add whole-grain cereal and a source of vitamin C such as berries to her morning yogurt.
- Snack on nuts and dried fruits instead of candy in the morning.
- Need to consume at least 5 to 6 ounces of protein foods in the diet to increase her daily iron consumption. Change her lunchtime sandwich to include 2 to 3 ounces of protein foods such as turkey and lean roast beef.
- Add a salad and/or vegetables with dinner to increase her vitamin C intake at dinner.
- Drink some vitamin C–rich orange or grapefruit juice along with her evening popcorn snack.

Two weeks later, Diane returns for a follow-up visit with the dietitian. She has made all of the dietary changes, but is concerned about her ability to consume this diet once she gets to college. She plans to be on the college's unlimited meal plan for her freshman year. The RDN gives Diane suggestions for her college meals, and they devise a list of the snacks that she can safely store in her dorm room. Diane makes an appointment to meet with the RDN for another diet assessment when she comes home for her Thanksgiving break.

The absorption of iron is controlled by iron status, the molecular form of the iron, and types of foods eaten together. Iron is stored as ferritin or hemosiderin and transported attached to transferrin. Iron functions in energy metabolism, and is needed for a healthy immune system and brain function. The RDA for iron is 18 milligrams per day for menstruating women and 8 milligrams per day for men and postmenopausal women. Heme iron is found in meat, poultry, and fish. Nonheme iron is found in plant foods, such as grains and vegetables. Adults with normal functioning intestinal tracts have little risk of developing iron toxicity from food. Iron toxicity from supplements greater than 20 mg/kg can develop. Hemochromatosis caused by a genetic mutation is associated with iron build-up in the body and possibly death. Iron deficiency results in iron-deficiency anemia. A deficiency of iron in children can impact their ability to learn and retain information.

Exploring Copper

LO 13.3 Describe the key functions, recommended intakes, food sources, and toxicity and deficiency symptoms associated with copper.

What Is Copper?

Copper (Cu) may bring to mind ancient tools, great sculptures, or American pennies (although pennies are no longer made of solid copper), but it is also associated with several key body functions. Copper is found in two forms in the body: the oxidized form called **cupric** (Cu^{+2}) and the reduced form called **cuprous** (Cu^+).

Copper Absorption and Transport

Copper is absorbed mostly in the small intestine. As with iron, the absorption of copper is based on the body's need for the mineral and the ability to free copper from food complexes during digestion with the aid of hydrochloric acid and the digestive enzyme pepsin in the stomach.

The absorption mechanisms for copper are not clear. However, the current understanding is that once copper is free, it is reduced to the cupric (Cu^{+2}) state by enzymes on the surface of the enterocyte and then absorbed across the brush border, mostly by active transport. After crossing the brush border, copper is either used by the enterocyte, stored attached to a zinc-containing protein called metallothionein, or transported across the basolateral membrane into the blood.

The bioavailability of copper can be enhanced by amino acids, especially those that contain sulfur. However, phytates in legumes and cereals bind copper and can reduce the bioavailability of copper, as they do to iron. Excess zinc can also reduce the biovailability of copper because zinc stimulates more metallothionein, which binds copper in the enterocyte. Because of their electron configuration, iron, calcium, molybdenum, and phosphorus compete with copper for absorption. Vitamin C supplements reduce the absorption of copper, at least in animals, and results in a copper deficiency.[20]

Absorbed copper crosses the basolateral membrane and attaches to the protein albumin to be transported through the portal vein to the liver. In the liver,

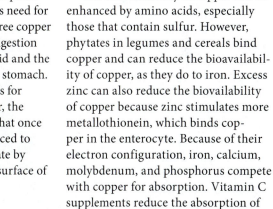

cupric The oxidized form of copper (Cu^{+2}).

cuprous The reduced form of copper (Cu^+).

continued

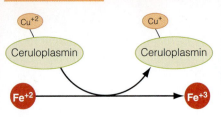

▲ **Figure 13.4 Ceruloplasmin Oxidizes Iron**
The copper-containing protein ceruloplasmin oxidizes ferrous iron (Fe^{+2}) to ferric iron (Fe^{+3}) before iron can bind to transferrin for transport in the blood.

copper is incorporated into another protein called **ceruloplasmin.** Very little copper, about 100 milligrams, is stored in the body. Most excess copper is excreted through the feces as part of bile.

Metabolic Functions of Copper

Copper is part of several metalloenzymes and proteins. Many of these proteins are essential for oxidation reactions and in reducing damage by free radicals. Copper-containing ceruloplasmin is the enzyme mentioned earlier that oxidizes iron from the ferrous form (Fe^{+2}) to the ferric form (Fe^{+3}) (**Figure 13.4**). If the diet is deficient in copper, the amount of copper-containing enzymes hephaestin and ceruloplasmin are reduced and iron accumulates in the intestinal cell rather than being attached to and transported by transferrin. A copper deficiency can thus result in iron-deficiency anemia.[21]

As part of the cytochromes, copper assists in energy production in the electron transport chain. And as part of the enzyme lysyl oxidase, copper links the proteins collagen and elastin together in connective tissue. Superoxide dismutase is a copper-containing enzyme that protects cells from free radical damage.

ceruloplasmin A protein found in the blood that transports copper.

In addition, copper also helps synthesize melanin (the dark pigment found in skin) and plays an important role as a cofactor in blood clotting and immune response.[22]

Daily Needs for Copper

The AI for copper for adult women and men is set at 900 micrograms of copper daily. U.S. women consume 1,000 to 1,100 micrograms, whereas men consume 1,300 to 1,500 micrograms daily, on average.

Food Sources of Copper

Organ meats (such as liver), seafood, nuts, and seeds are abundant in copper. Bran cereals, whole-grain products, and cocoa are also good sources (see **Figure 13.5**). Although potatoes, milk, and chicken are low in copper, they are consumed in such abundant amounts that they contribute a fair amount of copper to Americans' diets.

Copper Toxicity and Deficiency

Excessive intakes of copper supplements can cause stomach pain and cramps, nausea, diarrhea, vomiting, and even liver damage. The upper

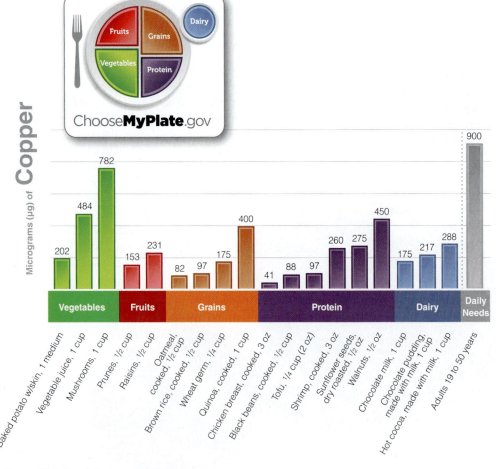

▲ **Figure 13.5 Food Sources of Copper**

level for copper for adults is set at 10,000 micrograms daily.

Copper deficiency is rare in the United States. Its symptoms resemble those of iron deficiency: fatigue and weakness. It has occurred in premature babies fed milk formulas, in malnourished infants fed cow's milk, and in individuals given intravenous feedings that lacked adequate amounts of copper.

Two genetic diseases affect copper metabolism. A rare genetic disorder, **Menkes' disease,** is a copper transport disorder. Copper accumulates in the kidney, brain, and liver and can cause developmental problems, osteoporosis, cardiovascular disease, and death. Another genetic disease, called **Wilson's disease,** prevents the body from excreting copper through the bile. An accumulation of copper in the brain and liver results in severe liver and brain damage if left untreated.

LO 13.3: THE TAKE-HOME MESSAGE
Copper is absorbed in the small intestine and transported attached to albumin. The bioavailability of copper is reduced by iron, zinc, molybdenum, calcium, phosphorus, and vitamin C supplements. Copper is part of ceruloplasmin, is a cofactor for metalloenzymes involved in energy production and the synthesis of connective tissue, and is part of the superoxide dismutase enzyme. The AI for copper is 900 micrograms for adults. Copper is found in seafood, nuts, and seeds. Copper toxicity is caused by some genetic diseases but deficiencies are rare.

Menkes' disease A genetic disorder that interferes with copper absorption.

Wilson's disease A rare genetic disorder that results in accumulation of copper in the body.

Exploring Zinc

LO 13.4 Describe the key functions, recommended intakes, food sources, and toxicity and deficiency symptoms associated with zinc.

What Is Zinc?

Zinc (Zn^{+2}) is found in very small amounts in almost every cell of the body, but mostly in bone and muscle. It is involved in the function of more than 100 metalloenzymes, including those used for protein synthesis.

Zinc Absorption and Transport

Like iron and copper, the absorption of zinc is controlled at the small intestine (**Figure 13.6**). Once it has been absorbed into the intestinal cell, it is bound to a protein called **metallothionine,** which stores zinc and temporarily prevents it from being absorbed into the portal vein. The body produces more metallothionine when zinc stores are high, to prevent toxicity, and less when zinc is deficient. If the zinc isn't needed, it diffuses into the lumen of the small intestine and is excreted through the feces. When it is needed, zinc stored in enterocytes is released from metallothionine and attaches to a transport protein for absorption across the basolateral membrane. The zinc is then released to attach to albumin for transport through the portal vein to the liver.

Zinc absorption can be reduced when high levels of nonheme iron are present in the intestinal tract. The use of iron supplements may be a factor in zinc status and diets high in fiber and phytates also reduce zinc absorption. Consuming animal protein improves zinc absorption.

Zinc Recycling

Zinc is found in the intestine as part of the pancreatic digestive juices. Because these juices are repeatedly excreted into and reabsorbed by the small intestine, zinc is recycled back to the pancreas to be reused. The zinc that is not recycled is excreted in the feces. Zinc can also be excreted in small amounts in the urine, sweat, and sloughed-off skin and hair.

Metabolic Functions of Zinc

Zinc plays a role in growth and development, in the immune system, and in the healing of wounds. It also influences taste and can help fight macular degeneration.

Zinc Is Needed for DNA Synthesis

Zinc is necessary for DNA and RNA synthesis. Zinc helps regulate gene expression by turning genes on and off, thus controlling transcription.[23] Delayed growth and maturation in children is a characteristic of zinc deficiency.

metallothionine A metal-binding protein rich in sulfur-containing amino acids that transports ions.

continued

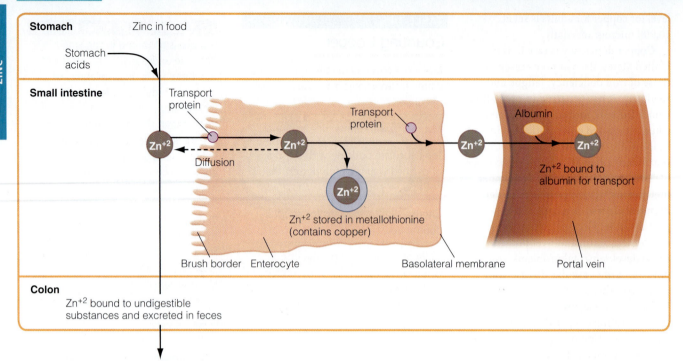

Stomach — Zinc in food

Stomach acids

Small intestine

Transport protein

Zn^{+2}

Diffusion

Transport protein

Zn^{+2}

Zn^{+2}

Zn^{+2} stored in metallothionine (contains copper)

Albumin

Zn^{+2}

Zn^{+2}

Zn^{+2} bound to albumin for transport

Brush border   Enterocyte

Basolateral membrane

Portal vein

Colon

Zn^{+2} bound to undigestible substances and excreted in feces

▲ **Figure 13.6 Zinc Absorption**
Zinc is absorbed into the enterocyte and attached to metallothionine for storage. When the body needs more zinc, it is released from metallothionine, transported across the basolateral membrane, and attached to albumin for transport through the body.

Zinc Supports the Immune System

Zinc affects a variety of key factors involved in maintaining a healthy immune system. For example, zinc is a component of thymic hormone, which controls and facilitates the maturation of lymphocytes and killer macrophages. Zinc also acts as an antioxidant and stabilizes cell membranes to provide a barrier to infection.[24] Without sufficient zinc, cell membranes become more susceptible to damage by free radicals and oxidation. Zinc helps reduce the inflammation that can accompany skin wounds, and helps wounds heal by being part of enzymes and proteins that repair skin cells and enhance their proliferation.[25]

Zinc lozenges are sometimes advertised to help reduce the severity and duration of the common cold. Whereas early research found little benefit to using them,[26] more recent research from Finland suggests zinc lozenges or syrup, if taken within 24 hours of the first sign of the sniffles, reduce a cold's severity and duration.[27] Zinc gluconate used as a nasal gel may also show promise, as it has lessened the duration[28] and the severity of cold symptoms in some cases.[29] Though the mechanism is still unclear, researchers suggest that zinc gels may reduce the duration of colds by blocking the viral infection at the site where cold viruses enter the body—the nasal passage. But not everyone is convinced. Possible side effects of the use of zinc nasal gels or lozenges include loss of smell, bad taste in the mouth, and nausea. More research is needed to understand the dosage and possible side effects before any recommendations can be made.

Zinc Improves Taste Perception

Zinc activates areas of the brain that perceive taste and smell. Its importance to appetite was first demonstrated in 1972 when researchers showed that taste disorders responded to zinc supplementation. Zinc has also been reported to influence taste preferences especially for salty foods.[30] This may be related to zinc's role in taste and smell.

Zinc May Prevent Age-Related Macular Degeneration

Research studies show that zinc may play a role in reducing the risk of age-related macular degeneration (AMD), a condition that hampers central vision. Zinc may work with an enzyme in the eyes that's needed to properly

Recent research suggests that zinc lozenges and nasal gels may help reduce the severity and duration of cold symptoms.

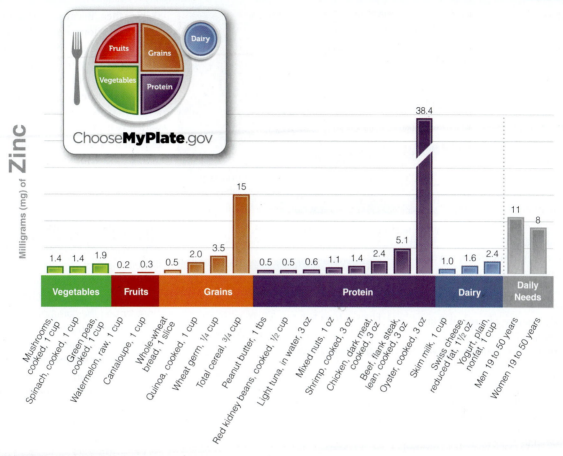

Figure 13.7 Food Sources of Zinc

Milligrams (mg) of Zinc

Vegetables	Mushrooms, cooked, 1 cup	1.4
Vegetables	Spinach, cooked, 1 cup	1.4
Vegetables	Green peas, cooked, 1 cup	1.9
Fruits	Watermelon, raw, 1 cup	0.2
Fruits	Cantaloupe, 1 cup	0.3
Grains	Whole-wheat bread, 1 slice	0.5
Grains	Quinoa, cooked, 1 cup	2.0
Grains	Wheat germ, 1/4 cup	3.5
Grains	Total cereal, 3/4 cup	15
Protein	Peanut butter, 1 tbs	0.5
Protein	Red kidney beans, cooked, 1/2 cup	0.5
Protein	Light tuna, in water, 3 oz	0.6
Protein	Mixed nuts, 1 oz	1.1
Protein	Shrimp, cooked, 3 oz	1.4
Protein	Chicken, dark meat, cooked, 3 oz	2.4
Protein	Beef, flank steak, lean, cooked, 3 oz	5.1
Protein	Oyster, cooked, 3 oz	38.4
Dairy	Skim milk, 1 cup	1.0
Dairy	Swiss cheese, reduced fat, 1½ oz	1.6
Dairy	Yogurt, plain, nonfat, 1 cup	2.4
Daily Needs	Men 19 to 50 years	11
Daily Needs	Women 19 to 50 years	8

use vitamin A for vision. Zinc may also help mobilize vitamin A from the liver to ensure adequate blood levels of this vitamin. Supplements that contain antioxidants along with zinc have been shown to reduce the risk of AMD. (For more information about the causes and treatment of AMD, see Chapter 9.)

Daily Needs for Zinc

The current RDA for adult men is 11 milligrams of zinc daily, whereas women need 8 milligrams daily. American adults, on average, are meeting their zinc needs. Men are consuming from 11 milligrams to over 14 milligrams daily and women are consuming 8 to 9 milligrams of zinc daily, on average.

Vegetarians, especially strict vegetarians, may need to ingest 50 percent more zinc compared to nonvegetarians. The bioavailability of zinc is lower in a vegetarian meal plan because they don't eat meat. The foods that vegetarians consume, such as grains and legumes that are high in phytates and staples of vegan diets, can bind with zinc, reducing its absorption in the intestinal tract and stores of zinc in the body.[31]

Food Sources of Zinc

Red meat, some seafood, and whole grains are excellent sources of zinc (see **Figure 13.7**). The dark meat in chicken and turkey is higher in zinc than the white meat. Because zinc is found in the germ and bran portion of grains, refined grains have as much as 80 percent less zinc than whole grains. This is yet another reason to favor whole-grain products over those made with refined grains.

Zinc Toxicity and Deficiency

The upper level for zinc in food and/ or supplements for adults is set at 40 milligrams daily. Consuming too much zinc, as little as 50 milligrams, can cause stomach pains, nausea, vomiting,

continued

Zinc continued

and diarrhea. Approximately 60 milligrams of zinc daily has been shown to lower body levels of copper by competing for absorption in the intestinal tract. This is an excellent example of how the overconsumption of one mineral can compromise the benefits of another. Excessive amounts, such as 300 milligrams of zinc daily, have been shown to suppress the immune system and lower HDL ("good") cholesterol.

A zinc deficiency can result from too much iron, which can interfere with zinc transport. The transport protein, transferrin, transports both zinc and iron. In an iron overload, transferrin becomes saturated with iron, which reduces the sites available for zinc transport. Iron transport is also impaired if transferrin is saturated with zinc.

A deficiency of zinc can cause hair loss, loss of appetite, impaired taste of foods, diarrhea, and delayed sexual maturation, as well as impotence and

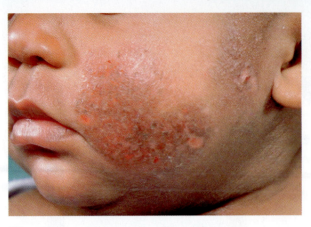

Skin rash is one of the symptoms of zinc deficiency.

TABLE TIPS

Improve Zinc Intake

Enjoy a tuna fish sandwich on whole-wheat bread at lunch for a double serving (fish and bread) of zinc.

Add kidney beans to a soup or salad.

Pack a small handful of mixed nuts and raisins in a zip-closed bag for a snack on the run.

Make oatmeal with milk for two servings of zinc in one bowl.

Add cooked green peas to casseroles, stews, soups, and salads.

skin rashes. Because zinc is needed during development, a chronic deficiency during childhood can slow and impair growth. Classic studies of groups of people in the Middle East showed that people who consumed a diet mainly of unleavened bread, which is high in zinc-binding phytates, experienced impaired growth and dwarfism.[32] Impaired growth may be partially reversed if zinc is restored in the diet.

LO 13.4: THE TAKE-HOME MESSAGE
Zinc is part of the RNA and DNA structure, functions in taste acuity, and helps prevent age-related macular degeneration. Zinc isn't effective in preventing the common cold but may reduce the duration of a cold. The RDA for zinc is 11 mg for adult males and 8 mg for adult females. Zinc is found in meat, fish, and whole grains. Zinc toxicity causes vomiting and diarrhea, suppresses the immune system, and lowers HDL cholesterol, whereas a zinc deficiency impairs growth, causes loss of hair and appetite, and delays sexual maturation.

Exploring **Selenium**

LO 13.5 Describe the key functions, recommended intakes, food sources, and toxicity and deficiency symptoms associated with selenium.

What Is Selenium?

The mineral selenium (Se) is a component of a class of proteins called

selenoproteins Proteins that contain selenomethionine.

selenomethionine An amino acid that contains selenium rather than sulfur.

selenoproteins, many of which are enzymes. Most dietary selenium is in the form of **selenomethionine.** Unlike iron and zinc, selenium absorption is based on the individual's needs. In fact, more than 85 percent of dietary selenium is absorbed mostly in the duodenum by passive diffusion.[33] Once absorbed, selenium is stored as selenomethionine or selenoprotein in a variety of tissues, including the liver, muscles, kidneys, and bone (**Figure 13.8**). Homeostasis of selenium is maintained by the kidneys, which excrete excess amounts through the urine.

Metabolic Functions of Selenium

Selenium plays a critical role in thyroid function and helps fight cancer via its antioxidant properties.

Selenium Is Required by the Thyroid

Three selenium-containing enzymes help regulate thyroid hormones in the body. These enzymes activate and deactivate thyroid hormone to maintain balance, and promote normal development and growth by regulating the thyroid gland.

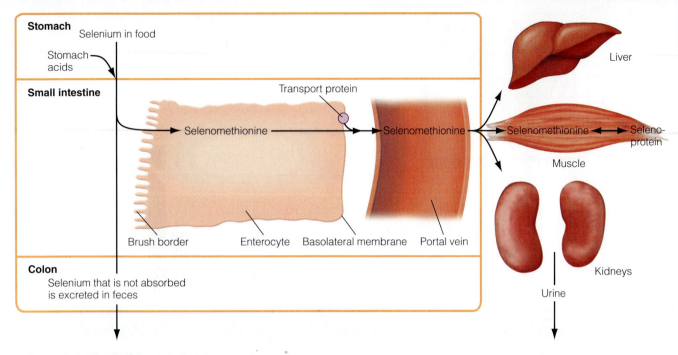

▲ **Figure 13.8 Metabolism of Selenium**
Selenium is easily absorbed, transported, and stored in the body, mostly as selenomethionine.

Selenium Plays an Antioxidant Role and May Help Fight Cancer

Selenoproteins, such as glutathione peroxidase, function as antioxidants that protect the cells from free radical damage. Research studies have suggested that deaths from cancers, such as lung, colon, and prostate cancers, are lower in groups of people who consume more selenium.[34] Selenium's antioxidant capabilities, and its ability to potentially slow the growth of tumors, are thought to be the mechanism behind its anticancer effects.[35] The FDA allows a Qualified Health Claim on food labels and dietary supplements that states, "Selenium may reduce the risk of certain cancers but the evidence is limited and not conclusive to date."[36]

Daily Needs for Selenium

The RDA for both adult females and males is set at 55 micrograms of selenium daily. American adults are more than meeting their needs—they consume about 80 to 160 micrograms daily, on average. The RDA is set to maintain optimal activity of the enzyme glutathione peroxidase. Most manufacturers do not include selenium on food labels unless the food has been fortified with the mineral. In this case, the label uses 70 micrograms as the standard for the percent Daily Value.

Food Sources of Selenium

Nuts, meat, seafood, cereal, grains, dairy foods, and fruits and vegetables can all contribute to dietary selenium (see **Figure 13.9**). However, the amount of selenium in foods depends upon the soil where the plants were grown and the animals grazed. For example, wheat grown in selenium-rich soil can have more than a tenfold higher amount of the mineral than wheat grown in selenium-poor soil.

Selenium Toxicity and Deficiency

Too much selenium can cause toxicity and a condition called **selenosis.** A person with selenosis will have brittle nails and hair, both of which may fall out. Other symptoms include stomach and

The content of selenium in dairy foods depends on the content of selenium in the plants cows are fed.

intestinal discomfort, a skin rash, garlicky breath, fatigue, and damage to the nervous system. A chronic intake of as little as 1 to 3 milligrams per day can result in toxicity. Thus, the upper level for selenium for adults is set at 400 micrograms daily to prevent the loss and brittleness of nails and hair.

Though rare in the United States, a selenium deficiency can cause **Keshan disease,** which damages the

selenosis The presence of toxic levels of selenium.

Keshan disease A disease related to a deficiency of selenium.

continued

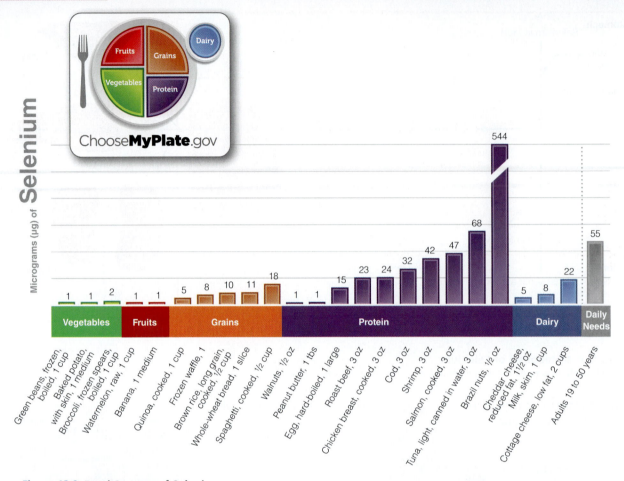

▲ **Figure 13.9** Food Sources of Selenium

TABLE TIPS

Seeking Out Selenium

Top a toasted whole-wheat bagel with a slice of reduced-fat Cheddar cheese for a hot way to start the day.

Spread peanut butter on whole-wheat crackers. Top each cracker with a slice of banana.

Top dinner pasta with broccoli for a selenium-smart meal.

Zap sliced apples, sprinkled with a little apple juice and cinnamon, in the micro-wave and top with vanilla yogurt for a tasty snack.

Spoon a serving of low-fat cottage cheese into a bowl and top with canned sliced peaches and almonds for a fabulous dessert.

heart. This disease typically only occurs in children who live in rural areas that have selenium-poor soil. However, some researchers speculate that selenium deficiency alone may not cause Keshan disease, but the selenium-deficient individual may also be exposed to a virus, which, together with the selenium deficiency, causes the damaged heart.[37]

Some reports suggest that selenium deficiencies may result in changes in thyroid hormone.[38] For example, there is a higher incidence of thyroiditis, such as the autoimmune thyroid disease called Hashimoto's, in individuals with lower levels of selenium.[39] This may be due to a decrease in activity of enzymes that require selenium as a cofactor within thyroid cells.

LO 13.5: THE TAKE-HOME MESSAGE
Selenium is part of selenoproteins, which act as antioxidants. Selenium also regulates thyroid function. Adults need 55 micrograms of selenium per day. All food groups contribute selenium, including nuts, meat, and seafood. Selenium toxicity causes brittle teeth and fingernails, garlic odor in the breath, gastrointestinal problems, and damage to the nervous system. A selenium deficiency can lead to Keshan disease and changes in thyroid hormone production.

Exploring **Fluoride**

LO 13.6 Describe the key functions, recommended intakes, food sources, and toxicity and deficiency symptoms associated with fluoride.

What Is Fluoride?

Fluoride (F^-) is the safe ionic form of fluorine, a poisonous gas. Fluoride is not classified as essential because the body does not require it for normal growth and development. However, it plays a critical role in developing strong teeth that are resistant to decay.

Fluoride is found naturally in plants and animals, and often added to the water supply. Almost all the fluoride consumed in the diet is absorbed in the small intestine and taken up by the bones and developing teeth.

Metabolic Functions of Fluoride

While no tissue or cellular process requires fluoride to function, fluoride has been shown to help maintain healthy teeth. Fluoride forms **fluoroapatite** by replacing the OH in hydroxyapatite crystals with fluoride. Fluoroapatite helps harden the outer layer of the tooth (the *enamel*) and makes the tooth more resistant to damage (see **Figure 13.10**). Over time,

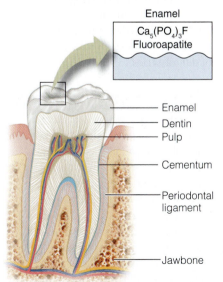

Enamel

$Ca_5(PO_4)_3F$
Fluoroapatite

— Enamel
— Dentin
— Pulp

— Cementum

— Periodontal ligament

— Jawbone

▲ **Figure 13.10 Structure of Fluoroapatite in Teeth**

acids produced by bacteria in the mouth, and from acidic foods and beverages, erode tooth enamel. Continual exposure of the teeth to these acids, especially during tooth formation, or if fluoride is lacking, can result in dental caries.

Fluoride from food, beverages, and dental products, such as toothpaste, can repair enamel that has already started to erode. Fluoride also interferes with the ability of the bacteria to metabolize carbohydrates, thus reducing the amount of acid they produce, and provides a protective barrier between the tooth and the destructive acids. Fluoride in the saliva continually bathes the teeth's surface, which helps remineralize the hydroxyapatite structure of the tooth and reduce the effect of the bacteria.[40] Consuming adequate amounts of fluoride is extremely important during infancy and childhood, when teeth are developing, and for maintenance of healthy teeth throughout life.

In the 1930s, scientists noticed lower rates of dental caries among individuals whose community water systems contained significant amounts of fluoride. Studies confirmed that the fluoride was the protective factor in the water. Since 1945, most communities have fluoridated their water, and today 67 percent of Americans live in communities that have a fluoridated water supply.[41] The increase in access to fluoridated water is the major reason there has been a decline in dental caries in the United States, and fluoridation of water is considered one of the ten greatest public health advances of the twentieth century.[42]

Fluoride also helps maintain strong bones by stimulating the osteoblasts. Fluoride in combination with calcium and vitamin D may increase bone mineral density and reduce the incidence of osteoporosis.

Tap water can be a good source of fluoride in communities that have fluoridated water.

Daily Needs for Fluoride

The AI for adult men has been set at 3.8 milligrams and 3.1 milligrams for adult women of fluoride daily. The Department of Health and Human Services estimates the optimal level of fluoridated tap water to prevent tooth decay is 0.7 milligrams per liter.[43] At this level, an individual would have to consume at least 15 cups of water daily, through either beverages or cooking, to meet fluoride needs (1 liter = 4.2 cups).

Currently, adults consume 1.4 to 3.4 milligrams of fluoride daily if they are living in communities with fluoridated water. The number drops to only 0.3 to 1.0 milligram consumed daily if the water isn't fluoridated.[44] In 2012 more than 74.6 percent of people were drinking fluoridated water.[45] This is close to the *Healthy People 2020* goal that 79.6 percent of people consume water that has the optimum level of fluoride recommended for preventing tooth decay.[46]

Food Sources of Fluoride

Foods in general are not a good source of fluoride. The best sources are

fluoroapatite The crystalline structure that results when hydroxyapatite has been changed by exposure of the tooth to fluoride.

continued

fluoridated water and beverages and foods made with this water, such as coffee, tea, and soups. Another source of fluoride can be juices made from concentrate using fluoridated tap water (remember, not all tap water contains fluoride). Water and processed beverages such as soft drinks account for up to 75 percent of Americans' fluoride intake.[47] Tea is also a good source of fluoride, as tea leaves accumulate fluoride. Because the decaffeination process involves the use of mineral water, which is naturally high in fluoride, decaffeinated tea has twice the amount of fluoride as the caffeinated variety.[48]

Most bottled waters sold in the United States have less than the optimal amount of fluoride. It is difficult to determine the fluoride content of many bottled waters because currently, fluoride amounts only have to be listed on the label if fluoride has been specifically added. Consumers need to check the label to see if the bottled water they purchase contains added fluoride.

Fluoride Toxicity and Deficiency

Having some fluoride is important for healthy teeth, but too much can cause

fluoride. **fluorosis** A condition caused by excess amounts of fluoride, resulting in mottling of the teeth.

fluorosis, a condition whereby the teeth become mottled (pitted) and develop white patches or stains on the surface (see **Figure 13.11**). Fluorosis creates teeth that are extremely resistant to caries but cosmetically unappealing.

Fluorosis occurs when teeth are forming, so only infants and children up to 8 years of age are at risk. Once teeth break through the gums, fluorosis can't occur. Fluorosis results from overfluoridation of water, swallowing toothpaste, or excessive use of dental products that contain fluoride. Some research suggests that fluorosis may be reversible, but more studies are needed to determine this.

Skeletal fluorosis can occur in bones when a person consumes at least 10 milligrams of fluoride daily for 10 or more years. This is a rare situation that may happen when water is mistakenly overfluoridated. Skeletal fluorosis

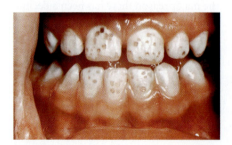

▲ **Figure 13.11 Fluorosis**
Teeth pitted by fluorosis.

can cause bone concentrations of fluoride that are up to five times higher than normal and result in stiffness or pain in joints, osteoporosis, and calcification of the ligaments.

The upper level for adults has been set at 10 milligrams to reduce the risk of fluorosis in the bones. Note, however, that the upper level for infants and children is much lower to prevent fluorosis in teeth. Infants in their first 6 months of age should ingest no more than 0.7 milligrams per day or 0.9 milligrams per day for infants 7 to 12 months old. Children from 1 to 3 years of age should not ingest more than 1.3 milligrams per day or 2.2 milligrams per day for children aged 4 to 8.

Because of fluoride's protective qualities, too little exposure to or consumption of fluoride increases the risk of dental caries.

LO 13.6: THE TAKE-HOME MESSAGE
Fluoride helps maintain the structure of bones and teeth and helps prevent dental caries. Adult males should consume 3.8 milligrams and women 3.1 milligrams of fluoride daily. The primary dietary source of fluoride is a fluoridated water supply and the consumption of foods and beverages prepared using fluoridated water. In children too much fluoride can result in fluorosis; in adults it can cause skeletal fluorosis. Too little fluoride increases the risk of dental caries.

Exploring **Chromium**

LO 13.7 Describe the key functions, recommended intakes, food sources, and toxicity and deficiency symptoms associated with chromium.

What Is Chromium?

Chromium (Cr) is the most recent mineral to be found necessary in humans.[49] Chromium is found in two ionic forms: **Trivalent chromium** (Cr^{+3}) is the active form of chromium found in food and **hexavalent chromium** (Cr^{+6}) is a toxic, carcinogenic form of the mineral produced from industrial waste.

Very little chromium is absorbed (less than 2.5 percent).[50] Once absorbed, the mineral is stored in a variety of tissues, including the liver, muscle, and spleen. Chromium can be excreted in the urine, especially when the diet is high in simple sugars.[51]

Metabolic Functions of Chromium

Chromium plays an essential role in how the body makes use of insulin. It also has an impact on prediabetes, metabolic syndrome, and weight.

Chromium Helps Insulin in the Body

The main function of chromium is to increase insulin's effectiveness in cells. The role of chromium in this mechanism is not clearly understood, but recent studies suggest that once insulin binds to the insulin receptor on the surface of the cells, chromium moves inside the cell and stimulates the transport of glucose across the cell membrane.[52] Chromium may also improve insulin's effects on the metabolism and storage of carbohydrates, fats, and protein in the body.

Because it works with insulin, some researchers believe that chromium may help individuals who have diabetes mellitus or prediabetes (glucose intolerance) to improve their blood glucose control. One small study suggests that a chromium supplement may reduce the risk of insulin resistance, and therefore, favorably affect the handling of glucose in the body.[53] Improving the body's sensitivity to insulin and maintaining a normal blood glucose level can possibly lower the incidence of type 2 diabetes in individuals at risk.[54] However, a large research study has yet to be reported that might confirm this theory.

Chromium May Prevent or Improve Metabolic Syndrome

Individuals with insulin resistance may not develop diabetes but could develop other health-related problems including metabolic syndrome, which comprises a cluster of risk factors including obesity, high lipid levels in the blood, hypertension, and hyperglycemia. Additionally, insulin resistance has been associated with cardiovascular disease.[55] Because chromium reduces insulin resistance, some researchers suggest that chromium supplements, particularly those that contain niacin, might reduce the symptoms of metabolic syndrome as well as lower blood sugar. Nutrigenomics could shed some light on these mechanisms and lead to new dietary strategies to prevent these insulin-resistance disorders.[56]

Based on this research, the FDA has allowed a Qualified Health Claim on

Chromium picolinate is often marketed as a weight-loss supplement; however, little scientific evidence supports this use.

chromium supplements. However, the supplement label must state that the evidence regarding the relationship between chromium supplements and either insulin resistance or type 2 diabetes is not certain at this time.[57]

Chromium Does Not Improve Body Composition

Although advertisements have sometimes touted chromium supplements as an aid to losing weight and building lean muscle, research doesn't support the claim. A review of over 20 research studies found no benefits from taking up to 1,000 micrograms of chromium daily.[58] In one specific study, ingesting a combination of chromium picolinate and conjugated linoleic acid for three months did not improve the weight and body composition of overweight young women.[59]

trivalent chromium The oxidized form of chromium (Cr^{+3}) found in food.

hexavalent chromium The oxidized form of chromium (Cr^{+6}) that is toxic.

continued

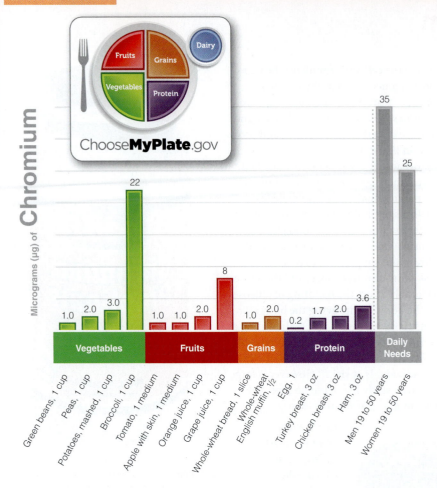

▲ **Figure 13.12** Food Sources of Chromium

TABLE TIPS

Cram in the Chromium

Toast a whole-wheat English muffin and top it with a slice of lean ham for a chromium-laden breakfast.

Add broccoli florets to salad for a chromium-packed lunch.

Try an afternoon glass of cold grape juice for a refreshing break. Add an apple for a double dose of chromium.

Combine mashed potatoes and peas for a sweet and starchy addition to dinner.

Split a firm banana in half, lengthwise, and spread a small amount of peanut butter on each side.

Daily Needs for Chromium

The AI for adult men ages 19 to 50 is 30 to 35 micrograms of chromium daily, whereas women need 20 to 25 micrograms daily, on average, depending upon their age. American men consume an estimated 33 micrograms of chromium from foods, and women consume 25 micrograms, on average, daily.[60]

Food Sources of Chromium

Many foods contain chromium, but the amount varies and is influenced by the amount of chromium in the soil. Whole grains are good sources of chromium, while refined grains contain much less. Meat, fish, and poultry and some fruits and vegetables can also provide chromium, whereas dairy foods are low in the mineral (see **Figure 13.12**).

Chromium Toxicity and Deficiency

Excess chromium, such as from supplements, may reduce the absorption, transport, and utilization of iron by binding to transferrin.[61] However, there are no known risks in humans from consuming excessive amounts of chromium from food or supplements, so no upper level has been set.

Chromium deficiency is very rare in the United States. Individuals who have a chromium deficiency show signs similar to those observed in diabetics, such as elevated blood glucose, and in people with cardiovascular disease, such as elevated fatty acids in the blood.[62] When a chromium deficiency has been shown to exist in individuals with type 2 diabetes, they experienced lower blood glucose levels and less insulin resistance when they were given chromium supplements. However, it is not clear if individuals with diabetes who do not have a chromium deficiency would benefit by taking a supplement.

LO 13.7: THE TAKE-HOME MESSAGE
Chromium may improve insulin function, the metabolism and storage of carbohydrates and fats, and metabolic syndrome, and may reduce prediabetes. The AI for adult men is 30 to 35 micrograms of chromium daily and women need 20 to 25 micrograms daily. Many plant foods contain chromium, depending on the soil levels. Chromium toxicity interferes with iron metabolism. Deficiencies of chromium are very rare.

Exploring Iodine

LO 13.8 Describe the key functions, recommended intakes, food sources, and toxicity and deficiency symptoms associated with iodine.

What Is Iodine?

Iodine (I) in the ionic form **iodide** (I^-) is an essential mineral. Like the fluoridation of community drinking water, the iodization of salt was a significant advance for public health in the United States. Prior to the 1920s, many Americans suffered from the iodine deficiency disease, **goiter** (**Figure 13.13**). A goiter epidemic in the midwestern United States prompted the campaign for mandatory iodization of salt. Once salt manufacturers began adding iodine to their product, incidence of the disease dropped. Today, rates of the disease are very low in the United States, though not in other parts of the world.

Metabolic Functions of Iodine

Iodine is essential for the thyroid, a butterfly-shaped gland that wraps around the trachea. The thyroid gland has evolved to trap iodine from the blood to make thyroid hormones and

▲ **Figure 13.13 Goiter**
Goiter refers to the enlarged thyroid gland caused by an iodine deficiency.

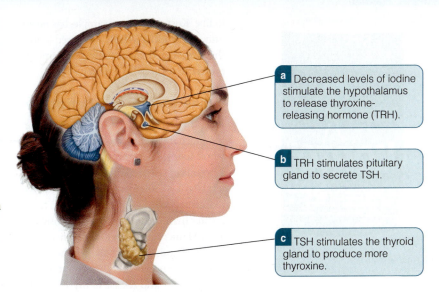

a Decreased levels of iodine stimulate the hypothalamus to release thyroxine-releasing hormone (TRH).

b TRH stimulates pituitary gland to secrete TSH.

c TSH stimulates the thyroid gland to produce more thyroxine.

▲ **Figure 13.14 The Thyroid Gland Produces the Hormone Thyroxine**

to store these thyroid hormones during times of iodine deficiency. Approximately 60 percent of thyroid hormones are comprised of iodine. The thyroid gland converts iodide to *tetraiodothyronine*, also referred to as T_4, or **thyroxine.** One of the iodide ions is removed from T_4 to form *triiodothyronine*, or T_3. The amount of T_4 produced by the thyroid is much greater than the amount of T_3, but T_3 is more potent. Both of these active thyroid hormones are released from the thyroid gland into the blood.

The powerful thyroid hormones affect the majority of cells. They help regulate metabolic rate, reproduction, and nerve, muscle, and heart function. Thyroid hormones also control the rate of ATP production in the TCA cycle. Children need thyroid hormones for normal growth of bones and brain development.[63]

The metabolism of the thyroid gland and the production of thyroxine are controlled by the hypothalamus. When the blood level of T_4 (thyroxine) is reduced, the hypothalamus responds by releasing **thyroxine-releasing hormone (TRH),** which stimulates the pituitary gland to produce **thyroxine-stimulating hormone (TSH).** TSH stimulates the thyroid to trap more iodide ions from the blood to produce more T_4. When the blood levels of T_4 rise, the hypothalamus shuts off the production of TRH and TSH to maintain thyroid hormone homeostasis. When the

diet is low in iodine, the blood levels of iodide ions become low and T_4 synthesis decreases, stimulating the process all over again (**Figure 13.14**).

Daily Needs for Iodine

The RDA for both adult men and women is 150 micrograms of iodine daily, an amount easily met by consuming seafood and iodized salt. In fact, Americans currently consume 230 to 410 micrograms of iodine daily, on average, depending upon their age and gender.

Food Sources of Iodine

The amount of iodine that occurs naturally in foods is typically low, approximately 3 to 75 micrograms in a serving, and is influenced by the amount of iodine in the soil, water, and fertilizers used to grow foods. Fish can provide higher amounts of iodine, as they concentrate it from

iodide The ionized form of iodine in the body (I^-).

goiter The enlargement of the thyroid gland, mostly due to iodine deficiency.

thyroxine The less active form of thyroid hormone, also known as *tetraiodothyronine* (T_4).

thyroxine-releasing hormone (TRH) A hormone secreted by the hypothalamus that stimulates the pituitary gland to release thyroxine-stimulating hormone (TSH).

thyroxine-stimulating hormone (TSH) A hormone released by the pituitary that stimulates the thyroid gland to trap more iodine to produce more thyroid hormone (T_4 and T_3).

continued

In the United States, most table salt is fortified with iodine.

seawater (**Figure 13.15**). Seaweed is also a highly concentrated source of iodine, with an average of 4,500 micrograms of iodine in one-quarter ounce of seaweed, or 3,000 percent of the Daily Value. Iodized salt provides 400 micrograms of iodine per teaspoon. Note that not all salt has added

iodine. Kosher salt, for example, has no additives, including iodine. Processed foods that use iodized salt or iodine-containing preservatives are also a source.

Iodine Toxicity and Deficiency

It is rare in the United States to consume too much iodine through the intake of whole foods. Diets that contain large amounts of seaweed may provide iodine intakes of 50,000 to 80,000 micrograms of iodine per day,[64] which is at least 45 times greater than the tolerable upper limit set at 1,100 micrograms per day. Consuming too much iodine can challenge the thyroid, impairing its function and reducing the synthesis and release of thyroxine. The result is similar to an iodine deficiency and hypothyroidism. Pregnant women should avoid ingesting too much iodine from iodized salt and prenatal supplements to prevent fetal damage.

An early sign of iodine deficiency is the enlarged thyroid gland known as *simple goiter*.[65] Consuming naturally occurring substances called **goitrogens,** found in foods such as rutabagas, cabbage, soybeans, and peanuts, can also result in a secondary deficiency and goiter if a person is iodine deficient. These antithyroid compounds reduce the absorption of iodide ions by the thyroid gland and decrease the amount of thyroid hormone released into the blood.

A deficiency of iodine during the early stages of fetal development can damage the brain of the developing baby, causing mental retardation. If the iodine deficiency is severe, **cretinism,** also known as *congenital hypothyroidism (congenital = born with, hypo = under, ism = condition),* can occur (**Figure 13.16**). Individuals with cretinism can experience abnormal sexual development, mental retardation, and dwarfism. Early detection of an iodine deficiency and treatment in women of

▲ **Figure 13.16 Cretinism**
Cretinism can result in a child born to a mother who was iodine deficient during the first few months of pregnancy when fetal development is the most active. The child can be born with stunted mental and physical development.

childbearing age is critical to avoid irreversible damage in their offspring.

LO 13.8: THE TAKE-HOME MESSAGE
Iodine is essential to make the thyroid hormones T_3 and T_4, which help regulate metabolic rate and stimulate growth and development. The RDA for both adult men and women is 150 micrograms of iodine daily. Iodine is found mostly in iodized salt, seafood, including shellfish, and dairy products. Iodine toxicity causes hyperthyroidism and hypothyroidism. Iodine deficiency during pregnancy causes mental retardation and cretinism in the offspring and goiter during adulthood.

goitrogens Substances in food that reduce the utilization of iodine by the thyroid gland, resulting in goiter.

cretinism A condition caused by a deficiency of thyroid hormone during prenatal development, resulting in abnormal mental and physical development in children.

Figure 13.15 chart

Microgams (μg) of **Iodine**

Food	Iodine (μg)
Tuna, canned in oil, 3 oz	17
Egg, large, 1	24
Turkey breast, 3 oz	34
Navy beans, cooked, 1/2 cup	35
Shrimp, 3 oz	35
Cod, 3 oz	99
Cheddar cheese, 1.5 oz	18
Milk, reduced fat, 1 cup	56
Yogurt, plain, low fat, 1 cup	75
Adults 19 to 50 years (Daily Needs)	150

Categories: Protein | Dairy | Daily Needs

▲ **Figure 13.15 Food Sources of Iodine**

Exploring **Molybdenum**

LO 13.9 Describe the key functions, recommended intakes, food sources, and toxicity and deficiency symptoms associated with molybdenum.

What Is Molybdenum?

Molybdenum (Mo) is part of several metalloenzymes involved in the metabolism of certain amino acids and oxidation-reduction reactions. For example, molybdenum is a cofactor for sulfate oxidase, the mitochondrial enzyme that converts sulfite (SO_3^{2-}) to sulfate (SO_4^{2-}) in the metabolism of methionine and cysteine.

Daily Needs for Molybdenum

The RDA for adult men and women is set at 45 micrograms of molybdenum daily. American women currently consume 76 micrograms and men consume 109 micrograms of molybdenum daily, on average.

Food Sources of Molybdenum

Legumes are excellent sources of molybdenum. Other molybdenum-rich foods include grains, nuts, dairy products, and leafy green vegetables.[66]

Molybdenum Toxicity and Deficiency

There is limited research on the adverse effects of too much dietary molybdenum in humans. In animal studies, too much molybdenum can cause reproductive problems and kidney disorders.[67] Because of this finding in animals, the upper level for molybdenum in humans has been set at 2 milligrams for adults.

A dietary deficiency of molybdenum has not been seen in healthy individuals.[68]

LO 13.9: THE TAKE-HOME MESSAGE
Molybdenum functions as a cofactor for protein synthesis, including DNA and RNA. The RDA for adult men and women is 45 micrograms daily. Molybdenum is found in legumes, whole grains, and nuts. Molybdenum is not toxic and a dietary deficiency has not been reported in humans.

Exploring **Manganese**

LO 13.10 Describe the key functions, recommended intakes, food sources, and toxicity and deficiency symptoms associated with manganese.

What Is Manganese?

Manganese (Mn) is a trace mineral that is either part of, or activates, many enzymes in the body. Much of the manganese in the body is found in bones and the accessory organs of the digestive tract, including the liver and pancreas.

Metabolic Functions of Manganese

This mineral acts as a cofactor for a variety of metalloenzymes involved in the metabolism of carbohydrates, fats, and amino acids. For example, in glycolysis, the conversion of pyruvate to oxaloacetate in the TCA cycle requires manganese. Manganese participates in the formation of the bone matrix and helps build cartilage that supports the joints.

Daily Needs for Manganese

The AI for manganese for adult women has been set at 1.8 milligrams, and at

continued

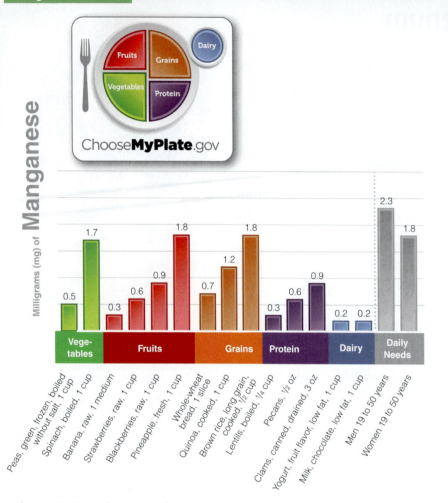

Milligrams (mg) of **Manganese**

Vegetables		Fruits				Grains				Protein				Dairy		Daily Needs	
0.5	1.7	0.3	0.6	0.9	1.8	0.7	1.2	1.8		0.3	0.6	0.9		0.2	0.2	2.3	1.8

- Peas, green, frozen, boiled without salt, 1 cup
- Spinach, boiled, 1 cup
- Banana, raw, 1 medium
- Strawberries, raw, 1 cup
- Blackberries, raw, 1 cup
- Pineapple, fresh, 1 cup
- Whole-wheat bread, 1 slice
- Quinoa, cooked, 1 cup
- Brown rice, long grain, cooked, ½ cup
- Lentils, boiled, ¼ cup
- Pecans, ½ oz
- Clams, canned, drained, 3 oz
- Yogurt, fruit flavor, low fat, 1 cup
- Milk, chocolate, low fat, 1 cup
- Men 19 to 50 years
- Women 19 to 50 years

▲ **Figure 13.17 Food Sources of Manganese**

Food Sources of Manganese

Manganese is prevalent in plant foods. Whole grains, nuts, legumes, tea, vegetables, and fruits such as pineapples, strawberries, and bananas are all robust sources of manganese (**Figure 13.17**). A teaspoon of ground cinnamon provides just under 0.5 milligram of manganese.

Manganese Toxicity and Deficiency

Manganese toxicity generally only occurs upon exposure to environmental pollutants, such as in manganese mining, battery manufacturing, and steel production.[70] For example, it has been

2.3 milligrams for men. Americans are easily meeting their manganese needs. Adult women consume over 2 milligrams of manganese daily, and adult men consume over 2.8 milligrams daily, on average, from the foods in their diet.[69]

reported that welders in the United States inhaled manganese in welding fumes due to lack of ventilation.[71] Toxicity can damage the nervous system and result in symptoms that resemble Parkinson's disease, including

Managing Manganese

Sprinkle whole-wheat toast with a dusting of cinnamon.

Combine cooked brown rice, canned and rinsed lentils, and chickpeas for dinner in a snap.

Spoon vanilla yogurt over canned crushed pineapples and sliced bananas for a tropical snack.

tremors, facial spasms, and difficulty walking.[72]

While toxicity is usually due to environmental pollutants, there have been reports of toxicity resulting from dietary intake. Manganese is found naturally in soil and under certain circumstances naturally high levels can be found in groundwater. A study of children in Canada who drank tap water with high levels of manganese showed lower IQ scores.[73] Most sources of water contain low levels (less than 10 µg/liter) of manganese. The Environmental Protection Agency (EPA) recommends that drinking water have no more than 50 µg/liter.[74] In addition, to protect against this toxicity, the tolerable upper level for dietary intake of manganese has been set at 11 milligrams daily.

A deficiency of manganese is rare in healthy individuals who consume a balanced diet. However, as with some other minerals, phytates can reduce the absorption of manganese. Excessive intake of other minerals from dietary supplements, including iron and calcium, may also reduce manganese absorption. Consuming a diet deficient in manganese can cause low serum cholesterol, a rash and scaly skin, and impaired growth in children.[75]

LO 13.10: THE TAKE-HOME MESSAGE
Manganese assists enzymes involved in energy metabolism, and functions as an antioxidant and in the synthesis of bone. The AI for men is 2.3 milligrams and women 1.8 milligrams daily. Legumes, nuts, and whole grains are good sources of manganese. Manganese is generally not toxic and deficiencies are rare.

Arsenic, Boron, Nickel, Silicon, and Vanadium: Are They Important to Health?

LO 13.11 Describe the potential roles, deficiency symptoms, food sources, and potential toxicity associated with arsenic, boron, nickel, silicon, and vanadium.

A few other minerals exist in the body, but their nutritional importance in humans has not yet been established. These minerals include arsenic, boron, nickel, silicon, and vanadium. Whereas limited research suggests that these may have a function in animals, there isn't enough data to confirm an essential role in humans.[76]

Arsenic may be needed in the metabolism of a specific amino acid in rats. A deficiency may impair growth and reproduction in other animals. The best food sources of arsenic are dairy products, meat, poultry, fish, grains, and cereal products. There are no adverse toxicity effects in humans from the organic form of arsenic found in foods. The inorganic form is poisonous for humans.

A deficiency of boron may be associated with reproductive abnormalities in certain fish and frogs, which suggests a possible role in normal development in other animals. Grape juice, legumes, potatoes, pecans, peanut butter, apples, and milk are all good food sources of boron. No known adverse effect from boron has been reported from foods. Some research suggests that high amounts of boron may cause reproductive and developmental problems in animals.[77] Because of this, the upper limit for human adults has been set at 20 mg daily, which is more than 10 times the amount American adults consume daily, on average.

Specific enzymes in the human body may need nickel. It is considered an essential mineral in animals. Grains and grain products, vegetables, legumes, nuts, and chocolate are good sources of nickel. No known toxicity of nickel has been shown in humans when consuming a normal diet. In rats, high exposure to nickel salts can cause toxicity, with symptoms such as lethargy, irregular breathing, and a lower than normal weight gain.[78] Because of this, the upper limit for adults is set at 1 mg daily for nickel salts.

Silicon may be needed for bone formation in animals. Grains, grain products, and vegetables are good sources of silicon. There is no known risk of silicon toxicity to animals from food sources.

Vanadium has insulin-like actions in animals. A deficiency of vanadium increases the risk of miscarriage. Vanadium can be purchased in supplement form, but mushrooms, shellfish, parsley, and black pepper are good food sources. There is no known risk of vanadium toxicity in humans by consuming foods. Too much vanadium has been shown to cause kidney damage in animals.[79] Because of the known toxicity in animals, the upper limit for adults is set at 1.8 mg daily.

LO 13.11: THE TAKE-HOME MESSAGE Other minerals, including arsenic, boron, nickel, silicon, and vanadium, may play a role in maintaining health, at least in animals. More research is needed in humans.

What Are Nutrient-Deficiency Anemias?

LO 13.12 Explain the causes and treatments for the various nutrient-deficiency anemias.

Do you donate blood more than two to four times a year? Are you a female of childbearing age, a vegetarian, or just don't eat right? If you answered *yes* to any one of these questions, you may be at risk of developing a nutrient-deficiency anemia. Unfortunately, you are not alone.

Anemia is a condition in which the blood lacks enough healthy, normal-sized red blood cells to deliver oxygen to the tissues. According to the National Heart, Blood, and Lung Institute, more than 3.5 million people have anemia.[80] Most of the more than 400 known anemias are caused by nonnutritional factors, including losing too

iron-deficiency anemia A type of anemia due to a lack of dietary iron or excessive loss of blood.

much blood, insufficient red blood cell production, or red blood cells being destroyed.

Lack of nutrient intake, malabsorption, or abnormal metabolism of certain nutrients can also cause anemia. The most common nutrient deficiencies that result in anemias are deficiencies of iron, folate, vitamin B_{12}, and vitamin B_6.

Anemias can be classified by the size of red blood cells. A complete blood count, or CBC, can provide a mean cell volume measurement identifying the anemia as *microcytic* (small) anemia, *normocytic* (normal) anemia, or *macrocytic* (large) anemia. Nutrient-deficiency anemias are usually either microcytic or macrocytic (**Figure 13.18**).

Microcytic Anemia Involves Red Blood Cells That Are Smaller than Normal

Microcytic anemia is a blood condition in which the mean cell volume of red blood cells is smaller than normal (*microcytosis)* and often *hypochromic* or

pale due to a lack of sufficient hemoglobin. The most common reason for microcytic anemia is having low iron stores in the body.

Iron-Deficiency Anemia

As the name suggests, **iron-deficiency anemia,** which is the most common form of anemia, results from insufficient iron stores in the body. An estimated 20 percent of women, 3 percent of men, and 50 percent of all pregnant women are iron deficient but may not have iron-deficiency anemia.[81] Anemia develops slowly when the normal levels of stored iron have been depleted and the number of red blood cells falls below normal. As the iron stores are decreasing, the bone marrow gradually produces fewer red blood cells. When the reserves of iron are depleted, there are fewer and abnormally smaller red blood cells.

Women, who have smaller stores of iron and who lose more blood (due to menstruation) than men, are at a higher risk. In men and postmenopausal women, iron deficiency is often the result of blood loss due to ulcers, increased use of aspirin, and specific

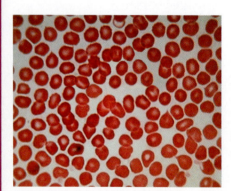

a Normal healthy red blood cells

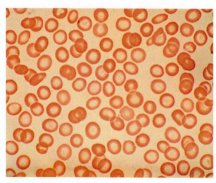

b Microcytic red blood cells affected by anemia

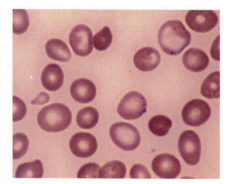

c Macrocytic red blood cells affected by anemia

▲ **Figure 13.18 Normal, Microcytic, and Macrocytic Red Blood Cells**
Microcytic red blood cells affected by anemia (b) are small and pale in color compared with normal red blood cells (a) due to lower heme concentration. Macrocytic red blood cells affected by anemia (c) are large, pale, and fewer in number compared with normal red blood cells due to the inability to normally divide.

Consuming a vitamin-C-rich food such as orange juice with iron supplements will improve iron absorption.

cancers such as colon, esophagus, and stomach cancer.

Signs and Symptoms of Iron-Deficiency Anemia

Mild iron-deficiency anemia may go unnoticed. The most common symptoms include fatigue, especially during physical exertion, due to the lack of red blood cells and, thus, the inability to carry sufficient oxygen to the muscle cells. Other possible signs may include pale skin color, irritability, shortness of breath, sore tongue, brittle nails, headache, a blue tinge to the whites of the eyes, and decreased appetite (especially in children).[82] In young children, a mild iron-deficiency anemia can result in intellectual impairment that is irreversible even after adding iron supplements to the diet.[83] Mild iron-deficiency anemia during pregnancy may cause premature births, low birth weight, and even maternal mortality.

Individuals who have been diagnosed with iron-deficiency anemia may also practice *pica*, a condition characterized by eating clay and other nonfood

items, including burnt matches and rubber bands.[84] Pica may exacerbate iron-deficiency anemia because the nonfood substances reduce the bioavailability of iron.

Testing for Iron-Deficiency Anemia

If you suspect you might have iron-deficiency anemia, a variety of simple blood tests can provide the correct diagnosis. Blood tests show a normal or low hemoglobin level, abnormal number, shape, or size of red blood cells, and the level of iron stored in the body.

A complete blood count (CBC) measures the hemoglobin level in the blood. A normal range for hemoglobin is 11.1 to 15.0 grams per deciliter. Anemia is diagnosed if the test reveals a hemoglobin level below 11.1. A CBC also determines the hematocrit, or the ratio of red blood cells to fluid in the blood. A normal hematocrit is between 32 and 43 percent red blood cells. If the tests reveal lower than normal hemoglobin, hematocrit, or both, the individual is diagnosed with anemia.

The CBC also provides a mean cell volume measurement that can establish whether red blood cells are microcytic or macrocytic.

Another test can be conducted to measure serum iron. This test directly measures the amount of iron in the blood, but it doesn't accurately reflect the stores of iron. To estimate iron stores, the **total iron-binding capacity (TIBC),** or transferrin levels, are measured. If iron-deficiency anemia exists, the total iron-binding capacity and the ability to transport more iron will be high.

Treatment for Iron-Deficiency Anemia

Iron supplements, along with an optimum intake of dietary iron, are usually necessary to correct iron-deficiency anemia and restore the iron reserves. Oral iron supplements in the ferrous, or Fe^{+2}, form, sold as ferrous sulfate, ferrous gluconate, or ferrous fumarate, are the most easily absorbed.[85] These supplements, taken for several weeks or even months, are best taken with orange juice or another vitamin C–rich substance to improve iron absorption. Recall that vitamin C makes iron more bioavailable. Avoid taking iron supplements with milk or antacids, which may interfere with the absorption of iron.

Vitamin B$_6$ and Microcytic Anemia

A deficiency of vitamin B$_6$ or pyridoxine may also result in microcytic anemia, although this is not as common as iron-deficiency anemia.[86] Recall from Chapter 10 that the active form of vitamin B$_6$, pyridoxal phosphate or PLP, acts as a coenzyme for more than 100 enzymes, most

total iron-binding capacity (TIBC) A blood test that measures the amount of iron that transferrin can bind. A higher TIBC indicates iron-deficiency anemia.

of which are involved in protein metabolism. PLP is required as a coenzyme in the synthesis of heme, the part of hemoglobin that is used to transport oxygen in the blood. If the diet is deficient in vitamin B_6, insufficient heme production occurs and results in hypochromic, microcytic anemia, the symptoms are undistinguishable from those of iron-deficiency anemia.

Macrocytic Anemia Involves Red Blood Cells That Are Larger than Normal

Macrocytic anemia is characterized by fewer, but abnormally large red blood cells (*macrocytosis*) that contain insufficient hemoglobin (see Figure 13.18). Macrocytic anemia is also referred to as *megaloblastic anemia* because the larger than normal cells cannot produce DNA quickly enough to divide and mature and the cells grow too large. The most common cause of nutritional macrocytic anemia is a deficiency of either folate or vitamin B_{12}.

Folate and Vitamin B_{12} Deficiencies

The mechanisms that result in macrocytic anemia are the same whether the diet is deficient in folate or vitamin B_{12}. The difference between a folate and a vitamin B_{12} deficiency is that the liver has abundant stores of vitamin B_{12} but the body doesn't store folate; thus, it takes longer to manifest macrocytic anemia due to vitamin B_{12} deficiency.

Remember that in Chapter 10 you learned that the function of folate is to transfer a single-carbon

macrocytic anemia A condition that results in abnormally large, pale, and fewer than normal red blood cells.

A leafy green salad topped with grilled chicken is a good source of both folate and vitamin B_{12}.

compound in the first step that converts homocysteine to methionine in DNA metabolism. If this step is impaired due to a lack of folate, the synthesis of DNA is disrupted and the red blood cells don't divide and increase in adequate numbers, causing macrocytic anemia. In addition to activating folate, vitamin B_{12} also activates coenzyme methylcobalamin, which is used in the conversion of homocysteine to the amino acid methionine, and in turn provides the methyl group used in DNA and RNA synthesis. Without adequate vitamin B_{12}, homocysteine levels accumulate and DNA synthesis is slowed, which results in macrocytic anemia.

Signs and Symptoms of Macrocytic Anemia

Similar to mild microcytic anemia, the condition may be asymptomatic, especially in younger individuals. The most common symptoms include loss of appetite, sore mouth and tongue, shortness of breath, fatigue, heart palpitations, and pale lips and eyelids.

Testing for Macrocytic Anemia

As with other forms of anemia, complete blood count (CBC) can be used to measure the mean cell volume or size of the red blood cell and the mean cell hemoglobin. In a normal CBC, the hemoglobin concentration will increase in proportion to the size of the cell, but in macrocytic anemia the hemoglobin concentration is less than expected. A mean cell volume greater than 100 fL (called *femtoliters)* indicates macrocytosis, or the presence of abnormally large cells (see Figure 13.18). Once macrocytosis has been confirmed, serum levels of folate and vitamin B_{12} are conducted to determine whether the cause is a folate or a vitamin B_{12} deficiency.

Treatment for Macrocytic Anemia

Individuals deficient in folate or vitamin B_{12} are prescribed supplements to overcome the anemia. If the macrocytic anemia is caused by a folate deficiency, one milligram per day of folate is usually the first line of treatment.[87] In macrocytic anemia due to a vitamin B_{12} deficiency, the individual is treated with vitamin B_{12} intramuscular injections.[88] A diet rich in folate, including green leafy vegetables and citrus, and animal products rich in vitamin B_{12}, is essential to support the supplementation and prevent a recurrence.

Pernicious Anemia

Pernicious anemia is a form of macrocytic anemia caused by the inability to absorb vitamin B_{12}. The cause is most often due to a lack of sufficient intrinsic factor secreted from the parietal cells in the stomach. This lack of intrinsic factor can be due to either gastritis or an autoimmune reaction in which the body's immune system attacks the parietal cells.[89] The symptoms include diarrhea or constipation, fatigue or light-headedness, loss of appetite, pale skin, shortness of breath, and problems concentrating. Serum vitamin B_{12} and the presence of antibodies against intrinsic factor or parietal cells are blood tests used to diagnose pernicious anemia. The treatment for pernicious anemia involves intramuscular shots of vitamin B_{12} given once per month to circumvent the malabsorption.[90]

LO 13.2: THE TAKE-HOME MESSAGE

Microcytic and macrocytic anemias can be caused by nutrient deficiencies. A deficiency of iron and vitamin B_6 can cause microcytic anemia. Folate and vitamin B_{12} deficiencies or malabsorption can cause macrocytic anemia, and malabsorption of vitamin B_{12} can result in pernicious anemia. A complete blood count is used to determine the form and cause of anemia, followed by treatment with supplements and an optimal diet to supply the lacking nutrient.

pernicious anemia A form of macrocytic anemia caused by a lack of intrinsic factor due to either gastritis or an autoimmune disorder.

Visual Chapter Summary

Lo 13.1 Trace Minerals Are Essential Inorganic Nutrients

Trace minerals are inorganic elements the body needs in small amounts. The bioavailability and absorption of trace minerals are affected by soil content, nutrient status, and the composition of the diet. The bioavailability of trace minerals depends on the individual's nutrient status, other foods eaten at the same time, and the form of the mineral. Once absorbed, several trace minerals, including iron and zinc, are recycled repeatedly for use in the body. For this reason, toxicity can be a concern. Trace minerals function as cofactors that activate metalloenzymes and provide structure to the body; they help hormones function; and they are part of proteins such as hemoglobin.

Lo 13.2 Iron

Iron absorption is tightly controlled and depends on the iron status of the individual, the form of iron in the food, and the types of foods eaten together. Iron is stored as ferritin or hemosiderin and transported attached to transferrin. Iron functions as part of the oxygen-carrying transport proteins—hemoglobin in the red blood cells and myoglobin in the muscles. As part of cytochromes in the electron transport chain, iron is involved in energy production.

The RDA for iron is 18 milligrams per day for menstruating women and 8 milligrams per day for men and postmenopausal women. Heme iron is found in meat, poultry, and fish. Nonheme iron is found in plant foods, such as grains and vegetables. Nonheme iron is the predominant source of iron in the diet but isn't absorbed as readily as is heme iron.

Adults with normal functioning intestinal tracts have little risk of developing iron toxicity from food. Iron toxicity from supplements greater than 20 mg/kg can develop and cause gastrointestinal distress. Hemochromatosis caused by a genetic mutation is associated with iron build-up in the body and possibly death. Iron deficiency is the most common nutrient deficiency in the world. A deficiency of iron in children can impact their ability to learn and retain information. Iron-deficiency anemia can cause fatigue and weakness.

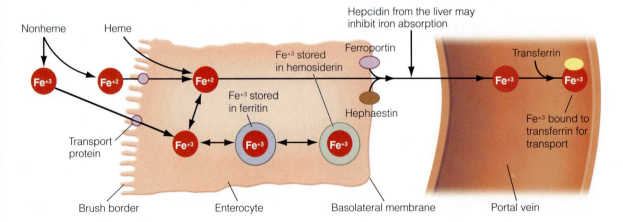

LO 13.3 Copper

Copper status is regulated by absorption in the small intestine. Copper is absorbed attached to albumin. Very little copper is stored and the excess is excreted through the bile into the feces. Copper is part of the protein ceruloplasmin, which converts ferrous iron to ferric iron. Copper is thus necessary for the synthesis of hemoglobin and red blood cells. Copper is a cofactor for metalloenzymes involved in energy production and in the synthesis of connective tissue. Copper is part of the superoxide dismutase enzyme, which reduces free radical damage in cells.

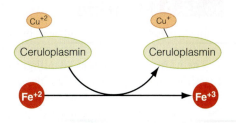

The AI for copper is 900 micrograms for adults. Copper is found in a variety of foods, especially seafood, nuts, and seeds. Some genetic diseases result in the accumulation of copper and cause tissue damage and even death if left untreated.

A deficiency of copper results in anemia and weakened bones and connective tissue.

LO 13.4 Zinc

Zinc plays a role in the structure of RNA and DNA, in taste acuity, and in helping prevent age-related macular degeneration (AMD). Zinc does not cure the common cold, but zinc lozenges or gels used in nasal passages may reduce the duration of a cold.

The RDA for zinc is 11 milligrams per day for adult males and 8 milligrams per day for adult females. Meat, fish, and whole grains are good sources of zinc.

Consuming too much zinc can cause vomiting and diarrhea, suppress the immune system, and lower HDL cholesterol. Eating too little can impair growth, cause loss of hair and loss of appetite, and delay sexual maturation.

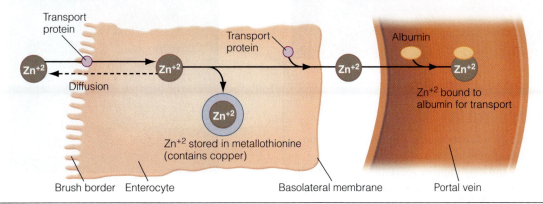

LO 13.5 Selenium

Selenium is a component of a group of proteins called selenoproteins, which act as antioxidants in the body and may help fight cancer. Selenium also regulates thyroid function.

The AI for adults is set at 55 micrograms of selenium per day. All food groups contribute selenium, including nuts, meat, and seafood.

Toxicity of selenium results in brittle teeth and fingernails, garlic odor in the breath, gastrointestinal problems, and damage to the nervous system. A deficiency of selenium can lead to Keshan disease, which damages the heart. Selenium deficiency may also result in changes in thyroid hormone production.

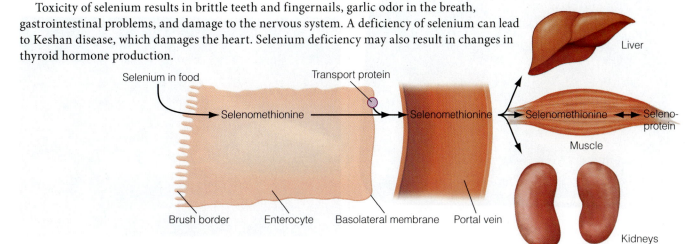

LO 13.6 Fluoride

Fluoride is not an essential nutrient, but it helps maintain the structure of bones and teeth and helps prevent dental caries.

The AI for adult males is 3.8 milligrams and 3.1 milligrams for women of fluoride daily. The primary dietary source of fluoride is a fluoridated water supply and the consumption of foods and beverages prepared using fluoridated water.

In children, consumption of too much fluoride during tooth development can result in fluorosis. In adults, too much fluoride can cause skeletal fluorosis, which results in joint stiffness or pain, osteoporosis, and calcification of the ligaments.

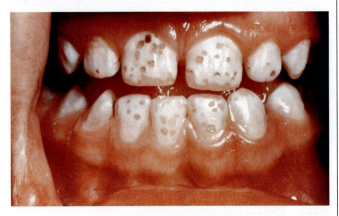

LO 13.7 Chromium

Chromium helps insulin function, may improve the metabolism and storage of carbohydrates, fats, and protein, may reduce prediabetes, and may improve metabolic syndrome. It has not been proven to enhance weight loss or build muscle mass during exercise. Adult men need 30 to 35 micrograms of chromium daily and women need 20 to 25 micrograms daily. Many plant foods contain chromium, depending on the soil levels. Chromium toxicity by taking supplements interferes with iron metabolism. Deficiencies of chromium are very rare in the United States.

LO 13.8 Iodine

Iodine is essential to make the thyroid hormones T_3 and T_4, which help regulate metabolic rate and stimulate growth and development. The RDA for adult men and women is 150 micrograms of iodine daily. Iodine is found mostly in iodized salt, seafood, including shellfish, and dairy products. A deficiency of iodine during pregnancy causes mental retardation and cretinism in the offspring. A deficiency of iodine during adulthood causes simple goiter, which is characterized by an enlarged thyroid gland. Iodine toxicity causes both hypothyroidism and hyperthyroidism.

LO 13.9 Molybdenum

Molybdenum is a cofactor for enzymes that synthesize proteins, including DNA and RNA. The RDA for adult men and women is 45 micrograms daily. Molybdenum is found in legumes, whole grains, and nuts. A dietary deficiency of molybdenum is rare and does not appear to be toxic in humans.

LO 13.10 Manganese

Manganese assists enzymes involved in energy metabolism, and functions in synthesis of bone and as an antioxidant. The AI for manganese is 2.3 milligrams for men and 1.8 milligrams for women daily. Manganese is found in legumes, nuts, and whole grains. A deficiency of manganese is rare in healthy individuals who consume a balanced diet. Some food components, such as phytates, or excessive use of supplements that contain iron and calcium, can reduce the absorption of manganese and cause a rash and dry, scaly skin, low serum cholesterol levels, and impaired growth in children. Toxicity can damage the nervous system and result in symptoms that resemble Parkinson's disease, including tremors, facial spasms, and difficulty walking.

LO 13.11 Other Minerals: Arsenic, Boron, Nickel, Silicon, and Vanadium

Other minerals, including arsenic, boron, nickel, silicon, and vanadium, may play a role in maintaining health. Arsenic in its organic form may be used for growth and both arsenic and boron may function in reproduction. Nickel may activate enzymes, silicon may be needed for bone formation, and vanadium may have insulin-like properties. More research is needed to understand the role each of these trace minerals plays in the human body.

LO 13.12 Microcytic and Macrocytic Anemia Can Be Caused by Mineral and Vitamin Deficiencies

Microcytic and macrocytic anemias can be caused by mineral and vitamin deficiencies. Symptoms are often similar for both forms of anemia. A deficiency of iron and vitamin B_6 can cause microcytic anemia, characterized by pale and smaller than normal red blood cells. A lack of dietary folate or vitamin B_{12} can cause abnormally large red blood cells that lack sufficient hemoglobin, called macrocytic anemia. Insufficient release of intrinsic factor either due to gastritis or an autoimmune disorder can cause a malabsorption of vitamin B_{12} and result in pernicious anemia. A complete blood count is used to determine the form and cause of anemia, followed by treatment with supplements and an optimal diet to supply the lacking nutrient.

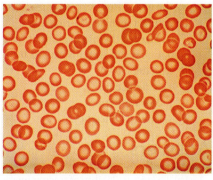

Microcytic red blood cells

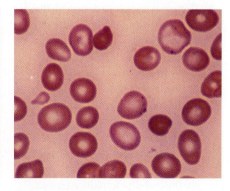

Macrocytic red blood cells

Terms to Know

- trace minerals
- metalloenzymes
- heme iron
- nonheme iron
- hemoglobin
- myoglobin
- ferric iron
- ferrous iron
- ferritin
- hemosiderin

- ferroportin
- hephaestin
- transferrin
- hepcidin
- hemochromatosis
- cupric
- cuprous
- ceruloplasmin
- Menkes' disease
- Wilson's disease
- metallothionine

- selenoproteins
- selenomethionine
- selenosis
- Keshan disease
- fluoroapatite
- fluorosis
- trivalent chromium
- hexavalent chromium
- iodide
- goiter
- thyroxine

- thyroxine-releasing hormone (TRH)
- thyroxine-stimulating hormone (TSH)
- goitrogens
- cretinism
- iron-deficiency anemia
- total iron-binding capacity (TIBC)
- macrocytic anemia
- pernicious anemia

MasteringNutrition™

To hear an MP3 chapter review, scan here or visit the Study Area in MasteringNutrition.

Check Your Understanding

1. The bioavailability of trace minerals is affected by
   a. the time of day you consume foods containing trace minerals.
   b. the form of the trace mineral.
   c. the protein content of your diet.
   d. the fat content of your diet.
2. The iron-containing protein that carries oxygen from the lungs to the tissues is called
   a. hemosiderin.
   b. myoglobin.
   c. hemoglobin.
   d. transferrin.
3. The primary storage form of iron in the body is called
   a. ferritin.
   b. transferrin.
   c. hemochromatosis.
   d. hemoglobin.
4. Copper is transported through the circulation by the blood protein called
   a. transferrin.
   b. albumin.
   c. hemoglobin.
   d. myoglobin.
5. A zinc deficiency may result in which of the following conditions?
   a. cretinism
   b. dental caries
   c. stunted growth
   d. the inability to reduce ferrous iron to ferric iron

6. Selenium may help prevent cancer due to its role as
   a. a toxin.
   b. an enzyme.
   c. an antioxidant.
   d. a supplement.
7. Which of the following statements is true regarding fluoride?
   a. Fluoride is considered an essential nutrient.
   b. Fluoride is found mostly in animal products such as meat and dairy products.
   c. Fluoride is part of the hydroxyapatite crystal that makes your teeth stronger and resistant to decay.
   d. Ingesting more than the recommended amount of fluoride increases your susceptibility to tooth decay.
8. Chromium increases the effectiveness of which hormone?
   a. thyroid-stimulating hormone
   b. insulin
   c. antidiuretic hormone (ADH)
   d. glucagon
9. The amount of manganese absorbed in the body is increased by
   a. a good source of phytates in the meal.
   b. the use of calcium supplements.
   c. the use of iron supplements.
   d. eating a manganese-rich diet.
10. The enlarged thyroid gland that is symptomatic of goiter is caused by
    a. iron deficiency.
    b. zinc deficiency.
    c. iodine deficiency.
    d. selenium deficiency.

Answers

1. (b) The bioavailability of trace minerals in the food you consume can vary

depending on the form of the mineral, your nutrient status, and the foods you choose to eat. The protein and fat content of the food does not influence trace mineral bioavailability, nor does the time of day the food is eaten.

2. (c) Hemoglobin is the iron-containing protein in red blood cells that carries oxygen. Hemoglobin exchanges oxygen with myoglobin, another protein found in muscle. Hemosiderin is the stored form of iron and transferrin is the protein that transports iron throughout the body.

3. (a) Ferritin is the primary storage form of iron in the body. Transferrin is the protein that transports iron. Hemochromatosis is a hereditary disorder in which the body absorbs and stores too much iron. Hemoglobin is found in red blood cells and contains heme.

4. (b) Albumin is the blood protein that transports copper. Transferrin transports iron, and hemoglobin and myoglobin are iron-containing proteins that participate in oxygen and carbon dioxide exchange.

5. (c) Zinc plays a significant role in growth and cell division. A deficiency of this trace mineral results in stunted growth. A deficiency of iodine during pregnancy results in cretinism. Fluoride makes the tooth enamel resistant to dental caries and copper functions as a cofactor to reduce ferrous iron to ferric iron.

6. (c) As part of selenoproteins, selenium functions as an antioxidant that protects cells from free radical damage.

7. (c). Fluoride, which is not considered an essential nutrient because

the body doesn't require it for normal growth and development, makes up part of the hydroxyapatite crystal that strengthens tooth structure and helps the tooth resist decay. It is found mostly in fluoridated water, tea, and seaweed. Consuming too much fluoride can cause fluorosis, a discoloration of the teeth.

8. (b) Chromium increases insulin's effectiveness in promoting glucose uptake by the cells. Iodine is needed to make thyroid hormones; ADH is the hormone that directs kidneys to minimize water loss and concentrate urine; and glucagon is the hormone that has the opposite effect to insulin, stimulating the release of glucose into the blood.

9. (d) Tissue levels of manganese are related to the amount present in your diet, thus eating a manganese-rich diet improves the amount of manganese absorbed. Phytates in food bind or inhibit the absorption of manganese, and other minerals in supplement form, such as iron and calcium supplements, decrease the absorption of manganese.

10. (c) Iodine deficiency results in goiter. Zinc deficiencies alter taste sensitivity; iron deficiencies cause microcytic anemia; and a deficiency of selenium may cause Keshan disease.

Answers to True or False?

1. **False.** Trace minerals are called *trace* because they are needed in small dietary amounts (less than 100 milligrams per day) and are found in small amounts in the body (less than 5 grams).

2. **False.** Although meat and seafood are rich sources of iron in the American diet, they are not the primary sources. Enrichment and fortification processes make many bread products and cereals good sources of iron, as are some vegetables.

3. **False.** Even though iron competes with other minerals, including zinc and copper, for binding to a transport protein in the small intestine, iron supplements do not appear to affect copper absorption or cause copper deficiency. Iron supplements do significantly reduce zinc absorption and could result in a zinc deficiency.

4. **False.** Zinc lozenges and gels do not prevent or cure the common cold. Some studies have reported that zinc lozenges or nasal gels may reduce the severity and duration of cold symptoms.

5. **True.** Excess selenium intake from dietary supplements is toxic. The symptoms include vomiting, diarrhea, fatigue, and hair loss.

6. **False.** Most bottled water sold in the United States does not contain fluoride. However, most tap water in the United States has been fluoridated.

7. **False.** Chromium supplementation does not appear to increase protein synthesis or have a beneficial effect on body composition or muscle mass.

8. **True.** While iodine is found in saltwater fish and in small amounts in dairy products, the only reliable source of iodine is iodized salt. Plants can be a good source of iodine, but only if they are grown in iodine-rich soil.

9. **True.** Two teaspoons of cinnamon contain 0.76 milligrams of manganese, or about 38 percent of the AI.

10. **False.** Vegetables are generally low in molybdenum. Other plant-based products such as legumes, nuts, and grains are considered good food sources of this trace mineral.

Web Resources

- To find out if your community water is fluoridated and how much fluoride is added, visit the Centers for Disease Control and Prevention's website, My Water's Fluoride, at http://apps.nccd.cdc.gov/MWF/Index.asp
- For more information on trace minerals, visit the U.S. Department of Health and Human Services' website at www.healthfinder.org
- For more information on iron and the symptoms associated with iron deficiency and iron overload, visit the Iron Overload Diseases Association at www.ironoverload.org
- Visit the American Cancer Society website for more information on selenium's role in cancer prevention at www.cancer.org
- For more information on thyroid health, visit the American Thyroid Association at www.thyroid.org
- For more information on the importance of minerals and mineral supplements, visit MedlinePlus, a service of the U. S. National Library of Medicine and the National Institutes of Health, at www.nlm.nih.gov/medlineplus

References

1. Institute of Medicine. 2001. *Dietary Reference Intakes: Vitamin A, Vitamin K, Arsenic, Boron, Chromium, Copper, Iodine, Iron, Manganese, Molybdenum, Nickel, Silicon, Vanadium, and Zinc.* Washington, DC: The National Academies Press.
2. Olivares, M. 2012. Acute Inhibition of Iron Bioavailability by Zinc: Studies in Humans.
3. Ibid.
4. Olivares, M., C. Castro, F. Pizarro, and D. L. de Romana. 2013. Effect of Increasing Levels of Zinc Fortificant on the Iron Absorption of Bread Co-Fortified with Iron and Zinc Consumed with a Black Tea. *Biological Trace Element Research* 154(3):321–325.
5. Donovan, A., C. N. Roy, and N. C. Andrews. 2006. The Ins and Outs of Iron Homeostasis. *Physiology* 21:115–123.
6. Fuqua, B. K., C. D. Vulpe, and G. J. Anderson. 2012. Intestinal Iron Absorption. *Journal of Trace Elements in Medicine and Biology* 26:115–119.
7. Gropper, S. S., and J. L. Smith. 2013. *Advanced Nutrition and Human Metabolism.* 6th ed. Belmont, CA: Wadsworth—Cengage Learning.
8. Ibid.
9. Wessling-Resnick, M. 2014. Iron. In *Modern Nutrition in Health and Disease.* A. C. Ross, B. Caballero, R. J. Cousins, K. L. Tucker, and T. R. Ziegler, eds. Philadelphia: Lippincott Williams & Wilkins.
10. Prado, E. L., and K. G. Dewey. 2014. Nutrition and Brain Development in Early Life. *Nutrition Reviews* 72(4):267–284.
11. Black, M. M. 2003. Micronutrient Deficiencies and Cognitive Function. *Journal of Nutrition* 133:3927S–3931S.
12. Institute of Medicine. 2006. *Dietary Reference Intakes: The Essential Guide to Nutrient Requirements.* J. J. Otten, J. P. Helwig, and L. D. Meyers, eds. Washington, DC: The National Academies Press.
13. U.S. Department of Agriculture, U.S. Department of Health and Human Services. 2010. Dietary Guidelines for Americans 2010. Washington, DC.
14. Ibid.

15. Britton, H. C., and C. E. Nossamn. 1986. Iron Content of Food Cooked in Iron Utensils. *Journal of the American Dietetic Association* 86:897–901.

16. Galy, B., D. Ferring-Appel, C. Becker, N. Gretz, H. J. Gröne, K. Schümann, and M. W. Hentze. 2013. Iron Regulatory Proteins Control a Mucosal Block to Intestinal Iron Absorption. *Cell Reports* 3(3):844–857.

17. Juurlink, D. N., M. Tenenbein, G. Koren, and D. A. Redelmeier. 2003. Iron Poisoning in Young Children: Association with the Birth of a Sibling. *Canadian Medical Association Journal* 168:1539–1542.

18. Dao, M. C., and S. N. Meydani. 2013. Iron Biology, Immunology, Aging, and Obesity: Four Fields Connected by the Small Peptide Hormone Hepcidin. *Advanced Nutrition* 4(6):602–617.

19. Centers for Disease Control and Prevention. 2013. *Hemochromatosis (Iron Storage Disease).* Available at www.cdc.gov. Accessed April 2014.

20. Collins, J. F. 2014. Copper. In *Modern Nutrition in Health and Disease.* A. C. Ross, B. Caballero, R. J. Cousins, K. L. Tucker, and T. R. Ziegler, eds. Philadelphia: Lippincott Williams & Wilkins.

21. Chen, H., G. Huang, T. Su, H. Gao, Z. K. Attieh, A. T. McKie, G. J. Anderson, and C. D. Vulpe. 2006. Decreased Hephaestin Activity in the Intestine of Copper-Deficient Mice Causes Iron Deficiency. *Journal of Nutrition* 136:1236–1241.

22. Collins. 2014. Copper. In *Modern Nutrition in Health and Disease.*

23. Institute of Medicine. 2001. *Dietary Reference Intakes: Vitamin A.*

24. Shankar, A. H., and A. S. Prasad. 1998. Zinc and Immune Function: The Biological Basis of Altered Resistance to Infection. *American Journal of Clinical Nutrition* 68:447S–463S.

25. Haase, H., and L. Rink. 2014. Multiple Impacts of Zinc on Immune Function. *Metallomics* doi:10.1039/C3MT00353A.

26. Farr, B. M., and J. M. Gwaltney. 1987. The Problems of Taste in Placebo Matching: An Evaluation of Zinc Gluconate for the Common Cold. *Journal of Chronic Disease* 40:875–879.

27. Singh, M., and R. R. Das. 2011. Zinc for the Common Cold. *Cochrane Database of Systematic Reviews* 16:CD001364.

28. Hulisz, D. 2004. Efficacy of Zinc Against Common Cold Viruses: An Overview. *Journal of the American Pharmacology Association* 44:594–603.

29. Zafer, K., N. Bayram, and T. Atik. 2007. Effect of Zinc Sulfate on Common Cold in Children: Randomized, Double-Blind Study. *Pediatrics International* 49:842–847.

30. Zepf, F. D., I. Sungurtekin, F. Glass, L. Elstrodt, D. Peetz, G. Hintereder, J. Kratzsch, et al. 2012. Differences in Zinc Status and the Leptin Axis in Anorexic and Recovered Adolescents and Young Adults: A Pilot Study. *Food and Nutrition Research* doi: 10.3402/fnr.v56i0.10941.

31. Institute of Medicine. 2001. *Dietary Reference Intakes: Vitamin A, Vitamin K, Arsenic, Boron, Chromium, Copper, Iodine, Iron, Manganese, Molybdenum, Nickel, Silicon, Vanadium, and Zinc.*

32. King, J. C., and R. J. Cousins. 2014. Zinc. In *Modern Nutrition in Health and Disease.* A. C. Ross, B. Caballero, R. J. Cousins, K. L. Tucker, and T. R. Ziegler, eds. Philadelphia: Lippincott Williams & Wilkins.

33. Sunde, R. A. 2014. Selenium. In *Modern Nutrition in Health and Disease.* A. C. Ross, B. Caballero, R. J. Cousins, K. L. Tucker, and T. R. Ziegler, eds. Philadelphia: Lippincott Williams & Wilkins.

34. Vinceti, M., G. Dennert, C. M. Crespi, M. Zwahlen, M. Brinkman, M.P. Zeegers, M. Horneber, et al. 2014. Selenium for Preventing Cancer. *Cochrane Database of Systematic Reviews* doi: 10.1002/14651858.CD005195.pub3.

35. Hurst, R., L. Hooper, T. Norat, R. Lau, D. Aune, D. C. Greenwood, R. Vieira, et al. 2012. Selenium and Prostate Cancer: Systematic Review and Meta-Analysis. *American Journal of Clinical Nutrition* 96(1):111–122.

36. FDA. 2012. *Summary of Qualified Health Claims Subject to Enforcement Discretion.* Available at www.fda.gov. Accessed April 2014.

37. Sunde. 2014. Selenium.

38. Turker, O., K. Kumanlioglu, I. Karapolat, and I. Dogan. 2006. Selenium Treatment in Autoimmune Thyroiditis: 9-Month Follow-Up with Variable Doses. *Journal of Endocrinology* 290:151–156.

39. Gartner, R., B. C. H. Gasnier, J. W. Dietrich, B. Krebs, and M. W. A. Angstwurm. 2002. Selenium Supplementation in Patients with Autoimmune Thyroiditis Decreases Thyroid Peroxidase Antibodies Concentrations. *Journal of Clinical Endocrinology and Metabolism* 87:1687–1691.

40. American Dental Association. 2013. *Fluoride and Fluoridation.* Available at www.ada.org. Accessed April 2014.

41. Brissette, S. 2011. Water Fluoridation: Has It Outlived It's Usefulness? Available at http://www.healthworldnet.com. Accessed July 2014.

42. Centers for Disease Control and Prevention. 2013. *Dental Fluorosis.* Available at www.cdc.gov. Accessed April 2014.

43. Federal Register. 2011. Proposed HHS Recommendation for Fluoride Concentration in Drinking Water for the Prevention of Dental Caries. Available at https://www.federalregister.gov. Accessed July 2014.

44. Institute of Medicine. 2006. *Dietary Reference Intakes: The Essential Guide to Nutrient Requirements.*

45. Centers for Disease Control and Prevention. 2013. *Community Water Fluoridation. General Fact Sheet Overview.* Available at www.cdc.gov. Accessed April 2014.

46. Centers for Disease Control and Prevention. 2012. *Fluoridation Basics.* Available at www.cdc.gov. Accessed April 2014.

47. American Dental Hygienists' Association. 2012. Fluoride Facts. Available at www.adha.org. Accessed July 2014.

48. Centers for Disease Control and Prevention. 2013. *Community Water Fluoridation.*

49. Mertz, W. 1993. Chromium in Human Nutrition: A Review. *Journal of Nutrition* 123:626–633.

50. Institute of Medicine. 2006. *Dietary Reference Intakes: The Essential Guide to Nutrient Requirements.*

51. Ibid.

52. Hoffman, N. J., B. A. Penque, K. M. Habegger, W. Sealls, L. Tackett, and J. S. Elmendorf. 2014. Chromium Enhances Insulin Responsiveness via AMPK. *Journal of Nutritional Biochemistry* 25(5):565–572.

53. Qiao, W., Z. Peng, Z. Wang, J. Wei, and A. Zhou. 2009. Chromium Improves Glucose Uptake and Metabolism Through Upregulating the mRNA Levels of IR, GLUT4, GS, and UCP3 in Skeletal Muscle Cells. *Biological Trace Element Research* 131(2):133–142.

54. Ibid.

55. Hummel, M., E. Standl, and O. Schnell. 2007. Chromium in Metabolic and Cardiovascular Disease. *Hormone and Metabolic Research* 39:743–751.

56. Lau, F. C., M. Bagchi, C. K. Sen, and D. Bagchi. 2008. Nutrigenomic Basis of Beneficial Effects of Chromium (III) on Obesity and Diabetes. *Molecular and Cellular Biochemistry* 317:1–10.

57. Suksomboon, N., N. Poolsup, and A. Yuwanakorn. 2014. Systematic Review and Meta-Analysis of the Efficacy and Safety of Chromium Supplementation in Diabetes. *Journal of Clinical Pharmacy and Therapeutics* 39(3):292–306.

58. Tian, H., X. Guo, X. Wang, Z. He, R. Sun, S. Ge, and Z. Zhang. 2013. Chromium Picolinate Supplementation for Overweight or Obese Adults. *Cochrane Database of Systematic Reviews* doi: 10.1002/14651858.CD010063.pub2.

59. Ibid.

60. Institute of Medicine. 2006. *Dietary Reference Intakes: The Essential Guide to Nutrient Requirements.*

61. Tian. 2013. Chromium Picolinate Supplementation for Overweight or Obese Adults.

62. Roussel, A. M., M. Andriollo-Sanchez, M. Ferry, N. A. Bryden, and R. A. Anderson. 2007. Food Chromium Content, Dietary Chromium Intake and Related Biological Variables in French Free-Living Elderly. *British Journal of Nutrition* 98:326–331.

63. Laurberg, P. Iodine. 2014. In *Modern Nutrition in Health and Disease.* A. C. Ross, B. Caballero, R. J. Cousins, K. L. Tucker, and T. R. Ziegler, eds. Philadelphia: Lippincott Williams & Wilkins.

64. Ibid.

65. Institute of Medicine. 2001. *Dietary Reference Intakes: Vitamin A.*

66. Ibid.

67. Institute of Medicine. 2001. *Dietary Reference Intakes: Vitamin A, Vitamin K, Arsenic, Boron, Chromium, Copper, Iodine, Iron, Manganese, Molybdenum, Nickel, Silicon, Vanadium, and Zinc.*

68. Ibid.

69. Ibid.

70. Long, Z., Y. M. Jiang, X. R. Li, et al. 2014. Vulnerability of Welders to Manganese Exposure—A Neuroimaging Study. *Neurotoxicology* doi: 10.1016/j.neuro.2014.03.007.

71. Ibid.

72. Barceloux, D. G. 1999. Manganese. *Clinical Toxicology* 37:293–307.

73. Bouchard, M. F., S. Sebastien, B. Barbeau, M. Legrand, M. Brodeur, T. Bouffard, E. Limoges, et al. 2010. Intellectual Impairment in School-Age Children Exposed to Manganese from Drinking Water. *Environmental Health Perspectives* 119:138–143.

74. Environmental Protection Agency. 2013. *Drinking Water Contaminants.* Available at http://water.epa.gov. Accessed April 2014.

75. Friedman, B. J., J. H. Freeland-Graves, C. W. Bales, et al. 1987. Manganese Balance and Clinical Observations in Young Men Fed a Manganese-Deficient Diet. *Journal of Nutrition* 117:133–143.

76. Institute of Medicine. 2001. *Dietary Reference Intakes: Vitamin A.*

77. Nielsen, F. H. 2009. Boron Deprivation Decreases Liver S-adenosylmethionine and Spermidine and Increases Plasma Homocysteine and Cysteine in Rats. *Journal of Trace Elements in Medicine and Biology* 23(3):204–213.

78. Institute of Medicine. 2001. *Dietary Reference Intakes: Vitamin A, Vitamin K, Arsenic, Boron, Chromium, Copper, Iodine, Iron, Manganese, Molybdenum, Nickel, Silicon, Vanadium, and Zinc.*

79. Ibid.

80. National Heart, Lung, and Blood Institute. 2013. *What Is Anemia?* Available at www.nhlbi.nih.gov. Accessed April 2014.

81. Centers for Disease Control and Prevention. 2012. *Anemia or Iron Deficiency.* Available at www.cdc.gov. Accessed May 2012.

82. National Institutes of Health. 2014. *Iron-Deficiency Anemia.* Available at www.nlm.nih.gov. Accessed April 2014.

83. Low, M., A. Farrell, B. A. Biggs, and S. R. Pasricha. 2013. Effects of Daily Iron Supplementation in Primary-School-Aged Children: Systematic Review and Meta-Analysis of Randomized Controlled Trials. *Canadian Medical Association Journal* 185(17):E791–E802.

84. Bay, A., M. Dogan, K. Bulan, S. Kaba, N. Demir, and A. F. Öner. 2013. A Study on the Effects of Pica and Iron-Deficiency Anemia on Oxidative Stress, Antioxidant Capacity and Trace Elements. *Human and Experimental Toxicology* 32(9):895–903.

85. Maghsudlu, M., S. Nasizadeh, G. R. Toogeh, T. Zandieh, S. Parandoush, and M. Rezayani. 2008. Short-Term Ferrous Sulfate Supplementation in Female Blood Donors. *Transfusion* 48:1192–1197.

86. Da Silva, V. R., A. D. Mackey, S. R. Davis, and J. F. Gregory III. 2014. Vitamin B$_6$. In *Modern Nutrition in Health and Disease.* A. C. Ross, B. Caballero, R. J. Cousins, K. L. Tucker, and T. R. Ziegler, eds. Philadelphia: Lippincott Williams & Wilkins.

87. Maakaron, J. E., and E. C. Basa. 2014. Macrocytosis Treatment and Management. Available at http://emedicine.medscape.com. Accessed April 2014.

88. Ibid.

89. PubMed Health. 2012. *Pernicious Anemia.* Available at www.ncbi.nlm.nih.gov. Accessed April 2014.

90. Antony, A. C. 2011. Megaloblastic Anemias. In *Cecil Medicine.* 24th ed. L. Goldman and A. Schafer, eds. Philadelphia: Saunders Elsevier.

14 Energy Balance and Body Composition

Learning Outcomes

After reading this chapter, you will be able to:

14.1 Define the terms energy balance, positive energy balance, and negative energy balance as they relate to body weight.

14.2 Explain the factors that contribute to total daily energy expenditure (TDEE), including basal metabolic rate (BMR), thermic effect of food (TEF), thermic effect of exercise (TEE), and adaptive thermogenesis.

14.3 Explain how energy expenditure is measured and calculate BMR and EER using equations and physical activity factors.

14.4 Define the term body composition, and explain the methods used to assess lean body mass and body fat.

14.5 Define the term healthy body weight, explain the methods used to estimate a healthy body weight, and describe how body weight and body fat can affect health.

14.6 List the criteria used to diagnose eating disorders and discuss the treatment options for disordered eating.

True or False?

1. Exercise isn't necessary to lose weight. **T**/**F**
2. Being skinny is always healthier than being overweight. **T**/**F**
3. Men burn more kilocalories than women. **T**/**F**
4. BMI can be used to determine if you are at a healthy weight, overweight, or obese. **T**/**F**
5. Storing fat around the hips is as unhealthy as storing it around the waist. **T**/**F**
6. Body composition is the same thing as body weight. **T**/**F**
7. Eating an excess 100 kilocalories per day will result in a weight gain of a pound a week. **T**/**F**
8. Skinfold calipers are the most accurate way to measure body composition. **T**/**F**
9. Disordered eating and eating disorders are the same thing. **T**/**F**
10. Eating disorders can be fatal. **T**/**F**

See page 540 for the answers.

Flip through a magazine, watch a little television, or spend some time online, and before long you'll find someone talking about how to lose or gain weight. Maintaining a healthy body weight is all about balance—that is, balancing the food and drinks you consume with the amount of kilocalories your body burns over time. While this equation seems simple enough, food intake is not the sole cause of an unbalanced equation. The environment and lifestyle choices we make also play a strong role.

In this chapter, we'll discuss the concept of energy balance, the methods used to assess energy intake and energy expenditure, and the factors that influence a healthy body weight and body composition.

What Is Energy Balance and Why Is It Important?

LO 14.1 Define the terms energy balance, positive energy balance, and negative energy balance as they relate to body weight.

The concept of **energy balance** can be boiled down to five simple words: energy in versus energy out. The amount of energy (in the form of kilocalories) consumed needs to equal the amount expended so that the body does not store the excess kilocalories as fat or break down stored fat for energy. This equation can be unbalanced by changing the amount of kilocalories you eat on one side of the equation or alter the amount of kilocalories burned on the opposite side of the equation. The result is a change in body weight and even body composition over time.

An Energy Imbalance Results in Weight Gain or Loss

Body weight remains constant when the energy equation is balanced. If energy intake is greater than the amount of energy expended, the body is in a state of **positive energy balance** (**Focus Figure 14.1**). In this situation, weight gain can occur from an increase in muscle mass, an increase in adipose tissue, or both. Positive energy balance is essential during growth periods such as pregnancy, infancy, childhood, and adolescence. Strength training requires a positive energy balance to increase muscle mass, and when the body is in a state of repair following surgery or an illness. However, nonpregnant, healthy adults will experience an unhealthy weight gain if they are in a regular state of positive energy balance. Even a small but chronic positive energy balance can result in weight gain over time. For every 3,500 excess kilocalories consumed, about a pound of body weight is gained. So if an individual takes in 100 excess kilocalories per day, he or she will gain a little less than one pound after one month, and about 10 pounds after one year. Most likely this weight gain will be stored as fat in the adipose tissue.

A **negative energy balance** occurs when the amount of energy ingested doesn't meet the energy output. Negative energy balance occurs if food intake is reduced, if more kilocalories are expended through exercise than are consumed in foods, or both. When less energy is consumed, energy needs are met by mobilizing energy reserves such as stored fat. The result of a negative energy balance is usually weight loss, mostly from adipose tissue. However, some of the weight loss may reflect a decrease in muscle mass, stored glycogen, and water.

energy balance The state at which energy (kilocalorie) intake from food and beverages is equal to energy (kilocalorie) output for BMR, physical activity, digestion and absorption, and body repairs.

positive energy balance The state in which energy intake is greater than energy expenditure. Over time, this results in weight gain.

negative energy balance The state in which energy intake is less than energy expenditure. Over time, this results in weight loss.

The Concept of Energy Balance

A chronic state of positive or negative energy balance will result in a change in body weight.

Energy balance is the relationship between the food we eat and the energy we expend each day. Finding the proper balance between energy intake and energy expenditure allows us to maintain a healthy body weight.

ENERGY BALANCE

When the kilocalories you consume meet your needs, you are in energy balance. Your weight will be stable.

ENERGY INTAKE = ENERGY EXPENDITURE = WEIGHT MAINTENANCE

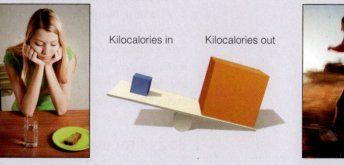

Kilocalories in   Kilocalories out

NEGATIVE ENERGY BALANCE

When you consume fewer kilocalories than you expend, your body will draw upon your stored energy to meet its needs. You will lose weight.

ENERGY INTAKE < ENERGY EXPENDITURE = WEIGHT LOSS

Kilocalories in   Kilocalories out

POSITIVE ENERGY BALANCE

When you take in more kilocalories than you need, the surplus calories will be stored as fat. You will gain weight.

ENERGY INTAKE > ENERGY EXPENDITURE = WEIGHT GAIN

Kilocalories in   Kilocalories out

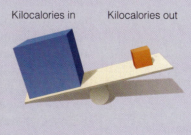

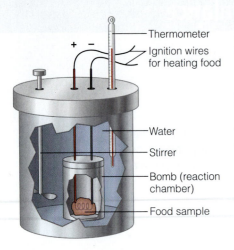

Thermometer
Ignition wires
for heating food
+ −

Water
Stirrer
Bomb (reaction
chamber)
Food sample

▲ **Figure 14.2 A Bomb Calorimeter Measures Energy in Foods**
A bomb calorimeter directly measures the kilocalorie content of food by measuring the heat released during combustion.

The energy balance equation appears to be quite simple. If we would simply consume the same number of kilocalories as we expend, we could maintain a healthful body weight. However, energy balance is more complex than it seems.

Food and Beverages Provide Energy In

As you learned in earlier chapters, the kilocalories that make up energy intake come from the carbohydrates, proteins, fats, and alcohol found in foods and beverages. The number of kilocalories found in a given food or beverage can be determined in one of two ways: either in a lab using a **bomb calorimeter,** or by calculating the grams of carbohydrate, fat, protein, and alcohol in the food.

A bomb calorimeter (**Figure 14.2**) measures the amount of heat produced when a given food is burned. The energy released when the chemical bonds in the food are broken raises the temperature of the water in the calorimeter. Because one kilocalorie is the heat required to raise the temperature of one kilogram of water one degree Celsius, the rise in water temperature indicates the amount of kilocalories in the food.

The burning of food also releases carbon and hydrogen, which combine with oxygen to form carbon dioxide and water. Hence, measuring the amount of oxygen consumed during combustion in the calorimeter provides an indirect measurement of the energy content of a food.

The body is not as efficient as a bomb calorimeter and does not completely digest or metabolize the fuels it consumes. The fuels that aren't oxidized to yield carbon dioxide and water are stored as either glycogen or body fat. The kilocalorie values obtained from a bomb calorimeter must be adapted to reflect the inefficiency of the body. For example, the heat of combustion of protein in meat is approximately 5.65 kilocalories per gram. But, because protein is only 97 percent digested and absorbed, the net kilocalories are actually 4.27 kilocalories per gram.[1] These corrected kilocaloric values are called **physiological fuel values** and reflect the kilocalories actually transformed into energy in the body. These are the kilocaloric values presented in food composition tables and databases.

Because bomb calorimeters are available only in laboratories, most individuals who want to estimate energy intake use nutrition analysis software or food composition tables to track and add up the kilocalories contained in meals. These resources provide the kilocalorie content of a given food as calculated by multiplying the grams of each energy nutrient in the food by the kilocalories contained in each gram (see the Calculation Corner).

Body Processes and Physical Activity Result in Energy Out

The other side of the energy equation is the expenditure of energy. Differences in *basal metabolism,* the *thermic effect of food* (TEF), *the thermic effect of exercise* (TEE), and *adaptive thermogenesis* mean that the energy needed throughout the day varies for every individual. Knowing your energy expenditure provides the basis for either establishing energy balance to maintain weight or creating an energy imbalance to gain or lose weight.

bomb calorimeter An instrument used to measure the amount of heat released from food during combustion; the amount of heat produced is directly related to the amount of kilocalories in a given food.

physiological fuel values The real energy value of foods that are digested and absorbed; they are adjusted from the results of bomb calorimetry because of the inefficiency of the body.

LO 14.1: THE TAKE-HOME MESSAGE Energy balance is the relationship between energy intake and energy expenditure. In positive energy balance, more kilocalories are consumed than are expended, resulting in weight gain. In negative energy balance, more kilocalories are expended than are consumed, resulting in weight loss.

Calculating the Energy Content of a Meal

Calculate the total energy content of this breakfast meal using the fuel values of 4 kilocalories per gram for carbohydrates and protein, and 9 kilocalories per gram for fat.

Food	Carbohydrate (g)	Protein (g)	Fat (g)		Kilocalories
½ cup cooked oatmeal	12	3	0	=	_____
½ cup nonfat milk	6	4	0	=	_____
½ cup orange juice	12	0	0	=	_____
2 slices whole-wheat toast	30	6	2	=	_____
1 tbs margarine	0	0	10	=	_____
8 fl oz coffee	0	0	0	=	_____
Total kilocalories				=	_____

a. Complete the table by calculating the total kilocalories for each food. Multiply the fuel value of each macronutrient by the number of grams found in each food. For example, ½ cup of cooked oatmeal would be calculated as follows:

Total kcal = (12 g carbohydrate $\times$ 4 kcal/g) + (3 g protein $\times$ 4 kcal/g) + (0 g fat $\times$ 9 kcal/g)

Total kcal = 60 kcal

b. After you have calculated the total kilocalories for each food, add the kilocalories for each food together to determine the total kilocalories for the meal.

How Is Total Daily Energy Expenditure Calculated?

LO 14.2 Explain the factors that contribute to total daily energy expenditure (TDEE), including basal metabolic rate (BMR), thermic effect of food (TEF), thermic effect of exercise (TEE), and adaptive thermogenesis.

The number of kilocalories necessary to balance the energy in with the energy out, called the **total daily energy expenditure (TDEE),** has several components.

Basal and Resting Metabolic Rate Contribute to TDEE

The energy needed to fuel the body's vital functions, such as pumping blood, expanding the lungs, and brain function, is known as its **basal metabolism** and is expressed as a **basal metabolic rate (BMR).** This is the amount of energy spent to meet the body's basic physiological needs when it's at physical, emotional, and digestive rest, but not asleep—in other words, the minimum amount of energy needed to keep your awake, resting body alive. If you sit on the couch to watch television, you aren't engaged in any physical activity but your cells are still active and require energy for basic functions.

Approximately 50 to 70 percent of your total daily energy kilocalories is determined by BMR (**Figure 14.3**). The factor that most affects BMR is **lean body mass (LBM).**

total daily energy expenditure (TDEE) The total kilocalories needed to meet daily energy requirements; based on basal metabolism, physical activity, the thermic effect of food, and adaptive thermogenesis.

basal metabolism The amount of energy expended by the body to meet its basic physiological needs, including muscle tone and heart and brain function.

basal metabolic rate (BMR) The measure of basal metabolism taken when the body is at rest in a warm, quiet environment, after a 12-hour fast; expressed as kilocalories per kilogram of body weight per hour.

lean body mass (LBM) Total body weight minus the fat mass; it consists of water, bones, vital organs, and muscle. LBM is the metabolically active tissue in the body.

Total Daily Energy Expenditure (TDEE)

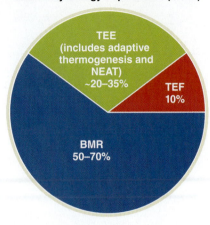

TEE
(includes adaptive thermogenesis and NEAT)
~20–35%

TEF
10%

BMR
50–70%

▲ **Figure 14.3 Requirements for the Total Daily Energy Expenditure**
The amount of total energy expended during a 24-hour period is comprised of an individual's basal metabolism, the thermic effect of exercise or physical activity, adaptive thermogenesis, and the thermic effect of foods. A sedentary individual will expend a larger percentage of energy from basal metabolism compared with an active person who would have a greater need for energy to fuel physical activity.

Once you crawl out of bed in the morning, the kilocalories you expend to stretch, take a shower, and get dressed are classified as TEE.

resting metabolic rate (RMR) The measure of the amount of energy expended by the body at rest and after approximately a 3- to 4-hour fasting period. This rate is about 6 percent higher than BMR.

thermic effect of exercise (TEE) This refers to the increase in muscle contraction that occurs during physical activity, which produces heat and contributes to the total daily energy expenditure.

non-exercise activity thermogenesis (NEAT) The energy expended for all activities not related to sleeping, eating, or exercise, including fidgeting, performing work-related activities, and playing.

Lean body mass is defined as the muscle, bone, and other nonfat tissue that makes up your body weight. Because lean body mass is more active tissue than body fat, it burns kilocalories at a higher rate than stored fat, even at rest. Thus, the more lean body mass you have, the greater your BMR—about 70 percent of your BMR is attributable to the metabolic activity of your LBM. Additional factors such as age, gender, body size, genes, ethnicity, emotional and physical stress, thyroid hormone levels, nutritional state, and environmental temperature, as well as caffeine and nicotine intake, affect BMR. **Table 14.1** explains each of these factors.

BMR, which is determined by an indirect measurement of the amount of oxygen consumed, is measured when a person is awake and cellular activity is the lowest. To get an accurate BMR measurement, your sympathetic nervous system cannot be stimulated. This is the reason a person's BMR is usually measured in a laboratory setting in the morning while the person lies motionless in a controlled (no shivering or sweating) environment after a 12-hour overnight fast. Neither the digestion of food nor physical activity (which both require energy) is factored into the BMR.

Because such precise circumstances are needed to measure BMR, it is a challenge to obtain. For this reason, the **resting metabolic rate (RMR)** is often used instead. The RMR is the amount of energy used by the body, measured when the person is lying calmly after only a 3- to 4-hour fasting period. The RMR is about 6 percent higher than the BMR, as it reflects increases in energy expenditure related to any recent food intake or physical activity.

Physical Activity or Exercise Burns Energy

While BMR accounts for the largest proportion of energy expenditure, the heat produced by contracting muscle during physical activity or exercise can contribute significantly to the amount of energy expended each day. Walking across campus, vacuuming your home, or pulling weeds in the garden are all activities that require energy above the minimum needed for BMR. This expenditure of kilocalories is referred to as the **thermic effect of exercise (TEE).** The amount of kilocalories you need each day for TEE depends on the activity itself, the amount of time you perform the activity, and how much you weigh. For instance, if two males run together at the same pace for an hour, but one male weighs 10 kilograms more than the other, the heavier male will burn 496 kilocalories compared with 400 kilocalories for his lighter running partner.

The kilocalories expended for TEE for sedentary people is less than half of their BMR. For very physically active individuals who have a greater muscle mass, TEE can be as much as double their BMR. In short, the more physical activity an individual incorporates into a daily routine, the more kilocalories he can consume to maintain energy balance. For example, two females who weigh the same and are similar in age both have a BMR of 1,200 kilocalories. One female is sedentary and her TEE is only 600 kilocalories, while the second female has a much higher TEE of 2,000 kilocalories because of her physically active lifestyle. Based on her TEE, the sedentary female can only consume 1,800 kilocalories per day (BMR + TEE) to maintain energy balance and not gain weight. In contrast, because of her higher TEE, the physically active female must eat 3,200 kilocalories per day to meet her energy requirements and not lose weight. Further, the amount of energy expended during physical activity goes beyond the activity itself. Exercise causes a small increase in energy expenditure for some time after the activity has stopped because of the recovery and adaptation the body undergoes following the exercise.[2]

In addition to the energy required to walk, talk, run, and climb stairs, TEE also includes the cost of energy to maintain posture and body position. This form of energy expenditure is called **non-exercise activity thermogenesis, or NEAT.** NEAT also includes the energy expended for fidgeting and other activities we don't

TABLE 14.1 Factors That Affect Basal Metabolism

Factor	Explanation
Lean body mass	Lean body mass, which is mostly muscle mass, is more metabolically active than fat tissue, so more kilocalories are needed to maintain it. Athletes who have a large percentage of lean body mass due to their increased muscle mass have a higher BMR than individuals who aren't athletic.
Age	For adults, BMR declines about 1 to 2 percent per decade after the early adult years but it increases by 15 percent during pregnancy. For children, BMR increases during times of rapid growth such as infancy and adolescence.
Gender	Women have less lean body mass, and typically have a higher percentage of body fat than men. This results in women having a BMR up to 10 percent lower than men's. Women also tend to have a smaller body size.
Body size	Taller individuals have a higher BMR due to increased surface area compared with shorter individuals. More surface area means more heat lost from the body, which causes the metabolism rate to increase to maintain the body's temperature.
Genes	Research suggests that genes may affect BMR, as individuals within families have similar metabolic rates.
Ethnicity	African-Americans have BMRs that are about 10 percent lower than those of Caucasians.
Stress	Hormones such as epinephrine, which are released during emotional stress, increase BMR. Physiological stress on the body caused by injury, fever, burns, and infections also causes the release of hormones that raise BMR. Heat loss from the body through wounds, as well as the response of the immune system during infection, increase BMR.
Hormones	An increase in thyroid hormone increases BMR, whereas too little of this hormone lowers BMR. Hormone fluctuations during a woman's menstrual cycle lower BMR during the phase before ovulation.
Starvation	Starvation and fasting for more than about 48 hours lower BMR.
Environmental temperature	Being very cold or very hot can increase BMR. The change is minimal if clothing or air temperature are adjusted.
Caffeine	Caffeine can raise BMR, but only slightly when consumed regularly in moderate amounts.
Drugs	Nicotine may increase BMR.* Stimulant drugs such as amphetamine and ephedrine increase BMR.

*Note: Smoking is not a weight-management strategy. Some people may think that replacing snacks with cigarettes helps them stay slim, but the health risks associated with smoking, such as lung cancer, heart disease, and stroke, make it a foolish habit. Anyone concerned about weight gain when quitting smoking can minimize the chances of this with exercise.

Data from Food and Nutrition Board, National Institute of Medicine, *Dietary Reference Intakes: The Essential Guide to Nutrient Requirements* (Washington, DC: The National Academies Press, 2006).

normally consider exercise. NEAT may play a key role in energy balance. Adults who fidget or are hyperactive tend to burn more kilocalories than people who are more docile.[3] While sitting in front of a computer all day does expend kilocalories, the amount is minimal.[4] Read Examining the Evidence: What Is NEAT about Fidgeting? for more information on the influence of NEAT on energy expenditure.

Energy Used for Digestion and Absorption Is Called the Thermic Effect of Food (TEF)

The digestive system requires kilocalories to digest and absorb the foods you eat, and the amount of energy required for this is called the **thermic effect of food (TEF).** The body uses energy to process the fuels and extract kilocalories during catabolism. Immediately after eating and for several hours after a meal, energy expenditure increases to provide ATP for chewing, peristalsis, digestion, absorption, and transport of nutrients. Approximately 10 percent of the kilocalories in food consumed is used for TEF. In other words, about 10 kilocalories in a 100-kilocalorie cookie are used to process the cookie. Likewise due to TEF, the gross kilocalories found in a food are slightly more than the net amount available for energy expenditures.

The type of nutrients consumed influences the TEF. For instance, a meal high in protein has the highest thermic effect (approximately 20 to 30 percent), probably because of the synthesis of body proteins after a protein meal. Carbohydrates have a greater TEF (5 to 10 percent) than fat (0 to 3 percent), most likely due to

thermic effect of food (TEF) The amount of energy expended by the body to digest, absorb, transport, metabolize, and store energy-yielding nutrients from foods.

What Is NEAT About Fidgeting?

Fidgeting is one aspect of the energy expenditure referred to as NEAT, or non-exercise activity thermogenesis.[1] The term NEAT, coined by cardiologist Dr. James A. Levine, is a component of TEE that refers to the energy we expend for everything we do while awake except eating or participating in structured exercise such as jogging, aerobics, or power walking. NEAT includes walking to work, dancing, gardening, and, yes, even fidgeting.

As a nation, the less often we move, the more obese we become.[2] Research has reported a strong correlation between a drop in NEAT and an increase in weight gain, specifically body fat.[3] Studies report that lean people who are sedentary stand and move 152 minutes longer per day than obese individuals do. And obese subjects sit 164 minutes per day (over 2.5 hours) more than lean subjects. In other words, people who are classified as obese have low NEAT.[4] Sitting, it would seem, increases your risk of obesity and all of the health risks associated with excess weight.

The amount of kilocalories burned by NEAT activities can vary substantially between individuals. Levine and colleagues report that NEAT can vary by almost 2,000 kilocalories per day.[5] What accounts for these large differences in daily energy expenditure? Let's examine the evidence.

Your Occupation Impacts NEAT

The advancement of technology has reduced NEAT by limiting the physical activity of jobs in the workplace. According to current research, working in a sedentary occupation is the main factor contributing to lower NEAT.[6] Among employed workers, men with sedentary jobs (secretaries, motor vehicle operators) were 22 percent less active and women were 30 percent less active than those with more active professions, such as farm or construction workers.[7] If you compare this to steps taken per day, a desk-bound man or woman takes only 5,000 to 6,000 steps a day. That

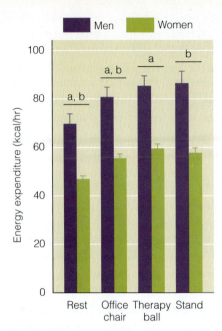

▲ **Figure 1** Energy expenditure in males and females expressed as kilocalories per hour during rest, office chair, therapy ball, and standing postures. Data are mean $\pm$ S.E.; $p < 0.05$ for means with the same letter.

Source: E. A. Beers, J. N. Roemmich, L. H. Epstein, and P. J. Horvath. 2008. "Increasing Passive Energy Expenditure during Clerical Work." *European Journal of Applied Physiology* 103:353–360. Copyright © by Springer. Reprinted with permission of Springer Science+Business Media.

compares with about 18,000 steps a day for the average man and 14,000 for the average woman in an Amish farming community.[8]

In controlled studies of sedentary adults, changes in the work environment that encourage NEAT, such as fidgeting and standing, have been shown to reduce weight gain. For example, standing rather than sitting is an example of passive work that burns more kilocalories. **Figure 1** illustrates the differences of energy expenditure in standing versus sitting during work. For those who find it difficult to stand during the workday, sitting on a therapy ball, which requires the individual to contract core muscles, may be another passive means to increase energy expenditure.[9]

Research is currently being conducted in a variety of office settings on the feasibility of using walking stations in the workplace, and the impact these stations may have on body composition, cognitive function, and job productivity. The use of walking desks should increase NEAT energy expenditure and may improve overall health in the workplace.

Walking slowly at the rate of about 1 mile per hour while working at your desk increases energy expenditure by about 200 kilocalories per hour compared with sitting at your desk.

Leisure Time and NEAT

Labor-saving devices and technology make it possible to squelch much leisure-time NEAT through the use of riding lawnmowers, electronically programmed vacuum cleaners, bread machines, microwave ovens, electric hammers, and handheld video games.[10,11] Consider your leisure-time hours after work or school and on the weekends. Do you surf the Internet or watch television for hours until bedtime, just moving the mouse or using the remote control? If this were your routine after work, the average energy expenditure for that sedentary activity would be about 70 kilocalories per hour.[12] What if you cleaned house, walked your dog after dinner, or worked in the garden as an alternative? Instead of 70 kilocalories per hour, you could burn 200 to 400 kilocalories per hour. This change in NEAT could potentially increase the amount of energy you burn by more than 800 kilocalories per day.

NEAT Changes with Food Intake

Research suggests that when you eat too much, NEAT increases or when you eat too little, NEAT decreases. This was illustrated in a study that overfed non-obese subjects 1,000 kilocalories per day for eight weeks. As expected, the subjects gained between 1.4 kilograms and 7.2 kilograms of weight. What was unexpected was that there was also an increase in NEAT, including changes in posture, fidgeting, and daily activities. The increase in NEAT seemed to be a factor in those who gained less weight than the others. The researchers concluded that the increase in NEAT helped resist additional weight gain even when subjects overate.[13]

Move and Walk More to Prevent Obesity

Even if you engage in regular structured exercise, your overall daily energy expenditure may be relatively low if you spend

Increase Your NEAT

Find a friend at work to walk with at lunch.

Stand or pace while talking on the telephone.

Put on your headset and listen to your favorite music while you walk during your morning break.

Set your NEAT goal to stand at least 2.5 hours per day.

Fold laundry while watching your favorite TV show.

Take the stairs instead of riding the elevator or escalator.

If you drive to work or school, park farther from the building.

Buy a pedometer to measure your steps; aim for 10,000 per day.

Adapted from J. Levine and S. Yeager, *Move a Little, Lose a Lot: New N.E.A.T. Science Reveals How to Be Thinner, Happier, and Smarter* (New York: Crown Publishers, 2009).

the rest of your time sitting. The secret to increasing your NEAT and burning more kilocalories during the day, especially during work hours, is to get up out of the chair and move more. Find ways to work simple movements into your day—tap your feet, pace while you talk on the phone, stand while you read, get up and walk to a coworker's desk instead of emailing. Any additional NEAT activities will help minimize the potential health risks of a chair-sitting lifestyle. See the Fitness Tips for helpful suggestions.

References

1. J. A. Levine. 2012. "Non-Exercise Activity Thermogenesis (NEAT)." *Best Practices in Research Clinical Endocrinology Metabolism* 16:679–702.

2. S. A. Lear, et al. 2014. "The Association between Ownership of Common Household Devices and Obesity and Diabetes in High, Middle, and Low Income Countries." *Canadian Medical Association Journal* doi:10.1503/cmaj.131090.

3. J. A. Levine and C. M. Kotz. 2005. "NEAT—Non-Exercise Activity Thermogenesis—Egocentric and Geocentric Environmental Factors vs. Biological Regulation." *Acta Physiologica Scandinavica* 184(4):309–318.

4. J. A. Levine, L. M. Lanningham-Foster, S. K. McCrady, et al. 2005. "Inter-Individual Variation in Posture Allocation: Possible Role in Human Obesity." *Science* 307:584–586.

5. Ibid.

6. J. A. Levine, W. M. W. Vander, J. O. Hill, and R. C. Klesges. 2006. "Non-Exercise Activity Thermogenesis: The Crouching Tiger Hidden Dragon of Societal Weight Gain." *Arteriosclerosis, Thrombosis, and Vascular Biology* 26:729–736.

7. D. R. Van Domelen, A. Koster, P. Caserotti, R. J. Brychta, K. Y. Chen, J. J. McClain, R. P. Trojano, et al. 2011. "Employment and Physical Activity in the U. S." *American Journal of Preventive Medicine* 41:136–145.

8. D. R. Bassett, P. L. Schneider, and G. E. Huntington. 2004. "Physical Activity in an Old Order Amish Community." *Medicine & Science in Sports & Exercise* 36:79–85.

9. S. J. Pederson, et al. 2013. "An E-Health Intervention Designed to Increase Workday Energy Expenditure by Reducing Prolonged Occupational Sitting Habits." *Work* DOI:10.3233/WOR-131644.

10. M. Hayes, M. Chustek, S. Heshka, Z. Wang, A. Pietrobelli, and S. B. Heymsfield. 2005. "Low Physical Activity Levels of Modern *Homo sapiens* among Free-Ranging Mammals." *International Journal of Obesity* 29:151–156.

11. Lear. 2014. "The Association between Ownership of Common Household Devices and Obesity and Diabetes in High, Middle, and Low Income Countries."

12. ChooseMyPlate. 2012. *How Many Calories Does Physical Activity Use?* Available at www.choosemyplate.gov. Accessed June 2012.

13. Levine. 2012. Non-Exercise Activity Thermogenesis (NEAT).

TABLE 14.2 Factors That Influence the Thermic Effect of Food

Factor	Effects on the Thermic Effect of Food
Type of fuel	Fat has the least effect on TEF; protein has the greatest effect.
Meal composition	Consuming all three macronutrients together produces a lower TEF than would be produced by protein or carbohydrates separately.
Fiber content	A high-fiber meal produces a lower TEF.
Age	TEF declines as we age.
Environmental temperature	Consuming a meal in a cold environment increases TEF.
Alcohol	Alcohol consumption increases TEF but reduces TEF if alcohol is consumed in a cold environment.
Intense exercise	TEF is higher following intense exercise.
Training status	Individuals who are trained athletes have a lower TEF than untrained individuals.
Obesity	Obese individuals have a lower TEF than normal-weight individuals.

Data from J. Kang, *Bioenergetics Primer for Exercise Science* (Champaign, IL: Human Kinetics, Inc., 2008).

The process of digesting and absorbing foods requires energy called the thermic effect of food.

the energy cost to convert glucose into glycogen. The energy cost of converting fat into stored triglycerides is minimal. Other factors that influence the TEF, such as composition of a meal, alcohol intake, age, and athletic training status, are presented in **Table 14.2**. A trained athlete appears to be able to digest and absorb food using fewer kilocalories than the untrained.[5] An obese individual may also have a reduced TEF. The reason for the decrease in TEF in obesity may be due to insulin insensitivity.[6] Note that the amount of kilocalories used for TEF is small compared with the amount expended by BMR and physical activity.

Energy Is Used for Adaptive Thermogenesis

Energy can also be expended by producing heat (**thermogenesis**). *Adaptive thermogenesis* is the body's regulation of heat production, influenced by environmental changes such as stress, temperature, or diet, which result in a change in metabolism. Shivering when the temperature drops is an example of adaptive thermogenesis.

Experts are still not sure how adaptive thermogenesis relates to total daily energy expenditure. The ability to regulate how much heat is produced from food energy rather than storing the kilocalories in fat tissue may be partly responsible for weight gain in overweight individuals versus their lighter peers. Some researchers believe adaptive thermogenesis explains why two people can have the same diet and exercise patterns but have completely different body compositions.

Figure 14.4 summarizes the factors on both sides of the energy balance equation that contribute to your total daily energy expenditure.

thermogenesis The generation of heat from the basal metabolism, digestion of food, and physical activity that provides necessary warmth; *adaptive thermogenesis* and *non-exercise activity thermogenesis (NEAT)* are other terms used to describe specific aspects of the generation of heat.

LO 14.2: THE TAKE-HOME MESSAGE About 50 to 70 percent of total daily energy expenditure (TDEE) is attributable to basal metabolic rate (BMR), the amount of energy spent to meet the body's basic physiological needs when it is at rest. The metabolic activity of lean body mass accounts for about 70 percent of BMR. In addition to BMR, TDEE includes the thermic effect of food (TEF), or the energy spent to digest and absorb nutrients from food, and the thermic effect of exercise (TEE), or the energy spent on physical activities. The thermic effect of exercise includes non-exercise activity thermogenesis (NEAT). Adaptive thermogenesis, another component of TEE, regulates the amount of heat produced when food is metabolized and may be responsible for reducing energy expenditure when food intake is reduced.

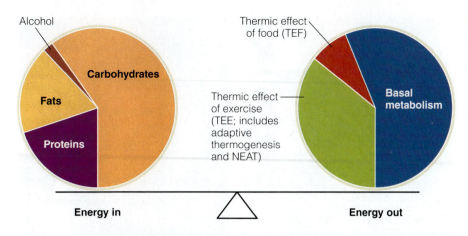

How Do We Measure Energy Expenditure?

LO 14.3 Explain how energy expenditure is measured and calculate BMR and EER using equations and physical activity factors.

Have you ever wondered how many kilocalories you burn walking to class or washing your car? Or how resting metabolic rate is calculated? Several methods have been developed to measure energy expenditure. Some of these methods require the skills of a trained technician using expensive equipment. Other methods involve simple equations and a calculator.

Direct and Indirect Calorimetry Measure Energy Expenditure

An individual's energy expenditure can be measured by *direct calorimetry* or *indirect calorimetry*. Both methods quantify the amount of energy produced during rest and physical activity.

Direct calorimetry measures the amount of heat the body generates and can be determined using a metabolic chamber in a specialized laboratory. Briefly, a metabolic chamber is an airtight room designed with the comforts an individual would need for normal daily living such as a bed, chair, TV, telephone, treadmill for exercise, and bathroom. The temperature and relative humidity in the room are controlled and the oxygen and carbon dioxide concentrations of the air supply and exhaust are measured for 24 hours. The concept is similar to the bomb calorimeter, but rather than measuring the amount of heat generated by burning food, this method measures the change in water temperature caused by heat that dissipates from a body sitting in an airtight chamber. Although this method provides a precise answer to the question of how many kilocalories an individual expends, for most people its use is too expensive and impractical.

The more practical and less expensive approach is to use an indirect measurement, called **indirect calorimetry,** to estimate the amount of energy expended. Indirect measurements sample the amount of oxygen consumed and carbon dioxide produced during exercise and for a specific amount of time. Metabolic calculations can then be done to determine energy expenditure. **Figure 14.5** illustrates two examples of indirect calorimetry: On the right is an example of indirect calorimetry during exercise using a metabolic cart often found in exercise science labs. On the left is an example of measuring energy expenditure at rest.

direct calorimetry A direct measurement of the energy expended by the body obtained by assessing heat loss.

indirect calorimetry An indirect measurement of energy expenditure obtained by measuring the amount of oxygen consumed and carbon dioxide produced.

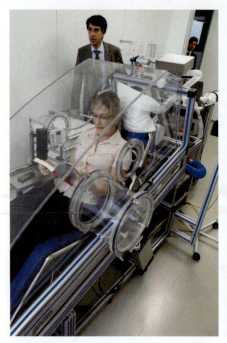 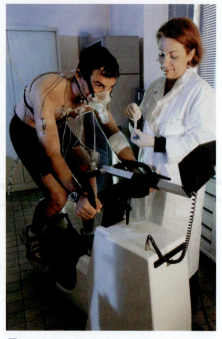

a Measuring metabolic rate at rest   **b** Measuring metabolic rate during exercise

▲ **Figure 14.5 A Metabolic Cart Indirectly Measures Energy Expenditure**
A metabolic cart measures the amount of oxygen consumed and carbon dioxide produced at rest (a) or during exercise (b). This information can then be used to indirectly calculate an individual's energy expenditure.

Simple Calculations Are Used to Estimate Energy Expenditure

Recall Table 2.2 from Chapter 2, which helped *estimate* energy needs for a 24-hour period using indirect calorimetry. This table was derived from the DRIs' estimated energy requirement. The **estimated energy requirement (EER)** is the average kilocalorie intake that is estimated to maintain energy balance based on a person's gender, age, height, body weight, and level of physical activity. The physical activity levels are separated into categories ranging from sedentary to very active, as shown in **Table 14.3**, and can be used along with a person's specific gender, age, height, and weight to compute individualized estimated energy requirements. One such calculation used by the DRI committee to estimate EER is presented in the Calculation Corner.[7] You can obtain an even more precise EER by assessing every

estimated energy requirement (EER) The average kilocalorie intake that is estimated to maintain energy balance based on a person's gender, age, height, body weight, and level of physical activity.

| | **Physical Activity Factor for** | |
Physical Activity Level	**Men**	**Women**
Sedentary	1.00	1.00
Low level of activity (walking approximately 2 miles per day at 3 to 4 miles per hour)	1.11	1.12
Active (walking approximately 7 miles per day at 3 to 4 miles per hour)	1.25	1.27
Very active (walking approximately 17 miles per day at 3 to 4 miles per hour)	1.45	1.48

TABLE 14.3 Physical Activity Factors for Men and Women

Data from Food and Nutrition Board, National Institute of Medicine, *Dietary Reference Intakes: The Essential Guide to Nutrient Requirements* (Washington, DC: The National Academies Press, 2006).

What's Your Estimated Energy Requirement (EER)?

You can estimate your energy requirement for kilocalories using this two-step calculation:

1. First, complete the information below.
   a. My age is _____.
   b. My physical activity during the day based on Table 14.3 is _____.
   c. My weight in pounds is _____ divided by 2.2 = _____ kilograms.
   d. My height in inches is _____ divided by 39.4 = _____ meters.

2. Using your answers from each part of step 1, complete the following calculation based on your gender and age.

   Males, 19+ years old, use this calculation:

   EER = [662 − (9.53 × _____)] + _____ × [(15.91 × _____) + (539.6 × _____)]

                          (a)   (b)   (c)   (d)

   Females, 19+ years old, use this calculation:

   EER = [354 − (6.91 × _____)] + _____ × [(9.36 × _____) + (726 × _____)]

                          (a)   (b)   (c)   (d)

3. Now calculate Will's EER. Will is 21 years old, weighs 180 pounds, and stands at 5 feet 11 inches tall. He describes his physical activity level as active. What is Will's estimated energy requirement?

> Scan this QR code with your mobile device to access practice math activities. You can also access the activities in MasteringNutrition™.

---

minute of movement and physical activity that you do throughout the day and, based on this, calculating the energy that you expend.

Another calculation often used is the Harris-Benedict equation, which also calculates RMR based on gender, age, height, and weight, and applies an activity factor to determine total daily energy expenditure. The drawback to this equation is that it does not include lean body mass, so it may not be accurate for individuals who are very muscular (for whom it underestimates kilocalorie needs) or who are very fat (for whom it overestimates kilocalorie needs). In those circumstances, other calculations, such as the Mifflin-St. Jeor equation, may be used in clinical settings.

LO 14.3: THE TAKE-HOME MESSAGE Energy expenditure can be measured by direct calorimetry using a metabolic chamber or by indirect calorimetry using a metabolic cart. Simple calculations can also be used to estimate energy expenditure using age, height, weight, and physical activity.

What Is Body Composition and How Is It Assessed?

LO 14.4 Define the term body composition, and explain the methods used to assess lean body mass and body fat.

Body tissues include bone, skin, muscle, fat, organs, and blood, which are comprised of the same basic nutrients: water, protein, minerals, and fat. The ratio of fat tissue to lean body mass is called **body composition.** This ratio, stated as a *percent body fat,* is particularly important for the sake of measuring health risks associated with too much body fat. It's essential to know what your body mass is composed of so as to take the necessary steps to achieve a healthy body weight and control health risks.

---

body composition The ratio of fat to lean tissue (muscle, bone, and organs) in the body; usually expressed as percent body fat.

Most Body Fat Is Stored in Adipose Tissue

Two types of fat make up total body fat: **essential fat,** which includes the fat found in the bone marrow, heart, lungs, liver, spleen, kidneys, intestines, muscles, and central nervous system; and stored fat, found in **adipose tissue,** or fat cells. Essential fat is just that—essential for the body to function. Women have four times (12 percent) more essential fat than men (3 percent) because of the fat deposits in breast tissue and surrounding the uterus. Every cell contains some fat, but most body fat is the storage fat found in adipose tissue.

Excess stored fat can be found as **subcutaneous fat** under the skin or as **visceral fat** around the internal organs. Subcutaneous and visceral fat insulate the body from cold temperatures and help protect and cushion the internal organs (**Figure 14.6**). Men and women store subcutaneous fat slightly differently, with men more likely to accumulate it in the belly, hips, and thighs, and women more apt to store it in the breasts, neck, and upper arms, as well as in the hips and thighs.

Adipose tissues release fat to be used as fuel when the body is in negative energy balance. An adipocyte shrinks as more fat is hydrolyzed from storage, and overall body weight is lost. When the body is in positive energy balance, fat accumulates in adipose tissue, the fat cells expand in size, and weight gain occurs.

Adipose tissue is described as *white fat* because of its creamy, white appearance. Another type of adipose tissue, called **brown adipose tissue (BAT),** is made up of specialized fat cells that contain more mitochondria and are rich in blood (**Figure 14.7**). While white adipose tissue is used as a storage depot for excess kilocalories, the function of BAT is to generate heat. Found primarily in infants, BAT protects infants from heat loss and cold. Recent research suggests that adults, especially older adults, have more BAT than once thought. Studies have shown that the more BAT an adult has, the lower their body mass index, suggesting that this active tissue plays an important role in adult metabolism.[8] This may be due to the fact that brown adipose tissue converts kilocalories into heat rather than storing them in the adipocyte.

essential fat A component of body fat that is necessary for health and normal body functions; includes the fat stored in the bone marrow, heart, lungs, liver, spleen, kidneys, intestines, muscles, and the lipid-rich tissues of the central nervous system.

adipose tissue Connective tissue that is the main storage site for fat in the body.

subcutaneous fat The fat located under the skin and between the muscles.

visceral fat The body fat associated with the internal organs and stored in the abdominal area.

brown adipose tissue (BAT) A type of adipose tissue, found primarily in infants, that produces body heat; it gets its name from the large number of mitochondria and capillaries responsible for the brown color.

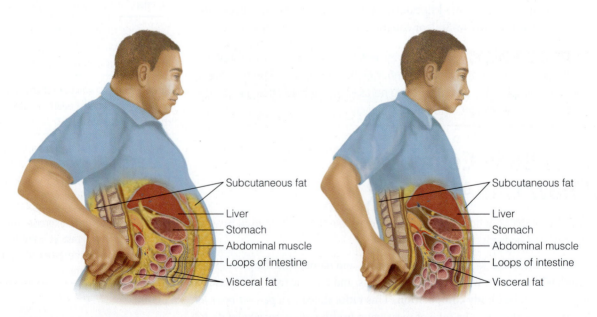

▲ **Figure 14.6 Visceral and Subcutaneous Fat Storage in the Body**
Visceral fat stored around the organs of the abdomen is more likely to lead to health problems than is subcutaneous fat sandwiched between the muscle and skin.

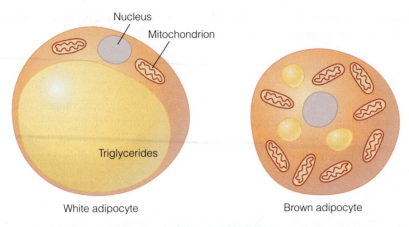

▲ Figure 14.7 **White Adipocyte and Brown Adipocyte**
Brown adipose tissue has significantly more mitochondria and less stored triglycerides than white adipose tissue.

Body Fat Distribution Affects Health

How much fat you carry isn't the only determinant of health risk—where you carry it also matters. Storing excess fat around the waist versus carrying it around the hips and thighs has been shown to increase the risk of heart disease, diabetes, and hypertension.[9] **Central or android obesity** occurs when excess visceral and subcutaneous fat is stored in the abdomen (**Figure 14.8**). This is sometimes referred to as an "apple-shaped" fat distribution pattern and is more common in men than in women. **Gynoid obesity** is due to excess subcutaneous fat stored in the lower part of the body around the thighs and buttocks. This "pear-shaped" fat distribution pattern is more frequently found in women than in men.

Because visceral fat is located near the liver, it is believed that fatty acids released from the fat storage area travel to the liver and can lead to insulin resistance, high levels of fat, low levels of the good HDL cholesterol, and high levels of LDL cholesterol in the blood, which all increase the risk of heart disease and diabetes. Insulin resistance also increases the risk for hypertension. Men, postmenopausal women, and obese people tend to have more visceral fat than young adults and lean individuals.

Body Fat Levels Affect Health

Carrying either too much or too little body fat can affect body functions and impair health. Everyone needs to have a certain amount of body fat to meet basic needs, but excess amounts of body fat can impact overall health. For this reason, specific body composition standards have been developed over the years from a variety of research to help individuals avoid health risk (**Table 14.4**). These body fat ranges,

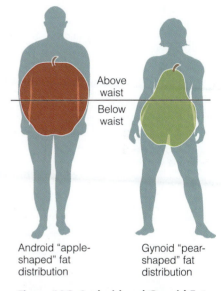

Android "apple-shaped" fat distribution

Gynoid "pear-shaped" fat distribution

▲ Figure 14.8 **Android and Gynoid Fat Distribution Patterns**
Men and women store subcutaneous fat differently. Men tend to store it in the upper body including the abdomen, chest, neck, and back—often referred to as "apple-shaped" fat distribution —while women tend to store subcutaneous fat below the waist including the buttocks, hips, and thighs for more of a "pear-shaped" appearance.

TABLE 14.4	Body Composition Reference Standards for Adult Men and Women	
	Men	**Women**
Essential fat	3 percent of total body fat	12 percent of total body fat
Desirable fatness for good health	10 to 20 percent body fat	16 to 26 percent body fat
Overfat	More than 25 percent body fat	More than 30 percent body fat

Data from W. D. McArdle, F. I. Katch, and V. L. Katch, *Sports and Exercise Nutrition*, 4th ed. (Baltimore: Lippincott Williams & Wilkins, 2012).

central or android obesity An excess storage of visceral fat in the abdominal area, indicated by a waist circumference greater than 40 inches in males and 35 inches in females; central obesity increases the risk of heart disease, diabetes, and hypertension.

gynoid obesity An excessive storage of body fat in the thighs and hips of the lower body.

which can be measured using a variety of indirect methods, are based on epidemiological studies of the general population of Americans.

Body Composition Is Assessed Indirectly

There are several indirect measurements used to estimate the percentage of body fat and lean body mass in the body. The most popular indirect techniques are found in laboratory settings and include hydrostatic weighing, air displacement, dual-energy X-ray absorptiometry (DEXA), bioelectrical impedance, and skinfold measurement (**Table 14.5**).

Percent Body Fat

Because fat mass has a lower density than either muscles or bones, it is possible to estimate body fat percentage from body volume. **Hydrostatic weighing** and **air displacement plethysmography** are two methods that use body volume to measure percent body fat. Hydrostatic weighing is based on the principle that an object immersed in water is buoyed up by a force equal to the weight of the fluid displaced by the object. In other words, if the density of an object is greater than the density of water, the object sinks. If the density of the object is less than water, the object floats. We can use this principle to determine body composition by measuring the difference in body weight in air compared with under water. With a 2 to 3 percent margin of error, hydrostatic weighing is considered one of the most accurate assessment tools. The BodPod, an air displacement plethysmography device that measures air rather than water displacement, is similarly accurate within 3 percent. Both hydrostatic weighing and the BodPod have pros and cons. While both are accurate, hydrostatic weighing takes longer; some people find it difficult to be submersed under water; and the equipment is usually only found in research facilities. The BodPod, on the other hand, is faster and it only requires you to sit quietly in a chamber. See the Calculation Corner for the equation used to determine body composition from either of these body volume methods.

   Dual-energy X-ray absorptiometry (DEXA) is the most accurate method of determining body composition; its margin of error is only 1 to 4 percent. DEXA is a noninvasive method that can estimate three body compartments: fat mass, lean body mass, and bone mass. This noninvasive method uses two low-energy X-ray beams: One detects all tissues including fat mass and bone mass and the other

Calculation Corner

Body Volume and Density
The body volume determined by either hydrostatic weighing or air displacement is mathematically converted to density and then to percentage of body fat using this equation:

Body density = body weight (kg)/body volume (L)

Percentage of body fat = (495/body density) − 450

Example: The body volume of an 83-kilogram male (182.6 pounds) was determined from hydrostatic weighing to be 79.4 L. Dividing body weight by body volume yields a body density of 1.0453. Body density can then be used to determine percent body fat as follows:

(495/1.0453) − 450
= 23.5 percent body fat

hydrostatic weighing A method used to assess body volume by underwater weighing.

air displacement plethysmography A procedure used to estimate body volume based on the amount of air displaced.

dual-energy X-ray absorptiometry (DEXA) A method that uses two low-energy X-rays to measure body density and bone mass.

TABLE 14.5 Ways to Measure Percentage of Body Fat

Air Displacement Plethysmography ▶ Using a BodPod

How It Is Done: A person's body volume is determined by measuring air displacement. The person sits in a special chamber (called the BodPod) and the air displacement in the chamber is measured. From this measurement, the percentage of body fat can be estimated.

Cost: $$$

Accuracy: 2–3% margin of error

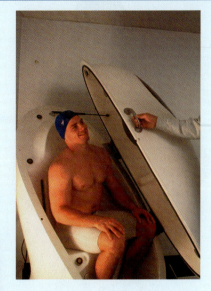

▲ Hydrostatic Weighing

How It Is Done: To determine the density of the body, a person is weighed both on land and suspended in a water tank. Fat is less dense and weighs less than muscle mass and this is reflected in the person's weight in the water. The difference of a person's weight in water and on land is then used to calculate the percentage of body fat.

Cost: $$

Accuracy: 2–3% margin of error

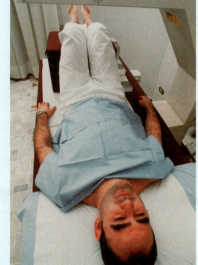

◀ Dual-Energy X-Ray Absorptiometry (DEXA)

How It Is Done: Beams of X-ray energy from two different sources are used to measure bone, fat, and lean tissue. The different types of tissue that the beams pass through absorb different amounts of energy. The percentage of body fat can be determined from the difference in the readings.

Cost: $$$

Accuracy: 1–4% margin of error

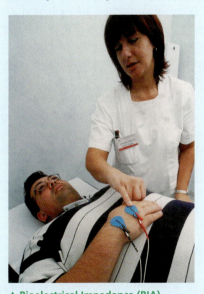

▲ Bioelectrical Impedance (BIA)

How It Is Done: An electric current flows through the body and its resistance is measured. Lean tissue is highly conductive and less resistant than fat mass. Based on the current flow, the volume of lean tissue can be estimated. From this information, the percentage of body fat can be determined.

Cost: $

Accuracy: 3–4% margin of error

Skinfold Thickness Measurements ▶

How It Is Done: Calipers are used to measure the thickness of fat that is located just under the skin in the arm, in the back, on the upper thigh, and in the waist area. From these measurements, percent body fat can be determined.

Cost: $

Accuracy: 3–4% margin of error

$ = very affordable
$$ = less affordable
$$$ = expensive

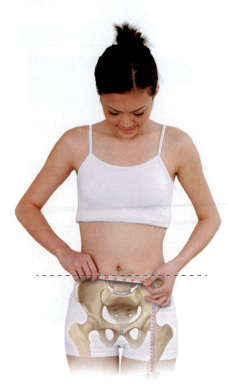

▲ **Figure 14.9 Measuring Waist Circumference**
The waist circumference measurement is taken at the top of the iliac crest (top of the hip bone), as shown by the dashed line.

detects only lean body mass. The computer then calculates the difference between lean body mass and fat mass to determine the percentage of body fat.

Bioelectrical impedance analysis (BIA) measures the resistance to a low-energy current as it travels through muscle and body fat. The current travels more quickly through lean body mass, which is high in body water and electrolytes, than through fat tissue. The resistance of the fat tissue is used to calculate body composition. BIA is not as accurate as body density tests and can be affected by age, hydration status, and consuming food and alcohol prior to the test.

Anthropometric (relating to body measurement) techniques are the simplest methods available and involve using a **skinfold caliper** to measure fat in various body locations. The metal calipers are used to pinch the subcutaneous fat at selected sites on the body. A trained technician grasps the skin and fat between the thumb and forefinger and pulls it gently away from the muscle. The caliper exerts a constant pressure while measuring the skinfold thickness in millimeters. These values are then used to calculate percent body fat. When conducted by a trained technician, skinfold caliper tests are fairly accurate.

Waist Circumference

Because abdominal fat can be particularly detrimental to health, measuring a person's **waist circumference** can quickly reveal whether he or she is at increased risk (**Figure 14.9**). A woman with a waist measurement of more than 35 inches or a man with a belly that's more than 40 inches around is at a higher risk for disease than people with slimmer middles. Carrying extra fat around the waist can increase health risks even if you are not overweight. In other words, a person who may be at a healthy weight based on their height, but who has excess fat around the middle, is at a higher risk for disease.

> **LO 14.4: THE TAKE-HOME MESSAGE** The body is composed of lean and fat tissue. Adipose tissue is classified as essential fat or fat that is stored as either subcutaneous or visceral fat. How much fat a person has and the placement of that fat can increase the risk of heart disease, diabetes, and hypertension, especially if the fat is distributed in the abdomen. Hydrostatic weighing, air displacement plethysmography, dual-energy X-ray absorptiometry, (DEXA), bioelectrical impedance analysis (BIA), and skinfold measurements are all techniques used to determine body composition. Measuring waist circumference can determine whether an individual has excess fat around the middle, which can increase the risk of several chronic diseases.

How Do We Estimate a Healthy Body Weight?

LO 14.5 Define the term healthy body weight, explain the methods used to estimate a healthy body weight, and describe how body weight and body fat can affect health.

The terms body weight and body composition are not synonymous. Body weight is defined as the total mass of a person expressed in either pounds (lb) or kilograms (kg). As you just learned, body composition is the percentage of body weight that is composed of fat and lean body mass. Even though the terms *body weight* and *body composition* do not measure the same component, they are often used interchangeably in the popular media.

Two common methods used to help individuals estimate whether their own percent body fat falls within a healthy range are height-weight tables and body mass

bioelectrical impedance analysis (BIA) A method used to assess the percentage of body fat by using a low-level electrical current; body fat resists or impedes the current, whereas water and muscle mass conduct electricity.

skinfold caliper A tool used to measure the thickness of subcutaneous fat.

waist circumference Measurement taken at the top of the iliac crest or hip bone; used to determine the pattern of obesity.

index (BMI). These reference standards are indirect estimates of body composition, and therefore somewhat imprecise, but they can be used as a rough guide to a healthy body weight for most people.

Height and Weight Tables Can Provide a Healthy Weight Range

Height-weight tables have been used since the 1940s in large-scale studies that were designed to investigate the relationship between body weight and disease. The most commonly used version was developed by the Metropolitan Life Insurance Company. The company published the Desirable Weights for Men and Women table in 1959 based on data collected from millions of policyholders. The most recent version of the table was published in 1999 and provides a recommended desirable weight range for a given height based on gender and frame size.

Several factors make the data used in these tables problematic. For example, the data does not represent the American population as a whole. The tables were originally designed with data from 25-to 59-year-olds, which means they may underrepresent older adults and individuals younger than 25 years of age. The original data was not standardized by the researchers. For instance, subjects self-reported their height and weight; the weights were measured at different times of the year; and there was no standard procedure regarding wearing shoes or clothing when taking the height and weight measurements. Lastly, the tables were constructed with the assumption that weight is associated with body fat. Today, mostly insurance companies use height-weight tables to determine mortality rates. Most health experts use body mass index rather than height-weight tables to determine healthy weight.

Body Mass Index Is a Useful Indicator of Healthy Weight for Most People

Body mass index (BMI) (**Figure 14.10**) is a convenient method of calculating body weight in relationship to height, and is a useful screening tool to determine an individual's risk of disease. It is calculated using either of the following formulas:

$$BMI = \frac{body\ weight\ (in\ kilograms)}{height^2\ (in\ meters)}$$

$$BMI = \frac{body\ weight\ ((in\ pounds) \times 703}{height^2\ (in\ inches)}$$

A BMI of 18.5 to 24.9 is considered a **healthy weight** based on height. A BMI between 25 and 29.9 is considered **overweight,** and a BMI above 30 is considered **obese.** As the BMI increases above 25, the risk of dying from diseases increases, although research shows that the risk is modest until a person reaches a BMI of 30.[10] Obese individuals have a 50 to 100 percent higher risk of dying prematurely than those at a healthy weight.[11] BMI has been shown to correlate with health risks associated with excess body fat, and an equation can be used to estimate body fat percentage from BMI (see the Calculation Corner).

While BMI can be useful in determining disease risks, it is important to note that BMI is not a *direct* measure of the percentage of body fat, and it doesn't specify if body weight is predominantly muscle or fat.[12] Therefore, athletes and people with a high percentage of muscle mass may have a BMI over 25, yet have a low percentage of body fat. Although these individuals are overweight based on their BMI, they are not "overfat" and unhealthy, and their muscular weight doesn't increase their health risk. In contrast, an older adult may be in a healthy weight range, but

body mass index (BMI) A calculation of body weight in relationship to height.

healthy weight A body weight in relationship to height that doesn't increase the risk of developing any weight-related health problems or diseases. A BMI between 18.5 and 24.9 is considered healthy.

overweight A body weight that increases risk of developing weight-related health problems; defined as having a BMI between 25 and 29.9.

obese A condition of excess body weight due to an abnormal accumulation of stored body fat; a BMI of 30 or more is considered obese.

A BMI between 18.5 and 24.9 is considered healthy. A BMI over 25 is considered over-weight, and a BMI over 30 is obese. A BMI under 18.5 is considered underweight, and can also be unhealthy.

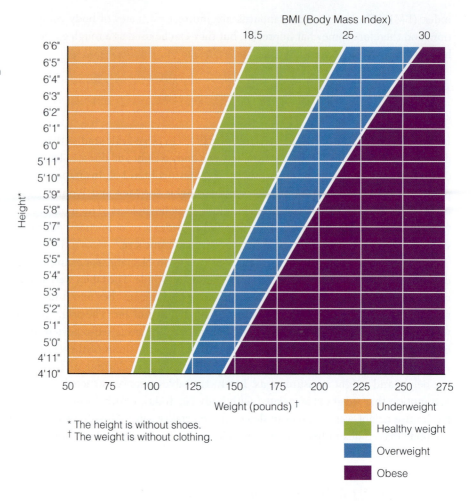

* The height is without shoes.
† The weight is without clothing.

This male gymnast stands 5 feet 5 inches tall and weighs 160 pounds. His BMI of 26.6 would place him in the overweight category without considering his low percentage of body fat.

steadily lose weight due to an unbalanced diet or poor health. This chronic weight loss is a sign of loss of muscle mass and the depletion of nutrient stores in the body, which increases health risks even though the BMI seems healthy. Also, because height is factored into the BMI, individuals who are very short—less than 5 feet—may have a high BMI, but, similar to athletes, may not be unhealthy.[13]

Combining indirect measurements is one way to get a better estimate of body composition. For example, a person who has both a BMI greater than 25 and a large waist circumference is considered at a higher risk for health problems than if he or she only had a high BMI but a low waist circumference (**Figure 14.11**).

There Are Health Risks Associated with Body Weight and Body Composition

Weighing too much or too little can both be harmful to health. Underweight adults, particularly older adults, can experience serious health risks, and an increased rate of obesity is directly related to higher rates of several chronic diseases among Americans.[14] Obesity is strongly correlated to several leading causes of death, including heart disease, type 2 diabetes, and cancer.

Calculation Corner

Converting BMI to Percent Body Fat

Now that you have learned how to calculate body mass index (BMI), how does this number correlate to the amount of stored body fat? Several researchers have presented equations that show a correlation between BMI and percent body fat in adults. One equation published in the *British Journal of Nutrition* was used to predict percent body fat from BMI.[1] The results of this research showed that the formulas, which are age and gender specific, can predict valid estimates of body fat comparable to prediction errors obtained from skinfold thickness measurements or BIA. The prediction equations do, however, overestimate percent body fat in obese individuals. Follow these steps to practice using these prediction equations.

1. If you are a female, use this formula: 1.2 (BMI) + 0.23 (age(y)) − 5.4
For example, a 21-year-old female with a BMI of 25 would calculate percent body fat as follows:

   1.2 (25) + 0.23 (21) − 5.4 = 30 + 4.83 − 5.4 = 29.43 percent body fat

2. A male would use this formula: 1.2 (BMI) + 0.23 (age(y)) − 16.2
For example, a 31-year-old male with a BMI of 21 would calculate percent body fat as follows:

   1.2 (21) + 0.23 (31) − 16.2 = 25.2 + 7.13 − 16.2 = 16.13 percent body fat

Now, using your own BMI, complete the calculation for percent body fat.

Note that these calculations do not consider ethnicity. The BMI–body fat relationship varies between different ethnic groups[2] and should be used in conjunction with other measurements such as waist circumference and percent body fat to provide a true picture of a healthy body weight.

References

1. P. Deurenbert, J. A. Weststrate, and J. C. Seidell. 1991. "Body–Mass Index as a Measure of Body Fatness: Age- and Sex-Specific Prediction Formulas." *British Journal of Nutrition* 65:105–114.
2. A. Luke. 2009. "Ethnicity and the BMI–Body Fat Relationship. *British Journal of Nutrition* 102:485–487.

Scan this QR code with your mobile device to access practice math activities. You can also access the activities in **Mastering**Nutrition™.

Extremely High Risk
BMI 40+ and high waist circumference

Very High Risk
BMI 30–39.9 and high waist circumference

High Risk
BMI 25–29.9 and high waist circumference
or
BMI 30–34.9 and low waist circumference

Increased Risk
BMI 25–29.9 and low waist circumference

Low Risk
BMI under 25

▲ **Figure 14.11 Using BMI and Waist Circumference to Determine Health Risk** Considering both BMI and waist circumference can give you a good idea of total risk levels for several chronic diseases.

Body weight can be a predictor for health risk because of its relationship to body composition. In general, heavier people tend to have a higher percentage of body fat. The higher the percent of body weight as body fat, the greater the health risks. For example, results from a recent study suggest that there is a significant rise in heart rate as adipose tissue accumulates, which may indicate an increased risk of hypertension.[15] Age was also found to be a factor in this study. Obese individuals aged 21 to 30 had heart rates similar to their non-obese peers (an average of 1.1 beats per minute higher), while obese individuals aged 51 to 60 had an average heart rate almost 7 beats per minute higher than their non-obese peers.

A healthy body weight doesn't increase the risk of developing any weight-related health problems or diseases. In contrast, being underweight or overweight can lead to numerous health risks. **Table 14.6** presents the criteria for defining the terms underweight, overweight, and obesity in adults.

Being Underweight Increases Health Risks

A BMI of less than 18.5 is considered **underweight** and is associated with a higher risk of anemia, osteoporosis and bone fractures, heart irregularities, and amenorrhea (loss of menstruation in women). Underweight older adults are at risk for low body protein and fat stores and a depressed immune system, which makes it more difficult to fight infections. Injuries, wounds, and illnesses that would normally

underweight Weighing too little for your height; defined as a BMI less than 18.5.

TABLE 14.6	Definitions of Underweight, Overweight, and Obesity in Adults

Classification	BMI (kg/m²)
Underweight	< 18.5
Normal weight	18.5–24.9
Overweight	25–29.9 (also defined as being 10 to 15 pounds above a healthy weight)
Obesity	30–39.9
Severe Obesity	> 40

improve in healthy individuals can cause serious medical complications, including death, in underweight individuals.[16]

Whereas some individuals have a BMI below 21 but are healthy, for others, a low body weight is symptomatic of malnutrition, substance abuse, or disease. Underweight and significant weight loss are also correlated to central nervous system problems such as depression and anxiety. The inability to fight off infection, trouble regulating body temperature, decreased muscle strength, and even an increase in the risk of prematurely dying are all associated with being underweight.

Certain diseases, such as cancer, inflammatory bowel disease, and celiac disease, can cause malabsorption and result in weight loss, leading to being underweight. Other inadvertent causes of underweight include certain medications, such as some antidepressants; osteoporosis; and blood pressure drugs, all of which can decrease appetite. Smoking and substance abuse can also lead to unhealthy weight loss.

Being Overweight Increases Health Risks

Overweight people, those with a BMI of greater than 25, have an increased risk for having heart disease, and the risk increases as BMI increases. A higher BMI can increase the risk of hypertension, stroke, heart disease, gallbladder disease, type 2 diabetes, osteoarthritis, joint stress, sleep apnea, and some cancers, including endometrial, breast, and colon cancer. Carrying extra body weight is so detrimental to health that for overweight individuals, losing as little as 10 to 20 pounds results in health benefits.[17]

Overweight people tend to have high blood levels of both triglycerides and LDL cholesterol, and less HDL cholesterol, which is an unhealthy combination for the heart. The insulin resistance that can develop over time in overweight individuals causes the pancreas to work harder to produce more insulin, and can eventually cause the organ to stop producing insulin altogether, leading to diabetes.

Being overweight is also a stepping-stone for developing obesity, and potentially even **severe obesity** (Table 14.7). Obesity can lead to congestive heart failure due to the inability of the heart to pump enough blood through the blood vessels. More than 80 percent of people with type 2 diabetes are overweight. Metabolic syndrome, a condition named for a group of risk factors associated with overweight and obesity, is seen more often in individuals who have android obesity. Excess weight raises the chance of developing a variety of cancers, including colon, breast, endometrial, and gallbladder cancer. Obesity correlates to osteoarthritis, a condition in which the tissue that protects the joints of the knees, hips, and lower back wears away. And finally, the risk of gallstones, sleep apnea, and reproductive problems increases with body weights above the standards established for health.[18]

severe obesity Defined as a BMI greater than 40 or more than 100 pounds over ideal body weight.

TABLE 14.7	Ways to Classify Obesity in Adults		
Obesity Is Classified by . . .			
Percent of body fat	Women: > 32%		
	Men: > 25%		
Distribution of body fat	Excess subcutaneous and visceral fat stored in the upper body (abdomen and waist); referred to as central or android obesity		
	▪ Waist circumference > 35 inches in women ▪ Waist circumference > 40 inches in men		
	Excess subcutaneous fat stored in the lower body (hips, buttocks, thighs); referred to as gynoid obesity		
	▪ Waist-to-hip ratio < 0.8 in women ▪ Waist-to-hip ratio < 0.95 in men		
Body mass index (BMI)	Women: > 30 kg/m^2		
	Men: > 25 kg/m^2		

Adapted from A. G. Kazaks and J. Stern, *Nutrition and Obesity. Assessment, Management, and Prevention* (Burlington, MA: Jones & Bartlett Publishing, 2013).

In Chapter 15 you will learn more about the relationship of weight to health and the safe methods used to achieve and maintain a healthy weight to reduce the risk of developing weight-related diseases.

LO 14.5: THE TAKE-HOME MESSAGE Height and weight tables and BMI are used to screen for overweight and obesity. Height-weight tables do not necessarily indicate a healthy weight for everyone. The body mass index (BMI) is a calculation of the ratio of weight to height and can be used to assess health risks. A BMI less than 18.5 is considered underweight and is associated with anemia, osteoporosis and bone fractures, heart irregularities, amenorrhea, depression, anxiety, depressed immune system, trouble regulating body temperature, and decreased muscle strength. A BMI greater than 25 is associated with an increased risk of heart disease, cancer, type 2 diabetes, metabolic syndrome, osteoarthritis, gallstones, sleep apnea, and reproductive disorders.

Health Connection

What Is Disordered Eating?

LO 14.6 List the criteria used to diagnose eating disorders and discuss the treatment options for disordered eating.

Attaining a healthy weight, whether it means gaining or losing a few pounds, is a worthwhile goal that can result in lowered risk of disease and a more productive life. However, patterns of eating that involve severe kilocalorie restriction, binge eating, purging, or other abnormal behaviors can be severely damaging to health. Whereas disordered eating and eating disorders are sometimes thought of as psychological rather than nutrition-related topics, it's important to be aware of them and recognize their symptoms.

The term **disordered eating** is used to describe a variety of eating patterns considered abnormal and potentially harmful. Refusing to eat, compulsive eating, binge eating, restrictive eating, vomiting after eating, and abusing diet pills, laxatives, or diuretics are all examples of disordered eating behaviors. **Eating disorders,** in contrast, are diagnosed when a person meets specific

disordered eating Abnormal and potentially harmful eating behaviors that do not meet specific criteria for anorexia nervosa and bulimia nervosa or binge eating disorder.

eating disorders Psychological illnesses that involve specific abnormal eating behaviors: anorexia nervosa (self-starvation) and bulimia nervosa (bingeing and purging).

TABLE 14.8	Diagnostic Criteria for Eating Disorders
Eating Disorder	**Diagnostic Criteria**
Anorexia nervosa	■ Restriction of energy intake relative to requirements leading to a significantly low body weight in the context of age, sex, developmental trajectory, and physical health ■ Intense fear of gaining weight or becoming fat, even though underweight ■ Disturbance in the way one's body weight or shape is experienced, excessive influence of body weight or shape on self-esteem, or denial of the seriousness of the current low body weight

Bulimia nervosa	■ Recurrent episodes of binge eating. An episode of binge eating is characterized by BOTH of the following:
	  ■ Eating in a discrete amount of time (within a 2-hour period) large amounts of food
	  ■ Sense of lack of control overeating during an episode
	■ Recurrent inappropriate compensatory behavior in order to prevent weight gain (purging)
	■ The binge eating and compensatory behaviors both occur, on average, at least twice a week for three months
	■ Self-evaluation is unduly influenced by body shape and weight
	■ The disturbance does not occur exclusively during episodes of anorexia nervosa

Binge Eating Disorder (BED)	■ Recurrent and persistent episodes of binge eating. An episode of binge eating is characterized by both of the following:
	  ■ Eating, in a discrete period of time, an amount of food that is definitely larger than most people would eat in a similar period of time under similar circumstances
	  ■ A sense of lack of control overeating during the episode (for example, a feeling that one cannot stop eating or control what or how much one is eating)
	■ Binge eating episodes are associated with three (or more) of the following:
	  ■ Eating much more rapidly than normal
	  ■ Eating until feeling uncomfortably full
	  ■ Eating large amounts of food when not feeling physically hungry
	  ■ Eating alone because of being embarrassed by how much one is eating
	  ■ Feeling disgusted with oneself, depressed, or very guilty after overeating
	■ Marked distress regarding binge eating is present
	■ The binge eating occurs, on average, at least once a week for three months
	■ The binge eating is not associated with the recurrent use of inappropriate compensatory behavior (for example, purging) and does not occur exclusively during the course of anorexia nervosa, bulimia nervosa, or avoidant/restrictive food intake disorder

Feeding or Eating Disorders Not Elsewhere Classified	■ Disordered eating behaviors that do not meet the criteria for anorexia nervosa, bulimia nervosa, or binge eating disorder, including orthorexia and night eating syndrome

Source: The Alliance for Eating Disorders Awareness. 2013. Available at www.allianceforeatingdisorders.com. Accessed May 2014.

criteria that include disordered eating behaviors as well as other factors (see Table 14.8). It is possible for someone to have disordered eating without having an actual eating disorder.

In the United States, approximately 20 million women and 10 million men struggle with eating disorders.[19] Adolescent and young adult females in predominantly white upper-middle- and middle-class families are the population with highest prevalence. However, eating disorders and disordered eating among males, minorities, and other age groups are increasing.[20, 21] Anyone can develop an eating disorder, regardless of gender, age, race, ethnicity, or social status.

Societal pressure to be thin and have a "perfect" figure is one factor that likely affects rates of disordered eating among girls and women. Images of models and celebrities with abnormally low body weights are portrayed as ideal, which frequently leads to body dissatisfaction among "normal" people. Thinness is too often associated with beauty, success, and happiness, and therefore many people believe that they cannot be beautiful, successful, or happy unless they are thin. Many females will try to achieve this perfect figure at any cost, including plastic surgery, liposuction, and engaging in disordered eating behaviors.

About 10 percent of all eating disorders occur in men. This may be an underestimate though, as many men, as well as women, feel ashamed or embarrassed and may hide their problem. In fact, the prevalence of eating disorders among both males and females is probably higher than reported. Researchers have found that men diagnosed with eating disorders have higher rates of other psychiatric illness like depression and anxiety

Societal pressure to be thin can cause people to feel fat when they look in the mirror regardless of their body weight. Dissatisfaction with one's body can lead to disordered eating behaviors.

disorders compared with men who do not have eating disorders.[22]

There are several different types of eating disorders, including anorexia nervosa, bulimia nervosa, and binge eating disorder. Each type of eating disorder has specific diagnostic criteria that make the eating disorder unique (see Table 14.8). Night eating syndrome is a form of eating disorder that is not described with specific diagnostic criteria in the *Diagnostic and Statistical Manual* of the American Psychiatric Association.

Anorexia Nervosa Results from Severe Kilocalorie Restriction

Anorexia nervosa is a serious, potentially life-threatening eating disorder that is characterized by self-starvation and excessive weight loss. People who suffer from anorexia nervosa have an intense fear of gaining weight or being "fat." This fear causes them to control their food intake by restricting the amount of food they consume, resulting in significant weight loss.

Many people with anorexia nervosa have a fear of eating certain foods, such as those that contain fat and sugar, or all foods. They believe that these foods will make them "fat," regardless of how little of them they eat. A distorted sense of **body image** is also present because sufferers usually see themselves as fat even though they are underweight. This misperception of body size contributes to the behavior of restricting food intake in order to lose (more) weight. For instance, someone with anorexia nervosa might eat only a piece of fruit and a small container of yogurt during an entire day. Some may also exercise excessively as a means of controlling their weight.

Although the highest rates of disordered eating patterns occur among females, males are not immune. Adolescents in particular can feel pressure to achieve a certain body image.

Numerous health consequences can occur with anorexia nervosa and some can be fatal. One of the most serious health effects is an electrolyte imbalance, specifically low blood potassium, which can occur if someone with anorexia also engages in episodes of purging. An electrolyte imbalance can lead to an irregular heart rhythm. Low blood potassium is the most fatal health effect among people

who have an eating disorder. Additionally, due to their extreme lack of body fat, internal body temperature drops and individuals with this disorder feel cold even when it is hot outside. In an effort to regulate body temperature, their body may begin to grow **lanugo** (downy hair), particularly on the face and arms.

The body of a person with anorexia nervosa is not getting enough nutrients. As a result, the body's processes begin to slow or shut down in an effort to conserve energy for its most vital functions. The person may begin to experience a decrease in heart rate and blood pressure, overall weakness and fatigue, hair loss, and a disruption of hormones resulting in amenorrhea (cessation of menstruation in women). The digestive process also slows down, which often results in constipation, bloating, and delayed gastric emptying. Dehydration, iron deficiency, and osteoporosis can also result from inadequate nutrient intake.

Bulimia Nervosa Involves Cycles of Binge Eating and Purging

Bulimia nervosa is another type of eating disorder that can be life-threatening. During times of binge eating, the person lacks control over eating and consumes larger than normal amounts of food in a short period of time. Following the binge, the person counters the excess food consumption with some type of purging. Many people assume that bulimics purge by vomiting, but self-induced vomiting

anorexia nervosa An eating disorder in which people intentionally starve themselves, causing extreme weight loss.

body image How you perceive your physical appearance.

lanugo Very fine, soft hair on the face and arms of people with anorexia nervosa.

bulimia nervosa An eating disorder characterized by consuming large quantities of food and then purging through vomiting, laxative and diuretic use, and/or excessive physical exercise.

People with bulimia nervosa often eat in secret.

is only one form. Purging can be described as any behavior that assists in "getting rid" of food to prevent weight gain or to promote weight loss. This can include vigorous exercise, abuse of diet pills, laxatives, or diuretics, and strict dieting or fasting.

As with anorexia nervosa, people with bulimia nervosa often suffer from depression and have low self-esteem. They may feel shame and guilt about their eating behaviors, and may try to hide their eating problems from others. Those who have bulimia nervosa are overly concerned with body shape and weight, but usually do not have the same distorted body image as someone with anorexia nervosa.

Most of the health consequences that occur with bulimia nervosa are associated with self-induced vomiting, such as tearing of the esophagus, swollen parotid glands (the salivary glands located on each side of the face in front of the ears), tooth decay and gum disease (due to stomach acid), and broken blood vessels in the eyes (due to pressure from vomiting). One sign of bulimia nervosa is often scar tissue on the knuckles of a person's fingers, which

forms from their being frequently used to induce vomiting. Electrolyte imbalance can occur with bulimia nervosa and can be fatal. People with bulimia nervosa may experience dehydration and constipation due to frequent episodes of binge eating and purging.

Laxative abuse can cause serious medical complications, depending on the type, amount, and length of time the person has used them. Laxatives used repeatedly can cause constipation, dehydration due to fluid loss in the intestines, electrolyte imbalances, fluid retention, bloody stools, and impaired bowel function.

Binge Eating Disorder Involves Compulsive Overeating

Binge eating disorder is characterized by recurrent episodes of binge eating without purging. People who have binge eating disorder eat without regard to physiological cues. They may eat for emotional reasons, which results in an out-of-control feeling while eating and physical and psychological discomfort after eating. Many people who struggle with this type of eating disorder will often eat in secret and feel ashamed about their behaviors.

The health effects of binge eating disorder are most commonly those that are associated with obesity because most people who struggle with binge eating disorder are of normal or heavier-than-average weight. Health effects may include high blood pressure, high cholesterol levels, heart disease, type 2 diabetes, and gallbladder disease.

Other Disordered Eating Behaviors Can Be Harmful

In addition to anorexia nervosa, bulimia nervosa, and binge eating disorder, there are other abnormal eating behaviors that can be harmful and require treatment. These include orthorexia, night eating syndrome, and pica.

Orthorexia is defined as an obsession with "healthy or righteous eating" and often begins with someone's simple desire to live a healthy lifestyle. Someone with orthorexia fixates on defining the "right" foods, and will spend just as much time and energy thinking about food as someone with anorexia nervosa or bulimia nervosa. While this person may not obsess about calories, they think about the overall health benefits and how the food was processed, prepared, etc. Various factors can contribute to this obsession for healthy foods, including hearing something negative about a food or food group, which then leads to completely eliminating the food or foods from their diet. Be aware that the restrictive nature of orthorexia has the potential to develop into anorexia nervosa.

Night eating syndrome is a unique combination of disordered eating, a sleep disorder, and a mood disorder.[23] Someone with this syndrome consumes the majority of daily kilocalories after the evening meal, as well as wakes up during the night, possibly even several times, to eat. In addition, the person typically does not have an appetite during the morning hours and consumes

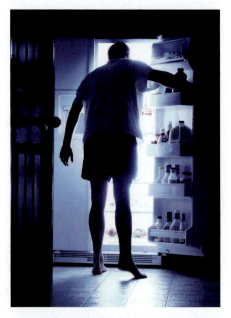

People with night eating syndrome may consume more than half their day's kilocalories between 8 p.m. and 6 a.m.

very little throughout the day. One study found that people with night eating syndrome consume 56 percent of their 24-hour kilocalorie intake between the hours of 8:00 p.m. and 6:00 a.m. This study also found that people with night eating syndrome generally do not binge eat with each awakening; rather, they eat smaller portions of food on several occasions throughout the night.[24]

Pica refers to a strong, persistent desire to eat, lick, or chew nonnutritive substances, such as clay, dirt, or chalk, for a period of at least 1 month. Consuming nonfood substances can cause serious medical complications such as intestinal obstruction, intestinal perforation, infections, or lead poisoning.

Because orthorexia, night eating syndrome, and pica do not meet the diagnostic criteria for anorexia nervosa, bulimia nervosa, or binge eating disorder, but still require treatment, they fall into the diagnostic category of "Feeding and Eating Disorders Not Elsewhere Classified." Other behaviors in this category include purging without binging, restrictive eating by people who are in a normal weight range despite having significant weight loss, binging and purging but not frequently enough to meet criteria for bulimia, and chewing and spitting out food instead of swallowing it.

Different Eating Disorders Have Some Traits and Signs in Common

A common trait of people with eating disorders is perfectionism. Unrealistic standards can produce a sense of failure and lowered self-worth. Many people who struggle with eating disorders are trying to gain some control in their lives. When external factors feel out of control, the person with an eating disorder gets a sense of security from being able to control personal food and weight issues. They may withdraw from social interactions because food is often

present and they do not feel comfortable eating around others. Depression and low self-esteem also exist among many people who have eating disorders.

Most college students today know someone with an eating disorder, but may not know how to help the person. Learning about eating disorders can help individuals understand why a friend or loved one can have destructive eating behaviors and be seemingly unaware of the damage, pain, or danger they can cause. Everyone should be aware of the warning signs of disordered eating behaviors so they can potentially identify them in friends and loved ones (Table 14.9). Take the Self-Assessment "Are You At Risk for an Eating Disorder?" to help you identify potentially problematic eating behaviors.

If you are concerned about someone, find a good time and place to gently express your concerns without criticism or judgment. Realize that you may be rejected or your friend may deny

the problem. Be supportive and let the person know that you are available if they want to talk to you at another time. You should also realize that there are many things that you cannot do to help a loved one or friend get better. You cannot force an anorexic to eat, keep a bulimic from purging, or make a binge eater stop overeating. It is up to the individual to decide when he or she is ready to deal with the issues in life that led to the eating disorder.

Eating Disorders Can Be Treated

The most effective treatment for eating disorders is a multidisciplinary team approach including psychological, medical, and nutrition professionals. All members of the team must be knowledgeable and experienced with eating disorders because it is a complex area; some health care professionals do not feel comfortable treating eating

TABLE 14.9	Warning Signs for Eating Disorders
Symptom	**Explanation/Example**
Weight is below 85% of ideal body weight	Refusal to accept and maintain body weight (even if it is within normal range)
Exercises excessively	Often exercises daily for long periods of time to burn kilocalories and prevent weight gain. May skip work or class to exercise.
Preoccupation with food, weight, and diet	Constantly worries about amount and type of food eaten. May weigh himself or herself daily or several times per day.
Distorted body image	Does not see himself/herself as he or she truly is. May comment on being fat even if underweight.
Refusing to eat	Will avoid food in order to lose weight or prevent weight gain. May avoid only certain foods, such as those with fat and sugar.
Loss of menstrual period	Periods become irregular or completely absent
Diet pill use or laxative use	Evidence of pill bottles, boxes, or packaging
Changes in mood	May become more withdrawn, depressed, or anxious, especially around food
Hair loss	Hair becomes thinner and falls out in large quantities
Avoids eating around others	Wants to eat alone. Makes excuses to avoid eating with others.

Are You at Risk for an Eating Disorder?

Mark the following statements True or False to help you find out.

1. I constantly think about eating, weight, and body size.

   True ☐   **False** ☐

2. I'm terrified about being overweight.

   True ☐   **False** ☐

3. I binge eat and can't stop until I feel sick.

   True ☐   **False** ☐

4. I weigh myself several times each day.

   True ☐   **False** ☐

5. I exercise too much or get very rigid about my exercise plan.

   True ☐   **False** ☐

6. I have taken laxatives or forced myself to vomit after eating.

   True ☐   **False** ☐

7. I believe food controls my life.

   True ☐   **False** ☐

8. I feel extremely guilty after eating.

   True ☐   **False** ☐

9. I eat when I am nervous, anxious, lonely, or depressed.

   True ☐   **False** ☐

10. I believe my weight controls what I do.

    True ☐   **False** ☐

Analysis

These statements are designed to help you identify potentially problematic eating behavior. These statements do *not* tell you if you have an eating disorder. Look carefully at any statement you marked as True and decide if this behavior prevents you from enjoying life or makes you unhealthy. Changing these behaviors should be done gradually, making small changes one at a time. Contact your student health services center or your health care provider if you suspect you need help.

---

disorders. A physician or other medical professional should closely monitor anyone who struggles with an eating disorder, as some eating disorders can be life-threatening. In severe cases, a physician may require the patient to be hospitalized as part of the treatment. A psychologist can help the person deal with emotional and other psychological issues that may be contributing to the eating disorder.

A Registered Dietitian Nutritionist can help someone with an eating disorder establish normal eating behaviors. Some nutritional approaches to eating disorders include identifying binge triggers, safe and unsafe foods, and hunger and fullness cues. Food journals are often helpful to identify eating patterns, food choices, moods, disordered eating triggers, eating cues, and timing of meals and snacks. Meal plans are also used in some instances to ensure adequate kilocalorie and nutrient intake among those with anorexia nervosa, and to help avoid overeating among those with bulimia nervosa or binge eating disorder.

Most people can recover from an eating disorder and may not have to struggle with it for the rest of their lives. When treatment is sought in the early stages, there is a better chance that the person will recover fully and have a shorter recovery process than someone who begins treatment after many years. Some people continue to have the desire to engage in disordered eating behaviors; however, they are able to refrain from actually doing these behaviors. Unfortunately, some individuals may never fully recover from an eating disorder. Caregivers must recognize that recovery is a process that often takes years and has no "quick fix."

LO 14.6: THE TAKE-HOME MESSAGE

Disordered eating is characterized by an abnormal eating pattern. Eating disorders include disordered eating behaviors and other specific diagnostic criteria. The most common eating disorders include anorexia nervosa, bulimia nervosa, and binge eating disorder. Eating disorders are most effectively treated with a multidisciplinary team of psychologists, physicians, and Registered Dietitian Nutritionists. A full recovery takes time but is possible, especially if the disorder is treated in the early stages.

Visual Chapter Summary

Lo 14.1 Energy Balance Is Achieved When Energy In Equals Energy Out

Energy balance is the relationship between energy consumed and energy expended. Body weight remains constant when energy intake equals energy expenditure. When more energy is consumed than expended, the body is in positive energy balance and weight gain occurs. When the intake of kilocalories falls short of energy needs or you expend more energy than you consume, the body is in negative energy balance and weight loss occurs.

ENERGY INTAKE = ENERGY EXPENDITURE

WEIGHT MAINTENANCE

Lo 14.2 Three Factors Contribute to TDEE

Total daily energy expenditure is based on basal metabolic rate (BMR), the thermic effect of food (TEF), and the thermic effect of exercise (TEE), or physical activities.

The BMR is influenced mainly by lean body mass, and is also affected by age, gender, body size, genes, ethnicity, emotional and physical stress, thyroid hormone levels, nutritional state, and environmental temperature.

The thermic effect of exercise (TEE) includes the energy required to walk, talk, run, exercise, and maintain posture while standing and sitting. One component of TEE, non-exercise activity thermogenesis, or NEAT, is the energy used for all activity that is not structured exercise, including unconscious muscle activity. Adaptive thermogenesis adds to TDEE by producing heat in response to environmental changes such as stress, temperature changes, or diet.

The thermic effect of food—energy used to process recently eaten foods—has a small but positive impact on total daily energy expenditure.

Total Daily Energy Expenditure (TDEE)

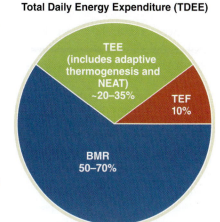

TEE (includes adaptive thermogenesis and NEAT) ~20–35%

TEF 10%

BMR 50–70%

Lo 14.3 Energy Expenditure Can Be Measured Directly or Indirectly

Energy expenditure can be measured directly with a metabolic chamber or indirectly based on oxygen consumed and carbon dioxide produced during activity. The estimated energy requirement (EER) can be calculated using an individual's age, weight, height, and physical activity level.

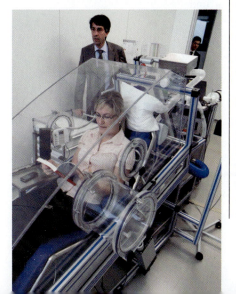

Lo 14.4 Body Composition Is Comprised of Lean Body Mass and Fat

Body composition refers to the ratio of fat to lean body mass and is measured as a percent body fat. Total body fat is comprised of essential fat, found in bone marrow, organs, muscles, and the central nervous system, and storage fat, found in adipose tissue. Stored fat can be visceral, located around the organs, or subcutaneous, located just beneath the skin. White adipose tissue is primarily a storage tissue; brown adipose tissue contains more mitochondria, is rich in blood, and generates heat.

The placement of body fat also affects overall health. Storing excess fat around the waist has been shown to increase the risk of heart disease, diabetes, and hypertension. The more visceral fat stored around the abdomen located near the liver, the greater the risk of insulin resistance, hyperlipidemia, and low levels of HDL cholesterol, all of which increase the risk of heart disease and diabetes.

The most accurate instrument to measure body composition is dual-energy X-ray absorptiometry (DEXA). Body composition is also estimated from body volume using hydrostatic weighing and air displacement plethysmography. Bioelectrical impedance analysis measures resistance by body fat; skinfold calipers estimate subcutaneous fat; and waist circumference measures android obesity.

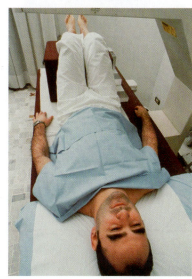

LO 14.5 BMI Is Used to Determine Body Weight and Health Risks

Reference standards have been developed as indirect measurements of a healthy body weight. Body mass index (BMI) is a calculation of body weight related to height and is correlated with disease risk. A BMI of 18.5 to 24.9 is considered healthy. A BMI from 25 to 29.9 is considered overweight and a BMI of 30 or greater is considered obese. A BMI lower than 18.5 is considered underweight.

Overweight and obesity increases the individual's risk of heart disease, hypertension, stroke, and hyperlipidemia. Other factors, including type 2 diabetes, metabolic syndrome, osteoarthritis, and certain cancers, are also associated with overweight and obesity, and the risk increases as BMI increases.

Too little body fat can affect body functions and impair health. A BMI of less than 18.5 is considered underweight and may be a sign of malnutrition.

Extremely High Risk
BMI 40+ and high waist circumference

Very High Risk
BMI 30–39.9 and high waist circumference

High Risk
BMI 25–29.9 and high waist circumference
or
BMI 30–34.9 and low waist circumference

Increased Risk
BMI 25–29.9 and low waist circumference

Low Risk
BMI under 25

LO 14.6 Disordered Eating and Eating Disorders Have Common Traits and Treatments

Disordered eating describes a variety of abnormal eating patterns, such as restrictive eating, binge eating, vomiting after eating, and abusing laxatives or diet pills. Eating disorders are diagnosed by meeting specific criteria that include disordered eating behaviors.

Anorexia nervosa is characterized by self-starvation and excessive weight loss. Bulimia nervosa involves repeated cycles of binge eating and purging. Binge eating disorders are characterized by binge eating without purging. Night eating syndrome is described as excessive kilocalorie intake in the evening and waking up during the night to eat.

The most effective treatment for eating disorders involves a multidisciplinary team approach including psychological, nutrition, and medical professionals.

Terms to Know

- energy balance
- positive energy balance
- negative energy balance
- bomb calorimeter
- physiological fuel values
- total daily energy expenditure (TDEE)
- basal metabolism
- basal metabolic rate (BMR)
- lean body mass (LBM)
- resting metabolic rate (RMR)
- thermic effect of exercise (TEE)
- non-exercise activity thermogenesis (NEAT)
- thermic effect of food (TEF)
- thermogenesis
- direct calorimetry
- indirect calorimetry
- estimated energy requirement (EER)
- body composition
- essential fat
- adipose tissue
- subcutaneous fat
- visceral fat
- brown adipose tissue (BAT)
- central (android) obesity
- gynoid obesity
- hydrostatic weighing
- air displacement plethysmography
- dual-energy X-ray absorptiometry (DEXA)
- bioelectrical impedance analysis (BIA)
- skinfold caliper
- waist circumference
- body mass index (BMI)
- healthy weight
- overweight
- obese
- underweight
- severe obesity
- disordered eating
- eating disorders
- anorexia nervosa
- body image
- lanugo
- bulimia nervosa

MasteringNutrition™

To hear an MP3 chapter review, scan here or visit the Study Area in MasteringNutrition.

Check Your Understanding

1. An individual who is regularly in negative energy balance will most likely
   a. lose weight.
   b. gain weight.
   c. maintain current body weight.
   d. burn more muscle weight than fat weight.

2. Kyle has a BMI of 27. He is considered
   a. underweight.
   b. overweight.
   c. at a healthy weight.
   d. obese.

3. Central or android obesity refers to
   a. the excess accumulation of fat around the hips and thighs.
   b. the excess accumulation of fat in the abdomen.
   c. the excess accumulation of fat in the arms and legs.
   d. the excess accumulation of subcutaneous fat.

4. The basal metabolic rate (BMR) refers to
   a. the amount of energy expended during physical activity.
   b. the amount of energy expended during digestion.
   c. the amount of energy consumed daily.
   d. the amount of energy expended to meet basic physiological needs that enable the organs and cells to function.

5. Fat surrounding the vital organs within the abdomen is called
   a. subcutaneous fat.
   b. visceral fat.
   c. brown adipose tissue.
   d. cellulite.

6. The method that uses the fact that lean tissue is denser than water to measure body composition is called
   a. air displacement plethysmography.
   b. bioelectrical impedance analysis.
   c. dual-energy X-ray absorptiometry.
   d. hydrostatic weighing.

7. For most adults, BMR accounts for _____ percent of the total daily energy expenditure.
   a. 15
   b. 30
   c. 50
   d. 60

8. Which of the following statements is true?
   a. Lean body mass is more metabolically active than fat tissue.
   b. Women generally have less essential fat than men.
   c. Nicotine depresses the BMR.
   d. African-Americans have BMRs that are about 10 percent higher than Caucasians'.

9. Will's breakfast contains 525 kilocalories. How many kilocalories will he expend (TEF) to process this meal?
   a. 5 to 10 kilocalories
   b. 50 to 100 kilocalories
   c. 125 to 140 kilocalories
   d. 150 to 175 kilocalories

10. Eating disorders include all of the following except
    a. bulimia nervosa.
    b. binge eating disorder.
    c. anorexia nervosa.
    d. night eating syndrome.

Answers

1. (a) Negative energy balance means the amount of energy intake is less than the energy output. If maintained over time, negative energy balance most likely results in weight loss.

2. (b) Because Kyle's BMI falls between 25 and 29.9, he is considered overweight. If his BMI was under 18.5, he would be underweight, whereas a BMI of 18.5 to 24.9 would put him in the healthy weight category. A BMI of 30 or higher is considered obese.

3. (b) Central obesity refers to the accumulation of excess fat in the stomach area and can be determined by measuring a person's waist circumference. Central obesity increases the risk of heart disease, diabetes, and hypertension. Excess accumulation of fat around the hips and thighs is called gynoid obesity.

4. (d) BMR refers to the minimum amount of energy needed to maintain cellular functions and keep blood circulating and lungs breathing. The amount of energy expended during physical activity is not factored into the BMR. The energy cost of digesting, absorbing, and processing food is called the thermic effect of food (TEF) and is also not part of BMR. The amount of energy consumed is part of the energy intake and doesn't factor into the BMR.

5. (b) Fat deposits that surround the vital organs within the abdomen are called visceral fat. Subcutaneous fat is sandwiched between the muscle and skin in various locations throughout the body. Brown adipose tissue is found in infants and children (and in adults in small amounts) and produces heat rather than storing excess fat. Cellulite is subcutaneous fat trapped in the connective tissue under the skin.

6. (d) Hydrostatic weighing is the method used to measure body composition based on the fact that lean tissue is denser than water. Air

displacement plethysmography is based on the amount of air the body displaces. Bioelectrical impedance measures the resistance of a current by body fat, and dual-energy X-ray absorptiometry measures body fat by passing X-rays through fat-free mass and fat mass.

7. (d) For most adults, BMR accounts for approximately 60 percent of the total daily energy expenditure. The more active you are, the less influence the BMR has on the total daily energy expenditure.

8. (a) Lean body mass is more metabolically active than fat tissue and requires more kilocalories to maintain. Women have four times as much essential fat as men. Nicotine raises the BMR and African-Americans have lower BMRs than Caucasians.

9. (b) The thermic effect of food costs approximately 10 percent of the total kilocalories to process a normal mixed meal. Ten percent of 525 kilocalories equals 52 kilocalories.

10. (d) All of these terms except night eating syndrome are considered a form of eating disorder. Night eating syndrome is a combination of disordered eating and a sleep and mood disorder.

Answers to True or False?

1. **True.** Technically, exercise isn't necessary to produce a negative energy balance. It is, however, the best approach to prevent a drop in basal metabolism, and to promote health benefits.

2. **False.** Having a BMI of less than 18.5 indicates a state of underweight. Being underweight increases the risk of serious health consequences, including anemia, heart irregularities, osteoporosis, amenorrhea, depression, and anxiety.

3. **True.** Males have a higher BMR than females mostly because they have more muscle mass and lower levels of essential fat. This higher BMR results in higher energy expenditure.

4. **True.** The *Dietary Guidelines for Americans* recommend using weight for height or body mass index calculations to estimate whether you are at a healthy weight.

5. **False.** Android obesity, or storing excess fat around the abdomen, puts an individual at higher risk for cardiovascular disease and diabetes than does gynoid obesity, which is the storage of excess fat around the hips.

6. **False.** Body weight measures the amount of total body fat plus lean body mass, but does not assess the amounts of each, while body composition indicates the ratios of body fat to total body weight and lean body mass to total body weight.

7. **False.** If you eat an extra 100 kilocalories per day for a week, that is equal to 700 additional kilocalories, not the 3,500 kilocalories needed to gain a pound.

8. **False.** The most accurate techniques for measuring body composition are the densitometry measurements, including underwater hydrostatic weighing, air displacement plethysmography, and DEXA scans. However, skinfold calipers are often the least expensive and most practical method for individuals measuring body composition in a gym or recreation center, rather than at a lab.

9. **False.** Disordered eating describes a variety of eating patterns considered abnormal and potentially harmful. Eating disorders are diagnosed by meeting specific criteria that include disordered eating behaviors as well as other factors. It is possible for someone to have *disordered eating* without having an actual eating disorder.

10. **True.** The long-term starvation of anorexia nervosa and consistent purging of bulimia nervosa (which can lead to electrolyte imbalance) can be fatal.

Web Resources

- For more on overweight and obesity, visit the Centers for Disease Control and Prevention at www.cdc.gov.
- For more information on assessing body composition and health risks, visit the National Heart, Lung and Blood Institute at www.nhlbi.nih.gov.
- Additional information on eating disorders and their prevention and treatment can be found at the National Eating Disorders Association at www.nationaleatingdisorders.org.

References

1. Merrill, A. L., and B. K. Watt. 1973. *Energy Values of Foods: Basis and Derivation.* Agricultural Handbook no. 74, Washington, DC: USDA.
2. Pedersen, S. J., P. D. Cooley, and C. Mainsbridge. 2013. An E-Health Intervention Designed to Increase Workday Energy Expenditure by Reducing Prolonged Occupational Sitting Habits. *Work* doi 10.3233/WOR-131644.
3. Levine, J. A., N. L. Eberhardt, and M. D. Jensen. 1999. Leptin Responses to Overfeeding: Relationship with Body Fat and Non-Exercise Activity Thermogenesis. *Journal of Clinical Endocrinology & Metabolism* 84:2751–2754.
4. Pederson. 2013. An E-Health Intervention Designed to Increase Workday Energy Expenditure by Reducing Prolonged Occupational Sitting Habits.
5. Apolzan, J. W., H. J. Leidy, R. D. Mattes, and W. W. Campbell. 2011. Effects of Food Form on Food Intake and Postprandial Appetite Sensations, Glucose and Endocrine Responses, and Energy Expenditure in Resistance Trained v. Sedentary Older Adults. *British Journal of Nutrition* 106(7):1107–1116.
6. Granata, G. P., and L. Brandon. 2002. The Thermic Effect of Food and Obesity: Discrepant Results and Methodological Variations. *Nutrition Reviews* 60(8): 223–233.
7. Food and Nutrition Board. 2005. *Dietary Reference Intakes for Energy, Carbohydrate, Fiber, Fat, Fatty Acids, Cholesterol, Protein, and Amino Acids (Macronutrients).* Washington, DC: National Academies Press.
8. Orava, J., L. Nummenmaa, T. Noponen, T. Viljanen, R. Parkkola, P. Nuutila, and K. A. Virtanen. 2014. Brown Adipose Tissue Function Is Accompanied by Cerebral Activation in Lean But Not in Obese

Humans. *Journal of Cerebral Blood Flow and Metabolism* doi: 10.1038/jcbfm.2014.50.

9. National Institutes of Health. 2000. *Clinical Guidelines on the Identification, Evaluation, and Treatment of Overweight and Obesity in Adults.* Available at www.nhlbi.nih.gov. Accessed May 2014.

10. Ibid.

11. Ibid.

12. Centers for Disease Control and Prevention. 2013. *Body Mass Index: Considerations for Practioners.* Available at www.cdc.gov. Accessed May 2014.

13. National Institutes of Health. 2000. *Clinical Guidelines on the Identification, Evaluation, and Treatment of Overweight and Obesity in Adults.*

14. Centers for Disease Control and Prevention. 2011. *Assessing Your Weight.* Available at www.cdc.gov. Accessed May 2014.

15. Shekharappa, R., J. S. Smilee, P. T. Mallikarjuan, K. J. Vadavathi, and M. P. Iayarajan. 2011. Correlation between Body Mass Index and Cardiovascular Parameters in Obese and Non-Obese in Different Age Groups. *International Journal of Biological and Medical Research* 2:551–555.

16. National Institutes of Health. 1998. *Clinical Guidelines on the Identification, Evaluation, and Treatment of Overweight and Obesity in Adults.* Available at www.nhlbi.nih.gov. Accessed May 2014.

17. Hammond, K. 2012. Intake: Analysis of the Diet. In L. Mahan, S. Scott-Stump, and J. L. Raymond, eds. *Krause's Food and Nutrition Care Process.* 13th ed. Philadelphia: Elsevier Saunders.

18. Centers for Disease Control and Prevention. 2013. *The Health Effects of Overweight and Obesity.* Available at www.cdc.gov. Accessed May 2014.

19. Wade, T. D., A. Keski-Rakonen, and J. Hudson. 2011. Epidemiology of Eating Disorders. In M. Tsuang and M. Tohen, eds. *Textbook in Psychiatric Epidemiology.* 3rd ed. New York: Wiley, 343–360.

20. Schoenefeld, S. J., and J. B. Webb. 2013. Self-Compassion and Intuitive Eating in College Women: Examining the Contributions of Distress Tolerance and Body Image Acceptance and Action. *Eating Behaviors* 14(4):493–496.

21. Räisänen, U., and K. Hunt. 2014. The Role of Gendered Constructions of Eating Disorders in Delayed Help-Seeking in Men: A Qualitative Interview Study. *British Medical Journal Open* 4(4):e004342.

22. Woodside, D. B., P. E. Garfinkel, E. Lin, P. Goering, A. S. Kaplan, D. S. Goldbloom, and S. H. Kennedy. 2001. Comparisons of Men with Full or Partial Eating Disorders, Men without Eating Disorders, and Women with Eating Disorders in the Community. *American Journal of Psychiatry* 158:570–574.

23. Birketvedt, G. S., J. Florholmen, J. Sundsfjord, B. Osterud, D. Dinges, W. Bilker, and A. Stunkard. 1999. Behavioral and Neuroendocrine Characteristics of the Night Eating Syndrome. *Journal of the American Medical Association* 282:657–663.

24. Ibid.

15 Weight Management

Learning Outcomes

After reading this chapter, you will be able to:

15.1 Explain why weight management is important to health and well-being.

15.2 Define the terms appetite, hunger, and satiety, and describe the physiological factors involved in regulating food intake.

15.3 Describe the role of hyperplasia and hypertrophy of adipocytes in the development of obesity.

15.4 Discuss the role of genetics and the environment in the development of underweight, overweight, and obesity.

15.5 Describe the role of diet and exercise in achieving a reasonable rate of weight loss.

15.6 Design a food and exercise plan to maintain a healthy weight.

15.7 Describe the role of diet and exercise in achieving a healthy weight gain.

15.8 Describe the role of weight-loss drugs and surgery for reducing obesity.

True or False?

1. Healthy weight loss occurs only with at least 2 hours of daily exercise. **T/F**

2. The body stops synthesizing fat cells after adolescence. **T/F**

3. Grazing throughout the day helps curb appetite and control body weight. **T/F**

4. Losing even 10 pounds can improve health. **T/F**

5. Genetics and the environment both affect body weight. **T/F**

6. Eating *more* vegetables and fruits can help an individual lose weight. **T/F**

7. Obesity is the result of consuming more energy than is expended. **T/F**

8. The nutrient that has the most effect on satiety is fat. **T/F**

9. You don't need to diet and exercise if you are taking a weight-loss drug. **T/F**

10. Bariatric surgery results in weight loss without restricting food intake. **T/F**

See page 580 for the answers.

In the last two decades, rates of overweight and obesity have exploded in the United States. In the early 1960s, fewer than 32 percent of Americans were overweight.[1] Today, that number has risen to an alarming 67 percent of Americans classified as overweight, and more than 33 percent of adults (about 72 million people) and 17 percent of children are obese.[2] Not surprisingly, as more and more individuals cross the threshold from a healthy body weight to being overweight, the topic has garnered much interest in popular culture. In fact, people often turn to social media sites such as Facebook, Pinterest, and Twitter to talk about weight management, and locate helpful tools to help manage their body weight.[3]

Despite its prevalence, people do not enjoy being overweight, and regularly spend large amounts of money in search of a "cure." In fact, Americans annually spend over $60 billion[4] on everything from over-the-counter diet pills to books, magazines, online support groups, and commercial dieting centers to help shed their excess weight. It has been estimated that 21 percent of the total U.S. health care budget is spent to treat the medical complications associated with being overweight.[5]

If you are currently struggling with your weight or know someone who is, don't despair. Weight loss takes work, but it is achievable. This chapter emphasizes the key components of how to achieve and sustain a healthy body weight.

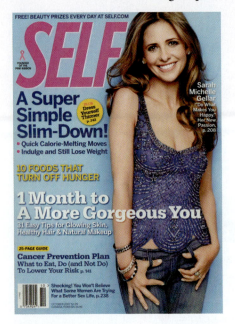

Weight management is such a hot topic in the United States that it is frequently covered by the mainstream media.

Why Is Weight Management Important?

LO 15.1 Explain why weight management is important to health and well-being.

The term **weight management** means maintaining body weight within a healthy range. Achieving a healthy body weight is essential for physical and emotional well-being. It helps you feel good about yourself, provides the energy you need to enjoy life, and lowers the risk of chronic disease.

Being Overweight or Underweight Carries Health Risks

As you learned in Chapter 14, a healthy weight is a body weight that doesn't increase the risk of developing any weight-related health problems or diseases.[6] For someone who is overweight, improving one's overall health profile can be achieved with a weight loss of as little as five to ten percent of body weight.[7] For example, if you currently weigh 200 pounds, a weight loss of 10 to 20 pounds can reduce your risk of hypertension, cardiac disease, and type 2 diabetes. In contrast, being underweight can also lead to numerous diseases and conditions. Individuals who are underweight are more likely to lack vital nutrients, such as calcium, which is important to maintain strong, dense bones. Being underweight increases the risk for osteoporosis later in life.[8] Sustaining a normal, healthy body weight can reduce this risk.

The AMA Considers Obesity a Disease

When Medicare first created a list of diseases that it would cover, obesity was not on the list. That changed in 2013 when the American Medical Association declared

weight management Maintaining a healthy body weight; defined as having a BMI of 18.5 to 24.9.

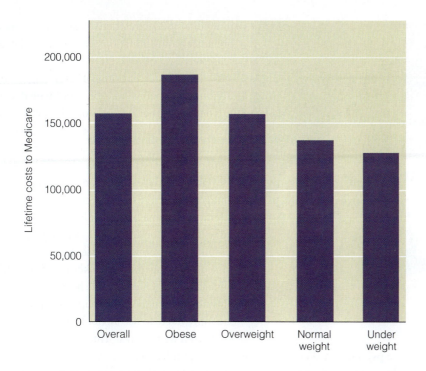

◀ Figure 15.1 The Lifetime Health Care Costs of Obesity Compared with Overweight, Normal Weight, and Underweight Adults

Source: D. N. Lakdawalla, D. P. Goldman, and B. Shang. 2005. "The Health and Cost Consequences of Obesity among the Future Elderly." *Health Affairs—Web Exclusive* W5-R30–W5-R41.

obesity a *multi-metabolic and hormonal disease state.*[9] This new classification of obesity as a disease may either focus more attention and resources on the problem, opening the door for the 90 million obese Americans to receive treatment for their obesity, or it may discourage their efforts to change.

At first glance, declaring obesity a disease makes good sense. This classification gives a clear warning of the health hazards of being overweight and may provide additional benefits. For example, declaring obesity a disease may make it easier for patients to receive weight-management counseling and encourage insurance companies to pay for weight-loss medications. More research funding may become available to address the obesity problem in the United States and potentially lessen the stigma of being obese.

However, there are also downsides. The cost of treating obesity will most likely skyrocket. As shown in **Figure 15.1**, the costs for treating obese individuals are several thousand dollars higher than for their lean counterparts. It has been estimated that each pound of extra body weight above normal could add up to $13 a year in added medical costs for men and up to $45 for women.[10]

Viewing obesity as a disease may also change the way medical professionals and overweight individuals approach weight management. It may encourage the use of more drugs and surgical procedures to address the obesity epidemic, rather than lifestyle changes. The obesity-as-a-disease message suggests that body weight is uncontrollable, like a chronic disease, and may hinder weight management efforts that focus on healthy eating and concern for body weight.

Being Overweight or Underweight Carries Social and Psychological Risks

Beyond the physical effects of carrying too much body weight, obese and overweight individuals are often at a social, educational, and economic disadvantage. Overweight people suffer more discrimination and are more likely to be denied job promotions and raises than normal-weight individuals.[11] Obese females are less likely to be accepted into college, especially higher-ranked schools.[12] Social situations, such as attending movies or sporting events, and travel on buses and airplanes may be limited for obese

Overweight and obese people are often embarrassed to exercise in a gym or change clothes in a locker room because of their body weight.

individuals due to restrictive seat sizes.[13] These prejudices and limitations can result in lower self-esteem.[14]

Popular perceptions of overweight individuals as being lazy or weak-willed can further affect their feelings of self-confidence and self-worth.[15] Images of slender models as the ideal in advertising and other media help perpetuate the notion that overweight individuals are less desirable. Living in an antagonistic environment may compromise attempts at achieving a healthy body weight. For example, obese and overweight people are less likely to exercise because they are embarrassed to change in the locker room or work out at a gym.[16] Obese people have higher rates of suicide than healthy-weight people[17] and are more likely to use alcohol and drugs when compared with their normal-weight peers.[18]

The psychological consequences of being underweight can be just as debilitating as being obese. Research has suggested that people who are underweight are at greater risk for irritability, anger, and depression.[19] For example, underweight males are reported to have a 12 percent increased risk of committing suicide compared with healthy-weight males.[20] People who are underweight can be more socially withdrawn compared with those with a healthy body weight.[21]

> **LO 15.1: THE TAKE-HOME MESSAGE** Weight management means maintaining a healthy weight to reduce the risk of specific health problems. Classifying obesity as a disease may improve treatment options but may also raise health care costs, increase drug and surgical procedures, and may hamper lifestyle changes to lose weight. Weight management may reduce the social and psychological effects of obesity and underweight, which includes discrimination, low self-esteem, depression, suicide, and alcohol and drug problems.

How Is Food Intake Regulated?

LO 15.2 Define the terms appetite, hunger, and satiety, and describe the physiological factors involved in regulating food intake.

Why do you feel hungry or full? There are a variety of factors that influence not only how much we eat, but also the type of food we choose to eat. These factors include strong physiological and psychological influences that go beyond the need for energy.

Appetite Often Triggers Eating for Unnecessary Reasons

Distinguishing between true hunger and **appetite,** or the desire to eat based on other factors, can be difficult. Have you ever groaned after a huge meal, "I'm so full!" only to turn around and eat a thick slice of apple pie with ice cream? Appetite is often stimulated even when we are satiated. This desire to eat the apple pie may be triggered by the smell, taste, texture, or color of the food, or by external cues such as time of day, social occasions, or other people. Appetite can also be triggered by learned behavior, and by emotions such as stress, fear, and depression. Identifying

appetite The desire to eat food whether or not there is hunger; a taste for particular foods and cravings in reaction to cues such as the sight, smell, or thought of food.

the triggers that affect your desire to eat is one of the key strategies in maintaining a healthy body weight.

Hunger and Satiation Affect the Desire to Eat and Stop Eating

Two strong physiological factors, hunger and satiety, affect the amounts of food individuals consume. **Hunger** is the physical sensation associated with the need or intense desire for food. Physiological signals such as low blood sugar or an empty stomach trigger hunger and searching for food. Once eating begins, hunger subsides as the feeling of fullness, or **satiation,** sets in and you stop eating. **Satiety** describes how you feel after a meal and before hunger is triggered again.

Satiety and hunger are both controlled by hormones produced in the brain and the gastrointestinal tract. In the brain, two regions of the hypothalamus control the trigger mechanisms that stimulate hunger and satiety: the *ventromedial nucleus* and the *lateral hypothalamus*. These regions receive signals from both inside and outside the brain. **Focus Figure 15.2** explains the signals that control hunger and satiation.

Satiety

Satiety is triggered in the ventromedial nucleus in response to a variety of physiological cues. After a meal, the stomach becomes distended, sending signals from stretch receptors in the lining of the stomach to the brain to suppress hunger. As protein, fatty acids, and monosaccharides reach the small intestine, two hormones, cholecystokinin (CCK) and peptide YY (PYY), are released, sending feedback to the hypothalamus to increase satiety and decrease hunger.[22] Once these nutrients are absorbed, the hormone insulin is released, which also results in a decrease in hunger.[23]

Other hormones, including leptin, produced in adipose tissue, influence satiety. The production of leptin is controlled by the obese gene (*ob*) and increases in amount as the fat stores increase. Leptin is a satiety signal. It acts on receptors found in the hypothalamus to decrease hunger and food intake, probably by inhibiting neuropeptide Y (NPY), a hormone that stimulates hunger. At the same time, leptin creates a negative energy balance by raising the body temperature, which in turn increases energy expenditure and stimulates the oxidation of fatty acids in the liver and muscles. Thus, leptin regulates the amount of fat stored in the adipose tissue.[24]

In addition to the influence of hormones, certain macronutrients, especially protein, influence satiety and reduce the intake of food. Researchers have reported that protein intake ranging from 15 to 30 percent of total kilocalorie intake significantly reduces food intake.[25]

Hunger

While the ventromedial nucleus affects satiety, the lateral hypothalamus controls hunger. The hormone ghrelin, produced in the gastric cells of the stomach, stimulates the lateral hypothalamus. Thus ghrelin has the opposite effect of leptin—it stimulates hunger. Ghrelin concentrations rise in the blood before a meal. Ghrelin travels through the blood to the hypothalamus, where it activates neuropeptide Y to stimulate hunger.

The production of ghrelin changes throughout the day. More ghrelin is produced between meals, during sleep, or when you fast. This increase in ghrelin production signals the hypothalamus that the body needs energy. Ghrelin levels drop following a meal, especially one that contains high amounts of carbohydrate and/or kilocalories. This drop in ghrelin levels signals satiety and decreases the urge to eat.

Lean individuals tend to have higher levels of ghrelin than individuals with more body fat, especially in the morning hours. Ghrelin levels increase when an

Hunger is stimulated by circulating hormones and signals from your intestinal tract.

hunger A strong sensation indicating a physiological need for food.

satiation The state of being satisfactorily full during a meal, which inhibits the ability to eat more food.

satiety The feeling of satiation or "fullness" after a meal before hunger sets in again.

The Brain Controls Hunger and Satiation

Two regions of the brain—the ventromedial nucleus and the lateral hypothalamus—control eating behaviors in response to hormones released from the stomach, pancreas, small intestine, adipocytes, and the hypothalamus. The ventromedial nucleus responds to hormones to stimulate satiety. Hunger is triggered by hormones that stimulate the lateral hypothalamus.

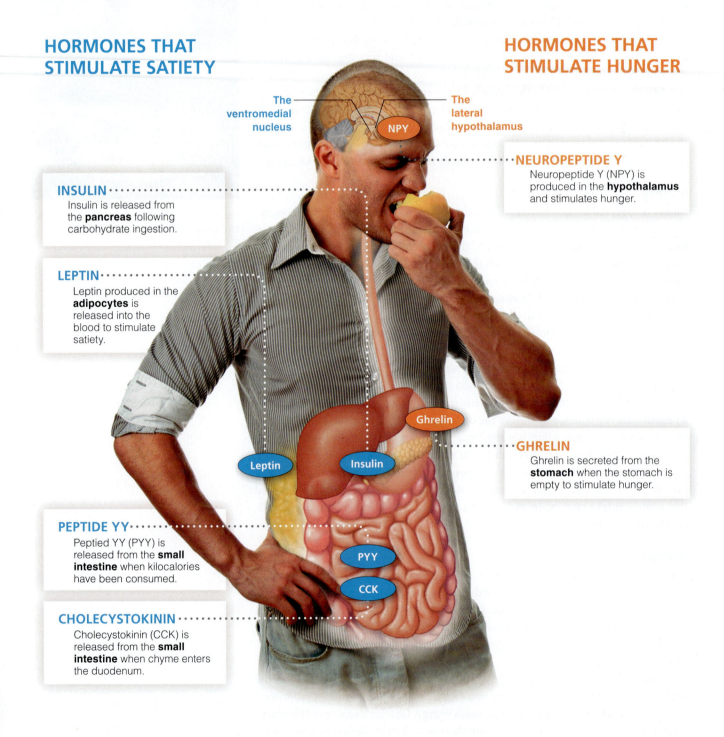

HORMONES THAT STIMULATE SATIETY

HORMONES THAT STIMULATE HUNGER

The ventromedial nucleus

The lateral hypothalamus

NPY

INSULIN
Insulin is released from the **pancreas** following carbohydrate ingestion.

NEUROPEPTIDE Y
Neuropeptide Y (NPY) is produced in the **hypothalamus** and stimulates hunger.

LEPTIN
Leptin produced in the **adipocytes** is released into the blood to stimulate satiety.

Ghrelin

Leptin

Insulin

GHRELIN
Ghrelin is secreted from the **stomach** when the stomach is empty to stimulate hunger.

PEPTIDE YY
Peptied YY (PYY) is released from the **small intestine** when kilocalories have been consumed.

PYY

CCK

CHOLECYSTOKININ
Cholecystokinin (CCK) is released from the **small intestine** when chyme enters the duodenum.

individual is on a low-kilocalorie diet, which may be one reason people on weight-reduction diets are hungry and find it difficult to lose weight.[26]

Leptin may also be partly responsible for hunger. When adipocytes shrink during weight loss, leptin levels drop. This reduction in leptin stimulates hunger and may drive the body to eat more to reestablish fat stores.

Certain vitamins and minerals have been shown to lower leptin concentrations and affect hunger levels. For example, zinc supplements have been reported to lower leptin in obese individuals and may be responsible for overeating.[27] On the other hand, ingesting too little vitamin A and C also appears to inhibit leptin secretion.[28] The mechanism of how vitamin and mineral intake affects the hormone leptin and hunger is still unclear.

> **LO 15.2: THE TAKE-HOME MESSAGE** Food intake is controlled by hunger, satiation and satiety, and appetite. Appetite is the desire for food controlled by psychological factors. Hunger is a strong physiological need for food and satiety is the physiological response to food intake, resulting in satisfaction. Hunger, satiation, and satiety are controlled by the hypothalamus and regulated by neuropeptides, hormones, and neural signals from the gastrointestinal tract and adipocytes. The hormones leptin and ghrelin play key roles in triggering hunger and satiety, with ghrelin triggering hunger and leptin triggering satiation.

How Do Fat Cells Form and Expand?

LO 15.3 Describe the role of hyperplasia and hypertrophy of adipocytes in the development of obesity.

The increase in the stores of body fat occurs in two ways: (1) fat cells (adipocytes) can expand to store more fat in a process known as **hypertrophy,** and (2) once a fat cell fills to capacity, it stimulates the production of more fat cells in a process known as **hyperplasia.** The excess cells build up into excess fat tissue, which is stored throughout the body (**Figure 15.3**).

The Number of Fat Cells in the Body Never Decreases

The average non-obese adult's body contains approximately 30 billion to 50 billion adipocytes, each of which holds between 0.4 and 0.5 micrograms of fat. Overweight or obese adults most likely have the same number of adipocytes as normal-weight adults but their fat cells are much larger, holding between 0.6 and 1.2 micrograms of fat. Thus, when a normal-weight adult gains weight, it is due to hypertrophy, or the expansion of the size of the fat cells. When an overweight or obese adult loses

hypertrophy An increase in size; in adipocytes, hypertrophy refers to the increase in size of the cells.

hyperplasia An increase in the number of cells due to cell division.

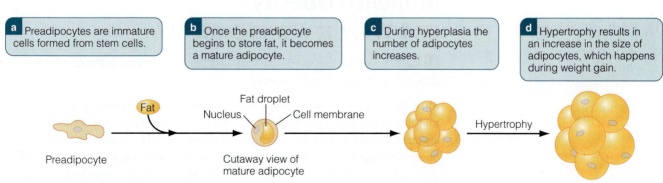

a Preadipocytes are immature cells formed from stem cells.

b Once the preadipocyte begins to store fat, it becomes a mature adipocyte.

c During hyperplasia the number of adipocytes increases.

d Hypertrophy results in an increase in the size of adipocytes, which happens during weight gain.

Fat droplet

Fat

Nucleus — Cell membrane

Hypertrophy

Preadipocyte

Cutaway view of mature adipocyte

▲ Figure 15.3 **The Formation of Adipocytes**

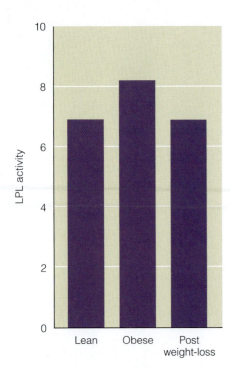

▲ **Figure 15.4 Lipoprotein Lipase Activity in Lean, Obese, and Post–Weight-Loss Adults**

Source: J. English. 2013. *Reversing Altered Metabolic Functions to Enhance Long-Term Weight Control.* Available at http://nutritionreview.org/2013/04/reversing-altered-metabolic-functions-enhance-longterm-weight-control/. Accessed May 2014.

weight, the size of the fat cell shrinks, but the number of cells does not. After weight loss, the smaller fat cells remain and can easily be filled up again when energy intake is greater than energy output. Although hyperplasia appears to slow with age,[29] the growth and production of fat cells continues throughout life. Every year about 10 percent of fat cells die and are replaced by new ones. The number of fat cells you create as a child remains with you for life.[30] Whether additional fat cells are formed as an adult and what turns on hyperplasia is still not clear.

Fat Cells Can Grow and Shrink

The size of fat cells is regulated by the enzyme lipoprotein lipase (LPL), which is made in the adipose tissue and lies on the surface of the adipocyte. As you learned in Chapter 5, LPL increases lipogenesis, or the accumulation of fat in the adipocyte. Another enzyme, called hormone-sensitive lipase (HSL), plays the opposite role in fat metabolism. HSL stimulates lipolysis, or the hydrolysis of triglycerides inside the adipocyte, and frees the fatty acids, which are then released into the bloodstream. It is the balance between fat being broken down (lipolysis) or synthesized (lipogenesis) that affects the size of the adipocyte. This is similar to a savings account—as you save money, the balance grows until you take it out and the balance shrinks.

The activity of LPL and HSL differs in overweight and lean individuals.[31] Heavier people have much more LPL activity, especially after eating (**Figure 15.4**). This makes it much easier to store energy from the meal. The activity of LPL increases following weight loss, which makes it much easier to regain lost weight.

Differences in LPL activity are also noted between genders.[32] In men, LPL is more active in the visceral, abdominal fat cells than in females, but females have higher LPL activity rates in the hips and thighs than do males. This is probably the reason women deposit more fat in the lower body and why adipose tissue in these areas is more stable and takes longer to lose. Overall, women oxidize more fat for fuel during exercise than men do and a male's LPL activity is higher following exercise than a female's. The reason for this remains unclear.

LO 15.3: THE TAKE-HOME MESSAGE The average adult body contains 30 billion to 50 billion adipocytes. Once adipocytes are formed, they can increase or decrease in size as fat storage needs change, but they can never decrease in number. Every year 10 percent of fat cells die and are replaced. The enzymes lipoprotein lipase and hormone-sensitive lipase influence the balance between lipolysis and lipogenesis, and thus the growing or shrinking of fat cells.

How Do Genetics and Environment Influence Obesity and Weight Management?

LO 15.4 Discuss the role of genetics and the environment in the development of underweight, overweight, and obesity.

Most health professionals now agree that obesity arises from the interaction of multiple genes (not just a single gene) with the environment, making weight management and the prevention of obesity challenging.[33] The relationship of genes to obesity was first demonstrated in studies on separated identical twins raised in different home environments who have similar weight gain and body fat distribution.[34] On the other hand, our genetic code has not changed since the obesity epidemic began. Therefore the environment in which we work and live must have a strong effect on body weight. This relationship is referred to as a **gene–environment interaction.** The question is, which is stronger, nature or nurture?

Nutrigenomics and Epigenetics May Influence Weight Control

Two new areas of study, **nutrigenomics** and **epigenetics,** may hold the answer to this question. The science of nutrigenomics has identified specific genes that are involved in the body's response to certain nutrients, such as how we absorb, store, or break down dietary fat, and can pinpoint the variation in the gene that may be responsible for the body's response. However, even with identical twins that have the same genetic makeup, the response to overeating or restricting kilocalories varies.

Researchers are still unclear what mechanism causes genes and nutrients to interact. This is where epigenetics comes into play. The term epigenetics describes the changes in gene activity and gene expression that occurs without changing the DNA sequence itself. The DNA in the body is wrapped around proteins called *histones,* much like wrapping thread around a spool. Both the DNA and the histones are covered with chemical tags that can react to signals within the body, such as diet, stress, toxins, and physical activity. This DNA-histone structure is called the epigenome (**Figure 15.5**). The epigenome tightly wraps or hides inactive genes. When the chemical tags react with diet or the environment, this reaction causes the

People who share genes often have similar body weights.

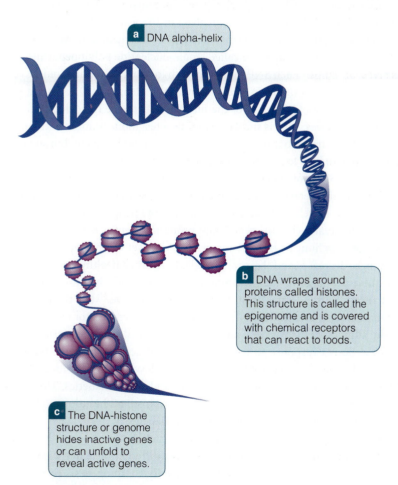

a DNA alpha-helix

b DNA wraps around proteins called histones. This structure is called the epigenome and is covered with chemical receptors that can react to foods.

c The DNA-histone structure or genome hides inactive genes or can unfold to reveal active genes.

▲ **Figure 15.5 The Epigenome**
The epigenome consists of DNA wrapped around proteins called histones and covered with chemical receptors or tags. The epigenome can hide inactive genes or unfold to reveal active genes.

gene–environment interaction The interaction of genetics and environmental factors that increases the risk of obesity in susceptible individuals.

nutrigenomics The study of how your genetic makeup interacts with your diet.

epigenetics The changes that may occur in gene activity and gene expression without altering the DNA sequence.

epigenome to partially unwind and expose the genes that were hidden, either turning the gene expression on or off.

Food is one factor that can cause the epigenome to partially unwind and expose inactive genes. Some vitamins, such as thiamin, riboflavin, and vitamin B_{12}, donate methyl groups during metabolic reactions. These methyl groups can attach to the chemical tags on the epigenome and activate or repress certain genes. For example, these gene expressions may trigger or inhibit fat synthesis, although how the mechanism works is still unknown.[35] In other words, while we can't alter the genetic makeup we are born with, we may eventually be able to control the factors that turn obesity genes on or off.

Genetics Can Influence Hunger, Satiety, and Insulin Response

Scientists currently associate more than 40 genetic variants with obesity.[36] Some of these genes influence how you store body fat, hunger and satiety patterns, and food intake.[37] The possibility of genes affecting hunger suggests that genetic differences in the level or the functioning of some hormones can influence a person's body weight and appetite.[38]

Earlier in the chapter, you learned that the hypothalamus regulates hunger and satiety by responding to signals from the adipocytes, the pancreas, the stomach, and the small intestine. These signals are conveyed to the brain by the hormones leptin, insulin, CCK, peptide YY, and ghrelin. The hypothalamus then instructs you to eat more or eat less. Multiple genes are involved in the way the body receives and responds to these signals, and even small changes in each gene can turn the gene "on" or "off." These small changes are called single-nucleotide polymorphisms, referred to as SNPs, or "snips." Each SNP represents a change in the building blocks of DNA, or a copy error. For example, in a gene with a SNP, a length of DNA might have the nucleotide thymine (T) in place of the nucleotide cytosine (C), which changes the way the gene behaves. This is similar to dialing a telephone number with one wrong digit. Most SNPs have no direct effect whatsoever on body weight, but some play an important role in how individuals respond to food intake.

There are SNPs of specific genes that affect eating behavior. For example, a SNP of the ghrelin gene may cause high levels of ghrelin (remember, ghrelin stimulates hunger) to be released, which may cause some people to overeat and become obese.[39] Individuals who are genetically prone to a leptin deficiency (remember, leptin suppresses hunger) become massively obese, yet when they are given leptin, their hunger decreases and their weight falls to within a healthy range.[40] Ironically, many obese people have adequate amounts of leptin, but the brain has developed a resistance to it, rendering its hunger control ineffective.[41] For these individuals, other mechanisms prevent leptin from functioning as a regulator of hunger.

The adipocytes also secrete another hormone called **adiponectin,** which improves the body's response to insulin, reduces fat accumulation in the liver and muscle, and enhances energy expenditure.[42] The levels of this hormone are higher in lean people but are low in obese individuals and type 2 diabetics. This difference may be explained by a single-nucleotide polymorphism of the adiponectin gene and may explain why obesity increases the risk for diabetes.

Genetics may also affect thermogenesis, which in turn impacts how kilocalories are expended in the body. Genes may cause different rates of thermogenesis in brown adipose tissue and in non-exercise activity thermogenesis (NEAT). When some individuals overeat, they burn rather than store excess kilocalories and are thus better able to manage their energy balance.[43] Many overweight individuals don't appear to have this compensatory mechanism.

adiponectin A hormone produced in the adipocytes that controls the body's response to insulin and may be involved in reducing the risk of obesity and type 2 diabetes.

Some researchers have described a genetic "**set point**" that determines body weight. This theory holds that the body fights to remain at a specific body weight and opposes attempts at weight loss. The body may even enable very easy weight gain when weight is lost in order to get back to this "set point." In other words, a person's weight remains fairly constant because the body "has a mind of its own." Given that the weight of Americans has disproportionately increased over the last few decades relative to previous decades, this theory either isn't true or the set point can be overridden.[44]

Some individuals also respond differently to their environment, suggesting that genetic differences can maintain obesity. When excessive amounts of food are available, some people store more fat, and in environments where food is scarce, they lose less fat compared with others.[45] If a person's environment and lifestyle stay the same, his or her weight should remain fairly stable. Likewise, if the environment and lifestyle shift to make it easier to gain weight, the body also shifts—it gains weight. Research comparing the Pima Indians in Arizona with their ancestors in Mexico reveals that the environment can impact genetically susceptible populations.[46] The Arizona Pima Indians share ancestry with the Mexican Pima Indians who migrated from a remote location in the northwestern part of Mexico. The original population of Mexican Pima Indians passed their genetic heritage on to their Arizona descendants, but not their lifestyle. The traditional Mexican Pimas lived a physically active lifestyle and ate a diet both rich in complex carbohydrates and lower in animal fats than that of the "Americanized" Pimas living in Arizona, who had a more sedentary lifestyle and consumed a fatty diet. Mexican Pimas had, on average, a BMI of about 25, compared with Arizona Pimas who had, on average, a BMI of over 33.[47] The traditional Pimas had a better chance of avoiding obesity because they lived in a healthier environment compared with the Pimas living in Arizona. This suggests that even if you have a genetic predisposition to being overweight, it's not a done deal. If you are determined to make healthy dietary choices and engage in regular physical activity, you can overcome your genetic predisposition.

Environmental Factors Can Increase Appetite and Decrease Physical Activity

Over the past few decades, the environment around us has changed in ways that have made it easier to incur a positive energy imbalance and gain weight. To explain how these two factors interact with each other, researchers have used the analogy that genes load the gun but an obesity-promoting environment pulls the trigger.[48] Environmental factors that seem particularly important include lack of time, an abundant food supply and portion distortion, and lack of physical activity. Take the Self-Assessment: Does Your Environment Impact Your Energy Balance? to reflect upon your environment and whether it may impact the lifestyle decisions you make throughout the day.

Lack of Time

Research shows that adults spend more time traveling to work and devote more of their daily hours to work than in previous decades.[49] This longer workday means there is less time to devote to everyday activities, such as food preparation. Today, almost a third of Americans' daily kilocalories come from ready-to-eat foods that are not prepared at home.[50] Between 1972 and 1995, the prevalence of eating out in the United States increased by almost 90 percent, a trend that is expected to increase steadily to the year 2020.[51] To accommodate this demand, the number of eateries in the United States has almost doubled, to nearly 900,000 food service establishments, during the last three decades.[52]

set point A weight-control theory that states each individual has a genetically established body weight. Any deviation from this point stimulates changes in body metabolism to reestablish the normal weight.

Research has shown that women who dine out five or more times weekly consume close to 300 kilocalories more on dining-out days than do women who eat at home.

Dining out frequently is associated with a higher BMI.[53] An Economic Research Service study in 2010 found an average increase in kilocalorie intake for adults of 134 kilocalories for every meal eaten away from home.[54] Eating out also reduces fruit and vegetable intake, and adds more fat, sugar, and alcohol.[55] The top foods selected when eating out, especially among college-aged diners, are energy-dense french fries and hamburgers.[56] Less-energy-dense, waist-friendly vegetables, fruits, and salads didn't even make the top choices on the list. For many people, dining out often is harming their diet by making energy-dense foods too readily available and displacing less-energy-dense vegetables and fruits.

An Abundant Food Supply and Portion Distortion

In the United States food is plentiful, there's a lot to choose from, and portion sizes are generous. All of these factors are associated with consuming too many kilocalories.[57]

Years ago, people went to a bookstore for the sole purpose of buying a book. Now they go to a bookstore to sip a vanilla latte and nibble on biscotti while they ponder which book to buy. Americans can grab breakfast at a hamburger drive-through, lunch at a museum, a sub sandwich at many gas stations, and a three-course meal of nachos, pizza, and ice cream at a movie theatre.

This access to a variety of foods is problematic for weight-conscious individuals. The appeal of a food diminishes as it continues to be eaten (that is, the first bite tastes the best and each subsequent bite loses some of that initial pleasure), but having a variety of foods available allows the eater to move on to another food once boredom sets in.[58] The more good-tasting foods that are available, the more a person eats. For example, during that three-course meal at the movie theater, once you're tired of the nachos, you can move on to the pizza, and when that loses its appeal, you can dig into the ice cream. If the pizza and ice cream weren't available, you would have stopped after the nachos and consumed fewer kilocalories.

As you learned from Chapter 2, the portion sizes of many foods, such as french fries and sodas, have doubled, if not tripled, compared with the portions listed on food labels. Consumers perceive "supersized" portions as bargains because they often cost only slightly more than the regular size. Research shows that people tend to eat more of a food, and thus more kilocalories, when larger portions are served.[59] In other words, when served a supersized soft drink, a person consumes more, if not all, of it even though a smaller drink would have provided the same level of satisfaction.

At home, the size of the serving bowl or package of food influences the amount that ends up on the plate. Serving from a large bowl or package has been shown to increase the serving size by more than 20 percent.[60] This means that you are more likely to scoop out (and eat) a bigger serving of ice cream from a half-gallon container than from a pint container. To make matters worse, most people don't compensate for these extra kilocalories by reducing the portions at the next meal.[61]

Portion sizes of french fries have more than doubled from the past. Choose the smaller size to reduce the ingestion of kilocalories.

Lack of Physical Activity

Americans not only eat about 300 more kilocalories daily (and have been doing so since 1985), they also expend less energy during their entire day.[62] The increase in "kilocalories in" and decrease in "kilocalories out" is a recipe for a positive energy imbalance and weight gain. Compared with years past, Americans expend less energy both at work and in the little leisure time that they have.

When your great-grandparents went to work in the morning in the 1940s, chances are good they headed out to the fields or off to the manual labor factory jobs. Your parents and older siblings, though, are more likely to head to an office and sit in front of a computer, and you will probably sit at a desk for much of your workday. This shift in work from jobs that required manual labor to jobs that are sedentary has been shown to increase the risk of becoming overweight or obese.[63] One study found that men who sit for more than six hours during their workday are at higher risk of being overweight than those who sit for less than an hour daily.[64]

Technology in the workplace now allows us to communicate with everyone without having to leave our desks. This means that people no longer have to get up and walk to see the colleague down the hall or the client across town. Researchers estimate that a 145-pound person expends 3.9 kilocalories for each minute of walking, compared with 1.8 kilocalories per minute sitting. Thus, walking 10 minutes during each workday to communicate in person with coworkers would expend 10,000 kilocalories annually, yet only about 5,000 kilocalories would be expended if the person sat in the office sending e-mails or calling colleagues on the phone. Over the course of a year, these extra 5,000 kilocalories not expended could add up to over a pound of body weight. After five years in the workforce, there would be around seven extra pounds of body weight sitting in the chair.

Increased amounts of "screen time" are contributing to decreased amounts of physical activity.

Another form of technology, the automobile, may negatively affect your weight-management goals. Earlier research on urban sprawl has shown that the greater the distance between home, school, or work, the more people drive and the less they engage in active living, such as biking or walking. In addition, the more you drive, the more you weigh.[65] For each hour you spend driving to work or school, the likelihood of obesity increases six percent, whereas for each half-mile walked per day, the likelihood of obesity is reduced by almost five percent.[66] This may be one of the factors in the increase in obesity rates among children. In a recent study in Canada, only 25 to 30 percent of children and youth reported walking or bicycling to school.[67] Changing these behaviors while providing a safe way for children to arrive at school requires creative solutions. One such solution is the "walking school bus." A walking school bus is similar to a car pool except students walk to school with one or more adults. Children arrive at school safely and increase their daily physical activity.[68]

Students who walk to school accompanied by their parents promote the concept of a "walking school bus."

As technology continues to advance and allows for less energy expenditure during the day, *planned* physical activity at another time of day must make up the difference. Unfortunately, more than 20 percent of Americans report no daily leisure-time physical activity.[69] Research shows that those aged 2 to 18 years old spend over 5 hours daily, on average, on a combination of "screen time" activities. These include watching TV, playing video games, and non-work/school–related computer time—even though experts have suggested limiting screen time to 2 hours daily.[70]

When people expend less energy during both work and play, weight gain becomes easier and the need for weight loss even greater. Combine this with an environment that is conducive to eating and it's not difficult to see why many people are becoming overweight or obese. Many Americans have to begin making conscious diet and lifestyle changes in order to lose weight, or at the very least, prevent further weight gain.

LO 15.4: THE TAKE-HOME MESSAGE Genetic influences, including the blood levels of leptin and ghrelin, play a role in obesity and weight management. Nutrigenomics has identified specific genes that are involved in how we absorb, store, or break down dietary fat. Epigenetics, or the change in gene activity and expression that occurs when the epigenome partially unwinds, may explain the effects on body weight when certain foods are eaten. Several current environmental factors—which provide easy access to a variety of energy-dense foods and at the same time decrease energy expenditure—encourage obesity.

Calculating Percentage of Weight Loss

If an overweight individual weighs 237 pounds at the beginning of a weight-loss program, what would he or she weigh after six months if the recommendations for healthy weight loss were followed?

Answer: The individual's initial weight minus 10 percent

$$237 \text{ lbs} - (237 \times 0.10) = 213.3 \text{ lbs}$$

Scan this QR code with your mobile device to access practice math activities. You can also access the activities in MasteringNutrition™.

How Can You Lose Weight Healthfully?

LO 15.5 Describe the role of diet and exercise in achieving a reasonable rate of weight loss.

The easiest way to avoid having to lose weight is to not gain weight in the first place. For those of you who need to shed pounds, there are several key principles that impact weight loss.

Strive for a Reasonable Rate of Weight Loss

According to the National Institutes of Health, overweight individuals should aim to lose about 10 percent of their body weight over a six-month period.[71] This means that the goal for an overweight, 180-pound person would be to shed 18 pounds in half a year, which would be about 3 pounds a month or ¾ pound weekly. Because a person must have an energy deficit of approximately 3,500 kilocalories to lose a pound of fat, a deficit of 250 to 500 kilocalories daily will result in a reasonable weight loss of about ½ to 1 pound weekly. Any diet that promises quicker weight-loss results is likely to restrict kilocalories to the point of falling short of nutrient needs. Practice calculating the amount of reasonable weight loss you can expect in the Calculation Corner.

Though there is no single diet approach that has been universally embraced, many health experts agree that a person needs to modify three areas of life for successful, long-term weight loss. These three areas are diet, physical activity, and behavior. Let's begin with the diet.

Remember That Kilocalories Count

When it comes to losing weight, two important words need to be remembered: Kilocalories count—no matter where they come from. An energy imbalance of too many kilocalories in and not enough kilocalories out causes weight gain, and reversing the imbalance causes the opposite: Taking in fewer kilocalories and burning off more results in weight loss. The dietary goal then, is to reduce the number of kilocalories consumed in foods. This can be done in several ways: by choosing lower-kilocalorie foods, by eating less food overall, or a combination of both.

However, cutting back too drastically on kilocalories is a culprit behind many failed weight-loss attempts. If a person skips meals or isn't satiated at each meal because of skimpy portions, the person will experience hunger between meals and be more inclined to snack on energy-dense foods. Thus a key factor for success during the weight-loss process is for the person to eat a healthy, balanced diet that provides fewer kilocalories, but is also *satisfying*. One strategy that many find helpful is to eat three small, nutritious meals throughout the day combined with a midmorning and a midafternoon snack. Eating more frequently keeps a person from getting too hungry and overeating at one sitting, while keeping meals small and nutrient dense ensures adequate nutrient intake without an overconsumption of kilocalories. Note that eating three small meals plus snacks is not the same thing as *grazing*. Grazing involves constant eating or nibbling throughout the day without allowing for feelings of hunger or satiation. This mindless eating behavior results in overconsumption of kilocalories and is considered a high-risk behavior for weight gain.[72]

Eat More Vegetables, Fruit, and Fiber

Research suggests that the volume (or bulk) of food due to its higher water and dietary fiber content consumed at a meal is very important. People tend to eat the same amount of food regardless of its energy density—that is, the amount of

Do Diets Rich in Carbohydrates Make Us Fat?

In recent years, there has been a renewed interest in altering the nutrient composition of diets to achieve weight loss. The recommended AMDR (Acceptable Macronutrient Distribution Range) is for 45 to 65 percent of daily kilocalories to come from carbohydrates, 20 to 35 percent of daily kilocalories to come from fat, and 10 to 35 percent of daily kilocalories to come from proteins. Some nutrition experts believe the healthier approach to weight loss is to increase protein consumption to as high as 45 percent of the total kilocalories, at the same time reducing carbohydrates to 25 percent of the total kilocalories.[1, 2] Some studies have reported that high-protein diets produce greater weight loss when compared with high-carbohydrate diets of the same kilocalorie content.[3] A diet lower in carbohydrate and higher in protein also was reported to prevent weight regain after weight loss had been achieved.[4]

The concept that carbohydrates are causing weight gain, and thus that reducing carbohydrates leads to weight loss, has been reported in popular media and explored by scientists. According to a 2013 meta-analysis, the increased intake in carbohydrate-rich, sugar-sweetened beverages correlates with the weight gain observed in both children and adults in recent decades.[5] This would suggest that as dietary intake of carbohydrates increases, so do our waistlines.

One big challenge is pinpointing the mechanism that might be responsible for weight gain with a higher carbohydrate intake. Some researchers argue that the culprit is insulin, while others suggest high-glycemic foods, such as those found in sugar-sweetened beverages, are the cause. A third theory is that carbohydrates alter appetite-suppressing hormones, causing hunger after a carbohydrate meal. Let's take a closer look at the evidence.

The Insulin Connection

As you learned in Chapter 4, the body requires insulin to process glucose. After a meal, insulin responds to the rise in blood glucose and aids in the transport of glucose inside the cell. The more dietary carbohydrate we consume, the more insulin we need to maintain normal blood glucose. But that's not the only function of insulin. This pancreatic hormone also promotes the synthesis of fatty acids, or lipogenesis, in the liver. Excess glucose not converted to glycogen in the liver, or used for energy, is converted to fatty acids and stored as fat. In theory, the more carbohydrate ingested, the more insulin the pancreas releases, the greater the potential for glucose to be stored as fatty acids in the adipocytes.

Insulin also prevents beta-oxidation of fatty acids by inhibiting lipolysis of stored fat in the adipose tissue, trapping fatty acids in the adipocyte.[6] Thus, the effects of insulin on lipid metabolism tend toward conservation of fat. To avoid elevated insulin levels, a diet lower in carbohydrates would be the logical conclusion.

Hunger Control and Carbohydrate Intake

The composition of the diet may impact the release of hunger-suppressing hormones. Recall that hunger is stimulated when ghrelin levels increase, or is reduced when leptin levels increase. In one study, total ghrelin levels were shown to decrease significantly when protein was consumed, compared with carbohydrates or lipids.[7] The researchers also noted that after three hours, ghrelin levels rebounded following carbohydrate intake but not following protein intake, suggesting that protein suppresses hunger for longer than does carbohydrate.

Ghrelin levels may be regulated by insulin, at least initially. In one study, a

higher carbohydrate intake, which increased the amount of insulin released, led in turn to a reduction in the amount of ghrelin in the blood.[8] Researchers suggest that this may be due to the impact of insulin on circulating ghrelin levels or be affected by whether the carbohydrates ingested were simple or complex carbohydrates.[9] The theory is that the release of ghrelin requires feedback after eating, which may be regulated by insulin.

Carbohydrate and protein may also affect the satiety hormone peptide YY. PYY levels have been shown to increase gradually without declining after consumption of a high-protein meal, whereas PYY levels peak and then begin to decline after consumption of a high-carbohydrate meal.[10] Researchers suggest that the increase in PYY following a high-protein/low-carbohydrate meal leads to more sustained feelings of satiety, and may play a role in promoting a reduction in overall food intake and weight loss.

Glycemic Index and Weight Loss

The typical Western diet, based on high-glycemic-index staples such as potatoes, bread, and enriched pasta, may affect hunger and ultimately body weight. Foods with a high glycemic index are digested quickly, which raises blood glucose, and increases insulin secretion to a greater extent compared with lower glycemic foods.

High-glycemic foods have been shown to stimulate hunger earlier than more complex carbohydrates with a low glycemic effect.[11] The increase in satiety with low-glycemic, high-fiber foods also results in lower kilocalorie intakes and potential weight loss.

Consuming a carbohydrate meal containing low-glycemic-index foods may also be effective in reducing total body fat. As noted above, increased levels of insulin may increase lipogenesis, and decrease lipolysis, thereby preserving body fat. A 2013 study measured the impact of a low-glycemic diet (average 49 on the glycemic index) compared with a high-glycemic diet (average 60 on the glycemic index) for 16 weeks. Results showed that at the end of the 16-week study, the low-glycemic group had dropped 4.4 percent of intra-abdominal fat compared with the high-glycemic group (**Figure 1**).[12] Another study reported that a low-glycemic diet is associated with a smaller waist circumference.[13] The results of these studies suggest that consuming low-glycemic foods reduces the impact of insulin on lipid metabolism and may enhance fat loss.

The evidence supporting the premise that carbohydrates may promote weight gain is promising; however, when researchers test the effects of isocaloric diets that contain either high carbohydrate/low fat or high protein/high fat, on weight loss, there was no advantage to the high-protein diet; the weight loss was similar.[14] In addition, restricting carbohydrates would reduce the quality of the diet. Until more conclusive evidence is presented, a healthy weight-loss diet should include whole grains, legumes, fresh fruits, and vegetables and limit high-glycemic refined carbohydrates.

References

1. J. McMillan-Price, P. Petocz, F. Atkinson, et al. 2006. "Comparison of 4 Diets of Varying Glycemic Load on Weight Loss and Cardiovascular Risk Reduction in Overweight and Obese Young Adults: A Randomized Controlled Trial." *Archives of Internal Medicine* 166:1466–1475.

2. N. H. Baba, S. Sawaya, N. Torbay, et al. 1999. "High Protein vs High Carbohydrate Hypoenergetic Diet for the Treatment of Obese Hyperinsulinemic Subjects." *International Journal of Related Metabolic Disorders* 23:1201–1206.

3. G. D. Foster, H. R. Wyatt, J. O. Hill, et al. 2003. "A Randomized Trial of a Low-Carbohydrate Diet for Obesity." *New England Journal of Medicine* 348:2082–2090.

4. M. P. Lejeune, E. M. Kovacs, and M. S. Westerterp-Plantenga. 2005. "Additional Protein Intake Limits Weight Regain After Weight Loss in Humans." *British Journal of Nutrition* 93:281–289.

5. V. S. Malik, A. Pan, W. C. Willett, and F. B. Hu. 2013. "Sugar-Sweetened Beverages and Weight Gain in Children and Adults: A Systematic Review and Meta-Analysis." *American Journal of Clinical Nutrition* 98(4):1084–1102.

6. S. M. Choi, D. F. Tucker, D. N. Gross, et al. 2010. "Insulin Regulates Adipocyte Lipolysis via an Akt-Independent Signaling Pathway." *Molecular Cellular Biology* 30(21):5009–5020.

7. K. E. Foster-Schubert, J. Overduin, C. E. Prudom, et al. 2008. "Acyl and Total Ghrelin are Suppressed Strongly by Ingested Proteins, Weakly by Lipids, and Biphasically by Carbohydrates." *Journal of Clinical Endocrinology and Metabolism* 93(5):1971–1979.

8. W. A. M. Blom, A. Stafleu, C. De Graaf, F. J. Kok, G. Schaafsma, and H. F. J. Hendriks. 2005. "Ghrelin Response to Carbohydrate-Enriched Breakfast Is Related to Insulin." *American Journal of Clinical Nutrition* 81(2):367–375.

9. F. R. Penaforte, C. C. Japur, L. P. Pigatto, P. G. Chiarello, and R. W. Diez-Garcia. 2013. "Short-Term Impact of Sugar Consumption on Hunger and Ad Libitum Food Intake in Young Women." *Nutrition Research and Practice* 7(2):77–81.

10. S. Wang, L. Yang, J. Lu, and Y. Mu. 2014. "High Protein Breakfast Promotes Weight Loss by Suppressing Subsequent Food Intake and Regulating Appetite Hormones in Obese Chinese Adolescents." *Hormonal Research in Paediatrics* DOI:10.1159/000362168.

11. S. B. Roberts. 2000. "High-Glycemic-Index Foods, Hunger, and Obesity: Is There a Connection?" *Nutrition Reviews* 58(6):163–169.

12. A. M. Goss, L. L. Goree, A. C. Ellis, P. C. Chandler-Laney, K. Casazza, M. E. Lockart, and B. A. Gower. 2013. "Effects of Diet Macronutrient Composition and Fat Distribution During Weight Maintenance and Weight Loss." *Obesity* 21(6):1139–1142.

13. J. Halkjaer, T. I. Sorensen, A. Tjonneland, et al. 2004. "Food and Drinking Patterns as Predictors of 6-year BMI-Adjusted Changes in Waist Circumference." *British Journal of Nutrition* 92:735–748.

14. M. Noakes, P. R. Foster, J. B. Keogh, A. P. James, J. C. Mamo, and P. M. Clifton. 2006. "Comparison of Isocaloric Very Low Carbohydrate/High Saturated Fat and High Carbohydrate/Low Saturated Fat Diets on Body Composition and Cardiovascular Risk." *Nutrition and Metabolism* DOI:10.1186/1743-7075-3-7.

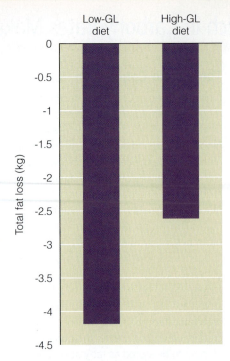

▲ **Figure 1 The Effects of a High versus Low Glycemic Diet on Fat Loss**
A low glycemic diet resulted in a greater loss of abdominal fat compared to a high glycemic diet.
Source: A. M. Goss, L. L. Goree, A. C. Ellis, P. C. Chandler-Laney, K. Casazza, M. E. Lockart, and B. A. Gower. 2013. "Effects of Diet Macronutrient Composition and Fat Distribution during Weight Maintenance and Weight Loss." *Obesity* 21(6):1139–1142.

kilocalories in the meal.[73] In other words, a meal or snack needs to be of sufficient size (high in volume or bulk) in order to fill you up or satisfy you. Healthy eating includes consuming low-energy-dense foods, rather than overeating energy-dense, low-volume foods such as candy, which can easily fill you *out* before they fill you *up*. You'll consume excess kilocalories before you become satiated. The reverse of this—consuming high-volume, low-energy-density, watery vegetables and fruits at meals and snacks—is associated with increased satiety and reduced feelings of hunger and kilocalorie intake—all helpful in weight management.[74] Try calculating the energy density of foods in the Calculation Corner.

In fact, consuming a large, high-volume, low-energy-density salad at the beginning of a meal can reduce the kilocalories eaten at that meal by over 10 percent.[75] Adding vegetables to sandwiches and soups increases both the volume

Calculation Corner

Calculating Energy Density

Energy density of foods can be calculated and compared using the method described by Barbara Rolls, PhD.[1] Divide the kilocalories in a serving of food by the weight in grams of a serving of the food. Try calculating the energy density from the labels of two different foods to determine which one is more energy dense.

a Ben & Jerry's Chubby Hubby Ice Cream   **b** Frozen Broccoli Florets

Nutrition Facts	
Serving Size ½ cup (111g)	
Servings per Container 4	
Amount Per Serving	
Calories 340	Calories from Fat 180
	% Daily Value*
Total Fat 20g	31%
Saturated Fat 10g	50%
Trans Fat 0g	
Cholesterol 55g	18%
Sodium 140mg	6%
Total Carbohydrate 33g	11%
Dietary Fiber 1g	4%
Sugars 25g	
Protein 7g	
Vitamin A 10% • Vitamin C 0%	
Calcium 10% • Iron 4%	
* Percent Daily Values are based on a 2,000 calorie diet. Your daily values may be higher or lower depending on your calorie needs	

Nutrition Facts	
Serving Size 1 cup (85g)	
Servings Per Container 3	
Amount Per Serving	
Calories 25	Calories from Fat 0
	% Daily Value*
Total Fat 0g	0%
Saturated Fat 0g	0%
Trans Fat 0g	
Cholesterol 0mg	0%
Sodium 10mg	0%
Total Carbohydrate 5g	2%
Dietary Fiber 3g	12%
Sugars 1g	
Protein 3g	
Vitamin A 15% • Vitamin C 60%	
Calcium 2% • Iron 2%	
* Percent Daily Values are based on a 2,000 calorie diet. Your daily values may be higher or lower depending on your calorie needs	

1. To calculate the energy density of Chubby Hubby ice cream, divide the kilocalories by the weight in grams.

2. Now calculate the energy density of the frozen broccoli florets using the label information:

Answer: Chubby Hubby: 340 kcals/111 g = 3.1.
Frozen broccoli florets: 25 kcals/85 g = 0.3.

Reference

1. B. J. Rolls and E. A. Bell. 2000. "Dietary Approaches to the Treatment of Obesity." *Medical Clinics of North America* 84:401–418.

Scan this QR code with your mobile device to access practice math activities. You can also access the activities in **Mastering**Nutrition™.

High-energy-dense foods

¾ cup chicken broth: **29** calories
½ cup chicken (white meat): **106** calories
1 cup noodles: **212** calories

347 total kilocalories

2 slices whole-wheat bread: **138** calories
4 oz ham: **125** calories
2 oz American cheese: **213** calories

476 total kilocalories

Low-energy-dense foods

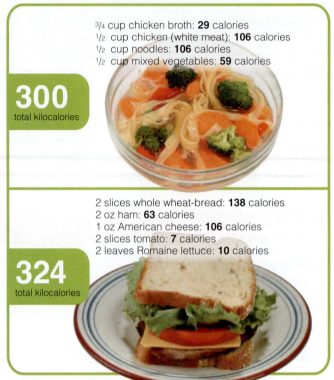

¾ cup chicken broth: **29** calories
½ cup chicken (white meat): **106** calories
½ cup noodles: **106** calories
½ cup mixed vegetables: **59** calories

300 total kilocalories

2 slices whole wheat-bread: **138** calories
2 oz ham: **63** calories
1 oz American cheese: **106** calories
2 slices tomato: **7** calories
2 leaves Romaine lettuce: **10** calories

324 total kilocalories

▲ **Figure 15.6 Adding Volume to Meals**
Adding high-volume, low-energy-dense foods like fruits and vegetables to sandwiches, soups, and meals can add to satiety and displace foods higher in kilocalories, two factors that can improve weight management.

TABLE TIPS
Eat More to Weigh Less

Eat more whole fruit and drink less juice at breakfast. The orange has more fiber and bulk than the OJ.

Make the vegetable portions on your dinner plate twice the size of the meat portion.

Have a side salad with low-fat dressing with a lunchtime sandwich instead of a snack bag of chips.

Order your next pizza with less pepperoni and more peppers, onions, and tomatoes. A veggie pizza can have 25 percent fewer kilocalories and about 50 percent less fat and saturated fat than a meat pie.

Cook up a whole-wheat-blend pasta instead of enriched pasta for your next Italian dinner. Ladle on plenty of tomato sauce and don't forget the big tossed salad as the appetizer.

---

of food consumed and meal satisfaction and helps displace higher kilocalorie items (**Figure 15.6**). Feeling full after eating a sandwich loaded with vegetables reduces the consumption of energy-dense potato chips. This is important because you don't need to eliminate chips from your diet if you enjoy them. Any food—from chocolate to chips—can be modest in kilocalories if eaten in modest amounts. Following these recommendations allows you to eat a variety of foods, but minimizing higher energy density foods lower in water content and dietary fiber, while emphasizing lower energy density options, will result in a satisfying diet and weight loss.

Table 15.1 provides examples of low-, moderate-, and high-energy-density foods.

Fiber also contributes to the bulk of vegetables and fruits and their ability to prolong satiety.[76] Overweight individuals have been shown to consume less dietary fiber and fruit than normal-weight people.[77] For these reasons, high-fiber foods are a key part of a weight-loss diet. The Table Tips provide easy ways to add these foods to your diet.

Eating more plant-based foods alters the microbes in gastrointestinal tract, which may be related to weight gain. Read the Examining the Evidence box "Microbiomes: Is There a Link to Obesity?" on page 562 to find out more.

Add Some Protein and Fat to Meals

Because protein has the most dramatic effect on satiety, high-protein diets tend to reduce hunger and can help in weight loss.[78] Because fat slows the movement of food out of the stomach into the intestines, it can also prolong satiety. Therefore,

TABLE 15.1 The Energy Density of Foods

▲ **Low**

These foods provide 0.7 to 1.5 kilocalories per gram and are high in water and fiber. Examples include most vegetables and fruits—tomatoes, cantaloupe, strawberries, broccoli, cauliflower, broth-based soups, fat-free yogurt, and cottage cheese.

▲ **Medium**

These foods have 1.5 to 4 kilocalories per gram and contain less water. They include bagels, hard-cooked eggs, dried fruits, lean sirloin steak, hummus, whole-wheat bread, and part-skim mozzarella cheese.

▲ **High**

These foods provide 4 to 9 kilocalories per gram, are low in moisture, and include chips, cookies, crackers, cakes, pastries, butter, oil, and bacon.

Adapted from B. J. Rolls and R. A. Barnett, *The Volumetrics Weight-Control Plan* (New York: HarperCollins Publishers 2000) and Centers for Disease Control and Prevention, *How To Use Fruits and Vegetables to Manage Your Weight,* 2012. Available at www.cdc.gov/healthyweight/healthy_eating/fruits_vegetables.html. Accessed May 2014.

adding some lean protein and healthy fat at all meals and even with snacks can help reduce hunger. This is not to say that carbohydrates should be severely restricted or eliminated; rather, it reinforces the basic fact that all macronutrients are necessary in the correct proportions.

Keep in mind also that adding high-saturated-fat foods such as whole milk, whole-milk cheese, fatty cuts of meat, and butter to the diet comes at the expense of cardiovascular health. A better bet would be to add lean meat, skinless chicken, fish, nuts, and oils, which are kinder to both a person's waist and heart. (Note: Unsaturated fat still contains 9 kilocalories per gram, so excessive amounts of nuts and oils, even though these are heart healthy, can quickly add excess kilocalories to the diet.)

Meals that contain lower energy dense foods, such as fruits and vegetables and whole grains, as well as some lean protein, and a modest amount of fat is a smart combination for weight loss, so a diet that contains all five food groups can be used to lose weight. Most importantly, this type of diet is well balanced and meets daily nutrient needs.

Reducing the intake of kilocalories a little at a time can add up to healthy weight loss. A 180-pound, overweight person who consumes 2,800 kilocalories daily can reduce his or her intake to 2,400 to 2,600 kilocalories, incurring a kilocalorie deficit of 200–400 kilocalories daily. He or she will then lose 10 pounds in about three months. Small changes, like switching from full-fat to nonfat dairy products or replacing an afternoon soda with a glass of water, can contribute to this kilocalorie reduction.

Increase Physical Activity to Lose Weight

Regular physical activity can not only add to the daily energy deficit needed for weight loss, but can also displace sedentary activity such as watching television, which often leads to mindless snacking on energy-dense foods.[79] Going for a walk

Microbiomes: Is There a Link to Obesity?

The term *microbiome* refers to the billions of microscopic organisms that live within an individual's body, including in the GI tract, on the skin, and in the lungs and genital tract. The majority of these microbes live in the large intestine and participate in a number of metabolic functions. For instance, intestinal bacteria are important to digestion and metabolism. They extract energy from undigested foods, synthesize vitamins, including vitamin K,[1] regulate fatty acid tissue composition, and control peptides secreted from the GI tract.[2]

The more than 1,000 different types of bacteria that live in the intestinal tract can vary between individuals independent of age, gender, ethnicity, or body mass index.[3, 4] Recently, scientists have suggested that when specific intestinal microbes are significantly high in the gut, obesity may result. If this is true, could we alter the type of bacteria in our intestinal tract and eliminate the obesity epidemic?

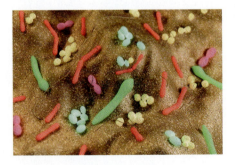

Effect of Diet on Intestinal Bacteria

Different diets, both long-term and short-term diet patterns, influence the types of intestinal bacteria that live in the GI tract and the types of genes expressed by those bacteria. These dietary changes influence the bacteria's metabolism and your body's immune functions by the fermentation of nutrients, altering the intestinal barrier to allow bacteria and other pathogens to enter the blood, and turning "on and off" your body's genes. Understanding the role of diet and the functions of intestinal bacteria may promote new approaches to reduce the incidence of obesity.

Intestinal bacteria change from birth to adulthood. Babies are born with a sterile intestinal environment containing no bacteria. The baby's GI tract is colonized by bacteria beginning soon after birth. The specific bacteria involved depend on how the infant is fed. Breast-fed infants have more *Bifidobacterium* and *Ruminococcus*, with significantly less *Escherichia coli*, *Clostridium difficile*, *Bacteroides fragilis*, and *Lactobacillus* than infants fed formula.[5] As soon as infants begin to eat solid food, the intestinal bacteria change in composition to that of an adult, with *Firmicutes* and *Bacteroidetes* as the predominant families of bacteria.[6]

Differences in diet may explain up to 57 percent of the differences in the type of intestinal bacteria.[7] Food provides nutrients for the bacteria to grow and some bacteria are more adept at metabolizing specific foods than others. For example, a change from a diet low in fat and high in fiber to a diet high in fat and sugar but low in dietary fiber increases the bacteria *Firmicutes* and decreases *Bacteroidetes*.[8] These changes happen quickly and can occur in just 24 hours.[9] Studies have reported that children in Europe who consume a low-fiber diet have little *Bacteroidetes* compared with children living in rural Africa and consuming a high-fiber diet.[10] Similar results have been reported in subjects eating a vegan or vegetarian diet. These subjects had significantly lower levels of *Bacteroidetes*, *Bifidobacterium*, *E. coli*, and *Enterobacteriaceae* than the subjects eating a normal mixed diet.[11] Vegetarians also have less of certain types of *Clostridium* bacteria.[12] What effect, if any, do these variations in microbiome have on obesity?

Intestinal Bacteria and Obesity

The first clue that there was a difference in the type of intestinal bacteria between obese and lean mice was the discovery that mice with a polymorphic leptin gene have different intestinal bacteria, compared with mice without this altered gene. Obese mice have a higher proportion of *Firmicutes* and significantly fewer *Bacteroidetes*.[13] Similar data has been published in humans, in which 12 obese human subjects were found to have a larger proportion of *Firmicutes* and very few *Bacteroidetes* compared with two lean subjects.[14] Other studies report a slightly different pattern, with obese individuals having a rise in *Lactobacillus* species belonging to the *Firmicutes* family and a drop in Bacteroidetes,[15] or lower *Bacteroidetes* with no change in *Firmicutes*.[16] Does this change in the type of intestinal bacteria cause obesity?

Just as the diet affects the different forms of bacteria that live in the GI tract, the presence of certain strains of intestinal bacteria can also influence metabolic functions in the human body—including obesity. Several theories have been proposed for the role of microbiomes in contributing to obesity. Different species of intestinal bacteria may control the amount of energy produced from nondigested food in the intestinal tract. For instance, an increase in *Firmicutes* and a drop in *Bacteroidetes* could increase the amount of energy produced. The *Firmicutes* bacteria are genetically prone to increase the digestion of polysaccharides, producing monosaccharides and short-chain fatty acids. These short-chain fatty acids attach to the epithelial cells lining the intestinal cells, which slows intestinal motility and transit. The receptor sites on the intestinal cells to which short-chain fatty acids attach may also stimulate hunger. Certain bacteria may also cause inflammation, and alter human genes that stimulate fat synthesis in the adipocyte.[17]

If we altered the diet of obese people in order to change the composition of intestinal bacteria, would they lose weight? Perhaps. One case study involved a morbidly obese male whose intestinal bacteria were 35 percent *Enterobacter*. This form of intestinal bacteria produces lipopolysaccharide endotoxins that, if they leak through the intestinal tract into the blood, can cause inflammation and contribute to obesity, at least in animal models. The subject in this case study was placed on a 9-week dietary regimen composed of whole grains, prebiotics, and traditional Chinese medicinal foods. After 9 weeks, the subject lost 66 pounds and reduced the *Enterobacter* population to 1.8 percent.[18] As the level of *Enterobacter* decreased, the inflammation and lipopoly-saccharide endotoxins also dropped.

The majority of the research reported thus far has been in animal models. Well-designed research in humans is needed to unravel the complex relationship between microbiomes and obesity. At this point, manipulating intestinal microbes should not substitute for diet and exercise as a weight-management tool.

References

1. N. Fei and L. Zhao. 2013. "An Opportunistic Pathogen Isolated from the Gut of an Obese Human Causes Obesity in Germ-Free Mice." *The ISME Journal* 7:880–884.
2. G. Musso, R. Gambino, and M. Cassader. 2010. "Obesity, Diabetes, and Gut Microbiota: The Hygiene Hypothesis Expanded?" *Diabetes Care* 33:2277–2284.
3. T. D. Leser and L. Molbak. 2009. "Better Living Through Microbial Action: The Benefits of the Mammalian Gastrointestinal Microbiota on the Host." *Environmental Microbiology* 11:2194–2206.
4. P. J. Turnbaugh, M. Hamady, T. Yatsunenko, B. L. Cantarel, A. Duncan, R. E. Ley, et al. 2009. "A Core Gut Microbiome in Obese and Lean Twins." *Nature* 457:480–484.
5. F. Turroni, C. Peano, D. A. Pass, E. Foroni, M. Severgnini, M. J. Claesson, et al. 2012. "Diversity of *Bifidobacteria* within the Infant Gut Microbiota." *PLoS ONE* 7:e36957.10.1371/journal.pone.0036957.
6. T. Yatsunenko, F. E. Rey, M. J. Manary, I. Trehan, M. G. Dominguez-Bello, M. Contreras, et al. 2012. "Human Gut Microbiome Viewed Across Age and Geography." *Nature* 486: 222–227.
7. C. Zhang, M. Zhang, S. Wang, R. Han, Y. Cao, W. Hua, et al. 2010. "Interactions between Gut Microbiota, Host Genetics and Diet Relevant to Development of Metabolic Syndromes in Mice." *ISME Journal* 4:232–241.
8. M. A. Hildebrandt, C. Hoffmann, S. A. Sherrill-Mix, S. A. Keilbaugh, M. Hamady, Y. Y. Chen, et al. 2009. "High-Fat Diet Determines the Composition of the Murine Gut Microbiome Independently of Obesity." *Gastroenterology* 137:1716–1724.
9. G. D. Wu, J. Chen, C. Hoffmann, K. Bittinger, Y. Y. Chen, S. A. Keilbaugh, et al. 2011. "Linking Long-Term Dietary Patterns with Gut Microbial Enterotypes." *Science* 334:105–108.
10. C. De Filippo, D. Cavalieri, M. Di Paola, M. Ramazzotti, J. B. Poullet, S. Massart, et al. 2010. "Impact of Diet in Shaping Gut Microbiota Revealed by a Comparative Study in Children from Europe and Rural Africa." *Proceedings of the National Academy of Science U.S.A.* 107:14691–14696.
11. J. Zimmer, B. Lange, J. Frick, H. Sauer, K. Zimmermann, A. Schwiertz, et al. 2011. "A Vegan or Vegetarian Diet Substantially Alters the Human Colonic Faecal Microbiota." *European Journal of Clinical Nutrition* 66:53–60.
12. K. Liszt, J. Zwielehner, M. Handschur, B. Hippe, R. Thaler, and A. G. Haslberger. 2009. "Characterization of Bacteria, Clostridia and Bacteroides in Faeces of Vegetarians Using qPCR and PCR-DGGE Fingerprinting." *Annals of Nutritional Metabolism* 54:253–257.
13. R. E. Ley. 2010. "Obesity and the Human Microbiome." *Current Opinions in Gastroenterology* 26:5–11.
14. R. E. Ley, P. J. Turnbaugh, S. Klein, and J. I. Gordon. 2006. "Microbial Ecology: Human Gut Microbes Associated with Obesity." *Nature* 444:1022–1023.
15. F. Armougom, M. Henry, B. Vialettes, D. Raccah, and D. Raoult. 2009. "Monitoring Bacterial Community of Human Gut Microbiota Reveals an Increase in *Lactobacillus* in Obese Patients and Methanogens in Anorexic Patients." *PLoS ONE* 4:e7125.10.1371/journal.pone.0007125.
16. J. P. Furet, L. C. Kong, J. Tap, C. Poitou, A. Basdevant, J. L. Bouillot, et al. 2010. "Differential Adaptation of Human Gut Microbiota to Bariatric Surgery-Induced Weight Loss: Links with Metabolic and Low-Grade Inflammation Markers." *Diabetes* 59:3049–3057.
17. I. Moreno-Indias, F. Cardona, and M. I. Queipo-Ortuño. 2014. "Impact of the Gut Microbiota on the Development of Obesity and Type 2 Diabetes Mellitus." *Frontiers in Microbiology* 5:190–200.
18. P. D. Cani, J. Amar, M. A. Iglesias, M. Poggi, C. Knauf, D. Bastelica, et al. 2007. "Metabolic Endotoxemia Initiates Obesity and Insulin Resistance." *Diabetes* 56:1761–1772.

and expending kilocalories rather than watching a movie while snacking on a bag of tortilla chips provides kilocaloric benefits beyond the exercise alone.

Individuals are advised to devote 60 to 90 minutes daily to moderate-intensity activities to aid in weight loss and prevent weight gain.[80] Moderately intense physical activity would be the equivalent of walking 3.5 miles per hour (Table 15.2). The longer your exercise session, the more oxygen is consumed after the exercise ends, which contributes to a higher sustained metabolic rate and more kilocalories burned throughout the day, even at rest.[81] Establishing an exercise program that incorporates cardiorespiratory and strength-training activities has even greater benefits, one of which is the increased metabolic rate that occurs with an increase in muscle mass. For more information on the influence of exercise on losing weight, see the Examining the Evidence box "Which Exercise Is Most Effective for Weight Loss?" on page 565.

TABLE 15.2   Kilocalories Used during Activities

Moderate Physical Activity	Approximate Kilocalories/Hour for a 154-lb Person*	Vigorous Physical Activity	Approximate Kilocalories/Hour for a 154-lb Person*
Hiking	370	Running/jogging (5 mph)	590
Light gardening/yard work	330	Bicycling (> 10 mph)	590
Dancing	330	Swimming (slow freestyle laps)	510
Golf (walking and carrying clubs)	330	Aerobics	480
Bicycling (< 10 mph)	290	Walking (4.5 mph)	460
Walking (3.5 mph)	280	Heavy yard work (chopping wood)	440
Weight lifting (general light workout)	220	Weight lifting (vigorous effort)	440
Stretching	180	Basketball (vigorous)	440

Note: *Calories burned per hour will be higher for persons who weigh more than 154 lbs (70 kg) and lower for persons who weigh less.

Adapted from *Dietary Guidelines for Americans, 2010.* 2012. Available at www.health.gov/dietaryguidelines/dga2010/DietaryGuidelines2010.pdf. Accessed May 2014.

Wearing a pedometer, like the one shown here, can help you track your steps. Remember to aim for 10,000 steps per day.

Research suggests that accumulating 10,000 steps daily, which generally is the equivalent of walking 5 miles, can help reduce the risk of becoming overweight.[82] Americans, on average, accumulate only 900 to 3,000 steps daily.[83] To reach 10,000 steps, most people need to make a conscious effort to keep moving. Using a pedometer can help you track the number of steps you take and let you know if you are hitting this target, or if you need to get up and move much more often. The Fitness Tips provide more suggestions on how to expend more energy during the day.

Establish Healthy Eating and Exercise Habits

Many incoming college freshmen worry more about gaining weight—the "freshman 15"—than about how they'll manage the combination of their course load and newfound freedom. The term "freshman 15" was coined to describe a gain in weight that some college students experience during their first year away from home. However, little data supports the theory. As with adults, freshman weight gain can be prevented by establishing healthy eating and exercise behaviors that lead to a healthy weight.

Behavior modification focuses on changing the eating behaviors that contribute to weight gain or impede weight loss. Several behavior modification techniques can be used to identify and improve eating behaviors. These techniques

FITNESS TIPS

Get UP and MOVE

Skip the text messages and walk to visit your friends on campus.

Don't go to the closest coffee shop for your morning latte; walk to the java joint that is a few blocks farther away.

Take a five-minute walk at least twice a day. A little jolt of exercise can help break the monotony of studying and work off some stress.

Accomplish two goals at once by cleaning your dorm room or apartment. A 150-pound person burns about 4 kilocalories for every minute spent cleaning. Scrub, sweep, or vacuum for 30 minutes and you could work off about 120 kilocalories.

Offer to walk your neighbor's pet daily.

behavior modification Changing behaviors to improve health outcomes. In the case of weight management, it involves identifying and altering eating patterns that contribute to weight gain or impede weight loss.

Which Exercise Is the Most Effective for Weight Loss?

Changes in body weight are affected by the amount of energy you expend compared with the amount of energy you consume creating an energy deficit. The current recommendations for successful weight loss and maintenance include adding exercise to your daily routine to help create this energy deficit. Exercise mobilizes energy stores, including fat stored in adipocytes, to fuel the exercise, ultimately reducing the size of adipocytes, increasing the ratio of lean body mass to fat mass, and positively impacting risk factors correlated with obesity.[1]

Exercise should be an integral part of any weight-loss or weight-maintenance program. The American College of Sports Medicine recommends that most adults should engage in moderate-intensity cardiorespiratory exercise of at least 225 to 300 minutes per week to sustain a healthy body weight and prevent weight gain.[2] However, some researchers advocate more intense exercise regimens to achieve a healthy weight loss. What are the potential weight-loss benefits of different types and intensities of exercise?

Aerobic Exercise and Weight Loss

Even though aerobic exercise provides numerous health benefits, including blood glucose control, reduced blood pressure, and an increase in high-density lipoproteins for overweight or obese subjects, clinical trials report only modest weight-loss effects related to the exercise itself.[3] Aerobic exercise is classified as exercise of low to moderate intensity that utilizes the aerobic reactions that produce ATP. Carbohydrates, fats, and protein all provide energy to perform aerobic-type exercise, which includes brisk walking, jogging, hiking, and cross-country skiing.

Recall from Chapter 8 that lipolysis, or the breakdown of stored fatty acids for energy production, occurs during aerobic metabolism. However, in the first few minutes of any moderate exercise, carbohydrates, creatine phosphate, and the 3 to 5 seconds' worth of stored ATP—not fat—provide most of the fuel.

As the aerobic metabolism begins to fully power up, lipolysis of stored fat and beta-oxidation of fatty acids increases, and will progressively exceed carbohydrates as the main fuel source. Does this mean that moderate aerobic exercise is the key to successful weight loss?

A classic three-month study reported the influence of diet and exercise on body composition in obese women. Ninety-one obese women were randomly assigned to diet only, exercise only, diet plus exercise, or control groups and those in the exercise groups were asked to complete 45 minutes of moderate-intensity cardiorespiratory exercise per day, five days a week. The results found that those in the diet plus exercise group lost the same amount of weight as those who only dieted.[4] The aerobic exercise–only group did not differ in weight loss from the control group at the end of the study. A more recent study found similar results. Subjects who increased the cardiorespiratory exercise to 50 minutes, five days a week without dieting, lost a similar amount of weight to those who restricted kilocalories without exercise.[5] In another study involving obese women, long-term, moderate-intensity aerobic exercise (without dieting) showed little beneficial change in body composition

compared with the diet-only group. Both groups lost an average of eight kilograms (about 17.5 pounds) over the course of 12 weeks.[6]

Over the course of a one-year study, subjects who performed aerobic exercise without dieting for 60 minutes a day, six days a week, lost only an average of 3.5 pounds over the year.[7] Unless the overall volume of accumulated time devoted to aerobic exercise is high, according to the experts, significant weight loss is unlikely from aerobic exercise alone.[8] However, as you already learned in this chapter, finding—or making—the time to exercise is a barrier for most adults. Perhaps the answer lies in short, intense bouts of anaerobic exercise?

Anaerobic Exercise and Weight Loss

Anaerobic exercise is more intense than aerobic, but it is also by necessity shorter in duration, because the intensity cannot be maintained as long as aerobic exercise. For instance, heavy weight lifting, sprinting, jumping rope, and climbing stairs are all examples of anaerobic, high-intensity exercise. As the intensity builds during anaerobic exercise, less fat is oxidized and more glycogen and blood glucose is used to produce energy.

Performing intermittent cycles of high-intensity exercise, also known as high-intensity intermittent exercise (HIIE) or high-intensity interval training (HIIT), has been shown to result in fat loss.[9] When HIIE is compared with aerobic exercise, HIIE shows a greater weight loss in some studies. For example, one 15-week study involved women partaking in either three 20-minute HIIE exercise sessions per week or a steady state exercise (SSE) at 60 percent of their maximum heart rate for 40 minutes three times per week. The HIIE group's exercise sessions consisted of 8 seconds of sprint cycling followed by 12 seconds of slow cycling repeated for 20 minutes. The HIIE subjects lost 2.5 kilograms, or 5.5 pounds, of subcutaneous body fat over the 15-week study, whereas women who performed SSE aerobic exercise for the 15 weeks experienced no change in body fat (**Figure 1**).[10] This fat loss was achieved with 50 percent less time exercising and a similar energy expenditure. Despite exercising for half the time compared with the SSE group, researchers suggested that the significant loss of body fat in the HIIE group might be due to the impact of high-intensity exercise on reducing hunger hormones and overall kilocalorie intake. Another explanation may be that high-intensity exercise enhances lipolysis and fatty acid oxidation. And finally, while the changes in lean muscle mass were not significantly different between groups, the high-intensity exercise group gained lean muscle, while the steady state group lost lean muscle. This is important for weight loss, as loss of lean muscle reduces basal metabolic rate, whereas an increase in active muscle tissue continues to burn more fatty acids even at rest.

One of the advantages of anaerobic exercise is that it burns more total kilocalories per minute than moderate, aerobic exercise. For instance, a 150-pound female who jogged at a pace of 12 minutes per mile would burn approximately 220 kilocalories in 30 minutes compared with running a 7-minute-mile pace, which would burn approximately 390 kilocalories in 30 minutes. Even though less fat is burned during anaerobic exercise, anaerobic exercise increases resting metabolic rate and lean muscle mass that continues to burn kilocalories (mostly fat kilocalories) after the exercise is complete, for up to 14 hours.[11]

Aerobic Exercise Combined with Resistance Training

If aerobic exercise utilizes fatty acids for energy but anaerobic exercise increases lean muscle mass and resting metabolic rate, why not combine the two in one exercise bout? In a recent study at Duke University, researchers followed 234 overweight and obese adults who were randomly assigned to an aerobic exercise group, a resistance-training group, or a group that performed both aerobic exercise and resistance training. The aerobic exercise group exercised the equivalent of 12 miles per week either on a treadmill or elliptical trainer. The resistance-training group lifted weights three days per week, three sets per day, with 8–12 repetitions per set. The aerobic exercise plus resistance-training group completed both protocols. After 10 weeks, the aerobic exercise group and the aerobic plus resistance-training group lost more total body weight and fat loss than the resistance-training group.[12] Interesting to note, however, is that the subjects in the combined group significantly reduced their waist circumference compared with the aerobic-only group or the resistance-training group.

Another study tested the hypothesis that short-term aerobic activity combined with anaerobic exercise might improve weight loss compared with aerobic activity alone. Sixteen obese subjects performed one of two exercise protocols. Group one performed an aerobic cycle workout for 30 minutes for a total of four weeks while group two completed a 25-minute aerobic workout followed by 5 minutes of anaerobic exercise for four weeks. Adding 5 minutes of anaerobic exercise achieved a significantly greater reduction in body fat compared with aerobic exercise alone.[13] Total body fat, visceral fat, and abdominal fat also appear to be significantly reduced with the addition of anaerobic resistance training. The addition of anaerobic resistance training may have produced greater lipolysis of stored body fat.

Choosing the Right Exercise for You

Not all individuals respond to the same type of exercise. Most research compares the group mean response of weight

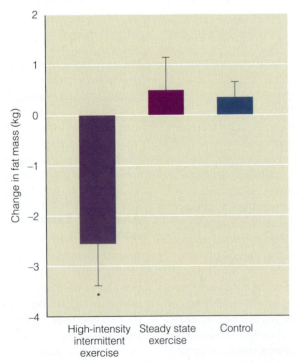

▲ **Figure 1** **The Effects of High-Intensity Intermittent Exercise on Fat Loss**

Source: E. G. Trapp, D. J. Chisholm, J. Freud, and S. H. Boutcher. 2008. "The Effects of High-Intensity Intermittent Exercise Training on Fat Loss and Fasting Insulin Levels of Young Women." *International Journal of Obesity* 32:684–691.

loss to exercise, not the individual variation. Just because one study failed to show results for the group of subjects doesn't mean it may not work for you. In other words, if you enjoy a specific type of exercise, and you find it effective in weight loss or maintaining a healthy weight—don't stop! Any exercise is better than not exercising at all.

In addition, both diet and exercise are essential to achieve the best results. The research is clear that achieving healthy weight loss requires not just exercise but dieting as well. In an 18-month study of 288 obese men and women, the results reported a significant drop in body fat and an increase in lean muscle mass when subjects participated in both exercise and a weight-loss diet compared with those who just exercised without dieting.[14] Thus, the combination of exercise and diet worked better than just exercise or just diet alone.

References

1. D. L. Swift, N. M. Johannsen, C. J. Lavie, C. P. Earnest, and T. S. Church. 2014. "The Role of Exercise and Physical Activity in Weight Loss and Maintenance." *Progress in Cardiovascular Diseases* 56(4):441–447.

2. C. E. Garber, B. Blissmer, M. R. Deschenes, B. A. Franklin, M. J. Lamonte, et al. 2011. "American College of Sports Medicine Position Stand. Quantity and Quality of Exercise for Developing and Maintaining Cardiorespiratory, Musculoskeletal, and Neuromotor Fitness in Apparently Healthy Adults: Guidance for Prescribing Exercise." *Medicine and Science in Sports and Exercise* 43(7):1334–1359.

3. W. Kemmler, M. Scharf, M. Lee, C. Petrasek, and S. von Stengel. 2014. "High versus Moderate Intensity Running Exercise to Impact Cardiometabolic Risk Factors: The Randomized Controlled RUSH-Study." *BioMed Research International* doi.org/10.1155/2014/843095.

4. A. C. Utter, D. C. Nieman, E. M. Shannonhouse, D. E. Butterworth, and C. N. Nieman. 1998. "Influence of Diet and/or Exercise on Body Composition and Cardiorespiratory Fitness in Obese Women." *International Journal of Sport Nutrition* 8(3):213–222.

5. L. M. Redman, L. K. Helbronn, C. K. Martin, A. Alfonso, S. R. Smith, and E. Ravussin. 2007. "Effect of Calorie Restriction With or Without Exercise on Body Composition and Fat Distribution." *Journal of Clinical Endocrinology and Metabolism* 92(3):865–872.

6. E. Hoppes and G. Caimi. 2011. "Exercise in Obesity Management." *Journal of Sports Medicine and Physical Fitness* 51(2):275–282.

7. A. McTiernan, B. Sorensen, M. L. Irwin, A. Morgan, Y. Yasui, R. E. Rudolph, et al. 2007. "Exercise Effect on Weight and Body Fat in Men and Women." *Obesity* 15(6):1496–1512.

8. D. L. Swift, N. M. Johannsen, C. J. Lavie, C. P. Earnest, and T. S. Church. 2014. "The Role of Exercise and Physical Activity in Weight Loss and Maintenance." *Progress in Cardiovascular Diseases* 56(4):441–447.

9. M. Heydari, J. Freund, and S. H. Boutcher. 2012. "The Effect of High-Intensity Intermittent Exercise on Body Composition of Overweight Young Males." *Journal of Obesity* doi:10.1155/2012/4804.

10. E. G. Trapp, D. J. Chisholm, J. Freud, and S. H. Boutcher. 2008. "The Effects of High-Intensity Intermittent Exercise Training on Fat Loss and Fasting Insulin Levels of Young Women." *International Journal of Obesity* 32:684–691.

11. C. Melby, C. Scholl, G. Edwards, and R. Bullough. 1993. "Effect of Acute Resistance Exercise on Post-Exercise Energy Expenditure and Resting Metabolic Rate." *Journal of Applied Physiology* 75(4):1847–1853.

12. L. H. Willis, C. A. Slentz, L. A. Bateman, A. T. Shields, L. W. Piner, C. W. Bates, et al. 2012. "Effects of Aerobic and/or Resistance Training on Body Mass and Fat Mass in Overweight or Obese Adults." *Journal of Applied Physiology* 113(12):1831–1837.

13. A. Salvadori, P. Fanari, P. Marzullo, F. Codecase, I. Tovaglieri, M. Cornacchia, et al. 2014. "Short Bouts of Anaerobic Exercise Increase Non-Esterified Fatty Acids Release in Obesity." *European Journal of Nutrition* 53(1):243–249.

14. K. M. Beavers, D. P. Beavers, B. A. Nesbit, W. T. Ambrosium, A. P. Marsh, B. J. Niclas, and W. J. Rejeski. 2014. "Effect of an 18-Month Physical Activity and Weight-Loss Intervention on Body Composition in Overweight and Obese Older Adults." *Obesity* 22(2):325–331.

used to identify weight gain behaviors include self-monitoring the behaviors by keeping a food log, controlling environmental cues that trigger eating when not hungry, and learning how to better manage stress.[84] Understanding the habits and emotions that drive your eating and exercise patterns is a key element of behavior modification. Once you have identified the less-than-healthy behaviors, you can replace them with new behaviors that promote weight loss and weight management.

A food log allows individuals to track the kinds of foods they eat during the day, when and where they eat them, their moods, and their hunger ratings. Based on this information, people can restructure their environment, how they respond to their environment, or both to improve the eating behaviors and manage their weight.

If you were to keep a food record, a typical day's log may be similar to the one in **Figure 15.7.** You might have habits that are common to people who struggle

Food Log

For: Hannah

Date: Monday, September 6

Food and drink	Time eaten	What I ate/ Where I ate it	Hunger level*	Mood †
Breakfast		Skipped it	3	G
Snack	11 a.m.	Oreo cookies, PowerAde from vending machine during morning class.	5	E
Lunch	1:30 p.m.	Ham and cheese sandwich, 2 large M&M cookies in student union cafeteria.	4	B
Snack				
Dinner	6:30 p.m.	Hamburger, french fries, salad at kitchen table	4	F
Snack	7 p.m. to 10 p.m.	Large bag of tortilla chips and entire bag of Pepperidge Farm Milano cookies while studying at kitchen table	1	I

*Hunger levels (1–5): 1 = not hungry; 5 = super hungry

† **Moods:**
A = Happy; B = Content; C = Bored; D = Depressed; E = Rushed; F = Stressed; G = Tired; H = Lonely; I = Anxious; J = Angry

▲ **Figure 15.7 Food Log**
Keeping track of when, where, and what you eat, as well as why you ate it, can yield some surprising information. Do you think you sometimes eat out of boredom or stress, rather than because you're hungry?

with their weight. These include skipping breakfast daily, which causes people to be very hungry in the late morning and increases impulsive snacking on energy-dense, low-nutrition foods from vending machines. A study of overweight women who typically skipped breakfast showed that once they started consuming cereal for breakfast, they indulged in less impulsive snacking.[85] Eating a bowl of high-fiber whole-grain cereal with skim milk (approximately 200 kilocalories) can help you bypass an 11 a.m. vending machine snack of 270-kilocalorie cookies and a 210-kilocalorie sports drink. This one behavior change would not only save a person 280 kilocalories in the morning, but reduce added sugar intake and add more nutrition to daily food intake. Additionally, adding a less-energy-dense salad at lunch could help increase satiety and displace at least one of the energy-dense cookies that people often grab with a sandwich.

Stress-induced eating associated with studying can be modified by a change in environment—for example, by going to the campus library, where eating is prohibited. In fact, removing access to snacks altogether is an excellent environmental change—once snacks are "out of sight" they are more likely to be "out of mind." Exercising before or after studying would be a healthier way to relieve stress than eating a bag of snacks. The Table Tips on page 560 list some additional healthy behaviors that can easily be incorporated into your life.

Based on the information presented in the Nutrition and Practice on page 569, what recommendations would you have for Victor in his quest to lose weight?

Nutrition in Practice: Victor

After his first year at college, Victor became concerned about his weight gain. He felt sluggish compared with a year ago. In fact, he even lost interest in playing pickup basketball with his friends. In an effort to increase his energy levels, he started going to the gym several times a week. When he got on the scale at the gym, he was shocked to learn that he had gained 20 pounds over the school year. He had never struggled with weight in high school, but he knows he has been eating bigger meals at college than at home because the food is good and he is on an unlimited food plan. When Victor discovered that his college employs a Registered Dietitian Nutritionist (RDN) who counsels both the faculty and students, he decided to make an appointment.

Victor's Stats:
- Age: 19
- Height: 5 feet 9 inches
- Weight: 185 pounds
- BMI: 27.3

Victor's Food Log

Food/Beverage	Time Consumed	Hunger Rating*	Location
Bacon and eggs with toast and butter	7 AM	3	Dining hall
Coffee (Mocha Supreme) and scone	10:30 AM	2	Coffee shop
Cheeseburger, fries, large cola	1:30 PM	5	Dining hall
Soft-serve ice cream, large, chocolate with fudge	4 PM	4	Dining hall
Fried chicken, mashed potatoes, corn, large cola	6:30 PM	3	Dining hall
Potato chips	10 PM	1	Study

*Hunger Rating (1–5): 1 = not hungry; 5 = super hungry.

Critical Thinking Questions

1. What would be a healthy weight for Victor?
2. Based on his food log, which waist-friendly food groups are inadequate in his diet?
3. What beverage recommendations would you make based on his food log?

Dietitian's Observation and Plan for Victor:

- Discuss the need to cut back on some excess kilocalories in his diet without causing him to be hungry during the day. To achieve this goal, he needs to add more low-energy-dense fruits, vegetables, and beverages to his meals and snacks to help him feel satiated and displace higher kilocalorie items at his meals and snacks.
- For breakfast have a whole-wheat bagel and a small amount of cream cheese and take a piece of fruit for his mid-morning snack rather than the scone.
- Replace the fries at lunch with a salad with low-kilocalorie dressing.
- Substitute a small low-fat frozen yogurt topped with fresh fruit for the large ice cream in the afternoon.
- Substitute a piece of fruit for the potato chips in the evening.
- Order a latte with skim milk instead of the higher kilocalorie mid-morning mocha coffee at the coffee shop.
- Drink water or nonkilocaloric beverages at all meals.

Two weeks later, Victor returns for a follow-up visit with the dietitian. He has lost a pound of weight and is excited! He has added more fruits and vegetables to his diet and, surprisingly, feels full. He no longer drinks sugary beverages during the day. The RDN works with Victor to choose leaner sources of protein at lunch and dinner. Victor agrees to try the turkey or veggie burger at lunch and grilled chicken at dinner. He makes another appointment to see the RDN in two weeks.

Adopt Some Healthy Habits

Don't eat out of boredom or stress; go for a jog instead.

Food shop with a full stomach and a grocery list. Walking around aimlessly while hungry means you are more likely to grab items on a whim.

The next time you pass a difficult course or get that long-awaited raise, celebrate without a plate. Replace the traditional restaurant dinner with a no-kilocalorie reward such as a new music download or a weekend hike.

Declare a vending machine–free day at least once a week, save money, and stop the impulsive snacking. On that day, pack two pieces of fruit as satisfying snacks.

LO 15.5: THE TAKE-HOME MESSAGE For successful, long-term weight loss, people can reduce their daily kilocalorie intake, increase their physical activity, and improve their eating behaviors. Adding low-energy-density, high-volume vegetables, fruit, and fiber along with some lean protein and healthy oils to the diet can help increase satiety and reduce unplanned snacking. Incorporating approximately 60 to 90 minutes of physical activity daily can facilitate weight loss. Establishing healthy eating and exercise habits by restructuring the environment to minimize or eliminate unhealthy eating can also help shed extra pounds.

How Can Weight Loss Be Maintained?

LO 15.6 Design a food and exercise plan to maintain a healthy weight.

Losing weight can be difficult, but not regaining the lost weight over time can be just as challenging. You or someone you know may be familiar with the typical weight-loss experience: the triumphant rush associated with dropping 10 pounds of weight, the disappointment that sets in when 15 pounds are regained, then a new round of hope when 10 of them are re-shed.

But don't be discouraged! Weight loss can be maintained when the right strategies are used. In a recent study of 3,000 individuals who had lost at least 30 pounds, researchers reported that 87 percent of the subjects who lost at least 10 percent of their body weight had maintained the weight loss when measured at 5 and 10 years.[86] The researchers reported that low-fat diets, avoiding overeating, being physically active, and daily self-weighing were successful strategies in maintaining the subjects' weight loss.

Diet and Exercise Can Aid in Maintaining Weight Loss

Consuming a healthy diet is as essential to weight-loss maintenance as it was to the weight loss. Individuals who lose weight often experience an **energy gap.** After weight loss, a person will have lower overall energy needs, as there is less body weight to maintain. The energy gap is the difference in daily kilocalories that are needed for weight maintenance before and after weight loss.[87] Researchers have estimated that the energy gap is about 8 kilocalories per pound of lost weight.[88] For example, someone who lost 30 pounds would need approximately 240 fewer kilocalories a day to maintain the new, lower body weight.

One problem with maintaining weight loss is that once the weight has been lost, individuals revert to the unhealthy eating habits that caused the excess weight in the first place. To adapt your eating patterns to the new body weight, limit the intake of fatty foods, monitor your kilocalorie intake, and follow a pattern of eating three small meals and two snacks a day. For many people, eating more frequent, smaller meals allows them to avoid becoming ravenous and overeating at the next meal. If weight loss continues even though you've reached your goal weight, gradually add about 200 kilocalories of healthy, low-fat, high-fiber foods to your daily intake until weight balance is achieved.

Another way to close the energy gap and help the body adjust to its new lower weight is to increase exercise. Because the environment we live in seems to encourage eating more than discourage it, researchers believe that increasing daily physical activity is likely the easier way to close the energy gap.[89] *Adding* something (physical activity) to one's lifestyle is often easier than *removing* something (kilocalories). Thus, the recommendation is to engage in 60 to 90 minutes of moderate physical activity daily in order to maintain weight loss.[90]

energy gap The difference between the numbers of kilocalories needed to maintain weight before and after weight loss.

Daily self-weighing may help maintain a healthy body weight.

Self-Weighing Is a Positive Strategy to Maintain Weight Loss

Daily or weekly self-weighing has often been discouraged to prevent increasing the risk of disordered eating, negative body image, mood disorders, or binge eating. Recent research refutes these claims and reports that daily self-weighing improved body satisfaction[91] and helped maintain weight loss.[92]

LO 15.6: THE TAKE-HOME MESSAGE People who lose weight are most likely to keep it off if they maintain the positive diet and lifestyle habits that helped them lose the weight. Exercise improves muscle mass, prevents a decline in basal metabolism, and helps overcome plateaus often associated with weight loss. Eating less and/or exercising more helps close the energy gap that occurs after weight loss.

What Is the Healthiest Way to Gain Weight?

LO 15.7 Describe the role of diet and exercise in achieving a healthy weight gain.

For people who are underweight, trying to gain weight can be as challenging and frustrating as trying to lose weight is for an overweight individual. The major difference is that the thin person rarely gets sympathy from others.

Like overweight individuals, those who are underweight experience an energy imbalance. In their case, however, they consume fewer kilocalories than they expend each day. Because those who wish to gain weight generally want to add muscle mass, rather than large amounts of fat, the challenge is to eat sufficient energy to meet their basal metabolic needs plus provide fuel for the exercise needed to stimulate muscle synthesis.

People who want to gain weight need to do the opposite of those who are trying to lose weight—they need to make each bite more energy dense. Adding at least

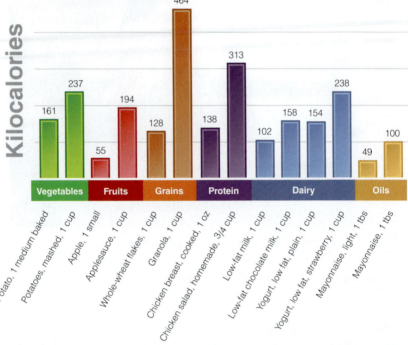

TABLE TIPS

Healthy Snacks for Healthy Weight Gain

Stash an 8-ounce container of 100 percent fruit juice (about 100 kilocalories) in your bag, plus one of the 150-kilocalorie snacks listed below for a quick 250-kilocalorie snack (food and juice combined) between meals.

Graham crackers, 5 crackers (2 ½" square)

Mixed nuts, 1 oz

Fig bars, 2-oz package

Pudding, individual serving sizes, 4 oz

Peanut butter on whole-wheat crackers (1 tbs peanut butter on 6 crackers)

500 kilocalories to their daily energy intake will enable them to add about a pound of extra body weight weekly.

Of course, someone who wants to gain weight should not just load up on high-fat, high-kilocalorie foods. The quality of the extra kilocalories is very important. Snacking on an extra 500 kilocalories of jellybeans adds 500 kilocalories of sugar and little nutrient value. Instead, these individuals should make energy-dense, nutritious choices from a variety of foods within each food group. For example, instead of eating a slice of toast in the morning, they should choose a whole-grain waffle. In a salad bar lunch, adding coleslaw provides 10 times the kilocalories of plain cabbage. **Figure 15.8** contrasts more- and less-energy-dense foods within each food group. Eating larger portion sizes at meals and energy-dense snacks during the day also adds kilocalories. The Table Tips provide easy and portable snack ideas.

Regular exercise and resistance training stimulates muscle growth and helps avoid excess fat storage. Remember that it takes time to gain weight and build sufficient muscle mass. Be patient and continue to choose healthy foods until you reach your goal weight.

LO 15.7: THE TAKE-HOME MESSAGE People who want to gain weight need to consume additional kilocalories through energy-dense foods so that they take in more energy than they expend. Adding nutrient-dense snacks between meals and increasing portion sizes during meals are easy ways to increase the number of kilocalories consumed. Add resistance exercise to build muscle mass and avoid excess fat storage.

What Are the Medical Interventions for Extreme Obesity?

LO 15.8 Describe the role of weight-loss drugs and surgery for reducing obesity.

For most people, the best path to a healthy body weight is to commit to improving their diet and exercising more. However, for some individuals, these measures are not enough to attain adequate weight loss. In fact, those who are extremely obese are at such a high risk for conditions such as heart disease and stroke, and even of dying, that a much more aggressive weight-loss treatment may be necessary. Extreme treatments for the extremely obese may include medications and/or surgery.

Weight-Loss Medications May Improve Weight Loss but Have Side Effects

Some prescription medications can help a person lose weight by either suppressing hunger or inhibiting the absorption of fat in the intestinal tract. The biggest risks associated with taking such drugs are often the potential side effects; because of this, they are almost always available only by prescription and must be taken under the care of a health care provider.

One hunger suppressant is the drug sibutramine (trade name Meridia), which reduces hunger and increases thermogenesis. The increased thermogenesis results in increased energy expenditure. However, the drug can also increase a person's heart rate and blood pressure, and therefore may not be appropriate for those who have

hypertension, which tends to occur often in overweight individuals.

The fat-absorption-inhibitor orlistat (trade name Xenical) is a prescription medication that inhibits an intestinal enzyme needed to break down fat. If fat isn't broken down, the body doesn't absorb the fat (and kilocalories). Up to about a third of the dietary fat in a meal is blocked and expelled in the stool. Orlistat needs to be taken at each meal and should be used with a diet that provides no more than about 30 percent of its kilocalories from fat. Because fat is lost in the stool, the drug can cause oily and more frequent stools, flatulence, and oily discharge.[93] Ironically, these side effects may help an individual adhere to a low-fat diet, as these effects are more pronounced if a high-fat meal is consumed.

A reduced-strength version of orlistat (brand named Alli) is approved as an over-the-counter medication for overweight adults 18 years and older. Alli, combined with a low-kilocalorie, low-fat diet and regular exercise, aids in modest weight loss. Because of the recent reports of rare, but serious, cases of liver damage in individuals using Xenical and Alli, both of these drugs must now carry warnings on their labels.[94]

A new weight-loss drug called Lorcaserin was recently approved by the FDA. This drug stimulates the release of serotonin, a neurotransmitter that stimulates satiety and may reduce food intake.[95] The drug was approved based on the results of the Behavioral Modification and Lorcaserin for Overweight and Obesity Management (BLOOM) study. Over 3,000 overweight and obese adult male and females were given Lorcaserin in a double-blind study over two years. The results showed that after one year, 47.5 percent of the subjects receiving Lorcaserin lost 5 percent or more of their

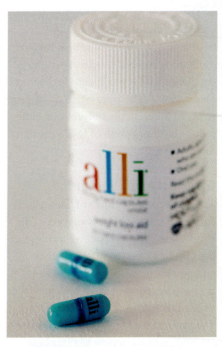

Alli promotes weight loss by reducing the digestion and absorption of fat.

original body weight, compared with 20.3 percent of the placebo group.[96] After two years, 67.9 percent of the Lorcaserin group had maintained their weight loss compared with 50.3 percent of the placebo group. This drug may cause side effects, including nausea, vomiting, constipation, diarrhea, upper respiratory tract and urinary tract infections, back pain, headache, and even memory loss and depression.[97]

Sometimes the side effects of weight-loss medications can be so serious that the medication must be withdrawn from the market. For instance, the FDA has prohibited the sale of supplements that contain ephedra (also called Ma huang), the plant source for ephedrine. Ephedrine has been shown to cause chest pains, palpitations, hypertension, and an accelerated heart rate. In 2003, baseball player Steve Bechler died at age 23 after taking a weight-loss supplement containing ephedrine during spring training. Ephedrine was determined to have contributed to his death.[98]

Bariatric Surgery Restricts Food Intake

Bariatric surgery has been shown to be an effective means of weight loss for moderately to severely obese people compared with low-kilocalorie diets and medication.[99] The term bariatric surgery refers to different procedures that either reduce the absorption of food or restrict food intake.

Gastric Bypass Surgery

The most common form of bariatric surgery is **gastric bypass surgery.** This surgical technique was developed in the middle of the twentieth century and quickly grew in popularity. The first gastric bypass surgery was performed in 1967 by Dr. Edward Mason, a surgeon at the University of Iowa.[100] By 1998, approximately 13,000 obese patients each year underwent gastric

bariatric surgery A surgical procedure that promotes weight loss by limiting the amount of food that can be eaten or absorbed.

gastric bypass surgery A type of bariatric surgery that reduces the functional volume of the stomach to minimize the amount of food eaten. Such surgeries are sometimes used to treat extreme obesity.

Al Roker, NBC's *Today Show* weatherman, lost approximately 140 pounds after gastric bypass surgery.

bypass to reduce the size of their stomachs. Ten years later that number had increased to over 190,000—more than a 1,400 percent increase.[101] During gastric bypass surgery, the stomach is reduced in size by making a small pouch at the

top of the stomach with surgical staples (see **Figure 15.9**). The stomach pouch is connected to the jejunum, bypassing the rest of the stomach and the upper small intestine. This reduces the size of the stomach so that it holds less than ¼ cup of food, and also reduces the small intestine's ability to absorb food. After the surgery, individuals need to consume small, frequent meals because the stomach pouch can only expand to a maximum of about 5 ounces, the size of a woman's fist. Bypass patients not only eat less because of their smaller stomachs, but also have higher levels of satiety and lower levels of hunger after the surgery. This loss of appetite is thought to be due to lower levels of ghrelin associated with the loss of stomach area.[102]

Because food is rerouted past the majority of the stomach and the duodenum, individuals can experience deficiencies of vitamin B_{12}, iron, and calcium. Recall from Chapter 10 that vitamin B_{12} needs to be separated from the protein in food before it can be absorbed. Also, intrinsic factor (IF) secreted from the gastric cells is needed for vitamin B_{12} to be absorbed, which is missing after surgery. To be absorbed, iron is converted from ferric iron to

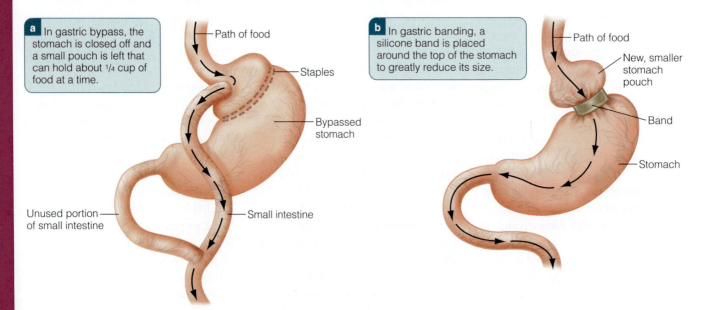

a In gastric bypass, the stomach is closed off and a small pouch is left that can hold about ¼ cup of food at a time.

Path of food

Staples

Bypassed stomach

Unused portion of small intestine

Small intestine

b In gastric banding, a silicone band is placed around the top of the stomach to greatly reduce its size.

Path of food

New, smaller stomach pouch

Band

Stomach

▲ **Figure 15.9 Gastric Bypass and Gastric Banding Surgical Procedures**
Bariatric surgery, including gastric bypass and gastric banding, restricts food intake and promotes malabsorption.

ferrous iron by hydrochloric acid secreted in the stomach. Bariatric surgery reduces the amount of hydrochloric acid released, which results in less iron available for absorption. Iron and calcium are also typically absorbed in the upper part of the small intestine, which is now bypassed. Vitamin B_{12} injections or supplements must be taken because of these deficiencies. Calcium and iron supplements, plus vitamin C, are prescribed immediately following surgery to help maintain a healthy balance.

Although weight loss varies from one individual to the next, the average weight loss with gastric bypass surgery is approximately 5 to 15 pounds per week for the first two or three months.[103] The weight loss gradually tapers off to about 1 to 2 pounds per week after the first six months. Other benefits of gastric surgery included the reduction of diabetes in 76.8 percent of patients, improved hyperlipidemia in more than 70 percent of patients, and the elimination of hypertension (in 61.7 percent) and sleep apnea (in 85.7 percent).[104]

Although dramatic amounts of weight loss can occur, there are also risks involved. About 10 percent of those undergoing gastric bypass surgery experience complications such as gallstones, ulcers, and bleeding in the stomach and intestines. Approximately 1 to 2 percent die from complications relating to the surgery.[105] After surgery, individuals need to be monitored long term by their doctor and nutrition professionals to ensure that they remain healthy and meet their nutritional needs.

Gastric Banding Surgery

A type of gastric surgery that's becoming more popular is a reversible procedure (unlike the permanent gastric bypass surgery), **laparoscopic gastric banding,** in which a silicone band is placed around the top of the stomach to create a small pouch with a very narrow opening at the bottom for the food to pass through. This delays the emptying of the stomach contents so that a person feels fuller longer. The doctor

can adjust the opening of the pouch by inflating or deflating the band. Weight loss with laparoscopic gastric banding is slower than with gastric bypass but the surgery is less invasive and the band can be removed if necessary. One study reported a weight loss of 58 percent after five years.[106]

LO 15.8: THE TAKE-HOME MESSAGE
Pharmacological and surgical approaches may be necessary for obese individuals. The current weight-loss drugs suppress appetite, reduce fat absorption, or increase serotonin production and satiety. Weight-loss drugs may have serious side effects. Gastric bypass surgery reduces the absorption of food and restricts food intake. Laparoscopic gastric banding is less invasive and reversible. This form of surgery creates a small stomach pouch that increases satiation.

laparoscopic gastric banding A type of gastric surgery that uses a silicone band to reduce the size of the stomach so that less food is needed to feel full.

Visual Chapter Summary

LO 15.1 Weight Management Is Important for Physical and Emotional Well-Being

Weight management means maintaining a healthy weight to reduce the risk of specific health problems. Social and psychological misperceptions and prejudices toward people who are obese or underweight may contribute to discrimination, low self-esteem, depression, suicide, and alcohol and drug problems. Classifying obesity as a disease may improve treatment options but may also raise health care costs, increase drug and surgical procedures, and reduce emphasis on lifestyle changes to lose weight.

LO 15.2 Food Intake Is Regulated by the Hypothalamus

Food intake is regulated by the physiological responses known as hunger and satiety. Hunger prompts the body to eat and subsides soon after eating begins. Satiety determines the length of time between meals or snacks. Appetite is psychological, not physiological, and can be affected by the sight, smell, taste, and thought of food, as well as emotions, environment, and social settings.

Hunger is controlled by the lateral hypothalamus and satiety is controlled by the ventromedial nucleus of the hypothalamus. Both areas of the brain respond to hormonal and neural signals from the GI tract. Certain hormones, including neuropeptide Y from the hypothalamus and ghrelin from the stomach, stimulate hunger. Other hormones, including cholecystokinin and peptide YY from the small intestine, insulin from the pancreas, and leptin from adipose tissue, increase satiety.

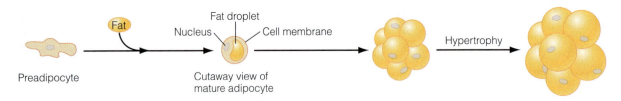

Preadipocyte

Fat

Nucleus

Fat droplet

Cell membrane

Cutaway view of mature adipocyte

Hypertrophy

LO 15.3 Fat Cells Form, Expand, and Shrink

Fat cells can increase in size to store additional fat (hypertrophy) and new fat cells can be produced (hyperplasia) to replace old cells and to create additional cells once existing ones fill to capacity. During weight loss, fat cells shrink but are not destroyed.

The enzymes lipoprotein lipase and hormone-sensitive lipase influence the balance between lipolysis and lipogenesis. Lipoprotein lipase activity stimulates lipogenesis and hormone-sensitive lipase activity stimulates lipolysis. LPL activity is greater in obese individuals; in men, LPL is more active in the abdominal fat cells than in females, but females have higher LPL activity rates in the hips and thighs than do males.

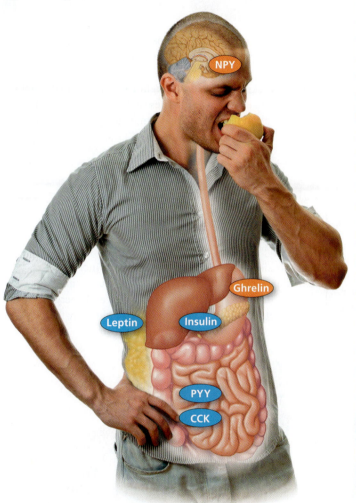

LO 15.4 Genetics and Environment Both Influence Obesity and Weight Management

An individual's genetic makeup can influence the predisposition or risk of becoming obese. Nutrigenomics has identified specific genes that influence how we absorb, store, or break down dietary fat. Epigenetics, or the change in gene activity and expression that occurs when the epigenome partially unwinds, may explain why certain foods affect body weight. Single-nucleotide polymorphisms of multiple genes influence the secretion of hunger-control hormones such as ghrelin and leptin. Genetic makeup also influences thermogenesis for maintaining a specific weight.

Obesity can be promoted by a gene–environment interaction in which genetically prone individuals have easy access to a variety of large portions of food and an environment that encourages a sedentary lifestyle. Environmental factors such as the lack of time, an abundant food supply and portion distortion, and lack of physical activity due to the advances in technology add to the risk of obesity.

LO 15.5 Losing Weight Healthfully Involves Eating Less and Exercising More

A healthy, reasonable rate of weight loss is losing 10 percent of body weight over a six-month period. Losing weight rapidly can cause a person to fall short of meeting nutrient needs. Many fad diets promise quick results but can be unhealthy for the long term.

Expending more kilocalories than consumed is the key to weight loss. Eating more low-energy-density, high-volume, high-fiber foods, such as vegetables and fruit, improves satiation, which results in fewer kilocalories consumed. Protein has the most dramatic effect on satiety. Eating high-protein foods such as lean meats, chicken, and fish at meals can help reduce hunger between meals. Because fat slows the movement of food out of the stomach into the intestines, it can also prolong satiety.

Routine physical activity and exercise can add to the daily energy deficit needed for weight loss. To aid in weight loss, over-weight individuals should partake in 60 to 90 minutes of moderate-intensity exercise daily and continue at least this amount of activity daily to maintain the weight loss.

Individuals who wish to lose weight must change the eating behaviors that contributed to weight gain or impeded weight loss. Self-monitoring of these behaviors by keeping a food record, controlling environmental cues that trigger eating when not hungry, and learning how to better manage stress are all behavior modification techniques that can be used by individuals who eat "out of habit" and in response to their environment.

LO 15.6 Behavior Modification Helps Maintain a Healthy Weight

Modifying your food intake to reflect lowered energy requirements is essential to weight-loss maintenance. After weight loss, there is an energy gap between the original body weight and the new healthy weight, which may be as high as 8 kilocalories per pound of lost body weight. The energy gap can also be adjusted with an increase in exercise of about 60 to 90 minutes per day. Self-weighing each day can improve body satisfaction and help maintain weight loss.

LO 15.7 Eat More Nutrient-Dense Foods and Exercise to Gain Weight Healthily

Individuals who wish to gain weight must increase kilocalorie intake and exercise to build muscle mass. Consuming larger portions at mealtimes and energy-dense snacks between meals can help with weight gain.

LO 15.8 Surgery and Pharmacological Aids May Be Necessary to Treat Extremely Obese Individuals

For extremely obese individuals who have tried diet and exercise and failed to achieve a healthy body weight, pharmacological and surgical treatments may be necessary. The current weight-loss drugs approved by the FDA suppress appetite, reduce fat absorption, or increase serotonin production and satiety. Weight-loss drugs may have serious side effects. Bariatric surgery procedures are designed to reduce the absorption of food or restrict food intake. Gastric bypass surgery involves reducing the stomach into a small pouch and connecting it to the jejunum, in order to bypass the rest of the stomach and the duodenum. Laparoscopic gastric banding, which uses an adjustable silicon band to create a small stomach pouch, is reversible and less invasive.

Gastric bypass

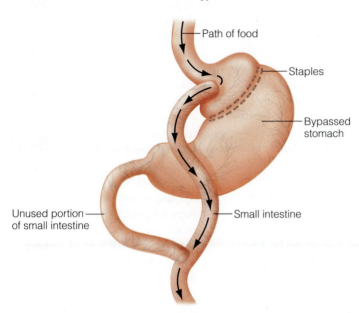

- Path of food
- Staples
- Bypassed stomach
- Unused portion of small intestine
- Small intestine

Gastric banding

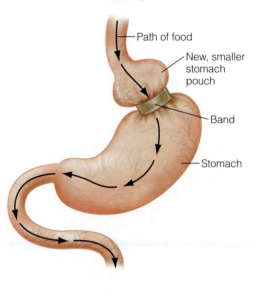

- Path of food
- New, smaller stomach pouch
- Band
- Stomach

Terms to Know

- weight management
- appetite
- hunger
- satiation
- satiety
- hypertrophy
- hyperplasia
- gene–environment interaction
- nutrigenomics
- epigenetics
- adiponectin
- set point
- behavior modification
- energy gap
- bariatric surgery
- gastric bypass surgery
- laparoscopic gastric banding

MasteringNutrition™

Scan to hear an MP3 Chapter Review in MasteringNutrition.

Check Your Understanding

1. The physiological need for food is called
   a. hunger.
   b. satiety.
   c. appetite.
   d. hyperplasia.
2. The section of the hypothalamus that controls hunger is called the
   a. ventromedial nucleus.
   b. lateral hypothalamus.
   c. hippocampus.
   d. pituitary gland.
3. When an individual loses body fat
   a. there is a decrease in the number of adipocytes due to hyperplasia.
   b. there is a decrease in the size of the fat cells due to hypertrophy.
   c. there is no change in the adipocytes, but subcutaneous fat is lost.
   d. the adipocytes shrink but the number of cells stays the same.
4. A rate of sustainable, healthy weight loss is ½ to 1 pound per week.
   a. True
   b. False
5. After a large meal of pasta and tomato sauce, the stomach is distended. Which hormone is released because of the distention of the stomach?
   a. cholecystokinin
   b. insulin

c. ghrelin
d. leptin
6. Which of the following can increase the risk of becoming overweight?
   a. having a parent who is obese
   b. consuming more meals at home than dining out
   c. reducing the amounts of "screen time" during the day
   d. decreasing the size of your food portions at meals
7. What is the best dietary approach to losing weight?
   a. eliminate all carbohydrates from the diet
   b. reduce kilocalorie intake and increase energy expenditure through physical activity
   c. consume foods high in both protein and fat to stimulate satiety
   d. limit fat intake to less than 5 grams per day
8. Mary Ellen was obese and lost 30 pounds during the last year by eating a well-balanced, kilocalorie-reduced diet and being physically active daily. To maintain her weight loss, she should continue to eat a healthy diet, monitor her eating behaviors, and
   a. accumulate 30 minutes of physical activity three times a week.
   b. accumulate 45 minutes of physical activity three times a week.
   c. accumulate at least 60 minutes of physical activity daily.
   d. accumulate more than 2 hours of physical activity daily.
9. Which of the following weight-loss medications may stimulate thermogenesis?
   a. Meridia
   b. Xenical
   c. Alli
   d. Lorcaserin
10. Which of the following surgical procedures can be reversed?
    a. gastric bypass surgery
    b. bariatric surgery
    c. laparoscopic gastric banding
    d. All of these surgical procedures are easily reversible.

Answers

1. (a) The physiological need for food is called hunger. Satiety is the feeling of fullness or satisfaction that sets in after eating begins, while appetite is defined as the desire for a food even in the absence of hunger. Hyperplasia is an increase in the number of fat cells.
2. (b) The lateral hypothalamus controls hunger, while the ventromedial nucleus is responsible for satiation. The hippocampus is a structure involved in memory consolidation. The pituitary gland, located beneath the hypothalamus, secretes many hormones important to homeostasis; it is not technically part of the brain.
3. (d) When the body loses fat, the adipocyte shrinks in size, but the number of fat cells remains constant. Adipocytes are the specialized cells that make up all adipose tissue, including subcutaneous fat. Hyperplasia is an increase in fat cells when the old cells have become saturated with fat and hypertrophy is the increase in the size of the adipocyte as it stores more fat.
4. (a) The average person can healthfully lose about ½ to 1 pound per week.
5. (a) A distended stomach causes the release of cholecystokinin, which is associated with the feeling of satiation and the ending of eating. Insulin is released once this carbohydrate-heavy meal is digested and absorbed into the blood. Ghrelin is released from the stomach when it is empty, and stimulates feeding. Leptin is secreted from the adipocyte and stimulates hunger when the fat cell shrinks.
6. (a) Having a parent who is overweight and/or obese may indicate that you have a genetic predisposition to becoming overweight. Increasing your regular physical activity by reducing screen time, eating more meals at home, and reducing food portions are methods that reduce your risk of becoming overweight.
7. (b) The best approach to losing weight is to reduce the total amount of kilocalories by reducing the amount of food consumed and increasing energy expenditure through physical activity. Consuming a diet that eliminated carbohydrates or contained high-protein, high-fat foods or less than 5 grams of fat per day would be unbalanced in nutrient content and could result in malnutrition.
8. (c) If Mary Ellen would like to keep the weight off, she should try to accumulate at least 60 to 90 minutes of physical activity daily.
9. (a) Merida or sibutramine increases thermogenesis and energy expenditure. Xenical, also known as orlistat, and Alli, the less potent over-the-counter weight-loss medication, inhibit fat absorption. Lorcaserin stimulates the release of serotonin and satiety.
10. (c) Laparoscopic banding surgery uses a silicone band placed around the top of the stomach to create a small pouch with a very narrow opening at the bottom for the food to pass through. This band can be removed if necessary. Gastric bypass surgery, a form of bariatric surgery, forms a small stomach that is connected to the jejunum, bypassing the rest of the stomach and upper small intestine. This form of surgery is not easily reversed.

Answers to True or False?

1. **False.** While the recommendation for weight loss is to accumulate at least 60 to 90 minutes of daily physical activity, the bottom line is that for weight loss to occur, more energy must be expended than is consumed. This can be accomplished by consuming less, exercising more, or a combination of both.
2. **False.** While the overall number of fat cells generally doesn't increase in adulthood, fat cell synthesis continues to replace old cells. Ten percent of fat cells are replaced with new cells every 10 years.
3. **False.** Grazing is considered a high-risk behavior for weight management because the foods that are typically chosen are low in protein and not

satiating. Individuals may also consume higher amounts of kilocalories by eating mindlessly rather than consuming planned, smaller meals.

4. **True.** Weight loss of as little as 10 pounds can improve health if an individual is overweight.

5. **True.** Nature and nurture both play a role in regulating body weight. Nature (genes) often sets the stage, while nurture (environment and personal behavior) directly affects weight management.

6. **True.** Increasing the volume of food and the fiber content of meals by eating *more* vegetables and fruits can improve appetite control, reducing kilocalorie intake and thus helping attain weight loss.

7. **True.** At its most basic, weight gain occurs because of a positive energy balance. However, genetics and the environment play strong roles.

8. **False.** Of all the nutrients, protein has the most powerful effect on satiety.

9. **False.** Most weight-loss supplement labels indicate that you need to eat a healthy diet and exercise regularly if you want to shed the pounds.

10. **False.** Bariatric surgery alters the gastrointestinal tract and requires permanent changes to eating habits.

Web Resources

- For more on overweight and obesity, visit the Centers for Disease Control and Prevention at www.cdc.gov/nccdphp/dnpa/obesity/index.htm
- For more information on weight control and physical activity, visit the Weight-control Information Network (WIN) at http://win.niddk.nih.gov/index.htm
- For more weight-loss shopping tips, recipes, and menu makeovers, visit the USDA's Nutrition and Weight Management website at www.nutrition.gov
- For more information on gastric bypass surgery, visit the American Society for Metabolic and Bariatric Surgery at www.asbs.org

References

1. Weight Control and Information Network. 2014. *Overweight and Obesity Statistics.* Available at http://win.niddk.nih.gov/statistics/. Accessed July 2014.
2. Ibid.
3. Li, J. S., T. A. Barnett, E. Goodman, R. C. Wasserman, and A. R. Kemper. 2012. Approaches to the Prevention and Management of Childhood Obesity: The Role of Social Networks and the Use of Social Media and Related Electronic Technologies: A Scientific Statement from the American Heart Association. *Circulation*, doi: 10.1161/CIR.0b013e3182756d8e.
4. Williams, J. 2013. *The Heavy Price of Losing Weight.* Available at www.money.usnews.com. Accessed May 2014.
5. Cornell University. 2012. *Obesity Accounts for 21 Percent of U.S. Health Care Costs, Study Finds.* Available at www.sciencedaily.com/releases/2012/04/120409103247.htm. Accessed May 2014.
6. Weight-Control Information Network. 2013. *Do You Know the Health Risks of Being Overweight?* Available at http://win.niddk.nih.gov/publications/health_risks.htm. Accessed May 2014.
7. Ibid.
8. Bialo, S. R., and C. M. Gordon. 2014. Underweight, Overweight, and Pediatric Bone Fragility: Impact and Management. *Current Osteoporosis Reports* doi:10.1007/s11914-014-0226-z.
9. American Medical Association. 2013. *AMA Adopts New Policies on Second Day of Voting at Annual Meeting.* Available at www.ama-assn.org/ama/pub/news/news/2013/2013-06-18-new-ama-policies-annual-meeting.page. Accessed May 2014.
10. Conover, Chris. 2013. *Declaring Obesity a Disease: The Good, the Bad, the Ugly.* Available at www.forbes.com/sites/theapothecary/2013/06/28/declaring-obesity-a-disease-the-good-the-bad-the-ugly. Accessed May 2014.
11. Saguy, A. C., D. Frederick, and K. Gruys. 2014. Reporting Risk, Producing Prejudice: How News Reporting on Obesity Shapes Attitudes about Health Risk, Policy, and Prejudice. *Social Science and Medicine* 111:125–133.
12. Richards, E. 2013. *College Admissions Bias Reflects Cultural Sterotypes.* Available at www.examiner.com/article/college-admissions-bias-reflects-cultural-stereotypes. Accessed May 2014.
13. U. S. News Report and Travel. 2014. *Who Is Too Fat to Fly? Airlines Are Working It Out.* Available at www.huffingtonpost.com/us-news-travel/too-fat-to-fly_b_2101347.html. Accessed May 2014.
14. Puhl, R. M., and C. A. Heuer. 2010. Obesity Stigma: Important Considerations for Public Health. *American Journal of Public Health* 100(6):1019–1028.
15. Hemmingsson, E. 2014. A New Model of the Role of Psychological and Emotional Distress in Promoting Obesity: Conceptual Review with Implications for Treatment and Prevention. *Obesity Review* doi: 10.1111/obr.12197.
16. Hong, Y., M. G. Ory, C. Lee, S. Wang, J. Pulczinksi, and S. N. Forjuoh. 2012. Walking and Neighborhood Environment for Obese and Overweight Patients: Perspectives from Family Physicians. *Family Medicine* 44(5):336–341.
17. Henriksen, C. A., A. A. Mather, C. S. Mackenzie, O. J. Bienvenu, and J. Sareen. 2014. Longitudinal Associations of Obesity with Affective Disorders and Suicidality in the Baltimore Epidemiologic Catchment Area Follow-Up Study. *Journal of Nervous and Mental Disease* 202(5):379–385.
18. Field, A. E., K. R. Sonneville, R. D. Crosby, et al. 2014. Prospective Associations of Concerns about Physique and the Development of Obesity, Binge Drinking, and Drug Use among Adolescent Boys and Young Adult Men. *JAMA Pediatrics* 168(1):34–39.
19. Calugi, S., M. El Ghoch, M. Conti, and R. Dalle Grave. 2014. Depression and Treatment Outcome in Anorexia Nervosa. *Psychiatry Research* 218(1-2):195–200.
20. Gao, S., J. Juhaeri, S. Reshef, and W. S. Dai. 2013. Association between Body Mass Index and Suicide, and Suicide Attempt among British Adults: The Health Improvement Network Database. *Obesity* 21(3):E334–E342.
21. Morris, P. F., and C. P. Szabo. 2013. Meanings of Thinness and Dysfunctional Eating in Black South African Females: A Qualitative Study. *African Journal of Psychiatry* 16(5):338–342.
22. Crespo, C. S., A. P. Cachero, L. P. Jiménez, V. Barrios, and E. A. Ferreiro. 2014. Peptides and Food Intake. *Frontiers in Endocrinology* doi: 10.3389/fendo.2014.00058.
23. Ibid.
24. Friedman, J. M. 2011. Leptin and the Regulation of Body Weight. *The Keio Journal of Medicine* 60(1):1–9.
25. Leidy, H. J. 2014. Increased Dietary Protein as a Dietary Strategy to Prevent and/or Treat Obesity. *Missouri Medicine* 111(1):54–58.
26. Pradhan, G., S. L. Samson, and Y. Sun. 2013. Ghrelin: Much More Than a Hunger Hormone. *Current Opinion in Clinical Nutrition and Metabolic Care* 16(6):619–624.
27. Garcia, O. P., D. Ronquillo, M. del Carmen, M. Camacho, K. Z. Long, and J. L. Rosado. 2012. Zinc, Vitamin A, and Vitamin C Status Are Associated with Leptin Concentrations and Obesity in Mexican Women: Results from a Cross-Sectional Study. *Nutrition and Metabolism* 9:59–79.
28. Ibid.
29. Spalding, K. L., E. Earner, P. O. Westermarck, S. Bernard, B. A. Buchholz, O. Bergmann, L. Blomqvist, et al. 2008.

Dynamics of Fat Cell Turnover in Humans. *Nature* 453:783–787.

30. Ibid.

31. English, J. 2013. *Reversing Altered Metabolic Functions to Enhance Long-Term Weight Control.* Available at http://nutritionreview.org/2013/04/reversing-altered-metabolic-functions-enhance-longterm-weight-control. Accessed July 2014.

32. Perreault, L., J. M. Lavely, J. M. Kittelson, and T. J. Horton. 2004. Gender Differences in Lipoprotein Lipase Activity after Acute Exercise. *Obesity Research* 12:241–249.

33. Heber, D. 2010. An Integrative View of Obesity. *American Journal of Clinical Nutrition* 91:280S–283S.

34. Polsky, S., V. A. Catenacci, H. R. Wyatt, and J. O. Hill. 2014. Obesity: Epidemiology, Etiology, and Prevention. In Ross, C. A., et al., eds. *Modern Nutrition in Health and Disease.* 11th ed. Philadelphia: Lippincott Williams & Wilkins.

35. Youngson, N. A., and M. J. Morris. 2013. What Obesity Research Tells Us about Epigenetic Mechanisms. *Philosophical Transactions of the Royal Society B.* Available at http://dx.doi.org/10.1098/rstb.2011.0337.

36. Herrera, B. M., S. Keildson, and C. M. Lindgren. 2011. Genetics and Epigenetics of Obesity. *Maturitas* 69:41–49.

37. Corella, D., and J. M. Ordovás. 2013. Can Genotype Be Used to Tailor Treatment for Obesity? State of the Art and Guidelines for Future Studies and Applications. *Minerva Endocrinologica* 38(3):219–235.

38. Centers for Disease Control and Prevention. 2013. *Public Health Genomics: Genes and Obesity.* Available at www.cdc.gov/genomics/resources/diseases/obesity/obesedit.htm. Accessed May 2014.

39. Polsky, et al. 2014. Obesity: Epidemiology, Etiology, and Prevention.

40. Bray, G., and C. Champagne. 2005. Beyond Energy Balance: There Is More to Obesity than Kilocalories. *Journal of the American Dietetic Association* 105:S17–S23.

41. Brodsky, I. 2014. Hormones and Growth Factors. In Ross, C. A., et al., eds. *Modern Nutrition in Health and Disease.* 11th ed. Philadelphia: Lippincott Williams & Wilkins.

42. Kriketos, A. D., S. K. Gan, A. M. Poynten, S. M. Furler, D. J. Chishol, and L. V. Campbell. 2004. Exercise Increases Adiponectin Levels and Insulin Sensitivity in Humans. *Diabetes Care* 27(2):629–630.

43. Polsky, et al. 2014. Obesity: Epidemiology, Etiology, and Prevention.

44. Ibid.

45. Sifferlin, A. 2013. *New Genes ID'd in Obesity: How Much of Weight Is Genetic?* Available at http://healthland.time.com/2013/07/19/news-genes-idd-in-obesity-how-much-of-weight-is-genetic/. Accessed May 2014.

46. Urquidez-Romero, R., J. Esparaza-Romero, L. S. Chaudhari, et al. 2014. Study Design of the Maycoba Project: Obesity and Diabetes in Mexican Pimas. *American Journal of Health Behaviors* 38(3):370–378.

47. Ravussin, E., M. Valencia, J. Esparza, P. Bennett, and L. Schulz. 1994. Effects of a Traditional Lifestyle on Obesity in Pima Indians. *Diabetes Care* 17:1067–1074.

48. Carr, K. A., H. Lin, K. D. Fletcher, et al. 2013. Two Functional Serotonin Polymorphisms Moderate the Effect of Food Reinforcement on BMI. *Behavioral Neuroscience* 127(3):387–399.

49. Fuglestad, P. T., R. W. Jeffery, and N. E. Sherwood. 2012. Lifestyle Patterns Associated with Diet, Physical Activity, Body Mass Index and Amount of Recent Weight Loss in a Sample of Successful Weight Losers. *International Journal of Behavioral Nutrition and Physical Activity* doi: 10.1186/1479-5868-9-79.

50. Ibid.

51. Saguy, et al. 2014. Reporting Risk, Producing Prejudice.

52. Fuglestad, et al. 2012. Lifestyle Patterns Associated with Diet, Physical Activity, Body Mass Index and Amount of Recent Weight Loss.

53. Wenwen, D., S. Chang, W. Huijun, W. Zhihong, W. Youfa, and Z. Bing. 2014. Is Density of Neighbourhood Restaurants Associated with BMI in Rural Chinese Adults? A Longitudinal Study from the China Health and Nutrition Survey. *BMJ Open* doi:10.1136/bmjopen-2013.

54. Todd, J., and R. M. Morrison. 2014. *Less Eating Out, Improved Diets, and More Family Meals in the Wake of the Great Recession.* Available at www.ers.usda.gov. Accessed May 2014.

55. Ibid.

56. Larson, N., D. Neumark-Sztainer, M. N. Laska, and M. Story. 2011. Young Adults and Eating Away from Home: Associations with Dietary Intake Patterns and Weight Status Differ by Choice of Restaurant. *Journal of the American Dietetic Association* 111:1696–1703.

57. Meyers, A., A. Stunkard, and M. Coll. 1980. Food Accessibility and Food Choice. *Archives of General Psychiatry* 37:1133–1135.

58. Rolls, B. 1986. Sensory-Specific Satiety. *Nutrition Reviews* 44:93–101.

59. Rolls, B. 2003. The Supersizing of America. *Nutrition Today* 38:42–53.

60. Wansink, B. 1996. Can Package Size Accelerate Usage Volume? *Journal of Marketing* 60:1–14.

61. Rolls, B., L. Roe, and J. Meengs. 2006. Larger Portion Sizes Lead to a Sustained Increase in Energy Intake over 2 Days. *Journal of the American Dietetic Association* 106:543–549.

62. French, S., M. Story, and R. Jeffery. 2001. Environmental Influences on Eating and Physical Activity. *Annual Reviews of Public Health* 22:309–335.

63. Ibid.

64. Mummery, W., G. Schofield, R. Steele, E. Eakin, and W. Brown. 2005. Occupational Sitting Time and Overweight and Obesity in Australian Workers. *American Journal of Preventive Medicine* 29:91–97.

65. Zhao, Z., and R. Kaestner. 2010. Effects of Urban Sprawl on Obesity. *Journal of Health Economics* 29(6):779–787.

66. Ewing, R., T. Schmid, R. Kinngsworth, A. Zlot, and S. Raudenbush. 2003. Relationship between Urban Sprawl and Physical Activity, Obesity, and Morbidity. *American Journal of Health Promotion* 18:47–57.

67. Larouche, R., J. Barnes, and M. S. Tremblay. 2013. Too Far to Walk or Bike? *Canadian Journal of Public Health* 104(7):e487–e489.

68. Heelan, K. A., B. M. Abbey, J. E. Donnelly, M. S. Mayo, and G. J. Welk. 2009. Evaluation of a Walking School Bus for Promoting Physical Activity in Youth. *Journal of Physical Activity and Health* 6(5):560–570.

69. Jopp, D., and C. Hertzog. 2010. Assessing Adult Leisure Activities: An Extension of a Self-Report Activity Questionnaire. *Psychological Assessment* 22(1):108–120.

70. Colley, R. C., D. Garriguet, K. B. Adamo, V. Carson, I. Janssen, B. W. Timons, and M. S. Tremblay. 2013. *Physical Activity and Sedentary Behavior during the Early Years in Canada: A Cross-Sectional Study.* Available at www.ijbnpa.org/content/pdf/1479-5868-10-54.pdf. Accessed July 2014.

71. National Institutes of Health. 2007. *Clinical Guidelines on the Identification, Evaluation, and Treatment of Overweight and Obesity in Adults.* Available at http://www.medstarfamilychoice.com/documents/guidelines/obesity.pdf. Accessed May 2014.

72. Colles, S. L., J. B. Dixon, and P. E. O'Brien. 2008. Grazing and Loss of Control Related to Eating: Two High-Risk Factors following Bariatric Surgery. *Obesity* 16:615–622.

73. Lissner, L., D. Levitsky, B. Strupp, H. Kalkwarf, and D. Roe. 1987. Dietary Fat and the Regulation of Energy Intake in Human Subjects. *American Journal of Clinical Nutrition* 46:886–892.

74. Tohill, B., J. Seymour, M. Serdula, L. Kettel-Khan, and B. Rolls. 2004. What Epidemiologic Studies Tell Us about the Relationship between Fruit and Vegetable Consumption and Body Weight. *Nutrition Reviews* 62:365–374.

75. Rolls, B., E. Bell, and E. Thorwart. 1999. Water Incorporated into a Food but Not Served with a Food Decreases Energy Intake in Lean Women. *American Journal of Clinical Nutrition* 70:448–455.

76. Burton-Freeman, B. 2000. Dietary Fiber and Energy Regulation. *Journal of Nutrition* 130:272S–275S.

77. Davis, J., V. Hodges, and B. Gillham. 2006. Normal-Weight Adults Consume More Fiber and Fruit than Their Age- and Height-Matched Overweight/Obese Counterparts. *Journal of the American Dietetic Association* 106:833–840.

78. Mattes, R., et al. 2005. Appetite: Measurement and Manipulations Misgivings. *Journal of the American Dietetic Association* 105(5):87–97.

79. Keim, N., C. Blanton, and M. Kretsch. 2004. America's Obesity Epidemic: Measuring Physical Activity to Promote an Active Lifestyle. *Journal of the American Dietetic Association* 104:1398–1409.

80. Saries, W., S. Blair, M. van Baak, et al. 2003. How Much Physical Activity Is Enough to Prevent Unhealthy Weight Gain? Outcome of the IASO Stock Conference and Consensus Statement. *Obesity Reviews* 4:101–114.

81. Knab, A. M., R. A. Shanely, K. Corbin, et al. Human Performance Laboratory, Kannapolis. 2011. A 45-Minute Vigorous Exercise Bout Increases Metabolic Rate for 14 Hours. *Medicine and Science in Sports and Exercise* 43(9):1643–1648.

82. Jakicic, J. and A. Otto. 2005. Physical Activity Consideration for the Treatment and Prevention of Obesity. *American Journal of Clinical Nutrition* 82:226S–229S.

83. Shape Up America! 2014. *10,000 Steps.* Available at www.shapeup.org/resources/10ksteps.html. Accessed May 2014.

84. Poston, W., and J. Foreyt. 2000. Successful Management of the Obese Patient. *American Family Physician* 61:3615–3622.

85. Rosenbaum, M., R. Leibel, and J. Hirsch. 1997. Obesity. *New England Journal of Medicine* 337:396–407.

86. Thomas, J. G., D. S. Bond, S. Phelan, J. O. Hill, and R. R. Wing. 2014. Weight-Loss Maintenance for 10 Years in the National Weight Control Registry. *American Journal of Preventive Medicine* 46(1):17–21.

87. Camps, S., S. Verhoef, and K. Westerterp. 2013. Weight Loss, Weight Maintenance, and Adaptive Thermogenesis. *American Journal of Clinical Nutrition* 97:990–994.

88. Hill, J., H. Thompson, and H. Wyatt. 2005. Weight Maintenance: What's Missing? *Journal of the American Dietetic Association* 105:S63–S66.

89. Ibid.

90. U.S. Department of Health and Human Services. 2005. *Report of the Dietary Guidelines Advisory Committee on the* Dietary Guidelines for Americans, 2005. Available at www.health.gov/DietaryGuidelines/dga2005/report. Accessed June 2014.

91. Steinberg, D. M., D. F. Tate, G. G. Bennett, S. Ennett, C. Samuel-Hodge, D. and S. Ward. 2014. Daily Self-Weighing and Adverse Psychological Outcomes: A Randomized Controlled Trial. *American Journal of Preventive Medicine* 46(1):24–29.

92. Thomas, et al. 2014. Weight-Loss Maintenance for 10 Years.

93. DeWald, T., L. Khaodhiar, M. Donahue, and G. Blackburn. 2006. Pharmacological and Surgical Treatments for Obesity. *American Heart Journal* 151:604–624.

94. Food and Drug Administration. 2010. *FDA Drug Safety Communication: Completed Safety Review of Xenical/Alli (Orlistat) and Severe Liver Injury.* Available at www.fda.gov/Drugs/DrugSafety/PostmarketDrugSafetyInformationforPatientsandProviders/ucm213038.htm. Accessed June 2012.

95. Redman, L. M., and E. Ravussin. 2010. Lorcaserin for the Treatment of Obesity. *Drugs Today* 46:901–910.

96. Smith, S. R., N. J. Weissman, C. M. Anderson, M. Sanchez, E. Chuang, S. Stubbe, et al. 2010. Behavioral Modification and Lorcaserin for Overweight and Obesity Management (BLOOM) Study Group. *New England Journal of Medicine* 363:245–256.

97. Brashier, D. B., A. K. Sharma, N. Dahiva, S. K. Singh, and A. Khadka. 2014. Lorcaserin: A Novel Antiobesity Drug. *Journal of Pharmacology and Pharmacotherapy* 5(2):175–178.

98. Yen, M., and M. B. Ewald. 2012. Toxicity of Weight-Loss Agents. *Journal of Medicinal Toxicology* 8(2):145–152.

99. Van Rossum, E. F. 2014. Bariatric Surgery: A Metabolic Solution or a Paradigm for Novel Treatment Options? *Netherlands Journal of Medicine* 72(4):183–185.

100. HaysMed. 2012. *The History of Gastric Bypass Surgery.* Available at www.haysmed.com/history-of-bariatric-surgery. Accessed May 2014.

101. Health Grades. 2011. *Health Grades 2011: Bariatric Trends in American Hospitals.* Available at www.healthgrades.com/business/img/HealthGradesBariatricSurgeryTrendsAmerHospReport2011.pdf. Accessed May 2014.

102. O'Brien, P. E., L. MacDonald, M. Anderson, L. Brennan, and W. A. Brown. 2013. Long-Term Outcomes after Bariatric Surgery: Fifteen-Year Follow-Up of Adjustable Gastric Banding and a Systematic Review of the Bariatric Surgical Literature. *Annals of Surgery* 257(1):87–94.

103. Padwal, R., S. Klarenbach, N. Wiebe, D. Birch, S. Karmali, B. Manns, et al. 2011. Bariatric Surgery: A Systematic Review and Network Meta-Analysis of Randomized Trials. *Obesity Reviews* 12(8):602–621.

104. Buchwald, H., Y. Avidor, E. Braunwald, M. D. Jensen, W. Pories, K. Fahrbach, and K. Schoelles. 2004. Bariatric Surgery: A Systematic Review and Meta-Analysis. *Journal of the American Medical Association* 292:1724–1737.

105. Crookes, P. 2006. Surgical Treatment of Morbid Obesity. *Annual Reviews of Medicine* 57:243–264.

106. Boza, C., C. Gamboa, G. Perez, F. Crovari, A. Escalona, F. Pimentel, et al. 2011. Laparoscopic Adjustable Gastric Banding (LAGB): Surgical Results and 5-Year Follow-Up. *Surgical Endoscopy* 25(1):292–297.

16 Nutrition and Fitness

Learning Outcomes

After reading this chapter, you be able to:

16.1 List and describe the five basic components of fitness.

16.2 Explain the main features of a successful fitness program.

16.3 Describe the role of carbohydrate, fat, and protein in exercise.

16.4 Discuss the timing of foods to consume before, during, and after exercise.

16.5 Describe the importance of vitamins and minerals for physical fitness.

16.6 Explain the relationship between fluid intake and fitness.

16.7 Describe the most common dietary supplements used in exercise and their side effects.

True or False?

1. Most people in the United States are physically fit. **T**/**F**

2. As little as 60 minutes of physical activity per week provides health benefits. **T**/**F**

3. Carbohydrate, fat, and protein provide energy during exercise. **T**/**F**

4. Low- to moderate-intensity exercise uses more fat than carbohydrate for fuel. **T**/**F**

5. Athletes should eat immediately after training. **T**/**F**

6. Vitamin and mineral supplements always improve athletic performance. **T**/**F**

7. Many athletes are at risk for iron deficiency. **T**/**F**

8. Everyone who exercises should consume sports drinks. **T**/**F**

9. You can never drink too much water. **T**/**F**

10. The NCAA classifies caffeine as a banned substance when consumed in high amounts. **T**/**F**

See page 623 for the answers.

Whether you are a weekend warrior, walking for fitness, or a triathlete, eating the right foods is just as important to your fitness and athletic performance as the exercise itself. Food preserves lean body mass, repairs cells, maximizes oxygen utilization, maintains strong bones, regulates all metabolic reactions, and provides the energy to contract muscles. The more you move, the more energy is required.

Imagine you are participating in a 5k race. To fuel your competition, energy is initially derived from the limited amount of ATP in the cells. As exercise progresses, it is the size of your carbohydrate stores, and the rate at which your cells are able to break down fat and produce ATP that determines the outcome of the race. Once the race ends, nutrients consumed at the right time and in the right amounts help the body recover and have enough energy stored to repeat the activity. Fueling your body with the proper balance of nutrients is necessary to achieve optimal fitness levels and optimal athletic performance.

In this chapter, we explore the components and health benefits of physical fitness, the role the various nutrients play in physical activity, and how nutrition relates to physical fitness and athletic performance. You do not have to be a competitive or trained athlete to find the information in this chapter beneficial. It is intended for anyone seeking to understand the relationship between nutrition and physical fitness and apply that knowledge to her or his life.

Running is a great way to improve cardio respiratory fitness.

physical fitness The ability to perform physical activities requiring cardiorespiratory endurance, muscle endurance, strength, and/or flexibility; physical fitness is acquired through physical activity and adequate nutrition.

physical activity Voluntary movement that results in energy expenditure.

exercise Any type of structured or planned physical activity.

What Is Physical Fitness and Why Is It Important?

LO 16.1 List and describe the five basic components of fitness.

What does it mean to be physically fit? Can you carry a heavy bag of groceries up a flight of steps without becoming winded, lift a heavy box from a shelf without straining a muscle, or feel invigorated after a long bike ride on the weekend? And are you at a healthy body weight? If the answer is yes to these questions, you match the definition of being physically fit. **Physical fitness** can be defined as good health or physical condition, primarily as the result of exercise and proper nutrition.

What does it take to achieve physical fitness? Do you have to participate in a specific exercise or can you become physically fit by being active? These two terms—exercise and physical activity—are often used interchangeably, but technically they are not the same thing. **Physical activity** refers to body movement that expends energy (kilocalories). Activities such as gardening, walking the dog, and playing with children can all be regarded as physical activity. **Exercise** is formalized training or structured physical activity, like step aerobics, running, or weight lifting. However, for our purposes in this chapter, the terms exercise and physical activity are used interchangeably.

Along with consuming a healthy diet, being physically active is one of the two critically important components of overall health and fitness. You cannot achieve optimal fitness if you ignore either of these areas.

Physical Fitness Has Five Components

Cardiorespiratory endurance, muscular strength, muscular endurance, flexibility, and body composition are the five basic components of physical fitness. All five components contribute to physical fitness.

Cardiorespiratory endurance is the ability to sustain cardiorespiratory exercise, such as running and biking, for an extended length of time. This requires that the heart, blood, and lungs provide enough oxygen and nutrients to the working muscles to avoid fatigue. Someone who can run a mile without being too out of breath to talk has good cardiorespiratory endurance. Someone who is out of breath after climbing one flight of stairs, on the other hand, does not.

Muscular strength is the ability to produce force for a brief period of time, while **muscular endurance** is the ability to exert force over a long period of time without fatigue. Together muscular strength and endurance produce muscular fitness. Increasing muscle strength and endurance is best achieved with **resistance training.** You probably associate muscle strength with bodybuilders or weight lifters, and it is true that these people train to be particularly strong. However, other athletes, such as cheerleaders and ballet dancers, also work hard to strengthen their muscles. Consider the strength it takes to lift another person above the head. Holding a person over the head for several minutes shows exceptional muscular endurance.

Flexibility is the range of motion around a joint. Improved flexibility is achieved with stretching. Athletic performance, joint function, and muscular function are all enhanced with improved flexibility. In addition, improved flexibility reduces the likelihood of injury. A gymnast exhibits high flexibility when performing stunts and dance routines. In contrast, people with low flexibility may not be able to bend over and touch their toes from a standing or sitting position.

Finally, **body composition** is the proportion of muscle, fat, water, and other tissues in the body. Collectively, these make up total body weight. Body composition can change without total body weight changing, because muscle takes up less space per pound than body fat. This is why an individual can lose inches without noticing a drop in body weight. Contrary to popular belief, body fat does not "turn into" muscle nor does muscle "turn into" body fat. Both muscle and fat can be lost with weight loss or increased with weight gain, but neither directly converts into the other.

Physical Fitness Provides Numerous Health Benefits

It is common knowledge that eating a balanced diet and exercising regularly helps maintain good health. It is also clear that even modest amounts of exercise provide health benefits, and the more you exercise, the more fit you'll be. However, despite the fact that the benefits of exercise are well known and well documented, only one in five adults living in the United States meets the recommendations for regular physical activity.[1]

How does physical activity maintain good health? It reduces the risk of developing chronic diseases like type 2 diabetes mellitus, some forms of cancer, and cardiovascular disease. Physical activity improves body composition, bone health, and immune function. Being physically active also enhances mental well-being, increases the likelihood of restful sleep, and helps reduce stress. **Table 16.1** lists some of the numerous health benefits that result from being physically active on a regular basis. Individuals have to be cautious, however, not to **overexercise** and increase the risk of injury.

To improve the health of American adults and children through regular physical activity, the U.S. Department of Health and Human Services developed the *2008 Physical Activity Guidelines for Americans.* This publication gives information and guidance on the types and amounts of physical activity that provide substantial health benefits for Americans aged 6 years and older. The recommendations are based on a review of scientific research on the benefits of physical activity, and conclude with the main idea that regular physical activity over time can produce long-term health benefits.[2]

cardiorespiratory endurance The body's ability to sustain prolonged exercise.

muscular strength The greatest amount of force exerted by the muscle at one time.

muscular endurance The ability of the muscle to produce prolonged effort.

resistance training Exercising with weights to build, strengthen, and tone muscle to improve or maintain overall fitness; also called strength training.

flexibility Ability to move joints freely through a full and normal range of motion.

body composition The relative proportions of muscle, fat, water, and other tissues in the body.

overexercise Excessive physical activity without adequate rest periods for proper recovery.

TABLE 16.1 The Benefits of Physical Fitness

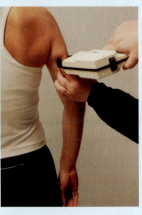

▲ Reduced Risk of Cardiovascular Disease

How It Works: Research has shown that moderate physical activity lowers blood pressure.[1] In addition, exercise is positively associated with high-density lipoprotein cholesterol (HDL).[2]

▲ Improved Body Composition

How It Works: Individuals with moderate cardiorespiratory fitness have less total fat and abdominal fat compared with people with low cardiorespiratory fitness.[3]

▲ Reduced Risk of Type 2 Diabetes

How It Works: Exercise helps control blood glucose levels by increasing insulin sensitivity.[4] This not only reduces risk for type 2 diabetes, but also improves blood glucose control for those who have been diagnosed with type 2 diabetes.

▲ Reduced Risk of Some Forms of Cancer

How It Works: Increased physical activity has been associated with a reduced risk of colon, breast, endometrial, and lung cancers. This reduced risk is likely the result of a reduction in overall body weight and other hormonal and metabolic mechanisms.[5]

Source: 1. B. Bushman. 2014. "Promoting Exercise as Medicine for Prediabetes and Prehypertension." *Current Sports Medicine Report* 13(4):233–239.

2. N. Sousa, R. Mendes, C. Abrantes, J. Sampaio, and J. Oliveira. 2014. "A Randomized Study on Lipids Response to Different Exercise Programs in Overweight Older Men." *International Journal of Sports Medicine* DOI: 10.1055/s-0034-1374639.

3. I. Janssen, P. T. Katzmarzyk, R. Ross, A. S. Leon, J. S. Skinner, D. C. Rao, J. H. Wilmore, et al. 2004. "Fitness Alters the Associations of BMI and Waist Circumference with Total and Abdominal Fat." *Obesity* 12:525–537.

4. J. W. Van Dijk, M. Venema, W. van Mechelen, C. D. Stehouwer, F. Hartgens, and L. L. van Loon. 2013. "Effect of Moderate-Intensity Exercise versus Activities of Daily Living on 24-Hour Blood Glucose Homeostasis in Male Patients with Type 2 Diabetes." *Diabetes Care* 36(11):3448–3453.

5. U.S. Department of Health and Human Services. 2008. *Physical Activity Guidelines Advisory Committee Report.* Washington, DC: ODPHP Publication No. U0049. Available from www.health.gov/paguidelines/Report/pdf/CommitteeReport.pdf. Accessed July 2014.

LO 16.1: THE TAKE-HOME MESSAGE Physical fitness is the state of being in good physical condition attained through proper nutrition and regular physical activity. The five components of physical fitness are cardiorespiratory endurance, muscular strength, muscular endurance, flexibility, and body composition. To achieve optimal fitness, all five components must be considered. The numerous health benefits of physical activity include reduced risk of several chronic diseases, including type 2 diabetes and cardiovascular disease; improved body composition, bone health, and immune function; more restful sleep; and reduced stress.

What Does a Successful Physical Fitness Program Look Like?

LO 16.2 Explain the main features of a successful fitness program.

Physical fitness programs generally incorporate activities that are based on the five components of fitness, including aerobic exercise, resistance training, and stretching. A successful fitness program should be tailored to meet the needs of the

TABLE 16.1 The Benefits of Physical Fitness

▲ Improved Bone Health

How It Works: Bone density has been shown to improve with weight-bearing exercise and resistance training, thereby reducing the risk for osteoporosis.[6, 7]

▲ Improved Immune System

How It Works: Regular exercise can enhance the immune system, which may result in fewer colds and other infectious diseases.[8]

▲ Improved Mental Well-Being

How It Works: Regular exercise protects against the onset of depression and anxiety disorders, reduces symptoms in people diagnosed with depression and anxiety, delays the incidence of dementia, and overall enhances mental well-being.[9]

▲ Improved Sleep

How It Works: People who engage in regular exercise often have better quality of sleep. This is especially true for older adults.[10]

6. L. A. Tucker, J. E. Strong, J. D. Lecheminant, and B. W. Bailey. 2014. "Effect of Two Jumping Programs on Hip Bone Mineral Density in Premenopausal Women: A Randomized Controlled Trial." *American Journal of Health Promotion* DOI: 10.4278/ajhp.

7. F. D. Saraví and F. Sayegh. 2013. "Bone Mineral Density and Body Composition of Adult Premenopausal Women with Three Levels of Physical Activity." *Journal of Osteoporosis* DOI: 10.1155/2013/953271.

8. D. Menicucci, A. Piarulli, F. Mastorci, L. Sebastiani, et al. 2013. "Interactions between Immune, Stress-Related Hormonal and Cardiovascular Systems Following Strenuous Physical Exercise." *Archives Italiennes de Biologie* 151(3):126–136.

9. U.S. Department of Health and Human Services. 2008. *Physical Activity Guidelines Advisory Committee Report*.

10. A. A. Akbari Kamrani, D. Shamsipour Dehkordi, and R. Mohajeri. 2014. "The Effect of Low and Moderate Intensity Aerobic Exercises on Sleep Quality in Men Older Adults." *Pakistan Journal of Medical Sciences* 30(2):417–421.

individual and performed consistently so that any gains in physical fitness are not lost. It is also important to incorporate activities that are enjoyable so that they are more likely to become a regular part of one's lifestyle. Someone who hates to jog, for example, is not likely to be consistent about going for a daily run.

Cardiorespiratory Exercise Improves Cardiorespiratory Endurance and Body Composition

Cardiorespiratory exercise, such as high-impact aerobics, stair climbing, and brisk walking, often involves continuous activities that use large muscle groups (abdomen, legs, and buttocks). This type of exercise is predominantly aerobic because it uses oxygen. During cardiorespiratory exercise, the heart beats faster and more oxygen-carrying blood is delivered to tissues.

How does this work? As exercise begins, the body requires more oxygen to break down nutrients for energy, so it increases blood flow (volume) to the working muscles. It accomplishes this by increasing heart rate and **stroke volume.** The body also redistributes blood from internal organs to maximize the volume of blood that is delivered to the muscles.

stroke volume The amount of blood pumped by the heart with each heart beat.

An individual's level of cardiorespiratory fitness can be measured by the maximum amount of oxygen the muscles can consume during exercise, or **VO₂max.** A person who is more physically fit has a higher VO₂max and can exercise at a higher intensity without fatigue than someone who is not as fit. A trained athlete, for example, might have a VO₂max of 50 to 80 milliliters per kilogram per minute (ml/kg/min), while a sedentary, unfit individual might have a VO₂max of 25 to 30 ml/kg/min.[3] Two of the highest VO₂max ever recorded were for two cross-country skiers, a male and a female, who measured 94 and 77 ml/kg/min, respectively.[4]

Cardiorespiratory conditioning, which includes making gradual increases in exercise intensity, helps increase VO₂max, and therefore improves cardiorespiratory endurance and overall physical fitness. In addition, cardiorespiratory exercise can help individuals maintain a healthy body weight and improve body composition by reducing body fat. Cardiorespiratory exercise also reduces stress, and lowers the risk of heart disease by maintaining normal cholesterol levels and lowering heart rate and blood pressure. As the heart becomes a more efficient pump, it does not have to work as hard with each beat.

Resistance training improves muscle strength and muscle endurance at any age.

Improving flexibility can help reduce muscle soreness and lower the risk of injury.

VO₂max The maximum amount of oxygen (ml) a person uses in one minute per kilogram of body weight.

cardiorespiratory conditioning Improvements in the delivery of oxygen to working muscles as a result of aerobic activity.

conditioning The process of improving physical fitness through repeated activity.

Strength Training Improves Muscle Strength, Muscle Endurance, and Body Composition

Strength (or resistance) training is designed to increase muscle mass, strength, and endurance. Maintaining adequate muscle mass and strength is important for everyone. Contrary to common belief, resistance training does not necessarily lead to large, bulky muscles. Many females, as well as males, use resistance training to define their muscles and improve their physical appearance and body composition.

In general, individuals should perform a low number of repetitions using heavy weights to increase muscle strength. To increase muscular endurance, perform a high number of repetitions using lighter weights. Heavier weights can also be used to improve muscular endurance by allowing short rest intervals between repetition sets.

Rest periods between sets of an exercise and between workouts are important to avoid overworking muscles and increasing risk of injury. Muscle that is not adequately rested may break down and not recover, leading to a loss of muscle mass. The amount of rest recommended during a workout depends on a person's fitness goals and level of **conditioning.** If increasing strength is the goal, long rest periods of 2 to 3 minutes between sets are best. If the goal is to increase muscular endurance, shorter rest periods of 30 seconds or less are recommended.

The general guideline for rest periods between workouts is two days, or a total of 48 hours, between workouts that use the same muscle groups. However, strength training can be performed daily as long as different muscles are used on consecutive days. For example, you can perform upper body strength training on one day, working your biceps, triceps, and pectoral muscles, and on the following day do leg lifts, squats, and lunges to work your lower body muscles.

Stretching Improves Flexibility

Most people associate flexibility with gymnasts or dancers, but everyone can benefit from being more flexible and enjoying a full range of motion. Improving flexibility can reduce muscle soreness and the risk of injury, as well as improve balance, posture, and circulation of blood and nutrients throughout the body. Stretching, such as through yoga, is the most common exercise used to improve flexibility.

The FITT Principle Can Be Used to Design a Fitness Program

FITT is an acronym for *frequency, intensity, time,* and *type*. The FITT principle provides an easy way to design a successful physical fitness regimen or conditioning program.

Frequency is how often an individual performs the activity, such as the number of times per week. **Intensity** refers to the degree of difficulty at which the activity is performed. Common terms used to describe intensity are low, moderate, and vigorous (high). One measure of intensity for cardiorespiratory exercise is **rating of perceived exertion (RPE),** in which the person performing the activity self-assesses the level of intensity. The RPE is based on your current level of fitness and your perception of how hard you are working. The scale ranges from 1 (rest) to 10 (maximal exertion). A range of 5 to 7 on the RPE scale (somewhat hard to hard) is recommended for most adults to achieve fitness. A more precise method of measuring intensity is using your **target heart rate.** Your target heart rate is the range (given in percentages of maximal heart rate) that your heart rate should fall within to ensure that you are training at your desired level of intensity. For example, a target heart rate of 60 percent would be considered low intensity compared with a target heart rate of 80 percent, which is considered high intensity. The Calculation Corner illustrates how to calculate your target heart rate. For weight training, intensity is referred to as **repetition maximum (RM).** For example, 1 RM is the maximum amount of weight that can be lifted once.

 Calculation Corner

Target Heart Rate

Target heart rate can be useful in determining the intensity level of cardiorespiratory exercise. One method used to calculate your target heart rate (THR) begins with calculating an estimate of your maximal heart rate (HRmax). Use the following formula to calculate an estimated HRmax.

$$206.9 - (\text{age in years} \times 0.67) = \text{estimated HRmax}$$

Before you can calculate your THR, you must first decide the intensity level at which you wish to exercise. Use the following as a guideline:

- Light/low intensity – 55% to 64% of HRmax
- Moderate intensity – 65% to 84% of HRmax
- High intensity – 85% to 95% of HRmax

Now, multiply your estimated HRmax by the desired intensity level to determine your target heart rate.

$$\text{THR} = \text{HRmax} \times \text{intensity level}$$

Example: John, a 45-year-old office manager, wants to know what his target heart rate should be as he begins his new training program.

1. Calculate John's estimated HRmax:

    $$206.9 - (45 \times 0.67) = 177 \text{ estimated HRmax}$$

2. Multiply John's estimated HRmax × intensity at 65% and 84% to determine his THR.

    $$177 \times 0.65 = 115 \text{ THR}$$
    $$177 \times 0.84 = 149 \text{ THR}$$

John's THR for moderate intensity is between 115 and 149 bpm. John can adjust his THR based on his RPE.

Scan this QR code with your mobile device to access practice math activities. You can also access the activities in **Mastering**Nutrition™.

Data from B. Bushman, ed., *ACSM's Complete Guide to Fitness & Health* 2011. Chicago: IL: Human Kinetics.

intensity The level of difficulty of an activity.

rating of perceived exertion (RPE) A subjective measure of the intensity level of an activity using a numerical scale.

target heart rate A heart rate in beats per minute (expressed as a percentage of maximum heart rate) achieved during exercise that indicates the level of intensity at which fitness levels can increase.

repetition maximum (RM) The maximum amount of weight that can be lifted for a specified number of repetitions.

Get Moving!

Schedule physical activity into your day, just like you would schedule a meeting, class, or work.

Find activities that you enjoy. Make exercise something you look forward to, so that you're more likely to keep it up.

Ask a friend or coworker to exercise with you. Many people are more likely to exercise if they have a partner to motivate them.

Track your exercise in a log or journal so you see how much you are getting and note improvement over time.

Take advantage of activities that are offered at your college or university, including club sports, intramurals, group fitness classes, and personal training sessions.

Be adventurous and try new activities. If you're used to jogging or going to the gym, try hiking or racquetball. Mixing up your routine will help prevent boredom.

duration The length of time that an activity is performed.

progressive overload principle A gradual increase in exercise demands resulting from modifications to the frequency, intensity, time, or type of activity.

hypertrophy To grow larger in size.

atrophy To shrink in size.

Time, or **duration,** is how long the activity is performed, such as a 30-minute run. And lastly, type means the specific activity performed.

The frequency, intensity, time (duration), and types of exercise that are right for a person depend partly on what goal the individual is trying to achieve. For individuals seeking health benefits, the *2008 Physical Activity Guidelines* state that as little as 60 minutes a week of moderate-intensity activity offers some health benefits.[5] However, a total amount of 150 minutes (2 hours and 30 minutes) a week of moderate-intensity aerobic activity provides substantial health benefits for adults by reducing the risk of many chronic diseases. To gain additional health benefits, such as a lower risk of colon and breast cancer, up to 300 minutes (5 hours) per week of moderate-intensity physical activity is recommended. Additionally, resistance training at a moderate or high intensity and that involves all major muscle groups should be performed two or more days a week.

Do you feel like you don't have the time to exercise? This is a common barrier that keeps many people from engaging in regular physical activity. The good news is that aerobic activity can be performed in sessions as short as 10 minutes to get some health benefits. Of course, the more activity performed, the greater the benefits. Taking advantage of short periods of time during the day for a brisk 10-minute (or longer) walk will help you meet the recommendations for physical activity.

Engaging in more vigorous-intensity activities, such as jogging or fast-paced swimming, for longer duration results in even greater health benefits. Individuals striving to maintain body weight and prevent gradual weight gain should participate in approximately 60 minutes of moderate- to vigorous-intensity activity on most days of the week, and avoid consuming excess kilocalories. Those striving to lose weight should participate in at least 60 to 90 minutes of daily moderate-intensity physical activity and adjust kilocalorie intake so that more kilocalories are expended than are consumed.

The Physical Activity Pyramid is another tool that can be used as a guide to meeting physical activity needs. It is designed to show examples of activities and how often they should be performed for optimal health and physical fitness (**Figure 16.1**). People with diabetes mellitus, high blood pressure, heart disease, and other chronic diseases should consult with a health care provider before participating in any exercise program, especially one to be performed at a vigorous intensity.

Individuals seeking improved physical fitness in addition to health benefits can follow the general recommendations outlined by the American College of Sports Medicine. These guidelines for cardiorespiratory endurance, muscular fitness, and flexibility for healthy adults are summarized in **Table 16.2** using the FITT principle.

Progressive Overload Can Help Improve Fitness over Time

During conditioning, the body gradually adapts to the activities that are being performed. Over time, if the activity is kept exactly the same, the body doesn't have to work as hard and fitness levels plateau as a result. To continue to improve fitness levels, the body must be challenged by performing different workout regimens on a regular basis. This can be done using the **progressive overload principle.** Modifying one or more elements of the FITT principle challenges the body in different ways so that the level of fitness improves. For example, someone trying to improve cardiorespiratory endurance might gradually increase both the pace and the duration of a run. To increase muscle strength, an individual might gradually increase the amount of weight being lifted.

As the body responds to the work it is being asked to do, it becomes more physically fit. The muscles increase in size (**hypertrophy**), endurance, and strength, and cardiorespiratory endurance and flexibility improve. However, if conditioning is executed improperly or nutrient intake is inadequate for physical activity, muscles can lose mass (**atrophy**), endurance, and strength, and cardiorespiratory fitness levels will suffer negative effects.

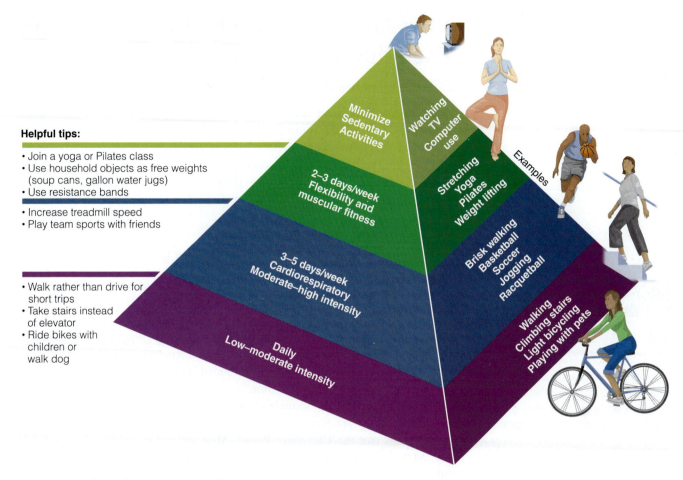

Helpful tips:

- Join a yoga or Pilates class
- Use household objects as free weights (soup cans, gallon water jugs)
- Use resistance bands

- Increase treadmill speed
- Play team sports with friends

- Walk rather than drive for short trips
- Take stairs instead of elevator
- Ride bikes with children or walk dog

Pyramid labels:

Minimize Sedentary Activities — Watching TV / Computer use

2–3 days/week Flexibility and muscular fitness — Stretching, Yoga, Pilates, Weight lifting

3–5 days/week Cardiorespiratory Moderate–high intensity — Brisk walking, Basketball, Soccer, Jogging, Racquetball

Daily Low–moderate intensity — Walking, Climbing stairs, Light bicycling, Playing with pets

Examples

▲ Figure 16.1 **Physical Activity Pyramid**

LO 16.2: THE TAKE-HOME MESSAGE Cardiorespiratory exercise improves cardiorespiratory endurance and body composition. Strength training can improve muscle strength and endurance as well as body composition. Stretching can enhance flexibility. An effective conditioning program can be designed using the FITT principle, which stands for frequency, intensity, time, and type of activity. The *2008 Physical Activity Guidelines* state that most people should aim for at least 60 minutes of moderate activity per week for some health benefits, while greater amounts of exercise are needed for substantial health benefits, weight loss, and to improve physical fitness. Applying the progressive overload principle to workouts helps individuals achieve optimal fitness levels.

TABLE 16.2	Using FITT to Improve Fitness		
	Cardiorespiratory Fitness	**Muscular Fitness**	**Flexibility**
Frequency	3–5 days per week	2–3 days per week	2–3 days per week
Intensity	64–95% of maximum heart rate	60–80% of 1 RM	To the point of feeling tightness or slight discomfort
Time	20–60 minutes per day (150 minutes per week), continuous or intermittent (minimum of 10-minute bouts)	8–10 different exercises performed in 2–4 sets, 8–12 repetitions	2–4 repetitions for each muscle group; hold static stretch for 10–30 seconds
Type	Brisk walking, jogging, biking, step aerobics	Free weights, machines with stacked weights, resistance bands	Stretching, yoga

Data from the American College of Sports Medicine. 2011. "Position Stand: Quantity and Quality of Exercise for Developing and Maintaining Cardiorespiratory, Musculoskeletal, and Neuromotor Fitness in Apparently Healthy Adults: Guidance for Prescribing Exercise," *Medicine & Science in Sports & Exercise* 43 (7):1334–1359.

What Does a Successful Physical Fitness Program Look Like? **593**

How Are Carbohydrate, Fat, and Protein Used during Exercise?

LO 16.3 Describe the role of carbohydrate, fat, and protein in exercise.

Food meets our nutrient needs for physical activity in two ways. Food supplies the energy, particularly from carbohydrate and fat, which the body needs to perform an activity. And food provides nutrients, predominantly from carbohydrate and protein, that help the body recover properly so that it can repeat the activity. The type of food used to supply energy depends on whether the physical activity is anaerobic or aerobic, reactions you learned about in Chapter 8. Let's review these energy-producing reactions.

Anaerobic Energy Production during Exercise

Recall that all body actions require energy in the form of adenosine troposphere (ATP) produced either aerobically (requiring oxygen) or anaerobically (without oxygen) from macronutrients in foods. Much of the energy production during cardiorespiratory exercise is aerobic. By contrast, anaerobic energy production is typically used for quick, intense activities that require strength, such as lifting weights; agility and speed, such as sprinting; or a sudden burst of power, such as jumping for a slam dunk during a basketball game.

During the first few seconds of physical activity the body relies heavily on anaerobic energy production from ATP and creatine phosphate (PCr) found in muscle cells (see the Chemistry Boost). Most anaerobic activities are fueled by the ATP and rely on creatine phosphate to resynthesize ATP—a total of about 10 seconds. Thus, the ATP-CP stored in the muscle can provide enough energy to fuel all-out exercise for about 10 seconds. If maximal exercise continues beyond 10 seconds, ATP will be recharged during anaerobic glycolysis.

Energy is released from ATP when the bond connecting the end phosphate is hydrolyzed from the ATP molecule, leaving adenosine diphosphate (ADP) (**Figure 16.2**). ADP is regenerated to ATP in the mitochondria of the cell when creatine phosphate donates a phosphate molecule. Creatine phosphate is a quick source of phosphate with a dual role in energy production. Energy is directly produced when the phosphate group is removed from the creatine phosphate molecule. This is an example of a catabolic reaction releasing energy. Energy is indirectly produced because the released phosphate group is donated to ADP, which regenerates ATP, and sets up another round of energy production.

The body produces a small amount of creatine from foods, including meat and fish, or creatine can be supplied to the body directly from dietary supplements. With the help of the liver and kidneys, creatine is converted to creatine phosphate and stored in skeletal muscle and other tissues, including the cardiac muscle and brain. The amount of creatine phosphate stored in the muscles is limited and becomes depleted after up to 10 seconds of maximum-intensity activity. Creatine phosphate is regenerated when the muscle cell is at rest, such as between sprints or in between sets during weight training, to prepare for the next exercise effort.

Aerobic Energy Production during Exercise

Just like creatine phosphate, the amount of ATP in cells is limited and can support only a few seconds of intense exercise, such as is needed to perform a 100-meter sprint. When the ATP and creatine phosphate stores are unable to meet sustained

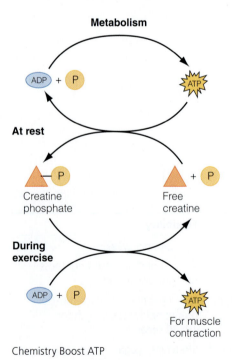

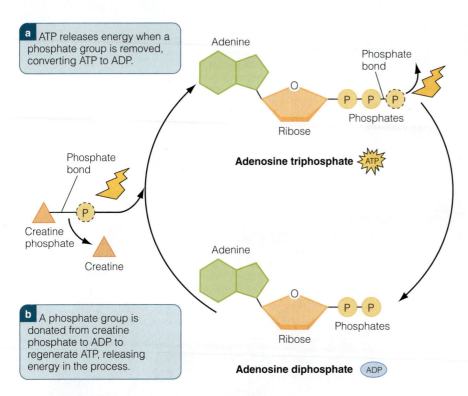

a ATP releases energy when a phosphate group is removed, converting ATP to ADP.

Adenine

Phosphate bond

Phosphates

Ribose

Adenosine triphosphate ATP

Phosphate bond

Creatine phosphate

Creatine

b A phosphate group is donated from creatine phosphate to ADP to regenerate ATP, releasing energy in the process.

Adenine

O

Ribose

Phosphates

Adenosine diphosphate ADP

◄ **Figure 16.2 Anaerobic Energy Metabolism**
During anaerobic metabolism, energy is released from the breakdown of ATP and creatine phosphate.

energy demands, breathing becomes heavier and oxygen intake increases. At this point the pace of exercise slows down and the body begins to rely more on aerobic production of ATP because the amount needed to support the quick bursts or sprints cannot be generated fast enough by anaerobic energy production. With oxygen in the cell, pyruvate formed from glucose during glycolysis is converted into acetyl CoA and is metabolized through aerobic metabolism to produce ATP.

The body relies on a mixture of carbohydrate, fat, and protein for energy during exercise, but the type and amount of these nutrients that are used depends on the intensity and duration of the exercise, the body's nutritional status, and the level of physical fitness. Remember that carbohydrate contributes to both anaerobic and aerobic energy production and fat contributes to the aerobic generation of ATP. Protein can be used for energy production when kilocalorie needs haven't been met. In exercise metabolism, the body prefers to use protein to promote muscle growth and recovery.

Carbohydrate Is the Primary Energy Source during High-Intensity Exercise

Carbohydrate is the predominant fuel used during high-intensity, short-duration, anaerobic exercise. Carbohydrate provides energy to the working muscle either through blood glucose, stored glycogen in the muscles and the liver, or the consumption of dietary carbohydrates (**Figure 16.3**). In adults, the amount of glycogen stored in the muscles ranges from about 200 grams to 500 grams. In addition, the liver stores around 60 to 120 grams of glycogen, which can be converted into glucose through glycogenolysis and released into the blood. The amount of glycogen that each person stores depends on many factors, including the person's nutritional intake and fitness levels.

The average adult body stores about 2,600 kilocalories of energy as glycogen, of which 2,000 kilocalories can be used. The rate at which glycogen stores are used

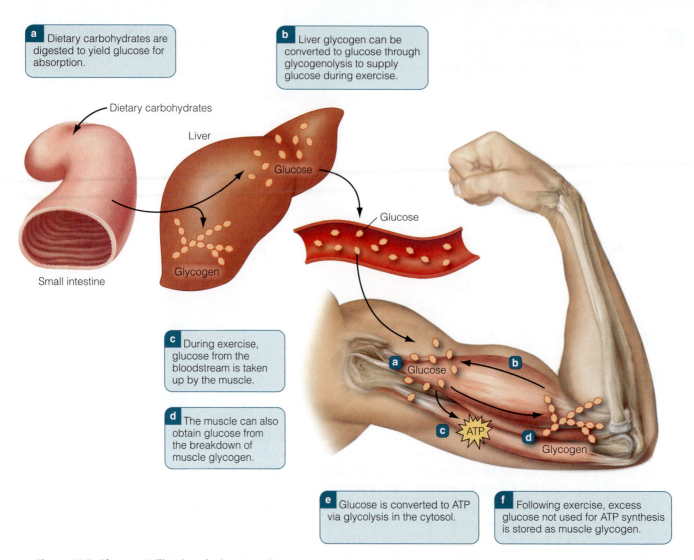

Dietary carbohydrates

Liver

Glucose

Glycogen

Small intestine

Glucose

Glucose

a Glucose

b

c ATP

d Glycogen

▲ Figure 16.3 **Glucose Utilization during Exercise**

Less glycogen is used as fuel compared to fat during low-intensity, long duration exercise.

depends on the intensity and duration of the exercise. If the exercise is of high intensity and short duration, glycogen stores are depleted in about 20 minutes, compared with low-intensity, long-duration exercise, during which glycogen stores can last up to 90 minutes.

Glucose derived from stored muscle glycogen is the preferred source for energy during exercise; however, liver glycogen stores are just as important. Glycogen stored in the liver is converted into glucose and delivered to the bloodstream to maintain normal blood glucose levels, both during periods of activity and at rest. Muscle cells first rely on glycogen stored in the muscles for energy during activity, but also blood glucose formed from the breakdown of liver glycogen. Liver glycogen is depleted faster when a person's muscle glycogen stores are suboptimal at the start of exercise.

Whereas muscle and liver glycogen provide glucose for the muscle cells during activity, blood glucose is also the energy source for the brain. If the brain does not receive the glucose to meet its energy needs, individuals may feel a lack of coordination or lack of concentration—two things no one wants to experience, especially during exercise or a sport competition.

Recall that during metabolism, pyruvate formed during glycolysis is reduced to lactate when the mitochondria lack sufficient oxygen to transform pyruvate into acetyl CoA. When lactate is produced at a low rate, as during aerobic metabolism, muscles can effectively clear it from the blood and use it as an energy source. For example, during low-intensity exercise, the body is able to oxidize the lactate that is produced by the muscle during glycolysis and therefore it does not accumulate in the working muscle tissue. The body also shuttles excess lactate to other tissues, such as the brain, heart, and liver, to prevent excessive accumulation in the muscle. Lactate from the muscle diffuses into the blood, is picked up by the liver, and enters the Cori cycle. In the Cori cycle (see Figure 8.8 in Chapter 8), lactate undergoes gluconeogenesis, is converted back to glucose, and is returned to the bloodstream to be used for energy again.

As exercise intensity increases, the energy demands are greater than the amount of ATP the cell can produce aerobically using available oxygen. As a result, more hydrogen ions are rapidly generated as glucose is anaerobically metabolized to pyruvate. These excess hydrogen ions combine with pyruvate to form lactate, which diffuses quickly into the blood. As exercise intensity continues, the levels of lactate and hydrogen ions increase as the body attempts to produce enough ATP to meet energy demands. The increase in hydrogen ions may negatively affect exercise performance due to a reduction in pH in the muscle cell. The good news is that the ability of the muscles to effectively use and shuttle lactate to other tissues improves with training. Lactate in the muscle will rise before it diffuses out of the cell into the blood where it is transferred to the liver to undergo transformation to glucose.

For many years, lactate in muscles was thought to be a cause of muscle fatigue, but now scientists report that lactate produced during anaerobic glycolysis can also be an important fuel during exercise. In several types of exercise, muscle is the major site of lactate production and removal. Some researchers believe that as exercise continues, there is a shift from lactate diffusing out of the muscle into the blood, to the muscle itself oxidizing lactate for energy in the mitochondria.[6] The rate at which muscles consume lactate for energy depends on the metabolic rate, the pH in the muscle, blood flow, and the fitness level of the individual.[7]

Intensity Affects the Use of Glucose and Glycogen

Muscles use glucose for energy no matter how intense the exercise. However, research shows that as the intensity of exercise increases, the percentage of energy derived from glucose and glycogen also increases.[8] Carbohydrates are the preferred energy source at high intensity levels because, unlike fat and protein, carbohydrate is efficiently oxidized for energy as the intensity of activity increases. At very high intensities, carbohydrates supply most of the energy in the form of muscle glycogen. Although carbohydrates are not the main energy source during prolonged low- to moderate-intensity exercise, they still provide some energy for the working muscles.

Duration Affects the Use of Glucose and Glycogen

In addition to intensity, the duration of exercise also affects the source and amount of carbohydrate used to fuel physical activity. At the start of low- to moderate-intensity exercise, stored muscle glycogen is the main source of energy. As muscle glycogen stores diminish, the liver also contributes its glycogen to be converted to glucose for energy and to prevent hypoglycemia. During prolonged exercise, the body relies more on blood glucose (generated from stored liver glycogen) and less on muscle glycogen as its carbohydrate source of energy.

In addition to affecting the source of carbohydrate, duration also affects how much carbohydrate is used. After about 20 minutes, as low- to moderate-intensity exercise continues, muscles rely less on glycogen and glucose and more on fat for fuel (more on this in a later discussion). Even when fat is being used for some energy production during exercise, the body always uses glycogen for energy as well, and if the intensity and duration of the exercise last long enough, muscle and liver glycogen stores become depleted and the activity can no longer be sustained at the same intensity. Many endurance runners refer to this as "hitting the wall."

Conditioning Affects the Use of Glucose and Glycogen

Research has shown that the amount of glycogen that the muscles can hold can be affected by training.[9, 10] When muscles are well trained, they have the ability to store 20 to 50 percent more glycogen than untrained muscles. More stored glycogen means more fuel for working muscles to use, which means individuals can exercise for a longer period of time and increase endurance. Just eating a high-carbohydrate meal before competition will not improve performance; individuals need to train their muscles *and* eat a high-carbohydrate diet regularly to maximize the effect.

Carbohydrate Requirement Depends on Exercise Duration

Recall that most adults should get 45 to 65 percent of their daily energy intake from carbohydrates. As we've already learned, the amount of carbohydrate needed to fuel physical activity depends greatly on the duration of the activity. Glycogen stores are continuously being depleted and replenished. For those who exercise often, eating carbohydrate-rich foods on a regular basis is important to provide the muscles with adequate glycogen. When glycogen stores are inadequate, the muscles have only a limited amount of energy available to support activity, which has been shown to reduce athletic performance and promote fatigue.[11, 12] Keep in mind that the glycogen storage capacity of both the muscles and the liver is limited. Once the muscles and liver have stored all of the glycogen possible, the body converts any excess glucose into fatty acids and stores it in the form of body fat.

Carbohydrate loading is one training strategy that athletes use to build up muscle glycogen stores before a competition. See Spotlight: Carbohydrate Loading for an explanation of this beneficial strategy for endurance athletes.

The best types of carbohydrates to eat during and immediately after exercise are simple carbohydrates, such as sports drinks, bars and gels, bananas, bagels, or corn flakes, because they are absorbed and enter the bloodstream quickly, and therefore can be used immediately for energy (glucose) or to replenish glycogen stores. Complex carbohydrates like whole-grain rice and pasta, oatmeal, and whole wheat are ideal to eat a couple of hours before exercise because they take longer to digest than simple carbohydrates and enter the bloodstream much more slowly, thereby providing a sustained source of energy. Remember, however, that complex carbohydrates are generally high in fiber, and too much fiber can cause bloating, gas, and diarrhea.

Fat Is the Primary Energy Source during Low- to Moderate-Intensity Exercise

Fat is supplied to muscles as an energy source in two forms: fatty acids stored in muscle tissue and free fatty acids in the blood derived from those stored in adipose tissue. Fatty acids in the muscle directly supply energy to the muscles, so they are used for energy during exercise before the fatty acids in adipose tissue. Recall from Chapter 8 that when the body breaks down stored body fat for energy (lypolysis), triglycerides in adipose tissue are first hydrolyzed into fatty acids and glycerol, and then released into the bloodstream. Circulating free fatty acids are taken up by the muscles and go through beta-oxidation inside the mitochondria to produce energy. Glycerol is taken up by the liver, where it is converted into glucose through gluconeogenesis to help maintain blood glucose levels and provide energy (see **Figure 16.4**).

carbohydrate loading A diet and training strategy that maximizes glycogen stores in the body before an endurance event.

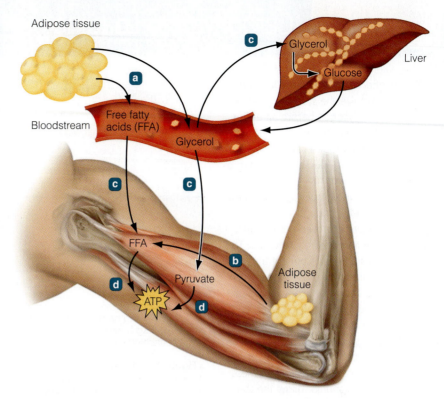

a The breakdown of triglycerides in the adipose tissue yields free fatty acids and glycerol, which diffuses into the bloodstream.

b Free fatty acids and glycerol are also hydrolyzed from intramuscular fat stores.

c Free fatty acids and glycerol are taken up by the muscle cell for energy. Glycerol may also enter the liver and produce glucose through gluconeogenesis. The glucose formed diffuses into the bloodstream.

d The free fatty acids undergo aerobic oxidation in the muscle cell to produce ATP. Glycerol is anaerobically transformed to pyruvate, which is converted into ATP through aerobic metabolism.

▲ **Figure 16.4 Fatty Acid and Glycerol Utilization during Exercise**

There are advantages to storing excess energy as fat rather than carbohydrate and protein. Fat is a more concentrated source of energy because it provides more than twice the kilocalories of carbohydrate or protein; this is because, unlike glycogen and protein, stored fat does not contain water. In addition, greater amounts of energy can be stored as fat because, while glycogen stores are limited, the capacity of fat cells is unlimited.

Intensity Affects the Use of Fat

Just as with carbohydrates, fat is used for energy during rest and aerobic exercise. The exercise intensity affects the source and amount of fat used. Recall that fatty acids require oxygen to be converted into energy (beta-oxidation). Therefore, the availability of oxygen is one of the most important factors for determining what nutrient the muscles use the most for energy.

During low- to moderate-intensity exercise, sufficient oxygen is available to oxidize fat efficiently enough to keep up with the demand for energy. Fat supplies nearly all of the energy required during low- to moderate-intensity activity, relative to the amount of carbohydrate and protein that is used. At low-intensity exercise, the body uses mostly free fatty acids in the blood (released from adipose tissue), rather than fatty acids stored in muscle, for energy. During moderate-intensity exercise, the body begins to use more fatty acids from muscle triglycerides and less fatty acids released from adipose tissue. At the same time, more muscle glycogen is used and contributes to about half of total energy.

As exercise intensity increases and greater demands are placed on the cardio-respiratory system, the availability of oxygen declines. With less oxygen, fatty acids cannot be converted into energy fast enough to meet the demand. Because glucose oxidation is more efficient than fat oxidation at higher intensities, muscles begin to rely less on fat and more on glucose for fuel.

The goal of carbohydrate loading is to maximize the storage capacity of muscle glycogen before an endurance event. Increasing the amount of stored muscle glycogen can improve an athlete's endurance performance by providing the energy to fuel activity at an optimal pace for a longer period of time.

Not all athletes or physically active people will have improved performance with carbohydrate loading, however. The people who are likely to benefit the most from this strategy are those who participate in endurance events or exercise that lasts more than 90 minutes. Examples of endurance events include marathons, triathlons, cross-country skiing, and long-distance cycling and swimming. Individuals who exercise or train for less than 90 minutes should follow the standard recommendations for carbohydrate intake for athletes to ensure adequate muscle glycogen stores. Research has also shown that women are less likely than men to have improved performance with carbohydrate loading because women oxidize significantly more fat and less carbohydrate and protein during endurance exercise compared with men.[1]

So how do athletes start carbohydrate loading? When this concept was

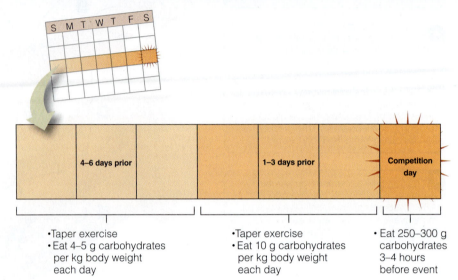

first developed, athletes began by training very hard for three to four days in addition to eating a low-carbohydrate diet (less than 5 to 10 percent of total kilocalories). This period was called the depletion phase and was thought to be necessary to increase glycogen stores during the next phase, called the loading phase. The loading phase involved three

to four days of minimal or no training while eating a diet high in carbohydrates. This resulted in higher muscle glycogen stores and better endurance performance.

Many people found the depletion phase hard to endure and would often experience irritability, hypoglycemia, and fatigue. In fact, today, many endurance

▲ **Figure 1** Carbohydrate loading involves tapering exercise and gradually increasing carbohydrate intake the week before a competitive event. On the day of the competition, a high-carb meal is eaten 3 to 4 hours before the event begins.

- • Taper exercise
- • Eat 4–5 g carbohydrates per kg body weight each day

- • Taper exercise
- • Eat 10 g carbohydrates per kg body weight each day

- • Eat 250–300 g carbohydrates 3–4 hours before event

Duration Affects the Use of Fat

In general, the use of fat for energy increases throughout the duration of low- to moderate-intensity exercise. During the first 15 to 20 minutes of exercise, fat utilization by the muscles increases at a slow rate due to the time required to oxidize fat for energy. During this time, free fatty acids in the bloodstream are taken up by the muscles and used for energy, which causes blood levels to drop. This in turn stimulates an increase in lypolysis, by way of the hormone epinephrine, and more fatty acids are hydrolyzed from adipose tissue and released into the bloodstream to provide (more) energy for the working muscles.

Once the duration of moderate-intensity activity exceeds 20 minutes, the level of fatty acids in the bloodstream becomes greater than normal as the body continues to use and release stored fat for energy. Because of this increase in blood levels, the body increases its use of fatty acids for energy.

athletes have modified this training strategy to exclude the depletion phase. Research has shown that depleting muscle glycogen stores is not necessary to increase the amount of stored muscle glycogen. However, there will be greater increases in muscle glycogen by initially depleting muscle glycogen stores.[2]

To begin a modified carbohydrate-loading regimen, athletes taper exercise about seven days prior to the event by doing a little less activity each day (**Figure 1**). This is often the hardest recommendation to follow because many athletes feel that they will be out of shape if they stop training before competition. But tapering exercise is necessary to increase muscle glycogen; otherwise, the body continues to burn glycogen for fuel rather than storing it to be used for energy during the upcoming event. One study showed that athletes can decrease training by 70 percent about one week prior to an endurance event without negatively affecting performance.[3]

In addition to tapering exercise, carbohydrate loading involves eating a high-carbohydrate diet that provides about 4 to 5 grams of carbohydrate per kilogram of body weight for the first three to four days. During the last three days of tapering exercise, carbohydrate intake is increased to 10 grams per kilogram of body weight. Lastly, a meal that is high in carbohydrate (providing about 250 to 300 grams),

Table 1	Sample Carbohydrate-Loading Menu			
Breakfast	**Lunch**	**Dinner**	**Snack**	
1 cup orange juice	2 slices oatmeal bread	3 cups spaghetti	1 cup vanilla	
½ cup Grape-Nuts cereal	3 oz turkey breast with lettuce, tomato	(6 oz uncooked)	yogurt	
1 medium banana	8 oz apple juice	1 cup tomato sauce	6 fig bars	
1 cup 2% milk	1 cup frozen yogurt	2 oz ground turkey		
1 English muffin		¼ loaf multigrain bread (4 oz)		
1 tbs jelly				
750 kilocalories	*750 kilocalories*	*1,300 kilocalories*	*500 kilocalories*	
85% carbohydrates	*65% carbohydrates*	*70% carbohydrates*	*80% carbohydrates*	

Total: 3,300 kilocalories: 75% carbohydrates (610 g), 15% protein (125 g), 10% fat (40 g)

Reprinted, with permission, from N. Clark, *Nancy Clark's Nutrition Guidebook*, 3rd ed. (Champaign, IL: Human Kinetics, 2008), p. 148.

moderate in protein, and low in fat should be consumed about 3 to 4 hours prior to the start of the event to further maximize glycogen stores.

Despite the emphasis on carbohydrate, athletes need to be sure not to compromise intake of protein and fat. They still need to include at least 0.8 grams of protein per kilogram of body weight (some athletes may require more protein) in their training diet, as well as about 20 to 25 percent of kilocalories coming from fat, preferably unsaturated fats.

Table 1 above is a sample one-day menu that might be used the day before an event. This menu is high in carbohydrate, adequate in protein, and low in fat.

References

1. J. Wismann and D. Willoughby. 2006. "Gender Differences in Carbohydrate Metabolism and Carbohydrate Loading." *Journal of the International Society of Sport Nutrition* 3:28–34.
2. W. H. Goforth, D. Laurent, W. K. Prusaczyk, K. E. Schneider, K. F. Peterson, and G. I. Shulman. 2003. "Effects of Depletion Exercise and Light Training on Muscle Glycogen Super-Compensation in Men." *American Journal of Physiology–Endocrinology and Metabolism* 285:E1304–E1311.
3. J. A. Houmard, D. L. Costill, J. B. Mitchell, S. H. Park, R. C. Hickner, and J. N. Roemmich. 1990. "Reduced Training Maintains Performance in Distance Runners." *International Journal of Sports Medicine* 11:46–52.

The body relies mostly on the energy produced from carbohydrate and fat during exercise. **Focus Figure 16.5** summarizes the preferred sources used to fuel muscular work based on the duration and intensity of the exercise.

Conditioning Affects the Use of Fat

An individual's level of conditioning can affect how much fat the body uses for energy. Endurance training results in an increase in the amount of fatty acids stored in the muscles, which can increase the amount of fat used for energy because it directly supplies fuel to the muscles. Training also causes muscle cells to produce new and larger mitochondria, which oxidize fatty acids to produce ATP. Lastly, training is thought to increase enzymes that aid in fatty acid oxidation. For these reasons, muscles that are well trained use more fat for energy than muscles that are not as well trained. Because they use more fat and less glycogen, conditioned individuals have the potential to increase endurance by "sparing" glycogen stores for later use.

Depending on the duration and intensity of the activity, our bodies may use ATP-CP, carbohydrate, or fat in various combinations to fuel muscular work. Keep in mind that the amounts and sources shown below can vary based on the person's fitness level and health, how well fed the person is before the activity, and environmental temperatures and conditions.

SPRINT START (0–3 seconds)
A short, intense burst of activity like sprinting is fueled by ATP and creatine phosphate (CP) under anaerobic conditions.

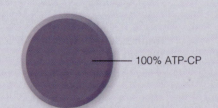

— 100% ATP-CP

100-M DASH (10–12 seconds)
ATP and CP provide energy for about 10 seconds of quick, intense activity, after which energy is provided as ATP from the breakdown of carbohydrates.

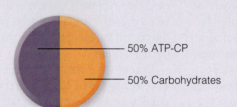

— 50% ATP-CP

— 50% Carbohydrates

1500-M RACE (4–6 minutes)
Energy derived from ATP and CP is small and would be exhausted after about 10 seconds of the race. At this point, most of the energy is derived from aerobic metabolism of primarily carbohydrates.

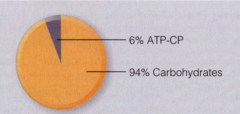

— 6% ATP-CP

— 94% Carbohydrates

10-KM RACE (30–40 minutes)
During moderately intense activities such as a 10-kilometer race, ATP is provided by fat and carbohydrate metabolism. As the intensity increases, so does the utilization of carbohydrates for energy.

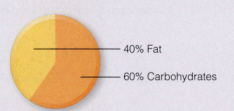

— 40% Fat

— 60% Carbohydrates

MARATHON (2.5–3 hours)
During endurance events such as marathons, ATP is primarily derived from carbohydrates, and to a lesser extent fat. A very small amount of energy is provided by the breakdown of amino acids to form glucose.

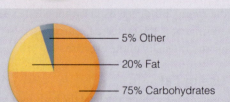

— 5% Other

— 20% Fat

— 75% Carbohydrates

DAY-LONG HIKE (5.5–7 hours)
The primary energy source for events lasting several hours at low intensity is fat (free fatty acids in the bloodstream, which derive from triglycerides stored in fat cells). Carbohydrates contribute a small percentage of energy needs.

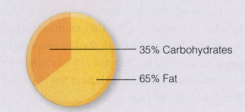

— 35% Carbohydrates

— 65% Fat

Recall that the body requires more oxygen to convert fatty acids into energy than it does to convert glucose into energy. This need for more oxygen creates more stress for the cardiovascular system. Conditioning the body through regular exercise results in the ability of the heart and lungs to deliver oxygen to working muscles more efficiently at higher intensity; thus, the oxidation of fatty acids for energy is greater.

The Amount of Fat Needed for Exercise

Dietary recommendations for fat intake are generally the same for active people as for the average adult population, with 25 to 30 percent of kilocalories coming from fat.[13] Remember from Chapter 5 that high intakes of saturated and *trans* fats have been linked to high cholesterol levels and heart disease. Physically active people sometimes assume that because they're in shape, they don't have to worry about these diseases. While it is true that physical activity grants some protection against heart disease, athletes and other fit people can also have high cholesterol, heart attacks, and strokes. Everyone, regardless of activity level, should limit saturated fat to no more than 10 percent of total kilocalories and consume primarily unsaturated fats in foods to meet the body's need for dietary fat.[14]

Some athletes, such as endurance runners and those in sports where low body weight is important, such as gymnasts and figure skaters, may feel they can benefit from a very low-fat diet (less than 20 percent). Though consuming too much dietary fat is a concern, limiting fat intake too much is also undesirable. Consuming less than adequate amounts of fat is more likely to result in inadequate consumption of kilocalories, essential fatty acids, and fat-soluble vitamins, which can negatively affect exercise performance.[15, 16]

Protein Is Primarily Used to Build and Repair Muscle

Protein is the nutrient most commonly associated with muscle and its relationship to physical activity, especially strength training. Recall from Chapter 6 that dietary and body proteins are broken down into amino acids and then reassembled into the various proteins that perform specific functions in the body, referred to as protein turnover. When protein synthesis occurs more often than breakdown, conditions are favorable for increases in muscle protein, which can translate to more muscle mass, strength, and endurance.

Exercise affects protein turnover by increasing the level of cortisol, a hormone associated with muscle protein breakdown during physiological stress, in the body. Nutritionally, protein synthesis can be achieved by consuming adequate dietary protein, in addition to carbohydrate and fat, because the amino acids and other nutrients are critical in promoting muscle growth (hypertrophy) and recovery after exercise. Protein synthesis is necessary to maintain or improve performance.

The Body Can Use Protein for Energy

Just as during rest, the body prefers to use carbohydrate and fat as its main energy sources during exercise. All active people use small amounts of protein for energy, but greater amounts are used when kilocalorie intake and carbohydrate stores are insufficient.

When dietary and body proteins are used for energy, they are broken down into amino acids that are then released into the bloodstream. The amino acids are carried to the liver, where they get converted through gluconeogenesis into glucose, which supplies the working muscles with energy. Remember that once amino acids are transformed to glucose, they cannot be changed back into amino acids. If the glucose is not used for energy, it is converted into fatty acids and stored as body fat.

If the body has to use a significant amount of protein for energy, that protein is not available to perform its vital functions and the rate of protein breakdown exceeds protein synthesis. Muscle atrophy is a likely consequence of protein breakdown when dietary intakes are inadequate to support physical activity. This commonly occurs in athletes who are trying to lose weight, those who need to "make weight" for a specific sport like wrestling, or in individuals who unintentionally do not eat enough to compensate for nutrients expended during physical activity.

Protein Needs Depend on the Level of Training

Many athletes and people who exercise assume that they need substantially more protein than people who do not exercise. Although it is true that those who are fit and physically active need more protein than those who are sedentary, their need is not significantly higher. The RDA for protein for most healthy adults, including recreational exercisers, is 0.8 grams per kilogram of body weight per day. Most people, including athletes, exceed this amount, with intake ranging from 0.9 to 2.3 grams per kilogram of body weight. Recreational exercisers can meet their need for protein with a balanced diet.

The increased protein needs of competitive and elite athletes, as well as bodybuilders, can also be met with a balanced diet. Endurance athletes are advised to consume 1.2 to 1.4 grams of protein per kilogram of body weight daily. People who primarily participate in resistance and strength activities may need to consume as much as 1.6 to 1.7 grams per kilogram of body weight daily.[17]

LO 16.3: THE TAKE-HOME MESSAGE Energy is provided by ATP-CP, carbohydrate, or fat, depending on the intensity and duration of exercise. Carbohydrate, in the form of blood glucose and muscle and liver glycogen, is the primary source of ATP during anaerobic, high-intensity, short-duration exercise. Fat is the main energy source during rest and aerobic, low-intensity, long-duration exercise. Protein provides the amino acids that are necessary to promote muscle growth and repair muscle breakdown caused by exercise.

How Does the Timing of Meals Affect Fitness and Athletic Performance?

LO 16.4 Discuss the timing of foods to consume before, during, and after exercise.

The timing and composition of meals and snacks before, during, and after exercise or athletic performance has a significant impact on energy stores, fatigue, and recovery time. For competitive athletes, modifying food intake to ensure optimal stores of liver and muscle glycogen before an athletic event is essential. In addition, the breakdown of muscle protein that can result from inadequate total energy and/or carbohydrate intake can lead to loss of muscle mass and strength, and lack of energy, which can negatively affect exercise performance.

Consumption of a precompetition meal depends on the time of the competition and how long food has to digest so that it doesn't negatively affect performance by causing cramps, bloating, or other discomforts. In general, larger meals (those that make you feel quite full) may take 3 to 4 hours to digest, whereas smaller meals (those that make you feel satisfied but not overly full) may take only 2 to 3 hours to digest. A liquid supplement or small snack may take about 30 minutes to 1 hour for digestion. For athletes competing in the early morning, a high-carbohydrate, low-fat dinner the night before will replenish glycogen stores that deplete during sleep, and

Consuming protein immediately after weight training enhances muscle recovery.

a small snack in the morning will provide the energy needed for performance. If an athlete competes in the afternoon, the morning meal becomes the critical feeding to pack muscle and liver glycogen stores. For a late afternoon or evening event, lunch should provide the carbohydrate necessary to top off the glycogen stores.

Endurance athletes or those who engage in high-intensity intermittent exercise, such as soccer, ice hockey, or basketball, are at risk of depleting glycogen stores during the event. Ingesting carbohydrate during the competition supports blood glucose levels and delays the depletion of glycogen stores.

Consuming the appropriate foods after exercise is important to support muscle recovery. During exercise, especially strength training, muscles are under a great deal of stress, which can result in overstretching and tearing of proteins and potential inflammation. After exercise, the body is in a catabolic (breaking down) state: Muscle and liver glycogen stores are low or depleted, muscle protein is broken down, and the immune system is suppressed.

Foods eaten after exercise affect how fast the body recovers, which in turn may affect how soon it is ready for the next workout or training session. This is especially important for competitive athletes who may train more than once per day.

These are general guidelines and may not apply to everyone. Individuals should experiment with their own eating and exercise schedule well before a workout or competition to know how long to wait before starting an activity.

Optimal Foods Before Exercise

A pre-exercise meal should contain adequate amounts of carbohydrate to maximize muscle and liver glycogen stores and maintain normal blood glucose levels. In general, the pre-exercise meal should contain 150 to 300 grams of carbohydrate (3 to 4.5 grams of carbohydrate per kilogram of body weight) and be consumed 3 to 4 hours prior to exercise (see **Table 16.3**). If the meal is small, about 400 to 500 kilocalories, it can be consumed 2 to 3 hours prior to exercise. If the meal is large and high in fat and protein, it may take 5 hours or more to digest. High-fiber carbohydrates and carbonated drinks should be avoided to prevent intestinal cramping and distress.

Consuming simple carbohydrates (1 gram per kilogram of body weight) immediately before exercise (about 15 to 30 minutes prior to the start), especially if the carbohydrate is in liquid form, such as sports drinks, may provide an advantage. The extra glucose gives muscles an immediate source of energy and spares glycogen stores, which allows for exercise for a longer duration or at a higher intensity without the body becoming tired as quickly.[18, 19]

Just as the body needs a continuous supply of carbohydrate, it also needs moderate amounts of protein throughout the day. Timing protein intake around activity has a significant impact on muscle preservation, growth, and recovery. Combining both protein *and* carbohydrate before exercise increases the muscle glycogen content in both the liver and the muscle more than eating carbohydrate alone.[20] With more glycogen in the liver and muscles, and proper training, endurance increases.

A pre-exercise meal must contain adequate amounts of carbohydrate.

TABLE 16.3 Timing and Amount of Macronutrients for Performance

Nutrient	Pre-Exercise	During Exercise		Postexercise Recovery
		Endurance	Ultra-Endurance	
Carbohydrate	150 to 300 g (3 to 4.5 per kg body weight)	30 to 60 g per hour	Up to 90 g per hour	Immediately after exercise 0.3 to 0.6 g per pound of body weight
Protein	Low protein	0	0	20 g of high-quality protein
Fat	Limit intake	0	0	Limit intake

Another benefit of consuming both protein and carbohydrate before exercise is that it results in greater protein synthesis after the exercise is over, compared with either protein or carbohydrate alone.[21] The making of new body proteins, including muscles, is necessary for optimal fitness and muscle preservation, repair, and growth.

Foods with a higher fat content take longer to digest than foods that are higher in carbohydrate and protein, and can lead to feelings of sluggishness or discomfort, which can impair performance. For this reason, high-fat foods should generally be avoided several hours before exercise. Of course this is a general guideline, and not all active people who consume higher fat foods before exercise experience difficulty.

Optimal Foods during Exercise

For exercise lasting longer than 1 hour, food intake during exercise should begin shortly after the start of exercise to maintain a blood supply of glucose, delay glycogen depletion, and reduce the perception of fatigue.[22] For long-lasting endurance activities, a total of 30 to 60 grams of carbohydrate should be consumed per hour.[23] Ultra-endurance athletes such as ultra-marathon runners or long-distance cyclists may need as much as 90 grams of carbohydrate per hour.[24]

Sports drinks and gels are one way to take in carbohydrate immediately before or during activity, but foods such as crackers and sports bars are also commonly eaten. Recent research has reported improved performance with a 6 percent carbohydrate mouth rinse for 5 to 10 seconds four times during a race.[25]

Glucose, sucrose, and maltodextrin are the best forms of carbohydrate to consume during exercise because the body absorbs them more quickly than other forms. Fructose, the sugar found in fruit and fruit juice, should generally be avoided during exercise because it may cause gastrointestinal problems or stomach discomfort in some individuals.[26]

Many sports drinks and gels contain only carbohydrate and electrolytes, while some also contain protein. For endurance athletes, consuming both carbohydrate and protein during exercise has been shown to improve net protein balance at rest as well as during exercise and postexercise recovery.[27] This net balance has, in turn, a positive effect on muscle maintenance and growth.

Optimal Foods after Exercise

Consuming carbohydrate after exercise helps replenish muscle and liver glycogen stores and stimulate muscle protein synthesis. The muscles are most receptive to storing new glycogen within the first 30 to 45 minutes after the end of exercise. Consuming 0.3 to 0.6 grams per pound of body weight of simple carbohydrates within that time frame will promote maximum glycogen storage.[28] Waiting longer than 1 hour results in less glycogen stored. Research shows that eating carbohydrate immediately after exercise also results in a more positive body protein balance.[29]

Consuming both protein and carbohydrate after exercise results in increased muscle protein synthesis. In addition, protein intake immediately after exercise rather than several hours later results in greater muscle protein synthesis. Research studies have shown that the addition of protein to carbohydrate intake causes an even greater increase in glycogen synthesis than either carbohydrate or protein alone, and therefore both nutrients should be consumed both before and after exercise.[30, 31]

Clearly, the body recovers more quickly after exercise when carbohydrate and protein are consumed in proper amounts before, during, and after exercise. Studies have shown that postexercise consumption of carbohydrate and protein in a ratio of approximately 4:1

Sports drinks can be a good source of carbohydrate during exercise.

(in grams) is ideal to stimulate muscle glycogen synthesis, repair muscle cells, stimulate protein synthesis, and promote faster recovery time.[32]

What is the best way to get these two nutrients? Most athletes and regular exercisers prefer to consume a liquid supplement that contains carbohydrate and protein rather than solid foods immediately after exercising. Whey protein (found in milk) is the preferred protein source because it is rapidly absorbed and contains all of the essential amino acids that the body needs. Commercial shakes and drinks containing whey protein are one option, but they can be expensive. A cheaper alternative is low-fat chocolate milk, which provides adequate amounts of carbohydrate and protein to assist in recovery.[33] For vegan athletes, rice protein supplements mixed with water have been shown to be effective for athletes following a resistance-training workout.[34] A liquid supplement or small snack consumed after exercise should be followed by a high-carbohydrate, moderate-protein, low-fat meal within the next 2 hours for optimum recovery.

The importance of carbohydrate and protein for recovery is clear. What about fat? Some people who load up on high-fat foods after a workout or competition experience fatigue that often results in less-than-optimal performance during the next workout.[35] Competitive athletes should always experiment with timing nutrient intake and consuming new foods and beverages during practice and not on the day of competition. Finding out that a particular food doesn't agree with you a few hours before an important race or event could be an unpleasant surprise. Apply these timing concepts to the athlete described in Nutrition in Practice on page 608.

Low-fat chocolate milk is a low-cost option to provide the whey protein and carbohydrate that help with muscle and glycogen synthesis after exercise. For vegan athletes, rice protein can be used effectively.

LO 16.4: THE TAKE-HOME MESSAGE Consuming the right balance of nutrients at the right time can improve exercise performance and recovery time. Pre-exercise meals should contain 150 to 300 grams of carbohydrate, and be low in protein and fat to promote faster digestion, and low in fiber to prevent intestinal problems. Fructose and higher fat foods should generally be avoided before exercise. During prolonged exercise, 30 to 60 grams of carbohydrates should be consumed per hour to delay glycogen depletion and support blood glucose. Immediately after exercise, simple carbohydrates plus protein should be consumed to replenish depleted glycogen and begin protein repair.

What Vitamins and Minerals Are Important for Fitness?

LO 16.5 Describe the importance of vitamins and minerals for physical fitness.

In addition to several other important functions, vitamins and minerals play a major role in the metabolism of carbohydrate, fat, and protein for energy during exercise. Some also act as antioxidants and help protect cells from the oxidative stress that can occur with exercise.

Some Vitamins and Minerals Contribute to the Processes of Energy Metabolism

Vitamins and minerals do not contain energy themselves, but some are key to catalyzing the release of energy held in the bonds of macronutrients. The B-complex water-soluble vitamins thiamin, riboflavin, niacin, pantothenic acid, biotin, and vitamin B_6 activate the enzymes that transform carbohydrates, proteins, and fats to ATP. Folate and vitamin B_{12} act together to maintain healthy red blood cells, which carry oxygen to the muscle used during aerobic metabolism. A deficiency in either of these two vitamins will result in fatigue and, potentially, anemia.

Nutrition in Practice: Stan

Stan plays left wing position on a Division I ice hockey team on the east coast. Stan doesn't have any particular dietary plan during the week and he doesn't like to eat before a game because it upsets his nervous stomach. After a game or practice, he is usually too tired to eat much and generally just grabs a bite to eat with friends. He notes that he often lacks the energy to get through an entire game or practice. Usually at the end of the third quarter he begins to feel fatigued. Stan understands how important his performance is to retaining his athletic scholarship, so he is committed to continuing his training over the summer break. Stan's summer training includes 10 to 15 hours weekly of weight training, sprints, and ice hockey drills, five days per week, two to three hours per day. His goal is to increase his strength, speed, and stamina on the ice before returning to school in the fall. Stan's coach recommended that he meet with the Registered Dietitian Nutritionist (RDN) assigned to the ice hockey team for advice before the fall semester begins, so as to develop a dietary plan to help him meet his goals.

Stan's Stats:
- Age: 20
- Height: 6 feet 0 inches
- Weight: 205 pounds
- BMI: 27.8
- % Body Fat: 9%

Stan's Food Log

Food/Beverage	Time Consumed	Hunger Rating*	Location
3 fried eggs with butter, 4 slices of bacon, 2 slices toast with 2 teaspoons margarine; 8 fluid oz orange juice	8 AM	5	Kitchen
16 ounces cola, large bean burrito	1:00 PM	4	Kitchen
16 ounces Gatorade; 3 Power Bars	3:00 PM (before practice)	3	Ice rink
4 slices pepperoni pizza (thick crust); 2 12-oz beers	7 PM (after practice)	5	Pizza restaurant with friends

*Hunger Rating (1–5): 1 = not hungry; 5 = super hungry.

Critical Thinking Questions

1. How many grams of carbohydrate should Stan be consuming daily?
2. Based on his food log, is Stan meeting his RDA for protein?
3. Is Stan's food timing appropriate for his exercise performance? What recommendations would you make to improve the timing of his meals and snacks to achieve his goals?

Dietitian's Observation and Plan for Stan:
- Discuss the importance of diet combined with resistance training to increase strength and speed, and to achieve optimal fuel stores, such as muscle and liver glycogen, before a game.
- Discuss the timing of eating pre-exercise, during exercise, and postexercise to provide fuel for training, muscle recovery, and strength development.
- Increase his kilocalorie intake to preserve muscle mass and provide energy to train with five nutrient-dense meals plus three snacks per day.
- Consume a pregame meal that contains at least 150 to 300 grams of carbohydrate about 3 to 4 hours prior to a game or intense practice.
- During the game, consume a liquid carbohydrate plus protein drink to maintain blood glucose, slow glycogen depletion, and provide fluid for hydration.
- Replenish his glycogen reserves after each game or practice to refuel for the next training session. Consume simple carbohydrates with protein immediately after the game to begin replenishing glycogen stores, followed later by a carbohydrate-rich dinner.
- To fully hydrate before a game, consume 400 to 600 ml of fluid 20 minutes before exercise, and 150 to 250 ml of fluid every 15 to 20 minutes during the game.

Two weeks later, Stan returns for a follow-up visit with the dietitian. Stan used the five-meal plus three snacks menu plan the RDN designed and feels stronger on the ice. The suggestions the RDN gave him fit his workout schedule and don't break his food budget. For example, rather than expensive protein powders, Stan drinks low-fat chocolate milk before resistance training and immediately after to provide the carbohydrate and amino acids necessary to rebuild muscle and improve his strength. Stan plans to continue his training and meal plan for the summer and makes an appointment to meet with the RDN for follow-up before the beginning of fall semester.

The mineral phosphorus is part of the energy currency adenosine triphosphate (ATP). A lack of phosphorus can lead to fatigue and weakness. The other minerals indirectly involved in energy production include iron and iodide. Iron (discussed further below) is an integral part of hemoglobin in red blood cells to carry and exchange oxygen with myoglobin in the muscle. And finally, the mineral iodide is necessary to produce thyroid hormone that controls metabolic rate and the rate at which the body produces energy.

Antioxidants Can Help Protect Cells from Damage Caused by Exercise

Muscles use more oxygen during exercise than at rest. As a result, the body increases production of free radicals that damage cells, especially during intense, prolonged exercise. Antioxidants, such as vitamins E and C, and selenium, are known to protect cells from the damage of free radicals. Vitamin C also assists in the production of collagen, which provides most of the structure of connective tissues like bone, tendons, and ligaments. This, in turn, can reduce the likelihood of developing strains, sprains, and fractures that may occur as a result of exercise.

Adequate intake of vitamins E and C through nutrient-rich foods has been linked to good health, which in turn can positively affect exercise and training. Research has not shown, however, that the use of antioxidants in levels above the RDA improves athletic performance, nor that it decreases oxidative stress in highly trained athletes.[36]

Deficiencies of Some Minerals Can Be of Concern for Highly Active People

In addition to their important roles in normal body functions and health, minerals are essential to physical fitness and athletic performance. In general, active people do not need more minerals than less active individuals. However, iron and calcium should be given special attention by some active people who may be at risk for deficiencies.

Iron

Iron is important to exercise because it is necessary for energy metabolism and transporting oxygen within muscle cells and throughout the body. Iron is a structural component of hemoglobin and myoglobin, two proteins that carry and store oxygen in the blood and muscle, respectively. If iron levels are low, hemoglobin and myoglobin levels can also fall, diminishing the blood's ability to carry oxygen to the cells. If this occurs during exercise, the result can be early fatigue. (Individuals with low iron levels can also feel tired even when they are not exercising.) Iron supplementation can improve aerobic performance for people with depleted iron stores.[37]

When iron levels are severely diminished, anemia can occur. Athletes and physically fit people are prone to iron-deficiency anemia for many reasons, including poor dietary intake or increased iron losses. Women can lose a lot of iron during menstruation, depending on their iron status and menstrual blood flow. This is one reason why female athletes are at a greater risk for iron-deficiency anemia than male athletes. Long-distance runners and athletes in sports where they must "make weight" have been noted to be at higher risk for iron-deficiency anemia. Athletes in other sports such as basketball, tennis, softball, and swimming also have a greater risk of suboptimal iron status.[38, 39]

Some people experience decreased levels of hemoglobin because of training, especially when the training is quite strenuous.

Female athletes are more prone to iron-deficiency anemia than male athletes.

Milk is an effective postexercise beverage that adds calcium, protein, and fluid to an athlete's diet.

During exercise, blood volume increases and concentrations of hemoglobin in the blood decrease. This is often referred to as **sports anemia**, or *pseudoanemia*, and is not the same as iron-deficiency anemia. Iron-deficiency anemia typically has to be treated with iron supplementation. Sports anemia can be corrected on its own because a body with sufficient iron stores can adapt to training and produce more red blood cells, which restores normal hemoglobin levels.

Another effect of exercise on iron is intravascular hemolysis (*hemo* = blood, *lysis* = breaking down), the bursting of red blood cells. Also called "foot strike hemolysis," this condition occurs when feet repeatedly hit a hard surface (the ground) during running, causing red blood cells to burst and release iron. The iron is recycled by the body and not lost, and therefore does not typically contribute to iron deficiency.

All individuals, whether they exercise or not, can maintain iron status by consuming adequate amounts of iron-rich foods, and supplements if necessary. Some vegetarian athletes are especially susceptible to iron deficiency and need to plan their diets appropriately so they consume adequate amounts of foods plentiful in iron. Many female athletes do not consume enough iron to meet their needs, which often leads to low iron levels. This is especially true for female athletes who exhibit disordered eating patterns. For more information, see the Spotlight: What Is the Female Athlete Triad? on page 611.

Calcium

Most people know about the importance of calcium to maintain bone health. Some people, including athletes, are particularly susceptible to broken bones and fractures. Having adequate calcium in the diet can reduce one's risk for these types of injuries. In addition, calcium affects both skeletal and heart muscle contraction, and hormone and neurotransmitter activity during exercise. It also assists in blood clotting in response to a cut or other minor hemorrhage, which may occur during exercise or competition.

Calcium is lost in sweat; the more individuals sweat, the more calcium they lose. One study concluded that exercise can increase bone mineral content (the mass of all minerals in bone) even when calcium intake is below the recommended intakes. The exercise effects on bone mineral density were sufficient to compensate for the calcium lost through sweating.[40]

While adequate calcium intake is essential, calcium supplements are not recommended unless intake from food and beverages does not meet the RDA. Choosing foods that are high in calcium, including fortified foods, can ensure that all individuals, including athletes, meet their needs for calcium.

Vitamin and Mineral Supplements Are Generally Not Necessary

Many athletes mistakenly believe that vitamins and minerals themselves supply energy, or that consuming extra vitamins and minerals can enhance performance. Previous studies have shown that multivitamin and mineral supplements are the supplements most commonly used by college athletes.[41] Can vitamin and mineral supplements really improve athletic performance? The answer is: not unless the body is already deficient in the nutrient. For people who consume enough vitamins and minerals in their diet, taking more than the RDA will not result in improved performance during exercise.[42]

Active people generally do not need more vitamins than sedentary people because vitamins can be used repeatedly in metabolic reactions. Everyone, not just

sports anemia Low concentrations of hemoglobin in the blood; results from an increase in blood volume during strenuous exercise.

The Female Athlete Triad

Christy Henrich joined the U.S. gymnastics team in 1986 weighing 95 pounds at 4 feet, 11 inches tall. Shortly after joining the team, Christy succeeded as a gymnast, but after a judge told her she needed to lose weight, she developed anorexia nervosa. Sadly, her weight plummeted to 47 pounds, and she died from multiple organ failure at the age of 22.

The anorexia that Christy battled is one part of the **female athlete triad,** a combination of interrelated health conditions existing on a continuum of severity: low energy availability, menstrual dysfunction, and low bone mineral density (**Figure 1**). Female athletes are often pressured to reach or maintain an unrealistically low body weight and/or level of body fat. This pressure contributes to the development of disordered eating, which helps to initiate the triad. The major concern with this disorder is that it not only reduces the performance of the athlete but may have serious medical and psychological consequences later in life.

Low Energy Availability or Disordered Eating

Athletes who wish to lose weight or maintain a low body weight may restrict their energy intake or develop abnormal eating behaviors. At one extreme are those who fulfill the diagnostic criteria for anorexia nervosa or bulimia nervosa. However, disordered eating occurs on a continuum and is not always so pronounced. At the other end are those who unintentionally take in fewer kilocalories than they need. They may appear to be eating

female athlete triad A syndrome of the three interrelated conditions occurring in some physically active females: low energy availability (often from disordered eating), amenorrhea, and decreased bone density or osteoporosis.

amenorrhea Absence of menstruation for at least three consecutive cycles.

▲ **Figure 1** Female athletes for whom body size or appearance is an issue, such as dancers, gymnasts, and skaters, are often particularly vulnerable to the female athlete triad.

a healthy diet—one that would be adequate for a sedentary individual—but their kilocalorie needs are higher due to their level of physical activity.

Many athletes mistakenly believe that losing weight by any method enhances performance and that disordered eating is harmless. Disordered eating can occur in athletes (both male and female) in all types of sports, but it is most common among athletes in sports where appearance is important, such as figure skating, gymnastics, and ballet, and sports in which individuals strive to maintain a low body weight, such as wrestling, rowing, and horse racing.

Menstrual Dysfunction or Amenorrhea

The failure to consume enough energy to compensate for the "energy cost" of the exercise can lead to disruption of the menstrual cycle.[1] **Amenorrhea,** the absence of at least three consecutive menstrual cycles, is the most extreme and recognizable form of disruption. Unfortunately, many females welcome the convenience of not menstruating and do not report it; however, this may put them at risk for reduced bone mass and increased rate of bone loss caused by decreased levels of estrogen in the body.[2]

Low Bone Mineral Density or Osteoporosis

Energy deficiency and decreased estrogen levels due to menstrual dysfunction contribute to bone loss and low bone mineral density. At its most extreme this causes premature osteoporosis, which puts the athlete at risk for stress fractures and hip and vertebral fractures, as well as the loss of bone mass that may be irreplaceable.[3]

Signs and Treatment

All individuals, including friends, teachers, and coaches, involved with at-risk athletes should be aware of the warning signs because the triad components are very often not recognized, not reported, or are denied. Warning signs include menstrual changes, weight changes, disordered eating patterns, cardiac arrhythmia, depression, or stress fractures. Those working with such athletes should provide a training environment in which athletes are not pressured to lose weight, and should be able to recommend appropriate nutritional, medical, and/or psychological resources if needed. Treatment of an athlete with this disorder is multidisciplinary, and needs to involve cooperation among the athlete's physician, dietician, psychologist, coach or trainer, family, and friends.

References

1. K. N. Brown, H. J. Wengreen, and K. A. Beals. 2014. "Knowledge of the Female Athlete Triad, and Prevalence of Triad Risk Factors." *Journal of Pediatric and Adolescent Gynecology* DOI: 10.1016/j.jpag.2013.11.014.
2. E. M. Lanser, K. N. Zach, and A. Z. Hoch. 2011. "The Female Athlete Triad and Endothelial Dysfunction." *Physical Medicine and Rehabilitation* 3(5):458–465.
3. M. T. Barrack, J. C. Gibbs, M. J. De Souza, N. I. Williams, J. F. Nichols, M. J. Rauh, and A. Nattiv. 2014. "Higher Incidence of Bone Stress Injuries with Increasing Female Athlete Triad–Related Risk Factors: A Prospective Multisite Study of Exercising Girls and Women." *American Journal of Sports Medicine* 42(4):949–958.

athletes, should obtain vitamins and minerals through foods before considering the use of supplements. As long as individuals consume adequate amounts of kilocalories by eating a wide variety of nutrient-dense foods, they are likely to meet vitamin and mineral requirements; thus, it is probably a waste of money to use vitamin and mineral supplements. In addition, excess intakes of some vitamins and minerals, especially from supplements, can be harmful (see Chapters 9, 10, 12, and 13). Anyone, including athletes, should consult with a physician or a Registered Dietitian Nutritionist before taking dietary supplements.

> **LO 16.5: THE TAKE-HOME MESSAGE** Vitamins and minerals play important roles in metabolism, and vitamins E and C can act as antioxidants. Some athletes need to pay special attention to their intakes of iron and calcium. Iron is important because of its role in transporting oxygen in blood and muscle. Iron deficiency is prevalent among athletes, especially females and vegetarians. Calcium intake is important for bone health and muscle contraction. Adequate amounts of all nutrients can be consumed in foods, so supplements are not usually necessary.

How Does Fluid Intake Affect Fitness?

LO 16.6 Explain the relationship between fluid intake and fitness.

As basic as it sounds, water is one of the most important nutrients during physical activity. Drinking too little fluid, or losing too much fluid and electrolytes through sweating, causes physiological changes that can negatively affect exercise performance and health. Early fatigue or weakness can occur when the body doesn't have sufficient amounts of water. Consuming adequate fluids on a regular basis, as well as monitoring fluid losses during physical activity, are key to maintaining optimal performance and preventing **dehydration** (also called *hypohydration*) and electrolyte imbalance.

Fluid and Electrolyte Balance and Body Temperature Are Affected by Exercise

During physical activity, the body loses more water via sweat and exhalation of water vapor than when it's less active. This lost water needs to be replaced during and after exercise to maintain normal fluid balance.

Electrolytes are also lost during exercise. Sodium and chloride and, to a lesser extent, potassium are contained in sweat. An electrolyte imbalance can cause heat cramps, as well as nausea, lowered blood pressure, and edema in the hands and feet, all of which can hinder performance. When electrolyte losses are within the range of normal daily dietary intake, they can easily be replaced by consuming foods rich in sodium, chloride, and potassium within 24 hours after exercise. If you prefer, you can replace electrolytes by drinking beverages that contain them, such as sports drinks.

During exercise, sweat releases the heat generated by the breakdown of nutrients to keep body temperature normal. The amount of fluid lost through sweating varies from person to person. Some people sweat heavily, while others may sweat very little. Regardless of how much you sweat, it is important that you don't allow your body to lose too much fluid without replacing it with water or other beverages.

Exercising in hot, humid weather results in more fluid being lost in breathing, which increases the body's need for fluids. However, if the air is very humid (that is, it contains a lot of water), sweat may not evaporate off the skin, and the body can't cool down. This can cause **hyperthermia,** and increase the risk of heat exhaustion or heat stroke. One significant warning sign of heat stroke is a complete lack of sweating. This happens when an individual is extremely dehydrated and cannot

Staying hydrated during physical activity is important to maintain electrolyte balance and help regulate body temperature.

dehydration Loss of water in the body as a result of inadequate fluid intake or excess fluid loss, such as through sweating; also called *hypohydration.*

hyperthermia A rise in body temperature above normal.

TABLE 16.4 Warning Signs of Heat Exhaustion and Heat Stroke

Heat Exhaustion	Heat Stroke
Profuse sweating	Red, hot, and dry skin (no sweating)
Fatigue	Rapid, strong pulse
Thirst	Rapid, shallow breathing
Muscle cramps	Throbbing headache
Headache	Dizziness
Dizziness or lightheadedness	Nausea
Weakness	Extreme confusion
Nausea and vomiting	Unconsciousness
Cool, moist skin	Extremely high body temperature (above 103°F [39.4°C], orally)

produce sweat, which prevents the release of heat and causes body temperature to rise. Other warning signs of heat exhaustion and heat stroke are shown in Table 16.4.

Many athletes and other active people may not realize that they can be at risk for **hypothermia,** which is just as serious as hyperthermia. Cold weather, especially if wet, can contribute to hypothermia when a person is exercising for a long period of time. Someone who is running at a slow pace in cold weather may produce very little heat, causing the body temperature to fall. Keep in mind that the body still sweats when exercising in cold weather, so meeting fluid needs is still important. Wearing adequate clothing and drinking fluids at least at room temperature or warmer helps prevent hypothermia.

Fluids Are Needed Before, During, and After Exercise

Many active people are aware that it's important to stay hydrated during exercise, but the need for water doesn't begin with the first sit-up or lap around the track. Meeting fluid needs before and after activity is important to maintain fluid and electrolyte balance and optimize performance.

Being hydrated prior to exercise is essential to performance. The timing and amount of fluid depends on the individual and their current hydration status. Too much fluid can cause bloating and result in excess urine produced during exercise. Too little fluid intake prior to exercise can result in dehydration during the exercise and a poor performance outcome. Most healthy adult women need 9 cups of water daily, while most healthy adult men need about 13 cups. This is a general guideline to follow for adequate hydration before exercise. Another way to determine estimated daily fluid needs is to divide body weight by 2. This reveals the number of ounces of fluid (8 ounces = 1 cup) needed daily, not including the additional needs associated with exercising.

Proper hydration during and after exercise is essential to replace sweat losses. As you learned in Chapter 11, you can determine fluid needs during exercise by weighing yourself both before and after an activity. After exercise, you should consume 20 to 24 fluid ounces (about 2 to 3 cups) of fluid for every pound of body weight lost (weight loss is mainly due to water loss).[43] The American College of Sports Medicine has specific recommendations for how much fluid to drink before, during, and after exercise. See Table 16.5 for these recommendations.

Some Beverages Are Better than Others

Beverages like tea, coffee, soft drinks, fruit juice, and, of course, water contribute to daily fluid needs. But what is the best type of fluid for preventing dehydration prior to and during activity? What about for rehydrating your body after activity? For these purposes, not all beverages are equal.

hypothermia A drop in body temperature to below normal.

TABLE 16.5	ACSM Hydration Recommendations	
When?	**How Much Fluid?**
4 hours before exercise	16–20 fl oz (2–2 1/2 cups)
10 to 15 minutes before exercise	8–12 fl oz (1–1 1/2 cups)
At 15- to 20-minute intervals when exercising less than 60 minutes	3–8 fl oz (3/8–1 cup)
At 15- to 20-minute intervals when exercising more than 60 minutes	3–8 fl oz (3/8–1 cup) sports beverage (5–8 percent carbohydrate with electrolytes)
After exercise for every pound of body weight lost	20–24 fl oz (2 1/2–3 cups)

Table from Simpson, Michael R., and Tom Howard. 2011. *Selecting and Effectively Using Hydration for Fitness.* Copyright © 2011 by the American College of Sports Medicine. Reprinted with permission.

Sports drinks are popular in the fitness world and are often marketed as tasty beverages to all groups of people, not just athletes. They typically contain 6 to 8 percent carbohydrate as well as sodium and potassium, two electrolytes that are critical in muscle contraction and maintaining fluid balance. The amount of electrolytes found in sports drinks will differ depending on the manufacturer. One purpose of sports drinks is to replace fluid and electrolytes after exercise that are lost through sweating, which is vital to prevent or treat muscle cramps associated with exercise. Sports drinks have been shown to be superior to water for rehydration, mostly because their flavor causes people to drink more than they would of just plain water.[44]

Sports drinks also provide additional carbohydrate to prevent glycogen depletion. This is beneficial during long endurance events or exercise when glycogen stores may be running low. Consuming a sports drink during exercise provides glucose, which can be used as an immediate energy source and prevent further decline in muscle glycogen stores. The amount of carbohydrate in sports drinks (6 to 8 percent) is formulated for optimal absorption, which makes them preferred over other beverages, such as soft drinks and fruit juice, that have higher concentrations and different types of carbohydrate.

However, not everyone needs sports drinks in order to stay adequately hydrated. For exercise that lasts less than 60 minutes, water can sufficiently replace fluids lost through sweating and food consumption following exercise can adequately replace electrolytes. Sports drink consumption can be beneficial for some people who exercise for less than one hour. But generally, a sports drink is most beneficial when physical activity lasts longer than 60 minutes, because fluids, electrolytes, and/or glucose are inevitably lost in greater amounts and need to be replenished to avoid fatigue and other negative effects on performance.[45] Sports beverages provide approximately 60 kilocalories for each 8-ounce cup, so remember that they can be a source of unwanted extra kilocalories.

Other beverages may be suboptimal for hydration during physical activity. Fruit juice and juice drinks contain a larger concentration of carbohydrate and do not hydrate the body as quickly during exercise as beverages with a lower concentration of carbohydrate (like sports drinks). However, fruit and vegetables juices can be a good choice to add simple carbohydrates and fluid after exercise. Carbonated drinks contain a large amount of water; however, the air bubbles from the carbonation can cause stomach bloating and may limit the amount of fluid consumed. In addition, fructose (the type of carbohydrate provided by carbonated soft drinks) is not as well absorbed as the glucose or sucrose that is found in sports drinks.

Though alcohol may seem like an unlikely choice for rehydration, some people may drink alcoholic beverages, such as beer, in order to quench thirst. But because alcohol is a

Fluids such as milk and fruit and vegetable juices can help meet daily water needs and make good postexercise beverage choices. Whole fruits and many other foods are also good sources of water.

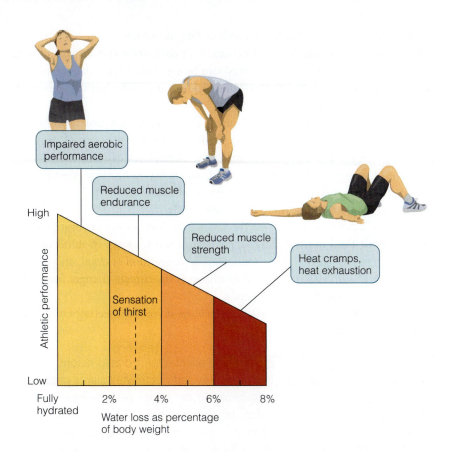

▶ **Figure 16.6** **Effects of Dehydration on Exercise Performance**
Failing to stay hydrated during exercise or competition can result in fatigue and cramps and, in extreme cases, heat exhaustion. Because the thirst mechanism doesn't kick in until after dehydration has begun, replacing fluids throughout physical activity is important.
Source: Adapted from L. Burke. 2007. *Practical Sports Nutrition.* Champaign, IL: Human Kinetics.

Impaired aerobic performance

Reduced muscle endurance

Reduced muscle strength

Heat cramps, heat exhaustion

High

Athletic performance

Sensation of thirst

Low

Fully hydrated   2%   4%   6%   8%

Water loss as percentage of body weight

diuretic, it can actually contribute to dehydration. Alcohol during performance can also impair judgment and reasoning, which can lead to injuries for both the exerciser and those nearby.

Caffeinated beverages, such as coffee, energy drinks, and some soft drinks, contribute to the DRI for water but are not optimal sources for meeting fluid needs for physical activity. Caffeine, a diuretic, should only be consumed in moderate amounts (less than about 300 milligrams, or the amount found in three 8-ounce cups of coffee, per day), because excessive intake can cause increased heart rate, nausea, vomiting, excessive urination, restlessness, anxiety, and difficulty sleeping.[46] However, recall from Chapter 11 that caffeine does not contribute to dehydration in individuals who regularly consume it. A discussion of caffeine as an ergogenic aid is presented in the Health Connection section on page 617.

Consuming Too Little or Too Much Fluid Can Be Harmful

As the body loses fluid during physical activity, it sends signals of thirst to stimulate fluid consumption. However, by the time an individual feels thirsty, he or she may already be dehydrated. **Figure 16.6** shows the effect of dehydration on exercise performance. Athletes need to know the warning signs of dehydration so they can respond by drinking adequate fluids and prevent health consequences and impaired exercise performance.

Becoming dehydrated over a short period of time, such as during a single exercise session or sports competition, can result in **acute dehydration.** Acute dehydration most commonly occurs if an individual is not adequately hydrated before beginning a hard exercise session, especially if that person has been sick, if it is extremely hot and humid, or if the temperature is significantly different from what the person is used to. To prevent acute dehydration, follow a regimented hydration schedule using water or sports drinks to hydrate before, during, and after exercise sessions or competition.

Chronic dehydration refers to being inadequately hydrated over an extended period of time, such as during several sports practices or games. The most common

acute dehydration Dehydration that sets in after a short period of time.

chronic dehydration Dehydration over a long period of time.

Are You Meeting Your Fitness Recommendations and Eating for Exercise?

Now that you know how to plan an effective fitness strategy and eat for optimal fitness and performance, think about your current dietary and exercise habits. Take this brief assessment to find out if your daily habits are as healthful as they could be:

1. Do you participate in at least 60 minutes of moderately intense physical activity during the week?

   Yes ☐   **No** ☐

2. Do you participate in strength training 2 to 3 times per week?

   Yes ☐   **No** ☐

3. Do you drink 6 to 12 ounces of fluid every 15 to 20 minutes during exercise?

   Yes ☐   **No** ☐

4. Do you drink a sports beverage after moderate or high-intensity exercise lasting longer than 1 hour?

   Yes ☐   **No** ☐

5. Do you consume carbohydrate and protein within 30 to 45 minutes after stopping exercise?

   Yes ☐   **No** ☐

Answer

If you answered "yes" to all of the questions, you are well on your way to optimal fitness. Participating in regular exercise, including aerobic exercise and strength training, helps you maintain optimal health and improves your level of fitness. Eating and drinking adequate nutrients also improves fitness. If you answered "no" to any of the questions, review this chapter to learn more on fitness and eating for exercise.

warning signs of chronic dehydration include fatigue, muscle soreness, poor recovery from a workout, headaches, and nausea. Very dark urine and infrequent bathroom trips (less than every 3 or 4 hours) can be signs of chronic dehydration. As with acute dehydration, following a regimented hydration schedule throughout the day helps prevent chronic dehydration.

When speaking of hydration and physical activity, we are usually concerned about consuming *enough* fluids so that we do not become dehydrated. However, consuming too much fluid without sufficient electrolytes can also be harmful. Symptoms of severe hyponatremia (review Chapter 11) occur more often in those who participate in endurance sports or prolonged exercise periods (greater than 4 hours), in which fluid and sodium loss is more likely.

If you are a distance runner, see the Calculation Corner for a hydration test to determine your fluid needs during long-distance races.[47] Keep in mind that you should perform this hydration test well before a competition or event, and perform the test again if your level of fitness improves or if the climate changes from when you initially determined your fluid needs.

Take the Self-Assessment at left to determine if you are meeting exercise and dietary recommendations.

LO 16.6: THE TAKE-HOME MESSAGE Being adequately hydrated before, during, and after exercise is important to sustain fluid and electrolyte balance and a normal body temperature. Inadequate hydration can impair performance. Water is the preferred beverage for hydration, but sports drinks can be beneficial during moderate- or vigorous-intensity exercise. Overhydration can be just as important to avoid as dehydration, but is more likely to occur among people engaging in endurance sports or prolonged exercise.

Calculation Corner

Fluid Needs for Distance Runners

The next time you take a 1-hour training run, use the following process to determine your fluid needs.

1. Make sure that you are properly hydrated before the workout. Your urine should be colorless.
2. Do a warm-up run to the point where you start to sweat, then stop. Urinate if necessary.
3. Weigh yourself on an accurate scale.
4. Run for 1 hour at an intensity similar to your targeted race.
5. Drink a measured amount of a beverage of your choice during the run to quench your thirst. Be sure to keep track of how much you drink.
6. Do not urinate during the run.
7. After you have finished the run, weigh yourself again on the same scale you used in step 3.
8. Calculate your fluid needs using the following formula:
   a. Enter your body weight from step 3 in pounds   _____
   b. Enter your body weight from step 7 in pounds   _____
   c. Subtract b. from a.   _____
   d. Convert the pounds of weight in c. to fluid ounces by multiplying by 15.3   _____
   e. Enter the amount of fluid you consumed during the run in ounces   _____
   f. Add e. to d.   _____

The final figure is the number of ounces of fluid that you must consume per hour to remain well hydrated.

Source: D. Casa. 2007. *USATF Self-Testing Program for Optimal Hydration*, from the USA Track and Field Web site. Copyright © 2007 by Douglas Casa. Reprinted with permission of the author.

Can Dietary Supplements Contribute to Exercise Performance and Fitness?

LO 16.7 Describe the most common dietary supplements used in exercise and their side effects.

Competitive athletes are always looking for an edge, and many turn to supplements in the hope of improving their performance. Supplement manufacturers may claim that their products enhance immunity, boost metabolism, improve memory, or provide some other physical enhancement. Because the Food and Drug Administration does not strictly regulate dietary supplements, the manufacturers do not have to prove the validity of these claims or the safety or efficacy of their products. As a result, many athletes risk their health and, in some cases, eligibility for competition by taking supplements that can be ineffective or even dangerous.

The term **ergogenic aid** describes any substance used to improve athletic performance, including dietary supplements. Although the makers of dietary supplements do not have to prove their products' effectiveness, researchers have examined several supplements and their effects on athletic performance. Studies have indicated that some dietary supplements have a positive effect on performance, while others do not. Further, some ergogenic aids cause serious side effects.

ergogenic aid A substance, such as a dietary supplement, used to enhance athletic performance.

Athletes sometimes take supplements, such as creatine phosphate or caffeine, to enhance their performance. Supplements are not strictly regulated by the FDA, so their quality and effectiveness can vary widely.

Creatine Improves Muscle Strength, Muscle Mass, and Anaerobic Metabolism during Some Activities

Creatine is one of the most well-known dietary supplements in the fitness industry today. In the early 1990s, research revealed that creatine supplementation increased creatine stores in the muscles (in the form of creatine phosphate), which increased the amount of ATP generated and improved performance during high-intensity, short-duration exercise.[48]

However, the data on whether creatine supplements enhance performance is mixed. Studies have supported the hypothesis that creatine supplementation improves athletic performance in high-intensity, short-duration activities such as weight training, when the body relies on anaerobic energy metabolism and increased muscle strength and muscle mass.[49] But research has shown mixed results in creatine supplementation improving sprint-running performance, with some studies showing improvement and others showing no benefit.[50, 51]

The most common side effect of creatine supplementation is water retention. However, when taken at higher than recommended doses for several months, there are reported cases of liver and kidney problems.[52] Anyone considering taking creatine supplements should check with a health care provider first.

Caffeine Improves Perception and Aerobic Metabolism

Caffeine used to be considered by athletes mostly in the context of its diuretic properties and resultant effect on hydration. Today, caffeine has gained popularity as an ergogenic aid among athletes, trainers, and coaches. Caffeine may decrease perception of effort by stimulating the central nervous system, directly affect the breakdown of muscle glycogen, and increase the availability of fatty acids during exercise, therefore sparing glycogen stores.

Studies on the effects of drinking caffeine prior to exercise have shown that caffeine enhances athletic performance, mostly during endurance events.[53] However, research has not shown that caffeine provides any benefit during short-duration activities, such as sprinting.[54]

Caffeine is considered a banned substance by some athletic associations when consumed in high amounts. For example, the National Collegiate Athletic Association (NCAA) classifies caffeine as a banned substance only when urine concentrations exceed 15 micrograms per milliliter. Because individuals weigh different amounts and metabolize caffeine at different rates, it is difficult to determine how many cups of coffee or another caffeinated beverage it would take to test positive for caffeine.

Bicarbonate Loading May Improve Anaerobic Metabolism during Exercise

Athletes who participate in anaerobic, high-intensity sports, including sprint cycling, 400- or 800-meter sprints, and swimming, strive to find ways to buffer lactate buildup during their event. Recall from Chapter 8 that anaerobic

metabolism involves the conversion of glucose to pyruvate. When there is insufficient oxygen, pyruvate is reduced to lactate and results in hydrogen ion buildup in the muscle cell and a drop in pH. The more acidic pH inhibits muscle contraction and the phosphorylation of ADP to form ATP, leading to muscle fatigue.

Sodium bicarbonate, or baking soda, has been reported to be one ergogenic aid that can buffer or neutralize the acid in the blood and improve performance.[55] Some research presented positive results when sodium bicarbonate was ingested pre-exercise. For example, ingestion of sodium bicarbonate significantly reduced fatigue in intermittent repeated sprint performance,[56] improved maximal sprint swimming performance,[57] and improved the number of accumulated repetitions in weight lifters.[58]

There are side effects with ingesting sodium bicarbonate. Some subjects have reported nausea, bloating, and gastric reflux within an hour of ingesting this ergogenic aid. Diarrhea, flatulence, and intestinal discomfort have also been reported.[59]

Amino Acid Supplementation Shows Some Benefit

Amino acid supplements have become a popular nutritional supplement marketed to athletes. For resistance-trained athletes, amino acid powders and pills have been proposed to enhance muscle synthesis and accelerate recovery following exercise. Endurance athletes ingest amino acid supplements to improve their physiological response during endurance exercise and training. Do these supplements work?

Numerous research studies have tested the benefits of ingesting branched-chain amino acid (BCAA) supplements (leucine, isoleucine, and valine) to enhance exercise performance. These studies have failed to demonstrate any benefit of BCAAs during exercise. However, some evidence suggests that these amino acids may improve muscle recovery after exercise and support the immune system.[60]

There are a few other amino acid supplements that show promise. Beta-alanine has been shown to buffer hydrogen ions produced during

Sports bars and shakes should supplement, not replace, whole, nutritious foods.

high-intensity intermittent exercise, and to improve endurance performance and lean body mass.[61] Carnitine reduces free radical formation during exercise, reduces muscle damage, and improves muscle recovery after exercise.[62] The amino acid leucine taken as a supplement after endurance exercise may improve protein synthesis and muscle recovery.[63] Glutamine supplementation may help maintain the immune system,[64] improve glucose utilization, and stimulate muscle glycogen synthesis postexercise.[65] Glutamine has not been shown to reduce muscle soreness or improve muscle repair.[66]

Sports Bars and Shakes May Provide Benefits

Sports bars and shakes are not defined as dietary supplements by the FDA because they are more like food and contain one or more macronutrients. However, people often refer to these items as supplements because they are typically eaten in addition to whole-food meals and snacks.

The main energy source in most commercial sports bars and shakes is carbohydrate, with protein and fat contributing smaller amounts of energy. The ratio of the macronutrients in these foods varies depending on

the purpose. Bars and shakes that are intended to provide energy for and recovery from exercise have a greater proportion of carbohydrates. Those that are promoted for muscle protein synthesis typically contain more protein than carbohydrate and fat. Vegetarians and some athletes who need additional sources of protein in their diet often use bars and shakes that are high in protein. Most bars and shakes also contain a variety of vitamins and minerals. These vitamins and minerals may not be necessary for individuals who consume regular, balanced meals or take a daily multivitamin.

Sports bars and shakes can be convenient for some individuals, but they are often expensive. An energy bar may be trendy and easy to stash in a book bag, but an old-fashioned peanut butter sandwich on whole-grain bread would cost less, fit a vegan athlete's diet, and be just as easy to carry. In addition, when athletes consume dietary protein within the recommended guidelines, there is little scientific evidence that adding more protein through sports bars and shakes enhance the physiological responses to exercise performance. Overall, it is best to limit intakes of commercial sports bars and shakes so that they don't become a substitute for whole, nutritious foods.

LO 16.7: THE TAKE-HOME MESSAGE Dietary supplements and ergogenic aids may enhance performance, but can have side effects. Creatine improves performance during high-intensity, short-duration exercise, and increases muscle strength and muscle mass, but causes water retention and may negatively affect liver and kidney function when taken at higher than recommended doses for several months. Caffeine may decrease perception of effort by stimulating the central nervous system, and improve endurance performance by sparing glycogen stores and increasing fatty acid utilization during exercise. The NCAA bans caffeine in high amounts. Sodium bicarbonate buffers the blood and improves anaerobic performance in some sports, but does cause unpleasant gastrointestinal side effects. Some amino acid supplements, including branched-chain amino acids, alanine, carnitine, leucine, and glutamine, may show some benefit in improving muscle recovery. Sports bars and shakes are convenient sources of energy, but are often more expensive than whole foods and should only be included as a minor part of an overall healthy diet. Athletes who consume dietary protein within the recommended guidelines do not benefit from additional protein intake.

Visual Chapter Summary

LO 16.1 Physical Fitness Includes Five Components for Health

Physical fitness, defined as good health or physical condition, includes five basic components: cardiorespiratory endurance, muscular strength, muscular endurance, flexibility, and body composition. Physical activity reduces the risk of developing type 2 diabetes, some forms of cancer, and cardiovascular disease. It improves body composition, bone health, immune function, mental well-being, and sleep, and reduces stress.

LO 16.2 A Successful Physical Fitness Program Uses FITT Principles

Fitness programs generally incorporate activities that are based on the five components of fitness, including aerobic exercise, resistance training, and stretching. FITT is an acronym for frequency (how often), intensity (degree of difficulty or effort), time (how long), and type (specific activity). Rating of perceived exertion (RPE) and target heart rate are used to measure intensity for cardiorespiratory exercise, while repetition maximum (RM) measures intensity for weight training.

A successful fitness program should be tailored to meet the needs of the individual and performed consistently so that any gains in fitness are maintained. The progressive overload principle of gradually increasing the exercise demands placed on the body will improve fitness levels over time.

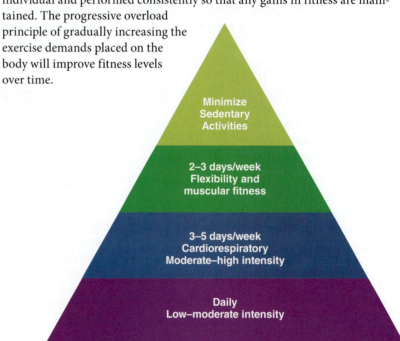

Minimize Sedentary Activities

2–3 days/week Flexibility and muscular fitness

3–5 days/week Cardiorespiratory Moderate–high intensity

Daily Low–moderate intensity

LO 16.3 Carbohydrate, Fat, and Protein Fuel Exercise

Carbohydrate, fat, and protein are all used by the body during exercise. The source of energy needed to fuel exercise depends on the intensity and duration of the activity, and an individual's current fitness level.

The body relies heavily on anaerobic energy from ATP and creatine phosphate (PCr) during the first few minutes of exercise. As exercise continues, the body relies on aerobic production of ATP mainly from carbohydrate and fat, obtained from blood glucose and stored glycogen, and fatty acids stored in muscle tissue and free fatty acids in the blood derived from lipolysis. Fat supplies nearly all of the energy required during rest and low- to moderate-intensity activity.

Protein primarily functions to maintain, build, and repair tissues, including muscle tissue. As long as the diet is adequate in total kilocalories, carbohydrate, and fat, only small amounts of protein are used for energy during exercise.

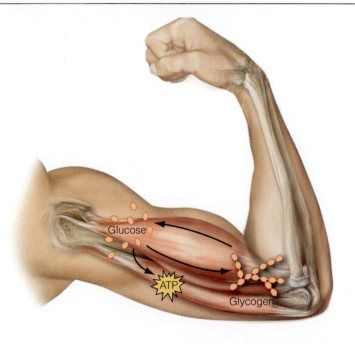

Glucose

ATP

Glycogen

LO 16.4 Timing of Meals Affects Fitness Performance

The timing of meals before, during, and after exercise impacts energy levels, performance, and recovery time. Consuming both carbohydrate (about 150 to 300 grams) and small amounts of protein up to 4 hours before exercise produces a greater increase in muscle glycogen synthesis, promotes greater endurance, and results in greater protein synthesis after exercise is over. Ingesting 1 gram of carbohydrate per kilogram of body weight 15 to 30 minutes prior to the start of exercise gives muscles an immediate source of energy, spares glycogen stores, and protects muscles from damage. For longer events, 30 to 60 grams of carbohydrate should be consumed per hour of activity. As much as 90 grams of carbohydrate per hour may be necessary for ultra-endurance events.

Consumed within the first 30 to 45 minutes postexercise, 0.3 to 0.6 grams of carbohydrate per pound of body weight helps replenish glycogen stores and stimulates muscle protein synthesis. Carbohydrate and protein in a ratio of 4:1 (in grams) after exercise results in increased muscle protein synthesis, with protein intake immediately following exercise resulting in greater muscle protein synthesis.

LO 16.5 Some Vitamins and Minerals May Improve Athletic Performance

Vitamins and minerals do not contain energy themselves, but some are key to catalyzing the release of energy held in the bonds of macronutrients. Thiamin, riboflavin, niacin, pantothenic acid, and vitamin B_6 assist as coenzymes in energy metabolism. Folate, vitamin B_{12}, and iron contribute to healthy red blood cells that indirectly participate in oxygen delivery to the cells for aerobic metabolism.

Antioxidants, such as vitamins E and C, can protect cells from damage by free radicals; however, consuming high levels of these in supplement form has not been shown to improve athletic performance or decrease oxidative stress. Female and vegetarian athletes are at greater risk of developing iron deficiency and should consume iron-rich foods regularly. Athletes also need to be sure their calcium intake is adequate to help reduce their risk of bone fractures during physical activity.

Athletes do not have greater needs for vitamins and minerals than do nonathletes, and intakes of vitamins and minerals above the RDA do not improve athletic performance. Supplements containing vitamins and minerals are not necessary when adequate amounts are obtained through consuming a variety of foods.

LO 16.6 Fluid Intake Affects Fitness and Performance

Being adequately hydrated before, during, and after exercise helps maintain fluid and electrolyte balance and normal body temperature. Sports drinks that contain a 6 to 8 percent concentration of carbohydrates, as well as electrolytes, are beneficial for moderate- to vigorous-intensity exercise to replace fluid and electrolytes and provide carbohydrates for fuel. For exercise that lasts less than 60 minutes, water can sufficiently replace fluids lost through sweating, and food consumption following exercise can adequately replace electrolytes. Caffeinated beverages, such as coffee, energy drinks, and some soft drinks, should be limited because excessive intake can cause increased heart rate, nausea, vomiting, excessive urination, restlessness, anxiety, and difficulty sleeping. Dehydration and overhydration should both be avoided because they can be harmful to health.

Impaired aerobic performance

Reduced muscle endurance

Reduced muscle strength

Heat cramps, heat exhaustion

High

Athletic performance

Low

Sensation of thirst

Fully hydrated   2%   4%   6%   8%

Water loss as percentage of body weight

LO 16.7 Some Dietary Supplements Can Contribute to Fitness

Dietary supplements are not strictly regulated for their safety and efficacy; individuals who choose to use them may be placing their health, and possibly their eligibility for competition, at risk. Some dietary supplements, such as creatine, caffeine, and sodium bicarbonate, are used as ergogenic aids to improve athletic performance. Creatine improves performance during high-intensity, short-duration exercise and increases muscle strength and muscle mass, but causes water retention and may negatively affect liver and kidney function when taken at higher than recommended doses for several months. Caffeine has been shown to improve endurance performance by sparing glycogen stores and increasing fatty acid utilization, and may decrease perception of effort, but has not shown any benefit in activities of short duration. The NCAA restricts caffeine during competition to less than 15 micrograms per milliliter of urine. Sodium bicarbonate buffers the blood and improves anaerobic performance in some sports, but does cause unpleasant gastrointestinal side effects. Some amino acid supplements, including branched-chain amino acids, alanine, carnitine, leucine, and glutamine, may show some benefit in improving muscle recovery. Sports bars and shakes are convenient sources of energy, but are often more expensive than whole foods and should only be included as a minor part of an overall healthy diet. Athletes who consume dietary protein within the recommended guidelines do not benefit from additional protein intake.

Terms to Know

- physical activity
- physical fitness
- exercise
- cardiorespiratory endurance
- muscular strength
- muscular endurance
- resistance training
- flexibility
- body composition
- overexercise
- stroke volume
- VO_2max
- cardiorespiratory conditioning
- conditioning
- intensity
- rating of perceived exertion (RPE)
- target heart rate
- repetition maximum (RM)
- duration
- progressive overload principle
- hypertrophy
- atrophy
- carbohydrate loading
- sports anemia
- female athlete triad
- amenorrhea
- dehydration
- hyperthermia
- hypothermia
- acute dehydration
- chronic dehydration
- ergogenic aid

MasteringNutrition™

Scan to hear an MP3 chapter review in MasteringNutrition.

Check Your Understanding

1. Which of the following is one of the five components of physical fitness?
   a. hydration
   b. cardiorespiratory endurance
   c. stress
   d. body mass index
2. Gradually increasing the exercise demands on the body is called
   a. cardiorespiratory endurance.
   b. VO_2max.
   c. progressive overload.
   d. hypertrophy.
3. Well-trained muscles have the ability to store
   a. an unlimited amount of glycogen.
   b. up to 100 grams of glycogen.
   c. up to 300 grams of glycogen.
   d. up to 500 grams of glycogen.
4. The body obtains most of its energy from _____ during low-intensity activity.
   a. muscle glycogen
   b. liver glycogen
   c. muscle protein
   d. fatty acids
5. Under what conditions does the body use significant amounts of protein for energy during exercise?
   a. inadequate kilocalorie and fluid intake
   b. inadequate carbohydrate and protein stores
   c. inadequate protein stores and fluid intake
   d. inadequate kilocalorie intake and carbohydrate stores
6. A pregame meal should be
   a. high in carbohydrate, low in fat.
   b. high in carbohydrate and high in fat.
   c. low in carbohydrate, high in fat.
   d. low in protein, high in fat.
7. Athletes should ingest a daily vitamin and mineral supplement

to improve their overall exercise performance.

   a. true

   b. false

8. A commercial sports drink might be beneficial because it

   a. provides electrolytes and carbohydrates, and contributes to hydration.

   b. is marketed to everyone, not just athletes.

   c. typically contains 12 to 16 percent carbohydrate.

   d. hydrates better than fruit juice and soft drinks.

9. An appropriate exercise recovery beverage would be

   a. a soft drink.

   b. coffee.

   c. low-fat chocolate milk.

   d. orange juice.

10. Endurance performance can be improved by using the ergogenic aid

   a. creatine monohydrate.

   b. sodium bicarbonate.

   c. caffeine.

   d. amino acid supplements.

Answers

1. (b) Cardiorespiratory endurance, muscular strength, muscular endurance, body composition, and flexibility are the five basic components of physical fitness. Hydration, stress, and body mass index are not components of physical fitness.

2. (c) The progressive overload principle allows an individual to improve his or her performance as the body adapts to increasingly difficult physical activity. Cardiorespiratory endurance is one aspect of physical fitness. VO$_2$max is the maximum amount of oxygen a person uses in one minute, and hypertrophy is the building of new muscle mass.

3. (d) Muscles that are well trained have the ability to store about 20 to 50 percent more glycogen than normal, or up to 500 grams; however, the storage capacity of all muscle glycogen is limited.

4. (d) Fatty acids are the main source of energy during low-intensity activity. As the intensity increases, the body uses fewer fatty acids and more glycogen for energy.

5. (d) The body uses larger amounts of protein for energy if overall kilocalorie intake is inadequate and if carbohydrate stores are low. Fluid intake does not affect the use of protein for energy during exercise.

6. (a) A meal before a game or workout should be high in carbohydrate to maximize glycogen stores and low in fat to prevent feelings of fatigue or discomfort.

7. (b) Ingesting vitamin or mineral supplements does not improve athletic performance. Athletes should focus on obtaining sufficient vitamins and minerals by consuming a variety of foods.

8. (a) Sports drinks supply fluids to rehydrate the body during and after exercise, electrolytes to replace those lost during sweating, and carbohydrate, which acts as an immediate source of energy that can potentially improve performance. Sports drinks typically contain 6 to 8 percent carbohydrate, which makes them a better beverage for hydration than drinks that contain more carbohydrate, such as fruit juice and soft drinks.

9. (c) Low-fat chocolate milk is a good exercise recovery beverage because it contains an appropriate ratio of carbohydrate and protein that is necessary for optimal recovery. Soft drinks, coffee, and orange juice provide the body with fluids, but lack other nutrients that are ideal for recovery after exercise.

10. (c) Caffeine has been shown to improve endurance performance by increasing fatty acid oxidation. Creatine monohydrate, sodium bicarbonate, and amino acid supplements may be more effective in anaerobic exercise.

Answers to True or False?

1. **False.** Fewer than half of all Americans meet recommendations for physical activity.

2. **True.** According to the *2008 Physical Activity Guidelines*, as little as 60 minutes of physical activity per week bestows health benefits, including improved bone health and lowered risk of certain diseases.

3. **True.** The body does use carbohydrate, fat, and protein for energy during exercise, but the amount of each that is used partly depends on the intensity of the exercise.

4. **True.** The body prefers to use fat as its primary fuel source during low-to moderate-intensity exercise.

5. **True.** Consumption of nutrients immediately after stopping exercise will improve recovery.

6. **False.** Taking vitamin and/or mineral supplements is only beneficial if an individual is deficient in vitamins or minerals.

7. **True.** Female and vegetarian athletes in particular are at higher risk for iron deficiency.

8. **False.** Sports drinks are generally beneficial only when exercise lasts for longer than 1 hour.

9. **False.** Overhydration can dilute the blood and alter the body's delicate fluid and electrolyte balance.

10. **True.** Caffeine is a banned substance at urine concentrations of more than 15 micrograms per milliliter.

Web Resources

- For more information on The President's Council on Fitness, Sports, and Nutrition, visit www.fitness.gov

- For more information on exercise, presented by the American Council on Exercise, visit www.acefitness.org

- For more information from the American College of Sports Medicine, www.acsm.org

- For more information on nutrition and fitness, visit the Academy of Nutrition and Dietetics, www.eatright.org

- For more information from the Sports, Cardiovascular, and Wellness Nutrition: A Dietetic Practice Group of the Academy of Nutrition and Dietetics, visit www.scandpg.org

- For more information on the National Collegiate Athletic Association, visit www.ncaa.org

References

1. Centers for Disease Control and Prevention. 2011. *One in Five Adults Meet Overall Physical Activity Guidelines.* Available at www.cdc.gov/media/releases/2013/p0502-physical-activity.html. Accessed July 2014.

2. U.S. Department of Health and Human Services. 2008. *Physical Activity Guidelines for Americans.* Available at www.health.gov/paguidelines. Accessed July 2014.

3. Kenney, W. L., J. H. Wilmore, and D. L. Costill. 2012. *Physiology of Sport and Exercise.* 5th ed. Champaign, IL: Human Kinetics.

4. Astrand, P., K. Rodahl, H. A. Dahl, and S. B. Stromme. 2003. *The Textbook of Work Physiology: Physiological Bases of Exercise.* 4th ed. Champaign, IL: Human Kinetics.

5. U.S. Department of Health and Human Services. 2008. *Physical Activity Guidelines for Americans.*

6. Cruz, R. S., R. A. de Aguiar, T. Turnes, R. Penteado Dos Santos, M. F. de Oliveira, and F. Caputo. 2012. Intracellular Shuttle: The Lactate Aerobic Metabolism. *Scientific World Journal* doi:10.1100/2012/420984.

7. Ibid.

8. Jensen, T. E., and E. A. Richter. 2012. Regulation of Glucose and Glycogen Metabolism During and After Exercise. *The Journal of Physiology* 590:1069–1076.

9. Costill, D., R. Thomas, R. Roberts, D. Pascoe, C. Lambert, S. Barr, and W. Fink. 1991. Adaptations to Swimming Training: Influence of Training Volume. *Medicine & Science in Sports & Exercise* 23:371–377.

10. Sherman, W., M. Peden, and D. Wright. 1991. Carbohydrate Feeding 1 Hour Before Exercise Improves Cycling Performance. *American Journal of Clinical Nutrition* 54:866–870.

11. Coyle, E. F., A. R. Coggan, M. K. Hemmert, and J. L. Ivy. 1986. Muscle Glycogen Utilization during Prolonged Strenuous Exercise When Fed Carbohydrate. *Journal of Applied Physiology* 61:165–172.

12. Jensen, et al. 2012. Regulation of Glucose and Glycogen Metabolism.

13. American College of Sports Medicine, American Dietetic Association, and Dietitians of Canada. 2009. Nutrition and Athletic Performance Joint Position Statement. *Medicine & Science in Sports & Exercise* 41:709–731.

14. Ibid.

15. Brownell, K. D., S. N. Steen, and J. H. Wilmore. 1987. Weight Regulation Practices in Athletes: Analysis of Metabolic and Health Effects. *Medicine & Science in Sports & Exercise* 19:546–556.

16. Horvath, P. J., C. K. Eagen, S. D. Ryer-Calvin, and D. R. Pendergast. 2000. The Effects of Varying Dietary Fat on the Nutrient Intake in Male and Female Runners. *Journal of the American College of Nutrition* 19:42–51.

17. American College of Sports Medicine, et al. 2009. Nutrition and Athletic Performance Joint Position Statement.

18. Yaspelkis, B. B., J. G. Patterson, P. A. Anderla, Z. Ding, and J. L. Ivy. 1993. Carbohydrate Supplementation Spares Muscle Glycogen during Variable-Intensity Exercise. *Journal of Applied Physiology* 75:1477–1485.

19. Coyle, E. F., J. M. Hagberg, B. F. Hurley, W. H. Martin, A. A. Ehsani, and J. O. Holloszy. 1983. Carbohydrate Feeding during Prolonged Strenuous Exercise Can Delay Fatigue. *Journal of Applied Physiology* 55:230–235.

20. Cermak, N. M., and L. J. van Loon. 2013. The Use of Carbohydrates during Exercise as an Ergogenic Aid. *Sports Medicine* 43(11):1139–1155.

21. Miller, S. L., K. D. Tipton, D. L. Chinkes, S. E. Wolf, and R. R. Wolfe. 2003. Independent and Combined Effects of Amino Acids and Glucose after Resistance Exercise. *Medicine & Science in Sports & Exercise* 35:449–455.

22. Temesi, J., N. A. Johnson, J. Raymond, C. A. Burdon, and H. T. O'Connor. 2011. Carbohydrate Ingestion during Endurance Exercise Improves Performance in Adults. *Journal of Nutrition* 141(5):890–897.

23. Ibid.

24. Burke, L. M., J. A. Hawley, S. Wong, and A. E. Jeukendrup. 2011. Carbohydrates for Training and Competition. *Journal of Sports Sciences* 29(1):S17–S27.

25. Rollo, I., and C. Williams. 2011. Effect of Mouth-Rinsing Carbohydrate Solutions on Endurance Performance. *Sports Medicine* 41(6):449–461.

26. Stellingwerff, T., and G. R. Cox. 2014. Systematic Review: Carbohydrate Supplementation on Exercise Performance or Capacity of Varying Durations. *Applied Physiology, Nutrition, and Metabolism* 25:1–14.

27. Koopman, R., D. L. Pannemans, A. E. Jeukendrup, A. P. Gijsen, J. M. Senden, D. Halliday, W. H. Saris, et al. 2004. Combined Ingestion of Protein and Carbohydrate Improves Protein Balance during Ultra-Endurance Exercise. *American Journal of Physiology–Endocrinology and Metabolism* 287:E712–E720.

28. Berardi, J. M., T. B. Price, E. E. Noreen, and P. W. Lemon. 2006. Post-Exercise Muscle Glycogen Recovery Enhanced with a Carbohydrate-Protein Supplement. *Medicine & Science in Sports & Exercise* 38(6):1106–1113.

29. Roy, B. D., M. A. Tarnopolsky, J. D. MacDougall, J. Fowles, and K. E. Yarasheski. 1997. Effect of Glucose Supplement Timing on Protein Metabolism after Resistance Training. *Journal of Applied Physiology* 82:1882–1888.

30. Rasmussen, B. B., K. D. Tipton, S. L. Miller, S. E. Wolf, and R. R. Wolfe. 2000. An Oral Essential Amino Acid-Carbohydrate Supplement Enhances Muscle Protein Anabolism after Resistance Exercise. *Journal of Applied Physiology* 88:386–392.

31. Zawadzki, K. M., B. B. Yaspelkis, and J. L. Ivy. 1992. Carbohydrate-Protein Complex Increases the Rate of Muscle Glycogen Storage after Exercise. *Journal of Applied Physiology* 72:1854–1859.

32. Zawadzki, et al. 1992. Carbohydrate-Protein Complex; Ivy, J. L., H. W. Goforth, B. M. Damon, T. R. McCauley, E. C. Parsons, and T. B. Price. 2002. Early Postexercise Muscle Glycogen Recovery Is Enhanced with a Carbohydrate-Protein Supplement. *Journal of Applied Physiology* 93:1337–1344.

33. Pritchett, K., and R. Pritchett. 2012. Chocolate Milk: A Post-Exercise Recovery Beverage for Endurance Sports. *Medicine and Sport Science* 59:127–134.

34. Joy, J. M., R. P. Lowery, J. M. Wilson, M. Purpura, E. O. De Souza, S. M. C. Wilson, D. S. Kalman, et al. 2013. The Effects of 8 Weeks of Whey or Rice Protein Supplementation on Body Composition and Exercise Performance. *Nutrition Journal* doi:10.1186/1475-2891-12-86.

35. Temesi, et al. 2011. Carbohydrate Ingestion during Endurance Exercise Improves Performance in Adults.

36. Mariacher, C., H. Gatterer, J. Greilberger, R. Djukic, M. Greilberger, M. Philippe, and M. Burtscher. 2014. Effects of Antioxidant Supplementation on Exercise Performance in Acute Normobaric Hypoxia. *International Journal of Sport Nutrition and Exercise Metabolism* 24:227–235.

37. DellaValle, D. M., and J. D. Haas. 2011. Impact of Iron Depletion without Anemia on Performance in Trained Endurance Athletes at the Beginning of a Training Season: A Study of Female Collegiate Rowers. *International Journal of Sport Nutrition and Exercise Metabolism* 21(6):501–506.

38. Gropper, S. S., D. Glessing, K. Dunham, and J. M. Barksdale. 2006. Iron Status of Female Collegiate Athletes Involved in Different Sports. *Biological Trace Element Research* 109:1–14.

39. DellaValle, et al. 2011. Impact of Iron Depletion.

40. Nasri, R., S. Hassen Zrour, H. Rebai, F. Neffeti, M. F. Najjar, N. Bergaoui, H. Mejdoub, and Z. Tabka. 2013. Combat Sports Practice Favors Bone Mineral Density among Adolescent Male Athletes. *Journal of Clinical Densitometry* doi: 10.1016/j.jocd.2013.09.012.

41. Darvishi, L., G. Askari, M. Hariri, M. Bahreynian, R. Ghiasvand, S. Ehsani, N. S. Mashhadi, et al. 2013. The Use of Nutritional Supplements among Male Collegiate Athletes.

International Journal of Preventive Medicine 4(Supplement 1):S68–S72.

42. Fry, A. C., R. J. Bloomer, M. J. Falvo, C. A. Moore, B. K. Schilling, and L. W. Weiss. 2006. Effect of a Liquid Multivitamin/ Mineral Supplement on Anaerobic Exercise Performance. *Research in Sports Medicine* 14(1):53–64.

43. Rosenbloom, C., and E. J. Coleman, eds. 2012. *Sports Nutrition: A Practice Manual for Professionals.* Chicago: IL: Academy of Nutrition and Dietetics.

44. Wilk, B., and O. Bar-Or. 1996. Effect of Drink Flavor and NaCl on Voluntary Drinking and Hydration in Boys Exercising in the Heat. *Journal of Applied Physiology* 80:1112–1117.

45. American College of Sports Medicine. 2007. Exercise and Fluid Replacement. *Medicine & Science in Sports & Exercise* 39(2):377–390.

46. National Institutes of Health. 2013. *Caffeine in the Diet.* National Institutes of Health Medline Plus Medical Encyclopedia. Available at www.nlm.nih .gov/medlineplus/ency/article/002445.htm. Accessed July 2014.

47. USA Track & Field. Press Release April 19, 2003. *USATF Announces Major Change in Hydration Guidelines.* Available at www .usatf.org/news/showRelease.asp?article=/ news/releases/2003-04-19-2.xml. Accessed July 2014.

48. Greenhaff, P. L., A. Casey, A. H. Short, R. Harris, K. Söderlund, and E. Hultman. 1993. Influence of Oral Creatine Supplementation on Muscle Torque during Repeated Bouts of Maximal Voluntary Exercise in Man. *Clinical Science* 84:565–571.

49. Antonio, J., and V. Ciccone. 2013. The Effects of Pre Versus Post Workout Supplementation of Creatine Monohydrate on Body Composition and Strength. *Journal of the International Society of Sports Nutrition* doi:10.1186/ 1550-2783-10-36.

50. Williams, J., G. Abt, and A. E. Kilding. 2014. Effects of Creatine Monohydrate Supplementation on Simulated Soccer Performance. *International Journal of Sports Physiology and Performance* 9(3):503–510.

51. Kreider, R. B., M. Ferreira, M. Wilson, P. Grindstaff, S. Plisk, J. Reinardy, E. Cantler, and A. L. Almada. 1998. Effects of Creatine Supplementation on Body Composition, Strength, and Sprint Performance. *Medicine & Science in Sports & Exercise* 30:73–82.

52. Hall, M., and T. H. Trojian. 2013. Creatine Supplementation. *Current Sports Medicine Reports* 12(4):240–244.

53. Hogervorst, E., S. Bandelow, J. Schmitt, et al. 2008. Caffeine Improves Physical and Cognitive Performance during Exhaustive Exercise. *Medicine & Science in Sports & Exercise* 49(10):1841–1851.

54. Brown, S. J., J. Brown, and A. Foskett. 2013. The Effects of Caffeine on Repeated Sprint Performance in Team Sport Athletes— A Meta-Analysis. *Sport Science Review* 22:25–32.

55. Saunders, B., C. Sale, R. C. Harris, and C. Sunderland. 2014. Effect of Sodium Bicarbonate and Beta-Alanine on Repeated Sprints during Intermittent Exercise Performed in Hypoxia. *International Journal of Sport Nutrition and Exercise Metabolism* 24:196–205.

56. Afman, G., R. M. Garside, N. Dinan, N. Gant, J. A. Betts, and C. Williams. 2014. Effect of Carbohydrate or Sodium Bicarbonate Ingestion on Performance during a Validated Basketball Simulation Test. *International Journal of Sport Nutrition and Exercise Metabolism* doi: http://dx.doi .org/10.1123/ijsnem.2013-0168.

57. Mero, A. A., P. Hirvonen, J. Saarela, J. J. Hulmi, J. R. Hoffman, and J. R. Stout. 2013. Effect of Sodium Bicarbonate and Beta-Alanine Supplementation on Maximal Sprint Swimming. *Journal of the International Society of Sports Nutrition* doi:10.1186/1550-2783-10-52.

58. Carr, B. M., M. J. Webster, J. C. Boyd, G. M. Hudson, and T. P. Scheet. 2013. Sodium Bicarbonate Supplementation Improves Hypertrophy-Type Resistance Exercise Performance. *European Journal of Applied Physiology* 113(3):743–752.

59. Afman, et al. 2014. Effect of Carbohydrate or Sodium Bicarbonate Ingestion on Performance.

60. Negro, M., S. Giardina, B. Marzani, and E. Marzatico. 2008. Branched-Chain Amino Acid Supplementation Does Not Enhance Athletic Performance But Affects Muscle Recovery and the Immune System. *Journal of Sports Medicine and Physical Fitness* 48(3):347–351.

61. Smith, A. E., A. A. Walter, J. L. Graef, et al. 2009. Effect of β-Alanine Supplementation and High-Intensity Interval Training in Endurance Performance and Body Composition in Men: A Double-Blind Study. *Journal of the International Society of Sports Nutrition* doi: 10.1186/1550-2783-6-5.

62. Huang, A., and K. Owen. 2012. Role of Supplementary L-Carnitine in Exercise and Exercise Recovery. *Medicine in Sport Science* 59:135–142.

63. Rowlands, D. S., A. R. Nelson, S. M. Phillips, J. A. Faulkner, J. Clarke, N. A. Burd, D. Moore, and T. Stellingwerff. 2014. Protein-Leucine Fed Dose Effects on Muscle Protein Synthesis after Endurance Exercise. *Medicine & Science in Sports & Exercise* doi: 10.1249/MSS.0000000000000447.

64. Kreider, R. B., C. D. Wilborn, L. Taylor, et al. 2010. ISSN Exercise and Sport Nutrition Review: Research and Recommendations. *Journal of the International Society of Sports Nutrition* doi: 10.1186/1550-2783-7-7.

65. Mason, B. C., and M. E. Lavallee. 2012. Emerging Supplements in Sports. *Sports Health* 4(2):142–147.

66. Ibid.

17 Life Cycle Nutrition
Pregnancy through Infancy

Learning Outcomes

After reading this chapter, you will be able to:

17.1 Describe the stages of pregnancy and some possible risks to fetal development.

17.2 Discuss the key diet and lifestyle factors associated with a successful pregnancy.

17.3 Identify key nutrient needs for women and potential complications in the first trimester of pregnancy.

17.4 Identify key nutrient needs for women and potential complications in the second trimester of pregnancy.

17.5 Identify key nutrient needs for women and potential complications in the third trimester of pregnancy.

17.6 List special concerns of younger, older, and low-income mothers-to-be.

17.7 Describe the benefits of breast-feeding.

17.8 Explain why infant formula is a healthy alternative to breast milk.

17.9 Discuss the nutritional needs of infants.

17.10 Explain when and how solid foods should be introduced to infants.

17.11 Explain how a food allergen causes a potentially life-threatening reaction.

True or False?

1. A man's health habits have little impact on his fertility. **T/F**

2. Drinking red wine is healthy during pregnancy. **T/F**

3. Morning sickness only happens between 8 A.M. and noon during the first trimester. **T/F**

4. Pregnant women shouldn't exercise. **T/F**

5. Commercially prepared infant formula is better for babies than breast milk. **T/F**

6. Breast milk helps boost a baby's immune system. **T/F**

7. Chubby babies should be put on diets. **T/F**

8. Infants never need dietary supplements. **T/F**

9. Commercially prepared baby food is always less nutritious than homemade. **T/F**

10. Infants should never eat highly allergenic foods, such as peanuts and peanut products. **T/F**

See page 669 for the answers.

When a woman is pregnant, her body facilitates the division, growth, and specialization of millions of new cells in her developing child. Nearly all of the raw materials for this rapid growth are provided by the nutrients found in food. A pregnant woman's diet, then, must be sufficient to maintain her health while fostering the proper growth and development of her baby.

A variety of lifestyle choices a woman makes before conception helps to give her baby a better chance for good health, at birth, and beyond. Dad's preconception habits, including what he eats and drinks, also play a role in the pregnancy.

This chapter highlights the specific nutrient requirements of pregnancy. We also explore the diet and lifestyle factors in both the mother and father that can help ensure successful conception and healthy fetal development, as well as the nutritional needs and concerns of infants in their first year of life. Let's begin by reviewing the stages of pregnancy and the mechanisms that allow the developing child to obtain nutrients from the mother.

What Are the Critical Periods of Prenatal Development?

LO 17.1 Describe the stages of pregnancy and some possible risks to fetal development.

A full-term pregnancy lasts about 39 to 40 weeks from **conception** to birth, and is divided into three roughly equal 13-week trimesters (tri = three, mester = month).[1] Prenatal development is divided into the embryonic and fetal periods. Many important physiological changes occur during the first weeks of pregnancy, even before a woman may be aware that she is expecting.

The Placenta Plays a Key Role in a Successful Pregnancy

The initial two weeks after conception is called the preembryo period, during which the fertilized egg, or **zygote,** travels down the fallopian tube to embed itself in the lining of the uterus (**Figure 17.1**). Once attached, the zygote immediately begins receiving nutrients from the mother. This enables both the fertilized egg (soon to be called an **embryo**) and the placenta to develop. The **placenta** is the site of common tissue between the mother and the embryo (later to be called a **fetus**) where nutrients, oxygen, and waste products are exchanged through the **umbilical cord** (**Figure 17.2**). Although maternal and fetal blood do not mix due to the double lining of cells in the placenta, this tissue allows the embryo to make use of the mother's mature organ systems to perform physiological functions for it while it is developing its own organs.

The placenta prevents the passage of red blood cells, bacteria, and many large proteins from mother to fetus. However, potentially harmful substances, such as alcohol, illicit drugs, and common prescription and over-the-counter medications are capable of crossing the placenta to the fetus. The placenta also releases hormones required to support the physiological changes of pregnancy, including the hormones that trigger labor and delivery.

Critical Periods of Fetal Development

Growth and development of the embryo and fetus follow predetermined paths. Cells multiply, differentiate, and establish functional tissues and organs during

conception The moment when a sperm fertilizes an egg.

zygote A fertilized egg during the first two weeks after conception.

embryo A fertilized egg during the third through the eighth week of pregnancy.

placenta The organ that allows nutrients, oxygen, and waste products to be exchanged between a mother and fetus.

fetus A developing embryo that is at least eight weeks old.

umbilical cord The cord connecting the fetus to the placenta.

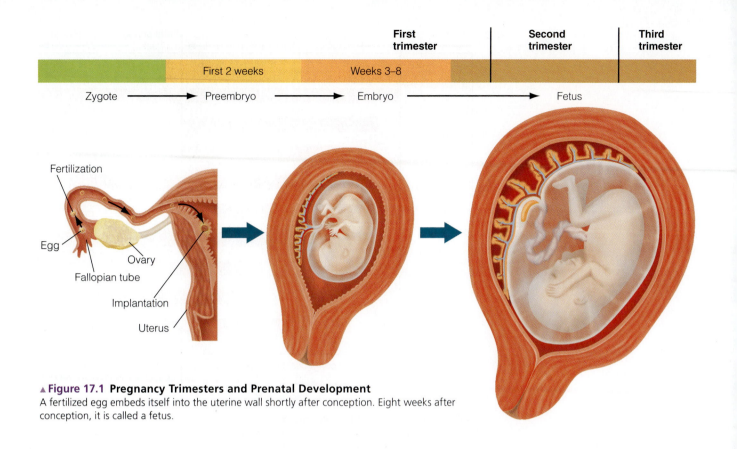

| First trimester | Second trimester | Third trimester |

| First 2 weeks | Weeks 3–8 |

Zygote → Preembryo → Embryo → Fetus

▲ **Figure 17.1 Pregnancy Trimesters and Prenatal Development**
A fertilized egg embeds itself into the uterine wall shortly after conception. Eight weeks after conception, it is called a fetus.

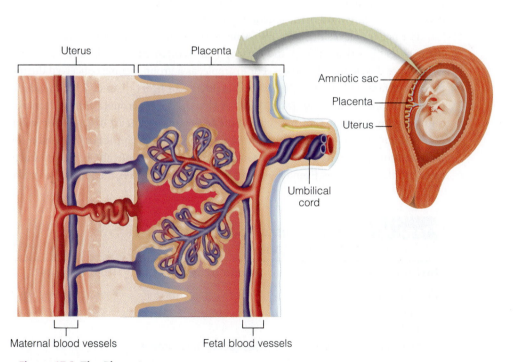

Uterus

Placenta

Amniotic sac

Placenta

Uterus

Umbilical cord

Maternal blood vessels

Fetal blood vessels

▲ **Figure 17.2 The Placenta**
The placenta is the site of common tissue between the mother and the embryo where nutrients, oxygen, and waste products are exchanged through the umbilical cord. The maternal blood vessels exchange nutrients and oxygen with the fetal vessels, and the fetal vessels deliver waste products for the maternal blood to carry away for excretion. Note that while substances diffuse between the two circulatory systems, no mixing of maternal and fetal blood occurs.

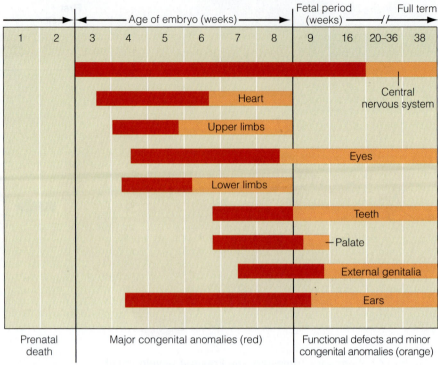

*Red indicates highly sensitive periods when teratogens may induce major anomalies.

▲ **Figure 17.3 Prenatal Development**
The damage caused by toxins or lack of nutrients during pregnancy can vary according to the stage of fetal development. Damage done during critical periods may be irreversible.

various **critical periods** in the first trimester of pregnancy (**Figure 17.3**). During this period of rapid cellular activity, the embryo and fetus are vulnerable to nutritional deficiencies, toxins, and other potentially harmful factors (also called insults).

The harm that results from the influence of a toxin or nutrient deficiency during periods of critical growth and development is often irreversible, and can influence future developmental stages. For example, as a group, people conceived during periods of famine have a higher overall incidence of heart disease, which tends to occur at an earlier age (see **Table 17.1**).[2] A shortfall of macronutrients and micronutrients during pregnancy may contribute to the onset of heart disease later in life by restricting organ growth. Suboptimal fetal growth may "program" a person for hypertension, impaired glucose tolerance, and altered lipid metabolism that affects their health as they age. Even when food supply is abundant, inadequate iron intake

critical periods Developmental stages during which cells and tissues rapidly grow and differentiate to form body structures.

TABLE 17.1	Increased Risks from Exposure to Famine during Gestation	
First Trimester	**Second Trimester**	**Third Trimester**
Glucose intolerance	Glucose intolerance	Glucose intolerance
Blood lipid profile associated with atherosclerosis	Kidney disease	
Coronary heart disease	Obstructive lung disease	
Stress sensitivity		
Obesity (women only)		
Breast cancer		

Data from T. Roseboom, S. de Rooj, and R Painter. 2006. "The Dutch Famine and Its Long-Term Consequences for Adult Health." *Early Human Development* 82(8):485–491.

in early pregnancy during the critical period for the central nervous system may cause poor cognitive development.[3]

Optimal maternal nutrition during critical periods of pregnancy may prevent or delay a child's risk of chronic diseases, such as heart disease and diabetes, later in life. There is growing evidence that maternal nutrition can alter how genes are expressed, and adverse events during critical periods of gestation can persist into adulthood.[4] This phenomenon is part of an emerging area of research into **metabolic or fetal programming.** The relationship between maternal nutrition, metabolic programming, and adult-onset chronic disease is supported by research examining inadequate nutrient intakes[5] as well as excessive calorie consumption. A woman who is obese at the time of conception has a greater risk of having a pregnancy affected by a birth defect or an infant with a greater fat mass that results in overweight in childhood.[6, 7]

LO 17.1: THE TAKE-HOME MESSAGE A healthy pregnancy lasts 39 to 40 weeks and is divided into three trimesters. The placenta is where oxygen, nutrients, and waste products are exchanged, though the maternal and fetal blood supplies do not mix. Toxins and insufficient nutrient intake may cause irreversible damage to the embryo or fetus. Proper nutrition positively influences the metabolic programming during pregnancy that may help limit future chronic conditions in the child.

What Nutrients and Behaviors Are Most Important to Support a Healthy Pregnancy?

LO 17.2 Discuss the key diet and lifestyle factors associated with a successful pregnancy.

You're probably aware of some of the suggested lifestyle changes pregnant women should make, including avoiding cigarettes and alcohol. Healthy preconception habits in future moms—and dads—are also important to support fertility and the healthiest pregnancy possible.

Prospective Fathers Should Practice Healthy Habits

A healthy baby is the product of two healthy parents, so fathers-to-be who make appropriate diet and lifestyle choices prior to conception help ensure the health of their offspring. A man's lifestyle choices may affect his fertility. Smoking cigarettes, drinking alcohol, illicit drug abuse, certain prescription medications, and obesity have been linked to decreased production and function of sperm.[8] Adequate intake of zinc and folate are linked to the production of healthy sperm, and antioxidants—such as vitamins E and C and carotenoids—may help protect sperm from damage by free radicals.[9]

Men should consume a balanced diet that contains adequate kilocalories to achieve and maintain a healthy weight and that provides a variety of fruits and vegetables (for the antioxidants, folate, and other beneficial nutrients), as well as whole grains, lean meats and dairy foods, legumes, and nuts (for zinc). Not smoking, and abstaining from alcohol or drinking only in moderation (no more than two drinks daily for men) are also beneficial behaviors. Future fathers who eat healthfully and practice other positive habits help to support their female partners' efforts to do the same.

Prospective fathers should practice healthy habits prior to conception.

metabolic or fetal programming The process by which the prenatal environment interacts with genetic and other factors to produce permanent change.

Before and During Pregnancy, Women Should Adopt a Healthy Lifestyle

Anyone who has run a marathon, or knows someone who has, is aware of the tremendous amount of effort and diligence it takes to train for the event. The commitment doesn't begin on the day of the race, but as far as a year in advance. In fact, the more time and effort the runner puts into preparing for the race, the better the results are likely to be.

Ask any woman who has had a baby and she will tell you that planning for, carrying, and delivering a healthy child was the marathon of her life. Achieving a healthy body weight, eating a nutritious diet, and practicing other healthy lifestyle habits are important for preconception health and fertility and for pregnancy.

Achieve and Maintain a Healthy Weight

Women who are capable of becoming pregnant should strive for a healthy weight before conception. Women who begin pregnancy at a healthy weight are likely to conceive more easily, have an uncomplicated pregnancy, and have an easier time nursing the baby.[10] Overweight or obese women may have a harder time getting pregnant, possibly due to irregular menstrual cycles. When they do become pregnant, they are at increased risk of complications, including hypertension and gestational diabetes.[11] Research indicates that women who begin pregnancy obese are also less likely to initiate breast-feeding and more likely to have shorter duration of any breast-feeding.[12]

Overweight and obese women also have a greater chance of requiring an induced labor or a cesarean section.[13] Being overweight can increase a woman's risk of hypertension, which increases the risk of several pregnancy complications, including preeclampsia, placental abruption (when the placenta separates from the wall of the uterus), and preterm delivery.[14] Children born to overweight or obese women are at greater risk of certain birth defects, preterm birth, and difficult deliveries because they tend to be larger.[15] These babies are also at a higher risk of developing childhood obesity[16] and, later in life, heart disease and diabetes.[17] Overweight or obese women should consider losing excess weight prior to conception to improve the chances of a healthier pregnancy and baby. Once an overweight or obese woman becomes pregnant, she should follow guidelines for the recommended weight gain based on her prepregnancy weight, and should not try to lose weight.

Underweight women also need to strive for a healthy weight before getting pregnant. A low prepregnancy BMI may indicate chronic nutritional insufficiency, and women with a low BMI may have a harder time conceiving. A woman who is underweight has a lighter weight placenta, which can interfere with her body's ability to deliver nutrients to the fetus. With less nutrition available, the risk of delivering a **low birth weight** baby, or a baby weighing less than 5 pounds, 8 ounces, increases. A low birth weight baby is usually born too early, and is at a higher risk of health problems, including developmental and intellectual disabilities, vision and hearing loss, and dying within the first year of life, than an infant born at a healthy weight.[18]

Underweight mothers are also at higher risk for delivering **small for gestational age (SGA)** babies, who may be born full term but weigh less than the 10th percentile of weight for gestational age. Although some babies are smaller because of genetics (their parents are small), most SGA babies are small because of growth problems that occur during pregnancy. The fetus may not have received the nutrients and oxygen needed for proper growth and development of organs and tissues.

Consume Adequate Folic Acid

Folic acid is needed to create new cells and help the baby grow and develop properly. Consuming the DRI of folic acid beginning at least one month prior to conception,

low birth weight Describes a baby weighing less than 5 ½ pounds at birth.

small for gestational age (SGA) Term for babies who weigh less than the 10th percentile of weight for gestational age.

TABLE 17.2 Fish Intake during Pregnancy

Pregnant and nursing women and women of childbearing age who may become pregnant should follow these guidelines for eating fish.

Do Not Eat	Limit	Enjoy
Shark Swordfish King mackerel Tilefish (golden bass or golden snapper)	Albacore (white) tuna to no more than 6 oz weekly Locally caught fish from nearby lakes, rivers, and coastal areas. Check local advisories regarding its safety before consuming it. If no advice is available for a particular species, eat up to 6 oz weekly. Don't consume any other fish during that week.	Eat 8 to 12 oz weekly of fish with low levels of methylmercury, such as: Canned light tuna Cod Catfish Pollack Salmon Scallops Shrimp Tilapia

Data from Food and Drug Administration. 2014. *Fish: What Pregnant Women and Parents Should Know.* Available at www.fda.gov. Accessed July 2014.

and preferably earlier, helps reduce the risk of neural tube birth defects (such as anencephaly and spina bifida, discussed in Chapter 10) in infants.[19] Neural tube birth defects occur within one month after conception—a time when a woman may not be aware that she's pregnant. For this reason, women who are capable of becoming pregnant should consume 400 micrograms of folic acid daily through supplements, fortified foods, or a combination (see Chapter 10). Women who have had a pregnancy affected by a neural tube defect should consult with their health care provider, as much higher daily doses of folic acid may help to prevent neural tube defects in future pregnancies.

Eat Safe Fish

The Food and Drug Administration (FDA) recommends that all women of childbearing age and young children should avoid certain fish with higher amounts of the methylmercury. This form of mercury can harm the developing nervous system of the fetus and young child. All fish contain some methylmercury, but some are much safer than others; **Table 17.2** summarizes the fish consumption guidelines for women.

Consume Moderate Amounts of Caffeine

During pregnancy, the caffeine a mother consumes from coffee, soft drinks, and energy drinks is passed on to her baby. Because the fetus cannot metabolize caffeine, it may linger in his or her body longer than in the mother's. Research results about the effects of caffeine on female fertility and fetal health are conflicting, but experts suggest limiting caffeine intake before and during pregnancy to 200 milligrams a day or less.[20] Depending on the amount of caffeine in certain beverages, this means limiting coffee, tea, and caffeinated soft drinks, including energy drinks, to a cup or two a day—or better yet, switching to decaffeinated versions of these drinks. See **Table 17.3** for the caffeine content in several common dietary sources.

Avoid Cigarettes

Cigarette smoking increases the risk of infertility in women, possibly making conception more difficult.[21] Prenatal exposure to cigarette smoke may stunt the fetus's growth and development, affect a child's future intellect and behavior, and increase the risk of birth defects, stillbirth, and premature birth, as well as **sudden infant death syndrome (SIDS),** after delivery.[22] Though there are thousands of substances

TABLE 17.3 Common Sources of Caffeine

Beverage	Caffeine (mg)
Coffee (8 oz)	
Brewed, drip	85
Brewed, decaffeinated	3
Espresso (1 oz)	40
Tea (8 oz)	
Brewed	40
Iced	25
Soft drinks (8 oz)	24
Energy drinks (8 oz)	80
Hot cocoa (8 oz)	6
Chocolate milk (8 oz)	5
Milk chocolate (1 oz)	6

Data from National Toxicology Program, Department of Health and Human Services. 2014. Caffeine. http://ntp.niehs.nih.gov; International Food Information Council (IFIC), www.foodinsight.org.

sudden infant death syndrome (SIDS) The unexplained death of an infant at less than 1 year of age.

Smoking during pregnancy is harmful to the mother and to the fetus.

As with smoking, drinking alcohol during pregnancy exposes the fetus to potentially toxic substances. Alcohol labels and cigarette packages are required by law to display the Surgeon General's warning about these dangers.

botanicals A part of a plant, such as its root, that is believed to have medicinal or therapeutic attributes.

in cigarettes and cigarette smoke that can harm the mother and the fetus, carbon monoxide and nicotine are particularly dangerous because they reduce the amount of oxygen that reaches the baby, thus intensifying adverse effects. Pregnant women who smoke cigarettes with regularity may weigh less and gain less weight during pregnancy than nonsmokers, which can contribute to a low birth weight baby.

Even secondhand smoke can affect the health of a mom-to-be and her infant. Exposure to passive smoke can affect the infant's ability to grow properly.[23] If possible, pregnant women, new mothers, and their children should avoid work, home, or social environments where they are exposed to secondhand smoke.

Don't Drink Alcohol

Because alcohol can affect a baby within weeks after conception, before a woman is aware that she is pregnant, the U.S. Surgeon General recommends that all women who may become pregnant abstain from alcohol.[24] As you read in Chapter 7, drinking alcohol during pregnancy can lead to fetal alcohol spectrum disorders (FASDs) in the baby. Children exposed to even low levels of alcohol during pregnancy can be born with learning and behavioral disabilities that last a lifetime. Because there is no known safe level of alcohol consumption, pregnant women should abstain completely to eliminate the chance of having a baby with these disorders.

Avoid Illicit Drugs

Marijuana, cocaine, and other illegal drugs can cross the placenta from the mother to the fetus. Illicit drug use during pregnancy may be linked to miscarriage, preterm delivery, high blood pressure, cognitive and behavioral problems, and other health issues. Babies born to cocaine-using mothers are more likely to have low birth weight and may have an increased risk of sudden infant death syndrome (SIDS).[25] After birth, babies whose mothers used illicit drugs during pregnancy may experience drug withdrawal symptoms, such as excessive crying, trembling, and seizures, as well as long-term health problems such as heart defects and behavioral and learning problems.

Women who use illicit substances, even occasionally, should speak with their health care provider about how to stop, preferably before pregnancy. They can also visit the National Drug and Alcohol Treatment Referral Routing Service at www .niaaa.nih.gov or phone 1-800-662-HELP (4357).

Beware of Botanicals

Whereas many pregnant women won't even consider taking over-the-counter drugs without clearance from their health care provider, they often don't have the same level of caution when it comes to taking botanical products as dietary supplements. **Botanicals** are plants (including herbs) or parts of a plant that are believed to have medicinal effects. Because these products are perceived to be "natural," people often assume they can take them without risk and may consider them safer than over-the-counter drugs. In fact, this isn't always true, and in some cases, botanicals can be harmful or even dangerous, especially during pregnancy. There is little conclusive scientific research on the safety and effectiveness of botanical products during pregnancy. Pregnant women should assume that all herbs and botanical supplements are unsafe and should always check with their health care provider before consuming them.

Blue cohosh is an herb that is sometimes used to induce labor, but has been associated with seizures, strokes,[26] and heart attacks[27] in newborns. In addition to blue cohosh, other supplements, such as juniper, pennyroyal, goldenseal, and thuja, as well as teas such as raspberry tea, may also cause contractions of the uterus, which can lead to a miscarriage or premature labor.

Generally speaking, most herbal teas sold on supermarket shelves are safe during pregnancy in moderate amounts, such as a cup or two daily. Green tea, which is not an herbal tea, contains a compound that inhibits folic acid. While it's unclear how strong the link between green tea intake and folic acid deficiency is, pregnant women should avoid excessive amounts of green tea to insure that there is sufficient folic acid for the embryo and fetus.[28]

Manage Chronic Conditions

Chronic conditions such as obesity, diabetes, hypertension, and phenylketonuria (PKU) can have a negative effect on the outcome of a pregnancy and therefore must be successfully managed before a woman conceives.

Diabetes mellitus increases the risk for maternal and fetal complications. An estimated 12.6 million (10.8 percent of) women in the United States aged 20 and

---

Self-Assessment

Are You Ready for a Healthy Pregnancy?

Both men and women should practice healthy habits before becoming parents. Take the following self-assessment to see if you need some diet and lifestyle fine-tuning before trying to get pregnant.

For Both Men and Women

1. Are you overweight?
   Yes ☐ **No** ☐

2. Do you smoke?
   Yes ☐ **No** ☐

3. Do you have more than 2 alcoholic drinks per day (men) or 1 drink per day (women) on a regular basis and do you consume 4 drinks or more within a two-hour span (women) or five or more drinks within the same time span (men)?
   Yes ☐ **No** ☐

4. Do you use any illicit drugs such as marijuana, cocaine, and/or Ecstasy?
   Yes ☐ **No** ☐

Additional Questions for Women Only

1. Do you drink alcohol?
   Yes ☐ **No** ☐

2. Do you take herbal supplements or drink herbal teas other than what's available on supermarket shelves?
   Yes ☐ **No** ☐

3. Do you drink more than 12 ounces of caffeinated coffee or energy drinks or four cans of caffeinated soft drinks daily?
   Yes ☐ **No** ☐

4. Do you eat albacore (white canned) tuna, swordfish, mackerel, tilefish, and/or shark?
   Yes ☐ **No** ☐

5. Do you consume less than 400 micrograms of folic acid daily from dietary supplements, fortified grains, or a combination?
   Yes ☐ **No** ☐

Answers

If you answered yes to any of these questions, review the previous section to find out how these diet and lifestyle habits can impact a pregnancy.

older have diabetes, and many are unaware of their condition.[29] Women with poorly controlled type 1 or type 2 diabetes are more likely to deliver an infant with a birth defect than are women without diabetes or those who enter pregnancy with normal glucose levels.[30] Optimal blood glucose control can help ensure a successful pregnancy. Medications used by women with diabetes should be evaluated before conception, as drugs commonly used to treat diabetes and its complications may be contraindicated or not recommended during pregnancy.

Women with preexisting, or chronic, high blood pressure are more likely to have certain complications during pregnancy than those with normal blood pressure. High blood pressure can harm the mother's kidneys and other organs, and it can cause low birth weight and early delivery.[31]

Women with the genetic disorder PKU can have healthy children as long as they are aware of and maintain strict adherence to their low-phenylalanine diet throughout their pregnancy. Women with poorly controlled PKU during a pregnancy put their baby at risk for delayed development, mental retardation, poor growth, heart defects, and other structural birth defects.

Women with chronic diseases who are contemplating pregnancy benefit from prepregnancy counseling. Dietary counseling is important before and throughout pregnancy and the postpartum (after-delivery) period.

LO 17.2: THE TAKE-HOME MESSAGE Good nutrition and healthy lifestyle habits are important for women *and* men before conceiving a child. Smoking, alcohol use and abuse, and overweight and obesity are some of the factors associated with decreased production and function of sperm. Conception is easier for women at a healthy weight. Women should consume adequate amounts of folic acid prior to getting pregnant and continue to take the suggested amount during pregnancy. Women should also avoid fish with potentially higher levels of methylmercury, and consume caffeine in moderation. They should also avoid cigarette smoking and secondhand smoke, alcohol, illicit drugs, and botanical supplements. Women should work closely with their health care professionals to manage preexisting medical conditions prior to conception. Proper nutrition and a healthy lifestyle before pregnancy help prevent certain birth defects and may reduce future health risks in both mother and child.

What Nutrients and Health Behaviors Are Important in the First Trimester?

LO 17.3 Identify key nutrient needs for women and potential complications in the first trimester of pregnancy.

The first trimester is marked by several developmental milestones. Organs begin to develop and function. The liver starts forming red blood cells, the heart begins beating, the limbs take shape, and the brain grows rapidly. During the first trimester, the head is actually much larger than the body to accommodate the developing brain. In spite of all the activity, the fetus weighs just a half ounce and measures only about three inches long by the end of the first three months; it still has a long way to go before birth.

Physiological Changes Occur in the Mother

The mother's body is also changing rapidly during the first trimester. Her breasts may be tender, and she may start to experience other effects of pregnancy, such

Ginger can help alleviate morning sickness for some women.

as a newly heightened sense of taste or smell, and seemingly random food cravings. She may also experience "morning sickness," or nausea, which is so common that women and health care professionals often use it as an initial sign of possible pregnancy.[32]

Morning Sickness

In spite of its name, "morning" sickness can occur at any time of the day. It usually begins during the first trimester and often ends by the twentieth week of pregnancy, although about 10 percent of women experience it longer.[33] The causes of morning sickness are unknown, but lower blood sugar during early pregnancy or fluctuating hormone levels, particularly increased estrogen, may play a role.[34] Estrogen may heighten a woman's perception of odors (experts sometimes refer to this as the "radar nose" of pregnancy), which leads to nausea and can trigger vomiting.

Though there are no known dietary deficiencies that cause morning sickness or dietary changes that can prevent it, some women find relief in eating small, frequent meals that are high in carbohydrates such as pasta, rice, and crackers, and avoiding an empty stomach. Salty foods such as potato chips combined with sour and tart beverages such as lemonade have been shown to help. Vitamin B_6 (100 milligrams or less daily) may also reduce the nausea and vomiting.[35] Because there is an upper limit for safe vitamin B_6 intake, pregnant women should consult their health care professional before increasing it.

Ginger consumption has also been shown to help ease morning sickness. However, ginger root may inhibit a specific enzyme in the body, causing potentially adverse effects, including interfering with blood clotting.[36] As with vitamin B_6, pregnant women should not consume ginger supplements or extracts without first consulting their health care provider.

Though morning sickness is uncomfortable, it usually does not harm the health of the woman or her fetus. However, in rare cases (less than 1 percent of pregnancies) some women experience a more severe form of morning sickness called **hyperemesis gravidarum** (hyper = overstimulated, emesis = vomiting, gravida = pregnant), which can cause serious complications, such as dehydration, electrolyte imbalances, and weight loss. Women with hyperemesis gravidarum often have to be hospitalized for treatment.

hyperemesis gravidarum Excessive vomiting during pregnancy that can lead to dehydration and loss of electrolytes.

▶ Figure 17.4 **Components of Weight Gain during Pregnancy for Healthy-Weight Women**
Healthy-weight women should gain 25 to 35 pounds during pregnancy.

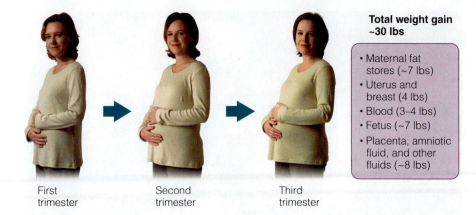

Total weight gain ~30 lbs

- Maternal fat stores (~7 lbs)
- Uterus and breast (4 lbs)
- Blood (3–4 lbs)
- Fetus (~7 lbs)
- Placenta, amniotic fluid, and other fluids (~8 lbs)

First trimester

Second trimester

Third trimester

The loss of appetite that often accompanies nausea can be harmful if it causes the mother to reduce her intake of nutritious foods. Whereas avoiding coffee, tea, and fried or spicy foods (common aversions for pregnant women) is fine, limiting consumption of fruits, vegetables, and whole grains, along with an inability to tolerate prenatal supplements, may result in certain nutrient deficiencies. When the fetus does not receive adequate amounts of an array of nutrients during pregnancy, organ growth may be limited.

Cravings

Pregnant women can have aversions to certain foods, and crave specific ones, too. Chocolate, citrus fruits, pickles, snack chips, and ice cream are foods that women commonly report craving when they are pregnant. There's no scientific basis for pregnancy food cravings, and there's no research that substantiates that women crave foods because their body needs certain nutrients, such as snack chips for the sodium or ice cream for calcium. However, there is no harm in occasionally indulging food cravings in moderation as part of a balanced diet.

There is potential harm, though, when women crave and consume nonfood substances. **Pica** is the abnormal, compulsive intake of nonedible items such as laundry starch, burnt matches, cornstarch, clay, dirt, paint chips, or baking soda. Pica has been associated with low blood levels of iron, which has led to the theory that pregnant women seeking out nonfood substances have an iron deficiency.[37] However, other research suggests that pica causes the iron deficiency in these women.[38] Consuming nonfood substances can lead to the ingestion of toxic compounds, such as lead, that could lead to lead poisoning and other ill effects in both the mother and the baby.[39]

Set Goals for Adequate Weight Gain

In a singleton (one baby) pregnancy, the fetus typically comprises about a third of the total weight gained and maternal tissues account for the remainder (**Figure 17.4**) The amount of overall weight a woman should gain during her pregnancy depends on her weight and health status prior to the pregnancy. Starting pregnancy with a healthy weight and gaining appropriately during pregnancy translates into a lower risk of complications for mother and child. Expert recommendations for pregnancy weight gain are based on a woman's pre-pregnancy BMI.[40] For example, women having a single baby who conceive at a healthy weight (with a BMI between 18.5 and 24.9) should gain 25 to 35 pounds, whereas underweight or overweight women have different weight gain goals (see **Table 17.4**).

TABLE 17.4	Recommended Weight Gain during Pregnancy
Prepregnancy Body Mass Index (BMI)	**Recommended Weight Gain (in Pounds)**
< 18.5	28–40
18.5–24.9	25–35
25–29.9	15–25
> 30.0	11–20

Source: Institute of Medicine. 2009. "Weight Gain during Pregnancy: Reexamining the Guidelines." Copyright © 2009 by the National Academy of Sciences, Courtesy of the National Academies Press, Washington, DC. Reprinted with permission.

pica Eating nonfood substances such as dirt and clay.

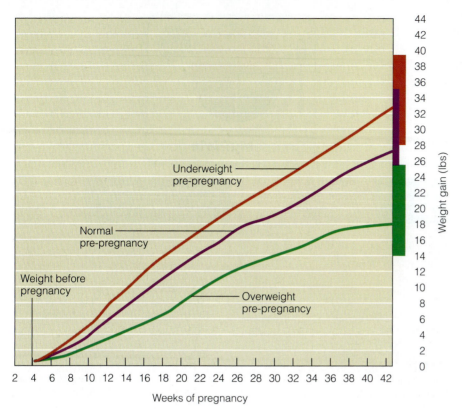

◄ **Figure 17.5 Patterns of Weight Gain**
A chart such as this is often used to monitor the rate of weight gain during pregnancy. Pregnant women should chart their weight gain every two to four weeks.

Source: Parent Link Centre, Alberta Children's Services. www.parentlinkalberta.ca/publish/474.htm. Accessed June 2012.

Patterns of weight gain, that is, the rate of weight gained per week of pregnancy after the first trimester as well as total weight gain, influence the outcome of the pregnancy, especially for twin and triplet pregnancies, which tend to be shorter than singleton pregnancies. Weight gain guidelines for pregnancy are designed to strike a balance between the baby's development and the mother's health. Appropriate weight gain during pregnancy provides for adequate growth so that the baby reaches a healthy weight of about 6.5 to 8.5 pounds, yet it does not increase the risk of complications during delivery or cause excess weight gain for the mother. Gaining excess weight makes it more difficult to lose the weight after delivery and increases the likelihood of the mother remaining overweight for many years afterward.[41] **Figure 17.5** shows healthy patterns of weight gain during a singleton pregnancy. Differences in the physiological response to pregnancy account for variations in weight gain. The recommended pattern of weight gain serves as a target and to identify women who should be evaluated for insufficient or excessive gain.

Most pregnancy weight gain occurs in the second and third trimesters and total weight gain recommendations assume that women gain between 1 and 4½ pounds during the first trimester.[42] Though the fetus grows steadily during the trimester, it's so small that there is no need for extra kilocalories in most pregnant women's diets. However, it has been suggested that women having more than one baby need about 500 additional kilocalories a day starting in the first trimester to help maximize fetal growth, as their pregnancies may not go to full term.[43]

Ensure Adequate Nutrient Intake throughout Pregnancy

Starting in the first trimester, a pregnant woman needs up to 50 percent more of certain vitamins and minerals than prior to pregnancy (**Figure 17.6**). How does a mom-to-be increase her intake of these nutrients in the first trimester and beyond?

A balanced 2,000-calorie diet can meet most pregnant women's nutrient needs during the first trimester. Additional healthy foods in the second and third trimesters help to satisfy increased requirements.

ChooseMyPlate.gov

Vegetables	Fruits	Grains	Protein	Dairy	Oils
2.5 cups	2 cups	6 oz eq	5.5 oz eq	3 cups	6 tsp

Nutrient	Recommended DRI for Nonpregnant Women Aged 19–50 Years	Recommended Nutrient Intake during Pregnancy
Protein	46 g	71 g
Carbohydrates	130 g	175 g (minimum)
Linoleic acid	12 g	13 g
Alpha-linolenic acid	1.1 g	1.4 g
Dietary folate equivalents	400 µg	600 µg*
Thiamin	1.1 mg	1.4 mg
Riboflavin	1.1 mg	1.4 mg
Niacin equivalents	14 mg	18 mg
Vitamin B$_6$	1.3–1.5 mg	1.9 mg
Vitamin B$_{12}$	2.4 µg	2.6 µg
Vitamin C	75 mg	85 mg
Vitamin E	15 mg	15 mg
Vitamin A	700 µg	770 µg
Vitamin D	15 µg	15 µg
Calcium	1,000 mg	1,000 mg
Magnesium	310–320 mg	350–360 mg
Copper	900 µg	1,000 µg
Iron	18 mg	27 mg†
Phosphorus	700 mg	700 mg
Zinc	8 mg	11 mg
Calories	**2,000–2,200‡**	**§**

* Supplemented and/or fortified foods are recommended.
† A supplement is recommended.
‡ Varies depending upon activity level and weight.
§ Doesn't increase until second and third trimester.

By including nutrient-dense foods and taking a daily dietary supplement that fills in dietary gaps for these important nutrients, and for others.

Folate

The DRI for folate is 400 micrograms daily; it's 600 micrograms daily throughout pregnancy. If a woman takes a dietary supplement with 400 micrograms of folic acid prior to conception and continues to take it while also consuming folic acid–fortified grains, it's reasonable to assume that she will satisfy her pregnancy folic acid needs. Foods rich in the naturally occurring form of this B vitamin—folate—are also helpful for meeting suggested pregnancy levels.

Iron

A woman's daily iron needs increase from 18 milligrams to 27 milligrams during pregnancy. Even though a woman loses less iron during pregnancy because she's not menstruating, and she absorbs up to three times more iron from foods than before she was pregnant, she must increase her iron intake for several reasons. She needs more iron to make additional red blood cells, which increase her oxygen-carrying capacity and help replace possible significant iron losses from bleeding during delivery. Iron is essential for fetal growth and development, and for the growth of the placenta. A woman also needs extra iron to prevent iron-deficiency anemia, a condition associated with premature delivery and an increased risk of dying for both mother and baby.[44]

A pregnant woman's increased iron needs are not easy to meet with food alone. Although meat, fish, poultry, and enriched grains supply iron, nearly all women need a dietary supplement to satisfy the suggested intake during pregnancy.[45] Women should not take iron supplements with foods that have components that inhibit its absorption, including milk products (calcium), high-fiber foods (phytate), and coffee and tea (polyphenolic compounds).

Prenatal supplements can help pregnant women meet their increased needs for iron, folic acid, and other essential nutrients.

Zinc and Copper

Because iron can interfere with the absorption of other minerals, a woman taking more than 30 milligrams of iron daily should also take 15 milligrams of zinc and 2 milligrams of copper to prevent a deficiency of these minerals.[46] Zinc is needed in protein metabolism and in the synthesis of DNA so that cells can replicate and differentiate. Copper, as part of enzymes, is needed in the production of energy, the synthesis of connective tissues, and in the transport and use of iron.

Calcium

Calcium needs do not increase during pregnancy. A pregnant woman absorbs more calcium during pregnancy, which offsets the amount of calcium needed by the growing fetus. However, many women fail to get adequate calcium before pregnancy to help build and preserve their own bone mass and to prevent osteoporosis later in life. More than half of women of childbearing age in the United States do not eat the suggested number of servings from the dairy, fruit, and vegetable groups as suggested by MyPlate, putting them at risk of inadequate intake for several nutrients, including calcium.[47]

Drinking milk, which is rich in calcium, is one way to ensure adequate calcium intake during pregnancy. Milk also contains protein, vitamins, including vitamin A, and minerals, such as phosphorus, all of which are needed by the mother and the growing baby. Most milk is also fortified with vitamin D (see below). Sugary drinks, such as regular soda, on the other hand, contain kilocalories, sugar, and not much else, and are not a good beverage choice for anyone, including mothers-to-be.

Vitamin D

Vitamin D is another important nutrient that women of childbearing age frequently underconsume. Suggested intakes for vitamin D don't increase during pregnancy, but many women are not getting enough vitamin D throughout their childbearing years. There is a high prevalence of low levels of serum vitamin D among women in the United States who are capable of conceiving a child. Insufficient vitamin D during pregnancy leads to poor absorption and use of calcium, which in turn hampers fetal bone formation. Maternal vitamin D deficiency during pregnancy has also been linked to preeclampsia, preterm birth, low birth weight, and gestational diabetes.[48] To avoid vitamin D deficiency, experts suggest consumption of adequate vitamin D from vitamin D–rich foods and dietary supplements, if necessary.

Other Nutrients of Concern during Pregnancy

Other nutrients are also of concern during the first trimester, and throughout pregnancy, especially if the mother is vegan, or doesn't eat the recommended daily servings from each food group. Choline, found in high amounts in animal foods, is important during pregnancy and breastfeeding. Choline is needed for healthy cells to divide and grow, especially in the brain.[49] Vegans who don't consume any animal products need to make sure that they are getting adequate amounts of vitamin B_{12} from reliable sources, such as dietary supplements and fortified foods. All pregnant women should be mindful about meeting their needs for alpha-linolenic acid, an essential fatty acid found in nuts, soybeans, and canola oil. Essential fatty acids are needed in the development of cell membranes and so are important in the formation of new tissues, particularly those of the central nervous system.[50]

Avoid Overconsumption of Vitamin A

While it's important that pregnant women meet their nutrient needs, it is equally important that they not consume too much of certain nutrients. Excessive amounts of preformed vitamin A (retinol) can increase the risk of birth defects, especially when taken during the first trimester (see Chapter 9). Women who take dietary supplements should consume no more than 5,000 IU (1,500 micrograms RAE) of preformed vitamin A daily, and should avoid other vitamin and mineral supplements with more than 100 percent of the Daily Value.

Sugar Substitutes

Even though very-low-calorie sweet foods such as diet sodas usually don't contain kilocalories, they are likely to contain sugar substitutes. During pregnancy, sugar substitutes may be used in moderation along with a balanced, nutrient-rich meal plan. Products that contain the sugar substitutes aspartame (Equal), sucralose (Splenda), acesulfame-K (Sunett), and saccharin (Sweet 'N Low) have been deemed safe to consume within the FDA's level of acceptable daily intake.[51] Women with PKU, however, should avoid using aspartame.

Foodborne Illness Is a Concern

During pregnancy, a woman's immune system is weakened and the fetus's immune system is undeveloped, which makes pregnancy a time of heightened susceptibility to foodborne pathogens. The bacterium Listeria monocytogenes, for example, may cause miscarriage, premature labor, low birth weight, developmental problems, and even infant death.

Some foods, such as raw and undercooked animal products, are more likely to carry pathogens and should be handled with care or avoided during pregnancy. Pregnant women should also avoid unpasteurized milk, cheese, and juices; and raw sprouts. You will learn more about foodborne pathogens and how to safeguard your food in Chapter 20.

Food that may carry pathogens, including raw animal foods such as sashimi, should be avoided by pregnant women for their own safety and the safety of their fetus.

> **LO 17.3: THE TAKE-HOME MESSAGE** Many women experience morning sickness and cravings during the first trimester. Women who begin their pregnancy at a healthy weight should gain from 25 to 35 pounds during pregnancy; underweight and overweight women will be advised to gain different amounts. The needs for many nutrients increase during pregnancy, but, with the exception of iron, most can be met with a balanced diet. For pregnant women to obtain the iron they need, a supplement is often prescribed. Pregnant women should avoid excess amounts of preformed vitamin A and use sugar substitutes in moderation. They should also avoid raw or undercooked animal foods and unpasteurized milk, cheese, and juice to reduce their chances of foodborne illness.

What Nutrients and Behaviors Are Important in the Second Trimester?

LO 17.4 Identify key nutrient needs for women and potential complications in the second trimester of pregnancy.

For many pregnant women, the nausea and fatigue of the first trimester subside during the second trimester, and appetite begins to increase. The baby is growing rapidly: Blood cells are forming in the baby's bone marrow, the body grows bigger than the head, the ears become prominent, the eyes blink, and the lips are capable of a sucking motion. The fetus weighs just under 2 pounds and is about 13 inches long by the end of this trimester.

The mother's body is also changing as her amniotic fluid and blood volume increase, her breasts get larger, and she stores more fat. During this period of growth, the mother should get adequate kilocalories, protein, and other nutrients, exercise on a regular basis if her pregnancy is healthy, and become more aware of potential pregnancy complications.

Consume Adequate Kilocalories, Carbohydrate, and Protein

The mother's kilocalorie needs increase at the beginning of the second trimester. Pregnant women need to eat the right amount of kilocalories to gain between a half and 1 pound weekly from this point until delivery.[52] Women who begin pregnancy at a healthy weight need an additional 340 kilocalories daily during the second trimester to achieve adequate weight gain; underweight women may need more kilocalories, and overweight women, fewer. A whole-wheat English muffin topped with peanut butter and some baby carrots (**Figure 17.7**) has about 340 kilocalories, as do many other healthy food combinations (see the Table Tips for some suggestions). Spending additional pregnancy kilocalories on whole and lightly processed foods provides the nutrients that a woman needs for pregnancy, including essential fatty acids, carbohydrates, fiber, calcium, zinc, iron, and protein.

Pregnant women need a minimum of 175 grams of carbohydrates per day (versus 130 grams for nonpregnant women) to supply the amount of glucose required for both the developing brain and the energy needs of the fetus, and to prevent ketosis in the mother. A balanced diet easily provides 175 grams of carbohydrate. A pregnant woman's protein needs also increase by about 35 percent, to about 71 grams daily, during the second and third trimesters. Three servings of dairy foods and about 8 ounces of meat, poultry, or seafood provide the protein most pregnant women need for the day.

Get Enough Exercise

Daily exercise during pregnancy can help improve sleep, lower the risk of hypertension and diabetes, prevent backaches, help relieve constipation, shorten labor, and allow women to return more quickly to their prepregnancy weight after delivery. Exercise may also provide an emotional boost by reducing stress, depression, and anxiety. Experts recommend healthy pregnant women get at least 150 minutes (2 hours, 30 minutes) each week of moderate-intensity aerobic activity, such as brisk walking, during and after their pregnancy. It is best to spread this activity throughout the week.[53] Pregnant women should check with their health care provider before exercising to see if it is appropriate.

Low-impact activities such as walking, swimming, and stationary cycling are best because they pose less risk of injury for both mother and baby. In contrast, high-impact activities, such as downhill skiing and basketball, could injure the baby and cause joint injuries for the mother (**Table 17.5**). As long as there are no

1 whole-wheat English muffin
2 tbs peanut butter
5 baby carrots

340 total kilocalories

▲ **Figure 17.7 Adding Kilocalories and Nutrients**
The extra kilocalorie and nutrient needs of the second and third trimesters can be met with additional nutrient-dense foods.

TABLE TIPS

340 Snacks

Create a "340 snack" with just five or fewer ingredients. Start with a whole or enriched grain. Complement it with servings from the protein, low-fat dairy, vegetable, or fruit food groups.

Spread 3 tablespoons of low-fat ricotta cheese on 2 brown rice cakes topped with a small sliced banana for a 340-kilocalorie pick-me-up.

Layer ¼ cup low-fat granola cereal and ¾ cup berries with 1 cup low-fat vanilla yogurt for a 340-kilocalorie refreshing yogurt parfait.

Layer 1 whole-wheat tortilla with ½ cup low-fat refried beans, 2 tablespoons salsa, ¼ cup shredded Cheddar cheese, and ¼ cup shredded lettuce. Roll up and enjoy.

TABLE 17.5	Safe and Unsafe Exercises during Pregnancy	
Safe Activities	**Unsafe Activities (Contact Sports and High-Impact Activities)**	
Walking	Hockey (field and ice)	
Stationary cycling		
Low-impact aerobics	Basketball	
	Football	
Swimming	Soccer	
Dancing	Gymnastics	
Jogging	Horseback riding	
	Skating	
	Skiing (snow and water)	
	Vigorous racquet sports	
	Weight lifting	

Adapted from American College of Obstetrics and Gynecology. 2011. FAQ: Exercise during Pregnancy. Available at www.acog.org. Accessed July 2014.

Walking is one form of exercise that is safe for both mother and baby, and helps reduce the risk of diabetes.

gestational diabetes Diabetes that occurs in women during pregnancy.

macrosomia Term for a large newborn, weighing more than 8 pounds, 13 ounces.

jaundice A yellowish coloring of the skin due to the presence of bile pigments in the blood.

health complications, pregnant women who already do vigorous-intensity aerobic activity, such as running, can continue doing so during and after their pregnancy provided they stay healthy and discuss with their health care provider how and when activity should be adjusted over time.[54] Exercising moms-to-be should take special care to avoid a significant increase in their body core temperature, and to drink plenty of fluids to avoid dehydration.[55]

Be Alert to Potential Complications: Gestational Diabetes and Hypertension

Women may develop complications during pregnancy that can endanger their health and the health of their child. Two potential problems, gestational diabetes and hypertension, often first make their appearance in the second trimester.

Gestational Diabetes

Gestational diabetes (gestation = pregnancy), high blood glucose levels during pregnancy, affects an estimated 2 to 10 percent of pregnancies in the United States after about the 20th week.[56] A pregnant woman should be tested for gestational diabetes during her second trimester. Though the cause of gestational diabetes is still unknown, the hormones from the placenta may cause insulin resistance in the mother, which in turn causes hyperglycemia. Extra blood glucose crosses the placenta, stimulating the baby's pancreas to make more insulin, which leads to the storage of excess glucose as fat and can result in **macrosomia** (macro = large, somia = body), or a large baby.[57] A larger than normal baby may be at risk of injury to its shoulders during delivery or may increase the risk of a cesarean delivery.[58] Because the fetus is producing extra insulin during its gestation, the baby may have elevated insulin levels after birth, causing a rapid drop in blood glucose levels, which can cause hypoglycemia.[59] Gestational diabetes also increases the risk of **jaundice** and breathing problems in newborns, and birth defects.[60]

Gestational diabetes typically goes away with delivery. However, immediately after pregnancy, 5 to 10 percent of women with gestational diabetes are found to have diabetes, usually type 2.[61] In addition, women with gestational diabetes and the babies they carry are at higher risk of developing type 2 diabetes, as well as hypertension and being overweight later on in life.[62] Women who have had gestational diabetes should be followed closely by their doctors after delivery.

Certain factors can increase a woman's risk for gestational diabetes:

- Being overweight
- Being over 25 years old
- Having a history of higher-than-normal blood glucose levels
- Having a family history of diabetes
- Being of Hispanic, African-American, Native American, or Pacific Islander descent
- Having previously given birth to a very large baby (> 9 pounds) or a stillborn baby
- Having had gestational diabetes in the past

According to the National Institute of Child Health and Human Development, if a woman has two or more of these risk factors, she is at high risk for developing gestational diabetes and should be tested earlier, during the first trimester of her pregnancy.[63] Having one risk factor indicates average risk, while having no risk factors indicates low risk.[64] Eating healthfully, maintaining a healthy weight, and exercising regularly can help reduce the risk of developing diabetes during pregnancy.

To achieve normal maternal blood glucose levels, women with gestational diabetes should receive nutritional counseling, by a Registered Dietitian Nutritionist when possible. Because gestational diabetes is a major risk factor for future maternal diabetes, it presents a "teachable moment" during which women can be alerted to take action to decrease risk.

Hypertension

Hypertension during pregnancy can damage the woman's kidneys and other organs and increase the risk of low birth weight and premature delivery.[65] Though some women have hypertension prior to conceiving, others develop it during their pregnancy. **Pregnancy-induced hypertension** includes gestational hypertension, preeclampsia, and eclampsia, each a progressively greater medical threat to mother and baby.

Gestational hypertension is more likely to occur halfway through pregnancy and be a precursor to preeclampsia, while another type of high blood pressure, chronic hypertension, is detected before 20 weeks of the pregnancy. Gestational hypertension may also be a sign of future chronic hypertension. Women who develop gestational hypertension should have their blood pressure monitored after they deliver.[66]

Preeclampsia, the most common kind of high blood pressure during pregnancy, occurs when the woman has hypertension and protein in her urine, which signals kidney damage.[67] As a result of elevated blood pressure and protein in the urine, women with preeclampsia may experience mild to severe swelling, or edema. Though some edema in a woman's feet and ankles is normal during pregnancy, the dramatic edema seen in preeclampsia is visible in her face and hands and can cause rapid weight gain. The cause of preeclampsia is not known, but we do know that it's dangerous to the baby because it prevents oxygen- and nutrient-rich blood from reaching the placenta.[68] Women at higher risk of developing preeclampsia include those who have hypertension prior to pregnancy or develop it during pregnancy, are overweight, under the age of 20 or over the age of 40, are carrying more than one baby, or have diabetes.[69] If left untreated, preeclampsia can lead to **eclampsia,** which can cause seizures in the mother and is a major cause of death of women during pregnancy.[70]

The only cure for preeclampsia and eclampsia is to deliver the baby. However, delivery too early (before 32 weeks) is unsafe for the baby. Bed rest, medications, and hospitalization are used to treat preeclampsia until the baby can be safely born.[71] Calcium supplements had been postulated to prevent preeclampsia, but research doesn't support this claim, especially if the mother's diet is adequate in calcium.[72, 73] Some research suggests that antioxidants, specifically vitamins C and E, may reduce the risk, but more research is needed to confirm a connection.[74]

LO 17.4: THE TAKE-HOME MESSAGE Pregnant women who conceive at a healthy weight should consume an additional 340 kilocalories daily during the second trimester. A varied selection of nutrient-dense foods helps to satisfy increased kilocalorie needs. Exercise can provide numerous benefits during pregnancy. Some women develop gestational diabetes and pregnancy-induced high blood pressure and need to be closely monitored by a health care professional.

What Nutrients and Health Behaviors Are Important in the Third Trimester?

LO 17.5 Identify key nutrient needs for women and potential complications in the third trimester of pregnancy.

During the third trimester, a woman who started pregnancy at a healthy weight should be eating 450 kilocalories more every day than before she became pregnant, and she should continue to gain between one-half and one pound weekly. (Adding a banana to the English muffin with peanut butter and carrots increases this

FITNESS TIPS

Exercising while Pregnant

Consult your health care provider before beginning or continuing an exercise program.

Begin slowly to avoid excessive fatigue and shortness of breath.

In warm weather, exercise in the early morning or evening to avoid becoming overheated.

Drink plenty of fluids to stay hydrated.

Report any problems or unusual symptoms such as chest pains, contractions, dizziness, headaches, calf swelling, blurred vision, vaginal discharge or bleeding, and/or abdominal pain immediately to your health care provider.

Source: U.S. Department of Health and Human Services. 2009. Tips for Pregnancy: Fit for Two. Available at http://win.niddk.nih.gov/publications/PDFs/fitfortwo.pdf.

pregnancy-induced hypertension High blood pressure resulting from pregnancy; includes gestational hypertension, preeclampsia, and eclampsia.

gestational hypertension Hypertension occurring during pregnancy in a woman without prior history of high blood pressure.

preeclampsia Serious medical condition developed late in pregnancy in which hypertension, severe edema, and protein loss occur.

eclampsia Seizures or coma in a woman with preeclampsia.

TABLE TIPS

Going from 340 to 450

What nutrient-dense foods could accompany a sandwich and a cup of milk? Consider adding an apple or banana to the snack.

A small handful of chopped nuts can top a yogurt parfait.

Melt a slice of cheese on a burger.

Garnish a green salad with an ounce of whole-grain croutons.

Sip a fruit smoothie made with 1 cup low-fat vanilla yogurt, a small banana, and 2 tablespoons wheat germ.

combination to about 450 kilocalories. Check out the Table Tips for more suggestions.) She is likely to have a harder time getting around due to her expanding body. By the end of the third trimester, climbing stairs may take her breath away and finding a comfortable sleeping position could take some maneuvering.

As the growing baby exerts pressure on the mother's intestines and stomach, she may experience "heartburn," which is actually acid indigestion. Heartburn happens when stomach acid makes its way into the esophagus. Hormonal changes may also slow the movement of food through the GI tract, and increase the likelihood of heartburn. To minimize discomfort, pregnant women should eat frequent, small meals rather than fewer, larger meals, and avoid foods that may irritate the esophagus, such as spicy or highly seasoned foods. They also shouldn't lie down immediately after meals, and they should elevate their head and shoulders during sleep to minimize reflux.[75]

Constipation is common near the end of pregnancy. The slower movement of food through the GI tract, coupled with a tendency for less physical activity, reduces regularity and causes a more sluggish large intestine. The high levels of iron in prenatal supplements can also contribute to constipation. Regular physical activity and a fiber-rich eating plan that features foods such as bran cereals, beans, whole grains, fruits, and vegetables, along with plenty of fluids, can help prevent or alleviate constipation.

LO 17.5: THE TAKE-HOME MESSAGE During the third trimester, a woman who began her pregnancy at a healthy weight needs an additional 450 kilocalories daily and should continue gaining about a pound per week. Heartburn and constipation commonly occur during the third trimester. Regular exercise, increasing fiber in the diet, and consuming plenty of fluids can help reduce constipation.

What Special Situations Do Younger, Older, or Low-Income Mothers-to-Be Face?

LO 17.6 List special concerns of younger, older, and low-income mothers-to-be.

Pregnancy and childbirth stress the body of a mother-to-be no matter what her age, but teenage moms, and those over the age of 35 may encounter certain health complications.

Teenaged Mothers Face Nutritional Challenges

The good news is that for several years, the birth rate for women under the age of 20 has been on the decline in the United States.[76] The bad news is that teenagers who become pregnant do so before their own bodies have had a chance to fully develop. Because an adolescent's body is still growing, she has higher nutrient needs than an adult woman. Adolescents are more likely to eat on the run, skip meals, eat nutrient-poor snacks, and consume inadequate amounts of whole grains, fruits, vegetables, and low-fat or fat-free dairy products. If a teen's diet lacks nutrients, such as iron, folic acid, kilocalories, and calcium, her baby's development, as well as her own, may be less than optimal.

A pregnant teen's inadequate diet can mean not only a low birth weight or SGA baby, but her own diminished health status.[77] Teenaged mothers are also more likely to develop pregnancy-induced hypertension and iron-deficiency anemia and

Nutrition in Practice: Susan

Susan was thrilled when she learned she was pregnant. Eager to start a family, she had recently given up cigarette smoking and started exercising regularly, walking after work every day and going on weekend bike rides and hiking trips with her husband. During her first prenatal visit, her physician referred Susan to a Registered Dietitian Nutritionist (RDN) for nutritional counseling and since then she has been following an individualized vegan meal plan. Despite suffering from morning sickness through the first two trimesters, Susan has continued to work full time. During her second trimester, Susan's physician prescribed a prenatal supplement, citing concern about Susan's vegan diet and her not obtaining adequate nutrition due to morning sickness. At her most recent prenatal visit, Susan told her doctor that she had recently started experiencing heartburn after supper and occasional constipation, and the doctor referred her to the RDN for another consultation.

Susan's Stats:
- Age: 27
- Height: 5 feet 6 inches
  Weight (pre-conception): 148 pounds
- Weight (34 weeks): 169 pounds
- BMI (pre-conception): 24

Susan's Food Log

Food/Beverage	Time Consumed	Hunger Rating*	Location
Fortified whole-grain cereal topped with blueberries and fortified soy milk; decaffeinated coffee with sugar substitute	6:30 A.M.	2	In kitchen at home
Whole-grain English muffin topped with peanut butter and shredded carrots; soy milk	9:30 A.M.	4	Staff break room
Black beans and brown rice with broccoli and carrots; spinach salad with vinaigrette dressing; diet soda	12:30 P.M.	5	Staff break room
Banana	3 P.M.	2	In the car driving to gym
Soy milk	4 P.M.	4	In the car on the way home
Vegetarian lentil soup; whole-wheat pasta topped with mushroom sauce and soy cheese; soy milk	6:30 P.M.	3	In the dining room at home
Soy yogurt sprinkled with wheat germ, raisins, and nuts	9 P.M.	2	In front of the TV at home

*Hunger Rating (1–5); 1 = not hungry; 5 = super hungry.

Critical Thinking Questions
1. Which foods in Susan's log are rich in these nutrients: fiber, vitamin B$_{12}$, folate, iron, zinc, and calcium?
2. How can Susan avoid or minimize heartburn and constipation?

Dietitian's Observation and Plan for Susan:
- Discuss the importance of optimal nutrient intake to maintain the recommended weight-gain pattern during pregnancy.
- To minimize heartburn, continue eating frequent, small meals, and avoid foods that may irritate the esophagus, such as spicy or highly seasoned foods. Discourage Susan from lying down immediately after meals and recommend keeping her head and shoulders elevated during sleep.
- Discuss the reasons why constipation is common near the end of pregnancy, and advise Susan to continue with regular exercise. Also recommend drinking plenty of fluids and consuming fiber-rich foods such as bran cereals, beans, whole grains, fruits, and vegetables, along with plenty of fluids.

Susan follows the RDN's suggestions for preventing heartburn and constipation and finds she has much less heartburn. Susan hopes to breastfeed her baby, so two weeks before her due date, Susan returns for a follow-up appointment with the dietitian to discuss her nutrient needs as a nursing mother. The dietitian advises Susan that she will need more fluid while she is breastfeeding—about 13 cups daily, most of which should be water. Once she delivers and starts breast-feeding, Susan will need an additional 330 kilocalories daily from nutrient-rich foods, so she can maintain her third-trimester eating plan for the first six months of her child's life.

Older mothers often deliver multiples—twins, triplets, or quads.

deliver premature babies, putting the baby at risk for health problems.[78] Teens may engage in unhealthy lifestyle habits such as smoking, drinking alcohol, and taking illicit drugs, all of which can compromise the baby's health. In addition, adolescents are less likely to receive adequate prenatal care than their older counterparts.[79] If she receives prenatal care, pays close attention to her nutrition, and avoids unhealthy habits, a teenaged mother can experience a normal, healthy pregnancy.

Older Mothers May Have Special Concerns

More women are having babies during their later childbearing years. The number of women who fall into this category has increased significantly in the last two decades: Since 1990, the number of births to women over age 35 has risen 40 percent. Today, births to mothers over age 35 represent over 35 percent of overall births in the United States. Fertility typically begins to decline in women starting in their early 30s, so getting pregnant may take longer, but when they do conceive, older women have a higher rate of multiple births. The more advanced age of women at childbirth accounts for about one-third of the rise in twin pregnancies over the previous 30 years.[80]

Though women in their 30s and 40s often experience normal, healthy pregnancies, they are at higher risk for certain complications, including diabetes and high blood pressure, and an older woman's fetus is more likely to be affected by Down syndrome or other birth defects.[81]

For the healthiest pregnancy possible, older mothers should try to achieve a healthy body weight prior to conception, avoid smoking, eat a balanced diet before and during pregnancy, and consume adequate amounts of folic acid before and throughout pregnancy. As with all pregnant women, older moms should limit their caffeine intake and avoid alcohol and illicit drugs. If they regularly take prescription or over-the-counter medications, they should check with their doctor to see if these are safe during pregnancy. See Table 17.6 for a summary of factors that relate to high-risk pregnancy.

TABLE 17.6	Factors That May Negatively Affect a Pregnancy
Factor	**Conditions Associated with Increased Risk**
Lifestyle	Smoking, alcohol, and abuse of illicit drugs; certain over-the-counter and prescription medications
	Use of botanical supplements and certain herbal teas
Age	Under age 20
	Over age 35
Weight	Prepregnancy: underweight, obese
	During pregnancy: insufficient or excessive weight gain
Health	Chronic diseases, including diabetes and hypertension
	Past history of a pregnancy affected by a birth defect, such as a neural tube defect
	Gestational diabetes, pregnancy-induced hypertension
Diet	Environmental contaminants (methylmercury, pica)
	Insufficient or excessive kilocalorie intake
	Nutrient deficiencies (folic acid, iron, calcium, vitamin D, B_{12})
	Foodborne illness
Socioeconomic status	Poverty
	Limited food supply
	Low educational level

Low-Income Mothers May Need Food Assistance

Adequate nutrition during pregnancy is critical for the health of both the mother and the child. The government program Special Supplemental Nutrition Program for Women, Infants, and Children (WIC) is designed to ensure that pregnant women and mothers with young children have access to nutrition information and nutritious foods during the most critical years of growth and development. WIC provides supplemental foods, health care referrals, and nutrition education for low-income pregnant and postpartum women, and children up to age 5 who are at nutritional risk and who meet the program's eligibility requirements.[82] Supplemental foods include iron-fortified infant formula and infant cereal, iron-fortified adult cereal, vitamin C–rich fruit or vegetable juice, eggs, milk, cheese, peanut butter, dried beans/peas, tuna fish, and carrots.[83]

Evaluation studies have shown that the WIC program has been playing an important role in improving birth outcomes and containing health care costs. The program improved the nutritional status of nearly 9 million WIC participants in 2012.[84] For example, the WIC program reduces the incidence of iron-deficiency anemia in women during pregnancy and after delivery, and helps improve babies' birth weights. It also leads to fewer premature births, fewer infant deaths, and increased prenatal care.[85] Every $1.00 spent on prenatal WIC participation for low-income women saves between $1.77 and $3.13 in health care costs within the first 60 days after birth.[86]

LO 17.6: THE TAKE-HOME MESSAGE Teens who become pregnant are at higher risk of developing hypertension and anemia and delivering a premature and low birth weight baby. Because a teen is still growing, she may have difficulty meeting both her own nutrient needs and her baby's, unless she is diligent about eating a well-balanced diet. Women over age 35 may have a harder time conceiving, are at higher risk for hypertension and diabetes during pregnancy, and have higher rates of babies born with developmental disabilities. The Special Supplemental Nutrition Program for Women, Infants, and Children (WIC) is a government-funded program that provides food assistance for nutritionally at-risk mothers during pregnancy, and for at-risk children through the first five years of life.

What Are the Benefits and Nutrient Needs of Breast-Feeding?

LO 17.7 Describe the benefits of breast-feeding.

A woman who has just given birth begins a period of **lactation,** that is, her body produces milk to nourish her new infant. The infant's suckling at the mother's nipple stimulates milk production. Nerve signals sent from the nipple to the hypothalamus in the mother's brain prompt the pituitary gland to release two hormones: prolactin and oxytocin. Prolactin causes milk to be produced in the breast, while oxytocin triggers a **letdown response,** which releases milk so the infant can receive it through the nipple[87] (see **Figure 17.8**).

The adage "breast is best" when nourishing an infant is still true. Through **breast-feeding,** or nursing, mothers provide food that is uniquely tailored to meet their infant's nutritional needs in an easily digestible form. Breast-feeding also provides many other advantages for both the mother and the baby.

lactation The production of milk in a woman's body after childbirth, and the period during which it occurs.

letdown response The release of milk from the mother's breast to feed a nursing baby.

breast-feeding The act of feeding an infant milk from a woman's breast.

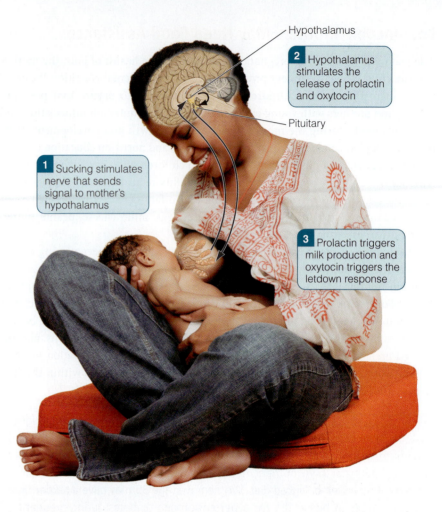

Hypothalamus

2 Hypothalamus stimulates the release of prolactin and oxytocin

Pituitary

1 Sucking stimulates nerve that sends signal to mother's hypothalamus

3 Prolactin triggers milk production and oxytocin triggers the letdown response

Breast-Feeding Provides Nutritional and Health Benefits for Infants

There are more than 200 compounds in breast milk that benefit an infant's health. Numerous research studies indicate that breast-feeding provides nutritional and health advantages that can last years beyond infancy.[88] Breast-feeding is one of the most important strategies for improving an infant's long-term health prospects.

Best for an Infant's Unique Nutrition Needs

The nutritional composition of breast milk changes as an infant grows. Right after birth, a new mother produces a carotenoid-rich, yellowish fluid called **colostrum** that has little fat but a lot of protein, vitamin A, and minerals. Colostrum also contains immune factors that help protect the infant from infections, particularly in the digestive tract.

Four to seven days later, actual breast milk begins to flow. Breast milk is high in lactose, fat, and B vitamins, and relatively low in fat-soluble vitamins, sodium, and other minerals. These nutrients are proportionally balanced to enhance their absorption. Breast milk contains the right amount of protein so as not to stress an infant's immature kidneys with excessive amounts of nitrogen waste products. The protein is also mostly in the form of alpha-lactalbumin, which is easier for the infant to digest.[89] The nutrient composition of breast milk continues to change as the baby grows and his or her needs change.[90]

Although breast-feeding is the recommended method of infant feeding and provides infants with necessary nutrients and immune factors, breast milk alone does not provide infants with an adequate intake of vitamin D. Breast

colostrum The fluid that is expressed from the mother's breast after birth and before the development of breast milk.

Determining Kilocalorie and Fat Content of Breast Milk

The daily energy needs of infants 0 to 6 months are typically met with a liter of breast milk. One liter of breast milk provides about 60 grams of carbohydrate, 9.1 grams of protein, and 31 grams of fat.

Approximately how many kilocalories are found in a liter of breast milk?

60 g carbohydrate $\times$ 4 kcal/g = 240 kcal

9.1 g of protein $\times$ 4 kcal/g = 36.4 kcal

31 g of fat $\times$ 9 kcal/g = 279 kcal

Answer: A liter of breast milk provides approximately 555 kilocalories.

The fat in breast milk contributes what proportion of the kilocalories?

Answer: From the above calculations, 279 kilocalories come from fat.

279 kcal from fat $\div$ 555 total kcal = 50.3 $\times$ 100 = 50%

Answer: Fat represents 50 percent of the total kilocalories found in breast milk.

Scan this QR code with your mobile device to access practice math activities. You can also access the activities in **Mastering**Nutrition™.

milk typically contains a vitamin D concentration of 25 IU per liter or less.[91] The American Academy of Pediatrics (AAP) recommends that all infants consume 400 IU of vitamin D per day, beginning soon after birth, because breast milk is low in vitamin D. Vitamin D supplementation should be continued unless the infant begins drinking at least one quart of vitamin D–fortified formula, or vitamin D–fortified whole milk, daily (after 12 months of age).[92]

Protection against Infections, Allergies, and Chronic Diseases

Breast milk provides the infant with a disease-fighting boost until the baby's own immune system matures. Research supports that breast-feeding decreases the risk and severity of diarrhea and other intestinal disorders, respiratory infections, meningitis, ear infections, and urinary tract infections.[93]

One particular protein in breast milk, lactoferrin, protects the infant against bacteria, viruses, fungi, and inflammation by binding with iron and making it unavailable to bacteria that need it to flourish.[94] Lactoferrin also inhibits the ability of bacteria to stick to the walls of the intestines, which impedes their growth.

Breast milk provides other beneficial compounds, such as antioxidants, hormones, enzymes, and growth factors that play a role in the development of the infant and protect the baby from pathogens, inflammation, diseases, and allergies.[95] Some research suggests that breast milk may also protect against sudden infant death syndrome (SIDS), asthma, leukemia, heart disease, and diabetes mellitus.[96]

Reduced Childhood Obesity Risk

Breast-feeding, especially if continued beyond six months, may help reduce the risk of childhood obesity. The reason for this isn't clear, but could be associated with the tendency of breast-fed infants to gain less weight during the first year of life than formula-fed infants. The lower weight gain may be due to breast-fed infants having more control over when they start and stop eating than their bottle-fed counterparts.[97]

Brain Development

Breast milk may help infants with intellectual development. When a lactating mother eats properly, her breast milk is rich in two unsaturated fatty acids, docosahexaenoic acid (DHA) and arachidonic acid (AA), which are important for the development of vision and the central nervous system, particularly the brain (see Chapter 5). Research suggests that breast-fed infants may have greater cognitive function than formula-fed babies,[98] which may be due in part to these two fatty acids. It's important to note that many commercial infant formulas also supply DHA and AA.

Breast-Feeding Provides Physical, Emotional, and Financial Benefits for Mothers

Breast-feeding not only provides optimal nutrition and immunological benefits for the baby, it helps improve the health of the mother and can be less expensive, safer, and more convenient than bottle-feeding. The health and emotional benefits of breast-feeding may last for years after it ends.

Pregnancy Recovery and the Risk of Some Chronic Diseases

In addition to stimulating the release of breast milk, the hormone oxytocin stimulates contractions in the uterus, which helps the organ return to its prepregnancy size and shape. Breast-feeding also reduces blood loss in the mother after delivery.[99] It may help some women better manage their weight after delivery. Breast-feeding women have a lower risk for type 2 diabetes, cancer of the breasts and ovaries, and postpartum depression.[100]

Expense and Convenience

Moms who breast-feed can save between $1,200–$1,500 in expenditures on infant formula in the first year alone,[101] far less than the amount she would spend to feed herself in order to nourish the baby properly on breast milk. In other words, making breast milk is less expensive than buying formula. Breast-feeding saves health care dollars, too. One study concluded that the national health care cost of not breast-feeding infants in their first year of life is as much as $13 billion dollars.[102]

There are other costs associated with formula-feeding beyond the price of the product and associated health care expenses. There is the cost to produce, package, and ship formula throughout the United States. There are also environmental costs associated with the 550 million formula cans and 800,000 pounds of paper and plastic packaging and waste that are disposed of in landfills each year, and costs associated with the energy needed to properly clean the feeding bottles.[103]

For the family, the environment, and society as a whole, breast-feeding uses fewer resources than formula-feeding. Feeding from the breast is more convenient than bottle-feeding because the milk is always sterile and at the right temperature, and there is no need to prepare bottles or infant formula. In addition, there is less cleanup associated with breast-feeding.

Stress Reduction and Bonding

Recent research suggests that exclusive breast-feeding is associated with a mother's reduced reactivity to psychological stress.[104] In addition, the close interaction between mother and child during nursing promotes a unique bonding experience. The physical contact helps the baby feel safe, secure, and emotionally attached to the mother.[105]

Breast-Feeding Is Recommended by Experts

Because of all of the benefits breast-feeding provides for mother and child, the AAP and the Academy of Nutrition and Dietetics recommend that women exclusively

The intimacy of breast-feeding promotes bonding between mother and child.

breast-feed for the first six months and then use a combination of appropriate foods and breast-feeding during the remainder of the first year of life, and breast-feed for longer, if desired. Currently, 77 percent of American women initiate breast-feeding when their infants are born, which is below the goal of 81.9 percent set for the nation in Healthy People 2020.[106, 107] However, only 49 percent still breast-feed their infants at six months and only 27 percent continue until the baby is one year of age.[108] The number of women breast-feeding in the United States falls short of the national goal of 60.6 percent of infants being breast-fed at six months and at least 34.1 percent still nursing at age 1.[109]

The breast-fed infant doesn't always have to consume breast milk directly from the breast. Milk can be expressed with a breast pump, refrigerated, and fed to the baby in a bottle by another caregiver at another time. This allows the mother to work outside the home or enjoy a few hours "off duty," and it allows others to feed the child. Expressed breast milk needs to be used within 24 hours, or it can be stored in the freezer for three to six months. The Spotlight: Breast-Feeding at Work Can Work addresses the dilemma of moms who want to breast-feed but who also want or need to return to work.

Breast-Feeding Mothers Have Special Nutrient and Lifestyle Needs

During the first six months of breast-feeding, the mother produces about three-fourths of a liter of breast milk daily. In the second six months, she produces a little over half a liter daily. During breast-feeding, a mother needs more fluid and more of certain nutrients.

Fluid and Nutrient Requirements

To meet her increased fluid needs, a breast-feeding woman should drink about 13 cups of fluid daily, and most of it should be plain water. Recall from Chapter 11 that most healthy nonpregnant women need 9 cups of water daily.

A breast-feeding woman's body requires 500 kilocalories daily during the first six months of lactating to make enough milk to feed her child. However, not all of these kilocalories have to come from the food she eats. Approximately 170 kilocalories are mobilized daily from fat that was stored during pregnancy, so she needs to eat about an extra 330 kilocalories to make up the difference.[110] This use of stored fat allows for a potential weight loss of about 2 pounds a month during the first six months of breast-feeding as long as the mother doesn't overeat.

After the first six months of breast-feeding, less energy is available from stored body fat, so a lactating woman needs to consume about 400 extra kilocalories daily to meet her needs.[111] A well-balanced diet similar to the one she consumed during pregnancy will meet her breast-feeding nutrient needs. Lactating women who are vegans should make sure that they consume adequate amounts of vitamin B_{12} from dietary supplements and fortified foods.

Lifestyle Habits

Anything that goes into a breast-feeding mother's body can potentially pass into her breast milk, and ultimately to her baby. Illicit drugs, such as cocaine, heroin, and marijuana, for example, can be transferred to a breast-fed infant and cause harm. Methylmercury, which a mother can overconsume if she eats certain fish, can also be harmful, so nursing mothers should adhere to the FDA's guidelines about fish to minimize the infant's exposure (refer to Table 17.2 on page 633).

Nursing women should limit coffee consumption and avoid alcohol and smoking. Caffeine can interfere with a baby's sleep and cause crankiness. Nursing women

Breast-Feeding at Work Can Work

For many women, the decision to breast-feed their infants is an easy one. The bigger challenge is how to juggle breast-feeding with returning to work or school.

Many women feel uncomfortable about breast-feeding or pumping breast milk outside the home, especially at their place of employment. Consider that about 50 percent of mothers with babies 1 year of age or younger are employed, and you can see that this reluctance is a big issue.[1] And the hesitation isn't just one-sided: Research shows that most companies don't offer support for working breast-feeding mothers, even though employer support for breast-feeding can extend the duration of a mother nursing her baby, which would benefit both mothers and babies.[2] The reality is that many women must choose between breast-feeding and a paycheck, and work usually wins out.

But this may be slowly changing. In 1998, the state of Minnesota mandated that its companies aid and support breast-feeding moms. From 1998 to 2002, the percentage of women still breast-feeding at six months more than doubled within the state.[3] Currently, 24 states in the United States have laws to support breast-feeding in the workplace.[4]

The Patient Protection and Affordable Care Act (also known as Health Care Reform) requires employers to provide reasonable break time and a private, non-bathroom place for nursing mothers to express breast milk during the workday, for one year after the child's birth. The new requirements became effective when the Affordable Care Act was signed into law on March 23, 2010. The law does not preempt state laws that provide greater protections to employees.[5]

Worksite support is not only healthy for the infant but, in many ways, healthy for the corporate bottom line. Supportive employers help to extend the duration of breast-feeding and so improve the health of both mother and baby. Because breast-fed infants are sick less often than formula-fed babies, annual health care costs are approximately $400 lower for breast-fed than for non-breast-fed babies.[6] Employees

Women can express breast milk using a breast pump and store the milk in the refrigerator or freezer for later use.

who are able to breast-feed are also happier, miss fewer workdays (whether for their own illness or to tend to a sick infant), are more productive, and show greater loyalty to the employer.[7] In fact, a company's commitment to supporting breast-feeding women can be used as a recruitment tool when seeking new workers. It is estimated that each $1 invested in a corporate breast-feeding program saves the company $3.[8]

Skilled lactation support and workplace policies can enable many mothers to plan to breast-feed on return to work.[9] Women who return to work while lactating need only minimal worksite resources to accommodate their breast-feeding. First, they need adequate break times throughout the day and access to a private, comfortable room with an electrical outlet in order to pump their breast milk. They also need a sink in which to wash their hands and the pumping equipment, and a refrigerator for storing the milk.[10]

Some companies have gone beyond these minimum requirements. For example, Johnson & Johnson initiated a company-wide breast-feeding program called Nurture Space. Employees who are new mothers, or their spouses or partners, receive a lactation

education kit that includes an instructional DVD, a breast-feeding guide, and other educational materials. They also receive a discount on a portable breast pump and free telephone consultations with a certified lactation consultant. At many Johnson & Johnson corporate locations there are Nurture Space rooms where breast-feeding mothers can comfortably express their milk during the workday.

References

1. Centers for Disease Control and Prevention. 2011. *Breast Feeding. Promotion and Support*. Available at www.cdc.gov/breastfeeding/promotion/employment.htm. Accessed July 2014.
2. W. Slusser, L. Lange, V. Dickson, C. Hawkes, and R. Cohen. 2004. "Breast Milk Expression in the Workplace: A Look at Frequency and Time." *Journal of Human Lactation* 20:164–169.
3. M. Johnson. 2008. Letter to the Editor: Twentieth Anniversary Issue. *Journal of Human Lactation* 22:14–15.
4. National Conference of State Legislatures. 2014. *Breastfeeding State Laws*. Available at www.ncsl.org/issues-research/health/breastfeeding-state-laws.aspx. Accessed July 2014.
5. U.S. Breast-Feeding Committee. 2011. *Workplace Support in Federal Law*. Available at www.usbreastfeeding.org/Employment/WorkplaceSupport/WorkplaceSupportinFederalLaw/tabid/175/Default.aspx. Accessed July 2014.
6. U.S. Breast-Feeding Committee. 2002. *Workplace Breast-Feeding Support*. Available at www.usbreastfeeding.org/Portals/0/Publications/Workplace-2002-USBC.pdf. Accessed July 2014.
7. O. A. Abdulwadud and M. E. Snow. 2007. "Interventions in the Workplace to Support Breast-Feeding for Women in Employment." *Cochrane Database of Systematic Reviews*. Issue 3. Article No. CD006177.
8. U.S. Breast-Feeding Committee. 2010. *Workplace Accommodations to Support and Protect Breast-Feeding*. Available at www.usbreastfeeding.org/Portals/0/Publications/Workplace-Background-2010-USBC.pdf. Accessed July 2014.
9. J. Kosmala-Anderson and L. M. Wallace. 2006. "Breast-Feeding Works: The Role of Employers in Supporting Women Who Wish to Breast-Feed and Work in Four Organizations in England." *Journal of Public Health* 28:183–191.
10. U.S. Breast-Feeding Committee. 2010. *Workplace Accommodations to Support and Protect Breast-Feeding*.

should also avoid alcohol, because it can appear in breast milk and inhibit milk production. They should not smoke, because nicotine can be passed on in breast milk and smoking is associated with a decrease in milk production and smaller weight gains in the baby.[112]

Breast milk can reflect the foods a mother eats and cause problems for the baby. For example, babies can become fussy if the mother has consumed certain spicy or gassy foods. The mother can abstain from that food, wait a few days, and then try it again. If the infant reacts the same way, it's best to stop eating that food while nursing.

In the past, medical experts and organizations such as the AAP advised avoiding highly allergenic foods, such as peanuts, while breast-feeding. However, there is a lack of evidence that avoiding allergens plays a significant role in the prevention of food allergy in infants. For infants at high risk of developing a food allergy (because a parent or sibling has food or other allergies), there is evidence that exclusive breast-feeding for at least four months compared with feeding cow's milk–based infant formula decreases the risk early in life.[113]

> **LO 17.7: THE TAKE-HOME MESSAGE** Breast-feeding helps reduce the risk for type 2 diabetes, certain cancers, and postpartum depression, and may help mothers return to their prepregnancy weight. Breast-feeding is the least expensive and most convenient way to nourish an infant, and helps the mother and baby bond. Human milk is rich in nutrients, antibodies, and compounds that protect the infant against infections, allergies, and chronic diseases, and it may enhance the child's cognitive development. Women are advised to breast-feed exclusively for the first six months of their baby's life, and then breast-feed to supplement solid food for the remainder of the first year, or longer if desired. A mother must increase her fluid and nutrient intake to help her body produce breast milk. Nursing mothers should limit caffeine consumption and avoid illicit drugs, alcohol, smoking, and overly spicy foods.

When Is Formula a Healthy Alternative to Breast Milk?

LO 17.8 Explain why infant formula is a healthy alternative to breast milk.

Commercial infant formula is the only healthy option to breast milk. Formula is designed to match the energy-nutrient composition of breast milk. For some women, formula-feeding is a personal preference. For others it is necessary, as breast-feeding may not be possible due to illness or other circumstances.

Some Women Are Not Able to Breast-Feed

Some health conditions or lifestyle choices make breast-feeding unsafe for an infant. Women taking prescription or over-the-counter medications should check with their health care provider to ensure that the medications are safe to consume while breast-feeding. Women who have untreated, active tuberculosis, who are infected with human T-lymphotrophic virus type 1 or type ll, or who have untreated brucellosis are among those who should not breast-feed.[114] An infant born with a genetic disorder, such as galactosemia or PKU, can't metabolize breast milk and needs specialized infant formula.[115] In developed countries, women who are infected with HIV (human immunodeficiency virus), the virus that causes AIDS, should not breast-feed, as this virus can be transmitted to the child through breast milk.

Infant formula is available in several forms and varies in cost and ingredients. Infant formula is strictly regulated by the FDA, so any formula on the market in the United States can be considered safe and reliable.

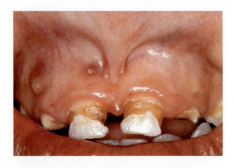

▲ **Figure 17.9 Early Childhood Caries**
When infants are given a bottle shortly before sleep, and their mouths are not sufficiently cleaned, the sugary beverage can pool in the mouth and dissolve immature tooth enamel.

early childhood caries Tooth decay from prolonged tooth contact with formula, milk, fruit juice, or other sugar-rich liquid offered to an infant in a bottle.

However, in developing countries, breast-feeding is the better option in spite of the potential danger. For HIV-infected women living in countries where there is inadequate food, an unsafe food and water supply, and/or frequent incidences of nutritional deficiencies and infectious diseases, the benefits of breast milk often outweigh the risks of HIV infection for the baby.

Formula Can Be a Healthy Alternative to Breast-Feeding

Commercial infant formula is developed to be as similar as possible to breast milk, and formula-fed infants grow and develop normally. The FDA regulates all infant formulas sold in the United States and has established specific requirements for the nutrients that the formula must contain.

Formula is typically made from cow's milk that has been altered to improve its nutrient content and digestibility. Soy protein–based formulas are free of cow's milk protein and lactose and can be used for infants who can't tolerate cow's milk protein–based formula or who are in vegan families. Hypoallergenic infant formulas are also available for infants who are unable to tolerate cow's milk or soy formulas. The AAP recommends that all formula-fed infants consume iron-fortified formulas to reduce the risk of iron deficiency during infancy.[116] Regular cow's milk should not be fed to infants, as it cannot meet the nutritional needs of the baby. Cow's milk lacks sufficient vitamin E, essential fatty acids, and iron, and provides more protein, sodium, and potassium than an infant's body can process.[117]

Commercially made infant formulas can be purchased as powder, as a concentrated liquid, or in ready-to-use forms. Powdered formula is the least expensive, while the ready-to-use form tends to be the most expensive. Care should be taken to mix the powder or concentrated liquid with the correct amount of water so the formula is not too diluted or too concentrated.

If the infant doesn't finish the bottle, the formula should be discarded, rather than saved for another feeding. The bacteria in the infant's mouth can contaminate the formula, and multiply to levels that could be harmful even if the formula is reheated. Constant reheating of the formula also destroys some of the heat-sensitive nutrients.[118] Formula should not be left out at room temperature for more than two hours, as bacteria can multiply to unhealthy levels.

Infants of any age should not be allowed to sleep with a bottle containing sugary liquids (milk, formula, fruit juice, soda, or other sweetened drinks), as this practice can lead to **early childhood caries,** sometimes called nursing bottle tooth decay (see **Figure 17.9**) and ear infections. Liquids from bottles tend to pool in the mouth during sleep. The normal bacteria in the mouth change the sugar to an acid, which gradually dissolves the immature enamel and allows tooth decay to occur.[119]

In addition, drinking from the bottle while lying down prevents liquid from fully draining from the eustachian tubes. The liquid buildup increases the risk of ear infections The American Academy of Pediatric Dentistry recommends against putting infants to sleep with bottles or sweetened pacifiers.[120] To prevent tooth decay, parents can massage and cleanse infant gums with a soft cloth after each feeding.

> **LO 17.8: THE TAKE-HOME MESSAGE** Commercially prepared infant formula is the only healthy option to breast-feeding. Commercially made formulas are modified from soy or cow's milk, and patterned after human breast milk. Cow's milk should not be given before age 1, as it is too high in protein and some minerals, and too low in fat. Powdered and concentrated formulas need to be mixed carefully so they are not too diluted or concentrated for the baby's digestive system. Avoid putting infants to sleep with baby bottles to help prevent early childhood tooth decay and ear infections.

What Are an Infant's Nutrient Needs and Why Are They So High?

LO 17.9 Discuss the nutritional needs of infants.

Parents and caregivers can be confident that adequate amounts of breast milk and commercial formulas will meet their infants' nutritional needs. Nevertheless, they benefit from knowing exactly what those nutrient needs are and why they are so high.

Infants Grow at an Accelerated Rate

During **infancy,** or the first year of life, a child experiences tremendous growth. Typically, an infant doubles his or her birth weight by about 6 months of age, and triples it by the age of 12 months. Length doubles around the end of the first year as well. Consider this growth rate in adult terms: An individual who weighs 100 pounds on January first would weigh 200 pounds by the end of June, and 300 pounds by New Year's Eve! An adult would have to eat an enormous amount of food every day to actually make this happen, but for infants, this is a normal rate of growth.

Health care providers use **growth charts** to track physical development progress. Typically, measures of head circumference, length, weight, and weight for length are used to assess growth. These measures are taken at each wellness check visit to the health care provider, about once a month for the first year. The information obtained from the measurements is plotted on a growth chart, placing the child into a **percentile.** Percentiles rank the infant with regard to other infants of the same age in a reference group. For example, a 4-month-old who is in the 25th percentile for weight for that age weighs less than 75 percent of 4-month-olds and weighs the same as or more than 25 percent[121] (see **Figure 17.10**). Regular checkups enable health care providers to identify and address any inconsistencies in patterns of growth.

Infants are doing much more than getting heavier and longer. Cognitive and social developments are also under way. As time goes by, infant communication skills go beyond crying, and by about 3 months of age a baby starts to smile. As a child gets older, preferences become clearer, too: for particular people (such as the mom), for specific activities (getting kisses or being held), and for certain foods (such as mashed bananas).[122]

An infant who does not receive adequate nutrition may have difficulty reaching developmental **milestones** (**Figure 17.11**), which can be thought of as checkpoints of physical, social, and cognitive development. Parents and pediatricians should work together to be sure that infants reach these checkpoints.

If a child doesn't reach the appropriate milestones, he or she may eventually develop a condition called *failure to thrive (FTT)*. A child with FTT is delayed in physical growth or size or does not gain enough weight. Poor appetite, poor diet, or a medical problem that has not yet been diagnosed can all cause FTT. Sometimes, FTT results from inappropriate care or neglect. Caregivers and health care providers need to be aware of the signs of this condition and watch for those signs in their children and patients.

Optimal infant nutrition is sometimes hindered by circumstance. In less-developed countries where poverty is the norm and food is scarce, problems such as protein-energy malnutrition (see Chapter 6) are common. Even in developed countries, problems with poor infant nutrition may affect growth. For example, infants fed juice, water, or cow's milk instead of adequate amounts of breast milk or iron-fortified formula may develop iron-deficiency anemia (see Chapter 13). Or, if a breast-fed infant does not begin consuming iron in solid foods by 4 to 6 months of age, his stores of iron run low, paving the way for anemia.

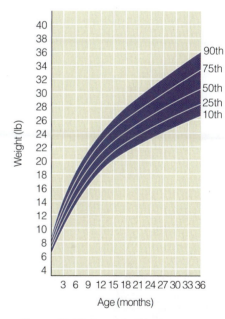

▲ **Figure 17.10 Growth Chart**
Growth charts can help determine if a child is growing at a healthy rate for her age.

infancy The age range from birth to 12 months.

growth charts Series of percentile curves that illustrate the distribution of selected body measurements in U.S. children.

percentile The most commonly used clinical indicator to assess the size and growth patterns of children in the United States. An individual child is ranked according to the percentage of the reference population he or she equals or exceeds.

milestones Objectives or significant events that occur during development.

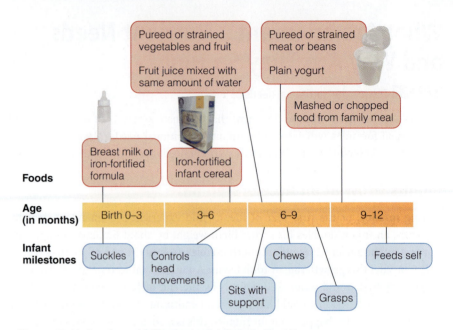

Figure 17.11 Foods and Milestones for Baby's First Year
During the first year after birth, an infant's diet will progress from breast milk or formula to age-appropriate versions of family meals.

Infants Have Specific Kilocalorie, Iron, and Other Nutrient Needs

Though every child is different, there are certain guidelines to follow to meet an infant's nutrient needs. For examples, infants under the age of 6 months require, on average, 108 kilocalories per kilogram of body weight every day.[123] Imagine a similar proportion of kilocalories at the scale of an adult who weighs 150 pounds (68 kilograms)—it would work out to 7,344 (68 kg × 108) kilocalories per day, more than twice the kilocalories required by some elite Olympic athletes!

Carbohydrate, protein, and fat needs change within the first year of life. Infants up to 6 months of age should consume 60 grams of carbohydrate per day, which increases to 95 grams per day at 7 to 12 months. Infants need about 9 grams of protein per day during the first six months of life, and 11 grams daily in the second six months. (The DRIs for infants are listed on the inside front cover of this textbook.) There's no need to limit fat in the first year of life, and doing so could negatively impact physical and mental growth and development. Babies should never be put on weight-loss diets.

Three nutrients must be added to an infant's diet: vitamin K, vitamin D, and iron. All newborns should receive an injection of vitamin K at birth to ensure that their blood clots in a timely fashion. This is necessary because infants are born with a sterile gut and lack the intestinal bacteria that produce vitamin K.[124]

The amount of vitamin D in breast milk is inadequate to prevent rickets, so infants should also receive 400 IU of vitamin D drops daily beginning during the first two months of life. Infants exclusively fed adequate amounts of vitamin D–fortified formula do not require additional vitamin D. Once they reach age 1, children can drink vitamin D–fortified milk instead of infant formula or breast milk; however, if they don't get enough vitamin D through foods, including fortified milk, they may still need supplementation. Exposure of the infant's skin to sunlight to obtain vitamin D is not recommended because it can cause sunburns and increases the risk of skin cancer.[125]

Iron-rich foods, such as enriched cereals, should be introduced at around 6 months, as the infant's stores of iron are depleted by this time. Premature infants, who have lower iron stores because they were born early, may need iron supplementation before age 6 months.[126]

Because vitamin B_{12} is naturally found only in animal foods, supplementation may be recommended if the infant is being breast-fed by a strictly vegan mother. If the child's water supply is nonfluoridated, or if bottled water is used for mixing formula, a fluoride supplement may also be necessary.[127]

An infant's fluid needs are nearly always met with adequate consumption of breast milk or formula. Extra fluid is only necessary in hot climates or to rehydrate following episodes of diarrhea, fever, or vomiting, when the body loses fluid and electrolytes. Extra fluid should still be limited even in these circumstances, as filling up on water might keep a baby from being hungry for nutrient-rich breast milk or formula.[128]

Beverages such as apple juice are a popular component of infant diets; however, the AAP suggests avoiding the introduction of juice until the child is a toddler, or waiting at least until 6 to 9 months of age before giving juice to infants, and limiting daily intake to 4 to 6 ounces.[129] Though juice provides many nutrients, it often displaces more nutrient-dense foods. Juices should be given only in moderation, and only 100 percent juice, not juice drinks, should be used.

> **LO 17.9: THE TAKE-HOME MESSAGE** Infants grow at a dramatic rate during the first year of life. Caregivers and health care providers can monitor infant growth by making sure the child achieves appropriate developmental milestones and by using CDC growth charts. Nutrient needs during the first year of life are substantial, and dietary supplements may be needed in certain circumstances.

When Are Solid Foods Safe to Introduce to Infants?

LO 17.10 Explain when and how solid foods should be introduced to infants.

Often, proud parents can hardly wait to show off how their baby is eating "real food." It is an exciting time, because eating **solid foods** represents infant maturity. Solid foods should be introduced at around 4 to 6 months of age.[130] However, parents should not suddenly decide to serve their baby steak! The infant must be nutritionally, physiologically, and physically ready to eat solid foods.

Solid Foods May Be Introduced Once Certain Milestones Are Met

Common sense tells us that as babies get bigger in size, they need more nutrients. Thus, an older, larger infant has higher nutrient needs than a younger, smaller one. Though breast milk can technically still provide most nutrients until age 4 to 6 months, introducing solid foods helps infants to meet their nutritional needs and develop feeding skills.

Before solid foods are introduced, the infant needs to be physiologically ready; that is, body systems must be able to process solid foods. At birth, and in early infancy, the GI tract and organs such as the kidneys cannot process solid foods. Even when an infant is nutritionally and physiologically ready for solid foods, he also must be physically ready. Physical readiness is specific to the individual child and depends on whether he or she has met the necessary developmental milestones. To determine physical readiness, the following questions must be answered:

- Has the **tongue-thrust reflex** faded? The tongue-thrust reflex protects infants against choking. The tongue automatically pushes outward when a substance is placed on it. The reflex fades at around 4 to 6 months of age.
- Does the infant have head and neck control? Without such control, the infant is at greater risk for choking on solids.

solid foods Foods other than breast milk or formula given to an infant, usually around 4 to 6 months of age.

tongue-thrust reflex A forceful protrusion of the tongue in response to an oral stimulus, such as a spoon.

- Does the infant swallow with ease?
- Is the infant able to sit with support?
- Does the infant have the ability to turn his or her head to indicate "I'm full!"?

When the answer to all of these questions is "yes," it is safe and realistic to begin offering solid foods. If the answer to any question is "no," parents and caregivers should wait until the infant does develop the appropriate skills.[131] Parents who have any doubts about their child's readiness for solid foods should consult with their pediatrician.

Solid Foods Should Be Introduced Gradually

Solid foods such as iron-fortified rice cereal, oatmeal, and pureed meats can be introduced to infants between 4 and 6 months of age.

Once an infant is ready for solids, foods should be introduced gradually to make sure the child isn't allergic or intolerant, and to increase acceptance as children learn to take food from a spoon. The best practice is to introduce only one new food per week.[132] Rice cereal heavily diluted with breast milk or infant formula is often offered to infants as a first food, so there is a familiar taste mixed in with the new taste. These is no scientific evidence regarding the best progression of foods for infants, although parents are often advised to leave fruits for last, so that babies become accustomed to foods that are less sweet. As long as a child isn't allergic to any food, and foods are introduced one at a time, the order of introduction of cereal, meat, fruits, and vegetables doesn't much matter in the long run.[133] Children should not have cow's milk of any type until after 1 year of age.

After introducing a new food, parents should wait at least two to three days to assess if the child is allergic.[134] Iron-fortified rice cereal, pureed meats, and pureed vegetables are the least likely to cause an allergic reaction. Allergic reactions may range from a very mild tingling sensation in the mouth or swelling of the tongue and the throat to difficulty breathing, hives, vomiting, abdominal cramps, diarrhea, a drop in blood pressure, and loss of consciousness or death. (See Health Connection: What Causes Food Allergies? on page 662 for an explanation of the mechanism of allergic reactions.) A baby's diet may include highly allergenic foods (such as cow's milk protein, egg, soy, wheat, peanuts, tree nuts, fish, and shellfish) once a few other foods are well tolerated first. To be safe, highly allergenic foods are best first introduced at home, rather than at a day care or at a restaurant.[135]

Phasing in solid foods should take place over a period of several months. Infants should eat pureed foods at first. As the infant's chewing and swallowing skills improve with practice, pureed foods can be replaced with soft, cooked foods. Refer again to Figure 17.11, which shows the progression in the infant's diet from breast milk or formula to age-appropriate versions of family meals.

Many parents wonder if they should make homemade baby food. This is an admirable idea, and gives the child exposure to fresh, unprocessed meals. However, many store-bought baby foods are of high quality and comparable to homemade. While some companies opt to add sugar, salt, or other less-desirable ingredients, others use organic produce or no preservatives or additives. One benefit of homemade food that everyone might agree upon is the financial savings—there are no added costs for fancy packaging and labels. The choice to use homemade or commercial baby food is up to the parent or caregiver.

Some Foods Are Not Appropriate for Infants

Not surprisingly, many foods are not appropriate for a baby. Some foods, like hot dog rounds or raw carrot slices, present a choking hazard and need to be cut into very small pieces or avoided altogether. Because infants have few teeth, foods should have a soft texture so they do not require excessive chewing; ideally, foods with texture should easily melt in the mouth, like a cracker. No matter what the food, infants should always be supervised by a responsible adult when eating.

Though some cultures and families have used honey-dipped pacifiers to calm infants for generations, this is a dangerous practice. Honey has been known to carry spores of Clostridium botulinum, which can lead to a fatal disease called **botulism.** Infants with botulism become lethargic, feed poorly, and suffer from constipation. They have a weak cry and poor muscle tone. Untreated symptoms may cause paralysis of the arms, legs, trunk, and respiratory muscles. The resulting respiratory failure is what makes this disease potentially deadly. Older children (1 year and older) and adults can consume honey without these concerns because their mature intestinal tracts are not as susceptible to the spores.[136]

Parents and caregivers also need to think twice before adding certain seasonings to their infants' foods. The high salt, sugar, and fat content of restaurant and processed foods, as well as our own habits in the kitchen and at the table have taught us to think that food only tastes "right" if it is salty, sweet, or buttery. Infants do not care if food is bland, and there is no nutritional benefit to enhancing foods with additional salt, sugar, and fat, such as butter or margarine. At this stage of the life cycle, infants are learning to find the natural flavors in whole foods to be satisfying, without added kilocalories, fat, or sodium.

Do babies need fiber to keep them "regular" like adults? Though fiber is useful for many reasons, too much can actually be harmful to an infant because it can whisk nutrients through the GI tract before they have a chance to be absorbed. At this time, no recommendations have been established for fiber during the first year of life.

LO 17.10: THE TAKE-HOME MESSAGE An infant must be physically and physiologically ready before being introduced to solid foods. Solid foods should be introduced gradually and cautiously. Choking hazards should be avoided, and children should always be supervised while eating. Avoid excessive amounts of seasonings such as salt, sugar, and butter in the infant's diet. Parents and caregivers must educate themselves about foods that are appropriate and those that are not in order to keep the infant safe and healthy.

botulism A rare but serious paralytic illness caused by the bacterium Clostridium botulinum.

What Causes Food Allergies?

LO 17.11 Explain how a food allergen causes a potentially life-threatening reaction.

One-year-old Adam was playing in the sandbox at the neighborhood playground, when his babysitter pulled a peanut butter cookie from her backpack. She broke off a small bite of the cookie and handed it to Adam, assuming that he must be hungry for his afternoon snack.

After a minute of chewing, Adam started to wheeze and have difficulty breathing. Then he vomited. The sitter quickly used her cell phone to call for emergency help. She gave the rest of the cookie to one of the paramedics who rushed Adam to the hospital. Unbeknownst to the sitter, Adam had developed a food allergy to peanuts.

A **food allergy** is an abnormal physical reaction of the immune system in response to the consumption of a particular food allergen. **Food allergens** are proteins that are not broken down during cooking or by the body's gastric juices and enzymes during digestion. Because they are not degraded, they enter the body intact, and can cause an adverse reaction by the immune system because the allergen is perceived as a foreign invader.

Food Allergies Are Immune System Reactions

A food allergy reaction occurs in two stages: the "sensitization stage" followed by the actual response, or "allergic reaction stage." In the first stage (**Figure 17.12**) a food allergen doesn't produce a reaction. Instead it sensitizes, or introduces, itself to the immune system. In response to the initial introduction of the food allergens, the immune system creates an army of antibodies that enter the blood. The antibodies attach to **mast cells** found in connective tissues, setting the stage for a potential future allergic reaction.

The reaction stage occurs when a person consumes the food allergen again.

The food allergen comes in contact with the mast cells carrying the antibody for the particular allergen. The mast cells release chemicals such as heparin and histamine that trigger a chain of reactions in the body. The areas in the body that manifest a food allergy reaction are those where mast cells are most prevalent, such as under the skin and in the mucosa. In very sensitive individuals, even a small amount of a food allergen—just one peanut, for example—can trigger an allergic reaction.[137] Reactions appear quickly after eating the food. In fact, an itchiness in the mouth may occur as soon as the food touches the tongue, and skin reactions and difficulty breathing may develop within minutes. After the food reaches the stomach and begins to be digested, vomiting and/or diarrhea may result. Once they enter the bloodstream, food allergens can cause a

food allergy An abnormal reaction by the immune system to a particular food.

food allergens Proteins that are not broken down by cooking or digestion and enter the body intact, causing an adverse reaction by the immune system.

mast cells Cells in connective tissue to which antibodies attach, setting the stage for potential future allergic reactions.

The eight most common food allergens are milk, eggs, fish, shellfish, tree nuts, peanuts, soy, and wheat.

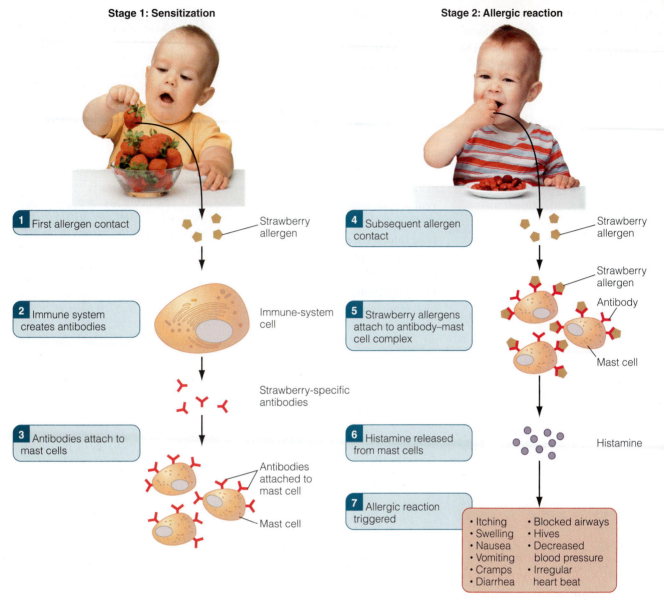

Stage 1: Sensitization

1 First allergen contact

Strawberry allergen

2 Immune system creates antibodies

Immune-system cell

Strawberry-specific antibodies

3 Antibodies attach to mast cells

Antibodies attached to mast cell

Mast cell

Stage 2: Allergic reaction

4 Subsequent allergen contact

Strawberry allergen

Strawberry allergen

Antibody

5 Strawberry allergens attach to antibody–mast cell complex

Mast cell

6 Histamine released from mast cells

Histamine

7 Allergic reaction triggered

- Itching
- Swelling
- Nausea
- Vomiting
- Cramps
- Diarrhea
- Blocked airways
- Hives
- Decreased blood pressure
- Irregular heart beat

▲ **Figure 17.12 Reactions to Allergens**
The reaction stage occurs when a person eats the food allergens for the second and subsequent times.

big drop in blood pressure. A severe allergic reaction can lead to **anaphylaxis,** a potentially life-threatening condition. Individuals with allergies or their caretakers often carry a syringe injector of epinephrine (adrenaline) to help treat a reaction. Epinephrine constricts blood vessels, relaxes the muscles in the lungs to help with breathing, and decreases swelling and hives.

Some Foods Are Highly Allergenic

Any food can cause an allergy, but 90 percent of food allergies are caused by eggs, cow's milk, peanuts, soy, wheat, tree nuts (such as walnuts), fish, and shellfish. The FDA requires that the food label

anaphylaxis Severe, life-threatening allergic reaction involving a sudden drop in blood pressure and constriction of the airways in the lungs, which inhibits the ability to breathe.

What Causes Food Allergies? **663**

state whether the product contains protein from any of these eight major foods known to cause an allergic reaction. The FDA is continually working with food manufacturers and consumer groups to improve public education about food allergies and the seriousness of anaphylactic reactions, in particular for the most common sources of food allergies.[138]

The proportion of children in the United States aged 0 to 17 with a reported food allergy rose from 3.4 percent in 1997–1999 to 5.1 percent in 2009–2011, according to the Centers for Disease Control and Prevention.[139] It's unclear why food allergies are rising

food intolerance Adverse reaction to a food that does not involve an immune response.

in children; however, some children do outgrow their food allergies. An estimated 80 to 90 percent of egg, milk, wheat, and soy allergies disappear by age 5 years,[140] and up to 20 percent of children with a peanut allergy will eventually outgrow it.[141] Food allergies that are not outgrown cannot be cured; only strict avoidance of food allergens and early recognition and management of allergic reactions to food help to prevent serious health consequences.

A food allergy is different from a **food intolerance.** The symptoms of a food intolerance, such as lactose intolerance, the inability to digest lactose, may mimic a food allergy, but a food intolerance does not involve the immune system.

LO 17.11: THE TAKE-HOME MESSAGE
Food allergies are on the rise in children, but the reason for the increased prevalence is not known. Food allergies are caused by proteins in foods called allergens, which are interpreted by the body as foreign and trigger bodily processes that cause breathing difficulties and could result in death. Any food can cause a food allergy, but most food allergies are caused by eggs, cow's milk, peanuts, soy, wheat, tree nuts, fish, and shellfish. Children may outgrow food allergies, but the only way to safely manage them is to avoid the offending allergen.

Visual Chapter Summary

LO 17.1 There Are Several Critical Periods of Prenatal Development

An average healthy pregnancy lasts about 39 to 40 weeks and is divided into three 13-week trimesters. The initial two weeks after conception is called the preembryo stage, and it's when the zygote implants into the uterine wall. The zygote gradually develops into an embryo during weeks three through eight. This is a critical developmental period when major congenital anomalies can occur if the embryo is exposed to insults. After eight weeks, the embryo is called a fetus. It is during this critical period of development that nutrients, oxygen, and waste products begin to be exchanged between the mother and fetus through the placenta. Proper nutrition and avoidance of known toxins, such as alcohol, are important to support the proper development of the embryo and the fetus.

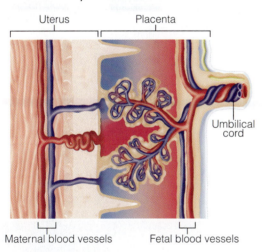

Uterus   Placenta

Umbilical cord

Maternal blood vessels   Fetal blood vessels

LO 17.2 Nutrient Intake and Healthy Behaviors Are Important for a Healthy Pregnancy

Future mothers and fathers should make healthy diet and lifestyle choices prior to pregnancy. For healthier sperm that are more likely to fertilize an egg, men should stop smoking, abstain from alcohol or drink only in moderation, strive for a healthy body weight, and consume a balanced diet. Prior to and during pregnancy, women should also abstain from alcohol, smoking, illicit drugs, and certain prescription and over-the-counter medications and supplements. They should also limit caffeine, and, before conception, strive for a healthy weight on a balanced diet. In addition, women should consume adequate amounts of folic acid to reduce the risk of neural tube defects. Women in their childbearing years should avoid fish that contain high amounts of methylmercury but eat fish considered safe by health experts. Women with preexisting conditions should work closely with their health care professional to manage them prior to and during pregnancy.

LO 17.3 Certain Nutrients Are Important during the First Trimester

A woman who starts her pregnancy at a healthy weight should gain 25 to 35 pounds during the course of her pregnancy. Women who are underweight or overweight prior to pregnancy, or who are carrying multiple fetuses, will have different weight gain goals. A woman's needs for many nutrients, including folate, iron, zinc, and copper, increase by up to 50 percent during pregnancy. With the exception of iron, for which a prenatal supplement is usually needed, most nutrient requirements can be met with a balanced diet. Care should be taken to avoid consuming too much preformed vitamin A (retinol), which can cause birth defects. Sufficient kilocalories, carbohydrates, protein, alpha-linolenic acid, and choline are necessary throughout pregnancy. Awareness of food safety is also important, as bacteria such as Listeria monocytogenes may cause miscarriage, premature labor, delivery of a low birth weight infant, developmental problems, or even infant death.

LO 17.4 Additional Carbohydrates and Protein Are Important during the Second Trimester

Many pregnant women find that the nausea and fatigue of the first trimester diminish during the second trimester, and appetite begins to return. The mother's kilocalorie needs also increase. Women who begin pregnancy at a healthy weight need about 340 more kilocalories daily than before becoming pregnant and should gain about a pound per week. Pregnant women need at least 175 grams of carbohydrate and 71 grams of protein as part of a balanced diet. The increased nutrient needs of the second trimester can be met with an array of nutritious foods. The risk of gestational diabetes and hypertension can be reduced during the second trimester with a healthy diet, daily exercise, and gaining the appropriate amount of weight.

1 whole-wheat English muffin
2 tbs peanut butter
5 baby carrots

340
total kilocalories

LO 17.5 Healthy Eating Behaviors and Weight Gain Are Important during the Third Trimester

During the last trimester of pregnancy, women who began pregnancy at a healthy weight should be consuming about 450 more kilocalories daily than before pregnancy, and continue to gain about 1 pound per week. Women who were underweight or overweight will need to eat more or less. The slower movement of food through the GI tract can contribute to heartburn and constipation. To minimize heartburn, pregnant women should eat smaller but frequent, healthy meals, eliminate spicy foods that may irritate the esophagus, and avoid lying down immediately after meals. Exercise and consuming fiber-rich foods, along with plenty of fluids, can help prevent or alleviate constipation.

Third trimester

Total weight gain ~30 lbs

- Maternal fat stores (~7 lbs)
- Uterus and breast (4 lbs)
- Blood (3–4 lbs)
- Fetus (~7 lbs)
- Placenta, amniotic fluid, and other fluids (~8 lbs)

LO 17.6 Younger, Older, or Low-Income Mothers-to-Be Face Special Challenges

Teenagers and women over age 35 may face additional challenges during pregnancy. Teenage mothers are at greater risk for pregnancy-induced hypertension, iron-deficiency anemia, and delivering premature and low birth weight babies. While many older women have healthy pregnancies, they are more prone to developing gestational diabetes and high blood pressure, and may begin their pregnancies with more health problems than younger women. Also, older women have a greater risk for having pregnancies affected by Down syndrome or other birth defects. Low-income women, who may not have access to quality health care and a steady supply of healthy food, are at greater risk of iron-deficiency anemia and premature and low birth weight infants.

LO 17.7 Breast-Feeding Benefits Both Mother and Child

Breast-feeding is the gold standard for feeding an infant. It provides physical, emotional, and financial benefits and convenience for the mother and nutritional and health benefits for the infant. Breast milk is rich in nutrients, antibodies, and other compounds that provide the infant with a disease-fighting boost until the baby's own immune system matures. Experts recommend that women exclusively breast-feed for the first six months of a baby's life and for as long after that as baby and mother desire. Breast-feeding mothers should eat an additional 330 to 400 kilocalories daily as part of a balanced diet to produce adequate amounts of nutrient-rich breast milk.

LO 17.8 Infant Formula Is the Only Healthy Alternative to Breast Milk

If an infant isn't breast-fed, the only healthy alternative is commercially made formula. Commercially made formulas are modified from soy or cow's milk, and patterned as much as possible after human breast milk. For some women, formula-feeding is a personal preference. For others it is necessary, as breast-feeding may not be possible due to illness or other circumstances. To prevent tooth decay and ear infections, infants should never be put to sleep with a bottle of infant formula, breast milk, or juice.

LO 17.9 Infants Have Specific Nutrient Needs

An infant typically doubles his or her birth weight by around 6 months of age, and triples it by 12 months. Poor infant nutrition interferes with proper growth and a child's ability to meet developmental milestones. Infants need approximately 108 kilocalories per kilogram of body weight during the first six months of life. All infants should receive a vitamin K injection at birth, and breast-fed infants need vitamin D supplements. Infants older than 6 months need to begin consuming iron through food sources, as their stored iron supply is depleted around this time.

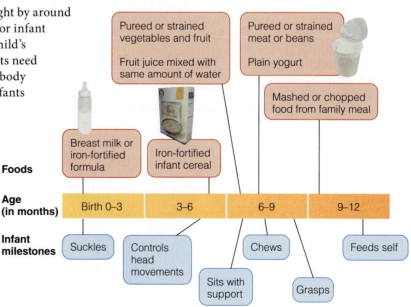

LO 17.10 Solid Foods Should Be Introduced Gradually after Certain Milestones Are Reached

An infant is ready to begin eating solid foods if the infant's birth weight has doubled, he has the ability to sit with support and can control his or her head and neck, his tongue-thrust reflex has faded, and his swallowing skills are mature. Once an infant is ready for solids, foods should be introduced gradually to make sure the child isn't allergic or intolerant. The best suggestion is to introduce only one new food per week. Choking hazards should be avoided, and children should always be supervised while eating. Avoid excessive amounts of seasonings such as salt, sugar, and butter in the infant's diet.

LO 17.11 A Food Allergy Is an Abnormal Immune Reaction

Food allergies are caused by specific proteins in foods that trigger an abnormal response by the immune system. The mast cells that respond to the allergen release heparin, histamine, and other chemicals that cause itching, swelling, hives, nausea, vomiting, constricted airways, and decreased blood pressure. A severe allergic reaction can lead to anaphylaxis and, potentially, unconsciousness and death. Epinephrine injections can counteract allergic reactions. Children may outgrow food allergies, but the only way to safely manage them is to avoid the offending allergen. Ninety percent of food allergies are caused by one of the eight most common food allergens: eggs, cow's milk, peanuts, soy, wheat, tree nuts, fish, and shellfish. The FDA requires labeling to indicate the presence of any of these ingredients.

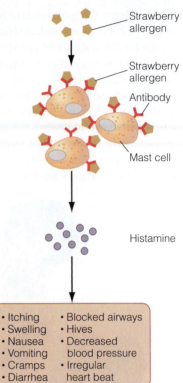

Strawberry allergen

Strawberry allergen

Antibody

Mast cell

Histamine

- Itching
- Swelling
- Nausea
- Vomiting
- Cramps
- Diarrhea
- Blocked airways
- Hives
- Decreased blood pressure
- Irregular heart beat

Terms To Know

- conception
- zygote
- embryo
- placenta
- fetus
- umbilical cord
- critical periods
- metabolic or fetal programming

- low birth weight
- small for gestational age (SGA)
- sudden infant death syndrome (SIDS)
- botanicals
- hyperemesis gravidarum
- pica
- gestational diabetes
- macrosomia
- jaundice

- pregnancy-induced hypertension
- gestational hypertension
- preeclampsia
- eclampsia
- lactation
- letdown response
- breast-feeding
- colostrum
- early childhood caries
- infancy

- growth charts
- percentile
- milestones
- solid foods
- tongue-thrust reflex
- botulism
- food allergy
- food allergens
- mast cells
- anaphylaxis
- food intolerance

Check Your Understanding

1. Sarah is trying to get pregnant. When should she start consuming 400 micrograms of folic acid every day to prevent neural tube birth defects?
   a. immediately
   b. during the first trimester
   c. during the second trimester
   d. during the last trimester

2. The production and function of sperm may decrease due to
   a. insufficient iron in the diet.
   b. insufficient copper in the diet.
   c. insufficient fat in the diet.
   d. obesity.

3. The definition of a low birth weight baby is one who is born weighing less than
   a. 5 ½ pounds.
   b. 6 ½ pounds.
   c. 7 ½ pounds.
   d. 8 ½ pounds.

4. Mary Ellen is pregnant and going out to a seafood restaurant for dinner. Which of the following fish should she *not* order because of its high methylmercury content?
   a. flounder
   b. shrimp
   c. swordfish
   d. lobster

5. A woman who began pregnancy at a healthy weight should gain _____ pounds during pregnancy.
   a. 15 to 25
   b. 20 to 30
   c. 25 to 35
   d. 30 to 40

6. During pregnancy, a woman's need for many nutrients increases. Which mineral requirement is most likely to go unsatisfied through diet alone?
   a. iron
   b. potassium
   c. sodium
   d. calcium

7. During the second trimester of pregnancy, a woman who began her pregnancy at a healthy weight should increase her daily kilocalorie intake by
   a. 340 kilocalories.
   b. 400 kilocalories.
   c. 440 kilocalories.
   d. 500 kilocalories.

8. Breast-feeding can have which of the following benefits for both mother *and* child?
   a. relief of intestinal disorders
   b. reduced risk of type 2 diabetes
   c. fewer respiratory infections
   d. lower chance of meningitis

9. Andy is a healthy, 3-month-old baby boy who is being breast-fed by his mother. Which of the following nutrients needs to be added to his diet?
   a. vitamin D
   b. potassium
   c. vitamin C
   d. calcium

10. Six-month-old Cathy is ready for solid foods. The one food that should not be introduced in her diet yet is
    a. oatmeal.
    b. rice cereal.
    c. pureed vegetables.
    d. cow's milk.

Answers

1. (a) Experts recommend that all women who are capable of becoming pregnant should consume 400 micrograms of folic acid daily to reduce the risk of neural tube birth defects, which occur during the first 30 days after conception. Folic acid is important throughout pregnancy, too.

2. (d) Obesity, along with smoking and alcohol abuse, is associated with the decreased production and functioning of sperm and may delay time to conception.

3. (a) A baby born weighing less than 5 ½ pounds is considered a low birth weight baby.

4. (c) The swordfish is off limits during pregnancy because of its high methylmercury content.

5. (c) A woman who begins pregnancy at a healthy weight should gain 25 to 35 pounds by the time she delivers.

6. (a) Because a pregnant woman's increased iron needs cannot be easily met through the diet, she will likely need a prescribed prenatal supplement. She can get the potassium, sodium, and calcium she needs by eating a balanced diet.

7. (a) A pregnant woman needs 340 extra kilocalories daily during the second trimester to meet her needs. During the third trimester, she needs an extra 450 kilocalories every day. She doesn't need additional daily kilocalories during the first trimester, but does have additional nutrient needs, so she should be sure to eat nutrient-dense foods.

8. (b) Breast-feeding reduces the risk of type 2 diabetes in both the mother and child. The other benefits—fewer intestinal disorders and respiratory infections, and lower risk of meningitis—affect the baby only.

9. (a) While breast milk is an ideal food for baby Andy, it doesn't contain enough vitamin D, so he should receive daily drops.

10. (d) Cathy should not have cow's milk until at least 1 year of age.

Answers to True or False?

1. **False.** A man's diet and other lifestyle habits, such as smoking and drinking alcohol, can affect his fertility.

2. **False.** Any type of alcohol, including red wine, can harm a growing fetus.

3. **False.** Though it's called morning sickness, nausea and vomiting can happen at any time of day, and may last past the first trimester.

4. **False.** Physical activity is beneficial for most mothers-to-be, though certain potentially dangerous activities need to be avoided.

5. **False.** Formula is a healthy alternative, but breast milk is nearly always best for a baby.

6. **True.** Antibodies in breast milk are passed from the mother to the baby,

which supports the infant's immune system.

7. **False.** Infants should never be put on a weight-loss diet. Babies need kilocalories and fat to support their rapid growth and development.

8. **False.** Most infants receive an injection of vitamin K at birth, and supplemental vitamin D is needed in an infant's diet.

9. **False.** Commercially prepared baby food is safe and nutritious.

10. **False.** There is no evidence that restricting known allergens in an infant's diet affects a child's food allergy risk.

Web Resources

- For more information on meal planning during pregnancy and lactation, visit ChooseMyPlate for pregnant and breast-feeding women at www.choosemyplate.gov/pregnancy-breastfeeding/pregnancy-nutritional-needs.html
- For more information on breast-feeding, visit the La Leche League International website at www.llli.org
- For more information on children and their dietary needs, visit the American Academy of Pediatrics at www.aap.org
- To obtain growth charts and guidelines for their use, visit www.cdc.gov/nchs/nhanes.htm
- For more information on food allergies, visit the Food Allergy and Anaphylaxis Network at www.foodallergy.org

References

1. The American Congress of Obstetrians and Gynecologists. The American College of Obstetricians and Gynecologists Committee on Obstetric Practice Society for Maternal-Fetal Medicine. 2013. *Definition of Term Pregnancy.* Available at www.acog.org/Resources_And_Publications/Committee_Opinions/Committee_on_Obstetric_Practice/Definition_of_Term_Pregnancy. Accessed May 2014.

2. Painter, R. C., S. R. de Rooij, P. M. Bossuyt, T. A. Simmers, C. Osmond, D. J. Barker, et al. 2006. Early Onset of Coronary Artery Disease after Prenatal Exposure to the Dutch Famine. *American Journal of Clinical Nutrition* 84:322–327.

3. Zajewska, H., M. Ruszczynski, and A. Chmielewska. 2010. Effects of Iron Supplementation in Nonanemic Pregnant Women, Infants, and Young Children on the Mental Performance and Psychomotor Development of Children: A Systematic Review of Randomized Controlled Trials. *American Journal of Clinical Nutrition* 91:1684–1690.

4. Tarry-Adkins, J. L., and S. E. Ozanne. 2011. Mechanisms of Early Life Programming: Current Knowledge and Future Directions. *American Journal of Clinical Nutrition* 94(6 Suppl):1765S–1771S.

5. Stover, P. J., and M. A. Caudill. 2008. Genetic and Epigenetic Contributions to Human Nutrition and Health: Managing Genome-Diet Interactions. *Journal of the American Dietetic Association* 108:1480–1487.

6. Poston, L., L. F. Harthoorn, and E. M. van der Beek. 2011. Obesity in Pregnancy: Implications for the Mother and Lifelong Health of the Child. A Consensus Statement. *Pediatric Research* 69:175–180.

7. Institute of Medicine. 2009. *Weight Gain during Pregnancy: Reexamining the Guidelines.* Available at www.ncbi.nlm.nih.gov. Accessed May 2014.

8. Mayo Clinic. 2012. *Male Infertility.* Available at www.mayoclinic.org/diseases-conditions/male-infertility/basics/causes/con-20033113. Accessed May 2014.

9. Young, S. S., B. Eskenazi, F. M. Marchetti, G. Block, and A. Wyrobek. 2008. The Association of Folate, Zinc and Antioxidant Intake with Sperm Aneuploidy in Healthy Non-Smoking Men. *Human Reproduction* 23:1014–1022.

10. Kaiser, L., and L. Allen. 2008. Position of the American Dietetic Association: Nutrition and Lifestyle for a Healthy Pregnancy Outcome. *Journal of the American Dietetic Association* 108:553–561.

11. National Institute of Diabetes and Digestive and Kidney Diseases. 2012. *Do You Know Some of the Health Risks of Being Overweight?* Available at www.win.niddk.nih.gov/publications/health_risks.htm#k. Accessed May 2014.

12. Viswanathan, M., A. M. Siega-Riz, et al. 2008. Outcomes of Maternal Weight Gain, Evidence Report/Technology Assessment No. 168. Agency for Healthcare Research and Quality. Rockville, MD.

13. Kaiser. Position of the American Dietetic Association: Nutrition and Lifestyle for a Healthy Pregnancy Outcome; Ramachenderan, J., J. Bradford, and M. Mclean. 2008. Maternal Obesity and Pregnancy Complications: A Review. *Australian and New Zealand Journal of Obstetrics and Gynaecology* 48:228–235.

14. Centers for Disease Control and Prevention. 2014. *Reproductive Health: Pregnancy Complications.* Available at www.cdc.gov/reproductivehealth/maternalinfanthealth/pregcomplications.htm. Accessed April 2014.

15. March of Dimes Foundation. 2014. *Overweight and Obesity during Pregnancy.* Available at www.marchofdimes.com/pregnancy/overweight-and-obesity-during-pregnancy.aspx. Accessed April 2014.

16. Kaiser, et al. 2008. Position of the American Dietetic Association: Nutrition and Lifestyle for a Healthy Pregnancy Outcome.

17. Tam, W. H., R. C. Ma, X. Yang, A. M. Li, G. T. C. Ko, A. P. S. Kang, et al. 2010. Glucose Intolerance and Cardiometabolic Risk in Adolescents Exposed to Maternal Gestational Diabetes. *Diabetes Care* 122:1229–1234.

18. March of Dimes Foundation. *Your Premature Baby.* Available at www.marchofdimes.com/baby/premature_indepth.html. Accessed April 2014.

19. U.S. Preventive Services Task Force. May 2009. *Folic Acid for the Prevention of Neural Tube Defects: U.S. Preventive Services Task Force Recommendation Statement.* AHRQ Publication No. 09-05132-EF-2. Available at www.uspreventiveservicestaskforce.org/uspstf09/folicacid/folicacidrs.htm. Accessed May 2014.

20. March of Dimes Foundation. 2012. *Caffeine in Pregnancy.* Available at www.marchofdimes.com/pregnancy/caffeine-in-pregnancy.aspx. Accessed May 2014.

21. March of Dimes Foundation. 2010. *Smoking during Pregnancy.* Available at www.marchofdimes.com/pregnancy/smoking-during-pregnancy.aspx. Accessed May 2014.

22. U.S. Department of Health and Human Services. U.S. Surgeon General. 2014. *The Health Consequences of Smoking—50 Years of Progress: A Report of the Surgeon General, 2014.* Available at www.surgeongeneral.gov/library/reports/50-years-of-progress. Accessed May 2014.

23. Kaiser, et al. 2008. Position of the American Dietetic Association: Nutrition and Lifestyle for a Healthy Pregnancy Outcome.

24. U.S. Department of Health and Human Services. 2005. *U.S. Surgeon General Releases Advisory on Alcohol Use in Pregnancy.* Available at www.surgeongeneral.gov/news/2005/02/sg02222005.html. Accessed November 2012.

25. Johns Hopkins Medicine. Health Library. *Illegal Drug Use and Pregnancy.* Available at www.hopkinsmedicine.org/healthlibrary/conditions/pregnancy_and_childbirth/illegal_drug_use_and_pregnancy_85,P01208. Accessed May 2014.

26. Dog, T. L. 2009. The Use of Botanicals During Pregnancy and Lactation. *Alternative Therapies* 15:54–58.

27. Jones, T., and T. Lawson. 1998. Profound Neonatal Congestive Heart Failure Caused by Maternal Consumption of Blue Cohosh Herbal Medication. *Journal of Pediatrics* 132:550–552.

28. National Institutes of Health. U.S. National Library of Medicine. 2013. *Folic Acid.* Available at www.nlm.nih.gov/medlineplus/druginfo/natural/1017.html. Accessed May 2014.

29. Centers for Disease Control and Prevention. 2011. *National Diabetes Fact Sheet.*

Available at www.cdc.gov/diabetes/pubs/pdf/ndfs_2011.pdf. Accessed May 2014.

30. Correa, A., S. M. Gilboa, L. M. Besser, L. D. Botto, C. A. Moore, et al. 2008. Diabetes Mellitus and Birth Defects. *American Journal of Obstetrics and Gynecology* 199(237):e231–e239.

31. March of Dimes Foundation. 2013. *High Blood Pressure during Pregnancy*. Available at www.marchofdimes.com/pregnancy/print/high-blood-pressure-during-pregnancy.html. Accessed April 2014.

32. Chan, R. L., A. F. Olshan, D. A. Savitz, A. H. Herring, J. L. Daniels, H. B. Peterson, et al. 2011. Maternal Influences on Nausea and Vomiting in Early Pregnancy. *Maternal and Child Health Journal* 15:122–127.

33. Ibid.

34. King, T. L., and P. A. Murphy. 2009. Evidence-Based Approaches to Managing Nausea and Vomiting in Early Pregnancy. *Journal of Midwifery and Women's Health* 54:430–444.

35. National Institutes of Health. U.S. National Library of Medicine. 2012. *Morning Sickness*. www.nlm.nih.gov/medlineplus/ency/patientinstructions/000604.htm. May 2014.

36. King, et al. 2009. Evidence-Based Approaches to Managing Nausea and Vomiting in Early Pregnancy.

37. Thihalolipava, S., B. M. Candalla, and J. Ehrlich. 2012. Examining Pica in NYC Pregnant Women with Elevated Blood Lead Levels. *Maternal and Child Health Journal* (Epub ahead of print.) Available from www.springerlink.com/content/f21128461441h738. Accessed April 2012.

38. Bakhireva, L. N., A. S. Rowland, B. N. Young, S. Cano, S. T. Phela, K. Artyushkova, et al. 2012. Sources of Potential Lead Exposure among Pregnant Women in New Mexico. *Maternal and Child Health Journal* (Epub ahead of print.) Available from www.springerlink.com/content/a606753211860514. Accessed April 2012.

39. National Institutes of Health. U.S. National Library of Medicine. 2012. *Pica*. Available at www.nlm.nih.gov/medlineplus/ency/article/001538.htm. Accessed May 2014.

40. Institute of Medicine. 2009. *Weight Gain during Pregnancy: Reexamining the Guidelines*.

41. Smith, S. A., T. Hulsey, and W. Goodnight. 2008. Effects of Obesity on Pregnancy. *Journal of Obstetric, Gynecologic, & Neonatal Nursing* 37:176–184.

42. Institute of Medicine. 2009. *Weight Gain during Pregnancy: Reexamining the Guidelines*.

43. Marcason, W. 2006. What Are the Calorie Requirements for Women Having Twins? *Journal of the American Dietetic Association* 106:1292.

44. Kaiser, et al. 2008. Position of the American Dietetic Association: Nutrition and Lifestyle for a Healthy Pregnancy Outcome.

45. Ibid.

46. Ibid.

47. Young, B. E., T. J. McNanley, E. M. Cooper, A. W. McIntyre, F. Witter, Z. L. Harris, and K. O. O'Brien. 2012. Maternal Vitamin D Status and Calcium Intake Interact to Affect Fetal Skeletal Growth in Utero in Pregnant Adolescents. *American Journal of Clinical Nutrition* 95:1103–1112.

48. Mazhar, S. B. 2012. Vitamin D Supplementation for Women during Pregnancy: RHL Commentary. *The WHO Reproductive Health Library*. Geneva: World Health Organization. Available at www.apps.who.int/rhl/pregnancy_childbirth/antenatal_care/nutrition/cd008873_mazharsb_com/en/. Accessed May 2014.

49. Jiang, X., J. Yan, A. A. West, C. A. Perry, O. V. Malysheva, S. Devapatla, et al. 2012. Maternal Choline Intake Alters the Epigenetic State of Fetal Cortisol-Regulating Genes in Humans. Federation of American Societies of Experimental Biology Journal 26:1995–2007.

50. Eijsden, M. V., G. Hornstra, M. F. van der Wal, T. G. M. Vrijkotte, and G. J. Bonse. 2008. Maternal n–3, n–6, and Trans Fatty Acid Profile Early in Pregnancy and Term Birth Weight: A Prospective Cohort Study. *American Journal of Clinical Nutrition* 87:887–895.

51. Kaiser, et al. 2008. Position of the American Dietetic Association: Nutrition and Lifestyle for a Healthy Pregnancy Outcome.

52. Institute of Medicine. 2009. *Weight Gain during Pregnancy: Reexamining the Guidelines*.

53. Centers for Disease Control and Prevention. 2012. *Physical Activity. Healthy Pregnant or Postpartum Women*. Available at www.cdc.gov/physicalactivity/everyone/guidelines/pregnancy.html. Accessed May 2014.

54. Ibid.

55. The American College of Obstetricians and Gynecologists. 2011. *Frequently Asked Questions. FAQ0119. Exercise during Pregnancy*. Available at www.acog.org/~/media/For%20Patients/faq119.pdf. Accessed May 2014.

56. U.S. Department of Health and Human Services. National Institute of Diabetes and Digestive and Kidney Diseases. National Diabetes Information Clearinghouse. 2011. *National Diabetes Statistics 2011*. Available at www.diabetes.niddk.nih.gov/dm/pubs/statistics/#fast. Accessed May 2014.

57. American Diabetes Association. 2012. Gestational Diabetes. Available at www.diabetes.org/diabetes-basics/gestational. Accessed April 2014.

58. German Institute for Quality and Efficiency in Health Care. 2011. Gestational Diabetes: Does a Routine Examination Help to Avoid Complications for Mother and Child? Available at www.ncbi.nlm.nih.gov/pubmed_health/PMH0010399. Accessed April 2014.

59. American Diabetes Association. 2012. Gestational Diabetes.

60. Ibid.

61. U.S. Department of Health and Human Services, et al. 2011. *National Diabetes Statistics 2011*.

62. Ibid.

63. American Diabetes Association. 2012. Standards of Medical Care in Diabetes. *Diabetes Care* 35:S4–S10.

64. American Diabetes Association. 2012. Gestational Diabetes.

65. The American College of Obstetricians and Gynecologists. 2011. *Frequently Asked Questions. FAQ034. High Blood Pressure during Pregnancy*. Available at www.acog.org/~/media/For%20Patients/faq034.pdf?dmc=1&ts=20120408T0131589597. Accessed May 2014.

66. Williams, D. 2011. Long-Term Complications of Preeclampsia. *Seminars in Nephrology* 31:111–122.

67. Chobanian, et al. 2003. Seventh Report of the Joint National Committee on Prevention, Detection, Evaluation, and Treatment of High Blood Pressure; American Academy of Family Physicians. 2010. Pregnancy-Induced Hypertension. Available at http://familydoctor.org/familydoctor/en/diseases-conditions/pregnancy-induced-hypertension.html. Accessed April 2014.

68. Ibid.

69. National Institutes of Health. U.S. National Library of Medicine. 2012. *Preeclampsia*. Available at www.nlm.nih.gov/medlineplus/ency/article/000898.htm. Accessed May 2014.

70. The American College of Obstetricians and Gynecologists. 2013. *Hypertension in Pregnancy*. Available at www.acog.org/~/media/Task%20Force%20and%20Work%20Group%20Reports/Hypertensionin Pregnancy.pdf. Accessed May 2014.

71. Chobanian, et al. 2003. Seventh Report of the Joint National Committee on Prevention, Detection, Evaluation, and Treatment of High Blood Pressure.

72. Solomon, C., and E. Seely. 2004. Preeclampsia: Searching for the Cause. *New England Journal of Medicine* 350:641–642.

73. Roberts, J., J. Balk, L. Bodnar, J. Belizan, E. Bergel, and A. Martinez. 2003. Nutrient Involvement in Preeclampsia. *Journal of Nutrition* 133:1684S–1692S.

74. Kaiser, et al. 2008. Position of the American Dietetic Association: Nutrition and Lifestyle for a Healthy Pregnancy Outcome; Roberts, et al. 2003. Nutrient Involvement in Preeclampsia.

75. Kaiser, et al. 2008. Position of the American Dietetic Association: Nutrition and Lifestyle for a Healthy Pregnancy Outcome.

76. Centers for Disease Control and Prevention. 2013. *Teen Birth Rates Drop, But Disparities Persist*. Available at www.cdc.gov/features/dsteenpregnancy. Accessed May 2014.

77. Casanueva, E., M. E. Rosello-Soberon, L. M. De-Regil, M. C. Arguelles, and M. I. Cespedes. 2006. Adolescents with Adequate Birth Weight Newborns Diminish Energy Expenditure and Cease Growth. *Journal of Nutrition* 136:2498–2501.

78. National Institutes of Health. U.S. National Library of Medicine. 2011. *Adolescent Pregnancy*. Available at www.nlm.nih.gov/medlineplus/ency/article/001516.htm. Accessed May 2014.

79. Ibid.

80. Centers for Disease Control and Prevention. 2012. *Three Decades of Twin Births in the United States, 1980–2009.* Available at www.cdc.gov/nchs/data/databriefs/db80 .htm#agedistribution. Accessed April 2014.

81. March of Dimes Foundation. 2008. *A Mommy After 35.* Available at www .marchofdimes.com/pregnancy/a-mommy- after-35.aspx. Accessed May 2014.

82. Food and Nutrition Service. 2013. *About WIC: WIC at a Glance.* Available at www .fns.usda.gov/wic/about-wic-wic-glance. Accessed May 2014.

83. Food and Nutrition Service. 2012. *WIC Food Packages—Regulatory Requirements for WIC-Eligible Foods.* Available at www .fns.usda.gov/wic/benefitsandservices/ foodpkgregs.htm. Accessed April 2014.

84. Food and Nutrition Service. 2012. *WIC Program: Total Participation.* Available from www.fns.usda.gov/pd/26wifypart.htm. Accessed May 2014.

85. Food and Nutrition Service. 2012. *About WIC: How WIC Helps.* Available at www .fns.usda.gov/wic/aboutwic/howwichelps .htm. Accessed April 2014.

86. Ibid.

87. Picciano, M. F., and S. S. McDonald. 2006. Lactation. In Shils, M. E., M. Shike, A. C. Ross, B. Caballero, and R. J. Cousins. *Modern Nutrition in Health and Disease.* 10th ed. Philadelphia: Lippincott Williams & Wilkins.

88. U.S. Department of Health and Human Services. Eunice Kennedy Shriver National Institute of Child Health and Human Development. 2013. *What Are the Benefits of Breast-Feeding?* Available at www.nichd .nih.gov/health/topics/breastfeeding/ conditioninfo/pages/benefits.aspx. Accessed May 2014.

89. James, et al. 2009. Position of the American Dietetic Association: Promoting and Supporting Breast-Feeding. *Journal of the American Dietetic Association* 109(11):1926- 1942; Lawrence, R. M., and R. A. Lawrence. 2011. Breast-Feeding: More Than Just Good Nutrition. *Pediatrics in Review* 32:267–280.

90. Picciano, et al. 2006. *Lactation.*

91. Casey, C. F., D. Slawson, and L. R. Neal. 2010. Vitamin D Supplementation in Infants, Children, and Adolescents. *American Family Physician* 81:745–748.

92. Wagner, C. L., F. R. Greer, and the Section on Breast-Feeding and Committee on Nutrition. 2008. Prevention of Rickets and Vitamin D Deficiency in Infants, Children, and Adolescents. *Pediatrics* 122:1142–1152.

93. James, et al. 2009. Position of the American Dietetic Association: Promoting and Supporting Breast-Feeding.

94. Bidlack, W., and W. Wang. 2006. Designing Functional Foods. In Shils, M. *Modern Nutrition in Health and Disease.* Philadelphia: Lippincott Williams & Wilkins.

95. Picciano, et al. 2006. *Lactation.*

96. James, et al. 2009. Position of the American Dietetic Association: Promoting and Supporting Breast-Feeding; Lawrence, et al. 2011. Breast-Feeding: More Than Just Good Nutrition.

97. U.S. Department of Health and Human Services. 2000. *HHS Blueprint for Action on Breast-Feeding.* Available at www .womenshealth.gov/breastfeeding/ government-in-action/hhs-blueprints-and- policy-statements. Accessed April 2014; Owen, C. G., R. M. Martin, P. H. Whincup, G. D. Smith, and D. G. Cook. 2005. Effect of Infant Feeding on the Risk of Obesity across the Life Course: A Quantitative Review of Published Evidence. *Pediatrics* 115:1367–1377.

98. Jedrychowski, W., F. Perera, J. Jankowski, M. Butscher, E. Mroz, E. Flak, et al. 2012. Effect of Exclusive Breast-Feeding on the Development of Children's Cognitive Function in the Krakow Prospective Birth Cohort Study. *European Journal of Pediatrics* 171:151–158.

99. U.S. Department of Health and Human Services (HSS). 2000. *HHS Blueprint for Action on Breast-Feeding.*

100. U.S. Department of Health and Human Services. Office on Women's Health. 2011. *Breast-Feeding. Why Breast-Feeding Is Important.* Available at www.womenshealth .gov/breastfeeding/why-breastfeeding-is- important/. Accessed May 2014.

101. U.S. Department of Health and Human Services. 2011. *The Surgeon General's Call to Action to Support Breast-Feeding.* Available at www.surgeongeneral.gov/ library/calls/breastfeeding/factsheet.html. Accessed May 2014.

102. Batrick, M., and A. Reinhold. 2010. The Burden of Suboptimal Breast- Feeding in the United States. *Pediatrics* 125:e1048–e1056.

103. Ibid.

104. Kim, P., R. Feldman, L. C. Mayes, V. Eicher, N. Thompson, J. F. Leckman, et al. 2011. Breast-Feeding, Brain Activation to Own Infant Cry, and Maternal Sensitivity. *Journal of Child Psychology and Psychiatry* 52:907–915.

105. U.S. Department of Health and Human Services. 2011. *The Surgeon General's Call to Action to Support Breast-Feeding.*

106. Centers for Disease Control and Pre- vention. 2013. Breast-Feeding Report Card—United States, 2013. Available at www.cdc.gov/breastfeeding/ pdf/2013breastfeedingreportcard.pdf. Accessed July 2014.

107. Department of Health and Human Ser- vices. 2010. Healthy People 2020. *Maternal, Infant, and Child Health.* Available at www.healthypeople.gov/2020/topics objectives2020/over_view.aspx?topicid=26. Accessed April 2014.

108. Centers for Disease Control and Prevention. 2013. Breast-Feeding Report Card—United States, 2013.

109. Ibid.

110. Institute of Medicine. Food and Nutrition Board. 2005. Dietary Reference Intakes for Energy, Carbohydrate, Fiber, Fat, Fatty Acids, Cholesterol, Protein, and Amino Acids. Washington, DC: The National Academies Press. Available at www.nal .usda.gov/fnic/DRI/DRI_Energy/energy_ full_report.pdf. Accessed May 2014.

111. Ibid.

112. Ward, R., B. Bates, W. Benitz, D. Burchfield, J. Ring, J. Walls, and P. Walson. 2001. The Transfer of Drugs and Other Chemicals into Human Milk. American Academy of Pediatrics Committee on Drugs. *Pediatrics* 108:776–784.

113. Thygarajan, A., and A. Wesley Burks. 2008. American Academy of Pediatrics Recommendations on the Effects of Early Nutritional Interventions on the Development of Atopic Disease. *Current Opinions in Pediatrics* 20:698–702.

114. American Academy of Pediatrics. Section on Breast-Feeding. 2012. Breast-Feeding and the Use of Human Milk. *Pediatrics* 129:e827–e841. Available at www.pediatrics .aappublications.org/content/129/3/e827 .full. Accessed May 2014.

115. Ibid.; Lawrence, et al. 2011. Breast-Feeding: More Than Just Good Nutrition.

116. Baker, R. D., F. R. Greer, and the Committee on Nutrition. 2010. Diagnosis and Prevention of Iron Deficiency and Iron-Deficiency Anemia in Infants and Young Children (0–3 Years of Age). Pediatrics 126:1040–1050.

117. National Institutes of Health. U.S. National Library of Medicine. 2011. *Cow's Milk – Infants.* Available at www.nlm.nih.gov/ medlineplus/ency/article/002448.htm. Accessed May 2014.

118. U.S. Department of Health and Human Services. U.S. Food and Drug Administration. 2013. *Food Safety for Moms-to-Be.* Available at www.fda.gov/ food/resourcesforyou/healtheducators/ ucm089629.htm. Accessed May 2014.

119. American Dental Association. 2012. Baby Bottle Tooth Decay. Available at www.ada .org/3034.aspx. Accessed April 2014.

120. American Academy of Pediatric Dentistry. 2011. Policy on Early Childhood Caries (ECC): Classifications, Consequences, and Preventive Strategies. Available at www .aapd.org/media/Policies_Guidelines/P_ ECCClassifications.pdf. Accessed April 2012.

121. National Center for Health Statistics. 2010. CDC Growth Charts: United States. Available at www.cdc.gov/growthcharts. Accessed April 2014.

122. Stettler, N., J. Bhatia, A. Parish, and V. A. Stallings. 2011. Feeding Healthy Infants, Children, and Adolescents. In Kliegman, R. M., R. E. Behrman, H. B. Jenson, and B. F. Stanton, eds. *Nelson Textbook of Pediatrics.* 19th ed. Philadelphia: Saunders Elsevier.

123. Institute of Medicine. Food and Nutrition Board. 2005. Dietary Reference Intakes for Energy, Carbohydrate, Fiber, Fat, Fatty Acids, Cholesterol, Protein, and Amino Acids.

124. Lawrence, et al. 2011. Breast-Feeding: More Than Just Good Nutrition.

125. Ibid.

126. Ibid.

127. Institute of Medicine. Food and Nutrition Board. 2005. Dietary Reference Intakes for Energy, Carbohydrate, Fiber, Fat, Fatty Acids, Cholesterol, Protein, and Amino Acids.

128. Stettler, et al. 2011. Feeding Healthy Infants, Children, and Adolescents.

129. American Academy of Pediatrics. *Infant Food and Feeding.* Available at www.aap.org/en-us/advocacy-and-policy/aap-health-initiatives/HALF-Implementation-Guide/Age-Specific-Content/Pages/Infant-Food-and-Feeding.aspx#none. Accessed May 2014.

130. American Heart Association, S. Gidding, B. Dennison, L. Birch, S. Daniels, M. Gilman, A. Lichtenstein, et al. 2006. Dietary Recommendations for Children and Adolescents: A Guide for Practitioners. *Pediatrics* 117:544–559.

131. Neelon, S. E. B., and M. Briley. 2011. Position of the American Dietetic Association: Benchmarks for Nutrition Programs in Child Care Settings. *Journal of the American Dietetic Association* 111:607–615.

132. Ibid.

133. American Academy of Pediatrics. 2013. *Switching to Solid Foods.* Available at www.healthychildren.org/English/ages-stages/baby/feeding-nutrition/Pages/Switching-To-Solid-Foods.aspx. Accessed May 2014.

134. Ibid.

135. Fleischer, D. M., J. M. Spergel, A. H. Assa'ad, and J. A. Pongracic. 2013. Primary Prevention of Allergic Disease through Nutrition Interventions. *Journal of Allergy and Clinical Immunology: In Practice* 1:29–36.

136. Centers for Disease Control and Prevention. 2010. Botulism. Available at www.cdc.gov/nczved/divisions/dfbmd/diseases/botulism/#what. Accessed April 2014.

137. National Institute of Allergy and Infectious Diseases. 2012. Food Allergy: An Overview. Available at www.niaid.nih.gov/topics/foodallergy/documents/foodallergy.pdf. Accessed April 2014.

138. Food and Drug Administration. 2005. Compliance Policy Guide. Section 555.250. Statement of Policy for Labeling and Preventing Cross-Contact of Common Food Allergens. Available at www.fda.gov/ICECI/ComplianceManuals/CompliancePolicyGuidance_Manual/ucm074552.htm. Accessed May 2014.

139. Centers for Disease Control and Prevention. 2013. *NCHS Data Brief Number 121: Trends in Allergic Conditions among Children: United States, 1997–2011.* Available at www.cdc.gov. Accessed July 2014.

140. American Academy of Pediatrics. 2013. *Food Allergies in Children.* Available at www.healthychildren.org/English/healthy-living/nutrition/Pages/Food-Allergies-in-Children.aspx. Accessed May 2014.

141. The Food Allergy and Anaphylaxis Network. 2014. *About Food Allergens.* Available at www.foodallergy.org. Accessed May 2014.

18 Life Cycle Nutrition
Toddlers through Adolescence

Learning Outcomes

After reading this chapter, you will be able to:

18.1 Describe the nutrient needs of toddlers and preschoolers.

18.2 Discuss how parents influence a child's food preferences.

18.3 Describe the nutrient needs of school-aged children.

18.4 Identify the nutrition-related issues facing school-aged children, including overweight and obesity.

18.5 Describe the nutritional needs of adolescents.

18.6 Discuss the nutritional issues that affect adolescents, including disordered eating.

18.7 Identify the health risks of obesity in children and teens.

True or False?

1. Toddlers grow at the same rate as infants. **T/F**
2. Toddlers and preschoolers are often too busy exploring to eat. **T/F**
3. Children can receive all the nutrients they need by drinking milk. **T/F**
4. Iron deficiency in young children is caused by eating too much chicken. **T/F**
5. Once a child refuses a new food, there is no point in offering it again. **T/F**
6. Young children often go on food "jags." **T/F**
7. The rise in childhood obesity is due entirely to fast food. **T/F**
8. Lunches served under the National School Lunch Program have to follow certain nutritional regulations. **T/F**
9. As long as teens drink diet soda, they don't have to worry about negative health effects. **T/F**
10. Most teens consume adequate amounts of calcium and iron. **T/F**

See page 702 for the answers.

As children age, their nutritional needs and eating habits evolve continually. While infants are relatively immobile much of the time, a toddler's life is an active one. Once children learn to stand and walk, the world is full of interesting things to explore, and sitting quietly at the table to eat meals and snacks isn't always high on a toddler's priority list. Just when parents think they have a handle on toddler nutrition, they find they are parenting an elementary school–aged child, which presents another set of nutritional challenges. And so it goes through the preteen and teen years.

While the ages and stages of child development are different, they do have a lot in common. Children of all ages should be encouraged to eat a balanced, varied diet, and the amount of food that's right for them. Good health for children also involves regular physical activity. In this chapter, we explore the unique nutrition needs of toddlers, preschoolers, school-aged children, and adolescents as they grow and change.

What Are the Nutritional Needs of Toddlers and Preschoolers?

LO 18.1 Describe the nutrient needs of toddlers and preschoolers.

Early childhood consists of two distinct age categories: **toddlers** (aged 1 to 3 years) and **preschoolers** (aged 3 to 5 years). Toddlers and preschoolers are still growing rapidly, but less rapidly than infants. During the second year of life the average weight gain is about 3 to 5 pounds, and the average height or length increase is about 3 to 5 inches.[1] As a result of their slowed growth, the appetites of toddlers diminish. A toddler's appetite may fluctuate, and caregivers may become concerned that the child isn't eating enough.

Toddlers and preschoolers require the same nutrients as older children and adults, but in different amounts. Toddlers and preschoolers tend to eat smaller amounts of food at one sitting, and may need to eat more frequently to satisfy their energy and nutrient needs. Parents may worry when children eat lightly for a day or two at a time, but it's likely that children are eating sufficient amounts as long as there are no prolonged dramatic changes in their health, including decreased energy level, diarrhea, nausea, vomiting, or changes in the child's hair, skin, or nails.

The chart shown in **Figure 18.1** is used to measure the growth of children at different intervals to determine an individual's rate of growth compared with standard growth curves for age and gender. Growth charts can be used to assess whether a child is developing at a rate comparable to other children of the same age and gender. In general, sudden changes in growth below the 10th percentile or above the 80th percentile may be cause for concern. See the Calculation Corner to practice reading a growth chart.

Young Children Need to Eat Frequent, Small Meals and Nutrient-Dense Foods

Toddlers are extremely active. Just watching them go from activity to activity can be exhausting for adults. To fuel their activity, toddlers need between 1,000 and 1,400 kilocalories per day from nutrient-dense foods. Toddlers eat small amounts and may need several meals and snacks. Meals and snacks should consist of small portions of protein-rich foods, including lean meat, poultry, seafood, and beans, and fruits, vegetables, milk, and whole grains, instead of

toddlers Children aged 1 to 3 years old.

preschoolers Children aged 3 to 5 years old.

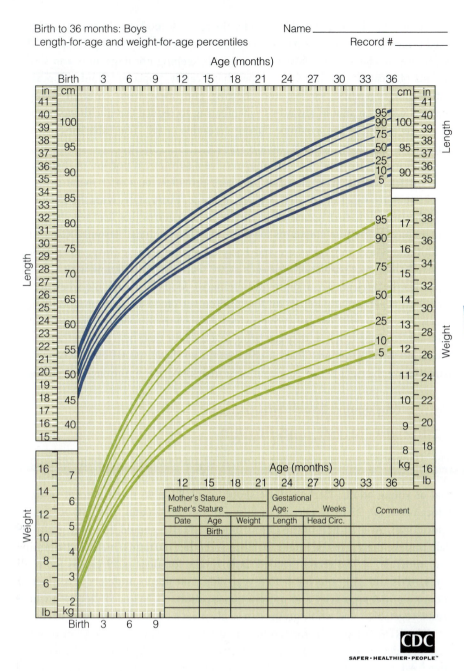

Birth to 36 months: Boys
Length-for-age and weight-for-age percentiles

Name _____

Record # _____

◄ **Figure 18.1 Growth Chart**
Growth charts can be used to assess whether a child is developing at a rate comparable to other children of the same age and gender.

Source: Developed by the National Center for Health Statistics in collaboration with the National Center for Chronic Disease Prevention and Health Promotion. 2000. Available at www.cdc.gov/growthcharts. Accessed July 2012.

Calculation Corner

Interpreting a Growth Chart

Properly interpreting a CDC growth chart is essential for monitoring a child's growth patterns. Marcus is 21 months old, weighs 32 pounds, and is 35 inches tall. Follow the steps below to determine where he falls on the growth chart.

Step 1. Select the appropriate chart for age and gender.

Step 2. Locate Marcus's age at the top of the chart.

Step 3. Locate Marcus's weight along the side of the chart.

Step 4. Mark where Marcus's age and weight meet.

Step 5. Locate Marcus's height (length) in inches along the side of the chart.

Step 6. Mark where Marcus's age and height meet.

What is Marcus's percentile for weight? for height?

Answer: Marcus is at the 90th percentile for weight. Ten percent of the population falls above Marcus's weight, and 90 percent below. He is also at the 90th percentile for height. Ten percent of the population falls above that, and 90 percent below.

Scan this QR code with your mobile device to access practice math activities. You can also access the activities in MasteringNutrition™.

lower-nutrient fare such as fried chicken nuggets, french fries, sugary drinks, cookies, and crackers.[2] (The Daily Food Plans for Preschoolers and Kids, discussed later in this chapter, can be used to determine specific numbers of servings for young children.)

Parents must be mindful about portion sizes for young children and avoid encouraging children to eat more than they need. One way to help ensure proper portion sizes is to use child-sized plates and cups, which are smaller and more appropriate for the quantity of food a child can fit into his stomach, and to allow the child to eat as much as he wants.

Children will eat different amounts at each meal. Parents should serve small portions, such as a few tablespoons of cooked pasta or vegetables, or an ounce or so of protein-rich foods such as chicken, to start. If a child wants more food, then she should have it. Caregivers looking after children with larger or smaller appetites should tailor portion sizes to each child's individual needs.

Using child-sized dishes at mealtimes can help caregivers monitor portion sizes.

TABLE TIPS

Prepare Tasty Treats for Toddlers

Fresh pear, peach, or plum, peeled and cut into very small pieces

Mini bagel, not toasted, cut into small pieces

Whole-grain pumpkin or bran muffin, cut into small pieces

Applesauce (no added sugar)

Yogurt with diced bananas

Remember: Young children should always be supervised while eating!

Having kids help in the kitchen is one way to get them interested in trying new foods and eating healthy meals.

To prevent choking in children under the age of 4, food should be cut into bite-sized pieces. Some foods are particularly problematic for very young children. The American Academy of Pediatrics recommends keeping hot dogs, nuts and seeds, chunks of meat or cheese, whole grapes, hard candy, popcorn, chunks of peanut butter, raw vegetables, raisins, and chewing gum away from children younger than 4.[3] Children should always sit when eating to reduce the likelihood of food becoming lodged in the windpipe during a stumble or fall. The Table Tips provide some ideas for healthy, toddler-friendly snacks.

Children who attend day care may receive a substantial portion of their daily food in that setting. In some cases, day-care providers may offer menu items or snacks that are superior to what is given at home. Every state, with the exception of Idaho (which doesn't license child-care centers) requires that licensed child-care centers meet minimum standards for nutrition. The National Resource Center for Health and Safety in Child Care and Early Education website (http://nrckids.org) posts all child-care regulations for each state.[4] Parents should know what is being offered at the day-care site and provide alternative foods for their child when necessary. This is particularly important for children with food allergies or food intolerances. Parents should ask day-care providers to alert them about special occasions, such as birthday parties, so they can bring in a treat for their own child if their child is allergic to certain foods. Even if children do not have special dietary concerns, parents have the right to be firm about what their child eats in the day-care setting.

Young Children Need Adequate Carbohydrate, Fat, and Protein

The *Dietary Guidelines for Americans, 2010* recommends offering children a variety of foods. The macronutrient composition of children's diets is similar to that of young adults: Carbohydrate should contribute 45 to 65 percent of daily kilocalories; fat, 25 to 35 percent of kilocalories; and protein, 10 to 30 percent of kilocalories. At least half of the grains in a child's diet should be whole grains to help achieve the suggested intake for fiber and other nutrients, including vitamins and minerals.[5, 6] The recommended daily intake for fiber is 19 grams for 1- to 3-year-olds and 25 grams for 4- to 8-year-olds. Like adults, toddlers need fiber to promote bowel regularity and prevent constipation.[7] A balanced diet with whole fruits, vegetables, and whole grains can easily meet a toddler's daily fiber needs.

The RDA for protein for toddlers is set at 1.1 grams per kilogram of body weight; it decreases to 0.95 gram per kilogram of body weight in school-aged children.[8] Adequate carbohydrate intake has a protein-sparing effect, allowing protein to be used for growth and tissue repair rather than for energy.

The recommendation for total daily fat intake is 30 to 35 percent of total kilocalories for children 2 to 3 years old, and 25 to 35 percent for children over age 4.[9] Dietary fat contributes to normal development of the brain and nerve cells, and is a concentrated source of energy to fuel growth. Fat is used for the synthesis of myelin, a substance that insulates nerve cells and aids in nerve conduction. Some neurons are fully myelinated at birth, such as those in the motor cortex that control the infant's ability to suckle. Intensive myelination continues as children fine-tune their vision, hearing, language, emotions, and physical capabilities during the first two years of life. Polyunsaturated and monounsaturated fats, found in foods such as fish, nuts, and vegetable oils, should be the dominant fats in the diets of children ages two and older. Solid fats, such as butter and lard, should be limited. In addition, children's diets should include a minimum of added sugars, found in sugar drinks, candy, and other refined-sugar foods.[10]

Young Children Need to Consume Adequate Calcium and Iron

Iron and calcium are particularly important to a young child's development. Iron is needed to prevent developmental delays, and calcium supports the rapid growth of bones.

Iron Needs

Children aged 1 to 3 need 7 milligrams of iron daily and those aged 4 to 8 require 10 milligrams.[11] The foods of infancy—breast milk, iron-fortified formula, and fortified infant cereals—are good sources of iron. As children start eating more adult foods, they require a variety of iron-rich foods to maintain their iron status. To help children meet their iron needs, parents and caregivers should offer iron-rich lean meats and poultry, and fortified grains such as breakfast cereal, on a daily basis and offer fewer iron-poor foods, such as juice and milk. If children get too large a percentage of their kilocalories from iron-poor cow's milk, iron-rich foods may be displaced.[12] The Table Tips list kid-friendly ways to enjoy foods that have plenty of iron.

Iron needs are highest during periods of rapid growth, and young children are more prone to iron deficiency because they are growing so fast. Iron deficiency is a condition resulting from too little iron in the body. Among children, iron deficiency is seen most often between six months and three years and it is the most common nutritional deficiency and the leading cause of anemia in the United States.[13] Among children living in the United States, an estimated 14 percent of 1- to 2-year-olds, and 4 percent of 3- to 4-year-olds, experience iron deficiency.[14] Worldwide, iron-deficiency anemia, the result of severe iron deficiency, affects an estimated 2 billion people, and young children and their mothers are the most often afflicted.[15]

Iron-deficiency anemia during infancy and early childhood can interfere with a child's cognition, behavior, and overall neurodevelopment, and leave lasting damage,[16] so it is crucial to ensure that children get sufficient iron in their diets.

Iron Toxicity

Although iron deficiency is a big concern in young children, it is possible to get too much iron, usually due to an overdose from iron-containing dietary supplements and medications. Children may be attracted to eating large amounts of pills with iron because they look like candy.[17] To prevent accidental iron poisoning, the FDA requires warning labels on iron-containing drugs and dietary supplements.[18] Parents and other caregivers should keep pills in containers with safety caps and out of reach of children.

Calcium Needs

Toddlers need calcium to develop healthy bones. Children between 1 and 3 years of age should consume 700 milligrams of calcium per day, and children aged 4 and 5 should consume 1,000 milligrams.[19] Eight ounces of any type of dairy milk, 8 ounces of yogurt, and 1 ½ ounces of hard cheese, such as Cheddar, each provide about 300 milligrams of calcium. If children do not drink cow's milk, soy beverages fortified with about 300 milligrams of calcium and other nutrients, such as vitamin D, are suitable substitutes.

Young Children Need to Consume Adequate Vitamin D

The American Academy of Pediatrics recommends that all children over the age of 1 year consume 10 micrograms (400 IU) of vitamin D daily.[20] Vitamin D is found in fortified milk, egg yolk, and certain types of fish. Two eight-ounce cups of milk and a variety of fortified foods, including eggs, breakfast cereal, and orange juice, daily can help to satisfy a child's vitamin D needs. If the child does not consume adequate amounts of vitamin D from foods, the AAP recommends vitamin D supplements to fill the gap.[21]

Young Children Need Adequate Fluid

A toddler's or preschooler's daily fluid recommendations are based on body weight. For example, a 21-pound child needs about 5 cups of fluid daily, while a 44-pound child needs about 8 cups. Drinking too much fluid may displace nutrient-dense solid foods and important nutrients such as iron and fiber. To ensure adequate amounts of nutrient-dense foods, caregivers should monitor a child's beverage intake and provide water, milk, and no more than six ounces of 100 percent juice daily, and avoid offering soda and other sugary drinks.

Young Children Can Grow Healthfully on Vegetarian Diets

Young children can grow and develop normally on a vegetarian diet, as long as it is balanced. Generally speaking, vegetarian diets are rich in whole grains, vegetables, and fruits, foods that experts encourage all children and adults to eat. Vegetarian diets may be high in fiber, which may prevent children from getting all the nutrients they need because fiber fills up their relatively small stomachs and they don't have room for other foods. Young children may need to eat several times throughout the day to get enough food to meet their energy and nutrient needs. As with any eating plan, a vegetarian child's diet should include adequate kilocalories, protein, calcium, iron, and zinc. Vegan children must supplement their diets with a daily source of vitamin B_{12}, found only in animal foods.[22] Vitamin B_{12} is available in dietary supplements and in certain fortified plant foods, such as breakfast cereal and soy beverages.

LO 18.1: THE TAKE-HOME MESSAGE Toddlers grow more slowly than infants, and have appetites that may fluctuate from day to day. Adults should offer children appropriate portion sizes. Toddlers need adequate amounts of kilocalories, carbohydrate, protein, fat, calcium, iron, vitamin D, fiber, and other nutrients, and must avoid excess iron. Caregivers also need to monitor a child's beverage intake and provide water, milk, and no more than six ounces of 100 percent juice daily while avoiding soda and other sugary drinks. Vegetarian toddlers need adequate calcium, iron, and zinc and a daily source of vitamin B_{12}.

How Can Adults Influence Young Children's Eating Habits?

LO 18.2 Discuss how parents influence a child's food preferences.

As a young child grows and feeds herself independently (see **Table 18.1**), the variety of healthy food choices should increase, too. Eating habits form early in life, and parents and other caregivers can help children establish a lifelong appreciation for a variety of nutrient-dense foods. Research shows that a child may need to be exposed to a food 10 to 15 times or more before accepting it.[23] Parents should not hesitate to offer healthy food like broccoli or brussels sprouts to their child because of their own dislike for these, and other, foods. Children often adapt to the foods made available to them.

TABLE 18.1	Food Skills of Young Children
Age	**Developmental Feeding Skill**
1–2	Child uses the big muscles of the arm and can tear and snap vegetables, help scrub, drink from a cup, and help feed self.
3	Child uses the medium muscles of the hand and can help pour, mix, shake, and spread foods. Child can crack nuts with supervision and feed self independently.
4	Child uses the small muscles of the fingers and can peel, juice, crack raw eggs, and use all utensils and napkins.
5	Child uses eye-hand coordination and can measure, cut with supervision, grind, and grate.

Shaping Early Food Preferences

According to Ellyn Satter, an expert on child feeding and nutrition, there is a division of responsibility when it comes to control of feeding.[24] The adult is responsible for what the child is offered to eat, as well as when and where the food is offered. The child, however, is responsible for whether he or she eats, and how much. Food issues and power struggles can occur when adults think that their job is not only to provide the food but also to make sure that the child eats it. Some parents encourage their children to "clean their plates," even though the children may have indicated that they are finished eating. This is a risky habit that encourages overconsumption of kilocalories, which could lead to obesity. Parents should allow children to stop eating once they are full.

Encourage children to enjoy a variety of healthy foods by involving them in preparing the family meal.

Small children may seem to have very narrow food preferences. Parents may think, "My child only likes chicken nuggets and fries," or "She hates all vegetables." Though it's true that toddlers may be selective in their eating, parents should not give up on encouraging them to try and to accept new foods, because it's likely that their food preferences will change with time.

Parents have tremendous influence on their child's food preferences. When parents act as a positive role model for nutritious food choices, it can help children learn to choose healthier foods.[25] Adults should load up their own plates with a variety of fruits and vegetables, lean protein sources, and whole grains, and snack on items like carrot sticks and apple slices between meals, so that children will be more likely to follow suit. Children often mimic adults' behaviors, including the unhealthy ones. A mom who only drinks diet soda for dinner, or a dad who insists that his 3-year-old eat asparagus but never puts it on his own plate, sends the child confusing messages. Involving children in the food shopping, menu selection, and preparation of meals is another way to encourage them to enjoy a variety of foods.

Food Jags

Food jags occur when a child refuses anything but a limited selection of foods. This behavior of getting "stuck" on a small selection of foods is quite common and normal in young children. Luckily, food jags are usually temporary. A child who only wants to eat pretzels and oranges, or refuses to eat anything green, will likely emerge from the phase within a few days or weeks.

food jags When a child will only eat the same food meal after meal.

Food jags, such as wanting to only eat one food (like macaroni and cheese), or avoiding certain foods, are common among toddlers.

If a parent or caregiver senses that the food jag is not going away, then the situation might require the parent to pay more careful attention to what the child is eating as well as what he or she is avoiding. Is the child really "eating only crackers" or is the parent forgetting that the child is also drinking milk and eating green beans and orange slices when they are offered? A parent or caregiver can keep a food diary of everything the child eats and drinks for a few days to help identify any problems. Sharing concerns (and the food diary) with the child's health care provider or a Registered Dietitian Nutritionist and asking for advice may prevent serious nutrient deficiencies in the long run.

In some cases, indulging the food jag may be the best option. If a child is stuck on something like pasta, a parent or caregiver can still offer a variety of foods within that category, such as whole-grain versions, or those with added nutrients, such as omega-3 fats.

MyPlate for Preschoolers is a tool that can help adults plan a healthy diet for this age group (see the Web Resources section at the end of this chapter).

LO 18.2: THE TAKE-HOME MESSAGE Although adults are responsible for what a child is offered to eat, the child is responsible for whether and how much he or she eats. Parents should serve toddlers and preschoolers age-appropriate portions, and shouldn't force them to clean their plates. Caregivers should be good role models when it comes to getting children to try new foods. New foods may need to be offered 10 to 15 times before a child accepts them. Food jags are normal and usually temporary.

What Are the Nutritional Needs of School-Aged Children?

LO 18.3 Describe the nutrient needs of school-aged children.

School-aged children, usually considered those between the ages of 6 and 12, still have plenty of growing to do, and the quality of their diet affects their growth. See Table 18.2 for the range of kilocalorie needs for children in this age group. During the school years, gross and fine motor skills become more refined, and children's growth rates are steady until the adolescent growth spurt. While school-aged

school-aged children Children between the ages of 6 and 12.

TABLE 18.2 Kilocalorie Needs for Children and Adolescents

| Age | Gender | Activity Level* | | |
		Sedentary	Moderately Active	Active
2–3 years (toddlers)	Male and female	1,000–1,200	1,000–1,400	1,000–1,400
4–8 years (preschoolers and school aged)	Female	1,200–1,400	1,400–1,600	1,400–1,800
4–8 years (preschoolers and school aged)	Male	1,200–1,400	1,400–1,600	1,600–2,000
9–13 years (school aged)	Female	1,400–1,600	1,600–2,000	1,800–2,200
9–13 years (school aged)	Male	1,600–2,000	1,800–2,200	2,000–2,600
14–18 years (adolescent)	Female	1,800	2,000	2,400
14–18 years (adolescent)	Male	2,000–2400	2,400–2800	2,800–3,200

*Note: These levels are based on Estimated Energy Requirements (EER) from the Institute of Medicine (IOM) Dietary Reference Intakes macronutrients report, 2002, calculated by gender, age, and activity level for reference-sized individuals. "Reference size," as determined by the IOM, is based on median height and weight for ages up to 18 years.

Source: HHS/USDA, 2010, *Dietary Guidelines for Americans, 2010.* Available at www.cnpp.usda.gov/publications/dietaryguidelines/2010/policydoc/appendices.pdf. Accessed May 2014.

children develop at different rates, they add, on average, 7 pounds and 2.5 inches per year.[26]

Due to the routine of school and being away from home, school-aged children do not eat as often throughout the day as toddlers and preschoolers. School-aged children have a greater capacity to consume more food, are better able to maintain their blood glucose longer, and tend to be less hungry between meals and snacks. Families, caregivers, and schools contribute to the nutritional needs of children. They can help ensure that children make healthy food choices, get regular exercise, and maintain a healthy body weight.

MyPlate Can Help Guide Food Choices

Most parents are not nutrition experts, and the idea of trying to meet their child's entire nutrient needs can be overwhelming and confusing. Fortunately, user-friendly versions of the Daily Food Plans and the extensive 10 Tips Nutrition Education System (see **Figure 18.2**) available at ChooseMyPlate.gov can help parents guide their children's choices. The SuperTracker creates a meal plan that shows what and how much the child should eat to meet his or her needs. It also provides

Cut back on kid's sweet treats

1 Serve small portions
2 Sip smarter
3 Use the check-out lane that does not display candy
4 Choose not to offer sweets as rewards
5 Make fruit the everyday dessert
6 Make food fun
7 Encourage kids to invent new snacks
8 Play detective in the cereal aisle
9 Make treats "treats," not everyday foods
10 If kids don't eat their meal, they don't need sweet "extras"

Be a healthy role model for children

1 Show by example
2 Go food shopping together
3 Get creative in the kitchen
4 Offer the same foods for everyone
5 Reward with attention, not food
6 Focus on each other at the table
7 Listen to your child
8 Limit screen time
9 Encourage physical activity
10 Be a good food role model

▲ **Figure 18.2 Tips and Daily Food Plans from ChooseMyPlate.gov**

Source: Adapted from USDA. 2011. *10 Tips Nutrition Education Series*. Available at www.choosemyplate.gov/healthy-eating-tips/ten-tips.html.

Track your daily food intake.

Track your physical activity.

See and analyze your progress.

Monitor your weight.

Create goals and get support.

▲ **Figure 18.3 The USDA's SuperTracker Offers Personalized Plans and Food Trackers**
The USDA's SuperTracker is an online diet and physical activity tool that helps you plan, assess, and analyze your daily food intake and activities.

Source: www.choosemyplate.gov.

ideas to help with meal planning (see **Figure 18.3**) as well as tips for making healthy foods fun for children.

The portions of the ChooseMyPlate.gov website about children encourage kids to:

- **Be physically active every day.**
- **Choose healthier foods from each group.** Every food group has foods that should be eaten more often than others. Choices from the vegetables, fruits, grains, protein, and dairy groups should be varied.
- **Eat more of some food groups than others.** The sizes of the food groups as highlighted in MyPlate indicate suggested relative proportions.
- **Eat foods from every food group every day.** The different colors of the food groups shown in MyPlate represent the five different food groups (and don't forget healthy oils).
- **Make the right choices for you.** ChooseMyPlate.gov gives everyone in the family personal ideas on how to eat better and exercise more.
- **Take it one step at a time.** Start with one new, good thing a day, and continue to add another new one every day.

Children with health-related issues or chronic diseases may not be able to follow the Daily Food Plans for Preschoolers and for Kids. For example, children with autism may become especially fixated on specific foods or be reluctant to try new foods. Overcoming these issues generally requires intervention and support from professionals who work with children with special needs, such as Registered Dietitian Nutritionists.

Nutrition in Practice: Max

Three-year-old Max has a very active life. He wakes up early in the morning. He enjoys his breakfast of banana chunks and some whole-grain cereal at the kitchen table. After a few bites of breakfast, he becomes distracted by the noise outside the window. He runs to see a neighbor mowing the grass. He asks to go outside and play with the family dog, Burt. Together they find all the puddles of water left by yesterday's rain shower. By noon, his father suggests that it's time to go to the kitchen and get something to eat, but Max isn't interested. There's too much to see, do, and explore before he has to lie down for his afternoon nap. It's not until his father starts calling for a pizza delivery later in the afternoon that Max suddenly becomes hungry.

Max's father, a single parent, has discovered that meal preparation is more challenging than he anticipated. He is worried that Max may be missing some essential nutrients from his diet, but he is not sure how to get his son to slow down and eat when he should. And since pizza has become a frequent menu item, the pizza parlor phone number is now on "speed dial." Max's father decides to seek the help of a Registered Dietitian Nutritionist for advice.

Max's Stats:
- Age: 3
- Height: 3 feet 1 inch
- Weight: 32 pounds

Max's Food Log

Food/Beverage	Time Consumed	Hunger Rating*	Location
Whole-grain cereal with milk and banana chunks	6:30 A.M.	5	Kitchen table
Pizza and cola	6 P.M.	5	Kitchen table

*Hunger Rating (1–5): 1 = not hungry; 5 = super hungry.

Critical Thinking Questions
1. What advice do you have for Max's father concerning feeding a toddler?
2. What do you think is the best strategy for ensuring that a toddler like Max gets adequate nutrition without putting him at risk for obesity?

Dietitian's Observation and Plan for Max:
- Discuss the importance of optimal nutrient intake to maintain the recommended growth pattern during childhood.
- Offer a variety of foods to help Max get the nutrients he needs from every food group.
- Encourage Max to participate in preparing family meals.
- Participate in family physical activity with Max. Regular exercise helps to prevent overweight and obesity.

The Registered Dietitian Nutritionist gave Max's father several strategies to improve Max's nutrient intake. During breakfast, Max now eats a fortified cereal with milk. At lunch, Max's father pops a whole-wheat English muffin into the toaster and spreads it with peanut butter topped with shredded carrots—Max's favorite. He takes Max to a local farmers' market and lets him choose some of the ingredients for their week's meals. Then, when preparing the evening meal, he gets Max involved washing vegetables and helping to assemble a salad.

School Lunches Contribute to Children's Nutritional Status

The National School Lunch Program (NSLP) provides nutritionally balanced lunches, many of which are available for a low cost or for free. In 2012, the NSLP offered more than 31.6 million lunches each day.[27] Providing healthy meals at school, particularly to children who may not be able to afford them without financial assistance, is one

The National School Lunch Program provides lunch for millions of school-aged children every day.

of the greatest successes of the NSLP. For some children, the food that they eat at school is the healthiest meal—perhaps the only meal—they eat all day.

Meals served as part of the NSLP are required to meet nutrition standards. As of 2010, NSLP nutrition standards have been updated to more closely match the Federal Dietary Guidelines for Americans.[28] For example, in keeping with expert health recommendations for children and adults, the percentage of total kilocalories from saturated fat is limited to 10 percent per meal for all age groups. Table 18.3 presents recommended levels for other nutrients.

Research suggests children who take part in the NSLP have lower intakes of sugar-sweetened beverages and a lower percentage of kilocalories from low-nutrient-density foods and beverages than nonparticipants. Overall, however, NSLP participation is not significantly related to students' BMI.[29] Students who eat school meals are more likely to consume vegetables and more milk products, not only in school but also during a 24-hour period.[30]

School meals have been carefully evaluated with one goal in mind: to provide students with healthy, nutritious meals. At the same time, school lunch services reflect a general trend in children's food preferences. The challenge is to provide healthier options that consist of whole, unprocessed foods that kids will eat and enjoy, while staying within budget.

Children who are not taking part in the NSLP need a healthy substitute. Given money to purchase lunch, children may select foods that are less nutrient dense than they need. It makes sense for the parent *and* the child to use MyPlate as a guide to pack a mutually agreeable, healthy, and appealing lunch for the child to take to school. When a child plans and makes his own lunch, it's more likely he will eat it. The Table Tips can help provide some useful ideas to improve the likelihood that a child actually eats the lunch that he or she helped pack.

The Importance of Breakfast

Research suggests a link between eating breakfast on a regular basis and a healthier body weight in children and adolescents.[31] When children skip breakfast, they lose out on an opportunity for good nutrition. Traditional breakfast foods, such as milk, fortified whole-grain breads and cereal, fruit, and eggs, are sources of important nutrients for kids. Breakfast-skippers may not make up for the nutrients they miss at breakfast during the rest of the day.

TABLE 18.3 Minimum Nutrient and Kilocalorie Levels for School Lunches (School Week Averages)			
Nutrients and Energy Allowances	**Minimum Requirements***		
	Grades K–5	**Grades 6–8**	**Grades 9–12**
Energy allowances (kilocalories)	550–650	600–700	750–850
Saturated fat (% of kilocalories)	less than 10	less than 10	less than 10
Sodium (mg)	640 or less	710 or less	740 or less

Source: USDA Food and Nutrition Service. Available at www.fns.usda.gov/sites/default/files/dietaryspecs.pdf. Accessed July 2014.

Some schools participate in the School Breakfast Program (SBP). Like the NSLP, the SBP provides nutritious meals to students at participating schools and in some residential child-care institutions, too. Eligible students receive free or reduced-price breakfasts. Participation in the SBP has grown in recent years. In 1989, 3.7 million students took part in the program on a given school day; in fiscal 2012, it was 12.8 million.[32] School Breakfast Program participants had significantly lower BMI than did nonparticipants.[33]

Hunger at any time of the school day can disrupt learning and behavior. There is evidence to suggest that habitual breakfast eating at home and school breakfast programs have a positive effect on children's academic performance; the clearest effects of the lack of a morning meal are seen on mathematic and arithmetic grades in undernourished children.[34]

If children don't have time to eat breakfast at home or don't receive breakfast at school, caregivers can provide nutritious morning meals for children to eat on the way to school or when they arrive. Another option is to offer a glass of milk or 100 percent fruit juice at home, and send the rest of breakfast to school with the child to have as a mid-morning snack. See the Table Tips for some on-the-go breakfast ideas.

Promoting Fruit and Vegetable Consumption in Children

Healthy People 2020 encourages Americans to eat more fruits and vegetables.[35] Suggested fruit and vegetable intake for children is based on their daily kilocalories, as produce is part of a balanced eating plan.[36] Many children, and their caregivers, are not consuming the recommended amount of fruits and vegetables every day. How do we get children to enjoy vegetables? In addition to providing well-prepared, fresh, and tasty vegetables, caregivers should give strong verbal encouragement, at school, at home, and in the community, to help children obtain their recommended servings.[37]

Parents can help establish healthy eating habits, such as filling half of their plate with fruits and vegetables at every meal, or starting each meal with a vegetable like sliced tomatoes, early in their children's lives. A little effort in planning meals that incorporate more produce in the family's diet can have big payoffs for the whole family. Parents can also substitute pureed vegetables in traditional dishes, like casseroles and breads, to increase vegetable intake and decrease energy density of foods.[38] Suggestions on increasing fruit and vegetable consumption are detailed in **Table 18.4**.

Children should be encouraged to eat fruit and vegetables every day.

Children with Food Allergy and Intolerance

An estimated 8 percent of U.S. children under age 18 have one or more food allergies.[39] Food allergy is an abnormal response to a food triggered by the body's immune system, while food intolerance is a digestive system response in which no antibodies are produced.[40] Symptoms of food allergy may include swelling, nausea, coughing, vomiting, drop in blood pressure, breathing difficulty, blackouts, and even death. Tree nuts and peanuts are the leading causes of deadly allergic reactions called anaphylaxis. Because peanut allergies can be dangerous for kids who have them, "peanut-free" zones are being established in schools across the country. In addition to the cafeterias, care must be exercised in multiple locations and events at the school, such as classroom parties and bake sales. Children who have contact with surfaces with peanuts in any way, including touching peanuts, using a peanut-containing skin care product, or breathing in peanut dust, such

	TABLE 18.4 TASTE: Increasing Fruits and Vegetables in the Family Meal	

T: Try something new at every eating occasion	▪ Add shredded carrots to casseroles, chili, lasagna, meatloaf, or soup. ▪ Drop berries into cereal, pancakes, or yogurt. ▪ Make fruit smoothies and veggie burritos. ▪ Use leftover veggies for salad, or add them to a can of soup. ▪ Keep grab-and-go snacks handy, such as boxes of raisins, trail mix made with dried fruit, or frozen 100% fruit bars. Cherry tomatoes and carrot sticks with hummus can be a tasty and refreshing veggie treat.
A: All forms of fruits and veggies count!	▪ Consider fresh, frozen, 100% juice, canned, and dried. ▪ Cook fruits and veggies in different ways, including steamed, slow-cooked, sautéed, stir-fried, grilled, and microwaved.
S: Shop smart	▪ Fresh produce in season is more affordable. Look for specials. ▪ Clean and cut up the produce, so it is ready to use. ▪ At a restaurant, substitute vegetables for high-fat side orders.
T: Turn it into a family activity	▪ Kids can skewer a shish-kabob or make pizza. ▪ A trip to a farmers' market is fun for kids and gets them interested in trying new fruits and vegetables.
E: Explore the bountiful variety	▪ Use salad bars or buffets to try new types of produce. ▪ When shopping, kids pick out a new produce item for the family meal.

Source: Table adapted from Fruits & Veggies—More Matters website, September 6, 2012. "T.A.S.T.E. Tips and Information for Moms." Copyright © 2012 by Produce for Better Health Foundation. Reprinted with permission.

as when in close proximity to other people eating peanuts, can experience an allergic reaction.[41]

Food allergies are not preventable. For children with food allergies, the only way to avoid allergic reactions is to avoid allergenic foods. It is important to carefully read the list of ingredients on the label of packaged foods and to ask about the ingredients in other prepared foods. Many allergens, such as peanuts, eggs, and milk, may appear unexpectedly in prepared foods. The Food and Drug Administration (FDA) requires U.S. food manufacturers to list the ingredients of prepared foods. In addition, they must use plain language to disclose whether their products contain (or may contain) any of the top eight allergenic foods—eggs, milk, peanuts, tree nuts, soy, wheat, shellfish, and fish.[42] Registered Dietitian Nutritionists with an expertise in food allergy can provide guidance on how best to avoid allergenic foods and how to plan nutritious diets for children with one or more food allergies.

LO 18.3: THE TAKE-HOME MESSAGE MyPlate can help people of all ages make food choices. School meals provide nourishment for many children at breakfast and lunch. Breakfast and lunch provide nutrients that benefit children's cognitive function, academic performance, school attendance rates, psychosocial function, and mood. Caregivers and other adults should be aware of the potential for a child's exposure to food allergens at home and at school.

What Nutrition-Related Issues May Affect School-Aged Children?

LO 18.4 Identify the nutrition-related issues facing school-aged children, including overweight and obesity.

School-aged children become increasingly independent; they develop self-care skills such as tying their own shoes or buckling their own seat belts. Part of going to school and making new friends includes exposure to other children's habits, including eating patterns. School-aged children may become more opinionated about their food preferences based on how they see their peers eat. However, parents and caregivers remain in charge of children's health and welfare, and they must be aware of nutrition-related issues including body weight, type 2 diabetes, and oral health. At this point in the life cycle, children acquire habits that they may keep for life, so encouraging a healthy lifestyle is essential. Parents and caregivers should capitalize on their role-model status.

School-Aged Children Are Experiencing Higher Rates of Obesity

More than 17 percent of U.S. youth are currently overweight or obese.[43] (See **Figure 18.4**.) The percentage of obese children aged 6–11 years in the United States has increased from 7 percent in 1980 to nearly 18 percent in 2010.[44]

Determining Childhood Overweight and Obesity

Beginning at two years of age, body mass index (BMI) is helpful for determining whether or not a child is overweight or obese. CDC growth charts are used to determine the BMI-for-age and sex percentile in children. Because children's body composition varies as they age and between males and females, health professionals use an age- and sex-specific method to determine BMI in those aged 2 to 19 years.[45]

In children and teens, overweight is defined as a BMI at or above the 85th percentile but lower than the 95th percentile, and obesity is defined as a BMI at or above the 95th percentile.[46] However, while BMI is a reasonable indicator of body fatness for most children and adolescents, it is not considered a diagnostic tool.[47] If a child has a high BMI for his age and sex, it remains to be seen if excess fat is the reason. Health care providers should perform further assessments, including skinfold thickness measurements, evaluations of diet, physical activity, and family history, and other appropriate health screenings.

Childhood overweight is more than a matter of extra "baby fat" and should be taken seriously. Children who are obese are likely to remain that way in middle or late childhood and adulthood, and may face serious consequences because of their weight.[48]

Multiple Factors Contribute to Childhood Overweight and Obesity

Several factors can contribute to childhood overweight and **childhood obesity** among U.S. school-aged children, including excessive consumption of kilocalories,

childhood obesity The condition of a child's having too much body weight for his or her height. Rates of childhood obesity in the United States are increasing.

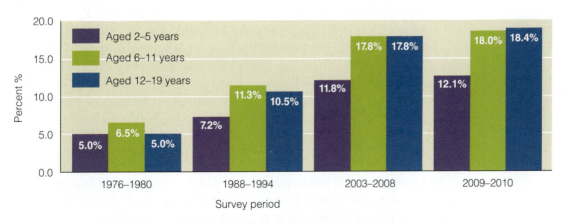

▲ Figure 18.4 Increase in Overweight among U.S. Children and Adolescents

Note: Overweight is defined as a BMI greater than or equal to the gender- and weight-specific 95th percentile from the CDC 2000 Growth Charts.

Source: Data from NCHS Health E-Stat. *Prevalence of Overweight among Children and Adolescents: United States, 2003–2004.* Available at www.cdc.gov/nchs/data/hestat/obesity_child_09_10/obesity_child_09_10.htm# Accessed July 2014.

genetics, a child's environment, a lack of physical activity, and outside influences like peers and the media; there is no single reason or single food or nutrient that is to blame.

Overconsumption of Kilocalories

Overweight and obesity are the result of a kilocaloric imbalance,[49] which can come, as we've seen, from many sources. Parents who are not educated about a balanced diet and the proper amount of food to serve school-aged children may easily overfeed them and children may become accustomed to eating past the point of satiation.[50] The increase in the prevalence of childhood obesity has coincided with an increase in portion sizes of foods both inside and outside the home. Children eat fewer family meals and more meals out, often at quick-service restaurants.[51] The relatively low levels of nutrients in restaurant food, including dietary fiber, and the high kilocalorie density, fat, and sugar content may contribute to excess energy intake in children.[52]

In addition to larger portions, children often have more access to energy-dense foods, which means they get more kilocalories per serving. These foods are typically processed products with added solid fats and added sugar. A recent study among children showed that a high-energy-dense diet is associated with a greater risk for excess body fat during childhood.[53]

Many children drink excess kilocalories. From 1989 to 2008, the percentage of children drinking sugary beverages increased from 79 percent to 91 percent, and kilocalories from sugary beverages increased by 60 percent in children aged 6 to 11, from 130 to 209 kilocalories per day. Sugary drinks, such as regular soda, juice drinks, and sports drinks, are the biggest source of added sugar in the diets of Americans aged 2 and older.[54] Even drinking excessive amounts of milk or 100 percent juice may lead to a kilocalorie imbalance that causes overweight and obesity.

Families typically have busy lifestyles, and snacking has become more prevalent as children miss regular mealtimes because of sports practice or other activities. Children consume 168 more kilocalories per day as snacks than they did in 1977, and, more than ever, snacks are sweetened beverages and salty and sweet foods.[55]

Genetics May Play a Role in Weight Gain

A small percentage of overweight or obesity in children can be attributed to genetic defects such as Prader-Willi syndrome and Down syndrome.[56] For the majority of children, however, the story is more complicated. Studies conducted with twin pairs show a strong connection for BMI between identical twins, suggesting a significant genetic influence on BMI.[57] Still, many people who have "obesity genes" fail to become overweight. During the past thirty years the human gene pool stayed the same, yet childhood obesity increased significantly. Changes in nutrition and physical activity over the past several decades have likely had the greatest impact on the present childhood obesity epidemic.[58]

The Family Environment

Parents and other caregivers are powerful examples for children, and they can guide them in making healthy food choices by being positive role models who eat a balanced diet, participate in regular physical activity, and get adequate sleep. Among children under age 3, the strongest predictor of adulthood obesity is parental obesity, which may be due in part to genetics, but is likely a by-product of learned personal health habits and the environment. The risk of becoming an obese adult is 50 percent if one parent is obese and 80 percent if both parents are obese.[59]

Parents also exert their influence on a child's propensity for overweight and obesity well before birth. Childhood obesity may start in the womb, a child's first environment. Maternal weight gain during pregnancy is a potential reason for a child's increased risk for overweight and obesity years after birth. When the mother overeats during pregnancy, the increased availability of energy may affect appetite, endocrine function, or energy metabolism of the baby for a lifetime.[60]

Family habits, including watching TV while eating dinner, not eating breakfast, and consuming more fast food than homemade food at home, are linked to higher BMI in children.[61] Parents may inadvertently reinforce a child's avoidance of unfamiliar foods if they respond to their picky child's behavior by giving up and offering only the child's favorite foods.[62] Conversely, trying to control children's food intake by pressuring them to eat healthy food, usually fruit and vegetables, restricting access to sweets and fatty snacks, and using food as a reward are likely to backfire. Restriction is directly associated with children's BMI. The more restrictive parents are in what, and how much, food they offer children, the greater the risk for a child's overeating in the absence of parental oversight.[63]

There is little doubt that school-aged children largely model their behavior after their family's. Childhood overweight treatment often takes the form of a family-based behavioral intervention in which parents are intricately involved.[64] Modeling healthy behaviors sends a strong message to children about what to value. When children see adults enjoying healthy foods and physical activity, they are more likely to do the same now and for the rest of their lives. Approaching healthy eating as a family fosters positive change in every member and helps to remove the stigma of overweight from the child. Parents and other caregivers play a crucial role in helping overweight children feel loved and accepted at any size and in control of their weight.

The Environment Outside the Home

The environments of children also include school, after-school child-care settings, recreational facilities, faith-based institutions, governmental agencies, and media and entertainment, and community and transportation infrastructure. Promoting lifestyle habits including healthy eating and regular physical activity on several fronts can reduce the risk of obesity. Government policies not traditionally thought of as health policies, such as those involving transportation, land use, education, agriculture, and economics, may affect health and obesity rates.[65] The U.S. government, along with other health organizations, is working to develop healthy environments by improving access to healthy and fresh foods, and by building walk paths, bike paths, and playgrounds in underserved communities.[66]

Most Children Don't Move Enough

Regular physical activity has many benefits for children, including helping them to attain and maintain a healthy weight as they grow.[67] Despite the importance of regular physical activity in promoting lifelong health and well-being, evidence shows that levels among youth are insufficient.[68]

One major factor that contributes to the decrease in physical activity in children is "screen time": time spent in front of a television, on computers, or on cell phones. Most children in the United States spend about 3 hours a day watching TV. Taken together, all forms of screen time add up to about 5 to 7 hours daily for children.[69] While a certain amount of screen time is necessary for homework, especially in older school-aged kids, excessive screen time, which is sedentary time, is unhealthy. Screen time may also result in increased energy intake, as children, and their parents, may snack and eat meals in front of the television or computer. In addition, TV food advertisements may influence families to purchase and eat kilocalorie-dense, low-nutrient foods.

Experts recommend limiting screen time for entertainment to 2 hours daily in children over age 2, but it's not always easy for parents to adhere to this guideline.[70] It's especially difficult to limit screen time when a child has a television in his

Does Sugar Cause Behavior Problems in Children?

Parents often wonder if dietary factors, such as sugar intake, are responsible for all or some of their children's behavior. Observing young children after they eat cake at a birthday party, for example, can lead one to wonder whether the sugar in the cake causes children to become hyper. In the United States, many young children are diagnosed with behavior-related conditions such as **attention deficit/hyperactivity disorder (ADHD)** (sometimes still called attention deficit disorder, or ADD). ADHD is a condition—generally identified in early childhood—in which children are inattentive, hyperactive, and impulsive.[1] Children with ADHD have difficulty controlling their behavior. An estimated 3 to 5 percent of children (about 2 million) in the United States have ADHD. Given the characteristics of the condition, it can be difficult and frustrating to manage for parents, caregivers, and teachers. It can be easy to assume that there is a connection between sugar, behavior, and ADHD.

Although the myth that sugar contributes to ADHD persists, there is no research to support this. In one study, children whose mothers felt they were sugar sensitive were given aspartame as a substitute for sugar. Half of the mothers

were told their children were given sugar, half that their children were given aspartame. The mothers who thought their children had received sugar were more critical of their behavior and rated them as more hyperactive than the other children.[2]

Based on the available research, the Academy of Nutrition and Dietetics has concluded that sugar doesn't have an effect on behavior or learning. Why, then, do children seem to become hyper when they have sugar? Some suggested explanations for this are that children are excited already because of a special occasion like a birthday party, or simply excited because they love treats!

The American Academy of Pediatrics has also confirmed that there is no

evidence that ADHD is caused by eating too much sugar, or by food additives, allergies, or immunizations.[3] With so many children and families affected by ADHD, more theories about the cause of ADHD have emerged in recent years. Attention disorders often run in families, so there are likely to be genetic influences.[4]

There is a range of treatments for ADHD. Medication, psychotherapy, and behavioral therapies, as well as diet restrictions, are among the many methods used to address the condition. Parents of children with ADHD may want to consult with a dietitian to help their child with nutritional issues, such as underweight due to side effects of medications that decrease appetite. Disruptive mealtimes may also be a concern (if untreated). Organizations such as the National Institute of Mental Health (www.nimh.nih.gov) and the American Academy of Child and Adolescent Psychiatry (www.aacap.org/index.ww) provide information for families with children who have ADHD.

References

1. PubMed Health. 2013. *Attention Deficit Hyperactivity Disorder.* Available at www.ncbi.nlm.nih.gov/pubmedhealth/PMH0002518. Accessed July 2014.
2. Ibid.
3. Position of the American Dietetic Association. 2012. "Use of Nutritive and Nonnutritive Sweeteners." *Journal of the Academy of Nutrition and Dietetics* 112:739–758.
4. B. Franke, et al. 2012. "The Genetics of Attention Deficit/Hyperactivity Disorder in Adults, A Review." *Molecular Psychiatry* 17:960–987. Available at www.nature.com/mp/journal/v17/n10/full/mp2011138a.html. Accessed July 2014.

attention deficit/hyperactivity disorder (ADHD) (previously known as attention deficit disorder, or ADD) A condition in which an individual may be easily distracted, have difficulty listening and following directions, difficulty focusing and sustaining attention, difficulty concentrating and staying on task, and/or inconsistent performance in school.

bedroom. A recent study found that 60 percent of children aged 10 to 14 had TVs in their bedrooms. A TV in the bedroom was associated with gaining about one extra pound per year for the four-year duration of the study, compared with not having a TV in the bedroom.[71] The American Academy of Pediatrics suggests that parents establish "screen-free" zones at home by allowing no televisions, computers, or video games in children's bedrooms, and by turning off the TV during dinner.[72]

Televisions, computers, and cell phones may interfere with a child's sleep, which may affect his weight. Many studies have examined the relationship between sleep duration and childhood obesity, and most suggest a link between inadequate sleep and overweight.[73] However, further studies are needed for a definitive answer on the topic.

Children aged 6 to 12 spend much of their day at school, and most of the time they are sitting in the classroom, which, like screen time, is a sedentary activity. Daily, quality physical education in schools can help students meet the 60-minutes-a-day guideline for exercise as outlined in the *2008 Physical Activity Guidelines for Americans*.[74] However, opportunities for regular physical activity are limited in many schools; daily physical education is provided in only 4 percent of elementary schools and 8 percent of middle schools in the United States.[75]

Media and Advertising Target Children

Food and beverage companies market extensively to children, even those as young as 2 years old.[76] According to the Institute of Medicine, food and beverage marketing influences children's food preferences, what they want to buy, and their overall diet.[77] Marketers are finding more ways to target children online and through smart phone applications, but television remains the top vehicle for food marketing to children. A 2009 study found that children who watched a TV program with food advertising ate 45 percent more food than children who watched a program with advertising for nonfood items.[78]

Let's Move! is a comprehensive initiative, launched by First Lady Michelle Obama, that encourages children to increase their physical activity.

Federal policymakers have begun to address the issue of marketing food products to children. An interagency group representing the Federal Trade Commission (FTC), U.S. Department of Agriculture, Food and Drug Administration, and Centers for Disease Control and Prevention have proposed voluntary nutrition guidelines for food companies, which state that marketing should bolster healthier choices, such as whole grains and produce, and that unhealthy fats, sugar, and sodium should be limited in foods marketed to youth.[79]

Friends Can Influence Food Preferences

As children age, they have greater access to their peers, and the way their peers' families eat and exercise. For children whose parents are inconsistent about offering healthy foods and getting regular exercise, peers can be positive role models. But peers may also negatively influence a child's food preferences. It's important for parents to lay a strong foundation of healthy habits at home so that kids know what's expected of them when they are away from the house. One of the best ways to establish expectations about behavior is to practice healthy eating and staying physically active as a family. Children need to know that each family conducts itself differently, and that, for their family, healthy living is a priority.

School-Aged Children Should Practice Good Dental Hygiene

The potential for tooth decay begins as soon as teeth emerge from the gums, so parents and caregivers must encourage tooth-friendly dental practices as early as possible. Unfortunately, many school-aged children do not practice adequate dental hygiene habits, and dental caries may result. In 2011, the Centers for Disease Control and Prevention (CDC) reported that tooth decay affects more than one-fourth of U.S. children aged 2 to 5 years.[80]

Untreated cavities in children can keep kids out of school, make concentration difficult, and hurt appearance, which may affect a child's quality of life. Left untreated, dental caries can cause serious health problems in addition to pain and discomfort.[81]

It's better to prevent dental caries than to treat them. Frequent ingestion of sugars and other carbohydrates, including fruit juices, and prolonged contact of these substances with teeth are particular risk factors in the development of caries, and should be limited.[82]

LO 18.4: THE TAKE-HOME MESSAGE School-aged children are more overweight now than ever before. Parents and other caregivers are strong models for health behaviors. A child's home environment is the one that exerts the most influence over his health behaviors now and in the future. Many other children's environments should be modified for healthier eating and more physical activity. Parents and caregivers should limit low-nutrient foods and promote physical activity in their children by encouraging them to be active, being active with them, and supporting their physical activities. Children should practice good dental hygiene, including a healthy diet and regular brushing and flossing, to prevent dental caries.

What Are the Nutritional Needs of Adolescents?

LO 18.5 Describe the nutritional needs of adolescents.

Adolescence is the stage of the life cycle between ages 9 and 19. With adolescence come many hormonal, physical, and emotional changes. Among the physical changes are a rapid **growth spurt,** and, for girls, the first menstrual period, or **menarche.** Growth must be supported with appropriate amounts of nutrients, as the requirements for most nutrients increases from childhood. Teens should choose nutrient-dense foods to meet their increased nutrient needs and optimize their development without consuming excess kilocalories.

The growth spurt of adolescence involves more than just getting taller. While height increases (adolescents attain about 15 percent of their adult height during this stage), weight also increases (they attain about 50 percent of their ideal adult weight), and bones grow significantly. Increases in lean muscle mass and body fat stores are also part of the adolescent growth spurt.

As with younger age groups, rates of overweight and obesity are increasing among adolescents. Results from the 2009–2010 National Health and Nutrition Examination Survey (NHANES) show that the percentage of overweight adolescents aged 12 to 19 increased from 11 to 17 percent.[83] In addition, more than half of young people in grades 9 to 12 do not regularly engage in vigorous physical activity. Daily participation in high school physical education classes dropped from 42 percent in 1991 to 18 percent in 2009.[84]

Adolescents Need Calcium and Vitamin D for Bone Development

Adolescents experience rapid bone growth. Almost half of **peak bone mass** is accumulated during adolescence. Most of the growth occurs in the **epiphyseal plate**

adolescence The developmental period between childhood and early adulthood (approximately ages 9 through 19).

growth spurt A rapid increase in height and weight.

menarche The onset of menstruation.

peak bone mass The maximum bone mass achieved.

epiphyseal plate The growth plate of the bone. In puberty, growth in this area leads to increases in height.

(**Figure 18.5**), the area of tissue near the end of the long bones. The growth plate determines the future length and shape of the mature bone. At some point during adolescence, bone growth stops. The plates close and are replaced by solid bone.[85] Adolescence is the last chance to maximize the potential of bone tissue. Adequate calcium and vitamin D intakes maximize bone development. Inadequate calcium intake is one factor that can lead to low peak bone mass and is considered a risk factor for osteoporosis.[86] The RDA for calcium is 1,000 milligrams for those aged 9 to 18. The RDA for vitamin D is 600 IU for all children over 1 year old.[87]

Getting enough dietary calcium is a concern for adolescents, particularly for females.[88] Just 15 percent of females aged 9 to 13 years and about 10 percent of those aged 14 to 19 meet the 1,300-milligram-a-day requirement.[89]

Teens don't take in enough calcium if they replace calcium-rich milk products with soft drinks, such as energy drinks and soda. Nearly all of the milk sold in the United States is fortified with vitamin D, so when teens don't drink milk, they miss out on a substantial source of this nutrient. For example, eight ounces of fortified milk supplies 100 I.U. of vitamin D, or 1/6 of a teen's daily requirement.

The Calculation Corner shows how to determine how much of a teen's daily calcium requirement is fulfilled by a glass of milk.

Adolescents Need Iron for Muscle Growth and Blood Volume

Iron needs are highest during growth spurts and after the onset of menstruation. Adolescents need more iron than younger children and most older adults to support muscle growth and increased blood volume. Adolescent girls need additional iron to replace monthly losses due to menstruation. The RDA for iron for females aged 14 to 18 is 15 milligrams per day; boys need 11 milligrams per day.[90] These recommendations are based on the amount of dietary iron needed to maintain adequate iron stores.

According to the USDA, the average daily iron intake from foods is about 15 milligrams a day in those aged 12 to 19 years.[91] Teens, particularly girls, may

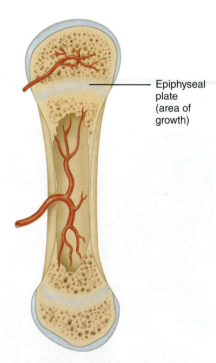

▲ **Figure 18.5 Epiphyseal Plate in Long Bone**
Adolescent bone growth takes place along the epiphyseal plate. Once the plate closes, lengthening of the bone stops.

Epiphyseal plate (area of growth)

Teen Table Tips

Read the Nutrient Facts panel on soda food labels to find out how many kilocalories are in a serving.

Listen to real-life stories of people who use weight-loss pills or other quick fixes to lose weight rather than eating in a healthy way to get results.

Locate trustworthy websites for information, such as http://kidshealth.org/teen/food_fitness.

Be a role model! Eat well, get enough rest, exercise, be realistic about dieting, and don't smoke.

Look for healthy options, such as salads and granola bars, at fast-food restaurants and in vending machines to make independent, healthy food choices.

Teen eating habits are often influenced by peers and social settings.

have inadequate iron intake if they restrict their overall food intake or avoid fortified grains, lean meats, seafood, nuts, and legumes. The symptoms of iron deficiency include weakness, fatigue, and a short attention span. Iron deficiency can also result in poor appetite, increased susceptibility to infection, and irritability. Iron-deficiency anemia is characterized by additional symptoms of paleness, exhaustion, and rapid heart rate. Several tests are used to diagnose iron-deficiency anemia, including hematocrit, hemoglobin, and serum ferritin.[92] In most cases, dietary iron supplements as part of a balanced diet are prescribed to replenish and maintain iron stores.[93]

LO 18.5: THE TAKE-HOME MESSAGE Adolescence brings many changes, including rapid physical growth that requires increased intake of most nutrients. Calcium and iron intake are particularly important during this period to ensure adequate bone and muscle growth, and support increased blood volume. Increased consumption of soft drinks and decreased milk consumption can compromise bone development. As part of a balanced diet, adequate consumption of lean meats, enriched grains, and legumes on a regular basis may improve iron stores in teens.

What Nutritional Issues Affect Adolescents?

LO 18.6 Discuss the nutritional issues that affect adolescents, including disordered eating.

Adolescence is a time of significant social and emotional change as well as tremendous physical growth and development. During the transition from childhood to adulthood, teens establish behaviors and make lifestyle choices, including what and how much they eat and exercise, that affect their health in the short term and the long run. Adolescents experience a strong desire for independence and individuality, and want to make their own decisions. Many earn their own money through a part-time job, and some have their own car, or other ways to get around. Increased financial means and mobility as well as more time spent away from home means teens are making more of their own food choices. Some teens exert their independence at the dinner table by adopting vegetarianism or veganism, or other more potentially restrictive ways of eating.

Outside Influences Play a Role

Parents and siblings, peers, sports figures and other celebrities, and images in traditional and social media influence adolescents. Teens may adopt damaging health habits in order to emulate what they see in the media or to fit in with their peer group. Social media have transformed the teenage years. It used to be that the pressures of high school could be left at the front door, and home was a safe haven from peer pressure. The advent of social media may increase pressure on teens to be thin or popular, or both. It's important for teenagers to feel that home is a safe, loving environment where they won't be judged and will be nurtured.

Strong family bonds are part of promoting healthier habits. Much has been made about the value of family meals on teen nutrition, but articles may overstate the specific link between family meals and teen eating behavior. Parents can model good behavior at the table and serve healthy foods at family meals, and it's often the only time of the day when family members speak face to face. However, it's difficult to isolate family mealtime benefits: Families that dine together most nights may also have other healthy behaviors. The good news is that when parent-child bonds are strong, dining together may contribute to fewer depressive symptoms and less tobacco, drug, and alcohol use in teens.[94, 95]

Adolescents Are Sometimes at Risk for Disordered Eating

As discussed in Chapter 14, teenagers may experience poor body image that could result in disordered eating. Disordered eating behaviors, such as anorexia nervosa and bulimia nervosa, are more prevalent among adolescent girls than adolescent boys, but are on the rise in males. An estimated 10 million men living in the United States will experience an eating disorder at some point during their lifetime, according to the National Eating Disorders Association.[96] One 2011 study described the rates of eating disorders, including anorexia nervosa, bulimia nervosa, and binge eating disorder, finding that the median ages for several types of disordered eating occurred at about 12 to 13 years of age. In addition, this study found that a large percentage of males as well as females experience anorexia nervosa and bulimia.[97]

Several risk factors may put teens at risk for eating disorders, including perceived or real pressure to be thin, paired with a distorted body image; low self-esteem; participation in activities such as figure skating, gymnastics, or wrestling, where body image and weight can be major issues; and personality traits such as perfectionism.[98]

It's not always possible, even for the most motivated and caring parents, to prevent disordered eating in teens. Experts recommend open communication about healthy eating. As a parent, voicing your pleasure at being strong as opposed to voicing your displeasure with your perceived flaws may help your children develop a good attitude toward their own bodies. Concentrating on good health, not thinness, may promote the idea that health is preferable to thinness.

Early intervention programs are crucial for those with disordered eating and it's important that caregivers recognize the signs of disordered eating. Interventions can increase the adaptability and coping skills of teens and family members to prevent eating disorders.[99]

Teens grapple with trying to fit in and must adjust to new bodies, new thoughts, new situations, and new experiences. All of this, along with the typical adolescent feeling of immortality, may encourage an adolescent to engage in risky tactics to reach a desired weight. Teens can sometimes adopt a variety of unhealthy habits, including eating very little food, skipping meals, smoking cigarettes, using diet pills, self-inducing vomiting, or using laxatives or diuretics, all of which can lead to disordered eating. In addition to body image issues, alcohol and drug use can adversely affect dietary intake of energy and nutrients.

LO 18.6: THE TAKE-HOME MESSAGE Adolescents want to have control over their food and lifestyle decisions. Peers and media also exert a strong influence. Adolescents are sometimes at risk of developing disordered eating patterns due to poor body image, emotional issues, or peer pressure. Because adolescents often live in the present, they may not think about the long-term health consequences of poor diet and lifestyle habits they adopt during their teen years.

What Are the Health Effects of Childhood Obesity?

LO 18.7 Identify the health risks of obesity in children and teens.

Childhood obesity can have multiple health consequences, including physical, mental, and even social problems. Generally speaking, the more obese the child is, the worse the potential health outcomes. Some effects of childhood overweight and obesity are apparent in youth, while many others may appear decades later.

The first step in helping an overweight child is to get the child evaluated by a health professional.

Childhood Obesity and Type 2 Diabetes Risk

One result of increased obesity among children is an associated increase in rates of type 2 diabetes. As you learned in Chapter 4, this previously adult-onset disease has begun to appear as a childhood-onset disease as well. Type 2 diabetes has been reported among U.S. children and adolescents with increasing frequency in the last two decades.[100] A recent report estimated that 15 percent of new diabetes cases among children and adolescents are type 2 diabetes.[101]

Childhood obesity and low levels of physical activity, as well as exposure to diabetes in utero, may contribute to the increase in type 2 diabetes during childhood and adolescence. Children and teens diagnosed with type 2 diabetes are often obese, have a strong family history for type 2 diabetes, and have insulin resistance. Native American youth have the highest prevalence of type 2 diabetes.[102]

Obese adolescents are more likely to have prediabetes, a condition in which blood glucose levels indicate a high risk for development of type 2 diabetes. An estimated 16 percent of teens aged 12 to 19 years have prediabetes, which often goes undiagnosed because clinical symptoms are not apparent.[103] Increasing diabetes and prediabetes rates among U.S. youth is of great concern, because these children will likely become adults who will live with diabetes for most of their lives and may develop diabetes-related complications, such as heart and kidney disease, nerve damage, and vision problems, at a much younger age than previously seen.

It's possible to delay and even prevent the onset of type 2 diabetes in at-risk obese youth. Lifestyle changes that remove unnecessary kilocalories supplied by low-nutrient foods, such as sugary drinks, increase nutrient-rich foods such as fruits, vegetables, whole grains, lean protein foods, and low-fat dairy, and increase physical activity can make a big difference in an obese child's chances for avoiding type 2 diabetes.[104]

What can families do to prevent type 2 diabetes? To start, identify those at highest risk. If a child's parents or grandparents have diabetes, it is critical to pay close attention to the child's health. Decreasing a child's risk factors, such as being overweight or sedentary, ought to be on the "to do" list as well. If a child is diagnosed with type 2 diabetes, early intervention and treatment are a must. The sooner the family learns what the child needs to eat and how to manage all other aspects of the disease, the better off the child will be.

For children who have type 2 diabetes, family support and encouragement are essential to their ability to successfully manage the disease. The entire family should consider eating in the same fashion as the child, because managing type 2 diabetes involves moderation, variety, and balance. Physical activity is also a major part of managing this disease, and everyone can take part in this as well. Taking a family walk or bike ride after dinner instead of turning on the TV, or enjoying weekend games of basketball or tennis, are excellent ways to teach the importance of exercise. The child is more likely to feel supported and succeed with keeping diabetes under control if everyone in the family is educated about what to do to help.

Other Risks Associated with Childhood Obesity

Beyond the risk of type 2 diabetes, obese children are more likely to have high blood pressure and high cholesterol, which are risk factors for cardiovascular disease (CVD). In one study, 70 percent of obese children had at least one CVD risk factor, and 39 percent had two or more.[105]

Overweight and obese children may suffer emotional problems in addition to physical ones. Research shows that obese children tend to experience more depression and have lower self-esteem compared with their nonoverweight peers.[106] Low self-esteem can create overwhelming feelings of hopelessness in some overweight children.[107] In addition, some children overeat to cope with problems or deal with emotions, such as stress, or to fight boredom or loneliness, which may intensify their weight issues. It's important to support overweight children in their daily lives and while they are in treatment. Research shows improved psychosocial functioning in children participating in weight-control treatments, and that these changes are typically independent of weight-loss outcomes.[108]

Perhaps one of the most obvious risks of childhood obesity is that it will continue into adulthood, bringing with it all of the risks associated with obesity in adulthood. Children and adolescents who are obese are likely to be obese as adults and are therefore more at risk for adult health problems such as heart disease, stroke, several types of cancer, sleep apnea, asthma, nonalcoholic fatty liver disease (NAFLD), and osteoarthritis.[109]

Reducing and Managing Childhood Overweight and Obesity

Childhood overweight is a multifactorial public health problem with personal, psychosocial, and financial ramifications. There is no single solution to reverse the rising tide of unhealthy weights among children in the United States, but there are plenty of reasons to try, one of which is that obesity in children can lead to costly medical problems later in life.[110]

There may be a need for better identification of childhood overweight and obesity at younger ages so that children can receive the help they need earlier in life. Health care providers, most often pediatricians, have the knowledge to identify children with high BMI-for-age percentiles and to recommend treatment. However, childhood obesity often goes undiagnosed. According to the American Heart Association, obesity was identified less often in children who were very young, and obese children who were not identified as such had a lower prevalence of weight evaluation and management. Children who were older at the time of their first clinical visit were more likely to receive counseling about physical activity and diet.[111]

Treatment goals for overweight children are to promote a healthy lifestyle and maintain weight, rather than attempt weight loss. Because children are still growing in height, maintaining weight while they continue to grow reduces the degree of overweight.[112] Encouraging overweight children to participate in regular physical activity helps them achieve the treatment goals. If a child's weight or BMI percentile does not improve as desired over three to six months of planned treatment, the provider and family should consider more intensive treatment.[113]

Parents who are concerned about their child's weight should consult first with the child's pediatrician. Putting a child on a restrictive diet, which may lack the essential nutrients children

need to grow and develop properly, may also encourage disordered eating in the long run. A Registered Dietitian Nutritionist can provide dietary counseling and help families implement the best eating plan for achieving and maintaining a healthy body weight for overweight and obese children.

The American Association of Pediatrics (AAP) has been focusing on preventing childhood obesity. Parental obesity and steep weight gain during early childhood help to identify children who might benefit from preventive measures. To reduce their children's risk of becoming overweight or obese, parents and caregivers need to be sure that children receive adequate nutrients without overloading on kilocalories, sugar, and fat, and that they participate in plenty of physical activity. The AAP recommends that parents and caregivers serve as role models when it comes to healthy eating and offer children healthy snacks such as vegetables, fruits, low-fat dairy products, and whole grains coupled with physical activity.

LO 18.7: THE TAKE-HOME MESSAGE

Overweight and obese children and adolescents are at greater risk for health problems. Increasing obesity rates are contributing to rising rates of type 2 diabetes and other health problems in children and teenagers. Causes of childhood diabetes include obesity, lack of exercise, and exposure to diabetes in utero. Changes in diet and exercise can reverse obesity, and may delay or prevent the onset of type 2 diabetes and other health problems.

Visual Chapter Summary

LO 18.1 The Needs of Toddlers and Preschoolers Are Met with Small, Nutrient-Dense Meals

Toddlers and preschoolers need frequent, small, nutrient-dense meals and snacks to consume adequate amounts of kilocalories and nutrients to fuel their growth and development. Young children need enough calcium and vitamin D to ensure healthy bone growth and adequate fiber and fluid for bowel regularity. Milk, water, and diluted 100 percent juice are better beverage choices than sugar-added drinks.

LO 18.2 Adults Influence Young Children's Eating Habits

Young children may be picky eaters and go on food jags, but these behaviors are normal and usually temporary. Caregivers should allow children to participate in food preparation and to choose the foods they eat from among several healthy options. New foods may need to be offered from 10 to 15 times before the child accepts them. Caregivers should act as role models by adopting the lifelong healthy eating habits they want to see in their children.

LO 18.3 MyPlate Helps School-Aged Children to Meet Their Nutritional Needs

The quality of the diet influences growth and development of school-aged children. School-aged children have the capacity to eat more and maintain blood glucose levels longer, and are less hungry between meals than younger children. Children who bring lunch from home should be involved in the planning and preparation of the lunch so they are more likely to consume it. Research shows that eating breakfast positively influences a child's energy levels, nutrient intake, and mental performance throughout the day.

LO 18.4 Obesity and Type 2 Diabetes May Affect Overweight Children

Obesity and type 2 diabetes are occurring at higher rates in children, particularly teens. Genetic and environmental factors, including poor dietary choices and inadequate exercise, are key sources of this problem. Children with type 2 diabetes are prone to several health problems.

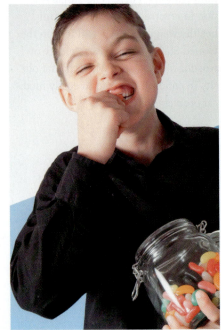

LO 18.5 Nutritional Needs of Adolescents Are Based on Hormonal and Physical Changes

Rates of overweight and obesity are increasing among adolescents. Adolescents require a nutrient-dense diet to meet their nutrient needs. Adolescents experience rapid bone growth, and adequate calcium and vitamin D intake supports this process. Overconsumption of soda may interfere with calcium intake if it displaces milk in the diet. Adequate iron intake is important for growth of lean muscle and blood volume. Girls' need for dietary iron increases after the onset of menstruation. Dieting, or limiting enriched grains, lean meats, and legumes, may result in inadequate iron intake.

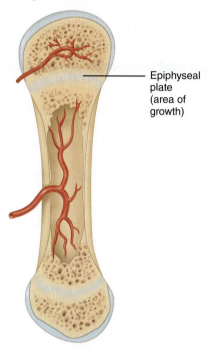

Epiphyseal plate (area of growth)

LO 18.6 Nutritional Issues That Affect Adolescents Are Due to Social and Emotional Changes

Adolescents are heavily influenced by peers, media, and other nonparental role models, which may lead them to adopt unhealthy eating and lifestyle habits, such as skipping meals, choosing unhealthy foods, dieting, or smoking. Adolescents are sometimes at risk of developing disordered eating patterns due to poor body image, emotional issues, or peer pressure.

LO 18.7 Childhood Obesity Has Several Health Effects

More children are overweight than ever before. Overweight and obese children are likely to stay that way into adulthood, putting them at greater risk for conditions such as heart disease and stroke. Type 2 diabetes is a result of rising obesity rates and affects an increasing number of children in the United States, particularly teens. Type 2 diabetes can damage the heart, kidney, nerves, and vision.

Terms to Know

- toddlers
- preschoolers
- food jags
- school-aged children
- childhood obesity
- attention deficit/ hyperactivity disorder (ADHD)
- adolescence
- growth spurt
- menarche
- peak bone mass
- epiphyseal plate

MasteringNutrition™

Scan to hear an MP3 chapter review in MasteringNutrition.

Check Your Understanding

1. When feeding toddlers and preschoolers, what is the best rule to remember?
   a. Decide for the child how much to eat at each meal.
   b. Offer small portions of a variety of healthy foods at each meal.
   c. Offer three tablespoons of food per year of age.
   d. Don't offer new foods.

2. During periods of rapid growth, young children are at a particular risk for developing
   a. iron deficiency.
   b. calcium toxicity.
   c. vitamin D toxicity.
   d. vitamin toxicity.

3. In order to foster healthy eating habits in children, caregivers should
   a. serve them only the foods they like.
   b. offer them a limited variety of foods.
   c. insist that they eat everything on their plate.
   d. allow them to stop eating when they are full.

4. MyPlate illustrates the _____ food groups that are the building blocks of a healthy diet.
   a. four
   b. five
   c. seven
   d. ten

5. Children are considered overweight if they have a BMI greater than or equal to the _____ percentile.
   a. 65th
   b. 75th
   c. 85th
   d. 95th

6. The American Academy of Pediatrics recommends that screen time be limited to no more than _____ daily.
   a. 1 hour
   b. 2 hours
   c. 3 hours
   d. 4 hours

7. There appears to be a relationship between the rise in childhood obesity and the increase in
   a. childhood cancers.
   b. eating disorders.
   c. type 2 diabetes.
   d. childhood cavities.

8. Which mineral supports healthy bone development and is particularly important during adolescence?
   a. calcium
   b. iron
   c. zinc
   d. copper

9. The need for iron increases during adolescence to support muscle growth and _____.
   a. blood volume
   b. bone development
   c. heart health
   d. kidney function

10. _____ may play a protective role in reducing the risk of disordered eating.
    a. Social engagement
    b. Restful sleep
    c. Emphasizing good health
    d. Regular physical activity

Answers

1. (b) A young child's appetite can fluctuate. Offer small portions of a variety of healthy foods at every meal and allow children to choose.

2. (a) Iron deficiency is the most common nutrient deficiency among young children. This is often due to an overly heavy milk diet.

3. (d) Caregivers should allow young children to stop eating when they are full. Forcing children to clean their plate may result in food struggles or overeating. Offer children new foods, not just what they are accustomed to.

4. (b) MyPlate illustrates these five food groups: vegetables, fruits, grains, dairy, and protein foods. They are the building blocks for a healthy diet using a familiar image—a place setting for a meal.

5. (c) Children with a BMI greater than or equal to the 85th percentile are considered overweight.

6. (b) To encourage more time for physical activity, the American Academy of Pediatrics recommends that screen time be limited to no more than 2 hours daily.

7. (c) Rates of type 2 diabetes among children, particularly teens, have risen along with rates of overweight and obesity.

8. (a) Adolescents need adequate amounts of calcium to support their growing bones.

9. (a) The need for iron is increased in adolescent girls to replace iron loss as part of the blood loss of menstruation.

10. (c) Parental emphasis of health rather than thinness may play a protective role in preventing disordered eating.

Answers to True or False?

1. **False.** Toddlers' growth slows down significantly compared with infants'. During the second year of life, a toddler may gain 3 to 5 pounds.

2. **True.** Between the ages of 1 and 4, small children are extremely active and may not be as interested in eating.

3. **False.** Milk is a source of important nutrients; however, it doesn't provide all the nutrients that growing children need. A variety of other foods are also needed to provide key nutrients for proper growth and development.

4. **False.** Iron deficiency may be caused by a limited diet that relies too heavily on milk or other iron-poor food sources.

5. **False.** Parents and caregivers may need to offer foods numerous times before a child accepts them.

6. **True.** Young children often refuse foods of a certain color, texture, or taste. Alternatively, they may get hooked on a particular food and eat only that item for a while.

7. **False.** Though high-fat, high-sugar foods often found in fast-food restaurants are part of the problem,

that's not the whole story. An overall poor diet with kilocalorie-dense foods and inadequate physical activity also contribute.

8. **True.** The school lunch and school breakfast programs must meet specific requirements in order to receive funding from the USDA.

9. **False.** Sodas, including diet sodas, provide nothing but kilocalories, and the teenage years are a nutritionally critical period.

10. **False.** Inadequate calcium and iron intakes are common among adolescents. Teens tend to prefer sugar-sweetened soft drinks to calcium-rich milk. Teens need iron to support muscle growth and increased blood volume. Adolescent females also need more iron than males to support the onset of menstruation.

Web Resources

- For more information on nutrition for preschoolers, visit www.choosemyplate.gov/preschoolers.html
- For more information on nutrition during the younger years, visit www.cdc.gov/healthyyouth/nutrition/facts.htm
- For more information on children's and teens' health, visit http://kidshealth.org
- To learn about practical tools for keeping kids at a healthy weight, visit We Can! at www.nhlbi.nih.gov/health/public/heart/obesity/wecan/index.htm
- For more about the USDA's School Lunch Program, visit www.fns.usda.gov/cnd/lunch
- For more information on increasing fruit and vegetable consumption, visit Fruits & Veggies—More Matters, at www.fruitsandveggiesmorematters.org

References

1. National Center for Health Statistics. 2000. *2000 CDC Growth Charts for the United States: Methods and Development.* U.S. Vital and Health Statistics, Health Resources Administration. Washington, DC: U.S. Government Printing Office. Available at www.cdc.gov/growthcharts/2000growthchart-us.pdf. Accessed April 2014.

2. Siega-Riz, A. M., D. M. Deming, K. C. Reidy, M. K. Fox, E. Condon, and R. R. Briefel. 2010. Food Consumption Patterns of Infants and Toddlers: Where Are We Now? *Journal of the American Dietetic Association* 110:S38–S51.

3. American Academy of Pediatrics. 2012. *Age-Related Safety Sheets: 6–12 Months.* Available at www.healthychildren.org/English/tips-tools/Pages/Safety-for-Your-Child-6-to-12-Months.aspx. Accessed April 2014.

4. National Resource Center for Health and Safety in Child Care and Early Education. 2014. State Licensing and Regulation Information. Available at http://nrckids.org. Accessed June 2014.

5. HHS/USDA. 2010. *Dietary Guidelines for Americans, 2010.* Available at www.health.gov/dietaryguidelines/dga2010/dietaryguidelines2010.pdf. Accessed April 2014.

6. Institute of Medicine. 2005. *Dietary Reference Intakes for Energy, Carbohydrate, Fiber, Fat, Fatty Acids, Cholesterol, Protein, and Amino Acids (Macronutrients).* Washington, DC: National Academies Press.

7. Ibid.

8. Ibid.

9. Ibid.

10. HHS/USDA. 2010. *Dietary Guidelines for Americans, 2010.*

11. Institute of Medicine. 2001. *Dietary Reference Intakes for Vitamin A, Vitamin K, Arsenic, Boron, Chromium, Copper, Iodine, Iron, Manganese, Nickel, Silicon, Vanadium, and Zinc.* Washington, DC: The National Academies Press.

12. Siega-Riz, et al. 2010. Food Consumption Patterns of Infants and Toddlers.

13. Centers for Disease Control and Prevention. 2011. *Iron and Iron Deficiency.* Available at www.cdc.gov/nutrition/everyone/basics/vitamins/iron.html. Accessed June 2014.

14. Centers for Disease Control and Prevention. 2013. *FastStats.* Available at www.cdc.gov. Accessed May 2014.

15. World Health Organization. 2014. *Micronutrient Deficiencies.* Available at www.who.int/nutrition/topics/ida/en/. Accessed June 2014.

16. Baker, R. D., F. R. Greer, and The Committee on Nutrition. 2010. Diagnosis and Prevention of Iron Deficiency and Iron-Deficiency Anemia in Infants and Young Children (0–3 Years of Age). *Pediatrics* 126:1040–1050.

17. National Institutes of Health. 2012. *Iron Overdose.* Available at www.nlm.nih.gov/medlineplus/ency/article/002659.htm. Accessed June 2014.

18. U.S. Food and Drug Administration. 2011. *Code of Federal Regulations Title 21. Sec. 101.17 Food Labeling Warning, Notice, and Safe Handling Statements.* Available at www.accessdata.fda.gov/scripts/cdrh/cfdocs/cfcfr/CFRSearch.cfm?fr=101.17. Accessed April 2014.

19. Institute of Medicine. 2010. *Dietary Reference Intakes for Calcium and Vitamin D.*

Washington, DC: National Academies Press. Available at www.iom.edu/reports/2010/dietary-reference-intakes-for-calcium-and-vitamin-D.aspx. Accessed April 2014.

20. Ibid.

21. Ibid.

22. Craig, W. J., and A. R. Mangels. 2009. Position of the American Dietetic Association: Vegetarian Diets. *Journal of the American Dietetic Association* 109:1266–1282.

23. Wardle, J., M.-L. Herrera, L. Cooke, and E. L. Gibson. 2003. Modifying Children's Food Preferences: The Effects of Exposure and Reward on Acceptance of an Unfamiliar Vegetable. *European Journal of Clinical Nutrition* 57:341–348.

24. Satter, E. 2012. *Ellyn Satter's Division of Responsibility in Feeding.* Available at www.ellynsatter.com/ellyn-satters-division-of-responsibility-in-feeding-i-80.html. Accessed April 2012.

25. Gibson, E. L., et al. 2012. A Narrative Review of Psychological and Educational Strategies Applied to Young Children's Eating Behaviours Aimed at Reducing Obesity Risk. *Obesity Review* Suppl. 1:85–95.

26. Kliegman, R. M., B. F. Stanton, J. St. Geme, N. F. Schor, and R. E. Behrman. 2011. *Nelson Textbook of Pediatrics.* 19th ed. Philadelphia: W. B. Saunders.

27. U.S. Department of Agriculture. Economic Research Service. 2013. *National School Lunch Program.* Available at www.ers.usda.gov/topics/food-nutrition-assistance/child-nutrition-programs/national-school-lunch-program.aspx#.U5iYn8aEQ58. Accessed June 2014.

28. Ibid.

29. Gleason, P., R. Briefel, A. Wilson, and A. Hedley Dodd. 2009. *School Meal Program Participation and Its Association with Dietary Patterns and Childhood Obesity.* Mathematica Policy Research, Inc. Contractor and Cooperation Report No. 55. Available at www.naldc.nal.usda.gov/download/35896/pdf. Accessed July 2014.

30. Gundersen, C., B. Kreider, and J. Pepper. 2012. The Impact of the National School Lunch Program on Child Health: A Nonparametric Bounds Analysis. *Journal of Econometrics* 166:79–91.

31. Szajewska, H., and M. Ruszczynski. 2010. Systematic Review Demonstrating That Breakfast Consumption Influences Body Weight Outcomes in Children and Adolescents in Europe. *Critical Reviews in Food Science and Nutrition* 50:113–119.

32. U.S. Department of Agriculture. Economic Research Service. 2013. *School Breakfast Program.* Available at www.ers.usda.gov/topics/food-nutrition-assistance/child-nutrition-programs/school-breakfast-program.aspx#.U7LxrcaEQ58. Accessed July 2014.

33. Gleason, et al. 2009. *School Meal Program Participation and Its Association with Dietary Patterns and Childhood Obesity.*

34. Adolphus, K., C. L. Lawton, and L. Dye. 2013. The Effects of Breakfast on Behavior and Academic Performance in Children and

Adolescents. *Frontiers in Human Neuroscience.* Available at www.ncbi.nlm.nih.gov/pmc/articles/PMC3737458/. Accessed June 2014.

35. Healthy People 2020. 2012. *Nutrition and Weight Status Objectives.* Available at www.healthypeople.gov/2020/topicsobjectives2020/objectiveslist.aspx?topicid=29. Accessed April 2014.

36. Centers for Disease Control and Prevention. 2013. *Fruits and Vegetables.* Available at www.cdc.gov/nutrition/everyone/fruitsvegetables/index.html?s_cid=tw_ob191. Accessed June 2014.

37. Prelip, M., M. Slusser, C. L. Thai, J. Kinsler, and J. T. Erausquin. 2011. Effects of a School-Based Nutrition Program Diffused Throughout a Large Urban Community on Attitudes, Beliefs, and Behaviors Related to Fruit and Vegetable Consumption. *Journal of School Health* 81:520–529.

38. Blatt, A. D., L. S. Roe, and B. J. Rolls. 2011. Hidden Vegetables: An Effective Strategy to Reduce Energy Intake and Increase Vegetable Intake in Adults. *American Society for Nutrition.* Available at http://ajcn.nutrition.org/content/93/4/756.full. Accessed July 2014.

39. Gupta, R., et al. 2011. *The Prevalence, Severity, and Distribution of Childhood Food Allergy in the United States.* Available at www.pediatrics.aappublications.org/content/early/2011/06/16/peds.2011-0204.full.pdf+html. Accessed June 2014.

40. Boyce, J. A., A. Assa'ad, A. W. Burks, S. M. Jones, H. A. Sampson, R. A. Wood, et al. 2010. Guidelines for the Diagnosis and Management of Food Allergy in the United States: Report of the NIAID-Sponsored Expert Panel. *Journal of Allergy and Clinical Immunology* 126:S1–S58.

41. National Institutes of Health. 2011. Food Allergies. *MedlinePlus Magazine* 6:24–25.

42. Food and Drug Administration. 2014. *Guidance for Industry: Questions and Answers Regarding Food Allergens, Including the Food Allergen Labeling and Consumer Protection Act of 2004 (Edition 4); Final Guidance.* Available at www.fda.gov/food/guidanceregulation/guidancedocumentsregulatoryinformation/allergens/ucm059116.htm. Accessed June 2014.

43. Ogden, C. L., M. D. Carroll, B. K. Kit, and K. M. Flegal. 2014. Prevalence of Childhood and Adult Obesity in the United States, 2011–2012. *Journal of the American Medical Association* 311(8):806–814.

44. Ibid.

45. Centers for Disease Control and Prevention. 2012. *Basics About Childhood Obesity.* Available at www.cdc.gov/obesity/childhood/basics.html. Accessed June 2014.

46. Ibid.

47. Centers for Disease Control and Prevention. 2011. *About BMI for Children and Teens.* Available at www.cdc.gov/healthyweight/assessing/bmi/childrens_BMI/about_childrens_BMI.html. Accessed June 2014.

48. Centers for Disease Control and Prevention. 2014. *Childhood Obesity Facts.* Available at www.cdc.gov/healthyyouth/obesity/facts.htm. Accessed June 2014.

49. Daniels, S. R., D. K. Arnett, R. H. Eckel, S. S. Gidding, L. L. Hayman, S. Kumanyika, et al. 2005. Overweight in Children and Adolescents: Pathophysiology, Consequences, Prevention, and Treatment. *Circulation* 111:1999–2002. Available at www.circ.aha-journals.org/content/111/15/1999.full. Accessed June 2014.

50. Centers for Disease Control and Prevention. 2013. *A Growing Problem.* Available at www.cdc.gov/obesity/childhood/problem.html. Accessed June 2014.

51. Daniels, S. R., M. S. Jacobson, B. W. McCrindle, R. H. Eckel, and B. McHugh Sanner. 2009. American Heart Association Childhood Obesity Research Summit Report. *Circulation.* 119:e489–e517. Available at http://circ.ahajournals.org/content/119/15/e489.full.pdf. Accessed June 2014.

52. Ebbeling, C. B., E. Garcia-Lago, M. M. Leidig, L. G. Seger-Shippee, H. A. Feldman, and D. S. Ludwig. 2007. Altering Portion Sizes and Eating Rate to Attenuate Gorging during a Fast-Food Meal: Effects on Energy Intake. *Pediatrics* 119:869–875.

53. Centers for Disease Control and Prevention. 2013. *A Growing Problem.*

54. HHS/USDA. 2011. *Dietary Guidelines for Americans, 2010.* Available at www.cnpp.usda.gov/publications/dietaryguidelines/2010/policydoc/chapter3.pdf. Accessed June 2014.

55. Piernas, C., and B. Popkin. 2010. Trends in Snacking among U.S. Children. *Health Affairs.* 29:398–404.

56. Shils, M. E., M. Shike, A. C. Ross, B. Caballero, and R. J. Cousins, eds. 2006. *Modern Nutrition in Health and Disease.* 10th ed. Baltimore: Lippincott Williams & Wilkins.

57. Dubois, L., K. O. Kyvik, M. Girard, F. Tatone-Tokuda, D. Perusse, J. Hjelmborg, A. Skytthe, F. Rasmussen, M. J. Wright, P. Lichtenstein, and N. G. Martin. 2012. Genetic and Environmental Contributions to Weight, Height, and BMI from Birth to 19 Years of Age: An International Study of Over 12,000 Twin Pairs. Available at www.plosone.org/article/info%3Adoi%2F10.1371%2Fjournal.pone.0030153. Accessed June 2014.

58. Skelton, J. A., M. B. Irby, and G. Miller. 2011. Etiologies of Obesity in Children: Nature and Nurture. *Pediatric Clinics of North America* 58(6):1333–1354. Available at www.ncbi.nlm.nih.gov/pmc/articles/PMC3224976/#!po=2.63158. Accessed June 2014.

59. American Academy of Child and Adolescent Psychiatry. 2011. *Facts for Families: Obesity in Children and Teens.* Available at www.aacap.org/galleries/FactsForFamilies/79_obesity_in_children_and_teens.pdf. Accessed April 2012.

60. Sridhar S. B., et al. 2014. Maternal Gestational Weight Gain and Offspring Risk for Childhood Overweight or Obesity. *American Journal of Obstetrics and Gynecology.* 211(3):259.e1–8. Available at www.ncbi.nlm.nih.gov/pubmed/24735804. Accessed June 2014.

61. MacFarlane A., V. Cleland, D. Crawford, K. Campbell, and A. Timperio. 2009. Longitudinal Examination of the Family Food Environment and Weight Status among Children. *International Journal of Pediatric Obesity* 4:343–352.

62. Scaglioni, S., C. Arrizza, F. Vecchi, and S. Tedeschi. 2011. Determinants of Children's Eating Behavior. *American Journal of Clinical Nutrition.* 94(6):2006S–2011S. Available at www.ajcn.nutrition.org/content/94/6_Suppl/2006S.full. Accessed June 2014.

63. Ventura, A. K., and L. L. Birch. 2008. Does Parenting Affect Children's Eating and Weight Status? *International Journal of Behavioral Nutrition and Physical Activity* 5:15–27.

64. Daniels, et al. 2009. American Heart Association Childhood Obesity Research Summit Report.

65. Centers for Disease Control and Prevention. 2011. Childhood Obesity in the United States. *Morbidity and Mortality Weekly Report (MMWR)* CDC Grand Rounds. 60(2):42–46.

66. Rahman, T., R. A. Cushing, and R. J. Jackson. 2011. Contributions of Built Environment to Childhood Obesity. *Mount Sinai Journal of Medicine* 78:49–57.

67. U.S. Department of Health and Human Services. Subcommittee of the President's Council on Fitness, Sports & Nutrition. 2012. *Physical Activity Guidelines for Americans Midcourse Report. Strategies to Increase Physical Activity among Youth.* Available at www.health.gov/paguidelines/midcourse/pag-mid-course-report-final.pdf. Accessed June 2014.

68. Centers for Disease Control and Prevention. 2013. *A Growing Problem.*

69. U.S. National Library of Medicine. National Institutes of Health. 2013. *Screen Time and Children.* Available at www.nlm.nih.gov/medlineplus/ency/patientinstructions/000355.htm. Accessed June 2014.

70. Ibid.

71. Gilbert-Diamond D., Z. Li, A. M. Adachi-Mejia, A. C. McClure, and J. D. Sargent. 2014. Association of a Television in the Bedroom with Increased Adiposity Gain in a Nationally Representative Sample of Children and Adolescents. *Journal of the American Medical Association Pediatrics* 168(5):427–434.

72. American Academy of Pediatrics. *Media and Children.* Available at www.aap.org/en-us/advocacy-and-policy/aap-health-initiatives/Pages/Media-and-Children.aspx#sthash.nh2WMY8b.dpuf. Accessed June 2014.

73. Harvard School of Public Health. n.d. *Sleep.* Available at www.hsph.harvard.edu/obesity-prevention-source/obesity-causes/sleep-and-obesity/#references. Accessed June 2014.

74. U.S. Department of Health and Human Services. 2008. *2008 Physical Activity Guidelines*

for Americans. Available at www.health.gov/paguidelines/pdf/paguide.pdf. Accessed June 2014.

75. U.S. Department of Health and Human Services. 2012. *Physical Activity Guidelines for Americans Midcourse Report. Strategies to Increase Physical Activity among Youth.*

76. Robert Wood Johnson Foundation. 2011. *Does Food and Beverage Marketing Influence Children's Food Choices?* Available at www.rwjf.org/content/dam/farm/reports/issue_briefs/2011/rwjf71703. Accessed June 2014.

77. Institute of Medicine. Committee on Food Marketing and the Diets of Children and Youth. 2005. *Food Marketing to Children and Youth. Threat or Opportunity?* Available at www.iom.edu/Reports/2005/Food-Marketing-to-Children-and-Youth-Threat-or-Opportunity.aspx. Accessed June 2014.

78. Robert Wood Johnson Foundation. 2014. Food and Beverage Marketing to Children and Adolescents. Available at www.rwjf.org/childhoodobesity/product.jsp?id=72193. Accessed June 2014.

79. Federal Trade Commission. 2011. *Interagency Working Group Seeks Input on Proposed Voluntary Principles for Marketing Food to Children.* Available at www.ftc.gov/opa/2011/04/foodmarket.shtm. Accessed June 2014.

80. Centers for Disease Control and Prevention. 2011. *Preventing Cavities, Gum Disease, Tooth Loss, and Oral Cancers at a Glance, 2011.* Available at www.cdc.gov/chronicdisease/resources/publications/AAG/doh.htm. Accessed June 2012.

81. Ibid.

82. American Academy of Pediatric Dentistry. 2012. *Policy on Dietary Recommendations for Infants, Children, and Adolescents.* Available at www.aapd.org/media/Policies_Guidelines/P_DietaryRec.pdf. Accessed June 2014.

83. Ogden, C. L., M. D. Carroll, B. K. Kit, and K. M. Flegal. 2012. Prevalence of Obesity and Trends in Body Mass Index Among U.S. Children and Adolescents, 1999–2010. *Journal of the American Medical Association* 307:483–490.

84. Centers for Disease Control and Prevention. 2011. School Health Guidelines to Promote Healthy Eating and Physical Activity. *Morbidity and Mortality Weekly Report* 60:5.

85. Institute of Medicine. 2011. *Dietary Reference Intakes for Calcium and Vitamin D*; KidsHealth.org. 2010. *Growth Plate Injuries.* Available from http://kidshealth.org/parent/medical/bones/growth_plate_injuries.html. Accessed April 2012.

86. Institute of Medicine. 2011. *Dietary Reference Intakes for Calcium and Vitamin D.*

87. Institute of Medicine, Food and Nutrition Board. 1997. *Dietary Reference Intakes for Calcium, Phosphorus, Magnesium, Vitamin D, and Fluoride.* Available at http://fnic.nal.usda.gov/dietary-guidance/dri-reports/calcium-phosphorus-magnesium-vitamin-d-and-fluoride.* Accessed June 2014.

88. Ross, A. C., J. E. Manson, S. A. Abrams, J. F. Aloia, P. M. Brannon, S. K. Clinton, et al. 2011. Clarification of DRIs for Calcium and Vitamin D across Age Groups. *Journal of the American Dietetic Association* 111(10):1467.

89. Bailey, R. L., et al. 2010. Estimation of Total Usual Calcium and Vitamin D Intakes in the United States. *Journal of Nutrition* 140(4):817–822.

90. Institute of Medicine. 2001. *Dietary Reference Intakes for Vitamin A, Vitamin K, Arsenic, Boron, Chromium, Copper, Iodine, Iron, Manganese, Nickel, Silicon, Vanadium, and Zinc.*

91. U.S. Department of Agriculture, Agricultural Research Service. 2012. *What We Eat in America, 2009–2010.* Available at www.ars.usda.gov/Services/docs.htm?docid=18349. Accessed June 2014.

92. U.S. Department of Health and Human Services. National Heart, Lung & Blood Institute. 2014. *How Is Iron-Deficiency Anemia Diagnosed?* Available at www.nhlbi.nih.gov/health/health-topics/topics/ida/diagnosis.html. Accessed June 2014.

93. U.S. Department of Health and Human Services. National Heart, Lung & Blood Institute. 2014. *How Is Iron-Deficiency Anemia Treated?* Available at www.nhlbi.nih.gov/health/health-topics/topics/ida/treatment.html. Accessed June 2014.

94. Meier, A., and K. Musick. 2014. Variation in Associations between Family Dinners and Adolescent Well-Being. *Journal of Marriage and Family* 76(1):13–23. Available at http://onlinelibrary.wiley.com/doi/10.1111/jomf.12079/abstract. Accessed June 2014.

95. *CASAColumbia.* 2012. *The Importance of Family Dinners VIII.* Available at www.casacolumbia.org/addiction-research/reports/importance-of-family-dinners-2012. Accessed July 2014.

96. National Eating Disorders Association. 2012. *Eating Disorders among Males.* Available at www.nationaleatingdisorders.org/silent-epidemic. Accessed June 2014.

97. S. Swanson, S. Crow, D., Le Grange, J. Swendsen, and K. Merikangas. 2011. Prevalence and Correlates of Eating Disorders in Adolescents. *Archives of General Psychiatry.* 68(7):714–723. Available at www.psychiatry-training.wiki.otago.ac.nz/images/a/af/Swanson11.pdf. Accessed June 2014.

98. H. Shaw, E. Stice, and C. B. Becker. 2009. Preventing Eating Disorders. *Child and Adolescent Psychiatric Clinics of North America* 18:199–207. Available at www.ncbi.nlm.nih.gov/pmc/articles/PMC2938770/. Accessed July 2014.

99. Berge, J. M., K. Loth, C. Hanson, J. Croll-Lambert, and D. Neumark-Sztainer. 2011. Family Life Cycle Transitions and the Onset of Eating Disorders: A Prospective Grounded Theory Approach. *Journal of Clinical Nursing* 21:1355–1363.

100. Centers for Disease Control and Prevention. 2013. *Children and Diabetes—More Information.* Available at www.cdc.gov/diabetes/projects/cda2.htm. Accessed June 2014.

101. Centers for Disease Control and Prevention. 2011. Childhood Obesity in the United States. *Morbidity and Mortality Weekly Report (MMWR)* CDC Grand Rounds. 60(2):42–46.

102. Centers for Disease Control and Prevention. 2013. *Children and Diabetes—More Information.*

103. Li, C., E. S. Ford, G. Zhao, and A. H. Mokdad. 2009. Prevalence of Prediabetes and Its Association with Clustering of Cardiometabolic Risk Factors and Hyperinsulinemia among US Adolescents: NHANES 2005–2006. *Diabetes Care* 32:342–347.

104. American Diabetes Association. 2014. *Preventing Type 2 Diabetes in Children.* Available at www.diabetes.org/living-with-diabetes/parents-and-kids/children-and-type-2/preventing-type-2-in-children.html. Accessed June 2014.

105. Freedman, D. S., Z. Mei, S. R. Srinivasan, G. S. Berenson, and W. H. Dietz. 2007. Cardiovascular Risk Factors and Excess Adiposity among Overweight Children and Adolescents: The Bogalusa Heart Study. *Journal of Pediatrics* 150(1):12.e2–17.e2.

106. De Neit, J. E., and D. I. Naiman. 2011. Psychosocial Aspects of Childhood Obesity. *Minerva Pediatrica* (6):491–505.

107. Mayo Clinic. 2013. *Childhood Obesity.* Available at www.mayoclinic.org/diseases-conditions/childhood-obesity/basics/causes/con-20027428. Accessed June 2014.

108. Daniels, et al. 2009. American Heart Association Childhood Obesity Research Summit Report.

109. Mayo Clinic. 2014. *Childhood Obesity Complications.* Available at http://www.mayoclinic.org/diseases-conditions/childhood-obesity/basics/complications/con-20027428. Accessed June 2014.

110. Centers for Disease Control and Prevention. 2011. Childhood Obesity in the United States. *Morbidity and Mortality Weekly Report (MMWR)* CDC Grand Rounds. 60(2):42–46.

111. Ibid.

112. Mayo Clinic. 2014. *Childhood Obesity Complications.* Available at http://www.mayoclinic.org/diseases-conditions/childhood-obesity/basics/complications/con-20027428. Accessed June 2014.

113. Barlow, S. E., and the Expert Committee Expert Committee. 2007. Expert Committee Recommendations Regarding the Prevention, Assessment, and Treatment of Child and Adolescent Overweight and Obesity: Summary Report. *Pediatrics* 120(4):164–192. Available at www.pediatrics.aappublications.org/content/120/Supplement_4/S164.full. Accessed June 2014.

19 Life Cycle Nutrition
Older Adults

Learning Outcomes

After reading this chapter, you will be able to:

19.1 Describe the demographics of aging in America and explain why Americans are living longer.

19.2 Describe common changes in bodily functions that occur as a result of the aging process.

19.3 Summarize the nutrient needs of older adults.

19.4 Discuss some of the nutrition-related health concerns common to old age.

19.5 Describe the social, economic, and psychological factors that can affect the health of older Americans.

19.6 Describe the risk factors for hypertension and the dietary interventions that help control it.

True or False?

1. Chronic disease is an inevitable part of aging. **T**/**F**
2. Heart disease is the number-one cause of death among older Americans. **T**/**F**
3. Inadequate dietary fiber leads many older adults to suffer from constipation. **T**/**F**
4. The population of those aged 65 years and older is declining in the United States. **T**/**F**
5. Many older individuals are more susceptible to osteoporosis due to insufficient intake of vitamin D. **T**/**F**
6. Too much vitamin A can increase the risk of bone fractures. **T**/**F**
7. Older adults rarely use dietary supplements. **T**/**F**
8. Older adults need fewer daily kilocalories than when they were younger. **T**/**F**
9. Food insecurity among elders is a nonissue in the United States. **T**/**F**
10. Alcohol abuse is extremely rare among older adults. **T**/**F**

See page 737 for the answers.

Aging is a natural, complex process associated with physical and psychological changes that eventually result in death. It's a process that begins during early middle age, which may be considered the years from 35 to 50, when bodily functions begin to gradually decline. Age 65 is often designated as the beginning of old age, but there is no single age at which people become old.[1] **Senescence,** another term for growing old, is defined as a process that begins at conception and ends at death.

Each aging experience is unique, and changes in bodily functions do not occur at the same rate or to the same degree in any two people. Perhaps the reason 65 is considered old is that traditionally, that's when many people retired from full-time employment, although now people are working well into their later years, and living longer in better health.

Although the older years are often seen as a positive time, chronic disease and disability may impose heavy health and financial burdens on people and diminish their quality of life. While the risk of illness increases with age, poor health is not inevitable.

In this chapter we'll discuss the physical, economic, and emotional aspects of aging, and the nutrient needs of older adults. We'll also examine the most common dietary challenges older adults face, and ways to minimize health risks and promote a healthier older age.

What Are the Demographics of Aging in America?

LO 19.1 Describe the demographics of aging in America and explain why Americans are living longer.

The potential **life span** of the human body hasn't changed much (it's currently around 120 years) during the last century. However, from 1900 to 2008, **life expectancy** at birth increased from 46 to 76 years for men and from 48 to nearly 81 years for women.[2] Fewer deaths from infectious disease at an early age, better nutrition, and advances in medicine, including medications and procedures to manage and treat chronic illness, have led to increased **longevity,** or duration of life.[3]

America's Population Is Getting Older and Is More Diverse

Given the rise in life expectancy, it isn't surprising that the United States' population is aging at a rapid rate. The large, so-called baby boomer generation—children born between 1946 and 1964—has reached their 60s and are expected to be the fastest growing segment of the population over the next decade. About 13 percent of the U.S. population, or one in seven people, are over age 65. In 2010, there were 40.3 million people 65 and older in the United States, up from 35 million in 2005.[4] By 2050, the number of Americans aged 65 and older is projected to be 88.5 million.[5] (**Figure 19.1**).

The 85-and-older population segment is also growing rapidly. The number of people in the oldest age group (85 years and older) is projected to grow from 5.8 million in 2010 to 8.7 million in 2030. In 2050, this group is projected to reach 19 million, and will account for about 4.3 percent of the U.S. population.[6]

As the total U.S. population becomes more diverse, so does the population of those aged 65 and older. According to the U.S. Census Bureau, by the year 2050, the percentage of older Americans who identify themselves as white is expected to drop by about 10 percent, while the percentages of older Americans who identify

aging Declines in bodily functions that accumulate with time, ultimately leading to death.

senescence Another term for aging.

life span The maximum age to which members of a species can live.

life expectancy The average length of life for a population of individuals.

longevity The duration of an individual's life.

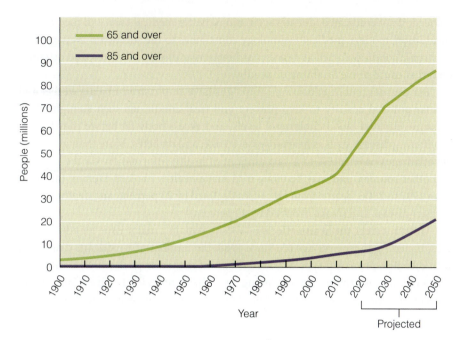

◄ **Figure 19.1 The Aging Population**
The number of older adults in the United States is expected to increase significantly during the next several decades.
Source: Data from www.agingstats.gov. 2012. Accessed July 2014.

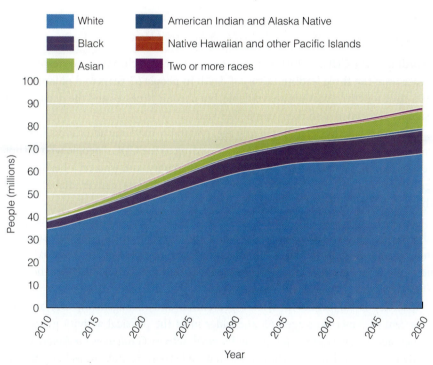

◄ **Figure 19.2 Projected U.S. Population Aged 65 and Over by Race: 2010–2050**
America's aging population will become more racially and ethnically diverse over the next several decades.

Note: Unless otherwise specified, data refer to the population who reported a race alone. Populations for each race group include both Hispanics and non-Hispanics, as Hispanics may be of any race.

Source: U.S. Department of Commerce, Economics and Statistics Administration. U.S. Census Bureau. 2010. *The Next Four Decades*. Available at www.census.gov/prod/2010pubs/p25-1138.pdf. Accessed July 2014.

themselves as Black or Asian are expected to rise by 12 percent and 9 percent, respectively (**Figure 19.2**). Although not shown as a separate group in Figure 19.2, the number of Hispanics aged 65 and older is projected to experience the sharpest population growth, tripling as a proportion of the population by 2030. Fully 42 percent of the population of Americans aged 65 and older will be of minority status in 2050.[7]

Improved Health Care and Disease Prevention Are Lengthening the Life Span

Medical advances and public health campaigns have greatly contributed to Americans' longer lives. The infectious and often deadly diseases of the 1900s, such as tuberculosis, pneumonia, polio, mumps, and measles, have been dramatically reduced, if not eradicated, due to vaccinations, better medical care, and medication. In addition, modern medical technology contributes to the successful management of chronic conditions such as cancer, cardiovascular disease, diabetes, and osteoporosis that could prove disabling or deadly.

For decades, public education campaigns have emphasized a balanced diet and regular physical activity to help prevent and treat conditions such as high blood pressure, elevated blood cholesterol levels, and excess body fat before they lead to debilitating disease such as heart disease, stroke, and diabetes. More than ever, people of all ages have access to a vast amount of health information via the Internet and other sources, and may be using it to make healthy choices. During the years from 1997 to 2006, deaths from all causes declined by 23 percent, and deaths related to heart disease and stroke dropped by 40 percent.[8]

Unfortunately, the health effects of obesity remain a major issue for adults of all ages, including those over age 65. Since 1980, the number of Americans diagnosed with diabetes, primarily type 2 diabetes, has more than tripled, which is linked to rising obesity, inactivity, and advancing age. The Centers for Disease Control and Prevention estimates that 25.8 million Americans have diabetes, and 7 million of them do not know it.[9]

Smoking, Poor Diet, and Physical Inactivity Contribute to the Leading Causes of Death among Older People

According to the CDC, in 2010, heart disease, cancer, and chronic lower respiratory disease were the three leading causes of death in people 65 years and older. Stroke was a close fourth.[10] Death is unavoidable, but chronic illnesses and the decline and disability associated with them can be reduced.

Adopting healthy behaviors at any age, preferably in young adulthood, helps to promote better health in the later years. According to the CDC, "people who do not use tobacco, who participate in regular physical activity, and who eat a healthy diet significantly decrease their risk of developing heart disease, cancer, diabetes, and other chronic conditions."[11]

Healthy habits, including following a diet plan low in saturated fat that provides the recommended servings of fruits and vegetables, lean protein sources, whole grains, and low-fat dairy, supplies beneficial nutrients, such as antioxidants and phytochemicals, that can decrease the risk of several chronic diseases and help to manage them.

Exercise is important in disease prevention and management, too, but just 16 percent of Americans aged 65 and older meet the physical activity guidelines for their age group as suggested in the *Physical Activity Guidelines for Americans*.[12] Inactivity may contribute to obesity and reduced strength, and excess body fat is a factor in the development of chronic diseases such as heart disease, certain types of cancer, stroke, and diabetes. Even with the physical changes that accompany aging, many people can remain physically active in their later years. Routine exercise improves sleep, flexibility, and range of motion, and can help postpone the decline in cognitive ability that naturally occurs in aging.[13] Working in the garden, mowing the lawn, walking a dog, and dancing provide health benefits. Older adults also benefit from strength-training activities such as lifting weights and calisthenics at least twice a week to help maintain muscle strength.[14]

Older adults in good physical shape may be able to live independently longer, reducing the need for assistance with activities of everyday living, thereby preserving quality of life and reducing health care costs. Prevention and management of chronic conditions with diet and exercise could save millions of health care dollars every year, and possibly improve the quality of life.

The number-one physical activity among older Americans is walking. Gardening is second most prevalent, followed by bicycling. Don't know what to get your grandparents for a birthday gift? Consider a pair of walking shoes.

The Centers for Disease Control's State of Aging and Health Report (also known as the National Report Card) assesses the health status and health behaviors of adults aged 65 years and older in the United States. The report for 2013 highlights the need to maintain the progress made on several health indicators and to increase our efforts to address other important health issues. Key indicators of health in older people help guide policy makers in developing strategies to improve the mental and physical well-being of Americans in their later years.[15] Older adults are encouraged to adopt healthier behaviors and obtain regular health screening to reduce the risk for many chronic diseases.

> **LO 19.1: THE TAKE-HOME MESSAGE** Life span is the maximum age to which members of a species can live, and longevity is the duration of an individual's life. Life expectancy has increased markedly in the United States since the 1900s. There are more older Americans than ever, and that population is expected to grow further. The U.S. population is living longer due to improved health care, disease prevention, and, for some, because of healthier lifestyle choices. Some of the leading causes of death among older adults are heart disease, cancer, and chronic lower respiratory diseases.

What Changes Occur as Part of the Aging Process?

LO 19.2 Describe common changes in bodily functions that occur as a result of the aging process.

As we age, changes occurring in individual cells cause changes in organ function and in a person's appearance. Cells die to make room for new cells. The age of a cell triggers cell death, and cell death also occurs as a result of damage from toxins. Cells can only divide so often, and eventually they die. In some organs, cells die and are not replaced. A reduced number of cells affects organ function.

Most age-related changes are gradual and their effects accumulate with time. The rate at which individuals change depends on genes, the environment, and lifestyle choices. Genetics determine the rate at which cells are maintained and repaired and can influence development of a number of chronic diseases, such as cardiovascular disease and cancer. Environmental factors such as oxidative stress, caused by excessive sun exposure or cigarette smoking, can cause cell damage and lead to cell mutation or death.

Important lifestyle choices, including diet and exercise, affect the rate of aging. A diet high in saturated fat and low in antioxidants and fiber can accelerate the aging process. Regular aerobic activity and strength training exercises help to better control blood pressure, levels of blood cholesterol, and glucose, among other health benefits. Excessive levels of stress may contribute to the aging process by making a person more susceptible to illness. Prolonged stress provokes higher levels of the hormone cortisol in the body. High cortisol levels can lead to increases in body weight, decreased immune function, and an increased inflammatory response.[16]

The **physiologic age** of a person can vary greatly from that person's **chronologic age,** and can reflect a wide range of changes that affect not only physical appearance but also body function and response to daily living. Overall, the changes that occur through aging involve a general slowing down of all organ systems due to a gradual decline in cellular activity. This slowing limits normal functions and makes individuals more susceptible to illness and death. Being aware of the most important physiological changes that occur with age can help individuals understand their nutritional implications.

physiologic age A person's age estimated in terms of body health, function, and life expectancy.

chronologic age A person's age in number of years of life.

Changes in Body Composition

Aging leads to changes in body composition that can affect overall health and nutrition status. Basal metabolic rate (BMR) starts to slow around age 30 largely due to a slowly declining muscle mass that slows metabolism. Many adults lose between 10 and 15 percent of their muscle mass and strength during their lifetime.[17] (**Figure 19.3**).

Sarcopenia, significantly reduced muscle mass and function, is caused by changes in muscle and nerve tissue that result from decreased physical activity. Day-to-day activities become more difficult, putting older adults at higher risk for falls and fractures, and preventing them from fully taking care of themselves. Although everyone experiences muscle loss, regular physical activity and optimal nutrition can slow or minimize the effects.

As a result of a lower BMI, reduced physical activity, or both, it's common for older adults to gain weight, usually fat tissue. Thirty-eight percent of males and 32 percent of females over age 60 living in the United States are obese.[18] Obesity increases the risk for cardiovascular disease, stroke, type 2 diabetes, certain kinds of cancer, osteoarthritis, and other health complications that reduce the quality of life. While many people in their 50s, 60s, and 70s grapple with excess body fat, those in their 80s and beyond may not weigh enough. Older adults may lose weight unintentionally, resulting in underweight. Chronic inadequate food intake may lead to malnutrition, reducing resistance to infections, as well as other adverse health outcomes, such as frailty, loss of independence, and functional decline.[19]

The aging process also affects bones and joints. With time, bones become less dense due to calcium loss. As a result, they are more prone to fracture. The significant estrogen losses caused by menopause accelerate bone loss. In addition, the body becomes less efficient at absorbing calcium from foods and dietary supplements, so there is less available to bones. Older people lose height because spinal vertebrae lose density and the disks between them get thinner, shortening the spine.

Our Immune Function Decreases as We Age

As a person ages, the function of the immune system decreases, reducing the body's ability to protect itself against bacteria and viruses, cancer, and autoimmune diseases, such as lupus and autoimmune hepatitis.

A decrease in immunity may be due in part to inadequate nutrient intake. The immune response depends on an adequate supply of nutrients such as protein, and an array of vitamins and minerals. Older adults, especially those who have limited food intake, may not consume adequate amounts of vitamins A, C, B_{12}, and E, as well as iron and zinc. Deficiency of key nutrients such as these in conjunction with advanced age can decrease the body's ability to fight illness.

Our Sensory Abilities Decline as We Age

In older age there is a progressive decline in vision, hearing, taste, and smell that becomes worse with time, but varies among older individuals. This decline in sensory abilities can result in decreased food and nutrient intake. For example, poor vision can make shopping for food and preparing meals more difficult. Hearing loss can lead to social isolation, solitary eating, and depression, which in turn may limit a person's interest in food.

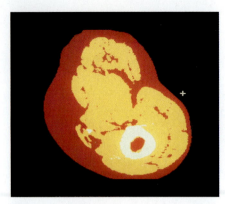

a Cross-section of a young adult's thigh

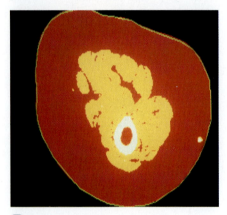

b Cross-section of an older adult's thigh

▲ **Figure 19.3 Aging Leads to Decrease in Muscle Mass**
Note the proportionally reduced muscle area (in yellow) of the older, sedentary adult in the bottom image compared with that of a younger, more active adult. Most people lose a significant amount of muscle as they age, some of which could be prevented by engaging in regular physical activity.

sarcopenia Age-related progressive loss of muscle mass, muscle strength, and function.

A decline in sense of smell may have an even greater impact on an individual's interest in food. Aging affects sense of smell, and so do certain medications and nutritional deficiencies. There is no treatment for loss of smell due to aging.[20] If a person's diet allows, they should flavor foods with some butter or olive oil, cheese, nuts, fresh herbs, mustard, hot pepper, spices, or lemon or lime juice.[21] Assisting older adults in maintaining an adequate and varied diet through the use of highly seasoned foods can help offset nutritional deficiencies and make meals enjoyable.

Gastrointestinal Changes Occur with Age

As a person ages, a number of changes occur within the gastrointestinal tract and its accessory organs that affect chewing, digestion, and nutrient absorption. One major change is a decline in saliva production, especially in the very old and in people who take certain medications. Decreased saliva production makes swallowing more difficult (a condition known as dysphagia) and may reduce taste perception. A lack of saliva also increases the risk of oral health problems, such as tooth decay and gum disease. Many elderly people may be missing teeth or wear ill-fitting dentures, which can make chewing difficult, limit food choices, and contribute to poor nutrition. Happily, the percentage of older adults who have retained most of their natural teeth has risen steadily over the past few decades. This trend is significant because the mouth reflects a person's health and well-being throughout life.[22]

Aging also causes changes in digestive secretions and motility of the stomach. Production of hydrochloric acid and pepsin declines, which can result in decreased absorption of certain nutrients. This reduction in secretions can contribute to the development of atrophic gastritis, which affects protein digestion, and can interfere with the absorption of nutrients, notably vitamin B_{12}.[23] Stomach emptying may also slow, reducing hunger and thus food and nutrient intake. A decline in gastrointestinal motility can contribute to constipation, gas, and bloating. Inadequate physical activity, a low-fiber diet, and low fluid intake exacerbate these problems.

Our Brain Function Changes as We Age

As people age, they change psychologically as well as biologically. An aging brain—and everything that entails, from the annoying inconveniences of age-related memory loss to more serious conditions like Alzheimer's disease and dementia—was once equated with neuron failure. Improved technology such as higher resolution magnetic resonance imaging (MRI) has generated a wealth of information about the physical changes in the aging brain. Scientists no longer believe that aging causes much in the way of brain cell loss. In fact, the body may generate new nerve cells in some parts of the brain as we age.[24]

The aging brain is far more resilient than was previously believed. Age-related changes in cognitive function vary considerably across individuals and across cognitive domains, with some cognitive functions appearing more susceptible than others to the effects of aging. So why do people become more forgetful or process new information more slowly? Experts cannot say for sure, but there is a decline in the levels of neurotransmitters, which allow for communication among brain cells, and aging typically means that blood flow to the brain decreases. Older people may react more slowly and take more time to accomplish tasks, but when given plenty of time, they react normally.[25] Cognitive impairment may affect a person's ability to care for himself or herself in several ways, including consuming an adequate diet and drinking enough fluid, which may further impair memory and other cognitive abilities.

What Are the Nutrient Needs of Older Adults?

LO 19.3 Summarize the nutrient needs of older adults.

Gender, health status, and level of physical activity all play a role in an older individual's nutrient needs. The Food and Nutrition Board of the Institute of Medicine, the experts who review nutrient research and determine the recommended dietary intakes (DRIs) for macronutrients and micronutrients, have devised two categories for older people: 51 years and older and 70 and older. **Figure 19.4** provides a graphic representation of the nutritional needs of older adults. A nutritious diet for elders includes adequate amounts of protein, complex carbohydrates, vitamins, and minerals, and possibly fewer kilocalories than during their younger years; **Table 19.1** summarizes the recommended dietary changes for older adults.

▶ **Figure 19.4 Older Adults Benefit from Good Nutrition and Physical Activity**
Older adults need to focus on nutrient-dense foods that contain adequate fiber, calcium, vitamin B$_{12}$, vitamin D, and many other nutrients. With a declining metabolic rate, seniors require fewer kilocalories. Food choices should emphasize fresh and lightly processed foods rich in complex carbohydrates, lean protein, and healthy fats. Older people also need to ensure adequate fluid intake, and regularly engage in physical activity.

Copyright 2011 Tufts University. For details about the MyPlate for Older Adults, please see http://nutrition.tufts.edu/research/myplate-older-adults.

MyPlate for Older Adults

Illustration by Betsy Hayes ©2011 Tufts University   http://now.tufts.edu/articles/eat-well-age-well

TABLE 19.1 Dietary Changes for Older Adults

Recommended Change	Rationale	Examples
Increase protein intake	Older people may need more protein to protect against lean tissue loss	Focus on lean sources of protein such as lean beef, skinless poultry, seafood, and legumes
Consume adequate amounts of nutrient-dense foods	Older adults continue to need vitamins, minerals, and phytonutrients	Choose foods in each food group that are low in added sugars and fats
Consume most carbohydrates in the complex form	Complex carbohydrate keeps blood glucose levels stable better than simple sugars	Eat whole grains, fruits, vegetables, and legumes daily; limit refined grains, sugary drinks, and desserts
Consume most fat as the unsaturated variety	Saturated fat increases heart disease risk; unsaturated fats help to reduce it	Include at least two seafood meals weekly; choose foods such as avocados, nuts, and olive and canola oils
Limit sodium intake to 1,500 milligrams daily	Decrease risk for high blood pressure	Eat more fresh and lightly processed foods; limit restaurant foods and packaged products
Consume adequate fiber	Helps prevent constipation and diverticulosis, and type 2 diabetes	Choose at least three servings of whole grains, such as whole-wheat bread, whole-grain cereals, and brown rice daily. Include legumes, whole fruits, and vegetables in meals and snacks
Consume adequate fluid	Decreased ability of kidneys to concentrate urine and decreased thirst mechanism can both increase risk of dehydration	Drink 1% low-fat or fat-free milk and water with and between meals; limit sugary, low-nutrient soft drinks
Increase intake of foods high in beta-carotene to meet vitamin A needs and limit dietary supplements with high levels of retinol (preformed vitamin A)	Higher amounts of retinol in the body can increase fracture risk	Choose brightly colored fruits and vegetables, including carrots, cantaloupe, broccoli, spinach, kale, and winter squash for beta-carotene
Increase intake of vitamin D–fortified foods	Lower ability to make the active form of vitamin D in the body decreases the absorption of calcium and phosphorus and increases the risk of osteoporosis	Choose vitamin D–fortified milk, yogurt, and breakfast cereals. Many older people will need a vitamin D supplement to satisfy suggested intakes
Increase intake of synthetic form of vitamin B_{12}	Decreased stomach acid reduces the absorption of naturally occuring vitamin B_{12} in foods	Choose vitamin B_{12}–fortified breakfast cereals and soy beverages. A daily multivitamin typically supplies the suggested amount of vitamin B_{12} for those 51 and older
Choose adequate amounts of iron-rich foods	To prevent iron deficiency, which is more common in people who don't eat iron-rich foods	Choose lean meat, fish, and poultry. Enjoy iron-fortified grains along with vitamin C–rich foods (such as citrus and tomatoes) to enhance iron absorption
Increase intake of zinc-rich foods	Zinc deficiency can suppress immune system and appetite	Choose zinc-fortified cereals, lean meats, poultry, legumes, and nuts
Increase intake of calcium-rich foods	Calcium needs increase with age. Adequate calcium intake helps protect against osteoporosis	Consume at least three servings of dairy foods daily. Older people may need a dietary supplement

Older Adults Need Fewer Kilocalories, Not Less Nutrition

Metabolic rate declines with age, and older adults typically need fewer kilocalories as time goes on. The decline in metabolism is a result of the natural loss of muscle mass (recall that muscle mass requires more energy for maintenance than fat mass). A lower metabolic rate combined with less physical activity reduces kilocalorie needs. (See the Calculation Corner for one way of estimating energy expenditure.) For example, a

Estimating Energy Expenditure Using the Harris-Benedict Equation

Sue, a 70-year-old retired nurse, walks 2 miles every day, as she has since she was 30. She is 5 feet 7 inches (170.2 cm) tall and maintains her weight at 154 pounds (70 kg). Use the Harris-Benedict equation below to determine her Estimated Energy Requirement (EER). How has Sue's EER changed from when she was 30 years old?

Answer

1. Use the Harris-Benedict equation for females to calculate Sue's RMR:

    RMR = 655.1 + (9.6 × weight in kg) + (1.8 × height in cm) − (4.7 × age in years)

    655.1 + (9.6 × 70 kg) + (1.8 × 170.2 cm) − (4.7 × 70) = 1,304.46 kcalories

    655.1 + 672 + 306.36 − 329 = 1,304.46

2. Next, apply the activity factor to determine total daily energy expenditure: Sedentary: 1.00; Low level of activity: 1.12; Active: 1.27; Very Active: 1.48

    1,304.46 × 1.12 = 1,461 kcalories

3. Now put the equations together to calculate her EER at age 30:

    655.1 + (9.6 × 70 kg) + (1.8 × 170.2 cm) − (4.7 × 30) = 1,492.46 kcalories

    1,492.46 × 1.27 activity factor = 1,895 kcalories

Compared with her needs at age 30, Sue now requires 434 fewer daily kilocalories. Most vitamin and mineral requirements remain the same for her, and some, such as for calcium and vitamin D, have increased since she was 30. Lower energy requirements mean that Sue should select nutrient-dense foods with fewer kilocalories to maintain her body weight.

Scan this QR code with your mobile device to access practice math activities. You can also access the activities in MasteringNutrition™.

70-year-old moderately active man needs about 400 fewer kilocalories—about the amount in a turkey sandwich—than his 40-year-old counterpart. By the age of 80, a sedentary female requires only about 1,600 kilocalories a day, which is 600 fewer kilocalories than she did when she was a moderately active 20-year-old.[26] Examining the Evidence: Does Kilocalorie Restriction Extend Life? explores the possible ramifications of decreased kilocalorie intake.

Though kilocalorie needs may be reduced, the need for most nutrients does not decline, and the need for certain nutrients increases. For many seniors it's challenging to get the nutrients they need on a more limited-kilocalorie budget, on a dietary plan designed to manage chronic conditions, or when they have a diminished appetite. Choosing nutrient-rich foods becomes even more important in aging because these foods supply the most nutrition for the least amount of kilocalories.

The Table Tips give some guidelines for healthy eating for older adults.

Older Adults Need Adequate Protein

Protein is essential for reducing the loss of lean tissue and muscle, helping to prevent bone tissue loss, and for tissue repair, wound healing, and immune function. According to the DRIs, protein requirements (expressed as grams per kilogram of body weight) do not change with age. However, because overall kilocalorie needs decline, individuals must obtain a relatively higher proportion of kilocalories from protein-rich foods. For healthy older people, the RDA is 0.8 grams per kilogram of body weight.[27] Although the role of dietary protein in the prevention of sarcopenia

Does Kilocalorie Restriction Extend Life?

In the last several decades, the number of centenarians, or people who have reached the age of 100, has increased around the world. Researchers are actively gathering information about where these people live, how they live, and what they eat to gain a better understanding of the factors that contribute to longevity. Longevity tends to run in families.[1] However, research suggests that lifestyle influences longevity.

Epidemiologists have studied populations with large numbers of centenarians, with the most notable and longest running study being conducted on the Japanese island of Okinawa, with the greatest number of centenarians per capita worldwide. The Okinawa Centenarian Study examined over 900 Okinawan centenarians and numerous other adults in their 70s, 80s, and 90s to identify factors associated with their increased life span.[2] The findings suggested that genetics and lifestyle habits explain why Okinawans remain healthy well into their senior years. A lower kilocaloric intake, part of the findings, was first reported in Okinawans in 1967 and researchers hypothesized that kilocaloric restriction was partly

responsible for their longevity. Okinawans have been shown to follow the "less is more" philosophy when it comes to eating, and regularly eat to the point where they are only 80 percent full.[3]

In animal studies, research about consuming significantly fewer kilocalories is mixed. Studies show that a kilocalorie-restricted diet can extend the lives of underfed rats up to 50 percent longer than those of rats given an unlimited supply of food.[4] However, another study on rhesus monkeys showed that those on restricted diets aged as quickly as their counterparts who were not restricted.[5] Human studies on kilocaloric restriction are limited, but one recent study found that restricting kilocalories reduced risk factors for diabetes and cardiovascular disease.[6]

How might eating less lead to a longer life? Nobody yet knows exactly how calorie restriction works at the cellular level, but experts hypothesize that it reduces oxidative damage through lower metabolism. Free radicals damage cellular material, including DNA. Damage accumulates with time, accelerating the "aging process."[7]

It's worth noting that kilocalorie restriction is not the sole distinguishing factor in the Okinawan diet. It is also rich in green leafy and yellow root vegetables, sweet potatoes, and soy, and is supplemented with fish. This plant-based diet is high in antioxidants, which may contribute to the inhabitants' extended life span. The health benefits that have been linked to the Okinawan diet and lifestyle are numerous and include decreased mortality from diseases of the heart and cancer as well as increased functional and cognitive capacity at older ages versus Americans.[8]

It's not possible to say whether kilocalorie restriction is the key to a longer life, nor yet what the ideal BMI is for humans.[9] People who are interested in kilocalorie restriction should consult a Registered Dietitian Nutritionist to establish a meal plan that meets their health goals. We do know that eating the right

number of kilocalories to achieve and maintain a healthy weight on a balanced diet can contribute to a better quality of life by supporting good health and preventing certain chronic conditions.

It's also important to consider lifestyle choices other than diet when it comes to longevity. Generally speaking, Okinawans are physically active into their later years, they have a long tradition of caring for one another's welfare, and their lifestyle is less stressful than that in mainland Japan,[10] factors that also contribute to well-being in the elderly everywhere.

References

1. B. J. Willcox. 2006. "Siblings of Okinawan Centenarians Exhibit Lifelong Mortality Advantages." *Journals of Gerontology Series A: Biological Sciences and Medical Sciences* 61:345–354.
2. D. C. Willcox, B. J. Willcox, H. Todoriki, J. D. Curb, and M. Suzuki. 2006. "Caloric Restriction and Human Longevity: What Can We Learn from the Okinawans?" *Biogerontology* 7:173–177.
3. Ibid.
4. D. Omodei and L. Fontana. 2011. "Calorie Restriction and Prevention of Age-Associated Chronic Disease." *Federation of European Biochemical Societies Letters* 585:1537–1542.
5. A. Maxmen. 2012. "Calorie Restriction Falters in the Long Run." *Nature: International Weekly Journal of Science* 488:569.
6. R. J. Ortiz-Bautista, et al. 2013. "Caloric Restriction: About Its Positive Metabolic Effects and Cellular Impact." (In Spanish). *Cirugía y Cirujanos* 459–464.
7. Ibid.
8. D. C. Willcox et al. 2006. "Caloric Restriction and Human Longevity: What Can We Learn from the Okinawans?"
9. A. Lorenzini. 2014. "How Much Should We Weigh for a Long and Healthy Life Span? The Need to Reconcile Caloric Restriction versus Longevity with Body Mass Index versus Mortality Data." *Frontiers in Endocrinology* 5:121. Available at www.ncbi.nlm.nih.gov/pubmed/25126085. Accessed July 2014.
10. J. Santrock, "Physical Development and Biological Aging." In M. Ryan, et al. (eds.) *A Topical Approach to Life-Span Development* (New York: McGraw-Hill Companies, Inc., 2008) 129–132.

remains unclear, a protein intake greater than that suggested by the DRI may enhance muscle protein anabolism and reduce progressive loss of muscle mass with age. Some experts recommend protein intake of 1.0 to 1.6 g/kg daily for healthy older adults.[28]

Older Adults Should Consume Adequate, Complex Carbohydrate

Older adults are encouraged to consume 45 to 65 percent of their total daily kilocalories as carbohydrates, which is no change from their younger years. However, because kilocalorie requirements decrease with age, older adults may need fewer carbohydrates. So, most of the carbohydrates adults consume should be the complex variety, which are nearly always found in foods with a higher nutrient density. Foods high in complex carbohydrate, such as whole grains, also contain more fiber than refined grains. Fiber helps prevent constipation and diverticulosis, and type 2 diabetes. The AI for fiber is 14 grams per 1,000 kilocalories. While fiber intake is related to calorie consumption, generally speaking, women 51 and older need 21 grams of daily fiber and men of the same age require 30 grams.[29] At meals and snacks, older adults should choose high-fiber foods, such as whole grains, fruits, and vegetables. Research suggests that most adults over the age of 51 do not meet the AI for fiber.[30]

Older Adults Need to Stay Hydrated

Consuming adequate amounts of fluid is important for older adults, especially those who take certain medications that cause their body to lose water, such as diuretics. There are several reasons why older people are more prone to dehydration. As we age, the body's ability to conserve water is decreased and the thirst mechanism becomes disturbed. People who don't eat enough watery foods, such as fruits and vegetables, or drink adequate fluid are likely to become mildly or severely dehydrated. Kidney disease and other chronic conditions, such as uncontrolled diabetes, increase dehydration risk.[31] Symptoms of dehydration include weakness, confusion, and fatigue, and may be dismissed as effects of aging, especially in the very old. Constipation is another side effect of dehydration.

Older adults have the same fluid requirements as younger people—13 cups a day, most of it as plain water—but they may not want to drink that much to avoid frequent trips to the bathroom. The incidence of urinary incontinence (the loss of bladder control) also increases with age due to prostate problems in men and weakened pelvic floor muscles in many women after pregnancy. Foods such as fruits and vegetables provide fluid and adults of all ages should be encouraged to eat five servings daily. All beverages, including coffee and tea, are considered fluid sources. Drinking water or milk with meals is a productive way to take in adequate fluid.

Older Adults Should Eat Moderate Amounts of Fat and Cholesterol

Fat provides kilocalories, supplies essential fatty acids, and is needed for the absorption of fat-soluble vitamins. Omega-3 fats are heart healthy, and the AHA recommends eating fish at least twice weekly.[32] However, a diet rich in saturated fat, *trans* fats, or both increases the risk for cardiovascular disease. In addition, because fat is kilocalorie-dense, eating too much fat may contribute excess kilocalories and lead to overweight and obesity. Healthy older people without evidence of heart disease, or unless otherwise advised by their doctor because of a medical condition, should aim for a diet with 20 to 35 percent of kilocalories from fat, with no more than 7 percent of kilocalories from saturated fat and 1 percent or less from *trans* fats. Total cholesterol intake should be no more than 300 milligrams per day for most people.[33]

Older Adults Need to Consume Adequate Vitamins A, D, and B$_{12}$

Though the recommended daily amount of vitamin A doesn't change for those over age 50, there is a concern that, because it can accumulate to toxic amounts in the body, consuming preformed vitamin A in excess of the RDA may increase the risk of osteoporosis and fractures (see Chapter 9). When choosing dietary supplements, such as a multivitamin, it's wise to choose products with the majority of vitamin A as beta-carotene rather than as retinol. The body will convert beta-carotene, which also acts on its own as an antioxidant, into vitamin A on an as-needed basis.

The beta-carotene found in many fruits and vegetables is a good source of vitamin A for seniors, as it won't contribute to vitamin A toxicity.

The skin's ability to begin the body's production of vitamin D from sunlight declines with age. Further, vitamin D absorption in the intestine declines, and the kidneys lose some ability to convert vitamin D to its active form.[34] The need for dietary vitamin D increases by 200 IU a day to 800 IU by age 71. Recall that vitamin D's main role is to help the body properly use calcium and phosphorus to strengthen bones, and that inadequate amounts of this vitamin can increase the risk of osteoporosis. It's difficult for most adults to get the recommended 600 IU of vitamin D from foods alone, and people over the age of 71 would most likely find it impossible. Vitamin D supplements help to fill in gaps in the diet, and are especially helpful for those who avoid vitamin D–fortified dairy products, such as milk and some yogurts. (Table 19.1)

The RDA for vitamin B$_{12}$ is the same for younger and older adults; however, because the stomach produces fewer acidic digestive juices as it ages, it's estimated that up to 30 percent of people over the age of 50 do not properly absorb the form of vitamin B$_{12}$ that naturally occurs in foods. They can, however, absorb the synthetic variety found in fortified foods and supplements, and the majority of older people should add these sources.[35] Proper nervous system function requires vitamin B$_{12}$, and prolonged deficiencies can lead to permanent nerve damage. Vitamin B$_{12}$, along with adequate amounts of folate and vitamin B$_6$, may keep levels of homocysteine normal in the bloodstream, helping to reduce the risk for heart disease and stroke.

Older Adults Need to Get the Right Amounts of Iron, Zinc, Calcium, and Sodium

Postmenopausal women, who are typically over age 50, need less dietary iron than they did in their younger years. While older people need less iron, they may become iron deficient if their diets do not supply adequate amounts of iron. Foods rich in iron, including meat, chicken, and seafood, are good choices for older people because they also supply protein, vitamins, and minerals to support good health. Older people are more prone to chronic conditions that can result in iron-deficiency anemia, such as an ongoing intestinal blood loss from an ulcer, cancer, and liver or kidney disease.[36] Iron deficiency can lead to fatigue, decreased physical activity, and impaired immunity.

Zinc is found in many of the same foods as iron, so if a person is iron deficient, he or she may also be short on zinc. Zinc is necessary for many bodily functions, including immunity, wound healing, and supporting a strong sense of taste and smell. Zinc deficiency may occur from inadequate zinc intake or absorption. Several chronic conditions, including diabetes, chronic liver disease, and chronic kidney disease, are associated with zinc deficiency. Research suggests many elderly people who live in food-insecure households are at risk for inadequate zinc intake.[37]

Calcium needs increase to 1,200 milligrams daily for women over the age of 50; a man's requirement is 1,000 milligrams daily until age 71, when it increases to 1,200 milligrams daily. Calcium absorption decreases by 10 to 15 percent in adulthood and continues to decrease with age, which is why recommended calcium intakes are higher for females older than 50 years and for both males and females older than 70 years. Surveys of calcium intake among people living in the United States suggest that women aged 51 to 70 years, and both men and women older than 70 years, fail to consume adequate amounts of calcium from food. However, many people take calcium supplements, which may increase their intake to the recommended levels.[38]

The body uses bone tissue as a reservoir for, and source of, calcium to maintain constant concentrations of calcium in blood, muscle, and intercellular fluids, and that calcium must be replenished on a daily basis.[39] Inadequate calcium intake increases the risk for osteoporosis. Experts estimated that, by 2020, half of all Americans over 50 will have weak bones unless we make changes to our diet and lifestyle.[40] Older adults should consume at least three servings of dairy foods daily, or the equivalent in calcium-fortified foods, such as soy beverages and orange juice. They may need a dietary supplement if they don't achieve these dietary goals on a daily basis.

Older Adults May Need to Decrease Sodium Intake

The 2010 *Dietary Guidelines for Americans* recommends that everyone over the age of 50 reduce daily sodium intake to 1,500 milligrams at the most to help reduce the risk of high blood pressure, which is more common with advancing age. People who have hypertension, or who have diabetes or chronic kidney disease, may need to make further modifications to their sodium intake.[41]

Older Adults May Benefit from Nutritional Supplements

Forty to 50 percent of men and women in the United States take multivitamin supplements on a regular basis.[42] Adults aged 60 or over are more likely than younger people to take dietary supplements to support the health of certain parts of the body, such as the heart, bones, joints, and eyes.[43]

The evidence for whether dietary supplements prevent chronic conditions is mixed. Clear health benefits appear with modest increases in consumption of omega-3s from fish oil supplements, including a reduction in the risk of sudden cardiac death. In addition, there is evidence that high-dose fish oil supplements may lower serum triglyceride levels.[44] But a recently published article contends that beta-carotene, vitamin E, and possibly high doses of vitamin A supplements increase mortality and that other antioxidants, folic acid and B vitamins, and multivitamin supplements have no clear benefit.[45] That conclusion may hinge on what experts consider a chronic disease. Definitions of chronic conditions tend to include few terms, such as heart disease and cancer, and overlook other chronic conditions that result from nutrient deficiencies, including iron-deficiency anemia, osteoporosis, and nerve damage. In one recent randomized controlled trial, considered the gold standard of studies, scientists demonstrated that taking a multivitamin significantly reduced the risk of cancer in some older men.[46] Because the study was conducted with well-nourished male physicians, it is not known whether the results apply to other types of people, including women and those more likely to have dietary insufficiencies.

Older people who, for whatever reason, don't get adequate servings from all of the food groups may benefit from personalized help with choosing vitamin and mineral

TABLE 19.2	Checklist for Talking about Nutritional Supplements
Questions about Nutritional Supplements to Ask a Health Care Provider	
Can I obtain the same nutrients in adequate amounts from my diet?	
Is taking a nutritional supplement an important part of my total diet, given my current intake?	
Are there any precautions or warnings I should know about (for example, is there an amount or "upper limit" I should not go above)?	
Are there any known side effects (such as loss of appetite, nausea, or headaches)? Do they apply to me?	
Are there any foods, medicines (prescription or over the counter), or other supplements I should avoid while taking this product?	
If I am scheduled for surgery, should I be concerned about the nutritional supplements I am taking?	

Source: Adapted from U.S. Food and Drug Administration. 2014. *Tips for Dietary Supplement Users.* Available at www.fda.gov/food/dietarysupplements/usingdietarysupplements/ucm110567.htm. Accessed August 2014.

supplements. Many elderly people are on medications that may deplete them of certain nutrients, and they may require dietary supplements even if their appetite is adequate. For example, proton-pump inhibitors, which reduce stomach acidity, reduce iron absorption and result in dangerously low levels of magnesium in the bloodstream.[47, 48]

Like anyone else, older adults should consult with their health care provider before they use nutritional supplements. They must read labels carefully to avoid exceeding the Tolerable Upper Intake Level. They should also consult with their pharmacist to see if their dietary supplements interact with any prescription or over-the-counter medication they consume. Using a checklist like the one in **Table 19.2** can help an individual have an effective conversation about nutritional supplements with a health care provider.

Older Adults Should Eat Right for Good Health and Disease Prevention

The best dietary strategy for aging adults to maintain good health and to prevent chronic diseases is to consume a varied, nutrient- and phytochemical-dense, heart-healthy diet.[49] Like their younger counterparts, many older Americans do not eat according to expert advice, and their diets may be too high in saturated fat, cholesterol, and sodium. When the diets of Americans 65 years of age and older were assessed in 2012 for compliance with the *Dietary Guidelines for Americans*, only 19 percent of those studied had diets that could be rated as "good." More than 65 percent of older Americans were eating diets that needed improvement and 13 percent were consuming diets rated as "poor."[50] **Table 19.3** summarizes the many diseases and conditions that a healthy diet may influence.

LO 19.3: THE TAKE-HOME MESSAGE Older adults typically require fewer kilocalories but not less nutrition than they did when they were younger. Meals and snacks should be nutrient dense to maximize nutrient intake. Adequate carbohydrate (including fiber) and protein intake are essential, and fat and cholesterol consumption should be moderate. Fruits and vegetables should be emphasized to ensure sufficient intake of beneficial antioxidants, phytochemicals, fluid, and fiber. Some vitamin and mineral consumption, including vitamins A, D, and B_{12} and the minerals iron, zinc, and calcium, should be particularly monitored to ensure adequate intake. Consuming adequate fluid is necessary to prevent dehydration and constipation. As much as possible, older adults should eat right to maintain their health.

TABLE 19.3 Eating Right to Fight Age-Related Diseases and Conditions

A varied, plant-based diet that supplies adequate macronutrients, fiber, and phytochemicals is the best diet defense against the conditions and chronic diseases associated with aging.

Condition/Disease	Disease-Fighting Compounds That May Help to Prevent It
Alzheimer's disease, Parkinson's disease	Antioxidants, vitamins C and E, and carotenoids
Anemia	Iron Folate Vitamin B_{12}
Cancer (colon, prostate, breast)	Fiber found in whole grains, fruits, vegetables Phytochemicals (phenols, indoles, lycopene, beta-carotene)
Cataracts, age-related macular degeneration	Vitamins C and E Lutein, zeaxanthin Zinc
Constipation, diverticulosis	Fiber Fluid
Heart disease	Vitamins B_6, B_{12}, and folate Omega-3 fatty acids Soluble fiber Phytochemicals in whole grains, fruits, vegetables
Hypertension	Calcium Magnesium Potassium
Impaired immune response	Iron Zinc Vitamin B_6 Protein
Obesity	Fiber as part of a balanced eating plan with the appropriate number of kilocalories to achieve and maintain a healthy weight
Osteoporosis	Calcium Vitamins D and K Protein
Type 2 diabetes	A healthy weight Chromium Fiber

What Are Some Nutrition-Related Health Concerns of Older Adults?

LO 19.4 Discuss some of the nutrition-related health concerns common to old age.

Aging is often associated with significant health problems and a diminished quality of life, especially in the very old. Almost 80 percent of older adults have one chronic condition, and half of all older adults have two or more.[51] Dealing with one or more chronic conditions can affect a person's ability to perform essential activities, including shopping for food and preparing meals, managing money, and taking medications as prescribed. As functional ability declines, people may lose even more abilities necessary to take care of themselves.[52]

About 36 percent of people age 65 and older in the United States report living with a disability, including trouble with living independently, moving around, and hearing. Living alone increases disability risk, and the risk increases further when that person living alone has no children or siblings, which is more common among those 85 years and older.[53]

Decreased Mobility Affects Many Older Adults

Some older adults, who may struggle with the activities of daily living, including carrying groceries, reaching over their heads, and stooping, can attribute the loss of function to sarcopenia. However, the most common causes of disability are **arthritis** (*arthr* = joint, *itis* = inflammation), back or spine problems, and heart problems, in that order.[54] Arthritis can cause pain, stiffness, and swelling in joints, muscles, tendons, ligaments, and bones. Getting out of bed, trying to open a jar, or climbing stairs can be challenging for those with arthritis. There are over 100 types of arthritis; *osteoarthritis, gout,* and *rheumatoid arthritis* are most common in older adults. Osteoporosis can also affect mobility in aging adults.

Osteoarthritis

Americans suffering from osteoarthritis number an estimated 27 million, of which nearly 34 percent are over the age of 65.[55] More than half of adults aged 65 and older have this type of arthritis. Osteoarthritis occurs when the cartilage, which covers the ends of the bones at the joints, wears down, causing the bones to rub together (see **Figure 19.5**). Repeated friction in the joint causes swelling, loss of motion, and pain. Osteoarthritis commonly occurs in the fingers, neck, lower back, knees, and hips. Exercises that increase flexibility, keep joints limber, and improve the range of motion can help maintain mobility in people with osteoarthritis. Losing excess weight also helps relieve some of the stress at the weight-bearing hip and knee joints.[56, 57]

Preliminary research has shown that the dietary supplements glucosamine and chondroitin sulfate, which are naturally found in cartilage, may provide some pain relief for some individuals with moderate to severe knee pain due to osteoarthritis, but had no effect in those with mild pain.[58] Individuals with osteoarthritis should speak with their health care provider to find out if they might benefit from using these supplements. For safety's sake, they should also discuss the use of all supplements, including herbs, with a health care provider prior to consuming them. Spotlight: Drug, Food, and Herb Interactions discusses the potentially harmful interactions between certain herbs, nutrients, and drugs.

Rheumatoid Arthritis

Rheumatoid arthritis, which occurs in at least 1.3 million U.S. adults, is an inflammatory disease of the joints that causes pain, swelling, and deformity.[59] Research suggests a link between diet and inflammation, and eating fish and foods rich in antioxidants may help ease the swelling seen in rheumatoid arthritis. Fish supply omega-3 fats, which play a role in modifying inflammation and pain, and people who don't eat at least two fish meals weekly should consult with their doctor about taking omega-3 supplements. Foods rich in antioxidants, including vitamins C and E, and phytonutrients, including flavonoids, may curb oxidation associated with inflammatory arthritis.[60] Compounds in cooked vegetables have been shown to possibly lower the risk of rheumatoid arthritis, and the fatty acids in olive oil may help reduce inflammation.[61]

▲ **Figure 19.5 Effects of Osteoarthritis**
Osteoarthritis can affect any joint. When multiple hand joints become affected, pain, swelling, and stiffness make routine tasks difficult to accomplish. Studies show that people who actively manage their osteoarthritis have less pain and function better.

arthritis Inflammation in the joints that can cause pain, stiffness, and swelling.

SPOTLIGHT Drug, Food, and Herb Interactions

The third National Health and Nutrition Examination Survey indicates that use of nonvitamin and nonmineral supplements such as herbs is increasing among the elderly.[1] There is concern, however, that the combining of herbal supplements with prescription and over-the-counter medications creates the potential for negative supplement–drug interactions. A growing concern among many physicians is that some herbal remedies such as ginkgo biloba and garlic may increase the risk of bleeding after surgery. St. John's wort, when combined with prescription antidepressant medications, may also produce negative effects.

Food can also interact with medications in several ways. For example, calcium can bind with tetracycline (an antibiotic), decreasing its absorption. For this reason, tetracycline shouldn't be taken with milk or calcium-fortified foods. In contrast, grapefruit juice increases the absorption of calcium channel–blocking agents,

Older individuals who are taking multiple medications must regularly review potential drug interactions with their doctor or pharmacist.

Potential Side Effects of Selected Herbs and Supplements

Herb/Nutrient	Purported Use	Potential Side Effects	Drug Interactions
Black cohosh	Reduce hot flashes and other menopausal symptoms	Possible headache and stomach discomfort	Interactions between black cohosh and medications has not been rigorously studied. Avoid if history of breast cancer or liver disease
Calcium	Prevent osteoporosis	Constipation; calcium deposits in body	Decreases the absorption of tetracycline, thyroid medication, iron, zinc, and magnesium, among others
Coenzyme Q-10	Hypertension, diabetes mellitus, congestive heart failure, increased energy levels	Nausea, vomiting, appetite loss	Do not combine with chemotherapy, antihypertensive drugs, and warfarin and red yeast
DHEA	To slow aging process, improve cognition, increase muscle mass and to improve sexual function	High blood pressure, liver problems, lower blood glucose levels	Corticosteroids decrease DHEA production in body; soy may decrease DHEA effectiveness; DHEA may increase effectiveness of insulin
Dong Quai root	Relieve menopausal symptoms, manage hypertension	Excessive bleeding due to blood thinning	Enhances the effectiveness of blood-thinning drugs and aspirin as well as vitamin E, garlic, and ginkgo biloba
Echinacea	Treat upper respiratory conditions, including the common cold	Rash, increased asthma, allergic reactions in sensitive individuals	May decrease effectiveness of immune-suppressing drugs (cyclosporine, corticosteroids)
Evening primrose oil	To reduce excema, inflammation, menopausal symptoms	Mild stomach and intestinal discomfort; headaches	May increase bleeding in people also taking blood thinners
Fish oil	Reduce the risk of heart disease, improve depression, dry eyes, glaucoma, age-related macular degeneration	Excessive amounts could suppress immunity in the elderly, increase bleeding risk, interfere with blood glucose control, belching, bad breath, heartburn, nausea, loose stools	Increases the risk of blood thinning in people who take blood-thinning medications and dietary supplements, such as vitamin E

U.S. Food and Drug Administration. 2014. *Tips for Older Dietary Supplement Users.* Available at www.fda.gov/food/dietarysupplements/ ConsumerInformation/ucm110493.htm. Accessed August 2014; National Institutes of Health, Office of Dietary Supplements. 2013. *Calcium.* Available at www.ods.od.nih.gov/factsheets/Calcium-HealthProfessional/#h10. Accessed August 2014; U.S. National Library of Medicine. National Institutes of Health. 2014. *Herbs and Supplements.* Available at www.nlm.nih.gov/medlineplus/druginfo/herb_All.html. Accessed August 2014. U.S. Food and Drug Administration. 2014. *Grapefruit Juice and Medicine May Not Mix.* Available at www.fda.gov/downloads/ ForConsumers/ConsumerUpdates/UCM292839.pdf. Accessed August 2014.

which are a type of medication often used to treat heart disease. Drugs can also interfere with the metabolism of certain substances in foods. An enzyme called monoamine oxidase metabolizes the compound tyramine, which is abundant in aged cheese, smoked fish, yogurt, and red wine. Certain medications called monoamine oxidase inhibitors, which may be prescribed to treat depression, prevent tyramine from being properly metabolized. High levels of tyramine in the blood can result in dangerously high blood pressure.

In addition to drug–herb interactions, prescription drugs can also interact with other prescription and over-the-counter drugs. Older individuals, who are often taking multiple medications, must regularly review with their doctor or pharmacist all of the potential interactions, particularly as they relate to food and dietary supplements. See the accompanying table for a list of potential interactions among herbs, nutrients, and medications.

Reference

1. R. S. Wold, S. T. Lopez, C. L. Yau, L. M. Butler, S. L. Pareo-Tubbeh, D. L. Waters, et al. 2005. "Increasing Trends in Elderly Persons' Use of Nonvitamin, Nonmineral Dietary Supplements and Concurrent Use of Medications." *Journal of the American Dietetic Association* 105:54–63.

Potential Side Effects of Selected Herbs and Supplements

Herb/Nutrient	Purported Use	Potential Side Effects	Drug Interactions
Garlic, garlic supplements	Lower blood cholesterol levels, reduce heart disease risk, lower blood pressure	Possible stomach and intestinal discomfort, bad breath	Don't mix with blood-thinning drugs and aspirin; garlic enhances the blood-thinning actions of medications and supplements such as vitamin E and ginkgo biloba
Ginkgo	Reduce memory loss, treat or prevent dementia	Possible stomach and intestinal discomfort, headache	Increases bleeding risk so do not combine with blood-thinning drugs and aspirin. Enhances the blood-thinning actions of vitamin E and garlic
Ginseng, American	Reduce fatigue, stress, boost immune system, general stimulant	May lower blood glucose levels, insomnia	Enhances the action of medications to lower blood glucose levels; stop taking at least 2 weeks prior to surgery. Increases blood thinning, so do not take with blood thinners such as warfarin, aspirin, and vitamin E
Grapefruit, grapefruit juice	Source of vitamin C	None known at this time	Increases the absorption of statin drugs to lower cholesterol, antihypertensive medication, some antianxiety and antiarrhythmia medications, and antihistamines
Hawthorn	Hypertension, congestive heart failure	Upset stomach, dizziness, headache	May not be combined with certain heart medications
Kava	Reduce anxiety, stress, insomnia	Possible severe liver damage, drowsiness, scaly yellow skin in long-term use	The FDA has issued a warning that kava supplements increase liver damage. Do not combine with drugs used for Parkinson's disease
St. John's wort	Reduce depression, anxiety, fatigue, menopausal symptoms	Insomnia, vivid dreams, restlessness, dizziness, headache, severe reactions to sun exposure	Interacts with several medications. May decrease effectiveness of antianxiety drugs, heart medications, and antidepressants
Vitamin E	Reduce the risk of heart disease	Excessive amounts can interfere with blood clotting, increasing the risk of hemorrhage	Can increase bleeding risk in those taking blood thinners and may reduce effectiveness of chemotherapy and radiation treatments
Vitamin K	Blood clotting, bone health	None known at this time	Reduces the effectiveness of blood-thinning medications; keep vitamin K intake and medication levels constant

Routine physical activity can help with arthritis by building muscles and increasing flexibility.

Routine physical activity can help those who suffer from arthritis. Exercise helps reduce joint pain and stiffness, and increases range of motion. It can also build muscles and increase flexibility. Swimming, aquatic exercises, and walking can all help older adults with arthritis.

Gout

Crystallization of excess uric acid within joints and soft tissues causes **gout,** an inflammatory arthritis. For many people, gout initially occurs as pain and swelling in the joints of the big toe. The needlelike uric acid crystals can also affect the insteps, ankles, heels, knees, wrists, fingers, and elbows.[62]

Gout is a growing health problem among older adults. Doctors may have difficulty diagnosing it because the symptoms can be vague, and gout often mimics other conditions.[63] A 2011 study shows that the prevalence of gout in the United States has risen over the last twenty years and now affects 8.3 million people—4 percent of all U.S. adults. In addition, more people than ever have elevated uric acid levels—some 43.3 million, or 21 percent of U.S. adults—and are thus at risk.[64]

Obesity, hypertension, diabetes, kidney disease, excessive alcohol intake, and a family history of gout are risk factors.[65] Managing gout means controlling weight; limiting purine-rich foods, such as meat, poultry, and fish; cutting back on saturated fat; limiting or avoiding alcohol, especially beer; limiting or avoiding foods with high-fructose corn syrup; eating more whole grains and fewer refined grains; choosing low-fat or fat-free dairy products; and drinking eight to 16 glasses of fluid daily, mostly as water.[66] People with gout should consult with a Registered Dietitian Nutritionist about the best diet to follow.

Osteoporosis

The bone disease osteoporosis can affect the mobility of older adults by increasing the likelihood of fracture and the thinning and hardening of the vertebrae, which reduce spine flexibility. Calcium loss from vertebrae results in a reduction in height and makes bending, reaching, and walking difficult. Older adults who suffer falls and fractures are often forced to walk with a walker for assistance or are confined to a wheelchair, making living independently and cooking and preparing healthy meals difficult. There is no cure for osteoporosis, but medications can slow bone loss and even build bone. These medications work best with a balanced diet rich in calcium and vitamins, dietary supplements as necessary, and regular weight-bearing exercise.

Eye Disease Is a Concern for Many Older Adults

Vision disorders are prevalent in older age. As described in Chapter 9, age-related macular degeneration is the most common cause of blindness in older Americans. Macular degeneration is a result of oxidative damage to the macula, the area of the retina that distinguishes fine detail. Deterioration of this area can make it more difficult to see and can eventually result in blindness.

Consumption of fruits and vegetables containing lutein and zeaxanthin, two carotenoid pigments, may be linked to a reduced risk for age-related macular degeneration. The carotenoids are part of the central region of the retina and may play a role in some aspects of vision. Increasing the concentration of these pigments in the eye may prevent the loss of sight caused by age-related macular degeneration. Lutein and zeaxanthin are found primarily in broccoli, corn, squash, and dark green leafy vegetables such as spinach and kale.[67]

Cataracts, cloudy spots on the lens of the eye, also cause loss of vision. The lens of the eye lies behind the iris and pupil and works much like a camera lens, focusing

gout A disease in which high levels of uric acid build up in the blood and cause inflammation in the joints. Chronic gout causes episodes of acute arthritis pain especially in the feet.

cataracts Clumps of protein that form on the lens of the eye, clouding vision.

light on the retina, where the image is recorded. The lens is made mostly of water and protein, which is arranged in a way that keeps the lens clear and allows light to pass through. As a person ages, some of the protein may clump together and form a cataract, reducing the sharpness of the image reaching the retina.[68]

In the United States, most cataracts are age related, affecting more than half of all Americans older than 65 to some degree.[69] A family history of cataracts increases the risk, as do diabetes, excessive alcohol intake, high blood pressure, obesity, and smoking.[70] Eating more antioxidant-rich foods may help to maintain good eye health, even once cataracts have been diagnosed. Older people should eat green, leafy vegetables and fruits such as blueberries, cherries, and raspberries on a regular basis. Eating fish regularly may also help prevent cataracts.[71]

Alzheimer's Disease Is a Serious Problem for Some Older Adults

Although it's normal for older adults to experience some cognitive changes, such as taking longer to learn new information, more serious mental declines are cause for concern. Some adults begin to forget where they live, have difficulty speaking, or become emotionally unstable. These individuals may be experiencing **dementia**—the loss of cognitive function and changes in behavior that interfere with a person's daily life and activities. Dementia ranges in severity. The most common form of dementia in older adults is **Alzheimer's disease.** This irreversible disease slowly damages the brain tissues and can progress over the years to severe brain damage. An estimated 5.1 million Americans have Alzheimer's disease, with most showing signs of the condition in their 60s.[72]

Alzheimer's disease leads to nerve cell death and tissue loss throughout the brain. With fewer nerve cells and synapses, the brain shrinks, affecting its ability to function. It appears likely that toxic changes begin to damage the brain a decade or more before symptoms appear.[73] Lifestyle choices may play a role in preventing Alzheimer's disease. Physical and mental inactivity, smoking, obesity, diabetes, hypertension, and depression are linked to the development of Alzheimer's disease. Researchers estimate that a 25 percent improvement in these conditions among the general population would prevent as many as 16.5 percent of Alzheimer's cases in the United States.[74]

Generally speaking, a lifestyle that supports heart health also supports brain health. A balanced diet with the recommended amounts of fruits, vegetables, and whole grains, as well as lean protein foods and low-fat dairy, helps to prevent clogged arteries that feed the heart and brain and provide the nutrients to support brain health. Higher dietary intake and circulating blood levels of omega-3 have also been related to a reduced risk for dementia and slower cognitive decline.[75, 76]

Elders with dementia are likely to need full-time care and shouldn't be allowed to take walks, jogs, or bike rides alone. However, accompanying an elder during any of these activities is a great way for two people to get some exercise. Those with dementia may experience mental deterioration, but they should be encouraged to stay active as long as possible to prevent physical deterioration.

Accompanying an elder during a walk is a great way for two people to get some exercise.

LO 19.4: THE TAKE-HOME MESSAGE Older adults face various health concerns that can have an impact on nutrition needs or that can be affected by nutrition. Decreased mobility is common in older age. Glucosamine and chondroitin sulfate supplements may help with the pain of osteoarthritis, and improving the diet can help control the symptoms of gout. Vision disorders, including macular degeneration and cataracts, are also common. Risk of developing eye disease may be reduced by a diet that includes foods rich in antioxidants and phytochemicals. Alzheimer's disease and other forms of dementia affect some older adults. Some evidence indicates that a balanced diet and omega-3 fats may help reduce the risk of dementia.

dementia A disorder of the brain that interferes with a person's memory, learning, and mental stability.

Alzheimer's disease A type of dementia.

What Socioeconomic and Psychological Issues Affect the Nutrition of Older Adults?

Describe the social, economic, and psychological factors that can affect the health of older Americans.

In addition to physical ailments, older people may have to deal with various social, psychological, and financial issues. Some older adults may not have enough money to live on and may have to choose among filling their prescriptions, buying food, or paying the rent. For individuals with inadequate financial resources, food insecurity and psychological and emotional difficulties can result.

Food Insecurity Has Nutritional Impacts

More people over the age of 65 than ever face poverty. In 2012, 3.9 million people in the 65 and older age group were in poverty (defined as at or below $15,730.00 for a household of two and at or below $11,170 for a person living alone),[77] up from 3.6 million in 2011.[78] Blacks and Hispanics are more likely than whites to experience poverty.[79] In light of these numbers, it's not surprising that nearly nine percent of American households with elders experience **food insecurity,** or the routine lack of sufficient food to feed those living there.[80]

Limited finances aren't always the cause of food insecurity. Some elders may be able to afford food but lack the physical means to obtain it, prepare it, or eat it (due to tooth loss).[81] Whatever the reason, food-insecure older adults run the risk of lower intakes for kilocalories and essential nutrients, and are more likely to be in poor or fair rather than good health.

Participation by older adults in food assistance programs can have both nutritional and nonnutritional benefits by reducing or preventing numerous poor outcomes associated with food insecurity, such as quality of life, health care expenses, and nutritional adequacy. For elders who must take medications with food, eating adequate amounts of nutritious food is especially important.

To help community advocates identify older adults potentially at risk for food insecurity, the American Academy of Family Physicians and other organizations created the Nutrition Screening Initiative (NSI). The NSI is designed to promote routine screening of older persons in both community and institutional settings through a network of dietitians, public health nutritionists, community workers, and physicians (see the Self-Assessment).[82]

Community Resources Exist for Older Adults

Government-supported food assistance programs that are available to the larger population, such as food stamps, also serve older adults; however, there are also federally funded food assistance programs specifically for older adults. These programs are funded under the 1965 Older Americans Act to provide support and services to individuals aged 60 and older.[83] The Act brought federal support to **Meals On Wheels,** making it one of the most significant volunteer programs in the country. Having the Meals On Wheels driver stop in daily assures that older adults receive nourishment and remain safe in their homes.[84] The goals of the Older Americans Act are to help seniors maintain good health, an adequate quality of life, and an acceptable level of independence.

In addition to Meals On Wheels, the Older Americans Act funds the Elderly Nutrition Program (ENP), which provides **congregate meals**—hot meals served at specified sites in the community, such as churches, synagogues, and senior centers.

food insecurity The chronic lack of sufficient food to nutritiously feed oneself.

Meals On Wheels A program that delivers nutritious meals to homebound older adults.

congregate meals Low- or no-cost meals served at churches, synagogues, or other community sites where older adults can receive a nutritious meal and socialize.

Are You at Nutritional Risk?

Circle the number in the right-hand column for the statements that apply to you (or someone you know, if you are taking the assessment for a friend or relative). Add up the circled numbers to determine your score.

I have an illness or condition that has made me change the kind and/or amount of food I eat.	2
I eat fewer than two meals per day.	3
I eat few fruits or vegetables or milk products.	2
I have three or more drinks of beer, liquor, or wine almost every day.	2
I have tooth or mouth problems that make it hard for me to eat.	2
I don't always have enough money to buy food.	4
I eat alone most of the time.	1
I take three or more different prescribed or over-the-counter drugs a day.	1
Without wanting to, I have lost or gained 10 pounds in the last six months.	2
I am not always physically able to shop, cook, and/or feed myself.	2
Total	_____

This guarantees that older adults receive a nutritious daily meal and provides an opportunity for them to socialize. Often, transportation to these meals is also available. The program brings consistency and quality to senior center programs.

Young people in the community can help make sure that older adults are familiar with and take advantage of the numerous services available to them. Consider "adopting" a senior neighbor or family member and, if necessary, help him or her locate these services.

Psychological and Emotional Conditions Can Affect Nutritional Health

Whereas many seniors live happy, fulfilled lives, some individuals can be affected by grief, depression, and loneliness as they lose family or friends, learn to live alone, or adjust to new environments, such as living with family or in an assisted living facility. Adults who are depressed or grieving may turn to alcohol and medications to deal with their feelings.

Depression and Grief

Depression affects more than 6.5 million of the 35 million Americans aged 65 years or older.[85] The loss of friends and loved ones, as well as chronic pain and concerns about their own health, can add to feelings of grief, sadness, and isolation. Depression can interfere with an older adult's motivation to eat, be physically active, and socialize—all of which can impact mental and physical health.

Depression in the elderly, especially the very old, may be difficult to detect. Common symptoms such as fatigue, appetite loss, and trouble sleeping can be part of the aging process or a physical illness, so depression may be confused with other conditions common to elders. Family and friends should be aware of the changes in elders' eating and lifestyle habits, and help elders seek treatment for depression, if necessary. Younger adults need to help elders reconnect with their communities after a loss and adjust to a new lifestyle. As mentioned, neighbors can "adopt an elder" who may be living alone

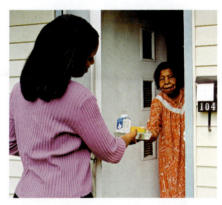

Programs such as Meals On Wheels provide hot meals to older adults who cannot leave their home.

Red Flags for Alcohol Abuse in Older Adults

Drinks to calm nerves, reduce stress or depression, or forget his or her troubles.

Gulps drinks.

Frequently has more than one drink a day.

Lies about or tries to hide his or her drinking habits.

Hurts self or others when drinking.

Needs increased amounts of alcohol to get high.

Feels irritable, resentful, or unreasonable when not drinking.

Has medical, social, or financial worries caused by drinking.

▲ **Figure 19.6 Red Flags for Alcohol Abuse in Older Adults**
Adapted from National Institute on Aging. 2012. *Alcohol Use In Older People.* Available at www.nia .nih.gov/health/publication/alcohol-use-older-people. Accessed May 2012.

and coordinate regular visits and delivery of meals. A quick visit by several supportive friends over the course of a month can go a long way to help seniors stay healthy.

Alcohol Abuse

Chronic health problems, loss of friends and loved ones, or financial stress can make alcohol an appealing sedative to temporarily ease discomfort or depression. An elderly person may drink more to self-medicate. Yet heavy drinking can exacerbate depression, which can lead to more drinking.[86] Also, because alcohol impairs one's judgment and interferes with coordination and reaction time, elders who have been drinking are at a higher risk for stumbling, falling, and fracturing bones.

With age, adults become more sensitive to alcohol, in part because of a decline in body water. Individuals with a lower percentage of body water will have a higher blood alcohol concentration (BAC) and thus feel its effects sooner. In addition, many prescription and over-the-counter medications should not be mixed with alcohol.[87] People over age 65 take, on average, two to seven medications daily,[88] and possibly one or more over-the-counter drugs as well, which can intensify alcohol's effects, diminish the effects of medication, or both.

Health care providers and family members may not recognize alcohol abuse in elders, mistaking it for the forgetfulness and disorientation of "normal aging."[89] **Figure 19.6** lists the red flags from the National Institute of Aging that may signal alcohol abuse in an older adult. The National Institute on Alcohol Abuse and Alcoholism recommends that adults over 65 who are healthy and do not take medications should limit alcohol consumption to seven drinks a week and no more than three drinks on a given day. People with health problems or who take certain medications may need to drink less or not at all.[90]

> **LO 19.5: THE TAKE-HOME MESSAGE** Financial challenges, emotional and psychological conditions, and alcohol abuse can impair the abilities of older adults to maintain healthy diets and lifestyles. Alcohol can also interfere with the actions of numerous prescription drugs. Many community resources exist to help elders cope with their life challenges. The Older Americans Act has been particularly effective at providing nutritional support to seniors.

What Is Hypertension?

LO 19.6 Describe the risk factors for hypertension and the dietary interventions that help control it.

Blood pressure is a measure of the force that blood exerts against the walls of arteries. With every beat, the heart pumps blood into the arteries, and to the rest of the body. Blood pressure is highest at the moment of the heart beat (measured as **systolic pressure**) and lower when the heart is at rest between beats (measured as **diastolic pressure**). An individual's blood pressure is expressed as a reading of systolic over diastolic pressure. A blood pressure reading of less than 120/80 mm Hg (millimeters of mercury) is considered normal.

Stages of Hypertension

High blood pressure is called **hypertension.** In most cases, hypertension develops over time. The first stage, prehypertension, occurs as blood pressure begins to rise above normal—that is, systolic blood pressure measures between 120 and 139 mm Hg or the diastolic reading reaches 80 to 89 mm Hg.[91]

If prehypertension is left untreated, it can advance to Stage 1 hypertension, which is characterized by a systolic pressure between 140 mm Hg and 159 mm Hg or a diastolic pressure of 90 mm Hg to 99 mm Hg. The most severe hypertension is Stage 2, which occurs when the systolic pressure rises to 160 mm Hg or higher or the diastolic pressure is 100 mm Hg or higher. Both numbers are important, but after age 50 the most common form of hypertension is when the systolic blood pressure is high and the diastolic pressure is within normal range.[92] **Table 19.4** summarizes the classifications of blood pressure.

Hypertension: The Silent Killer

High blood pressure increases the risk for heart attack, angina, stroke, kidney failure, and peripheral artery disease, and several studies link prehypertension to cardiovascular risk factors such as obesity, diabetes mellitus, and dyslipidemia.[93]

The percentage of Americans who have high blood pressure rose from about 26 percent in 2005 to more than 28 percent in 2009, a nearly 10 percent increase. As a group, older people have a higher rate of hypertension than their younger counterparts.[94] Generally speaking, most elderly people experience a moderate rise in blood pressure as they age for a variety of reasons, including that arteries, such as the aorta, become thicker and less flexible.[95] Individuals with chronic high blood pressure may develop an enlarged and weakened heart, because it has to work harder to pump enough oxygen- and nutrient-laden blood throughout the body. This can lead to fatigue, shortness of breath, and possibly heart attack.

Hypertension is referred to as the "silent killer" because there are no visible signs of the condition. The only way to be sure that blood pressure levels are within normal range is to regularly check blood pressure.

Hypertension Risk Factors You Cannot Control

Various factors affect the chances of developing hypertension; some are controllable and others are not. Family history, gender, race, and age are among the uncontrollable factors that influence the likelihood that a person will develop high blood pressure. Before age 55, men have a greater chance of having high blood pressure, while women are more likely to have high blood pressure after menopause.[96] Hypertension is more prevalent, and tends to occur earlier in life and be more severe, in African-Americans.[97]

systolic pressure The top number in a blood pressure reading that measures the pressure in the arteries when the heart muscle contracts.

diastolic pressure The bottom number in a blood pressure reading that measures the minimal arterial pressure during relaxation of the heart muscle when the ventricles fill with blood.

hypertension High blood pressure measuring140/90 mmHg or higher.

Having your blood pressure checked regularly is the only way to make sure you aren't developing high blood pressure.

TABLE 19.4 Classification of Blood Pressure

Category	Systolic Blood Pressure, mmHg	Diastolic Blood Pressure, mmHg
Normal	< 120 and	< 80
Prehypertension	120–139 or	80–89
Hypertension, Stage 1	140–159 or	90–99
Hypertension, Stage 2	≥ 160 or	≥ 100

Source: U.S. Department of Health and Human Services. National Institutes of Health. Heart, Lung, and Blood Institute. 2004. *Reference Card from the Seventh Report of the Joint National Committee on Prevention, Detection, Evaluation, and Treatment of High Blood Pressure (JNC 7).* Available at www.nhlbi.nih.gov/files/docs/resources/heart/phycard.pdf. Accessed July 2014.

Hypertension Risk Factors You Can Control

The good news is that there are more controllable risk factors for hypertension than uncontrollable factors.

Diet

Eating a balanced diet is a proven strategy to lower blood pressure. The DASH (Dietary Approaches to Stop Hypertension) diet is an eating plan based on research studies sponsored by the National Heart, Lung, and Blood Institute (NHLBI). The plan emphasizes fruits, vegetables, and low-fat dairy foods and includes whole grains, fish, poultry, beans, nuts, and seeds, while limiting sodium, sugar, and red meat. The DASH eating plan is relatively low in sodium and rich in potassium and other nutrients that help control blood pressure.[98] You can find the DASH eating plan online at www.nhlbi.nih.gov.

The initial DASH study found that subjects who followed the eating plan experienced a significant reduction in blood pressure compared with those who followed two other diets. Because all three diets in the study contained approximately 3,000 milligrams of sodium per day, researchers were unable to attribute the lowered blood pressure experienced by the DASH diet followers to a reduction in sodium intake. Rather, the researchers concluded that the blood pressure–lowering effect of the DASH diet was due to its abundance of fruits and vegetables, which provide healthy doses of potassium and magnesium, and because of its numerous servings of dairy foods, which are rich in calcium. The study concluded that dietary potassium, magnesium, and calcium can all play a role in lowering blood pressure.[99]

A follow-up to the DASH study, called the DASH-Sodium study, investigated whether reducing the amount of dietary sodium in each of the three diets could also help lower blood pressure. Not surprisingly, it did. While the result of this study showed that reducing dietary sodium from about 3,300 milligrams to 2,400 milligrams daily lowered blood pressure, the biggest blood pressure reduction occurred when sodium intake was limited to 1,500 milligrams daily.[100]

The DASH studies reinforced our understanding of sodium's role in blood pressure and showed that a largely plant-based diet with lean sources of protein significantly reduces hypertension. The authors of the Optimal Macronutrient Intake Trial to Prevent Heart Disease (OMNIHeart Trial) compared the effects on blood pressure of substituting protein (about half as plant protein) or unsaturated fat (mostly monounsaturated) for some of the carbohydrate in healthy diets such as DASH. The results of eating 10 percent more protein and 10 percent more kilocalories from monounsaturated fat reduced systolic blood pressure by an additional 1.4 mm Hg over the DASH diet.[101] The researchers concluded that all three diets (the DASH diet, as well as the higher-protein eating plan and higher monounsaturated fat versions in the OMNI diet) lowered blood pressure and thus cardiovascular risk.

Alcohol Consumption

Heavy and regular use of alcohol can significantly increase blood pressure. Older people who drink should do so in moderation, especially if they have high blood pressure. The American Heart Association recommends that men limit alcohol to no more than two drinks daily and women to one drink daily or less.[102]

Body Weight

Achieving and maintaining a healthy body weight can also markedly reduce the risk for hypertension. When you're overweight, your heart works harder to pump blood. Losing as few as 10 pounds can reduce blood pressure and/or prevent hypertension in many people with a body mass index of 25 or higher.[103]

Physical Activity

Regular physical activity—at least 30 to 60 minutes on most days of the week—can lower blood pressure by 4 to 9 millimeters of mercury (mm Hg).

Diet, alcohol consumption, body weight, and physical activity are all factors that you can control that influence blood pressure.

Nutrition in Practice: Ed

Ed recently retired at age 66. Although he grew up on a diet rich in saturated fats from meat and full-fat dairy foods, he has avoided these foods since his father survived a heart attack. Ed now consumes a largely plant-based diet of fruits, vegetables, legumes, and whole grains. However, Ed also has a sweet tooth, frequently dines out, and often enjoys a well-done steak. He was physically active during his school years, but became sedentary after college. He now goes for daily walks with his wife Ellie after dinner. During inclement weather, they go to the Y to strength-train and walk on the treadmill for 30 minutes. Despite watching his diet and exercising, Ed continues to carry 30 extra pounds. His fasting blood glucose is 120 mg/dl and cholesterol is 230 mg/dl. Blood pressure is 135/88. His family history reveals diabetes, heart-related diseases, osteoporosis, arthritis, and low thyroid. Ed suspects that he, too, is at risk for heart disease, but isn't sure that dietary changes at this point will make much of a difference. He decides to seek advice from his Registered Dietitian Nutritionist.

Ed's Stats:
- Age: 66
- Height: 5 feet 10 inches
- Weight: 200 pounds
- BMI: 28.7
- Fasting Blood Glucose: 120 mg/dl
- Total Cholesterol: 230 mg/dl
- Blood Pressure: 135/88 mm Hg

Ed's Food Log

Food/Beverage	Time Consumed	Hunger Rating*	Location
Fortified whole-grain cereal topped with blueberries and fortified nonfat milk; coffee with sugar	6:30 A.M.	2	In the kitchen
Black beans and brown rice with broccoli and carrots; spinach salad with vinaigrette dressing; coffee with sugar	12:30 P.M.	5	In the kitchen
Banana	3 P.M.	2	In front of the TV after an afternoon walk
Well-done rib-eye steak; green salad with vinaigrette; baked potato with sour cream and chives; glass of red wine; chocolate crème brulée for dessert; coffee with sugar	6:30 P.M.	3	At Ed's favorite steakhouse with friends

*Hunger Rating (1–5): 1 = not hungry; 5 = super hungry

Critical Thinking Questions
1. What behaviors is Ed doing right?
2. What changes should he make to improve his health?
3. What dietary advice would you give to Ed to help him to obtain the nutrients he needs while decreasing his risk for chronic disease?

Dietitian's Observation and Plan for Ed:
- Ed's BMI of 28.7 means he is overweight and his blood glucose reading of 120 m/dl indicates prediabetes. Ed's blood pressure is slightly elevated. The dietitian can work with Ed in establishing an individualized meal and exercise plan for reducing blood glucose, serum cholesterol, and body weight.
- A plant-based meal plan consisting of fruits, vegetables, legumes, and whole grains tends to be heart healthy. The meal plan includes a specified number of servings from each food group and distributed throughout the day, matching Ed's food preferences and lifestyle.
- Dining out can be challenging for individuals on any meal plan. Portion sizes tend to exceed those normally recommended. The dietitian can provide strategies for making heart-healthy food selections and controlling portions, while incorporating some favorite foods. Although Ed can still enjoy an occasional lean steak at his favorite restaurant, he may be sharing an entrée or have extra food to take home.
- Ed can benefit from a regularly scheduled exercise program. Physical activity will help him reduce the risk factors—elevated blood glucose, cholesterol, and blood pressure—associated with diabetes and heart disease. Exercise physiologists at the Y can monitor Ed's blood pressure as well as his progress in the exercise program.

TABLE 19.5	Take Charge of Your Blood Pressure!	
If You	**By**	**Your Systolic Blood Pressure* May Be Reduced by**
Reduce your sodium intake	Limiting dietary sodium consumption to no more than 2,400 mg daily	2–8 mm Hg
Follow the DASH diet	Consuming a heart-healthy diet that is abundant in fruits, vegetables, and low-fat dairy products; 58% carbohydrate, 15% protein, and 27% fat	8–14 mm Hg
Achieve and maintain a healthy body weight	Consuming the right number of kilocalories that allows you to maintain a normal, healthy BMI	5–20 mm Hg for every 22 lbs of weight loss
Stay physically active	Participating in aerobic exercise (such as brisk walking) 30 minutes per day most days of the week	4–9 mm Hg
Drink alcohol only in moderation	Limiting consumption to no more than 2 drinks daily for men and 1 drink daily for women	2–4 mm Hg

Note: *Controlling the systolic pressure is more difficult than controlling the diastolic pressure, especially for individuals 50 years of age and older. Therefore, lowering systolic pressure is the primary focus for lowering blood pressure. Typically, as systolic pressure goes down with diet and lifestyle changes, the diastolic pressure does, too.

Source: Data from A. V. Chobanian, et al. 2003. "The Seventh Report of the Joint National Committee on Prevention, Detection, Evaluation, and Treatment of High Blood Pressure," *Journal of the American Medical Association* 289:2560–2572.

People with prehypertension can avoid developing hypertension and bring their blood pressure down to safer levels with regular exercise.[104]

The research on high blood pressure is clear: Diet and lifestyle changes help reduce blood pressure and help prevent hypertension. Table 19.5 summarizes what you can do to control your blood pressure and reduce your risk of developing hypertension.

LO 19.6: THE TAKE-HOME MESSAGE

Hypertension risk increases with age, and it's on the rise because of the increasing number of older Americans in the United States. Older Americans should attempt to prevent and control hypertension to reduce the risk for heart attack and stroke. Some risk factors for hypertension, including obesity, alcohol intake, diet, and physical activity, are under personal control. The DASH diet, a plant-based eating plan with lean sources of protein, has been proven to reduce blood pressure.

Visual Chapter Summary

LO 19.1 The Demographics of Aging in America Are Changing

Improved health care, public health initiatives, and widespread access to health information have helped lead to a longer life expectancy for Americans. The average life expectancy for men in the United States is 76 years and for women, 81 years. By 2050, the number of Americans aged 65 and older is projected to be 88.5 million. While heart disease and cancer remain the leading causes of death in older Americans, people are living longer and better lives, in large part because of better medications and medical treatment. America's older population is also becoming more racially and ethnically diverse.

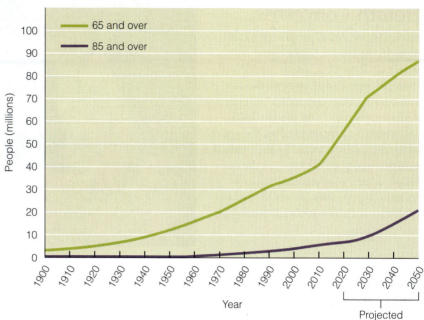

LO 19.2 Physical and Cognitive Changes Occur as Part of the Aging Process

The majority of age-related changes are gradual and accumulate over time. Physiological effects of aging include changes in body composition, including reduced muscle mass (sarcopenia) and increased body fat; a decrease in immune function; declining sensory abilities; gastrointestinal changes such as slower digestion; and changes in brain function, including memory loss and dementia. These changes can have a negative influence on the desire to eat and on the body's ability to extract nutrients from food.

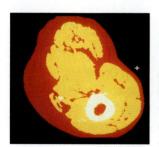
Young adult's thigh

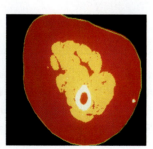
Older adult's thigh

LO 19.3 Nutrient Needs Change for Older Adults

Metabolism slows with age, so older adults need fewer kilocalories than their younger counterparts. Older adults should ensure that they get an adequate intake of high-quality lean protein, complex carbohydrates, and unsaturated fat, and that they consume enough fluid, vitamins D and B_{12}, and the minerals iron, calcium, and zinc, and decrease sodium intake. Vitamin D requirements increase by 200 IU at age 50 and by 400 IU at age 71.

LO 19.4 Older Adults Have a Variety of Nutrition-Related Health Concerns

About 36 percent of people age 65 and older in the United States report living with a disability, including trouble with living independently, moving around, and hearing. An estimated 27 million Americans suffer from osteoarthritis and nearly 34 percent are over the age of 65; others are affected by rheumatoid arthritis and gout, which is on the rise. Other nutrition-related health issues include osteoporosis, dementia, and eye problems such as macular degeneration and cataracts.

LO 19.6 Many Older Adults Have Hypertension

Hypertension is on the rise among older Americans. Age increases the risk for hypertension, but several positive lifestyle choices, including eating a balanced diet, limiting alcohol intake, and achieving and maintaining a healthy weight, help to keep blood pressure within normal range. The DASH diet is a plant-based diet with lean sources of protein that helps reduce hypertension. Staying physically active can help lower the risk of hypertension, as well as many other chronic conditions.

LO 19.5 Socioeconomic and Psychological Issues Can Affect the Nutritional Health of Older Adults

Older adults sometimes suffer from food insecurity due to financial hardship or physical disabilities. Federal food assistance programs specifically for older adults are funded under the 1965 Older Americans Act to provide support and services to individuals aged 60 and older. Loss of loved ones coupled with social isolation can lead to depression and grief in older adults. This may lead to a decreased motivation to eat as well as an increased reliance on alcohol.

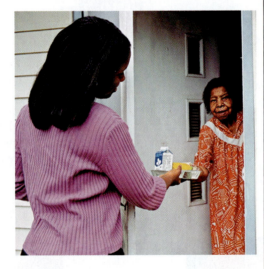

Terms to Know

- aging
- senescence
- life span
- life expectancy
- longevity
- physiologic age
- chronologic age
- sarcopenia
- arthritis
- gout
- cataracts
- dementia
- Alzheimer's disease
- food insecurity
- Meals On Wheels
- congregate meals
- systolic pressure
- diastolic pressure
- hypertension

MasteringNutrition™

Scan to hear an MP3 chapter review in MasteringNutrition.

Check Your Understanding

1. Which of the following refers to the loss of muscle that occurs with aging?
   a. senescence
   b. sarcopenia
   c. osteoarthritis
   d. dysphagia
2. Which of the following factors has contributed to the increased longevity of older Americans?
   a. a decrease in infant mortality
   b. rising health care costs
   c. advances in medical research
   d. increased incidence of dementia
3. With increasing age, the kidneys lose some ability to convert _____ into its active form.
   a. vitamin A
   b. vitamin B_{12}
   c. vitamin D
   d. vitamin K
4. Constipation in older adults can be a result of
   a. decreased GI motility.
   b. insufficient vitamin B_{12}.
   c. excessive fiber.
   d. too much fluid.
5. Older adults may benefit from adding zinc to their diet to
   a. help with weight loss.
   b. boost the immune system.
   c. promote bone growth.
   d. increase muscle mass.
6. Alzheimer's disease
   a. is an inevitable part of aging.
   b. is caused by a high-fat diet.
   c. leads to loss of memory.
   d. leads to thinning of the bones.
7. The risk of developing osteoporosis can be reduced by
   a. eating a diet high in fat.
   b. drinking plenty of fluids.
   c. engaging in weight-bearing exercise.
   d. taking herbal supplements.

8. The need for both _____ increases with age.
   a. water and lead
   b. calcium and vitamin D
   c. protein and lipids
   d. vitamin K and biotin
9. Which of the following best describes food insecurity?
   a. poor nutritional quality of food
   b. inadequate food distribution
   c. concerns about food safety
   d. lack of sufficient food
10. Congregate meals are
    a. meals delivered to the homes of older adults who are homebound.
    b. frozen meals that adults can purchase at the supermarket.
    c. hot meals that are served at specified sites in the community.
    d. meals served to members of churches or synagogues.

Answers

1. (b) Sarcopenia refers to a loss of muscle mass that occurs with aging. Senescence is the scientific term for the physical changes that occur with age. Osteoarthritis is an inflammation of the joints, and dysphagia is difficulty swallowing.
2. (c) Advances in medical research are a key reason for increased longevity. Infant mortality rates, though relevant to overall life expectancy, are not a direct factor in the longevity of older adults. Rising health care costs and the incidence of dementia are also irrelevant.
3. (c) Vitamin D is converted into its active form by the kidneys.
4. (a) As people age, GI motility slows, leading to problems with constipation. Vitamin B_{12} absorption decreases with age, but this does not affect GI motility. A high-fiber, high-fluid diet helps relieve constipation, it doesn't cause it.
5. (b) Adequate zinc is needed for a healthy immune system. Zinc has nothing to do with losing weight, promoting bone growth, or increasing muscle mass.

6. (c) Alzheimer's disease leads to memory loss. Although the exact≈mechanism for its development is unknown, it does not cause thinning of the bones and is not linked to a high-fat diet, nor is it inevitable.
7. (c) Osteoporosis can be slowed by engaging in regular weight-bearing exercise. A diet rich in calcium and vitamin D can also slow its progression.
8. (b) The need for both vitamin D and calcium is increased in older adults. Generally speaking, protein, fat, and water needs don't change with aging. Lead is a toxin and should never be consumed. Vitamin K and biotin are necessary for health, but are not needed in higher amounts by older adults.
9. (d) Food insecurity refers to the routine lack of sufficient food. It does not describe problems with the distribution, safety, or nutritional quality of food.
10. (c) Congregate meals are served to older adults at specific sites in a community. Although those sites may be churches, synagogues, or senior centers, participants do not need to be members. Meals served to older adults who are homebound are typically part of the Meals On Wheels program. The supermarket contains a variety of frozen meals that can be purchased by adults of all ages.

Answers to True or False?

1. **False.** Chronic disease development is not inevitable for many older people, although if you live to be very old, chances are you will develop at least one chronic condition. Healthy eating, physical activity, moderate alcohol intake, and not smoking are the best prevention for chronic conditions.
2. **True.** Heart disease remains the number-one cause of death in the United States among older adults.

3. **True.** A slowed gastrointestinal system in conjunction with low fluid and fiber intakes can lead to constipation in older adults.
4. **False.** The number of adults over the age of 65 continues to rise.
5. **True.** Vitamin D helps the body absorb calcium from foods and dietary supplements. Calcium is necessary for strong bones.
6. **True.** Vitamin A is stored in the body and too much can increase the risk for osteoporosis and fractures.
7. **False.** The use of dietary supplements is common among older people.
8. **True.** Because a person's metabolism slows naturally with age, older adults need less energy (kilocalories) than their younger counterparts.
9. **False.** Financial circumstances or reduced mobility can cause older adults to experience food insecurity, often for the first time in their lives.
10. **False.** Older adults sometimes turn to alcohol to deal with discomfort, loneliness, or boredom.

Web Resources

- For more general health information for older adults, visit www.cdc.gov/aging/aginginfo/index.htm
- For more information on herbs and interactions, visit the National Center for Complementary and Alternative Medicine, National Institutes of Health, at http://nccam.nih.gov
- For more information on Meals On Wheels, visit www.mowaa.org
- For information on legislative updates related to congregate meals and resources on diseases, elder rights, and nutrition, visit the Administration on Aging, part of the Administration for Community Living, at www.aoa.gov

- For information on good nutrition for all ages, visit the Academy of Nutrition and Dietetics (formerly the American Dietetic Association) at www.eatright.org

References

1. World Health Organization. 2014. *Definition of an Older or Elderly Person.* Available at www.who.int/healthinfo/survey/ageingdefnolder/en/. Accessed July 2014.
2. U.S. Census Bureau. 2012. *Table 105. Life Expectancy at Birth, by Sex, Age, and Race.* Available at www.census.gov/compendia/statab/2012/tables/12s0105.pdf. Accessed June 2012.
3. National Institutes of Health. National Institute on Aging. 2014. *Global Health and Aging.* Available at www.nia.nih.gov/research/publication/global-health-and-aging/living-longer. Accessed July 2014.
4. U.S. Department of Commerce, Economics and Statistics Administration. U.S. Census Bureau. 2011. *The Older Population: 2010.* Available at www.census.gov/prod/cen2010/briefs/c2010br-09.pdf. Accessed July 2014.
5. U.S. Department of Commerce, Economics and Statistics Administration. U.S. Census Bureau. 2010. *The Next Four Decades.* Available at www.census.gov/prod/2010pubs/p25-1138.pdf. Accessed July 2014.
6. Ibid.
7. Ibid.
8. Gregg, E. W., Y. J. Cheng, S. Saydah, C. Cowie, S. Garfield, L. Geiss and L. Barker. 2012. Trends in Death Rates among U.S. Adults With and Without Diabetes between 1997 and 2006. *Diabetes Care* 35(6):1252–1257. Available at http://care.diabetesjournals.org/content/35/6/1252.full. Accessed July 2014.
9. Centers for Disease Control and Prevention. 2012. *Heart Disease and Stroke Deaths Drop Significantly for People with Diabetes.* Available at www.cdc.gov/media/releases/2012/p0522_heart_disease.html. Accessed July 2014.
10. Centers for Disease Control and Prevention. 2012. *NCHS Data Brief.* Available at www.cdc.gov/nchs/data/databriefs/db99.htm. Accessed July 2014.
11. Centers for Disease Control and Prevention. 2013. *State of Aging and Health in America.* Available at www.cdc.gov/features/agingandhealth/state_of_aging_and_health_in_america_2013.pdf. Accessed July 2014.
12. Centers for Disease Control and Prevention. 2013. Adult Participation in Aerobic and Muscle-Strengthening Physical Activity—United States, 2011. *Morbidity and Mortality Weekly Report.* Available at www.cdc.gov/mmwr/preview/mmwrhtml/mm6217a2.htm?s_cid=mm6217a2_w. Accessed July 2014.
13. World Health Organization. 2002. *Keep Fit for Life.* Available at http://www.who.int/ageing/publications/keep_fit/en. Accessed July 2014.
14. Ibid.
15. Centers for Disease Control and Prevention. 2013. *State of Aging and Health in America.*
16. Mayo Clinic. 2013. *Stress Management.* Available at www.mayoclinic.org/healthy-living/stress-management/in-depth/stress/art-20046037. Accessed July 2014.
17. The Merck Manual Home Health Book. 2013. *Overview of Aging.* Available at www.merckmanuals.com/home/older_peoples_health_issues/the_aging_body/changes_in_the_body_with_aging.html. Accessed July 2014.
18. Centers for Disease Control and Prevention. 2013. *Prevalence of Obesity among Adults: United States, 2011–2012.* Available at www.cdc.gov/nchs/data/databriefs/db131.htm. Accessed July 2014.
19. Martin, C. T., J. Kayser-Jones, N. A. Stotts, C. Porter, and E. S. Froelicher. 2007. Risk for Low Weight in Community Dwelling Adults. *Clinical Nurse Specialist* 21:203–211.
20. U.S. National Library of Medicine. National Institutes of Health. 2013. *Smell—Impaired.* Available at www.nlm.nih.gov/medlineplus/ency/article/003052.htm. Accessed August 2014.
21. National Institute of Aging. National Institutes of Health. 2014. *Smell and Taste: Spice of Life.* Available at www.nia.nih.gov/health/publication/smell-and-taste. Accessed August 2014.
22. Centers for Disease Control and Prevention. 2013. *State of Aging and Health in America.*
23. University of Maryland Medical Center. 2013. *Vitamin B_{12} (Cobalamin).* Available at https://umm.edu/health/medical/altmed/supplement/vitamin-b12-cobalamin. Accessed August 2014.
24. The Merck Manual Home Health Book. 2013. *Overview of Aging.*
25. Ibid.
26. U.S. Department of Health and Human Services. 2010. *Dietary Guidelines for Americans, 2010.* 7th ed. Washington, DC: U.S. Government Printing Office.
27. Institute of Medicine, Food and Nutrition Board. 2002. *Dietary Reference Intakes for Energy, Carbohydrate, Fiber, Fat, Fatty Acids, Cholesterol, Protein, and Amino Acids.* Washington, DC: The National Academies Press.
28. Bernstein, M., and N. Munoz. 2012. Position of the Academy of Nutrition and Dietetics: Food

and Nutrition for Older Adults: Promoting Health and Wellness. *Journal of the Academy of Nutrition and Dietetics* 112:1255–1277.

29. Institute of Medicine, Food and Nutrition Board. 2002. *Dietary Reference Intakes for Energy, Carbohydrate, Fiber, Fat, Fatty Acids, Cholesterol, Protein, and Amino Acids.*

30. Institute of Medicine Food Forum. 2010. *Providing Healthy and Safe Foods as We Age: Workshop Summary.* Washington, DC: The National Academies Press.

31. Mayo Clinic. 2014. *Dehydration.* Available at www.mayoclinic.org/diseases-conditions/ dehydration/basics/risk-factors/con-20030056. Accessed August 2014.

32. American Heart Association. 2014. *Fish 101.* Available at www.heart.org/HEARTORG/ GettingHealthy/NutritionCenter/Fish-101_ UCM_305986_Article.jsp. Accessed August 2014.

33. American Heart Association. 2014. *Know Your Fats.* Available at www.heart.org/ HEARTORG/Conditions/Cholesterol/ PreventionTreatmentofHighCholesterol/ Know-Your-Fats_UCM_305628_Article.jsp. Accessed August 2014.

34. Bales, C., and C. Ritchie. 2006. The Elderly. In M. Shils, M. Shike, A. Ross, B. Caballero, and R. Cousins, eds. *Modern Nutrition in Health and Disease,* 10th ed. Philadelphia: Lippincott Williams & Wilkins.

35. Institute of Medicine, Food and Nutrition Board. 1998. *Dietary Reference Intakes: Thiamin, Riboflavin, Niacin, Vitamin B_6, Folate, Vitamin B_{12}, Pantothenic Acid, Biotin, and Choline.* Washington, DC: The National Academies Press.

36. Braden, C., and B. Brenner. 2013. *Chronic Anemia.* Available at www.emedicine. medscape.com/article/780176-overview. Accessed August 2014.

37. National Institutes of Health. Office of Dietary Supplements. 2013. *Zinc Fact Sheet for Health Professionals.* Available at www.ods.od.nih.gov/factsheets/Zinc-HealthProfessional/#en21. Accessed August 2014.

38. National Institutes of Health. Office of Dietary Supplements. 2013. *Calcium Fact Sheet for Health Professionals.* Available at www.ods.od.nih.gov/factsheets/Calcium-HealthProfessional/#en1. Accessed August 2014.

39. Institute of Medicine. Food and Nutrition Board. 2010. *Dietary Reference Intakes for Calcium, Phosphorus, Magnesium, Vitamin D, and Fluoride.* Washington, DC: National Academies Press.

40. National Institutes of Health Osteoporosis and Related Bone Diseases National Resource Center. 2012. *The Surgeon General's Report on Bone Health and Osteoporosis:*
What It Means to You. Available at www .niams.nih.gov/Health_Info/Bone/SGR/ surgeon_generals_report.asp. Accessed August 2014.

41. U.S. Department of Health and Human Services. 2010. *Dietary Guidelines for Americans, 2010.*

42. Bailey R. L., J. J. Gahche, C. V. Lentino, J. T. Dwyer, J. S. Engel, P. R. Thomas, et al. 2011. Dietary Supplement Use in the United States, 2003–2006. *Journal of Nutrition* 141:261–266.

43. Bailey R. L., J. J. Gahche, P. E. Miller, P. R. Thomas, and J. T. Dwyer. 2013. Why US Adults Use Dietary Supplements. *Journal of the American Medical Association—Internal Medicine* 173:355–361.

44. U.S. Food and Drug Administration. 2011. *Dietary Supplements: Tips for Older Dietary Supplement Users.* Available at www .fda.gov/Food/DietarySupplements/ ConsumerInformation/ucm110493.htm. Accessed May 2012.

45. Guallar, E., S. Stranges, C. Mulrow, L. J. Appel, and E. Miller. 2013. Enough Is Enough: Stop Wasting Money on Vitamin and Mineral Supplements. *Annals of Internal Medicine* 159(12):850–851. Available at www .annals.org/article.aspx?articleid=1789253. Accessed August 2014.

46. Gaziano, J. M., H. D. Sesso, W. G. Christen, V. Bubes, J. P. Smith, J. MacFadyen, J. Schvartz, et al. 2012. Multivitamins in the Prevention of Cancer in Men. The Physicians' Health Study II Randomized Controlled Trial. *Journal of the American Medical Association* 308:1871–1880.

47. Murray-Kolbe, L. E., and J. Beard. 2010. Iron. In P. M. Coates, J. M. Betz, M. R. Blackman, et al., eds. *Encyclopedia of Dietary Supplements.* 2nd ed. London and New York: Informa Healthcare, 432–438.

48. U.S. Food and Drug Administration. 2011. *Proton Pump Inhibitor Drugs (PPIs): Drug Safety Communication—Low Magnesium Levels Can Be Associated with Long-Term Use.* Available at www.fda.gov/Safety/ MedWatch/SafetyInformation/SafetyAlertsf orHumanMedicalProducts/ucm245275.htm. Accessed August 2013.

49. U.S. Department of Health and Human Services. 2010. *Dietary Guidelines for Americans, 2010.*

50. Loreck, E., R. Chimakurthi, and N. I. Steinle. 2012. Nutritional Assessment of the Geriatric Patient: A Comprehensive Approach toward Evaluating and Managing Nutrition. *Clinical Geriatrics* 20:20–26.

51. Centers for Disease Control and Prevention. 2011. *Helping People to Live Long and Productive Lives and Enjoy a Good Quality of Life: At a Glance, 2011.* Available at www
.cdc.gov/chronicdisease/resources/ publications/aag/aging.htm. Accessed August 2014.

52. Centers for Disease Control and Prevention. 2013. *State of Aging and Health in America.*

53. U.S. Department of Health and Human Services. Administration on Aging. n.d. *Aging Into the 21st Century.* Available at www .aoa.gov/AoARoot/Aging_Statistics/future_ growth/aging21/health.aspx. Accessed August 2014.

54. Centers for Disease Control and Prevention. 2009. *Prevalence and Most Common Causes of Disability among Adults—United States, 2005.* Available at www.cdc.gov/ mmwr/preview/mmwrhtml/mm5816a2.htm. Accessed August 2014.

55. Centers for Disease Control and Prevention. 2014. *Osteoarthritis.* Available at www.cdc .gov/arthritis/basics/osteoarthritis.htm. Accessed August 2014.

56. National Institute of Arthritis and Musculoskeletal and Skin Diseases. 2010. *Osteoarthritis.* Available at www.niams.nih .gov/Health_Info/Osteoarthritis/default.asp. Accessed May 2012.

57. Bijlsma, J. W., F. Berenbaum, and F. P. Lafeber. 2011. Osteoarthritis: An Update with Relevance for Clinical Practice. *The Lancet* 377:2115–2126.

58. Sawitzke, A. D., H. Shi, M. F. Finco, D. D. Dunlop, C. L. Harris, N. G. Singer, et al. 2010. Clinical Efficacy and Safety of Glucosamine, Chondroitin Sulfate, Their Combination, Celecoxib or Placebo Taken to Treat Osteoarthritis of the Knee: 2-year Results from GAIT. *Annals of the Rheumatic Diseases* 69:1459–1464.

59. American College of Rheumatology. 2012. *Rheumatoid Arthritis.* Available at www .rheumatology.org/practice/clinical/patients/ diseases_and_conditions/rheumatoid_ arthritis/. Accessed August 2014.

60. Mayo Clinic. 2013. *Nutrition and Healthy Eating.* Available at www.mayoclinic.org/ healthy-living/nutrition-and-healthy-eating/ expert-blog/diet-and-rheumatoid-arthritis/ bgp-20056187. Accessed August 2014.

61. Lahiri, M., C. Morgan, D. P. M. Symmons, and I. N. Bruce. 2012. Modifiable Risk Factors for RA: Prevention Better than Cure? *Rheumatology* 51:499–512.

62. National Institutes of Health. National Institute of Arthritis and Musculoskeletal and Skin Diseases. 2012. *Questions and Answers about Gout.* Available at www .niams.nih.gov/Health_Info/Gout/. Accessed August 2014.

63. Ibid.

64. Yanyan, Z., B. J. Pandya, and H. K. Choi. 2011. Prevalence of Gout and Hyperuricemia in the US General Population.

Arthritis & Rheumatology. Available at doi.wiley.com/10.1002/art.30520. Accessed August 2014.

65. Fletcher, J. 2012. *Gout Growing in U.S., Mostly in Men and Seniors.* Available at www.agingcare.com/News/gout-growing-in-men-and-seniors-147424.htm. Accessed May 2012.

66. Mayo Clinic. 2012. *Gout Diet: What's Allowed, What's Not.* Available at www.mayoclinic.org/healthy-living/nutrition-and-healthy-eating/in-depth/gout-diet/art-20048524. Accessed August 2014.

67. American Macular Degeneration Foundation. 2014. *Nutrition and Macular Degeneration.* Available at www.macular.org/nutrition-macular-degeneration. Accessed August 2014.

68. National Eye Institute. 2009. *Cataracts.* Available at www.nei.nih.gov/health/cataract/cataract_facts.asp. Accessed May 2012.

69. Johns Hopkins Medicine. *Cataracts FAQ.* Available at www.hopkinsmedicine.org/wilmer/conditions/cataracts_faq.html. Accessed August 2014.

70. Mayo Clinic. 2013. *Cataracts.* Available at www.mayoclinic.org/diseases-conditions/cataracts/basics/risk-factors/con-20015113. Accessed August 2014.

71. University of Maryland Medical Center. 2013. *Cataracts.* Available at www.umm.edu/health/medical/altmed/condition/cataracts#ixzz39RxPpOzJ. Accessed August 2014.

72. National Institutes of Health. National Institute on Aging. 2014. *Alzheimer's Disease Fact Sheet.* Available at www.nia.nih.gov/alzheimers/publication/alzheimers-disease-fact-sheet. Accessed July 2014.

73. U.S. Department of Health and Human Services. National Institute on Aging. 2014. *A Primer on Alzheimer's Disease and the Brain.* Available at www.nia.nih.gov/alzheimers/publication/2013-2014-alzheimers-disease-progress-report/primer-alzheimers-disease-and#characteristics. Accessed July 2014.

74. Barnes, D. E., and K. Yaffe. 2011. The Projected Effect of Risk Factor Reduction on Alzheimer's Disease Prevalence. *Lancet Neurology* 10:819–828.

75. Tan, Z. S., W. S. Harris, A. S. Beiser, R. Au, J. J. Himali, S. Debette, et al. 2012. Red Blood Cell Omega-3 Fatty Acid Levels and Markers of Accelerated Brain Aging. *Neurology* 78:658–664.

76. Gu, Y., N. Schupf, S. A. Cosentino, J. A. Luchsinger, and H. Scarmeas. 2012. Nutrient Intake and Plasma [Beta]-Amyloid. *Neurology* 78:1832–1840.

77. U.S. Department of Health and Human Services. Assistant Secretary for Planning and Evaluation. 2012. *2012 HHS Poverty Guidelines.* Available at www.aspe.hhs.gov/poverty/12poverty.shtml. Accessed August 2014.

78. U.S. Department of Commerce. Economics and Statistics Administration, U.S. Census Bureau. 2013. *Income, Poverty, and Health Insurance.* Available at www.census.gov/prod/2013pubs/p60-245.pdf. Accessed August 2014.

79. The Henry J. Kaiser Family Foundation. 2012. *Poverty by Race/Ethnicity.* Available at www.kff.org/other/state-indicator/poverty-rate-by-raceethnicity/. Accessed August 2014.

80. USDA ERS. Coleman-Jensen, A., et al. 2013. *Household Food Security in the United States in 2012, Table 2.* Available at www.ers.usda.gov/publications/err-economic-research-report/err155.aspx#.U_PmTFaA8U4.

81. Seligman, H. K., B. A. Laraia, and M. B. Kushel. 2010. Food Insecurity Is Associated with Chronic Disease among Low-Income NHANES Participants. *Journal of Nutrition* 140:304–310.

82. Sinnett, S. S., R. Bengle, A. Brown, A. P. Glass, M. A. Johnson, and J. S. Lee. 2010. The Validity of Nutrition Screening Initiative DETERMINE Checklist Responses in Older Georgians. *Journal of Nutrition for the Elderly* 29:393–409.

83. Administration on Aging. 2012. *Reauthorization of the Older Americans Act.* Available at http://aoa.gov/AoARoot/AoA_Programs/OAA/Reauthorization/docs/OAAreauth_summaries_stakehldrs.pdf. Accessed May 2012.

84. Meals On Wheels Association of America. 2012. Make the Case for Meals on Wheels. Available at www.mowaa.org. Accessed May 2012.

85. National Alliance on Mental Illness. 2009. *Depression in Older Persons Fact Sheet.* Available at www.nami.org/Template.cfm?Section=By_Illness&template=/ContentManagement/ContentDisplay.cfm&ContentID=7515. Accessed August 2014.

86. Ibid.

87. National Institutes of Health. National Institute on Alcohol Abuse and Alcoholism. 2014. *Harmful Interactions.* Available at www.pubs.niaaa.nih.gov/publications/Medicine/medicine.htm. Accessed August 2014.

88. National Institute on Aging. 2012. *Alcohol Use In Older People.* Available at www.nia.nih.gov/health/publication/alcohol-use-older-people. Accessed May 2012; U.S. Department of Health and Human Services. 2011. *Medication Review May Benefit Home Health Care Patients.* Available at http://healthfinder.gov/news/newsstory.aspx?docID=659205. Accessed May 2012.

89. National Institute on Aging. 2012. *Alcohol Use In Older People.*

90. National Institutes of Health. National Institute on Alcohol Abuse and Alcoholism. *Older Adults.* Available at www.niaaa.nih.gov/alcohol-health/special-populations-co-occurring-disorders/older-adults. Accessed August 2014.

91. U.S. National Library of Medicine. 2014. *High Blood Pressure.* Available at www.nlm.nih.gov/medlineplus/highbloodpressure.html. Accessed August 2014.

92. National Institute of Health. 2008. *Reference Card from the Report of the Joint National Committee on Prevention, Detection, Evauation, and Treatment of High Blood Pressure (JNC).* Available at www.nhlbi.nih.gov/files/docs/resources/heart/phycard.pdf. Accessed August 2014.

93. Zhang, W., and N. Li. 2011. Prevalence, Risk Factors, and Management of Prehypertension. *International Journal of Hypertension.* Available at www.ncbi.nlm.nih.gov/pmc/articles/PMC3205676/. Accessed August 2014.

94. Centers for Disease Control and Prevention. 2013. Self-Reported Hypertension and Use of Antihypertensive Medication Among Adults — United States, 2005–2009. *Morbidity and Mortality Weekly.* Available at www.cdc.gov/mmwr/preview/mmwrhtml/mm6213a2.htm?s_cid=mm6213a2_w. Accessed August 2014.

95. U.S. National Library of Medicine. National Institutes of Health. 2012. *Aging Changes in the Heart and Blood Vessels.* Available at www.nlm.nih.gov/medlineplus/ency/article/004006.htm. Accessed August 2014.

96. U.S. Department of Health and Human Services. National Institute on Aging. 2014. *High Blood Pressure.* Available at www.nia.nih.gov/health/publication/high-blood-pressure#risks. Accessed August 2014.

97. American Heart Association. 2012. *About High Blood Pressure.* Available at www.americanheart.org. Accessed August 2014.

98. National Institutes of Health. National Heart, Lung and Blood Institute. 2014. *What Is the DASH Eating Plan?* Available at www.nhlbi.nih.gov/health/health-topics/topics/dash/. Accessed August 2014.

99. Harsha, D. W., W. P. Lin, E. Obarzanek, N. M. Karanja, T. J. Moore, and B. Caballero. 1999. Dietary Approaches to Stop Hypertension: A Summary of Study

Results. *Journal of the American Dietetic Association* 99:S35–S39.

100. Sacks, F. M., L. P. Svetkey, W. M. Vollmer, L. J. Appel, D. Harsha, E. Obarzanek, P. R. Conlin, et al. DASH-Sodium Collaborative Research Group. 2001. Effects on Blood Pressure of Reduced Dietary Sodium and the Dietary Approaches to Stop Hypertension (DASH) Diet. *New England Journal of Medicine* 344(1):3–10.

101. Appel, L. J., F. M. Sacks, V. J. Carey, E. Obarzanek, J. F. Swain, E. R. Miller, P. R. Conlin, et al. 2005. Effects of Protein, Monounsaturated Fat, and Carbohydrate Intake on Blood Pressure and Serum Lipids: Results of the OMNIHeart Randomized Trial. *Journal of the American Medical Association* 294:2455–2464.

102. American Heart Association. 2012. *Understand Your Risk for High Blood Pressure.* Available at www.heart.org/HEARTORG/Conditions/HighBloodPressure/UnderstandYourRiskforHighBloodPressure/Understand-Your-Risk-for-High-Blood-Pressure_UCM_002052_Article.jsp. Accessed August 2014.

103. American Heart Association. 2014. *Weight Management and Blood Pressure.* Available at www.heart.org/HEARTORG/Conditions/HighBloodPressure/PreventionTreatmentofHighBloodPressure/Weight-Management-and-Blood-Pressure_UCM_301884_Article.jsp. Accessed August 2014.

104. Mayo Clinic. 2014. *High Blood Pressure (Hypertension).* Available at www.mayoclinic.org/diseases-conditions/high-blood-pressure/in-depth/high-blood-pressure/art-20046974. Accessed August 2014.

20 Food Safety, Technology, and Availability

Learning Outcomes

After reading this chapter, you will be able to:

20.1 Distinguish between foodborne infection and foodborne intoxication and provide an example of each.

20.2 Summarize strategies to prevent foodborne illness in the home, and when traveling.

20.3 Describe how the food supply is protected in the United States.

20.4 Compare the risks and benefits of food additives, and the use of hormones, antibiotics, and pesticides in both traditionally and organically grown food.

20.5 Describe what constitutes a sustainable food system.

20.6 Compare the benefits and risks of the use of biotechnology in our current food system.

True or False?

1. Foods that contain pathogens that cause foodborne illness always smell bad. **T/F**

2. Hand washing is more effective in preventing food contamination than using a hand sanitizer. **T/F**

3. A kitchen sponge is a prime environment for the breeding and spread of bacteria. **T/F**

4. Freezing foods kills the harmful bacteria. **T/F**

5. Leftovers that have been stored in the fridge for a week are safe to eat. **T/F**

6. As long as the expiration date hasn't passed, packaged food is always safe to eat. **T/F**

7. Food additives must demonstrate a "zero risk" of cancer to human beings in order to meet FDA approval. **T/F**

8. Pesticides can be washed off of produce with plain water. **T/F**

9. Foods grown organically that carry the USDA organic seal are free of pesticides. **T/F**

10. Genetically engineered foods are plentiful in the United States. **T/F**

See page 791 for the answers.

Have you ever thought about where food comes from before it appears on the supermarket shelf or how safe that food is for you? No matter what you are eating, it likely started out on a farm. Getting food safely from farms to your plate requires several steps and a huge amount of human and natural resources.

Thanks to monitoring and regulation by the FDA (Food and Drug Administration), USDA, and other government agencies, consumers in the United States enjoy a relatively safe food supply. However, despite well-intended efforts, foodborne illness continues to be a threat. In this chapter we discuss common foodborne illnesses, their causes, and how consumers can prevent them, how contaminants enter our food system, and what safety standards are in place to prevent that from happening.

As the world's population continues to increase, the pressure to produce more with limited natural resources has led to technological changes in the food system that not all consumers embrace. For example, genetic engineering can produce more and better foods, but some consumers have concerns about eating genetically modified food. Methods that reduce energy use and waste may enhance the sustainability of food systems, an issue that becomes more important as the world's population grows.

How Common Are Foodborne Illnesses and What Causes Them?

LO 20.1 Distinguish between foodborne infection and foodborne intoxication and provide an example of each.

Foodborne illness continues to be a major preventable public health threat even in industrialized countries. In the United States, foodborne illness causes 1 in 6 Americans (or 48 million people) to become ill every year, and about 128,000 are hospitalized.[1] These illnesses most commonly result in gastrointestinal symptoms such as cramps, diarrhea, and vomiting, but in extreme circumstances can result in death. Approximately 3,000 Americans die of foodborne disease every year.[2]

Pathogens and Toxins Cause Foodborne Illness

Foodborne illness is any infection or intoxication caused by consuming contaminated food. Foodborne illnesses can result in a broad array of symptoms such as headaches, nausea and vomiting, abdominal cramps, and diarrhea. In rare cases among high-risk individuals, foodborne illness may result in death. *Foodborne infection* is caused by consuming foods or beverages that are contaminated with disease-causing organisms, known as **pathogens.** Once ingested, the pathogens may grow in the intestinal tract of humans and cause illness. Pathogens that can make humans ill include bacteria, viruses, molds, parasites, and prions (**Table 20.1**).

Foodborne intoxication is caused by eating foods contaminated with a **toxin.** Some toxins are produced by harmful bacteria, but others can occur naturally in plants or seafood, or be the result of a chemical contamination. Some bacteria, including *Clostridium botulinum, Staphylococcus aureus,* and *Bacillus cereus,* produce toxins that cause intoxication. Viruses and parasites do not cause foodborne intoxication. Foodborne intoxication generally produces gastrointestinal symptoms such as nausea and vomiting more quickly than foodborne infections, and in some cases in as little as 30 minutes after consuming the contaminated food.[3]

foodborne illness Sickness caused by consuming pathogen- or toxin-containing food or beverages. Also known as foodborne disease or food poisoning.

pathogens Collective term for disease-causing organisms. Pathogens include microorganisms (viruses, bacteria) and parasites, and are the most common source of foodborne illness.

toxins Poisons that can be produced by living organisms.

| TABLE 20.1 | Pathogens That Cause Foodborne Illness |

Microbe	Where You Find It	How You Can Get It	What You May Experience
Viruses			
Noroviruses	In the stool or vomit of infected individuals	Fecal-to-oral transmission; eating ready-to-eat foods or drinking liquids contaminated by an infected person; eating contaminated shellfish; touching contaminated objects and then putting hands in mouth	Watery diarrhea, nausea, vomiting, flulike symptoms; possible fever. Symptoms can appear 24–48 hours after onset, last 24–60 hours, and are typically not serious.
Hepatitis A (HAV)	In the stool of infected individuals	Fecal-to-oral transmission; eating raw produce irrigated with contaminated water; eating raw or undercooked foods that have not been properly reheated; drinking contaminated water	Diarrhea, dark urine, jaundice, flulike symptoms that can appear 30 days after incubation, and can last 2 weeks to 3 months.
Bacteria			
Campylobacter jejuni	Intestinal tracts of animals and birds, unpasteurized milk, untreated water, and sewage	Drinking contaminated water or raw milk; eating raw or undercooked meat, poultry, or shellfish	Fever, headache, and muscle pain followed by diarrhea (sometimes bloody), abdominal pain, and nausea; appears 2 to 5 days after eating; may last 7 to 10 days; Guillain-Barré syndrome may occur
Clostridium botulinum	Widely distributed in nature in soil, water, on plants, and in the intestinal tracts of animals and fish. Grows only in environments with little or no oxygen.	Eating improperly canned foods, garlic in oil, vacuum-packaged and tightly wrapped food	Bacteria produce a toxin that causes illness by affecting the nervous system. Symptoms usually appear after 18 to 36 hours. May experience double vision, droopy eyelids, trouble speaking and swallowing, and difficulty breathing. Fatal in 3 to 10 days if not treated.
Clostridium perfringens	Soil, dust, sewage, and intestinal tracts of animals and humans. Grows only in little or no oxygen.	Called "the cafeteria germ" because many outbreaks result from eating food left for long periods in steam tables or at room temperature. Bacteria are destroyed by cooking, but some spores may survive.	Bacteria produce toxin that causes illness. Diarrhea and gas pains may appear 8 to 24 hours after eating; usually last about 1 day, but less severe symptoms may persist for 1 to 2 weeks.
Escherichia coli O157:H7	Intestinal tracts of some mammals, unpasteurized milk, unchlorinated water. One of several strains of *E. coli* that can cause human illness.	Drinking contaminated water, unpasteurized apple juice or cider, or unpasteurized milk; eating raw or rare ground beef or uncooked fruits and vegetables	Diarrhea or bloody diarrhea, abdominal cramps, nausea, and weakness. Can begin 2 to 5 days after food is eaten, lasting about 8 days. Small children and elderly adults may develop hemolytic uremic syndrome (HUS) that causes acute kidney failure. A similar illness, thrombotic thrombocytopenic purpura (TTP), may occur in adults.
Enterotoxigenic *Escherichia coli* (major cause of traveler's diarrhea)	Intestinal tracts of some mammals and unpasteurized dairy products. More common in developing countries.	Fecal-to-oral transmission; consuming stool-contaminated water and foods from unsanitary water supplies and food establishments	Diarrhea, nausea, vomiting, stomach cramping, bloating, fever, and weakness
Listeria monocytogenes	Intestinal tracts of humans and animals, milk, soil, leafy vegetables; can grow slowly at refrigerator temperatures	Eating ready-to-eat foods such as hot dogs, luncheon meats, cold cuts, fermented or dry sausage, other deli-style meat and poultry, or soft cheeses; drinking unpasteurized milk	Fever, chills, headache, backache, sometimes upset stomach, abdominal pain, and diarrhea; may take up to 3 weeks to become ill; may later develop more serious illness in high-risk individuals

(continued)

TABLE 20.1 Pathogens That Cause Foodborne Illness *continued*

Microbe	Where You Find It	How You Can Get It	What You May Experience
Salmonella (over 2,300 types)	Intestinal tracts and feces of animals; *Salmonella enteritidis* in eggs	Eating raw or undercooked eggs, poultry, and meat, unpasteurized milk and dairy products, and seafood; can also be spread by infected food handlers	Stomach pain, diarrhea, nausea, chills, fever, and headache usually appear 8 to 72 hours after eating. May last 1 to 2 days.
Shigella (over 30 types)	Human intestinal tract; rarely found in other animals	Fecal-to-oral transmission by consuming contaminated food and water. Most outbreaks result from eating food, especially salads, prepared and handled by workers with poor personal hygiene.	Disease referred to as "shigellosis" or bacillary dysentery. Diarrhea containing blood and mucus, fever, abdominal cramps, chills, and vomiting begin 12 to 50 hours from ingestion of bacteria; can last a few days to 2 weeks.
Staphylococcus aureus	On humans (skin, infected cuts, pimples, noses, and throats)	Consuming foods that were contaminated by being improperly handled. Bacteria multiply rapidly at room temperature.	Bacteria produce a toxin that causes illness. Severe nausea, abdominal cramps, vomiting, and diarrhea occur 1 to 6 hours after eating; recovery within 2 to 3 days.
Parasites			
Cryptosporidium parvum	In the intestines of humans and animals	Fecal-to-oral transmission; drinking contaminated water; eating contaminated produce	Stomach pains, diarrhea, cramps, fever, and vomiting
Cyclospora cayetanensis	Human stool	Fecal-to-oral transmission; drinking contaminated water; eating contaminated produce	Diarrhea, flatulence, stomach cramps, vomiting, fatigue
Giardia lamblia	In the intestines of humans and animals	Fecal-to-oral transmission; drinking contaminated water; eating contaminated produce	Diarrhea, stomach pains, flatulence
Trichinella spiralis	In undercooked or raw meats containing *Trichinella* worms	Raw or undercooked contaminated meat, usually pork or game meats	Nausea, vomiting, diarrhea, fever, aching joints and muscles

Data from Centers for Disease Control and Prevention (CDC). 2004. *Diagnosis and Management of Foodborne Illness: A Primer for Physicians*; CDC. 2012. *Norovirus*; CDC. 2014. *Hepatitis A Information for the Public*; CDC. 2006. *Traveler's Diarrhea*; Diagnosis and Management of Foodborne Illnesses: A Primer for Physicians. MMWR Recommendations and Reports 50 (January 2001):1–69; CDC. 2014. *Parasites: Food*. All available at www.cdc.gov. Food Safety and Inspection Service. 2013. *Foodborne Illness: What Consumers Need to Know*; Food Safety and Inspection Service. 2013. *Parasites and Foodborne Illness*. Both available at www.fsis.usda.gov.

Pathogens may be present in the raw ingredients of the food or may contaminate the food at any stage of the food system. For example, fruit flies have been shown to transfer *Escherichia coli* O157:H7 to apples under laboratory conditions.[4] *Escherichia coli* as well as several other disease-causing pathogens are found in the intestinal tract and fecal matter of humans or animals. Food may become contaminated with these pathogens if it comes into contact with fecal matter, and individuals can become infected by putting food or hands that have been in contact with fecal matter into their mouths. This is a common route of transmission of foodborne illness and is called the **fecal-to-oral transmission** route.

Even when a contaminated food is eaten, it may not result in foodborne illness. Many pathogens are killed in the mouth by antimicrobial enzymes and in the stomach by hydrochloric acid. In addition, the potential for a pathogen to cause illness depends on the amount that is consumed, the potency, and the nutritional and immune status of the person who consumes it. Pathogens that survive the natural defense systems of the body undergo an *incubation period* before the symptoms of illness begin. The delay in the time between when the pathogen is consumed and when it causes illness depends on the type and number of pathogens swallowed and can range from a few hours to few weeks (refer to Table 20.1 for a description of incubation periods). Bacterial infections can be diagnosed by specific laboratory tests

fecal-to-oral transmission The spread of pathogens by putting something in the mouth, such as hands or food, that has been in contact with infected stool.

for the causative organism through the culturing of stool samples in the laboratory. Parasites can be identified by examining stool samples under a microscope. Viruses are more difficult to identify under a microscope due to their small size, and they are also difficult to culture. To identify viruses, scientists test stool samples for genetic markers that indicate whether or not a particular virus is present.[5]

In the United States the majority of foodborne illness is caused by infection or intoxication from five pathogens: noroviruses, *Salmonella* (bacterium), *Clostridium perfringens* (bacterium), *Campylobacter* (bacterium), and *Staphylococcus aureus* (bacterium that produces a toxin).[6] Together these pathogens accounted for 91 percent of all domestically acquired cases of foodborne illness in the United States in 2011. **Norovirus** is currently responsible for more than half of all foodborne illness in the United States, making it the single most common cause of foodborne disease in this country.[7] The differences between various foodborne disease–causing pathogens are discussed next.

Viruses

The term **virus** denotes a microscopic infectious agent that contains genetic information (DNA or RNA) for its own replication. Viruses must have a living **host,** such as a plant or an animal, to survive. When an individual eats a plant or animal that is contaminated with a virus, the pathogen can invade the cells of the stomach and intestinal walls. The virus can then cause the cells' genetic material to start producing more viruses, ultimately leading to illness.[8]

Bacteria

Bacteria are singled-celled organisms that lack a nucleus. Thousands of types of bacteria are naturally present in our environment. If you were to swab your kitchen sink right now and look at the results under a microscope, you would find that there are about 16 million bacteria living on each square centimeter (less than half an inch) of the sink. Whereas viruses need a host to survive, bacteria can flourish on both living and nonliving surfaces, and can multiply on sponges, dishtowels, cutting boards and countertops, and in sinks. Given the right conditions, a single bacterium can produce colonies of billions of bacteria over the course of just one day.

Not all bacteria cause disease in humans, and some that live in the human gut are even beneficial for health.[9] The human gut harbors in excess of 1,000 different types of bacteria;[10] some of these produce small amounts of vitamins such as vitamin K and biotin, others aid in digestion of some nutrients, and still others help maintain the integrity of the lining of the gut. Harmful bacteria that enter the gut compete for resources with the beneficial bacteria and, depending on the amount of bacteria, the type of bacteria, and the condition of the human host, may result in illness.

Contamination of food by some types of bacteria causes it to spoil, while contamination of food by other types of bacteria may cause foodborne illness. Bacteria that cause food to spoil result in the deterioration of the quality of food but may or may not introduce pathogens that cause foodborne illness. Though most individuals do not become seriously ill after eating spoiled foods, these items can cause nausea and shouldn't be eaten. In contrast to spoiled foods, contaminated foods that contain bacterial pathogens may look and smell perfectly fine. It is not safe to eat food just because it "looks fine" or "smells OK."

Bacteria may be present on products when they're purchased at the grocery store, even when recommended safety procedures are followed. Raw meat, poultry, seafood, and eggs can all pick up and harbor bacteria during processing. Produce is not sterile either: Lettuce, tomatoes, sprouts, and melons—which are eaten raw—may carry pathogenic bacteria. Although they can grow in just about any food, bacteria

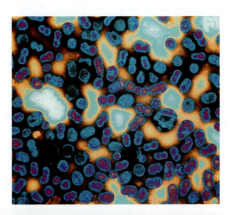

Viruses, such as the hepatitis A virus, need a host to survive and multiply.

norovirus The most common type of virus that causes foodborne illness. Can cause gastroenteritis, or the "stomach flu."

virus A microscopic organism that carries genetic information for its own replication; a virus can infect a host and cause illness.

host A living plant or animal (including a human) that a virus infects for the sake of reproducing.

bacteria Single-celled microorganisms without an organized nucleus. Some are benign or beneficial to humans, while others can cause disease.

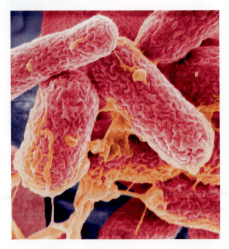

E. coli O157:H7 is the strain that causes most foodborne illness. Most other forms of *E. coli* are harmless.

grow particularly well on foods high in protein, such as meat, dairy foods, and beans. Even ready-to-eat foods that have been cooked may become cross-contaminated with bacteria from raw products or poor personal hygiene of food handlers.

The foodborne bacterium that causes the largest number of illnesses in the United States is *Salmonella*. *Salmonella* is found in the intestinal tract and feces of animals and in eggs. Most people infected with *Salmonella* experience diarrhea, fever, and abdominal cramps within 12 to 72 hours after eating the infected food. The illness usually lasts four to seven days. People in generally good health before becoming infected usually recover without treatment, but the infection becomes more severe in others. *Salmonella* infection is the most common cause of foodborne illness that results in hospitalization and death in the United States.[11]

One type of foodborne bacterium that is not as common, but is of particular concern, is *Escherichia coli* O157:H7. Although most strains of *E. coli* are benign, *E. coli* O157:H7 infection results in severe, even life-threatening illness for some individuals. *E. coli* O157:H7 infections can cause **hemolytic uremic syndrome** (*hemo* = blood, *lyti* = destroyed, *uremic* = too much urea in blood), which results in the destruction of red blood cells and damage to and eventual failure of the kidneys.[12] Contaminated ground beef has been the culprit behind most cases of foodborne illness caused by *E. coli* O157:H7. Because bacteria live in the gastrointestinal tracts of healthy cattle, they can easily come into contact with the meat of the animal during the slaughtering process and then get mixed in when the beef is being ground. *E. coli* is destroyed by heat, and most outbreaks occur when people eat undercooked meat, unpasteurized milk, or raw produce contaminated with the bacterium.

Molds

Molds are multicellular fungi that form a filamentous growth and thrive on damp surfaces. Spores give mold the color you see, and when airborne they spread very easily. Some molds cause allergic reactions and respiratory problems. A number of molds grow on foods such as breads, cheeses, and fruits, and not all of them are detrimental; some are used to make certain cheeses like Roquefort, blue, Gorgonzola, and Brie. Molds flourish in foods such as breads made without preservatives, because they prefer warmer temperatures and thrive at room temperature. Molds also grow on fruits and vegetables and in the refrigerator on jams, jellies, and even cured, salty meats, given enough time.

Some molds in the right conditions produce mycotoxins that can lead to food intoxication if ingested. One example of this is aflatoxin, a cancer-causing poison, which is sometimes found on moldy peanuts. To avoid mold growth in peanuts and other legumes, store them in a dry environment; avoid eating any legumes that have an off color. Many countries monitor foods for aflatoxin due to its potent disease-causing effects. Because of their visibility, molds are easy to identify and food that is moldy should be discarded. Cooking and freezing stop mold growth but do not kill the toxins present.[13]

Parasites

Parasites are small living organisms, occasionally in the egg or larval phase, that take their nourishment from hosts. They can be found in food and water and are often transmitted through the fecal-to-oral route.[14] The most common parasitic illness outbreaks in the United States have been caused by just a few types: *Cryptosporidium parvum*, *Cyclospora cayetanensis*, *Giardia lamblia*, and *Trichinella spiralis*. However, foodborne illness caused by parasites is much less common in the United States than is illness caused by other types of pathogens.[15]

Both *Cryptosporidium parvum* and *Cyclospora cayetanensis* can be found in contaminated water or food sources. *Giardia lamblia* is one of the most common

hemolytic uremic syndrome A rare condition that can be caused by *E. coli* O157:H7 and results in the destruction of red blood cells and kidney failure. Very young children and the elderly are at a higher risk of developing this syndrome.

molds Microscopic fungi that live on plant and animal matter. Some can produce mycotoxins, which are harmful.

parasites Organisms that live on or in another organism. Parasites obtain their nourishment from their hosts.

sources of waterborne illness. Hikers who drink unfiltered water from streams or lakes often become infected with the *Giardia* parasite. *Trichinella spiralis* (see photo) is an intestinal worm whose larvae (hatched eggs) can travel from the digestive tract to the muscles of the body. See Table 20.1 for a summary of these parasites and the foodborne illnesses they cause.

The parasitic roundworm *Trichinella spiralis.*

Prions

A **prion** is an infectious agent composed of an incorrectly shaped protein. Prions are responsible for diseases known as spongiform encephalopathies, such as bovine spongiform encephalopathy (BSE, or mad cow disease) in cattle and Creutzfeldt-Jakob disease (CJD) in humans. All known prion diseases affect the structure of brain and neural tissue and are untreatable. Consuming feed that contains prion-containing tissues of infected animals can infect cattle and other ruminant animals. Humans can be infected by consuming the meat or brain tissue of infected livestock.

Great Britain experienced an outbreak of BSE in the 1990s that resulted in cross-contamination of prion disease to humans. Since that time, the United States has taken specific steps to protect its citizens against beef contaminated with BSE. First and foremost, ruminant animals such as cattle and sheep, meat and meat products from ruminant animals, and animal feed that contains animal protein derived from countries that are at risk for BSE can no longer be imported into the United States. Also, feed for ruminant animals including cattle that is sold in the United States is banned from containing any mammalian protein. This type of feed has been identified as a major route of BSE transmission. Sick or lame cattle and specific tissues of cattle, such as the small intestines and spinal cord tissue, which have the greatest risk of containing the BSE agent, are banned from the human food supply. And lastly, techniques previously used when slaughtering cattle and separating the meat, which likely increased the potential for the animal's meat to become contaminated, have been prohibited.[16]

BSE is not irradicated, but the incidence of infection is sporadic and rare. Though approximately 150 people died of CJD after becoming infected from eating contaminated livestock in Great Britain in the 1990s, no human has ever been infected with CJD by eating infected meat in the United States. Since 2003 there have been only four cases of BSE reported in the U.S. cattle supply, including the most recent report of a dairy cow in California being infected with BSE in 2012.[17] In a press briefing, the USDA's chief veterinary officer said the cow's meat did not enter the food supply and the carcass was destroyed, so the risk to human health was minimal.[18] The World Organization for Animal Health (OIE) recently upgraded the United States' risk classification for BSE from controlled risk to negligible risk.[19]

Some Illnesses Are Caused by Natural Toxins

Many toxins that occur in plants and animals function as natural pesticides and assist in fending off predators. In many cases, these natural toxins are present in amounts too small to harm humans, but there are instances in which the toxins found in plant and animal foods can make a person seriously ill.

Marine Toxins

In addition to the pathogenic microbes that can be found in raw or undercooked seafood, naturally occurring **marine toxins** can cause illness if fish or other seafood is not cooked thoroughly. Moreover, cooking does not destroy some of these toxins.

Spoiled finfish, such as tuna and mackerel, can cause **scombrotoxic fish poisoning,** in which the spoilage bacteria break down proteins in the fish and

prion Short for proteinaceous infectious particle. Self-reproducing protein particles that cause degenerative brain diseases.

marine toxins Chemicals that occur naturally and contaminate some fish.

scombrotoxic fish poisoning A condition caused by consuming spoiled fish that contain large amounts of histamines. Also referred to as histamine fish poisoning.

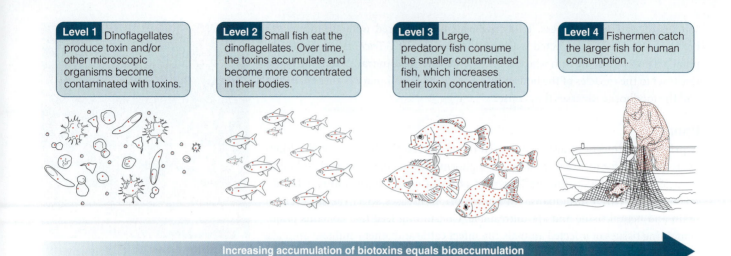

Level 1 Dinoflagellates produce toxin and/or other microscopic organisms become contaminated with toxins.

Level 2 Small fish eat the dinoflagellates. Over time, the toxins accumulate and become more concentrated in their bodies.

Level 3 Large, predatory fish consume the smaller contaminated fish, which increases their toxin concentration.

Level 4 Fishermen catch the larger fish for human consumption.

Increasing accumulation of biotoxins equals bioaccumulation

▲ **Figure 20.1 Bioaccumulation of Toxins**

generate histamine, which in turn can accumulate to harmful levels. Consuming fish that contain large amounts of histamine can cause symptoms such as diarrhea, flushing, sweating, and vomiting within 2 minutes to 2 hours.[20]

Large, predatory reef fish, such as barracuda and grouper, can sometimes be infected with ciguatoxins, which when eaten can cause **ciguatera poisoning.** In this case, toxins travel through the food chain and **bioaccumulate** in larger species (see **Figure 20.1**). Ciguatoxins originate in microscopic sea organisms called dinoflagellates, which are eaten by small tropical fish, which in turn are eaten by larger fish. When people consume the larger fish, the consumption of the accumulated concentrations of toxin can result in illness.[21] In addition to experiencing various gastrointestinal discomforts, individuals infected with ciguatera may have temperature sensation reversal in their mouth when they eat.[22] For example, hot liquids and hot foods feel cold, and vice versa.

Marine **neurotoxins** (*neuro* = nerve, *toxin* = toxic) can contaminate certain shellfish, such as mussels, clams, scallops, oysters, crabs, and lobsters, that typically live in the coastal waters of New England and the Pacific states. Neurotoxins are also produced by a particular reddish-brown-colored dinoflagellate. These reddish-brown dinoflagellates can become so abundant that the ocean appears to have red streaks, also known as red tides. Eating shellfish contaminated with neurotoxins can lead to **paralytic shellfish poisoning.** Symptoms include mild numbness or tingling in the face, arms, and legs, as well as headaches and dizziness. In severe cases muscle paralysis, the inability to breathe, and death could result.[23]

Toxins in Other Foods

Many plant foods naturally contain toxins in small amounts, and don't generally present problems when eaten in reasonable portions; however, consuming them in very large amounts could be harmful. For example, potatoes that have been exposed to light can develop a green tinge on the surface, which indicates that they contain increased amounts of **solanine,** a toxin that can cause fever, diarrhea, paralysis, and shock. Peeling potatoes and removing the green layer ensures that the potato can be safely eaten. Eating 2 to 5 milligrams of solanine per kilogram of body weight results in symptoms and eating 3 to 6 milligrams of solanine per kilogram of body weight may result in death.[24] The amount of solanine in potatoes is very small, on the order of about 0.2 milligrams per gram of potato. Eating approximately 1 pound of green potatoes would likely make a 100-pound person ill. Although some natural foods may contain toxic substances, the risk of actual harm is small.

ciguatera poisoning A condition caused by marine toxins that are produced by dinoflagellates and have bioaccumulated in fish that the affected person consumes.

bioaccumulate To build up the levels of a substance or chemical in an organism over time, so that the concentration of the chemical is higher than would be found naturally in the environment.

neurotoxins Toxins that affect the nerves and can cause symptoms including mild numbness or tingling in the face, arms, and legs, as well as headaches and dizziness. Severe cases of neurotoxicity could result in death.

paralytic shellfish poisoning A condition caused by a reddish-brown-colored dinoflagellate that contains neurotoxins.

solanine Toxin found in potato surfaces exposed to light that can cause fever, diarrhea, and shock if consumed in large amounts.

However, other foods contain toxins that are harmful even in trace amounts, and so should be avoided altogether. Certain wild mushrooms, for example, are poisonous; they contain toxins that can cause nausea, vomiting, liver damage, and death.

Chemical Agents Sometimes Cause Foodborne Illness

Consumers are becoming increasingly concerned about environmental damage caused by industrial and household chemicals. Traces of these substances can travel through the food chain and be ingested by people, posing numerous risks to health. Awareness of the potential environmental and health risks caused by these chemicals has led to a search for safer alternatives.

Polychlorinated Biphenyls (PCBs)

Polychlorinated biphenyls (PCBs) are chemicals that occur in the food supply due to industrial pollution. These chemicals were used as coolants and insulating fluids for transformers and capacitors, as flame retardants, and in the manufacture of plasticizers, waxes, and paper. Production of PCBs was banned in 1979 due to their high toxicity and inability to be broken down in the environment.[25]

Exposure to PCBs can cause cancer and have other adverse effects in animals, and may be carcinogenic in humans. PCB exposure in adults can cause skin conditions such as acne and rashes as well as liver damage. It is of particular concern for pregnant and lactating women because prenatal exposure and consumption of contaminated breast milk can damage a child's nervous system and cause learning defects. Also, because young children are smaller, exposure to PCBs has a proportionately greater effect on them than would the same level of exposure in adults.[26]

Although PCBs are no longer manufactured in the United States, they do not degrade and can therefore still make their way into the environment through releases from hazardous waste sites, the burning of commercial or municipal waste, and the improper disposal of consumer products, such as old television sets and electrical fixtures and devices.[27] PCBs in the air eventually return to our land and water by runoff in snow and rain and may bioaccumulate in larger predatory fish that live in polluted waters (see Figure 20.1).[28]

The EPA began regulating PCBs in drinking water in 1992, and the agency is working to lower the amount of PCBs in the environment.[29] Although the FDA routinely monitors PCB levels in the food supply, the toxin can be found in nonregulated food sources, such as locally caught fish. PCB contamination is the major chemical risk associated with eating fish. Consumers should therefore research and adhere to local fish consumption advisories. See the Table Tips for the EPA website that lists current advisories, as well as tips to minimize exposure to toxins and chemical agents in fish and seafood.

Methylmercury

Mercury occurs naturally, but is also produced as an industrial by-product or pollutant. An airborne form of mercury can accumulate on the surface of streams and oceans and be transformed by the bacteria in the water into the toxic form of methylmercury. Methylmercury toxicity is associated with nervous system damage in adults and impaired neurological development in infants and children.[30] Methylmercury may bioaccumulate in fish, seafood, and other wildlife and cause toxicity to humans if consumed in sufficient quantities. Larger fish, including shark, swordfish, king mackerel, and tilefish, contain high levels of mercury, so the FDA and EPA recommend that women who are or may become pregnant, women who are nursing, and young children should avoid consuming these fish.[31]

TABLE TIPS

Avoid Toxins and Chemical Agents in Fish and Seafood

Keep fish, especially finfish, such as fresh tuna, mackerel, grouper, and mahi mahi, chilled in the refrigerator to prevent spoilage and the formation of histamine toxins.

Never consume finfish or shellfish that is sold as bait, as these do not meet food safety regulations.

Observe all fish consumption advisories. To learn if an advisory is in place for the fish in your area, search for "Fish Consumption Advisories" at www.epa.gov.

If you fish recreationally, always check with the local or state health department for specific advice based on the local waters to avoid eating PCB-containing fish.

Eat a variety of types of fish to minimize the exposure to a particular toxin.

Adapted from Centers for Disease Control and Prevention. 2005. *Marine Toxins.* Available at www.cdc.gov/ncidod/dbmd/diseaseinfo/marinetoxins_g.htm; Agency for Toxic Substances and Disease Registry. Updated 2014. *ToxFAQ for Polychlorinated Biphenyls (PCBs).* Available at www.atsdr.cdc.gov/toxfaqs/tf.asp?id=140&tid=26; Environmental Protection Agency. Updated 2011. Persistent Bioaccumulative and Toxic (PBT) Chemical Program. n.d. *PBTs and You.* Available at www.epa.gov/oppt/pbt/pubs/pbtsandyou.htm.

polychlorinated biphenyls (PCBs) Synthetic chemicals that have been shown to cause cancer and other adverse effects on the immune, reproductive, nervous, and endocrine systems in animals. PCBs may cause cancer in humans.

Some People Are at Higher Risk for Foodborne Illness

Some individuals are at greater risk of contracting a foodborne disease than others. Older adults, young children, pregnant women, and those with a compromised immune system are more susceptible to contracting foodborne illness and suffering complications than the rest of the population. Shifting population demographics mean more and more Americans are at risk for foodborne illness. For example, about 14 percent of the U.S. population is currently 65 years of age or older. The number of Americans 65 years of age and older is projected to reach 21 percent by the year 2040.[32] In addition to age, any condition that weakens a person's immune system, such as HIV, AIDS, cancer, or diabetes, can increase his or her risk of contracting foodborne illness.[33]

The hormonal shifts that occur during pregnancy can affect a pregnant woman's immune system, making her more vulnerable to a potentially life-threatening illness caused by the bacterium *Listeria monocytogenes*. Infection with *Listeria* can result in miscarriage (see Spotlight: The Lowdown on *Listeria*). Certain deli meats, undercooked frankfurters, and ready-to-eat foods may carry listeriosis.

Age-related deterioration of the immune system increases the risk for foodborne illness. In addition, the level of gastric juice produced by the stomach declines with age, resulting in fewer foodborne pathogens being destroyed during digestion and greater risk of gastrointestinal infections and their complications. This puts the elderly at higher risk of dying from foodborne illness.[34] Individuals in institutional settings (such as nursing homes, hospitals, schools, and on cruise ships), where groups of people eat foods from the same source, are also at higher risk of foodborne illness. Improper food handling and poor hygiene practices of food service workers are often the causes of foodborne disease outbreaks in institutional settings.

LO 20.1: THE TAKE-HOME MESSAGE Foodborne illness is a serious public health problem. Foodborne illness is caused by consuming pathogens in contaminated food or drinks. Viruses and bacteria are the most common causes in the United States, although parasites and prions can also cause some foodborne illness. Toxins can occur naturally in foods and are also introduced as a result of chemical contamination of the environment. Chemicals such as polychlorinated biphenyls (PCBs) and methylmercury have been shown to bioaccumulate in fish as a result of environmental contamination. Certain populations, including the elderly, children, pregnant women, and those with compromised immune systems, are at higher risk of contracting foodborne illness and suffering complications.

What Strategies Can Be Used to Prevent Foodborne Illness?

LO 20.2 Summarize strategies to prevent foodborne illness in the home, and when traveling.

One of the best ways to prevent foodborne illness is to keep the pathogens that cause it from flourishing in foods. For example, in order for bacteria to thrive and multiply, they must have the proper conditions. These include (1) a source of nutrients (including glucose, amino acids, or vitamins and/or minerals), (2) moisture, (3) a pH above 4.6 (considered low acidity), (4) temperatures in the range of 40 to 140 degrees Fahrenheit, and (5) time (at least 20 minutes) to multiply.[35] Protein- and nutrient-rich animal foods, such as raw and undercooked meat, poultry, seafood,

The Lowdown on *Listeria*

Listeriosis, the illness caused by the bacterium *Listeria monocytogenes,* seriously affects approximately 1,600 individuals in the United Sates annually, with pregnant women being 10 times more likely than other people to become infected.[1] *Listeria* can reach the fetus through the placenta, be transmitted to the developing baby, and lead to severe illness, premature delivery, miscarriage, and stillbirth. Older adults and those with a weakened immune system are also at risk for becoming very sick or even dying.

Animals can harbor *Listeria,* which leads to contamination of meat and dairy foods. Pasteurization kills *Listeria*, so unpasteurized soft cheeses, such as Camembert, Brie, and blue cheeses, carry a higher risk of containing *Listeria*. Compared with hard cheeses such as Parmesan, these

Soft cheese can be contaminated with *Listeria*.

soft cheeses are less acidic and contain more moisture, two conditions that enhance bacterial growth. Even though cooking can also destroy *Listeria*, the lower cooking temperature used during the processing of soft cheeses isn't high enough to destroy this bacterium. Because contamination can occur after processing, many outbreaks have been associated with foods such as hot dogs, deli-style luncheon meats, Brie cheese, salami, and paté. *Listeria* can also continue to multiply at refrigerated temperatures.

The following tips can help pregnant women and other higher risk individuals reduce their likelihood of contracting *Listeria:*[2, 3]

- Reheat ready-to-eat luncheon meats, cold cuts, fermented and dry sausage, deli-style meat and poultry products, and hot dogs until they are steamy hot to kill any existing bacteria before you eat them.
- Wash your hands with hot, soapy water after touching these types of ready-to-eat foods, or any foods, for that matter. Thoroughly wash cutting boards, dishes, and utensils to avoid cross-contamination.
- Avoid soft cheeses such as feta, Brie, Camembert, blue-veined (blue)

cheese, and Mexican-style cheeses unless they are made with pasteurized milk. (Read the ingredients list to see if pasteurized milk was used.) You can safely eat hard cheeses, semi-soft cheese such as mozzarella, pasteurized processed cheeses, cream cheese, and cottage cheese.
- Avoid unpasteurized milk and foods made from unpasteurized milk.
- Avoid refrigerated smoked seafood such as smoked salmon (lox or nova style), trout, whitefish, cod, tuna, or mackerel unless they are used in an entrée such as a heated casserole. You can safely eat canned fish and shelf-stable smoked seafood.
- Avoid refrigerated paté or meat spreads. You can safely eat canned or shelf-stable varieties.
- Eat precooked or ready-to-eat perishable items before the expiration date on the food label.

References

1. Centers for Disease Control and Prevention. Updated 2013. Listeria *(Listeriosis).* Available at www.cdc.gov/listeria. Accessed July 2014.
2. Ibid.
3. USDA. Modified 2013. *Fact Sheets: Protect Your Baby and Yourself from Listeriosis.* Available at www.fsis.usda.gov. Accessed July 2014.

eggs, and unpasteurized milk, are the most common types of foods that provide conditions for rapid bacterial growth.

Bacteria thrive in moist environments, such as in raw chicken that is sitting in its juices. Dry foods, such as uncooked rice, sugar, flour, and cereals, do not usually support bacterial growth until they are hydrated with a liquid. However, infected utensils or hands can contaminate these foods. For example, a person with infected hands who takes a handful of cereal directly out of the box transfers bacteria onto the cereal. Although the bacteria may not multiply, they survive, and, once eaten, will grow in the moist environment of the GI tract, possibly resulting in foodborne illness.

Bacteria don't thrive in acidic foods (pH less than 4.6) such as vinegar and citrus fruits, so these foods seldom provide the conditions necessary for growth. However, animal protein has a higher pH and provides the right conditions for bacteria to flourish.

Bacteria multiply most abundantly between the temperatures of about 40°F and 140°F. At body temperature, or 98.6°F, bacteria can divide and double within 20 minutes, and multiply to millions in about 12 hours.[36] Because bacteria need such a short time period to multiply, it is important to realize that perishable food, such as raw meat, left at room temperature for an extended period can become a feast for bacterial growth.

Consumers can take various measures when consuming and handling food to reduce the risk of foodborne illness. These include preventing the growth of bacteria and destroying any pathogens that may be present. This can be done through the consistent practice of proper food consumption, handling, and storage strategies at home and while traveling.

Practice Food Safety at Home

An easy way to remember the important points of home food safety is by focusing on the "Core Four" of the Fight BAC! campaign of the nonprofit Partnership for Food Safety Education: Cleaning, Combating cross-contamination (or separating), Cooking, and Chilling (**Figure 20.2**).[37] You will learn more about the Partnership for Food Safety Education later in this chapter.

Clean Hands and Produce

Cleaning is one of the simplest ways to reduce the chances of microbial contamination, and proper hand washing is one of the most important overall strategies for preventing foodborne illness. If everyone practiced proper hand washing techniques, the incidences of foodborne illness could decrease by about half.[38] The Table Tips summarize proper hand washing techniques.

Proper hand washing refers to washing hands *thoroughly,* as well as washing hands *regularly.* This last part, regular washing, is where many people fall short. Germs accumulate on hands from a variety of sources throughout the day, and if

▲ **Figure 20.2 Fight BAC!**
The Fight BAC! symbol sums up the "Core Four" of keeping food safe in the kitchen: clean, combat cross-contamination (separate meats from ready-to-eat foods), cook thoroughly, and chill to a cold enough temperature.

hands are not regularly washed, these germs can infect the body after being passed into the mouth, nose, and eyes. Individuals also spread the germs to others by touching surfaces such as doorknobs. In a study conducted at Utah State University, over 100 participants were videotaped to observe their food handling practices. After reviewing the video, the researchers found that only 2 percent of the participants had washed their hands correctly, with warm soapy water and plenty of agitation and time. Though warm tap water isn't hot enough to kill microbes, it is superior to cold water for removing dirt, oil, and germs from hands.[39] The researchers also found that the average time the participants spent washing their hands was a mere 7 seconds, rather than the recommended minimum of 20 seconds.

In instances where hand washing is not an option, such as when traveling or eating on the run, using disposable wipes or hand gel sanitizers can be an excellent alternative. Only the alcohol-based products are effective in killing germs. The CDC recommends choosing products that contain at least 60 percent alcohol.[40] Individuals should keep hand sanitizers in the car, purse, desk drawer, and backpack so that proper hand hygiene can be practiced at all times. Office workers in particular can benefit from regular use of hand sanitizer. Studies conducted in the workplace have identified an astounding 25,127 germs per square inch on the average office phone, 3,295 germs per square inch on computer keyboards, and 1,676 germs per square inch on the average computer mouse![41]

In addition to hands, anything that touches food, such as knives, utensils, and countertops, should be thoroughly cleaned between each use. Cutting boards should be placed in the dishwasher or scrubbed with hot soapy water and rinsed after each use. Nonporous cutting boards made of plastic, marble, and tempered glass are easier to keep clean than the more porous wooden cutting boards or wooden surfaces. Cracked cutting boards should be discarded, as they can harbor pathogenic microbes and lead to cross-contamination. Kitchen sinks and cutting boards should be regularly sanitized by filling the sink with hot water and adding one teaspoon of bleach per quart of water. Let the board sit in the sanitizing liquid for a few minutes to kill the microbes, then rinse it thoroughly.

A kitchen sponge is an ideal environment for bacteria because it provides the ideal temperature, moisture, and nutrients (food particles). Household kitchen sponges and dishcloths have been shown to harbor more bacteria than toilet seats.[42] Consequently, sponges and dishcloths need to be replaced often and between replacements washed after each use in the hot cycle of the washing machine, preferably with bleach in addition to the soap. They can also be soaked in a bleach solution along with the cutting boards, run through the dishwasher (including the dry cycle), or placed in the microwave for one minute at its highest setting.[43] To avoid fire hazards when using the microwave method, be sure to apply it only to damp sponges and those without metal.

All fruits and vegetables should be thoroughly washed under running tap water before eating. Even foods like cantaloupe, which doesn't have an edible peel or rind, have been known to carry *Salmonella* and *E. coli*, and the microbe can be transferred from the peel or rind to the fruit by the knife used to cut it open. Washing firm fruit with a vegetable brush helps remove any dirt or microbes on its surface. Fruit should be washed *before* placing it on the countertop or cutting board to avoid picking up and spreading germs from the countertop. Washing fruits and vegetables offers the additional advantage of removing most of the pesticide residue that may be present. Pesticides are discussed in more detail later in this chapter.

The countertop sponge may very well be the most contaminated item in your kitchen. Food scraps, moisture, and room temperature can lead to a thriving bacterial colony on this common cleaning item.

Combat Cross-Contamination

Produce, especially if it's going to be eaten raw, should never come in contact with raw meat, poultry, or fish during the food preparation process. If these items do come in contact, they could **cross-contaminate** each other, meaning that microbes could

cross-contaminate The transfer of pathogens from a food, utensil, cutting board, kitchen surface, and/or hands to another food or object.

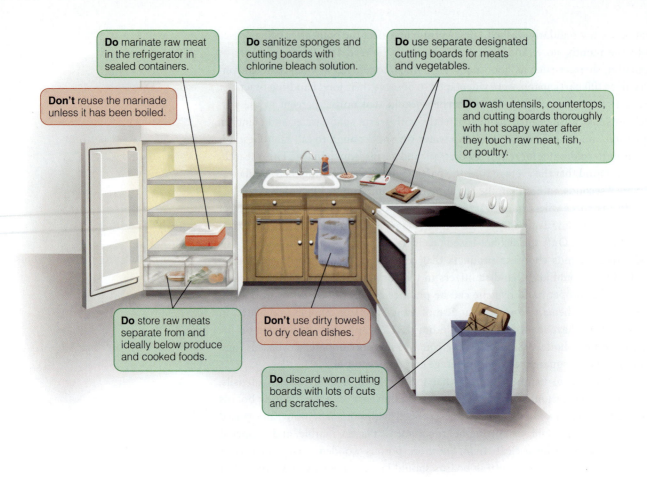

The following do's and don'ts appear in the figure:

Do marinate raw meat in the refrigerator in sealed containers.

Don't reuse the marinade unless it has been boiled.

Do sanitize sponges and cutting boards with chlorine bleach solution.

Do use separate designated cutting boards for meats and vegetables.

Do wash utensils, countertops, and cutting boards thoroughly with hot soapy water after they touch raw meat, fish, or poultry.

Do store raw meats separate from and ideally below produce and cooked foods.

Don't use dirty towels to dry clean dishes.

Do discard worn cutting boards with lots of cuts and scratches.

▲ **Figure 20.3** **The Do's and Don'ts of Avoiding Cross-Contamination**

a Cooked to internal temperature of 160°F

b Cooked to internal temperature of 135°F

▲ **Figure 20.4 Cook Meats Thoroughly to Kill Pathogens**
A hamburger needs to reach an internal temperature of 160°F to ensure that all foodborne pathogens are killed. Color is not an indication of "doneness."

be spread from one item to the other. Because raw meat, poultry, and fish contain microbes, they should be kept separate from ready-to-eat foods such as fruits and vegetables during food preparation and stored separately in the refrigerator. Uncooked meats, fish, and poultry should either be cleaned and frozen or stored in airtight containers on the bottom shelf of the refrigerator. This prevents contaminated drippings from coming in contact with cooked foods or raw fruits and vegetables. Marinades that are used to tenderize and flavor raw meats, poultry, or fish should never be reused as a basting or serving sauce. When purchasing groceries, raw meats should be bagged separately from produce. The knife and cutting board used to cut and prepare raw meat, poultry, or fish should not be used to slice vegetables or bread unless both have been thoroughly cleaned with hot soapy water. Ideally, separate cutting boards should be kept on hand for meat and nonmeat foods. All plates and bowls that have contained raw meats, poultry, and fish should be thoroughly washed before reuse. For example, at a barbecue, the plate that held the raw hamburgers should *never* be used to serve the cooked burgers unless it has been thoroughly washed between uses.

Another common source of cross-contamination occurs when soiled dishtowels are used to dry clean hands, dishes, or utensils. A towel that was used to wipe up raw meat juices or your hands can transfer those microbes to your clean dishes or utensils. You could easily coat those clean surfaces with a layer of germs. **Figure 20.3** summarizes some of the ways to combat cross-contamination in the kitchen.

Cook Foods Thoroughly

A common food safety misconception is that meat that looks brown is fully cooked. Look at the two hamburger patties in **Figure 20.4**. The brown patty on the bottom might look as thoroughly cooked as the pinker patty above, but it's not. The color of

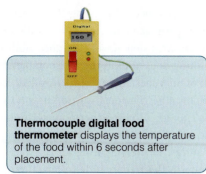

Thermocouple digital food thermometer displays the temperature of the food within 6 seconds after placement.

Thermometer fork combination thermometers allow you to stab and check. A device that measures the temperature in the food is located in the tines of the fork.

Thermistor digital food thermometers take approximately 10 seconds to display the temperature of the food on the dial.

Oven-safe bimetallic-coil thermometers are most useful when cooking thick foods such as roasts and turkeys. They are unique, as they can stay in the food during cooking.

▲ **Figure 20.5 Food Thermometers**
There are several types of food thermometers available for measuring the internal temperature of cooked foods. The thermometer should be inserted at least one-half inch deep into the food, and should be washed thoroughly after each use, and before insertion into any food.

TABLE 20.2	Safe Food Temperatures	
If You Are Cooking This Food	**The Food Thermometer Should Reach (°F)***
Ground Meat and Meat Mixtures	
Beef, pork, veal, lamb	160
Turkey, chicken	165
Fresh Beef, Veal, Lamb	145**
Poultry	
Chicken, turkey, whole or parts	165
Duck and goose	165
Fresh Pork	
Ham, raw	145**
Ham, precooked (to reheat)	140
Eggs and Egg Dishes	
Eggs	Cook until yolk and white are firm
Egg dishes	160
Leftovers and Casseroles	165

*The thermometer should be placed in the thickest part of the food item.

**Meat should rest for 3 minutes before consumption to ensure that pathogens are destroyed.

Adapted from USDA Food Safety and Inspection Service. 2013. *Kitchen Thermometers.* Available at www.fsis.usda.gov.

beef is largely determined by **myoglobin,** a protein that provides the purplish-red pigment in meat (and poultry). The denaturing of this protein is what causes meat to turn from pink to brown during cooking. However, if the meat starts out brown, this color change won't occur. Thus, a burger could look "done" when it may still be raw in places. Research has shown that hamburgers can look "well done" while only having reached an internal temperature of approximately 135°F.[44] Ground meat (beef, pork, veal, and lamb) must reach an internal temperature of 160°F to kill pathogens known to cause illness. There are also some lean or treated varieties of beef that can remain pink even though they have reached an internal temperature of 160°F.

Poultry color can also be misleading because it can remain pink after thorough cooking. This is caused by a chemical reaction that occurs in the poultry from gases in the oven that give the meat a pink tinge. Because younger birds have thin skins, the gases can react with their flesh more easily and make the meat look pinker than that of older birds. Also, nitrates and nitrites added to some poultry as a preservative can give poultry a pink tinge (see the discussion of food additives later in the chapter).[45]

The only way to determine if food has reached an internal temperature high enough to kill pathogens is to use a food thermometer. **Figure 20.5** shows several types of food thermometers available for use when cooking. **Table 20.2** provides a list of the internal temperatures that foods should reach to ensure that they are safe to eat.

Chill Foods at a Low Enough Temperature

Proper chilling and refrigeration of foods is essential to inhibit the growth of pathogens. But just how low must the temperature be? Foodborne bacteria multiply most rapidly in temperatures between 40°F and 140°F (or 5°C to 60°C), a range known as the "**danger zone.**" To keep foods out of the danger zone, hot foods must be kept *hot*, above 140°F, and cold foods need to be served *cold*, below 40°F, or even lower (see **Figure 20.6**). This means that when cooked foods like lasagna are on a buffet table, they should be sitting on a hot plate or other heat source that keeps their temperature above 140°F, while cold prepared foods such as potato salad should be kept at 40°F or below at all times.[46]

myoglobin A protein that provides the purplish-red color in meat and poultry.

danger zone The range of temperatures between 40°F and 140°F at which foodborne bacteria multiplies most rapidly. Room temperature falls within the danger zone.

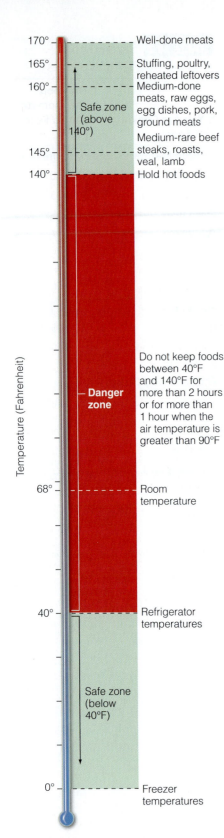

Temperature (Fahrenheit)

170° — Well-done meats
165° — Stuffing, poultry, reheated leftovers
160° — Medium-done meats, raw eggs, egg dishes, pork, ground meats

Safe zone (above 140°)

145° — Medium-rare beef steaks, roasts, veal, lamb
140° — Hold hot foods

Danger zone

Do not keep foods between 40°F and 140°F for more than 2 hours or for more than 1 hour when the air temperature is greater than 90°F

68° — Room temperature

40° — Refrigerator temperatures

Safe zone (below 40°F)

0° — Freezer temperatures

▲ **Figure 20.6 The Danger Zone**
Bacteria multiply rapidly in the "danger zone," between temperatures of 40°F and 140°F.

traveler's diarrhea A common pathogen-induced intestinal disorder experienced by some travelers who visit areas with unsanitary conditions.

Refrigerating foods for storage is another key aspect of keeping them chilled and inhibiting the growth and reproduction of pathogenic microbes. With the exception of the *Listeria* bacterium, cold temperatures *slow down* microbes' ability to multiply to dangerous levels; note that chilling does not kill them or completely stop their growth. To ensure that the growth of microbes on foods is controlled, refrigerator temperatures should be set at or below 40°F. The only way to know if the temperature in a refrigerator or freezer is low enough is to use a thermometer. Some refrigerators have built-in thermometers and separate appliance thermometers can be purchased at most grocery and discount stores. The temperature for the freezer should be set at 0°F or below. Food stays safe in the freezer indefinitely, though its quality may deteriorate. "Freezer burn" may occur if frozen food is not tightly wrapped and gets exposed to air. Freezer burn causes the texture of food to change, as it dries out and accumulates ice crystals. This results in a less pleasant taste and appearance, but it isn't harmful. Most microbes become dormant and are unable to multiply when they are frozen, but they aren't destroyed. When food is defrosted the microbes can multiply again under the right conditions.

Two hours is the critical time to remember. Perishables such as raw meat and poultry left out at room temperature (a temperature within the danger zone) for more than 2 hours may not be safe to eat. In temperatures above 90°F, such as in the kitchen in the summertime, foods shouldn't be left out at room temperature for more than 1 hour.[47] Leftovers should be refrigerated within 2 hours of being prepared. Large roasts and pots of soup or stews should be divided into smaller batches and placed in shallow pans in order to cool more quickly in the refrigerator. If these items have been left in the danger zone for too long, bacteria can not only grow, but may also produce toxins that are heat resistant. These toxins are not destroyed even if the food is cooked to a proper internal temperature, and could cause illness if consumed.[48]

Once food is refrigerated it shouldn't be held for more than a few days, even when kept at the proper temperature. A good rule of thumb is that leftovers can be in the refrigerator at 40°F or below for no more than four days. Remember, after *four* days in the refrigerator, leftovers are ready *for* disposal. Raw meats, poultry, and seafood can be safely kept in the refrigerator for a maximum of two days. A good food safety strategy is the acronym FIFO, which means "first in, first out." In other words, use food that has been in the refrigerator the longest first. **Table 20.3** lists the storage times for various foods. Don't eat food that you suspect may not be safe for any reason. If you are unsure about the safety of a food, remember this rhyme: *When in doubt, throw it out.*

Minimizing the risk for developing a foodborne illness requires a conscious effort to clean, cook, chill, and avoid cross-contamination to keep foods safe. Think about how many of these strategies you use in your own kitchen and use the Self-Assessment to help identify areas in which you may need to improve your food safety habits.

Practice Food Safety While Traveling

Travelers should follow food safety procedures to reduce the risk of illness while traveling abroad. Each year, up to 50 percent of international travelers have their trips interrupted by unpleasant intestinal side effects.[49] One type of *E. coli,* enterotoxigenic (*entero* = intestines, *toxi* = toxin, *genic* = forming) *E. coli,* is a common cause of **traveler's diarrhea.** Traveler's diarrhea causes watery diarrhea and gastrointestinal cramps and is primarily caused by consuming contaminated food, water, or ice. People visiting countries where proper sanitation is in question, including some developing countries in Latin America, Africa, the Middle East, and Asia,

TABLE 20.3 Safe Storage of Perishable Foods

Product	Storage Time after Purchase*
For Raw Foods	
Poultry	1 or 2 days
Beef, veal, pork, and lamb	3 to 5 days
Ground meat and ground poultry	1 or 2 days
Fresh variety meats (liver, tongue, brain, kidneys, heart, intestines)	1 or 2 days
Cured ham, cook-before-eating	5 to 7 days
Sausage from pork, beef, or turkey, uncooked	1 or 2 days
Eggs	3 to 5 weeks

	Unopened, after Purchase*	After Opening*
For Processed Product Sealed at Plant		
Cooked poultry	3 to 4 days	3 to 4 days
Cooked sausage	3 to 4 days	3 to 4 days
Sausage, hard/dry, shelf-stable	6 weeks/pantry	3 weeks
Corned beef, uncooked, in pouch with pickling juices	5 to 7 days	3 to 4 days
Vacuum-packed dinners, commercial brand with USDA seal	2 weeks	3 to 4 days
Bacon	2 weeks	1 week
Hot dogs	2 weeks	1 week
Luncheon meat	2 weeks	3 to 5 days
Ham, fully cooked, whole	7 days	3 days
Ham, canned, labeled "keep refrigerated"	9 months	3 to 4 days
Ham, canned, shelf-stable	2 years/pantry	3 to 5 days
Canned meat and poultry, shelf-stable	2 to 5 years/pantry	3 to 4 days
Leftovers		3 to 4 days

*Based on refrigerator home storage (at 41°F or below) unless otherwise stated.

Adapted from Food Safety and Inspection Service. 2013. *Keep Foods Safe! Food Safety Basics.* Available at www.fsis.usda.gov.

are at a higher risk of contracting it.[50] See the Table Tips for suggestions on how to avoid traveler's diarrhea and other forms of foodborne disease while traveling.

LO 20.2: THE TAKE-HOME MESSAGE Proper food handling and storage strategies, particularly cleaning, preventing cross-contamination, cooking to recommended temperatures, and chilling at recommended temperatures, can help reduce the risk of foodborne illness. Anything that comes in contact with foods, including hands, should be thoroughly washed, and produce should always be washed before eating it. Fruits and vegetables need to be kept separate from raw meats, poultry, and fish, and from any utensils that touch them. Checking the internal temperature of cooked food with a food thermometer is the only accurate way to tell if it is safe to eat. Perishables should be properly and promptly chilled to minimize the growth of bacteria. Raw meat, poultry, and seafood should be used within two days. Leftovers that are refrigerated should be discarded after four days. Extra caution is needed when traveling abroad to avoid foodborne illness.

How Do Your Food Safety Habits Stack Up?

Take the following quiz to find out.

How Often Do You	Always	Sometimes	Never
Wash your hands before preparing food?			
Scrub your fruits and vegetables under cold, running water before eating them?			
Use an insulated pouch with an ice pack to carry your perishable lunches and snacks, such as meat-filled sandwiches and/or yogurt and cheese?			
Wash your hands after using the bathroom?			
Throw out refrigerated leftovers after four days?			
Chop raw vegetables on a clean chopping board rather than the one you just used for raw meat, fish, or poultry?			
Use a thermometer to determine if the meat or poultry you are cooking is done?			

Answer

If you answered "Always" to all of the above you are practicing superior food safety skills. If you didn't, there's more you can do to reduce your chances of contracting a foodborne illness.

How Is the Food Supply Protected?

LO 20.3 Describe how the food supply is protected in the United States.

The sources and varieties of foods available to U.S. consumers has increased dramatically over the years. Keeping this vast and diverse food supply safe is the responsibility of farmers, food manufacturers, consumers, and the U.S. government. Several government agencies work together to ensure the safety of the U.S. food supply. The *Healthy People 2020* document and the 2010 *Dietary Guidelines for Americans* both highlight areas of concern related to food safety, with specific objectives aimed at improving safe food practices and decreasing foodborne illness outbreaks. In this section, we'll look at the food safety implications of our food system and the technologies available to expand and monitor our food supply. These include regulations as well as processes that occur from farm to table such as food preservation techniques, product dating, and irradiation. We'll start by looking at the government agencies that monitor our food supply, and then look at the contribution that food manufacturers make.

Several Government Agencies and Programs Protect the Food Supply

In 1906 Congress charged the USDA with responsibility for monitoring the safety of our nation's food. Today, several federal agencies share responsibility for food safety in the United States.[51] **Table 20.4** lists these agencies and summarizes the roles they

TABLE 20.4 Agencies that Oversee the Food Supply

Agency	Responsible For
USDA Food Safety and Inspection Service (FSIS)	Ensuring safe and accurately labeled meat, poultry, and eggs
Food and Drug Administration (FDA)	Ensuring the safety of all other foods besides meat, poultry, and eggs
Environmental Protection Agency (EPA)	Protecting you and the environment from harmful pesticides
Animal and Plant Health Inspection Service (APHIS)	Protecting against plant and animal pests and disease
The Centers for Disease Control and Prevention	Surveillance of foodborne disease

each play in safeguarding foods. The **Food Safety Initiative (FSI),** begun in 1997, coordinates the research, inspection, outbreak response, and educational activities of the various government agencies. The goal of the FSI is to make sure that government agencies work collaboratively. Rates of foodborne illness are lower today (up to 25 percent lower for several of the common pathogens) than they were just 10 years ago, largely due to the joint efforts of the USDA, CDC, FDA, EPA, and APHIS.[52]

An example of collaboration among these government agencies is FoodNet (www.cdc.gov/foodnet), which is a combined effort among the Centers for Disease Control and Prevention (CDC), the United States Department of Agriculture (USDA), the Food and Drug Administration (FDA), and ten state health departments. The program consists of active surveillance for foodborne diseases and related studies designed to help public health officials understand the cause and effect of foodborne diseases in the United States. The objectives of the program include determining the burden of foodborne illness in the United States, monitoring trends over time, assessing the incidence of foodborne illness and its relation to specific foods and settings, and developing interventions to reduce the overall burden of foodborne illness.

The CDC coordinates another program called PulseNet (www.cdc.gov/pulsenet), which is a national network of public health and food regulatory agency laboratories, including those at the CDC, USDA/FSIS, and the FDA, designed to identify and contain foodborne illness outbreaks. PulseNet participants perform **DNA fingerprinting,** a sort of molecular identification, on pathogenic bacteria. DNA fingerprinting uses the bacteria's unique genetic code to identify different strains of pathogens. These "fingerprints" are submitted electronically to a database at the CDC and the information is available on demand to public health and food regulatory agencies. Finding similar strains of a bacterium in both a person and a food suggests a common source and potential connection. If similar patterns emerge at the same time in different states, this could indicate a potential outbreak. Once a suspicious foodborne illness outbreak is reported and a source is identified, several government agencies then work together to contain the disease. The *E. coli* outbreak in spinach that occurred in the fall of 2006 is one example of how multiple government agencies work together to identify and contain an outbreak. The CDC, through its monitoring and surveillance programs, detected an outbreak of illness due to *E. coli* O157:H7 and immediately alerted the FDA. DNA fingerprinting was used by PulseNet to determine that all infected individuals had consumed the same strain of *E. coli*, and to trace the strain to bagged raw spinach grown in California. The fingerprinting also allowed the agencies to link the tainted food to reported illnesses in 26 states. Once the source of the outbreak was confirmed, the CDC

Food Safety Initiative (FSI) Coordinates the research, surveillance, inspection, outbreak response, and educational activities of the various government agencies that work together to safeguard food.

DNA fingerprinting A technique in which bacterial DNA "gene patterns" (or "fingerprints") are detected and analyzed to distinguish between different strains of a bacterium.

The FDA, CDC, and USDA worked together to combat an outbreak of *E. coli* O157:H7 in 2006 that was traced to bagged prewashed spinach.

issued an official health alert about the outbreak, and the FDA advised consumers to stop eating raw spinach. Before the outbreak was over, more than 200 people were infected, and more than half of them were hospitalized.[53, 54] Three individuals died and 31 developed hemolytic uremic syndrome from the outbreak. However, through the collaborative efforts and swift action of these federal and state agencies, the outbreak was contained in a short period of time and its impact was minimized.

Hazard Analysis and Critical Control Points (HACCP) is a program used to identify and control foodborne hazards that may occur in all stages of the food production process.[55] The HACCP approach was first conceived in the 1960s when the U.S. National Aeronautics and Space Administration (NASA) asked a private food manufacturer to design the foods for space flights. Since then, the FDA and USDA have mandated HACCP programs for seafood, juice, and meat processing in the United States. The use of HACCP is recommended, but not mandated, for other food industries as well. HACCP includes seven principles that focus on the analysis of potential hazards associated with foods and the identification of critical control points in the production of a food so that preventive measures can be put in place to minimize risks. For example, procedures for monitoring temperatures throughout a food's production need to be in place. Manufacturers also apply food preservation techniques to some foods to make them safer for consumers. We discuss these techniques later in the chapter.

Issues regarding food safety are also important at retail establishments. Grocery stores and restaurants must comply with FDA regulations. The Food Code is a reference document published by the FDA that local, state, and federal regulators use as a model for the development of their own food safety rules and to be consistent with national food regulatory policy. The Food Code provides practical, science-based guidance, including HACCP guidelines, and provisions to help purveyors minimize foodborne illness.[56]

Consumer food safety education is available through the Partnership for Food Safety Education (PFSE), a program designed to educate the public about safe food handling after purchase. Fight BAC! is one of the many consumer campaigns run by this program and is specifically geared toward educating children on food safety issues.

From the farmer to the consumer, everyone involved in the production and preparation of food plays a role in making sure the food we eat is safe. The food system comprises many steps: the processes and resources involved in growing, harvesting, processing, packaging, transporting, selling, and consuming food. Risks to both food safety and availability occur at each step in the food system. The **farm-to-table continuum** is a visual tool that shows how farmers, food manufacturers, transporters of food, retailers, and you, the consumer, can help ensure a safe food supply. **Figure 20.7** shows the steps in this continuum.

Food Manufacturers Use Preservation Techniques to Destroy Contaminants

In addition to government efforts to help prevent foodborne illness, food manufacturers also work to safeguard food. Food processing, preservation techniques, and irradiation help destroy contaminants and/or maintain a food's color and freshness. Product dating and coding can tell us if a food is still safe to eat and can identify recalled products.

Food preservation methods, some of which have been in use for thousands of years, include heating, canning, pickling, salting, drying, and freezing, and food manufacturers and consumers continue to use these methods to keep foods safe. At the same time, manufacturers' use of newer techniques such as irradiation and

farm-to-table continuum Illustrates the roles that farmers, food manufacturers, food transporters, retailers, and consumers play in ensuring that the food supply, from the farm to the plate, remains safe.

food preservation The treatment of foods to reduce deterioration and spoilage, and help prevent the multiplication of pathogens that can cause foodborne illness.

1 **Farm: Use good agricultural practices.** Farmers grow, harvest, sort, pack, and store their crops in ways that help reduce food safety hazards.

2 **Processing: Monitor at critical control points.** During processing, HACCP measures are implemented.

3 **Transportation: Use clean vehicles and maintain the proper temperature.** Food is kept at a proper temperature during transportation to reduce the growth of foodborne microbes.

4 **Retail: Follow the Food Code guidelines.** Retail outlets, including restaurants, grocery stores, and institutions (such as hospitals), use the Food Code guidelines to reduce the risk of foodborne illness.

5 **Consumer: Always follow the four Cs of food safety (clean, combat cross-contamination, cook, chill).** The consumer uses the four Cs to reduce the risk of foodborne illness.

◄ **Figure 20.7 The Farm-to-Table Continuum**
Every step in the farm-to-table continuum plays an important role in reducing microbes and the spread of foodborne illness.

chemical additives has expanded as consumers demand fast and convenient foods, new flavors, increased shelf life, and improved textures.

Pasteurization and Canning

Pasteurization is a process for destroying pathogenic bacteria in which liquid foods are heated to a prescribed temperature for a specified time. The process kills *E. coli*

pasteurization The process of heating liquids or food at high temperatures to destroy foodborne pathogens.

O157:H7, *Salmonella,* and *Listeria monocytogenes,* all of which can be present in raw milk. Pasteurization improves the quality of dairy products and keeps all products fresh for a longer period of time. In addition to dairy products, pasteurization is required for some juices like fresh apple juice and other foods. Unpasteurized juices must display a warning on the label to alert consumers.[57]

Canning is a process in which foods are packed into airtight containers and then heated to temperatures of 240°F to 250°F to kill microorganisms. The amount of exposure time to heat varies by the type of food, its acidity, and its density. Processing conditions are chosen to ensure that the foods are sterile while retaining the most nutrients.[58]

Commercial canning is regulated by the FDA and HACCP procedures, which virtually eliminates foodborne illness. However, improperly home-canned products can be the source of *Clostridium botulinum,* a foodborne bacterium that can survive in environments without air and that creates **spores** that are not destroyed at normal cooking temperatures (refer to Table 20.2 on page 753). A temperature higher than boiling (212°F) is needed to kill these spores.[59] Foodborne illness caused by the toxin produced by *Clostridium botulinum* can be dangerous because it results in paralysis of respiratory and other muscles.[60]

Two newer preservation methods used to keep foods fresh are **modified atmosphere packing (MAP)** and **high-pressure processing (HPP).** MAP is a process during which the manufacturer modifies the composition of the air surrounding the food in a package. The modification process decreases the amount of oxygen present in order to delay the decay of fresh produce. Used in foods such as packaged fruits and vegetables, MAP extends their shelf life and preserves their quality.[61] HPP is a method in which foods are exposed to pulses of high pressure, which destroys microorganisms. Foods such as jams, fruit juices, fish, vacuum-packed meat products, fruits, and vegetables can be treated with HPP.[62]

Irradiation

Foods can also be treated with ionizing radiation to kill pathogenic bacteria and parasites. During the process of **irradiation,** foods are subjected to a radiant energy source within a protective, shielded chamber called an *irradiator.* The energy from the radiant waves damages the DNA of the pathogens, causing defects in their genetic instructions. Unless the microbes can repair the damage, they die. Because pathogens differ in their sensitivity to irradiation, the process either kills all of them or greatly reduces their numbers, thus reducing the risk of foodborne disease.[63] In addition, irradiation can cause mutations in some bacteria and viruses and may lead to irradiation-resistant strains of these pathogens.[64]

Irradiation is a cold process and does not significantly increase the temperature or change the physical characteristics of most foods, which helps prevent nutrient loss. Also, just as foods cooked in a microwave do not retain microwaves, irradiated foods do not retain the energy waves used during the irradiation process.[65] Most of the irradiating energy passes through the food and the packaging without leaving any residue behind.[66]

Irradiation destroys bacteria such as *Campylobacter, E. coli* O157:H7, and *Salmonella* and helps control insects and parasites.[67] It does not destroy viruses, such as norovirus and hepatitis A, or the prion particles associated with mad cow disease (BSE). The nucleic acid of viruses is too small to be destroyed and prions do not have nucleic acid, which makes them resistant to irradiation at the doses approved by the FDA for foods. Irradiation can also stop the ripening process in some fruits and vegetables and reduce the number of food spoilage bacteria. Irradiated strawberries can last up to three weeks in the refrigerator, compared with only a few days for untreated berries.

canning The process of packing food in airtight containers and heating them to a temperature high enough to kill bacteria.

spores Hardy reproductive structures that are produced by certain bacteria and fungi.

modified atmosphere packaging (MAP) A food preservation technique that changes the composition of the air surrounding the food in a package to extend its shelf life.

high-pressure processing (HPP) A method used to pasteurize foods by exposing the items to pulses of high pressure, which destroys the microorganisms that are present.

irradiation A process in which foods are placed in a shielded chamber, called an *irradiator,* and subjected to a radiant energy source. This kills specific pathogens in food by breaking up the cells' DNA.

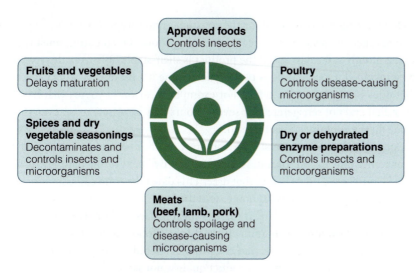

Approved foods
Controls insects

Fruits and vegetables
Delays maturation

Poultry
Controls disease-causing microorganisms

Spices and dry vegetable seasonings
Decontaminates and controls insects and microorganisms

Dry or dehydrated enzyme preparations
Controls insects and microorganisms

Meats (beef, lamb, pork)
Controls spoilage and disease-causing microorganisms

▲ **Figure 20.8 FDA-Approved Uses of Irradiation**
The international radura symbol must appear on all irradiated foods.

Food irradiation has been studied and tested for more than 50 years and remains the most researched food-related technology ever approved in the United States.[68] Irradiation has been used for years to sterilize surgical instruments and implants and to destroy disease-promoting microbes in foods served to hospital patients who have weakened immune systems. However, the use of irradiation in foods is not widespread due to consumer concerns and the expense of building the facilities.

Since 1986, all irradiated products must carry the international "radura" symbol, along with the phrase "treated by irradiation" or "treated with radiation" on the package (**Figure 20.8**). If a product such as sausage contains irradiated meat or poultry, these items must be listed as "irradiated pork" or "irradiated chicken" on the food label.[69] A label is not required if a minor ingredient, such as a spice, has been irradiated and used in the product.

Irradiation cannot be used with all foods. It causes undesirable flavor changes in dairy products, egg whites tend to become milky and liquid, fatty meats may develop an odor, and it causes tissue softening in some fruits such as peaches, nectarines, and grapefruits. Foods that are currently approved for irradiation in the United States include fruits and vegetables, herbs and spices, fresh meat, pork, and poultry, wheat flour, and white potatoes.[70]

Although irradiation has many advantages, it doesn't guarantee that a food is free from all pathogens, and some foods such as steak tartare (a dish that contains raw ground beef) should still not be eaten raw, even if they have been irradiated. Irradiation complements but does not replace the need for proper food handling practices by food growers, processors, and consumers.

Product Dating Can Help Determine Peak Quality

Food product expiration dates on almost all food products, with the exception of certain poultry, baby food products, and infant formulas, are provided voluntarily by food manufacturers and are not required by federal law. However, currently more than 20 states require some form of mandatory food product dating.

There are two types of food product dating: closed dating and open dating. **Closed** (or **coded**) **dating** refers to the packing numbers used by manufacturers that are often found on nonperishable, shelf-stable foods, such as cans of soup and fruit (see **Figure 20.9**). The manufacturer uses this type of dating to keep track of product inventory, rotate stock, and identify products that may need to be recalled.[71]

closed or "coded" dating Refers to the packing numbers that are decodable only by manufacturers and are often found on nonperishable, shelf-stable foods.

▲ Figure 20.9 **Closed and Open Food Product Dating**

Open dating is more useful for the consumer and is typically found on perishable items such as meat, poultry, eggs, and dairy foods. Open dating must include at least a month and a day, and if the product is shelf-stable or frozen, the year must also be included. Open dating is used to determine if a product is at its peak quality but does not refer to food safety. For example, a carton of yogurt that has been mishandled and not refrigerated for several hours may be unsafe to eat even though the date on the container hasn't passed.

Open-dated products must also contain a phrase next to the date that tells the consumer how to interpret it. If there is "Sell By" next to the date, the product should be purchased on or before that date. This date takes into consideration additional time for storage and use at home, so if the food is bought by the "Sell By" date it can still be eaten at a later date. If there is "Best if Used By" or "Use By" next to it, the date shows how long the manufacturer thinks a food will be of optimal quality. This does not necessarily mean that the product should not be used after the suggested date, as these dates refer to product quality, not safety.[72]

The Safety of the Water Supply Is Regulated

The Environmental Protection Agency (EPA) is the government body responsible for ensuring that consumers have a safe water supply; the Safe Drinking Water Act (SWDA) is the principal federal statute that affords that protection. Health-based standards are set by the EPA to protect the drinking water in the United States from unsafe amounts of contaminants. In most cases the EPA delegates to the states responsibility for ensuring that the health standards are met. Every year each state must produce an annual report on whether water systems within the state are meeting drinking water standards. The EPA collects and stores this information in a database called the Safe Drinking Water Information System (SDWIS). If there is an immediate threat to the health of consumers due to the violation of a drinking water standard, SDWA requires that public water systems notify consumers through the media or mail.[73]

LO 20.3: THE TAKE-HOME MESSAGE Several government agencies, including the FDA and USDA, share responsibility for food safety in the United States. HACCP is a food safety program used by the FDA, the USDA, and the food industry to identify and control hazards that may occur in any part of the food system. Manufacturers may use techniques such as pasteurization, canning, and irradiation to preserve food and destroy contamination. The FDA has approved the use of irradiation in the U.S. food supply even though some consumers have concerns about the safety of irradiated foods. Most food product dating is provided voluntarily, and can help determine peak quality but not food safety. The EPA is responsible for ensuring the safety of our water supply.

What Role Do Food Additives, Hormones, Antibiotics, and Pesticides Play in Food Production and Safety?

LO 20.4 Compare the risks and benefits of food additives, and the use of hormones, antibiotics, and pesticides in both traditionally and organically grown food.

open dating Typically found on perishable items such as meat, poultry, eggs, and dairy foods; must contain a calendar date.

food additives Substances added to food that affect its quality, flavor, freshness, and/or safety.

Food manufacturers use various types of **food additives** for many different reasons. Commonly used additives include preservatives (such as antioxidants and sulfites), nutrients, and flavor enhancers (such as MSG). Food producers also give food-producing animals hormones and antibiotics to improve the health and food yield of these animals, but they may cause unintentional side effects in consumers.[74] Other food producers use pesticides on plants to protect them and boost production.

Preservatives Prevent Spoilage and Increase Shelf Life

Most food additives are **preservatives** that are added to foods to prevent spoilage (usually by destroying microbes) and increase shelf life. The most common anti-microbial preservatives are salt and sugar. Salt has been used for centuries, particularly in meat and fish, to create a dry environment in which bacteria cannot multiply. Most (65 percent) of the salt consumed in the United States comes from processed and prepared foods that you find in grocery and convenience stores.[75] Sugar is used for the same preserving effect in products such as canned and frozen fruits and condiments.

Nitrites and nitrates are ionic salts, chemical compounds that result from the bonding of a positively charged ion to a negatively charged ion, that are added to foods to prevent microbial growth and are used in cured meats such as hot dogs and hams to prevent the growth of *Clostridium botulinum*. These chemicals give processed meats their pink color. The use of these salts has been controversial due to the fact that they form carcinogenic nitrosamines in the digestive tract of animals.[76]

The addition of antioxidants to foods can prevent an off taste or off color in a product that's vulnerable to damage by oxidation. Currently two vitamins are approved for use as food additives due to their actions as antioxidants: vitamin E and vitamin C. Vitamin E is fat soluble and often added to oils and cereals to prevent the fats in them from becoming rancid. Vitamin C is water soluble and is often added to cut fruit to prevent premature browning. Butylated hydroxyanisole (BHA) and butylated hydroxytoluene (BHT) are chemical antioxidants that are also used as preservatives. In some but not all experimental trials with animals, feeding high amounts of BHT and BHA caused increased risk of some cancers, but in other studies feeding animals high amounts of BHT and BHA caused decreased risk of some cancers.[77] There is little evidence to suggest that the low doses of BHT and BHA used as preservatives are harmful for humans, and these ingredients are on the FDA's **GRAS (generally recognized as safe)** list.

Sulfites are a group of antioxidants that are used as preservatives to help prevent the oxidation and browning of some foods and to inhibit the growth of microbes.[78] Sulfites are often found in dried fruits and vegetables, packaged and prepared potatoes, wine, beer, bottled lemon and lime juice, and pickled foods.

For most people sulfites pose no risk, but sulfites cause adverse reactions in some people. Individuals who are sensitive to sulfites may experience symptoms ranging from chest tightness, difficulty breathing, and hives to the more serious and potentially fatal anaphylactic shock. Studies suggest that the sulfur dioxide in the sulfites appears to cause these symptoms.[79] People at highest risk for negative reactions include people who suffer from asthma, those who are taking steroids, and those who have sensitive airways.

Due to the risk of adverse reactions in people who are sulfite sensitive, the FDA has prohibited the use of sulfites on fruits and vegetables that are served raw, such as in a salad bar, or are advertised as "fresh." The FDA requires that foods containing sulfite additives or ingredients treated with sulfites must declare "added sulfites" in the ingredients list on the label. Food sold in bulk, such as dried fruit treated with sulfites, must display the ingredients on a sign near the food. Because sulfites destroy the B vitamin thiamin, the FDA prohibits their use in enriched grain products and other foods that are good sources of this vitamin.[80]

Dried fruits often have sulfur dioxide or other sulfites added to them to preserve color and flavor. People with sulfite sensitivity should avoid products containing these additives.

preservatives Substances that extend the shelf life of a product by retarding chemical, physical, or microbiological changes.

nitrites and nitrates Substances that can be added to foods to function as a preservative and to give meats such as hot dogs and luncheon meats a pink color.

generally recognized as safe (GRAS) A designation given by the FDA to substances intentionally added to food, indicating that the substance is considered safe by experts and is exempted from further testing.

sulfites Preservatives used to help prevent foods from turning brown and to inhibit the growth of microbes. Often used in wine and dried fruit products.

TABLE 20.5	Commonly Used Food Additives	
Additive(s)	**Function(s)**	**Found In**
Alginates, carrageenan, glyceride, guar gum, lecithin, mono- and diglycerides, methyl cellulose, pectin, sodium aluminosilicate	Impart/maintain desired consistency	Baked goods, cake mixes, coconut, ice cream, processed cheese, salad dressings, table salt
Ascorbic acid (vitamin C), calcium carbonate, folic acid, thiamine (B_1), iron, niacin, pyridoxine (B_6), riboflavin (B_2), vitamins A and D, zinc oxide	Improve/maintain nutritive value	Biscuits, bread, breakfast cereals, desserts, flour, gelatin, iodized margarine, milk, pasta, salt
Ascorbic acid, benzoates, butylated hydroxyanisole (BHA), butylated hydroxytoluene (BHT), citric acid, propionic acid and its salts, sodium nitrite	Maintain palatability and wholesomeness	Bread, cake mixes, cheese, crackers, frozen and dried fruit, lard, margarine, meat, potato chips
Citric acid, fumaric acid, lactic acid, phosphoric acid, sodium bicarbonate, tartrates, yeast	Produce light texture and control acidity/alkalinity	Butter, cakes, cookies, chocolates, crackers, quick breads, soft drinks
Annatto, aspartame, caramel, cloves, FD&C Red No. 40, FD&C Blue No. 1, fructose, ginger, limonene, MSG, saccharin, turmeric	Enhance flavor or provide desired color	Baked goods, cheeses, confections, gum, spice cake, gingerbread, jams, soft drinks, soup, yogurt

Adapted from FDA. 2013. *Food Additives Status List*. Available at www.fda.gov.

Additives Are Used to Enhance Food Quality and Appeal

Food manufacturers also use additives to increase the quality or appeal of their products. Some additives improve food texture and consistency. Others enhance the nutrient content, color, or flavor of food. **Table 20.5** lists some commonly used nonpreservative additives and their functions in foods.

Additives to Enhance Texture and Consistency

Food additives can enhance the texture and consistency of food in a number of ways. Gums and pectins are often added to thicken yogurts and puddings. Emulsifiers improve the stability, consistency, and homogeneity of high-fat products like mayonnaise and ice cream. Lecithin is an example of an emulsifier that is often added to salad dressings. Leavening agents such as yeast or baking powder cause dough to rise before it's baked. Anticaking agents such as sodium aluminosilicate and calcium carbonate prevent products like powdered sugar that are crystalline in nature from absorbing moisture and lumping. Humectants such as propylene glycol increase moisture in products so that they stay fresh.

Additives to Improve Nutrient Content

Additives can be used to enhance a product's nutritional content, such as when refined grains are enriched and fortified with added B vitamins (folic acid, thiamin, niacin, and riboflavin) and iron. In some cases, such additions are mandated by the federal government; in other cases they are voluntarily added by food manufacturers. This was the case in 1996, when the FDA published regulations requiring the addition of folic acid to enriched breads, cereal, and other grain products in order to help decrease the risk of neural tube defects in newborns.

Additives to Improve Color

Additives can also enhance the color of foods. There are two main categories that make up the FDA's list of permitted colors. "Certifiable" color additives are man-made and are derived primarily from petroleum and coal. You can recognize these types of additives by the following prefixes: FD&C, D&C, or Ext. An example is FD&C Yellow, which is often found in cereals and baked goods. The second main category of color additives is obtained largely from plants, animals, or minerals. Examples include caramel and grape color extract.

Adverse physical or allergic reactions to color additives are rare, although FD&C Yellow No. 5 may cause itching and hives in some people. This additive is found in beverages, desserts, and processed vegetables and must be listed as an ingredient on food labels.

MSG to Enhance Flavor

Monosodium glutamate (MSG) is the sodium salt of glutamic acid, a nonessential amino acid, and is often used as a flavor enhancer in Asian foods, canned vegetables and soups, and processed meats. Consumers can buy it in a form that is similar in texture to salt. Although it doesn't have a strong taste of its own, it enhances sweet, salty, sour, and bitter tastes.

After an extensive review, the FDA classified MSG as "generally recognized as safe" (GRAS) and confirmed that MSG is safe to consume in the amounts typically used in processed foods and cooking (a typical meal that contains MSG has less than 0.5 gram). However, when consumed in large quantities such as 3 or more grams at a time, it may cause short-term reactions in people who are sensitive to it.[81] These reactions, which are called the **MSG symptom complex,** can include numbness, a burning sensation, facial pressure or tightness, chest pain, rapid heart beat, and drowsiness. In addition, people with asthma may have difficulty breathing after consuming MSG. For these reasons, the FDA requires that all foods containing MSG declare this ingredient on the food label.

Food Additives Are Closely Regulated by the FDA

Food additives are under strict regulation by the FDA, with consumer safety a top priority. The Federal Food, Drug and Cosmetic Act of 1938 gave the FDA authority to regulate food and food ingredients, including the use of food additives. The 1958 Food Additives Amendment further mandated that manufacturers document a food additive's safety and obtain FDA approval before using it in a food.[82]

Two categories of food additives were exempted from this amendment. The first category includes substances that were known to be safe before 1958 and were given **prior-sanctioned** status.[83] For example, because nitrates were used to preserve meats before 1958, they have prior-sanctioned status, but *only* for their use in meats. They can't be used in other foods, such as vegetables, without FDA approval. The second category includes substances that have a long history of being safe for consumption, such as salt, sugar, and spices, or have extensive research documenting that they are safe to consume, such as vitamins and MSG. These additives are categorized as GRAS and are exempt from FDA approval.[84]

The FDA continually monitors both prior-sanctioned additives and those with GRAS status to ensure that current research continues to support their safety. To remain on the GRAS list, an additive must not have been found to be carcinogenic in animals or humans. The 1958 Food Additives Amendment also included the **DeLaney Clause,** which was created to protect consumers from additives found to be carcinogenic. The clause states that no substances that have been shown to cause cancer in animals or humans at any dosage may be added to foods. However, with the present increases in technology and the ability to detect substances at very low levels, the clause is considered outdated. To address this issue the FDA deems additives safe if lifetime use presents no more than a one-in-a-million risk of cancer in human beings. If an additive is suddenly called into question, the FDA can prohibit its use or require that the food manufacturer conduct additional studies to ensure its safety.

monosodium glutamate (MSG) The sodium salt of glutamic acid, used as a flavor enhancer.

MSG symptom complex A series of reactions such as numbness, burning sensation, facial pressure or tightness, chest pain, rapid heart beat, and drowsiness that can occur in some individuals after consuming MSG.

prior-sanctioned Substances that the FDA had determined were safe for use in foods prior to the 1958 Food Additives Amendment.

DeLaney Clause Clause in the Food Additives Amendment mandating that additives shown to cause cancer at any level must be removed from the marketplace.

Some Food Additives Are Unintentional

The food additives discussed in the preceding sections are all **intentional food additives** used to improve the quality of food products. However, **unintentional food additives** may sometimes be indirectly added to a food. For example, very small amounts of substances used during packaging or processing may inadvertently end up in the food. The safety of packaging must therefore be determined by manufacturers to ensure that packing substances aren't harmful to the consumer. Unintentional additives may also include chemicals from processing or traces of compounds provided to food-producing animals. For example, dioxins used during the manufacture of bleached paper such as coffee filters may end up in coffee and other foods and beverages. Dioxins can accumulate in the food chain and are carcinogenic to animals. The FDA requires that dioxin levels in products be so low as to present no health risks to people.[85]

Natural bovine growth hormone, or its synthetic version, are sometimes injected into cows to increase milk production.

Hormones and Antibiotics Are Provided to Food-Producing Animals to Enhance the Food Supply

Hormones and antibiotics are two classes of compounds that are sometimes used to improve the health or output of food-producing animals. While the use of these substances is intentional, the resulting changes in the final food product are not, and these changes are a subject of controversy and consumer concern.

Bovine Growth Hormone

Bovine growth hormone (BGH), also known as bovine somatotropin, is produced naturally by cows. Some dairy farmers and ranchers treat their cattle with the naturally occurring form of BGH in order to produce animals that are leaner and produce more milk. Scientists can also produce a synthetic version of the hormone, **recombinant bovine somatotropin (rbST),** and cows injected with this form can produce up to 25 percent more milk than untreated cows.[86]

Consumer groups and Health Canada (the FDA equivalent in Canada) have questioned the long-term safety of rbST. Traces of both the synthetic and natural form of BGH remain in the meat and milk of cows. Also of concern is that milk from rbST-treated cows has higher levels of IGF-1, a hormone that normally helps some types of cells to grow.[87] The FDA's extensive review of the safety of the use of rbST has found no evidence that it poses any long-term health threat to humans.[88] However, consumer pressure due to concerns over the long-term safety of rbST has led to a decrease in the percent of milk produced in the United States from cows treated with rbST.

Other steroid hormones are sometimes used to increase the amount of weight that cattle gain and the amount of meat they produce, and to increase milk production in dairy cows. The FDA has approved the use of these hormones in cattle, as they have been shown to be safe at their approved level of use and not a health concern to consumers.[89] However, meat and milk that carry the USDA Organic seal cannot come from cows that were treated with growth hormones.

Antibiotics

Antibiotics are sometimes given to livestock and are generally used for three purposes: (1) to treat animals that are sick; (2) to prevent disease; and (3) to promote

intentional food additives Substances added intentionally to foods to improve food quality.

unintentional food additives Substances that enter into foods unintentionally during manufacturing or processing.

bovine growth hormone (BGH) A hormone that is essential for normal growth and development in cattle.

recombinant bovine somatotropin (rbST) A synthetically made hormone identical to a cow's natural growth hormone, somatotropin, that stimulates milk production. Also known as rbGH (recombinant bovine growth hormone).

antibiotics Drugs that kill or slow the growth of bacteria.

growth. When antibiotics are used properly in the treatment of sick animals and to prevent the spread of disease they are used for a relatively short period of time. However, when used to promote growth and increase the amount of meat and milk produced, they are used over a long period of time.

Pathogenic bacteria such as *Campylobacter, E. coli* O157:H7, and *Salmonella* are commonly found in the gastrointestinal tracts of animals without making them sick. The long-term use of antibiotics in animals can result in **antibiotic-resistant bacteria** strains in their intestinal tracts.[90] This practice poses a human health risk if a person contracts a foodborne infection from the resistant bacteria and is treated with the same antibiotic used to treat the animals. The antibiotic will not effectively treat the illness because resistance to the medicine has developed during its chronic use in the animals.

An example of antibiotic resistance posing a risk to human health occurred as a result of the discovery that the antibiotic fluoroquinolone could be used to successfully treat *Campylobacter,* which is commonly found in chickens. In 1995 the antibiotic began to be used regularly in poultry as a treatment and as a preventive. After a period of chronic use, the bacteria developed a resistance to the medicine. This resulted in *Campylobacter*-induced foodborne illness in humans whose infections were resistant to treatments with fluoroquinolone.[91]

The chronic intake of antibiotics can create additional strains of organisms, sometimes referred to as "super-bugs," that are resistant and cause the "overgrowth" of other bacteria in the animal. These surviving bacteria can flourish and multiply to high levels and treatment with typical antibiotics to control these surviving, resistant bacteria may be unsuccessful. This perpetuates the need for a higher dose of medication and/or a longer treatment period.

Label Terms Indicate How Animal Foods Are Produced

Both the FDA and USDA are the consumer watchdogs for food labeling, and labeling of animal food products is essential when it comes to determining how the animals were fed, housed, and treated. The label terms for meat and poultry are determined and defined by the USDA. The following list includes terms often found on prepackaged meat products:[92]

- **No Hormones (pork or poultry).** Hormones are not allowed in raising hogs or poultry. Therefore, the claim "no hormones added" cannot be used on the labels of pork or poultry unless it is followed by a statement that says, "Federal regulations prohibit the use of hormones."
- **No Hormones (beef).** The phrase "no hormones administered" may be approved for use on the label of beef products if no hormones have been used in raising the animals.
- **No Antibiotics.** May be used on labels for meat or poultry products if the animals were raised without antibiotics.
- **Certified.** Indicates that the USDA has evaluated a meat product for class, grade, or other quality characteristics (for example, "Certified Angus Beef").
- **Fresh Poultry.** Poultry that has never had an internal temperature below 26°F.
- **Free Range.** Producers must demonstrate that the animal has been allowed access to the outdoors.
- **Kosher.** Meat and poultry products that were prepared under the supervision of a rabbi.
- **Natural.** The food contains no artificial ingredient or added color and is only minimally processed; that is, using processes that do not fundamentally alter the raw product. The label must explain the use of the term natural (such as "no added colorings or artificial ingredients").

antibiotic-resistant bacteria Bacteria that have developed a resistance to an antibiotic such that they are no longer affected by antibiotic medication.

Farmers use pesticides on food crops to diminish the damage from pests such as weeds or insects.

Pesticides Are Widely Used in Agriculture to Improve Food Production

Pesticides are used to prevent plant disease and insect infestations and can be applied to crops in the fields or after harvest. These chemicals play an important role in food production by controlling threats to the food supply. Despite the beneficial role that they play in assuring consumers a wide variety of foods, concerns about pesticides in food persist. A year-long study in 1998 of the role of pesticides in U.S. agriculture concluded that a variety of pesticide technologies, including chemical methods, can be used to produce safe, productive, and profitable crops.[93]

Types of Pesticides

Several different types of pests can diminish or destroy crop yields, including weeds, insects, microorganisms (bacteria, viruses), fungi (mold), and rodents (rats and mice). **Herbicides** are a type of pesticide used to kill weeds, **insecticides** kill insects, **antimicrobials** are used on microorganisms, **fungicides** are used to destroy mold, and **rodenticides** poison and kill rodents. Each one of these pesticides is designed to target and destroy a specific type of pest.

Pesticides can be biologically or chemically based. Biologically based pesticides, such as biopesticides and sex pheromones, use material from animals, plants, bacteria, and some minerals and are typically less toxic than chemical pesticides.[94] Unlike chemical pesticides, biopesticides only harm a specific pest, and thus are not harmful to birds and other animals that may come into contact with them. For example, baking soda can be diluted with water and sprayed on plants to inhibit the growth of fungi without risk to animals or humans. Insect sex pheromones can be used to interfere with the reproduction of insects known to harm plants.

Chemically based **organophosphates** make up about half of all insecticides in the United States and are used on fruits, nuts, vegetables, corn, wheat, and other crops, as well as on commercial and residential lawns and plants. They are also used to help control mosquitoes and termites.[95] These pesticides kill pests by affecting their nervous systems, and exposure to humans may have effects on our nervous systems as well. The EPA reviewed the safety of organophosphates in 2006 and concluded that there is a reasonable certainty that the cumulative exposure to organophosphates in food and water to people living in the United States causes no harm.[96]

Antimicrobials, a special type of chemical pesticide that includes disinfectants and sanitizers, are used to destroy and control the spread of microorganisms on surfaces or objects, such as walls, countertops, and floors.[97] Sanitizers are often used in addition to washing with soap and water in food processing plants and in restaurants. Waterless, alcohol-based hand gels that are useful against pathogens are approved by the FDA for use in health care settings but are not approved for use in food service and retail establishments. Alcohol-based hand gels do not kill all types of pathogens, though using an antimicrobial hand gel is better than nothing when water and soap are not available for hand washing.[98]

The Risks of Pesticides

Chemically based pesticides are not without risks and because they are strong chemicals, they can cause unintended harm to animals, the environment, and even humans. Residues of these chemicals remain on fruits and vegetables that reach consumers, and infants and young children are particularly susceptible to their hazards. Research has shown that some pesticides, depending upon their level of toxicity and how much is consumed, may cause serious health problems, such as cancer, birth defects, and nerve damage.[99]

pesticides Substances that kill or repel pests such as insects, weeds, microorganisms, rodents, or fungi.

herbicides Substances that are used to kill and control weeds.

insecticides Pesticides used to kill insects.

antimicrobials Substances or a combination of substances, such as disinfectants and sanitizers, that kill or inhibit the growth of microorganisms.

fungicides Chemicals used to kill mold.

rodenticides Poisons used to kill rats, mice, and other rodents.

organophosphates A group of synthetic pesticides that adversely affect the nervous systems of pests.

To address these issues, *Healthy People 2020* includes an objective focused on reducing the number of health care visits related to pesticide exposure per year and advocates a reduction in the use of certain potentially dangerous pesticides.[100] In addition, the American Academy of Pediatrics has urged the U.S. government to improve public education, workplace training, science-based research, and the ongoing surveillance of pesticide usage.[101] In order to protect public health and the environment, the types of pesticides and how often they can be used, as well as the amount of residue that can remain on foods when they reach consumers, are heavily regulated in the United States.

EPA, USDA, and FDA Regulate Pesticides

The EPA requires extensive test data from pesticide producers demonstrating that pesticide products can be used with "a reasonable certainty of no harm." To determine this, the EPA uses a four-step human health **risk assessment** that includes hazard identification, dose-response assessment, exposure assessment, and risk characterization (see **Figure 20.10**).

The first step, hazard identification, identifies the potential hazards or ill effects that may develop after exposure to a specific pesticide. Tests looking at a wide range of side effects, from eye and skin irritations to more serious health effects such as cancer, are often performed on laboratory animals.

Because "the dose makes the poison," the second step, dose-response assessment, determines the dose levels at which adverse effects occur in animals and then uses this information to calculate a potentially equal dose in humans.

The third step, exposure assessment, determines all the ways that a person could typically be exposed to that specific pesticide. Most foods are grown with the use of pesticides, so one route of exposure is through eating food. Some pesticides applied to farmland make their way into drinking water supplies, which is another route of exposure. Exposure could also occur through inhalation or absorption through the skin when using household disinfectants or gardening pesticides around the home. The EPA has a separate program for assessing occupational risk and the level of exposure that pesticide applicators and vegetable and fruit pickers face due to the nature of their jobs.

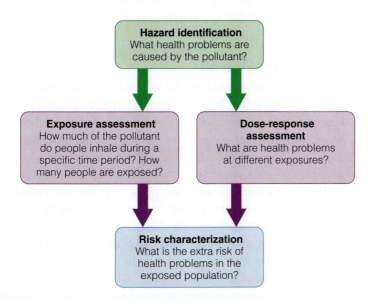

▲ Figure 20.10 **EPA's Four-Step Risk Assessment Process**
This four-step process is used by the EPA to assess risk of pesticides to humans.
Adapted from Environmental Protection Agency. 1991. *Risk Assessment for Toxic Air Pollutants: A Citizen's Guide*. Available at www.epa.gov/ttn/atw/3_90_024.html.

risk assessment The process of determining the potential human health risks posed by exposure to substances such as pesticides.

The fourth and last step, risk characterization, is the process of combining the hazard, dose-response, and exposure assessments to determine the pesticide's overall risk. Using the conclusions of a risk assessment, the EPA can make an informed decision regarding whether to approve a pesticide or chemical for use freely or with restrictions.[102]

Acceptable tolerance levels are set using a margin of safety due to the potential differences that exist between the effects of a pesticide on animals and its effect on humans, as well as differences among humans. A safety factor of tenfold or less, depending on the evidence, is added to protect the most vulnerable groups, such as infants and children, for whom the same amount of pesticide provides a larger dose per unit of body weight than for adults.[103] Thus, much effort goes into ensuring that the food supply is safe, yet affordable, so that consumers obtain foods that are nutrient dense while being exposed to a minimum amount of pesticide.

In addition to the EPA, the USDA and the FDA are also involved in regulating pesticides. The EPA is charged with approving pesticides for their specific usages, regulating how much of the pesticide can be used, and establishing acceptable tolerance levels. The USDA enforces the tolerance levels for meat, poultry, and eggs, and the FDA enforces tolerance levels for all other foods.[104]

Alternatives to Pesticides

One method that some growers use to manage pests in their crops is **integrated pest management (IPM),** which emphasizes the use of natural toxins. The goal of this approach is to use the most economical methods to control pests while causing the least risk of harm to the consumer, the crops, or the environment. Growers using the IPM approach use preventive measures, such as rotating crops, choosing pest-resistant strains of plants, and planting nonfood crops nearby to lure away pests.[105] When an infestation occurs, IPM programs use information about the life cycle of pests and nonsynthetic alternatives, such as biopesticides or the introduction of natural predators (specific insects that eat the unwanted pests), to limit damage. As a last resort, IPM growers use targeted spraying of chemical pesticides.

Most of the crops in the United States are grown using some form of IPM, by at least identifying pests before treating them.[106] However, because foods grown using IPM methods are not thus labeled, consumers cannot distinguish them from foods grown with the use of synthetic pesticides.

Minimizing Pesticides in the Diet

More than 80 percent of the pesticide residue remaining on the skins of fruits and vegetables can be removed simply by washing them with clean, running water and scrubbing them with a vegetable brush.[107] A study conducted by the University of California found that there was no difference in the amount of residue removed when the fruit was washed with plain water or with a commercial produce wash.[108] Peeling the skin from fruits and vegetables can help reduce pesticide residues and harmful microbes, but it also eliminates some of the fiber and micronutrients. For leafy vegetables such as cabbage and lettuce, the outer leaves can be removed and discarded to minimize risk. Consumers should also be aware that because of the strict pesticide guidelines in place in the United States, the amount of pesticide residue on fruits and vegetables should be below the EPA acceptable tolerance levels even *before* they reach the market.

Eating a variety of produce from a variety of locations also minimizes the consumption of any one type of pesticide. Although people who eat more fruits and vegetables potentially increase their exposure to pesticides, they still typically

acceptable tolerance levels The maximum amount of pesticide residue that is allowed in or on foods.

integrated pest management (IPM) Alternative to pesticides that uses the most economical and the least harmful methods of pest control to minimize risk to consumers, crops, and the environment.

Wash: Thoroughly wash and scrub all fresh fruits and vegetables under running water to dislodge bacteria and some of the pesticide residue. Running water is more effective for this purpose than soaking the fruit and vegetables.

Peel and trim: Peeling fruits and vegetables and discarding the outer leaves of leafy vegetables helps reduce pesticides. Trimming the visible fat from meat and the fatty skin from poultry and fish helps reduce some of the pesticide residue that remains in the fatty tissue of the animal.

Eat a variety of foods: Eating a variety of foods reduces the chance of being overexposed to any particular pesticide.

▲ Figure 20.11 **Reducing Pesticides in Foods**

have a lower risk of cancer than those who eat fewer fruits and vegetables.[109] Locally grown produce may contain fewer pesticides than shipped produce because it does not contain those applied to extend shelf life. See **Figure 20.11** for a summary of strategies to minimize pesticides in the diet.

Understand the Meaning of the Term Organic

Organic food production involves growing food using approved methods that integrate cultural, biological, and mechanical practices that conserve resources, promote ecological balance, and conserve biodiversity.[110] Organically grown foods are grown without the use of most synthetic pesticides, synthetic fertilizers, bioengineering, or irradiation. Only antibiotic-free or growth hormone–free animals can be used to produce organic meat, poultry, eggs, and dairy foods.[111] Consumers may choose organically grown foods over traditionally grown foods if they are concerned about their exposure to these things. Many consumers perceive organic foods to be healthier than their nonorganic counterparts and are willing to pay more for them. Consequently, consumer demand for organically grown products continues to increase. The annual growth rate of organically grown foods was 12 percent in 2013, the fastest growth rate realized for the past five years.[112] Organically grown foods are big business and annual sales of organically grown products topped $35 billion dollars in 2013, according to a survey on the organic food industry from the Organic Trade Association.[113]

The Organic Foods Production Act and the National Organic Standards (NOS) developed in 2002 by the USDA are intended to assure consumers that the organic foods they purchase are produced, processed, and certified consistent with national standards. Before the NOS were in place, over 50 organizations and state agencies had their own unique sets of organic standards and guidelines.[114] The NOS implemented under the USDA's National Organic Program provide specific criteria that food producers must meet during production, handling, and processing in order to label their products USDA *organic*. These standards define substances both approved for use and prohibited from use in organic food production. For

organic Being free of chemical-based pesticides, synthetic fertilizers, irradiation, and bioengineering. A USDA-accredited certifying inspector must certify organic foods.

example, organically grown foods cannot be grown using sewage sludge, and a USDA-accredited inspector must certify the farming and processing operations that produce and handle foods labeled as organic.[115]

Consumers who purchase organically grown and processed foods should not assume that they are pesticide free. Organically grown crops may come into contact with chemicals due to drift from wind and rainwater. Also, though organic farmers use IPM, and grow more disease- and pest-resistant plants, they can also use synthetic pesticides and biopesticides to control weeds and insects. The National Organic Program has created the National List of Allowed and Prohibited Substances that identifies substances that can and cannot be used in organic crop production. The list contains natural (biological) and synthetic substances that are allowed as well as natural substances that are prohibited. Included on the list of allowed substances are several synthetic pesticides, such as insecticidal soaps, microbials, botanicals, and minerals, while some natural substances, such as ash from the burning of manure, are prohibited from use in organic farming.[116]

There is little credible evidence to suggest that organically grown foods are safer or nutritionally superior to those grown using conventional methods.[117, 118] Organically grown foods differ from other foods in the ways they are grown, handled, and processed. These differences reduce exposures to pesticide residues, growth hormones, and antibiotic-resistant strains of bacteria, but do not result in significant differences to the nutrient content of food.[119] A well-balanced and varied diet can improve health regardless of whether the foods were grown organically or conventionally.

Labeling of organic foods is strictly regulated by the USDA and consumers can identify organically produced foods by looking for the USDA Organic Seal (Figure 20.12). Foods that display this seal or otherwise state that they are organic must contain at least 95 percent organic ingredients. There are other label claims and standards for foods that are 100 percent organic or made with organic ingredients. The labeling requirements are based on the percentage of a product's ingredients that are organic. See Table 20.6 for the standards that organic label claims must meet.

▲ Figure 20.12 **The USDA Organic Seal**
Foods that are labeled or advertised with the USDA Organic Seal must contain at least 95 percent organic ingredients.

LO 20.4: THE TAKE-HOME MESSAGE The FDA strictly regulates all compounds intentionally added to foods or provided to food-producing animals. Food additives have long been used for food preservation and are often used by modern manufacturers to preserve foods, enhance their color or flavor, or add to their nutrient content. Antioxidants, sulfites, and MSG are examples of additives used to preserve foods and enhance flavor. Growth hormone is often given to dairy cows to increase milk production. Animal feed containing low doses of antibiotics has been used to increase the growth of cattle, poultry, and pigs, but can lead to antibiotic-resistant strains of bacteria. All intentional food additives must be listed on food labels. Pesticides are used to destroy or mitigate pests and are strictly regulated by several government agencies. Consumers can minimize exposure to plant pesticides by washing produce under running tap water before consuming it, buying from producers that practice IPM, and eating a wide variety of foods. The USDA developed National Organic Standards (NOS) that help to assure consumers that foods labeled as USDA organic are grown without the use of most synthetic pesticides, synthetic fertilizers, bioengineering, or irradiation. There is little scientific evidence to support the idea that organically grown foods are more nutritious than foods grown using conventional methods.

TABLE 20.6 Various Levels of Organic

If the label says ▶

"Organic" and/or displays the USDA Organic seal

Then: The food contains at least 95 percent organic ingredients.

▲ **If the label says**

"100% Organic"

Then: The food must be composed entirely of organic ingredients. *Note:* These foods cannot contain sulfites and must declare the certifying agent. The USDA Organic seal may be displayed.

◀ **If the label says**

nothing about organic claims

Then: The food contains less than 70 percent (potentially 0 percent) organic ingredients.

◀ **If the label says**

"Made with Organic Ingredients"

Then: The food contains at least 70 percent organic ingredients.

What Is a Sustainable Food System?

LO 20.5 Describe what constitutes a sustainable food system.

There are currently more than 7 billion people in the world and that number is expected to increase by 2 billion people by 2050.[120] How will we provide safe and nutritious food for the growing number of people, given the limited resources available? This question deserves our attention and will require changes at all levels of our current **food system.**

A **sustainable** food system is one that can be maintained indefinitely. According to the position of the Academy of Nutrition and Dietetics, sustainable food systems conserve, renew, and protect natural resources; empower social responsibility to uphold the system; and are economically viable because they build community wealth (see **Figure 20.13**).[121] All food systems are impacted by social, political, economic, and environmental factors and depend on both human and natural resources. Sustainable food systems produce food using minimal natural resources, such as soil and water, are not depleted to grow food, and minimal

food system A food system includes all processes and infrastructure involved in feeding a population: growing, harvesting, processing, packaging, transporting, marketing, and consuming food.

sustainable Referring to a method of resource use that can be maintained indefinitely because it does not deplete or permanently damage the resource.

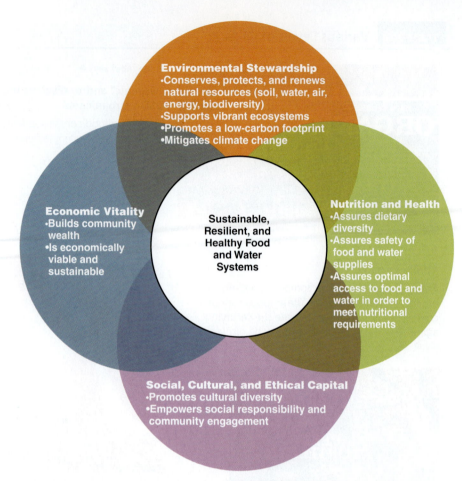

▲ **Figure 20.13 Sustainable, Resilient, and Healthy Food and Water Systems Framework**

Source: A. Tagtow, K. Robien, E. Bergquist, M. Mruening, L. Dierks, B. E. Hartman, et al. 2014. "Academy of Nutrition and Dietetics: Standards of Professional Performance for Registered Dietitian Nutritionists (Competent, Proficient, and Expert) in Sustainable, Resilient, and Healthy Food and Water Systems." *Journal of the Academy of Nutrition and Dietetics* 114(3):475–488.

energy is used to transport food to consumers. Thus, a sustainable diet contains foods that are produced in ways that are ecologically neutral.

Numerous natural resources, of two types, are used when growing crops and raising animals for food. *Internal natural resources* are used to produce foods. *External natural resources* are used to move food products from the farm to the consumer. Both internal and external resources generate natural and man-made by-products that affect the environment.

Preserving Internal Natural Resources Is the First Step toward Sustainability

Abuse of any of the natural resources required to grow foods can prevent sustainability. Soil, biodiversity, energy, and water are the key internal natural resources that must be preserved in a sustainable food system. **Table 20.7** describes several of the challenges associated with using internal resources, including land and water, to produce food, and various strategies that can be employed to protect the environment.

Soil

More than 99 percent of the food you eat depends upon the thin layer of topsoil that sits atop the Earth's crust.[122] It's not surprising, then, that numerous experts

TABLE 20.7 Environmental Effects of Food Production

The Effect	The Challenge	How Can We Minimize the Environmental Impact?
Land overuse	Excessive use of farming equipment, overtilling, and livestock overgrazing can all damage soil.	Proper land management and conservation methods of tilling can help preserve the land and replenish soil nutrients.
Soil erosion	Wind and rain can cause more than 1.5 billion tons of nutrient-rich topsoil to be blown and washed away each year. When fertile topsoil is lost, crop yield declines.	Proper crop covering and shielding from wind as well as proper tillage of the soil can dramatically reduce erosion.
Water depletion	Irrigation accounts for 80 percent of water consumption in the United States; hence, excessive irrigation can deplete naturally occurring groundwater.	Precision farming and the conscious reduction of overwatering can help preserve water.
Water runoff	After a rainfall (or watering of crops), the water runoff from farms can spread pesticides from crops and pathogens in animal manure to other fields, surface water, and downfield rivers and streams, contaminating these ecosystems.	Basins can be installed to collect the runoff water to prevent contamination prior to discharge to streams and rivers.
Airborne emissions	Emissions of ammonia and nitrogen (see below) in manure are released into the air. The ammonia released from these airborne emissions can settle on water surfaces, killing fish and encouraging the growth of toxic algae, both of which disrupt the natural ecosystem.	The proper handling of manure (see below) mitigates this problem.
Nitrate production	The production of nitrates from the nitrogen in manure can pollute surface water and groundwater that is used as drinking water.	Proper collection, stockpiling, and disposal of manure to minimize the leaching of nitrates into runoff and groundwater, as proposed in the latest EPA regulations, helps concentrated animal feeding operations (CAFOs) to safely manage manure.

Data from A. H. Harmon and B. L. Gerald. 2007. "Position of the American Dietetic Association: Food and Nutrition Professionals Can Implement Practices to Conserve Natural Resources and Support Ecological Sustainability." *Journal of the American Dietetic Association* 107:1033–1043; Department of Agriculture, Economic Research Service. Updated 2013. *Irrigation and Water Use.* Available at www.ers.usda.gov. Accessed November 2012; U.S. Environmental Protection Agency. 2009. *Ag 101: Beef Production.* Available at www.epa .gov/oecaagct/ag101/beef.html. Accessed January 2010.

are concerned about soil degradation. All land organisms ultimately depend upon the Earth's soil. Organisms within the soil, such as bacteria and other microorganisms, feed on the nutrients provided by animal waste products and decaying plant and animal matter. Plants use nutrients in the soil to grow, and to produce fruit, vegetables, nuts, and seeds. Humans and animals later obtain these same nutrients when they eat the plants and plant products.

Just as all organisms depend on healthy soil for survival, healthy soil depends on the organisms to anchor it in place and to keep it well oxygenated. Plant roots help hold soil in place, which protects it from water and wind erosion, and they also break up the soil to allow the dispersal of oxygen. As topsoil is formed and regenerated from decaying plants, organisms, animals, and rocks, a perpetual web of dependency is formed.

Problems arise when the topsoil can't be regenerated and/or is less fertile. When this happens plants cannot grow, the web is severed, and nourishment for all—the animals, microorganisms, plants, and you—suffers. The natural process of regenerating one inch of nutrient-rich topsoil takes more than 500 years.[123] Improper agricultural practices

Plants draw nutrients from the soil through their roots, which in turn help anchor the soil in place, preventing erosion.

that facilitate erosion of soil faster than it can be regenerated disrupt the entire web and food system.[124] However, research shows that crop rotation and other aspects of organic farming result in less soil erosion than conventional farming methods.[125]

Biodiversity

Achieving and maintaining biodiversity is an important part of a sustainable food system, and the extinction of even one member of the web can have dramatic consequences. Since 2006 the United States has seen the rapid decline in the honeybee population, termed *colony collapse disorder,* which has reduced the pollination, and therefore availability, of fruits, vegetables, and tree nuts (an estimated 30 percent of the foods that you eat need pollination to flourish).[126] Lack of biodiversity among aquatic systems is also a potential problem. More than 60 percent of commercial fisheries are overharvested, endangering the existence of more than 30 percent of native fish in North America.[127] As biodiversity is reduced, the variety and nutritional quality of foods available may also be reduced.

Energy

Research suggests that around 15 percent of the total energy consumption in the United States is used in the production, processing, transport, and preparation of our food.[128] Much of this is consumed as an external resource during processing and transport; however, some is used as an internal resource during the growth and production of food. For example, more energy (as well as land and water) is required to produce a meat-based diet than to produce a plant-based diet.[129] Every pound of animal protein generated from livestock requires approximately 6 pounds of plant protein in the form of feed.[130] Allowing livestock to graze on pasture rather than feeding them a grain diet would cut the amount of fuel needed to produce and transport feed grain in half. Producing chemical fertilizers and pesticides for crops also requires large amounts of fossil fuels.[131] Avoiding these chemicals and using natural fertilizers, such as animal manure, not only cuts the use of fossil fuel, but also can make soil more fertile.[132]

Water

According to the EPA, since the 1950s, the population in America has nearly doubled and our water consumption has more than tripled.[133] The average American uses 100 gallons—about 1,600 full glasses—of water each day.[134] By 2014 it is estimated that nearly every U.S. state will experience water shortages.[135]

This heightened demand for water is a danger not only to the environment but also to your health. You need water to survive; therefore, conserving water now to ensure a healthy supply in the future makes sense. There are several steps you and/or your family can take. Installing water-efficient appliances, including washing machines and dishwashers, helps cut down on water used for daily chores. If all households installed water-efficient appliances, the United States would save more than 3 trillion gallons annually.[136] Low-flow toilets and showerheads can also help save water, as can turning off the tap while washing dishes or brushing your teeth.

Locally Grown Food Requires Fewer External Natural Resources

External natural resources used to move food products from the farm to the consumer can contribute greatly to the environmental costs of food production. For

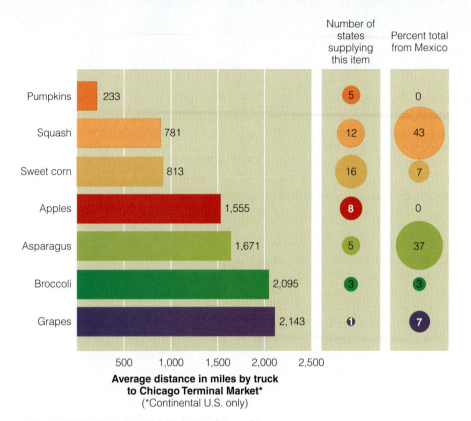

	Number of states supplying this item	Percent total from Mexico
Pumpkins — 233	5	0
Squash — 781	12	43
Sweet corn — 813	16	7
Apples — 1,555	8	0
Asparagus — 1,671	5	37
Broccoli — 2,095	3	3
Grapes — 2,143	1	7

Average distance in miles by truck to Chicago Terminal Market*
(*Continental U.S. only)

▲ **Figure 20.14 How Far Did Your Food Travel?**
You might be surprised to learn just how far some of your food travels to get to your local supermarket.

Adapted from R. Pirog, et al. 2002. "Food, Fuel, and Freeways: An Iowa Perspective on How Far Food Travels, Fuel Usage, and Greenhouse Gas Emissions." Leopold Center for Sustainable Agriculture. Available at www .leopold.iastate.edu/pubs-and-papers/2001-6-food-fuel-freeways.

example, the use of fossil fuels to grow, process, and transport food contributes to the release of carbon dioxide gas emissions. The carbon dioxide and other gases released when fossil fuels are burned for energy are referred to as *greenhouse gases*, as these gases absorb and trap heat in the air and re-radiate that heat downward. It is estimated that global temperatures could increase by 3.5 to 3.9 degrees Fahrenheit by 2100 due to these greenhouse gases.[137]

Carbon emissions associated with the transport of food from farm to supermarket are substantial, and consumers use additional fuel to drive to the supermarket and to prepare food at home. The lettuce, oranges, or cantaloupes that appear in supermarkets during the winter may have traveled 1,400 to 2,400 miles to reach consumers (see **Figure 20.14**).[138] The amount of fossil fuel used to transport that produce all those miles, coupled with the increase in carbon dioxide gas emissions into the air from burning that fuel, has enormous environmental costs. A study conducted in Iowa showed that produce made available from national sources and shipped in from various distances used 4 to 17 times more fuel and released 5 to 17 times more carbon dioxide gas emissions than produce that was locally produced (See Spotlight "Farmers' Markets").[139]

Natural resources aside, these fuel costs are factored into the price of the food, so they affect consumers' financial resources. An estimated 3 percent of your food dollars goes toward the cost of getting food from the farm to your plate, though fuel is used in other aspects of food production as well.[140] And as the price of fuel increases, the price that you pay for food increases. Thus, the farther your food has

Farmers' Markets

According to the USDA, farmers' markets are an integral part of the urban–farm linkage and their growth has continued to rise. The number of farmers' markets nationwide has increased from 1,755 in 1994 to 8,144 in 2013.[1] The USDA estimates that these markets generate approximately $1 billion in consumer spending each year. Most of this growth, a boon to local communities' economies, can be attributed to consumer interest in obtaining fresh products directly from the farm. In many cases consumers have the opportunity to personally interact with the farmer who grows the produce.

The USDA, in conjunction with the Agricultural Marketing Service (AMS), provides technical support to managers of farmers' markets by hosting conferences and training sessions throughout the country to present research findings and information on marketing strategies with agricultural producers, Extension economists, state Department of Agriculture personnel, and other parties interested in supporting direct farm marketing venues. Many farmers' markets accept WIC (Women, Infants, and Children) program food voucher coupons and provide nutrition education and food preparation demonstrations in conjunction with local and state health departments.

The USDA's AMS has also formed the Farmers Market Consortium, which is a public/private sector partnership dedicated to helping farmers' markets by sharing information about funding and resources available to them. The consortium publishes a Farmers Market Resource Guide that provides a centralized repository of information about federal and private resources that support farmers' markets. The USDA also publishes a National Farmers Market Directory that organizes farmers' markets by state and includes contact information, dates, and times of operation.

Produce sold at farmers' markets is available according to the season; although adapting to eating seasonally can be an adjustment, it is one that is more environmentally friendly because produce is not transported long distances for sale.

Farmers' markets vary by what can be sold but generally a product must be grown or raised or made (baked, canned, and so on) by the farm selling it. "Local" is also usually understood to mean food that comes from independent farmers and producers rather than from large corporations.

Costs at farmers' markets vary and sometimes produce may be more expensive than at a grocery store. Food bought in the conventional system where pesticides are used and the food is transported thousands of miles and stored in warehouses is heavily subsidized at all stages of production and produces costs not reflected in the purchase price. These costs include depleted fossil fuel reserves for fertilizer, cultivation, and transportation; water pollution from pesticide runoff; and the contribution of emissions to global warming.

Some products sold at farmers' markets are certified organic, while others use integrated pest management (IPM) or use organic methods but are not USDA certified. Farmers sell directly to consumers for a number of reasons and those who do generally care for their land and use sustainable growing practices to keep it healthy.

Farmers' markets are good for the local economy, the health of the land, and the health of the people. The USDA's farmers' market locator tells you where to find a farmers' market near you: http://search.ams.usda.gov/farmersmarkets.

Reference

1. USDA. Agricultural Marketing Service. Updated 2014. *Farmers Markets and Direct-to-Consumer Marketing*. Available at www.ams.usda.gov. Accessed July 2014.

Farmers' markets provide fresh produce to the consumer.

to travel, the more resources it uses, which not only has a negative effect on the environment, but also is a drain on your wallet.

Because of the environmental and financial costs of shipping foods over long distances, some people are becoming **locavores.** Locavores try to buy from local farms, farmers' markets, and roadside stands rather than supermarkets. They may have difficulty consuming 100 percent of their diet from local sources year round. For example, although Vermonters have access to fresh dairy foods 365 days a year, robust fruit and vegetable crops are hard to find under a foot of snow in the dead of winter. Depending on where they live, locavores may have to supplement with foods from the supermarket. Farmers' markets are an important resource for people who value food grown locally.

Many large supermarkets now sell locally grown produce. This combining of locally grown foods with conventionally grown foods allows consumers to do "one-stop shopping" rather than have to drive to farmers' markets, farm stands, or **community-supported agriculture (CSA)** pickups in addition to the supermarket. Corporate America is also making it easier to eat locally. Some large corporations and industrial complexes have weekly farmers' markets on their premises. Employees can shop for locally grown foods during the day and head home with the fixings for dinner.[141] The USDA recently awarded more than $5 million in grants to support local food connections between farmers and consumers, even in large cities, with its "Know Your Farmer, Know Your Food" initiative.[142]

Some individuals wrongfully assume that locally grown food is the same as sustainably grown food. A *sustainable diet* contains foods that meet your nutrient and health needs but can be produced for a long time without negatively impacting the environment.[143] Buying food from small local farms doesn't guarantee that the foods were grown in a sustainable way, nor does being from a distant farm mean that those farmers didn't practice sustainable agriculture.

LO 20.5: THE TAKE-HOME MESSAGE A sustainable food system is one that will survive over the long term. To maintain a sustainable food system, the natural resources used to produce, transport, and distribute the food are conserved instead of being destroyed or depleted. Minimal natural resources such as soil and water are depleted to grow the food and minimal energy is used to transport food to consumers. A sustainable diet contains foods that are produced in a way that is ecologically neutral. Natural resources are used internally to produce foods and externally to move foods from producers to consumers. Buying locally grown food decreases the amount of fuel needed to transport food and is one way to reduce the use of external natural resources in food systems.

locavore A person who eats locally grown food whenever possible.

community-supported agriculture (CSA) An arrangement where individuals pay a fee to support a local farm, and in exchange receive a weekly or biweekly box of fresh produce from the farm.

Is Genetically Engineered Food Safe?

LO 20.6 Compare the benefits and risks of the use of biotechnology in our current food system.

Historically, farmers have crossbred plants by trial and error, crossing two plants to produce a hybrid offspring with the desired combination of characteristics. For example, if one tree produced large apples with thinner skins, and another produced smaller, sour apples with thicker skins, an ancient apple farmer might have bred the two in the hope of producing a tree with large, fleshy, hardy fruit. This process is called **plant breeding.** Today's apples are an example of a plant food that has resulted from generations of deliberate crossbreeding. For thousands of years, humans crossbred different versions of the apple tree to produce more desirable offspring. The initial hybrids contain qualities from both parents, and it usually takes dozens of additional crosses and many years to separate the desirable traits from the less desirable ones. The ultimate result, though, is that modern apples look nothing like their small, sour ancestors.

plant breeding A type of biotechnology in which two plants are crossbred to produce offspring with desired traits from both.

biotechnology The manipulation of living organisms or their components to develop or manufacture useful products.

genome The total genetic information of an organism stored in the DNA of its chromosomes.

genetic engineering (GE) A biological technique that isolates and manipulates the genes of organisms to produce a targeted, modified product.

genetically modified organisms (GMOs) Organisms that have been genetically engineered to contain both original and foreign genes.

The apples of today are larger and sweeter than their ancestors, thanks to hundreds of years of selective breeding.

In the last two centuries, as scientists understood more about the workings of DNA and how to manipulate it, the process of breeding for particular characteristics has become faster and more controlled. Today, scientists use **biotechnology** to modify the actual **genomes** of plants and animals to create desired characteristics with great precision. American farmers routinely use selectively bred, genetically modified plants to create disease-resistant crops that produce larger, hardier fruits and vegetables and increase overall crop yields. The production of foods using plant or animal products that have been modified genetically helps to keep food costs low and availability high. In fact, the majority of fruits and vegetables on the market today are a product of genetic modification.[144]

Genetic Engineering Is the Latest Form of Biotechnology

Genetic engineering (GE) allows scientists to alter the genetic makeup of an organism by manipulating DNA sequences. In genetic engineering, or bioengineering, an exact gene or genes from the DNA sequence of an organism are isolated and inserted into the DNA of another species of organism to create the genetically modified product (**Figure 20.15**).

This cutting and splicing of genes into the genome of another cell is called recombinant DNA technology. Organisms that have been genetically engineered to contain both original and foreign genes are called **genetically modified organisms (GMOs).** These GMOs are used to grow genetically engineered (GE) plants that produce GE foods.

Farmers in the United States have adopted genetically engineered crops widely since their introduction in 1996. Soybeans and cotton genetically engineered with herbicide-resistant traits have been the most widely accepted crops. According to the USDA's National Agricultural Statistics Service (NASS), in 2013, 90 percent of the corn, 93 percent of the soybeans, and 90 percent of the cotton planted in the United States were genetically engineered varieties.[145]

Proponents Believe Genetic Engineering Can Produce More and Better Foods

Some people believe that GMOs may be part of the solution to the problem

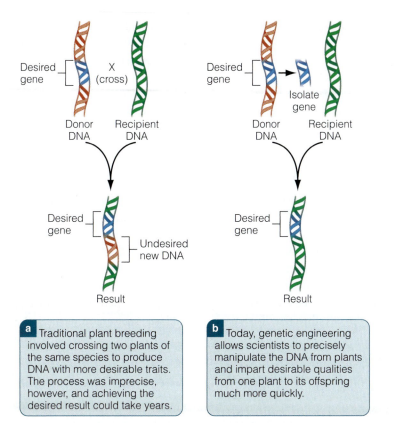

Desired gene — X (cross)

Donor DNA — Recipient DNA

Desired gene

Undesired new DNA

Result

Desired gene — Isolate gene

Donor DNA — Recipient DNA

Desired gene

Result

a Traditional plant breeding involved crossing two plants of the same species to produce DNA with more desirable traits. The process was imprecise, however, and achieving the desired result could take years.

b Today, genetic engineering allows scientists to precisely manipulate the DNA from plants and impart desirable qualities from one plant to its offspring much more quickly.

▲ **Figure 20.15 Plant Breeding versus Genetic Engineering**

of meeting the world population's need for food with limited resources. GMOs may help to increase the yield of crops, especially in countries that struggle to produce food, and provide options for improving the quality and quantity of foods available year round. Genetic engineering may also create new uses for plants in industries such as pharmaceuticals and manufacturing.

▲ **Figure 20.16 European Corn Borer Caterpillar**
Bt corn has been genetically engineered to produce a protein that is toxic to the larva of the European corn borer, the most damaging insect pest of corn in North America.

The original purpose of GE plants was to reduce the amount of pesticides used on food crops by engineering the plants themselves to be more resistant to pests. This would benefit both the health of consumers and the environment.[146] For example, the bacterium *Bacillus thuringiensis* (*Bt*), which is found naturally in soil, produces a toxin that is poisonous to certain pests but not to humans or animals. When the gene for this toxin is inserted into a crop plant, the plant becomes resistant to these pests.[147] Some corn crops in the United States contain the *Bt* gene, which makes them resistant to some insect pests (see **Figure 20.16**). Because chemical insecticides are not necessary, many benign insects are spared, and insect **biodiversity** is retained. Almost 15 percent of corn and cotton

harvested in the United States in 2012 were varieties genetically engineered to contain the *Bt* gene.[148]

Another goal of the first-generation GE products was to use this technology to improve a crop's tolerance to herbicides. With an herbicide-resistant version of a desired crop, a farmer can spray herbicide over a field to kill a variety of weeds without harming the crop.[149] According to the USDA, approximately 93 percent of soybeans planted in 2013 were genetically modified to be herbicide resistant.[150]

The second generation of GE products to hit the market was designed for increased shelf life and improved nutrient composition.[151] Tomatoes that stay firm and ripe longer were among the first genetically engineered foods to be sold to consumers. An example of genetically altering a plant to improve its nutrient profile is "golden rice." This rice has gene segments from a bacterium and a daffodil that encode the rice grain to make beta-carotene and to concentrate the levels of iron (see **Figure 20.17**). If planted by farmers and accepted by consumers in southeast Asia, "golden rice" could help eliminate the epidemic of vitamin A and iron deficiency in Asia and worldwide.[152] Another example is genetically modified, high-oleic-acid soybeans, which produce oil that is less prone to becoming rancid and thus is more stable when used for frying foods.

Genetic research has progressed to third-generation GE products that hold promise in the pharmaceutical, environmental, and industrial arenas. In fact, the first GE product created for commercial use was human insulin (needed by diabetics) produced by genetically engineered *E. coli* bacteria.[153] Plants can also be genetically modified

biodiversity The variability among living organisms on the Earth, including the variability within and between species and within and between ecosystems.

▲ **Figure 20.17 Genetically Engineered Golden Rice**
"Golden rice" is rich in both beta-carotene and iron, and is a product of genetic engineering.

to create substances with numerous medical uses, such as vaccines, antibiotics, anticlotting drugs, hormones, and substitutes for certain blood substances.[154] Scientists are currently experimenting with the concept of "growing" vaccines for measles, hepatitis B, and norovirus in produce.[155]

Some Consumers Have Concerns about GE Foods

Some consumers have concerns about the long-term safety of consuming GMOs and effects on the environment, including the introduction of allergens and toxins into foods, disruption of the ecosystem, and introduction of resistant weeds, as well as ethical dilemmas related to the splicing of genes from one organism into another.[156] A study at Cornell University in the late 1990s raised concerns that when milkweed leaves, which are the sole diet of monarch caterpillars, were heavily dusted with pollen from *Bt* corn, and then *exclusively* fed to monarch butterfly caterpillars, many of them died.[157] Critics of this finding said that this experiment didn't mimic a "real-life" setting. Most milkweed doesn't grow close enough to cornfields to collect significant amounts of corn pollen, especially since this heavy pollen typically doesn't travel far from its place of origin. Hence, it is unlikely that monarch caterpillars would feed primarily on milkweed that contains such an enormous amount of GE corn pollen. After conducting extensive research

coordinated by the USDA, researchers concluded that the monarch butterflies' exposure to GE corn pollen in a natural setting is minimal and so is not likely to be dangerous to these butterflies.[158, 159]

One significant concern consumers have about genetic engineering is the potential introduction of a food allergen into a GE product. Under the FDA's new biotech policy, companies must tell consumers on the food label when a product includes a gene from one of the common allergy-causing foods, unless it can show that the protein produced by the added gene does not cause allergies.[160] The following eight foods account for 90 percent of all food allergies: milk, eggs, peanuts, tree nuts, fish, shellfish, soy, and wheat.[161] The effects of introducing genes from these foods into other products should be carefully assessed before these products are released for human consumption.

Other concerns have arisen about the production of plant toxins, changes in the nutrient content and substances in foods, and the production of unsafe animal feed. **Table 20.8** lists the regulations the FDA has put in place to address these issues.

TABLE 20.8 Concerns and Regulations for GE Foods

Concern	FDA Regulation
Undesirable genetic modification	To avoid the creation of undesirable products, all genes used must not have prior evidence of encoding any harmful substances. The genes must also be stably inserted into the plant in order to avoid any rearranging of genetic information that would produce an undesirable substance.
Introduction of allergens	GE foods must be monitored for food allergens. Protein encoded from common allergen food sources (such as milk, eggs, fish, tree nuts, and legumes) should be presumed to be allergens and should be labeled as such on the GE food.
Excessive level of toxins	GE foods should not contain natural toxins at levels that are higher than those found naturally in plants.
Changes in nutrients	All GE foods should be monitored to assess unintentional changes in the nutrient levels in the plants and their ability to be utilized in the human body as compared with their conventional counterparts.
Creation of new substances	If the genes that are introduced into plants encode substances that are different in structure and function than those normally found in foods, these substances would need to be approved by the FDA, as would any other food additive. However, if these substances are GRAS or "substantially equivalent" to substances that already exist in foods, they do not need the FDA's premarket approval.
Unsafe animal feeds	Because a single plant type may be the predominant food source in an animal feed, all GE animal feeds must meet the same strict safety standards that are in place for food that is grown for humans.

Source: FDA. 2013. *Biotechnology: Genetically Engineered Plants for Food and Feed.* Available at www.fda.gov.

GE Foods Are Highly Regulated in the United States

Genetic engineering is more tightly regulated in the United States than any other technology. GE foods in the United States are regulated by the same three government agencies that regulate pesticides: the FDA, USDA, and EPA. The FDA ensures that GE foods are safe to eat and labeled if they contain a suspected allergen. The USDA ensures that the plants are safe to grow, while the EPA makes certain that the gene for any pesticide, such as that for *Bt* toxin, inserted into a plant is safe and won't have adverse environmental effects. Though these agencies work together to ensure the safety of GE foods, the FDA has the overall authority to remove any GE food that doesn't meet the same high safety standards that are set for its conventionally grown equivalent.[162]

The FDA must review and approve all GE products before they are allowed on the market. As part of this process, the FDA mandates that the developers of GE foods conduct extensive tests to ensure the safety of those foods. After testing is completed, the developer is required to send the FDA a report of the information pertaining to the product. The FDA reviews the documentation and seeks additional information as warranted. Once all FDA guidelines are satisfied, the food is considered safe and is allowed to enter the market. More than 50 GE foods, including canola oil, corn, cottonseed oil, potatoes, soybeans, squash, and tomatoes, have been evaluated by the FDA and are considered as safe as their conventional counterparts.[163] The FDA has yet to approve any GE meat or fish for human consumption, but at least one company has developed a GE salmon that grows faster than normal.[164]

Most consumers want genetically engineered foods to be labeled; however, the FDA has concluded that because there isn't any scientific evidence that GE foods differ from their conventionally grown counterparts, labeling isn't warranted.[165] The American Medical Association and the Society of Toxicology share this position.[166, 167] Canada follows the United States in this regard. If a manufacturer chooses to voluntarily label a product it may state that the product has been "genetically engineered." Mandatory labeling of GE foods is required in other countries across the world, including in the European Union, Japan, Australia, and New Zealand.[168]

Consumer acceptance of GE foods is increasing as a result of such foods becoming more common, their putative health benefits, and improved quality, but some consumers remain skeptical. In a survey of approximately 3,025 American adults conducted in October 2010, 60 percent said they were willing to eat genetically modified fruits, vegetables, and grain, but less than 40 percent said they were willing to eat genetically modified meat and fish. Over 90 percent of consumers polled said they felt that all genetically modified foods sold in the United States should be labeled.[169] Though many questions remain as to the long-term safety and impact of introducing GE foods into the world's food supply, GMOs offer attractive options for feeding the world's population now and in the future.

LO 20.6: THE TAKE-HOME MESSAGE

Traditional plant breeding and modern genetic engineering are types of biotechnology that alter an organism's genetic makeup to create a new plant or animal with more desirable traits. Many crops including corn, soybeans, and potatoes are currently available in the United States and are commonly used as ingredients in processed foods. Genetically engineered crops can be developed to be pest resistant, to provide additional nutrients, and to enhance flavor and quality. GE products are heavily regulated to minimize undesirable genetic modifications, the introduction of disease, and unfavorable nutrient changes in food, as well as to reduce the risk of creating potential food allergens, toxins, and unsafe feed for animals. Labeling is not currently mandatory for GE foods in the United States.

Visual Chapter Summary

LO 20.1 Foodborne Illness Is Caused by Pathogens and Toxins

Pathogens (viruses, bacteria, molds, parasites, and prions) are the primary causes of foodborne infection. Toxins produced by pathogens or present in food, either naturally or through chemical contamination, can cause foodborne intoxication. Noroviruses are the single largest cause of foodborne illness in the United States. The most common bacteria that cause foodborne illness are *Salmonella*, *Clostridium perfringens*, *Campylobacter,* and *Staphylococcus aureus.* Marine toxins and chemical contaminants, such as PCBs and methylmercury, can bioaccumulate to toxic levels in large fish. The elderly, children, pregnant women, and those with compromised immune systems are at higher risk of contracting foodborne illness and suffering complications.

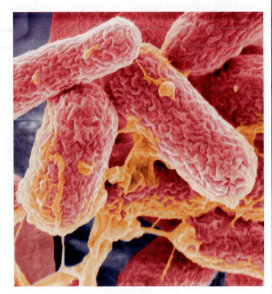

LO 20.2 Proper Food Handling Can Prevent Foodborne Illness

Proper food handling techniques during four critical steps—cleaning, combating cross-contamination, cooking, and chilling—can help reduce the risk of foodborne illness. Foodborne bacteria multiply most rapidly in temperatures between 40°F and 140°F (5°C to 60°C), a range known as the danger zone. Cold foods should be stored and served below 40°F, and hot foods must be kept above 140°F. The only sure way to tell if a food has reached a safe temperature is to measure it using a kitchen thermometer. Extra caution is needed when traveling abroad, particularly in developing countries, to avoid foodborne illness. As a general guideline to avoid foodborne illness while traveling, do not eat raw produce unless you wash and peel it first, and avoid drinking tap water or using ice made from tap water unless the water is boiled or treated with iodine or chlorine first.

LO 20.3 Everyone Plays a Role in Protecting Our Food Supply

Everyone, from the farmer to the consumer, plays an important role in food safety. Through the coordinated effort of the Food Safety Initiative, numerous U.S. government agencies work together to safeguard America's food supply against foodborne illness. Hazard Analysis and Critical Control Point (HACCP) procedures are used by both the FDA and USDA to identify and control foodborne hazards that occur in all stages of the food system. Food manufacturers use techniques such as pasteurization, canning, and irradiation to help keep food safe for extended periods of time. Food irradiation exposes a food item to a radiant energy source that kills or greatly reduces some pathogens. Food product dating is not a measure of food safety, but can be used to determine peak quality. The EPA monitors and regulates the safety of the water supply.

LO 20.4 Food Additives, Chemical Enhancers, and Pesticides Play a Role in Food Production and Safety

Food additives are used as preservatives, antioxidants, flavoring, coloring, and leavening agents; to maintain a food's consistency; and to add nutrients. Pesticides are substances that allow crop plants to flourish by killing or repelling damaging pests. Natural biopesticides and antimicrobials are less toxic than chemical pesticides such as organophosphates. Integrated pest management (IPM) is used by many farmers and is designed to use the most economical methods to control pests with the least risk of harm to the consumer, the crops, and the environment. The use of additives is regulated by the FDA and the use of pesticides is regulated by the FDA along with the EPA and USDA. Hormones and antibiotics are sometimes provided to food-producing animals to increase the yield of product. The FDA says the use of hormones and antibiotics is safe at its approved levels. Foods with the USDA organic seal are grown without the use of most synthetic pesticides, synthetic fertilizers, bioengineering, or irradiation. Only antibiotic-free or growth hormone–free animals can be used to produce organic meat, poultry, eggs, and dairy foods.

LO 20.5 A Sustainable Food System Conserves Natural Resources

A sustainable food system is one that can be maintained indefinitely because it conserves and protects natural resources, empowers social responsibility, and is economically viable. Food systems are impacted by social, political, economic, and environmental factors and depend on human and natural resources. Soil, biodiversity, energy, and water are key natural resources that must be preserved. Buying locally grown food decreases the amount of fuel needed to transport food and is one way to reduce the use of external natural resources in food systems.

LO 20.6 Biotechnology Is Used to Alter the Genetic Makeup of Foods

Biotechnology, such as plant breeding and genetic engineering, is the application of biological techniques to alter the genetic makeup of living cells in order to create a desired trait in an organism. Plant breeding creates disease-resistant crops and increases the yield of crops. Genetic engineering is a more precise technique in which a specific gene or genes are inserted into the DNA of another cell to create a genetically modified product. Genetic engineering is done to improve crop yields, reduce the use of pesticides, and in some cases enhance the nutritional value of foods. Genetically engineered foods are heavily regulated in the United States, but some consumers are concerned about the long-term effects of consuming these products. More and longer-term studies examining the effects of genetically engineered foods are needed.

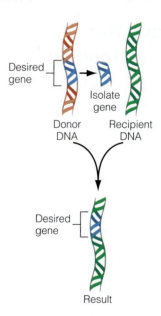

Terms to Know

- foodborne illness
- pathogens
- toxins
- fecal-to-oral transmission
- norovirus
- virus
- host
- bacteria
- hemolytic uremic syndrome
- molds
- parasites
- prion
- marine toxins
- scombrotoxic fish poisoning
- ciguatera poisoning
- bioaccumulate
- neurotoxins
- paralytic shellfish poisoning
- solanine

- polychlorinated biphenyls (PCBs)
- cross-contaminate
- myoglobin
- danger zone
- traveler's diarrhea
- food Safety Initiative (FSI)
- DNA fingerprinting
- farm-to-table continuum
- food preservation
- pasteurization
- canning
- spores
- modified atmosphere packaging (MAP)
- high-pressure processing (HPP)
- irradiation
- closed (or coded) dating
- open dating
- food additives

- preservatives
- nitrites and nitrates
- generally recognized as safe (GRAS)
- sulfites
- monosodium glutamate (MSG)
- MSG symptom complex
- prior-sanctioned
- DeLaney Clause
- intentional food additives
- unintentional food additives
- bovine growth hormone (BGH)
- recombinant bovine somatotropin (rbST)
- antibiotics
- antibiotic-resistant bacteria
- pesticides
- herbicides
- insecticides

- antimicrobials
- fungicides
- rodenticides
- organophosphates
- risk assessment
- acceptable tolerance levels
- integrated pest management (IPM)
- organic
- food system
- sustainable
- locavores
- community-supported agriculture (CSA)
- plant breeding
- biotechnology
- genomes
- genetic engineering
- genetically modified organisms (GMOs)
- biodiversity

MasteringNutrition™

To hear an MP3 chapter review, scan here or visit the Study Area in MasteringNutrition.

Check Your Understanding

1. Which of the following produce toxins that may cause foodborne illness?
   a. parasites
   b. viruses
   c. bacteria
   d. food additives
2. Which of the following pathogens is the most common cause of foodborne infection in the United States?
   a. *Clostridium botulinum*
   b. norovirus
   c. *Trichinella spiralis*
   d. *Escherichia coli* O157:H7
3. At what temperature, known as the danger zone, do bacteria readily thrive and multiply?
   a. any temperature above 40°F
   b. between 20°F and 120°F

   c. between 40°F and 140°F
   d. any temperature below 140°F
4. Which of the following food additives is on the FDA's GRAS list, is often added to enhance the flavor of savory foods, and causes adverse reactions among some individuals?
   a. nitrites
   b. sulfites
   c. monosodium glutamate
   d. vitamin E
5. Which of the following is the most likely source of mercury intoxication?
   a. green potatoes
   b. sardines
   c. large predatory fish
   d. unpasteurized milk
6. Which two government agencies oversee the safety of the majority of foods in the United States?
   a. United States Department of Agriculture (USDA) and Environmental Protection Agency (EPA)
   b. Centers for Disease Control and Prevention (CDC) and USDA
   c. USDA and Food and Drug Administration (FDA)
   d. FDA and EPA

7. Which of the following sets of four steps is part of the Fight BAC! campaign?
   a. cutting, cleaning, chopping, and chilling
   b. cleaning, combating cross-contamination, cutting, and chilling
   c. clearing, combating cross-contamination, cutting, and chilling
   d. cleaning, combating cross-contamination, cooking, and chilling
8. Which of the following preservation techniques destroys specific food-borne pathogens by breaking up the cells' DNA?
   a. irradiation
   b. pasteurization
   c. canning
   d. high-pressure processing
9. Which of the following is a justified reason for buying food grown and produced locally?
   a. Locally grown food is more nutrient dense than non–locally grown food.
   b. Locally grown foods are organic foods.

c. Locally grown foods are free from pesticides.

d. Locally grown foods use fewer natural resources than do non–locally grown foods.

10. A frozen chicken enchilada that has the USDA Organic seal on its label means which of the following?
   a. One hundred percent of the ingredients in the product are organic.
   b. No pesticides were used to grow the corn from which the tortillas were made.
   c. The chickens in the enchilada were grown without using antibiotics or growth hormones.
   d. The organic enchilada is better for you because it is nutritionally superior to a nonorganic chicken enchilada.

Answers

1. (c) Bacteria are the only pathogens that produce toxins and cause illness due to foodborne intoxication. Some but not all parasites, viruses, and bacteria cause illness due to foodborne infection. Food additives are common in food and should not cause illness. Food additives are either approved by the FDA prior to their use or have GRAS or prior-sanctioned status based on a history of safe consumption.

2. (b) Half of all foodborne illness is caused by infection due to the norovirus. Illnesses due to *Clostridium botulinum*, *Trichinella spiralis*, and *Escherichia coli* O157:H7 are much less common. *Clostridium botulinum* is a bacterium that causes foodborne intoxication, *Trichinella spiralis* is a parasite, and *Escherichia coli* O157:H7 is a bacterium that causes infection.

3. (c) Bacteria thrive and multiply best between the temperatures of 40°F and 140°F. Bacteria can grow or multiply on any living or nonliving surface or object, but also need a source of nutrients, moisture, time, and a pH above about 4.6 to thrive.

4. (c) Monosodium glutamate is a flavor enhancer and has GRAS status, but some people, including those with asthma, may experience symptoms such as numbness, a burning sensation, facial pressure or tightness, chest pain, and rapid heart beat after consuming MSG. Nitrites and sulfites and vitamin E are additives that help preserve food.

5. (c) Large predatory fish are the most common source of methylmercury. Predatory fish bioaccumulate methylmercury at high levels by absorbing it from polluted water and eating smaller fish that also contain it. Potatoes turn green after having been exposed to sunlight and may contain a toxin known as solanine. Unpasteurized milk may be a source of pathogens but is not a likely source of mercury.

6. (c) The USDA and FDA oversee the safety of most foods in the United States. Neither the CDC nor the EPA has direct regulatory oversight of the food supply.

7. (d) To prevent foodborne illness, it's important to employ proper food handling strategies when cleaning, combating cross-contamination, cooking, and chilling the foods in your meal.

8. (a) Irradiation involves using radiation to damage the DNA of pathogens. Pasteurization and canning both use high temperatures to kill pathogens, while high-pressure processing employs pulses of high pressure.

9. (d) Locally grown food requires fewer external natural resources in the form of fossil fuels from farm to your fork. However, just because a food is grown locally does not necessarily mean that it is grown organically, free from pesticides, or more nutrient dense than foods that are grown further from your home.

10. (c) The USDA Organic seal indicates that 95 percent of the ingredients in a food are grown organically and that food-producing animals used in the product were grown without the use of hormones or antibiotics. Some, but not all, pesticides may be used by organic farmers. There is little evidence that organically grown foods are more nutritious or safer for you than foods grown using conventional methods.

Answers to True or False?

1. **False.** A food may contain disease-causing bacteria or other contaminants, yet look and smell perfectly fine.

2. **False.** Hand sanitizer kills most disease-causing pathogens, as do soap and water. It is not necessary to wash your hands with soap and water if you use hand sanitizer.

3. **True.** A kitchen sponge provides the perfect medium for bacterial growth: moisture, nutrients, and room temperature.

4. **False.** Freezing doesn't kill bacteria but puts them in a dormant state. Once thawed, some bacteria can continue to grow and reproduce.

5. **False.** Leftovers should be thrown out if they're not consumed within three to five days.

6. **False.** Package dates refer to food quality, not safety.

7. **False.** The FDA deems food additives safe if they present a "negligible risk" of cancer to human beings with lifetime use.

8. **True.** A good scrub with cold, running water and a vegetable brush can remove most pesticide residue, and many germs, from produce.

9. **False.** Some synthetic pesticides have been approved for use on organic crops.

10. **True.** Corn, potatoes, and soybeans have been genetically modified to include a bacterial gene that makes them more resistant to insects since the 1990s. Labeling of genetically engineered foods is not mandatory in the United States, but many products contain genetically modified ingredients.

Web Resources

- For food safety education, visit www.fightbac.org
- For foodborne illness fact sheets, visit www.fsis.usda.gov/fact_sheets/ Foodborne_Illness_&_Disease_ Fact_Sheets/index.asp
- For more information on organic foods, visit www.ams.usda.gov/nop/ indexIE.htm
- For information on biotechnology, visit www.fda.gov/Food/ Biotechnology/default.htm

References

1. Centers for Disease Control and Prevention. Updated 2014. *CDC Estimates of Foodborne Illness in the United States.* Available at www.cdc.gov/foodborneburden. Accessed May 2014.
2. Ibid.
3. Centers for Disease Control and Prevention. Updated 2010. *Staphylococcal Food Poisoning.* Available at www.cdc.gov/nczved/ divisions/dfbmd/diseases/staphylococcal/. Accessed May 2014.
4. Center for Food Safety and Applied Nutrition. Updated 2013. *Preventive Control Measures for Fresh & Fresh-Cut Produce: Chapter IV: Outbreaks Associated with Fresh and Fresh-Cut Produce. Incidence, Growth, and Survival of Pathogens in Fresh and Fresh-Cut Produce.* Available at www.fda .gov/Food/ScienceResearch/ResearchAreas/ SafePracticesforFoodProcesses/ucm091265 .htm. Accessed July 2014.
5. Centers for Disease Control and Prevention. 2012. *Foodborne Illness, Foodborne Disease, (Sometimes Called "Food Poisoning").* Available at www.cdc.gov/foodsafety/facts .html. Accessed November 2012.
6. Centers for Disease Control and Prevention. 2011. *CDC Estimates of Foodborne Illness in the United States.*
7. Ibid.
8. Center for Food Safety and Applied Nutrition. Updated 2011. *Food Safety A to Z Reference Guide: U-V-W: Virus.* Available at www.fda.gov/Food/ ResourcesForYou/StudentsTeachers/ ScienceandTheFoodSupply/ucm215850 .htm. Accessed November 2012.
9. Sears, C. L. 2005. A Dynamic Partnership: Celebrating Our Gut Flora. *Anaerobe* 11:247–251.
10. Karlsson, F., V. Tremaroli, J. Nielsen, and F. Backhed. 2013. Assessing the Human Gut Microbiota in Metabolic Diseases. *Diabetes* 62(10):3341–3349.
11. Centers for Disease Control and Prevention. 2011. *CDC Estimates of Foodborne Illness in the United States.*

12. Centers for Disease Control and Prevention. Updated 2012. *E. coli (Escherichia coli).* Available at www.cdc .gov/ecoli/general/index.html. Accessed November 2012.
13. United States Department of Agriculture. Modified 2013. *Fact Sheet: Molds on Foods: Are They Dangerous?* Available at www.fsis .usda.gov. Accessed July 2014.
14. Food Safety and Inspection Service. Modified 2013. *Fact Sheet: Parasites and Foodborne Illness.* Available at www.fsis .usda.gov. Accessed July 2014.
15. Albrecht, J. A., and D. Nagy-Nero. 2009. Position of the American Dietetic Association: Food and Water Safety. *Journal of the American Dietetic Association* 109:1449–1460.
16. U.S. Department of Agriculture. 2012. *Hot Issues: BSE.* Available at www.aphis.usda .gov/animal_health/animal_diseases/bse/ index.shtml. Accessed November 2012.
17. Centers for Disease Control and Prevention. 2013. *BSE (Bovine Spongiform Encephalopathy, or Mad Cow Disease).* Available at www.cdc.gov. Accessed July 2014.
18. USDA. 2012. *Statement by USDA Chief Veterinary Officer John Clifford Regarding a Detection of Bovine Spongiform Encephalopathy (BSE) in the United States.* Release No. 0132.12, April 24, 2012. Available at www .usda.gov/wps/portal/usda/usdahome? contentidonly=true&conten tid=2012/04/0132.xml. Accessed July 2014.
19. United States Department of Agriculture. 2013. Statement from Agriculture Secretary Tom Vilsack Regarding World Organization for Animal Health (OIE) Upgrade of United States' BSE Risk Status. Statement Release no. 0106.13. Available at www.usda.gov/wps/portal/usda/ usdahome?contentid=2013/05/0106 .xml&contentidonly=true. Accessed May 2014.
20. Centers for Disease Control and Prevention. 2005. *Marine Toxins.* Available at www .cdc.gov/ncidod/dbmd/diseaseinfo/ marinetoxins_g.htm. Accessed July 2014.
21. Ibid.
22. Ibid.
23. Ibid.
24. National Toxicology Program, Department of Health and Human Services. 2005. *Executive Summary of Chaconine and Solanine.* Available at http://ntp.niehs.nih.gov. Accessed August 2012.
25. U.S. Environmental Protection Agency. 2012. *Polychlorinated Biphenyls (PCBs).* Available at www.epa.gov/epawaste/ hazard/tsd/pcbs/pubs/about.htm. Accessed November 2012.
26. Agency for Toxic Substances and Disease Registry. Updated 2014. *ToxFAQs™ for Polychlorinated Biphenyls (PCBs).* Available at www.atsdr.cdc.gov. Accessed July 2014.
27. U.S. Environmental Protection Agency. Updated 2013. *Polychlorinated Biphenyls*

(PCBs). Available at www.epa.gov. Accessed July 2014.
28. Ibid.
29. Environmental Protection Agency. 2006. *Consumer Fact Sheet on PCBs.* Available at http://water.epa.gov. Accessed July 2014.
30. Rice, K. M., E. M. Walker, Jr., M. Wu, C. Gillette, and E. R. Blough. 2014. Environmental Mercury and Its Toxic Effects. *Journal of Preventative Medicine & Public Health* 47(2):74–83.
31. Department of Health and Human Services and Environmental Protection Agency. 2004. *What You Need to Know about Mercury in Fish and Shellfish.* Available at www.fda.gov. Accessed July 2014.
32. Administration on Aging, U.S. Department of Health and Human Services. 2013. *A Profile of Older Americans 2013.* Available at www.aoa.gov. Accessed July 2014.
33. Albrecht, et al. 2009. Position of the American Dietetic Association: Food and Water Safety.
34. Buzby, J. C. 2003. Older Adults at Risk of Complications from Microbial Foodborne Illness. *FoodReview* 25:30–35.
35. United States Department of Agriculture Food Safety and Inspection Service. 2011. *Fact Sheets: Safe Food Handling.* Available at www.fsis.usda.gov/fact_sheets/danger_zone/ index.asp. Accessed June 2012.
36. USFDA. 2007. *Teacher's Guide for Middle Level Science Classrooms. Science and Our Food Supply.* Available at www.fda.gov/ food/resourcesforyou/studentsteachers/ scienceandthefoodsupply/ucm181842 .htm#main. Accessed August 2012.
37. Partnership for Food Safety Education. 2010. *Safe Food Handling: The Core Four Practices.* Available at www.fightbac.org/safe-food-handling. Accessed July 2014.
38. Center for Food Safety and Applied Nutrition. 2007. *Food Safety A to Z Reference Guide: Handwashing.* Available at www.fda .gov. Accessed November 2012.
39. Food Safety and Inspection Service. 2003. *The Food Safety Educator: Special Conference Issue: Thinking Globally, Working Locally.* Available at www.fsis.usda.gov/OA/educator/ educator8-1.htm. Accessed July 2014.
40. CDC. 2012. *Handwashing: Clean Hands Save Lives.* Available at www.cdc.gov/handwashing. Accessed November 2012.
41. BBC News. 2004. *Lifting the Lid on Computer Filth.* Available at http://news.bbc .co.uk/2/hi/health/3505414.stm. Accessed November 2012.
42. Food Safety and Inspection Service. 2003. *The Food Safety Educator.*
43. Sharma, M., J. Eastridge, and C. Mudd. 2009. Effective Household Disinfection Methods of Kitchen Sponges. *Food Control* 20(3):310–313[0].
44. Agriculture Research Service, Food Safety and Inspection Service. 1998. *Premature Browning of Cooked Ground Beef.* Available at www.fsis.usda.gov/OPHS/prebrown.htm. Accessed July 2014.

45. Food Safety and Inspection Service. Modified 2013. *The Color of Meat and Poultry.* Available at www.fsis.usda.gov. Accessed July 2014.

46. Food and Drug Administration. 2005. *Food Code.* Available at www.fda.gov/Food/FoodSafety/RetailFoodProtection/FoodCode/default.htm. Accessed November 2012.

47. Food Safety and Inspection Service. Modified 2013. *How Temperatures Affect Food.* Available at www.fsis.usda.gov. Accessed July 2014.

48. Ibid.

49. Centers for Disease Control and Prevention. 2006. *Travelers' Diarrhea.* www.cdc.gov. Accessed May 2014.

50. Centers for Disease Control and Prevention. 2013. *Travelers' Health: Food and Water Safety.* Available at www.nc.cdc.gov. Accessed May 2014.

51. Food and Drug Administration and U.S. Department of Agriculture. 2000. *A Description of the U.S. Food Safety System.* Available at www.fsis.usda.gov/OA/codex/system.htm. Accessed July 2014.

52. Centers for Disease Control and Prevention (CDC). 2011. Vital Signs: Incidence and Trends of Infection with Pathogens Transmitted Commonly through Food, 1996–2010. *Morbidity and Mortality Weekly Report* 60:749–755.

53. U.S. Food and Drug Administration. 2006. *Press Release: FDA Statement on Foodborne E. coli O157:H7 Outbreak in Spinach.* Available at www.fda.gov. Accessed July 2014.

54. U.S. Food and Drug Administration. 2007. *Press Release: DA Finalizes Report on 2006 Spinach Outbreak.* Available at www.fda.gov. Accessed July 2014.

55. Food and Drug Administration. 2001. HACCP: A State-of-the-Art Approach to Food Safety. *FDA Backgrounder.* Available at www.fda.gov. Accessed November 2008.

56. Food and Drug Administration. 2013. *Food Code.*

57. FDA. Updated 2013. *Talking about Juice Safety: What You Need to Know.* Available at www.fda.gov. Accessed May 2014.

58. FoodReference.com. n.d. *About Canned Food.* Available at www.foodreference.com/html/artcanninghistory.html. Accessed November 2008.

59. Tauxe, R. B. 2001. *Food Safety and Irradiation: Protecting the Public from Foodborne Infections.* Centers for Disease Control and Prevention, Emerging Infectious Diseases. Available at www.nc.cdc.gov. Accessed July 2014.

60. Centers for Disease Control and Prevention. Updated 2014. *Botulism.* Available at www.cdc.gov. Accessed May 2014.

61. Center for Food Safety and Applied Nutrition. 2001. *Analysis and Evaluation of Preventive Control Measures for the Control and Reduction/Elimination of Microbial Hazards on Fresh and Fresh-Cut Produce.* Available www.fda.gov. Accessed November 2012.

62. Finley, J., D. Deming, and R. Smith. 2006. Food Processing: Nutrition, Safety, and Quality. In Shils, M., M. Shike, A. Ross, B. Caballero, and R. Cousins. *Modern Nutrition in Health and Disease.* 10th ed. Philadelphia: Lippincott Williams & Wilkins.

63. Food and Drug Administration. Updated 2014. *Food Irradiation: What You Need to Know.* Available at www.fda.gov. Accessed July 2014.

64. Kindu, D., A. Gill, and R. Holley. 2013. Use of Low-Dose Irradiation to Evaluate the Radiation Sensitivity of *Escherichia coli* O157:H7, non-O157 Verotoxigenic *Escherichia coli*, and Salmonella in Phosphate-Buffered Saline. *Journal of Food Protection* 76(8):1438–1442.

65. Food and Drug Administration. Updated 2014. *Food Irradiation: What You Need to Know.*

66. Emmert, K., V. Duffy, and R. Earl. 2000. Position of the American Dietetic Association: Food Irradiation. *Journal of the American Dietetic Association* 100:246–253.

67. Food and Drug Administration. Updated 2014. *Food Irradiation: What You Need to Know.*

68. Emmert, et al. 2000. Position of the American Dietetic Association: Food Irradiation.

69. USDA. Modified 2013. *Irradiation and Food Safety Answers to Frequently Asked Questions.* Available at www.fsis.usda.gov. Accessed July 2014.

70. Centers for Disease Control and Prevention. Updated 2009. *Irradiation of Food: Frequently Asked Questions.* Available at www.cdc.gov. Accessed July 2014.

71. Lewis, C. 2002. Food Freshness and "Smart" Packaging. *FDA Consumer* 36:25–29.

72. USDA Food Safety and Inspection Service. Modified 2013. *Food Product Dating.* Available at www.fsis.usda.gov. Accessed July 2014.

73. Environmental Protection Agency. 2008. *It's Your Drinking Water: Get to Know It and Protect It!* Available at www.epa.gov/ogwdw/consumer/pdf/itsyours.pdf. Accessed November 2012.

74. Albrecht, et al. 2009. Position of the American Dietetic Association: Food and Water Safety.

75. Centers for Disease Control and Prevention (CDC). 2012. Vital Signs: Food Categories Contributing the Most to Sodium Consumption—United States, 2007–2008. *Morbidity and Mortality Weekly Report* 6:62–98.

76. Mirvish, S. S., J. Haorah, L. Zhou, M. L. Clapper, K. L. Harrison, and A. C. Povey. 2002. Total N-Nitroso Compounds and Their Precursors in Hot Dogs and in the Gastrointestinal Tract and Feces of Rats and Mice: Possible Etiologic Agents for Colon Cancer. *Journal of Nutrition* 132(Suppl):3526S–3529S.

77. National Toxicology Program, Health and Human Services. 2011. *12th Report on Carcinogens.* Available at http://ntp.niehs.nih.gov/?objectid=03C9AF75-E1BF-FF40DBA-9EC0928DF8B15. Accessed May 2012.

78. Center for Food Safety and Applied Nutrition. 2000. *Sulfites: An Important Food Safety Issue.* Available at www.cfsan.fda.gov/~dms/fssulfit.html. Accessed November 2008.

79. Papazian, R. 1996. *Sulfites: Safe for Most, Dangerous for Some.* Center for Food Safety and Applied Nutrition. Available at www.tequestafamilypractice.com/articles/Sulfite_Allergy.pdf. Accessed November 2012.

80. Center for Food Safety and Applied Nutrition. 2000. *Sulfites.*

81. USFDA. Updated 2013. *Questions and Answers on Monosodium Glutamate (MSG).* Available at www.fda.gov. Accessed July 2014.

82. FDA. Updated 2013. *Food Additives Status List.* Available at www.fda.gov. Accessed July 2014.

83. USFDA. Updated 2014. *Generally Recognized as Safe (GRAS).* Available at www.fda.gov. Accessed July 2014.

84. FDA. Updated 2013. *Food Additives Status List.*

85. Food and Drug Administration. 2012. *Questions and Answers about Dioxins and Food Safety.* Available at www.fda.gov. Accessed July 2014.

86. Center for Veterinary Medicine. 1999. *Report on the Food and Drug Administration's Review of the Safety of Recombinant Bovine Somatotropin.* Available at www.fda.gov/AnimalVeterinary/SafetyHealth/ProductSafetyInformation/ucm130321.htm. Accessed November 2012.

87. American Cancer Society. 2011. *Learn About Cancer: Recombinant Bovine Growth Hormone.* Available at www.cancer.org/cancer/cancercauses/othercarcinogens/athome/recombinant-bovine-growth-hormone. Accessed June 2012.

88. Center for Veterinary Medicine. 2002. *The Use of Steroid Hormones for Growth Promotion in Food-Producing Animals.* Available at www.fda.gov/AnimalVeterinary/NewsEvents/FDAVeterinarianNewsletter/ucm110712.htm. Accessed November 2012.

89. Ibid.

90. Centers for Disease Control and Prevention, National Antimicrobial Resistance Monitoring System. Updated 2014. *Antibiotic Use in Food-Producing Animals: Tracking and Reducing the Public Health Impact.* Available at www.cdc.gov. Accessed July 2014.

91. Iovine, N. M., and M. J. Blaser. 2004. Antibiotics in Animal Feed and Spread of Resistant *Campylobacter* from Poultry to Humans. *Emerging Infectious Diseases* DOI: 10.3201/eid1006.040403. Available at wwwnc.cdc.gov. Accessed July 2014.

92. USDA. Modified 2013. *Meat and Poultry Labeling Terms.* www.fsis.usda.gov. Accessed July 2014.

93. Committee on the Future Role of Pesticides in U.S. Agriculture. Board on Agriculture and Natural Resources. Board on Environmental Studies and Toxicology. National Research Council. 2000. *The Future Role of Pesticides in U.S. Agriculture.* Washington, DC: The National Academies Press.

94. U.S. Environmental Protection Agency. Updated 2014. *About Pesticides: What Is a Pesticide?* Available at www.epa.gov. Accessed May 2014.

95. Ibid.

96. U.S. Environmental Protection Agency. 2006. *Organophosphate Pesticides (OP) Cumulative Assessment: 2006 Update.* Available at www.epa.gov/oppsrrd1/cumulative/2006-op. Accessed May 2014.

97. U.S. Environmental Protection Agency. Updated 2012. *Antimicrobial Pesticides.* Available at www.epa.gov/oecaagct/tant.html. Accessed May 2014.

98. Food and Drug Administration. 2003. *FDA Fact Sheet on Hand Hygiene in Retail and Food Service Establishments.* Available at www.fda.gov/Food/GuidanceRegulation/RetailFood-Protection/IndustryandRegulatoryAssistanceandTrainingResources/ucm135577.htm. Accessed May 2014.

99. U.S. Environmental Protection Agency. Updated 2012. *Pesticides and Food: Health Problems Pesticides May Pose.* Available at www.epa.gov/opp00001/food/risks.htm. Accessed May 2014.

100. U.S. Department of Health and Human Services. 2012. *Healthy People 2020: Environmental Health Objectives.* Available at www.healthypeople.gov/2020/topicsobjectives2020/overview.aspx?topicid=12. Accessed November 2012.

101. American Academy of Pediatrics. 2012. Policy Statement on Pesticide Exposure in Children. *Pediatrics* 130(6):e1757–e1763.

102. U.S. Environmental Protection Agency. 2007. *Pesticides: Topical and Chemical Fact Sheets—Assessing Health Risks from Pesticides.* Available at www.epa.gov/pesticides/factsheets/riskassess.htm. Accessed November 2008.

103. U.S. Environmental Protection Agency. Updated 2014. *Pesticides: Regulating Pesticides—Laws and Regulations.* Available at www.epa.gov/pesticides/regulating/. Accessed May 2014.

104. U.S. Environmental Protection Agency. Updated 2012. *Pesticides and Food: How the Government Regulates Pesticides.* Available at www.epa.gov/pesticides/food/govt.htm. Accessed May 2014.

105. U.S. Environmental Protection Agency. Updated 2012. *Pesticides: Topical and Chemical Fact Sheets—Integrated Pest Management (IPM) Principles.* Available at www.epa.gov. Accessed May 2014.

106. Ibid.

107. Food and Drug Administration. Updated 2013. *Pesticide Q&A.* Available at www.fda.gov/food/foodborneillnesscontaminants/pesticides/ucm114958.htm. Accessed May 2014.

108. Krieger, R. I., P. Brutsche-Keiper, H. R. Crosby, and A. D. Krieger. 2003. Reduction of Pesticide Residues of Fruit Using Water Only or Plus Fit Fruit and Vegetable Wash. *Bulletin of Environmental Contamination and Toxicology* 70:213–218.

109. American Cancer Society. 2000. *The Environment and Cancer Risk.* Available at www.cancer.org. Accessed November 2008.

110. United States Department of Agriculture. Updated 2014. *National Organic Program.* Available at www.ams.usda.gov/AMSv1.0/nop. Accessed May 2014.

111. Ibid.

112. Organic Trade Association. 2011. *U.S. Organic Industry Overview.* Available at www.ota.com/pics/documents/2011OrganicIndustrySurvey.pdf. Accessed August 2012.

113. Ibid.

114. International Food Information Council. 2003. *USDA Launches Organic Standards.* Available at www.foodinsight.org. Accessed November 2008.

115. Agricultural Marketing Service, National Organic Program. Revised 2014. *National Organic Program Handbook: Guidance and Instructions for Accredited Certifying Agents and Certified Operations.* Available at www.ams.usda.gov/. Accessed July 2014.

116. Electronic Code of Federal Regulations. Updated 2014. *Title 7: Agriculture, Part 205—National Organic Program, Subpart G—Administrative: National List of Allowed and Prohibited Substances.* Available at www.ecfr.gov/. Accessed July 2014.

117. Dangour, A. D., K. Lock, A. Hayter, A. Aikenhead, E. Allen, and R. Uauy. 2010. Nutrition-Related Health Effects of Organic Foods: A Systematic Review. *American Journal of Clinical Nutrition* 92:203–210.

118. Smith-Spangler, C., M. L. Brandeau, G. E. Hunter, J. C. Bavinger, M. Pearson, P. J. Eschbach, V. Sundaram, et al. 2012. Are Organic Foods Safer or Healthier than Conventional Alternatives? A Systematic Review. *Annals of Internal Medicine* 157(5):348–366.

119. Ibid.

120. United Nations, Department of Economic and Social Affairs, Population Division. 2014. *Population Trends.* Available at www.un.org/en/development/desa/population/theme/trends/index.shtml. Accessed May 2014.

121. Tagtow, A., K. Robien, E. Bergquist, M. Mruening, L. Dierks, B. E. Hartman, et al. 2014. Academy of Nutrition and Dietetics: Standards of Professional Performance for Registered Dietitian Nutritionists (Competent, Proficient, and Expert) in Sustainable, Resilient, and Healthy Food and Water Systems. *Journal of the Academy of Nutrition and Dietetics* 114(3):475–488.

122. Brown, L. 2008. *Plan B 3.0. Mobilizing to Save Civilization.* New York: W.W. Norton & Company.

123. Environmental Protection Agency. Updated 2014. *What on Earth Is Soil?* Available at www.epa.gov/gmpo/edresources/soil.html. Accessed July 2014.

124. Tagtow, A. and Harmon A. 2009. *Healthy Land, Healthy Food and Healthy Eaters.*

Dieticians Cultivating Sustainable Food Systems. Available at www.uwyo.edu/winwyoming/pubs/healthyland%20healthyfood%20healthyeaters.pdf. Accessed May 2014.

125. Pimentel, D., P. Hepperly, J. Hanson, D. Douds, and R. Seidel. 2005. Environmental, Energetic, and Economic Comparisons of Organic and Conventional Farming Systems. *BioScience* 55:573–582.

126. United States Department of Agriculture. 2012. *Colony Collapse Disorder Progress Report.* Available at www.ars.usda.gov. Accessed May 2014.

127. Allendorf, F. W., O. Berry, and N. Ryman. 2014. So Long to Genetic Diversity, and Thanks For All the Fish. *Molecular Ecology* 23(1):23–25. doi: 10.1111/mec.12574.

128. Canning, P., A. Charles, S. Huang, K. R. Plenske, and A. Waters. 2010. Energy Use in the U.S. Food System. USDA, ERS, Economic Research Report. 94.

129. Pimentel, D., and M. Pimentel. 2003. Sustainability of Meat-Based and Plant-Based Diets. *American Journal of Clinical Nutrition* 78(3):660s-663s.

130. Ibid.

131. Heller, M. C. and G. A. Keoleian. 2000. *Life Cycle-Based Sustainability Indicators for Assessment of the U.S. Food System.* Ann Arbor, MI: Center for Sustainable Systems, University of Michigan. Available at http://css.snre.umich.edu/css_doc/CSS00-04.pdf. Accessed May 2014.

132. Harmon, A. H., and B. L. Gerald. 2007. Position of the American Dietetic Association: Food and Nutrition Professionals Can Implement Practices to Conserve Natural Resources and Support Ecological Sustainability. *Journal of the American Dietetic Association* 107(6):1033–1043.

133. Environmental Protection Agency. 2010. *Watersense.* Available at www.epa.gov/watersense. Accessed May 2014.

134. Ibid.

135. Holly, Robert. 2014. Experts Foresee Shortages as the Nation's Freshwater Supply Dwindles. *Midwest Center for Investigative Reporting.* Available at www.investigatemidewest.org. Accessed August 2014.

136. Ibid.

137. National Oceanic and Atmospheric Administration, National Climatic Data Center. 2008. *Global Warming Frequently Asked Questions.* Available at www.ncdc.noaa.gov/oa/climate/globalwarming.html#q1. Accessed January 2010.

138. Pirog, R., and K. Enshayan. 2002. *Food, Fuel, and Freeways: An Iowa Perspective on How Far Food Travels, Fuel Usage, and Greenhouse Gas Emissions.* Available at www.leopold.iastate.edu/pubs-and-papers/2001-06-food-fuel-freeways. Accessed May 2014.

139. Ibid.

140. ERS Report Summary. Economic Research Service. 2011. *USDA.* Available at www.ers.usda.gov/publications/

err-economic-research-report/err114.aspx#.U3-OdSi9Z8E. Accessed May 2014.

141. Harmon, et al. 2007. Position of the American Dietetic Association: Food and Nutrition Professionals Can Implement Practices to Conserve Natural Resources.

142. United States Department of Agriculture. 2013. *Know Your Farmer, Know Your Food.* Available at www.usda.gov/wps/portal/usda/knowyourfarmer?navid=KNOWYOURFARMER. Accessed May 2014.

143. Tagtow, A., et al. 2014. Academy of Nutrition and Dietetics: Standards of Professional Performance for Registered Dietitian Nutritionists (Competent, Proficient, and Expert) in Sustainable, Resilient, and Healthy Food and Water Systems.

144. United States Department of Agriculture. Modified 2013. *Biotechnology Frequently Asked Questions (FAQs).* Available at www.usda.gov/wps/portal/usda/usdahome?navid=AGRICULTURE&contentid=BiotechnologyFAQs.xml. Accessed May 2014.

145. Economic Research Service. Updated 2013. *Adoption of Genetically Engineered Crops in the U.S.* Available at www.ers.usda.gov/data-products/adoption-of-genetically-engineered-crops-in-the-us.aspx. Accessed July 2014.

146. McCullum, C. 2000. Food Biotechnology in the New Millennium: Promises, Realities, and Challenges. *Journal of the American Dietetic Association* 100:1311–1315.

147. Ibid.

148. Economic Research Service. Updated 2013. *Adoption of Genetically Engineered Crops in the U.S.*

149. Bren, L. 2003. Genetic Engineering: The Future of Foods. *FDA Consumer* 37:28–34.

150. Economic Research Service. Updated 2013. *Adoption of Genetically Engineered Crops in the U.S.*

151. Celec, P., M. Kukucková, V. Renczésová, S. Natarajan, R. Pálffy, R. Gardlík, J. Hodosy, et al. 2005. Biological and Biomedical Aspects of Genetically Modified Food. *Biomedicine & Pharmacotherapy* 59(10):531–540.

152. Bren, L. 2003. Genetic Engineering: The Future of Foods.

153. Ibid.

154. Celec, P., et al. 2005. Biological and Biomedical Aspects of Genetically Modified Food.

155. Ibid.

156. Kramkowska, M., T. Grzelak, and K. Czyżewska. 2013. Benefits and Risks Associated with Genetically Modified Food Products. *Annals of Agricultural and Environmental Medicine* 20(3):413–419.

157. Losey, J. E., L. S. Rayor, and M. E. Carter. 1999. Transgenic Pollen Harms Monarch Larvae. *Nature* 399:214. doi:10.1038/20338.

158. United States Department of Agriculture. 2007. *Q&A:* Bt *Corn and Monarch Butterflies.* Available at www.ars.usda.gov/is/br/btcorn. Accessed November 2012.

159. Jones, L. 1999. Genetically Modified Foods. *British Medical Journal* 318:581–584.

160. Food and Drug Administration. Updated 2013. *Biotechnology: Genetically Engineered Plants for Food & Feed.* Available at www.fda.gov/food/foodscienceresearch/biotechnology/. Accessed May 2014.

161. U.S. Food and Drug Administration. 2012. *Have Food Allergies? Read the Label.* Available at www.fda.gov/ForConsumers/ConsumerUpdates/ucm254504.htm. Accessed June 2012.

162. Food and Drug Administration. Updated 2014. *Questions and Answers on Food from Genetically Engineered Plants.* Available at www.fda.gov/food/foodscienceresearch/biotechnology/ucm346030.htm. Accessed May 2014.

163. Food and Drug Administration. Updated 2013. *Biotechnology: Genetically Engineered Plants for Food & Feed.*

164. Reuters. 2014. *USDA Is Still Weighing If Genetically Modified Salmon Is Safe to Eat.* Available at www.reuters.com/article/2014/03/13/us-usa-health-salmon-fda-idUSBREA2C23L20140313. Accessed May 2014.

165. Food and Drug Administration. Updated 2014. *Questions and Answers on Food from Genetically Engineered Plants.*

166. American Medical Association. 2012. *Policy H-480.958 Bioengineered (Genetically Engineered) Crops and Foods.* Available at www.ama-assn.org. Accessed July 2014.

167. Society of Toxicology. 2003. The Safety of Genetically Modified Foods Produced through Biotechnology. *Toxicological Sciences* 71:2–8.

168. Center for Food Safety. 2014. *Genetically Engineered Foods Labeling Laws.* Available at www.centerforfoodsafety.org/ge-map. Accessed May 2014.

169. Reuters. 2010. *National Survey of Healthcare Consumers: Genetically Engineered Food.* Available at www.justlabelit.org/wp-content/uploads/2011/09/NPR_report_GeneticEngineeredFood-1.pdf. Accessed May 2014.

21 Global Nutrition and Malnutrition

Learning Outcomes

After reading this chapter, you will be able to:

21.1 Define hunger and malnutrition, including overnutrition and undernutrition.

21.2 Discuss the factors that give rise to hunger and malnutrition in the United States.

21.3 Describe the causes of hunger and malnutrition worldwide.

21.4 Identify populations that are at greatest risk for malnutrition.

21.5 Explain several ways to reduce hunger.

21.6 Describe the health consequences of hunger.

True or False?

1. Hunger exists in every country in the world—including the United States. **T/F**

2. About one-seventh of the world's population does not have enough to eat. **T/F**

3. If you have a job, you will never experience food insecurity. **T/F**

4. Depression among mothers has been associated with food insecurity. **T/F**

5. Farmers already grow enough food to feed everyone on the planet today. **T/F**

6. Earthquakes can cause food shortages. **T/F**

7. Once you reach a certain age, you don't need to worry about malnutrition. **T/F**

8. Fortifying foods is a good idea, but it doesn't really affect malnutrition. **T/F**

9. You can't be obese and food insecure at the same time. **T/F**

10. The world's hunger problems would be solved if we just got food to everyone. **T/F**

See page 818 for the answers.

W̲e all know what "I'm hungry" feels like. After a long day, a grumbling or gnawing in the stomach, a feeling of fatigue, or maybe lightheadedness are all signs that tell us we need to eat. However, how many of us know what it is like to be hungry day in and day out, never to feel truly full, or to lose weight though we don't want to? Conversely, how many of us, though we satisfy our hunger, are actually malnourished without even realizing it?

Who are the malnourished people in the United States and the rest of the world? What are the effects of chronic hunger and malnutrition? And, once we understand the causes and scope of this problem, what can we do about it? Can one person's actions really help people who are hungry? In this chapter, we explore the conditions of hunger and malnutrition, their causes and effects, and potential solutions in the United States and around the world.

What Are Hunger and Malnutrition?

LO 21.1 Define hunger and malnutrition, including overnutrition and undernutrition.

Hunger is a discomfort caused by a lack of food paired with a desire to eat. **Malnutrition** is a lack of proper nutrition, caused by not having enough to eat, not eating enough of the right things, or being unable to use the food that one does eat. Children who are malnourished can't grow properly and have difficulty resisting disease. Malnutrition can cause problems with working and learning. Women who are malnourished during pregnancy risk giving birth to low-weight babies, and may have difficulty producing enough breast milk.[1]

Malnutrition may appear as **undernutrition,** in which a person gets too little of one or many needed nutrients, or as **overnutrition,** in which a person gets too much of one or many needed nutrients. Either condition may be caused simply by the level of food intake, or by other factors such as repeated infectious disease or poor absorption.[2]

Malnutrition Is a Problem in the United States and Worldwide

Multiple factors, including lack of food, disease, poverty, even overnutrition, contribute to malnutrition in the United States and around the world. In the United States, which is a **developed country,** malnutrition most frequently results from individual economic hardship and poverty. **Figure 21.1** shows the areas in the United States where food insecurity is most prevalent. In **developing** and **least developed** countries—collectively referred to as the developing world—poverty is also a factor, but situations such as war, civil unrest, and famine can also come into play.

Of a global population of 7 billion people, a minority—approximately 1 billion— live in developed countries[3] (**Figure 21.2**). The other 6 billion live in the developing world, where they lack many goods and services. The Food and Agriculture Organization of the United Nations estimates that there were 842 million undernourished people in the world in 2011–2013,[4] and in 2008, the World Bank reported that there were an estimated 1,345 million poor people in developing countries living on $1.25 a day or less.[5] That's less than many Americans pay for their regular cup of coffee in the morning. About 1 billion people lack access to safe drinking water.[6] An estimated 250,000 to 500,000 vitamin A–deficient children become blind every year, half of them dying within 12 months of losing their sight.[7] In the developing world about 50 percent of pregnant women and about 40 percent of

hunger An individual-level physiological condition that may result from food insecurity.

malnutrition A lack of proper nutrition, caused by not having enough to eat, not eating enough of the right things, or being unable to use the food that one does eat.

undernutrition A condition that may result when a person consumes too little of one or many nutrients.

overnutrition A condition that may result when a person consumes too much of one or many needed nutrients.

developed country A country that is advanced in multiple areas, such as income per capita, life expectancy, rate of literacy, industrial capability, technological sophistication, and economic productivity.

developing country A country that is growing in multiple areas, such as income per capita, life expectancy, rate of literacy, industrial capability, technological sophistication, and economic productivity.

least developed country A country that shows little growth in multiple areas, such as income per capita, life expectancy, rate of literacy, industrial capability, technological sophistication, and economic productivity.

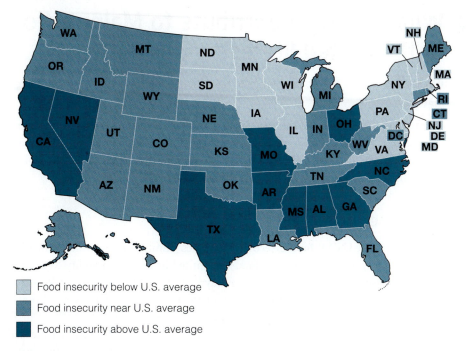

Food insecurity below U.S. average

Food insecurity near U.S. average

Food insecurity above U.S. average

▲ **Figure 21.1 Hunger in the United States**
Though some areas of the United States have higher rates of food insecurity and/or hunger, these conditions can happen anywhere. In this map, data for three years, 2010–2012, were combined to provide more reliable statistics at the state level.

Source: United States Department of Agriculture: Economic Research Service. Updated 2014. *Food Security in the U.S.: Key Statistics & Graphics*. Available at www.ers.usda.gov. Accessed June 2014.

preschool children are estimated to be anemic.[8] Low birth weight is a major determinant of mortality, morbidity, and disability in infancy and childhood and also has a long-term impact on health outcomes in adult life. In many developing countries the low birth weight rate is as high as 30 percent.[9]

LO 21.1: THE TAKE-HOME MESSAGE Malnutrition is a lack of proper nutrition, and may appear as undernutrition, overnutrition, or as a specific nutrient deficiency. Malnutrition is experienced by people in the United States and around the world, and is usually due to poverty, civil unrest, or other circumstances.

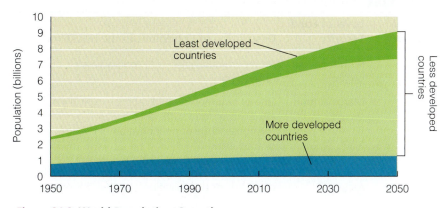

▲ **Figure 21.2 World Population Growth**
The majority of people in the world live in developing countries, and this number is expected to grow.

Source: United Nations Population Division. 2011. *World Population Prospects: The 2010 Revision, medium variant*. Available at http://esa.un.org. Accessed August 2014.

Are You at Risk for Hunger?

Take the quiz below to find out if you are at risk for hunger.
In the past 12 months:

1. Have you ever run out of money to buy food?

   Yes ☐ **No** ☐

2. Have you ever eaten less than you felt you should because there was not enough money to buy food or enough food to eat?

   Yes ☐ **No** ☐

3. Have you ever completely depleted your food supply because there was not enough money to buy replacement groceries?

   Yes ☐ **No** ☐

4. Have you ever gone to bed hungry because there was not enough food to eat?

   Yes ☐ **No** ☐

5. Have you ever skipped meals because there was not enough money to buy food?

   Yes ☐ **No** ☐

6. Have you ever relied on a limited number of foods to feed yourself because you were running out of money to buy food?

   Yes ☐ **No** ☐

Answers

If you have no "Yes" replies, you are food secure. If there are one to three "Yes" replies, you are at risk for food insecurity. If there are four or more "Yes" replies, you are likely in the low or very low food security category.

Source: Adapted from The Community Childhood Hunger Identification Project Survey. 1995; R. E. Kleinman, et al. 1998. "Hunger in Children in the United States: Potential Behavioral and Emotional Correlates," *Pediatrics* 101:3–10.

food insecurity A household-level economic and social condition of uncertain access to adequate food.

food security The degree to which an individual has regular access to adequate amounts of healthy foods.

What Factors Contribute to Malnutrition in the United States?

LO 21.2 Discuss the factors that give rise to hunger and malnutrition in the United States.

The United States is one of the wealthiest nations in the world,[10] yet many Americans cannot afford to buy meat and vegetables at a grocery store or dine out at a local restaurant. Hunger and malnutrition are very real problems across the United States, in inner cities, the suburbs, and in rural areas.

Food Insecurity in the United States

According to the USDA, **food insecurity** describes "limited or uncertain availability of nutritionally adequate and safe foods or limited or uncertain ability to acquire acceptable foods in socially acceptable ways."[11] The USDA Economic Research Service uses labels to convey the severity of food insecurity in the United States (**Table 21.1**).[12]

Food insecurity is common among older adults, who may suffer from decreased mobility in addition to inadequate financial resources. Older adults may also suffer from *food insufficiency* when they occasionally or persistently have too little food. Other populations, including individuals and families in rural and urban regions, experience *food poverty*: inconsistent access to food due to financial constraints or geographic circumstances.[13]

The Census Bureau conducts an annual survey of **food security,** in which it asks questions about anxiety over the household food budget, the quantity and quality of food eaten, and the instances of reduced food intake. The survey is regarded as a reliable indicator for assessing the well-being of households as well as measuring progress toward the *Healthy People 2020* goal of reducing food insecurity to 6 percent of U.S. households.[14]

In 2012, the USDA found that 14.5 percent of American households were food insecure at least some time during the year, including 5.7 percent with very low food security.[15] About 17.6 million people in the United States lived in food-insecure households in 2012; 10 million of those households include children. The

TABLE 21.1	Ranges of Food Security	
General Category	Level of Food Security	Description of Conditions in the Household
Food Security	High food security	No reported indications of food-access problems or limitations.
	Marginal food security	One or two reported indications—typically of anxiety over food sufficiency or shortage of food in the house. Little or no indication of changes in diets or food intake.
Food Insecurity	Low food security	Reports of reduced quality, variety, or desirability of diet. Little or no indication of reduced food intake.
	Very low food security	Reports of multiple indications of disrupted eating patterns and reduced food intake.

Source: Adapted from USDA Economic Research Service. 2014. Definitions of Food Security. Available at www.ers .usda.gov/topics/food-nutrition-assistance/food-security-in-the-us/definitions-of-food-security.aspx#.U44hJFwqYU4. Accessed June 2014.

number of people in the worst-off households, those classified as "very low food security," was unchanged from 2011 to 2012 at 5.7 percent.[16]

In addition, black and Hispanic households experienced food insecurity at higher rates than the national average, with 24.6 percent and 23.3 percent experiencing food insecurity, respectively. About 35.4 percent of single women heading up a household with children experienced food insecurity. Between 2010 and 2012, the five states with the highest food insecurity rates were Mississippi, Arkansas, Texas, Alabama, and North Carolina.[17] Various factors contribute to this problem, starting with poverty.

Poverty Causes Food Insecurity

Poverty is the principal cause of food insecurity in the United States. For people living in the inner cities, poverty can be a result of adverse cultural and behavioral factors that limit opportunities for employment. The revitalization of city centers can also make life too expensive for many poor residents, forcing them to move to suburban areas where housing is cheaper but jobs may still not be available. In rural areas, household income and education levels are generally lower. While unemployment rates are about the same as in cities, average earnings are substantially lower among rural workers.[18, 19] Many low-income families must choose between paying the rent and buying groceries—a tough decision, especially when there are young children in the home.

The U.S. Census Bureau calculates the number of people living in poverty using poverty thresholds, which are defined according to strict guidelines. The Census estimated that for 2012, the poverty rate was about 15 percent of the United States population.[20] The poverty rate in 2012 for children under age 18 was 21.8 percent. As of 2013, for a married couple, or a single mother plus a child, poverty means a household income below $16,057 per year. A family of four would be impoverished with an income below $23,624.[21]

Factors that lead to poverty include unemployment, lack of resources needed to get and keep a job (such as a car, a working telephone, and a permanent address), medical issues, and poor financial choices. Whatever the cause, poverty is often difficult to overcome. Lack of education or training, poor health, limited or no access to credit, and other obstacles can lock someone into circumstances with few prospects. In addition, people are often unaware of the resources available to assist them and do not know where to go or whom to ask for help.

In the United States, poor single parents and their children can experience food insecurity due to unemployment, low wages, or other circumstances that lead to financial hardship.

According to the USDA, those at the greatest risk of being food insecure are living in households with any or all of these life situations:[22]

- Household is headed by a single woman
- Household members are in a minority group
- Household income is below the poverty level
- There are children in the household
- Household is located in the inner city

These circumstances can contribute to poverty by producing additional disadvantages, such as increased exposure to crime and fewer employment opportunities. Lack of child care or expensive child-care arrangements impose additional stress and can drain an already-tight budget. Single mothers may feel "trapped" with very few employment options or lack of freedom to explore additional career paths because of obligations to their children. Single mothers with dependent children are more likely to experience times without adequate amounts of food than are families headed by a married couple.[23]

In today's competitive work environment, people without job skills typically have a harder time securing employment than those who are highly educated or

poverty Lacking the means to provide for material or comfort needs.

who have specialized skills. Consequently, it's not surprising that an individual's education level affects food insecurity—those without a high school diploma are more than six times as likely to experience food insecurity as those who have graduated from college.[24] Even employed individuals with advanced education may experience hunger if they are laid off, are unemployed for an extended period, or are unable to relocate for a job.

Additionally, people can sometimes be steadily employed in a low-wage full-time job, seasonal jobs, or in several part-time jobs, and still experience hunger. In fact, in 2012, about 10.9 million adults were classified among the **working poor**.[25] Though they had jobs, they still had incomes below the poverty line. High housing and utility costs can consume most of the household budget and leave little money for food. Individuals in these households may be living "paycheck to paycheck." An unexpected expense, such as an illness or a costly auto repair, can force them and their families to choose between paying the bills and consuming a healthy, adequate diet.

Food Deserts Contribute to Food Insecurity

Compounding the problem of poverty is the reality that those on low incomes often don't have markets or grocery stores with healthy options nearby. In inner cities and rural settings alike, **food deserts** make it difficult for people to feed themselves healthfully.[26] The CDC defines food deserts as areas without ready access to affordable fruits, vegetables, whole grains, lowfat milk, and other foods that make up the full range of a healthy diet.[27] Typically, fast-food restaurants and convenience stores, carrying less-healthful foods, abound in these areas. Food deserts exist all over the United States. You may be surprised, if you look at the USDA Food Desert Locator for your city, to see how prevalent they are. You can check it out by going to www.ers.usda.gov and searching for food desert locator.

People in poor, urban areas often find themselves in "food deserts," with little access to the fresh, healthy food found in supermarkets.

Illness, Disability, and Drug Abuse Can Also Lead to Hunger

Adults who are chronically ill or disabled are less likely to earn a steady income and are therefore at risk of having a poor diet. Nutritionally compromised individuals tend to be less productive at work and at increased risk for further illnesses. They may also lack the money or health care coverage to obtain proper medical care to improve their health. Having a chronic illness and routinely missing work to visit a physician can significantly reduce a paycheck, and thus available funds for food.

Mental illness can also contribute to or cause poverty, malnutrition, and hunger in the United States. According to the National Coalition for the Homeless, some 20 to 25 percent of individuals who are homeless are also mentally ill.[28] Mentally ill people, often including the homeless, can be difficult to reach, counsel, or help. They may be forced to rely on charity, church meals, or public assistance programs for most of their food. People who suffer from mental illness, such as anxiety disorders, phobias, depression, paranoia, schizophrenia, or some eating disorders, lose interest in eating or have decreased access to cooking facilities. Depression among mothers, particularly those in low-income families, has been associated with food insecurity in households.[29] Children living in these homes are more likely to routinely go without food or to rely on unhealthy diets, such as food from fast-food restaurants, and they are more likely to have mental health problems themselves.[30]

Drug abuse and alcohol abuse are also common causes of poverty and hunger, and, in extreme situations, homelessness. According to the U.S. Department of Housing and Urban Development, on a given night in January 2010, 34.7 percent of

working poor Individuals or families who are steadily employed but still experience poverty due to low wages or high dependent expenses.

food deserts Parts of the country, usually impoverished areas, where fresh fruit, vegetables, and other healthful whole foods are scarce, largely due to a lack of grocery stores, farmers' markets, and healthy-food providers.

all sheltered adults who were homeless had chronic substance use issues.[31] These individuals typically find it difficult to get and keep steady employment and to shop for and prepare nutritious food.

> **LO 21.2: THE TAKE-HOME MESSAGE** Food insecurity is the limited or uncertain access to foods of sufficient quality or quantity to live an active, healthy life and is divided into the subcategories of *low food security* and *very low food security*. Factors that contribute to hunger in the United States include poverty, unemployment, and illness. Food insecurity and hunger are particularly prevalent in households headed by a single mother, minorities, the poor, those living in inner cities, especially in food deserts, and among those with unstable or seasonal professions.

What Factors Contribute to Malnutrition around the World?

LO 21.3 Describe the causes of hunger and malnutrition worldwide.

Hunger and malnutrition in the developing world are often caused by a complex set of factors. Once again, poverty lies at the heart of the problem; however, war, political unrest, agricultural challenges, disease, or natural disasters can also cause food insecurity for large numbers of people, particularly in Asian and African nations.

Food Insecurity Worldwide

Worldwide, the food insecurity numbers are higher than in the United States. The United Nations Food and Agriculture Organization, which measures undernutrition, estimated that for the years 2011 to 2013, approximately 842 million people worldwide, or 12 percent of the world's population, were undernourished.[32] **Figure 21.3** shows where food insecurity hits across the globe.

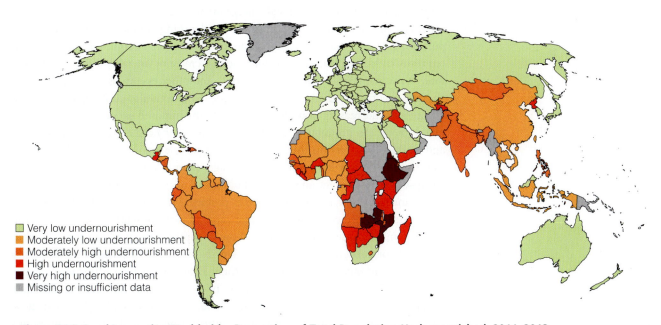

▲ **Figure 21.3 Food Insecurity Worldwide, Proportion of Total Population Undernourished, 2011–2013**
Food insecurity is a global problem. This map shows which areas of the globe are most profoundly affected.
Source: FAO, IFAD, and WFP. 2013. The State of Food Insecurity in the World 2013. Available at www.fao.org. Accessed August 2014.

Thanks to agricultural advances, the world's farmers can grow plenty of food. However, distribution problems and other factors keep some people from getting enough to stave off hunger.

What causes worldwide food insecurity? The rising costs of food, fuel, and fertilizer contribute to the problem.[33] Hunger and food insecurity exist despite the fact that current global food production exceeds the needs of the population. World agriculture produces 17 percent more kilocalories per person today than it did 30 years ago, which is enough to provide everyone in the world with at least 2,700 kilocalories per day.[34]

Discrimination and Inequality Promote Poverty

In many poor countries, discrimination and inequality exist at both the national and local levels. For example, at the national level, control over land and other assets is often unequal, so that even increased crop yields do not decrease food insecurity. Very few people in these countries own their own land, and a plentiful crop primarily benefits the landowner, not the farm laborer. Women, especially, suffer from discrimination.[35]

Cultural practices may also compromise access to food at the local or household level. In some cultures and within some families, the amount of food available to an individual is influenced by gender, control of income, education, birth order, and age.[36] Gender inequity is a serious problem worldwide. In many cultures women and girls are viewed as less valuable than men and boys, and they therefore receive less food and education. In sub-Saharan Africa six girls are enrolled in secondary school for every ten boys.[37] Accordingly, almost two-thirds of the 792 million illiterate adults in the world are women.[38] In every developing region, women tend to hold less secure jobs than men.[39]

Political Sanctions and Armed Conflicts Disrupt the Food Supply

Political **sanctions** and agricultural embargoes create food shortages by decreasing access to agricultural supplies, fuel, or crops. Shortages of these crucial items often hurt the average citizen more than the government they are meant to target.

One country or group of countries may use sanctions to postpone or replace military action and force political change on another government. Other goals for sanctions include restoring democracy, condemning human rights abuses, and punishing groups that protect terrorists or international criminals. Sanctions often result in harm to innocent people and can create or intensify a cycle of chronic food shortages. Higher prices for fuel, food, and other essentials may deprive average citizens of clean drinking water and food. Sanctions also contribute to a failing economy by decreasing household income. If the imposed sanction lowers the demand for certain products by blocking their import by other countries, businesses and workers that rely on this trade suffer negative economic effects. All of these factors can lead to widespread food shortages that, if left unchecked, may cause a collapse in food production and distribution and, ultimately, famine.[40]

Armed conflict is another serious problem. According to the World Food Programme, armed conflicts are a major cause of world hunger.[41] War and civil and political unrest cause hunger because of the disruption to agriculture, food distribution, and normal community activities. During the past two decades, the world has experienced an increase in regional conflicts. Examples include ethnic warfare, terrorism, and internal struggles for resources in countries such as Colombia, Ethiopia, Somalia, Sierra Leone, Congo, Sudan, and Syria. During wars and regional conflicts, government money is often diverted from nutrition and food distribution programs and redirected toward weapons and military support. Conflicts have caused a rise in global hunger and overwhelmed the efforts of humanitarian agencies. Political

sanctions Boycotts or trade embargoes used by one country or international group to apply political pressure on another.

turbulence can compromise humanitarian food distribution, making it difficult for food aid to reach the people in need. In some cases, assistance programs and aid workers may have to abandon war-torn areas and curtail their relief efforts.

Much Food Goes to Waste

One-third of all food produced is never consumed.[42] This food wastage represents a missed opportunity to improve global food security. According to the FAO, tons of food gets thrown out all along the food chain from farm to table, with larger losses occurring during agricultural production in developing countries, and at the consumer level in wealthier regions—like the eggplant you might leave on your plate at dinner.[43] Tackling the food waste problem involves reducing production to meet actual demand, directing surplus to regions in need, and responsibly recycling what can't be reused.

Many hunger relief programs work to provide food aid to needy nations. However, successfully delivering the food to those who need it is often challenging.

Natural Disasters and Depleted Resources Limit Food Production

Natural disasters such as droughts, floods, storms, earthquakes, crop diseases, and insect plagues can create food and water shortages in any country. In American communities, relief programs can help affected populations. In the developing world, the impact of natural disasters can completely devastate communities. Lack of communication and transportation systems, inadequate funding for relief programs, an inability to relocate populations from disaster-prone areas, and the incapacity to make homes and farms less vulnerable to destructive weather forces can all contribute to the problem.

Drought is the leading cause of severe food shortages in the developing world. When drought conditions exist or access to safe and clean drinking water is limited, **famine** and undernutrition result. This is particularly true in rural areas where people depend on agriculture for both food and income. Similarly, lack of water can force livestock owners to slaughter part of their herd or sell animals at "distress sales."[44]

Floods and excessive rain can also destroy food crops, and are major causes of food shortage. For example, in India, more than 70 percent of the annual rainfall occurs during the three months of monsoon season. Farmers must contend with water scarcity for nine months of the year only to be faced with crop failure later if monsoon rains are overly heavy.

The depletion of natural resources also causes reduced food production. Specific agricultural practices such as misuse of fertilizers, pesticides, and water may increase the yield in the short term, but they are unsustainable in the long term.[45] When the population of a poor country expands and food is in short supply, critical decisions are often made concerning the use of water, forest resources, and land. These choices often pit the needs of the people against concerns for the environment, threatening limited resources even more. Thus, a long-term investment in preserving natural resources could help reduce poverty and hunger.

Shortsighted farming techniques can take a heavy toll on crops and farmland.

Overpopulation Leads to Food Scarcity

The projected world population is 8.2 billion people by 2025, and 9.6 billion by 2050.[46] Much of this growth is taking place in the least developed regions, where

famine A severe shortage of food caused by weather-related crop destruction, poor agricultural practices, pestilence, war, or other factors.

the population is expected to increase from about 900 million people in 2013 to 1.8 billion in 2050.[47] Whenever rapid population growth occurs in areas that are strained for food production, the resulting **overpopulation** can take a toll on the local people's nutritional status.

People in the developing world tend to have more children due to poor health conditions. Because the infant and child death rate is so high, many children do not live to reach adulthood. Parents have more children to ensure that some of their offspring survive into adolescence. Large families are needed to work on farms to help generate income and to support older family members later in life.[48] This tendency contributes to the cycle of poverty and hunger because the economy cannot sustain such rapid population growth. The World Bank promotes gender equality and development to break this cycle, ensuring that girls and women in particular receive a basic education.[49]

Nutrition Transition Can Lead to Malnutrition

Ironically, malnutrition is not confined to those who are food insecure or even hungry. In countries that are becoming more prosperous, while people are getting more food to eat, they are not necessarily eating high-quality food. As nations get richer, with more access to a variety of foods, people who formerly ate meals full of vegetables and grains may shift over to diets higher in fat and sugar. And as workers move from rural locations to cities, they get less exercise in general. This so-called **nutrition transition** leads to overweight, obesity, and potentially malnutrition.[50]

LO 21.3: THE TAKE-HOME MESSAGE Factors that give rise to malnutrition around the world include poverty, discrimination, political sanctions and conflicts, poor agricultural practices, overpopulation, and nutrition transition.

Which Populations Are at Greatest Risk for Malnutrition?

LO 21.4 Identify populations that are at greatest risk for malnutrition.

Because of their increased nutritional needs, infants, children, and pregnant and lactating women are at higher risk for malnutrition than are other groups. Malnourished women are more likely to be ill, have smaller babies, and die at a younger age.[51] Furthermore, whenever infant and child mortality rates are high, birth rates are also high, as women tend to try to have more babies when they fear losing them.[52] This, of course, perpetuates the cycle of malnutrition and death. Finally, the ill and elderly populations are also at greater risk for malnutrition.

Pregnant and Lactating Women Are at Risk for Malnutrition

As you know from Chapter 17, nutrient requirements increase during pregnancy and lactation. Adequate nutrition during pregnancy greatly enhances the likelihood of having a healthy, full-term, normal-weight infant. Additionally, a healthy pregnancy increases the chances of the mother being able to lactate and breast-feed successfully.

Pregnant women need extra kilocalories and nutrients—in particular, protein, vitamins, and minerals—to support a healthy pregnancy. In general, during the first six months of a pregnancy, the majority of the additional kilocalories are used to nourish the mother as her body undergoes the changes necessary to support a

overpopulation When a region has more people than its natural resources can support.

nutrition transition A shift in dietary consumption and energy expenditure that may occur as people in developing countries shift from their traditional diet to diets higher in sugars, fat, and animal-source food.

pregnancy. During the last three months of a pregnancy, the majority of extra kilocalories are needed by the growing infant to supply the infant's reserves of protein, fat, and various micronutrients.[53] Improperly nourished pregnant women often give birth to malnourished infants.

Because human breast milk is the ideal nourishment for infants, women in the developing world are encouraged to breast-feed their babies. The global recommendation is for women to nurse their babies for the first six months and to continue nursing with supplemental foods into the child's second year of life.[54] One exception to this recommendation applies to women who are HIV positive, many of whom live in the poorest countries. Mothers with HIV risk passing the virus to their infants through breast milk, and therefore should be encouraged to use formula or a noninfected wet nurse to feed their babies instead of nursing children themselves. However, because many HIV-positive women live in poverty and can't afford these alternatives, they may still choose to breast-feed their children. In these cases, the benefits of providing the nutrients in the breast milk outweigh the risks of passing the HIV infection on to the baby.

Because of the increased nutrient needs associated with pregnancy, lactation, and early childhood growth, mothers and their young children are at particular risk for malnutrition.

Infants and Children Are Susceptible to Malnutrition

Infants are particularly susceptible to malnutrition because they are growing rapidly, have high nutrient requirements (per unit of body weight), and may be cared for by mothers who are malnourished themselves. Infants are dependent on their caregivers to give them adequate breast milk or formula.

After 6 months of age infants require solid food in addition to breast milk, which puts them at increased risk for malnutrition if food supplies are limited. As an infant transitions from an all–breast milk diet to a diet of breast milk plus solid foods, she or he is also at risk for improper weaning, which can lead to diminished growth during the first year of life and the potential for severe malnutrition during the second year of life.[55] In other cases babies may be given foods that are inappropriate, such as foods that are too high in protein or are difficult for an infant to chew. During the sixth to twelfth months of life, children may be more likely to be exposed to contaminated food and water, which may cause diarrhea and dehydration. When infants begin to crawl and walk, their risk of exposure to and thus infection by bacteria and parasites increases. Some parasitic infestations cause nutritional deficiencies directly. For example, hookworms suck blood from the lining of the gut, causing iron-deficiency anemia.

The risk of malnutrition continues from infancy into early childhood and may result from food shortages within the family or chronic disease. If there is a severe lack of protein in the diet, for example, children may develop kwashiorkor, as we saw in Chapter 6. Malnourishment also builds on itself: Children who are ill or malnourished have poor appetites—their normal hunger sensations are diminished. In some children maldigestion and malabsorption exacerbate the problem by increasing the loss of nutrients.

The loss of one or both parents from disease may also lead to decreased family income and a greater risk of malnourishment. For example, by 2010 AIDS had orphaned an estimated 10 million children in the developing world.[56] An estimated 34 million people in the world had HIV/AIDS in 2011, including 3.3 million children under age 15.[57] Most of these children were born to mothers with HIV or obtained the virus during infancy (via childbirth or breast-feeding).

The Ill and the Elderly Also May Suffer from Malnutrition

People who are chronically ill may have malabsorption problems that worsen their nutritional status. Liver and kidney disease can impair the body's ability to process and use some nutrients. Some cancer patients and many people with AIDS experience anorexia, which further complicates their treatment and their ability to eat.

Although older adults need fewer kilocalories due to a decrease in their metabolic rate and lower levels of physical activity, they have higher requirements for several minerals and vitamins. Older people may be at risk for nutrient deficiencies because of a decreased sense of taste and smell, immobility, malabsorption, or chronic illnesses. They are also at more risk for disease and disability due to an aging immune system than are younger individuals. Loneliness, isolation, poverty, missing teeth, confusion, or disinterest in cooking and eating also contribute to malnutrition. Many elderly people in developing countries are undernourished, emaciated, and anemic. In addition, most elderly people, whether in the United States or in other countries, live on a fixed income or have no income at all and must depend on family members to provide for them. In such cases, food is often stretched, and meals are smaller or are skipped altogether. All of these factors contribute to an increased rate of food insecurity and hunger in the older adult population.

Malnutrition Also Exists Among Those Who Are Overweight

Unfortunately, obesity among those who are food insecure is common. High-fat, high-kilocalorie diets are more affordable than diets based on lean meats, fish, vegetables, and fruits. There is a clear link in women between food insecurity and overweight and obesity. Research suggests that mothers often restrict their food intake during periods of food insufficiency to protect their children from hunger. These chronic ups and downs of food intake can contribute to obesity.[58]

People on limited incomes often shop for cheap foods because they can buy more. However, low-cost foods are often low-quality foods lacking nutrition. Fruit punch, for example, is about half the price of orange juice, and it is nutritionally inferior to orange juice. For those living on a limited budget, filling their cupboards with food, even if it is less-nutrient-dense food, takes precedence over choosing foods with nutritional value. If they live in a food desert, these people may not even have access to nutritious foods. As you have learned from previous chapters, a diet high in empty kilocalories and low in nutrient-dense foods can increase the risk of obesity *and* malnutrition.

> **LO 21.4: THE TAKE-HOME MESSAGE** Pregnant and lactating women, infants and children, and the ill and elderly are particularly vulnerable to the effects of malnutrition. People who are obese can also suffer from malnutrition.

How Can We Reduce Hunger?

LO 21.5 Explain several ways to reduce hunger.

In the United States, hunger relief efforts exist at many levels. At the local level, individuals, families, churches, and community relief agencies seek out and assist people who have insufficient resources. Examples of assistance include hot meals and free food provided by local shelters and food banks, as well as education and job training provided by local and state governments, nonprofit organizations, and faith-based organizations. See the Spotlight on America's Second Harvest for more information about food banks and how you can help. Some hunger relief efforts are undertaken at the corporate and governmental level. These organizations provide food aid and create economic opportunity for people who want to improve their lives. The USDA spent over $106 billion in 2012 on numerous food

Hunger among Us (and How You Can Help!)

Food insecurity may be closer than you think. In fact, you may have friends, relatives, or neighbors who've experienced hunger sometime in their lives.

In addition to the many food assistance programs available, people occasionally also use a **food pantry** or **emergency kitchen** to supplement the various food assistance programs.

America's Second Harvest, the largest hunger relief organization in the United States, was started to help individuals who are routinely without food. The mission of this organization is to eradicate hunger and ensure that no American goes to bed hungry. America's Second Harvest distributed nearly 52 million pounds of food from July 2012 through June 2013, through partnerships with over 300 food banks.[94] They redistribute excess and donated food and grocery items, work to increase public awareness of hunger, and advocate for those who are hungry.

Everyone—from children to adults—can help eradicate hunger.

America's Second Harvest stores surplus food from national food companies and other large donors in a centralized location. Volunteers travel to these food banks and gather and transport the donated foods to local food pantries. Volunteers and workers at a food rescue organization "rescue" prepared food, such as ready-to-eat surplus items from banquets, company and college cafeterias, and restaurants, that would otherwise go to waste.[95] Sometimes food rescue centers are located in the same building as food banks.

When it comes to fighting hunger in America, everyone needs to pitch in. You can help your needy neighbors in three ways: give funds, give food, and give time. Funds can be donated online at www.secondharvest.org. You can donate food by hosting a food drive. Finally, you can volunteer your time by helping out in your local community, perhaps by tutoring children on healthy eating practices, repackaging donated food, stocking shelves at a local food pantry, or transporting food to the hungry.

To find out where you can help, visit the America's Second Harvest website (www.secondharvest.org) and click on the volunteer link.

food pantry Community food assistance location where food is provided to needy individuals and families.

emergency kitchen A kitchen or a commercial food service that prepares for natural disasters, emergencies, or terrorist attacks.

assistance programs to feed Americans in need.[59] **Table 21.2** reviews some of the main programs.

In addition to the human (person-to-person) help provided by people and organizations, technology is also playing a role in alleviating malnutrition. As research and development provide new ways to pack more nutrition into food crops, hunger may be reduced. Enriched crops ultimately benefit hungry people by providing some of the common nutrients that are in low supply in current crops. The following discussion looks at a number of possible solutions to the problem of hunger around the world.

Improve Agriculture, Water Safety and Usage, and Sanitation

Agriculture plays an important role in the economy and food security of most developing countries. The long-term solution to hunger requires balancing the number of people in a country with the amount of food that can be locally

TABLE 21.2	Food Assistance Programs in the United States			
Program	**Eligibility**	**Description**	**Prevalence**	
Supplemental Nutrition Assistance Program (SNAP), (formerly the Food Stamp Program)	Low income (for a family of four, the net monthly income cannot exceed $1,988)	Individuals who are eligible for food stamps are issued a debit card to purchase specified foods, such as fruit, vegetables, cereals, meats, and dairy products, at their local authorized supermarket. (Items such as alcohol, tobacco, nonfood items, vitamins and medicines, and hot foods are not covered.)	In 2012, more than 46.6 million people per month in the United States	
Special Supplemental Nutrition Program for Women, Infants and Children (WIC)	At-risk low-income pregnant and lactating women, infants, and children less than 5 years old	The program provides nutritious, culturally appropriate food, including tortillas, brown rice, soy-based beverages, and a wide choice of fruits and vegetables, to supplement the diet. There are even some organic forms of WIC-eligible foods. The program also emphasizes nutrition education and offers referrals to health care professionals.	8.9 million women, infants, and children per month in 2012	
National School Lunch Program	Children with families with incomes at or below 130% of the poverty level are eligible for free meals and those with incomes between 130% and 185% of the poverty level are eligible for reduced-price meals	Eligible children receive free or reduced-price lunches each year. A subsidized breakfast is sometimes also available at schools.	More than 31 million American children in 2012	
Summer Food Service Program	Available to communities based on income data	Federal program that combines a meal or feeding program with a summer activity program for children	During the peak month of July 2013, more than 2.4 million children daily at 42,654 sites	
Child and Adult Care Food Program	Available to communities based on income data	Program provides nutritious meals to low-income children and senior adults who receive day care or adult care outside the home. There are income guidelines and specific menu requirements for program participation.	More than 3.3 million children and 120,000 adults receive meals and snacks each day as part of this program	
Congregate Meals for the Elderly and Meals on Wheels	Age 60 or over	The programs provide meals at a community site or delivered to the home.	More than one million meals per day served at sites across the country	

Source: Data from USDA, Food and Nutrition Service. 2014. www.fns.usda.gov; Meals on Wheels Association of America. 2013. www.mowaa.org.

produced. Increasing a country's capacity to feed its population by developing manageable systems for producing food benefits the worker, the landowner, and the community, even where poverty is widespread.[60] Crop sales generate income that travels through the economic system; this can significantly decrease poverty and help reduce hunger.

Agricultural Practices and Techniques

Biotechnology, specifically the production of genetically modified foods, can create crops with increased yields and pest resistance. Some staple crops, such as corn and rice, can be bioengineered to contain nutrients or precursors. For example, beta-carotene in "golden rice" is helping to alleviate vitamin A deficiency, which is the leading cause of blindness worldwide. Biotechnology can also improve the quality of plant foods by improving the taste or shelf life of fruits and vegetables.

On the other end of the spectrum, many farmers are turning to organic farming. In organic farming, as defined by the USDA, farmers do not use GMOs, or chemical pesticides or fertilizers. They do support animal health and welfare, provide outdoor access for animals, use only approved materials, receive annual onsite inspections, and separate organic from nonorganic food. They thus preserve natural resources and biodiversity and reduce pollution.[61]

As the soil on organic farms becomes balanced, the crops growing there tend to become healthier, and more disease resistant. While the yield from an organic farm may be lower than that of an industrial farm, organically grown plants tend to be more drought resistant.

Proper land management and appropriate crop selection can also help increase agricultural production. For example, in many countries productive land that could be used for food crops is frequently used for nonnutritive crops, such as tobacco or flowers. This is done to generate income through crop sales to industrialized nations. If some of this land were used instead to raise food crops for domestic consumption, such as high-protein beans, vegetables, grains, seeds, nuts, or fruit, instead of export crops, hunger could be reduced.[62] This argument applies to raising meat, as well. If farmers raised crops instead of animals for consumption, they could, generally speaking, feed more people.

Land ownership is directly related to food security and is a way of motivating farmers to make better decisions regarding irrigation, crop rotation, land fallowing (leaving land plowed, but unplanted), and appropriate soil management.[63] Land ownership is part of a long-term solution to a very complex problem. Part of this problem is that land ownership is not evenly distributed across most populations, and as mentioned above some landowners grow nonfood crops, such as tobacco, rather than crops that might feed local people. This situation is unlikely to change without *land reform,* in which governments create rules to reallocate land to landless people. In some countries there are grassroots programs under way that provide access to land for women and their families for the purpose of growing food and planting gardens.

Water and Sanitation

Providing safe water is critical in reducing hunger. Global freshwater consumption continues to rise at more than twice the rate of population growth,[64] creating health problems associated with lack of access to safe water and sanitation. Progress is being made to improve drinking water sources through programs that build wells and piped connections to dwellings; still, over 768 million people use unsafe drinking water sources, and 2.5 billion people (36 percent of the developing world's population) do not have improved sanitation facilities.[65]

The World Health Organization estimated in 2009 that 88 percent of all diarrheal illnesses in the world are attributable to inadequate water or sanitation.[66] The consequences of unsanitary conditions are enormous. Entire communities are often at risk for health problems from drinking contaminated water. A person who has diarrhea is at increased risk for malnutrition.[67]

Poor access to sufficient quantities of water is closely related to ecosystem conditions. About one-third of the world's

Better land management, appropriate crop selection, and biotechnology can all help eliminate hunger.

Access to clean drinking water is just as important as adequate nutrition for human health.

population lives in countries with moderate to high water stress, and problems of water scarcity are increasing, due in part to ecosystem depletion and contamination. Two out of every three persons on the globe may be living in water-stressed conditions by the year 2025 if the present global consumption patterns continue.[68] Water ecosystems are vital to the replenishment and purification of water resources, but development and land use have greatly affected the sustainability of many such systems.

Some innovative solutions are being proposed to alleviate the world's water problems. For example, in Tanzania, solar energy is being used to thermally purify the water supply.[69] Water is poured into plastic jugs that are placed on black-covered roofs and allowed to heat for several hours. Once the temperature of the water exceeds 50°C, it becomes safe to drink. The solar heat and UV rays effectively destroy common waterborne bacteria such as those that cause cholera, typhoid, and dysentery.

Preserving the health of both freshwater and coastal ecosystems is necessary and vital to the health and well-being of an increasing proportion of the world's population. Solutions to water management and protection include efforts at a number of levels. At the ecosystem level, protection of natural watersheds is necessary to ensure that the natural filtration and purification mechanisms continue. Integrated water management is another solution that includes the allocation of water resources on a shared and managed basis to governments, tourism, fisheries, and industries. Finally, water needs to be protected from contamination at all levels. This includes conservation and safe filtration and use at the household level, along with development and implementation of water monitoring and controls at the local, national, and global levels.[70]

Fortify Foods to Raise Nutrient Levels

Globally the most common micronutrient deficiencies include iodine, iron, and vitamin A. The fortification of staple foods with nutrients can help to alleviate these deficiencies. For food fortification to work, the staple foods must be shelf-stable, affordable, and consistently available in the food supply. Rice, cereals, flours, salt, and even sugar are examples of foods that can be successfully fortified.

Because food fortification is inexpensive, as well as enormously beneficial, fortification programs are being developed and implemented worldwide. Countries all across the globe fortify foods such as salt, flour, oil, sugar, and soy sauce with iron, iodine, and vitamin A.[71]

Promote Education

Education plays an important role in ensuring food security (see **Figure 21.4**). Educated people are more likely to have economic opportunities, and less likely to fall into the cycle of poverty. Literacy and education also build self-esteem and self-confidence, two qualities that help people overcome life's challenges.

Education also reduces poverty in other ways. For example, one study found that societies with a more educated population enjoyed:[72]

- Higher earning potential
- Improved sanitation
- More small businesses and rural enterprises
- Lower rates of infant mortality and improved child welfare
- Higher likelihood of technological advancement

The type and format of education varies depending on the needs of the people. To help solve hunger problems, education in the developing world ought to focus on including women and girls, and on literacy, technical knowledge, agricultural skills, horticulture, health education, and the development of natural resources. A focus

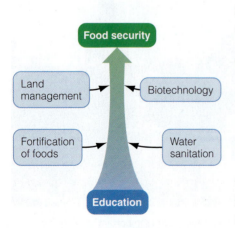

▲ **Figure 21.4 Factors in Food Security**

on agricultural education can help improve knowledge and skills and promote increased agricultural production. Educating women is of particular importance: It has been shown that population growth slows when women are educated.[73]

Generally, educators in the developed world should focus on land management, the importance of land reform, biotechnology, improved crop yields, boosting nutrient levels within crops, and continued development of drought-resistant and insect-repelling plants.

Assistance Programs across the Globe

Across the globe many large and small international organizations are working to end hunger. The World Food Programme, which has the goal of getting to "Zero Hunger," provides hundreds of thousands of tons of food per year to people in need, and this is only one of its programs—it also provides cash and vouchers to people who have access to food but not enough money to buy it, and it has programs to put people to work to improve their community and get paid in food.[74] Another large organization, UNICEF, channels money for humanitarian aid from people in developed countries to help feed children in need in developing countries. UNICEF was founded after the Second World War, to help children in war-torn countries, and it continues to do so today.[75]

The group Heifer International has the goal of ending poverty by providing families with animals such as sheep, goats, cows, or even flocks of ducks.[76] The idea is that families can become self-sufficient, and also sell surplus milk, eggs, and wool. The group also provides tools and training. Making families self-sufficient can help to lift them out of poverty.

The Peace Corps is another organization that helps people struggling with poverty, by helping communities develop in the areas of education, health, and the environment, among other things.[77] When people have the training they need, they become empowered to change their own situation.

> **LO 21.5: THE TAKE-HOME MESSAGE** Reducing or eliminating hunger benefits everyone. Local charities and community groups, corporations, and governments can provide aid and organize programs to alleviate hunger. Biotechnology and food fortification are two strategies that help provide healthier, hardier food crops with additional nutrients. Education of the world's population is also important, along with proper land management and proper crop selection. Several programs around the world help with global poverty and hunger.

Health Connection

What Are the Effects of Chronic Hunger?

LO 21.6 Describe the health consequences of hunger.

The effects of hunger can range from acute and reversible to chronic and irreversible. All human beings have an essential need for water and nutritious and adequate food in order to be healthy. When food or water is not available or is in limited supply, symptoms of nutrient deficiencies and emaciation become apparent. If the lack of food continues, it can prompt a downward health spiral that is hard to reverse (**Figure 21.5**).

In times of reduced kilocaloric intake, such as in times of fasting, famine, serious disease, or severe malnutrition, the body attempts to conserve energy and preserve body tissues by lowering basal metabolism. Over an extended period of time, however, the body needs to find a new source of energy and begins to break down its own tissue. This results in the reduction of stored fat and ultimately the

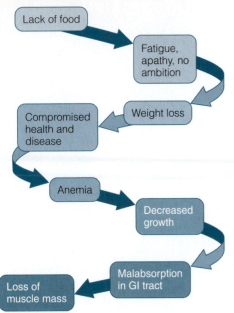

▲ Figure 21.5 Downward Spiral of Hunger and Malnutrition
Lack of food can lead to numerous other symptoms that compound the problem of hunger.

deterioration of internal organs and muscle mass. In prolonged starvation, adults can lose up to 50 percent of their body weight. The greatest amount of deterioration occurs in the intestinal tract and the liver; the loss is moderate in the heart and kidneys; and the least damage occurs in the brain and nervous system.[78]

Let's look at some individual effects of chronic hunger and malnutrition.

Children Suffer Impaired Growth and Development

If a child does not receive adequate kilocalories and nutrients while growing, his or her development will be affected. A child is likely to experience both physical and mental problems, including insufficient weight gain, improper muscle development, lowered resistance to infection,

growth stunting Impaired growth and development primarily manifested in early childhood and including malnutrition during fetal development. Once growth stunting occurs, it is usually permanent.

wasting The diminishment of muscle and fat tissue caused by extremely low energy intake from too little food and therefore too little energy; sometimes referred to as *acute malnutrition*.

growth stunting, and impaired brain development (**Figure 21.6**).[79] The bodies of children who are undernourished compensate for a lack of food by decreasing physical and mental growth. Children are more likely to show behavioral, emotional, and academic problems if they come from families that experience hunger and food insufficiency rather than from families that do not report hunger experiences.[80] In particular, long-term undernutrition is associated with increased anxiety, irritability, attention problems, and school absence and tardiness rates.[81, 82]

If hunger persists or occurs at early, crucial times of brain development, cognitive development is impaired.[83] Slowed brain growth could result in permanent lower intelligence and hindered learning ability. As a result, malnourished children may have a difficult time completing an elementary education, which has a measurable impact on income-earning ability later in life.

Even if the children are healthy enough to regularly attend school, hunger and malnutrition impair cognitive development.[84] Malnourished children also tend to be fatigued, inattentive, and unresponsive to their learning environment. Peers, teachers, and adult caregivers may neglect a child who does not respond to or interact with others.

Malnourished children grow poorly; globally, an estimated 161 million children experienced height stunting in 2012, and about 149 million of these children lived in Africa and Asia.[85] Deficiencies of energy, protein, iron, and zinc, as well as prolonged infection, have been implicated as causes. In 2012, about 40 million children under 5 years old in the developing world suffered from physical **wasting** (decreased weight for age) or *moderate acute malnutrition*.[86] Growth stunting has also been associated

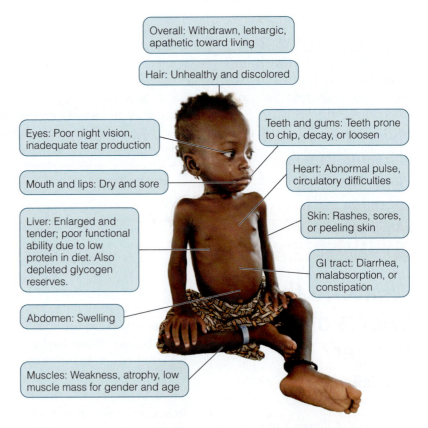

▲ Figure 21.6 Symptoms of Starvation
As hunger persists, physical symptoms set in and lead to further complications.

with long-term detrimental effects not only on development and immune function, but also on cognition and educational achievement.[87, 88]

Weakened Immunity Results in Disease

A malnourished individual has a weakened immune system, which increases his or her vulnerability to various infections. Fever, parasitic disease, pneumonia, measles, typhoid, cholera, and malaria are examples of conditions that can occur because of weakened immune systems and chronic malnutrition.

In 2012, 6.6 million children under the age of 5 died.[89] The World Health Organization estimates that about 45 percent of all childhood deaths in developing countries are associated with malnutrition. The most common causes of death in postneonatal children (that is, those who survive birth and the first 28 days of life) are pneumonia, diarrhea, and malaria, all of which have malnutrition as an underlying contributing factor.[90] **Table 21.3** summarizes the ramifications of these illnesses.

Diarrhea—caused by viruses, parasites, and other harmful microorganisms—can result in severe dehydration (loss of fluids and electrolytes). The gastrointestinal infections that cause diarrhea kill around 2.2 million people globally each year, mostly children in developing countries.[91] The use of contaminated water is a major cause of diarrhea.

Vitamin and mineral deficiencies and their resulting diseases are also serious concerns for people living in developing countries as well as for the impoverished in the United States. For example, more than 2 billion people, or more than one-third of the world's population, live with vitamin A, iron, or iodine deficiency.[92] These micronutrient deficiencies are sometimes referred to as "hidden hunger." **Table 21.4** lists the most common vitamin and mineral deficiencies observed in those who are malnourished.

TABLE 21.3	Common Illnesses in Malnourished Children	
Disease/Condition	**Cause**	**Effect**
Diarrhea	Pathogenic infections	Severe dehydration
Acute respiratory illness	Virus or bacteria	Pneumonia, bronchitis, colds, fast breathing, coughing, and fever
Malaria	Parasite (transmitted by a mosquito)	Flu, weakness, sweating, shivering, shaking, nausea, liver failure, infected red blood cells, and kidney failure or bleeding in the kidneys

TABLE 21.4	The Most Common Vitamin and Mineral Deficiencies	
Vitamin or Mineral	**Effects of Deficiency**	**Incidence**
Vitamin A	Eye disease, blindness	Vitamin A deficiency is the leading cause of preventable blindness in children in developing countries.
Iron	Iron-deficiency anemia	Extremely common worldwide. Anemia is most common among 7- to 12-month-old infants; toddlers and young children ($<$ 8 years of age); women of reproductive age; and anyone who has lost large amounts of blood.
Iodine	Goiter, cretinism	Iodine deficiency is the world's most prevalent, yet easily preventable, cause of brain damage. Up to 790 million people (13% of the world's population) have some form of iodine deficiency, goiter, or mental impairment caused by lack of iodine.
Folate	Macrocytic anemia	Folate deficiency is common among women of reproductive age; individuals with limited diets and reduced vegetable consumption; individuals who abuse alcohol; and obese individuals.
Vitamin B_{12}	Pernicious anemia	B_{12} deficiency is common among elderly men and women ($>$ 50 years of age); African-American adults; individuals who have malabsorption syndromes; and vegetarians who don't take enough B_{12} supplementation.

Infant and Child Mortality Rates Increase

Malnutrition is part of a vicious cycle that passes hunger and illness from one generation to the next. Unfortunately, many young women experience undernutrition during their own infancy and childhood. Girls who were low birth weight babies or were undernourished and ill during the first five years of life may be physically stunted and less able to support a healthy pregnancy when they become adults. The infants born to malnourished women are more likely to be malnourished themselves, to

experience chronic illness, and to have an increased risk of premature death.[93]

LO 21.6: THE TAKE-HOME MESSAGE
The effects of chronic malnutrition are devastating and can produce irreversible damage, depending on the stage of life. If malnutrition occurs during adulthood, the body tries to conserve nutrients and preserve its own organs, but eventually there could be irreversible organ damage. Physical effects of malnutrition in infants and children include stunted growth, impaired mental development and immunity, and higher likelihood of disease.

LO 21.1 Malnutrition Is a Problem throughout the World

Hunger and malnutrition are health conditions that can result from food insecurity. Despite abundant food production, many people in the United States and around the world suffer from chronic hunger, food insecurity, and malnutrition. People may get too few nutrients, and suffer from undernutrition, or they may eat too many or the wrong kind of nutrients, as in overnutrition. Less than one-sixth of the world's population lives in developed nations that have a high standard of living. Many of the world's residents live in developing or least developed countries and have access to fewer resources.

LO 21.2 Several Factors Contribute to Malnutrition in the United States

The USDA divides food insecurity into two subcategories: *low food security* and *very low food security*. In the United States, food insecurity and malnutrition can occur anywhere, including in rural areas, inner cities, and suburbs. Causes include poverty, disease or disability, lack of education, and inadequate wages. People living in food deserts are at risk of malnutrition. Mental illness and/or drug and alcohol abuse sometimes lead to homelessness, which in turn often results in hunger.

LO 21.3 Various Factors Contribute to Malnutrition around the World

Political sanctions, armed conflicts, crop failure, wasteful agricultural practices, and overpopulation factor into rates of hunger and malnutrition in many countries. When a country's economy is dependent on agriculture, natural disasters such as droughts, floods, diseases, and insect infestations can have a dire impact on food production and levels of hunger. Even when a country becomes more prosperous, its people may suffer from nutrition transition, a situation in which they get more, but not necessarily better, food.

LO 21.4 Pregnant and Lactating Women, Children, the Ill, and Older Adults Are at Greatest Risk for Malnutrition

Pregnant and lactating women have higher kilocalorie and nutrient needs. If they are improperly nourished, their infants may be, too. Infants and children in general have high nutrient needs because they are growing rapidly. They are dependent on their caregivers for food, making them more susceptible to food insecurity. Chronically ill people may have malabsorption problems. Older adults may be at risk for malnutrition because of higher needs for several micronutrients, decreased senses of smell and taste, chronic illness, compromised immunity, and lack of mobility.

LO 21.5 Providing Greater Food Resources Can Reduce Hunger

Biotechnology and food fortification are helping to reduce hunger worldwide by providing larger and more nutrient-dense food crops. Because deficiencies of iron, iodine, and vitamin A are most common, these are the nutrients most often used to fortify foods. Agricultural practices such as using genetically modified foods and organic farming can help to reduce hunger, and safe water and sanitation practices are crucial to reducing illness.

Community and faith-based organizations can help ease hunger by providing free food and meals and assistance programs to help people overcome poverty and food insecurity. Corporations and governments can invest in biotechnologies and education programs that provide more nutrient-dense foods and increase economic opportunity.

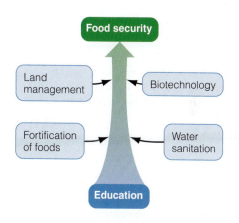

LO 21.6 Chronic Hunger Damages Your Health

Effects of chronic hunger include stunted growth, wasting, and impaired immune function, which increases disease risk, infections, anemia, and nutrient deficiencies. A nutrient deficiency can lead to serious, permanent health damage in both children and adults. Children who are malnourished are at increased risk for early death.

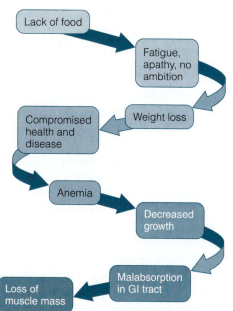

Terms to Know

- hunger
- malnutrition
- undernutrition
- overnutrition
- developed country
- developing country
- least developed country
- food insecurity
- food security
- poverty
- working poor
- food deserts
- sanctions
- famine
- overpopulation
- nutrition transition
- food pantry
- emergency kitchen
- growth stunting
- wasting

Check Your Understanding

1. Approximately how many people in the United States are food insecure?
   a. 11.3 million
   b. 14.8 million
   c. 50.1 million
   d. 16.2 million
2. Which of the following is a leading cause of famine?
   a. lack of technology
   b. lack of education
   c. natural disaster
   d. underpopulation
3. Which of the following states in the United States had one of the highest food insecurity rates between 2009 and 2011?
   a. Missouri
   b. Michigan
   c. North Dakota
   d. Mississippi
4. What does "hidden hunger" refer to?
   a. malnutrition in poor countries that no one knows about
   b. micronutrient deficiencies in the diet
   c. hunger in rich countries that people can't see
   d. lack of protein in the diet
5. Which of the following groups are especially vulnerable to illness?
   a. infants and young children
   b. adolescents
   c. adult men
   d. adult women
6. What is the projected world population for 2050?
   a. 7.8 billion
   b. 9.7 billion
   c. 6 billion
   d. 6.2 billion
7. A lack of which micronutrient has been implicated in causing blindness in children?
   a. vitamin K
   b. iodine
   c. iron
   d. vitamin A
8. Who are the "working poor"?
   a. workers classified as low income by the United States Department of Labor
   b. workers who have no steady employment
   c. workers who are employed but have incomes that fall below the poverty line
   d. workers who earn minimum wage
9. Which nutrients are most likely to be used to fortify food?
   a. vitamins D, E, and K
   b. sodium, potassium, and chloride
   c. magnesium, phosphorus, and sulfur
   d. iron, iodine, and vitamin A
10. How many people are killed each year by gastrointestinal infections that cause diarrhea?
   a. about 5.5 million
   b. about 800,000
   c. about 2.2 million
   d. about 3.2 million

Answers

1. (c) About 50.1 million people in the United States lived in food-insecure households in 2011.
2. (c) Natural disasters, such as drought, are a leading cause of famine. Lack of education would only be an indirect cause, at best. Biotechnology and underpopulation bear no relation to famine.
3. (d) Between 2009 and 2011, the five states with the highest food insecurity rates were Mississippi, Texas, Arkansas, Alabama, and North Carolina.
4. (b) Hidden hunger refers to micronutrient deficiencies, such as of vitamin A, iron, or iodine. This condition affects over 2 billion people in the world.
5. (a) Infants and young children have immature immune systems. Adolescents and adults have mature immune systems that are stronger and function better.
6. (b) The projected world population for 2050 is 9.7 billion.
7. (d) Vitamin A is implicated in preventable blindness.
8. (c) The working poor include individuals who are employed yet still have incomes below the official poverty line.
9. (d) Iron, iodine, and vitamin A are frequently used to fortify food because deficiencies of them are linked to many common and serious illnesses.
10. (c) About 2.2 million people are killed each year by the gastrointestinal infections that cause diarrhea.

Answers to True or False?

1. **True.** While hunger may be more severe in developing countries, it occurs all over the globe.
2. **True.** 842 million people are hungry.
3. **False.** Even those who have jobs sometimes experience food insecurity.
4. **True.** Depression among mothers, particularly those in low-income families, has been associated with food insecurity in households.
5. **True.** The world's agricultural producers grow enough food to nourish every man, woman, and child on the planet. The challenge is distributing their products evenly.
6. **True.** Natural disasters such as droughts, floods, storms, earthquakes, crop diseases, and insect plagues can create food and water shortages in any country.
7. **False.** Malnutrition can occur in anyone. Those at greatest risk include pregnant and lactating women, infants and children, and the ill and elderly.
8. **False.** Fortifying foods can provide numerous nutrients that some populations wouldn't otherwise obtain.
9. **False.** There is a clear link in women between food insecurity and overweight and obesity.
10. **False.** While getting food to hungry people is a short-term solution, the hunger issue is more complex. Reducing hunger over the long term involves improving agriculture, water use and sanitation, and education.

Web Resources

- To learn more about one organization that is fighting global poverty, visit CARE at www.care.org
- To find out how the Food and Agriculture Organization of the United Nations leads international efforts to defeat hunger, visit www.fao.org
- To learn more about an international children's group, visit the UNICEF website at www.unicef.org
- For more about the World Health Organization, visit www.who.org
- To learn more about how biotechnology is impacting food production in developing countries, visit www.sustaintech.org

References

1. World Food Programme. Hunger. 2014. *What Is Malnutrition?* Available at www.wfp.org. Accessed May 2013.
2. Food and Agriculture Organization of the United Nations. 2014. *Hunger Portal.* Available at www.fao.org. Accessed June 2014.
3. Population Reference Bureau. World Population Data Sheet. 2012. *Fact Sheet: World Population Trends 2012.* Available at www.prb.org. Accessed June 2014.
4. Food and Agriculture Organization. 2013. *Executive Summary. The State of Food Insecurity in the World. The Multiple Dimensions of Food Insecurity.* Available at www.fao.org. Accessed June 2014.
5. World Hunger Education Service. 2013. *World Hunger and Poverty Facts and Statistics. What Are the Causes of Hunger?* Available at www.worldhunger.org. Accessed June 2014.
6. WHO. The Health and Environment Linkages Initiative (HELI). 2014. *Water, Health and Ecosystems.* Available at www.who.int. Accessed June 2014.
7. World Health Organization. 2014. *Micronutrient Deficiencies: Vitamin A Deficiency.* Available at www.who.int. Accessed June 2014.
8. World Health Organization. 2014. *Micronutrient Deficiencies: Iron-Deficiency Anaemia.* Available at www.who.int. Accessed June 2014.
9. World Health Organization. 2014. *Feto-Maternal Nutrition and Low Birth Weight.* Available at www.who.int. Accessed June 2014.
10. The World Bank. 2014. *Data. GDP Per Capita ($US).* Available at http://data.worldbank.org. Accessed August 2014.
11. USDA. 2014. *Food Security in the U.S.* Available at www.ers.usda.gov. Accessed May 2014.
12. USDA. 2014. *Definitions of Food Security.* Available at www.ers.usda.gov. Accessed May 2014.
13. Food Bank for New York City. 2011. *Food Poverty in NYC.* Available at www.foodbanknyc.org. Accessed June 2012.
14. Healthy People.gov. 2014. *2020 Topics and Objectives: Nutrition and Weight Status.* Available at www.healthypeople.gov. Accessed June 2014.
15. USDA. Economic Research Service. 2013. *Household Food Security in the United States in 2012.* Available at www.ers.usda.gov. Accessed May 2014.
16. Ibid.
17. Ibid.
18. USDA. Economic Research Service. 2014. *State Fact Sheets.* Available at www.ers.usda.gov. Accessed May 2014
19. USDA. ERS. 2012. *Rural Economy & Population.* Available at www.ers.usda.gov. Accessed June 2014.
20. U.S. Census Bureau. 2013. *Poverty: Highlights.* Available at www.census.gov. Accessed May 2014.
21. United States Census Bureau. 2013. *Poverty: Poverty Thresholds.* Available at www.census.gov. Accessed May 2014.
22. USDA. 2014. United States Department of Agriculture, Economic Research Service. Key Statistics & Graphics. www.ers.usda.gov. Accessed June 2014.
23. Ibid.
24. USDA Economic Research Service. 2013. *Food Insecurity in Households With Children: Prevalence, Severity, and Household Characteristics, 2010-11.* Available at www.ers.usda.gov. Accessed June 2014.
25. U.S. Department of Labor, Bureau of Labor Statistics. 2014. *A Profile of the Working Poor, 2012.* Available at www.bls.gov. Accessed June 2014.
26. USDA. 2014. *Food Deserts.* Available at http://apps.ams.usda.gov. Accessed June 2014.
27. CDC Features. 2012. *A Look Inside Food Deserts.* Available at www.cdc.gov. Accessed June 2014.
28. National Coalition for the Homeless. 2009. *Mental Illness and Homelessness.* Available at www.nationalhomeless.org. Accessed June 2014.
29. Whitaker, R.C., S. M. Phillips, and S. M. Orzel. 2006. Food Insecurity and the Risks of Depression and Anxiety in Mothers and Behavior Problems in their Preschool-Aged Children. *PEDIATRICS* 118: e859-e868.
30. Ibid.
31. Substance Abuse and Mental Health Services Administration. 2011. *Current Statistics on the Prevalence and Characteristics of People Experiencing Homelessness in the United States, July 2011.* Available at http://homeless.samhsa.gov. Accessed May 2014.
32. Food and Agriculture Organization of the United Nations. 2013. *The State of Food Insecurity in the World.* Available at www.fao.org. Accessed May 2014.
33. Food and Agriculture Organization of the United Nations. 2013. *Undernourishment Around the World in 2013.* Available at www.fao.org. Accessed June 2014.
34. World Hunger Education Service. 2013. *2013 World Hunger and Poverty Facts and Statistics.* Available at www.worldhunger.org. Accessed June 2014.
35. Doss, Cheryl, et al. 2013. Gender Inequalities in Ownership and Control of Land in Africa. Washington, DC: International Food Policy Research Institute. Available at www.ifpri.org. Accessed June 2014.
36. Smith, L. C., and L. Haddad. 2000. *Explaining Child Malnutrition in Developing Countries: A Cross-Country Analysis.* Washington, DC: International Food Policy Research Institute. Available at www.ifpri.org. Accessed May 2014.
37. UNESCO. 2012. *Key Messages and Data on Girls' and Women's Education and Literacy.* Available at www.unesco.org. Accessed May 2014.
38. Ibid.
39. United Nations. 2014. *Millennium Development Goals and Beyond 2015.* Available at www.un.org. Accessed May 2014.
40. Petrescu, Ioana M. 2010. *The Humanitarian Impact of Economic Sanctions.* Available at www.essex.ac.uk. Accessed May 2014.
41. World Food Programme. 2012. *Hunger. What Causes Hunger?* Available at www.wfp.org. Accessed May 2014.
42. Ibid.
43. United Nations Environment Programme. 2013. *Food Waste Harms Climate, Water, Land and Biodiversity.* Available at www.unep.org. Accessed June 2014.
44. World Food Programme. 2012. *Hunger. What Causes Hunger?*
45. Mission 2014: Feeding the World. 2014. *Ineffective/Inadequate Agricultural Practices.* Available at www.mit.edu. Accessed May 2014.
46. United Nations, UN News Centre. 2013. World Population Projected to Reach 9.6 Billion by 2050—UN Report. Available at www.un.org. Accessed May 2014.
47. Ibid.
48. Scott, B., E. W. Counts, M. Medora, and C. Woolery. 1998. The Dietitian's Role in Ending World Hunger: As Citizen and Health Professional. *Topics in Clinical Nutrition* 13:31–45.
49. The World Bank. 2011. *Getting to Equal: How Educating Every Girl Can Help Break the Cycle of Poverty.* Available at www.worldbank.org. Accessed May 2014.
50. Schmidhuber, J., and P. Shetty. 2005. *The Nutrition Transition to 2030. Why Developing Countries Are Likely to Bear the Major Burden.* Available at www.fao.org. Accessed June 2014.
51. Freedom from Hunger. 2014. *World Hunger Facts.* Available at www.freedomfromhunger.org. Accessed June 2014.
52. Reivilo, K. 1990. How Does Infant Mortality Affect Birth Rates? *Duodecimo* 106:1187–1189. (Article in Finnish) Available at www.ncbi.nlm.nih.gov. Accessed May 2014.

53. King, F. S., and A. Burgess. 1993. *Nutrition for Developing Countries.* 2nd ed. Oxford, England: Oxford Medical Publications, Oxford University Press.

54. World Health Organization. 2002. *The Optimal Duration of Exclusive Breast-Feeding: A Systematic Review.* Geneva: World Health Organization. Available at www.who.int. Accessed May 2014.

55. King, et al. 1993. *Nutrition for Developing Countries.*

56. Dickson, Shey Nsagha, Ngowe Ngowe Marcelin, Jules Clement Nguedia Assob, and Anna Longdoh Njundah. 2013. A Public Health Model and Framework to Mitigate the Impact of Orphans and Vulnerable Children Due to HIV/AIDS in Cameroon. *World Journal of AIDS* 4:27–37. Available at www.scirp.org/journal/wja. Accessed June 2014.

57. UNICEF. Childinfo. Updated 2013. *Statistics by Area. HIV/AIDS.* Available at www.childinfo.org. Accessed June 2014.

58. Food Research and Action Center. 2011. *Why Low-Income and Food-Insecure People Are Vulnerable to Overweight and Obesity.* Available at http://frac.org. Accessed May 2014.

59. USDA. 2013. *The Food Assistance Landscape: FY 2012 Annual Report.* Available at www.ers.usda.gov. Accessed May 2014.

60. Food and Agriculture Organization of the United Nations. 2013. *The State of Food Insecurity in the World.* www.fao.org. Accessed May 2014.

61. USDA Organic Agriculture. 2014. Available at www.usda.gov. Accessed May 2014.

62. Lappe, F. and J. Collins. 1998. *World Hunger: Twelve Myths.* 2nd ed. New York: Grove Press.

63. Ibid.

64. Bazza, M., and R. Najib. 2003. Towards Improved Water Demand Management in Agriculture in the Syrian Arab Republic. Available at www.fao.org. Accessed June 2014.

65. WHO/UNICEF. 2013. *Water, Sanitation and Hygiene.* Available at www.unicef.org. Accessed May 2013.

66. WHO. Media Centre. 2009. Reducing Childhood Deaths from Diarrhoea. News Release. Available at www.who.int. Accessed May 2014.

67. WHO. Media Centre. 2013. *Diarrhoeal Disease. Fact Sheet no. 330.* Available at www.who.int. Accessed May 2014.

68. United Nations. 2012. International Decade for Action 'Water for Life' 2005–2015. *Water Scarcity.* Available at www.un.org. Accessed May 2014.

69. BBC News, Africa. 2006. Using the Sun to Sterilize Water. Available at http://news.bbc.co.uk. Accessed May 2014.

70. The Health and Environment Linkages Initiative. 2008. *Water, Health, and Ecosystems.* Available at www.who.int. Accessed June 2012.

71. Global Alliance for Improved Nutrition. 1996. *Why Food Fortification?* Available at www.gainhealth.org. Accessed June 2012.

72. Cleland, J. G., and J. K. Van Ginneken. 1988. Maternal Education and Child Survival in Developing Countries: The Search for Pathways of Influence. *Social Science and Medicine* 27:1357–1368.

73. Population Reference Bureau. 2012. *Human Population: Women: Factors Affecting Family Size.* Available at www.prb.org. Accessed June 2014.

74. World Food Programme. 2014. Fighting Hunger Worldwide. Available at www.wfp.org. Accessed June 2014.

75. UNICEF. 2013. UNICEF in Emergencies and Humanitarian Action. UNICEF's Role in Humanitarian Action. Available at www.unicef.org. Accessed September 2014.

76. Heifer International. 2014. About Heifer International. Available at www.heifer.org. Accessed September 2014.

77. Peace Corps. 2013. Fast Facts. Available at www.peacecorps.gov. Accessed September 2014.

78. Beers, M., R. Porter, T. Jones, J. Kaplan, and M. Berkwits, eds. 2006. Starvation. In *The Merck Manual of Diagnosis and Therapy, Section 1—Nutritional Disorders, Chapter 2: Malnutrition Topics.* Available at www.einet.net. Accessed June 2012.

79. World Food Programme. 2014. *Hunger. What Is Malnutrition?* Available at www.wfp.org. Accessed May 2014.

80. Kleinman, R. E., et al. 1998. Hunger in Children in the United States: Potential Behavioral and Emotional Correlates. *Pediatrics* 101:3–10.

81. Scanlon, K. S. 1989. (Thesis) Activity and Behavior Changes of Marginally Malnourished Mexican Pre-Schoolers. Storrs, CT: University of Connecticut.

82. Mora, J. O. 1979. Nutritional Supplementation, Early Stimulation, and Child Development. In J. Brozek, ed. *Behavioral Effects of Energy and Protein Deficits.* Bethesda, MD: U.S. Department of Health, Education, and Welfare (NIH).

83. Jyoti, D., E. A. Frongillo, and S. J. Jones. September, 2005. Food Insecurity Affects School Children's Academic Performance, Weight Gain, and Social Skills. *Journal of Nutrition* 135:2831–2839.

84. WHO. 2014. *Nutrition. Micronutrient Deficiencies. Iron-Deficiency Anaemia.* Available at www.who.int. Accessed May 2014.

85. World Health Organization. Global Health Observatory Data Repository. 2012. *Joint Child Malnutrition Estimates (UNICEF-WHO-WB): Global and Regional Trends by UN Regions, 1990–2025. Stunting: 1990–2025.* Available at www.apps.who.int. Accessed June 2014.

86. World Health Organization. 2012. *Nutrition. Supplementary Foods for the Management of Moderate Acute Malnutrition in Infants and Children 6–59 Months of Age.* Available at www.who.int. Accessed May 2014.

87. Branca, F., and M. Ferrari. 2002. Impact of Micronutrient Deficiencies on Growth: The Stunting Syndrome. *Annals of Nutrition and Metabolism* 46(Suppl 1):8–17.

88. Walker, S. P., S. M. Chang, C. A. Powell, and S. M. Grantham-McGregor. 2005. Effects of Early Childhood Psychosocial Stimulation and Nutritional Supplementation on Cognition and Education in Growth-Stunted Jamaican Children: Prospective Cohort Study. *The Lancet* 366:1804–1807.

89. World Health Organization. Media Centre. 2012. *Children: Reducing Mortality.* Available at www.who.int. Accessed May 2014.

90. Ibid.

91. World Health Organization. 2012. *Water Sanitation Health. Water-Related Diseases. Diarrhoea.* Available at www.who.int. Accessed May 2014.

92. CDC. 2014. *IMMPaCt - International Micronutrient Malnutrition Prevention and Control Program.* Available at www.cdc.gov. Accessed June 2014.

93. UNICEF. 2014. *India: The Children: Nutrition.* Available at www.unicef.org. Accessed June 2014.

94. Second Harvest Food Bank. 2014. *How We Work.* Available at www.shfb.org. Accessed June 2014.

95. Ibid.

Appendices

When learning about the science of nutrition, it is important to understand basic principles of metabolism and to know the molecular structures of important nutrients and molecules. Chapter 8 of the text provides a detailed discussion of the major metabolic processes that occur within the body. This appendix gives additional information and detail on several metabolism pathways and biochemical structures of importance.

Metabolism Pathways

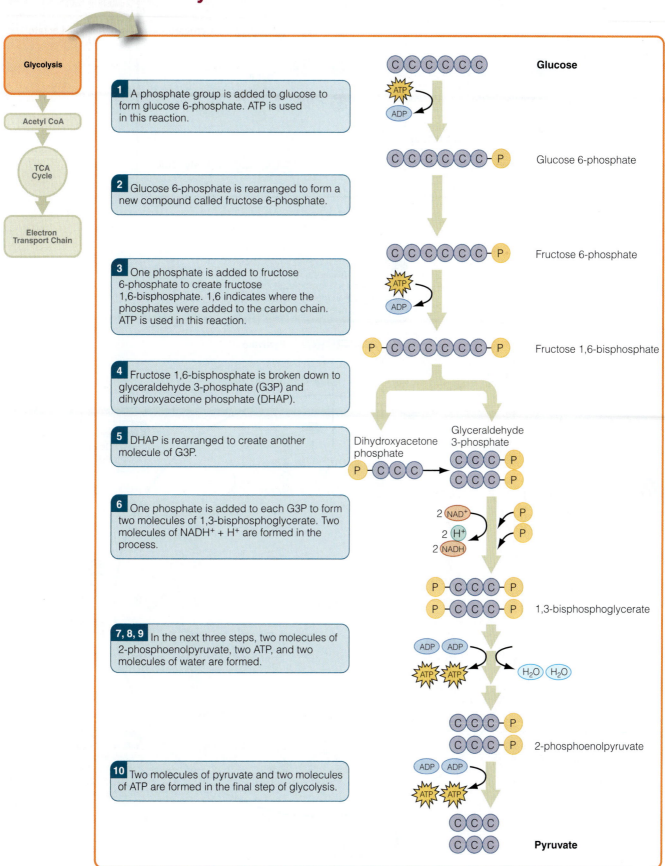

Glycolysis

Acetyl CoA

TCA Cycle

Electron Transport Chain

1 A phosphate group is added to glucose to form glucose 6-phosphate. ATP is used in this reaction.

2 Glucose 6-phosphate is rearranged to form a new compound called fructose 6-phosphate.

3 One phosphate is added to fructose 6-phosphate to create fructose 1,6-bisphosphate. 1,6 indicates where the phosphates were added to the carbon chain. ATP is used in this reaction.

4 Fructose 1,6-bisphosphate is broken down to glyceraldehyde 3-phosphate (G3P) and dihydroxyacetone phosphate (DHAP).

5 DHAP is rearranged to create another molecule of G3P.

6 One phosphate is added to each G3P to form two molecules of 1,3-bisphosphoglycerate. Two molecules of NADH+ + H+ are formed in the process.

7, 8, 9 In the next three steps, two molecules of 2-phosphoenolpyruvate, two ATP, and two molecules of water are formed.

10 Two molecules of pyruvate and two molecules of ATP are formed in the final step of glycolysis.

Glucose

Glucose 6-phosphate

Fructose 6-phosphate

Fructose 1,6-bisphosphate

Dihydroxyacetone phosphate

Glyceraldehyde 3-phosphate

1,3-bisphosphoglycerate

2-phosphoenolpyruvate

Pyruvate

▲ **Figure A.1 Glycolysis Pathway.**

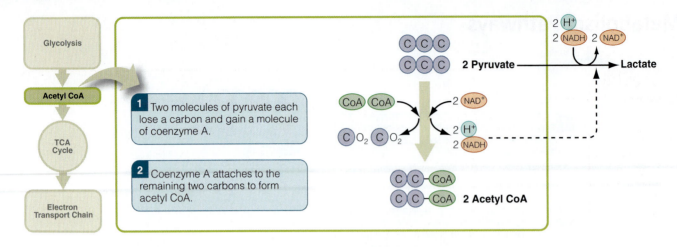

▲ Figure A.2 Acetyl CoA Pathway.

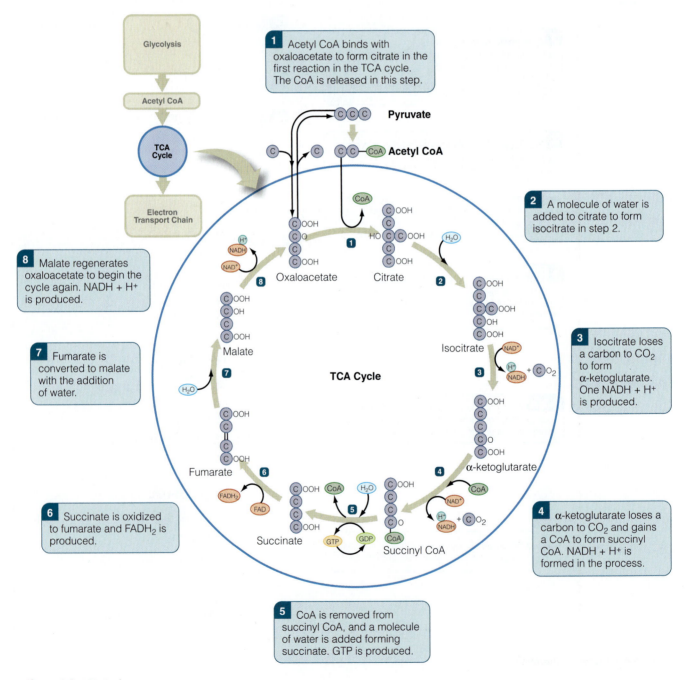

▲ Figure A.3 TCA Cycle.

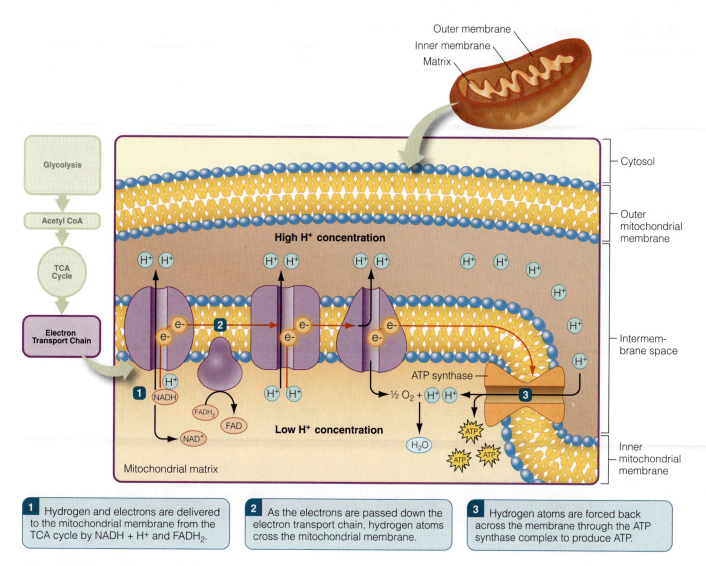

Outer membrane
Inner membrane
Matrix

Glycolysis

Acetyl CoA

TCA Cycle

Electron Transport Chain

Cytosol

Outer mitochondrial membrane

High H⁺ concentration

Intermembrane space

ATP synthase

Inner mitochondrial membrane

Low H⁺ concentration

½ O₂ + H⁺ H⁺

H₂O

ATP

Mitochondrial matrix

NADH

NAD⁺

FADH₂

FAD

1 Hydrogen and electrons are delivered to the mitochondrial membrane from the TCA cycle by NADH + H⁺ and FADH₂.

2 As the electrons are passed down the electron transport chain, hydrogen atoms cross the mitochondrial membrane.

3 Hydrogen atoms are forced back across the membrane through the ATP synthase complex to produce ATP.

▲ Figure A.4 **Electron Transport Chain.**

a Sources of energy use and production in the different metabolic pathways

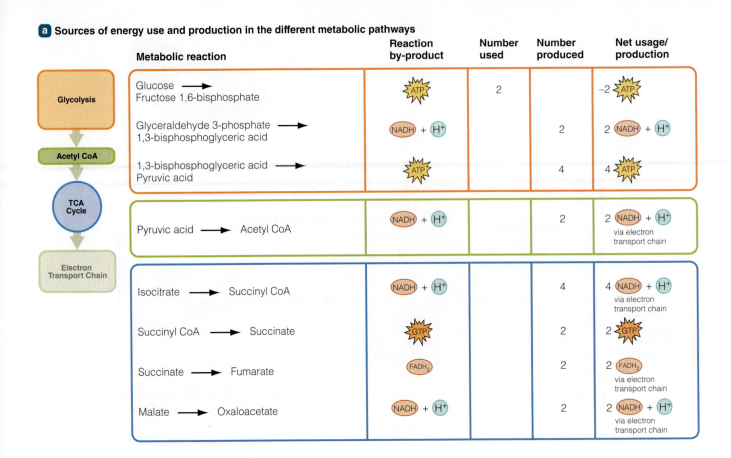

	Metabolic reaction	Reaction by-product	Number used	Number produced	Net usage/ production
Glycolysis	Glucose ⟶ Fructose 1,6-bisphosphate	ATP	2		−2 ATP
	Glyceraldehyde 3-phosphate ⟶ 1,3-bisphosphoglyceric acid	NADH + H⁺		2	2 NADH + H⁺
	1,3-bisphosphoglyceric acid ⟶ Pyruvic acid	ATP		4	4 ATP
	Pyruvic acid ⟶ Acetyl CoA	NADH + H⁺		2	2 NADH + H⁺ via electron transport chain
	Isocitrate ⟶ Succinyl CoA	NADH + H⁺		4	4 NADH + H⁺ via electron transport chain
	Succinyl CoA ⟶ Succinate	GTP		2	2 GTP
	Succinate ⟶ Fumarate	FADH₂		2	2 FADH₂ via electron transport chain
	Malate ⟶ Oxaloacetate	NADH + H⁺		2	2 NADH + H⁺ via electron transport chain

b Energy balance sheet for glucose oxidation

Reaction by-product	Number produced	Number of ATP produced per product	Net usage/ production
ATP	4 − 2 = 2	1	2 × 1 = 2 ATP
NADH + H⁺ from glycolysis	2	2 to 3	2 × 2 = 4 or 2 × 3 = 6 ATP
NADH + H⁺ from TCA cycle	8	3	8 × 3 = 24 ATP
GTP	2	1	2 × 1 = 2 ATP
FADH₂ via electron transport chain	2	2	2 × 2 = 4 ATP

Balance of energy from the oxidation of one unit of glucose: 36 to 38 ATP

▲ **Figure A.5** Products of Metabolic Pathways.

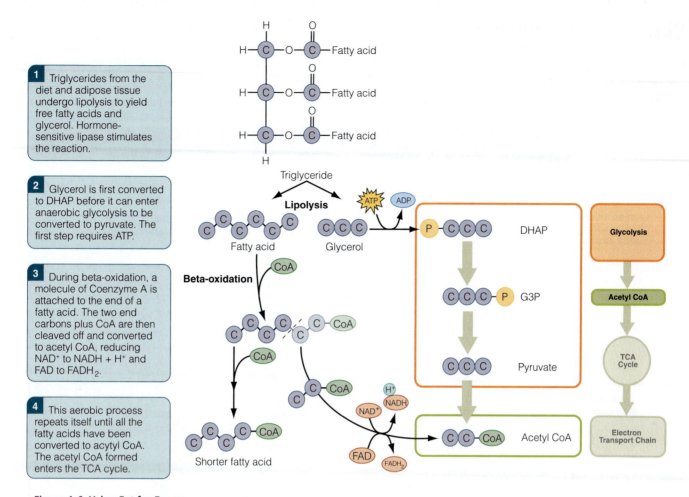

1 Triglycerides from the diet and adipose tissue undergo lipolysis to yield free fatty acids and glycerol. Hormone-sensitive lipase stimulates the reaction.

2 Glycerol is first converted to DHAP before it can enter anaerobic glycolysis to be converted to pyruvate. The first step requires ATP.

3 During beta-oxidation, a molecule of Coenzyme A is attached to the end of a fatty acid. The two end carbons plus CoA are then cleaved off and converted to acetyl CoA, reducing NAD^+ to $NADH + H^+$ and FAD to $FADH_2$.

4 This aerobic process repeats itself until all the fatty acids have been converted to acytyl CoA. The acetyl CoA formed enters the TCA cycle.

▲ **Figure A.6 Using Fat for Energy.**

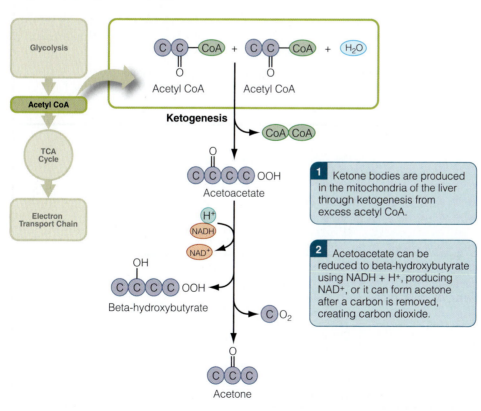

1 Ketone bodies are produced in the mitochondria of the liver through ketogenesis from excess acetyl CoA.

2 Acetoacetate can be reduced to beta-hydroxybutyrate using $NADH + H^+$, producing NAD^+, or it can form acetone after a carbon is removed, creating carbon dioxide.

▲ **Figure A.7 Ketone Bodies.**

Biochemical Structures

Amino Acid Structures

Amino acids all have the same basic core but differ in their side chains. The following amino acids have been classified according to their specific type of side chain.

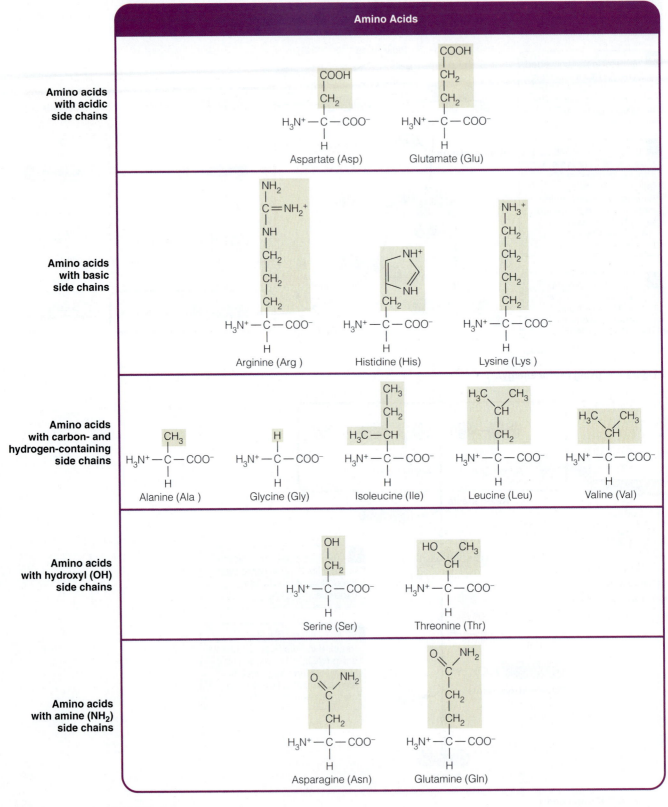

▲ **Figure A.8** **Amino Acid Structures.**

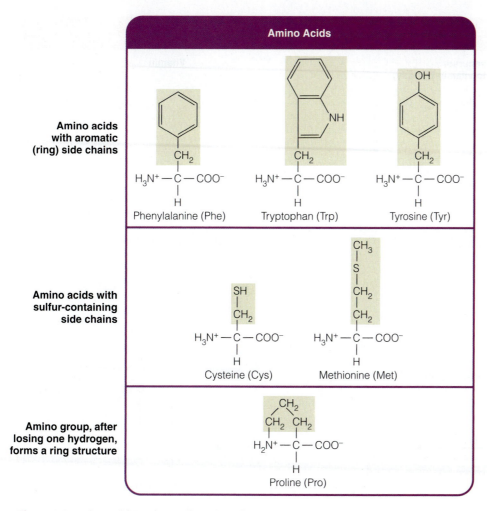

Amino Acids

Amino acids with aromatic (ring) side chains

Phenylalanine (Phe) Tryptophan (Trp) Tyrosine (Tyr)

Amino acids with sulfur-containing side chains

Cysteine (Cys) Methionine (Met)

Amino group, after losing one hydrogen, forms a ring structure

Proline (Pro)

▲ Figure A.8 Amino Acid Structures. *(Continued)*

Vitamin Structures and Coenzyme Derivatives

Many vitamins have common names (for example, vitamin C, vitamin E) as well as scientific designations (for example, ascorbic acid and α-tocopherol). Most vitamins are found in more than one chemical form. Many of the vitamins illustrated here have an active coenzyme form; review both the vitamin and coenzyme structures and see if you can locate the "core vitamin" structure within each of the coenzymes. The vitamins found in food or supplements are not always in the precise chemical form needed for metabolic activity, and therefore the body often has to modify the vitamin in one way or another. For example, many of the B vitamins are phosphorylated, meaning that they have a phosphate group attached.

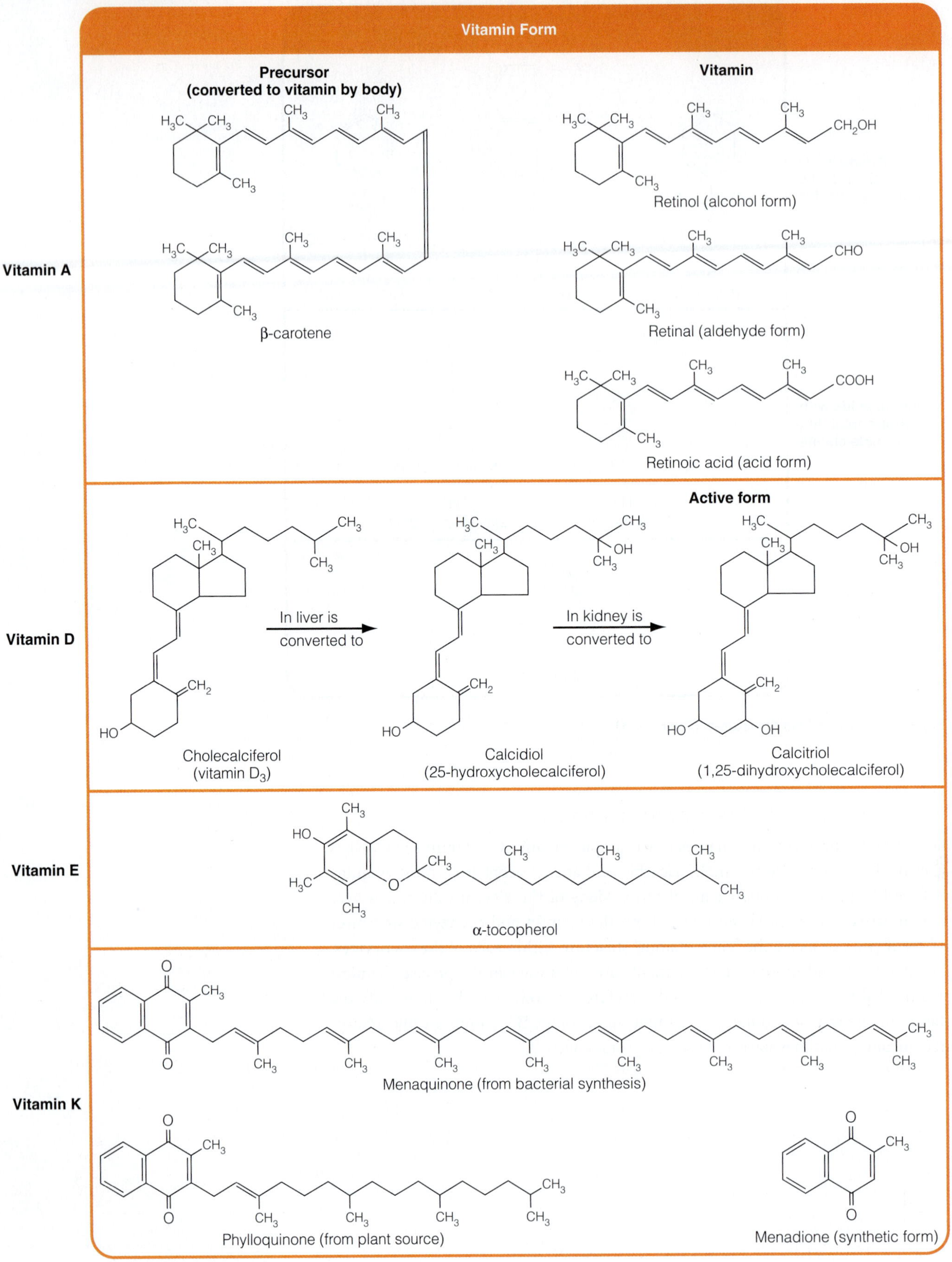

▲ **Figure A.9 Fat-Soluble Vitamins.**

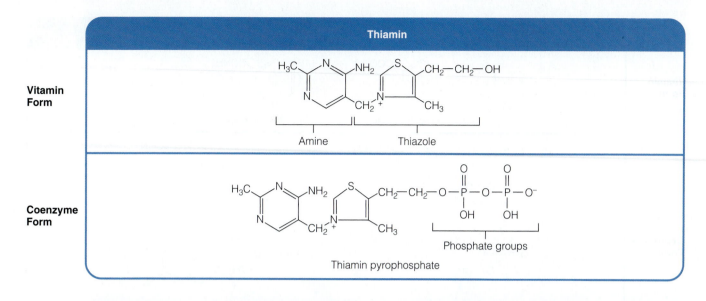

Thiamin

Vitamin Form

Amine | Thiazole

Coenzyme Form

Phosphate groups

Thiamin pyrophosphate

Riboflavin

Vitamin Form

Riboflavin

Coenzyme Form

FMN | AMP

Pyrophosphates

Flavin adenine dinucleotide (FAD)

▲ Figure A.10 **Water-Soluble Vitamins and Their Coenzymes.**

Niacin

Vitamin Form

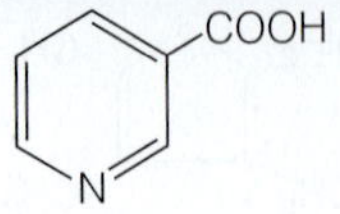

Nicotinic acid

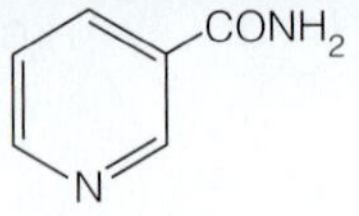

Nicotinamide

Coenzyme Form

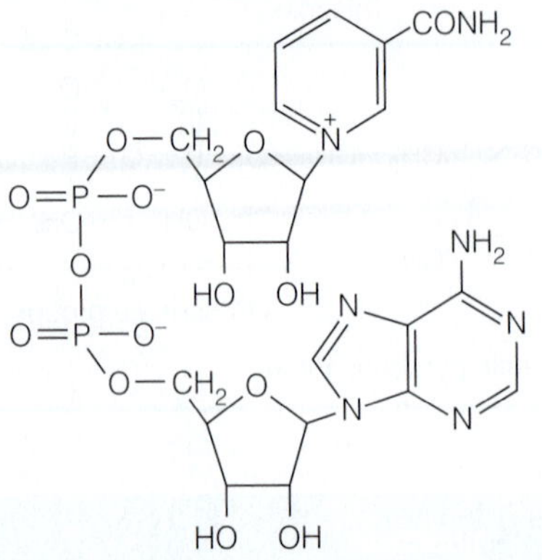

Nicotinamide adenine dinucleotide (NAD$^+$)

or

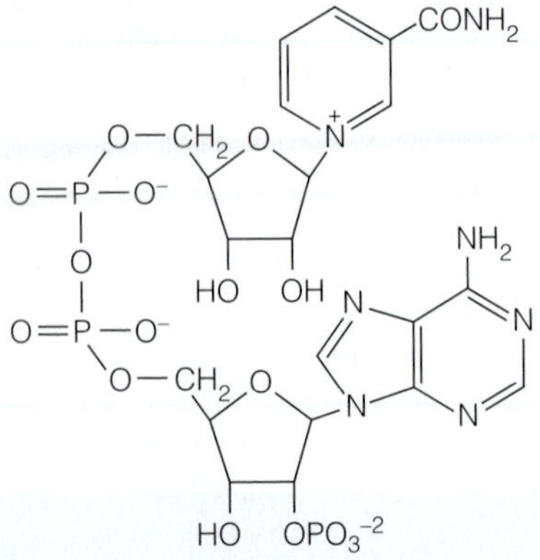

Nicotinamide adenine dinucleotide phosphate (NADP$^+$)

Pantothenic acid

Vitamin Form

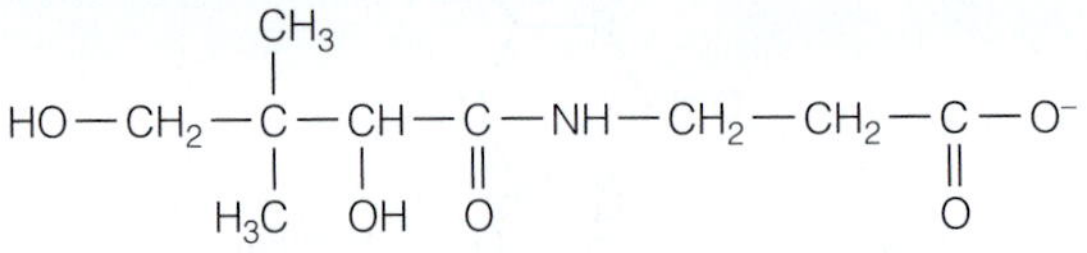

$$HO-CH_2-\underset{\underset{H_3C}{|}}{\overset{\overset{CH_3}{|}}{C}}-\underset{\underset{OH}{|}}{CH}-\underset{\underset{O}{\|}}{C}-NH-CH_2-CH_2-\underset{\underset{O}{\|}}{C}-O^-$$

Pantothenic acid

Coenzyme Form

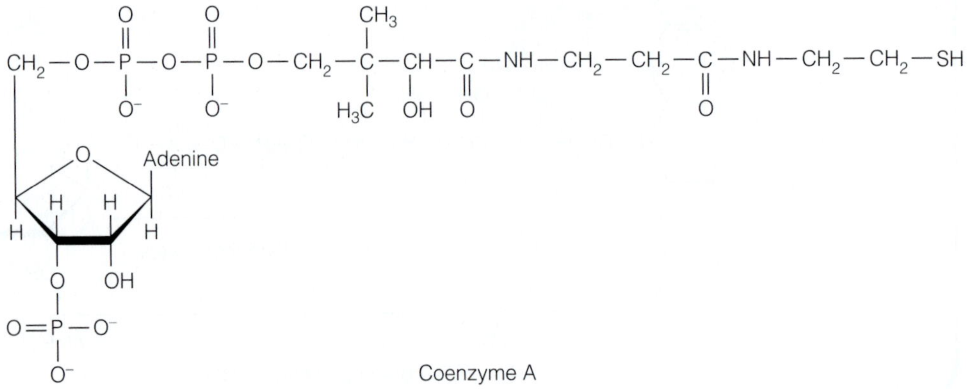

Coenzyme A

▲ **Figure A.10 Water-Soluble Vitamins and Their Coenzymes.** *(Continued)*

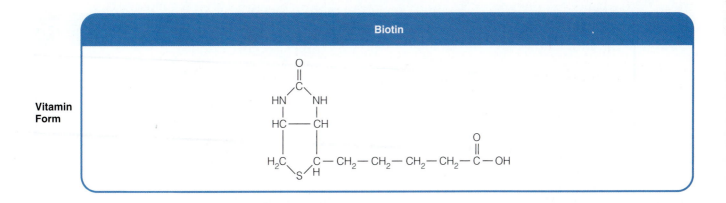

Biotin

Vitamin Form

Vitamin B₆

Vitamin Form

Pyridoxine (PN)

Pyridoxal (PL)

Pyridoxamine (PM)

Coenzyme Form

Pyridoxine 5′ phosphate (PNP)

Pyridoxal 5′ phosphate (PLP)

Pyridoxamine 5′ phosphate (PMP)

Folate

Vitamin Form

Pteridine

PABA

Glutamate

Coenzyme Form

Tetrahydrofolate

▲ Figure A.10 **Water-Soluble Vitamins and Their Coenzymes.** *(Continued)*

Vitamin B₁₂

Vitamin Form

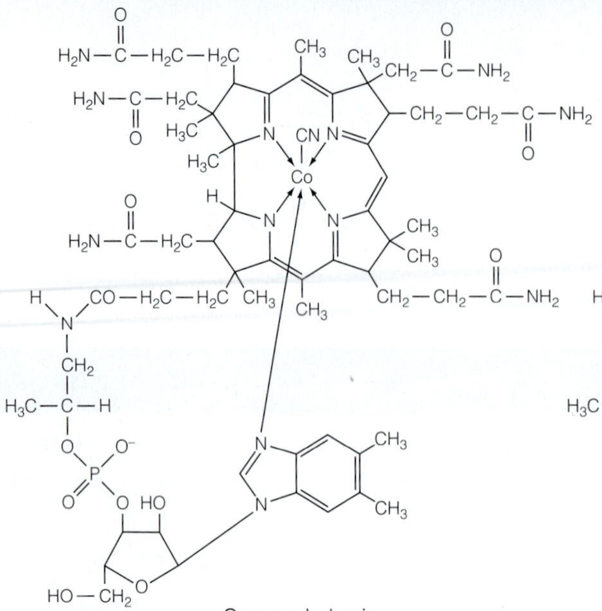

Cyanocobalamin

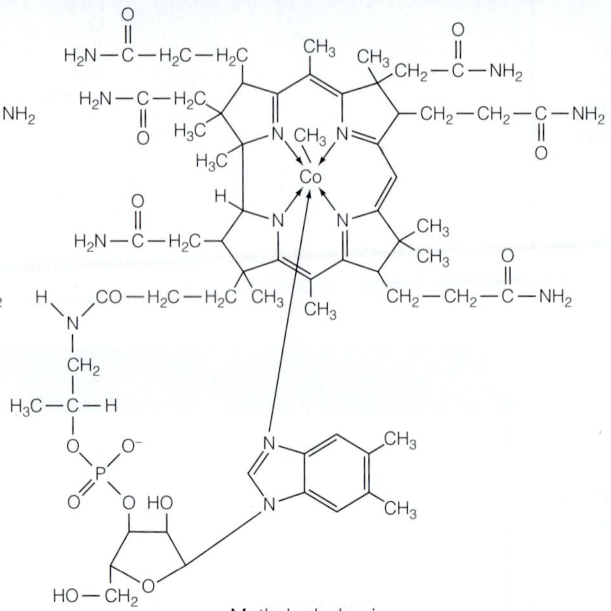

Methylcobalamin

Vitamin C

Vitamin Form

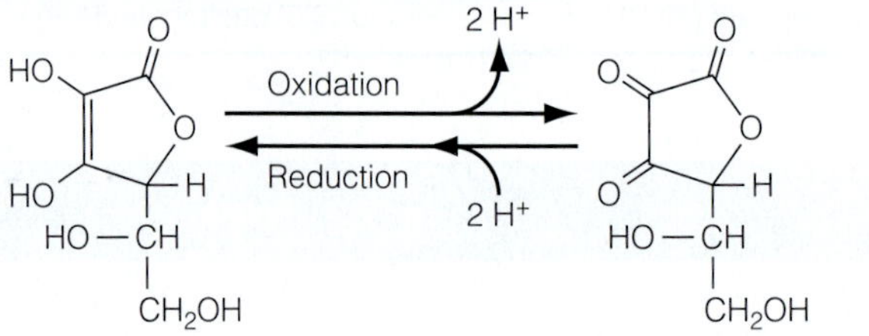

2 H⁺

Oxidation

Reduction

2 H⁺

Ascorbic acid

Dehydroascorbic acid

Choline

Vitamin Form

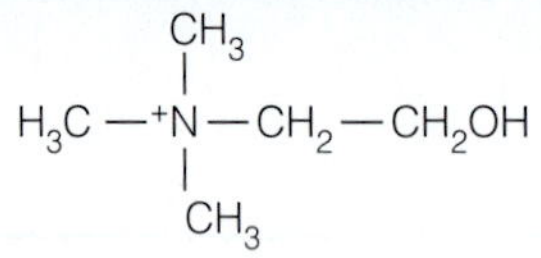

▲ Figure A.10 Water-Soluble Vitamins and Their Coenzymes. *(Continued)*

Calculation and Conversion Aids

Commonly Used Metric Units

millimeter (mm) : one-thousandth of a meter (0.001)
centimeter (cm) : one-hundredth of a meter (0.01)
kilometer (km) : one-thousand times a meter (1,000)
kilogram (kg) : one-thousand times a gram (1,000)
milligram (mg) : one-thousandth of a gram (0.001)
microgram (μg) : one-millionth of a gram (0.000001)
milliliter (ml) : one-thousandth of a liter (0.001)

Conversion Factors

Use the following table to convert U.S. measurements to metric equivalents:

Original Unit	Multiply By	To Get
ounces avdp	28.3495	grams
ounces	0.0625	pounds
pounds	0.4536	kilograms
pounds	16	ounces
grams	0.0353	ounces
grams	0.0022	pounds
kilograms	2.2046	pounds
liters	1.8162	pints (dry)
liters	2.1134	pints (liquid)
liters	0.9081	quarts (dry)
liters	1.0567	quarts (liquid)
liters	0.2642	gallons (U.S.)
pints (dry)	0.5506	liters
pints (liquid)	0.4732	liters
quarts (dry)	1.1012	liters
quarts (liquid)	0.9463	liters
gallons (U.S.)	3.7854	liters
millimeters	0.0394	inches
centimeters	0.3937	inches
centimeters	0.0328	feet
inches	25.4000	millimeters
Inches	2.5400	centimeters
Inches	0.0254	meters
feet	0.3048	meters
meters	3.2808	feet
meters	1.0936	yards
cubic feet	0.0283	cubic meters
cubic meters	35.3147	cubic feet
cubic meters	1.3079	cubic yards
cubic yards	0.7646	cubic meters

International Units

Some vitamin supplements may report vitamin content as International Units (IU).

To convert IU to:

> Micrograms of vitamin D (cholecalciferol), multiply the IU value by 0.025.
> Milligrams of vitamin E (alpha-tocopherol), multiply the IU value by 0.67 if vitamin E is from natural sources. Multiply the IU value by 0.45 if vitamin E is from synthetic sources.
> Vitamin A: 1 IU = 0.3 μg retinol or 0.3 μg RAE or 0.6 μg beta-carotene

Retinol Activity Equivalents

Retinol activity equivalents (RAE) are a standardized unit of measure for vitamin A. RAE account for the various differences in bioavailability from sources of vitamin A. Many supplements will report vitamin A content in IU, as shown above, or in retinol equivalents (RE).

1 μg RAE = 1 μg retinol
    12 μg beta-carotene

To calculate RAE from the RE value of vitamin carotenoids in foods, divide RE by 2. Divide the amount of beta-carotene by 12 to convert to RAE.

For vitamin A supplements and foods fortified with vitamin A, 1 RE = 1 RAE.

Folate

Folate is measured as dietary folate equivalents (DFE). DFE account for the different factors affecting bioavailability of folate sources.

1 μg DFE = 1 μg food folate
    0.6 μg folate from fortified foods
    0.5 μg folate supplement taken on an empty
     stomach
    0.6 μg folate as a supplement consumed with a meal

To convert micrograms of synthetic folate, such as that found in supplements or fortified foods, to DFE:

$$\mu\text{g synthetic folate} \times 1.7 = \mu\text{g DFE}$$

For naturally occurring food folate, such as spinach, each microgram of folate equals 1 microgram DFE:

$$\mu\text{g folate} = \mu\text{g DFE}$$

Niacin

Niacin is measured as niacin equivalents (mg NE). NE reflects the amount of preformed niacin in foods or the amount that can be formed from a food's content of the amino acid niacin.

To calculate mg NE from a meal:

If you know the tryptophan and preformed niacin in a meal: (tryptophan × 1,000 ÷ 60) + preformed niacin = mg NE

If you know the total amount of protein in a meal but not the tryptophan content: (0.011 × g of protein) × 1,000 ÷ 60 + preformed niacin = mg NE

Length: U.S. and Metric Equivalents

¼ inch = 0.6 centimeters
1 inch = 2.5 centimeters
1 foot = 0.3048 meter
30.48 centimeters
1 yard = 0.9144 meter
1 millimeter = 0.03937 inch
1 centimeter = 0.3937 inch
1 decimeter = 3.937 inches
1 meter = 39.37 inches
1.094 yards
1 micrometer = 0.00003937 inch

Weights and Measures

Food Measurement Equivalencies from U.S. to Metric

Capacity

⅓ teaspoon = 1 milliliter
¼ teaspoon = 1.23 milliliters
½ teaspoon = 2.5 milliliters
1 teaspoon = 5 milliliters
1 tablespoon = 15 milliliters
1 fluid ounce = 30 milliliters
¼ cup = 59 milliliters
⅓ cup = 79 milliliters
½ cup = 118 milliliters
1 cup = 237 milliliters
1 pint (2 cups) = 473 milliliters
1 quart (4 cups) = 0.95 liter
1 liter (1.06 quarts) = 1,000 milliliters
1 gallon (4 quarts) = 3.79 liters

Weight

0.035 ounce = 1 gram
1 ounce = 28 grams
¼ pound (4 ounces) = 113 grams
1 pound (16 ounces) = 454 grams
2.2 pounds (35 ounces) = 1 kilogram

U.S. Food Measurement Equivalents

3 teaspoons = 1 tablespoon
½ tablespoon = 1½ teaspoons
2 tablespoons = ⅛ cup
4 tablespoons = ¼ cup
5 tablespoons + 1 teaspoon = ⅓ cup
8 tablespoons = ½ cup
10 tablespoons + 2 teaspoons = ⅔ cup
12 tablespoons = ¾ cup
16 tablespoons = 1 cup
2 cups = 1 pint
4 cups = 1 quart
2 pints = 1 quart
4 quarts = 1 gallon

Volumes and Capacities

1 cup = 8 fluid ounces
½ liquid pint
1 milliliter = 0.061 cubic inch
1 liter = 1.057 liquid quarts
0.908 dry quart
61.024 cubic inches
1 U.S. gallon = 231 cubic inches
3.785 liters
0.833 British gallon
128 U.S. fluid ounces
1 British Imperial gallon = 277.42 cubic inches
1.201 U.S. gallons
4.546 liters
160 British fluid ounces
1 U.S. ounce, liquid or fluid = 1.805 cubic inches
29.574 milliliters
1.041 British fluid ounces
1 pint, dry = 33.600 cubic inches
0.551 liter
1 pint, liquid = 28.875 cubic inches
0.473 liter
1 U.S. quart, dry = 67.201 cubic inches
1.101 liters
1 U.S. quart, liquid = 57.75 cubic inches
0.946 liter
1 British quart = 69.355 cubic inches
1.032 U.S. quarts, dry
1.201 U.S. quarts, liquid

Energy Units

1 kilocalorie (kcal) = 4.2 kilojoules
1 megajoule (MJ) = 239 kilocalories
1 kilojoule (kJ) = 0.24 kcal
1 gram carbohydrate = 4 kcals
1 gram fat = 9 kcals
1 gram protein = 4 kcals

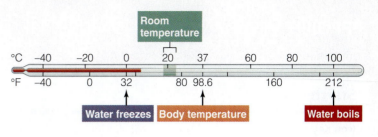

Temperature Standards

	°Fahrenheit	°Celsius
Body temperature	98.6°	37°
Comfortable room temperature	65–75°	18–24°
Boiling point of water	212°	100°
Freezing point of water	32°	0°

Temperature Scales

To Convert Fahrenheit to Celsius

[(°F − 32) × 5]/9

1. Subtract 32 from °F
2. Multiply (°F − 32) by 5, then divide by 9

To Convert Celsius to Fahrenheit

[(°C × 9)/5] + 32

1. Multiply °C by 9, then divide by 5
2. Add 32 to (°C × 9/5)

Starch

One starch choice has 15 grams of carbohydrate, 3 grams of protein, 1 gram of fat, and 80 calories.

Icon Key

✔ = Good source of fiber

! = Extra fat

🧂 = High in sodium

Food	Serving Size	Food	Serving Size
Bread		Muesli	¼ cup
Bagel	¼ large bagel (1 oz)	Puffed cereal	1 ½ cups
! Biscuit	1 biscuit (2 ½ inches across)	Shredded wheat, plain	½ cup
		Sugar-coated cereal	½ cup
		Unsweetened, ready-to-eat cereal	¾ cup

Breads, loaf-type

Food	Serving Size
white, whole-grain, French, Italian, pumpernickel, rye, sourdough, unfrosted raisin or cinnamon	1 slice (1 oz)
✔ reduced-calorie, light	2 slices (1 ½ oz)

Breads, flat-type (flatbreads)

Food	Serving Size
chapatti	1 oz
ciabatta	1 oz
naan	3 ¼-inch square (1 oz)
pita (6 inches across)	½ pita
roti	1 oz
✔ sandwich flat buns, whole-wheat	1 bun, including top and bottom (1 ½ oz)
! taco shell	2 taco shells (each 5 inches across)
tortilla, corn	1 small tortilla (6 inches across)
tortilla, flour (white or whole-wheat)	1 small tortilla (6 inches across) or ⅓ large tortilla (10 inches across)
Cornbread	1 ¾-inch cube (1 ½ oz)
English muffin	½ muffin
Hot dog bun or hamburger bun	½ bun (¾ oz)
Pancake	1 pancake (4 inches across, ¼ inch thick)
Roll, plain	1 small roll (1 oz)
! Stuffing, bread	⅓ cup
Waffle	1 waffle (4-inch square or 4 inches across)

Cereals

Food	Serving Size
✔ Bran cereal (twigs, buds, or flakes)	½ cup
Cooked cereals (oats, oatmeal)	½ cup
Granola cereal	¼ cup
Grits, cooked	½ cup

Grains (Including Pasta and Rice)

Unless otherwise indicated, serving sizes listed are for cooked grains.

Food	Serving Size
Barley	⅓ cup

Bran, dry

Food	Serving Size
✔ oat	¼ cup
✔ wheat	½ cup
✔ Bulgur	½ cup
Couscous	⅓ cup
Kasha	½ cup
Millet	⅓ cup
Pasta, white or whole-wheat (all shapes and sizes)	⅓ cup
Polenta	⅓ cup
Quinoa, all colors	⅓ cup
Rice, white, brown, and other colors and types	⅓ cup
Tabbouleh (tabouli), prepared	½ cup
Wheat germ, dry	3 Tbsp
Wild rice	½ cup

Starchy Vegetables

All of the serving sizes for starchy vegetables on this list are for cooked vegetables.

Food	Serving Size
Breadfruit	¼ cup
Cassava or dasheen	⅓ cup
Corn	½ cup
on cob	4- to 4 ½-inch piece (½ large cob)
✔ Hominy	¾ cup
✔ Mixed vegetables with corn or peas	1 cup
Marinara, pasta, or spaghetti sauce	½ cup
✔ Parsnips	½ cup
✔ Peas, green	½ cup
Plantain	⅓ cup

Potato

Food	Serving Size
baked with skin	¼ large potato (3 oz)
boiled, all kinds	½ cup or ½ medium potato (3 oz)

Source: From Choose Your Foods: Exchange Lists For Diabetes. © Academy of Nutrition and Dietetics. Adapted and reprinted with permission.

Food	Serving Size
! mashed, with milk and fat . . . . .½ cup	
French-fried (oven-baked)* . . . . .1 cup (2 oz)	
✔ Pumpkin puree, canned, no sugar added . . . . .¾ cup	
✔ Squash, winter (acorn, butternut) . . . . .1 cup	
✔ Succotash . . . . .½ cup	
Yam or sweet potato, plain . . . . .½ cup (3 ½ oz)	

Crackers and Snacks

Note: Some snacks are high in fat. Always check food labels.

Crackers

animal . . . . .8 crackers
✔ crispbread . . . . .2 to 5 pieces
                                     (¾ oz)
graham, 2 ½-inch square . . . . .3 squares
nut and rice . . . . .10 crackers
oyster . . . . .20 crackers
! round, butter-type .6 crackers
saltine-type . . . . .6 crackers
! sandwich-style, cheese or peanut butter filling . . 3 crackers
whole-wheat, baked . . . . .5 regular 1 ½-inch
          squares or
          10 thins (¾ oz)
Granola or snack bar . . . . .1 bar (¾ oz)
Matzoh, all shapes and sizes . . . . .¾ oz
Melba toast . . . . .4 pieces (each
          about 2 by
          4 inches)

*Note: Restaurant-style French fries are on the **Fast Foods** list, **page C-11**.

Food	Serving Size
Popcorn	
✔ no fat added . . . . .3 cups	
!! with butter added . . . . .3 cups	
Pretzels . . . . .¾ oz	
Rice cakes . . . . .2 cakes	
(4 inches across)	

Snack chips

baked (potato, pita) . . . . .about 8 chips
         (¾ oz)
!! regular (tortilla, potato) . . . . .about 13 chips
         (1 oz)

! count as 1 starch choice + 1 fat choice (1 starch choice plus 5 grams of fat)

!! count as 1 starch choice + 2 fat choices (1 starch choice plus 10 grams of fat)

Note: for other snacks, see the **Sweets, Desserts, and Other Carbohydrates** list, **page C-4**.

Beans, Peas, and Lentils

The choices on this list count as 1 starch choice + 1 lean protein choice.
✔ Baked beans, canned . . . . .⅓ cup
✔ Beans (black, garbanzo, kidney, lima, ...½ cup
navy, pinto, white), cooked or canned, drained and rinsed
✔ Lentils (any color), cooked . . . . .½ cup
✔ Peas (black-eyed and split), cooked . . . . .½ cup
or canned, drained and rinsed
🧂✔ Refried beans, canned . . . . .½ cup

Note: Beans, lentils, and peas are also found on the **Protein** list, **page C-6**.

Fruits

One fruit choice has 15 grams of carbohydrate and 60 calories.

Icon Key
✔ = Good source of fiber
! = Extra fat
🧂 = High in sodium

Food	Serving Size
Fruits	

The weights listed include skin, core, seeds, and rind.

Food	Serving Size
Apple, unpeeled	1 small apple (4 oz)
Apples, dried	4 rings
Applesauce, unsweetened	½ cup
Apricots	
canned	½ cup
dried	8 apricot halves
fresh	4 apricots
	(5 ½ oz total)
Banana	1 extra-small banana, about 4 inches long (4 oz)
✔ Blackberries	1 cup
Blueberries	¾ cup
Cantaloupe	1 cup diced
Cherries	
sweet, canned	½ cup
sweet, fresh	12 cherries (3 ½ oz)
Dates	3 small (deglet noor) dates or 1 large (medjool) date

Food	Serving Size
Dried fruits (blueberries, cherries, cranberries, mixed fruit, raisins)	2 Tbsp
Figs	
dried	3 small figs
✔ fresh	1 ½ large or 2 medium figs (3 ½ oz total)
Fruit cocktail	½ cup
Grapefruit	
fresh	½ large grapefruit (5 ½ oz)
sections, canned	¾ cup
Grapes	17 small grapes (3 oz total)
✔ Guava	2 small guava (2 ½ oz total)
Honeydew melon	1 cup diced
Kiwi	½ cup sliced
Loquat	¾ cup cubed
Mandarin oranges, canned	¾ cup

Food	Serving Size	Food	Serving Size
Mango	½ small mango (5 ½ oz) or ½ cup	dried (prunes)	3 prunes
Nectarine	1 medium nectarine (5 ½ oz)	fresh	2 small plums (5 oz total)
✓ Orange	1 medium orange (6 ½ oz)	Pomegranate seeds (arils)	½ cup
Papaya	½ papaya (8 oz) or 1 cup cubed	✓ Raspberries	1 cup
Peaches		✓ Strawberries	1 ¼ cup whole berries
canned	½ cup	Tangerine	1 large tangerine (6 oz)
fresh	1 medium peach (6 oz)	Watermelon	1 ¼ cups diced

Fruit Juice

Food	Serving Size
Apple juice/cider	½ cup
Fruit juice blends, 100% juice	⅓ cup
Grape juice	⅓ cup
Grapefruit juice	½ cup
Orange juice	½ cup
Pineapple juice	½ cup
Pomegranate juice	½ cup
Prune juice	⅓ cup

Pears
canned	½ cup
✓ fresh	½ large pear (4 oz)

Pineapple
canned	½ cup
fresh	¾ cup
Plantain, extra-ripe (black), raw	¼ plantain (2 ¼ oz)

Plums
canned	½ cup

Milk and Milk Substitutes

One carbohydrate choice has 15 grams of carbohydrate and about 70 calories. One fat choice has 5 grams of fat and 45 calories.

Food	Serving Size	Choices per Serving
Milk and Yogurts		
Fat-Free (skim) or Low-Fat (1%)		
milk, buttermilk, acidophilus milk, lactose-free milk	1 cup	1 fat-free milk
evaporated milk	½ cup	1 fat-free milk
yogurt, plain or Greek; may be sweetened with an artificial sweetener	⅔ cup (6 oz)	1 fat-free milk
Chocolate milk	1 cup	1 fat-free milk + 1 carbohydrate
Reduced-fat (2%)		
milk, acidophilus milk, kefir, lactose-free milk	1 cup	1 reduced-fat milk
yogurt, plain	⅔ cup (6 oz)	1 reduced-fat milk
Whole		
milk, buttermilk, goat's milk	1 cup	1 whole milk
evaporated milk	½ cup	1 whole milk
yogurt, plain	1 cup (8 oz)	1 whole milk
chocolate milk	1 cup	1 whole milk + 1 carbohydrate
Other Milk Foods and Milk Substitutes		
Eggnog		
fat-free	⅓ cup	1 carbohydrate
low-fat	⅓ cup	1 carbohydrate + ½ fat
whole milk	⅓ cup	1 carbohydrate + 1 fat
Rice drink		
plain, fat-free	1 cup	1 carbohydrate
flavored, low-fat	1 cup	2 carbohydrates
Soy milk		
light or low-fat, plain	1 cup	½ carbohydrate + ½ fat
regular, plain	1 cup	½ carbohydrate + 1 fat
Yogurt with fruit, low-fat	⅔ cup (6 oz)	1 fat-free milk + 1 carbohydrate

Note: Unsweetened nut milks (such as almond milk and coconut milk) are on the **Fats** list, **page C-8**.

Nonstarchy Vegetables

One nonstarchy vegetable choice (½ cup cooked or 1 cup raw) has 5 grams of carbohydrate, 2 grams of protein, 0 grams of fat, and 25 calories.

Icon Key

✔ = Good source of fiber

! = Extra fat

[S] = High in sodium

Nonstarchy Vegetables

Amaranth leaves (Chinese spinach)

Artichoke

Artichoke hearts (no oil)

Asparagus

Baby corn

Bamboo shoots

Bean sprouts (alfalfa, mung, soybean)

Beans (green, wax, Italian, yard-long beans)

Beets

Broccoli

Broccoli slaw, packaged, no dressing

✔ Brussels sprouts

Cabbage (green, red, bok choy, Chinese)

✔ Carrots

Cauliflower

Celery

Chayote

Coleslaw, packaged, no dressing

Cucumber

Daikon

Eggplant

Fennel

Gourds (bitter, bottle, luffa, bitter melon)

Green onions or scallions

Greens (collard, dandelion, mustard, purslane, turnip)

Hearts of palm

✔ Jicama

Kale

Kohlrabi

Leeks

Mixed vegetables (without starchy vegetables, legumes, or pasta)

Mushrooms, all kinds, fresh

Okra

Onions

Pea pods

Peppers (all varieties)

Radishes

Rutabaga

[S] Sauerkraut, drained and rinsed

Spinach

Squash, summer varieties (yellow, pattypan, crookneck, zucchini)

Sugar snap peas

Swiss chard

Tomato

Tomatoes, canned

[S] Tomato sauce (unsweetened)

Tomato/vegetable juice

Turnips

Water chestnuts

Note: Salad greens (like arugula, chicory, endive, escarole, lettuce, radicchio, romaine, and watercress) are on the **Free Foods** list, **page C-9**.

Sweets, Desserts, and Other Carbohydrates

One carbohydrate choice has 15 grams of carbohydrate and about 70 calories. One fat choice has 5 grams of fat and 45 calories.

Icon Key

✔ = Good source of fiber

! = Extra fat

[S] = High in sodium

Food	Serving Size	Choices per Serving
Beverages, Soda, and Sports Drinks		
Cranberry juice cocktail	½ cup	1 carbohydrate
Fruit drink or lemonade	1 cup (8 oz)	2 carbohydrates
Hot chocolate, regular	1 envelope (2 Tbsp or ¾ oz) added to 8 oz water	1 carbohydrate
Soft drink (soda), regular	1 can (12 oz)	2 ½ carbohydrates
Sports drink (fluid replacement type)	1 cup (8 oz)	1 carbohydrate
Brownies, Cake, Cookies, Gelatin, Pie, and Pudding		
Biscotti	1 oz	1 carbohydrate + 1 fat
Brownie, small, unfrosted	1 ¼-inch square, ⅞-inch high (about 1 oz)	1 carbohydrate + 1 fat

Food	Serving Size	Choices per Serving
Cake		
angel food, unfrosted	¹/₁₂ of cake (about 2 oz)	2 carbohydrates
frosted	2-inch square (about 2 oz)	2 carbohydrates + 1 fat
unfrosted	2-inch square (about 1 oz)	1 carbohydrate + 1 fat
Cookies		
100-calorie pack	1 oz	1 carbohydrate + ½ fat
chocolate chip cookies	2 cookies, 2 ¼ inches across	1 carbohydrate + 2 fats
gingersnaps	3 small cookies, 1 ½ inches across	1 carbohydrate
large cookie	1 cookie, 6 inches across (about 3 oz)	4 carbohydrates + 3 fats
sandwich cookies with crème filling	2 small cookies (about ⅔ oz)	1 carbohydrate + 1 fat
sugar-free cookies	1 large or 3 small cookies (¾ to 1 oz)	1 carbohydrate + 1 to 2 fats
vanilla wafer	5 cookies	1 carbohydrate + 1 fat
Cupcake, frosted	1 small cupcake (about 1 ¾ oz)	2 carbohydrates + 1 to 1 ½ fats
Flan	½ cup	2 ½ carbohydrates + 1 fat
Fruit cobbler	½ cup (3 ½ oz)	3 carbohydrates + 1 fat
Gelatin, regular	½ cup	1 carbohydrate
Pie		
commercially prepared fruit, 2 crusts	⅙ of 8-inch pie	3 carbohydrates + 2 fats
pumpkin or custard	⅛ of 8-inch pie	1 ½ carbohydrates + 1 ½ fats
Pudding		
regular (made with reduced-fat milk)	½ cup	2 carbohydrates
sugar-free or sugar- and fat-free (made with fat-free milk)	½ cup	1 carbohydrate

Candy, Spreads, Sweets, Sweeteners, Syrups, and Toppings

Food	Serving Size	Choices per Serving
Blended sweeteners (mixtures of artificial sweeteners and sugar)	1 ½ Tbsp.	1 carbohydrate
Candy		
chocolate, dark or milk type	1 oz	1 carbohydrate + 2 fats
chocolate "kisses"	5 pieces	1 carbohydrate + 1 fat
hard	3 pieces	1 carbohydrate
Coffee creamer, nondairy type		
powdered, flavored	4 tsp.	½ carbohydrate + ½ fat
liquid, flavored	2 Tbsp	1 carbohydrate
Fruit snacks, chewy (pureed fruit concentrate)	1 roll (¾ oz)	1 carbohydrate
Fruit spreads, 100% fruit	1 ½ Tbsp.	1 carbohydrate
Honey	1 Tbsp	1 carbohydrate
Jam or jelly, regular	1 Tbsp	1 carbohydrate
Sugar	1 Tbsp	1 carbohydrate
Syrup		
chocolate	2 Tbsp	2 carbohydrates
light (pancake-type)	2 Tbsp	1 carbohydrate
regular (pancake-type)	1 Tbsp	1 carbohydrate

Condiments and Sauces

Food	Serving Size	Choices per Serving
Barbecue sauce	3 Tbsp	1 carbohydrate
Cranberry sauce, jellied	¼ cup	1 ½ carbohydrates
Ⓢ Curry sauce	1 oz	1 carbohydrate + 1 fat
Ⓢ Gravy, canned or bottled	½ cup	½ carbohydrate + ½ fat
Hoisin sauce	1 Tbsp	½ carbohydrate
Marinade	1 Tbsp	½ carbohydrate
Plum sauce	1 Tbsp	½ carbohydrate
Salad dressing, fat-free, cream-based	3 Tbsp	1 carbohydrate
Sweet-and-sour sauce	3 Tbsp	1 carbohydrate

Note: You can also check the **Fats** list and **Free Foods** list for other condiments.

Doughnuts, Muffins, Pastries, and Sweet Breads

Food	Serving Size	Choices per Serving
Banana nut bread	1-inch slice (2 oz)	2 carbohydrates + 1 fat
Doughnut		
cake, plain	1 medium doughnut (1 ½ oz)	1 ½ carbohydrates + 2 fats
hole	2 holes (1 oz)	1 carbohydrate + 1 fat
yeast-type, glazed	1 doughnut, 3 ¾ inches across (2 oz)	2 carbohydrates + 2 fats
Muffin		
regular	1 muffin (4 oz)	4 carbohydrates + 2 ½ fats
lower-fat	1 muffin (4 oz)	4 carbohydrates + ½ fat
Scone	1 scone (4 oz)	4 carbohydrates + 3 fats
Sweet roll or Danish	1 pastry (2 ½ oz)	2 ½ carbohydrates + 2 fats

Frozen Bars, Frozen Dessert, Frozen Yogurt, and Ice Cream

Food	Serving Size	Choices per Serving
Frozen pops	1	½ carbohydrate
Fruit juice bars, frozen, 100% juice	1 bar (3 oz)	1 carbohydrate
Ice cream		
fat-free	½ cup	1 ½ carbohydrates
light	½ cup	1 carbohydrate + 1 fat
no-sugar-added	½ cup	1 carbohydrate + 1 fat
regular	½ cup	1 carbohydrate + 2 fats
Sherbet, sorbet	½ cup	2 carbohydrates
Yogurt, frozen		
fat-free	⅓ cup	1 carbohydrate
regular	½ cup	1 carbohydrate + 0 to 1 fat
Greek, lower-fat or fat-free	½ cup	1 ½ carbohydrates

Protein

One lean protein choice has 0 grams of carbohydrate, 7 grams of protein, 2 grams of fat, and 45 calories.

Icon Key

✔ = Good source of fiber

! = Extra fat

🅢 = High in sodium (based on the sodium content of a typical 3-oz serving of meat, unless 1 oz or 2 oz is the normal serving size)

Food	Serving Size	Food	Serving Size
Lean Protein		sardines, canned	2 small sardines
Note: 1 oz is usually the serving size for meat, fish, poultry, or hard cheeses.		tuna, fresh or canned in water or oil and drained	1 oz
Beef: ground (90% or higher lean/10% or lower fat); select or choice grades trimmed of fat: roast (chuck, round, rump, sirloin), steak (cubed, flank, porterhouse, T-bone), tenderloin	1 oz	🅢 smoked: herring or salmon (lox)	1 oz
		Game: buffalo, ostrich, rabbit, venison	1 oz
		🅢 Hot dog with 3 grams of fat or less per oz. Note: May contain carbohydrate.	1 hot dog (1 ¾ oz)
🅢 Beef jerky	½ oz	Lamb: chop, leg, or roast	1 oz
Cheeses with 3 grams of fat or less per oz	1 oz	Organ meats: heart, kidney, liver Note: May be high in cholesterol.	1 oz
Curd-style cheeses: cottage-type (all kinds); ricotta (fat-free or light)	¼ cup (2 oz)	Oysters, fresh or frozen	6 medium oysters
Egg substitutes, plain	½ cup	*Pork, lean*	
Egg whites	2	🅢 Canadian bacon	1 oz
Fish		🅢 ham	1 oz
fresh or frozen, such as catfish, cod, flounder, haddock, halibut, orange roughy, tilapia, trout	1 oz	rib or loin chop/roast, tenderloin	1 oz
salmon, fresh or canned	1 oz	Poultry, without skin: chicken; Cornish hen; domestic duck or goose (well-drained of fat); turkey; lean ground turkey or chicken	1 oz

Food	Serving Size	Food	Serving Size

🧂 Processed sandwich meats with 3 grams of fat.....1 oz
   or less per oz: chipped beef, thin-sliced deli
   meats, turkey ham, turkey pastrami

🧂 Sausage with 3 grams of fat or less per oz........1 oz

   Shellfish: clams, crab, imitation shellfish, ...1 oz
     lobster, scallops, shrimp

   Veal: cutlet (no breading), loin chop, roast ....1 oz

Medium-Fat Protein

One medium-fat protein choice has 0 grams of carbohydrate,
7 grams of protein, 5 grams of fat, and 75 calories.

Note: 1 oz is usually the serving size for meat, fish, poultry, or hard cheeses.

   Beef trimmed of visible fat: ground beef..........1 oz
     (85% or lower lean/15% or higher fat),
     corned beef, meatloaf, prime cuts of beef
     (rib roast), short ribs, tongue

   Cheeses with 4 to 7 grams of fat per oz: ....1 oz
     feta, mozzarella, pasteurized processed
     cheese spread, reduced-fat cheeses

   Cheese, ricotta (regular or part-skim) ....¼ cup (2 oz)

   Egg . . . . .1 egg

   Fish: any fried. . . . . .1 oz

   Lamb: ground, rib roast .1 oz

   Pork: cutlet, ground, shoulder roast . . . . .1 oz

   Poultry with skin: chicken, dove, pheasant, ...1 oz
     turkey, wild duck, or goose; fried chicken

🧂 Sausage with 4 to 7 grams of fat per oz. . . . . .1 oz

High-Fat Protein

These foods are high in saturated fat, cholesterol, and calories and may
raise blood cholesterol levels if eaten on a regular basis. Try to eat 3 or
fewer choices from this group per week.

Note: 1 oz is usually the serving size for meat, fish, poultry, or hard cheeses.

   Bacon, pork . . . . .2 slices (1 oz each
                     before cooking)

🧂 Bacon, turkey. . . . . .3 slices (½ oz each
                     before cooking)

   Cheese, regular: American, blue-veined, ...1 oz
     brie, cheddar, hard goat, Monterey jack,
     Parmesan, queso, and Swiss

! Hot dog: beef, pork, or combination . . . . .1 hot dog (10 hot
                     dogs per
                     1 lb-sized
                     package)

   Hot dog: turkey or chicken. . . . . .1 hot dog
                     (10 hot dogs per
                     1 lb-sized
                     package)

   Pork: sausage, spareribs .1 oz

🧂 Processed sandwich meats with 8 grams of . . . . . . .1 oz
   fat or more per oz: bologna, hard salami, pastrami

🧂 Sausage with 8 grams fat or more per oz: . . . . .1 oz
   bratwurst, chorizo, Italian, knockwurst,
   Polish, smoked, summer

Protein

Icon Key

✔ = Good source of fiber

! = Extra fat

🧂 = High in sodium (based on the sodium content of a typical 3-oz serving of meat, unless 1 oz or 2 oz is the normal serving size)

Food	Serving Size	Choices per Serving

Plant-Based Protein

Because carbohydrate and fat content varies among plant-based proteins, you should read the food labels.

	Food	Serving Size	Choices per Serving
	"Bacon" strips, soy-based	2 strips (½ oz)	1 lean protein
✔	Baked beans, canned.	1/3 cup.	1 starch + 1 lean protein
✔	Beans (black, garbanzo, kidney, lima, navy, pinto, white), . . .	½ cup	1 starch + 1 lean protein
	cooked or canned, drained and rinsed		
	"Beef" or "sausage" crumbles, meatless	1 oz	1 lean protein
	"Chicken" nuggets, soy-based	2 nuggets (1 ½ oz).	½ carbohydrate + 1 medium-fat protein
✔	Edamame, shelled	½ cup	½ carbohydrate + 1 lean protein
	Falafel (spiced chickpea and wheat patties)	3 patties (about 2 inches across) .	1 carbohydrate +1 high-fat protein
	Hot dog, meatless, soy-based.	1 hot dog (1 ½ oz)	1 lean protein
✔	Hummus	1/3 cup.	1 carbohydrate + 1 medium-fat protein
✔	Lentils, any color, cooked or canned, drained and rinsed	½ cup	1 starch + 1 lean protein
	Meatless burger, soy-based	3 oz	½ carbohydrate + 2 lean proteins
✔	Meatless burger, vegetable and starch-based	1 patty (about 2 ½ oz)	½ carbohydrate + 1 lean protein
	Meatless deli slices.	1 oz	1 lean protein
	Mycoprotein ("chicken" tenders or crumbles), meatless.	2 oz	½ carbohydrate + 1 lean protein
	Nut spreads: almond butter, cashew butter, peanut butter, . . .	1 Tbsp.	1 high-fat protein
	soy nut butter		
✔	Peas (black-eyed and split peas), cooked or canned, ...	½ cup	1 starch + 1 lean protein
	drained and rinsed		
🧂✔	Refried beans, canned	½ cup	1 starch + 1 lean protein
	"Sausage" breakfast-type patties, meatless	1 (l½ oz)	1 medium-fat protein
	Soy nuts, unsalted	¾ oz	½ carbohydrate + 1 medium-fat protein
	Tempeh, plain, unflavored	¼ cup (1 ½ oz)	1 medium-fat protein
	Tofu	½ cup (4 oz)	1 medium-fat protein
	Tofu, light	½ cup (4 oz)	1 lean protein

Fats

One fat choice has 5 grams of fat and 45 calories.

Food	Serving Size	Food	Serving Size
Unsaturated Fats—Monounsaturated Fats		*Salad dressing*	
Almond milk (unsweetened)	1 cup	reduced-fat (Note: May contain carbohydrate.)	2 Tbsp
Avocado, medium	2 Tbsp (1 oz)	regular	1 Tbsp
Nut butters (*trans* fat-free): almond butter, cashew butter, peanut butter (smooth or crunchy)	1 ½ tsp	*Seeds*	
		flaxseed, ground	1 ½ Tbsp
Nuts		pumpkin, sesame, sunflower	1 Tbsp
almonds	6 nuts	Tahini or sesame paste	2 tsp

Unsaturated Fats—Monounsaturated Fats

Food	Serving Size
Almond milk (unsweetened)	1 cup
Avocado, medium	2 Tbsp (1 oz)
Nut butters (*trans* fat-free): almond butter, cashew butter, peanut butter (smooth or crunchy)	1 ½ tsp
Nuts	
almonds	6 nuts
Brazil	2 nuts
cashews	6 nuts
filberts (hazelnuts)	5 nuts
macadamia	3 nuts
mixed (50% peanuts)	6 nuts
peanuts	10 nuts
pecans	4 halves
pistachios	16 nuts
Oil: canola, olive, peanut	1 tsp
Olives	
black (ripe)	8
green, stuffed	10 large
Spread, plant stanol ester-type	
light	1 Tbsp
regular	2 tsp

Unsaturated Fats—Polyunsaturated Fats

Food	Serving Size
Margarine	
lower-fat spread (30 to 50% vegetable oil, *trans* fat-free)	1 Tbsp
stick, tub (*trans* fat-free), or squeeze (*trans* fat-free)	1 tsp
Mayonnaise	
reduced-fat	1 Tbsp
regular	1 tsp
Mayonnaise-style salad dressing	
reduced-fat	1 Tbsp
regular	2 tsp
Nuts	
pignolia (pine nuts)	1 Tbsp
walnuts, English	4 halves
Oil: corn, cottonseed, flaxseed, grapeseed, safflower, soybean, sunflower	1 tsp

Food	Serving Size
Salad dressing	
reduced-fat (Note: May contain carbohydrate.)	2 Tbsp
regular	1 Tbsp
Seeds	
flaxseed, ground	1 ½ Tbsp
pumpkin, sesame, sunflower	1 Tbsp
Tahini or sesame paste	2 tsp

Saturated Fats

Food	Serving Size
Bacon, cooked, regular or turkey	1 slice
Butter	
reduced-fat	1 Tbsp
stick	1 tsp
whipped	2 tsp
Butter blends made with oil	
reduced-fat or light	1 Tbsp
regular	1 ½ tsp
Chitterlings, boiled	2 Tbsp (½ oz)
Coconut, sweetened, shredded	2 Tbsp
Coconut milk, canned, thick	
light	⅓ cup
regular	1 ½ Tbsp
Coconut milk beverage (thin), unsweetened	1 cup
Cream	
half-and-half	2 Tbsp
heavy	1 Tbsp
light	1 ½ Tbsp
whipped	2 Tbsp
Cream cheese	
reduced-fat	1 ½ Tbsp (¾ oz)
regular	1 Tbsp (½ oz)
Lard	1 tsp
Oil: coconut, palm, palm kernel	1 tsp
Salt pork	¼ oz
Shortening, solid	1 tsp
Sour cream	
reduced-fat or light	3 Tbsp
regular	2 Tbsp

Free Foods

A "free" food is any food or drink choice that has less than 20 calories and 5 grams or less of carbohydrate per serving.

Icon Key

✔ = Good source of fiber

! = Extra fat

🧂 = High in sodium

Food	Serving Size	Food	Serving Size
Low Carbohydrate Foods		*Salad dressing*	
Candy, hard (regular or sugar-free) . . . . 1 piece		fat-free. . . . . 1 Tbsp	
Fruits		fat-free, Italian . . . . 2 Tbsp	
Cranberries or rhubarb, sweetened . . . . ½ cup with sugar substitute		Sour cream, fat-free or reduced-fat . . . . 1 Tbsp	
Gelatin dessert, sugar-free, any flavor		*Whipped topping*	
Gum, sugar-free		light or fat-free. . . . . 2 Tbsp	
Jam or jelly, light or no-sugar-added . . . . 2 tsp		regular . . . . 1 Tbsp	
Salad greens (such as arugula, chicory, endive, escarole, leaf or iceberg lettuce, purslane, romaine, radicchio, spinach, watercress)		**Condiments**	
Sugar substitutes (artificial sweeteners)		Barbecue sauce . . . . 2 tsp	
Syrup, sugar-free . . . . 2 Tbsp		Catsup (ketchup) . . . . 1 Tbsp	
Vegetables: any **raw** nonstarchy vegetables . . . . ½ cup (such as broccoli, cabbage, carrots, cucumber, tomato)		Chili sauce, sweet, tomato-type . . . . 2 tsp	
Vegetables: any **cooked** nonstarchy vegetables . . . . ¼ cup (such as carrots, cauliflower, green beans)		Horseradish	
		Hot pepper sauce	
Reduced-Fat or Fat-Free Foods		Lemon juice	
Cream cheese, fat-free . . . . 1 Tbsp (½ oz)		Miso . . . . 1 ½ tsp	
Coffee creamers, nondairy		*Mustard*	
liquid, flavored . . . . 1 ½ tsp		honey. . . . . 1 Tbsp	
liquid, sugar-free, flavored . . . . 4 tsp		brown, Dijon, horseradish-flavored, wasabi-flavored, or yellow	
powdered, flavored . . . . 1 tsp		Parmesan cheese, grated . . . . 1 Tbsp	
powdered, sugar-free, flavored. . . . . 2 tsp		Pickle relish (dill or sweet). . . . . 1 Tbsp	
Margarine spread		*Pickles*	
fat-free. . . . . 1 Tbsp		🧂 dill . . . . 1 ½ medium pickles	
reduced-fat . . . . 1 tsp		sweet, bread and butter. . . . . 2 slices	
Mayonnaise		sweet, gherkin . . . . ¾ oz	
fat-free. . . . . 1 Tbsp		Pimento	
reduced-fat . . . . 1 tsp		Salsa . . . . ¼ cup	
Mayonnaise-style salad dressing		🧂 Soy sauce, light or regular . . . . 1 Tbsp	
fat-free. . . . . 1 Tbsp		Sweet-and-sour sauce . . . . 2 tsp	
reduced-fat . . . . 2 tsp		Taco sauce . . . . 1 Tbsp	
		Vinegar	
		Worcestershire sauce	
		Yogurt, any type. . . . . 2 Tbsp	

Free Foods

Icon Key

✔ = Good source of fiber

! = Extra fat

🧂 = High in sodium

Food	Serving Size	Food	Serving Size
Drinks/Mixes		Water	
🧂 Bouillon, broth, consommé		Water, flavored, sugar-free	
Bouillon or broth, low sodium		**Seasonings**	
Carbonated or mineral water			
Club soda		Flavoring extracts (for example, vanilla, almond, or peppermint)	
Cocoa powder, unsweetened (1 Tbsp)		Garlic, fresh or powder	
Coffee, unsweetened or with sugar substitute		Herbs, fresh or dried	
Diet soft drinks, sugar-free		Kelp	
Drink mixes (powder or liquid drops), sugar-free		Nonstick cooking spray	
Tea, unsweetened or with sugar substitute		Spices	
Tonic water, sugar-free		Wine, used in cooking	

Combination Foods

One carbohydrate choice has 15 grams of carbohydrate and about 70 calories.

Icon Key

- ✓ = Good source of fiber
- ! = Extra fat
- S = High in sodium

Icon	Food	Serving Size	Choices per Serving
	Entrees		
S	Casserole-type entrees (tuna noodle, lasagna, spaghetti with meatballs, chili with beans, macaroni and cheese)	1 cup (8 oz)	2 carbohydrates + 2 medium-fat proteins
S	Stews (beef/other meats and vegetables)	1 cup (8 oz)	1 carbohydrate + 1 medium-fat protein + 0 to 3 fats
	Frozen Meals/Entrees		
S	Burrito (beef and bean)	1 burrito (5 oz)	3 carbohydrates + 1 lean protein + 2 fats
	Dinner-type healthy meal (includes dessert and is usually less than 400 calories)	about 9–12 oz	2 to 3 carbohydrates + 1 to 2 lean proteins + 1 fat
	"Healthy"-type entree (usually less than 300 calories)	about 7–10 oz	2 carbohydrates + 2 lean proteins
	Pizza		
S	cheese/vegetarian, thin crust	¼ of a 12–inch pizza (4½–5 oz)	2 carbohydrates + 2 medium-fat proteins
S	meat topping, thin crust	¼ of a 12–inch pizza (5 oz)	2 carbohydrates + 2 medium-fat proteins + 1½ fats
S	cheese/vegetarian or meat topping, rising crust	⅙ of 12–inch pizza (4 oz)	2½ carbohydrates + 2 medium-fat proteins
S	Pocket sandwich	1 sandwich (4½ oz)	3 carbohydrates + 1 lean protein + 1 to 2 fats
S	Pot pie	1 pot pie (7 oz)	3 carbohydrates + 1 medium-fat protein + 3 fats
	Salads (Deli-Style)		
	Coleslaw	½ cup	1 carbohydrate + 1½ fats
	Macaroni/pasta salad	½ cup	2 carbohydrates + 3 fats
S	Potato salad	½ cup	1½ to 2 carbohydrates + 1 to 2 fats
	Tuna salad or chicken salad	½ cup (3½ oz)	½ carbohydrate +2 lean proteins + 1 fat
	Soups		
S ✓	Bean, lentil, or split pea soup	1 cup (8 oz)	1½ carbohydrates + 1 lean protein
S	Chowder (made with milk)	1 cup (8 oz)	1 carbohydrate + 1 lean protein + 1½ fats
S	Cream soup (made with water)	1 cup (8 oz)	1 carbohydrate + 1 fat
S	Miso soup	1 cup (8 oz)	½ carbohydrate + 1 lean protein
S	Ramen noodle soup	1 cup (8 oz)	2 carbohydrates + 2 fats
S	Rice soup/porridge (congee)	1 cup (8 oz)	1 carbohydrate
S	Tomato soup (made with water), borscht	1 cup (8 oz)	1 carbohydrate
S	Vegetable beef, chicken noodle, or other broth-type soup (including "healthy"-type soups, such as those lower in sodium and/or fat)	1 cup (8 oz)	1 carbohydrate + 1 lean protein

Fast Foods

One carbohydrate choice has 15 grams of carbohydrate and about 70 calories.

Icon Key

✔ = Good source of fiber

! = Extra fat

🧂 = High in sodium

Food	Serving Size	Choices per Serving
Main Dishes/Entrees		
Chicken		
🧂 breast, breaded and fried*	1 (about 7 oz)	1 carbohydrate + 6 medium-fat proteins
breast, meat only**	1	4 lean proteins
drumstick, breaded and fried*	1 (about 2 ½ oz)	½ carbohydrate + 2 medium-fat proteins
drumstick, meat only**	1	1 lean protein + ½ fat
🧂 nuggets or tenders	6 (about 3 ½ oz)	1 carbohydrate + 2 medium-fat proteins + 1 fat
thigh, breaded and fried*	1 (about 5 oz)	1 carbohydrate + 3 medium-fat proteins + 2 fats
thigh, meat only**	1	2 lean proteins + ½ fat
wing, breaded and fried*	1 wing (about 2 oz)	½ carbohydrate + 2 medium-fat proteins
wing, meat only**	1 wing	1 lean protein
🧂✔ Main dish salad (grilled chicken type, no dressing or croutons)	1 salad (about 11 ½ oz)	1 carbohydrate + 4 lean proteins
Pizza		
🧂 cheese, pepperoni, or sausage, regular or thick crust	⅛ of a 14-inch pizza (about 4 oz)	2 ½ carbohydrates + 1 high-fat protein + 1 fat
🧂 cheese, pepperoni, or sausage, thin crust	⅛ of a 14-inch pizza (about 2 ¾ oz)	1 ½ carbohydrates + 1 high-fat protein + 1 fat
🧂 cheese, meat, and vegetable, regular crust	⅛ of a 14-inch pizza (about 5 oz)	2 ½ carbohydrates + 2 high-fat proteins
Asian		
🧂 Beef/chicken/shrimp with vegetables in sauce	1 cup (about 6 oz)	1 carbohydrate + 2 lean proteins + 1 fat
Egg roll, meat	1 egg roll (about 3 oz)	1 ½ carbohydrates + 1 lean protein + 1 ½ fats
Fried rice, meatless	1 cup	2 ½ carbohydrates + 2 fats
Fortune cookie	1 cookie	½ carbohydrate
🧂 Hot-and-sour soup	1 cup	½ carbohydrate + ½ fat
🧂 Meat with sweet sauce	1 cup (about 6 oz)	3 ½ carbohydrates + 3 medium-fat proteins + 3 fats
🧂 Noodles and vegetables in sauce (chow mein, lo mein)	1 cup	2 carbohydrates + 2 fats
Mexican		
🧂✔ Burrito with beans and cheese	1 small burrito (about 6 oz)	3 ½ carbohydrates + 1 medium-fat protein + 1 fat
🧂 Nachos with cheese	1 small order (about 8 nachos)	2 ½ carbohydrates + 1 high-fat protein + 2 fats
🧂 Quesadilla, cheese only	1 small order (about 5 oz)	2 ½ carbohydrates + 3 high-fat proteins
Taco, crisp, with meat and cheese	1 small taco (about 3 oz)	1 carbohydrate + 1 medium-fat protein + ½ fat
🧂✔ Taco salad with chicken and tortilla bowl	1 salad (1 lb, including tortilla bowl)	3 ½ carbohydrates + 4 medium-fat proteins + 3 fats
🧂 Tostada with beans and cheese	1 small tostada (about 5 oz)	2 carbohydrates + 1 high-fat protein
Sandwiches		
Breakfast Sandwiches		
🧂 Breakfast burrito with sausage, egg, cheese	1 burrito (about 4 oz)	1 ½ carbohydrates + 2 high-fat proteins
🧂 Egg, cheese, meat on an English muffin	1 sandwich	2 carbohydrates + 3 medium-fat proteins + ½ fat

*Definition and weight refer to food **with** bone, skin, and breading.

Definition refers to above food **without bone, skin, and breading.

Food	Serving Size	Count As
Egg, cheese, meat on a biscuit	1 sandwich	2 carbohydrates + 3 medium-fat proteins + 2 fats
Sausage biscuit sandwich	1 sandwich	2 carbohydrates + 1 high-fat protein + 4 fats
Chicken Sandwiches		
grilled with bun, lettuce, tomatoes, spread	1 sandwich (about 7 ½ oz)	3 carbohydrates + 4 lean proteins
crispy, with bun, lettuce, tomatoes, spread	1 sandwich (about 6 oz)	3 carbohydrates + 2 lean proteins + 3 ½ fats
Fish sandwich with tartar sauce and cheese	1 sandwich (5 oz)	2 ½ carbohydrates + 2 medium-fat proteins + 1 ½ fats
Hamburger		
regular with bun and condiments (catsup, mustard, onion, pickle) . .	1 burger (about 3 ½ oz)	2 carbohydrates + 1 medium-fat protein + 1 fat
4 oz meat with cheese, bun, and condiments. . . . . (catsup, mustard, onion, pickle)	1 burger (about 8 ½ oz)	3 carbohydrates + 4 medium-fat protein + 2 ½ fats
Hot dog with bun, plain	1 hot dog (about 3 ½ oz)	1 ½ carbohydrates + 1 high-fat protein + 2 fats
Submarine sandwich (no cheese or sauce)		
less than 6 grams fat	1 6-inch sub	3 carbohydrates + 2 lean proteins
regular	1 6-inch sub	3 carbohydrates + 2 lean proteins + 1 fat
Wrap, grilled chicken, vegetables, cheese, and spread	1 small wrap (about 4 to 5 oz)	2 carbohydrates + 2 lean proteins + 1 ½ fats

Sides/Appetizers

Food	Serving Size	Count As
French fries	1 small order (about 3 ½ oz)	2 ½ carbohydrates + 2 fats
	1 medium order (about 5 oz)	3 ½ carbohydrates + 3 fats
	1 large order (about 6 oz)	4 ½ carbohydrates + 4 fats
Hashbrowns.	1 cup/medium order (about 5 oz) . . .	3 carbohydrates + 6 fats
Onion rings	1 serving (8 to 9 rings, about 4 oz) . .	3 ½ carbohydrates + 4 fats
Salad, side (no dressing, croutons or cheese)	1 small salad	1 nonstarchy vegetable

Beverages and Desserts

Food	Serving Size	Count As
Coffee, latte (fat-free milk).	1 small order (about 12 oz)	1 fat-free milk
Coffee, mocha (fat-free milk, no whipped cream)	1 small order (about 12 oz)	1 fat-free milk + 1 carbohydrate
Milkshake, any flavor	1 small shake (about 12 oz).	5 ½ carbohydrates + 3 fats
	1 medium shake (about 16 oz)	7 carbohydrates + 4 fats
	1 large shake (about 22 oz).	10 carbohydrates + 5 fats
Soft-serve ice cream cone	1 small	2 carbohydrates + ½ fat

Alcohol

One alcohol equivalent or choice (½ oz absolute alcohol) has about 100 calories. One carbohydrate choice has 15 grams of carbohydrate and about 70 calories.

Alcoholic Beverage	Serving Size	Choices per Serving
Beer		
light (less than 4.5% abv)	12 fl oz	1 alcohol equivalent + ½ carbohydrate
regular (about 5% abv)	12 fl oz	1 alcohol equivalent + 1 carbohydrate
dark (more than 5.7% abv)	12 fl oz	1 alcohol equivalent + 1 to 1 ½ carbohydrates
Distilled spirits: (80 or 86 proof): vodka, rum, gin, whiskey, tequila	1 ½ fl oz	1 alcohol equivalent
Liqueur, coffee (53 proof).	1 fl oz	1 alcohol equivalent + 1 carbohydrate
Sake.	1 fl oz	½ alcohol equivalent
Wine		
champagne/sparkling	5 fl oz	1 alcohol equivalent
dessert (sherry)	3 ½ fl oz	1 alcohol equivalent + 1 carbohydrate
dry, red or white (10% abv)	5 fl oz	1 alcohol equivalent

Note: The abbreviation "% abv" refers to the percentage of alcohol by volume.

Academic Journals

International Journal of Sport Nutrition and Exercise Metabolism
www.humankinetics.com/IJSNEM

Journal of Nutrition
www.jn.nutrition.org

Nutrition Research
www.journals.elsevierhealth.com/periodicals/NTR

Nutrition
www.nutritionjrnl.com

Nutrition Reviews
http://onlinelibrary.wiley.com/journal/10.1111/
%28ISSN%291753-4887

Obesity
http://onlinelibrary.wiley.com/journal/10.1111/
%28ISSN%291753-4887

International Journal of Obesity
www.nature.com/ijo

Journal of the American Medical Association
http://jama.ama-assn.org

New England Journal of Medicine
www.nejm.org

American Journal of Clinical Nutrition
www.ajcn.org

Journal of the Academy of Nutrition and Dietetics
www.adajournal.org

Aging

Administration on Aging
www.aoa.gov

American Association of Retired Persons (AARP)
www.aarp.org

Health and Age
Sponsored by the Novartis Foundation for Gerontology &
The Web-Based Health Education Foundation
www.healthandage.com

National Council on Aging
www.ncoa.org

International Osteoporosis Foundation
www.iofbonehealth.org

National Institute on Aging
www.nia.nih.gov

*NIH Osteoporosis and Related Bone Diseases National
Resource Center*
www.niams.nih.gov

American Geriatrics Society
www.americangeriatrics.org

National Osteoporosis Foundation
www.nof.org

Alcohol and Drug Abuse

National Institute on Drug Abuse
www.nida.nih.gov

National Institute on Alcohol Abuse and Alcoholism
www.niaaa.nih.gov

Alcoholics Anonymous
www.alcoholics-anonymous.org

Narcotics Anonymous
www.na.org

National Council on Alcoholism and Drug Dependence
www.ncadd.org

National Clearinghouse for Alcohol and Drug Information
http://ncadi.samhsa.gov

Canadian Government

Health Canada
www.hc-sc.gc.ca

Canadian Council of Food and Nutrition
www.nin.ca

Agricultural and Agri-Food Canada
www.arg.gc.ca

Canadian Food Inspection Agency
www.inspection.gc.ca/english/toce.shtml

Canadian Institute for Health Information
www.cihi.ca

Canadian Public Health Association
www.cpha.ca

Canadian Nutrition and Professional Organizations

Dietitians of Canada, Canadian Dietetic Association
www.dietitians.ca

Canadian Diabetes Association
www.diabetes.ca

National Eating Disorder Information Centre
www.nedic.ca

Canadian Paediatric Society
www.cps.ca

Disordered Eating/Eating Disorders

American Psychiatric Association
www.psych.org

Harvard Eating Disorders Center
www.mcleanhospital.org/programs/klarman-eating-disorders-center

National Institute of Mental Health
www.nimh.nih.gov

National Association of Anorexia Nervosa and Associated Disorders (ANAD)
www.anad.org

National Eating Disorders Association
www.nationaleatingdisorders.org

Eating Disorder Referral and Information Center
www.edreferral.com

Overeaters Anonymous
www.oa.org

Weight Managementhttp://wmdpg.org/

Exercise, Physical Activity, and Sports

American College of Sports Medicine (ACSM)
www.acsm.org

American Physical Therapy Association (APTA)
www.apta.org

Gatorade Sports Science Institute (GSSI)
www.gssiweb.com

National Coalition for Promoting Physical Activity (NCPPA)
www.ncppa.org

Sports, Cardiovascular, and Wellness Nutrition (SCAN)
www.scandpg.org

President's Council on Physical Fitness and Sports
www.fitness.gov

American Council on Exercise
www.acefitness.org

IDEA Health & Fitness Association
www.ideafit.com

Food Safety

Food Marketing Institute
www.fmi.org

Agency for Toxic Substances and Disease Registry (ATSDR)
www.atsdr.cdc.gov

Food Allergy and Anaphylaxis Network
www.foodallergy.org

Foodsafety.gov
www.foodsafety.gov

USDA Food Safety and Inspection Service
www.fsis.usda.gov

Consumer Reports
www.consumerreports.org

Center for Science in the Public Interest: Food Safety
www.cspinet.org/foodsafety/index.html

Center for Food Safety and Applied Nutrition
www.fda.gov/Food/FoodSafety

Food Safety Project
www.extension.iastate.edu/foodsafety

Organic Consumers Association
www.organicconsumers.org

Infancy and Childhood

Administration for Children and Families
www.acf.hhs.gov

The American Academy of Pediatrics
www.aap.org

Kidshealth: The Nemours Foundation
www.kidshealth.org

National Center for Education in Maternal and Child Health
www.ncemch.org

Birth Defects Research for Children, Inc.
www.birthdefects.org

USDA/ARS Children's Nutrition Research Center at Baylor College of Medicine
www.kidsnutrition.org

Centers for Disease Control—Healthy Youth
www.cdc.gov/healthyyouth

International Agencies

UNICEF
www.unicef.org

World Health Organization
www.who.int/en

The Stockholm Convention on Persistent Organic Pollutants
www.pops.int

Food and Agricultural Organization of the United Nations
www.fao.org

International Food Information Council
www.ific.org

Pregnancy and Lactation

San Diego County Breastfeeding Coalition
www.breastfeeding.org

National Alliance for Breastfeeding Advocacy
www.naba-breastfeeding.org

American College of Obstetricians and Gynecologists
www.acog.org

La Leche League
www.lalecheleague.org

National Organization on Fetal Alcohol Syndrome
www.nofas.org

March of Dimes Birth Defects Foundation
http://modimes.org

Professional Nutrition Organizations

Academy of Nutrition and Dietetics (AND)
www.eatright.org

American Cancer Society
www.cancer.org

American Dental Association
www.ada.org

American Heart Association
www.americanheart.org

American Medical Association
www.ama-assn.org

Center for Science in the Public Interest
www.cspinet.org

The American Society for Nutrition (ASN)
www.nutrition.org

Dietitians in Integrative and Functional Medicine
www.complementarynutrition.org

The Institute for Functional Medicine
www.functionalmedicine.org

North American Association for the Study of Obesity (NAASO)
www.naaso.org

The Society for Nutrition Education
www.sne.org

American College of Nutrition
www.americancollegeofnutrition.org

American Obesity Association
www.obesity.org

American Council on Science and Health
www.acsh.org

American Diabetes Association
www.diabetes.org

Institute of Food Technologists
www.ift.org

ILSI Human Nutrition Institute
www.ilsi.org

Trade Organizations

American Meat Institute
www.meatami.com

National Dairy Council
www.nationaldairycouncil.org

United Fresh Fruit and Vegetable Association
www.uffva.org

U.S.A. Rice Federation
www.usarice.com

U.S. Government

Agricultural Research Service
www.ars.usda.gov

The USDA National Organic Program
Agricultural Marketing Service
www.ams.usda.gov

U.S. Department of Health and Human Services
www.hhs.gov

Food and Drug Administration (FDA)
www.fda.gov

Environmental Protection Agency
www.epa.gov

Federal Trade Commission
www.ftc.gov

Office of Dietary Supplements
National Institutes of Health
http://dietary-supplements.info.nih.gov

Nutrient Data Laboratory
Beltsville Human Nutrition Research Center, Agricultural
Research Service
www.ars.usda.gov/nutrientdata

National Digestive Diseases Information Clearinghouse
http://digestive.niddk.nih.gov

The National Cancer Institute
www.cancer.gov

The National Eye Institute
www.nei.nih.gov

The National Heart, Lung, and Blood Institute
www.nhlbi.nih.gov/index.htm

National Institute of Diabetes and Digestive and Kidney
Diseases
www.niddk.nih.gov

National Center for Complementary and Alternative
Medicine
http://nccam.nih.gov

U.S. Department of Agriculture (USDA)
www.usda.gov

Centers for Disease Control and Prevention (CDC)
www.cdc.gov

National Institutes of Health (NIH)
www.nih.gov

Food and Nutrition Information Center
Agricultural Research Service, USDA
www.nal.usda.gov/fnic

National Institute of Allergy and Infectious Diseases
www.niaid.nih.gov

Weight and Health Management

North American Association for the Study of Obesity
(NAASO)
www.obesityresearch.org

The Vegetarian Resource Group
www.vrg.org

American Obesity Association
www.obesity.org

Anemia Lifeline
www.anemia.com

The Arc
www.thearc.org

Bottled Water Web
www.bottledwaterweb.com

Food and Nutrition
Institute of Medicine
www.iom.edu/Global/Topics/Food-Nutrition.aspx

The Calorie Control Council
www.caloriecontrol.org

TOPS (Take Off Pounds Sensibly)
www.tops.org

Shape Up America!
www.shapeup.org

World Hunger

Center on Hunger, Poverty, and Nutrition Policy
http://nutrition.tufts.edu

Freedom from Hunger
www.freefromhunger.org

Oxfam International
www.oxfam.org

WorldWatch Institute
www.worldwatch.org

The Hunger Project
www.thp.org

U.S. Agency for International Development
www.usaid.gov

Feeding America
www.feedingamerica.org

Food First
www.foodfirst.org

Glossary

1,25-dihydroxycholecalciferol The active form of vitamin D, also called calcitriol, that is formed in the kidney by adding a second hydroxyl group on the first carbon to 25-dihydroxycholecalciferol.

5-methyltetrahydrofolate (5-methyl THF) The most active form of folate.

7-dehydrocholesterol (provitamin D₃) The compound in the skin that is converted to precalciferol by UV light from the sun; synthesized in the liver from cholesterol.

25-hydroxycholecalciferol The compound formed in the liver by adding a hydroxyl group to the 25th carbon of cholecalciferol.

A

absorption The process of moving nutrients from the GI tract into the circulatory system.

absorptive state The period after you eat when the stomach and small intestine are full and anabolic reactions exceed catabolic reactions.

acceptable macronutrient distribution ranges (AMDRs) A healthy range of intakes for the energy-containing nutrients—carbohydrates, proteins, and fats—expressed as a percentage of total daily energy. The AMDRs for adults are 45 to 65 percent carbohydrates, 10 to 35 percent protein, and 20 to 35 percent fat.

acceptable tolerance levels The maximum amount of pesticide residue that is allowed in or on foods.

acetaldehyde One of the first compounds produced in the metabolism of ethanol. Eventually, acetaldehyde is converted to carbon dioxide and water and excreted.

acetaldehyde dehydrogenase (ALDH) The enzyme that converts acetaldehyde to acetate; this is the second step in oxidizing ethanol in the liver.

acetyl CoA A two-carbon compound formed when pantothenic acid combines with acetate.

acid-base balance The mechanisms used to maintain body fluids close to a neutral pH so the body can function properly.

acidosis A condition in which the blood pH is too low, generally due to excessive hydrogen ions.

active transport The process of absorbing nutrients with the help of a carrier molecule and energy expenditure.

acute Describes a sudden onset of symptoms or disease.

acute dehydration Dehydration that sets in after a short period of time.

added sugars Sugars that are added to processed foods and sweets.

adenosine diphosphate (ADP) A nucleotide composed of adenine, ribose, and two phosphate molecules; it is formed when one phosphate molecule is removed from ATP.

adenosine triphosphate (ATP) A high-energy molecule composed of adenine, ribose, and three phosphate molecules; cells use this to fuel all biological processes.

adequate intake (AI) The *approximate* daily amount of a nutrient that is sufficient to meet the needs of similar individuals within a population group. The Food and Nutrition Board uses AIs for nutrients that do not have enough scientific evidence to calculate an RDA.

adipocytes Cells in adipose tissue that store fat; also known as fat cells.

adiponectin A hormone produced in the adipocytes that controls the body's response to insulin and may be involved in reducing the risk of obesity and type 2 diabetes.

adipose tissue Connective tissue that is the main storage site for fat in the body.

adolescence The developmental period between childhood and early adulthood (approximately ages 9 through 19).

aerobic A reaction that requires oxygen.

age-related macular degeneration (AMD) A disease that affects the macula of the retina, causing blurry vision and, potentially, blindness.

aging Declines in bodily functions that accumulate with time, ultimately leading to death.

air displacement plethysmography A procedure used to estimate body volume based on the amount of air displaced.

albumin A protein produced in the liver and found in the blood that helps maintain fluid balance.

alcohol A class of organic compounds that contain one or more hydroxyl groups attached to carbons. Examples include ethanol, glycerol, and methanol. Ethanol is often referred to as "alcohol."

alcohol abuse Continuing to consume alcohol even though the behavior has created social, legal, and/or health problems.

alcohol dehydrogenase (ADH) One of the alcohol-metabolizing enzymes, found in the stomach and the liver, that converts ethanol to acetaldehyde.

alcoholic hepatitis Stage 2 of alcoholic liver disease, in which the liver becomes inflamed.

alcoholic liver disease A degenerative liver condition that occurs in three stages: (1) fatty liver, (2) alcoholic hepatitis, and (3) cirrhosis.

alcoholism A chronic disease characterized by craving for and elevated tolerance to alcohol, inability to control alcohol intake, and dependency on alcohol to prevent withdrawal symptoms; also referred to as *alcohol dependence.*

alcohol poisoning When the BAC rises to the point that a person's central nervous system is affected and his or her breathing and heart rate are interrupted.

alcohol tolerance When the body adjusts to long-term alcohol use by becoming less sensitive to the alcohol. More alcohol needs to be consumed in order to get the same euphoric effect.

aldosterone A hormone secreted from the adrenal glands in response to reduced blood volume; aldosterone signals the kidneys to reabsorb sodium, which increases blood volume and blood pressure.

alkalosis A condition in which the blood pH is too low due to a low concentration of hydrogen ions.

allergen A substance, such as wheat protein, that causes an allergic reaction.

alpha-ketoglutarate A compound that participates in the formation of nonessential amino acids during transamination.

alpha-linolenic acid A polyunsaturated essential fatty acid; part of the omega-3 fatty acid family.

alpha-tocopherol (α-tocopherol) The most active form of vitamin E in the body.

Alzheimer's disease A type of dementia.

amenorrhea Absence of menstruation for at least three consecutive cycles.

amine group The nitrogen-containing part (NH_2) connected to the central carbon of an amino acid.

amino acid pools Limited supplies of amino acids that accumulate in the blood and cells; amino acids are pulled from the pools and used to build new proteins.

amino acids The building blocks of protein. There are 20 amino acids composed of carbon, hydrogen, oxygen, and nitrogen.

amino acid score The composition of essential amino acids in a protein compared with a standard, usually egg protein.

amylopectin A branched chain of polysaccharides found in starch.

amylose A straight chain of polysaccharides found in starch.

anabolic An energy-requiring process in which smaller molecules are combined to form larger molecules.

anabolic reactions Metabolic reactions that combine smaller compounds into larger molecules.

anaerobic A reaction that does not require oxygen.

anaphylaxis Severe, life-threatening allergic reaction involving a sudden drop in blood pressure and constriction of the airways in the lungs, which inhibits the ability to breathe.

anencephaly A neural tube defect that results in the absence of major parts of the brain and spinal cord.

angiotensin I and II The active protein in the blood that causes vasoconstriction in the blood vessels and triggers the release of aldosterone from the adrenal glands, which raises blood pressure.

angiotensinogen A precursor protein produced in the liver and found in the blood; it is converted to the active form called angiotensin.

anions Negatively charged ions.

anorexia nervosa An eating disorder in which people intentionally starve themselves, causing extreme weight loss.

antibiotic-resistant bacteria Bacteria that have developed a resistance to an antibiotic such that they are no longer affected by antibiotic medication.

antibiotics Drugs that kill or slow the growth of bacteria.

antibodies Proteins that bind to and neutralize pathogens as part of the body's immune response.

antidiuretic hormone (ADH) A hormone secreted by the pituitary gland when blood volumes are low; ADH reduces the amount of water excreted through the kidneys, constricts the blood vessels, and raises blood pressure; also known as vasopressin.

antimicrobials Substances or a combination of substances, such as disinfectants and sanitizers, that kill or inhibit the growth of microorganisms.

antioxidants Substances that neutralize harmful oxygen-containing free radicals that can cause cell damage. Vitamins A, C, and E and beta-carotene are antioxidants.

anus The opening of the rectum, or end of the GI tract.

appetite The desire to eat food whether or not there is hunger; a taste for particular foods and cravings in reaction to cues such as the sight, smell, or thought of food.

arachidonic acid An omega-6 fatty acid formed from linoleic acid; it is used to synthesize the eicosanoids, including leukotrienes, prostaglandins, and thromboxanes.

ariboflavinosis A deficiency of riboflavin characterized by, stomatitis, glossitis, and cheilosis.

arthritis Inflammation in the joints that can cause pain, stiffness, and swelling.

ascorbic acid The active form of vitamin C.

atherosclerosis Narrowing of the coronary arteries due to buildup of debris along the artery walls.

atrophic gastritis Chronic inflammation of the stomach.

atrophy To shrink in size.

attention deficit/hyperactivity disorder (ADHD) (previously known as attention deficit disorder, or ADD) A condition in which an individual may be easily distracted, have difficulty listening and following directions, difficulty focusing and sustaining attention, difficulty concentrating and staying on task, and/or inconsistent performance in school.

avidin A protein in raw egg whites that binds biotin.

B

bacteria Single-celled microorganisms without an organized nucleus. Some are benign or beneficial to humans, while others can cause disease.

balance The diet principle of providing the correct proportion of nutrients to maintain health and prevent disease.

bariatric surgery A surgical procedure that promotes weight loss by limiting the amount of food that can be eaten or absorbed.

basal metabolic rate (BMR) The measure of basal metabolism taken when the body is at rest in a warm, quiet environment, after a 12-hour fast; expressed as kilocalories per kilogram of body weight per hour.

basal metabolism The amount of energy expended by the body to meet its basic physiological needs, including muscle tone and heart and brain function.

behavior modification Changing behaviors to improve health outcomes. In the case of weight management, it involves identifying and altering eating patterns that contribute to weight gain or impede weight loss.

beriberi The thiamin deficiency that results in weakness; the name translates to "I can not."

beta-carotene One of the provitamin A carotenoids.

beta-oxidation A series of metabolic reactions in which fatty acids are oxidized to acetyl CoA; also called *fatty acid oxidation*.

bicarbonate A negatively charged alkali ion produced from bicarbonate salts; during digestion, bicarbonate ions are released from the pancreas to neutralize HCl in the duodenum.

bile A secretion produced in the liver and stored in the gallbladder. It is released through the common bile duct into the duodenum to digest dietary fat.

binders Compounds such as oxalates and phytates that bind to minerals in foods and reduce their bioavailability.

binge drinking The consumption of five or more alcoholic drinks by men, or four or more drinks by women, in about two hours.

bioaccumulate To build up the levels of a substance or chemical in an organism over time, so that the concentration of the chemical is higher than would be found naturally in the environment.

bioavailability The degree to which a nutrient is absorbed from foods and used in the body.

biodiversity The variability among living organisms on the Earth, including the variability within and between species and within and between ecosystems.

bioelectrical impedance analysis (BIA) A method used to assess the percentage of body fat by using a low-level electrical current; body fat resists or impedes the current, whereas water and muscle mass conduct electricity.

biological value The percentage of absorbed amino acids that are efficiently used to synthesize proteins.

biotechnology The manipulation of living organisms or their components to develop or manufacture useful products.

biotinidase An enzyme in the small intestine that releases biotin from food to allow it to be absorbed.

blackouts Periods of time when an intoxicated person cannot recall part or all of an event.

bleaching When light enters the eye and interacts with rhodopsin, splitting it into *trans*-retinal and opsin.

blood alcohol concentration (BAC) The amount of alcohol in the blood. BAC is measured in grams of alcohol per deciliter of blood, usually expressed as a percentage.

blood lipid profile A measurement of blood lipids used to assess cardiovascular risk.

body composition The relative proportions of muscle, fat, water, and other tissues in the body.

body image How you perceive your physical appearance.

body mass index (BMI) A measurement calculated using the metric formula of weight in kilograms divided by height in meters squared; used to determine whether an individual is underweight, at a healthy weight, or overweight or obese.

bolus A soft mass of chewed food.

bomb calorimeter An instrument used to measure the amount of heat released from food during combustion; the amount of heat produced is directly related to the amount of kilocalories in a given food.

bone mineral density (BMD) The amount of minerals, in particular calcium, per volume in an individual's bone.

botanicals A part of a plant, such as its root, that is believed to have medicinal or therapeutic attributes.

botulism A rare but serious paralytic illness caused by the bacterium *Clostridium botulinum*.

bovine growth hormone (BGH) A hormone that is essential for normal growth and development in cattle.

bran The indigestible outer shell of the grain kernel.

breast-feeding The act of feeding an infant milk from a woman's breast.

brown adipose tissue (BAT) A type of adipose tissue, found primarily in infants, that produces body heat; it gets its name from the large number of mitochondria and capillaries responsible for the brown color.

buffers Substances that help maintain the proper pH in a solution by accepting or donating hydrogen ions.

bulimia nervosa An eating disorder characterized by consuming large quantities of food and then purging through vomiting, laxative and diuretic use, and/or excessive physical exercise.

C

calciferol The family of vitamin D compounds.

calcitonin A hormone secreted by the thyroid gland that lowers blood calcium levels.

calcitriol The active form of vitamin D, also referred to as 1,25-dihydroxycholecalciferol.

calcium (Ca^{2+}) One of the most abundant divalent cations found in nature and in the body.

cancer A general term for a large group of diseases characterized by uncontrolled growth and spread of abnormal cells.

cancer initiator A carcinogen that initiates the mutation in DNA; these mutations cause the cell to respond abnormally to physiological controls.

cancer promoter A substance that induces a cell to divide and grow rapidly, and reduces the time that enzymes have to repair any damage or mutation; examples of cancer promoters are dietary fats, alcohol, and estrogen.

canning The process of packing food in airtight containers and heating them to a temperature high enough to kill bacteria.

carbohydrate loading A diet and training strategy that maximizes glycogen stores in the body before an endurance event.

carboxyl or **acid group** The organic group attached to an amino acid that is composed of one carbon, one hydrogen, and two oxygen atoms (COOH).

carboxylation The chemical reaction in which a carboxyl group is added to a molecule.

carcinogen Cancer-causing substance, including tobacco smoke, air and water pollution, ultraviolet radiation, and various chemicals.

carcinogenesis The process of cancer development.

cardiac arrhythmia A disturbance in the beating and rhythm of the heart; can be caused by excessive alcohol consumption.

cardiac myopathy Condition in which the heart becomes thin and weak and is unable to pump blood throughout the body; also called disease of the heart muscle.

cardiorespiratory conditioning Improvements in the delivery of oxygen to working muscles as a result of aerobic activity.

cardiorespiratory endurance The body's ability to sustain prolonged exercise.

cardiovascular disease (CVD) A general term for diseases of the heart and blood vessels.

carnitine A vitamin-like substance used to transport fatty acids across the mitochondrial membrane to properly utilize fat.

carotenodermia The presence of excess carotene in the blood, resulting in an orange color to the skin due to excessive intake of carrots or other carotene-rich vegetables.

carotenoids The family of provitamin compounds that includes beta-carotene. Also a group of yellow, red, and orange pigments found in plants; three of them are precursors to vitamin A. The body stores carotenoids in the liver and in fat cells.

catabolic An energy-releasing process that breaks larger molecules into smaller parts.

catabolic reactions Metabolic reactions that break large compounds into smaller molecules.

catalysts Substances that aid and speed up reactions without being changed, damaged, or used up in the process.

cataract A common eye disorder that occurs when the lens of the eye becomes cloudy.

cataracts Clumps of protein that form on the lens of the eye, clouding vision.

cations Positively charged ions.

cecum A pouch at the beginning of the large intestine that receives waste from the small intestine.

celiac disease Genetic disease that causes damage to the small intestine when gluten-containing foods are eaten.

cell differentiation The process of a less specialized immature cell becoming a specialized mature cell.

cell division The process of dividing one cell into two separate cells with the same genetic material.

cellulose A nondigestible polysaccharide found in plant cell walls.

central or android obesity An excess storage of visceral fat in the abdominal area, indicated by a waist circumference greater than 40 inches in males and 35 inches in females; central obesity increases the risk of heart disease, diabetes, and hypertension.

ceruloplasmin A protein found in the blood that transports copper.

cheilosis A noninflammatory condition of the lips characterized by chapping and fissuring.

chemical digestion Breaking down food through enzymatic reactions.

chief cells Specialized cells in the stomach that secrete an inactive protein-digesting enzyme called pepsinogen.

childhood obesity The condition of a child's having too much body weight for his or her height. Rates of childhood obesity in the United States are increasing.

chloride (Cl⁻) Major anion in the extracellular fluid.

chlorophyll The green pigment in plants that absorbs energy from sunlight to begin the process of photosynthesis.

cholecalciferol (vitamin D₃) The form of vitamin D found in animal foods, supplements, and formed from precalciferol in the skin. This is the form absorbed from the skin into the blood.

cholecystokinin (CCK) A hormone released by the duodenum that stimulates the gallbladder to release bile.

cholesterol A common sterol found only in animal products and made in the liver from saturated fatty acids.

choline A vitamin-like substance that is a precursor for the neurotransmitter acetylcholine, which is essential for healthy nerves. Also a component of the phospholipid lecithin.

chronic Describes a symptom or condition that lasts over a long period of time.

chronic dehydration Dehydration over a long period of time.

chronologic age A person's age in number of years of life.

chylomicron A type of lipoprotein that carries digested fat and other lipids through the lymph system into the blood.

chyme The semiliquid, partially digested food mass that leaves the stomach and enters the small intestine.

ciguatera poisoning A condition caused by marine toxins that are produced by dinoflagellates and have bioaccumulated in fish that the affected person consumes.

cirrhosis Stage 3 of alcoholic liver disease, in which liver cells die and are replaced by scar tissue.

cis The configuration of a fatty acid in which the carbon chains on each side of the double bond are on the same side.

closed or "coded" dating Refers to the packing numbers that are decodable only by manufacturers and are often found on nonperishable, shelf-stable foods.

clotting factors Substances involved in the process of blood clotting, such as prothrombin and fibrinogen.

coagulation The process of blood clotting.

cobalamin The vitamin involved in energy metabolism and the conversion of homocysteine to methionine; another name for vitamin B₁₂.

coenzymes Organic substances, often vitamins, that bind to an enzyme to facilitate enzyme activity; unlike enzymes, coenzymes can be altered by the chemical reaction.

cofactors Similar to a coenzyme, a substance that binds to an enzyme to help catalyze a reaction. The term cofactor generally refers to a metal ion, while a coenzyme is usually an organic molecule such as a vitamin.

collagen A protein found in connective tissue, including bones, teeth, skin, cartilage, and tendons.

colon Another name for the large intestine.

colostrum The fluid that is expressed from the mother's breast after birth and before the development of breast milk.

community-supported agriculture (CSA) An arrangement where individuals pay a fee to support a local farm, and in exchange receive a weekly or biweekly box of fresh produce from the farm.

complete protein A protein that provides all the essential amino acids, along with some nonessential amino acids. Soy protein and protein from animal sources are complete proteins.

complex carbohydrates A category of carbohydrates that contain many sugar units combined. Oligosaccharides and polysaccharides are complex carbohydrates.

conception The moment when a sperm fertilizes an egg.

condensation A chemical reaction in which two molecules combine to form a larger molecule, and water is released.

conditionally essential [amino acids] Those nonessential amino acids, such as tyrosine and glycine, that become essential (and must be consumed in the diet) when the body cannot make them.

conditioning The process of improving physical fitness through repeated activity.

cones Light-absorbing cells responsible for color vision.

congeners Fermentation by-products or additives in alcohol that may contribute to hangover symptoms.

congregate meals Low- or no-cost meals served at churches, synagogues, or other community sites where older adults can receive a nutritious meal and socialize.

consensus Agreed-upon conclusion of a group of experts based on a collection of information.

constipation The infrequent passage of dry, hardened stools.

control group In experimental research, the group that does not receive the treatment but may be given a placebo instead; used as a standard for comparison.

Cori cycle The metabolic pathway in the liver that regenerates glucose from lactate released from the muscle.

cortical bone The hard outer layer of bone.

cortisol A hormone produced by the adrenal cortex that stimulates gluconeogenesis and lipolysis.

C-reactive protein (CRP) A protein found in the blood that is released from the cells during inflammation; used as a marker for the presence of atherosclerosis.

creatine phosphate (PCr) A compound that provides a reserve of phosphate to regenerate ADP to ATP.

cretinism A condition caused by a deficiency of thyroid hormone during prenatal development, resulting in abnormal mental and physical development in children.

critical periods Developmental stages during which cells and tissues rapidly grow and differentiate to form body structures.

Crohn's disease A form of ulcerative colitis in which ulcers form throughout the GI tract and not just in the colon.

cross-contaminate The transfer of pathogens from a food, utensil, cutting board, kitchen surface, and/or hands to another food or object.

crypts Glands at the base of the villi; they contain stem cells that manufacture young cells to replace the cells of the villi when they die.

cupric The oxidized form of copper (Cu^{2+}).

cuprous The reduced form of copper (Cu^+).

cytochromes Protein complexes that move electrons down the electron transport chain; they contain the minerals iron and copper.

cytokines Substances that damage liver cells and lead to scarring.

cytosol The fluid portion of the cell where anaerobic metabolism takes place.

D

daily values (DVs) Reference values developed by the Food and Drug Administration and used on nutrition labels to describe the amount of a nutrient provided in one serving of the food.

danger zone The range of temperatures between 40°F and 140°F at which foodborne bacteria multiplies most rapidly. Room temperature falls within the danger zone.

deamination The removal of the amine group from an amino acid.

dehydration Loss of water in the body as a result of inadequate fluid intake or excess fluid loss, such as through sweating, diarrhea, or vomiting; also called *hypohydration*.

DeLaney clause Clause in the Food Additives Amendment mandating that additives shown to cause cancer at any level must be removed from the marketplace.

dementia A disorder of the brain that interferes with a person's memory, learning, and mental stability.

denature To alter a protein's shape, either its secondary, tertiary, or quaternary structure, which prevents its function; the chains of amino acids remain linked together by peptide bonds.

dental caries Tooth decay.

deoxyadenosylcobalamin The coenzyme form of vitamin B_{12} that converts intermediate substances in the TCA cycle.

developed country A country that is advanced in multiple areas, such as income per capita, life expectancy, rate of literacy, industrial capability, technological sophistication, and economic productivity.

developing country A country that is growing in multiple areas, such as income per capita, life expectancy, rate of literacy, industrial capability, technological sophistication, and economic productivity.

diabetes mellitus A medical condition whereby an individual either doesn't have enough insulin or is resistant to the insulin available, resulting in a rise in blood glucose levels. Diabetes mellitus is often called diabetes.

diarrhea The abnormally frequent passage of watery stools.

diastolic pressure The bottom number in a blood pressure reading that measures the minimal arterial pressure during relaxation of the heart muscle when the ventricles fill with blood.

dietary folate equivalents (DFE) A measurement used to express the amount of folate in a food or supplement.

Dietary Guidelines for Americans Guidelines published every five years by the Department of Health and Human Services and the United States Department of Agriculture that provide dietary and lifestyle advice to healthy individuals aged 2 and older to maintain good health and prevent chronic diseases. They are the basis for the federal food and nutrition education programs.

Dietary Reference Intakes (DRIs) Reference values for nutrients developed by the Food and Nutrition Board of the Institute of Medicine, used to plan and evaluate the diets of healthy people in the United States and Canada. It includes the Estimated Average Requirement (EAR), the Recommended Dietary Allowance (RDA), the Adequate Intake (AI), and the Tolerable Upper Intake Level (UL).

digestion A process that breaks down food into individual molecules small enough to be absorbed through the intestinal wall.

diglyceride A remnant of fat digestion that consists of a glycerol with two attached fatty acids; also the form of fat used as an emulsifier in food production.

dipeptide A chain of two amino acids joined together by a peptide bond.

direct calorimetry A direct measurement of the energy expended by the body obtained by assessing heat loss.

disaccharide Simple sugar that consists of two sugar units combined. The three most common disaccharides: sucrose, lactose, and maltose.

disordered eating Abnormal and potentially harmful eating behaviors that do not meet specific criteria for anorexia nervosa and bulimia nervosa or binge eating disorder.

distillation The evaporation and then collection of a liquid by condensation. Liquors are made using distillation.

diuretics Substances that increase the production and secretion of urine; they are often used as antihypertensive drugs.

diverticula Small bulges at weak spots in the colon wall.

diverticulosis The existence of diverticula in the lining of the large intestine or colon.

DNA fingerprinting A technique in which bacterial DNA "gene patterns" (or "fingerprints") are detected and analyzed to distinguish between different strains of a bacterium.

double-blind placebo-controlled study An experimental study in which neither the researchers nor the subjects in the study are aware of who is receiving the treatment or the placebo.

dual-energy X-ray absorptiometry (DEXA) A method that uses two low-energy X-rays to measure body density and bone mass.

duration The length of time that an activity is performed.

early childhood caries Tooth decay from prolonged tooth contact with formula, milk, fruit juice, or other sugar-rich liquid offered to an infant in a bottle.

eating disorders Psychological illnesses that involve specific abnormal eating behaviors: anorexia nervosa (self-starvation) and bulimia nervosa (bingeing and purging).

eclampsia Seizures or coma in a woman with preeclampsia.

edema The accumulation of excess water in the spaces surrounding the cells, which causes swelling of the body tissue.

eicosanoids Hormonelike substances in the body. Prostaglandins, thromboxanes, and leukotrienes are all eicosanoids.

eicosapentaenoic acid (EPA) and docosahexaenoic acid (DHA) EPA (C20:5n–3) and DHA (C22:6n–3) are omega-3 fatty acids that are synthesized in the body and found in cold-water fish. These compounds may be beneficial in reducing heart disease.

electrolytes Ions such as sodium, potassium, chloride, and calcium in the blood and within the cells that are able to conduct electrical current when they are dissolved in body water.

electron transport chain The final stage of energy metabolism. NADH or $FADH_2$ transports high-energy electrons from glycolysis and the TCA cycle to the cytochromes in the electron transport chain, resulting in the formation of ATP and water.

elimination Excretion of undigested and unabsorbed food through the feces.

elongation The phase of protein synthesis in which the polypeptide chain grows longer by adding amino acids.

embryo A fertilized egg during the third through the eighth week of pregnancy.

emergency kitchen A kitchen or a commercial food service that prepares for natural disasters, emergencies, or terrorist attacks.

empty calories Kilocalories that provide little nutrition, such as those found in candy.

emulsifier A compound that keeps two incompatible substances, such as oil and water, mixed together.

emulsify To break large fat globules into smaller droplets.

endocytosis A type of active transport in which the cell membrane forms an indentation, engulfing the substance to be absorbed.

endosperm The starchy inner portion of a cereal grain.

endotoxins Damaging products produced by intestinal bacteria that travel in the blood to the liver and initiate the release of cytokines.

energy The capacity to do work.

energy balance The state at which energy (kilocalorie) intake from food and beverages is equal to energy (kilocalorie) output for BMR, physical activity, digestion and absorption, and body repairs.

energy density A measurement of the kilocalories in a food compared with the weight (grams) of the food.

energy gap The difference between the numbers of kilocalories needed to maintain weight before and after weight loss.

energy-yielding nutrients The three nutrients that provide energy to the body to fuel physiological functions: carbohydrates, lipids, and protein.

enriched grains Refined grain foods that have folic acid, thiamin, niacin, riboflavin, and iron added.

enterocytes Absorptive epithelial cells that line the walls of the small intestine.

enterogastrones A group of GI tract hormones, produced in the stomach and small intestine, that controls gastric motility and secretions.

enterohepatic circulation The process of recycling bile from the large intestine back to the liver to be reused during fat digestion.

enzymes Substances, mostly proteins, that increase the rate of chemical changes or catalyze chemical reactions; also called biological catalysts.

epidemiological research Research that studies the variables that influence health in a population; it is often observational.

epigenetics The changes that may occur in gene activity and gene expression without altering the DNA sequence.

epiglottis Cartilage at the back of the tongue that closes off the trachea during swallowing.

epinephrine A hormone produced by the adrenal glands that signals the liver cells to release glucose; also referred to as the "fight-or-flight" hormone.

epiphyseal plate The growth plate of the bone. In puberty, growth in this area leads to increases in height.

epithelial cells Cells that line the cavities in the body and cover flat surfaces such as the skin.

ergocalciferol (vitamin D₂) The form of vitamin D found in plants and dietary supplements.

ergogenic aid A substance, such as a dietary supplement, used to enhance athletic performance.

esophagus Tube that connects the mouth to the stomach.

essential [amino acids] The nine amino acids that the body cannot synthesize; they must be obtained through dietary sources.

essential fat A component of body fat that is necessary for health and normal body functions; includes the fat stored in the bone marrow, heart, lungs, liver, spleen, kidneys, intestines, muscles, and the lipid-rich tissues of the central nervous system.

essential fatty acids The two polyunsaturated fatty acids that the body cannot make and therefore must be eaten in foods: linoleic acid and alpha-linolenic acid.

essential nutrients Nutrients that must be consumed from foods because they cannot be made in the body in sufficient quantities to meet its needs and support health.

estimated average requirement (EAR) The average daily amount of a nutrient needed by 50 percent of the individuals in a similar age and gender group.

estimated energy requirement (EER) The average kilocalorie intake that is estimated to maintain energy balance based on a person's gender, age, height, body weight, and level of physical activity.

estrogens The hormones responsible for female sex characteristics.

ethanol The type of alcohol, specifically *ethyl alcohol* (C_2H_5OH), found in alcoholic beverages such as wine, beer, and liquor.

exchange lists A diet-planning tool that groups foods together based on their carbohydrate, protein, and fat content. One food on the list can be exchanged for another food on the same list.

exercise Any type of structured or planned physical activity.

experimental group In experimental research, the group of participants given a specific treatment, such as a drug, as part of the study.

experimental research Research involving at least two groups of subjects receiving different treatments.

extracellular fluid (ECF) The water found outside the cell, including the intravascular fluid and the interstitial fluid.

F

facilitated diffusion The process of absorbing nutrients with the help of a carrier molecule.

famine A severe shortage of food caused by weather-related crop destruction, poor agricultural practices, pestilence, war, or other factors.

farm-to-table continuum Illustrates the roles that farmers, food manufacturers, food transporters, retailers, and consumers play in ensuring that the food supply, from the farm to the plate, remains safe.

fat-soluble vitamins Vitamins that dissolve in fat and can be stored in the body.

fat substitutes Substances that replace added fat in foods; they provide the creamy properties of fat for fewer kilocalories and total fat grams.

fatty acid The most basic unit of triglycerides and phospholipids; fatty acids consist of carbon chains ranging from two to 80 carbons in length.

fatty liver Stage 1 of alcoholic liver disease, in which fat begins to build up in the liver cells.

fecal-to-oral transmission The spread of pathogens by putting something in the mouth, such as hands or food, that has been in contact with infected stool.

female athlete triad A syndrome of the three interrelated conditions occurring in some physically active females: low energy availability (often from disordered eating), amenorrhea, and decreased bone density or osteoporosis.

ferment (fermentation) The process by which yeast converts sugars in grains or fruits into ethanol and carbon dioxide.

ferric iron The oxidized form of iron (Fe^{3+}).

ferritin A protein that stores iron in the intestine.

ferroportin A protein found on the basolateral surface of the enterocyte that transports iron out of the enterocyte into the portal vein.

ferrous iron The reduced form of iron (Fe^{2+}).

fetal alcohol spectrum disorders (FASDs) A range of conditions that can occur in children who are exposed to alcohol in utero.

fetal alcohol syndrome (FAS) The most severe of the fetal alcohol spectrum disorders (FASDs); children with FAS display physical, mental, and behavioral abnormalities.

fetus A developing embryo that is at least eight weeks old.

fiber Food components that humans cannot digest. Most are carbohydrates.

flatulence Production of excessive gas in the stomach or the intestines.

flavin adenine dinucleotide (FAD) A coenzyme form of riboflavin that functions as an electron carrier in energy metabolism.

flavin mononucleotide (FMN) A coenzyme form of riboflavin, which functions in the electron transport chain.

flavonoids Food pigments that act as antioxidants and may help reduce the risk of chronic diseases; flavonoids are found in many fruits, vegetables, tea, and wine.

flavoproteins Protein complexes that move electrons down the electron transport chain; they contain the B vitamin riboflavin.

flexibility Ability to move joints freely through a full and normal range of motion.

fluid balance The difference between the amount of water taken into the body and the amount of water excreted.

fluoroapatite The crystalline structure that results when hydroxyapatite has been changed by exposure of the tooth to fluoride.

fluorosis A condition caused by excess amounts of fluoride, resulting in mottling of the teeth.

folic acid The form of folate often used in vitamin supplements and fortification of foods.

food additives Substances added to food that affect its quality, flavor, freshness, and/or safety.

food allergens Proteins that are not broken down by cooking or digestion and enter the body intact, causing an adverse reaction by the immune system.

food allergy An abnormal reaction by the immune system to a particular food.

foodborne illness Sickness caused by consuming pathogen- or toxin-containing food or beverages. Also known as foodborne disease or food poisoning.

food deserts Parts of the country, usually impoverished areas, where fresh fruit, vegetables, and other healthful whole foods are scarce, largely due to a lack of grocery stores, farmers' markets, and healthy-food providers.

food guidance systems Visual diagrams that provide a variety of food recommendations to help a person create a well-balanced diet.

food insecurity A household-level economic and social condition of uncertain access to adequate food.

food intolerance Adverse reaction to a food that does not involve an immune response.

food jags When a child will only eat the same food meal after meal.

food pantry Community food assistance location where food is provided to needy individuals and families.

food preservation The treatment of foods to reduce deterioration and spoilage, and help prevent the multiplication of pathogens that can cause foodborne illness.

food safety initiative (FSI) Coordinates the research, surveillance, inspection, outbreak response, and educational activities of the various government agencies that work together to safeguard food.

food security The degree to which an individual has regular access to adequate amounts of healthy foods.

food system A food system includes all processes and infrastructure involved in feeding a population: growing, harvesting, processing, packaging, transporting, marketing, and consuming food.

fortified foods Foods with added vitamins and minerals; fortified foods often contain nutrients that are not naturally present in the food or that are in higher amounts than the food contains naturally.

free radicals Unstable molecules that contain an unpaired electron; free radicals can damage the cells of the body and possibly contribute to the increased risk of chronic diseases.

fructose The sweetest of all the monosaccharides; also known as fruit sugar or levulose.

functional fiber The nondigestible polysaccharides that are added to foods because of a specific desired effect on human health.

functional foods Foods that may provide additional health benefits beyond the basic nutrient value.

fungicides Chemicals used to kill mold.

G

galactose A monosaccharide that links with glucose to create the disaccharide found in dairy foods.

galactosemia The genetic disorder characterized by high levels of galactose in the blood due to the inability to convert galactose to glucose.

gallbladder A pear-shaped organ located behind the liver. The gallbladder stores bile produced by the liver and secretes the bile through the common bile duct into the small intestine.

gallstones Stones formed from cholesterol in the gallbladder or bile duct.

gastric bypass surgery A type of bariatric surgery that reduces the functional volume of the stomach to minimize the amount of food eaten. Such surgeries are sometimes used to treat extreme obesity.

gastric inhibitory peptide (GIP) A hormone produced by the small intestine that slows the release of chyme from the stomach.

gastric pits Indentations or small pits in the stomach lining where the gastric glands are located; gastric glands produce gastric juices.

gastrin A stomach hormone released after eating a meal that stimulates the release of hydrochloric acid.

gastritis Inflammation of the lining in the stomach.

gastroenteritis Inflammation of the lining of the stomach and intestines; also known as stomach flu.

gastroesophageal reflux disease (GERD) The backward flow of stomach contents into the esophagus due to improper functioning of the LES, resulting in heartburn.

gastrointestinal (GI) tract A long tube comprised of the organs of the digestive tract. It extends from the mouth through the esophagus, stomach, and small and large intestines to the anus.

gene The basic biological unit in a segment of DNA that contributes to the function of a specific protein.

gene–environment interaction The interaction of genetics and environmental factors that increases the risk of obesity in susceptible individuals.

gene expression The processing of genetic information to create a specific protein.

generally recognized as safe (GRAS) A designation given by the FDA to substances intentionally added to food, indicating that the substance is considered safe by experts and is exempted from further testing.

genetic engineering (GE) A biological technique that isolates and manipulates the genes of organisms to produce a targeted, modified product.

genetically modified organisms (GMOs) Organisms that have been genetically engineered to contain both original and foreign genes.

genome The total genetic information of an organism stored in the DNA of its chromosomes.

germ The vitamin-rich embryo, or seed, of a grain.

gestational diabetes Form of diabetes that may develop during pregnancy in women who were not previously diagnosed with diabetes.

gestational hypertension Hypertension occurring during pregnancy in a woman without prior history of high blood pressure.

ghrelin A hormone produced in the stomach that stimulates hunger.

glossitis Inflammation of the tongue.

glucagon The hormone secreted from the alpha cells of the pancreas that stimulates glycogenolysis and gluconeogenesis to increase blood levels of glucose.

glucogenic amino acids Amino acids that can be used to form glucose through gluconeogenesis.

gluconeogenesis The formation of glucose from noncarbohydrate sources such as glucogenic amino acids, pyruvate, lactate, and glycerol.

glucose The primary monosaccharide and primary energy source for the body.

glycemic index (GI) A rating scale of the likelihood of foods to increase the levels of blood glucose and insulin.

glycemic load (GL) The amount of carbohydrate in a food multiplied by the amount of the glycemic index of that food.

glycerol The three-carbon backbone of a triglyceride.

glycogenesis The process of assembling excess glucose into glycogen in the liver and muscle cells.

glycogenolysis The hydrolysis of glycogen to release glucose.

glycogen The storage form of glucose in animals, including humans.

glycogen storage disease A genetic disorder characterized by the inability to break down glycogen due to the lack of glucose 6-phosphatase.

glycolysis The breakdown of glucose; for each molecule of glucose, two molecules of pyruvate and two ATP molecules are produced.

glycosidic bond A bond that forms when two sugar molecules are joined together during condensation.

goblet cells Cells throughout the GI tract that secrete mucus.

goiter The enlargement of the thyroid gland, mostly due to iodine deficiency.

goitrogens Substances in food that reduce the utilization of iodine by the thyroid gland, resulting in goiter.

gout A disease in which high levels of uric acid build up in the blood and cause inflammation in the joints. Chronic gout causes episodes of acute arthritis pain especially in the feet.

growth charts Series of percentile curves that illustrate the distribution of selected body measurements in U.S. children.

growth hormone A hormone that regulates glucose metabolism by increasing glycogenolysis and lipolysis.

growth spurt A rapid increase in height and weight.

growth stunting Impaired growth and development primarily manifested in early childhood and including malnutrition during fetal development. Once growth stunting occurs, it is usually permanent.

gynoid obesity An excessive storage of body fat in the thighs and hips of the lower body.

H

hangover A collective term for the unpleasant symptoms, such as a headache and dizziness, that occur after drinking an excessive amount of alcohol; many of the symptoms are caused by high levels of acetaldehyde in the blood.

health claims Claims on food labels that describe a relationship between a food, food component, dietary ingredient, or dietary supplement and a disease or health-related condition.

Healthy People 2020 A set of disease prevention and health promotion objectives for Americans to meet during the second decade of the twenty-first century.

healthy weight A body weight in relationship to height that doesn't increase the risk of developing any weight-related health problems or diseases. A BMI between 18.5 and 24.9 is considered healthy.

heart attack Permanent damage to the heart muscle that results from a sudden lack of oxygen-rich blood; also called a myocardial infarction (MI).

heme iron Iron that is part of a heme group found in hemoglobin in the blood, myoglobin in muscles, and in the mitochondria as part of the cytochromes.

hemochromatosis A blood disorder characterized by the retention of an excessive amount of iron.

hemoglobin The oxygen-carrying, heme-containing protein found in red blood cells.

hemolytic uremic syndrome A rare condition that can be caused by *E. coli* O157:H7 and results in the destruction of red blood cells and kidney failure. Very young children and the elderly are at a higher risk of developing this syndrome.

hemopoiesis The formation of red blood cells.

hemorrhage Excessive bleeding or loss of blood.

hemorrhoid Swelling in the veins of the rectum and anus.

hemosiderin A protein that stores iron in the body.

hepatic portal vein A large vein that connects the intestinal tract to the liver and transports newly absorbed nutrients.

hepatic vein The vein that carries the blood received from the hepatic portal vein away from the liver.

hepcidin A hormone produced in the liver that regulates the absorption and transport of iron.

hephaestin A copper-containing enzyme that catalyzes the conversion of ferrous to ferric iron before attaching to transferrin for transport.

herbicides Substances that are used to kill and control weeds.

hexavalent chromium The oxidized form of chromium (Cr^{6+}) that is toxic.

hexose A sugar that contains six carbons; glucose, galactose, and fructose are all hexoses.

high-density lipoproteins (HDLs) Lipoproteins that remove cholesterol from the tissues and deliver it to the liver to be used as part of bile and/or to be excreted from the body. Because of this, HDL is known as the "good" cholesterol.

high-pressure processing (HPP) A method used to pasteurize foods by exposing the items to pulses of high pressure, which destroys the microorganisms that are present.

homocystinuria A genetic disorder characterized by the inability to metabolize the essential amino acid methionine.

hormones Molecules, usually protein- or lipid-based, that initiate or direct specific actions from one organ to another. Insulin, glucagon, ADH, and estrogen are examples of hormones in the body.

hormone-sensitive lipase The enzyme that catalyzes lipolysis of triglycerides.

host A living plant or animal (including a human) that a virus infects for the sake of reproducing.

hunger An individual-level physiological condition that may result from food insecurity.

hydrochloric acid (HCl) A strong acid produced in the stomach that aids in digestion.

hydrogenation Adding hydrogen to an unsaturated fatty acid to make it more saturated and solid at room temperature.

hydrolysis A chemical reaction that breaks the bond between two molecules with water. A hydroxyl group is added to one molecule and a hydrogen ion is added to the other molecule.

hydrophobic "Water fearing." In nutrition, the term refers to compounds that are not soluble in water.

hydrostatic weighing A method used to assess body volume by underwater weighing.

hydroxyapatite The crystalline salt structure that provides strength in bones and teeth. Calcium and phosphorus are the main minerals found in the structure.

hypercalcemia Abnormally high levels of calcium in the blood.

hyperchloremia Abnormally high level of chloride in the blood.

hyperemesis gravidarum Excessive vomiting during pregnancy that can lead to dehydration and loss of electrolytes.

hyperkalemia Abnormally high levels of potassium in the blood.

hypernatremia Excessive amounts of sodium in the blood.

hyperphenylalanemia Elevated levels of blood phenylalanine due to a lack of the enzyme phenylalanine hydroxylase.

hyperphosphatemia Abnormally high level of phosphorus in the blood.

hyperplasia An increase in the number of cells due to cell division.

hypertension High blood pressure; defined as a systolic blood pressure higher than 140 mm Hg and/or a diastolic blood pressure greater than 90 mm Hg.

hyperthermia A rise in body temperature above normal.

hypertonic Having a high solute concentration.

hypertriglyceridemia The presence of high levels of triglycerides in the blood. Defined as triglyceride levels between 400 and 1,000 milligrams per deciliter.

hypertrophy An increase in size; in adipocytes, hypertrophy refers to the increase in size of the cells.

hypervitaminosis A condition resulting from the presence of excessive amounts of vitamins in the body; also referred to as *vitamin toxicity*.

hypervitaminosis D A condition resulting from excessive amounts of vitamin D in the body.

hypocalcemia Abnormally low levels of calcium in the blood.

hypochloremia Abnormally low level of chloride in the blood.

hypoglycemia A blood glucose level that drops to lower than 70 mg/dl.

hypokalemia A dangerously low level of blood potassium.

hyponatremia A dangerously low level of sodium in the blood that can result from water intoxication or a lack of sodium during heavy exercise.

hypophosphatemia Abnormally low level of phosphorus in the blood.

hypothermia A drop in body temperature to below normal.

hypothesis An idea or explanation proposed by scientists based on observations or known facts.

hypotonic Having a low solute concentration.

hypovolemia Low blood volume.

I

ileocecal valve The sphincter that separates the small intestine from the large intestine.

immunity The state of having built up antibodies to a particular pathogen so that pathogen enter the body, it is destroyed by the antibodies.

impaired glucose tolerance A condition whereby a fasting blood glucose level is higher than normal, but not high enough to be classified as having diabetes mellitus. Also called *prediabetes*.

incomplete protein A protein that is low in one or more of the essential amino acids. Proteins from plant sources tend to be incomplete.

indirect calorimetry An indirect measurement of energy expenditure obtained by measuring the amount of oxygen consumed and carbon dioxide produced.

infancy The age range from birth to 12 months.

inorganic Describing compounds that do not contain carbon.

inositol A water-soluble compound synthesized in the body that maintains healthy cell membranes.

insecticides Pesticides used to kill insects.

insensible water loss The loss of body water that goes unnoticed, such as by exhalation during breathing and the evaporation of water through the skin.

insoluble fiber A type of fiber that isn't dissolved in water or fermented by intestinal bacteria.

insulin The hormone secreted from the beta cells of the pancreas that stimulates the uptake of glucose from the blood into the cells.

insulin resistance The inability of the cells to respond to insulin.

integrated pest management (IPM) Alternative to pesticides that uses the most economical and the least harmful methods of pest control to minimize risk to consumers, crops, and the environment.

intensity The level of difficulty of an activity.

intentional food additives Substances added intentionally to foods to improve food quality.

international units (IU) A system of measurement of a biologically active ingredient such as a vitamin that produces a certain effect.

interstitial fluid The fluid that surrounds cells. It is the main component of extracellular fluid.

intracellular fluid (ICF) The fluid found in the cytoplasm within the cells; it represents the largest fluid compartment in the body.

intravascular fluid The fluid found inside the blood vessels and the lymph fluid.

intrinsic factor (IF) A glycoprotein secreted by the stomach that results in the absorption of vitamin B_{12}.

iodide The ionized form of iodine in the body (I^-).

iodopsin The compound found in the cones of the eye that is needed for color vision.

iron-deficiency anemia A type of anemia due to a lack of dietary iron or excessive loss of blood.

irradiation A process in which foods are placed in a shielded chamber, called an *irradiator,* and subjected to a radiant energy source. This kills specific pathogens in food by breaking up the cells' DNA.

irritable bowel syndrome (IBS) An intestinal disorder resulting in abdominal discomfort, pain, diarrhea, constipation, and bloating; the cause is unknown.

isoflavones Naturally occurring phytoestrogens, or weak plant estrogens, that function in a similar fashion to the hormone estrogen in the human body.

J

jaundice A yellowish coloring of the skin due to the presence of bile pigments in the blood.

K

keratinization The accumulation of the protein keratin in epithelial cells, forming hard, dry cells unable to secrete mucus due to vitamin A deficiency.

Keshan disease A disease related to a deficiency of selenium.

ketoacidosis A form of metabolic acidosis, or pH imbalance due to excess acid, that occurs when excess ketone bodies are present in the blood; most often seen in individuals with untreated type I diabetes.

ketogenesis The formation of ketone bodies from excess acetyl CoA.

ketogenic Describing molecules that can be transformed into ketone bodies.

ketone bodies The by-products of the incomplete breakdown of fat.

ketosis The condition of increased ketone bodies in the blood.

kilocalorie The amount of energy required to raise the temperature of 1 kilogram of water 1 degree centigrade; used to express the measurement of energy in foods; 1 kilocalorie is equal to 1,000 calories.

kwashiorkor A state of PEM where there is a severe deficiency of dietary protein.

L

laboratory experiment A scientific experiment conducted in a laboratory. Some laboratory experiments involve animals.

lactate A three-carbon compound generated from pyruvate when mitochondria lack sufficient oxygen.

lactation The production of milk in a woman's body after childbirth, and the period during which it occurs.

lactose A disaccharide composed of glucose and galactose; also known as milk sugar.

lactose intolerance When maldigestion of lactose results in symptoms such as nausea, cramps, bloating, flatulence, and diarrhea.

lactose maldigestion The inability to digest lactose due to low levels of the enzyme lactase.

lanugo Very fine, soft hair on the face and arms of people with anorexia nervosa.

laparoscopic gastric banding A type of gastric surgery that uses a silicone band to reduce the size of the stomach so that less food is needed to feel full.

large intestine The lowest portion of the GI tract, where water and electrolytes are absorbed and waste is eliminated.

lean body mass (LBM) Total body weight minus the fat mass; it consists of water, bones, vital organs, and muscle. LBM is the metabolically active tissue in the body.

least developed country A country that shows little growth in multiple areas, such as income per capita, life expectancy, rate of literacy, industrial capability, technological sophistication, and economic productivity.

lecithin A phospholipid made in the body that is integral in the structure of cell membranes; also known as phosphatidylcholine.

letdown response The release of milk from the mother's breast to feed a nursing baby.

licensed dietitian nutritionist (LDN) An individual who has met specified educational and experience criteria deemed by a state licensing board necessary to be considered an expert in the field of nutrition. An RDN would meet all the qualifications to be an LDN.

life expectancy The average length of life for a population of individuals.

life span The maximum age to which members of a species can live.

lignin A noncarbohydrate form of dietary fiber that binds to cellulose fibers to harden and strengthen the cell walls of plants.

limiting amino acid An essential amino acid that is in the shortest supply, relative to the body's needs, in an incomplete protein.

linoleic acid A polyunsaturated essential fatty acid; part of the omega-6 fatty acid family.

lipases A group of lipid-digesting enzymes.

lipid A category of carbon, hydrogen, and oxygen compounds that are insoluble in water.

lipogenesis The process that converts excess glucose into fat for storage.

lipoic acid A vitamin-like substance used in energy production; it may also act as an antioxidant.

lipoprotein Capsule-shaped transport carrier that enables fat and cholesterol to travel through the lymph and blood.

lipoprotein lipase (LPL) An enzyme that hydrolyzes triglycerides in lipoproteins into three fatty acids and glycerol.

liver The largest organ in the body, located in the upper abdomen. This organ aids digestion by secreting bile.

locavore A person who eats locally grown food whenever possible.

long-chain fatty acids Fatty acids with a chain of 12 carbons or more.

longevity The duration of an individual's life.

low birth weight Describes a baby weighing less than 5½ pounds at birth.

low-density lipoproteins (LDLs) Lipoproteins that deposit cholesterol in the walls of the arteries. Because this can lead to heart disease, LDL is referred to as the "bad" cholesterol.

lower esophageal sphincter (LES) The muscular ring located between the base of the esophagus and the stomach.

Lp(a) protein A lipoprotein containing LDL cholesterol found in the blood; this lipoprotein has been correlated to increased risk of heart disease.

lumen The channel or inside space of a vessel such as the intestine or artery.

lymph fluid Fluid that circulates through the body in lymph vessels and eventually enters the bloodstream.

lymphatic system A system of interconnected spaces and vessels between the tissues and organs that contains lymph and circulates fat-soluble nutrients throughout the body.

M

macrocytes Large cells such as a red blood cell.

macrocytic anemia A form of anemia characterized by large, immature red blood cells.

macronutrients Organic nutrients, including the energy-containing carbohydrates, lipids, and proteins, and water that the body needs in large amounts.

macrosomia Term for a large newborn, weighing more than 8 pounds, 13 ounces.

magnesium (Mg^{2+}) A major divalent cation in the body.

major minerals Minerals needed in amounts greater than 100 milligrams per day. These include sodium, chloride, potassium, calcium, phosphorus, magnesium, and sulfur; also referred to as macrominerals.

malabsorption A problem associated with the lack of absorption of nutrients through the intestinal tract.

malnourished A condition that results when the body does not receive the right amount of essential nutrients to maintain health; overnourished and undernourished are forms of malnutrition.

malnutrition The long-term outcome of consuming a diet that is either lacking in the essential nutrients or contains excess energy; an imbalance of nutrients in the diet.

maltose A disaccharide composed of two glucose units joined together.

maple syrup urine disease (MSUD) A genetic disorder characterized by the inability to metabolize branched-chain amino acids; symptoms include a maple syrup smell in the urine.

marasmus A state of PEM where there is a severe deficiency of kilocalories, which perpetuates wasting; also called starvation.

marine toxins Chemicals that occur naturally and contaminate some fish.

mast cells Cells in connective tissue to which antibodies attach, setting the stage for potential future allergic reactions.

mastication Chewing food.

Meals on Wheels A program that delivers nutritious meals to homebound older adults.

mechanical digestion Breaking down food by chewing, grinding, squeezing, and moving food through the GI tract by peristalsis and segmentation.

medical nutrition therapy The integration of nutrition counseling and dietary changes, based on individual medical and health needs, to treat a patient's medical condition.

medium-chain fatty acids Fatty acids with a chain of six to 10 carbons.

megadose An amount of a vitamin or mineral that's at least 10 times the amount recommended in the DRI.

megaloblasts Large, immature red blood cells.

menadione (vitamin K$_3$) The synthetic form of vitamin K used in animal feed and dietary supplements.

menaquinone (vitamin K$_2$) The form of vitamin K produced by bacteria in the colon.

menarche The onset of menstruation.

Menkes' disease A genetic disorder that interferes with copper absorption.

messenger RNA (mRNA) A type of RNA that copies the genetic information from the DNA and carries it from the nucleus to the ribosomes in the cell.

metabolic or fetal programming The process by which the prenatal environment interacts with genetic and other factors to produce permanent change.

metabolic pathway A sequence of reactions that convert compounds from one form to another.

metabolic water Water that is formed in the body as a result of metabolic reactions. Condensation reactions are an example of a chemical reaction that results in the production of water.

metabolism The sum of all chemical reactions in the body.

metalloenzymes Active enzymes that contain one or more metal ions that are essential for their biological activity.

metallothionine A metal-binding protein rich in sulfur-containing amino acids that transports ions.

methylcobalamin The coenzyme form of vitamin B$_{12}$ that converts homocysteine to methionine.

micelle Transport carrier in the small intestine that enables fatty acids and other compounds to be absorbed.

microcytic hypochromic anemia A form of anemia in which red blood cells are small and pale in color due to lack of hemoglobin synthesis due to vitamin B$_6$ deficiency.

micronutrients Essential nutrients the body needs in smaller amounts: vitamins and minerals.

microsomal ethanol oxidizing system (MEOS) The second metabolic pathway for oxidizing ethanol, used at higher intakes of alcohol; it also participates in metabolizing drugs.

microsomes Small vesicles in the cytoplasm of liver cells where oxidative metabolism of alcohol takes place.

microvilli Tiny projections on the villi in the small intestine.

milestones Objectives or significant events that occur during development.

mineralization The process of adding minerals, including calcium and phosphorus, to the collagen matrix in the bone, which makes the bone strong and rigid.

minerals Inorganic elements essential to the nutrition of humans.

mitochondrion A cellular organelle that releases energy from carbohydrates, proteins, and fats to make ATP; *pl.* mitochondria.

moderate The diet principle of providing reasonable but not excessive amounts of foods and nutrients.

moderate drinking According to the *Dietary Guidelines for Americans*, up to one drink per day for women and up to two drinks a day for men.

modified atmosphere packaging (MAP) A food preservation technique that changes the composition of the air surrounding the food in a package to extend its shelf life.

molds Microscopic fungi that live on plant and animal matter. Some can produce mycotoxins, which are harmful.

monoglutamate The form of folate absorbed through the cells of the small intestine.

monoglyceride A remnant of fat digestion that consists of a glycerol with only one fatty acid attached to one of the three carbons.

monosaccharide Simple sugar that consists of a single sugar unit. The three most common monosaccharides: glucose, fructose, and galactose.

monosodium glutamate (MSG) The sodium salt of glutamic acid, used as a flavor enhancer.

monounsaturated fatty acid (MUFA) A fatty acid that has one double bond.

MSG symptom complex A series of reactions such as numbness, burning sensation, facial pressure or tightness, chest pain, rapid heart beat, and drowsiness that can occur in some individuals after consuming MSG.

mucus Secretion produced throughout the GI tract that moistens and lubricates food and protects membranes.

muscular endurance The ability of the muscle to produce prolonged effort.

muscular strength The greatest amount of force exerted by the muscle at one time.

myelin sheath The tissue that surrounds and protects the nerves.

myoglobin The oxygen-carrying, heme-containing protein found in muscle cells.

MyPlate A food guidance system that illustrates the recommendations in the *Dietary Guidelines for Americans* and the Dietary Reference Intakes (DRIs) nutrient goals.

N

naturally occurring sugars Sugars such as fructose and lactose that are found naturally in foods.

negative energy balance The state in which energy intake is less than energy expenditure. Over time, this results in weight loss.

neural tube defects Any major birth defect of the central nervous system, including the brain, caused by failure of the neural tube to properly close during fetal development.

neurotoxins Toxins that affect the nerves and can cause symptoms including mild numbness or tingling in the face, arms, and legs, as well as headaches and dizziness. Severe cases of neurotoxicity could result in death.

niacin equivalents (NE) A measurement that reflects the amount of niacin and tryptophan in foods that can be used to synthesize niacin.

nicotinamide A form of niacin that is found in food and as a topical cream in treating acne.

nicotinamide adenine dinucleotide (NAD$^+$) A coenzyme form of niacin that functions as an electron carrier and can be reduced to NADH during metabolism.

nicotinamide adenine dinucleotide phosphate (NADP$^+$) A coenzyme form of niacin that functions as an electron carrier and can be reduced to NADPH during metabolism.

nicotinic acid A form of niacin found in foods and sometimes prescribed to lower LDL cholesterol.

night blindness The inability to see in dim light or at night due to a deficiency of retinal in the retina.

nitrites and nitrates Substances that can be added to foods to function as a preservative and to give meats such as hot dogs and luncheon meats a pink color.

nitrogen balance The difference between nitrogen intake and nitrogen excretion.

nonessential [amino acids] The 11 amino acids the body can synthesize and that therefore do not need to be consumed in the diet.

nonessential nutrients Nutrients that can be made in sufficient quantities in the body to meet the body's requirements and support health.

non-exercise activity thermogenesis (NEAT) The energy expended for all activities not related to sleeping, eating, or exercise, including fidgeting, performing work-related activities, and playing.

nonheme iron Iron that is not attached to heme.

norepinephrine A hormone produced by the adrenal glands that stimulates glycogenolysis and gluconeogenesis.

normal blood pressure A systolic blood pressure less than 120 mm Hg (the top number) and a diastolic blood pressure less than 80 mm Hg (the bottom number). Referred to as 120/80.

norovirus The most common type of virus that causes foodborne illness. Can cause gastroenteritis, or the "stomach flu."

nutrient content claims Claims on the food label that describe the level or amount of a nutrient in the food. Terms such as *free, high, reduced,* or *lite* are examples of nutrient content claims.

nutrient density A measurement of the nutrients in a food compared with the kilocalorie content; nutrient-dense foods are high in nutrients and low in kilocalories.

nutrient requirements The amounts of specific nutrients needed to prevent malnutrition or deficiency; reflected in the DRIs.

nutrients Compounds in foods that sustain body processes. There are six classes of nutrients: carbohydrates, fats (lipids), proteins, vitamins, minerals, and water.

nutrigenomics The study of how your genetic makeup interacts with your diet.

nutrition The science that studies how nutrients and compounds in foods nourish the body and affect body functions and overall health.

nutritional genomics A field of study of the relationship between genes, gene expression, and nutrition.

Nutrition Facts panel The area on the food label that provides a list of specific nutrients obtained in one serving of the food.

nutritionist A generic term with no recognized legal or professional meaning. Some people may call themselves a nutritionist without having any credible training in nutrition.

nutrition transition A shift in dietary consumption and energy expenditure that may occur as people in developing countries shift from their traditional diet to diets higher in sugars, fat, and animal-source food.

O

obese A condition of excess body weight due to an abnormal accumulation of stored body fat; a BMI of 30 or more is considered obese.

obesity For adults, having a BMI greater than 29.9.

observational research Research that involves systematically observing subjects to see if there is a relationship to certain outcomes.

oils Lipids that are liquid at room temperature.

oligosaccharides Three to ten units of monosaccharides combined.

omega-3 fatty acid A family of polyunsaturated fatty acids with the first double bond located at the third carbon from the omega end.

omega-6 fatty acid A family of polyunsaturated fatty acids with the first double bond located at the sixth carbon from the omega end.

open dating Typically found on perishable items such as meat, poultry, eggs, and dairy foods; must contain a calendar date.

organic Describing compounds that contain carbon or carbon–carbon bonds. Being free of chemical-based pesticides, synthetic fertilizers, irradiation, and bioengineering. A USDA-accredited certifying inspector must certify organic foods.

organophosphates A group of synthetic pesticides that adversely affect the nervous systems of pests.

osmolality A measurement of the concentration of solutes per kilogram of solvent in a solution.

osmosis The diffusion of water or any solvent across semipermeable membranes from a weak concentration of solutes to a more concentrated solute.

osmotic gradient The difference in concentration between two solutions on each side of the permeable cell membrane.

osmotic pressure The pressure that prevents the solutes in a solution from drawing water across a semipermeable membrane.

osteomalacia The adult equivalent of rickets, causing muscle and bone weakness, and pain.

osteopenia A condition in which the bone mineral density is lower than normal but not low enough to be classified as osteoporosis.

osteoporosis A condition in which bones become brittle and porous, making them fragile due to depletion of calcium and bone proteins.

overexercise Excessive physical activity without adequate rest periods for proper recovery.

overnourished The condition of having consumed excess energy or nutrients.

overnutrition The state of consuming excess nutrients or energy.

overpopulation When a region has more people than its natural resources can support.

overweight A body weight that increases risk of developing weight-related health problems; defined as having a BMI between 25 and 29.9.

oxaloacetate The starting molecule for the TCA cycle.

oxidation A chemical reaction in which oxygen combines with other substances, resulting in the loss of an electron.

oxidation reaction A reaction in which an atom loses an electron.

oxidative phosphorylation The metabolic pathway in the mitochondria in which ATP is formed using energy from the oxidation-reduction reactions in the electron transport chain.

oxidative stress A condition whereby free radicals are being produced in the body faster than they are neutralized.

P

pancreas A large gland located behind the stomach that releases digestive enzymes after a meal. The pancreas also secretes the hormones insulin and glucagon, which control blood glucose.

paralytic shellfish poisoning A condition caused by a reddish-brown-colored dinoflagellate that contains neurotoxins.

parasites Organisms that live on or in another organism. Parasites obtain their nourishment from their hosts.

parathyroid hormone (PTH) The hormone secreted from the parathyroid glands that activates vitamin D formation in the kidney.

parietal cells Specialized cells in the stomach that secrete the gastric juices hydrochloric acid and intrinsic factor.

passive diffusion The process of absorbing nutrients freely across the cell membrane.

pasteurization The process of heating liquids or food at high temperatures to destroy foodborne pathogens.

pathogens Collective term for disease-causing organisms. Pathogens include microorganisms (viruses, bacteria) and parasites, and are the most common source of foodborne illness.

peak bone mass The maximum bone mass achieved.

peer-reviewed journal A journal in which scientists publish research findings, after the findings have gone through a rigorous review process by other scientists.

pellagra A disease resulting from a deficiency of niacin or tryptophan.

pepsin The active protease that begins the digestion of proteins in the stomach.

pepsinogen The inactive protease secreted by the chief cells in the stomach; this enzyme is converted to the active form called pepsin in the presence of HCl.

peptide A chain of amino acids.

peptide bonds The bonds that connect amino acids, created when the acid group of one amino acid is joined with the nitrogen-containing amine group of another amino acid through condensation.

peptide YY A hormone produced in the small intestine that reduces hunger.

percentile The most commonly used clinical indicator to assess the size and growth patterns of children in the United States. An individual child is ranked according to the percentage of the reference population he or she equals or exceeds.

peripheral neuropathy Damage to the peripheral nerves causing pain, numbness, and tingling in the feet and hands, and muscle weakness.

peristalsis The forward, rhythmic motion that moves food through the digestive system. Peristalsis is a form of mechanical digestion because it influences motion, but it does not add chemical secretions.

pernicious anemia A form of anemia caused by a lack of intrinsic factor needed for absorption of vitamin B_{12}, forming large, immature red blood cells.

pesticides Substances that kill or repel pests such as insects, weeds, microorganisms, rodents, or fungi.

pH A measure of the acidity or alkalinity of a solution. The measurement indicates the concentration of hydrogen ions in body fluids.

pharynx The area of the GI tract between the mouth and the esophagus; also called the throat.

phenylketonuria (PKU) A genetic disorder characterized by the inability to metabolize the essential amino acid phenylalanine.

phospholipids A category of lipids that consist of two fatty acids and a phosphorus group attached to a glycerol backbone. Lecithin is an example of a phospholipid found in food and in the body.

phosphorus (P) The second most abundant mineral in the body.

photosynthesis A process by which plants create carbohydrates using the energy from sunlight.

phylloquinone (vitamin K_1) The form of vitamin K found in plants.

physical activity Voluntary movement that results in energy expenditure.

physical fitness The ability to perform physical activities requiring cardiorespiratory endurance, muscle endurance, strength, and/or flexibility; physical fitness is acquired through physical activity and adequate nutrition.

physiologic age A person's age estimated in terms of body health, function, and life expectancy.

physiological fuel values The real energy value of foods that are digested and absorbed; they are adjusted from the results of bomb calorimetry because of the inefficiency of the body.

phytochemicals Naturally occurring substances in fruits, vegetables, and whole grains that protect against certain chronic diseases.

phytostanols A type of plant sterol similar in structure to cholesterol.

phytosterols Naturally occurring sterols found in plants.

pica Eating nonfood substances such as dirt and clay.

placebo An inactive substance, such as a sugar pill, administered to a control group during an experiment.

placenta The organ that allows nutrients, oxygen, and waste products to be exchanged between a mother and fetus.

plant breeding A type of biotechnology in which two plants are crossbred to produce offspring with desired traits from both.

plaque The hardened buildup of cholesterol-laden foam cells, platelets, cellular waste products, and calcium in the arteries that results in atherosclerosis.

polar Having a pair of equal and opposite charges; water is a polar molecule because oxygen has a negative charge and hydrogen has a positive charge.

polychlorinated biphenyls (PCBs) Synthetic chemicals that have been shown to cause cancer and other adverse effects on the immune, reproductive, nervous, and endocrine systems in animals. PCBs may cause cancer in humans.

polyglutamate A form of folate that naturally occurs in foods.

polypeptide A chain consisting of ten or more amino acids joined together by peptide bonds.

polysaccharides Many sugar units combined. Starch, glycogen, and fiber are all polysaccharides.

polyunsaturated fatty acid (PUFA) A fatty acid with two or more double bonds.

portion The quantity of a food usually eaten at one sitting.

positive energy balance The state in which energy intake is greater than energy expenditure. Over time, this results in weight gain.

postabsorptive state The period when you haven't eaten for more than four hours and the stomach and intestines are empty. Energy needs are met by the breakdown of stores.

potassium (K^+) Main cation in the intracellular fluid.

poverty Lacking the means to provide for material or comfort needs.

preeclampsia Serious medical condition developed late in pregnancy in which hypertension, severe edema, and protein loss occur.

preformed vitamins Vitamins found in food.

pregnancy-induced hypertension High blood pressure resulting from pregnancy; includes gestational hypertension, preeclampsia, and eclampsia.

preschoolers Children aged 3 to 5 years old.

preservatives Substances that extend the shelf life of a product by retarding chemical, physical, or microbiological changes.

previtamin D_3 (precalciferol) The compound that is formed from 7-dehydrocholesterol when sunlight hits the skin.

primary malnutrition A state of being malnourished due to poor diet, consuming either too much or too little of a nutrient or energy.

primary structure The first stage of protein synthesis after transcription when the amino acids have been linked together with peptide bonds to form a simple linear chain.

prion Short for proteinaceous infectious particle. Self-reproducing protein particles that cause degenerative brain diseases.

prior-sanctioned Substances that the FDA had determined were safe for use in foods prior to the 1958 Food Additives Amendment.

probiotics Live microorganisms, which, when administered in adequate amounts, confer a health benefit on the host.

progressive overload principle A gradual increase in exercise demands resulting from modifications to the frequency, intensity, time, or type of activity.

prohormone A physiologically inactive precursor to a hormone.

proof A measure of the amount of ethanol contained in alcoholic beverages.

proportionality The relationship of one entity to another. Vegetables and fruits should be consumed in a higher proportion than dairy and protein foods in the diet.

propulsion The process that moves food along the gastrointestinal tract during digestion.

proteases Protein-digesting enzymes that can break the peptide bonds linking amino acids together.

protein digestibility corrected amino acid score (PDCAAS) A score measured as a percentage that takes into account both digestibility and amino acid score and provides a good indication of the quality of a protein.

protein-energy malnutrition (PEM) A lack of sufficient dietary protein and/or kilocalories.

proteins Large molecules, made up of chains of amino acids, found in all living cells; the sequence of amino acids is determined by the DNA.

protein turnover The continual process of degrading and synthesizing protein.

protooncogenes Specialized genes that turn on and off cell division.

provitamin A vitamin precursor that is converted to a vitamin in the body.

public health nutritionists Individuals who may have an undergraduate degree in nutrition but who are not Registered Dietitian Nutritionists.

pyridoxal The aldehyde form of vitamin B_6.

pyridoxal phosphate (PLP) The active coenzyme form of vitamin B_6.

pyridoxamine The amine form of vitamin B_6.

pyridoxine The alcohol form of vitamin B_6.

pyruvate A three-carbon molecule formed from the oxidation of glucose during glycolysis.

Q

quackery The promotion and selling of health products and services of questionable validity. A quack is a person who promotes these products and services in order to make money.

quaternary structure The fourth geometric pattern of a protein; formed when two or more polypeptide chains cluster together, forming a final rod-like or ball-like structure.

R

rancidity The spoiling of lipids through oxidation.

rating of perceived exertion (RPE) A subjective measure of the intensity level of an activity using a numerical scale.

recombinant bovine somatotropin (rbST) A synthetically made hormone identical to a cow's natural growth hormone, somatotropin, that stimulates milk production. Also known as rbGH (recombinant bovine growth hormone).

recommended dietary allowance (RDA) The recommended daily amount of a nutrient that meets the needs of nearly all individuals (97 to 98 percent) in a similar age and gender group. The RDA is set higher than the EAR.

rectum Final 8-inch portion of the large intestine.

reduction reaction A reaction in which an atom gains an electron.

refined grains Grain foods that are made with only the endosperm of the kernel. The bran and germ have been removed during milling.

registered dietitian nutritionist (RDN) A health professional who is a food and nutrition expert; RDNs obtain a college degree in nutrition from an Academy of Nutrition and Dietetics–accredited program, and pass a national exam to become a Registered Dietitian Nutritionist.

renin An enzyme secreted by the kidneys that participates in the renin-angiotensin system; renin increases blood volume, vasoconstriction of the blood vessels, and blood pressure.

repetition maximum (RM) The maximum amount of weight that can be lifted for a specified number of repetitions.

resistance training Exercising with weights to build, strengthen, and tone muscle to improve or maintain overall fitness; also called strength training.

resistant starch A type of starch that is not digested in the GI tract but has important health benefits in the large intestine.

resting metabolic rate (RMR) The measure of the amount of energy expended by the body at rest and after approximately a 3- to 4-hour fasting period. This rate is about 6 percent higher than BMR.

retinal The aldehyde form of preformed vitamin A.

retinoic acid The acid form of preformed vitamin A.

retinoids The term used to describe the family of preformed vitamin A compounds.

retinol The alcohol form of preformed vitamin A.

retinol activity equivalents (RAE) The unit of measure used to describe the total amount of all forms of preformed vitamin A and provitamin A carotenoids in food.

retinol binding protein (RBP) A protein made in the liver that transports retinol through the blood to the cells.

retinyl ester The ester form of preformed vitamin A found in foods and stored in the body.

rhodopsin A compound found in the rods of the eye that is needed for night vision. It is comprised of *cis*-retinal and the protein opsin.

ribosomes Organelles found in the cytosol that read the mRNA and build the protein in the proper sequence during elongation.

rickets A vitamin D deficiency in children resulting in soft bones.

risk assessment The process of determining the potential human health risks posed by exposure to substances such as pesticides.

rodenticides Poisons used to kill rats, mice, and other rodents.

rods Light-absorbing cells responsible for black-and-white vision and night vision.

R protein The protein secreted from the salivary glands that binds vitamin B_{12} in the stomach and transports it into the small intestine during digestion.

S

saliva Secretion from the salivary glands that softens and lubricates food, and begins the chemical breakdown of starch.

salivary amylase A digestive enzyme that begins breaking down carbohydrate (starch) in the mouth; other important enzymes during carbohydrate digestion include pancreatic amylase, maltase, sucrase, and lactase.

salivary glands Cluster of glands located underneath and behind the tongue that release saliva in response to the sight, smell, and taste of food.

sanctions Boycotts or trade embargoes used by one country or international group to apply political pressure on another.

sarcopenia Age-related progressive loss of muscle mass, muscle strength, and function.

satiation The state of being satisfactorily full during a meal, which inhibits the ability to eat more food.

satiety The feeling of satiation or "fullness" after a meal before hunger sets in again.

saturated fatty acid A fatty acid in which all of the carbons are bound with hydrogen.

school-aged children Children between the ages of 6 and 12.

scientific method A process used by scientists to gather and test information for the sake of generating sound research findings.

scombrotoxic fish poisoning A condition caused by consuming spoiled fish that contain large amounts of histamines. Also referred to as histamine fish poisoning.

scurvy A disease caused by a deficiency of vitamin C and characterized by bleeding gums and a skin rash.

secondary malnutrition A state of being malnourished due to interference with nutrient absorption or metabolism.

secondary structure The geometric shape of a protein caused by the hydrogen ions of amino acids linking together with the amine group, causing the straight chain to fold and twist.

secretin A hormone secreted from the duodenum that stimulates the stomach to release pepsin, the liver to make bile, and the pancreas to release digestive juices.

segmentation Muscular contractions of the small intestine that move food back and forth, breaking the mixture into smaller and smaller pieces and combining it with digestive juices.

selectively permeable Describes the feature of cell membranes that allows some substances to cross the membrane more easily than other substances.

selenomethionine An amino acid that contains selenium rather than sulfur.

selenoproteins Proteins that contain selenomethionine.

selenosis The presence of toxic levels of selenium.

senescence Another term for aging.

serving size A recommended portion of food that is used as a standard reference on food labels.

set point A weight-control theory that states each individual has a genetically established body weight. Any deviation from this point stimulates changes in body metabolism to reestablish the normal weight.

severe obesity Defined as a BMI greater than 40 or more than 100 pounds over ideal body weight.

short-chain fatty acid A fatty acid with a chain of two to four carbons.

sickle-cell anemia A blood disorder caused by a genetic defect in the development of hemoglobin. Sickle-cell anemia causes the red blood cells to distort into a sickle shape and can damage organs and tissues.

side chain The part of an amino acid that provides its unique qualities; also referred to as the R group.

simple carbohydrates Carbohydrates that consist of one sugar unit (monosaccharides) or two sugar units (disaccharides).

skinfold caliper A tool used to measure the thickness of subcutaneous fat.

small for gestational age (SGA) Term for babies who weigh less than the 10th percentile of weight for gestational age.

small intestine The long coiled chamber that is the major site of food digestion and nutrient absorption.

social drinking Moderate drinking of alcoholic beverages in social settings within safe limits.

sodium (Na⁺) The major cation in the extracellular fluid.

sodium-potassium pump A protein located in the cell membrane that actively transports sodium out of the cell in exchange for potassium ions.

solanine Toxin found in potato surfaces exposed to light that can cause fever, diarrhea, and shock if consumed in large amounts.

solid foods Foods other than breast milk or formula given to an infant, usually around 4 to 6 months of age.

solubility The ability to dissolve into another substance.

soluble fiber A type of fiber that dissolves in water and is fermented by intestinal bacteria. Many soluble fibers are viscous and have thickening properties.

solvent A liquid in which substances dissolve to form a new solution. Water is called the universal solvent because it can dissolve a variety of substances, including minerals and glucose.

specific heat A measurement of the energy required to raise a gram of a substance, such as water, 1 degree Celsius.

sphincter A circular ring of muscle that opens and closes in response to nerve input.

spina bifida A serious birth defect in which the spinal cord is malformed and lacks the protective membrane coat.

spores Hardy reproductive structures that are produced by certain bacteria and fungi.

sports anemia Low concentrations of hemoglobin in the blood; results from an increase in blood volume during strenuous exercise.

starch The storage form of glucose in plants.

sterols A category of lipids that contains four connecting rings of carbon and hydrogen. Cholesterol is the most common sterol.

stomach A J-shaped muscular organ that mixes and churns food with digestive juices and acid to form chyme.

stomatitis Inflammation of the mucous lining of the mouth.

stool Waste produced in the large intestine; also called *feces*.

stroke A condition caused by a lack of oxygen to the brain that could result in paralysis and possibly death.

stroke volume The amount of blood pumped by the heart with each heart beat.

structure/function claims Claims on the label that describe the role of a nutrient or dietary compound that is proposed to influence the structure or function of the human body. For example, "Calcium builds strong bones" is a structure/function claim.

subcutaneous fat The fat located under the skin and between the muscles.

substrate A substance or compound that is altered by an enzyme.

sucrose A disaccharide composed of glucose and fructose; also known as table sugar.

sudden infant death syndrome (SIDS) The unexplained death of an infant at less than 1 year of age.

sugar substitutes Alternatives to table sugar that sweeten foods for fewer kilocalories.

sulfate (SO₄) The oxidized form of the mineral sulfur.

sulfites Preservatives used to help prevent foods from turning brown and to inhibit the growth of microbes. Often used in wine and dried fruit products.

sustainable Referring to a method of resource use that can be maintained indefinitely because it does not deplete or permanently damage the resource.

systolic pressure The top number in a blood pressure reading that measures the pressure in the arteries when the heart muscle contracts.

T

target heart rate A heart rate in beats per minute (expressed as a percentage of maximum heart rate) achieved during exercise that indicates the level of intensity at which fitness levels can increase.

tertiary structure The third-level shape of a protein; occurs when the side chains of the amino acids, most often containing sulfur, form bridges, causing the protein to form even stronger bonds than in the secondary structure; these bonds form loops, bends, and folds in the molecule.

thermic effect of exercise (TEE) This refers to the increase in muscle contraction that occurs during physical activity, which produces heat and contributes to the total daily energy expenditure.

thermic effect of food (TEF) The amount of energy expended by the body to digest, absorb, transport, metabolize, and store energy-yielding nutrients from foods.

thermogenesis The generation of heat from the basal metabolism, digestion of food, and physical activity that provides necessary warmth; *adaptive thermogenesis* and *non-exercise activity thermogenesis (NEAT)* are other terms used to describe specific aspects of the generation of heat.

The United States pharmacopeial convention (USP) A nonprofit organization that sets quality standards for dietary supplements.

thiamin pyrophosphate (TPP) The coenzyme form of thiamin with two phosphate groups as part of the molecule.

thirst mechanism A complex interaction between the brain and the hypothalamus triggered by a loss of body water; the interaction leads to a feeling of thirst.

thyroxine The less active form of thyroid hormone, also known as *tetraiodothyronine* (T_4).

thyroxine-releasing hormone (TRH) A hormone secreted by the hypothalamus that stimulates the pituitary gland to release thyroxine-stimulating hormone (TSH).

thyroxine-stimulating hormone (TSH) A hormone released by the pituitary that stimulates the thyroid gland to trap more iodine to produce more thyroid hormone (T_4 and T_3).

toddlers Children aged 1 to 3 years old.

tolerable upper intake level (UL) The maximum daily amount of a nutrient considered safe in a group of similar individuals.

tongue-thrust reflex A forceful protrusion of the tongue in response to an oral stimulus, such as a spoon.

total daily energy expenditure (TDEE) The total kilocalories needed to meet daily energy requirements; based on basal metabolism, physical activity, the thermic effect of food, and adaptive thermogenesis.

total iron-binding capacity (TIBC) A blood test that measures the amount of iron that transferrin can bind. A higher TIBC indicates iron-deficiency anemia.

toxicity The level of nutrient intake at which exposure to a substance becomes harmful.

toxins Poisons that can be produced by living organisms.

trabecular bone The inner structure of bone, also known as spongy bone because of its appearance. This portion of bone is often lost in osteoporosis.

trace minerals Minerals needed in amounts less than 20 milligrams daily. These include iron, zinc, selenium, fluoride, chromium, copper, manganese, and molybdenum; also referred to as microminerals.

trans The configuration of a fatty acid in which the carbon chains are on opposite sides of the double bond.

transamination The transfer of an amino group from one amino acid to a keto acid to form a new nonessential amino acid.

transcobalamin The protein that transports vitamin B_{12} in the blood.

transcription The first stage in protein synthesis, in which the DNA sequence is copied from the gene and transferred to messenger RNA.

trans **fat** Substance that contains mostly *trans* fatty acids, a result of hydrogenating an unsaturated fatty acid, causing a reconfiguring of some of its double bonds. A small amount of *trans* fatty acid occurs naturally in foods from animal sources.

transfer RNA (tRNA) A type of RNA that transfers a specific amino acid to a growing polypeptide chain in the ribosomes during the processes of translation and elongation.

transferrin An iron-transporting protein.

translation The second phase of protein synthesis; the process of converting the information in mRNA to an amino acid sequence in the ribosomes.

transport The process of moving absorbed nutrients throughout the body through the circulatory and lymph systems.

transport proteins Proteins that carry other substances, mainly nutrients, through the blood to various organs and tissues. Proteins can also act as channels through which some substances enter your cells.

traveler's diarrhea A common pathogen-induced intestinal disorder experienced by some travelers who visit areas with unsanitary conditions.

tricarboxylic acid cycle (TCA) A cycle of aerobic chemical reactions in the mitochondria that oxidize glucose, amino acids, and fatty acids, producing hydrogen ions to be used in the electron transport chain, some ATP, and by-products carbon dioxide and water.

triglycerides A type of lipid commonly found in foods and the body; also known as fat. Triglycerides consist of three fatty acids attached to a glycerol backbone.

tripeptide A chain of three amino acids joined together by peptide bonds.

trivalent chromium The oxidized form of chromium (Cr^{3+}) found in food.

type 1 diabetes Autoimmune form of diabetes in which the pancreas does not produce insulin.

type 2 diabetes Form of diabetes characterized by insulin resistance.

Type I osteoporosis Osteoporosis that results from lowered estrogen levels women experience during menopause. This type of osteoporosis is characterized by rapid bone loss.

Type II osteoporosis Osteoporosis that occurs in both men and women; characterized by the slow loss of bone mass over time due to aging.

U

ulcer A sore or erosion of the stomach or intestinal lining.

ulcerative colitis A chronic inflammation of the colon or large intestine that results in ulcers forming in the lining of the colon.

umbilical cord The cord connecting the fetus to the placenta.

undernourished A condition in which the individual lacks sufficient energy or is deficient in quality or quantity of essential nutrients.

undernutrition A state of inadequate nutrition whereby a person's nutrient and/or energy needs aren't met through the diet.

underweight Weighing too little for your height; defined as a BMI less than 18.5.

unintentional food additives Substances that enter into foods unintentionally during manufacturing or processing.

unsaturated fatty acid A fatty acid in which there are one or more double bonds between carbons.

upper esophageal sphincter The muscular ring located at the top of the esophagus.

urea A nitrogen-containing waste product of protein metabolism that is mainly excreted through the urine via the kidneys.

V

vary The diet principle of consuming a mixture of different food groups and foods within each group.

vegetarian A person who avoids eating animal foods. Some vegetarians only avoid meat, fish, and poultry, while others (vegans) avoid all animal products, including milk, eggs, and cheese.

very low-density lipoproteins (VLDLs) Lipoproteins that deliver fat made in the liver to the tissues. VLDL remnants are converted into LDLs.

villi Small, fingerlike projections that line the interior of the small intestine.

virus A microscopic organism that carries genetic information for its own replication; a virus can infect a host and cause illness.

visceral fat The body fat associated with the internal organs and stored in the abdominal area.

vitamin D₃ binding protein (DBP) A protein made in the liver that transports vitamin D through the blood to the cells.

vitamins Thirteen essential, organic micronutrients that are needed by the body for normal functions, such as regulating metabolism and assisting in energy production, growth, reproduction, and overall health.

VO₂ max The maximum amount of oxygen (ml) a person uses in one minute per kilogram of body weight.

W

waist circumference Measurement taken at the top of the iliac crest or hip bone; used to determine the pattern of obesity.

warfarin An anticoagulant drug given to prevent blood from clotting.

wasting The diminishment of muscle and fat tissue caused by extremely low energy intake from too little food and therefore too little energy; sometimes referred to as *acute malnutrition*.

water balance A state of equilibrium when the intake of water equals the amount of water excreted.

water intoxication A potentially dangerous medical condition that results from drinking too much water too quickly, also known as *hyperhydration*; can lead to hyponatremia and possible death.

water-soluble vitamins Vitamins that dissolve in water; they generally cannot be stored in the body and must be consumed daily.

weight management Maintaining a healthy body weight; defined as having a BMI of 18.5 to 24.9.

Wernicke-Korsakoff syndrome A severe brain disorder associated with chronic excessive alcohol consumption; symptoms include vision changes, loss of muscle coordination, and loss of memory; the cause is a thiamin deficiency.

whole grains Grain foods that are made with the entire edible grain kernel: the bran, the endosperm, and the germ.

Wilson's disease A rare genetic disorder that results in accumulation of copper in the body.

working poor Individuals or families who are steadily employed but still experience poverty due to low wages or high dependent expenses.

X

xerophthalmia Permanent damage to the cornea causing blindness due to a prolonged vitamin A deficiency.

Z

zoochemicals Nonnutritive animal compounds that play a role in fighting chronic diseases.

zygote A fertilized egg during the first two weeks after conception.

Index

Credits

Photo Credits

Chapter 1 Chapter Opener: boggy22/Getty Images; **p. 4:** Karin Dreyer/ Blend Images/Corbis; **p. 5:** Roy Johnson/dbimages/Alamy; Corbis Super RF/Alamy; **p. 6:** Taylor S. Kennedy/National Geographic; Steve Smith/Purestock/SuperStock; **p. 7:** Pearson Education, Inc.; **p. 10:** Peter Bernik/Shutterstock; **p. 12:** Darqué/ Photocuisine/AGE Fotostock; **p. 13:** D. Hurst/Alamy, Purestock/Getty Images; **p. 14:** Don Smetzer/Alamy; **p. 17:** Dr. Tim Evans/Science; **p. 19:** SourceAuremar/Fotolia; **p. 23:** Pearson Education, Inc.; Bill Aron/PhotoEdit Inc.; **p. 24:** Biophoto Associates/ Science Source; **p. 27:** US Food and Drug Administration; **p. 29:** Kristin Piljay/ Pearson Education, Inc.; **p. 30:** Karin Dreyer/Blend Images/Corbis; Peter Bernik/ Shutterstock; **p. 31:** Don Smetzer/Alamy, Auremar/Fotolia; **p. 32:** US Food and Drug Administration

Chapter 2 Chapter Opener: Ariel Skelley/Blend/Corbis; **p. 38:** Dorling Kindersley, Ltd; **p. 39:** Jupiterimages/Creatas/360/Getty Images; **p. 40:** Jiri Hera/ Fotolia, Joe Gough/Fotolia; **p. 42:** Institute of Medicine; United States Department of Agriculture; **p. 45:** Samuel Borges/Shutterstock; **p. 48:** Peter Cavanagh/Alamy; **p. 54:** Richard Megna/Fundamental Photographs; **p. 57:** Radius Images/Alamy; **p. 58:** Pearson Education, Inc.; **p. 60:** Monkey Business/Fotolia; **p. 62:** Pearson Education, Inc.; **p. 63:** Pearson Education, Inc.; **p. 65:** Kristen Piljay/Pearson Education, Inc./Pearson Science; Pearson Education, Inc.; **p. 66:** Kristen Piljay/ Pearson Education, Inc./Pearson Science; Kristin Piljay/Pearson Education, Inc.; **p. 67:** Kristin Piljay/Pearson Education, Inc.; **p. 68:** Pearson Education, Inc.; **p. 69:** Radius Images/Alamy; Institute of Medicine; United States Department of Agriculture; **p. 70:** Dorling Kindersley, Ltd; Kristin Piljay/Pearson Education, Inc.

Chapter 3 Chapter Opener: Image Source/Getty Images; **p. 77:** Tom Grill/ Corbis; **p. 78:** Japack/AGE Fotostock; **p. 79:** wavebreakmedia/Shutterstock; **p. 81:** David Musher/Science Source; Steve Gschmeissner/Science Source; Don W. Fawcett/Science Source; Maridav/Shutterstock; **p. 83:** Tom Grill/Corbis; **p. 84:** Kristin Piljay/Pearson Education, Inc.; **p. 86:** Tom Grill/Corbis; **p. 87:** Red Chopsticks/ AGE Fotostock; **p. 95:** John Lund/Tiffany Schoepp/Blend Images/Boost/Corbis; **p. 97:** Joana Lopes/Shutterstock; **p. 98:** Images-USA/Alamy; **p. 99:** Dr. E. Walker/ Science Photo Library/Science Source; Southern Illinois University/Science Source; **p. 100:** Koki Iino/Getty Images; **p. 102:** Cristovao/Shutterstock; **p. 103:** David Musher/Science Source; **p. 104:** BananaStock/AGE Fotostock; **p. 105:** Tom Grill/ Corbis; **p. 106:** John Lund/Tiffany Schoepp/Blend Images/Boost/Corbis

Chapter 4 Chapter Opener: Marco Mayer/Fotolia; **p. 115:** Kristin Piljay/Pearson Education, Inc.; **p. 116:** Kristin Piljay/Pearson Education, Inc., Inc.; **p. 118:** Barbro Bergfeldt/Fotolia; **p. 119:** Foodcollection/Getty Images; **p. 121:** KO Studio/Shutterstock; **p. 126:** Yuri Arcurs/Shutterstock; Flashon Studio/Shutterstock; **p. 128:** Valentyn Volkov/Shutterstock; **p. 129:** Dragon_fang/Shutterstock; **p. 130:** Elenathewise/Fotolia; **p. 132:** zstock/Fotolia; **p. 137:** Pearson Education, Inc.; **p. 138:** Ingram Publishing/ Alamy; Pearson Education, Inc.; Kristin Piljay/Pearson Education, Inc.; **p. 142:** Kristin Piljay/Pearson Education, Inc.; **p. 144:** Pearson Education, Inc.; **p. 145:** Official White House photo by Pete Souza; **p. 149:** Moodboard Premium/Glow Images; **p. 150:** Science Source; **p. 151:** Supri Suharjoto/Shutterstock; **p. 152:** Yuri Arcurs/Shutterstock; **p. 153:** zstock/Fotolia; **p. 154:** Pearson Education, Inc.; Science Source

Chapter 5 Chapter Opener: Ekaterina Shlikhunova/Getty Images; **p. 162:** Ryan McVay/Photodisc/Getty Images; **p. 164:** gemenacom/Fotolia; **p. 166:** Charles Brutlag/ Shutterstock; **p. 168:** Comstock Images/Stockbyte/Getty Images; **p. 174:** David M. Phillips/Science Source; **p. 180:** Dianne McFadden/Shutterstock; **p. 181:** Shebeko/ Shutterstock; **p. 186:** Kristin Piljay/Pearson Education, Inc.; **p. 189:** Brand X Pictures/ AGE Fotostock; Pearson Education, Inc.; **p. 190:** Pearson Education, Inc.; **p. 194:** Biophoto Associates/Science Source; **p. 196:** Helen Sessions/Alamy; Ligia Botero/ Photodisc/Getty Images; **p. 197:** Comstock/Stockbyte/Getty Images; Pearson Education, Inc.; **p. 199:** Stockbyte/Jupiter Images; **p. 201:** Shebeko/Shutterstock; Mariano Heluani/ Shutterstock; **p. 202:** Biophoto Associates/Science Source

Chapter 6 Chapter Opener: liv riis-larsen/Alamy; **p. 208:** Proles Productions/ AGE Fotostock; **p. 212:** SoFood/Alamy; **p. 214:** John Lund/Tiffany Schoepp/ Blend Images/Boost/Corbis; **p. 218:** Oliver Meckes/Nicole Ottawa/Pearson

Education, Inc.; **p. 220:** PhotoAlto/Alamy; **p. 221:** Dr. P. Marazzi/Science Source; **p. 222:** Juergen Berger/Science Source; **p. 225:** Ruth Jenkinson/Dorling Kindersley, Ltd.; Pearson Education, Inc.; Monkey Business Images/Shutterstock; **p. 227:** Elke Dennis/Shutterstock; **p. 229:** Pearson Education, Inc.; **p. 230:** Stockstudios/ Shutterstock; **p. 231:** Macdaddy/Dreamstime/Pearson Education, Inc.; Elena Elisseeva/Shutterstock; **p. 233:** Pearson Education, Inc.; **p. 234:** Kristen Piljay/ Pearson Education, Inc.; **p. 237:** Farah Abdi Warsameh/AP Images; Dai Kurokawa/ EPA/Newscom; **p. 238:** Elenathewise/Fotolia; **p. 239:** David R. Frazier Photolibrary, Inc./Alamy; **p. 240:** My Vegan Plate by Reed Mangels, PhD, RD; Lindsey Siferd; The Vegetarian Resource Group; www.vrg.org; **p. 241:** Michaeljung/Shutterstock; **p. 243:** PhotoAlto/Alamy; Monkey Business Images/Shutterstock; Elena Elisseeva/ Shutterstock; **p. 244:** Pearson Education, Inc.; My Vegan Plate by Reed Mangels, PhD, RD; Lindsey Siferd; The Vegetarian Resource Group; www.vrg.org

Chapter 7 Chapter Opener: Food Passionates/Corbis; **p. 252:** Syracuse Newspapers/Jim Commentucci/The Image Works; **p. 253:** Foodcollection/Getty Images; Pearson Education, Inc.; Yukata/Fotolia; johnfoto18/Shutterstock; **p. 254:** Jupiterimages/Photolibrary/Getty Images; **p. 255:** Digital Vision/Getty Images; **p. 257:** Jim Varney/Science source; **p. 259:** wavebreakmedia/Shutterstock; **p. 260:** David R. Frazier Photolibrary, Inc./Alamy; **p. 261:** Fuse/Getty Images; **p. 262:** Image Source/ Corbis; **p. 264:** Unpict/Fotolia; Danny Hooks/Fotolia; AmpFotoStudio.com/Fotolia; Antonio MuAoz Palomares/Getty Images; Pali Rao/Vetta/Getty Images; OlegSam/ Shutterstock; Iofoto/Shutterstock; Joy Brown/Shutterstock; **p. 265:** Richard Megna/ Fundamental Photographs; **p. 266:** Arthur Glauberman/Science Source; **p. 268:** Pearson Education, Inc.; **p. 269:** OlVic/Shutterstock; **p. 270:** Pearson Education, Inc.; **p. 273:** Joe Koshellek/MCT/Newscom; **p. 274:** Jupiterimages/Photolibrary/ Getty Images; Digital Vision/Getty Images; **p. 275:** Joe Koshellek/MCT/Newscom; Image Source/Corbis; wavebreakmedia/Shutterstock

Chapter 8 Chapter Opener: fatchoi/Getty Images; **p. 283:** Bloomimage/ Corbis; **p. 290:** Don Mason/Blend Images/Alamy; **p. 293:** Andres Rodriguez/Alamy; **p. 301:** Rudchenko Liliia/Shutterstock; **p. 304:** Sniegirova Mariia/Shutterstock; April_89/Fotolia; **p. 308:** Chris Rout/Alamy; **p. 309:** Andy Dean Photography/ Shutterstock; **p. 311:** Andy Dean Photography/Shutterstock; Rudchenko Liliia/ Shutterstock

Chapter 9 Chapter Opener: Joe Biafore/Getty Images; **p. 317:** Stockbyte/ Getty Images; Mtsyri/Shutterstock; **p. 319:** Best View Stock/Alamy; **p. 321:** National Eye Institute; **p. 325:** Pearson Education, Inc.; **p. 326:** Pearson Education, Inc.; **p. 328:** Elena Schweitzer/Shutterstock; **p. 329:** Sarsmis/Shutterstock; **p. 330:** Siri Stafford/Digital Vision/Getty Images; **p. 332:** Science Source; Timmary/Shutterstock; **p. 333:** Brand X/AGE Fotostock; **p. 334:** James Stevenson/Science Source; **p. 336:** Gustoimages/Science Source; **p. 337:** Seth Joel/Photographer's Choice/Getty Images; **p. 338:** John Smith/Photolibrary/Getty Images; **p. 340:** Michael Littlejohn/ Prentice Hall, Inc./Pearson Education, Inc.; Jacek Chabraszewski/Fotolia; Biophoto Associates/Science Source; **p. 341:** Frank and Helena/Cultura/Glow Images; **p. 343:** Ian O'Leary/Dorling Kindersley, Ltd.; **p. 344:** Rachel Epstein/Photo Edit; **p. 346:** Dee Breger/Science Source; SPL/Science Source; Cristina Pedrazzini/Science Source; **p. 347:** Suzannah Skelton/Getty Images; **p. 348:** Jupiterimages/Getty Images; Kristin Piljay/Pearson Education, Inc.; **p. 349:** U.S. Pharmacopeial Convention; **p. 350:** NEED SOURCE; **p. 351:** Stockbyte/Getty Images; Mtsyri/Shutterstock; **p. 353:** Kristin Piljay/Pearson Education, Inc.

Chapter 10 Chapter Opener: Laura Clay-Ballard/Getty Images; **p. 365:** Joe Gough/Fotolia; **p. 367:** Ralph Morse//Time Life Pictures/Getty Images; **p. 368:** Jjava/ Fotolia; **p. 369:** Biophoto Associates/Science Source; SPL/Science Source; **p. 371:** D. Hurst/Alamy; Elena Elisseeva/Shutterstock; **p. 373:** Dr. M.A. Ansary/Science Source; Smileus/Shutterstock; **p. 374:** Justin Lightley/Photographer's Choice/Getty Images; **p. 375:** Richard Semik/Shutterstock; **p. 376:** MaxPhotographer/Shutterstock; **p. 378:** FoodCollection/Photolibrary/Getty Images; **p. 380:** Tim Ridley/Dorling Kindersley, Ltd.; Biophoto Associates/Photo Researchers/Getty Images; **p. 381:** Brand X Pictures/AGE Fotostock; **p. 382:** AmpFotoStudio/Shutterstock; **p. 384:** wavebreakmedia/ Shutterstock; **p. 385:** 28/Ocean/Corbis; Pearson Education, Inc.; **p. 386:** Tetra Images/ Alamy; **p. 388:** Edyta Pawlowska/Shutterstock; **p. 389:** Brand X/AGE Fotostock; SPL/ Science Source; **p. 390:** St. Mary's Hospital Medical School/Science Source; Jason Stitt/

Tolerable Upper Intake Levels (ULs)

Life Stage Group	Vitamin A (μg/d)[a]	Vitamin C (mg/d)	Vitamin D (μg/d)	Vitamin E (mg/d)[b,c]	Niacin (mg/d)[c]	Vitamin B_6 (mg/d)	Folate (μg/d)[c]	Choline (g/d)
Infants								
0–6 mo	600	ND[d]	25	ND	ND	ND	ND	ND
6–12 mo	600	ND	38	ND	ND	ND	ND	ND
Children								
1–3 y	600	400	63	200	10	30	300	1.0
4–8 y	900	650	75	300	15	40	400	1.0
Males								
9–13 y	1,700	1,200	100	600	20	60	600	2.0
14–18 y	2,800	1,800	100	800	30	80	800	3.0
19–30 y	3,000	2,000	100	1,000	35	100	1,000	3.5
31–50 y	3,000	2,000	100	1,000	35	100	1,000	3.5
51–70 y	3,000	2,000	100	1,000	35	100	1,000	3.5
>70 y	3,000	2,000	100	1,000	35	100	1,000	3.5
Females								
9–13 y	1,700	1,200	100	600	20	60	600	2.0
14–18 y	2,800	1,800	100	800	30	80	800	3.0
19–30 y	3,000	2,000	100	1,000	35	100	1,000	3.5
31–50 y	3,000	2,000	100	1,000	35	100	1,000	3.5
51–70 y	3,000	2,000	100	1,000	35	100	1,000	3.5
>70 y	3,000	2,000	100	1,000	35	100	1,000	3.5
Pregnancy								
14–18 y	2,800	1,800	100	800	30	80	800	3.0
19–50 y	3,000	2,000	100	1,000	35	100	1,000	3.5
Lactation								
14–18 y	2,800	1,800	100	800	30	80	800	3.0
19–50 y	3,000	2,000	100	1,000	35	100	1,000	3.5

Note: A Tolerable Upper Intake Level (UL) is the highest level of daily nutrient intake that is likely to pose no risk of adverse health effects to almost all individuals in the general population. Unless otherwise specified, the UL represents total intake from food, water, and supplements. Due to a lack of suitable data, ULs could not be established for vitamin K, thiamin, riboflavin, vitamin B_{12}, pantothenic acid, biotin, and carotenoids. In the absence of a UL, extra caution may be warranted in consuming levels above recommended intakes. Members of the general population should be advised not to routinely exceed the UL. The UL is not meant to apply to individuals who are treated with the nutrient under medical supervision or to individuals with predisposing conditions that modify their sensitivity to the nutrient.

[a] As preformed vitamin A only.

[b] As α-tocopherol; applies to any form of supplemental α-tocopherol.

[c] The ULs for vitamin E, niacin, and folate apply to synthetic forms obtained from supplements, fortified foods, or a combination of the two.

[d] ND = Not determinable due to lack of data of adverse effects in this age group and concern with regard to lack of ability to handle excess amounts. Source of intake should be from food only to prevent high levels of intake.

Data from: DIETARY REFERENCE INTAKES series, National Academies Press. Copyright ©1997, 1998, 2000, 2001, and 2011, by the National Academy of Sciences. These reports may be accessed via www.nap.edu. Courtesy of the National Academies Press, Washington, DC. Reprinted with permission.

Tolerable Upper Intake Levels (ULs)

Elements

Life Stage Group	Boron (mg/d)	Calcium (mg/d)	Copper (µg/d)	Fluoride (mg/d)	Iodine (µg/d)	Iron (mg/d)	Magnesium (mg/d)[e]	Manganese (mg/d)	Molybdenum (µg/d)	Nickel (mg/d)	Phosphorus (g/d)	Selenium (µg/d)	Vanadium (mg/d)[f]	Zinc (mg/d)	Sodium (g/d)	Chloride (g/d)
Infants																
0–6 mo	ND[d]	1,000	ND	0.7	ND	40	ND	ND	ND	ND	ND	45	ND	4	ND	ND
6–12 mo	ND	1,500	ND	0.9	ND	40	ND	ND	ND	ND	ND	60	ND	5	ND	ND
Children																
1–3 y	3	2,500	1,000	1.3	200	40	65	2	300	0.2	3	90	ND	7	1.5	2.3
4–8 y	6	2,500	3,000	2.2	300	40	110	3	600	0.3	3	150	ND	12	1.9	2.9
Males																
9–13 y	11	3,000	5,000	10	600	40	350	6	1,100	0.6	4	280	ND	23	2.2	3.4
14–18 y	17	3,000	8,000	10	900	45	350	9	1,700	1.0	4	400	ND	34	2.3	3.6
19–30 y	20	2,500	10,000	10	1,100	45	350	11	2,000	1.0	4	400	1.8	40	2.3	3.6
31–50 y	20	2,500	10,000	10	1,100	45	350	11	2,000	1.0	4	400	1.8	40	2.3	3.6
51–70 y	20	2,000	10,000	10	1,100	45	350	11	2,000	1.0	4	400	1.8	40	2.3	3.6
>70 y	20	2,000	10,000	10	1,100	45	350	11	2,000	1.0	3	400	1.8	40	2.3	3.6
Females																
9–13 y	11	3,000	5,000	10	600	40	350	6	1,100	0.6	4	280	ND	23	2.2	3.4
14–18 y	17	3,000	8,000	10	900	45	350	9	1,700	1.0	4	400	ND	34	2.3	3.6
19–30 y	20	2,500	10,000	10	1,100	45	350	11	2,000	1.0	4	400	1.8	40	2.3	3.6
31–50 y	20	2,500	10,000	10	1,100	45	350	11	2,000	1.0	4	400	1.8	40	2.3	3.6
51–70 y	20	2,000	10,000	10	1,100	45	350	11	2,000	1.0	4	400	1.8	40	2.3	3.6
>70 y	20	2,000	10,000	10	1,100	45	350	11	2,000	1.0	3	400	1.8	40	2.3	3.6
Pregnancy																
14–18 y	17	3,000	8,000	10	900	45	350	9	1,700	1.0	3.5	400	ND	34	2.3	3.6
19–50 y	20	2,500	10,000	10	1,100	45	350	11	2,000	1.0	3.5	400	ND	40	2.3	3.6
Lactation																
14–18 y	17	3,000	8,000	10	900	45	350	9	1,700	1.0	4	400	ND	34	2.3	3.6
19–50 y	20	2,500	10,000	10	1,100	45	350	11	2,000	1.0	4	400	ND	40	2.3	3.6

Note: A Tolerable Upper Intake Level (UL) is the highest level of daily nutrient intake that is likely to pose no risk of adverse health effects to almost all individuals in the general population. Unless otherwise specified, the UL represents total intake from food, water, and supplements. Due to a lack of suitable data, ULs could not be established for vitamin K, thiamin, riboflavin, vitamin B₁₂, pantothenic acid, biotin, and carotenoids. In the absence of a UL, extra caution may be warranted in consuming levels above recommended intakes. Members of the general population should be advised not to routinely exceed the UL. The UL is not meant to apply to individuals who are treated with the nutrient under medical supervision or to individuals with predisposing conditions that modify their sensitivity to the nutrient.

[d] ND = Not determinable due to lack of data of adverse effects in this age group and concern with regard to lack of ability to handle excess amounts. Source of intake should be from food only to prevent high levels of intake.

[e] The ULs for magnesium represent intake from a pharmacological agent only and do not include intake from food and water.

[f] Although vanadium in food has not been shown to cause adverse effects in humans, there is no justification for adding vanadium to food, and vanadium supplements should be used with caution. The UL is based on adverse effects in laboratory animals, and this data could be used to set a UL for adults but not children and adolescents.

Data from: Reprinted with permission from the Dietary Reference Intakes series. Copyright 1997, 1998, 2000, 2001, 2005, 2011 by the National Academies of Sciences, courtesy of the National Academies Press, Washington, D.C. These reports may be accessed via www.nap.edu.